TILL TIME'S LAST SAND

TILL TIME'S LAST SAND

A History of the Bank of England
1694–2013

David Kynaston

BLOOMSBURY

LONDON · OXFORD · NEW YORK · NEW DELHI · SYDNEY

Bloomsbury Publishing
An imprint of Bloomsbury Publishing Plc

50 Bedford Square   1385 Broadway
London   New York
WC1B 3DP   NY 10018
UK   USA

www.bloomsbury.com

BLOOMSBURY and the Diana logo are trademarks of Bloomsbury Publishing Plc

First published in Great Britain 2017

© David Kynaston 2017

David Kynaston has asserted his right under the Copyright,
Designs and Patents Act, 1988, to be identified as Author of this work.

Every reasonable effort has been made to trace copyright holders of
material reproduced in this book, but if any have been inadvertently overlooked
the publishers would be glad to hear from them. For legal purposes the Acknowledgements on
pp. 850–1 constitute an extension of this copyright page.

British Library Cataloguing-in-Publication Data
A catalogue record for this book is available from the British Library.

Library of Congress Cataloguing-in-Publication data has been applied for.

ISBN: HB: 978-1-4088-6856-0
         TPB: 978-1-4088-6857-7
         ePub: 978-1-4088-6858-4

2 4 6 8 10 9 7 5 3 1

Typeset by Integra Software Services Pvt. Ltd.
Printed and bound in Great Britain by CPI Group (UK) Ltd, Croydon CR0 4YY

To find out more about our authors and books visit www.bloomsbury.com.
Here you will find extracts, author interviews, details of forthcoming events
and the option to sign up for our newsletters.

Thus at thy helm of Gold, thy short-liv'd Pride,
No abler, trustier pilot-hand could guide:
That fair Foundation Royal, that (if my
Too poor Propheticks may dare speak so high)
Beyond her yet too narrow lease shall stand
With its unshaken head, till time's last sand;
Whose circulating warmth shall never cease,
At once the nerves of War and veins of Peace:
Commerce, Arts, Arms, all her own fair increase,
A Treasury, from whose diffusive mine
Our glebe shall fatten, and our Throne shall shine.

From Elkanah Settle, 'Augusta Lachrymans:
a Funeral Tear to the Memory of the Worthy and
Honour'd Michael Godfrey, Esq.' (1695)

I once had the temerity to ask a central banker the secret of his craft. 'It all depends,' he said, 'on making the right-sounding noises at the right time.' He then abruptly changed the subject, and started discussing with patently spurious animation the prospects of Sussex in the County Cricket Championship.

'Lombard Lane', *Punch*, 14 August 1963

Contents

Preface

I was honoured to be asked in 2009 by the then governor, Mervyn King, to undertake a single-volume history of the Bank of England. Other commitments and unavoidable circumstances have delayed the book's preparation, but the work itself has been both challenging and enjoyable. From the start we were agreed that I would retain complete independence of judgement; and the Bank has admirably kept to its word. We were also agreed that this would be a book for the general reader, not the specialist, and I am very conscious that – for all its length – this is a far from comprehensive account of the Bank's activities over the years. The reader who wishes to go wider and deeper should in the first instance consult the notable series of books on specific periods of the Bank's history: Sir John Clapham (1944) on 1694 to 1914; Richard Sayers (1976) on 1891 to 1944; John Fforde (1992) on 1941 to 1958; and Forrest Capie (2010) on the 1950s to 1979. In addition, on the domestic side of the Bank, the reader wanting more should go to W. Marston Acres (1931) for the first two centuries or so and to Elizabeth Hennessy (1992) for 1930 to 1960. I have drawn heavily on the pioneering work of all these historians, as I also have on my own four-volume history of the City of London, for each volume of which I did a considerable amount of archival research at the Bank. At the end of writing this book, I find myself thinking – not for the first time – of the haunting words that Richard Sayers wrote on completing his history: 'I am all too aware of its imperfections and shortcomings, and can only plead, in the phrase of Hippocrates and Chaucer, "so short the life, so long the craft to learn".'

March 2017

It Must Now Necessarily be a Bank

'The Commissioners for the new Bank came this morning to Mercers' Chapel, where the books were opened,' noted the dogged chronicler Narcissus Luttrell on Thursday, 21 June 1694. ''Tis said,' he added, 'the subscriptions already amount to £300,000.' Luttrell was right: the capital-raising process for the putative Bank of England was off to a cracking start. In addition to King William and Queen Mary (jointly contributing £10,000, the maximum permitted), other first-day subscribers included the first lord of the Treasury (Lord Godolphin, £4,000), a clockmaker (John Ebsworth, £1,000), a salter (John English, £500), an apothecary (Nicholas Gambier, £600), a host of merchants, and a 'gentleman' from 'the town of St Albans in the county of Hertfordshire' (John Gape, £500). The following Tuesday a friend told the political philosopher John Locke that he had subscribed £300 – which, Locke then informed another friend, 'made me subscribe £500' – while even before that, on the 25th, one of the opponents of the new institution had faced up to painful reality. 'I am informed,' the Duke of Leeds wrote from his Yorkshire fastness to his London bankers, 'That subscriptions to the Bank do fill so fast, that their is at this day near 700'000 subscribed, so that it must now nesesarily be a bank. I therfore desire that you will subscribe foure thousand pound for mee ...' The overall target was £1.2 million (25 per cent payable in cash), and it was reached at Mercers' Hall in Cheapside on the tenth day, 2 July, with the last of the 1,268 subscribers being Judith Shirley of Preston in Sussex, staking a modest £75.[1]

Three men above all had been responsible for getting the Bank (as the Bank of England would in time be familiarly called) to this promising point. William Paterson, a remarkable and resilient Scot, is best described as a 'projector' – or, in the words of one of his biographers, someone 'more skilful at promoting his plans than at executing his projects, and more interested in his own self-advancement than in carrying through the consequences of his ideas'. In any case, whatever the motivation, it was Paterson who had the persistence and the flair to put the idea of an English bank of credit – note issuing and able to lend to the state, unlike the Dutch model – firmly on the table. Such a bank would, he insisted in his key pamphlet *A Brief Account of the Intended Bank of England*, be 'for the convenience and security of great Payments, and the better to facilitate the circulation of Money, in and around this great and oppulent City'. By 1694, and probably earlier, his two key allies were Charles Montagu, a difficult but hugely able Treasury minister who marshalled the political support, and Michael Godfrey, a substantial merchant who did much the same in the City of London. On 25 April, the much contested Bill that became generally known as the Tonnage Act passed through both Houses of Parliament. Among other things it declared that if half the pledged sum of £1.2 million was lent to the state at 8 per cent by the start of August, the subscribers were to be incorporated under the Great Seal as 'the Governor and Company of the Banke of England'.[2]

There followed the successful subscription of late June and early July, ensuring that it would be a certainty. On 5 July, three days after the books had closed, an announcement in the *London Gazette* summoned all subscribers of £500 or more to meet on the 10th at 8am at Mercers' Hall. There, after swearing that the sum subscribed had been their 'own proper money', they were to 'give in Riting, Rolled up, the Names of Two Such Persons as they think fit', one to be governor of the new bank, the other deputy governor. The election duly happened, resulting in Godfrey (an £8,000 subscriber) being named deputy governor, with another prominent City merchant, Sir John Houblon (a £10,000 subscriber), as governor. Next day the process was repeated, with twenty-four of the subscribers being chosen as the Bank's first set of directors. Governor, deputy governor and most of the directors then assembled at Mercers' Hall just over a fortnight later, on the afternoon of Friday, 27 July, for their first 'Court', hours after the Bank's Charter had been formally sealed at the Lincoln's Inn Fields house of Sir John Somers, lord keeper of the Great Seal. The immediate issue faced by the fledgling body was to determine the appropriate method 'of giving Receipts for running Cash':

> Upon putting the Question after a long Debate, It was Resolved, That these three Methods shall be observed & none other
> 1st To give out Running=Cash=Notes, and to endorse on them what is paid off in part
> 2nd To keep an Accompt with y^e Creditor: in a Book or Paper of his owne
> 3rd To accept Notes drawn on y^e Bank
> And it is Ordered that no Creditor shall use any two of the said methods ...

The second option was in effect pass-book banking, the third option cheque-book banking; but almost certainly the preferred option was the first – a recognition of (in Derrick Byatt's 1994 words, referring to the goldsmith-bankers who had emerged in London since the 1630s) 'the advantage to commerce generally of the goldsmith's note payable to a named depositor or order (later, or bearer)'. And 'thus,' he added, 'was laid the foundation stone for the Bank's series of note issues down the centuries'.[3]

On the occasion of an earlier anniversary, the 250th in 1944, a more celebrated historian of the Bank, Sir John Clapham, opened his account with a sentence that would become much quoted: 'The establishment of the Bank of England can be treated, like many historical events both great and small, either as curiously accidental or as all but inevitable.' And he went on: 'Had the country not been at war in 1694, the government would hardly have been disposed to offer a favourable charter to a corporation which proposed to lend it money. Had Charles Montagu, a Lord of the Treasury, and from [May] 1694 Chancellor of the Exchequer, not thought that, out of several scores of financial schemes submitted to him, this was on the whole the most promising, there would again have been no charter or perhaps quite a different one.' Context is often all, and perhaps peculiarly so in the case of this quasi-accidental institution that would achieve a rare permanence.

The cardinal context was indeed war – specifically, the Nine Years' War against France that followed on from William and Mary's accession to the throne in 1688, a war that resulted in public expenditure during the 1690s running at well over twice the level it had in the 1680s. Taxation naturally increased, up to around £4 million a year by the mid-1690s, but that still left an annual shortfall of some £2 million. Given that the King had no intention of making what he saw as a premature peace – and given the underlying truth of the political economist Charles Davenant's contemporary observation that 'the whole Art of War is in a manner reduced to Money', so that 'that Prince, who can best find Money to feed, cloath, and pay his Army, not he that has the most Valiant Troops, is surest of Success and Conquest' – the need to fill the gap was, to put it mildly, urgent. What to do? With means of repayment increasingly non-existent, and a range of short-term expedients already tried, the obvious answer was long-term borrowing: the beginning, in effect, of the funded (aka national) debt. Lottery tickets and lottery-like tontine annuities were tried, with mixed success, before finally the 'special bonds' solution: namely, £1.2 million bonds, not only (in the words of the financial historian Larry Neal) 'carrying a guaranteed eight per cent rate of interest and funded from specific taxes assigned to that purpose by Parliament', but 'sold only to subscribers in the proposed new Bank of England'. This did not quite meet the shortfall, but crucially it meant that the King's will could be done and the war continue.

Not that the King's will was quite what it had been, given that 1694 was only six years after England's 'Glorious Revolution' – that decisive shift towards constitutional monarchy and in due course something starting to resemble parliamentary democracy, a shift that William himself had no alternative but to accept as the price of his kingship. Undoubtedly, the Bank itself was one of the most palpable immediate consequences of the revolution; and it was explicitly in relation to this new institution and its likely financial muscle that on 8 July, six days after the subscription books had closed, the future Duke of Chandos, James Brydges, candidly informed his Jacobite-inclined father that 'the opinion of most persons here as well as strangers abroad' was that there was now 'no likelihood' of the government of the day 'ever changing in favour of King James'. There was also by this time a specifically party political aspect: whereas the Tories stood foursquare for the primacy of land and were instinctively hostile to the City and all its financial wiles – incomprehensible, dangerous, even republican – the increasingly powerful Whigs were developing a political economy that (in the words of Steve Pincus, historian of England's 'First Modern Revolution') 'embraced urban culture, manufacturing, and economic imperialism'. In short, the Bank was 'a Whig creation against Tory resistance', a creation that marked the triumph of the commercially minded and the unsentimental forces of the new.[4]

Arguably paramount among those forces was what was rapidly emerging by the late seventeenth century as a profound financial revolution, parallel to the political one. Key elements included a rapidly growing securities market, now poised to trade in long-term government debt; Lloyd's insurance, with Edward Lloyd in 1691 moving his coffee house from near the river to Lombard Street in order to be close to the General Post Office, a prime source of shipping intelligence; and an increasingly enmeshed web of bankers and merchants, enjoying a symbiotic and mutually beneficial relationship. The glaring absence was clearly a national bank, call it the Bank of England. But as to precisely what sort of animal it was at the point of creation in July 1694, that was less clear-cut.

Partly through the legislation, partly through the Charter and partly through what was tacitly understood, the following (baldly summarised) seems to have been the case: that the Bank, in return for its £1.2 million loan, not only received 8 per cent annual interest and a £4,000 annual management fee, but a range of privileges, including a) seldom accorded joint-stock status; b) in effect limited liability; c) the right to maximise its profits through undertaking a general banking business, including through issuing paper money, taking deposits, lending on mortgages and dealing in bills of exchange as well as gold and silver; and d) the right to choose its own top personnel. The deal was not quite open sesame – the Charter was guaranteed for only eleven years, the Bank was not yet formally the government's banker, and it did not yet have a monopoly on either joint-stock banking or note issue – but this was still a pretty attractive package.[5]

Looked at in the round, from a larger viewpoint as well as just the Bank's, the temptation is to see the whole process as smooth, Whiggish (literally) and inevitable, all coming together to form a virtuous circle. 'The state's blessing afforded general circulation to the Bank's notes,' comments Felix Martin on this 'public/private' partnership. 'The commercial ownership and management of the Bank improved the state's creditworthiness.'[6] Yet ultimately, as economists and even economic historians sometimes forget, it takes people to make something work – and people, mercifully, are neither uniform nor predictable.

———

Who, to start with, were the 1,268 initial subscribers? We know quite a lot.[7] One hundred and ninety 'esquires' contributed 25 per cent of the total £1.2 million; 201 merchants contributed 21 per cent; sixty-three titled aristocrats contributed 15 per cent; almost 70 per cent of subscribers contributed under £1,000; 12 per cent of the subscribers were women, responsible for about 6 per cent of the capital; some 123 of the subscribers were Huguenots (£104,000), but only about half a dozen were Jews (£4,100); and although the lists did feature a range of tradesmen and artisans, including carriers, clothworkers, embroiderers, farmers, mariners and wharfingers, generally the subscribers (in the words of Anne Murphy) 'belonged to the mercantile middle classes of London', albeit with 'important ancillary contributions from lawyers, office-holders, and clergy of the Church of England'. Barely 2 per cent of the capital was subscribed for from abroad; over 87 per cent of the subscribers lived in London, Middlesex, Surrey and Hertfordshire; and almost 55 per cent of the subscribers were based in the City itself, the historic square mile. As to motivation, what Jonathan Swift would recall as 'the bait of large Interest' was almost certainly the prime inducement, at a time of war and dislocation drawing in 'a great Number of those whose Money by the Dangers and Difficulties of Trade lay dead upon their hands'. Or as the anonymous author of *Remarks upon the Bank of England* would recall in 1706, 'the *8 per Cent.* Alone, (when the Legal Interest was but 6, and the clear produce of Land seldom 4) was of itself a sufficient Encouragement to this Undertaking; especially considering that this was Exempt from Taxes, to which other Money, and Stock, and Land was liable'. Even so, for many of the subscribers it was not *just* about the 8 per cent – it was also about getting in on the ground floor of an incorporated joint-stock company with rich financial potential. 'They were attracted,' as Sir Albert Feavearyear wrote many years later, 'by the opportunity which the foundation of the first joint-stock bank in England provided of taking a hand in the business of banking, a business which in the last fifty years had raised up more junior clerks and scriveners to be wealthy aldermen than had any other in treble the time. Most of the subscribers, in short, were speculators, men of "quality" and men of business, who saw a chance of big dividends.'[8]

Some of the keenest to enjoy those dividends were almost certainly the original directors, about whom we again have a reasonable degree of background knowledge.[9] The great majority were City-based merchants of considerable substance; about a third were merchants trading with Portugal merchants, concentrating largely on the wine trade; half a dozen were of Huguenot background, while there was also a significant Dutch connection; about half were from the dissenting interest; and there existed an overwhelming affiliation with the Whigs. An exception was Sir William Gore, a Tory alderman whose turnover the following year was estimated at an impressive £64,000, helped by his Court connections securing him profitable contracts supplying the armed forces; but politically more typical was Sir Thomas Abney, a future Whig MP for the City who had made his way up in the mercantile world after originally being a linen draper and would eventually give his name to a north London cemetery. Probably the chief merchant prince among the new directors – and possibly even in the City as a whole – was Gilbert Heathcote. The eldest son of a Chesterfield ironmonger, and by the 1690s a West Indies and Baltic merchant of immense wealth, he is described by his biographer as 'one of the inner group' that had promoted the Bank's chartering and flotation – an activity that he would not have spent valuable time on purely out of sentiment or for the public good, to judge by Alexander Pope's subsequent deathless couplet: 'The grave Sir Gilbert holds it for a rule / That every man in want is knave or fool ...'

There was no doubting, though, who was the main man, and indeed the main family, in July 1694. 'It was a mighty pretty sight,' recorded Samuel Pepys back in the 1660s, 'to see old Mr Houblon whom I never saw before, and all his sons about him; all good Merchants.' So they were, mainly in Mediterranean trade (especially Iberian), and two of the brothers, Sir James and Abraham, were among the first directors while another brother, Sir John Houblon, became at the age of sixty-two the first governor. The brothers were fourth-generation Walloon immigrants, their great-grandfather having been the son of a Lille merchant who in the 1560s had found asylum in England from Catholic persecution; their political sympathies were moderate Whiggish (John himself being MP for Bodmin); and they were all major subscribers to the new institution. Pepys's particular friend was James – 'a pretty serious man', thought the diarist on their first encounter, though soon 'a man I love mightily'. Unquestionably the three brothers were all very wealthy men: after dining with James, Pepys noted that none of the food or wine had originated from anywhere closer than Persia, China and the Cape of Good Hope, and another diarist, John Evelyn, observed after a similar occasion that the merchant lived '*en prince*'. But all the evidence suggests that this was also a family with, perhaps because of its distinctive Protestant roots, a strong sense of duty and public responsibility; and when Sir John died in 1712 in the Threadneedle Street house (site of the present Bank) where he had lived and worked, he was found – at least according to the family biographer – in his chamber in the attitude of prayer.

Solid, unimaginative, breathing the air for the most part of a somewhat limited circle that seldom questioned its own worth or purpose, merchants would continue to dominate the leadership and governance of the Bank of England for the next two centuries and more. Yet it is too easy to be condescending. In 1711, introducing the members of the imaginary Spectator Club, the essayist Richard Steele described one of them, Sir Andrew Freeport. 'A Merchant of great Eminence in the City of London', he was a man 'acquainted with Commerce in all its Parts' who, as a favourite jest, 'calls the Sea the *British Common*'. Sir Andrew, reflected Steele in his portrait, was proof of the proposition that 'a General Trader of good Sense, is pleasanter Company than a general Scholar', having 'a natural unaffected Eloquence', so that 'the Perspicuity of his Discourse gives the same Pleasure that Wit would in another Man'.[10] Sadly, it is not always possible to get as close as one would like to the words of the real-life merchants. Much more ample is the evidence of their deeds, including their deeds at what was not yet remotely a central bank; and it is by their deeds that these practical men must largely be judged.

PART ONE

1694–1815

I

Services to the Nation

Business began for real during the week starting 30 July 1694. That day, the directors decided that the Bank's Common Seal was to represent 'Britania sitting and looking on a Bank of mony' – a decision that in turn meant that Britannia would henceforth appear on all the Bank's printed notes. That same Monday, the directors appointed the first nineteen 'Servants of this House', including a 'Secretary and Sollicitor' (John Ince), a 'First Accomptant' (Thomas Mercer) and a 'First Cashier' (John Kendrick): these were the three key staff appointments (though Kendrick lasted only a few weeks), anticipating how until well into the twentieth century the Bank in a day-to-day sense would essentially be run along tripartite lines, under the secretary, the chief accountant and the chief cashier. Over the next few months, most of the infant institution's business concerned funding the government, mainly through the original subscription to the Bank. Crucially, the £1.2 million loan promised to the Treasury was paid not in coin, but in paper – at first in the form of so-called 'sealed bills', then in the form of 'running cash notes' issued by the Bank. The Bank was thus from the start an engine to create credit, albeit an engine inevitably somewhat resented by London's goldsmith-bankers, who nevertheless often still found it convenient to have an account there. No doubt they read the runes, and despite the odd setback the price of Bank stock steadily rose during the autumn and into 1695. It was also telling that by December the Bank was based in larger premises, having taken out a lease – though initially only for a cautious eleven years, the period of the Charter – on Grocers' Hall, governor Houblon's livery company. 'A very convenient place,' Daniel Defoe would note in the

1720s about this enclosed building roughly halfway between Poultry and Lothbury, 'and considering its situation, so near the [Royal] Exchange, a very spacious, commodious place.'[1]

The Bank's enjoyment of its new home may have been marred during 1695 by a flurry of anti-Bank broadsheets and pamphlets. *Reasons Humbly Offer'd to The Honourable House of Commons, By Eminent Merchants and Citizens of the City of London: Shewing The Inconveniences that may arise by the Bank* was the restrained title of one, apparently co-authored by the prominent Tory goldsmith-banker Richard Hoare and accusing the Bank of being poised to 'Engross most of the Ready Money in and near the City of *London*, which is the Heart of Trade, and so will amount in effect to a Monopoly'; an anonymous pamphleteer claimed that the Bank's note issue was 'almost a Fraud on the Subject'; while according to the equally anonymous author of *Angliae Tutamen: or the Safety of England*, 'the great Dividends the *Bank* has already made, and is preparing to make … tell all the World in honest *English*, that one Part of the Nation preys upon t'other', with the author broad-mindedly adding that 'if we could extract Profits from Foreigners 'twould do well, but from one another, enriches not the Publick one jot'. Even John Locke had his doubts. 'The money in the Bank is, and I conclude always will be, managed by London merchants,' he declared to Whig friends in February, prompting him to predict that as a result 'the greatest part of our trade will in a little while by secret combinations be got into a few hands', whereas 'money might be better distributed into the country, and other ports, and trading parts of England'. Amid all this, the Bank's main defender was its deputy governor, Michael Godfrey, responsible for *A Short Account of the Bank of England*. Lower interest rates, an enhanced price for land, a financial strengthening of the monarchy – these were among the many 'services to the nation', he insisted in a detailed exposition, that the Bank was already providing and would continue to provide. Godfrey also challenged the goldsmith-bankers: 'If there be an advantage to be made by the running cash of the kingdom, it's fitter for the Bank to have it; which consists of thirteen hundred persons, and who employ it to serve the nation in general, by lowering the interest of money; than that it should be given to a few private men, who have already made use of it, so much to the nation's prejudice.' In short, he concluded, the Bank 'will and must be preserved and maintained, because of its great use to the whole realm'.[2]

Duly justifying its existence, the Bank continued through 1695 to lend to the government: either directly to the Treasury – with the Bank receiving in return exchequer 'tallies' (sticks of notched wood that were in effect IOUs) – or more indirectly by discounting (which is to say purchasing) tallies and Navy paper (bills based on the security of the English Navy). Two human dramas, meanwhile, played out. The first involved the Bank's original 'projector', William Paterson, who had been elected as one of the original directors but by early 1695 was almost certainly getting itchy feet. His latest scheme was for another bank, to be called the Orphans' Bank, and on 12 February his colleagues at Grocers' Hall informed him unequivocally that 'his proceeding in the business of the Orphans Estate, in Conjunction with those he told the Court were known enemies of the bank, is not becoming a Director of this Court, but a Breach of his Trust'. A few days later, Paterson claimed that the Orphans' Bank, dealing in land not trade, would be no threat to the Bank of England; but by the end of the month he was gone. The other human drama stemmed from the decision in May to establish an agency in Antwerp in order to pay the troops in Flanders, with a small sub-committee, including Michael Godfrey, James Houblon and Sir William Scawen, being 'empowered to goe over to Antwerpe'. Two months later, on 17 July, the deputy governor found himself in the trenches in the company of his monarch, watching the siege of Namur at all too close quarters:

> *William:* Mr Godfrey, you ought not to run these hazards; you are not a soldier; you can be of no use to us here.
> *Godfrey:* Sir, I run no more hazard than your majesty!
> *William:* Not so; I am where it is my duty to be, and I may without presumption commit my life to God's keeping; but you—.

At which point, relates Macaulay in his immortal account, a cannon ball from the ramparts laid Godfrey's head at William's feet. Bank stock immediately fell 2 per cent, once the news reached London; and Scawen, who apparently had been standing only two yards away, was elected as the new deputy governor.[3]

He and his colleagues now confronted the exceptionally challenging circumstances of 1696 – in effect, a two-pronged attack on the very existence of the Bank, or at the least its credibility. The first prong derived from the consequences of the Recoinage Act of January that year: although necessary in its own terms, in order to tackle the scandalously debased condition of England's silver coin, the solution – recalling and reminting all silver coin – inevitably led to the Bank itself becoming seriously short of specie and soon finding it difficult to meet demands for cash. Hoare would later deny the charge, but some of his fellow goldsmith-bankers did not hesitate in their attempt to wreak maximum damage, culminating on 6 May when they, according to Macaulay, 'flocked to Grocers' Hall and insisted on immediate payment': that is, of bullion (silver or gold) for bills and notes issued by the Bank that they had been assiduously storing ahead of this orchestrated démarche. At which point, the directors 'refused to cash the Notes which had been thus maliciously presented', whereas 'other creditors, who came in good faith to ask for their due, were paid'. Put another way, there had been a run on the Bank – and partial suspension of payments. A week later, on the 13th, Scawen gravely informed the General Court (a meeting of the Bank's stockholders) that 'a greater demand is made att present than is possible att present to be answer'd by the money coined'; and that 'if any person be under any uneasinesse for want of his money, The Bank is willing to Give such person Good Tallies [IOUs] for his notes'. Whereupon, it was not only resolved that 'every Member of the Corporation who has any goldsmiths notes should be desired to bring them into the Bank & Change them for Bank Notes', but also 'recommended to all the Members to keepe their Cash & Transact all their businesse in the Bank'.[4]

The other prong was the Land Bank threat. Conceived specifically as a rival to the Bank of England, and supported largely by the 'country' interest (anti-Whig, anti-City), the Land Bank had as its central premise a note issue on the security of land. 'How a Land Bank shall supply the King with ready money I doe not well see,' reflected Locke on 14 February, shortly after a House of Commons committee had both agreed to a national land bank going ahead and (in Narcissus Luttrell's words) 'ordered that none concerned in the Bank of England have any thing to doe in it'. To this the Bank responded proactively, offering to lend the government the same amount (£2.56 million) promised by the Land Bank, but at a lower rate of interest. The offer, however, was rejected, and on 10 March the Commons accepted its committee's recommendation. 'The Governour informed the Court,' recorded the General Court's minutes on 29 April in detailing the Bank's reponse, 'that tho' the Act of Parliam^t was passed [on 27 April] for the Establishing of a Land Bank, yet that the Bank of England doe still remaine in good Creditt – And that the Court of Directors have and will doe all things in their power for the Interest of the Bank.' Fighting talk, but these were bad days, and on 4 May, just forty-eight hours before the run on the Bank caused by the recoinage crisis, there appeared a would-be prophetic pamphlet called *The Trial and Condemnation of the Land Bank at Exeter Change for murdering the Bank of England at Grocers' Hall*. The level of personal abuse was high even by the standards of the day – there were references to Sir John Houblon's 'obstinacy and blunders', Sir William Gore's 'shuffling tricks', Sir Gilbert Heathcote's 'cynicalness and self conceit' – and just at this moment the prospect of a Grocers' Hall corpse seemed far from impossible.⁵

In the event, the would-be rival proved one of the more spectacular flops in financial history. 'People generally despair of the Land Bank and think it will come to nothing,' observed Lord Godolphin (until recently first lord of the Treasury) shortly after the subscription books opened on 4 June – and within weeks the whole thing was dead in the water, with barely £7,000 subscribed. Even so, the Bank was still in a very tight spot, given the larger national situation. 'The months of July and August 1696,' notes one historian, 'were the most desperate of the war'; and on 15 August it needed a masterly speech by the governor to persuade the General Court to vote through a £200,000 loan to the government. Although he fully acknowledged that the Bank continued to suffer from that 'want of Specie which at this time is the common Calamity of the whole nation', the essential fact was, he went on, that the government now acknowledged the Bank as indispensable, with the Lords of the Treasury having 'informed the Court of Directors (which is a great truth) that neither the Government nor the trade of England can be carried on without Creditt, and that they knowe if the Creditt of the Bank be not maintained, no other Creditt can be supported'. Nevertheless, the so-called 'patriotic' loan further intensified the Bank's shortage of cash (gold or silver coin), and by October the price of Bank stock was down to 60 (having stood at par at the start of the year), with the Bank resorting to understandable delaying tactics. 'All Notes of £5 and under,' resolved the directors, 'be paid off in full alphabetically, beginning upon Wednesday the 28th day of October instant with Notes payable to names of A and B, and so on Wednesday of every week two letters through the alphabet.' Meanwhile, the government's need for cash to pay the troops remained acute, and by early December, a few months after he had created the first issue of Exchequer bills, the chancellor Charles Montagu decided further to chance his arm, proposing his so-called 'engrafting' scheme: that the outstanding tallies (IOUs) would be added to the Bank's stock through a new subscription, with the Bank being paid interest on those tallies. 'He is very confident in his Scheme,' John Freke, a Whig barrister, reported to Locke on 5 December, adding that 'last night he went to the Directors of the Bank to propose it to them'. Would Montagu get his way? Freke did not know, but had 'no doubt' that he would 'threaten them' if 'they would not comply'. Perhaps he did, but it seems that the Houblon faction (a nephew, brother-in-law and cousin being directors, as well as the three brothers) in particular stood firm, apparently apprehensive that engrafting would not only overburden the Bank but also reduce their personal stakes; and on the 7th the General Court rejected the scheme.[6]

There ensued during the early weeks and months of 1697 some arguably risky brinkmanship, as the Bank took the opportunity to exercise a significant degree of leverage and in the process consolidate its long-term future. In essence, having first at the start of the year declined outright to lend some £2½ million, the Bank did now consent to take £1 million of short-term debt off the government's hands through a capital-enlarging 'engrafting' process – but only in return for four key conditions being met: that the original Charter should be extended to 1711; that the Bank should be exempt from taxation; that the government would initiate measures against the counterfeiting of Bank notes, which was becoming a serious problem (such forgery was later made a capital offence); and above all that, in the Bank's own words as it formulated its demands, 'no other Bank or any Constitution whatever in the nature of a Bank, be Erected or Established, permitted or allowed, within this Kingdome, during the continuance of the Bank of England'. The Bank did not quite get everything its own way – with the Commons insisting that 'at all future Elections there shall not be chosen above two-thirds of those who were Directors the previous year' – but overall the legislation passed that spring marked a decisive victory for the fledgling institution in its relationship with government.

The resulting capital enlargement, involving government creditors exchanging their short-term debt (tallies) for Bank stock, led to a significant social broadening of the Bank's shareholders, with first-time proprietors including a Plaistow waterman (John Wells, £625) and a Horsley Down mealwoman (Martha Thomson, £250); while the Bank's newly strengthened position saw the price of Bank stock rapidly climbing back towards par. The first elections under the new dispensation took place in July, with Scawen being chosen as governor and Nathaniel Tench as deputy governor; and two months later, the Treaty of Ryswick marked the end of the Nine Years' War.[7] This particular conflict was over, but one of its most important by-products was here to stay.

The pleasures of peace did not last very long. Even as they were still 'looking back with Horrour on the heavy Load of Debts they had contracted', recalled Jonathan Swift in 1711 about the English people during the aftermath of the Nine Years' War, they, 'without giving themselves time to breath, would again enter into a more dangerous, chargeable, and expensive War'. This new war was the War of the Spanish Succession, lasting from 1702 to 1714 – and another opportunity for the Bank to show its prowess in war finance, especially through loans to a predictably strapped state. 'The government which is chiefly supplied by them, can scarce expect for the future to be supported without them,' observed in 1706 one pamphleteer, the Duke of Marlborough's chaplain John Broughton, of its apparently ever-increasing dependency on the men running the Bank. That dependency was intensified from 1707, when in effect the Bank took over responsibility for circulating new issues of Exchequer bills secured on taxes, a service it performed not only for a handsome allowance for bills outstanding, but also with the precise interest on bills left entirely to its own discretion. 'What extraordinary profit must have accrued to the bank by this operation, every one must perceive,' noted with grudging admiration the political economist Sir James Steuart over half a century later, adding that 'almost the whole accumulated interest paid, became a pure profit to the bank, as well as a great augmentation of the national debt'.

In addition, 1707 was the year of the Act of Union, involving the Bank in a less profitable service to the state. The agreement, far from popular north of the border, included the provision that the Scots, as an 'equivalent' for their contribution to repaying England's national debt, would receive some £100,000 in cash and £300,000 in Exchequer bills; and that summer, a heavily guarded party of twelve wagons, accompanied by three Bank officials, made its way from London to Edinburgh. There they were met by four English commissioners, including James Houblon, son of the former Bank director Sir James. 'A good share of ye Mob are very Angry,' he reported to his brother on 5 August after the wagons' arrival, '& threw Stones at ye Bank-Officers & Coachmen.' Apparently the mob believed that the wagons contained ammunition. Such was the uncertain standing of Exchequer bills that the commissioners had to request the Bank to send a further £50,000 in coin, resulting in a second convoy (again attended by three Bank officials) later in the summer. The tailpiece to the story involved an unseemly squabble. Back in London, the wagon drivers demanded from the Bank an extra £22 per man; the Bank's offer of an extra £10 was refused; the secretary, John Ince, complained to the Treasury that the drivers were 'very rude and troublesome'; and although the documentation runs out at this point, no doubt a compromise was reached.

Meanwhile, a war famous for its resonant battle names (Blenheim 1704, Ramillies 1706, Oudenarde 1708, Malplaquet 1709) continued to drag on – and just as a decade earlier, the Bank took advantage of the Whig government's need for immediate funds to secure for itself a new, enhanced agreement. Embedded in legislation in 1708–9, there were three key aspects from the Bank's point of view: first, its Charter was extended to 1733, almost a quarter of a century away; second, its monopoly over joint-stock banking was strengthened, at the same time confining private banking to organisations of six partners or fewer; and third, its authorised capital was doubled to £4.4 million, immediately resulting in a highly successful subscription process at

Grocers' Hall. None of this meant that the Bank had suddenly become a universally accepted, let alone welcomed, institution. 'The malignity of the Bank is of that extent that I know not well where to begin my account of it,' declared in 1708 the anonymous author of a public letter to an MP, *Arguments against Prolonging the Bank, Showing the Dangerous Consequences of it to our Constitution and Trade*. Still, in terms of prevailing sentiment, in the City anyway, that same year a London correspondent of Thomas Pitt at Madras surely had the right of it. 'The Bank,' he wrote, 'not only in my own opinion but of all my acquaintance, is thought the surest estate, and scarce any money'd man but has a share which he looks upon as his nest egg.'[8]

What sort of place was the Bank by the time this new deal was struck? 'I looked into the Great Hall,' Joseph Addison would note a year or two later in the *Spectator*, 'and was not a little pleased to see the Directors, Secretaries and Clerks, with all the other Members of that Wealthy Corporation, ranged in their several stations, according to the Parts they act in that just and regular Oeconomy.' The directors remained predominantly merchants, typified by Francis Eyles, a Wiltshire clothier's son who became a prominent Levant and colonial merchant and, having been elected a director in 1697, served as governor for what was becoming the usual two-year term, in his case 1707 to 1709. But in terms of the conduct of the Bank's day-to-day business, the people who really mattered during these formative years were not 'the Direction' (as it came to be called) but its first generation of permanent, full-time staff.

Inevitably their numbers increased (over sixty by 1700), though it would be a long time before their total reached three figures; as for their functions, the clerical staff were mainly divided into those working in the Accountant's Office, those in the Cashier's Office, those in the Secretary's Office, those in the Discount Office, and the tellers. The heaviest burden probably lay on the last group: over twenty of them by the early 1700s, situated in the handsome banking hall at Grocers' Hall, and in effect the public face of the bank – accepting deposits and loan payments, cashing notes and bills, and from 1704 subject to a detailed four-page 'Orders for the Observance of the Tellers of the Bank'. Theirs was demanding work, not helped by poor-quality coinage and the ever-present danger of forgery of paper instruments of exchange, and one of the many specific stipulations was that 'the Teller Indorse the persons name to whom they pay mony on Notes payable to Order, and if unbeknown the place of his abode'. There were also of course non-clerical staff, comprising by 1704 two messengers and doorkeepers, one gate-porter, two house-porters, one house-cleaner, one gardener and six watchmen, with the gate-porter provided by this time with 'a crimson cloth gowne lined with orange, and a large Bamboo cane with a silver head'. Discipline was generally strict: not only were 'the servants of the House' (whether clerical or non-clerical) under threat of instant dismissal for failure to comply with the rules of the Bank, but they were required on pain of suspension to report on any fellow-employees guilty of 'prophaneness, immorality, loose or scandalous living' in their personal conduct; and although the pay was respectable (the average teller getting around £55 a year, somewhat above what a schoolmaster earned), Anne Murphy's verdict that 'on balance the majority of the Bank's employees would have found its management practices to be more about the stick than the carrot' is surely correct. Still, there were always the consolations of home: an evocative 1704 list shows that although a handful of the most senior staff lived at the Bank, Thomas Jones could retreat to 'his Mothers a Coffeehouse in Starre-Court in Breadstreete', William Deards to 'his owne house in Naggshead Court in Bartholomew Lane by ye Exchange', Robert Lloyde to 'the Middle Temple in Essex Court in the Staircase No. 4 up one paire of staires at Mr. Scroopes chamber', and Thomas Cowell to 'Hony Lane market, at ye Bell a Publick House'.[9]

What exactly, then, *was* the nature of the Bank's day-to-day business during its first fifteen or so years? Elements of mystery remain, but essentially what it did – as a private (as opposed to public) bank, in addition to its ever-closer connection with government – was to provide a range of indispensable services for the London mercantile community. These services included issuing banknotes and other paper credit instruments; providing deposit, account and payment transfer facilities; making carefully selected loans; and discounting bills of exchange. As for services on behalf of government, over and above making regular loans and advances as well as its facilitating role in relation to Exchequer bills, the Bank did not yet manage the long-term national debt. But it did increasingly act as banker to what Clapham calls 'the great national accounts', such as 'during Marlborough's wars the Paymaster of the Army, the Paymaster of Guards and Garrisons, the Treasurer of the Ordnance Office and the Treasurer of the Navy'. All in all, whether for the mercantile community or for government, but especially for the latter, it was a profitable business; and between 1697 and 1709, the annual dividend payment to stockholders invariably amounted to at least 7 per cent and was often significantly more.

One should not exaggerate the reach of the early Bank of England – after all, for much of the eighteenth century it was quite often referred to as the 'Bank of London'. Moreover, unlike the appreciably older Bank of Amsterdam, the Bank 'did not', to quote the historians Larry Neal and Stephen Quinn, 'dominate the local bill market, it did not act as a large-scale clearing house, and no bills were required to pass through it'. Instead, notwithstanding its other services to the mercantile community, it was a 'note-issuing bank, committed to serving the British Treasury'. Undoubtedly a key aspect of that service was the part the Bank played in helping the development of what other historians have called 'credible commitment' – that key post-1688 evolution of an institutional structure by which the new dispensation of parliamentary government could be more widely trusted than had ever been the case in the age of Crown-dominated public finance. Or put more specifically, the Bank's role in almost all new loans to government was soon so central that in effect it acted as guarantor of responsible behaviour, not least in relation to the prompt payment of interest. Yet at the time, it must be re-emphasised, not everyone saw the Bank in such a favourable, public-interest light. 'Its status was contested, its monopoly at risk, and it remained highly vulnerable to the whim of Parliament': even after the 1709 enhanced deal, Murphy's salutary words still apply.[10] And indeed the Bank at this point had still to face perhaps the biggest threat of all to its very existence.

The sequence of events that eventually led to that threat began in 1710 – a year of intense political drama, with the Bank under the take-no-prisoners leadership of Sir Gilbert Heathcote (governor from

1709) positioned uncomfortably close to the drama's centre. The larger context helps to explain the febrile atmosphere. Public finances under increasing strain, bad harvests, a seemingly endless war (with Heathcote stubbornly insisting to Godolphin, back in office as first lord of the Treasury, that any peace failing to secure war aims in Spain would be 'a rotten peace'), Queen Anne in the ninth year of her reign believing the time at last ripe to get rid of the detestable Whigs – all this, and Dr Henry Sacheverell too. On 27 February the trial began (for seditious libel) of this eloquent high churchman and fierce anti-Whig; within days the Sacheverell Riots were under way; and the mob – intent on looting and burning Grocers' Hall – was thwarted only by the arrival of the Grenadier Guards, whose Captain Orrell had reputedly declared, 'Gentlemen, it is better to have all the [dissenting] meeting-houses destroyed than the Bank.' Sacheverell himself was virtually acquitted, and the Tories by early summer had the wind firmly in their sails, to the alarm of the money men.

Over the next few months, the Bank twice tried to halt political change and twice failed. The first intervention came on 15 June, with Heathcote and three colleagues personally informing the Queen of their 'desire', following the dismissal of the Earl of Sunderland from the government, that 'she would make no further alterations in the ministry which much affect all the public credit'; some seven weeks later, a further Bank deputation, this time to the Treasury and seeking to shore up the position of Godolphin (a pro-Bank moderate Tory who had become increasingly close to the Whigs), only had the effect of goading Anne into dismissing him. That same deputation also demanded an assurance against an early dissolution of the Commons – and again the Bank's wishes were ignored, with an October election resulting in a Tory landslide. Did Heathcote repent at all of the Bank's interventions? Probably not. 'If we err'd,' he confided to a prominent Whig, 't'was in failure of our judg'ments, and God of his mercy grant that that may be the case, but I cannot help being still of the same mind.'[11]

That autumn the politics of the City could hardly have been more charged, with Heathcote in the thick of it. In late September, in the midst of a controversial count and a riot at the mayoral Common Hall, Heathcote was chosen as the next lord mayor; the following month, in the City's parliamentary election, he was one of the four Whig candidates (all of them present or past Bank directors, and three

of them, including Heathcote, sitting MPs) swept aside by the four
Tory candidates (including Sir Richard Hoare), after a five-day poll
marked by, in the words of one historian of the City, 'an atmosphere
of rhetorical and physical violence unmatched since the Revolution'.
The Bank itself continued to dig in its heels and make life as difficult
as possible for Robert Harley's new Tory government – not only still
refusing to discount bills of exchange for military pay officers, but
also now refusing to discount overseas bills of exchange. 'It is only
pique and revenge of Heathcote's and his party who now govern the
Bank absolutely,' a banker-ally of Harley informed him in November,
almost certainly accurately.

The game-changer was the news just before Christmas that Lord
Stanhope's army had surrendered at Brihuega – in effect, spelling an
end to any serious hopes of conquering Spain and of thereby avoiding
Heathcote's 'rotten peace'. By early 1711 there was a palpable spirit of
compromise and co-operation between the Tory government and the
Whig-supporting Bank, much helped by a successful internal rebellion
against Heathcote during the last few months of his governorship, a
rebellion apparently led by two former governors, John Ward and Sir
James Bateman. Even so, at the annual election in April of new directors,
Tories in the City still tried to stage a coup, leading to a much heavier
turn-out by stockholders than usual. The coup failed – in Clapham's
words, 'the crowds of proprietors voted for the men they knew' – and
accordingly it was very much the old Whiggish guard that was returned,
including Nathaniel Goulde as governor and John Rudge as deputy
governor, both of whom had joined the Court back in the 1690s. A more
successful Tory initiative was the formation later in 1711 of the South
Sea Company, intended from the start as a counterweight to the Bank
and designed in essence as a vehicle for converting into perpetual annuities a large chunk of the government's floating debt, with the vaunted
South Sea trading-company aspect being little more than a façade.
Revealingly, and befitting his reputation as a pragmatic operator, Harley
went to great lengths to ensure that the Bank did not feel unduly threatened by the new creation. He was well aware that a rapprochement with
the heart of the monied interest, even if that interest was still defiantly
Whiggish, was too important to be thrown away lightly.[12]

Over the rest of the decade, the Bank largely consolidated its position. In July 1713, three months after the Treaty of Utrecht had at last

ended a war that had seen the national debt triple in size to £52 million, a new act extended the Charter to 1743 in return for the Bank agreeing to circulate a further £1.2 million of Exchequer bills. Politically, the dominant fact was increasingly the Queen's ailing health and fears of a Jacobite-supporting French invasion, leading to at least two significant runs on the Bank. But when Anne did die in August 1714, the Hanoverian succession proceeded, to the Bank's relief, entirely peacefully; and though in May 1715 the Jacobite plan was apparently for 'three mobs to assemble at Smithfield, proclaim the Pretender, seize the Bank of England and set it on fire, assassinate some of the Chief Magistrates (including Sir Gilbert Heathcote) and raise a general insurrection', not only did that dramatic scenario fail to unfold, but later in the year, during the failed actual Jacobite rebellion, the Bank found itself under little serious pressure. Indeed, it was in 1715 itself that the Bank's remit was crucially extended, with the government asking it to handle a supply loan of £910,000 – the first major step in the Bank establishing control over long-term government borrowing. What about the South Sea Company? Relations between it and the Bank were generally reasonable, with the Bank even coming in effect to act as the upstart company's bankers; but by the autumn of 1719 the directors of that company were, in Clapham's words, 'planning great and daring ventures'.[13]

In essence, as its scheme evolved that winter, the South Sea Company (SSC) proposed to take over the national debt (excluding that part owed to the Bank and the East India Company) in return for making a substantial one-off payment into the Exchequer – cash that would enable a financially hard-pressed government to redeem other long-term public debt, including that held by the Bank. What was in it for the SSC? Why might it be so advantageous to have a major swathe of the national debt converted into newly issued shares in the Company? Accounts of the ensuing infamous South Sea Bubble have tended to emphasise the motive of stock market speculation and manipulation; but the historian Richard Kleer has argued that the ambitious debt-conversion project of 1720 had an equally powerful motivation: namely, an attempt by the SSC 'to direct vast new amounts of public money through its coffers and at the same time deprive the Bank of England of most its public cash flow' – so that ultimately, further argues Kleer, the Company would 'supplant the Bank of England and assume the latter's longstanding status as the state's principal lender'. 'Longstanding' is perhaps an exaggeration, given the Bank was still barely a quarter of a century old, but it is a compelling interpretation of what the Bank itself undoubtedly perceived as a very real and very present threat. 'Now they stand ready,' observed Daniel Defoe at the time about the architects of the scheme, 'as occasion offers, and profit presents, to stock-job the nation, cozen the Parliament, ruffle the Bank, run up and down stocks, and put the dice upon the whole town.'[14]

Battle between the SSC and the Bank was joined in late January and early February, as the two rivals bid against each other – and, indeed, seriously over-bid – for the right to convert government debt. It was a hectic few days. On the afternoon of 27 January, the SSC presented a £3½ million offer before the Commons; that same afternoon, the Bank (whose directors had met earlier in the day at Waghorn's Coffee House) offered up to £5½ million for the privilege of enabling holders of long-term government debt to convert into Bank stock. The intrinsic economics may not have been sound, comments John Carswell in his authoritative narrative of the South Sea Bubble, but 'for the Bank the devising of a counter-proposal seemed a matter of life and death'. Then on 1 February the SSC returned to the table with an offer that was not only worth up to £7½ million, but included a promise (directly aimed against the Bank) to circulate £1 million of Exchequer bills without charging interest or a management fee. Meanwhile, the Bank itself was now broadly sticking to its £5½ million offer, no longer enough; and next day, the 2nd, against the wishes of the rising Whig politician Robert Walpole, the Commons accepted the SSC's proposal, immediately causing the price of its stock to rise in Exchange Alley from 129 to 160. Morale at Grocers' Hall slumped. 'I could hear only a few broken words,' reported James Milner, a merchant and MP, about a visit to the Bank probably not long afterwards. '"Buy long annuities, lock up our cash, distress, upstarts, revenge and ruin, &c."'

But elsewhere, as winter gave way to spring and early summer, the SSC – and a plethora of companies formed in the wake of its apparent coup – bubbled away merrily. 'Surprizing scene in Change Alley,' noted an observer by early June. 'S. Sea in the morning above 900 … Professions & shops are forgot, all goe thither as to the mines of Potosi. Nobility, Ladys, Brokers, & footmen all upon a level. Great equipages set up, the prizes of things rose exorbitantly. Such a renversement of the order of Nature as succeeding ages can have no Idea of.' As for its battle with the Bank, predictably the SSC continued to make all the running – partly through muscling into the Bank's customary domain of circulating Exchequer bills, partly through arranging to bring into circulation significant amounts of its own bonds, or in Kleer's words 'laying the groundwork for a push to displace Bank notes from their position as the nation's premier fiduciary currency'. Indeed, so generally rattled was the Bank that in May it committed what Clapham calls the 'grave mistake' of following the example of the SSC by starting to lend on the security of its own stock, so that over the next few months more than £1 million was lent by the Bank to its own proprietors – a not unimportant contribution to the prevailing credit inflation. And for the SSC itself, it must have been a sweet moment when in July the Bank was among the holders of the redeemable national debt that now put those redeemables at the Company's disposal, in the Bank's case up to the value of £300,000: not huge perhaps, but hugely symbolic.[15]

In fact, the tide was already starting to turn. Parliamentary action in June against the bubble companies impacted also on the SSC, whose share price peaked at just over 1,000 by the end of the month, before steadily subsiding to 775 by the start of September and 520 a fortnight later. 'All is floating, all falling, the directors are curst, the top adventurers broke,' observed a contemporary that month; for one gifted young artist, William Hogarth, his first great subject was at hand, with his subsequent print of *The South Sea Scheme* showing Self Interest breaking Honesty on the wheel, Villainy flogging Honour, and Trade lying ragged and abandoned.

That autumn of 1720, as the SSC's price continued southwards, to 290 at the start of October and 170 by mid-October, before picking up a little, the Bank's role in starting to resolve what was a general crisis of public credit is not easy to chart with certainty. During negotiations from 15 to 23 September that eventually led to the so-called 'Bank Contract' under the overall auspices of Walpole, the Bank (with the indomitable Heathcote to the fore) imposed two key conditions for agreeing to circulate £3 million in SSC bonds: first, that the Company would henceforth keep its cash with the Bank – or, as Heathcote put it, 'if the South Sea Company be wedded to the Bank, he ought not to be allowed to keep a mistress'; and second, that the Bank would be allowed to exchange for South Sea stock its £3.8 million of redeemable debt. 'In effect,' comments Kleer, 'this meant that the Bank would keep its existing cash flow and get access to the whole of the new flows associated with the debt-conversion project,' which in turn meant that 'the Bank would also retain its current position as the government's chief credit purveyor'. The next few weeks were difficult: such was the market's gloomy post-Bubble state that subscriptions to the newly created Bank Contract stock fell well short of the intended £3 million; the Bank itself was under pressure from a serious run, even as it called in loans and increased its bullion stock; while among many merchants and others now going down was Sir Justus Beck, a leading director of the Royal Exchange and a former director of the Bank. 'How terrible a calamity the fall of South Sea Stock has produced in a few days,' lamented Joseph Moyle, writing on 12 October to his cousin Humphry Morice, a Bank director and a Whig MP, big in the Africa trade (gold, ivory, slaves) and very friendly with Walpole. Even so, there was probably some truth in what Moyle then added: 'I am however very glad that the Bank made so noble a stand in such ticklish times, and has showed themselves, as indeed they are, the only Support of credit, and the true Balance of the nation's interest.'[16]

Further twists and turns lay ahead in what became a protracted process, not least after the Bank itself in November had controversially repudiated the Bank Contract, on the possibly dubious – and certainly belated – grounds of changed circumstances. Eventually, in October 1722, the so-called 'Bank Treaty' saw the Bank agreeing to pay (through the issue of new stock) £4.2 million for £200,000 per annum of the SSC's 'Exchequer annuity', at last enabling the SSC to get back into the black and start to pay off its bond debt. The SSC was saved – but would never again be a major financial force. As for public credit more generally, the Bank signed earlier that year an important new contract with the Treasury over the circulation of Exchequer bills; while, despite the fiasco of the SSC itself, the beneficial fact was that the conversion of a mass of illiquid annuities into liquid and tradable South Sea annuities left the legacy of a hugely enhanced secondary market, above all for government debt. There was also of course a personal dimension to the Bubble's aftermath. Among those found guilty by the House of Commons in 1721 for having been partly responsible for the dramatic chain of events was Sir Theodore Janssen, a founder-director of the Bank and on the Court as recently as 1719. 'I had no hand in contriving the scheme,' he protested to MPs; and although he had his estate confiscated, he was permitted to retain £50,000 out of his considerable fortune – some consolation as he lived out his last twenty-seven years until his death in 1748, the last of the men of 1694.[17]

Daniel Defoe in 1724 not only described the Bank's home in Grocers' Hall as 'a very spacious, commodious place'. He also noted admiringly that 'here Business is dispatched with such Exactness, and such Expedition and so much of it too, that it is really prodigious; no Confusion, nobody is either denied or delayed Payment, the Merchants who keep their cash there, are sure to have their Bills always paid, and even Advances made on easy Terms, if they have Occasion'. In short: 'No Accounts in the World are more exactly kept, no place in the World has so much Business done, with so much Ease.' It was a glowing tribute to an organisation that during the post-Bubble decade was becoming increasingly indispensable, not least to government. Managing a large part of the national debt, taking responsibility for underwriting and paying the interest on Exchequer bills on the annual taxes, making short-term loans (to the paymaster general of the forces, to the treasurer of the Navy, above all to the lords of the Treasury during these largely peaceful years under Walpole's 'Robinocracy'), managing a range of government securities (following on from the 1717 establishment of a sinking fund), responding to the Macclesfield scandal of 1725 (involving the impeachment of a lord chancellor) by taking charge of all Chancery monies and securities – in these and many other ways, including in relation to private commerce, the Bank justified its place in national life as, to quote the historian Paul Langford, 'a uniquely favoured corporation'.

Unsurprisingly, dividends were reassuringly solid, from 1721 to 1733 invariably between 5½ and 6 per cent, prompting John Hanger, governor during the Bubble and still a director, to reflect in 1731 that 'the prosperity of the Bank' was 'very agreeable to me'. Hanger himself was by this time among some 8,000 or more stockholders, with foreigners (especially Dutch) owning perhaps some 17 per cent of the capital stock, but still with the overwhelming majority of the Bank's proprietors being individuals living in London or the Home Counties – above all members of the City's prosperous mercantile community, including of course many merchants, but also bankers and brokers. As for the directors, if there was between the mid-1720s and early 1730s a single dominant figure, it was probably no longer Heathcote (even though he served a second term as governor, 1723–5) but Samuel Holden, a director from 1720 and governor between 1729 and 1731. He was also a leading merchant, governor of the Russia Company for twelve years from 1728, MP for the rotten borough of East Looe in Cornwall, friendly with Walpole, and a prominent nonconformist, being chairman of the Dissenting Deputies Committee, albeit (in a biographer's words) 'conspicuously reluctant to run a noisy public campaign for the repeal of the Test and Corporation Acts'. Altogether Holden's was a life of the utmost respectability; and when he died in 1740, still a Bank director, he left £80,000 and instructions that 'what of my estate may exceed £60,000 (exclusive of Land) be distributed in charitable uses at the discretion of my wife and children [two unmarried daughters] such as promoting true religion, sobriety, Righteousness and Godliness'.[18]

In reality, not everything in the final phase at Grocers' Hall was quite as well ordered as it might have been. A rash of scandals, internal as well as external, began with a trio in 1721: during what turned out to be a terminal illness, William Stubbs, one of the most trusted cashiers, drew fictitious bills via his son John, also working at the Bank; a fraudulent transfer of £350 of Bank stock, involving a Jewish broker called Moses Waag, eventually led to two members of staff vainly pursuing him across much of Europe; and a Cambridge-educated medical student called George Nicholas, who had fallen into criminal company, was found guilty of altering the value of a handwritten banknote, leading to a death sentence subsequently commuted to transportation for life. Note forgery also featured in the 1724–5 cases of Philip Lodgeing and Francis Kyte, with the latter's punishment being to stand in the pillory on Little Tower Hill; and as a result of these and similar cases, an agreement was reached with the paper-maker Henry Portal, of Whitchurch in Hampshire, to supply 'Paper for Bank Notes of the like Goodness or fitter for their Service than the paper now used', though it would be a considerable time yet before a similar upgrade was made to printing methods for the notes. Security concerns also motivated the decision in 1728 to start issuing promissory notes 'at three Days' Sight', which in practice proved less than adequate time for rightful owners to notify the Bank of forgery or theft, and ten years later the period of grace would be extended to seven days' sight.

By then there had been the two scandals of 1731. The first was bad enough, involving a clerk in the Accountant's Office, William Maynee, found guilty of having for several years 'carried on a fraudulent prac-tice in the business of Accountable Receipts', leading to Bank losses of £4,420 and for Maynee himself an appointment at Tyburn, at which place of hanging he 'begged pardon of the Court of Directors, prayed for the prosperity of the Bank, and died very penitent'. The second scandal was worse. 'I think it a little hard to have your business encroach more this year upon you than ever it did since I was so happy to be your wife as not to allow you time to come down oftener than once a week, but as it is I must submit to it & live in hopes of better days,' Mrs Katherine Morice wrote in September 1728 to her husband from her paren-tal home in Wandsworth, before adding: 'I have thus long harangued upon this subject.' She was the second wife of Humphry Morice, then in the middle of his term as governor. Three years later, in November 1731, Morice suddenly died – at which point it was discovered that he had discounted with the Bank a whole series of fictitious bills in order to secure advances of nearly £29,000, quite possibly in order to buy a peerage from Walpole. Would the merchant's widow now repay to the Bank the money obtained by such 'unwarrantable practices'? No, decided Katherine; and it would be many years after her death in 1743 that the Bank managed to recover even as much as £12,000.[19]

But for his own death, Morice would have been present a few weeks later on 16 December 1731 when the Court of Directors, conscious of the Bank's recent growth and potential for future growth, not to mention enhanced status, took a fundamental decision: to end nego-tiations with the Grocers' Company over a fresh lease and instead to go ahead with building a new, bespoke home for the Bank. Four of the older directors (including Heathcote, who himself would die barely a year later) dissented; but the decision was final, confirmed by the General Court's unanimous vote in January 1732 to erect 'a new publick office for the Bank upon the Bank's estate in Threadneedle Street'. Appropriately, the site had been acquired from the widow of the Bank's first governor, Sir John Houblon, whose mansion house was soon afterwards demolished; and, amid considerable competition, the architect chosen for the job was George Sampson, probably getting the nod because of his plan's adherence to the principles of classical composition (or what Daniel Abramson in his definitive history of the Bank's architecture calls 'the classical standards of anthropomorphic composition and beauty as enunciated by Vitruvius'). The construction process ran some eight months behind schedule, but on 5 June 1734 – virtually forty years on from those formative summer days – the Bank opened for business at its new premises.[20]

A Great Engine of State

'The Bank was comfortable,' Sir John Clapham would write about the 1730s – that decade of almost unbroken peace, of Sir Robert Walpole still managing for the most part to let sleeping dogs lie. One City man, the public-spirited MP and marine insurance underwriter Sir John Barnard, was less comfortable. Urging that the key to national prosperity and lower taxation lay in reducing the interest on the national debt, he put forward in March 1737 a plan that envisaged a reduction from 4 to 3 per cent, including on the government's debt to the Bank. That institution, he told the Commons, was a 'powerful and rich company' whose stockholders 'of late years' had 'in some measure become masters of the public credit of the nation'; and he plausibly predicted that they would 'certainly oppose, with all their might, a scheme concerted for the ruin of their company, and for making every particular man in it lose at least 50 per cent of what he may then call himself worth'.

That was on the 14th, and over the next six weeks or so a short, intense squall played out. 'The House of Commons this day confirmed that the national debts shall be reduced to 3 per cent, against which the moneyed men clamour exceedingly, and this day there was a run on the Bank,' noted the Earl of Egmont in his diary on 30 March, as gold began to drain from the Bank. The following evening he heard the latest from his brother: 'He said he had been in the city, where the run continued on the Bank and every face appeared confounded; that the stocks continued to fall; that the Bank directors held a court this morning to depute a committee to Sir Robert Walpole ...' Things had barely improved a week later, with another observer, Sir Thomas

Robinson, recording on 7 April that 'the Stocks begin to rise again, but the run still continues on the Bank, and they pay in silver all demands above 50 pounds'. All now turned on Walpole: albeit privately sympathetic to Barnard's scheme, he decided that the City's – including the Bank's – opposition was too fierce to be challenged. By the 21st he was reported as being 'determined to throw it out'; and just over a week later, on the 29th, he ensured that Barnard's Bill was decisively rejected by the Commons. 'Great rejoicings were made in the City,' noted Egmont next day, adding that not only was Barnard 'burnt in effigy', but the cry went up 'Long live Sir Robert Walpole for ever.'[1]

Five years later, the country was at war again (the War of the Austrian Succession), Walpole had lost power, the state needed money, and it was time for that ritualistic dance that was the periodic renewal of the Bank's Charter. 'Resolved,' stated the minutes of the Court of Directors in March 1742,

> That it is the opinion of this Court, That the Bank may advance the sum of Twelve Hundred Thousand Pounds for the Service of the Publick, on their present Annuity of One Hundred Thousand Pounds payable the 1ˢᵗ of August 1743, in Order to purchase a Term of 21 Years longer from that time for the Existence of the Corporation of the Bank, and a prolongation of their Priviledge of Exclusive Banking for the same time, together with a Confirmation of all the Clauses and other Priviledges granted them by their Charter, or Acts of Parliament, *now in force*, and with such further Advantages as shall be hereafter Agreed on …

In the event, the Treasury successfully held out for a £1.6 million loan as the price of renewal, taking the government's debt to the Bank to a total of £10.7 million; the Bank in turn increased its own capital by £840,000, taking it up to a total of £9.8 million; and that telling phrase 'exclusive banking' was duly incorporated in the 1742 Act, its first appearance in an English statute. Yet arguably 1742 was more significant in the Bank's history because it was from this year that, in a war context, there began a series of publicly subscribed long-term loans to the government that were entered at the Bank in special subscription ledgers and, more generally, were entirely administered by the Bank.[2] Put another way, the demands of war finance were starting to become too big for the Bank to be able to continue its role as a principal direct supplier to government. Rather, its future now lay in facilitating, in organising, in enabling; and as such, it rapidly became indispensable to the functioning of a national financial war machine that was soon the envy of all rival powers.

It was the course of the war, and specifically the defeat of the Allies at Fontenoy, that gave the green light to the Jacobite rebellion of 1745 under the leadership of the 'Young Pretender'. On 21 September, Prince Charles Edward Stuart's Highlanders defeated Hanoverian troops at Prestonpans, news of which caused serious alarm in London, including the almost inevitable run on the Bank – 'a hurry' that the *Gentleman's Magazine* subsequently sought to explain: "Twas said to be occasioned by the *Papists* and *Jacobites*, with design to hurt credit as much as was in their power and to get gold to send to the rebels; in which the directors wisely disappointed them, by ordering payment in silver.' Paying demands for cash with silver shillings and sixpences was a tactic out of the 1720 playbook, but on the 26th the directors also ordered that 'no Bills of Exchange be discounted which have more than a Month to run, and those only with such persons who keep Cash with the Bank'. The key intervention, though, came later that day:

> Several very eminent merchants of *London*, considerable traders and proprietors of the publick funds, met, about noon, at *Garraway's* coffee-house [reported the *Gentleman's Magazine*], and with the utmost alacrity came to the following agreement, for supporting the public credit. 'We the undersign'd merchants and others, being sensible how necessary the preservation of public credit is at this time, do hereby declare, that we will not refuse to receive bank notes in payment of any sum of money to be paid to us. And we will use our utmost endeavours to make all our payments in the same manner'; and by five next afternoon 1140 had sign'd it.

This Change Alley démarche did much to restore confidence during the autumn, but it was not quite the end of the story. By 4 December the Young Pretender had reached Derby, causing a fresh wave of metropolitan panic; and just over a week later, in order to boost the Bank's depleted bullion reserve, the directors called in 20 per cent from those who had subscribed to the 'last subscription for circulating Exchequer Bills'. The following month, January 1746, saw a £1 million loan to government, a tacit recognition that the Bank needed to do its bit in the suppression of the Scottish rebels; in February the stockholders (aka proprietors) voted that a not hugely handsome £1,000 be contributed to a City fund 'for the relief, support and encouragement of His Majesty's forces'; and two months later, the rebellion ended bloodily enough at Culloden.[3] The Hanoverian settlement, and all the mercantile prosperity that flowed from it, was at last safe.

The Treaty of Aix-la-Chapelle in 1748 finally brought the war to an end, by which time the national debt had risen to some £77 million, with all its attendant servicing costs, compared to £46 million before the war. The chancellor was the much underrated Henry Pelham, who in the course of 1749 steered through Parliament a bill to reduce the interest on the 4 per cent Funds to 3½ per cent from 1750 and then to 3 per cent from 1757. The landed interest naturally welcomed the prospect of lower taxes, the moneyed interest for the moment stayed its hand, the Bank was apparently not consulted, and the deadline set for fundholders to signify their consent to Pelham's scheme was the end of February 1750. Everyone knew that the crux would be the attitude of the three moneyed companies (the South Sea Company and the East India Company as well as the Bank itself): although the debt due to them comprised barely a quarter of the overall funded debt, the justifiable assumption was that individual fundholders would look to the companies for guidance and almost certainly follow their example.

By the time the Bank's General Court assembled on the morning of 31 January 1750 at Merchant Taylors' Hall in Threadneedle Street, the equivalent bodies of the other two companies had already indicated a significant degree of resistance. The governor, William Hunt, began proceedings by recommending that 'their Debates on the Proposals be carried on with Calmness of Temper and Respect to one another as becomes Gentlemen who have but one view or Design which is the Prosperity and Safety of their Corporation'. The directors themselves do not seem to have participated in the ensuing discussion, while a

contemporary press report revealed that among the Bank's proprietors arguing for an acceptance of the scheme was the great Jewish
financier Samson Gideon, a key Pelham ally. The report also revealed
the outcome: 'After some Debates, the Majority (which was at least
Five to One) were against the Question.' Given that a lower rate of
interest meant lower profits for what was still a private organisation,
this was not on the face of it a surprising outcome.

Could Pelham turn it round? His other key ally was the indomitable Barnard, who a week after the Bank's overwhelming negative
brought out a pamphlet, *Considerations on the Proposals for Reducing
the Interest on the National Debt*, that cogently argued both a
moral-cum-political case (the unfortunate implications of flouting the
authority of Parliament) and a financial case (that 3 per cent was now
the normal market rate of interest, enabling the government if necessary
to raise a loan to pay off those who did not come in). 'Tom Telltruth',
calling himself 'a Bank Proprietor', grumbled in a letter to the *General
Advertiser* on 19 February – 'the Generality of the publick Contracts
hitherto made between the Legislature and the Bank, have been to the
Prejudice of the Bank Proprietors' – but by the time the General Court
reassembled at Merchant Taylors' Hall on the 27th, the resistance was
already starting to weaken. At that meeting, Hunt made it clear that
the view of the Court of Directors was in favour of accepting Pelham's
proposals; Gideon again took a prominent role in the debate; and in
the words of the *General Advertiser*'s report, 'the question being put,
it was by a very great Majority carried in the Affirmative'.

The inner story of the Bank's volte-face is impossible to uncover.
'It would be nice to know,' wistfully reflects one historian, 'what arts
Gideon used to turn the lion of January into the lamb of February.' But,
in any case, the success of Pelham's scheme was now assured; and in
1752 much of the national debt was consolidated into one fund which
became known as 'Consols', with their entire management entrusted to
the Bank. For whatever mixture of motives, the proprietors – a significant minority of them foreign, mainly Dutch, although not voting
unless prepared to travel to London – had done a good day's work.[4]

Indeed, Pelham's scheme could hardly have been more timely,
for it was not long before the fife and drum were heard again. The
Seven Years War (1756–63) had of course its splendidly patriotic,
empire-building aspect – 'Our bells are worn threadbare with ringing

from victories,' observed Horace Walpole at one point – and was in many ways a tribute to the development since the 1690s of the state's financial sinews of power, not least through the offices of the Bank. Some, though, continued to worry about the ever-steeper rise in the national debt, up to £139 million by the end of hostilities, a rise that inevitably much increased the Bank's daily workload. As ever, war put pressure on the Bank's holdings of gold and silver, so that in 1759 notes for £10 and £15 were issued for the first time (the previous lowest denomination being £20) in an attempt to relieve that pressure. And in the event, the financial crisis that many had been dreading came not during the war, but in its immediate wake.

The 1763 crisis, starting to unfold within months of the Peace of Paris being signed in February, was essentially Continental in origin – above all, the collapse of some twenty of Amsterdam's major mercantile houses, in turn leading to a series of bankruptcies in London. Almost certainly the consequences could, but for the Bank, have been far worse. 'The British merchants,' declared David Macpherson in his 1805 *Annals of Commerce*, 'acted with the most honorable liberality by giving large credit to their [European] correspondents ... and even sending large remittances for their support, which they were enabled to do by the no less liberal determination of the Bank of England and the principal bankers to support payment of their own bills'; while, according to George Chalmers in his 1812 *Comparative Strength of Great Britain and Ireland*, the Bank during the crisis discounted bills of exchange in large amounts, in effect supplying emergency credit. Quantitative analysis by the historian Michael Lovell supports these assertions: even though its reserve ratio (the ratio of bullion to notes in circulation) fell to an alarming 6.9 per cent by August 1763, compared to almost 52 per cent a year earlier, the Bank's high level of discount operations during the crisis unambiguously indicates that, in Lovell's words, 'it stood by willing to provide aid in large proportions' – that, in fact, it was 'serving as lender of last resort', probably for the first time. Did this represent a deliberate policy shift? There is nothing in the minutes of the Court of Directors to confirm that this was the case; and Lovell may well be right when he suggests that the liberal approach reflected the behaviour of an institution now instinctively feeling more secure in its position, as well as less apprehensive about its ability to maintain convertibility into cash (gold or silver) on its notes. Either way, acting as lender of last resort marked a signal moment: whether consciously or otherwise, it was the Bank's 'first step' (to quote Lovell again) 'towards the adoption of the powers and responsibilities of central banking'.[5]

Contemporary observers occasionally let themselves go. The Bank of England, claimed the *London Chronicle* in 1765, was the 'grandest, as well as the most commodious repository of wealth and business in Europe, if not the whole world'. Still, it was a grandness that, financially speaking, had to be taken largely on trust, given that before the 1790s the Bank was muteness itself when it came to explaining and detailing its activities and ambitions to the outside world. Almost two centuries later, the economist Joseph Schumpeter would reflect on this 'reticence of its official spokesmen who, even when they were forced to say something, did their best to confine themselves to innocuous trivialities that would give as little scope to hostile criticism as possible'. After noting that 'practitioners of business are rarely able to formulate their own behaviour correctly', he went on:

The Bank had few friends. Control is now [*circa* 1950] a popular word. It was the reverse of popular in the epoch of intact capitalism. To say openly that the Bank was trying to control the banking system, let alone to manage the general business situation, would have evoked laughter if not indignation: the thing to say was that the Bank was modestly looking after its own business; that it simply followed the market; and that it harbored no pretensions at controlling anything or anybody. Moreover, in the formative stage of its policy, it would have been madness to assume in so many words the responsibilities that we now attribute to a central bank as a matter of course. This would have meant commitments which the Bank could not have been sure of being able to fulfil. Moreover, any spectacular announcement of policy would have brought down upon directors hosts of unbidden advisers, every one of them convinced that he knew much better what the Bank ought to do – and there would have been the danger of public outcries for legislation to force the Bank to take, or to refrain from taking, particular courses of action.

It was a reticence that Adam Anderson for one sympathised with. In his pioneering 1764 survey, *An Historical and Chronological Deduction of the Origin of Commerce*, his section on the Bank of England included this tellingly cautionary passage:

> Some might possibly be so much farther inquisitive, as to form Conjectures, (for they can be no other) concerning the proportion which the *Quantum* of ready Cash always necessary to be reserved in this or any other public or private Bank ... We can see no Benefit which can arise by any such minute Enquiries, to the Generality of Men; neither do we apprehend them proper to be enquired into at all, without there should arise any reasonable Suspicion for Fraud. For, as it has been a political Observation of long standing, *That even the reputation of great and powerful Monarchies and States often subsists more by common Fame or Opinion than by real Strength or Ability*, so it may more strictly and properly be applicable to a *Bank* and *Bankers* ...[6]

Perhaps inevitably, and for a mixture of reasons, the eighteenth century remains the part of the Bank's history we know the least about; but it is still possible to summarise its main day-to-day functions during its first half-century or so in Threadneedle Street.

A starting point is its management of almost three-quarters of the national debt, a task involving considerable administrative complexity – or, at the least, attention to detail – in return for an annual management fee. By 1774, in addition to managing the debt owed by the state to the Bank itself as a corporation (amounting to £11.7 million), the Bank had responsibility for five classes of loan: in essence, acting as the government's agent by on the one hand registering ownership and transfers of stock, on the other hand distributing interest, usually half-yearly. As itemised by J. E. D. Binney in his invaluable study of British public finance in the late eighteenth century, these five loan stocks were: the Civil List 3 Per Cents of 1726; 3 Per Cent Consolidated stock (Consols), whose market price was 'the yardstick by which government credit was customarily measured'; the 3 Per Cents Reduced; the 3½ Per Cents of 1758 (whose rate of interest was due to reduce to 3 per cent in 1782); and the 4 Per Cents of 1760–2 (again due to reduce to 3 per cent in 1782). The Bank in 1774 also managed the so-called 'Long Annuities', which derived from the ninety-nine-year annuities of 1761 and were due to expire in 1860. Importantly, the Bank from the late 1760s also provided a bespoke marketplace, the newly built Brokers' Exchange (also known as the Rotunda), in order to stimulate trading in the national debt and thereby a sufficiently liquid secondary market – in turn facilitating the issuance of new debt in the highly probable event that it should be needed. Significantly, the Bank's transfer and dividend offices, where the public went to register stock transactions and to collect dividends, were physically close to the Rotunda; and the historian Anne Murphy is surely right to suggest that this publicly accessible and highly visible mixture of market liquidity and 'a one-stop shop' for the efficient execution of 'all business relating to the public debt' made a key contribution to the enhanced credibility of public credit. In short, 'the Bank was undeniably a space in which public credit was put on display and the financial integrity of the state was demonstrated'.[7]

That said, the area of the Bank's real dominance in relation to government lay in *short-term* lending – an area where there was little doubt which party enjoyed the thick end of the wedge. 'The Exchequer Bill contract,' complained a government informant in 1754, 'is signed annually in July and is advantageous to the Bank; because as they are Cashiers to the Exchequer, and have seldom less in their hands than a million of Exchequer Cash, they lend the Government their own Money. For this they lodge in the Tellers hands, by way of Security, Exchequer Bills for the Value.' Admittedly, government received each year a reliable £1–3 million, as the Bank agreed to take and circulate Exchequer bills up to a certain maximum; but given the Bank's increasingly central position as the government's bank (with accounts held there by the middle of the century including for the Army, Navy and Ordnance, as well as for many collectors of revenue), it was a not unreasonable charge that the Bank was in effect lending the government's own money *to* the government. Moreover, the annual process of renewing 'the Subscription for the Circulation' was in itself an undeniably nice little earner for the Bank's inner circle. 'The Subscription has been filled for the most Part, by People in the Management and their Favourites,' observed the Dutch financier Nicholas Magens in 1753. 'Those who have interest to procure it commonly dispose of it at a handsome advance, before even they have paid in their subscription money … it being thought no Risque.' Other ways in which the Bank was able to provide government with ready money included taking Navy and Ordnance bills, while it was also willing to make substantial advances (almost £5 million in 1777) on the two most reliable taxes, 'Land and Malt', with government paying back the advances as those taxes were collected.[8] In sum, the Bank's short-term financial help may have been self-interested to a degree; but from the state's point of view it could hardly have discharged its responsibilities without that help.

Another Bank activity that by the second half of the eighteenth century increasingly had 'public' implications concerned the money supply. Outside London, it was country-bank notes that were the main medium of exchange, in line with the rapid growth of provincial private banks (up to nearly 400 by the 1790s); but in London significant payments usually involved Bank of England notes, though occasionally the notes of London private banks. Importantly, the latter notes were convertible to Bank of England notes, which were themselves convertible to gold on demand – what has been called the Pre-classical Gold Standard, functioning from 1717 (when Sir Isaac Newton, master of the Royal Mint, introduced a revised gold–silver ratio in such a way as to put Britain on a de facto gold standard) through to almost the end of the century. From a Bank perspective, it was a far from straightforward regime to operate. The export of bullion may have been illegal, but in practice, as Elisa Newby observes in her pioneering study of the Bank's gold reserve policy in this era, 'British monetary gold was withdrawn from the Bank and smuggled to the continent when the exchanges were unfavourable and the price of gold abroad was higher than at home.' And she goes on: 'Disruptions in gold supply and shipping conditions, especially during warfare on the sea, made the gold convertibility rule a challenging task to follow. Bank runs and financial panics were relatively common and demand for gold was at its highest during political disruption. If there were simultaneous gold supply blockades, the Bank of England was in danger of exhausting its gold reserves.'[9]

What, then, was the relationship, if any, between the Bank's note issue on the one hand and its 'cash' (that is, gold) holding on the other? 'Is it now, or was it ever your Understanding or Opinion, that the Bank of England, kept Cash equal, or nearly equal, to the Amount of the Sums secured by all the Bank Notes in Circulation?' a parliamentary inquiry in the 1790s asked Samuel Hoare, a prominent London banker who was also a shareholder in the Bank of England. 'No,' answered Hoare. 'My opinion is, that they generally preserved a Proportion, as 3 to 5, that is, if they had three Millions Sterling they might Issue five Millions Paper in Times of Security.' Responding to the same inquiry, a Bank director and former governor, Samuel Bosanquet, reflected something of the strain involved, noting that 'it is possible for the Bank to be in a much safer Situation, with a much smaller Sum in Specie when Public Affairs are prosperous, than with a much larger Sum and an apprehension that that Sum is draining away'. And: 'Whenever there is an Influx of Bullion into the Country, the Bank have nothing to fear; when a Drain takes place from the Country, is in general the Period for them to be alarmed.' The sense of apprehension was eloquent, and Clapham reckons that towards the end of the century anxiety usually set in when the Bank's gold reserves fell significantly below £5 million, out of a national bullion stock of perhaps £15–20 million. Given which, a reply in the affirmative might have been expected when the inquiry asked the governor of the day, Daniel Giles, whether the Bank had 'any system of measures' for acquiring bullion. Instead, Giles merely replied: 'When it is advantageous to bring it in, individuals will bring it.' Or, as Clapham comments, that was a remark exemplifying what had become 'the established policy of letting external forces play on the Bank rather than attempting to guide them'.[10] No doubt there was the occasional exception – not least the vigorous response to the 1763 crisis – but the broader truth seems to hold.

That response in 1763 had taken the form of liberal discounting (buying) of bills, and indeed it was particularly from the 1760s that the Bank's discount business really grew as a core and increasingly profitable activity that at the same time was invaluable to the functioning of the City. 'As a general rule,' notes Clapham, 'it felt bound to oblige anyone – any business person that is – introduced by a Director [of the Bank] and offering paper with "two good London names" on it. It might show reluctance to do business with particular firms for precise reasons, and it never dealt in very long-dated bills; but apart from that it was open-handed … the greatest and most accessible haven of refuge for storm-tossed traders and, at the last, bankers also.' So, a much appreciated, indeed indispensable, 'haven of refuge', offering short-term credit (usually thirty or sixty days) at 5 per cent (for most of the century the legal maximum rate of interest). Even so, Clapham's phrase about 'particular firms for precise reasons' is also suggestive. Here the key witness is Sir Francis Baring, as a young man the founder in 1763 of what became the prestigious merchant bank Baring Brothers & Co, and on his death in 1810 described as 'unquestionably the first merchant in Europe'. Towards the end of his life, he recalled how 'before the Revolution [of 1789 in France] our Bank (of England) was the centre upon which all credit and circulation depended, and it was at that time in the power of the Bank to affect the credit of individuals in a very great degree of refusing their paper'. Who had their paper refused? Presumably it could be a range of people and firms, for a range of reasons, but the historian Stanley Chapman has no hesitation in making a key identification. 'Through the eighteenth century,' he observes in his history of the highly successful Raphael banking-cum-stockbroking family, 'the Bank of England stood at the apex of commercial credit in England and world trade, and the Bank's directors were known to be anti-Semitic. There was no secret about this; it was a recognised feature of their policy.'[1] Almost certainly he is right. A degree of anti-Semitism – perhaps never virulent, but seldom entirely absent – would be an integral part of the Bank's culture for its first two and a half centuries, and arguably even a little longer.

What else did the Bank do (or not do)? The other main activity was private loans, prior to the 1760s usually producing an income greater than that from discounting. Importantly, these loans were neither to small businesses nor to fund the embryonic Industrial Revolution. Rather, as Clapham explains: 'Described as private, the chief of these loans were really of a semi-public character. Very few names of individual borrowers are to be found in the Court Books in normal times. The great borrower was, as it always had been, the East India Company ...' Other regular loans, sometimes indeed in the form of running loans, were to the South Sea Company, the Hudson's Bay Company and the Royal Bank of Scotland. By contrast, in terms of another potential area of business, the Bank by the late eighteenth century seems to have been still some way from having made itself into the automatic banker's bank. 'Only a minority, and a rather small minority at that, of the London bankers certainly had drawing accounts in Threadneedle Street in 1774,' notes Clapham, adding that 'not quite half had such accounts in 1794'. That development awaited. Yet, taking the Bank's activities as a whole during its formative Threadneedle Street decades, the Scottish economist Adam Smith was surely justified in reaching in 1776 his celebrated verdict – a verdict that pointed clear-sightedly to how the institution's future would ultimately lie in the public rather than the private realm. After calling the Bank 'the greatest bank of circulation in Europe', he went on in his seminal *An Inquiry into the Nature and Causes of the Wealth of Nations*:

> The stability of the bank of England is equal to that of the British government. All that it has advanced to the publick must be lost before its creditors can sustain any loss. No other banking company in England can be established by act of parliament, or can consist of more than six members. It acts, not only as an ordinary bank, but as a great engine of state.[12]

What about the directors themselves? Thanks to the diligence of W. Marston Acres, whose findings appeared in *Notes and Queries* during the darkest days of the Second World War, we know some-thing – though in some cases not very much – about each of the 133 men who were directors of the Bank at some stage between 1735 and 1792 inclusive. Their average age on becoming a director was 43.9 years old, with the youngest being 25, the oldest 77; if they became governor, the average age on attaining that office was 56.7, with the youngest being 40, the oldest 71; and the average length of time between becoming a director and finally stopping being a director was 19.7 years, with those lengths varying between one year or less and 56 years. As for occupation, this is identified by Acres for just over half of them, with fifty-six being merchants, while among the other eleven, three were bankers, one was an ironmaster, one was a barrister, one was a wholesale grocer and one was a Blackwall Hall factor. So far so more or less predictable, but fortunately it is possible, on the basis of Acres and other sources, to flesh out the picture further.

Inevitably, family connections and influence continued to be strong, though no single family quite matched the example of the Houblons from the Bank's pioneering era. Take three families: the Rapers, the

Thellussons and the Thorntons. Matthew and Moses Raper were the
two sons of Matthew Raper, an ironmonger who was himself briefly
a director of the Bank in the 1710s. The younger son Moses was a
silk merchant, became a Bank director in 1716 in his mid-thirties, left
the Court in 1742 and on his death six years later was president of
Guy's Hospital; his brother Matthew became a director in 1730 in
his mid-fifties and died in harness in 1748, having made perhaps his
biggest mark on public life as treasurer of the Unitarian Chapel in
Newington Green. For the Thellussons, it was not just family but
a whole intricate network around them. Peter Thellusson came to
London from Paris as a young man in the early 1760s, established a
highly successful merchanting business, and was closely linked with
his fellow-Huguenot Martyn Fonnereau (a director 1771–83 and
himself the grandson of a director) in the victualling of the garrison at
Gibraltar; while Peter's eldest son Peter Isaac grew up in his father's
business and was elected a director in 1787 in his mid-twenties, having
four years earlier married Elizabeth Cornwall, daughter of a former
Bank director (John Cornwall) and cousin of a clutch of Thorntons,
all of them present or future directors. The Thorntons themselves
were seemingly ubiquitous. Robert Thornton, 'a merchant of London
and of Clapham' (Acres), was the eldest son of a Hull merchant and
served as a director from 1732 until his death at the start of 1748;
later that year, his younger brother Godfrey, likewise a merchant,
became a director, before his own death in 1752; Godfrey's third son,
also Godfrey, was elected a director in 1772 and in due course governor; and from 1780 another Thornton director (and future governor)
was his cousin Samuel – born in 1754, eldest son of the remarkable
merchant John Thornton (a founder of the evangelical movement
and said on his death in 1790 to have been the second richest man in
Europe), and himself a partner in the family firm from 1776, allotted a
one-third share of his father's profits.

Of course, the larger question remains. Was the Bank directorate, as it evolved through the eighteenth century, a broadly 'open'
or a broadly 'closed' body of men? Certainly it was closed to Jews,
notwithstanding their increasing importance in the City, as exemplified by Samson Gideon; more generally, Daniel Abramson has offered
an unflattering picture of a Court that by the end of the century 'no
longer consisted of ambitious, daring, new City of London men', but

instead 'represented the City's oligarchic establishment', as 'webs of inter-marriage conserved wealth and status within a limited circle of families'.[13] That verdict may be a little harsh, underestimating the quality as well as sense of duty of some of the individual directors, yet it is probably fair enough about the rather ossifying direction of travel.

What about, though, these Bank men and society at large? Here, Abramson's claim that 'from being the embodiment of dynamic capitalist innovation, the Bank of England's directorate evolved into almost a quasi-aristocratic backwater' is surely a stretch, at least as far as the period up to the 1790s is concerned. Undoubtedly 'money' and 'land' were moving closer together during the eighteenth century, though often experiencing a chequered, fractured sort of relationship; but analysis of the 133 directors suggests that there was still a certain distance between the two. Take the question of whom the directors married. Of the twenty-three for whom we have reasonably precise information, eleven married into the London business world (the daughter of a London merchant, the daughter of a London haberdasher, the daughter of a 'citizen and vintner of London', and so on), compared to only six marrying into what seem to have been gentry-cum-aristocratic families (the daughter of the first Earl of Scarborough, the daughter of Henry Thompson of Kirby Hall, Yorkshire, and so on). Moreover, most of the missing 110 were far likelier to have married into the former category than the latter. Or take the question of where the directors lived. Undeniably there was the occasional flavour of country house and rolling acres (Lilling Hall, Yorkshire or Waltham Place, Berkshire or Spondon, Derbyshire or Thorpe, Norfolk); but much more common was a prosperous suburban or quasi-suburban location (Fleetwood House, Stoke Newington or Wall Street, Hackney or Dacre House, Lee or unspecified residences at such places as Clapham, East Sheen, Richmond, Highgate and Hendon).[14]

Nor, in terms of exercising a broader sway, did many directors become MPs: only fifteen out of the 133 did so. However, a man from the Bank was sometimes just what the government of the day – or, more specifically, the Treasury – badly needed in order to boost its financial authority and expertise. In April 1759 the senior secretary to the Treasury, James West, sent his chief, the Duke of Newcastle, a briefing note on possible City candidates for the vacant Cornish seat of Camelford. They included two Bank directors, Charles Savage (a former governor) and Bartholomew Burton (the current deputy governor). Savage, alas, had 'no inclination to come into Parliament, and tho' a good Whig and very rich, has peevishness and singularity in many things to a high degree'; instead, the choice ultimately fell on Burton, 'a very good sensible man', albeit 'I do not think of any great weight in the City'. Probably a more substantial Bank MP was William Ewer, a Turkey merchant who became a director in 1763 and governor in 1781, while sitting for Dorchester between 1765 and his death in 1789. He is recorded as subscribing during the 1770s very large sums to government loans; and in his final Commons speech, in May 1788, he presented a petition of London merchants exalting the national benefits derived from the slave trade.[15]

A happier remembrance is those directors with a rich hinterland. James Theobald, for instance, was a substantial timber merchant and a director from 1743 to 1756; but his passions were his multi-faceted activities as a natural historian and his leading role in the Royal Society, 'generously contributing' (in a biographer's words) to its 'knowledge and activities for over 33 years'. The passions of Gustavus Brander, who spent much of his life as a merchant operating out of White Lion Court, Cornhill, are caught in his 1787 obituary in the *Gentleman's Magazine*. Describing him as 'a very considerable Bank-stock-holder', it went on: 'He was for several years [1761–79] a Director of the Bank; but, having inherited the accumulated fortune of his uncle Mr. Speaker, he indulged his favourite pursuits in literature and the fine arts.' And it cited as a particularly notable acquisition 'the magnificent chair in which the first emperors of Germany used to be crowned'. The truly systematic acquirer, though, was Lyde Browne, a prosperous Foster Lane merchant and silver refiner who was a director between 1768 and his death in 1787. One of the age's most assiduous pursuers of antique sculpture, gathered together about 200 strong at his home (Cannizaro House in Wimbledon), he eventually sold much of his collection to Catherine the Great. Yet for Ruth Guilding, author of a recent authoritative study of the collectors of antique sculpture, he is a far from admirable figure. Calling Browne 'a businessman in antiquary's clothing', she writes of how he 'joined the ranks of the connoisseurs and boasted of the antique sculptures housed in his museum at Wimbledon, but then traded them like the merchant that he was' – an 'easy, mercenary attitude' that 'challenged the whole idea of connoisseurship'. And she quotes as self-condemnatory his frank observation: 'All Virtu will be bought in future for present enjoyment, and to be parted with when satiated with the possession thereof.'

Every now and then, the authentic voice of the typical City man – commonsensical, sceptical, unassuming, prosaic, pragmatic – comes through loud and clear. Charles Palmer was a merchant who became a director in 1739, then governor in 1754, and left the Court in 1763, retiring to Pinner. But he maintained close links with the Bank, writing regularly over the next few years to a trusted senior clerk, Thomas Hulley. A few extracts from the letters speak of an almost timeless sensibility. On the formation of the Rockingham government:

> As to this great revolution in the Ministry and the further changes that may be expected to be made, I do not trouble myself much about them. The late outs are now the inns and will do all they can to keep themselves where they are, and those they have outed will do their utmost to pay them in their own coin, and thus our political affairs are likely to go, and have gone, all my time, and I see no likelihood of its being otherwise.

On Rockingham's fall a year later:

> I am obliged for your news of a new Administration. I do not find that it is quite settled yet, but I suppose it must be soon. A state of uncertainty is a bad one on all accounts, both public and private.

On the press:

> I long to hear news that I may make some sort of dependence upon, for I have not been in the way lately of hearing anything but what the newspapers tell me, and that does not go for much with me.

On a summer stay in Tunbridge Wells, taking the waters:

> We have had several showers and to-day it seems to be set in for rain; but I shall not wish it to continue much longer than to-day for

this is a terrible place in continued wet weather. Here is a pritty deal of company, but not near so much as last year, and but little quality.

And again:

By the help of fine weather, which we now have, and a good horse to carry me abroad in it, and some few old acquaintances I have met with here, added to my own family (not to speak of the pleasure I take in being an idle spectator and admirer of the Gay World) my time rubs on pritty well.

And finally, that same increasingly hot August, after commiserating with Hulley for being 'shut up and stew'd in a public office in London':

But we ought, and must indeed, affect the philosopher so far as to endeavour as much as we can to make the lott that falls to our share in the world as easy and light as may be, and leave the rest to time and fate.[16]

———

Palmer was writing in 1765, the year after the Bank's Charter was renewed for a further twenty-one years. It does not seem on the whole to have been a particularly contentious process, with the Treasury getting if anything the better of the bargain. The Bank agreed to advance £1 million on Exchequer bills at 3 per cent; it also agreed to make an outright gift to the Exchequer of £110,000, with no interest attached; and Charles Jenkinson, who as joint secretary to the Treasury had helped to draft the bill, would subsequently reveal how 'an eminent merchant' and Bank proprietor, Sir William Baker, had at the time 'strongly opposed' the 'bargain', though perhaps only in private, 'on the ground of its being too hard a one for the Bank'. From the Bank's point of view, a significant plus in the legislation was a tighter wording about fraudulent transfers of stock – a concern recently highlighted by the systematically fraudulent activities of a broker called John Rice, who had eventually fled to the Continent, where he was pursued by representatives of the Bank and of the South Sea Company, before being arrested at Cambrai in January 1763, put on trial at the Old Bailey and compelled to pay the ultimate penalty.[17]

The rest of the 1760s were uneventful, but as usual the next financial crisis was not far away. That of 1772 was possibly the most fraught since the South Sea Bubble, and during its most acute phase the *London Chronicle* offered an all-too-plausible analysis. 'The present calamity,' declared the paper in late June, 'is owing to several concurring circumstances, the chief of which is generally reckoned to be a pernicious practice, that has been encreasing for some years, and which of late has been carried to a great height, that of drawing bills on London on fictitious credit for the purpose of raising money.' Earlier in the year, the Bank had in fact sought to limit discounts and thereby check speculation, earning it some anonymous public abuse about virtuous traders being malignly 'oppressed by one man or a set of men who devote a few hours in the day to business and call themselves Directors'; but during June itself, as panic and emptiness grew almost hourly following the failure on the 10th of the London banking house Neale & Co (whose leading partner, Alexander Fordyce, had particularly intimate connections with the Scottish banking and commercial world), the Bank reprised its 1763 policy and began to discount more liberally. In the wake of the collapse of the major Edinburgh house of William Alexander and Sons (which held the contract for the export of tobacco to France), the very worst day was Monday the 22nd, as one of the City's most respectable private banks, Glyn and Hallifax, was compelled to stop payments, fortunately only temporarily. 'It is beyond the power of words to describe the general consternation of the metropolis yesterday,' reported the *Evening Post* next day. 'No event for these thirty years past has been remembered to have given so fatal a blow to both our trade and credit as a nation. An universal bankruptcy was expected; the stoppage of every banker's house in London was looked for. The whole city was in an uproar: the whole city was in tears.' At this point the Bank accelerated its discounting dramatically: whereas between January and May there had been only nine occasions when the daily business had exceeded £200,000, on 23 June the day's business was £387,756, and on 25 June it was £529,265 – 'nearly as much,' notes Clapham, 'as in the busiest whole week of 1763'. That same day, the 25th, the seriously over-ambitious and over-extended Scottish bank Douglas, Heron & Co, commonly known as the Ayr Bank, was forced to suspend payments, described by one historian as 'a major catastrophe for Scotland, since many influential people, both landed and mercantile, were either shareholders or customers of the bank'.

Much helped by the Bank's discounting policy, the worst of the crisis was over by early July, though a series of bankruptcies continued for the rest of the year; as for two of the main protagonists, the Ayr Bank foolishly declined the Bank's terms to help re-establish its credit and eventually gave up business in 1773, but Alexanders accepted from the Bank a credit of £160,000 and resumed payments in mid-July. 'You will find it impossible,' an anonymous but well-informed observer had warned the Ayr Bank in an open address published in the *London Chronicle*, 'to carry on your business as a Banking Company independent of the Bank of England, that being the great source of the British funds and credit, without whose countenance and occasional aid, no banker nor merchant even in London, can do business with safety and profit.'[18]

A further indication of the Bank's indispensability came soon after the crisis. Over three-quarters of a century earlier, the great recoinage of 1696 had been essentially concerned with silver, not gold, which by the 1770s was, in Clapham's apposite words, 'badly worn'. Accordingly, legislation in 1773–4, in which the good offices of the Bank seem to have been largely taken for granted, involved its bullion office receiving and replacing gold guineas, half-guineas and quarter-guineas that had been cut and defaced, thereby denoting that they were light or counterfeit. Eventually, at least 6½ million such guineas were received – and, to quote Clapham again, 'what was now in effect the British standard coinage was put into admirable order'. The mid-1770s also saw the start of yet another war: the American War of Independence. Its immediate cause (the dumping on the American market of tons of unsold tea) has been described by one American historian as 'the direct result of the East India Company's gross irresponsibility', so perhaps it might have been better in retrospect if the Bank had managed in 1773 to resist the government's demand to lend it £1.4 million against Exchequer bills in order that it could bail out the overstretched Company. Initially the new war made relatively little financial impact, but that all changed from 1778, as in turn France, Spain and Holland became involved. By early in the new decade the 3 per cents were rarely above 60, Bank stock struggled to be much above par, and the national debt was rising rapidly. All of which was presumably of some concern to George Washington, who throughout the war continued to be a Bank of England stockholder.[19]

He might also have noted with interest the events of June 1780. On Friday the 2nd a 60,000-strong crowd, headed by Lord George Gordon, marched on Parliament to present a petition, sponsored by the Protestant Association, demanding the repeal of recent legislation relieving some of the penal laws against Roman Catholics. Over the next few days London trembled, amid multiple disturbances, acts of physical intimidation and the storming of prisons. The Gordon Riots culminated on the night of 'Black Wednesday', the 7th, as the mob sought to take the Bank, whose protection lay in the hands of a guard placed in the nearby Royal Exchange. Thomas Holcroft related the outcome in his contemporary account:

They made two attempts upon the Bank; but were so much intimidated by the strength with which they beheld it guarded that their attacks were but feebly conducted. They were led on to the first by a brewer's servant on horseback, who had decorated his horse with the chains of Newgate [which had been destroyed on the 6th, with all the prisoners released]; but were repulsed at the first fire from the Military, and their second succeeded no better. They made an effort to break into the Pay Office likewise, and met the same fate. Several of them fell in these skirmishes, and many more were wounded, as the importance of these places made it necessary to shew but little lenity.

The first assault was probably at around 11 o'clock at night, and the second in the small hours. Taking part in repulsing the former attempt was the radical City politician John Wilkes in his capacity as a London militiaman ('killed two rioters directly opposite to the Great Gate of the Bank', he recorded), while the latter assault was described by the *London Chronicle*:

A large party of the rioters went down Cheapside in order to attack the Bank, several of them armed with muskets. When they got to Poultry the Horse and Foot Guards were drawn up and stopped them. The rioters fired on the soldiers, and the soldiers returned the fire for several minutes, and killed about eight people and wounded

a great many. The mob was so great that they beat off the Horse
Guards, but the Foot, by keeping a constant fire, dispersed them.

Altogether, over 200 rioters were shot dead in the capital's streets
that night, while possibly as many died later from their wounds.
London's historian Jerry White justifiably calls it the city's 'most
terrible crisis in the modern period, not exceeded until the wartime
blitz 160 years later'; and unsurprisingly, less than a fortnight after
that memorable night, the Bank's Committee of Treasury 'considered
of the necessity of some defence & security to be established at the
Bank'. The upshot was the Bank Picquet: a military guard consisting
of a detachment from the Brigade of Guards, mounted almost every
night (except during the Second World War) at the Bank, until its
eventual withdrawal in 1973, some 70,000 nights later. As an immediate expression of gratitude the Bank in August 1780 'gave an elegant
entertainment at the Queen's Arms Tavern in St Paul's Churchyard
to all the officers who have been on duty at the Bank or elsewhere in
the City during and since the late riots' – a dinner that, continued the
London Chronicle, 'consisted of a turtle (which alone cost 23 guineas), a dozen haunches of venison and the first dainties in season,
together with all sorts of wines'.[20]

If riots came and went, the war was less obliging, and the following summer, five years early but owing everything to the financial
burden on the state of the continuing American conflict, it was agreed
between government and Bank that the Charter should be renewed
for a further twenty-six years (four fewer than the Bank had originally demanded) in return for a £2 million loan at 3 per cent against
Exchequer bills. Unusually, there ensued a full-scale debate in the
Commons, with the prime minister, Lord North, vigorously defending not only the bargain, but renewal itself. 'The Bank, he said, had
been established for near ninety years, and had been conducted in all
that time with so much wisdom, so much advantage to the nation, and
so much credit to itself, that he could not imagine there was one man
living, who, after the long experience of its utility, would deny that it
was the duty of parliament to cement and strengthen the connection
and union between the Bank and the public as much as possible.' As
for those unhappy with the new Charter's terms and even wanting to
replace the Bank:

They knew not the solid advantages resulting to the public from its connection with the present company, they saw not the difficulty that must now attend the attempt to incorporate a new one; at present the Bank, from long habit and the usage of many years, was a part of the constitution, or if not a part of the constitution, at least it was to all important purposes, the public exchequer; all the many business of the Exchequer being done at the Bank, and as experience had proved, with much greater advantage to the public, than when it had formerly been done at the Exchequer.

The Bank of England as an integral part of the British constitution was not a concept that appealed to Yorkshire's MP Sir George Savile, eighth baronet and an independent-minded Whig. Mocking North for having 'spoken of the connection that subsisted between the public and the Bank with a degree of warmth, as if he had been describing conjugal love', and declaring his belief that 'the Bank business was to him something like magic', he argued forcibly that 'this moment, when public credit was crippled', was far too premature for renewal. Other speakers had their say, few of them particularly well informed, but the exception was the MP for Dorchester, who happened to have recently become governor. Pronouncing that the Bank had 'offered fairly and handsomely' in negotiating the terms of renewal, and insisting that its profits 'arose from the industry, the hazard, and management of the directors of the Bank', William Ewer went on to express his conviction that 'the public had no more right to those profits than to the profits of the private trade of any individual, or of any private banking company'. What about Savile's 'magic' accusation? 'Good God,' expostulated Ewer, 'could public business be so little known, that at this time of day it should be supposed that the Bank could coin whatever sum they wanted?' And, somewhat more tactfully, he sought to allay concerns that such a lengthy renewal would make the Bank dangerously independent of government:

The public were by far the best customers the Bank had. Their credit, their power of accommodating government, arose solely from their being the cashiers of the public ... If, at any time, the directors acted so ill, so imprudently, or so rashly, as to refuse granting to government every assistance in their power, as often as the occasion of the state rendered such assistance necessary, government would have it in its power to continue the Bank the cashier of the public no longer ...

North and Ewer duly carried the day: a decisive vote (109–30) in favour of renewal on the proposed terms saw the Bank's future assured until 1812.[21]

The war was effectively over by the early weeks of 1783, but that was still a year of crisis. The Bank's bullion reserve, having plunged from £4.2 million in August 1780 to £2 million by August 1782, continued to deteriorate, down to £1.3 million by February 1783 (compared to a rising note circulation of £7.7 million) and heading further south. A decade and a half later, a Bank director, Samuel Bosanquet, would explain the larger context, as well as the decisive action that the Bank then took, refusing for about six months to make its customary advances to government:

> The drain of cash proceeded from the great extension of commerce which followed the peace, and which occasioned so considerable an export of the commodities of this country that the circulation was hardly sufficient to support it. It was evident that if this drain could be supported for a short time the influx of wealth that must follow from the return of the Exports would amply compensate for the preceding drain, and so it turned out. The Bank Directors, therefore, without opening the state of affairs to the Administration, took a bold step of their own authority, and refused to make the advances on the loan of that year; this answered the purpose of making a temporary suspension in the amount of the drain of the specie. The time at which they had the most ground of alarm was not when their cash was at the lowest, but about April or May, when they refused to advance on the loan, and although in October their cash was lower than before [down by August to £590,000] yet they had such reason to expect a turn in their favour by a favourable alteration of the exchanges, that they were under much less apprehensions than they were in the Spring.

The Bank, it seems, had played a difficult hand with considerable adroitness.

That certainly is the reading by Sir Albert Feavearyear, in his magisterial history of *The Pound Sterling*, of the Bank's temporary refusal to finance a large portion of the government's loan. 'The remainder of that loan,' he explains, 'was therefore thrown immediately upon the resources of the market. This had the effect of tightening money and of curbing the tendency to over-speculation. The exchanges turned in favour of the country and the foreign drain ceased. Later in the year, although their reserve had fallen lower still, the directors were so much more confident of the position that they freely advanced money to relieve the strain upon houses which were feeling the effects of the falling market.' Plausibly enough, Feavearyear contends that this was 'the first occasion upon which the Bank definitely attempted to exercise some control of the money market'. And again he elucidates: 'It discovered a principle which has been of great service on many occasions since, namely that when speculation is reaching a dangerous level credit should be progressively contracted until a definite fall of the market sets in; but when this occurs there need be no more fear, and advances may be made freely to soften the fall.'[22]

From the mid-1780s the dominant politician was the remarkable – and remarkably determined – William Pitt the Younger. In 1786 he not only introduced an improved sinking fund (privately describing himself as 'half mad with a project which will give our supplies the effect almost of magic in the reduction of debt'), but prevailed upon the Bank to charge significantly less (£450 per million instead of £562 10s) for managing the national debt. Over the next few years it was a tense enough relationship, including a sparky moment in July 1790 when 'the Chairs' (that is, governor, deputy governor and former governors) who formed the Committee of Treasury reluctantly accepted a block of Exchequer bills, but at the same time stated that they 'wished it to be thoroughly understood that they meant this loan as a temporary assistance to government and not to be renewed on any account'. The real stand-off came soon afterwards. Pitt towards the end of 1790 put forward the argument that the balances of unclaimed dividends left in the Bank's hands, amounting to some £547,000, belonged by rights not to the Bank but to 'the temporary use of the public', which is to say the government; the Bank flatly disagreed; and one of its MP directors, Samuel Thornton, made the strongest possible protest in the Commons, calling Pitt's claim 'a stab to public credit'. Neither side blinked during the early months of 1791, with the Bank fortified by a supportive memorandum from an impressively international range of 'proprietors of the Public Funds' as well as 'Agents of many respectable foreigners extensively inter-ested in these Funds'. The Bank followed this up in March with a petition on the 15th to the Commons that described Pitt's proposal as a raid upon the 'property of individuals without their consent and without their knowledge', before on the 24th it decided to play its trump card – the publication of a list of unclaimed dividends dating from before September 1780, predictably causing a huge 'press to obtain payment' from dividend owners anxious not to let the govern-ment get their money. The eventual outcome, formally endorsed by both sides in May, was a compromise: the Bank offering interest free a 'perpetual loan' of £500,000, in return for Pitt abandoning his Bill about unclaimed dividends. The Tory prodigy may have possessed a 'damned long obstinate top lip' (in George III's words) and may indeed have generally held the upper hand in the relationship; but on this occasion the Bank had just about managed to keep him in check.[23]

By this time the French Revolution, with all its manifold conse-quences, was under way. For three years, despite lurid accounts of events across the Channel, the British economic mood was largely buoyant, much helped by the booming cotton industry; but by the autumn of 1792 the outlook was perceptibly changing, not least in the City. A poor wheat harvest, country banks issuing implausibly large amounts of paper money, the threat of war, rising bankruptcies – these and other factors caused in November a brief but sharp panic among the brokers, jobbers and speculators who thronged Exchange Alley. Nor was the Bank itself in the best possible place that winter. Its bullion reserve, sometimes called its 'treasure', was on another downward curve, dipping below £5 million, while anxiety about French-inspired revolu-tionary radicalism (centred on the London Corresponding Society) led to its bespoke military guard, so much disliked and perhaps envied by the City authorities, being doubled in strength.[24] Then, on 21 January 1793, Louis XVI was executed; and eleven days later, on 1 February, France declared war on Britain. For the Bank, poised to enter its second century, some wholly uncharted waters lay ahead.

3

A Steady and Unremitting Attention

The physical Bank of 1793, whether as a building or as a working environment, was very different to what it had been in its original Threadneedle Street incarnation almost sixty years earlier. In large part this reflected the institution's growing workload and accompanying rise – steady if not yet spectacular – in staff numbers:[1]

1734	110
1763	246
1783	345
1793	418

The changing physical character of the Bank, though, was not just down to size of staff. It was also determined by two remarkable architects, Robert Taylor and John Soane.

First, however, there was George Sampson's Bank, a relatively modest affair surrounded by two churches, three taverns and as many as twenty private houses. 'The frontage of the new premises was not more than 80 feet,' notes Marston Acres, 'extending from St. Christopher's Church on the west to the Crown Tavern on the east, and the depth of the site cannot have exceeded 300 feet in the direction of Lothbury. The only outside windows were above the main entrance in Threadneedle Street, and at the west end of the Hall overlooking the churchyard of St. Christopher.' Inside the building, features included a nod to the Bank's origins, in the form of a life-size white marble statue of King William III erected on 1 January 1735, and the imposing Pay Hall – crowded six days a week by merchants and others converting coins into banknotes (or vice versa), making deposits or withdrawals, and (less often) collecting dividends, with high, grille-topped counters separating these customers from the tellers and clerks. 'The primacy of the Pay Hall,' observes Daniel Abramson about what was by far the largest occupied space in Sampson's Bank, symbolised 'the paramount importance the Bank placed on its commercial banking activities.' There were of course other aspects to the new building, not least the directors' parlours or meeting rooms ('sumptuously appointed,' Abramson notes, 'with fine wood panelling and marble chimney-pieces') and the Accountant's Office, the heart of the book-keeping back office and deliberately kept apart from the areas of public access. 'On the level of spatial planning Sampson's Bank of England helped instrument the Bank's trustworthiness,' reflects Abramson. 'At the level of architectural style the building also represented virtue. A classically planned and proportioned building like the Bank of England possessed a power-ful authority.'[2]

By the time that Robert Taylor succeeded Sampson as the Bank's architect in 1764, the need for physical expansion was manifest, even after a certain amount of new building in the late 1740s. Taylor himself in an earlier life had been a sculptor, including creating the figure of Britannia for the Pay Hall, but during the 1750s he had taken off as an architect, specialising in villas and townhouses for the City's wealth-iest. 'Skillful industry, dauntless self-denial, oeconomy of money and time' would be the defining characteristics recalled at his death, and in addition to his intellectual and cultural sophistication (including strong Continental influences) he was renowned for his relentlessly detailed quality control over his subordinates. As the Bank's architect, he designed and saw through a major programme of expansion, mainly between the mid-1760s and the mid-1770s. Taylor's programme, much of it simultaneously executed, had four main components. On the other side of Threadneedle Street, in front of the main entrance to the Royal Exchange, he erected on the triangular site two four-storey blocks, the Bank Buildings, whose offices were used by other busi-nesses and which was in effect a pioneering speculative development on the Bank's part; to the north, beyond the Accountant's Office, he built a four-storey Library, mainly for the purpose of records storage;

to the north-west, close to the Pay Hall, he constructed an elegant suite of new rooms for the directors, of which the centrepiece was the Court Room, handsomely decorated and thrice the size of the previous Court Room; above all, on the eastern side of the existing premises, he built a whole new wing that almost doubled the Bank's overall size and comprised not only the great circular Rotunda for dealings in government stock, but also four spacious and identical new Transfer Offices (including two devoted to 3 Per Cent Consols). Taylor's was, by any standards, a prodigious achievement. And when the French finance minister Calonne, well known as a patron of the arts, visited these additions to the Bank, he pronounced them to be 'the first architecture of London', with the only exception being Wren's St Paul's.[3]

Taylor, knighted in 1783, would remain the Bank's architect until his death in 1788. The start of the 1780s saw of course the Gordon Riots, a profound shock to the Bank authorities; and in the aftermath of the violent disturbances, they came to the conclusion that the tower of the thirteenth-century church of St Christopher-le-Stocks, situated on Threadneedle Street immediately to the west of the Bank, might well be all too tempting a vantage point for a future mob to storm the Bank from. Accordingly, amid perhaps surprisingly little controversy, the Bank purchased the church in 1781 for the sum of £4,462 4s and then, between 1782 and 1784, had it knocked down and replaced by a new group of buildings – the Bank's own west wing – reaching as far as the corner of Princes Street. New offices in this wing, with Taylor again to the fore until his death, included the Dividend Warrant Office and the Reduced Annuities Office; but on the site of St Christopher's burial ground, which the Bank had pledged not to build over, was instead now the Garden Court, under which bodies for a time continued to be buried. Tree lined, and not unspacious, it broke 'the formality of architectural lines', observed Thomas Malton in his 1792 *Picturesque Tour* of the City, adding that the garden provided 'unexpected pleasure in this busy commercial scene'.

The west wing may not have been Taylor at his best, striking as it did, in Abramson's disappointed words, 'a dissonant note with its boxy, disconnected aggregate of parts'. Yet, taking his near quarter-century as a whole, he had played an integral part in (Abramson again) 'the fundamental institutional and architectural transformation of the Bank of England into a large-scale, public, monumental workplace'. A year before his death, a correspondent of the *Gentleman's Magazine* could only express wonder at 'the amazing rapidity' of the institution's 'modern expansion and extended accommodation to the moneyed interest and commercial world'; five years before that, in 1782, an implicit sense of its daily public importance comes through in *The Bank of England's Vade Mecum: or Sure Guide*, a small book written by 'A Gentleman of the Bank, &c'. Its purpose was made clear on the title page (so that 'the greatest Strangers to the Bank, may with Certainty and Propriety do all they want, without being obliged to ask any Questions of any Persons whatever'); two helpful copper-plate plans showing the Bank's layout were included; and the main focus was on 'the hall department', that is the Pay Hall, described as 'particularly' the part of the Bank 'found to be not sufficiently understood', but which was 'certainly the principal Place, where all Money Matters, Notes, Bills, Drafts, &c are transacted'. Most of the treatise was a helpful, matter-of-fact guide to conducting business in the Bank. For example:

> If you want *Bank Notes* for Cash, pay your Money to any one of the Tellers, at their Tables, marked (3) in the Plan and tell him what Note or Notes, you want for it; he then gives you a Ticket, which you present through the little Rails to one of the Clerks, who sit under the Letter A on the Right Hand Side of the Dial, and they will accommodate you. But if you want a Parcel of Notes, take a Slip of Paper, which you will generally find ready, at the Desk marked (1), and write down what you want, and take it to Letter A with the Ticket ... Then the Clerks at Letter A will accordingly make out your Notes, which you must be particularly careful to get signed by one of the *Cashiers*, who sit under the Dial (as before mentioned), before you take them away, and this must always be done with every new Note you receive.

Addenda indicated 'where to apply to the Gentlemen Stock-brokers, to have Business of that Sort transacted, or where to receive their different Dividends', in other words in Taylor's eastern wing ('As soon as you enter the Court-yard of the Bank, from Thread-needle-Street, – you will to the Right Hand see a Door, ascended to by four Stone Steps, with the Words transfer offices wrote over the Door ...'). But the anonymous gentleman of the Bank reserved his greatest weight for his 'General Remarks':

> Let every one please to observe, that when he has paid his Money to the Tellers, and receives a Ticket for his *Money paid in*, never to take that Ticket away, but carry it to the Place it is designed for.
> The Public are earnestly desired to pay due Attention to the above Remark, as it very frequently happens, that people take these Tickets away, for want of knowing better, and give themselves a great deal of Trouble; for if the Tickets are carried away, the Business they came to do, is left undone.

The self-published treatise, sold by booksellers who included Messrs Richardson and Urquhart at the Royal Exchange, cost 1 shilling, and within a year was running to a second edition.[4]

Taylor died on 27 September 1788, and only three days later the Committee of Treasury noted that eleven people 'were offered for his place of Architect'. On 15 October the Committee of Building reached its 'unanimous' choice: John Soane. Aged thirty-five, and youngest of seven children of a journeyman-bricklayer, he had trained under George Dance (architect of the Mansion House) and over the previous ten years had been involved in the post-Riots rebuilding of Newgate Prison, had started to become known for his country-house designs, had married the niece of a wealthy builder, and – perhaps most significant of all – had become friendly with one of the Bank's most influential directors, Samuel Bosanquet.[5] It was a bold but inspired choice. 'The underlying dynamic of Soane's career,' considers Abramson, 'involved his attempts to conjoin the two divergent strands of his early education, one favouring conventional classicism and the other poetic picturesqueness. The force of Soane's best designs derived from his unwillingness to allow one tendency to triumph over the other.' The new man soon got to work across a range of projects – as early as December 1788 successfully laying before the Committee of Building 'a plan for taking off part of the Room designed for the Cheque Office, to be converted into a safe place for depositing the Transfer Books of the £3 p Cent. Reduced Office' – but undoubtedly his crucial early achievement, calling on some assistance from Dance, was the Bank Stock Office, situated just to the north of the

Bartholomew Lane vestibule and completed in 1793. 'This was one of Soane's most remarkable interiors, the prototype of his other banking halls and of many of his other interiors,' Giles Waterfield would write in 1989 in celebration of its re-creation. 'Its use of a thin, highly stretched Classical vocabulary, its avoidance of mass, and its ingenious employment of new material epitomise the novelty of the architect's approach.' Monumental, austere, Roman: it spoke of a company proudly poised to celebrate its first centenary.[6]

To be a clerk in the eighteenth-century Bank – possible in the first place only through being the son of a Bank clerk or being nominated by a Bank director – was not on the whole to find oneself on the road to riches. Salaries began at £50 a year, barely enough to live on, though extra work during busy periods, or in connection with the administration of public lotteries, was remunerated, while the pay was reasonable enough for the older clerks. Pensions tended to be on a grace-and-favour basis (though usually granted), and in any case there was no set retirement age; as for holidays, the notion of mandatory annual leave was not yet in place. What the Bank did provide, however, was security of employment and, for the senior clerks anyway, relatively short working hours (often 9 to 3), enabling them to find additional paid work later in the day in City shops or businesses. How hard did they work when they were in Threadneedle Street? 'I am sorry to find you met with difficultys in setting your last day's work,' one clerk, Thomas Ormes, convalescing in Waltham Abbey, wrote in 1762 to another clerk, Thomas Hulley. 'Indeed I do not wonder at it, as its expected that one person *must* do the business of two, and I am inclined to think the Fates have doomed us to be slaves to the Bank, our state being very little better. How often have we complained of this our hard lot, and still have the mortification of expecting no relief.' There is some evidence that Ormes may have been one of life's grumblers; but the probability is that the policy of deliberate overmanning – so that at times of pressure or crisis there would always be sufficient experienced clerks at hand – had not yet come into play.

Inevitably there were breaches of discipline or cases of unacceptable slackness: a clerk, Edward Stone, discharged in 1736 for habituating a tavern with a gaming table 'at which he used to play'; another, Thomas Dowdeswell, suspended in 1747 for arriving at the Bank 'disordered with liquor'; or in 1782 the seven Consols Office clerks who dined too well in Lime Street, failed to return to the Bank, subsequently explained that it had been raining and were lucky to get away with a reprimand. Irregularities, meanwhile, ranged from the relatively mild to the wholly grave, with the latter category including two particularly egregious cases during the middle decades. In May 1741 it was discovered that John Waite, a cashier who had been a 'servant of the House' (as the phrase went) for almost twenty years, had absconded with 133 East India Company bonds for £100 each. 'About five foot eight inches high, well-set, round visaged, small grey eyes, very light eyebrows and eyelashes, and of a most remarkable fresh complexion' was the description at once posted in the *London Gazette*, with the Bank's reward for the successful apprehension of Waite soon raised from £200 to £500. Eventually, a year and a half later, he was arrested in Dublin; and though at the subsequent Old Bailey trial he was acquitted on a legal technicality, his inexorable former employers managed to get him rearrested for a debt of £13,300, leaving him in due course to spend the rest of his days in the Fleet Prison. The other case concerned William Guest. The son of a Worcestershire clergyman, he secured a clerkship in 1763 through the recommendation of the director Peter Du Cane, soon becoming a teller in the Pay Hall. Unfortunately for him, a fellow-teller, John Leach, noticed that, for no apparent good reason, he had the habit of separating recently minted coins from older ones; and it quite soon transpired that Guest had been systematically extracting gold from new guineas and using an ingenious machine of his own invention to make a fresh milled edge on those coins. Reported to the Court of Directors in July 1767 as being in custody 'on a violent suspicion of diminishing the current coin of the Kingdom', he was summarily dismissed from the Bank's service. And three months later, after a trial at the Old Bailey, he met his end at Tyburn – where at the public hanging he was, recorded the *London Magazine*, 'dressed in decent mourning with a club wig on', and 'his whole deportment was so pious, grave, manly, and solemn, becoming the gentleman and Christian, as to draw tears from the greatest part of the numerous spectators'.[7]

It would be wrong to dwell overlong on the miscreants, for the probability is that at any one time the overwhelming majority of the Bank's staff were honest and more or less conscientious. Two men above all showed the way, becoming in turn, through their long service and through their dedication, the very heartbeat of the Bank. The first was Daniel Race, who entered in 1719, became joint chief cashier in 1739, then sole chief cashier in 1759, which he remained until a few months before his death in October 1775 at his house in Clapton. He was buried at St Luke's, Old Street, where his memorial tablet (written by a Bank director, Thomas Plumer) warmly praised 'a man of plain appearance' who was 'in every respect the man of business, the gentleman, the philosopher, the Christian'. He had, Plumer went on, 'the clearest ideas and soundest judgement, most unblemished integrity, singular diligence, attention and regularity in every branch of his department: wonderful calmness of temper, affability of manner, unruffled by times or persons; himself always composed, and by his candour composing the most troublesome: remarkably correct, and in a manner faultless himself, yet indulgent to the faults of others, as far as consisted with his own duty ...' Or in the words of one of the lines of verse on an engraving of the portrait of Race commissioned by the directors shortly before his retirement, he had 'the coolest Reason allied to keenest Wit'. The other exemplar was Abraham Newland. One of twenty-five children of a Southwark miller and baker, he entered the Bank as a seventeen-year-old in 1748, rising to become chief cashier in 1778, and like Race remaining so until shortly before his death, which in his case was in November 1807. In his position, over the course of almost thirty years, he slept every night in the Bank, though after business hours he would sometimes retreat to his semi-rural Highbury cottage to take tea and perhaps play the violin, before returning in the evening to Threadneedle Street. After his death, a journalist would call Newland's 'a life less marked by enterprize than by enduring patience and plodding perseverance', adding that 'the progress of a horse in a mill is but a faint type of such an existence'; but Newland himself, remembered by intimates as a cheerful companion not averse to a glass with friends, would never for a moment have doubted the high and serious purpose of his unwearying daily round.[8]

The year of Race's retirement, 1775, is not an especially notable one in the Bank's history, but it is the first time we get any real sense of how things looked from the top. Becoming governor that year was Samuel Beachcroft, a merchant whose father Matthews Beachcroft (also a merchant) had been governor in the 1750s. He started a working journal, mercifully legible, and a selection of entries between April and November 1775 speak for themselves about the mixture of diverse concerns that seem to have occupied much of his time:

13 April. Read the petition of Jn° Sharp, & Giles Collins for advance of Gratuity – Rejected.

14 April. Appointed M^r Le Gros to serve the Bank with half their coals.

2 May. Reprimanded Mr Smith, partner of Smith Wright & Gray, for misbehaviour of His House by sending bad Silver, & giving other hindrances to our Clerks. He promised in future to alter their method & behave better.

11 May. Agreed with Palmer the upholsterer for a pair Green Moreen Curtains & Pullies to the Bullion Office for £9.

15 June. Reprimanded Mr Tudman for taking a Bank Note that was forged, & cautioned the Out Tellers in regard to the inspection of all Notes in Future.

30 June. Waited on Lord North, who informed the Dep^y & Myself that the Exch^r Bills on the Supplys 1775 £250,000 wou'd be Issued this Year sooner than usual, & desir'd us to take the Sense of our Court upon advancing said sum at 3 p C^t.

12 July. Order'd Mr Newland to acquaint all the Cashiers & other Officers upon receipt of any Stolen Bank Note, forged Note &c immediately to mark them that they may be sworn to upon any necessity.

Reprimanded Mr Vickery for misbehaviour to Mr Thomas Bowen & order'd him to make a proper Apology, & bring a Letter from him to that purpose.

4 August. Mr Pearson and Mr Nowell appeared on behalf of Benj Nowell suspended 2 June last, & said his affairs being involv'd & the Loss of a Wife had brought him to drink, that he had settled all his affairs to pay in three year, that they wou'd continue his Security & pray'd for his being reinstated; Nowell promised to behave well, when I told him wou'd bring it before the Court next Thursday.

7 September. Order'd Mr Taylor to Color one of the Sky Lights by way of trial to prevent the great glare of light on the Books in the Transfer Offices.

14 November. Reprimanded several Officers for being concern'd in Lottery Offices, upon promise of never being concern'd again after this Lottery they were pardon'd, but told on any future offence they must be discharged.

17 November. Order'd Mr Jewson [Charles Jewson, a troubled figure who was briefly chief cashier between Race and Newland] to acquaint the Tellers never to take any Money in Bags by the weight without counting it, & if any person takes money away without telling it to acquaint them it is at their own risk, as we shall not make good any deficiency.

Beachcroft kept his diary going for the rest of the customary two-year term, and a couple of entries for 1776 nicely convey the 'low' and the 'high', that timeless contrast in Bank life:

21 May. Order'd Mr Jewson to allow the Weighers of the Light Guineas some porter & bread & cheese daily at one oClock, but by no means to suffer any ale house boy to attend.

22 November. The Dep^y Govr & Myself waited upon Lord North, desiring to be inform'd if any requisitions had been made for money from Lord Howe [in charge of Britain's North American fleet during the American War of Independence], stating our present situation & if any immediate want to desire some means might be used to prevent it; his Lordship answer'd he shou'd inquire into the matter, believ'd they wou'd not want any till about February, but cou'd not promise, however wou'd do what he cou'd to prevent it.[9]

Beachcroft's diary is suggestive, but even more so is the Committee of Inspection that the directors launched in 1783 to inquire into the Bank's internal workings. The trigger may well have been the Commission for Examining Public Accounts, in the context of the end of the War of American Independence, but it might also have tied in with internal fraud – especially the case of Charles Clutterbuck, a clerk discovered in July 1782 to have been filling in for his own nefarious purposes the blank forms that were used to prepare banknotes.[10] Either way, the following spring, amid temporarily unavailing efforts to bring Clutterbuck (who had absconded abroad) to justice, the Court of Directors established a Committee 'to inspect & enquire into the mode & execution of the Business as now carried on in the different departments of the Bank'.[11] It comprised three directors – Samuel Bosanquet (Soane's future supporter), Thomas Dea, Benjamin Winthrop – and apart from a lengthy summer break ('as some of the Committee were going out of Town') met regularly between March 1783 and March 1784, collecting evidence and writing six reports. The senior of the trio, and probable driving force, was Bosanquet, who for his own purposes kept a running aide-memoire touching on some of their findings and deliberations. Early on, he noted three wants: there was 'a great want of subordination in the Hall throughout'; 'a proper Check upon the Clerks who post in the Drawing Office to detect any error that may creep in by posting to a wrong account – is much wanted in the Accountant's Office'; and 'there wants a check upon the Clerks of the cash book in issuing Bank Notes'. As for some of the individual clerical staff, his judgements were unsparing. Boult: 'an old Gentleman almost worn out – not very sharp'. Gardner: 'a poor hand – obstinate & prejudiced to the old mode'. Bridges: 'a chattering Fellow'. Wilde: 'great abilities – but drinks & then muddled & lost'. Hutton: 'capable but won't be directed'. Fenning: 'obstinate'. Gandon: 'a sulky young man'. Occasionally he offered undiluted praise (Fonton: 'a very good regular clerk'), but more typical was his brusque verdict on Abraham Vickery, head of the 3 Per Cent Consols Office and the object of Beachcroft's reprimand in 1775: 'don't attend as well as he should' and 'lives too high'.

Much of the evidence presented to Bosanquet's Committee was essentially descriptive. Newland, for instance: 'Whatever Gold is purchased by the Bank & taken in at the Bullion Office is the next day brought to the Chief Cashier's Office, weighed, the Account examined & the Gold placed in the Warehouse 'till finally deposited in the Vaults.' Or Cowper, the principal Clerk attending the Exchequer, on 'the Mode in which they pay away the Bank Notes': 'One Clerk has charge of the Notes & another keeps a book in which the number & other particulars of them have been previously entered in numerical order, under the several heads of Tens, Twentys, Fiftys & up to a Thousand; the Clerk who has charge of the Notes looks out such as are demanded, & then calls out to the Clerk who keeps the book their number & Value, who seeing that they agree with the particulars in his book, marks them off, adding the name of the person to whom they are paid.' Or William Watkins, principal gate-porter, explaining how the fifteen watchmen under his direction 'assemble at the Bank at 6 o'clock in the evening in the Winter & at 7 in the Summer', whereupon:

> The Watch is immediately set for the night, 5 being allways on duty in the following stations –
> Fore-yard.
> Passage looking into the Mid-yard by the Bullion Office.
> Back-yard by the Library & passages near it.
> Old Church-yard under the Windows of the Great Parlour.
> They are relieved every 2 hours, & the 10 not on duty accommodate themselves as to Rest or refreshment in the best manner they can, within the Bank.

Quite often the Committee went to look for itself, for example going twice into the Accountant's Office, where on the second occasion its members

> saw the whole process of entering & posting the Bills & Notes discounted, & the manner of writing off the payments as they become due: The labour being very great occasions its being carried on to a late hour before finished, as the enterers can seldom begin to journalize the Bills 'till near 2 o'clock. Each Bill or Note discounted, being journalized, is afterwards posted in Discount Ledgers to the Account of the person by whom it is payable: At the same time, the Warrants from the Discount Office are journalized in another Journal, & then posted to the Account of the Discounter in the same Ledgers – being the books that are brought in every morning & laid upon the Table in the Parlour.
> In order to subtract from the Accounts in these Ledgers the sums that go off daily, the Article book, kept by the Clearers in the Hall,

containing an Account of all Bills & Notes discounted sent out every day for payment, is (as soon as done with by the Clearers) brought into the Accountants Office; & all the Bills & Notes sent out that day are collected from it in a book, under the name of each discounter; *which is a most laborious operation* ...

Occasionally there were grumbles. John Payne, chief accountant and a friend of Dr Johnson, 'took occasion to represent that all the Transfer Offices, through their not having any chimnies or other apertures for the admission of fresh Air, are so unwholesome as greatly to prejudice the health of the Persons employed in them'; Walton, a supervisor in the 3 Per Cent Reduced Office, drew attention to 'the confined State of the Office, so inadequate to the business carried on in it that the Clerks are obliged to put the Books upon one another, there not being space sufficient in the Office to lay them separately'; and Padman of the Library complained that it was 'very cold & damp', that 'there will very soon be no convenient room for an addition of more books', and that 'there is a vast number of files of money tickets & other apparently useless papers'. Next day the Committee inspected the Library, where having 'examined the State of the Books in each Story, which they found by no means to be in a perishing condition, but the paper very dry', they 'took notice that the Windows were all shut close, although it was a fine day ...'

Bosanquet and his colleagues had much on their collective mind during a year of pretty intensive work, with perhaps three aspects in particular being at or near the top of their agenda: banknotes; gratuities; and clerks acting as stockbrokers.

Banknotes had been at the heart of the recent Clutterbuck scandal, and one of the Committee's earliest steps was to call in a cashier, the 'almost worn out' Boult, and elicit his opinion 'on the practicability of a plan, which they had thought of, of accommodating the Public with Bank Notes ready made out', by which means 'the business of issuing Bank Notes in the Hall would be transacted with a much greater degree of security as well as facility than at present'. Sadly, 'Mr Boult did not seem clearly to comprehend how such a plan was to be executed.' Next day, the Committee tried out their scheme on another experienced cashier, the 'obstinate' Gardner; he 'at first made some objections', but 'did not state any one which seemed well founded;

his objections arising principally from the apprehension of having so considerable a Charge committed to his care'. By happy contrast, the Committee gained support from the official who really mattered, the chief cashier, with Newland a few weeks later reiterating his view that 'the Scheme was a very good one, very practicable, & in his opinion not liable to any objections'. Accordingly, the Committee success-fully recommended the use of 'ready-made' notes, while at the same time strongly urging that all notes should be printed within the Bank, which duly became the case from 1791.

As for gratuities, these seem to have been common in most depart-ments. Etheridge of the Bullion Office, for example, explained that in most years they varied between £40 and £130, adding that 'the money so received is divided, three quarters between the two Chiefs equally, the remainder to the Junior'; while in some departments they could total as much as several hundred pounds a year. Payne for his part took the high moral ground – 'he has allways refused them, conceding it totally inconsistent with his Station to accept of any, as it is undoubt-edly his duty to do the business of the Publick with the Bank, without receiving any emolument from them for so doing' – but cumulatively it was clear that tips from customers were generally welcome. And the Committee plausibly concluded not only that these gratuities led to 'dissatisfaction & heart-burnings amongst the Clerks themselves, from the unequal distributions in some of the Offices', but also, 'what is a matter of much more serious consequence', a disturbing pattern in staff behaviour of 'partialities & unjust preferences, towards the Publick', in other words a natural favouring of those customers who were the big tippers.

The question of clerks in the Transfer Offices doubling up as stock-brokers in the nearby Rotunda (or Brokers' Exchange) had been a thorny one since the early 1770s, when the practice was explicitly forbidden but seemingly continued nevertheless. The Committee of Inspection was determined to get at the existing truth of the matter. Robert Browning, an irascible Dorsetshire man who was second in charge at the Bank Stock Office and the poet's grandfather, stoutly denied that any of the clerks in his office 'act as Brokers in their own persons', but did accept that they 'buy & sell Stock for their friends through the means of a Broker who generally allows them ⅔ds, & sometimes a larger proportion, of the Commission'; Bibbins

of the same office stated that the clerks employed brokers to buy or
sell stock for their friends, explaining that 'most of them are upon
such good terms with the Brokers that they rarely, if ever, charge them
any brokerage'; while Turner, head of the 3 Per Cent Reduced Office,
conceded of his clerks that 'some of them do act as Brokers & may be
likewise concerned in Jobbing'. The next key witness was that high
liver Abraham Vickery. 'Common rumour says Mr Vickery & M^r
Salmon [a Stock Exchange broker] are partners – that Vickery makes
out many of the Tickets himself – that there is a little boy of Salmons
who is always stationed in front of Vickery's Seat, & carries about
his Tickets,' privately noted Bosanquet, adding that 'he acts improperly & over rough with the Clerks'. Certainly Vickery was rough
enough when on New Year's Eve 1783 he gave evidence, pronouncing that he had 'informed all the Clerks under him that, when called
before the Committee, he should openly & candidly declare all he
knew concerning their conduct' – a threat he proceeded to fulfil,
telling the Committee that, in terms of his clerks acting as brokers,
'he believes several of them do to no inconsiderable amount'. As for
himself, however, he was adamant, baldly stating that he was 'in no
ways concerned in partnership with Mr Salmon or any other Broker',
and denying that he had ever acted as a broker or a jobber himself. So
it continued into 1784. 'He does not act as a Broker, but takes care to
be always at his book & never goes into the Market, nor does he job,'
declared Francis Fonton of his own impeccable behaviour in the 3
Per Cent Consols Office; his colleague Poppleton 'acknowledg'd that
he acts as a Broker, but said he does not often go into the Market',
promising that he would not do so in future; and several clerks from
the 4 Per Cent Consols Office admitted that they sometimes acted as
brokers, though usually in 'a very trifling way'. The eventual upshot
was a resolution, passed by the Court of Directors in August 1784,
'that no clerk of the Bank should act as a Stockbroker under pain of
immediate dismission from his employment', while if any clerk was
still in partnership with a stockbroker he must 'immediately discon-
tinue the connexion'. Notices to that effect, painted in large letters,
were accordingly posted in the Rotunda and each of the Transfer
Offices.

These three areas of concern were not the only ones. The Committee
also demanded that current Bank ledgers should no longer be left out

all night open on desks; that the lockers that generally kept the Bank's books should be much less flimsily constructed; that access to vaults containing bills and notes should be much more tightly controlled; and above all that the senior men should raise their game. 'Very extraordinary' was the Committee's verdict on the disturbing revelation that the chiefs of the departments and the heads of the offices were usually the first each day to quit the Bank, 'leaving the charge of everything to the vigilance and honesty of junior clerks'; and the Committee insisted that henceforth those at the top were to be 'held accountable for the conduct of those immediately under them'. Altogether, it was a commendably root-and-branch exercise that Bosanquet and his two fellow-directors undertook in 1783–4. And their sixth and final report ended with all due sonority:

> When we contemplate the immense importance of the Bank of England not only to the City of London, in points highly essential to the promotion & extension of its Commerce, but to the Nation at large, as the grand Palladium of Publick Credit, we cannot but be thoroughly persuaded that an Object so great in itself & so interesting to all Ranks of the Community, must necessarily excite care & solicitude in every breast, for the wise administration of its Affairs, but principally & directly in theirs who are entrusted with the immediate management of them.

'We deem it therefore superfluous,' they concluded, 'to say a single word to the Court with a view of inculcating a religious Veneration for the glorious fabrick, or of recommending a steady and unremitting attention to its sacred Preservation.'

All too soon, however, there was another scandal, another committee. Samuel Bosanquet may have judged Francis Fonton 'a very good regular clerk', but in September 1790 he was found guilty of forging stock receipts for his own financial gain, leading to his hanging in November. That same month a Special Committee was appointed, resulting in March 1791 in the promulgation of seventeen 'Rules and Orders' relating to the daily conduct of every clerk. These included much more rigorous attendance requirements; an injunction that each clerk should conduct himself 'with zeal and activity to the business allotted him', paying 'implicit obedience to the directions of his superiors in office'; a similar exhortation to behave to the public 'with the utmost civility and assiduity without giving a preference to any, but serving each person in his proper turn'; and a series of specific demands, such as not to move freely between offices, not 'on any account' to employ a non-Bank person on Bank business, not without permission to 'allow any person to have access to books or papers belonging to the Bank, or to furnish extracts thereof, or information of any kind relating to the business of the House', not to make unauthorised erasures in Bank books (ledgers), and not only to report to the chief cashier or chief accountant knowledge of any 'unfaithfulness, fraud, error, or any indirect practices against the interest of the Bank committed by any person whatever', but to 'use every endeavour to prevent or detect the same'. There were also similarly stern injunctions for the Bank's senior men; in addition the Special Committee successfully recommended both the recruitment of at least eight day porters to enhance internal security and the taking in hand of the Library, still 'encumbered with much useless lumber' in the shape of cancelled banknotes and redundant old books. This task, sensibly added the Committee, was to be undertaken by 'a few active young men', for the three existing librarians, all long in the tooth, were 'seldom disposed to spend any great part of their time in a building where at some seasons they must expect to find it cold and damp'.[12]

Rome was not built in a day, and January 1792 saw the unwelcome discovery that two clerks, Richard Hands and Shadrach Shaw, had been systematically defrauding the Bank through forged stock transfers, disguising their crime by using their own money to pay dividends to the real owners. Although Hands got away, Shaw found himself being sentenced at the Old Bailey to seven years' transportation; and, in a perhaps surprisingly generous gesture, the Bank sent £50 to the captain of the *Royal Admiral* 'for extra expenses which he will incur in affording some comforts and conveniences to Shadrach Shaw who is to go to Botany Bay as a convict on board such ship'. Before their fall from grace, Hands and Shaw would have been just in time to see the handsome outfits worn by the newly recruited day porters, in the event eleven of them. 'The said Day Porters to be furnished with coats and badges,' recorded the Court minutes in May 1791, with the high probability that this was when what became a familiar and famous uniform (salmon-pink tailed jacket, red waistcoat, black trousers, silk

top hat) began to be worn. Who designed it? At least one Bank historian has speculated that John Soane may well have had a leading hand
in the choice of livery; and given that over the years it would set off
so well against his great banking halls, only the pedantic or curmud-
geonly might wish to find evidence showing otherwise.[13]

4

An Elderly Lady in the City

In 1797 a Scottish MP called Alexander Allardyce penned *An Address to the Proprietors of the Bank*. Noting that he himself had become a proprietor 'some years ago', he related how on doing so he had sought to find out about the management of the institution in which he now had a financial stake. 'As to the state of affairs of the Bank, it was a perfect mystery, said to be known only to the Court of Directors. Every body said, that the Bank must be possessed of an immense hoard of wealth, which was continually increasing; but, when asked for what this hoard and its accumulations were intended, nobody could tell but the Directors, and they were not accustomed to answer questions of that nature.' Allardyce willingly conceded – as over the years did most of the Bank's critics – that 'the present Directors are men of integrity and honour', but the sense of exasperation was palpable. In fact, even as Allardyce wrote, the fundamentals were changing. The war with France that began in February 1793 and lasted a generation not only precipitated monetary turmoil, but also placed the Bank and its affairs beneath an unprecedented public gaze.

Turmoil certainly characterised the first few months of the war. 'An alarming effect upon the public credit was brought by the check given to our trade and manufactures,' noted the director Samuel Thornton in January 1794 in his private overview of the previous year. 'But for the successful interference of Parliament, by the issue and loan of a new species of Exchequer bills, the effect would have been fatal to the mercantile part of the community.' Even so, he added, 'the number of bankruptcies in the last year exceeds all former example'. Thornton himself had been a member of an eleven-strong ad hoc City committee that in April had urgently pressed on Pitt the large-scale issue of Exchequer bills, which sound but hard-pressed merchants and traders could discount at once at the Bank; before that, amid what was one of the century's most serious financial and commercial crises (already brewing during the winter of 1792–3), credits from the Bank had helped in March to save some of the City's key merchants. According to Sir Francis Baring's retrospective account of the crisis, these credits involved a significant change of policy. 'In the distress of 1793,' he explained, 'they [the Bank] committed a fatal error by deciding that all merchants and traders were entitled to their proportion of accommodation as the Bank was a public body and ought not to discriminate between individuals.' Put another way, houses now receiving their 'proportion of accommodation' included Jewish houses – unwelcome to Baring, but a signal moment in the City's development as an international financial centre, with war poised to recruit to London from Germany and the Low Countries an array of talented outsiders (many of them Jewish) from Nathan Rothschild downwards.

Yet was the Bank, in purely financial terms, being too liberal in its approach, notwithstanding the severity of the crisis? 'If not the whole by farr the greater part of the accommodation intended for the merchant Bankers & traders resident within the Kingdom of Great Britain (by the bye a pretty comprehensive description) must as surely come from the Coffers of the B. of E. without the Least necessity for any application for the consent of the directors as if the Court of Directors had with the most unbounded Liberality of sentiment offered to advance the whole money,' Benjamin Winthrop, a former and future director ('give me credit for the purity of my motives'), wrote darkly to the Committee of Treasury in early May ahead of the implementation of the Exchequer bills scheme, even as parliamentary critics claimed loudly that the Bank was not doing enough. And Winthrop found instruction if not consolation in history: 'King Alfred divided his Loaf with the Pilgrim but he did not make an offer of his whole Loaf to the Pilgrim.' In fact, the scheme worked a treat, as did the introduction of the £5 note (a temporary measure that proved to have staying power), and Winthrop's fears were unfounded; but the crisis as a whole was yet another reminder of the difficulty of pleasing everyone.[1]

The war itself inevitably put fresh strains on the Bank's already difficult relationship with the relentlessly demanding Pitt. He for his part was ultimately prepared to defend the Bank when necessary – even on one occasion telling the Commons that it was 'a private trading company' that would regard any attempt to have a governor and deputy governor cross-examined by the House as 'highly unjust and violent' – but generally treated it with a large degree of ruthlessness and at times deviousness. The relationship's worst year was 1795, as the war's financial pressures deepened. In January the governor and deputy governor, Godfrey Thornton and Daniel Giles respectively, 'waited on Mr. P.' (in the latter's words) 'to acquaint him that it was their wish to bring to his consideration that he would so settle his arrangements of Finance for the present year so as not to depend on any further assistance from the Bank beyond the 4 millions already agreed upon & that the advances on the Treasury bills cannot be allowed at any time to exceed the sum of five hundred thousand pounds'; by June the Bank was threatening to withhold all further advances on Treasury bills; in July it warned gravely about its liabilities starting dangerously to exceed its reserves of specie; and in August it refused a request for a further advance on Exchequer paper, with Giles, now governor, reminding Pitt that 'a provident care for their Establishment must precede all other Objects'. Giles, indeed, seems to have had a gratifyingly combative streak, in October even asking Pitt face to face whether he actually knew how the nation's reserves of gold stood; to which, according to the Committee of Treasury's discreetly pencilled minutes, the great man 'really took shame to himself for having never formed any idea on that subject so as to leave him to judge of it with any accuracy'.

In fact, the Bank's treasure by this time was rapidly shrinking, not least in the context of the French government's determined attempt to restore its own gold standard after the collapse of the assignat. What to do? Winthrop, a director again, had his say in a characteristic letter to Giles at the start of December. Arguing that 'the unexampled Efflux of Specie & Bullion from the Bank in the course of the last Six Months' was likely to continue or even intensify, and declaring that the Bank's own 'Safety' was 'a Consideration in my Mind far superior & paramount to all others', he urgently called for the Bank 'to endeavour to contract our Advances to Government at this time'. In the middle of a patriotic war, that was always going to be easier said than done; but four weeks later, on New Year's Eve, the Bank did seek to retrench, with the directors resolving 'to adopt some Measures

that will be effectual to enable the Court at all times to restrain the
Amount of the Discounts within such Limits as they shall from Time
to Time prescribe', in practice through a system of weekly limits.[2]
The directors had a far from easy line to tread: tightening commercial
credit might easily trigger alarm and in turn another financial crisis;
yet doing nothing to check the flight of gold was hardly an attractive
alternative.

The year 1796 proved a predictably stressful one, with an internal drain on gold replacing the external drain and taking the Bank's
treasure, which had stood at some £7 million back in 1794, down to
below £2 million by the autumn. For the City as a whole, though, the
greater preoccupation – and bone of contention – was the Bank's new
discount-restriction policy. In February a group of Bank proprietors
lodged a complaint, only to be informed haughtily by the Committee
of Treasury that it was 'quite unusual in the Bank to give particular
reasons for any measures which they, after mature deliberation, may
think fit to adopt'; and when in April a City committee (that included
the versatile financier Walter Boyd, close to Pitt and no friend of the
Bank) sought to establish a board of twenty-five members that would
be authorised by Parliament and issue promissory notes, 'for the
express purpose of furnishing to trade a temporary assistance which
the Bank of England do not find it convenient, or perhaps do not
think themselves sufficiently authorised, under their present powers,
to give', the Bank made a dead set against it and successfully persuaded
Pitt to offer it no encouragement. Not that the Pitt/Bank relationship was suddenly harmonious. Take the memorial that the directors
presented to him in late July after they had agreed, with intense reluctance, to his latest pressing request for a substantial advance:

> They beg leave to declare, that nothing could induce them, under
> the present circumstances, to comply with the demand now made
> upon them, but the dread that their refusal might be productive of a
> greater evil, and nothing but the extreme pressure and exigencies of
> the case can in any shape justify them for acceding to this measure,
> and they apprehend, that in so doing, they render themselves totally
> incapable of granting any further assistance to Government during
> the remainder of this year, and unable even to make the usual
> advances on the land and mort for the ensuing year ...

'Money is extremely scarce in the City,' noted next week the diarist Joseph Farington (not a City man, but with his ears close to the ground), adding, 'Bank Directors much out of humour with Pitt'. By autumn the prevailing City mood was one of anxiety and grumbling. 'The apprehension of an invasion of this country seems to have taken possession of men's minds so strongly that even in every company it becomes a subject of conversation,' reported *The Times* in September, an apprehension naturally contributing much to the hoarding of gold, as guineas were withdrawn rapidly from the country banks as well as from the Bank itself. As for grumbling, supplementing anxiety, Farington received an instructive visit at the start of October from a Mr Berwick, woollen draper as well as Cornhill banker:

> There are great difficulties in the City from a want of money, – He blames in some degree some of the Directors of the Bank, who are supposed to be unfriendly to government, and who may have an interest in promoting occasional difficulties. – He also said that the *Capital* of the Bank is not proportioned to the business done, which is a cause of hesitation in discounting there from an apprehension that if the times become precarious from the alarms of invasion &c. a run might be made which the Bank could not answer, not having specie equal to its discounts or in such proportion as to secure its safety in such an emergency.

Despite the success of Pitt's so-called Loyalty Loan in December – the Bank showing the way by contributing £1 million, plus £½ million from individual directors – neither government nor people, City nor Bank, entered 1797 in optimistic mood.[3]

'I have found my health decline through anxiety and application,' reflected Samuel Thornton in January, writing his customary retrospective of the previous year. 'The duties I have to fulfil at the Bank, and the office of deputy governor upon which I am entering [he was due to take up the position in the spring], call indeed for all my attention.' So they already did, and so they increasingly would. The early weeks of 1797 were essentially more of the same – rumours of imminent invasion, flight of gold, money tight – before a dramatic endgame began during the last full week of February. A series of country banks stopped payment; specie drained from the Bank at the rate of some £100,000 a day; a substantial enemy fleet was sighted off Beachy Head, a sighting that did its damage before proving false; the price of Consols tumbled; and a handful of the Bank's main men – usually including governor Daniel Giles, deputy governor Thomas Raikes, veteran director Samuel Bosanquet and Thornton himself – were in seemingly ceaseless conclave with Pitt, giving him regular updates about the loss of gold, as the treasure threatened to dip below £1 million. Thus on Tuesday the 21st the Bank's deputation, having explained 'exactly to him how the Cash [specie] is circumstanced', urged 'that he may, if possible and proper, strike out some means of alleviating the public alarms, and stopping this apparent disposition in people's minds for having a large deposit of Cash in their houses'; three days later, the Bank's representatives waited on Pitt not only to impart the latest alarming bullion figures (£130,000 withdrawn that Friday), but 'to ask him how far he thought the Bank might venture to go on paying Cash, and when he would think it necessary to interfere before our Cash was so reduced as might be detrimental to the immediate service of the State'. The ball, in other words, was firmly placed in Pitt's court – and next morning, Saturday the 25th, as news reached London that French troops had landed at Fishguard, he resolved to take decisive action, probably to the relief of the Bank.[4]

Events over the rest of the weekend moved with notably clockwork precision. Pitt later on Saturday despatched a message to King George III at Windsor, urgently asking him to return to London the next morning; noon on Sunday saw a meeting of the Privy Council, attended also by Giles and his three colleagues, at which the decision was reached to suspend cash payments; and at the Bank on Sunday evening, eleven directors (including the lord mayor, Brook Watson) assembled to wait for the formal communication from the Privy Council. This duly arrived at half-past seven, containing an Order in Council stating that it was the 'unanimous Opinion' of that body that it was 'indispensably necessary for the Publick Service, that the Directors of the Bank of England, should forbear issuing any Cash in Payment until the Sense of Parliament can be taken on that Subject, and the proper Measures adopted thereupon, for maintaining the Means of Circulation, and supporting the Publick and Commercial Credit of the Kingdom at this important Conjuncture'. Whereupon, after Abraham Newland had been called in and 'directed to pay

Obedience' to the new dispensation, the lord mayor was 'desired to send round to all the Bankers in the City this Evening a Copy of the Injunction of the Privy Council'. Overnight, printed circulars were prepared for posting at the doors of the Bank – containing not only the text of the Order in Council, but a resolute and reassuring message from the Bank itself in consequence of that Order:

> The Governor, Deputy Governor, and Directors of the BANK of ENGLAND, think it their Duty to inform the Proprietors of BANK STOCK, as well as the PUBLICK at large, that the general Concerns of the BANK are in the most affluent and prosperous Situation, and such as to preclude every Doubt as to the Security of its Notes.
>
> The directors mean to continue their usual Discounts for the Accommodation of the Commercial Interest, paying the Amount in Bank Notes, and the Dividend Warrants will be paid in the same Manner.

A new, paper-money era was beginning, though amid huge uncertainty and with no one knowing – or even able plausibly to guess – for how long.

The lord mayor on the Sunday evening was also requested to ask the City's bankers to meet at the Mansion House at 11 o'clock on Monday morning. There, they carried a resolution, almost at once bearing about a thousand signatures, that had deliberately strong echoes of 1745 in its statement that, in order to 'prevent embarrassments to Publick Credit' and 'to support it with the utmost Exertions at the present important Conjuncture', the signatories 'do most readily hereby declare, that we will not refuse to receive Bank Notes in Payment of any Sum of Money to be paid to us, and we will use our utmost Endeavours to make all our Payments in the same Manner'. Other similar meetings and declarations, almost all intensely patriotic in tone, rapidly followed in many cities and towns; and the contemporary evidence strongly suggests a broad acceptance in these weeks of Bank of England notes even if they were no longer backed by gold, with the notes themselves soon including £1 and £2 denominations. One inevitable consequence was at the supply end. 'Before the present urgency there were 5 printing presses used in printing Bank notes,' whereas '*now* there are 16 presses employed night & day, and

14 more are to be added,' recorded Farington as early as 16 March. Legislation, meanwhile, gave full sanction to the new situation, with the Restriction Bill of 9 March (becoming law on 3 May) indemnifying the Bank against the direct consequences of suspension of cash payments. Predictably, if perhaps illogically, many now hoarded what gold they had left; and less than three weeks after suspension, Samuel Thornton confessed to his brother-in-law, Lord Balgonie, that 'I wish I could comply with your request & send you a bag of gold, but no such thing is to be obtained …'

The Bank was also busy in these weeks supplying witnesses to the 'secret' parliamentary committees investigating the events leading up to suspension. 'When did you first perceive a diminution of the usual quantity of Bank Notes in circulation?' the Commons Committee asked its first witness, Thomas Raikes, on 4 March, less than a week after the event. 'I cannot recollect,' replied the deputy governor, and his next few answers were not all that much more helpful:

Did that diminution take place, to any considerable degree, before the Bank began to lessen their Discounts? – I fancy not.

Did the diminution of the Discounts and of the Bank Notes in circulation, correspond with each other? – Yes; except so far as it might be affected by the emission of Bank Notes for the payment of dividends.

Did the diminution of Discounts, by the Bank, produce any difference with respect to discounts by private Bankers, and other persons usually discounting bills? – I presume it did.

What difference did it produce? – It is not within my cognizance, further than that the less accommodation the Bank give to the Public, the less Bank Notes will be in the hands of the Bankers.

The next witness was Pitt himself. 'I certainly thought, from all that passed, that they felt the necessity of the measure on public grounds,' he responded when asked about the attitude of the Bank directors to suspension. 'But,' he carefully added, 'I certainly do not mean to represent them as recommending or advising the measure.' The governor, Daniel Giles, was also asked: 'According to the best judgement you could form at that time, founded upon all the circumstances affecting the interest of the Bank, did you think such a measure necessary? – I thought it was prudential.' Other witnesses included Walter Boyd, who launched a full-scale attack on the Bank's December 1795 change of discount policy ('has diminished the powers of commercial houses, and diminished the value of public securities'), while from Threadneedle Street, after Raikes on being recalled had insisted that it was 'the alarm of invasion' that above all had caused 'the present drain', the remaining three witnesses were Benjamin Winthrop, Godfrey Thornton and Samuel Bosanquet. Winthrop put it on record that 'I was always fearful that such very large advances to Government might at some time or other operate very prejudicially to the Bank, and therefore on many occasions, as an individual Director, I have been against such advances'; Thornton feebly replied, 'The causes are unknown to me,' when asked to explain the unusual demand for specie; and Bosanquet cogently outlined the big picture as seen from the Bank's Court Room:

> Is it not always in the power of the Directors of the Bank to restrict the amount of their Advances to Government, and to enforce the reduction of those Advances? – Undoubtedly it is; but not without taking measures which may be very detrimental in their consequences. I do not recollect a single Advance of any importance, which has been consented to for the use of Government, for a considerable time past, but where the consequences of refusing it did not appear to the Directors to be liable to the fatal consequence of bringing on a public alarm, by injuring the national credit.

'And this,' explained Bosanquet, 'they judged likely to be of more fatal consequence than any inconvenience which could arise to the Bank from making the Advance.'[6]

The Commons naturally also debated the turn of events, specifically the Bank Restriction Bill. The most resonant contribution (retrospectively anyway) came on 24 March, from the Whig politician and Irish playwright Richard Brinsley Sheridan, always happy to portray Pitt's Tory government in an unfavourable light:

> He made a fanciful allusion to the Bank, as an elderly lady in the City, of great credit and long standing, who had lately made a *faux pas* which was not altogether inexcusable. She had he said unfortunately

fallen into bad company, and contracted too great an intimacy and connexion at the St James's end of the town. The young gentleman, however, who had employed all his arts of soft persuasion to seduce this old lady, had so far shown his designs, that by timely breaking off the connexion, there might be hopes for the old gentlewoman once more regaining her credit and injured reputation.

The Bank's main spokesman in the Commons was Samuel Thornton, who three days later ignored Sheridan's jest but insisted that 'no minister, nor any authority on earth, ever had or ever should control the conduct of the directors of the Bank in giving accommodation to individual merchants by way of discount', adding that 'the directors were the best judges to what extent their issue of paper should be made, which must be regulated by prudence ...' His words cut no ice with Sir William Pulteney, MP for Shrewsbury and reputedly the wealthiest man in Britain. In a fierce speech on 7 April he advocated 'putting an end to the monopoly of the Bank of England'; argued that 'its antiquity alone has had a great effect, and the imposing mystery which has hitherto been observed in the conduct of its affairs, has created an awe and veneration, which the human mind must, for a time, have some difficulty to overcome'; and went on:

But the late events, have, in a great measure, dispelled this charm: the Bank of England has been obliged to disclose the state of its affairs, the veil is drawn up, and we see nothing of that fancied magnificence which, till now, made a wonderful impression. It can never again, I believe, assume the same place in the imagination of the public.

The debate ended that day with a short pained speech from Thornton, explicitly repudiating Pulteney. 'The restriction did not arise from the operations of the Bank itself, but from other causes, which he was not at liberty to describe,' he stated; while 'as to the compact which was said to subsist between government and the Bank, during the years in which he had been connected with the Bank, he knew of no partiality whatever ...'[7]

The suspension of payments in gold was undeniably a huge national event, and the great political cartoonist James Gillray was quickly on the case. On 9 March a cartoon entitled 'MIDAS, Transmuting all into GOLD PAPER' went on sale at Mrs Hannah Humphrey's print shop in St James's, above which Gillray occupied a room. As arresting as anything that he drew, it showed Pitt vomiting banknotes and shitting money into the Bank of England. A fortnight later, Sheridan in the Commons indulged in his bit of fancy; and on 22 May, in the immediate context of Pitt under criticism for seeking to secure yet another substantial loan from the Bank, there appeared Gillray's celebrated cartoon, 'POLITICAL RAVISHMENT, or The Old Lady of Threadneedle Street in danger!' It depicted the freckly beanpole Pitt seeking to ravish a gaunt old lady dressed in banknotes and sitting on a locked box containing the Bank's treasure; while, as he did his worst, she was crying, 'Murder! murder! Rape! murder! – Oh you Villain! what have I kept my Honor untainted so long, to have it broke up, by you at last? – Oh Murder! Rape! Ravishment! Ruin! Ruin! Ruin!!!'[8] A nickname, by Gillray out of Sheridan, was thus born, lasting at least two centuries and in the process giving to the Bank an affectionate familiarity that no public relations campaign could have hoped to achieve.

On and off, but mainly on, Britain would continue to be at war with France for the next eighteen years, until Wellington's hard-fought victory at Waterloo. Jane Austen's near-silence on the subject may have suggested otherwise, but across Britain these were frequently tumultuous, even fearful years, wonderfully caught in Jenny Uglow's panoramic survey *In These Times* (2014). At the Bank, shortly before Christmas 1803 and following the appointment the previous month of a select committee, the Court of Directors was assured that 'a Plan has been concocted, whereby, they [the Committee] have reason to hope, not only the many valuable Articles, which are allways in the Custody of the Bank, but also such of the original Books and Papers, as appear most necessary to be preserved, may be secured from danger, during the confusion which is to be apprehended from an Invasion'. Personal vicissitudes were many, even for those accustomed to the dignity of the Court Room. 'With a fortune diminished by two-thirds of its amount,' mused Samuel Thornton at the start of 1812 in the context of having been compelled to sell his Albury Park estate in Surrey, 'I hope still to live with contentment, and though not in splendour, yet in comfort.' More generally, the Bank played a key role in the often underestimated (then and later) British war machine – a role acknowledged in 1800 by the almost entirely uncontentious twenty-one-year renewal of its Charter, taking it from 1812 to 1833 at the acceptable price of an interest-free £3 million loan to government for six years.[9]

What, then, specifically was the Bank's contribution to the war effort? Arguably it had six main aspects: first, amid the pound sterling's continuing inconvertibility, the issuing of paper money on a large scale, with the £1 and £2 denominations putting banknotes into the hands of the general populace for the first time; second, managing the hugely enlarged national debt, up from £245 million at the start of the war to £834 million by the end; third, managing much of the government's day-to-day money, an increasingly complex task; fourth, the time-honoured function of providing, relatively uncomplainingly, temporary advances to government, running for much of the duration at a reasonably manageable six to seven millions a year; fifth, managing the government loan process, vital to the financing of the war and usually involving competitive tenders from contractors, with the Treasury in practice heavily reliant on the disinterested guidance of the governor and deputy governor of the day; and sixth, stimulating commercial credit (largely through its discounting activities), not least so that, in a deeply uncertain trading world, merchants could guard against future shortages by stockpiling goods in their warehouses.

It was this sixth aspect that was by far the most controversial, especially after the commercial boom of 1808–10 got out of hand, with predictable results. Had the Bank, asked its critics, abused the freedom of non-convertibility? A trio of modern verdicts are helpful. Ian Duffy, the economic historian who has made the closest study of the Bank's discounting policy during what came to be known as the restriction period (that is, the suspension of cash payments), accepts that the Bank's refusal to reduce advances in early 1810 was mistaken; but at the same time he argues that this refusal was a tacit and honourable acknowledgement that its December 1795 policy of rigid rationing had been an error, leading to severe commercial and financial difficulties, even perhaps to suspension itself. More generally, Elisa Newby has valuably emphasised how these eighteen years were inevitably taxing times, as 'the war, high government expenditure, trade blockades and bad harvests made the formulation of monetary policy a difficult task'. Yet despite all this, she observes, the Bank's notes were accepted as payment throughout, while the fact that interest rates (for both long- and short-term borrowing) remained below 6 per cent graphically indicated the monetary policy's market credibility. A final word goes to a politician as well as historian, Kwasi Kwarteng: 'Despite the steep increase in [government] borrowing, the fact that the paper pound essentially held its value [depreciating only 30 per cent between 1797 and 1815] was an extraordinary piece of financial management on the part of any central bank. The Bank of England had organised government borrowing, but it had not put money into circulation. In modern parlance, the Bank maintained a tight control of the money supply, in stark contrast to the French and American revolutionary regimes.'[10]

An important and time-consuming by-product of the paper-money era – especially with so many people unaccustomed to banknotes now having them in their pockets – was large-scale forgery and the related crime of 'uttering' (deliberately possessing and circulating) counterfeit notes. 'If some steps are not taken to counteract this alarming increase in the circulation of forged paper,' a Plymouth correspondent warned the Bank only four years after suspension, 'we are apprehensive that it may prevent the negotiating of your notes altogether.' Or as a partner from the Bank's solicitors, the firm that soon became known as Freshfields, put it in 1809: 'The fabrication and circulation of forged bank notes has lately become so systematic a matter of business that the security of the circulating medium of the country is seriously menaced and unless prompt and active measures are taken to detect and punish the offenders, the most serious consequences may be the result.' The Bank's reaction to the problem was vigorous, undertaking in most years between 1800 and 1815 at least thirty prosecutions for forgery, having not stinted in its system of financial rewards in order to get to that point. A significant proportion of prosecutions ended in the death penalty, though legislation in 1801 permitted those pleading guilty to uttering the lesser sentence of fourteen years of transportation.

Inevitably, letters from convicted prisoners, appealing for mercy and/or charity (usually pecuniary), poured in. How did the Bank, whose Committee for Law Suits met regularly from 1802, respond? 'Deliberate and rational' is Deirdre Palk's verdict, based on her pioneering analysis of this often wretched correspondence and what ensued. 'To those, male or female, who were condemned to die, it would make only the cold response that it was not its business to interfere. Nor would it support others petitioning the Home Secretary or monarch. Having gone through the expensive and difficult process of prosecuting capitally those it believed to be a serious threat to the nation's, and its own, security, it stood back, justified in its actions. On the other hand, the Bank showed tolerance towards those who were going to be removed from the country.' In particular, she notes, 'the Bank was willing to respond with generosity to women convicts while they remained in prison and when they went on board the transport ships'; while in general 'it responded favourably to requests from women, and unfavourably to requests from men'. Financial relief was above all what most women asked for – and, according to Palk, 'this was what they got in abundance', often in the form of weekly payments, usually after the Bank had sent investigators to Newgate to check the genuineness of the request. 'The reasons given were distress, hunger, little children to support, lack of clothing, no husband or friends to give support, no one to visit them. Men were not so likely to be in this condition, or so the Gentlemen of the Bank believed.'[11]

The paper-money era, and the attendant rise of counterfeiting, also meant that the focus was on the banknotes themselves. 'Until means are discovered of rendering the Forgery of Bank Notes utterly impracticable,' observed a landscape engraver, John Landseer, in 1797, 'it should seem to be a duty the Bank Directors owe to the Public and to themselves to render it as difficult as possible.' Perhaps the Bank should have taken responsibility for coming up with its own solution, but instead it asked the public at large to put forward proposals for a so-called 'inimitable' note – a course of action that led to some 400 suggestions reaching the Bank during the whole restriction period. Sadly, the quest proved unavailing, with a future governor recalling in the 1830s that 'the multiplicity of proposed schemes, the absurdity of many and the inefficiency of others had tended to embarrass and protract the subject rather than add any useful information'; even among those proposals that had some initial plausibility, there proved to be no 'inimitable' note that the Bank's engraver was not capable of copying. As for the Bank's existing notes – or 'Newlands' as they were often called, in reference to the chief cashier, whose name appeared as the payee on all notes until his retirement in 1807 – some new security measures were undoubtedly adopted during these years, in addition to the traditional use of white watermarked paper, but there was some truth in the claim of a miniature painter called J. T. Barber Beaumont. Of 'inferior workmanship to common engraved shop-bills' was his unfavourable judgement, soon after the end of the war, on the Bank's notes; and furthermore, he added, they could be forged 'by any one who can use a camel's hair pencil'.[12]

Famously, the paper-money era engendered more than its fair share of debate among economists and bankers. The first phase occurred in the early 1800s, against the background of a sharp rise in the cost of food and an unfavourable turn in the foreign exchanges. *A Letter to the Right Honourable William Pitt, on the Influence of the Stoppage of Issues in Specie at the Bank of England* was the title of Walter Boyd's combative pamphlet, published in early 1801. Boyd argued that 'there is the highest probability that the increase of Bank Notes is the principal cause of the great rise in the price of commodities and every species of exchangeable value'; declared that 'the real resources of the country are now, and always have been, too solid and extensive to require the aid of forced paper-money, that dangerous quack-medicine'; professed himself 'intimately convinced' that 'the resumption of payments in specie at the Bank' would be 'perfectly consistent' with 'the truest interest' of 'the Bank itself'; and depicted the Bank's directors as facing since 1797 an 'almost irresistible temptation', given that the 'impression upon their minds, that every fresh addition to their circulating paper was a new service rendered', chimed so naturally with 'the still more powerful and certain conviction that it was, at the same time, an addition to the sources of profit to the Bank'.

Later that year came a direct refutation from Sir Francis Baring, who back in 1797, not long after suspension, had publicly identified the Bank as the lender of last resort – while 1802 saw a heavyweight contribution from Henry Thornton. He was an MP, an economist, a City banker and a younger brother of Samuel (who himself the previous year had optimistically noted that 'my own strength and vigour will be recruited as soon as my responsible situation of Governor to the Bank shall be ended'). *An Enquiry into the Nature and Effects of the Paper Credit of Great Britain* had at its heart a paradox. On the one hand, it stoutly defended the Bank, not only highlighting its independence of government but finding 'an additional ground of confidence' in it, namely:

> that the numerous proprietors who chuse the directors, and have the power of controlling them (a power of which they have prudently forborne to make any frequent use), are men whose general stake in the country far exceeds that particular one which they have in the stock of the company. They are men, therefore, who feel themselves to be most deeply interested not merely in the increase of the dividends or in the maintenance of the credit of the Bank of England, but in the support of commercial as well as public credit in general. There is, indeed, both among them and among the whole commercial world, who make so large a portion of this country, a remarkable determination to sustain credit, and especially the credit of the bank ...

On the other hand, the remorseless logic of Thornton's treatise tended towards what soon became known as the 'bullionist' position, at whose heart lay the belief – for some an almost messianic belief – that it was the quantity of money that determined prices. 'His loyalty to the Bank of England led him to accept too readily the view that the premium on gold was due to a decline in trade due to bad harvests,' reflected the economist J. Keith Horsefield many years later. 'Nor did he recognise that his explanation of the necessity to suspend cash payments – a panic demand for gold at home superimposed upon an unfavourable balance of trade – was in itself inadequate to justify the continuance of the suspension. His theoretical demonstration was perfectly clear, and only his reliance on the practical good sense of the Bank can have prevented his applying it to the facts.'[13]

The debate then died down for some six or seven years, while the Bank continued to apply its practical good sense. The reason for the debate's return was mainly economic (in particular another unfavourable turn on the exchanges, throwing fresh doubt on the strength of the currency in a paper-money regime), but it also owed something to the remarkable stockjobber-turned-economist David Ricardo. 'All the evils in our currency', he stated in a pungent piece in the *Morning Chronicle* in August 1809, were 'owing to the over-issues of the Bank, to the dangerous power with which it was entrusted [since 1797] of diminishing at its will, the value of every moneyed man's property, and by enhancing the price of provisions, and every necessary of life, injuring the public annuitant, and all those persons whose incomes were fixed, and who were consequently not enabled to shift any part of the burden from their own shoulders'. Ricardo undoubtedly came to hold a dim view of the Bank, delighting in nicknaming it dismissively 'the company of merchants' – which was true enough, though underestimating the very real concern about conflicts of interest if that institution elected out-and-out bankers to its Court of Directors. In any case, not long afterwards, the Commons agreed to appoint what became known as the Bullion Committee, with the three active members comprising its chairman Francis Horner, the rising Tory politician William Huskisson and the widely esteemed Henry Thornton.[14]

Taking evidence between February and May 1810, the Committee had several sessions with the governor, John Whitmore, and deputy governor, John Pearse. In all likelihood neither enjoyed the experience, but they held firm to their position that (in the governor's words) 'the Bank never force a note into circulation, and there will not remain a note in circulation more than the immediate wants of the public require'. And they explained that when it came to making a discounting decision, the three key considerations were 'the amount already given to the individual', 'the solidity of the paper' and 'the appearance of its being issued for commercial purposes'. Indeed, insisted Whitmore, 'the Bank does not comply with the whole demand upon them for discounts, and they are never induced, by a view to their own profit, to push their issues beyond what they deem consistent with the public interest'. More than once the two men found themselves having to stall – 'I desire time to consider that question … I would wish for time to consider that question … I cannot say, for want of advices …' – while Whitmore was adamant that 'I decline answering questions as to opinion.' Perhaps inevitably, that included anything relating to the possible future of cash payments, with both men playing the deadest of bats. Following the proceedings especially closely was Ricardo, and on Whitmore being asked a hypothetical question and replying that 'never having weighed the subject with any reference to the price of Bullion, I am not prepared with an opinion how a merchant would act in such a case', he privately noted, 'Is not this a confession that he has not considered a most important question in political economy, particularly necessary to be well understood by a Bank director?'

The most powerful criticism of the Bank came from Sir Francis Baring, no longer able – following the recent tide of speculation amid an apparent loosening of monetary policy – to support suspension and the wide discretionary powers that that had given to the Bank:

> There are many instances of clerks not worth £100 establishing themselves as merchants, and receiving (since the restriction) an accommodation from the Bank, by discounting what is called good bills to the amount (probably) of five or £10,000; such a demand I am inclined to consider as created by the Bank, and not arising out of a regular course of trade, such as would exist if the restriction was removed. This circumstance is important, if my opinion, that the circulation of the country cannot be perfectly safe until the restriction is removed, is well founded.

'I think the Bank would not be disposed to extend their issues beyond three-fourths part of its present amount,' Baring added, 'if the restriction was removed.' To these and similar charges, Jeremiah Harman, a director since 1794, was unwilling to concede an inch:

> Do you not apprehend that there is a disposition in persons keeping accounts at the Bank, to apply for a larger extent of discount than it is on the whole expedient for the Bank to grant? – Very many do, and we treat them accordingly.
>
> Do you not think that the sum total applied for, even though the accommodation afforded should be on the security of good bills to safe persons, might be such as to produce some excess in the quantity of the Bank issues if fully complied with? – I think if we discount only for solid persons, and such paper as is for real *bona fide* transactions, we cannot materially err.

The final Bank witness was John Humble, principal clerk of the Bullion Office (which according to him 'used formerly to be called the Warehouse'). 'Can you state to the Committee,' he was asked, 'the quantity, or nearly the quantity, of gold bullion imported, that has been deposited in your office in the course of the last year?' 'I have no conception of it,' he replied. 'Could you not state from your books the amount of sales of gold of all sorts for the last year?' To this he was more helpful: 'Probably we might.'

Horner, Huskisson and Thornton (by now an explicit bullionist) produced their report in June. The key recommendation was that cash payments should be resumed in 1812; and their treatment of the Bank was firm but measured, noting at the outset that suspension in 1797 had been 'not a measure fought for by the Bank, but imposed upon it by the Legislature for what were held to be urgent reasons of State policy and public expediency'. The fundamental argument was straightforward:

> It was a necessary consequence of the suspension of cash payments, to exempt the Bank from that drain of Gold, which, in former times, was sure to result from an unfavourable Exchange and a high price of Bullion. And the Directors, released from all fears of such a drain, and no longer feeling any inconvenience from such a state of things, have not been prompted to restore the Exchanges and the price of Gold to their proper level by a reduction of their advances and issues.

Unfortunately, suggested the report, the Bank had been too stuck in its ways, failing to alter its policy, based on familiar 'sound and well adjusted principles', in the light of the unfamiliar post-1797 situation. The three wise men helpfully summarised that policy:

> The Bank Directors, as well as some of the merchants who have been examined, shewed a great anxiety to state to Your Committee a doctrine, of the truth of which they professed themselves to be most thoroughly convinced, that there can be no possible excess in the issue of Bank of England paper, so long as the advances in which it is issued are made upon the principles which at present guide the conduct of the Directors, that is, so long as the discount of mercantile Bills are confined to paper of undoubted solidity, arising out of real commercial transactions, and payable at short and fixed periods.

Furthermore, the report went on:

> It was natural for the Bank Directors to believe, that nothing but benefit could accrue to the public at large, while they saw the

growth of Bank profits go hand in hand with the accommoda-
tions granted to the Merchants. It was hardly to be expected of the
directors of the Bank, that they should be fully aware of the consequences that might result from their pursuing, after the suspension
of cash payments, the same system which they have found a safe
one before. To watch the operation of so new a law, and to provide
against the injury which might result from it to the public interests,
was the province, not so much of the Bank as of the Legislature.

Ultimately, the discretionary trust, established as a result of suspension, was one 'which it is unreasonable to expect that the Directors
of the Bank of England should ever be able to discharge', given that
'the most detailed knowledge of the actual trade of the Country,
combined with the profound science in all the principles of Money
and circulation, would not enable any man or set of men to adjust,
and keep always adjusted, the right proportion of circulating medium
in a country to the wants of trade'. The magisterial summing-up came
later in the paragraph:

> The Directors of the Bank of England, in the judgement of Your
> Committee, have exercised the new and extraordinary discretion
> reposed in them since 1797, with an integrity and a regard to the
> public interest, according to their conceptions of it, and indeed a
> degree of forbearance in turning it less to the profit of the Bank
> than it would easily have admitted of, that meant the continuance
> of that confidence which the public has so long and so justly felt
> in the integrity with which its affairs are directed, as well as in the
> unshaken stability and ample funds of that great establishment.
> That their recent policy involves great practical errors, which it is
> of the utmost public importance to correct, Your Committee are
> fully convinced; but those errors are less to be imputed to the Bank
> Directors, than to be stated as the effect of a new system, of which,
> however it originated, or was rendered necessary as a temporary
> expedient, it might have been well if Parliament had sooner taken
> into view all the consequences.

The Bank may still have been in some sense a private body (to the
extent, indeed, that the Bullion Committee meekly gave way over the

Bank's insistence that it need not be required to reveal the total of its private discounts); but inasmuch as it was to be regarded as a public institution – increasing by the year – the whole question of discretion was shaping up as the battleground of the future.[15]

More immediately, the question was whether Parliament would side with the economists or with the practical men. 'A strong political contention has arisen about our paper currency,' observed Samuel Thornton at the start of 1811, adding that 'parties are very nearly balanced'. Finally, in May, a four-day debate in the Commons decided the matter. From the Bank, Alexander Baring (a director since 1805) asserted that 'the mass of the evil was to be found in the national debt, and not in the circulating medium', while Samuel Thornton 'disclaimed the idea that the Bank issued paper to an unlimited amount', pointed out that 'the discounting of bills was not the only means of issuing their paper, much being issued on government securities', and 'expressed his conviction that there would be no limit to the distress and embarrassment that must follow the restoration of cash payments, under circumstances like the present'; from the bullionists, William Wilberforce expressed disappointment with the evidence of the Bank directors ('their eyes were not opened to the magnitude of the duties they were called on to discharge'); and from the politicians, the decisive contribution was that of Spencer Perceval, like Pitt both prime minister and chancellor of the exchequer, according to whom the adoption of the Bullion Report 'would be tantamount to a declaration that they would no longer continue those foreign exertions which they had hitherto considered indispensable to the security of the country'. In other words, there was a war still on, its outcome remained deeply uncertain, and the unavoidable fact was that resuming cash payments – however theoretically desirable – would seriously jeopardise getting hold of specie in order to pay armies and fleets, to subsidise allies and to pay for food imports in the context of Napoleon's Continental Blockade. Indeed, if Horner's resolution in May 1811 to end the Bank restriction 'two years from the present time' had been passed, that would have taken effect in 1813, just when (observes Clapham) 'Napoleon was beating Russians and Prussians at Lützen and Bautzen'. But Horner's resolution was rejected, the Commons instead resolved that cash payments should be resumed six months after the end of the war, and for the time being the Bank was allowed to continue doing its best or worst. Ricardo meanwhile could only fume. 'I trust the day is not far distant,' he had written in the *Morning Chronicle* following the publication of the Bullion Committee's report, 'when we shall look back with aston-ishment at the delusion to which we have so long been subject, in allowing a company of merchants, notoriously ignorant of the most obvious principles of political oeconomy, to regulate at their will, the value of the property of a great portion of the community.'[16]

Fortunately the great economist was not privy to the Bank's records in October 1811, revealing difficulty in maintaining a quorum at the Court and seven directors (including Alexander Baring, Stephen Thornton and a future governor, Cornelius Buller) being rather acerbically asked 'when their attendance could be depended upon'. Even so, the government's reliance upon the Bank during these last few years of the war was as heavy as ever, as again and again it sent supplicant letters begging the purchase of surplus Exchequer bills. Perceval's successor as chancellor was Nicholas Vansittart – known as 'Van' and somewhat unfairly the laughing-stock of the advanced school of financiers under Huskisson, who called him 'old Mouldy'. A request from Van on 16 May 1815, just weeks before Waterloo and asking the governor and deputy governor to enable the purchase of £2 million of Exchequer bills, had all the well-worn phrases: 'Lord Liverpool [prime minister] and I had hoped ... I am, however, sorry to find myself under the necessity of requesting ... I feel it my Duty earnestly to recommend this Application to the favourable consid-eration of your Court.' As usual, the application was successful; and Clapham's evocative phrases about the Bank's 'reluctant yet stubborn' support of the chancellor of the day, backing him 'faithfully, if some-times with groans', almost certainly capture the relationship exactly.[17]

The war was far from being John Soane's restriction period, as his physical transformation of the Bank continued apace. Two crucial decisions were taken and implemented in the mid-1790s: to acquire land to the north, pushing up to the edge of Lothbury; and to turn the whole of the Bank into a continuous walled island site, exuding security, solidity and permanence – invaluable qualities at a time of considerable radical agitation. Thereafter, it was full steam ahead. In 1797 he began the Residence Court, home to key officials and their families; in 1798–9, having quite recently rebuilt the 4 Per Cent Office, he built the Consols Transfer Office, along rather more orthodox classical lines than the Bank Stock Office; and over the next few years there followed the New Library, the New Accountant's and Cashier's Offices, and the Lothbury Court, with the last showing Soane at his most simultaneously picturesque and monumental, albeit largely concealed from the visitor's gaze. Soane's classical masterpiece, though, was Tivoli Corner. This was built on the north-west corner between 1805 and 1807, was wholly in public view and possessed a uniqueness authoritatively described by Daniel Abramson:

> A marvel of geometry mediating a difficult site, its pyramidal elevation and complexly alternating projections and recessions reached back through two centuries of European Baroque architecture. A century of the classical British picturesque, beginning with Vanbrugh, also climaxed with the Tivoli Corner's ebullient skyline and richly shadowed layers of space. The Tivoli order's full-bodied Roman Corinthian richness – here with complete garland and bucrania frieze – juxtaposed against the angular plainness of the Grecian inflected attic seemed to propose a modern classical amalgam.

Soane also took the opportunity during the 1800s to expand and remodel the suite of directors' parlours, including the addition of the Governor's Court, and to construct the 130-foot Long Passage, linking the Bank's public spaces near the southern front to its more private areas to the north. Altogether, it was a prodigious achievement by one man; and it was neither idle boasting nor special pleading when Soane affirmed in 1803 that 'the business of the Bank is my first consideration'.

For their part, the directors deserve credit for the backing they gave him, especially given that – initially at least – Soane's approach was far from universally applauded. In May 1796, at a meeting of the Architects' Club with Soane absent, satirical verses were read aloud (subsequently printed, eventually leading to a libel case) that, among other charges, accused Soane of having vandalised Taylor's Rotunda; while later in 1796 three dining acquaintances of the diarist Joseph Farington castigated his work at the Bank as 'affected and contemptible'. Undoubtedly some directors harboured reservations, on the grounds partly of expense (sometimes running at upwards of £40,000 a year) and partly of taste, with the Committee for Building perhaps somewhat nervously in 1797 conveying its wish to Soane for 'some ornament but not too much'. Two things helped Soane. The first was his increasingly close links over the years with many of the individual directors, who employed him as their personal architect; the other was a growing general sense of the sheer scale and impressiveness of what he was doing. A culminating moment came in June 1814, when Tsar Alexander I took time during his visit to London to inspect the Bank, with the architect by his side, at the end of which the Tsar, reported the press, 'complimented Soane in a very particular manner on the grandeur of the work and shook him most cordially by the hand'. Few contemporaries denied the grandeur; as *Leigh's New Picture of London* put it four years later, 'this immense pile of building is more extensive in its range of offices, and more eminent for its architectural ornament, and interior arrangement, than any single public office in the metropolis'.[18]

Soane was probably unstoppable, war or no war, but without the conflict there certainly would not have been a Bank Volunteer Corps. It was formed in 1798, was given the responsibility of defending the Bank as a reinforcement of the Picquet, and had its moment in the sun on the first Monday of September 1799, as recorded by Farington:

> Bank Association Colours I went to see delivered in Lords Cricket ground [then in Dorset Square] by Mrs Saml Thornton, wife of the Governor of the Bank, to Lieut. Coll. Whitmore, Commander of the Corps. – The *Captains* are all Directors of the Bank, the Lieutenants & Ensigns Principal Clerks of the Bank. There were upwards of 400 in the line. The Colours were delivered about ¼ before one oClock after a Sermon read by the Chaplain. – The Corps then performed many evolutions admirably well till past 3 oClock. The Company separated about 4 oClock, after many hundred spectators had been partakers of refreshment prepared in 18 Marquees, beside the Pavilion.

The quartermaster was none other than Soane, and it was through his invitation that Farington that evening went to the Bank itself, where he 'saw the Bank Directors, and the whole Corps, seated after dinner, drinking patriotic toasts. – The Rotunda contained several tables, a Company with the Officers sat at each table. Other Companys were in the Dividend rooms.' Clearly the Corps was a mirror image of the day-to-day Bank in its respect for hierarchy, together with a strong streak of paternalism, and just over a week later the diarist gleaned some further information:

> Bank Clerk told me today that the Directors provided breakfast for each Company of their Volunteers at Coffee Houses at 8 oClock after they had exercised, – and they went to the Offices at 9. – On the Kings birth day the Directors presented each of them, 500 in number, with 6 guineas each as a compliment to buy suit of cloaths &c.

In practice, until they were disbanded in July 1814, the Bank Volunteers saw little in the way of serious action; but during much of 1803–5 they stood ready to guard the Bank's gold, should invasion happen and the treasure have to be despatched elsewhere.[19]

Such was the wartime Bank's enlarged workload that, unsurprisingly, staff numbers rose sharply, as can be seen in the table.

	Clerical	Porters &c.
1793	394	24
1796	430	28
1797	542	28
1805	752	49
1810	829	73
1815	933	77

Who were these increasingly numerous clerks? Anne Murphy, on the basis of a close study of the recruitment process between 1800 and 1815, finds that the great majority had no familial connection with the Bank; that without that connection it remained necessary to be recommended by a director; that the primary motive was a steady job together with job security; that applicants tended to be around twenty years old; that none was Catholic; that social background was often somewhere between higher artisan and general 'middling';

and that relatively few new recruits arrived at the Bank with particularly well-developed skills in handwriting or accounting or 'telling'
money – that, in other words, they would largely be expected to learn
on the job. As for the wider fraternity they now joined, Murphy
offers a striking but convincing assessment of the national contribution made by what she calls 'the largest concentrated white-collar
workforce in the world':

> Much like a civil service, together the Bank's clerks constituted a
> body of knowledge and experience that remained constant while
> directors and governors of the Bank came and went. Each operated
> in a specialised capacity in offices supervised by senior colleagues,
> and heavily coordinated with each other, thus making work at the
> Bank akin to that in a large factory. Individually, the jobs those
> clerks performed were mundane and repetitive but collectively the
> feat they achieved, that of managing the national debt and providing
> banking and discount facilities for London's business and financial
> community, was nothing short of extraordinary. They dealt with
> thousands of transactions every month, managed records relating
> to a huge balance sheet, made sense of the system of public debt,
> provided effective and efficient liaison with the Exchequer, managed
> much of London's bullion inflows and oversaw the processes for
> the manufacture and circulation of banknotes. Moreover, this was
> a labour force that, until the advent of the automated bookkeeping
> machine and the typewriter, and indeed arguably until the advent
> of the computer, could not be replaced or even significantly aided
> by technology. Their work was done by hand in processes that
> involved the endless recording of details in ledgers and checking
> and double-checking to ensure the integrity of the records.

That unremitting work (perhaps helped a little more by technology
than Murphy allows) may not always have been properly appreciated; but in May 1815, during the last weeks of war, the Committee
of Inspection for the Drawing Office &c recommended that 'the
Wages of the Clerks in the post Bill Office be advanced £30 each, in
Consideration of the great weight of Business, the risque they run in
paying Bills improperly, and receiving no benefit from their Situations,
exclusive of their Wages'.[20]

As during the eighteenth century, the major blemish was – despite a continuing tightening of regulations – the occasional but disturbing case of serious fraud. Robert Aslett had joined the Bank in 1778 and soon become a protégé of Abraham Newland, so much so that when in 1799 he was appointed second cashier it was generally assumed that he would in due course succeed Newland as chief cashier. Indeed, such were Newland's growing infirmities that Aslett by the early 1800s was virtually managing the business of the Cashier's Office, causing him to succumb in 1802–3 to the temptation of large-scale embezzlement, principally of Exchequer bills. 'His looks were pale, sorrowful and emaciated,' noted a reporter as he appeared at the inevitable Old Bailey; and though he avoided the gibbet, some seventeen years of imprisonment lay ahead, until a pardon from the Bank in 1820 on condition that he left the country. No such escape for Philip Whitehead, a former clerk in the Cashier's Office who in 1812 was hanged for forgery, having pretended to his victim still to be in the employment of the Bank when in fact he had been effectively dismissed for a combination of extravagant living and Stock Exchange speculation. His sister Sarah reacted badly, over the next quarter of a century going daily to the Bank and asking for her brother, with her invariable black dress earning her the sobriquet 'the Bank Nun' from the mainly kindly clerks.

One of those may have been Samuel Harrison, who in 1805 as a would-be entrant in his early twenties had been 'examined by a Committee, my religion enquired into and whether I was a member of any political club, then had to count £100 silver coin, and cast up columns of figures'. He was no Rousseau, but his autobiographical notes, written in annual diary form probably many years later, have their moments:

1806. The 26th July was my first day at the Bank. I was installed in the Bank Note Office, and had to enter and fill up £1 and £2 notes. 200 were the morning's work. I had to join the Bank Volunteers.

1809. At the Bank, in consequence of several Elections of Clerks, I had many juniors and got into the Drawing Office. At the close of this year, the writing of the numbers and dates on the Bank Notes was superseded by hand machines which printed them. This work not being to the taste of all, I willingly undertook, and eventually got fixed in the Numbering Office. Leaving daily at three o'clock,

we had sometimes to work on Sundays to supply the demand of
£1 Notes, so much gold being sent to Spain to supply the English
Army there.

1810. I agreed to be one of the Godfathers to my friend Feldwick's
first child, a son and heir. I found a large party assembled. It was
here I first met Catherine Harpley with her sisters Bessie and Jane
then unmarried. My dear Kate soon struck me as being the wife I
wanted; lively and good-tempered, a nice spanking girl ... My court-
ship was conducted according to my nature, in a somewhat cold and
sensible manner. Whether this told against me, or the animosity of
the family, I was suddenly struck down by a concise and abrupt
dismissal.

1811. Several of the Bank Clerks used to dine at the Woolpack
in St Mildred's Court; we paid 1/6 each and had a joint cooked
expressly, and once a week we had a pint of wine each and got an
extra hour from the office. There were about twelve of us; some were
very amusing, full of jokes and puns. The hilarity was so uproari-
ous the landlord begged us to be more orderly. On the 25th May
we had a holiday, and, with a friend each, dined at Blackheath. We
had subscribed 6d a week until 15/- each was collected. We called
ourselves the Bonny Vivants; I was treasurer and chairman with the
privilege of making up deficiencies.

At last, in 1813, he met Kate Harpley again, and this time got the
go-ahead from her father. 'On the appointed day [3 April], without
anybody knowing at the office, I quietly slipped out, met the wedding
party, was married and then returned to the Bank while the rest amused
themselves driving in the Park. Then we met again to dinner at White
Conduit House. In the afternoon there was a heavy fall of snow which
is considered a good omen.' So it was, and the following year, 'at 50
minutes past one in the morning of February 12th', a daughter was
born. 'The pleasure to the parents of a first child is indescribable, but
the necessity arises of more stay-at-home habits, and, very possibly,
sleepless nights,' recalled Harrison wryly enough. 'The high price of
provisions, bread 1/5 the quartern and butter 1/11 a pound, with coals
65/- the ton, and the probable termination of the war with France
stopping the overtime at the Bank, made me somewhat modify my
pleasure of seeing the beginning of a family of children to support.'[21]

PART TWO

1815–1914

5

All the Obloquy

The year 1815 marks one of those attractively straightforward lines in the sands of modern British history: not only the end of the war, but the start of almost a century of peace (broadly speaking), of Britain's rise to becoming the workshop of the world, of London's increasing dominance as an international financial centre, exporting capital to all quarters of the globe. All that is essentially true; yet for at least three decades, until the 1850s, it felt to contemporaries a far more chequered, fraught and uncertain process. Certainly these were difficult decades for the Bank, finding itself uncomfortably often at the sharp end of sustained and widespread criticism, as what became a distinctively Victorian monetary settlement was slowly and painfully forged.

Against a larger background of severe economic depression and high unemployment, allied to pent-up resentment about the Bank's undeniably handsome profits during the war, criticism was under way within months of Waterloo. 'That an account should be laid before a General Court,' demanded a proprietor in December 1815, 'of the amount of the surplus profits of this Company', a demand 'warmly' supported by David Ricardo; but on the governor, William Mellish, brusquely informing the Bank's stockholders that 'the Company had all along placed great confidence in their Directors, and that if any reason were harboured for wishing to withdraw it, he begged that their accusation might be spoken out', the motion was lost on a show of hands 'by about two to one'. The verdict of the political economist James Mill, writing next day to Ricardo, was plain enough: 'I should treat all the excess above the due remuneration for

their public services, as money got upon false pretences, which the
law treats as swindling.' Ricardo himself entirely agreed – 'I think
the Bank an unnecessary establishment getting rich by those profits
which fairly belong to the public,' he had written not long before to
another eminent economist, Thomas Malthus – but probably no one
was hotter on the subject than the Whig MP and businessman Pascoe
Grenfell. The deposits of public money at the Bank were, he told
the Commons in February 1816 in the course of proposing a select
committee to look into its arrangements with government, 'wholly
unproductive to the public, but productive of profit and advantage
to the Bank', quite apart of course, he added, from the excessive cost
of the Bank's management of the public debt, as well as the 'immense
increase in Bank profits' as a result of the paper-money era. 'I am not,'
he insisted, 'advising the establishment of a second great national
bank'; but he had no hesitation in contrasting on the one hand a
country during the last twenty years 'groaning under the weight and
burthen of taxation – vexed, harassed, and tormented, by a swarm of
petty, paltry, teazing taxes', with on the other hand the fact that 'we
should be squandering upon this wealthy, this opulent company, so
large, so vast, so extravagant a remuneration' – a contrast, he went
on, that 'excites in us feelings of disgust and indignation'. From the
government benches, Lord Castlereagh (mindful no doubt that the
post-war abolition of income tax would make ministers particularly
dependent on loans from the Bank) argued that 'any unnecessary
inquiry' into the Bank's affairs would be 'to its prejudice, and, so
far, to the prejudice of the country, by affecting the public credit';
while, directly on the Bank's behalf, Alexander Baring declared
that his 'main objection to the motion arose from the exaggeration with which it was prefaced, and the sort of spirit with which
it was proposed', sentiments echoed by William Manning (a recent
governor, and father of the cardinal), who 'stated that, including all
the responsibility and expenses, the Bank only charged the public,
for the expense of managing the funds, eightpence in the £100'.
Grenfell's motion was duly defeated, 81–44; and a year later, when he
tried again, the result was similar, 90–40, notwithstanding his well-
researched claim that 'the profits of the Bank within the last twenty
years, in addition to the usual dividend of seven per cent, amounted
to the sum of 27 millions' – albeit he 'did not mean to impute any

censure to the Bank that made these gains', but rather he 'found fault only with the government that tolerated them'.[1]

All this was hardly, from the Bank's point of view, brilliant mood music for determining the big one: whether to resume cash payments, and if so, when.

'Much difficulty occurs about our currency,' noted Samuel Thornton at the start of 1816, adding that it was 'the general wish that the Bank should resume its cash payments as soon as possible'. May that year saw a full-scale Commons debate and vote, and again it was Baring and Manning to the fore. The former, calling himself 'as great an enemy as any man to the restriction act in itself', wanted the House to 'intrust the whole to the discretion of the Bank, and depend upon its zeal, and its desire of answering the expectations of the country, so conformable with its own interests', at the same time asserting that 'two years were necessary to enable the Bank to supply specie in sufficient quantity for the circulation of the country'; while the latter took a similar line, emphasising that the watchword had to be 'caution'. The Commons duly voted to extend restriction until July 1818, but not before a fierce attack from the Whig MP George Tierney:

> However demure the Bank directors might look, and whatever professions they might make, they seemed resolved to act in opposition to those looks and professions; they had still upon their countenances all the beautiful simplicity and innocence they had worn for the last nineteen years – always pretending to be ready to pay in gold, yet, when the time came, always finding some reason to keep their money in their own hands. He entertained great personal respect for the directors individually; but, speaking of them collectively, he could not help saying that they seemed very desirous of retaining in their hands the annual gain of £800,000.

Still, two years was perhaps not so long in the overall scheme of things, and William Huskisson in February 1817 told the Commons that he 'rejoiced to see the period approaching in which cash payments would be resumed'.

It was not to be. By that autumn the exchanges had turned decisively against England and gold began inexorably to drain away, with indeed increasing rapidity from early 1818, fuelled also by successive bad harvests necessitating substantial imports of wheat; and in May 1818 the Tory government pushed through a further one-year post-ponement of resumption. As usual the Bank came in for criticism, prompting Thornton to protest in the Commons that circumstances had been beyond its control. 'The resumption of cash payments would,' he explained in his customary hurt tones about the entirely honour-able motives of his colleagues and himself, 'make them comparatively independent men – for they would then be no longer subject to those questions which were daily pressed upon them, and those asperities that were hourly used towards them.' Huskisson meanwhile kept his eye firmly on his long-term goal, befitting his increasing reputation as the intellectual driving-force behind Lord Liverpool's ministry and in effect speaking for a rising generation of commercially minded middle-class economic liberals. For him, and those who thought like him, one of the decisive advantages of returning to the gold standard was that it would be so properly regulated from the outset that there could be no possi-bility of mismanagement – let alone greed – on the part of Thornton *et al.* 'The Bank,' he assured Liverpool in July 1818 in visionary manner, 'would be the great Steam Engine of the State to keep the Channel of the Circulation always pressing full, and the power of converting its Notes at any time into Gold Bullion at 78s per ounce the Regulator and Index of the Engine, by which the extent of its operations and the sufficiency of the supply would be determined & ascertained.'[2]

If that was essentially a utilitarian perspective, there was also emerging strongly by this time a powerful radical-cum-humanitarian critique of the Bank, fuelled in significant part by the continuing vain search for an 'inimitable' banknote and the sharp rise in Bank prose-cutions for forgery (up from 63 in 1815 to 260 by 1818), together with subsequent hangings (some two dozen in 1818). It proved a fruitful artistic subject. *A peep into the old rag shop in Threadneedle Street* was the title of an anonymous print published in September 1818, showing the unfortunate, meanly dressed possessor of a forged note pleading on his knees for mercy, while the Bank's prosperous directors sit in judgement at a nearby table. 'Take him out, Thomas!!! he has a d——d hanging look,' orders one director to a minion; 'Away with the Vagabond! do you think we sit here for nothing?' says another; a third merely slumbers; and a fourth deigns to inspect the note, before declaring, 'Upon my soul I have my doubts … We had better declare it bad.' Soon afterwards, in January 1819, the great George Cruikshank (later Dickens's illustrator) produced his uncompromising 'Bank Restriction Note', adorned with skulls, convict ships and gibbets, as well as Britannia gobbling up a naked infant. So too with radical journalists, above all the brilliant, tireless and shamelessly exaggerating William Cobbett. 'This villainous Bank has slaughtered more people than would people a *State*,' he exploded in the *Political Register* a few months after Cruikshank's gruesome parody.

> With the rope, the prison, the hulk and the transport ship, this Bank has destroyed, perhaps, fifty thousand persons, including the widows and orphans of its victims. At the shop of this crew of fraudulent insolvents, there sits a *council* to determine, which of their victims shall live, and which shall swing! Having usurped the royal prerogative of coining and issuing money, it is but another stop to usurp that of pardoning or of causing to be hanged!

For its part, understandably unwilling not to protect the integrity of its notes, the Bank could only hope to ride out the storm, no doubt aware that justice for the little men was sometimes rough. 'We talked of Bank note Forgeries,' recorded Joseph Farington in January 1819 after sitting at dinner next to the son of a City alderman. 'Price said, that it is well known that the principal Forgers reside at Birmingham; that they are well known to the Bank Directors but sufficient evidence against them has not been obtained.'³

On the larger question of resumption itself, the next few months would see a remarkable sequence of events unfold. At the Bank's urging – based on the argument that it was 'a matter of the highest Importance that the Public shall not be deluded with an Expectation which is not likely to be realized' – the government appointed secret committees of inquiry in both the Commons and the Lords, which duly held hearings between mid-February and the start of May. The Bank's more experienced witnesses (including Jeremiah Harman and Samuel Thornton, as well as governor George Dorrien and deputy governor Charles Pole) continued to refuse to commit themselves. 'It is very difficult to say when the Bank could with propriety resume its cash payments, it must always be judged of by experience,' Dorrien told the Commons committee (chaired by Robert Peel). 'Fixing a

period, and not adhering to it, always creates a great deal of dissatisfaction and disappointment in the public mind,' added Harman;
and he stressed that such was the state of the foreign exchanges 'what
further time may be necessary must depend on circumstances not
under our control', though of course 'we always look on the bright
side of things'. By contrast, two younger, more recently elected directors, William Haldimand and William Ward (in his leisure time a
high-scoring batsman), revealed themselves as appreciably more open
to the prospect of early resumption, with Ward arguing that a return
to gold would result in a change of commercial 'habits', and in particular in fewer 'extravagant speculations' than during the restriction
period. The committees recommended a definite return to gold within
four years, but in the end it would come down to government resolve
and parliamentary opinion.

'A strong and decisive effort can alone redeem our character and
credit,' insisted Liverpool to doubters; his fellow-Tories Peel and
Huskisson were especially determined to seize the moment; on 20
May the Bank made a formal representation to the Commons, declaring – in the face of 'all the obloquy, which has been so undeservedly
heaped upon the establishment' – that restriction had given it 'duties
to the community at large, whose interest in a pecuniary and commercial relation, have in a great degree been confided to their discretion';
and four days later there began a two-day debate in the Commons to
settle the matter. Amid what the historian Boyd Hilton has described
as a 'curiously unreal' atmosphere, Peel not only warned that if 'the
circulating medium was to be left to the discretion of the Bank directors, uncontrolled by any consideration but that of their own profits,
it would become impossible to estimate the extent of the mischief that
might ensue', but also asserted unambiguously that the time had come
for Parliament to 'recover' from the Bank 'the authority which it had
so long abdicated'; Manning counter-warned that 'if the House with-
drew its confidence from the Bank at a moment like the present, they
[the Bank] could not be answerable for the consequences'; Ricardo
had some knockabout fun, accusing the Bank of being 'a cautious and
timid body' possessing 'total ignorance of the principles of political
economy'; and in a dramatic denouement, amid 'loud and universal
cries of hear, hear!', George Canning for the Tories successfully called
on the House to make 'an undivided vote' for resumption within four

years, in order 'to show the public that the House was in earnest in its attempts to restore the ancient standard' – though not without Manning 'reserving to himself ... the right of stating his objections to the proposed measures on a future occasion'.[4]

The politicians had triumphed, defying the wishes of not just the Bank but the City as a whole. After all, Nathan Rothschild, the square mile's new titan, could hardly have been more direct in his evidence to the Commons secret committee, anticipating 'a great deal of mischief' in the event of early resumption, given that 'money will be so very scarce, every article in this country will fall to such an enormous extent, that many persons will be ruined'; while shortly before the crucial Commons debate some 400 to 500 of the City's merchants, bankers and traders had signed a petition along similar lines. 'They all dreaded the pressure of monetary stringency,' in Hilton's words, and 'very few could see the ultimate commercial benefits of deflation and a "sound" currency'. How much were they (and indeed the Bank's leadership) motivated by broader pragmatic economic concerns? Or by fear for their own commercial survival? Or simply by a natural conservatism, having become comfortably used to the paper-money dispensation? Perhaps all one can usefully say is that no doubt it was a mixture of all three. As for the politicians, there were also arguably three principal motives at work. First, as developed by the bullionist theoreticians (who had done much of the intellectual heavy lifting for resumption in their 1810 report), a belief in the superior commercial morality of gold as opposed to paper, not least its anti-speculative aspect; second, the understandable conviction that by placing gold at the centre of the monetary system, automatically regulating and stabilising its daily workings, this would greatly reduce the Bank's unwelcome scope for discretion; and third, as probably only perceived by a select few, a view of the return to gold as transformative for London's place in the bigger global picture. On that last motive, Huskisson had set out his thinking in his visionary memo to Liverpool the previous July:

I have no doubt that with the extent of our commercial dealings and operations of Exchange, which make this Country the Emporium not only of Europe but of America North & South, the Bank of England would make London the chief Bullion Market of the World ... The facility it would give to Trade in affording them the means of promptly rectifying the Exchange with any particular Country, and probably in the particular Coin of that very Country to which it might be desirable to remit Bullion, could not fail to form one of those inducements which would make London the *settling House* of the Money transactions of the World.

In time, of course, this would become a vision fully and proudly shared by the Bank and the City, almost believing that they had had the idea in the first place; but in 1819 that time was not yet.

The next year or two proved difficult for almost all concerned, as the boom of 1818 gave way to an intense economic trough accompanied by considerable popular disaffection – including 1820's Cato Street conspiracy, a plan both to assassinate the Tory Cabinet and to seize the Bank. For its part, the Bank during the months after the resumption vote remained grumpy enough, refusing Liverpool's request for advances on a loan and generally showing a frosty attitude to government, until eventually Vansittart felt compelled to begin peace talks with three key directors (Harman, Thornton and Haldimand). Postponement of resumption was not on the table – Liverpool was adamant that to do so would amount in practice to a 'perpetual restriction' – but Van did promise to repay £5 million; and by November 1819 Huskisson was able to inform his wife that 'all the difficulties with the Bank are adjusted'. During 1820 the Bank made large purchases of bullion, helped by favourable exchanges; and by February 1821 its treasure had reached £11.9 million, more than ever before, prompting it to decide that if the return to gold was going to have to happen anyway by 1823, this was the moment to do it. Accordingly, payments in cash were resumed in May – almost a quarter of a century after the fateful turn of events in 1797 – and, simultaneously, small notes (£1 and £2) were withdrawn. The role may not have been quite of its own choosing, but the moment was now at hand for the Bank to prove itself 'the great Steam Engine of the State'.[5]

It was very shortly before resumption that the twenty-seven-year-old George Warde Norman, not yet a partner in the family firm of timber merchants, was elected a director. As he gazed around the Court

Room during his early weeks and months, and listened to proceedings, he was largely unimpressed. Not only were governor Charles Pole and deputy governor John Bowden 'utterly without the scientific knowledge which a Director of the present day would be expected to possess', he recalled in the late 1850s, but most of the other senior directors, sitting also on the Committee of Treasury, were 'persons of still humbler grade of intellect'. He then named names: 'Jeremiah Harman, who had long ruled the Bank with almost despotic sway, was ignorant, pompous, prejudiced, and overbearing. The opinion of a junior, if opposed to his, he hardly thought of answering, excepting by an exhibition of scorn and contempt. Manning and Mellish, amiable but feeble, Dorrien feeble but less apparently amiable, in fact a nobody. Pearse a man of some sense, but little knowledge.' What about Samuel Thornton, who had become a director back in 1780 and would remain on the Court until eventually stepping down in 1836? 'He was a man of strong mind and general ability,' reflected Norman. 'His ability was conspicuous in all he said. Unfortunately he was by nature sly and a thorough intriguer. He liked secret paths and crooked ways and it was with the utmost difficulty one ever arrived at a knowledge of his real wishes and opinions.'

In what was clearly a mixed-ability class, there were nevertheless some notable figures. The cricketing William Ward, quite apart from saving the present-day Lord's ground from speculative development in the mid-1820s, was an incisive presence on the Court until a reversal in his fortunes compelled retirement in 1836; Norman himself was a serious economist, whose youthful pamphlet on the question of timber duties prompted Thornton to sponsor his election; and William Cotton (elected 1822) was a conscientious social reformer and a man of parts, as displayed not least by his invention in the 1840s of an 'automaton balance', capable of weighing and separating light gold coins from those of standard weight, in the process doing much to preserve the eyesight of the Bank's weighing clerks. Perhaps the most notable director, though, was John Horsley Palmer. Born in 1779 into a London merchanting background, he became a director in 1811, having established himself as an East India merchant, and emerged in the course of the 1820s as the Bank's dominant voice. 'Love of business and ability to bear any quantity of it, and above all a force of will, which I never saw exceeded in any man,' were identified by Norman as his key characteristics. 'When he had made up his mind it was all but impossible to turn him and his resolute advocacy of his opinions bore down all opposition.' Fortunately, also noted Norman, 'he had much sound sense'.

Like quite a number in the larger mercantile community, Palmer's merchanting background included an active interest in the slave trade. How common was that in the case of Bank directors? A helpful snapshot comes from looking at the twenty-one directors who attended Court on 31 July 1834 – the day before the previous year's Slavery Abolition Act came into force, ending slavery in the British Empire – and identifying how many of them subsequently received compensation. As far as one can tell, the answer is five: relatively small amounts (under £7,000) for Palmer himself and Timothy Curtis (governor in the late 1830s); some £50,000 each for Sir John Rae Reid (governor after Curtis) and Humphrey St John Mildmay (Barings' representative on the Court); and some £100,000 for Rowland Mitchell (a Lime Street merchant who had joined the Court in 1832 and would leave it in 1841 after his business failed). It requires much fuller research, though, to reach any definitive conclusions.[6]

The slavery question aside, Anthony Howe's illuminating prosopographical study enables one to make various generalisations about the composition of the Court during the second quarter of the century – a Court that still met in Taylor's Court Room, though with the addition since 1805 of a wind-dial (connected with a vane on the roof) giving the direction of the wind, vital information to merchants in the age of sailing ships. As ever, well over four-fifths were indeed still merchants, with bankers as such still firmly excluded on the grounds of possible conflicts of interest; the particular bias of many of those merchants was towards the Russia and West India trades; a not wholly insignificant minority of directors had close links with British industry, especially the metal and mining sectors; recruitment still tended to come from influential City families (prompting Howe's comment that 'by and large this was no world for Dick Whittingtons'); new directors were often in their early to mid-thirties, seldom having received a university education; and – perhaps just starting to be recognised in what was becoming an age of reform in the wider world – the strict rotation of the governorship, with length of service since election the sole criterion, was little incentive for an able, restlessly ambitious merchant to put himself forward for the Court. As for the social position of these directors, Howe convincingly emphasises that 'it would be wrong to exaggerate the aristocratic lifestyle within the Court, which contained many men whose social horizons were firmly contained within the metropolis, with the pattern of sociability of an urban *haute bour-geoisie*, with London houses and occasional retreats to country and coast'. A letter that Samuel Thornton sent to John Soane in August 1825 speaks volumes. 'Being here with some friends from the North who are desirous to see the improvements that are making in Windsor Castle I shall be greatly obliged if you can give me an introduction to Mr Wyatville [the architect carrying out the work] if Etiquette does not prevent you,' the Bank's aged director wrote somewhat nervously from Chobham Place in Bagshot. 'I shall of course abstain from going,' he went on, 'when there is the least probability of any of the Royal Family visiting the premises & be anxious to accord to any rules.'

Soane himself was by now on his final stretch. Between 1818 and 1823 he renovated Taylor's 4 and 5 Per Cent Offices, unifying (in the warm words of the nineteenth-century critic Richard Brown) 'the classical delicacies of the Greek and Roman designs with the play-fulness of the Gothic'; and between 1824 and 1828 he reconstructed the whole of the 370-foot south front, after a successful appeal to the directors that if they followed his advice and chose the more expen-sive option (rebuilding as opposed to merely repairing) the gratifying outcome would be that 'the whole of the exterior of this extensive pile erected at so many different times and under so many different circumstances will appear uniform, simple, and characteristic'. The rebuilding included in 1825 the front entrance, prompting soon after-wards a plea to Soane from 'A Proprietor of Bank Stock':

The new Front you have given to the Bank, is an honor to the Country and the age; but I would beg leave, with the kindest feel-ings, to point your attention to the wretched state of the pavement in front of it – one half is paved with very middling flags; the other – with blocks of granite of very irregular surface. Do pray have it amended, to correspond with the glorious architecture.

Eventually, almost eighty and with eyesight failing, Soane felt no alternative but to call time – two years after his belated knighthood – on an astonishing, transformative tenure. 'During a period of forty five years, my best endeavours have been anxiously and unremittingly exerted in the faithful discharge of the important trusts reposed in me,' he wrote to the directors in October 1833, resigning from 'a situation which has so long been the pride and boast of my life'. And though over the years they had sometimes quibbled about costs, the directors were surely being sincere when in reply they thanked him for his 'unremitted zeal' on the Bank's behalf – zeal that had done much to create for that institution an image of certainty and monumentality, discouraging to critics and inquirers alike.[7]

'In consequence of the return to cash payments at the Bank, and the great diminution of work, many clerks, mostly old and unfit, were pensioned,' recalled Samuel Harrison about the step-change of the early 1820s. 'Nearly 200 went. Some applied to go, among these Geldald, who on his salary of £200 got as much as £100 a year with 16 years' service. He commuted this for £1,000 down.' Higher up the food chain, these years saw not only two successful government debt conversions (£150 million of 5 per cent stock converted to 4 per cent; £70 million of 4 per cent stock reduced to 3½ per cent), but also the altogether more problematic 'deadweight' scheme. A forty-five-year annuity to cover the cost of military and naval pensions, it proved a no-go with the investing class, before the Bank reluctantly assumed from government a share of responsibility. More generally, this early post-resumption phase was a time of 'high bullion reserves and low profits' (in Clapham's phrase), with two interesting developments: a flurry of substantial mortgages, especially to the landed class (£300,000 to the Duke of Rutland, £200,000 to the Marquis of Bath, £130,000 to the Duke of Devonshire); and the start of a serious business relationship with Nathan Rothschild, the master of bullion operations. A huge boon, meanwhile, from the end of the paper-money era was the collapse in forgeries and prosecutions, following the withdrawal of small notes, and it was a further relief when in 1824 a new form of banknote could be issued, whose 'numerical sum' would, reported the *London Gazette*, be 'visible in the substance of the paper in Roman letters on waved lines', thereby significantly enhancing security. Not that fraud suddenly disappeared from the scene. Henry Fauntleroy, a partner in the West End private bank Marsh, Stracey & Co, was arrested that autumn on the grounds of large-scale fraudulent transfers of government stock, going back to 1815; it emerged at the trial that the principal motive was revenge ('they shall smart for it'), after the Bank had begun to refuse his bank's acceptances; the gallows followed; and it cost the Bank some £265,000 to replace the fraudulently transferred stocks.[8]

Fauntleroy met his maker on the last day of November 1824, almost exactly a year before the City was hit by arguably the most acute of the several financial crises of the first half of the century. The collapse of an absurdly overblown boom in ill-judged foreign loans and company promotions, speculative overtrading in imported commodities, rashness on the part of the country banks, the Bank's credit policy veering between complacent expansion (fuelled in some measure by the perceived need to make up for lost paper-money income) and over-sharp contraction – all these factors undoubtedly played a part in the humdinger 1825 crisis. 'The abundance of money has led to a variety of speculations in England, and scarcely a week has passed but some new company was founded to direct a wild projected adventure,' reflected Thornton as early as New Year's Day. 'What must be the cure of this mania time only can show.' Part of the problem as 1825 unfolded was a signal lack of co-ordination between government and Bank, even as bullion drained steadily away, down from almost £12 million the previous August to £3.6 million a year later; and when in autumn 1825 the Bank did start belatedly to reduce its note issue and ration its discounts, the effect was a sudden and almost total collapse of credit generally. 'There is a tremendous pressure upon this town, & I suppose almost *all* the Bankers are more or less distressed,' J. J. Gurney (a member of the great Norfolk banking family) found in mid-November on a visit to the capital. 'The root of the difficulty is in the Bank of England, where they are extremely restricting their discounts with a view to producing a favourable effect on the exchanges, so as to prevent their being run upon for gold.' And he added darkly: 'It seems strange that the pecuniary facilities of the whole realm should thus depend on the management of a small despotic Committee.'[9]

The pace quickened from early December, with runs on country banks under way and the Bank, reversing its recent policy, starting to discount largely. An especially piquant drama was played out at the City private bank Pole, Flinton, Free, Down & Scott, whose elderly senior partner, Sir Peter Pole, was connected by marriage to the Bank's governor, Cornelius Buller. That bank, in generally poor shape and not helped by its extensive country banks agency, had been suffering from a run since the 1st; and on Sunday the 4th Buller persuaded his fellow-directors to lend it £400,000. For an intensely relieved Marianne Thornton ('from the deepest sorrow, we are all at once the happiest of the happy'), sister of the young partner Henry and niece of Samuel, it proved a false dawn. News on the 8th of the failure of Wentworth & Co, a leading Yorkshire bank, prompted a severe run on the country banks; and Poles on Monday the 12th stopped payment, intensifying the general sense of crisis in the City. That week, the Court met almost every day, and some years later the veteran director Jeremiah Harman would make a celebrated claim about how the Bank during those desperate days sought to restore credit:

> We lent by every possible means, and in modes that we never had adopted before; we took in stock as security, we purchased exchequer bills, we made advances on exchequer bills, we not only discounted outright, but we made advances on deposit of bills of exchange to an immense amount; in short by every possible means consistent with the safety of the Bank; and we were not upon some occasions over nice; seeing the dreadful state in which the public were, we rendered every assistance in our power.

Perhaps there was a degree of exaggeration – for instance, it was not until Wednesday the 14th that the Bank abruptly jettisoned its policy of refusing discounts on bills longer than ninety-five days – but the substance probably holds; while, at the other end of town, the Cabinet on the 15th authorised the issue of £1 notes, on condition that such issue was 'understood to be strictly temporary'.

Next day, Friday the 16th, the situation remained critical. That morning, the diarist Mrs Arbuthnot and her husband (a Treasury minister) were put in the picture – charged and fractious – by the member of government closest to the City:

> Mr Herries told us that such had been the extraordinary demand for gold to supply the country bankers & to meet the general run upon them that the Bank of England was completely drained of its specie & was reduced to 100,000 sovereigns ... The Bank expects to be obliged to suspend cash payments tomorrow, and they want the Government to step forward to their assistance & order the suspension. Lord Liverpool is unwilling to do this & wishes the Bank to do it upon their own responsibility. By Mr Herries's account there seems to be considerable irritation between the Govt & the Governors of the Bank ... Rothschild has made most gigantic efforts to assist the Bank & he told Mr Herries that, if he had been applied to sooner, he wd have prevented all the difficulty. As it is, if they can hold out till Monday or Tuesday, he will have enormous sums over in sovereigns from Paris, & the pressure will be entirely relieved ...

The exact timing and extent of Rothschild's contribution would be disputed over the years, but there is evidence that even on that Friday he managed to get paid into the Bank a significant amount of bullion, possibly as much as £300,000. In any case, that evening the Cabinet met and eventually, after five hours, reached a political compromise about the Bank's demand. The key figure was Wellington, who on the one hand reluctantly acceded to Huskisson's insistence that the Bank should not be allowed to exploit the crisis as a way of going off gold, and on the other persuaded his colleagues that Huskisson's wish to deprive the Bank of its Charter, should it be forced to stop cash payments, was absurd. 'He told Lord Liverpool,' recorded Mrs Arbuthnot about the resolute Iron Duke, 'that while there was life there was hope; that there was a chance of the Bank standing & while that chance remained, he wd not despair; that the Government were bound to support them to the very utmost of their power ... for that their interests were those of the country.'

Over the weekend, the Bank managed to avoid suspension of cash payments – possibly helped by the chance discovery, according to a well-worn story that may or may not have been true, of a large box of unissued £1 notes, but certainly assisted by a fresh supply from the printers of £5 and £10 notes. By Monday, or Tuesday at the latest, Rothschild had come through with major tranches of gold from France; and by Christmas Eve the run on the Bank's reserves was conclusively over. 'For the extraordinary exertions of the clerks,' remembered Samuel Harrison about some of the Old Lady's most demanding weeks, 'they were rewarded with a gratuity each of £10 and £20. I missed by a half-year's service coming under the latter category though working as much as any.'[10] The cost of the crisis had been – and would continue to be – severe, involving amid much else the collapse of numerous country banks. The Bank itself had just about survived unscathed, but it did not take a Nostradamus to predict that a major overhaul of the nation's banking system, including the Bank's place in it, would soon be under way.

Liverpool himself took the initiative as early as January 1826. England's existing banking structure was, he informed governor Buller, 'unsound and delusive', in which 'the effect of the law at present is to permit every system of banking *except* that which is *solid* and *secure*'. He proposed therefore two main structural changes: first, that the Bank would have to give up its historic monopoly on joint-stock banking, in order to allow the creation of joint-stock banks with greater financial resources and stability than the country banks, confined to a maximum of six partners; and second, that the Bank itself should establish branches in the provinces, thereby further reducing the influence of the country banks. In both cases the Bank reluctantly agreed, though in the former successfully insisting that the new joint-stock banks should be confined to areas sixty-five miles or more outside London. As for the latter, it seems to have been a matter of some internal debate. 'My opinion was that the branches would give increased stability to the currency generally,' recalled Norman three decades later. 'That they would augment the necessity for, and the importance of, the Bank of England, which was then at a low ebb, and that they would furnish large profits to the proprietors.' Accordingly, 'I carried my point in spite of the opposition of most of the seniors and of the Committee of Treasury.'[11]

Those two major changes may have been forced on the Bank, but soon the Bank itself was seeking to be more proactive, even to stake – as it had seldom or never done before – the intellectual high ground. Following an initiative by William Ward, 1827 saw the rescinding of the resolution that the directors had put forward in 1819 to the parliamentary committee on resumption – a resolution that had obstinately denied that the note issue could have any impact on the foreign exchanges. Then, over the next few years, John Horsley Palmer really came to the fore, as deputy governor from 1828 and governor from 1830. His contribution was threefold: resisting a Huskisson plan to introduce a form of bimetallism (that is, a monetary system in which the currency is backed by silver as much as it is by gold), effectively arguing that the Bank already possessed enough silver bullion to overcome panics and 'combinations made to their prejudice'; pushing increasingly hard (as far as political circumstances allowed) for the note issue to be centralised upon the Bank; and above all, starting to implement what would become known as the 'Palmer Rule' – essentially, a currency principle by which the Bank's deposits and note circulation would fluctuate in relation to its holding of specie, in effect seeking to further the Bank's operational independence from government, while at the same time being entirely consistent with Palmer's conception of the Bank as fundamentally a public rather than a private institution. George Warde Norman, although as an economist uneasy about the specifics of the principle itself, did not underestimate Palmer's achievement. Whereas, he reflected, 'the absurdities of the Harmans &c of former days as to the uselessness of adverting to the state of the exchanges in managing the Bank of England' had 'disgusted sensible men and made them regard the Bank as a great overgrown job, deserving of being consigned to the Limbo of things', it was Palmer by contrast who 'first abandoned the rule of thumb system of management, or rather the absence of all rule', and 'devised a principle which although not quite sound, had at any rate some reference to sense and reason, and he thus won for us many and powerful adhesions'.

Palmer's strength of will came fully into its own during 1830, as the Wellington government sought, against a darkening economic backdrop, to end the 65-mile restriction on the new joint-stock banks. Wellington's chancellor was the capable Henry Goulburn, whose biographer notes that Palmer 'proved to be as formidable and skilful a defender of a strong position as Wellington had been on many a battlefield'. Eventually in April, after two months of correspondence and meetings, negotiations were suspended, but not before Goulburn had told Palmer to his face that 'he [Goulburn] thought it to be quite practicable to obtain the formation of a new Bank, which would be willing to undertake the management [of government business] without any charge for that agency, considering itself sufficiently compensated by the collateral advantages which it would derive from the countenance & support of Government' – a threat that the newly elected governor seems to have ignored. In September, not long before the fall of the ministry, the two men talked again. Might the government be willing, asked Palmer, to give, prior to the establishment of any further joint-stock banks, a 'fair trial' to extending the circulation of the Bank's notes? Might the government also be willing to restrict heavily those new banks in the issuing of their own notes? To both questions, Goulburn answered in the negative, leaving a difficult relationship to end with neither side happy.[12] Even so, as both men were well aware, the Bank's Charter was up for renewal in only three years, and inevitably these and related matters would soon be revisited.

Before then, there was the small matter of a profound political crisis over the extension of the franchise. In October 1831 the House of Lords rejected the Whig government's Reform Bill, leading to widespread riots, including loss of life at Bristol – where an attempt was made to blow up the Bank's recently opened branch. Then the following spring came the dramatic 'May Days', as the anti-reform Wellington sought to form a government. By Sunday the 13th, a placard devised by the leading radical Francis Place – 'to Stop the Duke, Go for Gold' – was widely on display in London. Hectic scenes ensued over the next two days. 'The demand for gold at the Bank is increasing,' reported *The Times*'s 'Money-Market and City Intelligence' on Monday evening. 'The counter in the Cashier's office at which sovereigns are obtained, was beset during the whole day with applicants.' And the following evening, after another day of 'a steady demand for gold': 'Every man of common understanding is convinced that the gold in the Bank will be exhausted in a week if a Tory Ministry is appointed in the face of the obstinate determination against it on the part of the people.' The Bank itself, quite apart from making substantial purchases of bullion, took action on Wednesday the 16th. 'Under the peculiar circumstances of the moment,' as Palmer explained to the Court next day, a notice was issued stating that the Bank was 'ready to receive applications for Loans upon the deposit of Bills of exchange, Exchequer Bills, East India Bonds, or other approved Securities' – a significant panic-averting move. By the end of the week it was clear that Wellington was not going to be able to form a ministry, and by early June the Great Reform Act was a reality. How decisive had Place's intervention been? Accounts have differed, not helped by the Bank's continuing reluctance in the 1830s to disclose figures, though according to one informed calculation as much as £1.6 million of gold drained away in the course of a week or so; and Michael Brock, in his authoritative history of the reform crisis, reflects that the key politicians 'may well have known that the figures popularly given for the Bank's reserves were too high'.[13]

The 'Go for Gold' drama was barely over before, on 29 May 1832, a parliamentary committee – which included Peel, Goulburn and the chancellor of the exchequer, Lord Althorp – began taking evidence in connection with the renewal of the Bank's Charter. Sole witness for the first four days was Palmer (entering his third year as governor), who lost little time in stating his Rule:

What is the principle by which in ordinary times the Bank is guided in the regulation of their issues? – The principle, with reference to the period of a full currency, and consequently a par of exchange, by which the Bank is guided in the regulation of their issues (excepting under special circumstances) is to invest and retain in securities, bearing interest, a given proportion of the deposits, and the value received for the notes in circulation, the remainder being held in coin and bullion; the proportions which seem to be desirable, under existing circumstances, may be stated at about two-thirds in securities and one-third in bullion; the circulation of the country, so far as the same may depend upon the Bank, being subsequently regulated by the action of the Foreign Exchanges.

Perhaps the most telling sequence, though, came after Palmer had agreed with a questioner that the Bank should be 'a bank of discounts only in cases of emergency':

Is not the accommodation of discount to the commerce of the country, one of the main objects for which the Bank has ever been instituted, and for which all banks are instituted? – As an exclusive Bank of issue in the capital, it appears to me that it cannot beneficially conduct a discount account to any great extent with individuals, except in times of discredit. When the circulation is full, a competition with the bankers would in all probability lead to excess …

Then you consider that it ceases to become the paramount duty of the Bank, because there are other bodies, in the shape of private bankers, and so on, that do it? – Yes, who employ the circulation.

What do you consider as the principal function which it is the duty of the Bank to perform? – To furnish the paper money with which the public act around them, and to be a place of safe deposit for the public money, or for the money of individuals who prefer a public body, like the Bank, to private bankers.

Are not those functions the functions of a Government rather than a private company? – That is for the Government to determine.

Other Bank witnesses included the former governors Harman, growling six years on from the joint-stock legislation that he was 'always jealous of the measure', and John Richards, dismissing concerns about the Bank's lack of transparency and declaring that 'the best security you have is to get individuals of integrity to manage it'. Among non-Bank witnesses, a powerful sense came through of major City figures closing ranks around its indispensable if sometimes unloved institution. 'Speaking generally, it is exceeding well managed,' insisted Samuel Gurney, the square mile's dominant bill broker; 'I feel the management, and I know that it is good,' agreed Nathan Rothschild; while George Grote – private banker, the City's main pro-reform spokesman during the political crisis, and future historian of Greece – explained how in times of difficulty 'a man can get to the Bank without that special, permanent, and exclusive connexion which he preserves with his own Banker, and which cuts him off from all other Bankers'. Particular attention was paid to the evidence of Samuel Jones Loyd, by now emerging among the City's private bankers as *the* intellectual heavyweight on monetary subjects:

Is not the Bank of England as much an engine of Government, and an establishment performing the functions of Government, as it is an engine performing the functions and connected with the interests of a private company? – The Bank of England is a body issuing currency, which is the public currency of the country, and at the same time performing Banking business …

May not the Bank, as a Company in which a great body of Proprietors are interested, have a separate interest from those of the country at large? – I conceive such a thing to be possible …

Should you anticipate a better system of management of the circulation of the country if Government had more immediate control than it has over the circulation of the Bank of England? – I am inclined to think not.

But a last word goes to another private banker with likewise a mind of his own, George Carr Glyn. 'Is your intercourse with the Bank almost daily?' he was asked. 'Hourly, I may say,' replied Glyn. And: 'Do you find any facilities afforded in your transactions with the Bank? – Every facility.'

Just over a year later, in August 1833, the Bank's Charter was duly renewed, in effect for a minimum of another eleven years. From the Bank's point of view, the terms featured one definite minus, one arguable minus and two definite pluses. Permitting joint-stock banks in London (and thereby abandoning the 65-mile restriction) would, the Bank vainly petitioned the House of Lords shortly before the Bill was enacted, 'have the effect of destroying the present character of the Bank of England and forming it into a Bank of competition'; but politically speaking, following the 1832 Reform Act, a further reduction of the Bank's monopoly was perhaps inevitable. The more arguable minus was the Bank Act's stipulation that the Bank henceforth be required to provide the Treasury with a weekly return of its total of bullion, securities, circulation and deposits, with a monthly average to appear in the *London Gazette* – undoubtedly repugnant to some at the Bank, though as Norman had conceded to the committee, the Court was 'much divided' on the question of publishing the amount of bullion in the Bank's possession. By contrast, the two unequivocal pluses were firstly the provision liberating the Bank's discount rate from the 5 per cent maximum embodied since 1713 in anti-usury legislation – an important moment in the Bank's embryonic development of credit control; and secondly, the clause that made all Bank notes above £5 legal tender (except at the Bank itself or at its branches, where gold was still payable), a measure likely to reduce future internal drains of bullion. Altogether, eight years after the horrors of the 1825 crisis had left the Bank badly exposed, it was in a better place than it might have been. While as for the continuing vexed private/public relationship, it might have taken comfort from the words of Althorp introducing the legislation: 'I feel confident, that persons standing so prominent as the Bank Directors will be as completely controlled by public opinion as if they were acting under legal responsibility.'[14]

By this time the Bank's branches were a well-established part of the provincial banking scene. Back in 1826, responding to the government shake-up of the banking structure, the Bank had moved quite quickly into action, with branches opened by the end of the year in Gloucester (where there had been a particularly widespread failure of country banks), Manchester and Swansea; these were followed in 1827 by Birmingham, Liverpool, Bristol, Leeds and Exeter, in 1828 by Newcastle, and in 1829 by Hull and Norwich. Subsequently, over the next decade and a half, branches were opened in 1834 at Plymouth and Portsmouth, and in 1844 at Leicester, while the unprofitable Exeter and Swansea branches were closed in 1834 and 1839 respectively – ultimately followed by Gloucester (1849), Norwich (1852), Leicester (1872) and Portsmouth (1913), leaving eight branches at the start of the First World War. These new Bank branches were not universally welcome in their localities – 'Of all men who are sinned against by this uncalled-for interference on the part of the Bank of England,' complained the *Exeter Flying Post* in December 1827, 'none are less deserving it than the bankers of our own City' – and in each case it was down to the branch's agent and deputy agent, salaried but receiving on top a percentage of net profits, to manage a sometimes difficult situation. Perhaps the most important branch was Birmingham, headed by George Nicholls for its first eight years. In his mid-forties when he took on the position, Nicholls had spent much of his adult life at sea, as an officer of the East India Company, as well as being a Poor Law reformer and a canal engineer. The evidence is that he ran the branch only reasonably efficiently, while the work itself failed to satisfy a restless, questing spirit. 'Mere banking – that is, the receipt and payment of money and the discount of bills – is of all the associations with which it has been my lot to be connected,' he would reflect in his autobiography, 'the least interesting and intellectual; I think I may also add, the most narrowing and restrictive in its influence on character.'[15]

For both government and Bank, the prime purpose of the branches was to expand the Bank's note issue in the provinces, at the expense above all of the note issue of the country banks, and generally to give the Bank greater control over circulation as a whole. 'To effect this,' explains Dieter Ziegler, a leading historian of the Bank's branches, 'the main device was the introduction of the so-called "circulation accounts", or "three per cent accounts", a privileged discount account for those banks which abandoned their issuing right and circulated Bank of England notes only. Up to the amount of the former note circulation – with a minimum of 14 per cent below this figure – these banks were entitled to re-discount at their Bank of England branch at three per cent.' And, adds another historian, David Moss, 'from the contracting bank's point of view, the guaranteed supply of notes, backed by the Bank's gold reserves, reduced the risk of failure during a monetary crisis when confidence in the banking system was low and country notes could be held in poor esteem'. On paper it was a mutually attractive arrangement, but in practice, amid continuing local jealousies, it worked out better in some branches than others. Liverpool achieved the greatest success with these privileged circulation accounts, to the extent that provincial banknotes were displaced there altogether by 1840; Birmingham did pretty well, at least for a time; while elsewhere was mixed. By the early 1840s, through these accounts and other means (including the offer to provincial banks of ordinary open accounts with the Bank), the Bank had gone some way, but far from the whole way, to meeting its objective: during the first half of 1841, as many as 281 private banks and 91 joint-stock banks were still issuing their own banknotes; and of total banknotes being circulated in the provinces, around £6.3 million had been issued by the country banks and around £3.7 million by the joint-stock banks, with the Bank itself responsible for around £4 million – less than one-third.[16]

The branches were also supposed to make money for the Bank. Palmer may have claimed in his 1832 evidence that the Bank had established them 'without any profit to the Bank of England, the object being to give solidity and strength to the whole circulation of the country', but six years earlier the Bank's Committee for Branch Banks had explicitly stated that opening branches in the provinces would be 'for the benefit of the Bank as well as to the interest of the public and the Government', while of course Norman had bullishly anticipated that 'they would furnish large profits to the proprietors'. In reality, that turned out to be, admitted Norman, 'an exaggerated view'; yet at the same time, during the 1830s and into the 1840s anyway, the income from branch discount business often exceeded that from Threadneedle Street's discount business, notwithstanding that branch agents often chafed at the tight controls imposed upon them by Head Office, while several branches – including Newcastle, Gloucester, Bristol, Hull and Plymouth – struggled for a long time to make any sort of profit. Altogether, the measured optimism in September 1843 of the Committee for Branch Banks, recommending to the Court the opening of a branch in rapidly industrialising Leicester, was probably fair enough: 'The Committee do not contemplate a large profit in the first instance, but they have reason to believe that the Branch will pay its expenses with a surplus and with a fair prospect of increasing profit.'[17]

In March 1834, less than a year after the renewal of the Bank's Charter and the accompanying loss of its London monopoly over joint-stock banking, the London and Westminster Bank (direct forerunner of the modern NatWest) opened in Throgmorton Street for deposit-taking business. It received a cool welcome from the City establishment – not least from the Bank, which through a protracted legal tussle tried to clip its powers, refused until 1842 to open a drawing account for it, and for a time would not even discount bills payable at the new bank. The Bank's attitude won few friends, with *The Times* as early as 1834 identifying 'a petty jealousy and meanness' that was 'unworthy not only of men filling a high public trust, but of men of character'. By contrast, the Bank's relationship during the same years with the Bank of Ireland was more one of stern mentor, as England's embryonic central bank did its best to guide Ireland's (founded in 1783). 'The elevated position occupied by the Bank of Ireland as the chartered Bank of that country and which it doubtless wishes to maintain imposed on it not the care of its own Credit only but the protection of the Banking and Commercial Security of Ireland, generally,' the older institution's governor, James Pattison, reminded in December 1836 his counterpart in Dublin; 'and it is therefore indispensable,' he went on, 'that more extended views should be taken by that Corporation and it should as regards the Security of that Country occupy in Ireland a similar station to that which this Bank sustains in relation to the security of England.'[18]

Pattison himself – somewhat reluctant Liberal MP for the City, and described by the financial journalist David Morier Evans as looking less like a Bank director than 'a respectable country farmer', with 'his bluff face, his long flapped black coat, his drab smalls [breeches] and gaiters, ornamented with small bright buttons' – was writing during anxious times. American trade and its financing had been booming, but the rapid and alarming downturn of the American economy from earlier in 1836 resulted in a crisis that lasted the best part of a year – a crisis that at the London end was played out in three main phases and intimately concerned the Bank as well as the leading 'American' houses: principally, Barings, Morrison Cryder, Browns (based in Liverpool) and the three Ws (Wiggins, Wilsons and Wildes).

'The Governor of the Bank pretends to be or really is most alarmed about the gold going to America and the amount of American bills in circulation,' was the report in July 1836 of Joshua Bates, the dour Bostonian who was for many years the main man at 8 Bishopsgate, home of Barings. Two months later, the Bank decided to take overt action against the American houses, temporarily refusing to discount their paper – a manoeuvre condemned by Bates as 'shabby' – before in late October the governor called in the partners of each firm and formally told them that 'the extensive Credits hitherto given to the Bankers of the United States and others, either as open Credits or in anticipation of the Sale of States Securities in this Country, are objectionable so far as the Bank of England is concerned ...' Bates was convinced that the Bank, in its understandable concern to restore its dwindling bullion reserves, had got it wrong, complaining that 'it is useless for the Bank to make war on Bills of exchange'; but in the Bank itself during the closing weeks of 1836 a rival focus was an internal disciplinary matter. 'The circumstances connected with the origin, progress and communication to the Public of the Report respecting the House of George Wildes & Co' was the subject of the report on 14 December of the Committee of Inspection of the Drawing Office &c,

following the spread of false rumours six days earlier, rapidly reaching the press, that the undoubtedly over-extended Wildes had failed. The report found

that Mr Smith of the Bill Office was the first to name the House as having failed; that Mr Whitford, the Principal of the Bill Office, having heard from Mr Worthington, who was told by one of the Out Tellers, that the House had failed, on giving instructions to the Clerks to expedite their business imprudently named the failure of the House as the reason of his doing so, without having made due inquiry into the fact; that Mr Ormes, who is a Junior Clerk in the Establishment, on hearing in the Bill Office, that the House had stopped payment, within 20 Minutes communicated the information to a Stock Broker in the Rotunda of the name of James Woolley, and as he states, that he did it in confidence, and told Woolley that it was in confidence, it is evident that he knew, he was not justified in making the communication Public.

For Ormes, his big mistake had been to trust Woolley – 'a school-fellow of mine', he revealed under examination. He and Smith were compelled to resign, with the latter writing forlornly to the Court:

I have been in the Establishment upwards of 26 Years, – 24 years of which Period I have attended at the Bill Office, as early as ½ past seven and occasionally as early as seven oClock in the Morning (Sundays excepted) and have to the best of my Ability discharged the Duties of my Situation with zeal and fidelity. I am now in the fiftieth year of my Age with my Health seriously impaired and my Eye sight defective.

Accordingly, he asked the Court 'to make some Provision during the remainder of my Life'; and some provision, though not handsome, was indeed made.[19]

Against the background of an unnervingly steady flow of bad news from across the Atlantic, the second phase of the crisis was under way by March 1837, with an especially sharp City commentary being provided by George Carr Glyn, seriously concerned that too many of the Bank's directors were 'impregnated with political economy doctrines', an approach he contrasted with the 'practical knowledge' of Horsley Palmer, fortunately still a director. 'I may tell you,' he confided in a correspondent at the Bank of Liverpool, 'that had it not been for the firmness of Horsley Palmer & the Deputy Governor [Timothy Curtis], the Governor and his party in the Court would have brought down every American house.' 'I really think,' he added, 'the Governor is mad upon this subject. He and I have been brought into disagreeable collision.' Later in March, two of the Bank of Liverpool's directors came down to London, where they stayed at St Paul's Coffee House and wrote to the governor, warning of 'the great embarrassment which prevails in Lancashire both in the Mercantile and Manufacturing interest, arising chiefly from the want of confidence occasioned by the doubt and discredit thrown upon American paper', so that 'unless immediate steps are taken to restore confidence and mercantile credit, we must soon inevitably witness the most awful crisis ever known in this or any other Country'. 'We are sure,' hopefully concluded their petition to Pattison (due shortly to vacate the governor's chair), 'that it must be particularly gratifying to you at the close of your administration of the affairs of the most important institution in the World, to be instrumental in preserving the Country from the calamities with which it is now threatened.' That was on the 21st, and it is clear that the Bank's directors were deeply divided, with Norman among those instinctively but nervously on the side of leaving the more reckless American houses to their fate. 'I can see very serious difficulties in the way of assistance from the Bank and very serious objections upon principle to any such measure,' his close friend Samuel Jones Loyd wrote to him on the 25th in stiffening mode. Eventually in April, after the government had declined to intervene, the Court took a deep breath and agreed to save Wildes, the most stretched of the three Ws and unable to offer any collateral – a decision no doubt made easier by the fact of Curtis now being governor, with the similarly pragmatic Sir John Rae Read as his deputy.[20]

The final phase was not long following. By May remittances from the United States were still notable by their absence, many bills were arriving only to be dishonoured, and even those bills accepted were proving problematic. 'Has known the business in US all his life & has been in London 16 years, never knew such a state of things before,' noted James Morrison on the 21st after a conversation with Bates, while Glyn soon afterwards accurately mirrored the City's keen desire that the Bank further assist the still desperately struggling three Ws, telling the Bank of Liverpool that 'we all entertain the strongest hopes of the Bank taking the decisive step and determining to carry these houses'. The crunch came at the very end of May and beginning of June. Wilsons and Wiggins formally besought the Bank for relief, blaming 'the temporary and almost universal suspension of credit throughout the principal commercial Cities of the United States'; 'the Bank deliberating on the W's – and all consternation dismal forebodings no sleep all night,' recorded Morrison in his diary; 'from what Mr Palmer tells me, I fear the result', related Glyn. His forebodings were justified. The Court requested Curtis and Reid to lay before the prime minister (Lord Melbourne) and his chancellor (Thomas Spring Rice) the Wilsons/Wiggins applications for relief, but insisted that they state to the politicians 'the apprehension of many of the Directors, from the character of the accounts received from America, of the eventual solvency of the Houses in question'. The politicians declined to get involved. And, by a single vote (according to Glyn's information, presumably from Palmer), the Court decided against extending relief: the three Ws would never trade again. In effect, although some small firms fell in their wake, that lanced the boil of the crisis, especially after the Bank later in June gave significant help to both Morrison Cryder and Browns. But it was a crisis that, taken as a whole, had significantly damaged the Bank's reputation, not least for unity and consistency. 'Floundering about from one expedient to another, so as to resemble nothing but a ship at sea, without rudder or compass, exciting the pity of those who are placed beyond their influence, and the terror of those who are within its reach': such was the verdict of *The Times*'s City editor at the end of June, and although exaggerated it had an undeniable kernel of truth.[21]

The Bank was in a different sort of jeopardy in January 1838. On a freezing night, with snowbound streets almost impassable, virtually the whole of the Royal Exchange burned down – the fire having been discovered, too late, in its north-west corner, only twenty-one feet from the Bank. Luckily, the wind that night was blowing from the north-east, not the south-east, while vigorous action, not least on the part of William Mellish (in the closing months of his forty-six-year directorship), saved Taylor's Bank Buildings to the west of the Exchange. Soon afterwards, in April, governor Curtis took the decision to expel the stockbrokers from the Rotunda, linked possibly to the destruction of brokers' offices in the recent fire and consequent overcrowding of the Rotunda, but possibly also to the unfortunate Ormes/Woolley episode. Either way, this did not make the governor flavour of the month among the stockbrokers, and three years later they enjoyed their revenge, as the floor of the Stock Exchange, in nearby Capel Court, bellowed out three cheers on the news of his firm's failure. Plans by this time were well afoot for a new and enlarged Royal Exchange, complete with plaza in front; and one consequence was the soon regretted demolition of the Bank Buildings. Complementing the new Royal Exchange – officially opened in October 1844 by Queen Victoria, who during her reign apparently never visited the Bank – was the wonderful (and still standing) statue of Wellington on horseback. In 1836 the Committee of Treasury had declined to help with the cost of its erection, 'the Bank not being in the habit of contributing to such objects'; but two years later the Bank relented, to the extent of 100 guineas.[22]

Timothy Curtis, meanwhile, was also to the fore, though no longer governor, in an embarrassing but telling episode during the summer of 1839. For a mixture of reasons, including lax control and a drain on sterling in order to pay for wheat imports, the Bank's bullion by the last week in July stood at barely £3.7 million, just over a fifth of the circulation and manifestly inadequate. It is possible that the Bank turned initially to Rothschilds, no longer under the guidance of Nathan, who had died three years earlier; but, in any case, by 19 July it was looking elsewhere, approaching Barings for assistance in negotiating a £2 million credit from the Bank of France, as formally given the go-ahead by the Court next day. Barings agreed to help, and soon Tom Baring joined Curtis in Paris for the negotiations with a syndicate of Paris bankers acting on behalf of the Bank of France. The agreement was eventually signed on 1 August, providing the Bank of England with £2 million in bills and thus avoiding the danger of having to suspend cash payments. The diary entry of a veteran timber broker, Charles Churchill, nicely caught the City reaction to the turn of events: 'The Bank of England raise the rate of disC to 5 p C^t & negotiate an arrangement with the Bank of France to draw 2 Millions, by way of a Check to the Exchanges!! The Bank of England & accommodation Bills!! What next.'

The dismay was unmistakable, but at least it lacked the venom of the Rothschild reaction, after its Paris house had apparently tried to get involved in the negotiations but left it too late. Writing from there on the day the agreement was signed, Nathan's brother James recalled that in 1825 'we arranged for such large quantities of gold to be brought in and thereby saved the Bank'; noted that 'now it is Baring who is the recipient of everything'; argued that the Bank 'should at least share out', so that 'the business is properly distributed'; and reserved his deepest ire for Curtis, nothing less than 'a two-faced scoundrel'. Relations between Rothschilds and the Bank would continue to deteriorate, to the point where Nathan's son Lionel took the decision in 1843 to close their account there. But for Curtis himself, sending a report back to Threadneedle Street at the end of the negotiations, the lesson of the episode was the desirability of establishing 'a direct intercourse and interchange of good services' between the Bank of England and its French counterpart. 'Such an arrangement,' he went on,

> might be of the highest advantage to the Bank of England in freeing it in the first place from the necessity of applying to individuals on business when it may be desirable to operate on the foreign exchanges in the second, and therefore in giving greater facility to the intended action, from the powerful means it would place at the disposal of the Bank of England, and thereby from the immediate and unobserved influence which such friendly and confidential relations between the two establishments would tend to produce when the situation of either Bank might require the aid and assistance of the other.[23]

No one of course yet talked about 'central banks', but it was still a significant anticipatory moment in the history of central bank co-operation.

That was for the relatively distant future. Later in 1839, the Manchester Chamber of Commerce – speaking as the voice of provincial industry rather than metropolitan finance – issued a report (endorsed by the influential *Morning Chronicle*) specifically blaming the Bank for having caused unnecessary commercial distress through monetary contraction, at a time when the state of trade was essentially sound. The response of one of the Bank's directors, Norman, was to start preparing a lengthy defence of the Bank's recent conduct, to be delivered to its proprietors early in 1840. 'They are bound as faithful Stewards of the interest of the Proprietors, and as beside intrusted with important obligations towards the public at large,' he asserted of his colleagues and himself, 'to declare it to be their unequivocal opinion, that the old system of silence and reserve on their part is no longer applicable, and that great injury would arise to the corporation and the community, was it any longer persisted in to the former extent.' The uncomfortable but unavoidable fact was, he continued, 'that the Bank of England in all occasions, seems to be the general object of hostility': 'These attacks in some few instances are directed against the personal integrity of the Court of Directors, but more commonly charge them with gross ignorance and incompetence, and represent the Bank itself as a pernicious, or at best useless, Institution.' The Bank appeared to be entering the new decade in a distinctly exposed, vulnerable position; and although nearly a century and a half old, and for all the lucidity of Norman's ensuing analysis (including the admission that 'had it been possible to foresee at the commencement of last Year all that has subsequently occurred, The Court of Directors can have no hesitation in saying that their measures would not have been exactly what they have been', prompting the scribbled note 'very true' on Horsley Palmer's copy), the general outlook was at best murky.[24]

The Bank's travails during the second half of the 1830s had especially serious implications for Palmer and his celebrated Rule, placing both on the defensive. Naturally he took to print, publishing as early as 1837 *The Causes and Consequences of the Pressure upon the Money-Market* – in which pamphlet he pinned the blame for the ongoing monetary instability almost wholly on the new joint-stock banks, by now numbering around a hundred, with as many as forty-two established during 1836 alone. 'It is needless,' declared Palmer, 'to attempt to describe the competition that grew out of this excessive multiplication of banks: its effects were exhibited in a great and undue, and even rash extension of paper-money and credits ... The commonest observer

must have seen the gathering clouds, and dreaded the consequences.'
What about the Rule itself, so far honoured as much in the breach as
in the observance? 'The proportion of one-third of bullion with reference to the liabilities of the Bank at the period of a full currency' was,
he insisted, 'never intended to apply under any extraordinary events
that might arise,' adding that 'in such times it would become the duty
of the Bank to reduce their securities without delay'. Palmer's protestations failed to convince Samuel Jones Loyd, who within weeks
issued a counter-pamphlet, not only accusing the former governor of
'a mere arbitrary mode of making up an account to exhibit a desired
result', but advancing an attractively clear-cut argument:

> The Bank, it must be observed, acts in two capacities; as a manager
> of the circulation, and as a body performing the ordinary functions
> of a banking concern. The duties of these two characters, though
> very often united in the same party, are in themselves perfectly
> distinct. In the principle [that is, the Palmer Rule] laid down by the
> Bank for its own guidance, the separate and distinct nature of these
> two characters has not been sufficiently attended to.

Accordingly, proposed Loyd, 'if the two natures of the Bank of England
were completely dissociated, each would proceed to the discharge of
its respective functions with more simplicity and efficiency, unencum-
bered by the conflicting tendencies and opposite action of its former
companion'; and under which system, involving a rigid separation of
the Bank's issuing and banking functions, 'the amount of paper issued
shall be represented by an amount of securities which never varies,
and an amount of specie which is left to fluctuate with the fluctuations
of the amount of notes out'.

Over the next few years, the late 1830s and into the early 1840s,
two clear schools of thought took shape: the pro-Palmer 'banking'
school that sought to give discretionary powers to bankers over the
volume of currency; and the pro-Loyd 'currency' school that explicitly warned against such powers. The Bank's recent track record
hardly helped the former school, and by 1842, in his survey of *Banks
and Bankers*, Daniel Hardcastle was bluntly stating that Palmer's
Rule was 'effective against a Bank of issue, but not effective against
a Bank of deposit also'. The decisive factor was political will. Prime

minister since 1841 was the stern-minded Sir Robert Peel, arguably
the principal driving force behind the 1819 decision over the resumption of cash payments, a move essentially designed to reduce the
Bank's freedom of action; and having witnessed since then a series of
monetary mishaps, usually involving feverish speculation followed
by financial crisis, he was determined to force the banking system,
including the Bank itself, on to a path as straight and narrow as he
could make it. Everything came together in 1844: the Bank's Charter
was liable for renewal; many of the Bank's directors had long lost
confidence in the efficacy of the Palmer Rule, perhaps even in their
own discretionary abilities; Peel himself was thoroughly convinced
of the merits of Loyd's 'currency' school; and in William Cotton
he and his chancellor, Henry Goulburn, had a governor (abetted by
Benjamin Heath as deputy governor) with whom they could work.
'I must say,' publicly declared Peel with apparent sincerity after a
round of positive and broadly harmonious negotiations during the
early months of the year, 'that I never saw men influenced by more
disinterested or more public-spirited motives than they have evinced
throughout our communications with them.'[25]

Peel's warm words came in the course of a lengthy speech to the
Commons on 6 May, setting out and justifying his proposals.[26] In
essence they were sixfold: separation of the Bank's note-issuing function from its banking operations; restrictions on other banks of issue;
a fixed fiduciary issue of £14 million (that is, the amount of notes
that might be issued against securities); above that limit, a fixed ratio
between notes and bullion; £180,000 less annually to the Bank for its
management of the national debt; and the weekly publication of the
Bank's accounts. The reception was generally positive. 'There can be
little objection raised to the *principle* of the proposed plan,' asserted
a few days later the recently founded *Economist*; 'sound & solid &
generally approved of,' noted the timber broker Churchill; while
according to the diarist Charles Greville, 'Peel has gained immense
credit by his measure (and speech) about the Bank.'

Among the Bank's proprietors, though, opinion was more divided.
At two special meetings of the General Court, on 7 and 13 May, at
least four strong dissenting voices were heard. Timperon stated ('in
a low tone of voice') that 'if it rested with him he would send the
proposal of the Ministers to the winds'; Fielder, recalling bitterly that

'the Government paid not a farthing of Fauntleroy's frauds, which have all been paid by the Bank', declared that once again 'the Bank had been hardly dealt with, that they had not had fair play'; Cook (speaking 'amidst much interruption') claimed that the directors 'were totally unfit to defend the interests of the proprietors', being 'tied down by the Government'; and Younger likewise 'hoped the proprietors would make a stand, and not suffer themselves to be dictated to, or be made, as they had been, the 'scape-goats'. The key speeches on the other side of the argument came from Hammond and, perhaps inevitably, Samuel Jones Loyd. Praising the separation of departments, the former set out a financially attractive vision of the directors now given 'an opportunity of directing their attention more to the Banking Department, and making it more profitable', so that 'he had no doubt that that branch of the business would extend, unfettered by the trammels of the other branch, with great advantage to the proprietors'; while from a loftier, less mercenary perspective, the latter, speaking in response to 'many calls', termed the proposed legislation 'the measure of a truly statesmanlike mind, characterized as it was by a manly adoption of great principles and enlarged views of the public interest', adding that 'there might be some difficulty in working out the measure, but it would be well carried out by those of whom the Bank could justly boast, who would work the measure in a manner to promote the interests of the Bank'. Significantly, these fine uplifting words came after Loyd had waved a big stick. Rejection of the government's proposals would lead, he warned, to a 'monetary system of the country' that 'would assume a totally new and distinct form, which would terminate in a manner not less beneficial to the interests of the country, but infinitely less beneficial to the interests of this corporation'. In any case, from whatever mixture of motives, the proprietors voted overwhelmingly to accept, with 'only three hands held up against'.[27]

Thereafter, it was not quite all plain sailing. Horsley Palmer was the last man to concede defeat readily, and at the end of May he wrote to Peel, asking him to increase the fiduciary limit to £16 million. Then a week later, on 7 June, the senior partners of the City's private banks met to consider a memorial to Peel that expressed themselves 'apprehensive that the absolute limitation of the issue to £14,000,000, without any power of expansion being reserved, whether that amount be in itself a proper amount or not, will create a general feeling of uneasiness throughout the country', in due course 'leading to a general withdrawal of legitimate accommodation' – in short, causing yet another financial and/or commercial crisis. 'I strongly suspect that Mr Palmer is very much at the bottom of this movement,' a disconcerted Cotton wrote on the 10th to Goulburn. 'He has been trying to influence members of the Court and I shall not be surprised if he brings forward some resolution which may probably place me in a Minority, but I will make the best fight I can and I shall be supported by the intelligence if not by the members of the Court.' In the event, though next day the majority of City bankers signed and presented their memorial to Peel, the former governor did not seek to mobilise fellow malcontent Bank directors – perhaps because, despite Cotton's anxiety, he did not quite have the numbers.

Peel, anyway, was unmoved, and very soon afterwards, on the 13th, the Bill had its decisive second reading in the Commons, amid a fair degree of apathy. During the debate, the Whig politician Benjamin Hawes warned that having what was increasingly tantamount to 'a single bank of issue' would lead to the Bank being 'ruled by the Government of the day' and getting 'mixed up with party politics', producing 'all the evils which resulted from such a course in America'; Goulburn, after referring to 1825 (when 'the country had nearly been reduced to a state of barter') and to 'the misfortunes' of 1839, and explaining that 'the principle of this measure was, to make the currency, consisting of a certain proportion of paper and gold, fluctuate precisely as if the currency were entirely metallic', insisted that 'if there was one thing more than another guarded against in this measure, it was, that the Government should have no control over the Bank'; John Masterman, private banker and Conservative MP for the City, 'thought it was a difficult point to settle that fourteen millions was to be the exact amount of money required at any particular period, or under any circumstances'; and the loudest cheer was reserved for Colonel Sibthorp, the famously reactionary member for Lincoln, when he declared that 'if he had £100,000 in money he would rather entrust it to country bankers than to the monopolising Bank of England'. None of which stopped a 185–30 vote in the Bill's favour, so that within weeks the Bank Charter Act was duly in existence, almost at the very moment of the Bank's 150th anniversary.

The creators of the new dispensation undoubtedly knew their history, going back to the 1790s. 'The main object which Sir R. Peel and myself had in the arrangement made in 1844,' Goulburn would recall, 'was to ensure the convertibility of the Bank note and to prevent as far as was in our power a return of the calamitous circumstances which had resulted from the suspension of cash payments of which we were both old enough to have witnessed the commencement and the close.' At the heart of that analysis lay an unshakeable belief in the superior virtues of gold – virtues that, if consistently adhered to, would dampen down speculation and ensure financial and commercial stability; while in ministerial eyes the prospect that the Bank would henceforth be kept in check, administering the gold standard along strictly non-discretionary lines, merely completed the virtuous circle. Yet of course the underlying reality was more complex. Not only did the narrowness of the Bank's remit give it the opportunity to achieve a technical mastery over monetary matters that few outsiders would be able to challenge, but the very inflexibility of the fiduciary limit (somewhat against Cotton's wishes) would make future crises more likely – as predicted by Horsley Palmer, and inevitably compelling politicians to look to Threadneedle Street for guidance.

Even so, the godfather of the Act was relaxed enough. 'H. Palmer has sent me his letter, *if it proves anything* it proves only that 14 million on Securities is too much,' Samuel Jones Loyd wrote in August 1844 to George Warde Norman, still on the Court and perhaps secretly not unsympathetic to somewhat more flexible notions than either Loyd's or Peel's. 'For a just decision on this point,' went on the wealthiest banker of the day, 'you Gentlemen of the Bank are exclusively responsible; and if you go wrong a la lanterne with you all.'[28]

6

The Effects of Tight Lacing

'I do most sincerely congratulate you and Sir Robert Peel on the good which has already resulted from the bold & comprehensive measure of the last session,' William Cotton – in many ways the co-architect of the Bank Charter Act – wrote to Henry Goulburn in January 1845 shortly before stepping down as governor. 'I think it is generally admitted by the great money dealers,' he added, 'that the effect of the measure up to the present time has been eminently beneficial.' Much of Cotton's valedictory letter was about the financial aspect to the Bank of the working out of the Act; but he ended with some sentiments hard to imagine coming from the pen of many Victorian governors:

You will I am sure rejoice with me in knowing, that, for many years, we have not had so small a number of prisoners in gaol at this season of the year. In the manufacturing districts the past year has been profitable beyond any former example. Some of the Cotton-spinners have, I understand, made a profit of £100,000. I wish they would devote a tithe of their profits to improve the spiritual & temporal condition of those who have been working for them.

Closer to home, a key concern for Cotton and his successors, in the new world of the Bank Charter Act, was what would be known in due course as Bank rate. Given that the Act meant that the Bank's power over its note issue was now much reduced, the obvious concomitant was to put the discretionary emphasis instead on short-term interest rates; and indeed it was later in 1844 that the decision was taken

to fix the discount rate on a weekly basis, with the Committee of
Treasury noting that such an approach would be 'essential for the
proper management of the circulation'. More generally by this time,
the second quarter of the century, a new phase had been developing
in the Bank's relationship with the money market – especially from
1830, when the Bank had consented to bill brokers, forerunners of
the discount houses, opening discount accounts with it, formally
embedding an arrangement by which these specialist dealers in bills of
exchange could come to the Bank and exchange bills for Bank notes.
'The realisation by the Bank of England,' reflects W. M. Scammell,
historian of the London discount market, 'of its own position as the
ultimate source of cash; of the need for a means of channelling cash to
the economy in times of need; and the conscious choice of the discount
market as that means, marks a definite step in the direction not only
of the modern discount market but of the modern banking system as
a whole.' Over the next three decades, the 1830s through to the 1850s,
the discount market expanded considerably, largely on the back of the
'call loan' system, by which the rapidly growing joint-stock banks
lent large sums to the bill brokers; and the Bank's relationship with
those bill brokers, now armed with a right to rediscount at the Bank,
would become far from unproblematic.[1]

    This was so not least during the immediate years after the 1844
Act, as the Bank – now invested with apparently complete freedom
on the banking side of things – discombobulated the money market
by pursuing an unexpectedly competitive discounting policy on its
own behalf. The Bank's directors, commented the *Bankers' Magazine*
in April 1845, were 'now anxious to push their business, as bankers,
to an extent hitherto quite unknown to their system of management';
and undoubtedly the policy played a part in stimulating the growth
of easy money and fuelling the railway mania, at its peak that year.
By 1846 stormclouds were on the horizon, as the mania conclusively
burst and the repeal of the Corn Laws took place against a background of rapidly deteriorating corn supplies (European and Irish
crops failing, the English harvest poor), requiring by the end of the
year rising imports of increasingly expensive wheat and the start of
a serious drain of gold. The Bank would subsequently be much criticised for its seemingly irresponsible discounting policy, coupled with
equally aggressive short-term lending, with Wilfred King, pioneering

historian of the discount market, reflecting in the 1930s that 'the
frantic railway speculations did not, apparently, raise even the faint-
est doubt in the minds of the Bank directors as to the expediency of
their free policy, far less any suspicion that it might be the actual cause
of the prevalent excesses'. It is possible, though, that such criticism
was not wholly fair; and in the fullest examination yet of the causes
of the 1847 crisis, H. M. Boot has argued not only that the Bank's
'new' discount policy was in reality appreciably more passive than
has generally been assumed, but that anyway 'the low market rates
of discount charged between 1844 and 1846 were not the result of the
Bank's discounting activities but of the large inflow of bullion arising
from the strong balance of payments surplus of these years'. Even so,
Clapham probably has the right of it. 'Corn and railways; these were
at the back of the crisis of 1847 – corn and railways, and to a certain
though disputable extent the Bank's new competitive policy and its
failure to realize the amount of control that it might exercise over the
market.' And in a striking metaphor true to the nautical preoccupations of the merchant directors: 'The Bank had not whistled for the
wind that brought up the storm, though it had carried on too long
with no reef in its topsails, and by example had encouraged others to
do the same.'[2]

The 'too long' criticism especially applied to the early – and in retrospect disastrous – months of 1847 itself. Notwithstanding the stark
fact of falling reserves between the start of the year and early April
(note reserves down from £8.2 million to £3.7 million, and bullion
down from £14.3 million to £9.6 million), the Bank signally failed to
tighten its monetary policy, prompting *The Times* to note on 7 April
that 'the extraordinary apathy of the Bank of England from January
last up to the stage we have now reached in our monetary affairs
is beginning to excite universal comment, and to be regarded with
universal apprehension'. The far from flattering explanation for this
policy failure is revealed in George Warde Norman's autobiography:

During the course of the year [1847] I did not fail to impress upon
the Court my views of the propriety of acting earlier, and more
efficiently by raising the rate of discount. I did this especially by a
formal motion in March of this year, by which and my subsequent
conduct, I acquired no little obloquy and unpopularity on the part

of certain members of the Court, some of whom had overtraded and regarded an easy state of the money market as vitally important to them. The fact that I was out of business, and could thus look without alarm as to my private interest upon the storm raging around, did not tend to make my counsels more acceptable.

'Among my fiercest objurgators,' added Norman, was the former governor James Pattison, 'with whom I had one regular shindy, having put up with a great deal, before I thought it right to stand upon my defence.'

The volte-face, when it came, was abrupt and, because it had been delayed so long, more severe than it would otherwise have been. First, on 8 April the Bank raised its minimum discount rate to 5 per cent (compared to 4 per cent since January and the historic low of 2½ per cent the previous autumn). Then, immediately afterwards, it took (in Feavearyear's words) 'violent action':

In London only very short bills were taken at 5 per cent, and others were charged at 5½ per cent or 6 per cent, while at the branches the Bank fell back on the old-fashioned method of restricting discounts, agents being told to cut the amount of paper taken in by half. There was some peremptory calling in of advances, and £1,275,000 of Consols were sold for cash and bought back for the account.

Unsurprisingly, all this induced widespread panic about the shortage of available credit, as the pressure on bill brokers like Overend Gurney became intense and trade at large more or less ground to a halt. To an extent, of course, the about-turn did its job, with doubts disappearing for the moment about the Bank's ability to maintain convertibility, as its ratio of bullion reserves to deposits recovered from under 20 per cent in mid-April to well over 30 per cent by early June; but at the same time, with substantial gold outflows still continuing in order to pay for imported grain, the cost of credit remained inordinately high. So much so that in early July a 'Petition of the Merchants, Bankers, and Traders of London against the Bank Act' was presented to government, describing the 'extent of monetary pressure' as 'without precedent in the memory of the oldest living merchant' and, as the petition's title suggested, blaming the City's woes on the 1844 Act – of which, it had been said in April, only three defenders were left in the square mile. Staunchest of all defenders remained Samuel Jones Loyd, who that summer did not hesitate to pin the blame on the Bank's earlier failure to protect its banking reserve of notes during the months of unavoidable bullion drain. 'I could at any time,' he wrote in June to the Whig chancellor of the exchequer Sir Charles Wood, 'convulse Manchester by gross mismanagement of my banking business – and the Bank of England, acting with infinitely larger powers, can and recently has convulsed the whole Country by mismanagement of its banking affairs.' Against this, he insisted, 'the Bill never pretended to afford any protection'.[3]

The new factor in play by the second half of the summer was the much improved corn situation – welcome to most, but producing havoc in the corn trade, as the price of wheat almost halved. The Bank's recently elected governor, William Robinson, was senior partner of the merchants W. R. Robinson & Co; and on 19 August his firm's bankers Prescott, Grote & Co, alerted to 'imprudent operations in Corn', spent most of the day inspecting the books. Naturally the bankers wanted to avoid the failure of a house in such a 'high position', but eventually (stated their subsequent report) they were 'compelled to inform Mr Robinson, that they could not assist him, as they took an unfavourable view of his affairs':

> It would seem that we have entertained a very erroneous impression of the amount of Mr Robinson's private property; we entertained the idea, from whence we derived we know not, that he was a Man worth upwards of £100,000, independent of his business; whereas it would appear his private property, including his Directorial qualification [his holdings of Bank stock] and a landed Estate in Gloucestershire, cannot be estimated at more than £25,000. His capital in the business is not more than £22,000; the stoppage of the House we fear is inevitable.

So it was, and with his firm went Robinson's governorship, being replaced in due course by his deputy, James Morris. The sense of shock in the City was profound – 'it has created an extraordinary sensation', reported one eye-witness on 24 August – while, according to an unsympathetic Loyd, the governor's fall was due to 'extensive Corn

Speculations, entered into and very foolishly conducted by his Son and partner and not properly controlled by himself', though Norman more generously reflected that 'his official duties have kept him from his counting-house in critical times'.

Worse followed in September, with a whole run of mercantile failures, including two firms closely associated with Bank directors: Gower, Nephews & Co (merchants over-committed in Mauritius sugar estates) and Reid, Irving & Co (East and West India merchants); and as a direct result, both Abel Lewes Gower and Sir John Rae Reid had to follow Robinson's example and walk the plank, temporarily leaving three vacancies on the Court. Compounding the crisis atmosphere was the stoppage, with liabilities of over £2.6 million, of the bill brokers Sanderson & Co. Never, declared on 24 September one well-informed City figure, John Abel Smith, had he known such 'general alarm, discord, and distrust'; five days later *Punch* published a pointed cartoon, 'The Effects of Tight Lacing on the Old Lady of Threadneedle Street', showing the Bank (its gold reserve less than £9 million) about to go pop unless the constraints of the Bank Charter Act were relaxed.[4]

Things did not improve in October, with Magniac, Jardine & Co informing Hong Kong on the 11th that 'since the departure of the last mail the money difficulties have been progressively becoming worse, & the additional failures of important mercantile houses have been to an alarming extent'. A list followed, and then came the crux:

> You may suppose how severely such disasters must cripple the means of other houses, while, though the resource of the Bank of England have been liberally afforded to the extent of its safety, the pressure has been so great as to compel the Directors occasionally to suspend assistance entirely, and other usual sources of accommodation are locked up. We confess we cannot see how the evil is to be arrested, unless by Government interference with the stringency of the currency act, of which there appears to be no present prospect. Want of confidence is extreme.

Two days later saw the first significant bank failure (Abingdon Old Bank), before on Saturday the 16th there assembled at the chancellor's all the key players: Wood himself, the prime minister (Lord John

Russell), the colonial secretary, governor Morris, deputy governor Henry James Prescott, his brother the private banker W. G. Prescott, the Bank directors Norman and Cotton, and the inevitable Loyd. 'The Governor stated,' noted the record kept by W. G. Prescott, 'that it was quite within the means of the Bank of England, as far as that establishment itself was concerned, to carry out the provisions of Peel's Bill [that is, maintaining convertibility], but that they could not consistently with their own position as Bankers afford further extensive aid.' Accordingly, explained Morris, 'they would afford what aid they could, but their present power of assistance was in fact limited to the amount of their daily receipts'. Eventually, after Loyd had stressed that 'no aid which did not effect the restoration of confidence would be of any service', all were agreed that 'there was no remedy for this within the law' – and accordingly, 'after much discussion the conclusion was arrived at that the government might direct an unlimited issue of Bank Notes by the Bank of England on condition that no advance was made by them under a high rate of Interest'.

For the moment, though, no action was taken. And during the following week, Monday the 18th to Friday the 22nd, other provincial banks (including the Royal Bank of Liverpool) stopped payment; the money market 'suffered severely' (with 9 and 10 per cent commonly charged on best short bills, and one merchant telling another, 'I would not advise you to take bills on Barings even'); the Stock Exchange remained 'a scene of continued alarm and excitement'; deputations from all over the country steadily poured into Downing Street; and at the Bank itself, which had lent well over £2 million since mid-September, the banking reserve was down by the Friday to £2.3 million, of which only £1.6 million was in London.[5]

Saturday the 23rd began with John Horsley Palmer writing from his home at Hurlingham House a lengthy letter to Sir Robert Peel, no longer in office but still a powerful political presence. Not quite resisting the obvious I-told-you-so temptation, the former governor reminded Peel that in 1844 he had pointed out to him and Goulburn 'the possibility of such a discredit as we are now sustaining'; asserted that since that fateful year 'every endeavour has been made to carry out the principles of the Bill with no other effect than the creation of that general panic which pervades the whole Country'; claimed that the Bank was now 'placed in a critical position unable to sustain the increased demand without endangering its own safety, or by refusing the requisite accommodation to mercantile solvent firms, incurring the hazard of an universal stoppage'; implicitly called on Peel to support a relaxation of the Act; and finally, after declaring that 'the enormous sacrifice of property daily made by the mercantile community is literally heart-rending', concluded with all due solemnity: 'In my 50 years experience I never witnessed so perilous a position as that in which the Country is now placed. The reports from the North today are full of danger.'

In Downing Street, meanwhile, similar sentiments were being expressed by a high-level City deputation, before at noon Morris and Norman waited on the ministers:

> The Governor stated that in his opinion, the Bank was still in a position to maintain itself within the limits of the Act of 1844, but that he did not feel confident that this could be done without resorting to some active measures such as a Sale of Securities, or, the limiting accommodation in the way of Discounts.
>
> Lord John Russell and the Chancellor of the Exchequer considered any restrictions in the way of Discount &c &c to be highly inexpedient and expressed a strong wish, that the Bank should act liberally today, with an emphatic assurance that happen what might, the letter authorising a possible deviation from the Law of 1844 should be sent to the Bank on Monday morning.

Such was the Bank's own record of a historic meeting, at which Morris had come as close as he could to asking for suspension of the Act without actually doing so. 'The Question was put to me over and over again whether we were able to take care of the Bank,' he would recall about that and previous conversations with ministers. 'I always stated that, so far as the Bank itself was concerned, we had no Difficulty; but that, whether Her Majesty's Government might have any political Reasons, such as Fear of Mills being stopped, or Riots in the Country, was a Question for them to decide, and one which we could not answer.' In any case, after whatever version of winks and nudges, a Treasury letter to the Bank was duly published on 25 October. This in effect suspended the Act, with Russell and Wood encouraging the Bank to grant as much accommodation as it needed to, free of concerns (including financial concerns, with the promise by government of an indemnification arrangement) about increasing the fiduciary issue above the legal maximum – a freedom which indeed it had been practising since the oral assurance of Saturday. 'The deed is done; and I hope it will succeed, but, I never did anything so unwillingly in my life,' the reluctant Wood wrote that Monday to Loyd. 'I am very curious to know the effect in the city. I am afraid that it will be too much approved.'[6]

In the event, de facto suspension did the trick immediately. 'It was only after the Government suspended clause II of the Bank Act and allowed the Bank to issue notes to an unlimited quantity that the situation was brought under control,' observes Boot. 'The Government's action effectively convinced the money market that the Bank's reserve was inexhaustible. Once convinced of this, private institutions recognised themselves to be highly over-liquid and within a few days money was readily offered on the money market. By the end of November the market rates of discount had fallen to 6 per cent and there were complaints of difficulty in employing money.' Altogether, commented Disraeli characteristically in the speech that he would claim made him Conservative leader, the process had been the equivalent to the liquefaction of St Januarius' blood – 'the remedy is equally efficient and equally a hoax'. Yet even as the general outlook rapidly improved, leading to the suspension being removed after only a month, there were those expressing regret. 'It will be impossible to destroy a feeling which for many years must pervade the public mind,' sternly predicted the *Economist* at the end of October, 'that the pressure must only be severe enough, and the demands loud enough, in order to procure a suspension of any restriction which may exist.' Others focused on how the deep commercial crisis – one that had brought down over thirty-three important mercantile houses in London alone, with liabilities of over £8 million – had happened in the first place. Committees of inquiry of both the Commons and the Lords were under way by February 1848, and inevitably much blame was attributed to the Bank for both its overly competitive discounting policy and its tardiness in changing tack. The Bank Charter Act itself, though, was still regarded by the Whig government as necessary to preserve, as indeed it was by the Bank.

What about the Bank's larger responsibilities? Had the experience of the crisis changed its own conception of them? Not according to Morris. 'I consider that with the powers that have been given to the Bank of England,' the governor declared in the course of his evidence, 'they are no more bound to support commercial credit than any other bankers are, except, that being a more powerful body, and having greater means, they are enabled to accomplish that object to a larger extent.' And so too Cotton: 'I think the Bank of England should be conducted upon the same principle as any other Bank is conducted.' Even so, the eventual report of the Commons Committee made it all too clear that post-1847 this was likely to become a minority view, *whatever* the logical implications of the Act:

> It is true that there are no restrictions imposed by law upon the discretion of the Bank, in respect to the conduct of the Banking as distinguished from the Issue Department. But the Bank is a public institution, possessed of special and exclusive privileges, standing in a peculiar relation to the Government, and exercising from the magnitude of its resources, great influence over the general mercantile and monetary transactions of the country. These circumstances impose upon the Bank the duty of a consideration of the public interest, not indeed enacted or defined by law, but which Parliament in its various transactions with the Bank has always recognized and which the Bank has never disclaimed.[7]

Given the Morris/Cotton evidence, those last few words may have been a bit of a stretch; but given also that the Bank had acted as lender of last resort as long ago as the 1760s, the phrase 'has always recognized' told a larger truth, albeit temporarily disguised during those somewhat errant – and arguably cussed – two and a half years before the crisis broke.

———————

The 1847 crisis also put squarely on the agenda the question of the Bank's governance. As early as May that year, Russell was suggesting to Wood the desirability of governors serving longer than the usual two (occasionally three) years; but it was really the failure and enforced resignation in August of governor Robinson that raised the stakes. 'It must expedite the period for those general discussions and arrangements respecting the future management of the Bank which could not under any circumstances have been long delayed,' Loyd at once wrote to Wood. 'A brother Banker of considerable eminence called on me today to ascertain my opinion whether this was not the proper time for a public movement in the City respecting a permanent Governor of the Bank, well paid, and unconnected in his private capacity with business. I recommended him to remain quiet.' Then came the intervention of *The Times*'s City editor on 14 September, two days before the General Court's half-yearly meeting. He called for the election of a permanent governor ('one who shall have familiarised himself with the broad practical philosophy of commerce and finance, holding no plurality of directorships, free from the narrow views and daily anxieties of a local business, unbiased by the consciousness that the duties of a banker must often clash with the momentary gains of a trader, and uncontaminated by the petty but always active jealousies of commercial rivalry'); condemned the present method of choosing directors ('the aristocratic plan of selecting the junior members of firms who inherit a mercantile name and fortune, but rarely or never the shrewdness and energy by which the name and the fortune were originally won, has been tried long enough to render its continuance intolerable'); and observed that 'a disposition on the part of the institution towards self-reformation would be gladly hailed'.

At the General Court itself, the proprietor who made the running was Parry de Winton:

> The unfortunate position of the gentleman who lately occupied the chair in the direction was a matter of notoriety. If the circumstance to which he now alluded was one which only happened occasionally, he should have looked upon it as purely accidental, for every man was liable to misfortune; but when he looked back during a period of 18 years, he found that out of nine persons who had passed the chair six had fallen into a state of insolvency. Now, he would ask any proprietor present what would have been thought thirty years ago if a governor of that establishment had been called before a court of bankruptcy to answer his creditors? It was a discredit to the Bank that such things should be allowed to occur, and they formed in

the eyes of the mercantile world a sight as bad as would be that of the Bishop of London standing before a Bow-street magistrate for petty larceny. *(Laughter.)* The proprietors must try to prevent the recurrence of this evil, for, if they did not, they might depend on it, the matter would be taken out of their hands.

Accordingly, de Winton wanted the governor to be elected for at least four years and to be 'a gentleman of settled habits of thought, of a dignified bearing, of talent, and, by retirement from business, he should be free from all personal pecuniary distractions'; and he demanded a special meeting of proprietors to discuss the whole issue of the election of directors. This, governor Morris emphatically refused, while Loyd made a powerful speech insisting that any visible sign of disagreement between management and proprietors would be deeply damaging to the Bank and indeed to the City. The General Court thus ended inconclusively; but within days Wood was informing Loyd that he had written to Morris and Norman urging that the Bank's constitution 'be altered so as to get a better set of men into the direction and to provide for the situation of Governor being filled by persons chosen for some better reason than that of being next in succession'.[8]

The events of the next few weeks allowed little time for questions of governance, but towards the end of the year the Committee of Treasury prepared a report, ready for consideration in January by the directors as a whole. 'The Court are aware,' it reminded them, 'that it has been the custom to expect each Director in rotation to offer himself to fill the offices, first of Deputy Governor and then of Governor; and Directors not willing so to offer themselves have, with few exceptions [including Norman], retired from the Direction.' This, however, 'has occasioned (and might again occasion) the withdrawal from the Court of many valuable Members'; and therefore, 'for this and other reasons to which it is not necessary more particularly to allude, The Committee of Treasury are of opinion that Gentlemen should be selected to fill the Chairs [the governorship and deputy governorship] upon some other principle than that of rotation' – that, instead, the principle should be 'the persons who may be deemed most qualified, without regard to their seniority in the Direction'. Although silent on the question of a permanent governor, the report argued that a further advantage of this reform would be ending the tendency to elect directors 'below the middle age', given that it would no longer be necessary to wait a set period of years before becoming governor, and thus 'the field for the choice of suitable Candidates [to become directors] would be enlarged'. Moreover, likewise in the interests of widening the field, the report advocated 'no longer to require as an indispensable condition that Candidates [for directorship] should be actually engaged in business, although, at the same time, they are still of opinion that persons who have been members of Commercial Houses should alone be selected'. The Court duly accepted all these proposals, subsequently endorsed by the General Court in March 1848; and, even if hardly revolutionary, they undoubtedly, taken in the round, put the Bank in potentially a better state to cope with the demands of the second half of the century.

Anthony Howe's examination of the changing composition of the Court – comparing the twenty-seven directors elected between 1848 and 1873 to the twenty-three directors elected between 1833 and 1847 – suggests in practice a sluggish pace of change. Governors did get appreciably older (59.5 years old at the start of their tenure, compared to 53.2), but directors barely so (35.2 years old at point of election, compared to 34.8); while in terms of the hereditary aspect, there were only three sons of directors in the earlier cohort, but five in the later. Merchants meanwhile remained the dominant occupational group, but whereas in the first cohort there were eighteen merchants to three merchant bankers, the respective figures in the second cohort were thirteen to nine, reflecting the increasing importance of merchant banking in the City at large, with one of those nine being Alfred de Rothschild, elected in 1868 as the Bank's first Jewish director. Out-and-out commercial bankers, whether private or joint-stock, continued – despite their obvious potential expertise – to be barred from the Bank's direction, seemingly (though never or seldom explicitly stated) on the traditional grounds of potential conflicts of interest. As for other characteristics, the Bank's directors were not yet on the whole overwhelmingly wealthy (only four of the 1848–73 cohort leaving fortunes of over £½ million, though that was four more than the previous cohort); but they were becoming better educated (half of the later cohort going to Oxford) and increasingly politically active (no fewer than ten of the directors in 1863 also being MPs, still mainly of Liberal rather than Tory persuasion, reflecting perhaps the

City's deep Whig roots). Were they also moving socially upwards? To a degree, perhaps. 'As near the true idea of aristocratic perfection as is permitted to imperfect mortality,' was how an American visitor in the 1860s would describe the Hampshire country house of the merchant banker Tom Baring, a director between 1848 and 1867; while in the early 1870s it was estimated that ten directors possessed landed estates of 2,000 acres or more. Even so, Bonamy Dobree, on the Court between 1835 and 1863, was probably more typical. Becoming deputy governor and then governor in the late 1850s, this Tokenhouse Yard merchant continued doggedly to fulfil his London duties, as a governor of Charterhouse School as well as of Guy's Hospital; and not long afterwards, a contemporary would nicely describe the Dobrees as 'immensely wealthy & seem to have a very nice position, not among swells, substantial but not fashionable'.[9]

If 1847 was the year of commercial and financial crisis, 1848 was the year of threatened revolution. The Bank took no chances. On Friday, 7 April, with the great Chartist demonstration due to take place at Kennington Common on the 10th, all able-bodied members of staff were sworn in as special constables, followed on the Sunday by the rapid preparation of extra defences – so that on the day itself the Bank was, in the *Morning Chronicle*'s words, 'not only defended by an extra garrison, but its parapets were surmounted with a breast-work of sand bags, so placed as to defend and cover the besieged, but allowing apertures sufficiently large to permit him to take deadly aim upon his assailants'. That Monday morning, an anxious Stock Exchange Committee was informed that 'the Bankers in Lombard Street [which had become shorthand for the money market] were sending over their Securities to the Bank of England'; while outside the Bank a large crowd of spectators 'most vociferously cheered' whenever soldiers entered the building. In the event, there was no trouble – whether from the 12,000-strong Chartist contingent who marched down Bishopsgate on their way to London Bridge and Kennington, or subsequently from the massed demonstrators, who quietly dispersed instead of marching on Westminster. The episode marked, undeniably, a turning-point of modern British history. 'England has only to be quiet,' wrote confidently next day the *Morning Chronicle*'s City editor, 'and the trade of the world must centre in her.'[10]

The 1850s duly turned out to be the transformative decade. 'The world,' reflected Joshua Bates of Barings on his birthday in October 1852, 'seems very prosperous since the discovery of Gold in California & Australia, & the extension of railways & navigation by Steam are working great changes in the world.' He was right. British exports doubling, the international economy's holy trinity of capital, goods and labour flowing in unprecedented quantities around most of the known world, the City of London as the ever more indispensable hub of that global wheel, providing as it did unrivalled entrepôt facilities, credit accommodation and access to capital – these were indeed transformative times, inevitably presenting challenges as well as opportunities to the world's leading bank, in some ways still an institution learning on the job.[11]

Arguably it was in the 1850s that the Bank began to stop trying to be all things to all men. Although it opened in 1855 its 'Western branch', in Mayfair's Burlington Street, its policy in the provinces was increasingly one of retrenchment, with across the branches after 1848 'not a single one' (to quote Ziegler) 'whose turnover of bankers' bills of exchange exceeded its pre-1844 level'. More generally, the clear need felt by the business world at large was for greater consistency from the Bank, certainly to judge by the heartfelt evidence in 1848 of Joseph Pease, a prominent railway owner and industrialist, to one of the parliamentary committees. 'It being connected in some way or other with the government,' he said, explaining his frustration with its 'ambiguous' position, 'it frequently appears to me to act as a private individual would act, and then at other times it appears to act as having certain national objects to sustain or difficulties to meet; so that a country tradesman, like myself, has no idea what the policy of the Bank is.' The Bank's response, in relation to the all-important money market, was to start distancing itself. 'After the 1847 crisis,' notes King in his history of the discount market, 'the Bank's open market activities definitely ceased to have any quality which could possibly be described as "aggressive" ... Within a short period its discount business could hardly be deemed competitive at all – it was competitive only when there was a definite shortage of discount facilities elsewhere.' Put another way, the Bank was behaving more

like a central bank, standing above the fray, and less like a commercial
rival, while always trying to make sure that Bank rate was not too far
removed from market rate. The process may or may not have been
entirely deliberate, but altogether the Bank (in King's words) 'evolved
a technique which would enable it to play the role of impartial regulator and disciplinarian of a market which was moving rapidly towards
a high degree of organization, cohesion and centralization'.[12]

The 1850s also saw the emergence of a long-term thorn in the Bank's
flesh. When William Gladstone became chancellor in 1852, he did so
having already imbibed from his master, Peel, a very distinct historical
perspective, one that he would put on paper near the end of his life in
retrospective justification of his strongly critical attitude towards the
Bank. He asserted that back in the seventeenth century 'the state was
justly in ill odour as a fraudulent bankrupt' in its relations with the
City; and that after the Glorious Revolution of 1688, when 'in order
to induce moneyed men to be lenders' the state 'came forward under
the countenance of the Bank as its sponsor', there developed a 'position of subserviency which it became the interest of the Bank and the
City to prolong'. Thus according to Gladstone, in return for 'amicable
and accommodating measures towards the government ... the government itself was not to be a substantive power in matters of finance,
but was to leave the money power supreme and unquestioned'. Since
then, Peel himself of course had fought the good fight, in 1819 and
1844, while Gladstone by the mid-1850s was explicitly envisaging the
creation of a 'Ministry of Finance' under whose authority the Bank
would have to bow. The first outright clash came in 1854 – involving certain longstanding conventions allowing the Bank to benefit
through the timing of payments to it of dividends on the national debt
– and saw Gladstone displaying what his first great biographer, John
Morley, would call 'a toughness, stiffness, and sustained anger that
greatly astonished Threadneedle Street'. The chancellor was adamant
that (as he told the deputy governor) 'public monies continue to be
public monies until ... disbursed'; and although he won this particular
battle, thereafter he never forgave the Bank for what with some justification he regarded as its obstructive attitude.

Nor, further afield, was the Bank hugely popular around this time
with the Bank of France. Experiencing in October 1855 a serious
drain of gold, Paris asked London for a loan of between £2 million

and £3 million in the precious yellow stuff; but regrettably, explained the governor, Thomas Weguelin, in his reply, the Bank Charter Act did not permit the Bank to employ its reserve in support of foreign currencies. 'Allow me to add,' concluded Weguelin, 'that it would have given me the highest satisfaction, if I could have had the means of conducting an arrangement in favour of the Bank of France similar to that in which the Bank of England was indebted to its assistance in the year 1839.'[13] No doubt he was sincere, but it was still a significantly retrograde step for embryonic central bank co-operation.

The Bank itself was also under some continuing bullion pressure by this time, and Bank rate was at 7 per cent when in the autumn of 1856 almost all the directors responded to Weguelin's request and gave their individual views on the subsequent workings of the 1844 Act and whether they would recommend any changes to it. Predictably, Horsley Palmer yielded not an inch – 'I have entertained an unfavourable opinion of the Act of 1844 from the period of its enactment and which is confirmed by its operation to the present time' – but he was in a distinct minority:

Productive of great advantages and has fully answered the main purposes for which it was devised. *(Sheffield Neave, deputy governor)*

Has worked admirably and been productive of vast benefit to the Public. *(John Hanson)*

Highly beneficial in its operation, by maintaining the convertibility of the Bank Note, and in preventing any discredit of the paper circulation of the Country. *(Thomas Smith)*

I should *strongly* advocate its renewal for a term of years *as it now stands. (James Currie)*

Crises and Panics will arise under any system, whether Metallic or any other; and in my humble opinion founded on long and extensive connection with Commercial affairs, I am satisfied the Act has greatly mitigated those that have occurred during its existence, and to which they were in no degree owing. *(James Malcolmson)*

Weguelin himself, forwarding the replies to the chancellor (by now the generally more accommodating Sir George Cornewall Lewis), contrasted the safety of the Bank's reserve with that of the very rapidly growing joint-stock banks. Citing the Joint Stock Bank of London

– £30 million of deposits, £3 million capital, £31 million 'invested in one Kind of Security or another', thereby 'leaving only £2,000,000 of Reserve against all this mass of liabilities!' – he asserted that 'it is impossible to foresee the consequences of the failure of one of these large establishments'; and that, he claimed not altogether implausibly, was a subject that 'more pressingly requires the attention of Parliament' than 'any alteration' in the 1844 Act.

The governor's tactic failed, and from March to July 1857 a select committee of the Commons took evidence on how the Bank Charter Act had played out in practice. Weguelin and Neave (the new governor from April) were the Bank's two main witnesses, with the former the more articulate, not least as he conceded, contrary to the literal interpretation of the Act, that the Bank's banking department was the 'pivot of the whole banking system of the country' and thus should eschew active competition with other financial institutions, let alone any form of speculation. Gladstone pressed him at one point:

Will you describe to the Committee what you consider to be the difference between the Bank of England and a private banker with regard to the management of their deposits? – The chief difference, perhaps the only difference, is that the Bank of England makes a much larger reserve than a private bank finds it necessary to do.

So that the Bank of England has to apply prudential considerations of a public order to cross and qualify to a certain extent the simple pursuit of profit? – That is so.

It must therefore be a matter of great difficulty at times for the Court of Directors, having the interest of the Bank proprietors to attend to on the one hand, and these public considerations on the other, to balance the one against the other? – No; I have been a Director of the Bank of England for 20 years, and I can never yet remember a discussion in the Bank Court in which the interests of the proprietors were considered irrespective of the public interests.

Still if I understand you rightly, it is the fact, that to a certain extent under certain circumstances, the interests of the proprietors have to give way to what you deem prudential considerations immediately connected either with the welfare of the State or with the welfare of commerce at large? – I think that the interests are identical; I do not think that the Bank Court could manage its affairs well for the interests of its proprietors, and at the same time manage them badly for the interests of the public. The interests of the public are the same as the interests of the proprietors, namely, that the Bank should be in an effective position of the highest possible credit.

Is the Committee then to understand that there is a real, or that there is only an apparent conflict of interest between the two? – I think that there is only an apparent conflict of interest between the two; and that has been the invariable opinion of the Bank Court.

What, asked another questioner, about the bullion aspect? 'I think the result has been satisfactory,' answered Weguelin. 'In no case has our reserve declined below 3 millions; and on the whole, I think, there has been no anxiety in the public mind with regard to the state of our reserve.' It was not a reply that satisfied the up-and-coming journalist and commentator Walter Bagehot, though at this point, writing in June, he blamed the legislation rather than the Bank itself:

> The bullion which the Act of 1844 compels the Bank to keep is, to speak absurdly, bullion in a straight waistcoat. It appears to be tied up for something, and there is no confidence that it can be made available for the actual liabilities of the concern ... We have seen that even while the notes are in good credit, the bullion might be reduced to less than one seventh of the liabilities. In general the Bank ought not, I imagine, to hold less than one third of its liabilities in bullion; it ought never, perhaps, to have less than one fourth. Occasions might arise in which they should have more than either.

After all, as Bagehot concluded, 'the great wish on the part of the English people as to currency and banking is to be *safe*'.[14]

Within months, the Bank was facing the first major crisis for all of ten years – a crisis occasioned largely by the collapse of American banks and railroads. It was, as so often, an autumnal affair. 'We clearly are going to have a heavy Squall & we must take in every reef we can,' governor Neave, laid up at home in Hampstead, wrote on 9 October 1857 to his deputy, Dobree, shortly after Bank rate had gone up from 5½ to 6 per cent and shortly before it jumped to 7. From the start, the Bank's primary focus was on the discount houses. 'My almost only fear is whether the great Bill Brokers are in such a position to bear a considerable drain on their resources,' one senior director, Thomson Hankey, confided to Dobree on the 20th, the day after Bank rate had been raised again, this time to 8 per cent, the rate imposed during the 1847 crisis; and Hankey was right to be fearful, especially after the failure a week later of the Borough Bank of Liverpool, prompting the joint-stock banks to recall their call money from the money market, which in turn left the discount houses struggling to finance their bill portfolios and having to look to the Bank for help. King of the discount houses was Overend Gurney, whose David Barclay Chapman, senior partner since the recent death of Samuel Gurney, dropped in to Threadneedle Street on the 29th in order, noted Dobree in his diary, 'to know whether they could rely on the Bank for unlimited assistance if pressed'. As usual, Norman (in his fourth decade as a director) kept Loyd (now Lord Overstone) in the picture. 'The bill brokers', he reported in late October, 'now find themselves up to the ears in their Bills' and 'expect the old Lady to cash every thing'; while by Guy Fawkes Day, with Bank rate hoisted to 9 per cent, 'things in the City' were 'very sick, and more likely to be worse than better', so that 'we may again see Lombard St knocking at the door in Downing St'. Saturday, 7 November brought the news that Dennistoun, Cross & Co, an important firm of American bankers and exchange brokers based in Liverpool, London, Glasgow, New York and New Orleans, had stopped payment – news that Neave and Dobree presumably took with them late that afternoon when they went to the Foreign Office at the request of the foreign secretary, Lord Clarendon, who was under pressure from Emperor Napoleon III to be told what was going on in London and likely to transpire. 'The Governor replied [recorded Dobree] that as regarded the Bank of England's Position it was one of considerable anxiety: that the Figures of the Bank as nearly as possible corresponded with those existing at the memorable period in October 1847 when the celebrated Letter authorised an unlimited issue of Notes on Securities: that the difficulties of the Moment were gravely aggravated by the total Suspension of all Credit in the U States …'[15]

Then came the week of third time pays for all. On the late afternoon of Monday, 9 November, with Bank rate up to 10 per cent, Neave and Dobree were summoned to see Lewis in Downing Street. 'Chancellor stated that a Deputation from Glasgow was to have an interview with him Tomorrow. Asked in general Terms whether or no the Bank of

England have any thing to suggest in regard to the Action of the Bill of 1844. The Gov^{or} replied that they had none.' Such was the first of the week's three key meetings, with neither side blinking. Next day the significant event was recorded in Dobree's terse diary entry – 'Gurney's asked for a dis: of 30 day Bills 400m [that is, mille, the old-fashioned term for thousand]. Granted' – before the crisis was further ratcheted up on Wednesday the 11th by two dramatic developments: the stoppage of the City of Glasgow Bank (causing huge consternation in that city) and the failure of the discount house Sandersons, with liabilities of at least £3½ million. By late afternoon governor and deputy governor, accompanied by Weguelin, were again in Downing Street. Lewis asked 'if the time had arrived to adopt the measure resorted to in 1847', mentioning that earlier in the day Chapman had urged him to do so; to which Neave and his colleagues replied that 'the period had not arrived for such a Step' and that 'a strong opinion was entertained by the Court of Directors to maintain the Bill of 1844 at any sacrifice'. As they left the room, Neave remarked to his deputy that his impression was that the government 'were prepared to issue 50 Letters and all they wished was that the Governors should make such a request'. The decisive third meeting was not long coming. Thursday the 12th saw discounting virtually non-existent, the joint-stock banks unwilling or unable to make any advances, two major discount houses (Gurneys and Alexanders) under severe pressure, the Bank's own banking reserve down to under £1 million: unsurprisingly, Neave and Dobree were in Downing Street by 2 o'clock. After some discussion – during which Neave admitted that certain directors were starting to waver, but refused either to reveal names or to make a formal request – it was Lewis of his own accord who produced the Treasury letter once again in effect temporarily suspending the 1844 Act.[16]

The relief produced by its publication was not quite so instant as in 1847, but even so it broadly turned the tide, notwithstanding the American house George Peabody & Co (forerunner of the merchant bank Morgan Grenfell) having a week later to borrow at least £250,000 from the Bank in order to keep going. A trio of immediate codas to the crisis was telling. One was Norman's reluctant pragmatism, for almost certainly he was the anonymous director – 'a consistent and heretofore staunch supporter of the Bill and well capable of judging the actual condition of affairs,' as Neave explained to Lewis at their final meeting – who on the crucial Thursday morning 'declared to his great regret that he saw no safety to the Bank or to the Mercantile Interest but in a relaxation of the restrictive Clause'. Second was the revelation, by an Overstone informant, that very soon after the letter's publication Chapman had 'avowed to his friends that he had threatened to compel the Bank to stop unless the Directors should obtain from Government a suspension of the Act'. And the third came from Overstone himself, who on the 24th, two days after Lewis had rather ingenuously told him that prior to suspension 'no pressure was applied to the government which they could not have resisted as easily as an application for a postponement of the hop duty', and that 'the pressure which was applied to them was the pressure of *facts*', sent a reply amply suggestive of unfinished business on the Bank's part:

> The Bill brokers have been in the habit of holding probably from 15 to 20 Millions of Money *at call*!! The whole of this sum they invest in the discount of Bills and in advances upon Goods and Produce. – When general pressure arises, and calls for Money are made upon them by all their depositors – they have no source from which to meet these calls, except that of rediscounting at the Bk of England. Hence the enormous demands upon the Bank – The Bill-brokers cease to discount – they send overwhelming masses of Bills to the Bank – and if this process sustains the slightest check – they at once exclaim, the world must stop payment, because there is an inadequate supply of money. In one, the last day before the Letter, Gurneys obtain 800 from the Bank!! and then they go to the Gov^t to urge the suspension of the Law, because the Bank is exhausted and can do nothing for trade. Either this system must be broken down, or it will in its turn break down any and every Monetary system which can be established …[17]

Crises notwithstanding, the Court's doors were always open – if the timing was right and the face fitted. 'Mr W. Goschen called to ask if there would be any objection to his son being considered a candidate for the Bank direction,' recorded Dobree on New Year's Day 1858 following a visit from the elderly co-founder of the successful merchant bank Frühling & Goschen. His son was George Joachim Goschen, just twenty-seven but already a partner in the family firm, and he duly became a Bank director that spring. Quickly tagged 'the fortunate youth' by the City at large, he published three years later *The Theory of the Foreign Exchanges*, an instant classic owing at least something to his assurance to its readers that 'the object proposed is by no means to propound any dogmatic theories'; in 1863 he was returned unopposed as a Liberal member for the City, having been nominated by two fellow Bank directors; and two years later he became vice-president of the Board of Trade, compelling him to retire from business and relinquish his position at the Bank.

Back in January 1858, a week after Goschen senior had put out his feeler, it was the turn of Horsley Palmer, who the previous spring had stepped down from the Court after a combative and often successful, but in the end somewhat marginalised, forty-six years. He explained to Dobree the new set-up of Dent, Palmer & Co (somewhere on the border between merchants and merchant bankers) following his own retirement – essentially, that the senior partner would be the sixty-year-old Thomas Dent, but with a major role for his own forty-five-year-old son Edward Howley Palmer, whose capital in the house would be at least £60,000. Accordingly, Palmer senior (who would die only a few weeks later) had two requests to make of the deputy governor. First, in relation to Dent, that 'it would be very desirable he should be chosen as Director of the B^k of England & for which Mr D has declared himself a Candidate, and if his Age should not be deemed a disqualification & he should be recommended by the Comm^e of Treasury'; second, in relation to his son, that 'should Mr Dent not be accepted a Candidate (on a/c of his Age), then in such Case Mr Edw H. Palmer would be a Candidate'. Horsley Palmer's suspicion was correct: Dent was indeed considered too old – and accordingly Edward Howley Palmer joined Goschen that spring as one of the new directors.[18]

By then, Neave and Dobree had appeared thrice before the Select Committee on the workings of the 1844 Act, reconvened in the wake of the previous autumn's crisis. Inevitably, Neave was pressed hard about the exact circumstances during the critical week:

What would have been the effect upon the Bank, if the Act of 1844 had not been suspended by the Treasury letter? – The Bank had evidently gone beyond what a mere ordinary joint-stock banker would have done. The Bank would not have risked what she did, if she had been certain that by no possibility would Government give any relief; but feeling that she was bound, as a public institution, to make common cause with commerce, she certainly gave greater assistance. If she had only had to think of herself, and selfishly to protect herself, she would have refused discounts at an earlier period altogether ...

Then, as I understand you, the Bank acted upon the conviction that the Treasury would suspend the Act, in case of difficulty? – I think it must have weighed with them within the last few days, that the Government would probably interfere, if the action of the Bank was unsuccessful.

And again, later in the same February 1858 session of evidence, with Sir Francis Baring (a former chancellor) continuing to put the questions:

A few days before it was issued, did you, on the part of the Bank, represent to the Chancellor of the Exchequer the necessity of issuing such a letter? – No; we did not take upon ourselves to urge upon him a measure for which we considered the Government entirely responsible; but we gave him every information from which he could make a correct judgement.

You went as near the wind as you could, I suppose? – No; I do not use that expression 'near the wind'; but we gave him every information which we possessed ourselves.

You did not give him your advice or opinion, but you gave him the facts? – We gave him all the facts.

It fell to the Committee's chairman, Edward Cardwell, to ask Neave whether, in terms of the suspension of the Act, 'it might not be as well to leave the power with you as to throw it upon the Executive Government'. To which Neave carefully replied, 'I would place it chiefly in the hands of the Government.' A final exchange followed: 'That the responsibility would, in your opinion, be too great if it were cast upon you? – I think the Bank would rather be without it.' Given that in day-to-day practice the Bank had been able since 1844 to exercise a significant degree of discretionary monetary control, almost certainly more than Peel would have wished or intended, Neave's was a sensible – and politically realistic – reply.

The Committee itself reported in July, with only two members dissenting from its recommendation (tacitly accepted by the Commons, which failed to debate the report) to retain the Act as it stood. 'A new generation were taking charge who saw no practical difficulty in operating under the Act, particularly since they realized that it would be suspended if necessary,' would be the helpful gloss of Elmer Wood in as the 1930s, adding that anyway 'the problem of monetary control was becoming less pressing as the supply of gold increased'. Even so, the 1858 report had its tantalising might-have-been – namely, an appendix considering the merits of implementing Ricardo's proposal (in a posthumously published pamphlet) for a National Bank of Issue, distinct from the Bank of England. The decisive voice against came from Lord Monteagle, the former chancellor Thomas Spring Rice. Such a bank, 'charged also with banking functions on Government account', would, he insisted, 'rest on no defensible principle whatsoever'; and he resoundingly declared that 'the honour and independence of the Bank of England, and the sense of duty invariably manifested by that great Corporation in fulfilling the trust confided to it by Parliament, furnishes a security which may not always be found in a mere executive department of the State, bound to obey the commands of a superior authority'.[19]

For Neave personally, no less than for Overstone, what had really stuck in his gullet about the previous year's crisis was what he saw as the grossly irresponsible conduct of the discount houses. On 11 March 1858 the Court met to decide whether to forbid bill brokers from discounting any bills at the Bank whatever, but instead only to be eligible (at the Bank's strict discretion) for advances; and by the governor's casting vote, this policy was carried, controversial from the start. *The Times* signalled its approval – 'if those houses choose to receive money at call to an unlimited extent, they must themselves bear the responsibility of being at all times prepared to meet the engagements into which they may enter', no longer able to rely 'on their immediate ability in times of sudden pressure to throw the onus of any difficulty on the Bank' – but the *Economist* was far more doubtful, contending that the new approach not only failed to take into account 'the character of the house or the quality of the bills it may offer', but might be dangerously inflexible in times of monetary strain. Neave himself, however, had no doubts about its justice, as he explained to the Select Committee within days of the announcement:

> The object is to keep the resources of the Bank more within her own compass, and not to give the opportunity to the discount brokers, who accumulate such very large sums in their hands, to rely entirely and totally for cashing their bills upon the Bank of England. When those [mainly the joint-stock banks] who have deposited money with them want it, the discount brokers have been in the habit of considering that they could repay their loans at an hour's notice by merely coming over to the Bank, and asking for the cash to do it with. The immense drain upon the Bank in the last panic has shown that that power is an inconvenient one.

Did this really mean that the Bank would not necessarily be lender of last resort to the discount houses? Not according to Wood, who argued that 'the main object of the rule was to threaten the brokers vaguely, with the idea of forcing them to maintain reserve balances at the Bank'; while Bagehot at the time, writing in the *Economist* in early April, asserted, 'I own that I question whether the rule recently laid down will much diminish the real advances which the Bank of England will think itself obliged to make during a crisis of difficulty,' even if the bill brokers could no longer approach the Bank directly and had to secure accommodation from the Bank via their own bankers.[20]

Which is not to say that the bill brokers themselves were not immediately resentful, feelings that deepened as the money market began to show signs of tightening in early 1860. Overend Gurney took it hardest. 'M' Gurney had an interview with the Governors to urge a Relaxation of the Bank's Exclusion of Discount Houses,' noted Dobree (by now governor) at the end of January. 'The Gov' did not give him the smallest hope that an Appeal to the Court would be attended with any success.' A dramatic denouement unfolded in April, starting between the 9th and 11th with Overend Gurney deploying its powerful Quaker connections in the City to make £1.6 million of withdrawals (all in £1,000 notes) from the Bank and soon openly boasting, a Stock Exchange source informed Dobree, of their intention 'to reduce the Bank's Reserve to the lowest possible Amount'.

Monday the 16th saw the conflict further escalate. 'If the Rule excluding the dis Houses should be modified,' the message went to Dobree through an intermediary, 'the Notes withdrawn & still locked up in Lombard St shall be returned to the Bank "*tonight*".' The governors refused 'to entertain any such proposal'; but next morning there arrived on Dobree's desk a sinister anonymous message: 'Overends can pull out every note you have, from actual knowledge the writers can inform you that with their own family assistance they can nurse seven millions!!' This proved, however, the final threat, for later that day Dobree learned that the firm had told John Masterman (City MP and banker) that 'if it would be considered a conciliatory step on their part, they will at once return to the Bank the Million, Five Hundred & Fifty Thousand Bank Notes locked up in Lombard St' and that 'they are sorry for what they have done'. On Wednesday the notes were indeed returned to the Bank, 'identical but all cut into halves'; and next day a relieved Court 'approved of the Course pursued by the Gov^rs in this disreputable Affair'.

Were Overend Gurney truly repentant? When, a couple of months later, two directors of the Sheffield and Hallamshire Bank spent the best part of a week in the City calling on leading figures, their highlight was a visit to the 'Corner House', on the corner of Lombard Street and Birchin Lane, where they found 'Mr Gurney junior the most intelligent & business like, & Gentlemanly Person, we had up to this time met with':

> He entered on the subject of their controversy with the Bank of England & said – that he thought this subject was not understood by the public – who thought that the question was solely between Bank of England and Overends, whereas it was between the Bank of *England* and the *Commercial public*. The latter would have to pay in *inconvenience* & the *price of money* for the restrictions now in force.
>
> If the Bank of England did not relax, Peel's act would again have to be broken; but – not by *them*, but by the *Bank of England*, for its own salvation.

'We now do business on the principle known & acknowledged *of taking care of ourselves*,' added Henry Edmund Gurney; and he stressed again to his suitably impressed visitors, 'all must take care of themselves in any future Panics'.[21]

By this time the Bank's less than favourite politician was back at the Treasury, with the Bank once again finding itself quickly on the back foot. John Hubbard, governor in the mid-1850s, had suffered particularly at Gladstone's hands – friends though the two men were through religious affinity – and at the end of 1860 he wrote to Dobree complaining of the chancellor's continuing 'aggression' and regretting that 'the defenders of the Bank bulwarks have demolished them at the first blast of the trumpet sounded by this modern Joshua'. A few weeks later, the trumpet sounded louder than ever, as Gladstone on 31 January 1861 sent Dobree and his deputy (Alfred Latham) a ten-page letter detailing his proposals for the management of the national debt over the next twenty-five years, involving a significant reduction in the Bank's annual remuneration. 'A veritable skinflint' was Neave's private reaction, writing to Dobree on 5 February; but next day the Court reluctantly acceded, with the governors informing Gladstone that the directors did so 'mainly because the combined management of the National Debt, and of the collateral Departments of Issue and Banking, enable them to exercise a very important economy in the labor charge, and in the other expenses of Bank administration'. The proprietors still had to ratify the decision, and a General Court met on the 7th to do so. 'They were called upon to make a sacrifice it was true,' argued Prescott, 'but in return for that sacrifice they would secure the good will of the country, and the permanence for 25 years of the arrangement, which he regarded as a valuable consideration'; though for R. Mills 'the proposal was unjust' and 'his submission was certainly unaccompanied with any feeling of cordiality'. Gladstone's victory was further cemented in 1861 by his successful creation of the Post Office Savings Banks, their deposits (accessible to the Treasury) reaching £15 million as early as 1870. 'I had an object of first-rate importance, which has been attained,' he would reflect with satisfaction shortly before his death in 1898. That object was, he went on, 'to provide the minister of finance with a strong financial arm, and to secure his independence of the City by giving him a large and certain command of money'.[22] Gladstone never wavered from his conviction that the Bank was a vested interest, at best only semi-reformed; and his relationship with it was destined, like his relationship with Queen Victoria, to remain star-crossed.

In the financial world at large, the next few years, especially 1863 and 1864, were far from Gladstonian in spirit, as a sustained bull market raged and the City was awash with speculative froth, including an array of new-fangled finance companies. Somewhere near the heart of the action was Overend Gurney, whose response to the Bank's exclusion had been to diversify radically away from its core business, becoming shipbuilders, shipowners, grain traders, ironmasters, railway financiers and probably much else. Too many of these new lines, though, involved ill-judged lock-up investments, and by July 1865 it was probably as a desperate final throw that it converted to a limited liability company, seeking to concentrate again on its traditional discounting business. 'It is an extraordinary change,' reflected the private banker Robert Fowler. 'They have lost a good deal of money, but they must have a splendid business at bottom.' The following winter, they sought to borrow money from Glyn Mills at a special rate on securities which seemed to that bank's Bertram Currie of uncertain value. When he ventured to express qualms, Henry Edmund Gurney retorted indignantly: 'Do you presume to question the credit of Overend, Gurney and Co?'[23] But by the spring of 1866, it was not only Currie who was asking the question.

The memorable Overend Gurney crisis was played out during the second week of May.[24] By Wednesday the 9th, with the money market in a lather, the key question on everyone's lips – or at least everyone in the know – was whether Overend Gurney would be rescued by the Bank, which had appointed a committee of three wise men (Kirkman Hodgson, a recent governor, and two private bankers) to scrutinise the books. On the 10th their answer became known to all: the business was essentially rotten and there could be no possibility of the Bank offering a helping hand. The formal announcement of the stoppage was made late that afternoon. 'The fatal day, the long expected day has come & O.G. has put up his shutters,' Currie informed his father. 'For some weeks I have ventured to predict this event ... The panic is pretty smart & and beats 47 or 57 ... I think some of the new Banks will have a hard time & financial companies & contractors must go right & left.'

It was indeed the third big crisis in twenty years, and next morning – the City's Black Friday – *The Times* anticipated that the shock of Overend Gurney's failure 'will, before this evening closes, be felt in the remotest corners of the kingdom'. The atmosphere was certainly bad enough in the City itself, recorded by the partners of Prescotts as 'a day of most intense excitement and panic, in fact such a day has never been experienced in the memory of any one', while *The Times* described 'throngs heaving and tumbling about' as by noon 'the tumult became a rout' and 'the doors of the most respectable Banking Houses were besieged'. Gladstone was still chancellor, still an austere Peelite to the core, yet he could not but take notice when he received that morning a hasty scribbled note from Bagehot (by now the esteemed editor of the *Economist*) about 'a complete collapse of credit in Lombard Street and a greater amount of anxiety than I have ever seen', anxiety accentuated by several serious stoppages. The Bank for its part, responding manfully to what was a serious credit crunch, lent to banks, discount houses and merchants in the course of the day the very considerable amount of £4 million; but the pressure on Gladstone to authorise yet another de facto suspension of the 1844 Act came less from the governor (Lancelot Holland, a linen-yarn manufacturer) than from a series of urgent deputations, including country bankers as well as what Gladstone in his diary called 'a stream of City magnates'. As in 1847, as in 1857, it was essentially psychological relief that was craved, and once again a Treasury letter did the necessary. 'The Government allowing the Bank to issue Notes at 10% gave relief,' recorded the young banker Richard Biddulph Martin at the close of Saturday, 12 May, '& the panic subsided to a great extent.' Bank rate remained at 10 per cent until August, and there was a handful of further significant banking stoppages, but the crisis itself was over.

Had it been solely for objective financial reasons that the Bank had let Overend Gurney go down? Certainly those reasons were compelling enough. 'The Governor took the view,' reflects King in his history of the discount market, 'that the Bank could not assist one concern unless it was prepared to assist the many others which were known to be in a similar plight.'[25] Yet remembering the history of an intensely strained relationship from at the latest 1857, culminating in 1860 in the infamous £1½ million gun held at the Bank's head, it is hard not to feel that other considerations – conscious or unconscious – were involved. After all, the mid-Victorian City was in many ways a club, run along strictly hierarchical lines; and it would never do if that club's ex officio chairman allowed such blatantly disrespectful behaviour to go unpunished.

Matters of Conduct and Behaviour

'London was still London,' recalled many years later the American writer Henry Adams about the world capital that as a young man he had encountered in 1858. 'A certain style dignified its grime; heavy, clumsy, arrogant, purse-proud, but not cheap; insular but large; barely tolerant of an outside world, and absolutely self-confident ... Every one seemed insolent, and the most insolent structures in the world were the Royal Exchange and the Bank of England.'

Inside those four walls, the Victorian Bank remained physically very much Soane's creation, though his successor, C. R. Cockerell, built a new Dividend Warrant and Pay Office, followed in 1849–50 by a new Private and Public Drawing Office, the latter giving the Bank's commercial customers a handsome and up-to-date banking hall comparable to those of the burgeoning joint-stock banks. Probably not all that many of the staff fell in love with the place, but one who did so was Herbert de Fraine, arriving as a clerk in the 1880s:

It was a magnificent conglomeration, due to the piecemeal acquisition of the site. Nothing could have been less like the stream-lined office block of today [the 1950s]. You could seldom go direct from place to place, and dead ends seemed almost a rule ... Most of the Bank was only one storey high, and many of the offices had domes or lanterns, with the solid roof supported by columns or caryatides. Separating the buildings were the Garden and various courts and yards, including the Bullion Yard and the Well Yard.

Looked at from above, the roof was peppered with domes, skylights and lanterns, in the midst of which towered the great dome of the Rotunda. There were no windows on the street on any of the four sides ...

The Pay Hall (called by de Fraine 'the Great Hall') still had at one end its original statue of King William III in Roman garb; Soane's Transfer Offices were 'all beautifully proportioned, all beautifully light', each with its 'graceful features'; Cockerell's Drawing Office was 'majestic'; the parlour featured an 'exceptionally fine' ceiling, three fireplaces with 'grates of burnished steel', and at each end a 'triple arcade supported by Corinthian columns of wood'; and altogether in the Bank's many offices 'the general impression was one of space, light and harmony', so that 'as a young man I was overwhelmed by their quiet dignity, which was even enhanced by the perfection of detail'.

Yet that quiet dignity could never be taken for granted. A revealing moment occurred in May 1867, when a large demonstration in Hyde Park, calling for an extension of the franchise, prompted an urgent, little-publicised meeting between the governor and Colonel Burnaby, commanding the Grenadier Guards at the Tower:

It appeared that the Bank were in possession of about 120 Muskets and Bayonets and the same number of Pistols, with various Pikes, Cutlasses &c: the same being kept in the Porters' Armoury. In addition to these, the Volunteers' Armoury contained about 150 Enfield muzzle loading Rifles with bayonets. In the Magazine were 1000 rounds of ball cartridge for the muskets, and the same number of rounds for the pistols. There was however no ammunition for the Enfield Rifles. At the suggestion of Col. Burnaby, and by the Governor's direction, the Secretary wrote a letter on that day to the Officer commanding the Grenadier Guards at the Tower, requesting that 10,000 rounds of Breech loading Ball cartridge, and 10,000 of muzzle loading do. [i.e. ditto] with caps, might be supplied to be kept in Store at the Bank. This Ammunition including 11,000 caps was duly supplied from the Royal Arsenal at Woolwich ...

The Bank's understandable concern for its security as well as its dignity seldom faltered; and in 1883 it was the turn of the 'Out-Door Porters and Street-Keepers' to receive their orders from the deputy governor:

They shall attend during the time the Gates are open, to keep the approaches to the Bank clear, to prevent cabs and omnibuses standing near the Gates to ply for fares, and generally to prevent and remove any obstruction or annoyance to persons having business at the Bank.

One man shall be constantly stationed at the Front Gate, another at the Gate in Prince's Street, and the third shall patrol round the Bank, giving special attention to the Gates in Lothbury and Bartholomew Lane …

In case of a crowd passing, or any unusual collection of persons in the street, the Street-Keeper will at once close the Outer Iron Gates, and caution the Gate-Porter on duty inside that he may be prepared to close the Inner Gates, and to give notice by means of the Electric Bell to the Head Gate-Keeper, or, if the emergency requires it, to obtain immediate assistance from the nearest point where it may be available.

Still, most of the time it was quiet and orderly enough, especially of course at night. That was certainly the case on the evening when the young Spanish philosopher George Santayana was invited by an acquaintance – the officer commanding the guard – to take dinner at the Bank. The date was 1901, but it could have been at least twenty or thirty years earlier:

The room into which I was ushered had a dingy Dickensian look of solidity grown old-fashioned and a bit shabby. There was a walnut mantelpiece with a small clock and two candlesticks without candles; heavy black walnut chairs, with horse-hair bottoms and a table set unpretentiously, with thick white plates and thick glasses. But there was a pleasant fire in the grate, and the rather superannuated butler served us an excellent absolutely English dinner: mock-turtle soup, boiled halibut with egg-sauce: roast mutton: gooseberry tart and cream, and anchovies on toast; together with one bottle of claret and one of port.[1]

The Bank during the mid- to late nineteenth century may in a commercial banking sense have been increasingly dwarfed by the giant joint-stock banks, which were willing (unlike the Bank and many of the long-established private banks) to pay interest on deposits. Even so, its own range of activities and responsibilities, whether for its 'private' purposes or in the larger 'public' interest, continued to grow. In 1864 the Bank entered the Bankers' Clearing House, which meant, noted a report three years later on the Private Drawing Office, that henceforth the Bank was 'enabled to offer the same advantages to Customers as those afforded by the other Clearing Bankers'; while, in terms of acting as the bankers' bank, typical figures in the late 1860s showed London bankers' balances at the Bank running at over £7 million, amounting to one-third of the Bank's private deposits. Soon afterwards, in 1871, the Bank's assiduous secretary, Hammond Chubb, itemised some significant indicators since 1853: Bank notes issues annually up from £9 million to £13 million; 'a considerable increase in the number of gold coins weighed in the Weighing Office, and in the amount of silver counted in the Tellers' Office'; the number of accounts in the Drawing Office up by more than 600, with the average balance nearly doubled; securities deposited by customers up from £4.9 million nominal value to £19.9 million, 'the greater part bearing Coupons for half-yearly collection'; and 'the management of all the India Stocks and Promissory Note Loans has been undertaken, as well as a great part of the Banking Business of the India Office, formerly managed at the East India House', not to mention the printing of India currency notes, stock certificates and so on being added to the work of the Printing Department. Indeed, there was from the late 1860s, as Clapham notes, 'a steady access of colonial, municipal, and other business for bodies corporate' – business that was 'safe and certain' and of a sort that the Bank was 'well qualified to handle'.[2]

Despite the overall increase of activities, the size of the Bank's staff (including at the branches) remained notably constant: 908 in 1832, 883 in 1854, 899 in 1880. Chubb, writing in 1871, had no doubt about the key role played by 'the introduction and use of mechanical labour', citing as examples 'the system of "Surface Printing" in Bank Notes, the printing signatures to Bank Notes and Warrants, the employment of mechanics in the Accountant's Bank Note Office, an increased use of printing in special forms and cheques; and, latterly, the application of printing to the Dividend Books and Warrants'. His detailed case-study, in which he took manifest pride, concerned the Accountant's Bank Note Office:

> There was first in 1860 the introduction of mechanics as 'posters', and subsequently in 1861 as 'ledger examiners'. These were aided in their work by the simple 'stamping pen', with moveable dates. In 1862 the system of employing uncovenanted [in effect apprentice] clerks as sorters of Bank Notes was commenced. By degrees the system was extended, and a further step was taken in 1863 by the use of stamping and numbering machines, and finally by the abolition of some duplicate work in 1868. But this is not all. The Inspectors of notes still stand at the number fixed in 1853, notwithstanding the larger number of notes – a result which has been obtained by a better organization in the Inspectors' Department, but chiefly by the arrangements made in recent years, under which the clerks in several of the Banking Offices inspect the notes passing through their hands. The system was first applied to the Private Drawing Office, and ultimately to the Pay Hall; a slight payment being made to the clerks in these Offices to cover the increased risk.

'Thus, by the adoption of these measures, which followed one another as circumstances would admit,' concluded Chubb in his report to the governor about 'the Expenses of the Bank', the office 'has been brought to its present condition, in which its arrangements are more simple, the performance of the work is more efficient, and the cost is far less than it has ever been in modern times.'[3]

Banknotes themselves were of declining relative importance during the second half of the century – rivalled by the growing use of cheques and the ever-greater popularity of gold sovereigns and half-sovereigns – but they still mattered hugely, while remaining to the world at large the most visible symbol of the Bank. Increasingly, as intended by the Bank Charter Act, the Bank's notes enjoyed a near-monopoly of the note issue in England and Wales, hastened from the late 1870s by the remorseless takeover of country banks by the large, non-issuing joint-stock banks – so that by the end of the century provincial banknotes accounted for only 7 per cent of the circulation of banknotes in England, with the rest being Bank of England notes. Those notes themselves were of a new type from 1855:

printed by letterpress, with a shaded watermark; on distinctively thin, crisp paper; payable only to 'the Bearer on Demand'; on and featuring a spear-carrying Britannia of somewhat Pre-Raphaelite mien, as depicted by the artist Daniel Maclise. Forgery now became significantly more difficult, though in 1862 there was a major scare with the discovery of the theft of a large quantity of banknote paper (and paper for printing rupees) from Messrs Portals' Laverstock Mills in Hampshire, which had led to forged £5 notes, all printed on genuine banknote paper, being presented at the Bank. The main culprits were eventually identified, leading to a trial at the Old Bailey in 1863 and heavy sentences; but never tracked down was the woman, invariably dressed in black, who would wait at Waterloo Station for the packages of stolen paper, before disappearing with them over Waterloo Bridge in a horse-drawn cab. 'We need to write a novel,' commented the Bank's solicitor Henry Freshfield, with a nod to the recent Wilkie Collins bestseller, 'and call it *The Woman in Black*.'[4]

A decade later came another fraud, another trial – and considerable embarrassment.[5] An American called George Bidwell, aided by his brother Austin and two accomplices, managed in the early months of 1873 to sell to the Bank's Western branch in Burlington Gardens over £100,000 worth of forged bills of exchange. The branch's manager was Colonel Peregrine Madgwick Francis, who had previously run the Hull branch, and he was undone by some highly accomplished fraudsters and no doubt a significant element of negligence. 'It appears as if the bank managers,' recalled George Bidwell, 'had heaped a mountain of gold out in the street and had put up a notice, "Please do not touch this," and then had left it unguarded with the guileless confidingness of an Arcadian.' The fraud was eventually discovered; at the ensuing trial that summer at the Central Criminal Court, all four were found guilty; and they each received a life sentence, though in the event being released between 1887 and 1891. The Bank itself recovered almost all the money lost, but *The Times* estimated the cost – borne by the Bank – of pursuing, capturing and prosecuting the offenders at as high as £46,000. As another paper commented, 'If the Bank of England can be so easily misled there is no question that minor establishments may be victimised.'

It was a more innocent scene in G. E. Hicks's wonderfully detailed and characterful painting *Dividend Day at the Bank of England*, a popular hit of the 1859 Royal Academy Exhibition if less esteemed by the critics. Until 1869, when postal transmission was reluctantly authorised by the Bank following political pressure, it remained the inviolable practice that all dividend warrants on stock inscribed in the Bank's books (whether government stock or the Bank's own stock) had to be physically handed across its counters in the Dividend Office to the individual stockholders or their authorised representatives, who could then present them for payment in the Rotunda; and even after 1869, until in 1910 the receipt of dividends on personal attendance was almost entirely abolished, the practice still continued in some considerable numbers, as remembered in the 1920s by Arthur Rowlett, a veteran clerk:

> The Dividends were paid from 9 till 4, the great bulk of the public attending on the 5th and two following days of January, April, July and October, when the principal public funds became payable. On arrival at the Bank at 8.45 a little crowd of people were found waiting, the precursors of 'all sorts and conditions of men' and women who steadily thronged the counters till closing time. Within all was ready in the Dividend Office, freshly cut quill pens and new blotting paper laid ready for the motley crowd which soon filled the Office. Two Scotland Yard detectives were in attendance all day in case of pocket-picking or any other delinquency. The costumes were mostly of the Sunday best, and many ancient and venerable beaver hats were in evidence. Many quaint characters one calls to mind. Here we see the communicative stockholder who retails all his family history and ailments. There is the mysterious individual who whispers into the ear of the paying clerk his name and amount of Stock. On the one hand is the forgetful person who can only remember that he wants 'a pink paper for five pounds.' On the other hand is the stupid man who on being asked his name says 'Two 'undred Consols,' and when required to state the title of his Stock says 'John Jones.' Here is the family party with a luncheon basket, evidently making the occasion one for a joy-day in London. There we see the joint Stockholders who, suspicious of each other, come together and never let one another out of sight. And, most unpopular, the man who takes about five minutes to sign his name, and always arrives

at five minutes to four for ten years' arrear dividends which take
nearly an hour to pay ...

Or as the *Comic Almanack* had put it back in 1841, almost twenty
years before Hicks painted his warrant-chewing dog, unnoticed amid
all the jostle:

> What a crowd! What a crush!
> What a row! What a rush!
> What screaming, and tearing, and noise –
> Of cabmen and footmen, policemen and bus-men,
> And poor little run-over boys! ...
> Oh! It's Dividend Day!
> Oh! It's Dividend Day!
> And all sorts of queer incongruities:
> Old men and young maids, deaf ears and bright eyes
> Are coming to claim their annuities ...
> It's Dividend Day at the Bank.[6]

The overwhelming majority of the Bank's staff occupied a clerical
position, with up to one-sixth of vacancies being reserved for sons of
those who had been clerks at the Bank for more than fifteen years.
Otherwise, the main criteria for election to a clerkship were character and capacity (though it still remained necessary to find a director
willing to exercise the power of nomination), as well as of course being
male. 'The general behaviour of the candidates, the nature of their testi-
monials, and their replies to the questions put to them regarding their
habits and occupations' were identified by the Court in 1844 as indispensable considerations; as for capacity, the examination procedure
in place from the early 1850s comprised writing from dictation about
thirty lines of an article taken from *The Times*, performing two reasonably simple interest sums, and (in the presence of the Committee for
Examining Clerks for Election) working out a further sum in interest.
'Although the system has unquestionably tended to raise the standard of Clerks,' observed an 1865 memo almost certainly by Chubb,
'it has, on the other hand, failed to keep out some who have proved

very ill-fitted for the Bank service'; and henceforth would-be clerks were also to do a test simulating the most common work of junior clerks, namely 'entering Warrants in the Dividend Books, or entering Cheques in the Cash and Bill Books'.

Three years later, in 1868, an internal report on the clerks and their departments gives us some names and some flesh. Starting with the Accountant's Bank Note Office, where the individual verdicts by its Principal, Daniel Hill, suggest a more mixed picture than that model of modernised efficiency soon afterwards drawn by Chubb:

A valuable officer, but afflicted with lameness. *(George Reynolds)*
Indefatigable, zealous, conscientious. *(George Betts)*
Persevering, intelligent, speaks German. Ideas rather contracted.
    (Richard Baily)
Clever, useful, excitable, ready at figures. *(Charles Earles)*
A good conscientious clerk, negligent in appearance. *(Alfred
    Appleton)*
Excellent moral character, a promoter of ragged schools. *(Edward
    Gribble)*
Gentlemanly, intelligent, considerable ability. *(Edmund Gill)*
Conscientious, exemplary, useful in training young clerks, but too
    timid for anything beyond routine business. *(Lewis Mayer)*
Author of 'Laing's Theory of Business'. His talents might be more
    usefully employed than at present. *(John Laing)*
Industrious, attentive, illiterate. *(Edward Oliver)*
Well conducted, but very weak & nervous. *(William Bawtree)*
Gentlemanly, wants energy. *(Daniel Reid)*
Good clerk, not brilliant. *(Charles Williams)*
Average. *(Henry Halsey)*
Gentlemanly, attentive. *(Francis Langford)*
Good abilities, but liable to be careless & uncertain. *(Charles Edis)*
Moderate ability, conceited. *(Richard May)*
Well meaning, but remarkably thoughtless. *(Thomas Critchett)*
Average abilities, lethargic. *(Frederic Stretton)*

Elsewhere, to take some examples of clerks almost at random, Henry Dixon junior in the Consols Office was 'quick, active & clever' but 'apt to make mistakes by too rapid a discharge of his duties'; Henry Rennell in the New £3 Per Cent Office was 'steady, attentive, & regular'; John Bawtree in the Power of Attorney Office was 'very careful and assiduous'; Thomas Hill in the Chancery and Exchequer Office was 'better educated than the rest, but unfortunately very incorrect in keeping the Accounts'; Herbert Crickmay in the Branch Banks Office was 'rapid' with 'good abilities', but 'somewhat too off-hand'; George Grey in the Private Drawing Office was 'a medium clerk' who 'has not maintained his character'; Secundus Pryce Jones in the Public Drawing Office was of 'average ability' and 'rather nervous'; Alexander Goudge in the Bill Office was 'a hard working plodding Clerk and well conducted'; Gilbert Allum in the General Cash Book Office was 'slower than formerly – says he does not feel so able for a heavy day's work'; and so on.[7] But of course, what was going on in their heads, as to a great or lesser extent they fulfilled their duties, we shall never know.

Two partial exceptions are clerks who have come down to us because of their sons. One was Robert Browning, father of the poet as well as son of the long-serving, ill-tempered Bank clerk who rose to be a department head – with all three unhelpfully having the same Christian name. Born in 1782, the middle Browning was probably still in his teens when he was sent to St Kitts in order to help manage the plantation holdings of his dead mother's family, with the chance of a substantial inheritance. What then transpired was related by his son in 1846 in a letter to the future Elizabeth Barrett Browning:

> If we are poor, it is to my father's infinite glory, who, as my mother told me last night, as we sate alone, 'conceived such a hatred to the slave-system in the West Indies, that he relinquished every prospect,' supported himself, while there, in some other capacity, and came back, while yet a boy, to his father's profound astonishment and rage ... My father on his return, had the intention of devoting himself to art, for which he had many qualifications and abundant love – but the quarrel with his father, – who continued to hate him till a few years before his death, – induced him to go at once and consume his life after a fashion he always detested. You may fancy, I am not ashamed of him.

So the Bank it was, which he entered in 1803 and where he stayed for a full half-century (mainly in the Dividend Room of the Consols

Office), but devoting most of his energies to his many sketchbooks and his extensive library, as well as apparently becoming an authority on sermons. 'Not a very able Bank official but clever and much liked' would be the verdict in the 1880s, some twenty years after his death, of the chief accountant of the day.

The other father of fame was William Marshall, whose son Alfred became a major economist and an inspiration for John Maynard Keynes. He was born in 1812; managed to enter the Bank in 1830 despite being the son of a downwardly mobile financial failure; started his own family life near the tanneries of Bermondsey, before moving to suburban Clapham; and in the Bank eventually rose in 1870 to become a cashier (though never chief cashier) before retiring in 1877. 'A tough old character, of great resolution and perception, cast in the mould of the strictest Evangelicals, bony neck, bristling projecting chin,' recalled Keynes less than affectionately. 'The nearest objects of his masterful instincts were his family, and their easiest victim his wife; but their empire extended in theory over the whole womankind, the old gentleman writing [before his death in 1901] a tract entitled *Man's Rights and Woman's Duties*.'[8]

At any one time, there was never any doubt about who – below the level of governor, deputy governor and directors, but often just as important – were the two kingpins: the chief cashier and the chief accountant, usually in that order. The chief cashier, explained Herbert de Fraine in his recollections of the late-Victorian Bank (but broadly applicable to the nineteenth century as a whole), 'controlled all the Cash Offices, and his own office conducted all their correspondence':

It looked after the Charity Commissioners, the Ecclesiastical Commissioners, the National Debt Commissioners, and so on and so on, dealt with Treasury Bills and handled the issue of public loans. The offices under this Chief were the Discount Office, which discounted bills for the public, and the Bill Office, which collected bills as they became due, and dealt with the 'Clearing' and the Out-tellers. Then there was the Private Drawing Office, which kept the accounts of private firms and individuals, and the Public Drawing Office, which kept the accounts of all Government Departments, such as the Paymaster-General, the Post Office, etc.

The Chief Cashier also controlled the Bank's Treasury. Here, under strong-room conditions, and under dual control, was kept the stock of Notes and coin needed for the Bank's day-to-day transactions. Under him were the Bullion Office, the Gold Weighing Room, and the Great Hall. Half of the Hall was occupied by the Issue Office, to which the public came to exchange Notes for gold. The other end was the In-tellers Office, where silver, received in bulk from the bankers, was 'garbled' [that is, removing counterfeit, damaged or worn coins] and checked.

'The second Chief, the Chief Accountant,' added de Fraine, 'controlled all the various Stock Offices and conducted all their correspondence. The most important of these were the Consols Office, the Bank Stock Office and the India Stock Office. Here were kept the "Books" of each stock, giving full details of every holding, and here Transfers were made, to be subsequently entered in the "Books".'

In the course of the nineteenth century, perhaps no chief cashier was quite as dominant as Abraham Newland had been until his retirement in 1807, but there were still some notable figures. Thomas Rippon (1829–35) died in harness at his residence in the Bank, having reputedly taken only one holiday (of three days) during his fifty-three years of service, 'stating' (explained an obituary) 'that green fields and country scenery had no charms for him'; William Miller (1864–6) was an ardent advocate of the decimal system, managing to introduce it into the bullion department and informing a parliamentary committee that 'the use of decimal arithmetic, independently of the greater security for accuracy, would enable the Bank of England to dispense with one clerk in twelve'; and George Forbes (1866–73) was a highly capable Aberdonian who, in a letter to the *Economist* shortly before his promotion, lucidly explained the annual cycles of bullion flowing in and out of the Bank, largely dependent on agricultural factors. The longest tenure (1835–64) belonged to Matthew Marshall (no relation of William), during which the division of the Bank was made – though on an accounting rather than an organisational or infrastructural basis – into Banking and Issuing Departments, as laid down by the Bank Charter Act. The son of an Amersham solicitor, Marshall had entered the Bank in 1810 at the age of nineteen and would die in 1873 at Amersham House, Beckenham.

Overlapping as chief accountant for much of the time (1831–58) was William Smee, and the chances are that the two men worked closely together, given that both were founders and trustees of the Gresham Life Assurance Society. Smee himself, who after fifty-seven years' service died still in post at the age of eighty-one, had three sons: William, the eldest, who lived with his father at the Bank and rose to become secretary to the Committee of Treasury, before a railway smash on the Brighton line in 1852 so severely injured him that he resigned and emigrated to Australia; Frederick, the youngest, who was at the Bank from 1842 to 1876, predictably enough working mainly in the Chief Accountant's Office; and Alfred, a doctor who in 1840 became the Bank's first medical officer, soon afterwards invented a new ink ('Bank Black') that for over a century would be used for writing the Court minutes, and generally became well known for his work in electro-metallurgy, almost certainly contributing to the 1855 note. The ink was perhaps a more mixed blessing – 'it was almost as thick as soup, smelled of vinegar, and using it was rather like writing with mud,' noted John Giuseppi in the 1960s, on the basis of personal experience – but the Smees were clearly among the more remarkable of the many Bank families.[9]

What was life like in the Victorian Bank? Speaking to the Genealogical Society in 1949, Giuseppi offered a reassuring perspective:

While from time to time evidence appears of some dissatisfaction, of complaints that salaries were not keeping pace with rising prices, there was never at any time anything in the nature of an ill-disposed staff. The steady, sober clerk of some fifteen to twenty years' service was, in fact, by modern standards, reasonably well off. He had his house, usually at a comparatively low rental, a domestic staff of two, occasionally three, trained servants: his children could be educated at 'select' establishments where the tone at any rate was high, and usually a sound knowledge of the three 'r's' was inculcated. If he rose to be a Principal he might keep his carriage. A 'Gentleman of the Bank' ranked high in the City.

Even so, as Giuseppi intimated, it was not all sweetness and light. *Punch* in 1842, with presumably some exaggeration, reckoned the Bank's clerks to be 'the hardest worked' and 'the worst paid' in all of London; when two years later the salaries of the younger clerks were significantly increased, this was done at no extra overall cost, through the simultaneous abolition of the additional £30 after thirty-five years of service. For a long time the rising cost of living was a constant gripe, typified by the 1865 memorial to directors in which 558 members of staff declared that they had 'much difficulty in meeting their unavoidable expenses and maintaining their social respectability, in consequence of the very high price of provisions, the advance in house rents, and the generally diminished value of fixed incomes'. That did the trick, resulting in a substantially improved pay scale (ranging from £70 a year for eighteen-year-old clerks to £280 for clerks of forty-five and upwards), although in 1872 the Court was less convinced by a similar clerks' memorial, with a director (apparently residing in Kensington) producing a detailed report. 'Potatoes,' he found, 'are certainly dearer than they were in 1865 and 1866, but perhaps next year they will be as cheap as ever.' He was a little more generous when it came to washing: 'I cannot find out that there is any increased charge under this head. I pay precisely the same now as I did in 1865. The wholesale price of common soap is rather less; but as the wages of the servant-of-all-work class are rather higher, I will allow an increase of 10 per cent on this item.' Meat was another matter. 'Since 1865, beef, mutton, ox and sheep tongues, of excellent quality, have been introduced from Australia, and retailed, without bone, at 6d to 7d per lb., and nothing can be nicer for occasional use.'[10]

Nevertheless, taken as a whole, pay and conditions were reasonable enough by the 1870s. Following a bleak period between the mid-1830s and the mid-1840s, when the Bank's traditional 'holy-days' were virtually abolished, a system of annual leave was gradually put in place and expanded, in due course varying from fifteen to twenty-one days depending on length of service. A fixed scale of pensions, meanwhile, had been in place since the 1830s, broadly comparable to those operating in government departments; and in 1870 the retirement age was formally set at sixty-five. More generally, there was an increasing awareness during the third quarter of the century that, for the Bank to operate to maximum efficiency, its 'higher duties' would, as Chubb explained in his 1871 report, require 'an increase of Salary to those to whom the higher duties were entrusted' – to which policy, he added, 'may be attributed many of the advanced additional salaries now paid, especially to the several classes in the Drawing Offices, the Security Clerks in the Bill Office, and certain positions in the Bank Note and other Offices'.

Chubb in his 1871 report also focused on an important change that had taken place around the middle of the century in the Bank's day-to-day working methods:

> Prior to 1850, an enormous mass of almost mechanical work was performed by Clerks; and, under the system then pursued, correctness was insured, as far as practicable, in large branches of the business by a duplicate system of account-keeping. The old method of entering cancelled Bank Notes in the Cash Book Office, is a fair instance of the mechanical duties then performed; and the Ledgers in the Drawing Office will serve as an example of the method of check referred to. One Ledger was kept by the Cashiers, and another by the Accountants, and a periodical comparison of them enabled a mutual correction of errors to be carried out. It is, perhaps, needless to say, that this system permitted a minimum of intelligent exertion on the part of any Clerk ...

It was, in short, 'a cumbrous system of checks' that had been 'relied upon for the general correctness of the work in many of the Banking Offices, rather than, as now, the efficient performance of their duties by intelligent and carefully selected Clerks'. Writing in 1898, a retired clerk, William Shand, agreed that the mid-century 'reformation of the Bank' had been 'not before it was needed', likewise adducing the condition of 'the P.D.'s' (the Private and Public Drawing Offices), and specifically the 'very queer' and 'abominably managed' system of book-keeping in the Public Drawing Office, that he had got to know in 1842 before being transferred for some years to the Newcastle branch:

> The Cash Books were ill-kept. Great piles were slumped together and posted to the ledgers in accumulations, to which the letter 'P.S.' were affixed, meaning 'part side', or part of the side of the cash book. The alterations were numerous in the figures, and consequently in

the additions and totals. The figures of the totals sprawled over the page and became sometimes so illegible that to make them readable they must necessarily be big. Blotting paper was insufficient; of sand there was plenty – so much so that the backs of the ledgers were often split by the leverage of the boards operating on a fulcrum of silica lying within and about the sewing, so as to tear away the covers.

The only purpose these ledgers served was to show how much money was at credit of the accounts, so that any overdrafts might be avoided. But this was a rare chance in the public accounts and, in fact, we were allowed to keep the books as we liked. The Principals never interfered.

The real books of the Bank, for permanent use, were kept upstairs, in a dismal place, and there the pass-books were written up the day after the transactions had taken place. So it happened every morning that a messenger was sent down to us, to come up with our ledgers to agree the totals. We got our messengers to take them on their backs, and I well remember following a snuffy old porter in livery along the garden walk towards a staircase which led up to the galleries in the roof, which were dignified by the name of the Back Drawing Office – where the men belonged to the Accountant's side. They were a rum lot. Ragged, if not dirty, with sleeves sometimes turned up to the elbow, in an appalling atmosphere ...'[11]

Inevitably, the post-1850 approach was uncomfortable for some, especially in certain areas after the Bank's entry to the Clearing House in 1864. 'There is no doubt that the work of the Drawing Office has undergone a radical change both in its nature and extent, and that more intelligence and activity are required on the part of the Clerks,' noted an 1867 report on the Private Drawing Office. 'Many of them under the old system performed their duties with satisfaction, but now are manifestly unequal to the strain which the more pressing requirements of the day demand ...' Accordingly, the recommendation was that eleven clerks be removed 'to less onerous positions in quieter offices'. For most clerks though, certainly most younger ones, it was surely a reformation for the better, with Hill the following year in his report on the Accountant's Bank Note Office gratified to identify 'more direct individual responsibility on the part of the clerks, who feel deeper interest in their duties from conviction that nothing is demanded of them which is not of real importance'. All that said, one should not exaggerate the pace or ubiquity of change. At this stage, Chubb's vaunted mechanisation still had strict limits; huge, unwieldy ledgers – often of over a thousand folios, enclosed in half-inch-thick cardboard covers decorated with green sailcloth – remained for many years yet the staple of the Bank's permanent records of transactions; in 1874 there was a celebrated episode as the Drawing Office launched an investigation, lasting four or five weeks, into a difference of three-pence on the Private Accounts section; and when de Fraine entered the Bank in 1886, his first task was to deal with Bank notes returned from circulation – some 60,000 a day, involving clerks standing at desks and manually dividing them, one by one, into two sections, the 'Fives' and the 'Tens and High Sums', before they were then sorted, again one by one, according to date and number.[12]

In reality, moreover, the Victorian Bank was never, whether before or after 1850, as orderly and purposeful as those in charge might have wished. Between 1837 and 1845 alone, at least three acrimonious disputes between clerks were noted in the Court minutes: in one, an argument about the quality of the food led to post-prandial blows and a nosebleed; in another, the hurling of a large bill case, accompanied by 'very gross & low abuse', resulted from the refusal to part with an inkstand; and in a third, the tussle over an office stool led to a severe blow in the face, rendering the recipient 'incapable of resuming his work for the remainder of the day'. Or take the formative impressions of W. Courthope Forman and C. H. Goodman, both of whom started work in 1866 in the Private Drawing Office. A 'busy hive', indeed, found Forman, but with 'a good many quaint insects':

There was a youngish gentleman on the ledgers, who made remark-ably clever caricatures and sketches in pen and ink, sometimes even upon the covers of the sacred books. There was a little rotund, elderly gentleman, with a short temper and a colossal skull, who frequently murdered the Queen's English in a manner that was a real delight. There was a middle-aged gentleman who ran a sort of farm in the suburbs, and brought a whiff of country to the Drawing Office, with the produce he offered there for sale; and yet another (said to have a connection in the hosiery line), who brought ties, and handkerchiefs, and fancy socks, and sold them to the highest bidder. Then there was a nice, rosy, bald-headed old gentleman, still apparently doing junior work, who dozed over his books on summer afternoons, then, leaning over a glazed partition behind him, one or other of us would gently tickle his bald spot with the feathers of a quill pen, till at last, wide awake and goaded to desperation, he would smite his 'mighty dome' with his palm, exclaiming, to our delight, 'Oh! damn those flies'! Our mission accomplished, like red indians, we would steal quietly away. Then there was an irate gentleman on a waste-book, whom we thought mad, and who eventually became so. Behind him it was an entertainment to stand as he cast up the columns of his book aloud, at a terrific pace, sandwiching the most profane oaths between the figures. And, lastly, I must not forget that curious character that seemed to have stepped from the pages of Dickens; that lugubrious looking person, in tightly buttoned, ill-fitting frock coat of shiny black, with wrinkling trousers to match, who presided over the Pass Books. He wore a rusty chimney-pot hat, but ill kept, which he never took off; indeed, tradition said that he slept in it, or even, that like a caul, it was born with him.

Goodman for his part was struck by the lack of decorum of his new colleagues ('not only were some of them rather rough but the tone of conversation of many was very coarse'), as well as by the amount of drinking that went on ('in at least one desk was a wine bin where you could get accommodation'). Nor seemingly was the prevailing atmosphere any more prim and proper by the early 1880s, to judge by the experience of Allan Fea, a young clerk who would eventually become a full-time writer:

In those days [he would recall almost half a century later] the Private Drawing Office, to which I was handed over, was more like a big school play-ground than anything else. From the fossil cashiers down to the callow 'unattached', all seemed to enter wholeheartedly upon the game of enlivening the passing official hours: universal chaff and merriment, with little or no heed of the ponderous contents of weighty ledgers or the balancing intricacies of 'Waste Books'. Balancing feats on more acrobatic lines, however, demanded a certain amount of thought and concentration when those formidable volumes were called into requisition as handy tests of muscular fitness, or proof of boasted sinew. Other mild sport was improvised in the way of 'cock-shies', wherein somebody's 'topper' was offered up for sacrifice for want of a genuine cocoanut. Wrestling matches, also, were popular, those contesting usually involving considerable wreckage of official furniture and fittings, including the glass chimneys of gas-jets, ink-pots, and sundry such accessories. Those endowed with histrionic skill held forth, providing a varied programme modulating from a solemn pulpit sermon to an Adelphi hero's soliloquy broadcast to the 'gods' more eloquently far than the aerial transmission of these times. A faithful rendering of the chairman at The Oxford [music hall] also was usually greeted with rapturous applause ...

Presumably, in the Bank as a whole, it was not a case of overgrown schoolboys having jolly japes the entire time; yet, given that most other parts of the Victorian City (above all the Stock Exchange) tended to be inward-looking and ultimately conformist, for all the surface eccentricities and 'characters' it was probably true across the Bank as a whole that, in Fea's words, 'any marked peculiarity or pedantic inclination about a fellow was soon spotted, and very much brought up in evidence against him for ever after'.[13]

As usual, there was no shortage of rules and exhortations from above, almost all of them aimed at greater regularity of conduct. In 1847, any clerk 'appearing at his office in a state of intoxication' was to be 'dismissed the service'; in 1850, immediate dismissal was also laid down as the punishment for 'all clerks who are henceforth found to be engaged in betting, in subscribing to sweepstakes, or in gambling transactions of any kind'; in 1851, the 'Heads of Office' explicitly forbade 'the admission or use of Beer, Wine or any Spirituous Liquor by the clerks throughout the Bank' (though with an exception made for porters and 'the Mechanics on weekly wages'); in 1853, the governor ordered that 'in future all the clerks in the House in signing their names or initials to any book or document relating to the service of the Bank will do so in a plain, distinct, and legible hand and without any flourish'; and that same year, 'the Authorities' let it be known that 'having seen a disposition upon the part of certain Bank clerks to wear moustaches, they strongly disapprove of the practice', adding that if necessary 'measures will be resorted to which may prove of a painful nature'. Or take the coda that followed the detailed 'explicit regulations' contained in the 1884 version of 'Rules and Orders to be Observed by the Clerks of the Bank of England':

> There are matters of conduct and behaviour which are not less important, though they cannot be so dealt with. Thus it is required of every person in the service of the Bank that he behave himself honourably in all the private and social relations of life, and that his general conduct, whether within the Bank or not, be that of a gentleman and a man of principle ... Discipline throughout the Bank is strictly enforced, and any insubordination is severely visited. It is essential and required of each Clerk that he be punctual in his duties, and intelligent in the performance of his work; and also that he should observe propriety in his dress and in his general habits.
>
> The Governors have so often had before them cases of great distress arising from early or imprudent marriages on the part of the younger clerks, that they think it necessary to warn them earnestly against such a course. They leave the question to the judgment of those whom it concerns: but if embarrassment, as is almost sure to be the case, arises from imprudent conduct in this respect, the Court have decided that they will afford no pecuniary relief, and Clerks must bear in mind that irretrievable embarrassment, from whatever course, involves the loss of their position.

By this time, moreover, clerks on their election to the Bank also received what was known as 'The Governor's Charge' (probably introduced in 1812):

> Your Salary is sufficient to maintain you in a suitable manner if expended with strict economy and a reasonable measure of self-denial ...
>
> You are warned against contracting habits of dissipation, and you are enjoined to be careful in the selection of your companions, and to maintain a respectable character in all relations of life.
>
> The Library, which has been formed within the Bank for the use of the Clerks, affords facilities for reading at small expense, and it will furnish a resource for the leisure hours.

Governors came and went, but a governor of a particularly high moral tone was William Lidderdale. 'It has become evident to the Governor that the cause of most of the troubles which have befallen Messengers and Porters, and of very much of the ill-health from which many of them have suffered, is to be found in present or past habits of intemperance,' stated a notice posted on his behalf in July 1890 by the chief accountant. 'In the Porters' and Messengers' own interests, therefore, the Governor gives distinct warning that any men brought before him for want of sobriety will be severely dealt with.'[14]

In practice, when it came to disciplinary action, one's overall impression is that the Bank tried if possible to be merciful to transgressors and to give them another chance. The fate in the late 1850s of Ernest Stephens was instructive. A young clerk in the Accountant's Bank Note Office, he was up before the Committee of Inspection first in February 1858, when he was found guilty of having certified that he had checked notes when in fact he had not; but having expressed his 'sorrow and a sense of shame' for his 'neglect', he got away with a 'severe reprimand' from the governor. Barely a year later, however, he was back in the dock:

On the 7th May it was the duty of Stephens to read the file containing the £100 Notes sorted and entered in the course of the day, in number about 1800. He should have requested some other clerk to take the books in which they had been entered and check the entries as he (Stephens) read over the Notes. It was then the duty of each to sign the check books and the file, the one as having read and the other as having checked the same. All this Stephens neglected to do. He selected no partner, but simply took the pile of Notes, tied it up as though it had been read and checked, and then signed the label on the outside of the file and the end of each check book with his own name and the names of two other clerks as having read and checked the Notes in question.

This time, inevitably, he was 'called upon to send in his resignation' – which at least meant that, unlike being outright dismissed, he would be able to find a berth elsewhere in the City. Then, just over two years later, in July 1861, occurred the 'extremely difficult' case of Richard Denison of the Bill Office, a case prompted by this twenty-six-year-old clerk applying to the Bank for a loan of £200. On inquiry, it emerged not only that he had been during his four and a half years at the Bank 'generally careless and wanting in zeal and attention', albeit showing 'a slight improvement lately', but that he had got himself in a pretty pickle:

> In November, he married a widow, in whose house he previously lodged, and whose husband had died about a year and a half before that time. Prior to his marriage he had the distinct assurance both from herself and her mother, that she was quite free from debt, and that the furniture of the house, with slight exceptions, was her own. Very shortly after his marriage however, he discovered that his wife's former husband had died insolvent – that she was considerably in debt, and that the furniture was the property of her brother-in-law, who immediately commenced an action for its recovery. Another brother-in-law who, it appears, is a professional money-lender, then advanced the sum claimed on the furniture, which advance Denison was to pay off by instalments, but this money is now called in, and Denison is threatened with imprisonment … His wife has one child by her former husband, and another child, by her present husband, is just born.

What was to be done? 'The young man has no friends who can aid him, and urges that he has no course, if assistance be withheld, but to go to prison or to hide himself. The Committee [of Investigation] believe him to be the victim of evil disposed persons, from whom he is well inclined, if he can, to free himself.' The eventual conclusion was that 'had Denison's previous character been praiseworthy', and had it been possible to ascertain more clearly 'the amount of his liabilities', then 'they would have been strongly inclined to recommend that the advance should have been made'; but in the circumstances the Committee felt compelled to recommend that Denison 'be called upon to hand in his resignation forthwith'.[15]

Much of the responsibility for staff relations attached to the secretary, and it seems that in the long-serving Hammond Chubb the staff had a firm but sympathetic chief. Forman in his reminiscence of the late 1860s evokes him vividly:

> I was sent to work on the 'Stock Side', and while there had experience of what was called 'the Shutting', when for some days the public

were excluded and the clerks prepared lists of Stockholders in duplicate or triplicate; I forget which ... In the morning, to each clerk
was given a packet of slips on which were the names and addresses
of Stockholders, and the amounts of their holdings. Here one might
be lucky or unlucky. A slip might, for instance, be inscribed: John
Smith, 12 Rye Lane, Peckham, £200, or it might have the names of a
dozen trustees whose addresses were lengthy, and whose 'godfathers
and godmothers in their baptism' had been inordinately generous.
But, lucky or unlucky, your portion of slips finished you were free
for the day. This led to great carelessness in writing, everything being
sacrificed to pace. To make matters worse, we had sweepstakes of 6d
or 1s a sheet among ourselves ... At eighteen my hand was boyish
and unformed, and quickly degenerated sadly. My 'sheets' were,
doubtless, shocking. However, 'shutting' being over, I thought no
more about them till, one day, a week or so later, I was sent for by
the Secretary, a small gentleman of mournful mien and suave address.
When he interviewed me, turning upon me 'a countenance rather in
sorrow than in anger', he looked not unlike a mediaeval saint in a
painted window, substituting, of course, for robe and halo, a black
frock coat and grey trousers. 'He washed his hands with invisible
soap' (a habit of his) while he gently dressed me down, and then, so
to speak, rubbed my nose in those unfortunate 'sheets' written in the
'Shutting'. 'Sheets' that had been returned as illegible by Somerset
House, and which looked, I confess, as if an irresponsible spider had
dipped his legs in ink and pranced gaily up and down the paper.

'Well,' added Forman, 'I was never invited to take a stool in the
Secretary's office'; but almost certainly under Chubb's say-so, the
Bank kept him on, and he was soon transferred to the Western
branch.

Not long afterwards, in late 1870, Chubb reported on the 'peculiarly painful' case of Robert Gerard. Elected a clerk in July 1866, and
now almost twenty-four, he was the son of a clerk at the Bristol branch
who had died in 1862. 'During the early part of Gerard's Service, he
was absent very seldom. He was a good, well-conducted Clerk, and
earned for himself an excellent character throughout the house.' In
1867 he got scarlet fever; in 1868 'his attendance was very regular';
and then, early in 1869, 'he showed distinct symptoms of want of

mental power, which showed itself in a feeling of almost horror for the Bank', and he missed almost the whole year. Alfred Smee in May 1870 tried out Gerard on 'some simple duties', but he 'soon broke down'; between August and October he was only intermittently present, though when at the Bank he 'conducted himself exceedingly well, showing himself capable of performing all the ordinary work of the Office'; and finally, in early November, he sent Chubb a letter which 'showed symptoms of a return of his previous state of mind'. The humane secretary summed up the sad case:

> His Mother, Mrs Gerard, was left with six children and very limited means ... It is known that Gerard felt very acutely the position in which his Mother was placed, and believed that, as the eldest Son, a grave responsibility rested upon him. There is some reason to believe his present state had its origin in the fever of 1867, or rather of his coming to work before he was really strong enough to work. But whether this did affect his brain or not, those who know something of his family and have had opportunities of watching him, believe that he has given way under the constant strain of mind arising from his efforts to aid his Mother and his family.

Accordingly, Chubb recommended that Gerard's name be removed from the list of clerks, but that a donation of £100 be made to his mother.[16]

In broader terms, it is fair to depict the Victorian Bank as an increasingly paternalistic organisation, seeking to create for its staff a secure, stable and morally improving environment in which to spend their working lives. Take three emblematic developments, the first of them described by the *Illustrated London News* in May 1850:

> On Wednesday afternoon, a handsome reading-room, which has just been formed for the Bank of England Library and Literary Association, instituted by the directors for the use of the clerks, was opened by Thomson Hankey, junior Esq., Deputy-Governor of the Bank. There was a very numerous meeting of the members; when the Chief Cashier, as President, and the Chief Accountant, the Treasurer of the Institution, moved and seconded a vote of thanks to the Court of Directors for the handsome manner in which they

had fitted up the Library, and for the liberal support which had been accorded the Association.

Several hundred of the staff were soon members of the library, paying an annual subscription of 10 shillings, at a time when the concept of the public library was still only slowly taking hold; and members were allowed to borrow two books, with an especially strict time limit (eight days) for novels. The second development followed shortly, with the founding in 1854 of the Bank Provident Society – essentially a savings society that also undertook life assurance business, and whose 4 per cent interest on premiums paid was guaranteed by the directors. Finally, there was the whole stomach-rumbling question of the inner man. In 1881 a detailed memo (probably written by Chubb) on lunch arrangements found that, of the 650 clerks in the Bank, some 110 to 130 managed to knock up a scratch meal within the building, about 100 stayed in their offices and got porters to fetch something from outside, and the rest went out for lunch. The memo continued:

That the present arrangements are unsatisfactory in every way is admitted on all sides. They are unsatisfactory to the Clerks, many of whom earnestly desire some means by which their wants can be simply but decently met. The underground Drawing Office kitchen is a most uninviting room – it is close to the cooking place, lavatories, etc; the food may be good, but it is roughly served, and the surroundings are so disagreeable that it is repugnant to men of any refinement. In the case of those who remain in the Offices, the meal furtively eaten behind a desk cover cannot be desirable; and though many no doubt will always desire to go outside The Bank during the ½ hour, it is known that the places where a cheap good meal can be obtained are becoming fewer each year and it is felt, especially as regards the younger clerks, that the alternative of obtaining what they require within the walls would be better for their health and keep them from the temptations of the Bars and Wine rooms.

As regards the Porters, the present practice is equally unsatisfactory. During much of the morning they are engaged on duties, which though, in a measure, recognised, are wholly undefined and cannot be supervised: it leads them to go out of The Bank to buy what is required, and it gives rise to the very objectionable practice of their making money out of the Clerks, with whom it begets a certain undue familiarity. The time occupied by the porters in this way cannot be estimated, but it is undoubtedly very great: and indeed it is a question whether if these duties were taken from them, the number might not be reduced.

Altogether, concluded the memo, if 'a General Luncheon Room' were introduced, and 'if the room were bright and the service well conducted', this 'might lead, in many cases, to a higher tone amongst the Clerks'. Chubb then circulated a notice, eliciting strong support for the concept of 'fitting up Dining Rooms within the Bank, in which, at a cost to cover actual expenses only, gentlemen could have lunch or light dinner'; and by 1884 a fully fledged staff canteen was in existence, though known by the more dignified title of the Luncheon Club.[17]

What the Victorian Bank was not was a meritocracy. In 1869 the Court ordered that 'the practice, now becoming prevalent, of private canvassing of Directors, through their personal friends, on the part of Clerks seeking to be appointed to vacant offices, be prohibited'; but almost certainly this had little effect, and some twenty years later a young, ambitious and capable clerk like de Fraine found that 'no one believed any effort would help towards promotion in the Service':

The only way to 'get on' was to pull strings with Directors or Chiefs of Departments. As one caustic colleague said to me, 'It doesn't matter what you *are*; it's what you can persuade the other fellow to *think* you are.' I saw the string-pulling in action several times, the men who were on to a good thing being perfectly frank about their progress. One told me that on approaching his Director he received the suggestion, amounting to a command, that he should show a keen interest in the House – join the Volunteers, for instance, or stand for the Luncheon Club or Clerks' Library Committees. He followed this advice, and in a few weeks was seconded as 'Assistant' (a hitherto non-existent post) to a Principal in another office. From that moment he never looked back, and eventually became a Personage.

Still, an institution does not need to be meritocratic in order to have a very clear appreciation of its own worth and a very clear attitude towards the outside world. A reply in November 1845 to one Joseph Hartnell of Hawkhurst in Kent, who had had the temerity to write directly to a former governor, might have been sent at any time in the ensuing half-century and was just the sort of missive that Henry Adams would have imagined emanating from behind those 'insolent' walls:

I beg to inform you in reply to your letter of the 27th Inst. to Mr Palmer, that the present balance to the credit of your acc^{t} is £920.14.0 and to request that your pass Bk may be forwarded by Post for the purpose of being made up.

Be good enough in future to address your official communications to 'The Chief Cashier of the Bank of England'.[18]

8

Money Will Not Manage Itself

'THE GREAT IMPORTANCE OF THE LATE MEETING OF THE PROPRIETORS OF THE BANK OF ENGLAND' was the *Economist*'s punchy headline on 22 September 1866, and it quoted at length from the speech of the Bank's governor, Lancelot Holland, looking back on the Overend Gurney crisis some four months earlier:

> This house exerted itself to the utmost – and exerted itself most successfully – to meet the crisis. We did not flinch from our posts. When the storm came upon us, on the morning on which it became known that the house of Overend and Co had failed, we were in as sound and healthy a position as any banking establishment could hold; and on that day and throughout the succeeding week we made advances which could hardly be credited …
>
> We could not flinch from the duty which we conceived was imposed upon us of supporting the banking community, and I am not aware that any legitimate application for assistance made to the this house was refused.

The paper's editor was Walter Bagehot, who spelled out the momentous lender-of-last-resort implications of the Bank's welcome sense of responsibility – '*If* no other reserve is kept but that of the Bank, and *if* the Bank at a crisis are bound to lend all that any one asks on good security, how large ought not that reserve to be, and how careful ought not the Bank to be of it?' – before ending by congratulating Holland and his colleagues 'on the safe issue of a period of great anxiety, and great responsibility, such as few men have to meet during their lives, and still fewer would consent to meet, when so little personal gain can conceivably be obtained by it'.

Two of those colleagues were Thomson Hankey and George Warde Norman, directors since 1835 and 1821 respectively, and neither the type to succumb to flattery. Hankey was preparing a treatise on *The Principles of Banking*, and that autumn of 1866 he wrote his preface, pulling no punches:

> The *Economist* newspaper has put forth what, in my opinion, is the most mischievous doctrine ever broached in the monetary or Banking world in this country; viz., that it is the proper function of the Bank of England to keep money available at all times to supply the demands of Bankers who have rendered their own assets unavailable. Until such a doctrine is repudiated by the Banking interest, the difficulty of pursuing any sound principle of Banking in London will be always very great. But I do not believe that such a doctrine as that Bankers are justified in relying on the Bank of England to assist them in time of need is generally held by the Bankers in London.

Although his book was not officially published until the new year, the *Economist* responded in early December. Citing the most recent figures, showing the Bank's reserve standing at £10.5 million (relative to deposits of £25.1 million), Bagehot asked: 'Can any one fancy the sudden and to shareholders inexplicable reduction in the dividend of the joint stock banks, and the equal catastrophe to the income of private bankers, if they began to hoard bars or cash on a scale approaching this or resembling it?' Accordingly, he went on, the Bank 'alone has the means to meet a sudden emergency, and it must use those means, or it will fail in the universal ruin'. Norman entered the lists just before Christmas. 'That the Bank of England should keep the whole unused reserve of the country seems to me an arrangement at once impracticable, and unsound in principle,' he wrote to the *Economist* in defence of Hankey. 'How is it possible that the directors should know, at any given time, the aggregate demand that may be made upon their resources, and provide accordingly?' The old man's letter could hardly have been gloomier. 'With each oscillation of the financial pendulum,' he noted with reference to the two most recent crises (1857 as well as 1866), 'the pressure appears to become more sudden and intense'; and he blamed everyone but the Bank – above all, though he did not need to name them, the joint-stock banks that had become so large during his time – for the dark prospect that lay ahead: 'If the present system of holding immense amounts at call in London without corresponding reserves be persisted in, no banking arrangements can meet the difficulty in times of extreme pressure. The result is obvious and inevitable, and I fully expect that younger men than myself will witness such a financial catastrophe as we have never yet seen nor can now imagine.'[1]

The question of the Bank's responsibilities was once again firmly on the table. Inasmuch as the Bank had a collective opinion, it seems over the next few years to have settled somewhere between the Bagehot and Hankey poles – to judge, anyway, by a parliamentary intervention in 1869. The catalyst was that most parsimonious of all Victorian chancellors, Robert Lowe, who not long before a Commons debate in May publicly asked, 'What have I to do with the money-market?', and equally publicly answered, 'It must take care of itself.' In the chamber he explicitly tackled the *Economist*'s demand that it was his duty 'to keep a large balance in the Bank of England in order that it may be able to exercise control over the market', a demand that he repudiated:

> It is the duty of the Chancellor of the Exchequer to take care of the taxpayer and the revenues intrusted to his charge, and it is not his duty to put money into the Bank merely for the benefit of the share-holders of the Bank of England – which, after all, is really a private banking institution – or to enable the Bank to assist traders, or to set up storm signals announcing the coming of panics …
>
> There is no monarch set up by any other department of business to warn those engaged in it of dangers to come; they must look out for themselves, and I don't see that Government should go out of its way merely to strengthen a great institution like the Bank of England.

An immediate response came from Robert Crawford, not only a Liberal MP but also the recently elected governor. Observing that Lowe's recent remark about the money market taking care of itself had caused 'a considerable amount of consternation' in the City, and adding that the City was 'the centre of the commercial interests of the country, and as the Government acted upon that centre so would the public interests throughout the country be more or less affected', he then turned to the Bank itself:

> It was not the business of the Bank of England to find funds for the commercial community, nor had it been at any time. The business of the Bank of England was to take care of the funds intrusted to it, and to employ the money for the benefit of the proprietors. As to the 'storm signals' to which his right hon. friend had referred, the Bank of England did hoist storm signals, and, more than that, having the power, it used it in rectifying what otherwise might at the time be an unfortunate state of things.

Crawford finished with a peroration that almost certainly lacked nothing in sincerity. 'He held that the Bank of England in past times had exercised the vast power which it held with great benefit to the public *(hear, hear)*, and as long as he was in the position which he happened to fill he would do all in his power not to disparage but to make effective the services which the Bank of England have always rendered. *(Hear, hear)*'[2]

Neither Hankey nor Bagehot was done. In November 1872 the veteran director (and former governor) wrote to *The Times*, referring darkly to how 'a recent writer on the subject considers it an error for the Bank of England not to keep a larger available reserve of bullion to meet the wants of the country whenever any unusual demand for gold occurs', and went on: 'Now, in reply to such an opinion, I venture to say that the Directors of the Bank of England neither have nor ought to have any more control over the reserve of bullion in this country than have any other bankers or any money dealer in England.' Indeed, Hankey saw 'no reason' why the Bank 'should increase the amount of money left unemployed in order to allow other banking establishments and other large traders in London to use up their own ready money more closely, believing that in case of need they may always avail themselves of the resources of the Bank of England, which resources are not kept for any such purpose'. Bagehot's riposte, in the next issue of the *Economist*, appeared below a wholly predictable headline: 'THE DANGEROUS OPINIONS OF A BANK DIRECTOR'. And in the article itself, after noting that a) 'for the purpose of gold exportation it is of no use to look to the resources of other London bankers', that b) 'the only real source at which gold on a large scale can be obtained if wanted is the reserve of the Banking department of the Bank of England', and that c) the consequence of the Franco-Prussian War of 1870 had been to knock out Paris as a rival 'great European exchange centre', leaving London as 'the sole such centre', he reiterated his argument: 'The Bank of England is the bankers' bank. Its reserve is the *ultimate*; our means of meeting a foreign payment depend on the magnitude of that final fund. The country must not go without a reserve while the London bankers and the Bank of England are squabbling who shall keep it.' Moreover, he insisted, the apparent rule or custom by which the Bank kept about one-third of its deposits in cash was now anachronistic: 'The nature of the demands upon the Bank of England has changed. The amount of foreign money now in London, the amount of the foreign liabilities of England, the amount of money which may be *drawn out* of the Banking department at any moment, is excessively increased.'

By this time, Bagehot had almost finished writing one of the great City books: *Lombard Street*. Subtitled *A Description of the Money Market*, and published in the summer of 1873 (almost simultaneously with a new edition of Hankey's *Principles*, with the author conceding no ground in his latest preface), it fleshed out in wonderfully vivid and persuasive style the two key arguments in relation to the Bank's policy that he had been expounding for at least seven years. One, of course, was that the Bank should do everything in its power to protect its reserve. For, as he explained:

A panic is sure to be caused if that reserve is, from whatever cause, exceedingly low. At every moment there is a certain minimum, which I will call the 'apprehension minimum', below which the reserve cannot fall without great risk of diffused fear; and by this I do not mean absolute panic, but only a vague fright and timorousness which spreads itself instantly, and as if by magic, over the public mind. Such seasons of incipient alarm are exceedingly dangerous, because they beget the calamities they dread. What is most feared at such moments of susceptibility is the destruction of credit; and if any grave failure or bad event happens at such moments, the public fancy seizes on it, there is a general run, and credit is suspended.

So what, then, was that 'apprehension minimum'? In present-day
conditions, he reckoned, there was no alternative but to plump for the
historically high figure of £10 million – below which 'the important and
intelligent part of the public which watches the Bank reserve becomes
anxious and dissatisfied'. But ideally, he went on, the reserve should
be significantly higher, no less than £11½ million and preferably of the
order of £14–15 million. Bagehot's other key theme concerned what
the Bank should do if, despite its best efforts, there was a recurrence in
the future of financial panic. His answer was straightforward – that 'in
time of panic it must advance freely and vigorously to the public out
of the reserve' – and he set out his twin rules: that 'these loans should
only be made at a very high rate of interest'; and that 'at this rate
these advances should be made on all good banking securities, and as
largely as the public ask for them'. As for those who maintained that
the Bank's reserve might not be enough for all such loans, Bagehot's
reply was bracingly clear: 'The only safe plan for the Bank is the brave
plan, to lend in a panic on every kind of current security, or every sort
on which money is ordinarily and usually lent. This policy may not
save the Bank; but if it do not, nothing will save it.'[3]

How much did *Lombard Street* shift the dial? During the middle
years of the twentieth century, as historians and occasionally practitioners reflected on the evolution of modern central banking, the
consensus formed that to a significant degree it had done so. 'After
Bagehot,' reckoned R. S. Sayers, 'no one could again put forward the
doctrine of 1844 in all its nakedness,' and instead the Bank's 'special
position' was 'taken for granted', in other words as 'the holder of the
single reserve, the ultimate source of support for the country's financial structure in times of difficulty'; to another economic historian,
E. Victor Morgan, Bagehot's vanquishing of Hankey in the court of
public opinion 'may be said to mark another and final stage in the
assumption by the Bank of the responsibilities of lender of last resort'.
Yet the reality was perhaps somewhat more complicated. For one
thing, it was a striking fact (highlighted by Hugh Rockoff in the 1980s)
that the Bank's reserve signally failed to increase during the decade
and a half after *Lombard Street*, in half of those years averaging less
than during the early 1870s and presumably, at least in part, reflecting a reluctance to damage the Bank's profitability; for another thing,
the Bank in practice showed itself wholly unwilling to take Bagehot's

advice and commit *publicly* to being the lender of last resort in times of panic or crisis, perhaps because of an understandable reluctance to surrender the dimension of moral hazard.

Indeed, it is even possible that the widely held assumption that most of the Bank's newer directors were instinctively if tacitly on Bagehot's side of the argument, broadly speaking, may be mistaken – in the sense, anyway, of sharing Bagehot's almost febrile urgency about the larger financial situation. Suggestive evidence comes from William Lidderdale, a director since 1870, writing to a partner in Liverpool a few months after the book's publication:

> That our Banking and Monetary system in this Country is of an overcomplicated & interdependent nature which makes difficulties in any important quarter a serious matter for every one, is a fact upon which none of us are likely to differ. The system of taking enormous sums on deposit at call or short notice, on which interest has to be paid & which there is almost a necessity to employ if serious losses are to be avoided, is one which carries risk on its face. Mr Bagehot says things *are* so & that it is useless trying to change the system, & then throws upon the Bank of England the onus of providing a reserve adequate to the needs of all its competitors as well as regular customers.

Crucially, however, Lidderdale insisted that the system could take the strain; and he asserted that 'so far as concerns the big Joint Stock Banks, they most undoubtedly have remembered their lesson & materially improved their practice in the last 6 years'. Such an attitude is doubly instructive, given that Lidderdale was appreciably less complacent and more independent-minded than many of his colleagues. Not that Bagehot himself would have been surprised. Memories of the 1866 crisis may have been all too vivid in his own mind, Paris in the early 1870s may have vanished as a helpful counterweight to London, the sheer volume of the City's liabilities as well as assets may have been daily growing – and yet:

> It is not easy to rouse men of business to the task. They let the tide of business float before them; they make money or strive to do so while it passes, and they are unwilling to think where it is going.

Even the great collapse of Overends, though it caused a panic, is beginning to be forgotten. Most men of business think – 'Anyhow this system will probably last my time. It has gone on a long time, and is likely to go on still.' But the exact point is, that it has *not* gone on a long time. The collection of these immense sums in one place and in few hands is perfectly new.

In short, 'money will not manage itself'.[4]

In addition to questions of policy, Bagehot offered one other major reform thrust: the improved governance of the Bank. 'The Bank directors,' he argued, 'are not trained bankers; they were not bred to the trade, and do not in general give the main power of their minds to it. They are merchants, most of whose time and most of whose real mind are occupied in making money in their own business and for themselves.' Thus, he went on:

> We have placed the exclusive custody of our entire banking reserve in the hands of a single board of directors not particularly trained for the duty, – who might be called 'amateurs,' – who have no particular interest above other people in keeping it undiminished – who acknowledge no obligation to keep it undiminished – who have never been told by any great statesman or public authority that they are so to keep it or that they have anything to do with it – who are named by and are agents for a proprietary which would have a greater income if it *was* diminished, – who do not fear, and who need not fear, ruin, even if it were all gone and wasted.

Accordingly, argued Bagehot, 'we should diminish the "amateur" element; we should augment the trained banking element; and we should ensure more constancy in the administration'. Specifically, he recommended two things: a permanent deputy governor, who would be 'a trained banker' having 'no business save that of the Bank'; and, in terms of the Court as a whole, that 'the London bankers' should no longer be 'altogether excluded':

> The old idea was that the London bankers were the competitors of the Bank of England, and would hurt it if they could. But now the London bankers have another relation to the Bank which did not

then exist, and was not then imagined. Among private people they are the principal depositors in the Bank; they are therefore particularly interested in its stability; they are especially interested in the maintenance of a good banking reserve, for their own credit and the safety of their large deposits depend on it. And they can bring to the court of directors an experience of banking itself, got outside the Bank of England, which none of the present directors possess, for they have learned all they know of banking at the Bank itself. There was also an old notion that the secrets of the Bank would be divulged if they were imparted to bankers. But probably bankers are better trained to silence and secrecy than most people. And there is only a thin partition now between the bankers and the secrets of the Bank. Only lately a firm failed of which one partner was a director of the London and Westminster Bank, and another a director of the Bank of England. Who can define or class the confidential communications of such persons under such circumstances?

Neither suggestion seems to have been discussed, let alone countenanced, by the Bank itself; and although the Court had seen a certain broadening since the late 1840s with the election of various merchant bankers, these were far from the 'trained' commercial bankers that Bagehot had in mind. Again, it was Lidderdale who offered a private commentary:

You have [he wrote in October 1873 to his Liverpool correspondent, who had dared to raise a moral eyebrow in the context of the Bank lifting its rate to 7 per cent against the background of bad news from both America and Europe] a very curious notion about the action of the *Merchants* who occupy seats at the Bank Court – the effect of alterations of rate is generally much less felt in their business than in Banking arrangements, & people who do the latter on a large scale are much more constantly face to face with questions of self interest ... Then many Directors, men like Morris, Latham, Hankey, Hubbard, Huth, Campbell, the present Governor Greene, & Gibbs are personally in a position so little touched by anything which goes on in the Bank that it cannot be a matter of material interest what the rate is. Certainly no body of men have a right to claim superiority to even unconscious promptings of self

interest, but I am bound to say that I have never seen more honest
endeavours to decide in the true interest of the Bank, even when I
have differed with the majority.'

In politics, in cricket, in Threadneedle Street, the cult of the disinterested amateur was only just approaching its apogee.

Even so, one can overdo the Bagehotian exasperation, shading
into scorn. The men who ran the Bank during the final third of the
century were for the most part serious, conscientious and intelligent,
usually with a highly developed sense of the practical. Take a handful
of examples. Robert Crawford in 1869, a few months after becoming governor, declined the offer of a baronetcy, on the grounds (he
informed Rothschilds) that 'a man in business ought not to be Sir
Robert'; Benjamin Buck Greene (governor, 1873–5), of a firm trading largely in Mauritian sugar, was a thoroughly sound operator, a
member of the Bank's inner councils for many years, and renowned
for his private collection of statistics relating to its accounts; J. W.
Birch (governor, 1879–81), senior partner of a Hispano-English
merchanting firm (Mildred, Goyenesche & Co), was described in a
contemporary profile as 'a shrewd man of business, impatient of the
refinements of theorists, careful of facts, and, therefore, as a necessary
consequence, judicious in a crisis'; while Sir Mark Collet (governor,
1887–9) was, as senior partner of the steadily rising merchant bank
Brown, Shipley & Co, a capable, hugely experienced figure, as well
as being brother-in-law of George Warde Norman and a benevolent,
closely involved grandfather to young Montagu Norman.

In a category of his own was Henry Hucks Gibbs (governor, 1875–7)
of the merchant bank Antony Gibbs & Sons, a man of energy and
versatility, if not always directed sufficiently to the gently declining
fortunes of his own firm. He was a vigorous correspondent (despite
the loss of his right hand in a gun accident); he had a keen interest in
architecture, books, pictures and genealogy, not to mention ecclesiastical politics; he was an authority on card games (especially ombre) as
well as matters of currency; and, befitting a dedicated philologist, he
contributed much of the letter 'C' to the *Oxford English Dictionary*.
In the closing months of 1877, no longer governor but still a director
(as he would remain until 1900), he engaged in some typically direct
correspondence with an Oxford professor, Bonamy Price, on the

subject of the Bank's reserve. Price at one point attacked the ignorance and narrow-mindedness of 'City oracles, who are emphatically practical men', prompting Gibbs not only to launch a defence of practical man – 'a man who, knowing the theory, has personally seen it in practice – who knows not only the theoretic forces, but can take into account the friction of external circumstances which modifies them' – but also to state bluntly to the professor that 'your theory is right and good, but your practice is defective'. 'Pray', he declared later in what turned into a marathon letter, 'don't father upon the Bank of England the follies of others, the slipshod stuff of sciolists, the nonsense of newspapers …' And he ended with a resounding, difficult-to-answer affirmation about who knew best:

> When it is necessary to rectify a disproportion, present or foreseen, between Reserve and Deposits, we cannot wait till the evil is upon us, and neither you nor any one else has ever given us the slightest reason why we should so wait.
>
> Of that disproportion and that necessity, the only persons who have the faintest means of judging are those who have before them the ever-changing character of the Deposits and the ever-changing condition of the Reserve, viz., the Directors of the Bank of England; and the only lever which they have in the ultimate resort, the only force which can efficiently act on the Reserve, is the rate of discount. *Experto crede!*[6]

'Trade does not revive – Credit is shaken – our Finances are not in good order – our Foreign Relations are overcast with dark clouds and threatening Thunder …' The gloomy commentary came from Lord Overstone, writing to his old friend George Warde Norman (no longer a director) on 19 October 1878. It was just over a fortnight after the spectacular failure of the City of Glasgow Bank, reckoned by Clapham to be 'perhaps the most discreditable British banking catastrophe of the century', involving as it did not just undue risk-taking, but systematic fraud and the subsequent imprisonment of directors. In what was the only major financial crisis of the 1870s and 1880s, the next few months saw many provincial banks under significant pressure, while in the City the mood was apprehensive enough that shortly before Christmas one of the Rothschilds – presumably Alfred, in his additional capacity as a Bank director – went to the chancellor, Sir Stafford Northcote, and asked him if, before he departed from town, he would leave a signed letter in effect suspending the Bank Charter Act, with the letter to be used at once should necessity arise. In the event, potentially fourth time around since 1844, suspension was not required, but what otherwise was the Bank's role in alleviating the crisis? Historians are agreed that it was generally supportive, helped by the reserve being in a state sufficiently strong that Bagehot (who had died the previous year) would have approved, but there is debate as to what degree it acted as lender of last resort. Michael Collins contends for a high degree, on a de facto basis, given that it was the Bank that 'substantially met the increased demand for cash and near-cash assets' during the crisis; Dieter Ziegler is more sceptical, pointing to how 'the Bank was almost completely separated from the provincial banks', so that 'even during the weeks of crisis there was no significant increase in the Bank's holding of bills of exchange and loans on bills at the [Bank's] provincial branches'.[7]

More generally, the 1878 crisis has been seen by some as a fateful turning-point in British banking and indeed economic history – the crisis whose legacy was to shift bank assets away from industrial loans and towards more liquid securities.[8] One commentator, Will Hutton, puts the Bank itself at the historical heart of the fractured City/industry relationship:

In the 1870s [he wrote in 2011] the UK was faced with the same decision as Germany – how to get banks to step up lending to industry as industrialisation moved up a gear. Bismarck set up the Reichsbank in 1876, mandated to finance German banks as they stepped up their industrial lending; the new German central bank would provide banks with the necessary finance and stand ready to buy back any commercial loans they made if they went sour or if for any reason banks needed cash fast.

Successive governors of the Bank of England refused to do the same. This would be financially unsound and politicise the central bank, ran the argument. The Bank of England would only supply cash to the banking system in exchange for gold-standard government debt, not corporate debt. And it would never create credit. In the 1870s, British banks began to go bust. To save themselves, more than 1,000 merged, creating today's highly concentrated banking system, while disengaging from the industrial lending. No explanation of British decline and German industrial pre-eminence is complete without understanding the Bank of England's approach to industrial financing.

It is a fascinating and suggestive critique, but needs further detailed research to become authoritative. Moreover, in truth, Ricardo's company of merchants had *always* had an international rather than national orientation, in the sense that the City's most powerful commercial interests, which they represented, almost invariably related to overseas trade and business. Of course, there was the odd exception – James Currie for instance, governor in the mid-1880s, was a distiller in Bromley – but for those merchants and merchant bankers who continued to dominate the Court, they naturally tended to look to points west, south and east rather than north.[9]

All this was especially so from the 1870s, as a whole new phase opened up in the internationalisation of the City. The key moment was the Franco-Prussian War at the start of the decade, with its manifold consequences including the non-convertibility of the franc for eight years (confirming sterling as the unrivalled medium of settlement), the Bank of France's suspension of specie payments (leaving London as the only world bullion market), and more generally the flow to London from other countries of 'hot money' (seeking instantly higher returns) that so agitated Bagehot. Increasingly through the decade, as most of Europe moved to a gold standard and the sums of money passing through London became ever greater, the cumulative and interlocking logic was irresistible: sterling, backed by the Bank's adherence to the gold standard, as *the* international currency; the City as *the* place where the world's trade was financed and settled; and Lombard Street itself as *the* short-term money market of unrivalled liquidity and security. 'If England be the heart of international trade and cosmopolitan finance, and London be the heart of England, the City is the heart of London,' declared the leading journalist T. H. S. Escott in his 1879 survey of *England: Its People, Polity, and Pursuits*; and in a bravura set-piece passage, he convincingly depicted the Old Lady herself as lying at the very heart of the City's unrivalled financial machinery:

Outside and beyond the specially national functions which the
Bank is bound to discharge in being the banker of the Government,
the issuer of notes that, under certain conditions, are legal tender
and therefore national currency, in taking charge of Government
securities and paying the dividends thereon to the holders, and in
discharging the other various offices of a bank for the public, there
are other multifarious functions which it is compelled by its position to fulfil. Bills from all parts of the world are drawn payable
in London, as in other capitals, because it is convenient to have
recognised places at which the international trading balances and
the balance between the markets and traders of different countries
may be settled; while, by mere force of geographical circumstances, London has, in a special degree, drifted into the position
of international Clearing-House of the world, and the banking
functions connected with it are largely, though not exclusively,
discharged by the Bank of England, which is known as the bankers' bank at home. This is not all. In the final resort, when balances
remain to be discharged as between one nation and another, after
all the complicated mechanism of bills set off against each other
has accomplished its utmost, they must be paid in gold. There is
no other means of settling the final outcome of the mass of transactions in international commerce except through the precious
metals – gold and silver; and while silver is mainly employed in
the East, gold is chiefly used in the West. London consequently,
as the convenient centre that may be drawn upon from all parts
of the world, must possess a stock of gold sufficient to meet the
demands that may be made on it. The Bank of England, as the
banker of the nation, is the custodian of this treasure; and being
thus constituted a bullion storehouse, to it flow all supplies of the
precious metal that reach our shores. Circumstances have thus
caused it to become a dealer in bullion as well as a banker. The
Bank of England, in fact, discharges wider than national banking
functions. Along with the joint stock and private banks by which
it is surrounded, and with which its relations are close and intimate – for as the central institution it keeps the reserves of the
other banks as well as its own – it represents the banking of the
metropolis, and therefore, in the final issue, of England. Owing
to England's world-wide commercial relations, this same banking

system, and the subsidiary agencies by which it is buttressed, acts as the general international Clearing House; and bearing in mind the duties that further devolve on it from the fact that London is the great bullion centre, we can form some faint idea of the multiplicity and complexity of its operations, and the vastness of the weight which presses on the central pivot around which the entire commercial and financial system revolves.

A word of caution is necessary. For all its concern about ensuring the convertibility of sterling (albeit a concern sometimes compromised by the perceived need to make acceptable profits for the Bank's shareholders), it would be an exaggeration to say that the Bank in any real day-to-day sense actively managed the *international* gold standard. Moreover, contact with other national (not yet 'central') banks seems to have remained distinctly spasmodic for the rest of the century. Even so, in terms of the international orientation, it is worth quoting from an interview given by Birch in 1887, six years after the end of his governorship but while he was still a director:

When I entered the Bank [in 1860] I remember in our discussions as to raising or lowering the Bank rate we were always talking about the balance of trade and trade returns. We know now that the balance of trade has very little to do with our international balancing. The great thing which governs us is the enormous transactions on the Stock Exchange, in France, in Germany, and in the United States. These are the operations we have to follow most carefully. We have to observe the course of the foreign exchanges, and they are more carefully watched than they used to be. We have also to follow the movements of gold, and within the Bank we are not simply working *le jour pour le jour*, but we try to look ahead and forecast what is likely to result from the negotiation of public loans, not only in this country but on the Continent. For instance, if a loan is contracted in Germany for the Argentine Republic it is more than probable that if gold is required, it will be taken not from Germany, but from England.

What about, in this new dispensation, the impact on domestic trade and industry of all the Bank rate changes necessary to maintain convertibility? The interviewer (for the *Journal of the Institute of Bankers*) failed to ask the question; but, if he had, it is unlikely that Birch would have seen it as any more than a desirable – but not crucial – consideration.[10]

Instead, during these two decades, the 1870s and the 1880s, the major monetary controversy concerned the arcane subject of bimetallism: in other words, the increasingly noisy school of thought arguing that, against a post-1873 background of world economic depression and a falling general price level, including the price of silver, the only realistic solution was for the leading nations, above all Britain, to return to a bimetallic standard – that is, abandoning the monometallism of the gold standard and thereby permitting the free coinage of silver in addition to gold. By 1881 the Bimetallic League was under way, with its two most prominent members being the former governors Henry Hucks Gibbs and Henry Riversdale Grenfell (a copper merchant, with close links to Welsh mining), both still directors. Five years later, as trade depression deepened, the government agreed to appoint a Gold and Silver Commission; and the governor, Currie, asked his directors for their private views, which they gave during the winter of 1886–7. A handful (Gibbs and Grenfell inevitably to the fore) saw merit in the double standard, but the overwhelming majority, whether merchants or merchant bankers, preferred to stick with the reassuring certainties of the status quo:

I am most decidedly of opinion that it would be very unwise to make any alteration in our currency laws, by which gold of a fixed standard and quality in England, and, I believe, in all of the Colonies, is and has been for many years in existence. (*Thomson Hankey*)

My opinions have never inclined in the least to the side of, as it seems to me, an unpractical and dangerous economic fallacy. (*R. W. Crawford*)

If there were any advantage to England in Bimetallism, which I deny, it would never do for her to rely upon any international agreement whatever. (*Benjamin Buck Greene*)

I prefer to make the best of existing circumstances rather than surrender our single standard with the advantages it possesses. (*William Lidderdale*)

It must be wiser to adhere to our present system of currency rather than 'take a leap in the dark', and enter upon an experiment the result of which no one can possibly foresee. (*Charles Goschen*)

To sum up the situation in a few words, London being the centre of the financial world, we have to be doubly careful to protect our stock of gold. *(Alfred de Rothschild)*

I have the pleasure to rank myself on the side of the firm mono-metallists. *(Lord Revelstoke)*

I do not believe Bimetallism would be a cure for the so-called depression in trade. *(Everard Hambro)*

Significantly, there was concurrence from two of the directors with strong industrial links, namely the linen-yarn manufacturer Lancelot Holland (governor twenty years earlier) and Henry Blake, a civil engineer who was London partner of the Birmingham-based James Watt & Co:

I believe it to be an impossibility to fix a permanent ratio at which gold and silver shall be interchangeable all over the world; and I should expect that any attempt to do so would fail, in spite of national agreements, which cannot possibly become universal ...

The monometallic currency in Great Britain based upon a gold standard is admitted by general consent to be as perfect, if not more so, than that of any other country; and this, coupled with the universal trade which England possesses, and other reasons, makes London the chief centre of exchange for the settlement of commercial transactions ...

The Bank did not formally present its collective judgement; but, asked by the Royal Commission in May 1887 if his bimetallist views represented 'the preponderating views amongst the directors', Gibbs had no alternative but to accept that he was 'in a small minority'. Not that he gave up the battle. 'I believe that the notion that England's prosperity is due to our having a single gold standard is merely a vain imagination,' he declared at the following April's Bimetallic Conference. 'What a futile and miserable foundation on which to build the commercial greatness of England!'[11] In the event, after the Royal Commission's report later in 1888 had failed to come down decisively on one side or the other, it became apparent during 1889 that there was as yet no parliamentary majority for bimetallism; and as long as the City, headed by the Bank, was broadly antagonistic, that was almost certainly not going to change.

The Bank certainly called most of the shots in the expanding new field of colonial loans, with Australasia the prime example. 'It is almost essential that inscription of New Zealand Stock should be done through the Bank of England, if it is to be made a success,' noted New Zealand's representative in London, Sir Julius Vogel, in 1875, while the following year he reflected that 'the fact of the Bank of England managing the loans will enhance the estimation in which they are held' and that 'it will be difficult to overrate the collateral advantages arising from the employment of such an institution as the Bank of England'. The Colonial Stock Act of 1877 made colonial loans possible, and next year the Bank made its first issue for a colonial government (New Zealand), followed in 1884 by issues for Queensland and New South Wales. For its part, the Bank did not take on the responsibilities of loan agent solely out of imperial sentiment. 'The Bank consider,' reported Queensland's man in London shortly before that state's loan, 'that if they give their prestige to any Colony by affording facilities for the inscription of its Stock they are entitled to the profit connected with the issue of the loan.' Moreover, over the rest of the 1880s, a distinct high-handedness tended to characterise the Bank's approach. In 1888 for instance, Collet as governor not only insisted on New Zealand having a three-year loan moratorium – during which time it was to pursue an 'urgent need for retrenchment and for an increase of revenue', which he held to be 'of vital importance to the wellbeing of the Colony and to the full restoration of its credit' – but was similarly stern in the course of a meeting with Queensland's representative, who reported back to Brisbane after a less than enjoyable visit to Threadneedle Street: 'That gentleman [Collet] dwelt very strongly on the subject of the rapidly increasing debt of Queensland, and the delicate position in which the Bank of England is placed by the heavy responsibility attaching to the placing of these many Queensland loans on the market at short intervals.' Furthermore: 'The Governor requested me to represent to my Government the desirability of discontinuing this system, and hinted very strongly that if it were continued it would be necessary for his Board to take steps to rid the Bank of that responsibility.' Unsurprisingly, all this engendered a degree of resentment; and it was perhaps telling that the cipher code for the Bank used at this time by both New

South Wales and Queensland was the less than flattering 'bastard'. Even so, as Bernard Attard observes in his study of the colonial loan process, 'direct attacks on the Bank's good faith could only have disastrous consequences', and 'the consequences of the Bank of England declining to float a loan were never far from the minds of Colonial Treasurers'.[12]

The late-Victorian Bank could also seem a formidable presence when it came to politicians. An invaluable witness was the Treasury's Edward Hamilton, a marvellously watchful diarist who accompanied successive chancellors on visits to the parlour. In September 1886 it was the turn of Lord Randolph Churchill. A year earlier, while at the India Office, he had declared to the viceroy that the 'financial knowledge' of Rothschilds was 'as great as that of the Bank of England is small'; but now his mood was rather different. 'Tenders for Treasury Bills [a recent innovation that was becoming increasingly important to the short-term funding of the government] afforded a good opportunity of introducing him to the Governor & Deputy Governor with whom the Chanc of the Exchequer ought to be on good terms,' recorded Hamilton. 'He seemed quite nervous about presenting himself ...' Almost certainly this was the episode when Lord Randolph was reduced, in his son's words, to 'hovering for half an hour outside in a panic of nervousness'. Once inside, however, things went smoothly enough:

> We sit [noted Hamilton] round the Governor's table. The Cashier & two others bring in the Tenders, open & sort them. The Governor then proceeds to read them out. The cashiers then give roughly the average price at which our requirements can be met by three months Bills & six months Bills ... Today we wanted about 2 millions, & as nearly a million falls due in 6 months Bills next December we took one million in three months Bills at about 2¼% per annum, & the other million in 6 months Bills at about 2¾% p.a. One of course defers to the judgement of the Governor & Deputy Governor; but it is generally a simple & straightforward business ... Randolph Churchill said he was interested in the ceremony. The Bank of England is certainly a grand institution. After we had done our business we had luncheon. The working of the Bank Act very appropriately formed a subject of discussion.

'One of course defers' – four words conveying a wealth of mean-ing. Or as Hamilton had reflected of a similar occasion a year earlier, 'one must practically follow the advice of the Governor & Deputy Governor', even though 'I am not satisfied with the bargain I made.' Politicians came and went, and the Bank was intensely careful not to be drawn into party controversy, but there was one eminent politi-cian towards whom its private view was now consistently negative, reflecting a larger shift in the City's political mood as well as specific institutional memory. 'At luncheon in the Bank parlour one generally hears grumbles, if not expletives, about Mr G,' recorded Hamilton in January 1888 after a visit. 'Mr G' was of course Gladstone, still the Liberal leader in his late seventies. 'One Director,' added Hamilton, 'said he intended to send Mr G a naive advertisement of an enter-prising undertaker, who expressed surprise that people should go on living a life of trouble to themselves and others when they could be comfortably interred for £3 ...'[13]

There were warmer feelings towards George Joachim Goschen, Churchill's successor and the only former Bank director ever to have become chancellor (1887–92). His first great moment of reli-ance on the Bank was in the spring of 1888, as he sought to convert almost £600 million of British government 3 per cent stock to 2½ per cent. The circumstances were propitious – cheap money, dear securities, Goschen's own high reputation in the City – but only four years earlier a debt-conversion scheme had failed unexpectedly. 'The Chanc of the Exchequer is fortunate in having a very sensible Governor of the Bank (Collet) and a shrewd hard headed Deputy Governor (Lidderdale) with whom to consult,' noted Hamilton in early March, and not long afterwards Goschen publicly announced his scheme. This time it came off triumphantly, with Lidderdale in due course expressing to Goschen the Bank's pride in having contributed to 'the complete success of a financial operation of such unprecedented magnitude', an operation that earned Collet a knighthood. For those at the Bank never in line for honours, though, the work involved was huge and continuous for weeks if not months – 'beyond all precedent' in the words of Collet himself, while the principal of the Transfer Offices broke down under the round-the-clock strain. 'I had no love for it,' admitted Allan Fea many years later:

The great thing, I remember, was to knock off as many addressed envelopes as possible, and the speed records were easily carried off by Scotsmen, for I believe it was 'piece-work' – pay on the hop-picking system – the greater the bulk the taller the pile of solid cash. I must confess I didn't make much myself over the job. The novelty of nocturnal scribbling soon palled ... I, therefore, escaped into the open-air whenever I could alight upon a plausible, though obviously shiftless excuse, and like the moral story of Hogarth's 'Good and Bad Apprentice', left the diligent to earn his own reward.

A further recollection came from another former Bank clerk, Arthur Rowlett. This was of the 'courtly, white-haired old gentleman with Gladstonian collar and white choker' who 'refused to recognise' Goschen's conversion. 'He always appeared on the same day and at the same hour, and asked for his Dividends on 3 per cent Consols. When told they were now 2½ per cent he shook his head, walked to the middle of the Office, looked at the clock, compared the time with his gold hunter, and then walked slowly out. This proceeding he repeated regularly each quarter for about fifteen years until he died ...'[14]

Yet if the Bank remained indispensable, perhaps increasingly so during the 1870s and 1880s, it was hardly omnipotent. This was especially so in the money market, where the big commercial joint-stock banks, their deposits continuing to rise at a far greater pace than the Bank's, enjoyed considerable clout. 'It is felt on all sides that the old system of paternal government is passing away,' one informed City practitioner wrote to the *Economist* in December 1874, adding that 'the Bank of England, which once distanced every competitor, is now only *primus inter pares*'. The key problem was that of making Bank rate effective in the market, an especially pressing concern with the development in the mid-1870s of the so-called Greene–Gibbs policy (named after the two successive governors of those years), involving the systematic use of Bank rate to protect the reserve. 'The Bank of England,' explained Gibbs to his Oxford correspondent in 1877, 'has but one weapon, the rate, wherewith they defend their own position, and make those who want to borrow money pay a little more for it, inducing, by the rise of interest, the foreigners to minister to the provisions of the Act of '44, and send more note-producing gold into our coffers.' Gibbs was honest enough to concede that the Bank no longer had the power 'to command and control the market', but even so, he went on:

> Our rate is a real power; and as to export of gold, it is so also. So long as the bankers have *with us* more in balance *than what is necessary for them to work with*, they can of course buy gold and export it, whatever the rate of discount in the Bank; but we, of course, know by practice how far they can go; and, when they can go no farther, our rate is an all-controlling engine. Nor are we powerless while they have a surplus balance with us, for of course a timely disposal of some of our Consols or other securities takes the spare money off the market, and makes the Banker of Bankers ('*Shah-in-Shah*') the real arbiter.

Over the next decade or so the question of making the rate effective continued to exercise the Bank's best minds. Three distinct approaches gradually evolved: first, as intimated by Gibbs, an increasingly frequent resort to open-market operations, selling securities (usually Consols) 'spot' for immediate delivery and repurchasing them forward, thereby impacting as desired on the reserve base of the commercial banks; second, gradually withdrawing the controversial 1858 rule and fostering closer relations with the discount houses, by now instinctively more co-operative than the commercial banks; and third, in relation to those banks, seeking to subdue antagonism by slowly retreating from the Bank's own commercial business, a policy not always easy to sell to the Bank's own shareholders. All three approaches helped, but the problem was far from solved by the end of the 1880s.[15]

There were signs of relative weakness in other areas too, most visibly the famous 1875 episode in which Benjamin Disraeli at 10 Downing Street, eager that the British government buy a major stake in the Suez Canal Company, cold-shouldered the Bank and instead turned to Rothschilds to put up the £4 million.[16] Possibly there was a legitimate constitutional doubt whether the government could raise that sum from the Bank without the authority of Parliament (not sitting), but almost certainly Disraeli saw Rothschilds as the more dynamic outfit in an urgent situation. Ten years later, in July 1885, the Bank again found itself outflanked by that merchant bank, this time at the behest of Lord Salisbury's government, choosing the issuer of the London portion of a £9 million loan to Egypt guaranteed by the British, French and German governments.[17] 'We were prepared,' insisted a pained governor, Currie, in his reply to Salisbury's letter giving the disappointing news, 'to carry out the issue in the centres of the guaranteeing powers with, we believe, the greatest advantage to the Egyptian Government.' Within weeks, moreover, Currie was writing again, this time to the chancellor, Sir Michael Hicks Beach, after a recent meeting at which Hicks Beach had, in Currie's words, 'informed us [the governor and his deputy] that it had been hinted that the government might have offers for the supply of their "Ways and Means" advances from some other source than The Bank of England'. A lengthy *cri de coeur* ensued:

> The expediency of the Government entertaining offers of loans from other Banks than The Bank of England cannot be decided by a consideration of the present or any exceptional condition of the Money Market.
>
> The Bank of England, as the Banker of the State, is by statute empowered to make loans to the Government under provisions which apply to it exclusively. The Advances under different Statutes, which The Bank is enabled to make in preparation of the dividends, or to meet deficits in the Revenue at other periods, are always made at exceptionally low rates of interest – lower considerably upon the average than could possibly be charged by any other Banks guided by the rate they could obtain in the open Market, or upon discount of bills spontaneously offered to them.
>
> The Bank of England supplies the Government on exceptionally favourable terms because it regards the Government as its largest and, under every point of view, its most important customer, and believing hitherto that (with the exception of Treasury and Exchequer Bills) the Government invariably resorted to The Bank for the pecuniary advances indispensable to the punctual fulfilment of the engagements of the State, The Bank has always held itself bound to the extent of its power to render the assistance required by the Treasury in any exigency and under any condition of the Money Market.
>
> Acting upon this sense of obligation, The Bank have at times encountered serious inconvenience and loss in order to enable them

to comply with the requirements of the Government; selling, for instance, at a large sacrifice, portions of their public securities.

That there is at times a large amount of unemployed capital in the Money Market is certain, and there is no reason why the Treasury should not reap the benefit to be derived from its use. Treasury Bills were devised for the very purpose of enabling the Government to avail itself of these occasional redundancies of cash, and the experience of the present year demonstrates how successfully the instrument has worked in supplying the Exchequer with considerable sums at unprecedentedly low rates of interest.

The Bank at times holds large amounts of these Treasury Bills; and when the state of the Money Market has been at any time such as to cause fewer tenders to be made than would cover the requirements of the Government, The Bank has invariably come forward to supply the deficiency, although it may not have considered it advisable to tender at the time.

A statement could easily be framed exhibiting over a series of years the very moderate rates charged by The Bank upon advances to the State compared with the Market rate of discount or with The Bank's charge to its ordinary Customers.

'In conclusion,' wrote Currie, 'I would observe that the practice which has hitherto prevailed enables the State to depend upon The Bank of England for any Advances it may require, at all times, upon the most favourable terms; whereas offers from any other Bank would probably only be made under exceptional circumstances when it suits the interests of that Bank to make them.' And he finished with what he clearly trusted was his killer point: 'It must be borne in mind that any transactions between the Treasury and a Joint Stock Bank would certainly be known, whereas those subsisting between the Treasury and The Bank are accompanied with a secrecy greatly to the advantage of the State.' To the extent that the Bank did indeed retain its monopoly of Ways and Means advances (short-term loans by the Bank to government to enable the latter to balance its immediate books), the governor's missive worked; but the very fact of the letter was troubling enough.

'The Declining Power of The Bank of England' was the title of a leading article in the *Bullionist* in early 1890. Noting that the official rate of discount had been 6 per cent for several weeks, 'yet this high rate has failed to attract gold, as it would have done in years gone by, when the power of The Bank of England had not been diminished substantially', the paper argued that the Bank had not only lost control over 'the Home Discount Market' – 'partly by its own antiquated methods of procedure and practice, and partly because of the active operation and greater liberality of its powerful competitors, the large joint-stock banks' – but was also by this time significantly less influential in relation to 'foreign money markets', with London 'not the monopolist of gold which it once was', as increasing quantities of gold went instead to Germany and the United States. In consequence of all of which, declared the *Bullionist*, the Bank 'finds itself in tight places'.[18]

By now the buck stopped with Currie's successor but one, William Lidderdale, who in his mid-sixties had become governor the previous year. His own background was part Scottish, part Merseyside, and since the 1860s he had been the London partner of the Liverpool-based merchants Rathbone Brothers, developing in the process a distinct scepticism about the much trumpeted virtues of the City. He also had a clear-sighted view of the Bank's weaknesses, and during the first seven months or so of 1890 took significant action on a handful of fronts, all designed to strengthen Bank control. These included raising its price for gold from Paris and no longer making importers of large bars bear the charge for melting; securing deposits from the new county councils; managing more closely the India Council's considerable balances; seeking to co-ordinate the market actions of the Bank and the Treasury; pushing for greater business with the provincial banks; and jettisoning the last remnants of the 1858 rule, thereby readmitting the discount houses to regular borrowing and rediscount facilities at the Bank. This vigorous approach won praise. 'It is said,' noted Hamilton in August 1890, 'that Lidderdale is considered in the City to be the best Governor the Bank has ever had (not excepting Collet). He always knows his mind, & his judgement is very good.' But Lidderdale himself was far from satisfied with the larger situation, writing a few weeks later to the Treasury's Sir Reginald Welby:

> I don't think any one who has not sat for 2 years in the Governor's chair during the last decade can realise fully – the dependence of

the English Banking system upon the Bank – the difficulty that this dependence creates in our management. Banking liabilities have enormously increased, not so Bankers' reserves, & this makes our burden much heavier than before & leads to fluctuations in rates quite out of proportion to actual movement of currency.

Lidderdale's particular grievance concerned the joint-stock bankers and their tendency to remove without warning their already inadequate balances from the Bank; as for bankers as a whole, he frankly told Welby that 'a less public-spirited class ... I do not know'.[19] In the event, however, it was to be the hubris of a merchant banker that would put him to the ultimate test.

'Went to the Bank, things queer!' noted Goschen in his diary on about 10 October 1890. 'Some of the first houses talked about. Argentine, etc, have created immense complications. Uncomfortable feeling generally.' Over the next few weeks it emerged – though not to public knowledge – that the City house in most serious trouble was Barings, second in prestige only to Rothschilds but guilty of having rashly over-committed itself in the Argentine (site of a lethal blend of political chaos and financial mismanagement), and whose head was Edward ('Ned') Baring, elevated to the peerage as Lord Revelstoke five years earlier. A man of considerable ability but also high self-importance and poor judgement, he had been a director of the Bank since 1879; and it is possible that in 1887 he had had a moment with the governor of the day, James Currie, with the latter writing to him, 'I am sorry that you express a feeling that the Junior Members of the Court [that is, including Revelstoke himself] have practically nothing whatever to do with the management of the affairs of the Bank.'[20]

What became known as the Baring Crisis – in time as the first Baring Crisis – began for real on Saturday, 8 November.[21] Early that morning, the merchant banker Everard Hambro, one of Revelstoke's two closest friends in the City and likewise a Bank director, called first on Nathaniel ('Natty') Rothschild (who in 1885 had been elevated to the peerage at the same time as Baring), in order to put him fully in the picture, and then on Revelstoke himself, who bleakly informed him that he would be able to say on Monday whether or not Barings could go on. In response, Hambro told Revelstoke that the only person who could help him now was the governor; and, befitting a crisis that would be played out almost entirely behind closed doors, he arranged that Lidderdale should come to Hambros in the afternoon so that he could discreetly see Revelstoke. At that meeting – before which Lidderdale scribbled a note to Goschen asking him to come to the Bank first thing on Monday – Revelstoke and a fellow-partner presented to the governor and Hambro 'a preliminary statement of their affairs', in Lidderdale's retrospective words, 'which rendered it uncertain whether the Firm would have any surplus after payment of their liabilities'. In an unsurprisingly strained atmosphere, the governor, who had probably only discovered that day that Barings was in such dire, life-or-death straits, contented himself with observing that he needed further particulars and would wait until Monday to see whether Barings could continue. Already, though, he must have begun to see that the consequences of Barings going down were almost unthinkable: not only would the collapse of the City's leading accepting house (that is, merchant bank), the world leader in trade finance, inevitably bring down an array of other firms, including all the discount houses, but the very status of the bill on London would be endangered and thus the pre-eminence of the City as an international financial centre.

Lidderdale occupied Sunday by taking his small son to London Zoo, but next morning was ready to receive the chancellor. 'To the Governor of the Bank,' recorded Goschen:

Found him in a dreadful state of anxiety. Barings in such danger that unless aid is given, they must stop. — — [that is, Revelstoke] came in while I was there; almost hysterical. Governor and he both insisted that the situation could only be saved if Government helped ... Picture drawn of the amount of acceptances held by various Banks, which would have to stop. All houses would tumble one after the other. All credit gone. I entirely understood their reasoning, but remembering action taken in France when [in 1889] Comptoir d'Escompte was in difficulties, I said the great houses and banks in London must come together and give the necessary guarantees. This was declared impossible if the Government didn't help.

The chancellor then called on two other (unnamed) bankers, who were likewise adamant that government help was necessary. 'Both quite demoralised,' noted Goschen. 'Lidderdale much more of a man and keeping his head, though certainly he pressed me hard.' That evening and into the small hours, after he had attended the lord mayor's annual Mansion House banquet for bankers and merchants, Goschen agonised. 'If I do nothing and the crash comes I shall never be forgiven: if I act, and disaster never occurs, Parliament would never forgive my having pledged the National credit to a private Firm.' At last, his 'night thoughts' convinced him of the difficulty as well as undesirability of seeking to carry direct aid in Parliament: 'How defend a supplemental estimate for a loss of half a million! And would not immediate application put the whole fat in the fire?' The City, in short, would apparently have to rely on itself.[22]

Over the next three days, Tuesday to Thursday, there were four main aspects-cum-developments. Firstly, neither Goschen nor Lidderdale giving ground, with the governor still insistent that the Bank could act only within a larger umbrella provided by government; secondly, the Bank persuading the Russian government not to make the £1½ million withdrawal from Barings due on the 11th; thirdly, after Lidderdale on the Monday had urged Goschen to get him involved, Natty Rothschild emerging as a constructive figure, not only leaning on the Bank of France to lend £3 million in gold to reinforce the Bank's badly stretched reserves, but exercising informal pressure on his good friend the prime minister, Lord Salisbury, to take a less passive approach to the crisis; and fourthly, the real key, Lidderdale deciding to appoint a two-man committee to determine whether Barings was solvent in the long run, in other words whether it was worthy of rescue. The committee comprised the octogenarian director Benjamin Buck Greene and the leading banker Bertram Currie, the latter happening to be Revelstoke's other particularly close City friend, the two men going back many years. 'I don't like to come & see you & hardly think I ought to write,' a highly emotional Revelstoke wrote to Currie after the appointment was made, 'but I cannot help sending one line in my wretched agony to implore you to do what you can. I know you will & I am sure you feel for us all in our nightmare.'[23]

Friday the 14th, the decisive day, unfolded in three acts. The first took place at the Bank, where it became clear that in the view of Greene and Currie, notwithstanding Barings' urgent need for a huge cash loan of up to £9 million, 'if sufficient time be given for realizing the assets ... the Firm will be left with a substantial surplus after discharging their liabilities'. 'I must frankly say,' Greene himself would subsequently write to Lidderdale about his memories of that morning, 'that as the amount required was so large ... I considered the shutters must go up soon after I reached The City, instead of which on delivery of the report to my surprise you instantly said "They must be carried on ...".' At the same time, it was also becoming clear that, after almost a week of successful news management, the City at large was beginning to give way to outright panic. At about noon John Daniell, senior partner of Mullens the government brokers, rushed into the Bank, beseeching Lidderdale with his arms aloft: 'Can't you do something, or say something, to relieve people's minds? They have made up their minds that something awful is up, and they are talking of the very highest names – the very highest!' During the next hour, Barings' bills started to pour into the Bank, as hardly anyone else would purchase them, though the Bank itself was naturally anxious that, with the value of those bills plummeting, it stood to make a serious loss when it came to reselling them; and at about two o'clock, with the entire credit of the City at peril, Lidderdale slipped quietly out of the Princes Street door.

He took a circuitous route until he secured a hansom cab to drive him to Downing Street. There he did not meet Goschen, who was committed to speak in Dundee that evening and believed he had to fulfil the engagement in order to avoid panic. Instead his place was taken by W. H. Smith (first lord of the Treasury), soon accompanied by Salisbury. For at least an hour there was give from neither side. At one point Salisbury offered authority to suspend once again the Bank Charter Act; but this the governor (as he was to recall) 'emphatically refused', declaring that 'reliance on such letters was the cause of a great deal of bad banking in England'. Eventually, Lidderdale played his highest card:

I told Lord Salisbury I could not possibly go on with the matter at the Bank's sole risk; that the Bank had been taking in Baring's Bills all the week, pending the investigation; that they were probably coming in fast now that alarm had set in, and that unless

Government would relieve us of some of the possible loss, I should
return at once and throw out all further acceptances of the Firm.

This threat carried the day, as Salisbury and Smith in effect gave
Lidderdale just under twenty-four hours to save Barings, promising
that government would meet half the loss resulting from the Bank
taking in Barings' bills up to early afternoon on Saturday. By 5 o'clock,
mercifully spared the traffic gridlock of late-Victorian London, the
governor was back at the Bank for the day's final act.

Bertram Currie was one of those waiting for him, as Lidderdale
summoned an immediate meeting in his room and declared his intention of launching a guarantee fund for Barings, in effect a 'lifeboat',
with the Bank itself putting up the first million pounds. Currie quickly
responded by saying that his own bank, Glyn Mills, would contribute
half a million provided that Rothschilds did the same. Moments later
Natty Rothschild entered the room. Would he agree? 'He hesitated
and desired to consult his brothers,' recalled Currie, 'but was finally
and after some pressure persuaded to put down the name of his firm
for £500,000.' What pressure? According to Hamilton, his ear close to
the ground, it required Lidderdale to say bluntly to Rothschild: 'We
can get on without you.' What would have transpired if Rothschild
had called Lidderdale's bluff is an unanswerable question. But he
did not, and the success of the guarantee fund was assured: over the
next half-hour the City's elite rushed to contribute. Subscribers to
the first list included Raphaels (£250,000), Antony Gibbs and Brown
Shipley (£200,000 each), and Smith Payne & Smiths, Barclays (still a
private bank), Morgans and Hambros (£100,000 each). That evening,
Lidderdale met representatives of the five leading joint-stock banks,
who put themselves down for £3¼ million. Essentially, the fund
indemnified the Bank against any losses arising out of advances made
to Barings to enable it to discharge its liabilities; and the certainty was
that Barings – and the City – would now be saved.[24]

'The Bank of England has added to its historic services to the State
and to the commercial community by prompt and courageous action
which has averted a lamentable catastrophe,' applauded *The Times*
next day. 'Thanks are due to the present energetic administration of
the Bank, not only for providing for a vast reinforcement of the stock
of gold to meet the possibility of the exceptional demands that arise

out of panic, but for stepping out of the ordinary routine of business to prevent the downfall of one of the greatest and most respected of English financial houses ...' In the event, not all was sweetness and light over the following week, with Lidderdale for his part distinctly unhappy about the response from north of the border. 'I am ashamed of my countrymen,' he wrote on Tuesday, 18 November to the London manager of the Bank of Scotland:

£250^m [that is, £250,000] each from the three most important Scotch Banks as a contribution towards our effort to avert a national disaster! You Scots Bankers are dependent upon the Bank of England for the prompt return of the large sums employed in this market, and for the safety of a considerable part of the security you hold against that money. If the Bank of England had failed to save Barings, not a bill you hold would have been beyond question.

Next day, Wednesday the 19th, it seemed for a few hours in the City as if the guarantee fund had never been, with one well-informed banker, John Biddulph Martin, relating in his retrospective account a loaded encounter:

A rumour, more or less well founded, that the joint stock banks had announced that they would call in all loans from the Stock Exchange, caused almost a panic in the morning; it was certain that the Governor of the Bank of England called the managers in and told them that if they would not give their customers reasonable accommodation, they must not themselves look to the Bank in case of need. Thereupon they let it be known that they would make advances as usual, and a general improvement all round took place immediately. This seemed to be the turning point, and the crisis was at an end.

So it was; and at the end of the year, Lidderdale received a formal deputation from the Committee of the Stock Exchange, expressing admiration in their address for 'the masterly ability with which the measures of yourself and the Court of Directors were carried out in the negotiations in this Country and abroad' – and 'more especially' for 'the firm and decisive manner, in which your great influence as

Governor was so wisely and courageously exercised, that a panic of unparalleled dimensions was averted'. Lidderdale's reply was characteristic: 'I shall always remember with pride and satisfaction that, in the opinion of such a body as yours, in a moment of danger I was able to do my duty.'

The successful resolution of the crisis did not preclude the odd external criticism, notably – and perhaps predictably – from the *Economist*. For one thing, there was the issue of moral hazard, for another thing there was the question of being too big to fail. Neither phrase was in the contemporary vocabulary, but that was the gist of the paper's critique in its issue dated 22 November: the guarantee, it argued, had been 'rather too far reaching'; and it expressed anxiety about a precedent being set in which, after a sufficiently large financial institution had over-committed itself 'to the extent of a sufficient number of millions', this would automatically mobilise the banking system as a whole 'to tide them over their difficulties'.[25] What contemporary analysis tended not to focus on was a comparison of the 1866 and 1890 crises – in particular, why the Bank had chosen to rescue Barings less than a quarter of a century after it had decided to leave Overend Gurney to its fate, even though Overends did in time pay its creditors. The answer lay partly in the objective and more or less accurate assessments made at the time about the larger damage that would be caused by the failure of those houses; but it also lay partly in more subjective considerations. Overend Gurney prior to 1866 had spectacularly blotted its copybook in the Bank's eyes, whereas Barings in 1890 was supremely the establishment's – political and social as well as financial – *inside* house. More than almost all his colleagues, Lidderdale may have been a semi-outsider in the City; yet as governor of the Bank he could not help but be, like Barings, at the very centre of a whole nexus of assumptions, influence and connections. Ultimately, the lesson of the crisis was that the establishment would always do its best to look after its own; and nowhere more than in the City, still in many ways an intimate and village-like place, did it pay to be fortunate in one's friends.

Wonderfully Youthful
in Spirit – Considering

The Baring Crisis had, among other things, thrown into sharp, Bagehot-like relief the question of the Bank's palpably inadequate reserves of gold, less than £11 million as the crisis broke.[1] Amid a plethora of 'schemes' in the air, Lidderdale had typically strong views, as related by Hamilton after a conversation in the early days of 1891:

> He was prepared to try the experiment of £1 notes ... but he doubted if the addition by this means of more gold in the bank cellars would be any great gain ... The only way of increasing the spare cash of this country, the smallness of which was our real danger, was to take steps whereby the Joint Stock Banks would be made to keep larger balances; and the least objectionable manner of securing this end would probably be to require them to publish frequently their balances ... Lidderdale is prepared to go on as Governor for a third year, notwithstanding that it means a considerable private loss: he is wrapped up in the work at the Bank, and is fully alive not only to the interest but to the importance of the post. I don't think he greatly appreciates the Chancellor of the Exchequer, of whose extreme sensitiveness and at times want of courage he complains. I admitted that it was a pity Goschen was thin-skinned. 'Thin-skinned,' said Lidderdale. 'Why, he has no skin at all; he is nothing, but nerves and bones.'

The governor later in January sought to fortify the chancellor – complaining about the country's 'very inadequate Banking Reserves', highlighting the invidiousness of the Bank's position given that the larger its own reserve 'the less Bankers like to keep *their* money unused', and even expressing quasi-regret for having helped the bankers the previous autumn, calling them 'a stiff-necked & rebellious race each caring only for his own corporation' – with the result that Goschen in late January made a major speech at Leeds on the whole thorny subject. After noting the relative smallness of English bullion reserves compared to those in France, Germany and the United States, as well as the fact that London being the world's only free gold market left it peculiarly exposed, and declaring that it was 'a false system and a dangerous system to rely significantly upon the aid the Bank of England can give in a crisis', he put forward three key proposals: that the banks should maintain greater cash reserves (presumably, albeit unstated, at the Bank of England); that the banks should reveal the extent of their reserves more frequently; and that the reintroduction of £1 notes would, by taking the place of sovereigns in people's pockets, have the effect of increasing the amount of gold at the Bank of England.

The story of the next year was of the failure of Goschen's plan (apart from the banks agreeing to monthly – but not weekly – publication of their balance sheets), a failure partly attributable to his own lack of resolve, but mainly to hardening opposition from an instinctively conservative, change-averse City. The leader of the resistance was Bertram Currie, arguing throughout that banks entrusting greater reserves to the Bank benefited only one institution, the Bank itself. 'That the Bank should desire to increase the balances of its customers is natural and laudable,' he wrote in May to the governor in the course of a less than good-tempered correspondence, 'but how the public, other than the holders of Bank Stock, are to be benefited, I fail to see.' To which Lidderdale (who indeed stayed on for a third year) responded: 'Somebody who once was sick wanted to be a Monk, but changed his mind on recovery. Similarly, the Bankers increased their balances after the Leeds speech ... but this soon became too much for their virtue.' Unfortunately, Lidderdale's heavy-handedness was part of the problem, with Hamilton observing soon afterwards that he had been 'preaching at the Joint Stock Banks again'. Nor did it help the governor that the scheme had such patchy support from his own colleagues. 'Notwithstanding that the measure has the cordial approval of the Governor himself, the majority of the Court appears to be very lukewarm about it, if not hostile to it,' recorded Hamilton later that year after conversations with 'sundry' Bank directors. 'It is a case of "laissez nous faire". "We have got on well enough up till now, why not leave us alone?"' Indeed, Lidderdale's own soundings revealed a substantial minority (eleven out of twenty-six) explicitly hostile, with a future governor, the merchant Samuel Gladstone, declaring that 'Mr Goschen's proposal would have as much effect on foreign exchanges as King Canute's orders had on the waves of the sea,' while a former governor, Edward Howley Palmer, offered a historical warning about the practicality of small notes, referring gravely to 'the danger and risk to the working classes of the forgeries which existed so extensively when they were last in circulation'. The governor's tone, reporting back to Goschen on his findings, was understandably weary: 'Do you expect enthusiastic support from the Bank to anything? We are not a very youthful body of men, though wonderfully youthful in spirit – considering.'

By early 1892, the scheme was effectively dead, its demise further ensured by a lack of support from the shadow chancellor, the abrasive Sir William Harcourt. 'I don't find that the City at all share your admiration of Lidderdale,' he wrote that winter to Hamilton. 'I have had letters from persons whom you would recognise as being of the highest authority who regard the recent scheme as a mere Bank of England job to increase the profits of the Bank of England …' Even so, if £1 notes were no longer up for debate for the foreseeable future, that was far from the case in terms of the central reserve. During the 1880s there had been little appetite for challenging Bagehot's conclusion that there was no plausible alternative to a single-reserve system; but it was a significant pointer when the *Bankers' Magazine* asserted in March 1892 that instead of banks concentrating all their reserves at the Bank, 'we shall have to revert to the older methods – to causing each bank to maintain an adequate cash reserve of its own'. Or as Currie privately reflected some months later, 'the time for living under the patronage of the Bank of England seems to be passing & the other Banks would act wisely in recognising this fact & in making provision for future troubles before they arrive'. Over the next two decades, the question of the reserve would stubbornly – and sometimes tediously – persist; and it came to symbolise the shifting balance of power not only between the Bank and the rapidly growing joint-stock clear-ing banks (capital of over £50 million by 1891, compared with £35 million ten years earlier, and almost a thousand more branches), but also in some sense between a deeply entrenched City establishment and an unwelcome bunch of muscle-flexing upstarts often with strong provincial roots.[2]

More generally, despite widespread praise for its role in resolving the Baring Crisis, the first half of the 1890s was a far from happy time for the Bank. 1892 saw a Charter renewal in which the Bank found itself distinctly squeezed by the Treasury in terms of payment for its day-to-day services; governor from that year until 1895 (a third year added because of his deputy's serious illness) was David Powell, a rather unimaginative, obstinate merchant; and his governorship almost exactly coincided with Harcourt's tenure as chancellor in the Liberal ministries of first Gladstone and then Lord Rosebery. 'The Bank will, I see, need to be carefully handled,' reflected Hamilton after a visit to Threadneedle Street in August 1893. 'They have not got over (what they consider to be) the hard bargain which we drove with them last year, and there is not a single Director who is politically friendly towards the Government.' Careful handling was never the chancellor's forte, spoiling anyway as he was for a showdown with what he regarded as one of the last great unreformed vested interests; and the following week, while on holiday, Hamilton was presumably dismayed to receive a Harcourt special:

In your absence I have fought a great fight with the dragons of the Bank parlour.

I sent for the Governor who came supported by that valiant champion Deputy Governor Wigram. After some polite beating about the bush we came to close quarters on the rate of interest on Ways & Means advances.

I blandly threw out a ½ per cent above the rate on deficiency advances which at the present discount rates would have been 2½ p.c.

The two pundits looked at one another in blank dismay and revealed the fact that they had come with instructions to ask 3½ p.c.; thereupon I poured upon them the vials of my wrath; I showed them that such a rate had never been paid when the Bank Rate was 4%; I asked them with indignation how they dare behave in such a way to a customer who kept an average balance of £5,000,000 in their hands; I told them point blank that nothing would induce me to listen to such an exorbitant demand and I said it would become my duty to enquire what 'other persons' there were in the City of London who might be ready & willing to accommodate HM's Govt at a reasonable rate. I said I had hitherto been unwilling to open a Govt account elsewhere than at the B of England but that such demands might make it necessary to look in other quarters for reasonable accommodation. This was quite enough to indicate the proximity of New Court [home of Rothschilds] to Threadneedle St and they trembled at the notion of the Ch of the Exch dealing with Jews less extortionate than themselves. After I had exhibited this bug bear sufficiently I was prepared to dismiss them with the question whether I was to take their proposal as an ultimatum, upon which the ferocious Powell hinted that I might write and suggest 3% and they would give it anxious consideration.

The two gentlemen who looked for all the world like the picture of the money lenders at Windsor then retired. The valiant Wigram looked daggers – but used none.

I accordingly wrote a polite note splitting the difference which has been graciously acceded to, they endeavouring to cover their retreat by alleging 'the change in the condition of the money market' as the reason of their climbing down …

A few days later, Harcourt was in no more forgiving mood, informing Hamilton that the Bank's 'scandalous conduct' was something he would not forget, accusing it of having 'practically robbed the public of ¾% on £2,000,000', promising that he would have 'as little dealings as I can help with these gentlemen in the future', and again raising the tactic of borrowing from Rothschilds in order to 'show up these Bank gentlemen to the public for what they are'.[3]

At which delicate point 'certain irregularities', as the recurrent phrase went, were discovered in the Chief Cashier's Office – a phrase that masked what was arguably the Bank's worst ever internal scandal.[4] The culprit was the chief cashier himself, Frank May, autocratic holder since 1873 of that powerful post. 'Mr May,' an admiring profile in the *Bankers' Magazine* had noted in the late 1880s, 'is said to despise what is known as popularity, and, still more, the insincerity of word and manner sometimes made to the charge of men who flinch from what may be their strict, although unpleasant, duty to their fellow-workers'; earlier in 1893, he had been one of three authors of an internal report on the Bank's administration, highlighting the twin problems of 'the irregularity of the work, which is subject to periods of considerable pressure and slackness, not only within the year but within the day', and 'the employment, for some of the duties in the Bank, of a class of persons not always well fitted for such duties'. May's transgression, it emerged from a report submitted by Lidderdale, Greene and James Currie to the Committee of Treasury in November 1893, had been for several years past to make large unauthorised advances – with recipients, it would subsequently transpire, including the City editor of *The Times* and May's own son, of the stockbrokers Coleman & May, intimately involved with the investment trust companies that had flourished on the back of the late 1880s boom but subsequently perished amid the protracted fallout from the Baring Crisis. For the time being, Powell and his colleagues were able to hush up the cause of May's abrupt departure from the Bank – 'a surprise,' mildly commented the *Financial Times*, calling him 'the stationary point round which revolved the ring of ephemeral Governors' – but for the governor of the day, Powell, there was no avoiding an interview with the dreaded Harcourt, who naturally (noted Hamilton) 'spoke his mind out very strongly' in 'rather too hectoring a tone' when told the circumstances. Indeed, although the Bank itself had decided that May's offences were not actionable, Harcourt was even minded for a time to refer the case to the public prosecutor, until persuaded by his mandarins, including Hamilton, that this might seriously damage the Bank's reputation.[5]

Eventually, however, the fourth estate had its say. 'A Paralytic Bank of England' was the unfriendly title of a seventeen-page blast by A. J. Wilson, appearing in his *Investors' Review* at the start of 1894 after several weeks of swirling rumours. 'Little of the true condition of the Bank can be known until daylight is let in on its accounts,' he declared:

> The Bank publishes no balance-sheet – nothing whatever except the meagre weekly returns. There is no outside audit of its books;

its stockholders have no control whatever over the management. Under the charter shareholders are supposed to meet and elect directors and governors at stated periods, but this power has dwindled into mere routine or pantomime. The 'House List', as it is called, is always elected as a matter of course, so that the board is really co-optative. It is thus, in great measure, 'a family party'. The son follows the father, the nephew the uncle, or a lucky marriage brings with it a seat at the board. At best tradition prevails, and the new director is never a banker, rarely a man trained in the hard school of competitive business.

Emphasising the danger of making May the scapegoat, Wilson itemised in some detail the close connections of several Bank directors with various investment trust companies, accusing them of having 'dabbled in the dirty waters of the City', and generally condemned the Bank for 'its isolated position, its business ineptitudes, and its appalling absence of anything like consistent, or even decently intelligent, direction'. For the institution itself, this was an intensely uncomfortable experience. 'London was humming with his stories about Threadneedle-street,' reported the *Daily Chronicle* a day or two later about the impact of Wilson's article, 'and, fearful to tell, newsboys were exhibiting sensational posters, and doing a brisk trade on the strength of them, under the very noses of the dignified gentlemen in livery who stand outside the Bank.' Wilson himself, speaking to the paper, was in trenchant mood:

The Bank of England is protected by the prestige of 200 years' existence and of a great national institution. Why, its prescriptive right of keeping its position in the dark is looked upon as a sort of guarantee of infallibility. What can you expect of such a system? Any human institution which gets divorced from the general movement of things goes mouldy and moth-eaten in time until a breath of life comes along from the world ...

The first thing to be done is to let in the light. Not one bank manager in ten, I venture to say, could make head or tail of the weekly statement which is issued by the Bank. A balance-sheet is never presented from year's end to year's end. There is no outside audit and no representative of the chief customers of the Bank – namely, the bankers of the country – on the governing body. Can anyone in his senses contend that this is a proper footing for a vast national institution in the present day? ...

The best of Governors is never able to make any permanent impression upon the management of the Bank's business. They all come and go, these Governors, like mere cogs in a wheel. Routine controls them in most things, and where routine is master abuses thrive ... The Government ought to step in at once and get the affairs of the Bank thoroughly overhauled, so that everything may be brought to the light. There is nothing else for it that I can see, unless the country is to wait with hands folded for the inevitable catastrophe.

Soon afterwards there appeared a classic *Punch* cartoon by John Tenniel. Entitled 'A Dirty Crossing', it depicted the inevitable old lady peering down at 'Mismanagement' below her dress, and saying, 'O DEAR, O DEAR! I WISH I WERE OUT OF THIS NASTY MESS!' That was on 8 January; and though *The Times* the same day sought to offer a sense of perspective – 'the Bank directors are not gods, but they are not black-beetles either' – Harcourt soon afterwards treated Powell to another earful, demanding to know 'what changes in the system of the management of the Bank are in contemplation'.

The immediate upshot was a power struggle, with Hamilton ascertaining later in January that Everard Hambro, supported by Charles Goschen (the former chancellor's younger brother) and some of the junior directors, was proposing to change the Committee of Treasury from an ex officio body of past governors to one elected from the directors as a whole. 'It is believed,' he noted, 'that the present ex-governors are too averse to so radical a step to admit of its being taken.' So they were; and after Powell had been careful to circulate to all directors a letter to him from Henry Hucks Gibbs insisting that 'it is wholly beneath the dignity of the Court that any of its members should be influenced by the ignorant comments of the Press', the Court voted on 1 February against Hambro's initiative. Instead, the emphasis was put on a different sort of internal reform, with the creation by April of an Audit Department supervised by an Audit Committee, the latter comprising the deputy governor and five directors. By then the proprietors, at their regular half-yearly General Court, had given Powell and his colleagues a vote of confidence, after the governor had provided some hard information about May's misdemeanours, including his speculations on the Stock Exchange, and had informed them that the Bank had set aside £250,000 to meet possible losses. 'There may have been some fault in the system,' conceded Powell, 'but the directors have always had the best interests of the Bank thoroughly at heart, and they have tried, and will always try in the future, to do their best.'[6]

Altogether, it was not brilliant timing for the bicentenary that July; and Herbert de Fraine ruefully remembered how the staff, convinced they would each receive an anniversary gift of one whole year's salary, in fact got nothing at all – 'absolutely shattering' to those who had pinned all their financial hopes on a lump sum, and without a word of explanation either. There would be disappointment too at the top, as recorded by Harcourt's son in March 1895, just as Powell was preparing to step down: 'The wife of the Governor of the Bank of England (who looked like a Regent St prostitute) came to see Ch Ex [Harcourt] this morning to ask that some "honour" should be given to him on his retirement from the Bank ...'[7] Harcourt's reply is sadly not recorded, but in any case the surprise visit proved fruitless.

In the event, the bicentenary was marked by something entirely different – the employment from the summer of 1894 of about two dozen women, initially to sort and count banknotes. The motive was largely financial, part of cost-cutting in the wake of the harsh 1892 settlement; and the explicit rule was that all new female recruits were to be aged between eighteen and twenty-four, were to be unmarried or widows, and 'will be required to resign their appointments on marriage'. 'Our path', recalled Janet Hogarth (later Courtney), the Oxford-educated first superintendent of women clerks, 'wasn't always smooth':

> Those were the early days of women's entry into business and they were not accorded a wide welcome – one can't wonder at it. They did indeed displace men ... So my sympathy goes out retrospectively to the elderly clerks and superintendents who tried to make out that we were inefficient, though we did with a staff of forty [the number of female clerks by 1896] what had before occupied sixty, and got away for the most part punctually at 4 p.m. instead

of being kept till 6 p.m. to adjust a lost balance. 'Balance out' was seldom the cry as I got to the end of totting up the day's total. Yet high officials were informed that we had 'failed' over work that had never been given to us, or that our health record was faulty, or our thoughts wandering, or what not. More than once we were in danger of extinction. But Mr [James] Currie remained our firm friend, and a free lunch did away with most of the health trouble. I remember his coming in to ask me whether that, or an extra £10 a year, would be most beneficial. I said firmly, 'The lunch – if you give them the money they'll spend it on hats and go on eating buns just the same.'

In 1898 some of Hogarth's charges qualified as typists; but broadly speaking the Bank remained until 1914 a male domain, as did the City at large, with Hogarth herself not unhappy to leave in 1906 and become librarian of the *Times* Book Club. 'In the end I grew weary even of the comfort and the consideration – we were too closely segregated and confined to one narrow outlet. Ambition had little scope. Sex disability seemed likely always to bar preferment.' That was undoubtedly true, yet the very existence of female clerical staff had made a significant difference to the late-Victorian Bank. The key witness is the notably dispassionate de Fraine. Noting that their 'advent was very unreasonably resented', he argues that this 'infiltration' was in its effect 'much more far-reaching than was, I imagine, foreseen by anybody': 'It meant in fact the end of all the old easy-going methods. It would be of no use in future a Principal's not knowing what sort of staff he had in the office, or even what numbers he employed.' And de Fraine adds that 'actually the tightening-up was long overdue, as must have been perfectly well known to everybody'.[8]

During the City's increasingly prosperous mid-1890s, epitomised by the frantic speculation in 1895 in South African gold-mining shares that led to remarkable scenes in the Stock Exchange's 'Kaffir Circus', few Bank staff of either sex, and indeed possibly not all that many directors, concerned themselves unduly with the notoriously recondite question of bimetallism. Back in 1892 there had been an inconclusive international conference at Brussels, with no formal Bank representation; in 1895, the year that Miss Prism warned Cecily (in Oscar Wilde's *The Importance of Being Earnest*) that 'even these metallic problems have their melodramatic side', the Bimetallic League again pushed hard, leading to a memorial from the newly formed Gold Standard Defence Association, though with relatively few Bank signatories; and finally, in 1897, the controversy enjoyed more or less its final fling.

The background, from the Bank's perspective, was partly the way in which increased global economic activity meant an end to its temporary abundance of gold (itself much stimulated by the influx of new gold from the Rand), and partly the impact in July 1897 of a visiting American pro-silver delegation to London, led by Senator Wolcott, banging the old drum of an international bimetallist agreement. Neither the chancellor, Sir Michael Hicks Beach, nor the governor, Hugh Colin Smith, was willing to budge in any fundamental way from the monometallist faith; but at the end of July the latter did inform the former that, following their conversation, the Bank was 'prepared to carry out what is laid down as permissible in the Bank Charter – namely, to hold one-fifth of the bullion held against the Note issue in silver, provided always that the French Mint is again open for the free coinage of silver and that the prices at which the silver is procurable and saleable are satisfactory'. Some seven weeks later, at a meeting of the General Court, Smith in effect informed the world at large of this 'one-fifth' concession – and the consequence was an immediate City storm. A prominent merchant banker, Robert Benson, at once sold his Bank stock, as did Gladstone's future biographer, the Liberal politician John Morley; Hamilton reflected that 'the reception of the announcement, which is regarded as an imprudent flirtation of the "Old Lady" with bimetallism, shows how exceedingly sensitive the great City world is about any suspicion of tampering with our currency system'; the *Financial Times* declared that the Bank had 'no business to be coquetting with bi-metallism at their time of life'; and the Committee of London Clearing Bankers passed 'with practical unanimity' a resolution condemning the Bank's proposal. The reasons for that initiative would remain unclear – Benson at the time reckoning that many of the directors had been 'entirely ignorant of the Governor's action', that of 'a wharfinger & not a banker' – but in any case the storm proved to be of the teacup variety, with the government making clear by October its wholesale rejection of the bimetallist agenda.[9]

These were also the years of cheap money, with Bank rate at only 2 per cent from February 1894 to September 1896, further reducing the Bank's already squeezed income. How to increase it? The obvious answer was to grow the Bank's business in its provincial branches (several now housed in splendid buildings, such as Hardwick's Italian-style Leeds branch), an approach that would also do at least something to redress the balance in relation to the ever-vaster resources and thus potential leverage of the joint-stock banks. It was a policy that engendered predictable resentments. 'We do not complain about fair competition but this is fostered by free money costing the lender nothing at all,' one leading provincial banker, Beckett Faber of Beckett & Co, asserted in May 1896 to the Central Association of Bankers. 'How can we country bankers who pay well for our deposits meet such competition as this? Our loans are taken from us; our bills no longer exist in our cases and our current accounts are "touted" for ...' Faber finished with a dark warning: 'The time is already arriving, if it has not already arrived, when the Bank of England must choose whether to be the banker for the Government or a commercial bank. It cannot be both ...' Over the next year or so the Bank did hold out the occasional olive branch, at one point promising Faber it would instruct its agents not to compete 'unduly' with their neighbours. But from March 1897 the man in overall charge of the branches was Ernest Edye, one of the more driven figures in the Bank's history, operating semi-autonomously and producing in his first seven years an annual average profit of some £145,000, almost double what it had been over the previous nine years. 'I hear from all sides that at the Branches they have adopted an aggressive and an irritating policy,' a well-informed London bill broker told a visiting country banker in May 1899, adding that 'I suppose they have too much regard for the power of the London Banks to go on similar lines here.' That may well have been true; but the underlying reality by this time was not only that the great joint-stock banks had been getting vexed by the Bank's competitive policy in the provinces, but also that they had become, by virtue of their enormous balances, so dominant in the London money market that they naturally wished for a tangible expression of that power. What better stick with which to beat the Old Lady than gold reserves? Later that summer both the Central Association of Bankers and the Committee of the London Clearing

Bankers voted to set up committees on the subject; and in August the *Bankers' Magazine* floated the idea of the joint-stock banks keeping their own bullion reserve at the Bank – but 'withdrawable only by the associated banks, and held apart from the uncontrolled discretion of the Bank of England'.[10]

That autumn saw the start of the Boer War. 'The clearest and most dramatic instance of the operation of the world-wide forces of international finance,' would be J. A. Hobson's famous verdict soon afterwards on its causes; and over the years historians have sought to establish – often on slender empirical evidence – connections, whether in the City or in the official mind, between London as the world's only free gold market, the unsatisfactory state of the bullion reserve and the long-term ensuring of a regular supply of gold from South Africa. Yet even if there is no smoking gun, and even if one concedes (as one should) that there was a significant non-economic dimension to government policy, it is hard to deny the proximity of the two facts that South Africa meant gold and that gold had become the very pivot of the City's existence. Certainly, during the febrile days of October 1899, the City was firmly to the fore of popular support for the war, culminating in a mass meeting at the Guildhall loudly backing the Tory government's strong line. Among those making speeches were Samuel Gladstone the present governor, his predecessor but one A. G. Sandeman ('the merchants of the City of London and of Great Britain are very adverse to having their affairs unsettled by war, but when the occasion arises, when the necessity is seen, as in this case, they rise as one man'), and William Lidderdale, who in a more nuanced speech regretfully saw no alternative and called for 'a merciful victory'.

Meanwhile, discussion continued for some time about the gold reserves question, until early in 1900 the Union Bank of London's Felix Schuster, emerging as a dominant figure in the banking world, announced that it could not be systematically considered again until after the war. That did not stop him, speaking a few months later at the Institute of Bankers, from offering some broader thoughts:

What we require is co-operation, and not legislation. More harmonious working together, although we compete with one another; more harmonious working towards one common end is absolutely necessary, not only between outside bankers, but between us and

the Bank of England. In every foreign country, I believe, the State
Bank has on its Board representatives of all the other great Joint
Stock institutions in the banking world. The State Banks are practically managed, or supervised, by those whose special experience lies
in the banking line. I hardly think that such a thing is practicable
here – I would not advocate it for a moment – that is not in my
mind; but I should think some means could be devised by which the
Bank of England, instead of holding itself rather aloof from other
banks, should periodically meet us and tell us what their views of
the situation are, and that we should from time to time discuss a
common policy, and act harmoniously with one another, instead of
acting in the dark, as we are doing now, quite unaware of what may
be in the minds of the Bank of England ...'[11]

In short, though Schuster refrained from spelling it out, the time was
fast approaching for the company of merchants to accept, at last, him
and his joint-stock counterparts as first-class citizens.

The financing of the conflict did not on the whole enhance the
Bank's authority. 'An addition to Consols' rather than 'a separate
Stock' was, governor Gladstone advised Hicks Beach in February
1900, 'the best way for Government to raise the money to pay for
this South African War'; but counselled also by Sir Ernest Cassel,
the great cosmopolitan financier, Hicks Beach decided that a separate
stock would appeal to a significantly broader public. The governor
– senior partner of the East India merchants Ogilvy, Gillanders &
Co, a first cousin of William Ewart Gladstone, and described by a
leading bill broker as 'unfortunately very self-opinionated' – did not
react well. 'In conclusion,' ended his response to Hamilton in early
March on the draft prospectus for the £30 million loan, 'I feel regret
that the loan is not to be raised by an addition to Consols and would
have preferred a terminable 3% annuity at par to a 2¾% one at a
heavy discount ...' Nor was he any less disgruntled when, just as the
prospectus was published, Hicks Beach summoned to his presence
not just Gladstone himself but the City's top bankers. 'In my humble
opinion,' he told Hamilton, 'their patriotism is a mere matter of price
– make that attractive enough and there will be no danger of the loan
not being subscribed.' In the event the 'Khaki' loan proved a roaring success, with the chief cashier (H. G. Bowen, May's successor)

reporting that 'scores of clerks are here every night until 10, 11, 12 and even ½ past one o'clock' – work that would have been less demanding (albeit less profitable) if Gladstone had not successfully resisted the Treasury's suggestion that applications could be made to the main London clearing banks as well as to the Bank itself: 'I hope it will not be pressed. It is not necessary & therefore undesirable: please leave this paragraph alone & turn a deaf ear to the suggestions of other Bankers.'[12]

The war's second loan, raising almost £10 million, came towards the end of the summer and again was not without some ill-feeling. Once more, Gladstone took with Hicks Beach a strongly pro-Consols line ('would be more popular with the City and the public than any other form'); and once more the chancellor was swayed by Cassel, this time settling on Exchequer bonds. Significantly, in an initiative apparently owing little to the governor, just over half of the new loan was placed in advance in America, in the knowledge that this would attract large quantities of gold to London, at a point when the Bank's reserve was at its lowest for the time of year for seven years. The Treasury's view was that that advance placing should have been stated in the prospectus, but, noted Hamilton, 'the Bank of England are averse to this, and think we can arrange the matter by closing the list as soon as the sum required has been applied for'. The upshot was intense City criticism, with the Bank not only accused of withholding material information but also of angering some key players through its surely reasonable decision to close the lists as soon as it knew that the balance had been subscribed. 'The Bank of England!' privately groaned one leading merchant banker. 'If that old institution is not reorganised on some better basis it will bring us into trouble yet.'

Things proceeded rather more smoothly for the rest of the war, including major tranches of Consols (at last) being issued in April 1901 and April 1902, raising between them over £86 million. Both were thoroughly international operations, involving a New York syndicate headed by Morgans and a London syndicate headed by Rothschilds, with the Bank helping to arrange matters, as well as each time itself taking up several millions.[13] Even so, for those in the City who kept a close eye on such things, it was already clear enough from the circumstances of the earlier loans that the Bank now needed to raise its game.

'The Bank all through gave an extraordinary impression of wealth, quality, permanence,' recalled Janet Hogarth, evoking how 'it was almost unbelievably soothing to sit in a quiet upper room with walls about two feet thick, looking into a soundless inner court, with nothing to do but lay out bank-notes in patterns like Patience cards, learning all about the little marks on them, crossing them up in piles like card-houses, sorting them into numerical order, counting them in sixties and finally entering their numbers in beautiful ledgers made of the very best paper, as if intended to last out the ages'. Yet for her, with a particularly strong sense of the possibilities of life outside Soane's walls, the accumulated weight of the years cut both ways:

> The Bank was full of eighteenth-century, and even earlier, survivals. The dress of its gate porters, the 'nightly watch' going round with Guy Fawkes lanterns (I once asked them, when I met them at 4 o'clock on a summer Saturday afternoon, why they did this and they seemed hardly to know, except that it was an immemorial custom); the company of Guards coming in at sunset, their sentinels stationed in the courtyard; the Bank cats which a parsimonious Governor put down by docking their 'allowance'; the great bars of gold and silver in the fortress-like bullion vaults, brought in from Lothbury under guard through an archway which looked as if it ought to have a portcullis; the almost human gold-weighing machines, which spat out light sovereigns sideways and let the rest fall in a steady stream into copper vessels like coal pans – all the significant evidence of Britain's wealth and British solidity, so picturesque, so historic, so reassuring and, in the long run, so unbearably tedious. I used to wish a bomb would explode and wreck the Bank as the only way to get out of it ...

That was not a perspective shared by de Fraine, unambiguously proud of the Bank's historic traditions. In 1898, having already worked in several offices (including at the Law Courts branch, which had been opened in 1881), he was posted to the Chief Cashier's Office, staying there until 1907 and finding it a pleasingly unhurried contrast to the 'rough and tumble' of the Bill Office, 'where the great thing was to get the cheques *into* the Clearing House, and where there was always a small staff hunting out "differences" which were bound to occur owing to the frantic speed with which we had to make entries'. He also found the functions of the Chief Cashier's Office enjoyably various, with in his case the work involving 'a spell on "The Books"', in other words collating all the figures necessary each week for the Committee of Treasury (meeting on Wednesdays) and the Court of Directors (meeting on Thursdays):

> These Books, showing in detail all the figures of the week's working, became my responsibility in due course. They were so numerous that I had to have a messenger to help me carry them. They were put beside the Governor's chair in the Parlour a few minutes before the time of the meeting, and I had to have them removed immediately afterwards. It was also my job to take in a Book to the Governor, and another to the Deputy Governor, every morning, showing the previous day's transactions. I was on 'The Books' for two years, and thus got to know by name at least a few of the Directors, which didn't fall to the lot of most of the Old Lady's brood.

During these two years, de Fraine introduced in the Bank ('a little behind the times, perhaps') the first graphs, making it easier for the governor of the day to grasp more easily the implications of the returns. 'In time, there were quite a number, and he kept them in a special upright box standing by the side of his chair, which I saw every day.'[14]

Was that pre-1914 governor presiding over something recognisably akin to what later generations would call a 'central bank'? In at least four distinct respects, the answer is surely in the negative:

A public body? For all its many important wider responsibilities, most of the time willingly shouldered, the Bank remained before the First World War a part-public, part-private institution, wholly making its own senior appointments and largely unaccountable to government or Parliament. 'The Bank of England is trying to serve two masters,' persuasively argued the *Financial News* in 1893, shortly before the May scandal broke:

One of these masters is the body of its own shareholders, whose dividends depend upon the amount of discount business done by the Bank, and who do not like to see their prospects injured by the successful competition of the open market; and the other is the vast interest of British credit, represented in the City mind by the amount of gold in the Bank's vaults. The policy of the directors, as exemplified in their latest exploit of reducing the minimum official rate to 3 per cent, is too obviously the policy that animated Mr Facing-both-ways in Bunyon's allegory. They want to get some of the business which now drifts into other channels, and they do not want to encourage withdrawals of bullion by foreign customers. As usual in similar attempts, they have adopted a compromise course which is not at all certain to achieve either of the desired ends …

The paper called in strong terms for the Bank's precise character to be more clearly defined. In practice, however, little was done in that direction over the next twenty years; as for the Bank's daily operations over that period, John Pippenger's detailed analysis has shown that, despite its ultimate and abiding commitment to maintaining convertibility into gold, the necessity of continuing to make profits and thus to pay dividends significantly affected policy. 'Like a normal commercial bank,' he explains, 'the Bank of England reduced reserves and the proportion [of reserves to deposits] as interest rates increased. The tendency to reduce the proportion as interest rates rose and raise it as nominal income increased meant that the Bank followed conflicting policies over the business cycle.'[15]

Attentive to the broader national economy? In reality it seems to have been entirely up to the Bank itself to what extent it prioritised the concerns of the UK economy. Certainly there was little government interference. 'In pre-war days,' recalled Sir Otto Niemeyer (a major figure at both the Treasury and the Bank) in 1929, 'a change in Bank rate was no more regarded as the business of the Treasury than the colour which the Bank painted its front door.' Yet on the part of British industry itself, certainly by the 1900s, a striking critique was starting to emerge. 'That the constant and violent fluctuations in the Bank of England rate of discount are injurious to trade and commerce,' declared in 1907 a motion at the annual meeting of the Association of Chambers of Commerce, carried once the mover had agreed to substitute the more tactful 'frequent' for 'constant and violent'; later that year, the Association pushed for three representatives of the state to be co-opted on to the Bank's Court, in order to judge whether Bank policy was 'conducive to the welfare of the country and the advantage of trade and business'. Of course, the Bank was not wholly oblivious to the domestic implications of Bank rate rises made in order to protect its reserves or to forestall trouble. Indeed, it seems that sometimes, 'out of tenderness for home trade' (to quote R. S. Sayers), the Bank resorted to other, less damaging devices than Bank rate, such as intervention in the gold market, in order to raise rates in the money market. Even so, in the most thorough examination we have of the issue, another historian, Dieter Ziegler, has found relatively little evidence, on either a micro or a macro level, of such 'tenderness' – and, in particular, he stresses the absence of any appetite on the Bank's part to use interest rates in a helpfully counter-cyclical way.[16]

Exercising control over the City? Not helped by its high turnover of governors, and despite Lidderdale's man-of-the-hour moment in 1890, the Bank did not yet exercise over the rest of the City a huge amount of moral suasion, or what would subsequently be known as the governor raising his eyebrows. Indeed, it is probably fair to say that at this stage the widespread perception in the City was that the Bank was run along distinctly backward, old-fashioned lines – a perception hardly encouraging a sense of deference. 'A very bad day,' recorded the working diary in March 1900 of the bill brokers Smith St Aubyn:

> Money absolutely unobtainable. We were obliged to go to the Bank for £115,000. They say that they will charge 5% for advances as they want their loans repaid by the market, & they also refuse to discount short bills. This is a distinct attempt of Gladstone's the Governor to extort usury from the market. In consequence of this individual's action we took 15[m] down to S, P & S [the bank Smith, Payne & Smiths] who discounted them for us at 4%.

'The sooner Gladstone returns to his petroleum tanks the better,' concluded the entry, 'as this is simply another instance of the misuse of public money by *him*.'[17]

Co-operating with other national banks? 'At first sight the Bank was an extraordinarily insular institution,' observes Sayers in his magisterial overview of 'The Bank and its world' between 1890 and 1914. 'Neither Governors nor officials made any visits to other countries on official business, and visitors to the Bank from other countries were ordinarily paying only courtesy visits. Very rarely a "top hat" letter would come in French from the Bank of France, but knowledge of foreign languages was not regarded as a necessary qualification for anyone in the Bank's service.' It was, insists Sayers, an 'illusory' appearance, given that the Bank well knew that nothing so intimately affected its 'guardianship of the gold standard' as 'the current of world events'. Nevertheless, as he fully concedes, there was little if any of the almost continuous dialogue and often co-operation with other national banks that would characterise long stretches of the post-1914 era. The deputy governor may in December 1900 have written to the newly appointed director general of the Bank of Italy, offering 'felicitations' and assuring him that 'nothing shall be wanting' on the Bank of England's part to keep relations with the Bank of Italy 'on as pleasant a footing in the future as they have been in the past', but the actual relationship with this and other national banks was altogether more distant. Occasionally there was an exception – in 1898 the Bank agreed with the Bank of France to help German banks in difficulty and thus ease pressure in the Berlin money market; during the difficulties of 1907, the Bank was grateful for assistance from the Bank of France – but that was all it was. Instead, on a more day-to-day basis, 'the theory was,' reflects Sayers, 'that through the action of the banking system the Bank would sense the tides of world affairs and, in so far as personal knowledge was necessary, the Directors with their varied and widespread business connections could answer any questions the Governor had to ask'.[18]

One should not exaggerate. Notwithstanding all four disclaimers, the fact was that the pre-1914 Bank saw itself – quite rightly – as something very special globally as well as nationally, and not just purely a commercial organisation. A nice reflection of underlying assumptions surfaced in September 1900, as the Boxer Rebellion raged in China and the Bank optimistically envisaged the eventual restoration there of 'peace and quietude'. 'The Bank,' a surprisingly forthcoming director confided in the financial press about that happy eventuality,

'would be appointed the vehicle for the transfusion of Western civilisation into that ancient community, and they would enjoy the honour
of being bankers to two-thirds of the human race. Dividends were a
very interesting and satisfactory point with them; but these national
connections and services greatly added to the value of their proprietary stock.'[19]

No one expressed the seemingly immutable gold standard verities more eloquently than John Maynard Keynes retrospectively
(calling the Bank the conductor of the world's financial orches-
tra) or Winston Churchill at the time. Addressing his Manchester
constituents in April 1908, the newly appointed president of the
Board of Trade evoked a world destined soon to disappear, a world
of broadly open economies in equilibrium with each other, and with
a benign, all-seeing Bank of England at its eternal beating heart:

> In the transactions of States scarcely any money passes. The goods
> which are bought and sold between great powers are not paid for
> in money. They are exchanged one with the other. And if England
> buys from America or Germany more than she has intended to buy,
> having regard to our own productions, instantly there is a cause
> for the shipments of bullion, and bullion is shipped to supply the
> deficiency. Then the Bank rate is put up in order to prevent the
> movements of bullion, and the rise of the Bank rate immediately
> corrects and arrests the very trade which has given rise to the dispar-
> ity. *(Hear, hear.)*
>
> That is the known established theory of international trade,
> and everyone knows, every single business man knows, it works
> delicately, automatically, universally, and instantaneously. It is the
> same now as in January 1906 [the date of the Liberal landslide at
> the general election], and it will be the same as it is in 1908 when the
> year 2000 has dawned upon the world. As long as men trade from
> one nation to another and are grouped in national communities you
> will find the differences of free trading are adjusted almost instan-
> taneously by shipments of bullion corrected by an alteration in the
> Bank rate.

Sadly, it is only very occasionally during this quarter-century or so
before 1914 that the records enable one to see the Bank fully in action,

outlining the circumstances and weighing up the options before it decides to take a particular course of action. Probably the closest we come is through letters that the veteran and highly respected director Benjamin Buck Greene sent to colleagues in the mid-1890s, in the specific context of the Japanese government having deposited at the Bank a huge indemnity payment following its victorious war against China. 'I am curious to see what is to happen to the Japanese Money,' Greene wrote in November 1895 to Mark Collet, fellow-member of the Committee of Treasury as well as of the Court:

> No doubt we shall lose control of the greater part though still with us. If a persistent attempt be made to employ money must go to nowhere – & yet until it leaves the Country somebody must hold it without interest.
>
> The U.S.A. are again shipping gold – & if she continues the same Currency policy she may issue more gold Bands [Bonds?] to share the same fate in due time for which they have to pay interest – but as they can afford it it does not signify to them.
>
> The payment by the Hong Kong & Shanghai Bank of a further 2 Millions made a temporary flutter in the market – but now it looks as if we shall have what is called increased 'ease' again & next month gold will return from the internal Currency.

The following autumn, in September 1896 the day after a Bank rate rise, and too infirm himself to be in the City, Greene was writing from his home near Reading to governor Sandeman:

> If the 5½ Millions of gold we have lost since the 22nd July had been taken away by the Japanese and exported, thereby reducing their deposits by that amount, it would not have signified so much and any movement on our part would have been less necessary. How long it will remain with us or in this Country, we know not, therefore on looking at our position in the event of its withdrawal it seems that the time had come or nearly so to consider the question.
>
>   Our total deposits stood on the 9th Ins^{t} at £57,365^{m}
>   Reserve   "   " 32,380^{m}
>   Proportion   56.9 [per cent]

Take away the Japanese deposit of £12,523^{m} without disturbing any other account we should have £44,842^{m}. Reducing our Reserve by same am^{t} to £19,857^{m}, [we should have] Proportion to 44.1, which I think under Existing Circumstances is about the minimum we should aim at to let it go to without taking action …

As we do not know yet what is to become of it [the Japanese money] we ought to legislate as if it were certain to be exported directly or indirectly at any moment and though perhaps your move yesterday [increasing Bank rate] was not urgent it was at any rate safe while we do not yet know to what amount the present drain may extend & particularly in view of the decline we usually have in our Reserve after about the 22 Sep^{t}. Of course there are other Variations that may crop up and require consideration. The Bank of France has lost Gold since the 19th Augt to the Extent of nearly two Millions Sterling.

I do not think your move will interfere at present with the demand upon you for discounts (though the outside Market may be better) unless you put up your unpublished rates which perhaps would check them.

In answer to your question I do not think at present it would be useful or desirable to take cheap money off the Market, the Bankers are too rich for that having still large balances with us, besides having so much more money in their tills than they used to have …

A coda comes from Sandeman himself, who three months later wrote to the chancellor, Hicks Beach, asking if he would 'obtain for us some precise information as to the intentions of the Japanese Government in connexion with the large amount which they have at the present moment on deposit with us', adding that 'lately the Japanese Government had withdrawn a certain amount in gold for export'. 'It has been done,' noted the governor, 'in a very discreet manner, but, should these withdrawals assume large proportions, and become generally known, they might easily create alarm,' that is, in the money market. The Treasury obliged, but probably only to a degree, to judge by the letter that Sandeman sent soon afterwards, in January 1897, to Hamilton: 'I am much obliged for your suggestions as to means that might be adopted for ascertaining something definite as to the Japanese intentions, from the Legation, but I fear it would not do to reopen the question now, as we have already declined to depart from our "traditions".[20]

If that was presumably a reference to traditional relationships with customers, an even more inviolable tradition remained that of the rotation of governors. Every now and then the notion was floated of a permanent governor, for instance by Hamilton to Lidderdale shortly after the Baring Crisis: 'He said, on the whole "no". It was difficult enough now to get good men to serve as Directors, and if you deprived them of the chance of occupying the *chair*, which to many was a coveted distinction, you would probably get even less good men to enter the Bank.' It is impossible to be certain how fair that was as an estimate of the calibre of the Bank's direction; but through the prosopographical research of Youssef Cassis we can at least make certain generalisations about the nature of the Court between 1890 and 1914. Cassis finds that merchants (as opposed to merchant bankers) still occupied nearly half the positions; that it was still very English and Anglican; that it still had a strongly hereditary element, with Evelyn Hubbard even explicitly stating that he had 'inherited' his directorship from his father; that its political affiliation was almost unflaggingly Conservative or Liberal Unionist; that by some way the most popular club to belong to was the Carlton, followed by the Athenaeum; and that in terms of society as a whole there were some directors enjoying considerable prestige, including the Roehampton set living in substantial residences, but others, for instance the wine merchant Albert Sandeman, who were far from social high-flyers.

There was perhaps no such thing as the 'typical' director, but a certain flavour comes through in *Vanity Fair*'s mid-1890s profile of Henry Cosmo Bonsor, who had been elected to the Court in 1885 and would not depart until 1929:

He is an Eton boy (who played in the football Eleven and rowed in the Boats), a Director of the Bank of England, a County Alderman for Surrey, a Lieutenant for the City of London, a Justice of the Peace and Deputy-Lieutenant for Surrey, and he has sat in the Commons for the North-East, or Wimbledon, Division of Surrey since December 1885 ... Chairman of the South-Eastern Railway and of Watney and Company Limited, and a partner in Combe and Co (brewers), he is perhaps best known as the popular and energetic

Treasurer of Guy's ... He is a man of great daring, even to the extent of brown boots, a billycock hat, and a cheery good-natured person ... With all his business he still finds time to be a sportsman. He is suspected of knowing something about racehorses; he has been seen at Monte Carlo; he can play an occasional rubber; and if the grouse on the Yorkshire moors do not like him they are much appreciated in the wards of Guy's Hospital. Altogether he is a thoroughly good fellow.

He is still a boy: of more than six feet; and though he is a Freemason he is a typical Englishman who disdains white gloves.

An occupational breakdown of the governors themselves – in turn impacting on the composition of the Committee of Treasury – is revealing. Of the dozen governors between 1890 and 1914, all but one or two were from essentially 'mercantile' firms – and seldom possessing any obvious banking expertise. One of the Edwardian governors was said to use his room at the Bank to receive his travellers with their samples; while in October 1902, when the governor was Augustus Prevost of the declining firm of merchants Morris, Prevost & Co and his deputy was Samuel Morley of the warehousemen I & R Morley, one merchant banker, fairly or unfairly, let himself go. 'The Governors are charming fellows,' Herbert Gibbs wrote to his father Lord Aldenham (the former Henry Hucks Gibbs, no longer a director), '& I would leave them in charge of a roast chestnut business with the most absolute confidence, but the same rules do not quite apply to the centre of the Commercial centre of the world.'[21]

All things considered, it was probably fortunate that the Bank by the early twentieth century also had an emerging cadre of high-class functionaries. The exemplar was undoubtedly Gordon Nairne. Born in 1861, and employed first at the Kirkcudbright branch of the National Bank of Scotland, he entered the Bank's service in 1880 on the nomination of Thomson Hankey. He rose rapidly and in 1902 became chief cashier, by this time acknowledged as the senior position to chief accountant. Between then and the war, culminating in his knighthood in June 1914, he was almost certainly year in, year out the single most important figure at the Bank, apart from occasionally the governor or deputy governor, being renowned for his attention to detail, his close supervision of those below him and his severe disciplinary streak. He was not, as Sayers nicely puts it, 'the man to foster an innovation not engaging his sympathies'; and shortly before the war, when the Bank tentatively experimented with recruiting university graduates as permanent staff, it seems to have been Nairne who made sure that this initiative did not get very far, dismayed as he was by careless handwriting not up to the Bank's standard.[22] Put another way, it did not yet pay – and would not for a long time whether in the Bank or in the wider City – to wear one's intelligence on one's sleeve.

The first full year of peace after the Boer War, and of telephones installed in the Bank, featured two notable episodes. May 1903 saw a £30 million loan for the Transvaal, marked by chaotic scenes outside the Bank – queues four deep from the Threadneedle Street doorway to the Bartholomew Lane entrance – on the day it issued the prospectus. The loan was massively oversubscribed, and Lee Goodier, working in the Chief Cashier's Office, would recall that 'my working hours during the ten days the work on this lasted totalled more than 158':

> We began on Thursday, the 7th May, by working from 9 a.m. until midnight, and finished with a day of fourteen hours on Monday, the 18th. Our longest day was on the 12th, a Tuesday when, starting at 9 a.m. we worked until 5.50 on the following morning, 20 hours 50 minutes, beginning the next day's work at 9 a.m. It was decided to finish early on that Wednesday only because of the physical exhaustion of the Staff. We were reduced to kicking each other under the desks to keep each other awake and in the circumstances the risk of serious errors was considered too great.

Some six months later, on 24 November, shots were fired at the future author of *The Wind in the Willows*. Born in 1859, the son of a lawyer, Kenneth Grahame had joined the Bank in 1878, rising to become secretary in 1898, successor but one to Chubb, and remembered by de Fraine as 'popular but distant'. The 1903 drama was described next day by the *Financial Times*:

A respectably dressed man of medium height and ordinary appearance, apparently some thirty years of age, who subsequently gave the name of George Frederick Robinson, entered the Bank and made his way to the Discount Office, where he asked to see Sir Augustus Prevost, the ex-Governor. The man was shown into the Library, where the Secretary, Mr Grahame, inquired as to his business.

Robinson tendered what appeared to be a scroll containing a petition, and asked Mr Grahame to read it, but the latter replied that he had not time. Robinson remarked, 'Oh, then, you will not read my petition!', pulled out a revolver and fired three shots at Mr Grahame, dancing about and attitudinising wildly as he did so. Luckily the Secretary was near the door, and was able to escape, locking the door behind him, leaving his assailant a prisoner.

The police were summoned, and there was something of a dilemma as to the best method of securing so dangerous an intruder, but the ingenious suggestion of one of the clerks to turn the fire hose on him was promptly adopted. On the door being cautiously opened to admit the hose, Robinson fired a fourth shot, again, fortunately, without hitting anybody. A well-directed stream of water, under high pressure, instantly knocked him over, and he was quickly secured and handcuffed, though in the struggle damage was done to the room. The revolver was thrown through a bookcase, and a chair was also smashed in the *mêlée* ...

'Mr Grahame, we are glad to say, suffered no injury at all,' concluded the report. 'He is absolutely at a loss to account for the attack, and it is believed that Robinson was in a demented state and quite unaccountable for his actions, though there is some suggestion that he expressed Anarchist ideas.'

Less than five years later, in June 1908, Grahame would abruptly leave the Bank. His letter of resignation referred to 'constant strain' and a 'deterioration of brain and nerve'; but the Bank's medical officer could find on examination little supporting evidence, and he was accorded a pension of only £400 a year. Why did he decide to go? There is some evidence that he had had a run-in with one of the directors, culminating in the secretary saying to him, 'You're no gentleman'; if so, the director may well have been Walter Cunliffe, a notorious bully. In any case, four months after he left Threadneedle Street, the adventures of Ratty *et al* were revealed to the world, and Grahame joined the literary immortals.[23]

He had already while at the Bank published *The Golden Age* (a childhood memoir, reportedly a favourite book of the Kaiser's), and during the mid-1900s there was seldom any respite from the gold reserves question. In February 1904 the Institute of Bankers heard Alfred Cole, a plain-speaking merchant who had been a Bank director since 1895, tell the assembled company that, in order to increase the country's gold reserves, the banks 'must agree that, instead of calling in their loans temporarily, they must all keep permanently larger balances at the Bank of England'; some two years later, the new Liberal chancellor, H. Asquith, briefly considered setting up a broad-based royal commission to examine the whole issue. 'It is quite true I have spoken to 2 or 3 City men about the gold inquiry,' he told Hamilton. 'In what other way one is to get any independent opinion of any value, I fail to see. The truth is all these people, & not least the Bank directors, are as jealous of one another as a set of old maids in a Cathedral town.' Later in 1906, at a big City dinner that July at the Ritz, the major speech was made by Viscount Goschen, almost half a century after he had joined the Court before becoming a politician. In a classic piece of elder statesmanship, he cogently outlined the options:

> The bankers ought to hold more reserves themselves. The Bank of England ought to hold more gold. *(Hear, hear.)* I see the majority are in favour of making the shareholders of the Bank of England responsible for the increased cost. Well, that is the question. I am not controversial; after dinner I will never be controversial; but I am putting the various alternatives. There is the Bank of England or there are the bankers. Then there is the Government. Perhaps there will be greater unanimity there, because now the representatives of the Bank can join with the representatives of the bankers in saying it is the Government who ought to bear the increased cost. Well, gentlemen, those are difficult questions, but I do think it would be worthy of the City of London – that it would be worthy of this great community who are responsible for the finance of the country – if they could agree to go upon some plan by which, perhaps by mutual sacrifice, by mutual compromise, by wise counsels, they might discover some method by which the present position might be remedied.

'It was significant,' noted the *Financial News* in its report, 'that there was dead silence, in an audience largely composed of bankers, when he spoke of the possible duty of the joint-stock banks in this connection, loud applause when he suggested the Bank of England as an alternative sufferer, and vehement cheers when the Government was mentioned as a last resort.'

As it happened, the events of the next year and a half, including a mini-crisis and a more testing crisis, brought the issue even more to the fore. The mini-crisis was in the autumn of 1906, against a background of feverish speculation in New York and an increasingly worrying drain of gold from London across the herring pond. 'Threadneedle Street has, of course, arrived at the season when the demands upon it from abroad are usually keenest, and naturally a Reserve of under 19 millions makes the market sensitive to every rumour of possible further withdrawals,' observed the *Financial Times* on Friday, 19 October, after Bank rate had been increased from 4 to 5 per cent; later that day, it was put up to 6 per cent, precipitated by a heavy demand for gold from Egypt, following a bumper cotton crop there. Eventually the danger passed, but in January 1907 Schuster's emerging rival as the great joint-stock banker of the day, the combative Edward Holden of London City and Midland Bank, put forward a complicated scheme by which the joint-stock banks would have a gold reserve created for themselves – a scheme that the *Economist* roundly condemned, declaring that the joint-stock banks 'do not scruple to ask that the Bank of England and the public should be fleeced for their benefit, but their profits are to be held sacred'. The bankers themselves were far from united, and soon afterwards the London Joint Stock Bank's Charles Gow expressed himself satisfied with the existing constitutional arrangements: 'The Bank of England is by our system the holder of the only gold reserve in the Country which is of practical use, that is to say, which can be drawn upon in need, and which can be replenished by the action of the exchanges influenced by the Bank rate.'[24]

The real crisis came that autumn, again in the context of American irrational exuberance, with the failure on 22 October of the important Knickerbocker Trust Co the catalyst for near-panic in London, compounded from the 28th by the severe drain of gold from London to the States. Bank rate went up on the 31st from 4½ to 5½ per cent,

but the drain still continued. Then, on Monday, 4 November, the
governor, William Campbell, walked into the Bank, inspected the
figures, and did two things. First, wholly off his own bat, he raised the
rate to 6 per cent, a 'Governor's rise' that much impressed the newest
director, Mark Collet's grandson Montagu Norman. And second, he
sent for Lord ('Natty') Rothschild, head of the London house, and
asked him to secure via Rothschilds in Paris a major tranche of gold
from the Bank of France. With the reserve dipping dangerously below
£20 million, this was duly done by Tuesday. Yet, as large withdrawals
of gold by New York continued, Campbell and his colleagues saw no
alternative on Thursday the 7th but to raise Bank rate to 7 per cent,
its highest level since 1873. Soon afterwards, the American authorities at last got a grip on the situation, through the issuing of Treasury
securities; and over the rest of the year, with the worst of the crisis
over, gold flowed into London. 'Does the raising of the Bank Rate
ever fail to attract gold and change the course of exchanges?' the US
Senate's National Monetary Commission would subsequently ask the
Bank. 'Experience seems to prove,' it reassuringly answered, 'that the
raising of the Bank Rate to a sufficient level never fails to attract Gold,
provided the higher rate is kept effective.' Or as the tag now went in
the money market, '7 per cent brings gold from the moon.'[25]

On the eternal question, and despite the recent alarms, nothing
much happened over the next few years, which included the cautious
governorship of the coffee merchant Reginald Johnston, grandfather
not of a future governor but of a famous cricket commentator. His
successor, from the spring of 1911, was Cole, an altogether larger figure
and determined to resolve the gold-reserve impasse. So it seemed were
the bankers also, and that summer it was as if peace was suddenly
breaking out. 'I am one of those who have always refused to believe
that the interests of the bankers are opposed to those of the Bank of
England,' Cole on 21 July, one of the hottest days of a ferociously hot
spell, told the lord mayor's banquet:

There is no conflict of interests between the banks and the central
institution, and I have hailed with the utmost satisfaction a proposal
that has been made unanimously by the representatives of the
London Clearing Bankers that will bring the Governor of the Bank
into more direct personal relations with the Clearing Banks. The

resolution is that there should be quarterly meetings of the representatives of the London Clearing Banks at the Bank of England …

The timing was propitious, given the fast-moving events just about to happen – events that Cole would subsequently relate to the Court:

On Saturday, the 22nd July, I received a telegram in the country [Cole's out-of-town home being West Woodhay House near Newbury] from the Chief Cashier stating that Sir Edward Holden had sent over to the Bank as he wished to see me on important business. When he heard I was absent he proposed to motor down to call on me. I replied by telegram that I could see him at any time on the following day, Sunday, the 23rd, but my telegram was not in time to reach him on the Saturday. I arranged to see him at the Bank on Monday morning. He then informed me that, in his opinion, the condition of the affairs of the Yorkshire Penny Bank was serious … Sir Edward Holden informed me that he had communicated with the Chairman of the Union of London and Smiths Bank and the National Provincial Bank; also that he had prepared a scheme by which the business of the Yorkshire Penny Bank should be taken over by a group of Bankers, if those Bankers would agree to raise a capital of £2,000,000 sterling so as to ensure the safety of the Yorkshire Penny Bank on a reconstituted basis. He asked me as Governor of the Bank to assist him in raising the Capital.

On the Monday, at a meeting at the Bank attended by Cole, Holden and Schuster among others, 'it was decided to proceed on the lines of Sir Edward Holden's scheme'; and over the rest of the week, Cole and Holden worked 'day and night' to prevent a 'debacle' that would 'lay in ashes the whole of Yorkshire and a great deal of Lancashire', to quote Holden's reports to the chancellor, David Lloyd George. Between them, Cole and Holden succeeded in rescuing the Penny Bank, with the leading joint-stock banks injecting £2 million of working capital and the Bank heading a guarantee fund of £1 million.[26] All in all, it seemed that Holden, Schuster and the others had at last arrived on the stage as acknowledged – not least by the Bank – members of the City elite.

The new spirit of amity lasted only until 1913. That February, shortly before the end of his governorship, Cole for the final time took

the chair of the by now well-established quarterly meeting between
the Bank and the leading joint-stock bankers; and he proceeded, with
supporting statistical evidence, to argue that although the Bank had
done its bit in maintaining a respectable proportion of cash to liabilities, the bankers had not followed its example. The upshot was the
formation of a new Clearing Bankers' Gold Reserves Committee
(CBGRC), to be chaired by Lord Aldwyn, the former Hicks Beach.
It had made little progress by January 1914, at which point Holden in
his annual address to shareholders dropped his bombshell: in essence,
that his bank would henceforth increase the holdings of gold in its
own vaults, independently of the Bank – a move instantly and widely
viewed as an assertion of a larger independence. Schuster meanwhile
continued to plug away at his idea of strengthening the central reserve
through establishing a secondary gold reserve – comprising an agreed
proportion of each bank's liabilities – that was in the Bank's physical
custody. For if, he contended, 'we each of us say we will maintain
sufficient gold reserves of our own, then we assume a responsibility to the community which is not properly ours, and we relieve the
Bank of England from the responsibility which is theirs'. At this
point, critically, Cole's successor, Cunliffe, failed to persuade a wait-
ing-on-events Court to allow him to attend the CBGRC – no doubt
with the directors well aware of his potentially damaging tactless-
ness. In any case, the slighted bankers now came together, and that
summer Schuster, Holden and Herbert Tritton of Barclays laid before
the CBGRC their joint scheme by which the banks would secure
Parliament's assent to their holding 5 per cent of their liabilities in
gold. 'He had had a strong aversion to any legislative requirements
being mooted,' explained Tritton in a short speech that said much.
'But after the action of the Bank of England in refusing to participate
in the discussion and formulation of a scheme, he had concluded that
the line of least resistance was to … leave nothing to the discretion or
goodwill of the Bank of England …'[27]

That was on 22 July 1914, while a largely unconcerned Bank
pursued – like a largely unconcerned City – the daily round. The
overwhelming majority of the Bank's 700 or so officials and clerks in
Threadneedle Street continued to work under either the chief cashier
or the chief accountant: those in the former category including the
ninety in the Private Drawing Office, the fifty in the Bill Office, the

twenty-seven in the Public Drawing Office, the twenty-seven in the Dividend Pay Office, the eighteen in the Securities Office, the fifteen in the Issue Office, the ten in-tellers; those in the latter category including the fifty-seven in the Dividends Office, the forty-five in the Consols Office, the thirty-two in the Bank Note Office, the thirty-one and twenty-eight in the Colonial and Corporation Stock and Bank Stock Offices ... Sometimes the work was heavy, often it was not. A final glimpse of the pre-war Bank comes from the *Financier*'s profile in 1910 of the Stock Transfer Office:

> In each 'pulpit' sit two stern-looking gentlemen, looking uncommonly like schoolmasters watching over a large class. And, in point of fact, that is exactly what they are, for their only business seems to be that the staff are not playing cards, or 'noughts and crosses', or 'blind man's buff', instead of checking and entering the transfers in the books. Time must hang very heavily on their hands during the long hours between 10 and 4! But at 3.55 principals and clerks are alike very busy, for then begin hasty preparations for departure. Here is the program: 3.55, coat-brushing; 3.57, hat-brushing; 3.59, putting on gloves; 4, hats on, and – exeunt omnes.[28]

Two Bank directors and the current governor were among those who in the winter of 1911–12 gave evidence to the Committee of Imperial Defence, conducting an inquiry into the financial and commercial consequences if war broke out between England and Germany. The first director was the energetic Frederick Huth Jackson of the merchant bank Frederick Huth & Co. 'To suspend the export of gold even for twenty-four hours might be to jeopardise our position as the principal bankers of the world,' he insisted; and generally he argued that provided London got through the first few days of war then all would be well, because by raising Bank rate it would be able to call in gold from all quarters of the globe. The other director was Lord Revelstoke, son of the main culprit of 1890 and now head of the resuscitated Barings. Predicting that a declaration of war 'would create such chaos as would result in the ruin of most, if not of all, accepting houses', he declared that 'the only way to remedy such a state of affairs would be a moratorium'. Whereupon this exchange followed:

> And a moratorium not in the realm of the Bank of England, but between private individuals and banks in this country; that is the sort of moratorium you mean, is it not? – No moratorium could affect the Bank of England, of course. The Bank of England really is the source of the whole credit of the British Empire.

The governor was Cole, who like Huth Jackson strongly deprecated any idea of a wartime embargo on the export of gold, given that it was the 'free market for gold' that more than anything had made London 'the international banking centre of the world'; and, after optimistically asserting that 'the City as a whole would escape any great financial disaster' if the worst did happen, he concluded with some reassuring rhetoric about how, in terms of defending the gold standard, 'the adjustment of the discount rate to meet the ever-varying circumstances of each moment' was a mechanism that had 'never failed us in the past' and 'might be relied on in almost any conceivable eventuality, so long as we retained command of the sea'.[29]

In the summer of 1914, it all played out for real. 'The general feeling seems to be that there will not be war on the Continent, but it is by no means certain,' Brien Cokayne, another Bank director and a partner in the merchant bank Antony Gibbs, informed a correspondent on Monday, 27 July, with Serbia having just rejected Austria's ultimatum. But the City as a whole was now starting to get distinctly nervous, compounded by the joint-stock banks – in a way that they would find difficult to defend afterwards – not only in a panicky way calling in loans from discount houses and Stock Exchange firms, but starting to withdraw gold from the Bank in significant quantities. As for the Bank itself during the first half of the week (which included the news on Tuesday afternoon that Austria had formally declared war), it did its best to provide liquidity to the money market, with Natty Rothschild somewhat grudgingly noting on Wednesday the 29th that it had been 'advancing money against gold shipments from New York which is the wisest thing they have done for a long time'. That same day, a Treasury party went to the Bank to meet Cunliffe, Cole and a trio of senior merchant bankers. 'The opinion of the Governor, confirmed by the other Directors present,' noted the Treasury's permanent secretary, Sir John Bradbury, 'was that the Bank of England was in a very strong position, and that any special steps would be unnecessary, and indeed harmful as tending to excite apprehensions.' 'The Bank,' he added, 'had the situation in hand.' And 'opinion was also expressed that it were better that the Governor should not go to visit the Chancellor of the Exchequer lest alarming inferences be drawn'. In short, steady as she goes – or, as another Treasury official, Basil Blackett, put it in his diary, the message from the Bank was that 'all was quite comfortable, though Bank Rate would be put up to 4 p.c. tomorrow by way of precaution'.[30]

And so it was put up, on Thursday, 30 July, the day that in the City's inner parlours serious unease turned into an awareness that there was now an outright financial crisis. That awareness was also starting to spread more widely. 'A very bad day,' recorded the bill brokers Smith St Aubyn. 'People are getting really alarmed and are flocking to the Bank of England to change notes for gold.' They were indeed, with again the joint-stock banks playing a less than helpful (if perhaps understandable) role. 'There is a general run on all the banks,' the general manager of Lloyds, Henry Bell, told the eminent financial journalist Sir George Paish, adding that 'customers are asking for gold, but we are paying out in notes and telling them to go to the Bank of England to change them'. On which news, recorded Paish, 'I hurried round to the Bank of England and there found an immense queue waiting to cash their notes': 'They filled the Issue Department of the Bank and spilled out, four deep, through the courtyard, down Threadneedle Street and half way up Princes Street. Hundreds and hundreds of people waiting as patiently as possible to see if their money was still safe!'[31]

Inside the Bank, it was now largely down to Walter Cunliffe, governor since the previous year, a director since 1895 and founder with his two brothers of the firm of Cunliffe Bros, concentrating mainly on accepting. A large man with a walrus moustache, he was asked once how he knew which bills to approve, to which he replied as a true City man, 'I smell them.' Rude, arrogant and a bully, he was hardly the most popular of men – 'a little of Mr Cunliffe's society fills me up for the year,' a Bank director, E. C. ('Teddy') Grenfell of Morgan Grenfell, remarked in 1908. A small flavour comes through in the curt letter he sent in October 1912 from the Bank, while deputy governor, to someone at Kensington Palace. It reads *in toto*: 'I shall be much obliged if you will kindly return at your convenience, the catalogue of my silver which I sent you in April last.' There was, though, a more positive side, as Grenfell, for all his innate distaste, acknowledged some years after the 1914 crisis. Cunliffe had, he wrote, 'an intimate knowledge of banking, bill broking, Stock Ex, accepting & though not the greatest expert in all, yet he combined the knowledge of these spheres of finance to an unique degree'. Moreover, he also had a 'wonderful physique enabling him to work as few younger men could do'. Against that, 'he had no gift of public speaking, was always at a loss for words, had very bad manners & suspected everyone who differed with him, of having ulterior motives'. And of course, seemingly unable to help himself, 'he was rude & abrupt with his colleagues, the bankers & the ministers'.[32] All in all, the governor may or may not have been the man for the hour, but he was certainly not burdened with self-doubt about being the man of the hour.

The City's worst two days were now at hand. On Friday, 31 July – with Austria mobilising against Russia, the Stock Exchange closed until further notice and the Bank rapidly losing gold to a drain that was both internal and external – Bank rate was doubled from 4 to 8 per cent. 'A most untimely shock to the public's nerves,' would be the verdict of the financial journalist Hartley Withers in his 1915 book *War and Lombard Street*. 'Many, who had never heard of Bank Rate before, became aware that something unprecedented and dire had happened in the world of finance.' Meanwhile, that Friday, 'the courtyard and the Issue Department of the Bank of England presented a remarkable spectacle', in the words of *The Times* reporter, confirmed by the man from the *Financial Times*, who found 'a queue of people, some 200 to 250 strong, resignedly awaiting their turn to obtain access to the magical counter where cash [that is, gold sovereigns] was being poured forth in a steady stream':

There was no visible sign of alarm among the besiegers; rather the matter was treated in the light of a humorous episode … This cheerful demeanour even spread to the usually ultra-sober officials, who were stirred to unprecedented activity, and a quantity of good-natured chaff and banter passed between them and many unsuspecting clients, who, all unconscious of the position, strolled into the Bank with a nonchalant and proprietary air, only to be unceremoniously placed in their legal positions in the queue.

'Gold, gold, gold, gold,
Bright and yellow; hard and cold.'

This was undoubtedly what was wanted, and when a red-cloaked official shouted ironically, 'Silver! Anybody want silver? Plenty of silver going cheap,' a dead silence followed, and on many faces was to be observed a sardonic smile. No, cheap silver was not wanted, and the outflow of the precious yellow metal continued ...

'We were so hard pressed,' recalled one Bank clerk, 'that none of us on the Issue Office Counter got out to lunch; instead we had to be content with sandwiches and whiskies and sodas sent down from the Club.'

That afternoon, unbeknown to most, Cunliffe went to the Treasury to see Lloyd George and his senior officials. 'Very angry,' noted Blackett, 'with the Joint Stock Banks for acting against & not with the Bank of England'; and, accusing the bankers of having 'caused the panic', he called on the chancellor not just to suspend the Bank Charter Act, but if necessary to suspend cash payments and to introduce a moratorium. The Treasury demurred about the double suspension, and it was agreed to see how much gold the Bank – its reserve down to £17 million – lost next day, with £5 million as the tipping point for at least suspending the Act. As to larger questions of British foreign policy, Cunliffe made it very clear where the Bank and the City stood. 'The Governor of the Bank of England,' noted Lloyd George's confidant Lord Riddell in his diary that day, 'said to me with tears in his eyes, "Keep us out of it. We shall all be ruined if we are dragged in!"'[33]

Saturday, 1 August featured, amid much else, the money market more than ever on the rack; the clearing banks still more or less refusing to pay out sovereigns; an even longer queue than the previous day's straggling from inside the Bank into its courtyard; Cunliffe returning to the Treasury, warning that the Bank's reserve was likely to be down by the end of the day to £11 million, and taking away with him a 'chancellor's letter' permitting suspension, if need be, of the Act; Bank rate being hiked by a further two points up to the traditional 'crisis rate' of 10 per cent; and the governor at last managing to get the joint-stock banks to agree to stop calling in loans from the discount houses. Cunliffe – what one might call good Cunliffe – was in his element, nicely caught in Blackett's description of an informal moment at the Treasury as they waited for the letter to be finalised:

> The Governor, who was as cool as ever, was chatting about Bank matters & mentioned the Officer commanding the Guard. I asked if that was the Bank Guard & he said yes. Bradbury [the Treasury's Sir John Bradbury] remarked that he would not need a Guard in a few days [a reference to the Bank's rapidly vanishing gold reserve] & the Governor's smile was a delight in tune with the funniness of the joke. While talking with me, he remarked, with a twinkle, that he had had the misfortune to run out of £5 notes this morning. His manner was a rare contrast to the frantic excitement of two members of the Cabinet whom I met just after.
>
> The letter secured, the Governor returned to the Bank, leaving me to telephone to Nairn[e] that 'the Governor has just started back with all he wanted'. This was the nearest he came all day to telling a soul (except the Deputy Govr) [R. L. Newman, known in the Bank as 'the port-wine man' because of his firm's merchanting speciality] that he had got the fateful letter.

It was left to a youngish director, though, to record the great cardinal fact of the day. 'Germany *v.* Russia,' noted Montagu Norman flatly but meaningfully in his sparsely filled diary.

That Saturday marked the end of what Richard Roberts in his authoritative account of the 1914 financial crisis calls the 'breakdown' phase. How had the Bank performed? Arguably its Bank rate policy was, by the end of the week anyway, counter-productive, with the youthful John Maynard Keynes arguing in his retrospective a month or so later that in the 'special circumstances' a 10 per cent rate was the worst of both worlds, not only failing to attract gold from abroad but also severely undermining confidence. Where the Bank did well, earning praise from both contemporary commentators and subsequent historians, was in its provision of liquidity to the discount houses and thus in turn to the banks: over the fortnight from 20 July, computes Roberts, its combined discounts and advances rose almost fourfold, from £12 million to £44.8 million. 'Following the splendidly cool policy it has adopted throughout the crisis,' noted the *Financial Times*'s money market report for 31 July, 'the Bank of England was a free lender.' Or in Roberts's summarising words, 'despite deteriorating relations with the major banks, the Bank of England went on liberally providing liquidity to the market and relieving the situation'.[34]

Sunday, 2 August was, from the Bank's point of view, an uneventful day – albeit with no sighting of the governor relaxing at London Zoo – before early on Monday the 3rd, fortuitously enough a bank holiday, about 150 of the City's leading bankers and merchants gathered in the Court Room, with Cunliffe presiding. The meeting had its moments of drama – Bell of Lloyds at one point shaking his fist at the governor – but there was general agreement (though with Cunliffe himself dubious) that the banks needed to be closed for a further three days in order to enable adequate measures to be taken. The request was passed on to Lloyd George, who agreed, while arrangements were also made to implement a moratorium on bills of exchange, thereby providing immediate relief to the merchant banks. Those things settled, the major financial debate of the day was about the Bank's wish (backed by the banks) to be able to suspend cash payments – that is to say, the convertibility of notes into gold – as well as the 1844 Act. This was the cue for a decisive intervention by the thirty-one-year-old Keynes, by now ensconced at the Treasury. 'It is difficult to see how such an extreme and disastrous measure,' he wrote to Lloyd George, 'can be justified,' given how much it would 'damage our prestige as a free gold market'. All this, however, was overshadowed by the diplomatic situation. That afternoon, against a background of the German ultimatum to Belgium and its rejection, the foreign secretary, Lord Grey, made his historic statement in the Commons that in effect committed Britain to military action. Writing to a former Morgans partner, Grenfell commented that 'war seems to be an absolute certainty'.[35]

Keynes apparently swayed Lloyd George, who during the late afternoon and early evening of Tuesday, 4 August attended the first session of the Treasury's protracted 'War Conference' while the banks were shut. Also present were other key politicians and what the minutes described as 'representative bankers and traders', including Cunliffe, Newman and Cole from the Bank. The governor was involved in two characteristic exchanges, the first concerning Bank rate. It was due to be lowered on Friday to 6 per cent, but on Holden's insistence it was agreed to reduce it to 5. Might 'one or two banks attempt to exploit this?' wondered the chancellor (with the joint-stock bankers out of the room). 'Lame ducks, in other words,' observed the unforgiving Revelstoke. To which Cunliffe roundly responded: 'If there are lame ducks it does not matter to us. We have to help them over the stile. We cannot afford to let one bank go – not the smallest in the country.' The other exchange, perhaps involving the governor in a degree of economy with the *actualité*, was with an unnamed colleague of Holden's:

> *A Banker:* I understand one of the difficulties today is that the Bank of England cannot help us because they are afraid of a run on the gold supply. It is really a question for the Governor of the Bank of England whether he wants people to come and ask for specie and not get it.
>
> *The Governor:* It is not true that if the Bank is open today I could not pay my way in gold.
>
> *A Banker:* I am very glad to hear it.
>
> *The Governor:* And if you could see the accounts of the Bank which the Chancellor of the Exchequer has seen, you would be surprised that there is so much fuss.

The Bank, in other words, had suddenly changed tack; and of course Cunliffe's desire not to suspend cash payments, if it could possibly be helped, was sincere and deep rooted. But at the same time, the question of abandoning the gold standard had become the new symbol of a long-running power struggle between the Bank and the bankers. Fortified by the support of Lloyd George and the Treasury, the governor was not someone – at this of all times – to underplay his hand.

Later that evening, the British ultimatum to Germany expired. For the Bank as for the City, the guns of August meant that life would never be quite the same again. Back in January 1912, soon after Norman Angell's highly influential treatise *The Great Illusion* had gone into its sixth edition, a crowded Institute of Bankers had heard a paper from its author on 'The Influence of Banking on International Relations'. At its core was the thesis that finance and commerce were now so inextricably entwined, crossing all national boundaries, that the price of war between nation states must be so high as to make the prospect inconceivable. 'It is very evident that Mr Norman Angell has carried this meeting almost entirely with him,' observed one speaker during the discussion. But at the very end Huth Jackson, president of the Institute as well as a director of the Bank, sounded a note of caution:

'It is all very well to get the bankers on your side, but that is not sufficient. What you have to do is to get the whole body of all the peoples
in the world on your side.' And he concluded: 'But, gentlemen, bear in
mind one thing, and that is that until you get that thing done, there is,
I am afraid, little prospect of any change in the international position –
that is to say, war will still remain a possibility.'[36] Two and a half years
later, events proved him horribly right: surrounded by frightened
monarchies and restless masses, by the unreason of nationalism, not
even the safest, most secure institution in the world was invulnerable.

PART THREE

1914–1946

The Kipling Man

'As I was passing the Bank of England, I met Hendy and a friend of his and they were just going to be shown over the Bank, so asked me to go with them,' recorded a young Australian on the last Friday of August 1914:

We went into the weighing room, where every sovereign that has been in circulation is put through a machine & weighed, – the light coins dropping one side and the right weights on the other. These machines each weigh 60 coins per minute and all day there are over 100 machines working. Sovereigns & ½ sov⁵ are scattered all over the floor and the men walk over them just as if they were dirt. We were shown a small scuttle-full of sovs and were told that we could have them if we could take them away, but one can hardly lift them, – they're so heavy.

Next we visited the store-room where all the notes & gold are stored, the gold all being in canvas bags, each bag containing £1,000 sovs, & they are all stacked so that the money can be counted at a glance. The notes are all tied in small bundles of about 500 to 1000 notes in each. We saw the richest spot on the earth viz a little safe about 2 ft 6 in square where the £1,000 notes are kept, and were given two bundles of these, each bundle containing 500 notes, so that for ½ a minute of my life, I have been a millionaire.

After this novel experience we were very lucky and got special permission to go to the bullion room. Here, all the gold bars each weighing about 80 lbs odd & worth £1700 are stored when they arrive. They are pure gold (24 carat) and although very small are exceedingly heavy. It is only a very small room with thick walls and the bars are packed on trollies. The amount of gold bar at present there was worth over £4,000,000. I never expect to see so much money in such a small space again.

It all seemed timeless and reassuring, but of course in the world outside the war was almost a month old. And indeed, ten days before the diarist's visit, the secretary had posted on 18 August a telling notice with regard to the Bank Picquet: 'The Military Authorities think it necessary that, in place of the countersign now prevailing in the Bank, namely, two stamps with the foot, in future there should be a different password each night.'[1]

In that outside world, the great financial crisis of 1914 continued to be played out during the days and weeks after the declaration on war on 4 August. The key immediate development was Lloyd George's decision to issue Treasury currency notes for £1 and 10 shillings – a decision that, in the words of Richard Roberts, not only 'rendered redundant the need for the suspension of the Bank Act', but 'by staunching a possible internal gold drain, clinched the case for the retention of specie convertibility'. Why Treasury as opposed to Bank notes? Ultimately there was no alternative, given that the Bank's Printing Department was already working flat out producing enough £5 notes for the reopening of the banks on Friday the 7th; but inevitably the Bank regretted the development, with the Court soon afterwards expressing its view that the Treasury's note issue should in the fullness of time be issued by the Bank. The other significant initiative during those febrile early days of war, as the summit conference at the Treasury continued on Wednesday the 5th and Thursday the 6th, was the decision to broaden Sunday's moratorium on bills of exchange into a more general one-month moratorium (eventually extended to three months), in effect offering protection to the commercial world against banks calling in loans. For their part, the concern of the banks was that major account holders might transfer deposits to the Bank; but Cunliffe reassured them, saying that he had rejected a £100,000 account because 'I thought it was not cricket.'[2]

In due course the 'Containment' phase of the financial crisis moved into the 'Revival' phase, culminating in the reopening of the Stock Exchange in January 1915. Perhaps nothing was more important than the measures – in which the Bank was intimately involved in the planning stages, especially through the person of the former governor Alfred Cole – to restore to life the discount market and to save the accepting houses (that is, the merchant banks). The details were complicated, but the crux in relation to the former was the Bank's willingness, under government guarantee against loss, to abandon its traditional practice of buying only the 'finest' commercial bills. Instead, as the veteran financial commentator W. R. Lawson put it soon afterwards, 'practically the Bank lowered its standard from first-class to second, and even third-class bills'. As for the latter aspect, rescuing those accepting houses not in a position to pay once bills matured, the Bank was prepared to lend at 2 per cent above Bank rate, with the helpful promise that it would not seek repayment until a year after the war ended. The Bank during these early months also advanced substantial sums to government – some £83 million by the end of the year – as well as naturally playing a significant role in the first War Loan, issued in mid-November for £350 million at 3½ per cent. Cunliffe, overridden by the Treasury, would have preferred a more generous coupon; and he was proved right, as the issue flopped, despite fulsome political and journalistic propaganda about its high take-up. The reasons for the fiasco, amounting to a £113 million short-fall, have been closely analysed by Jeremy Wormell, who among other factors identifies errors in timing and structuring as well as pricing. In any case, Cunliffe at this point took the big view and acted decisively: with the Bank having already at the outset subscribed for £40 million, he now covertly came in for the remaining £113 million – typically without troubling to consult his colleagues.[3]

Indeed, the governor in wartime seems to have been on his own turf even more bullying in manner than in peacetime, to judge by the letter that a leading banker, Robert Martin Holland of Martins, sent to him as early as 19 August. Martin Holland that morning had gone to the Bank to consult Nairne about the terms of a forthcoming issue of Treasury bills. 'He referred it to you,' wrote the banker, 'and you requested me to come and see you, and then proceeded in the presence of Sir Gordon Nairne to address me in a way that would have been unjustifiable if between a master and his servant.' Subsequent correspondence revealed that Cunliffe had believed that Martin Holland was seeking to induce him 'to enter into some ring of the Bankers to force the price of Treasury Bills against the Government'. But for the government itself, and the chancellor in particular, Cunliffe during these early stages of the war was their indispensable go-to man in the City, especially valued for his ability to bang together the heads of the squabbling bankers. 'His sense of humour, which he concealed under a dour almost surly countenance, was an encouragement in those trying days,' affectionately recalled Lloyd George:

He was fond of little practical jokes to lighten the dismal anxieties of our common burden. He affected a deep resentment at our issuing the £1 notes as Treasury and not Bank of England Notes. He scoffed at the inferiority of our issue in the quality of its paper and its artistry as compared with the crisp £5 note of the Great Bank over which he presided. I can see his impressive figure with its rolling gait, coming one morning through the door of the Treasury Board Room. He had a scornful look on his face. He came up to my desk with a mumbled greeting, solemnly opened the portfolio he always carried, and pulled out a bedraggled £1 Treasury Note, dirty and barely legible. He said: 'Look at that. It came into the Bank yesterday in that condition. I told you the paper was no good – far better to have left it to us.' He had scrubbed the note in order to reduce it to this condition of defacement for the pleasure of ragging me. I told him so and he laughed. His manner was not propitiatory to strangers, but when you got to know him he was a genial, kindly man, and I liked him. I relied on his shrewdness, his common sense and instinct.

'The best way to avoid a panic is to meet the situation like lions,' Cunliffe himself had assured the Treasury's Bradbury on the first day of hostilities, and some three months later he received an honour that few of his predecessors had known, let alone while still in office. 'I like the Governor – a regular John Bull of the farmer type, but wonderfully shrewd & level-headed,' Asquith at No 10 confided to an intimate in early November following a meeting about the imminent issue of the War Loan. 'When the others had gone, I told him (he is called Cunliffe) that the King had agreed to give him a peerage, and that I proposed to announce it at the Guildhall on Monday. He was not the least *émotionné* & simply said – "Well, I obey orders".'[4]

The war was not on the whole a happy or comfortable time at the Bank. A nagging worry throughout was the retention of adequate numbers of qualified men. In October 1914 permission was given to staff to join the National Volunteer Reserve, but only 'on condition that they are not required to sign any enrolment form which will render them liable to be called up for service by the Military Authorities without the Bank's consent having first been obtained'; and the following May a governor's order stated that 'so many Members of the Staff have gallantly volunteered that, with the increased National duties which the Bank have had to undertake, it is quite impossible to spare any more'. Volunteering gave way of course to conscription, and as the war dragged on more and more pensioners returned, more and more temporary appointments were made – and more and more women were recruited, with their numbers rising to well over a thousand as the men went to the Front. Before the war there had been complete physical segregation of the sexes, but now just a wood-and-glass screen kept them apart; and Cunliffe was so disconcerted by some of the colourful dresses he encountered that a new rule confined permissible colours to navy, black and very dark grey. More generally, the wartime spirit seems by 1918 to have been flagging quite badly. In April a notice inveighed against the 'disgraceful practice' of 'thefts of Toilet paper and Soap in certain of the lavatories'; in October another notice urged economy in the use of electric lights ('At irregular intervals all lights will be switched off-and-on twice, in rapid succession, as a reminder that any lights burning unnecessarily must be extinguished'); and between times, that summer, a 'Committee of Delegates' not only laid before the governor its specific complaints about pay failing to keep up with wartime inflation, but warned that the larger mood in the Bank was one of 'a great unrest'. It is clear enough that the failure was one of an inadequate human touch. 'All through these dark years there was a grim silence on the part of the authorities,' recalled Wilfred Bryant, a senior clerk, soon after the end of hostilities. 'I shall always regret the fact that on the anniversaries of the opening of the War, when we met and sang together *en masse* the National Anthem in the Lothbury Courtyard, no words from official

lips were ever uttered of sympathy, appreciation, and encouragement
... But, alas! the authorities seem to have looked upon us as mere
machines.' And he went on: 'We always lived from hand to mouth.
Our domestic interests at home were never thought of. Sunday duty
was often not officially announced till the last thing on Saturday night
... Such pin-pricks pierced into our very marrows.'⁵

At a more *haute finance* level, there were for the Bank perhaps two
overarching wartime facts. The first, amid the comprehensive breakdown of the international gold standard, was that although sterling
continued in principle to be convertible, in practice the gold standard
was more or less suspended, not least because of intensely difficult
shipping conditions. The other cardinal fact was the shifting balance of
power between Bank and Treasury. 'I remember Lord Cunliffe saying
to me during the first few days of the war that while the war lasted the
Bank would have to regard itself as a department of the Treasury,' was
Bradbury's recollection; and in all sorts of ways – including approval
of new issues, the power to requisition securities, and Treasury bills
effectively replacing Bank rate as the arbiter of short-term interest rates
– it proved an accurate prediction of the westerly drift. So too with
war loans, where the Bank had some success (notably with the huge
£2,000 million 5 per cent loan of January 1917) in skilfully preparing the market but was generally overshadowed by the Treasury; to
a significant degree that was even the case in the almost continuously
problematic area of the dollar exchange – absolutely vital to the war
effort, given that (in Victor Morgan's subsequent words) 'upon the
maintenance of an adequate supply of dollars at a reasonable price
depended the whole vast purchasing programme of food, materials
and munitions for ourselves and our Allies'. All that said, the Bank
did have one unique if highly secret contribution to make. So secret
indeed that Cunliffe's successor, Brien Cokayne, did not even know of
its existence until shortly after becoming governor, despite three years
as deputy governor. His informant was Admiral Sir Robert Hall, in
charge of Naval Intelligence, who told him (recorded Cokayne) that
'for a long time past' the Bank's Printing Department had been undertaking '*very* secret & important work for the Admiralty'. Hall declined
to disclose the exact nature of the work, but the new governor agreed
that it should continue, 'from the stand point of the Nation & the
Bank'. Some four decades later, Herbert de Fraine, who had become

principal of the Department three years before the war, spilled the beans: in essence, the work was the printing of forgeries of German documents, done under high-security conditions and delivered by taxi each Sunday morning to Hall himself. 'In due course,' noted de Fraine, 'he told us gratifying news of the success of our product – which, however, had needed a little attention at other hands to make it less "fresh from the printer."'[6]

For Cunliffe personally, wartime was good so long as his close ally stayed at 11 Downing Street. In February 1915 they enjoyed a harmonious week together in Paris, at a major conference on Allied finance. 'When a question arose as to a transhipment of gold the Governor of the Bank of France expressed himself with great fluency,' recalled Lloyd George. 'I then said: "The Governor of the Bank of England will state the British view on the subject". [Cunliffe] rose slowly, and after a few preliminary puffs he said: "We do not mean to part with our gold", and then subsided into his seat.' The chancellor would also remember the governor's reluctance to accompany him on a visit to Béthune, under occasional bombardment: 'He said: "A predecessor of mine was killed visiting the trenches at Namur. But he was there on business with the King, and the City said, 'Poor fellow!' but if I were hit in the stomach at Béthune they would all say, 'D—d fool – what business has he to go there?'"' The great blow to Cunliffe was the government reshuffle in May 1915, causing Lloyd George one morning to be interrupted in his shaving by his maid, who told him that the governor was downstairs wanting to see him. 'I went down. The old boy blundered out, "I hear they want you to leave the Treasury. We cannot let you go!" and then he quite broke down, and the tears trickled down his cheeks.' To Asquith soon afterwards, Cunliffe was equally – and unavailingly – beseeching. 'I couldn't,' related the prime minister, 'get anything out of him, except "We don't want to lose our man! Don't take our man away from us!"'

The new chancellor was Reginald McKenna, very sure of his own abilities, unwilling to accept advice and soon at loggerheads with the governor. Against a background of Cunliffe threatening to resign, Asquith tried during the summer to mediate, telling McKenna that Cunliffe had 'rendered us invaluable service during the past year' and that, for all his 'limitations of outlook and faults of temper', his 'deliberate judgement' was 'always well worth taking into account' and that he was 'perfectly straight'. The governor stayed in post, but the relationship was permanently damaged. McKenna, according to the retrospective account of Lord Beaverbrook, would 'frequently urge upon Cunliffe the necessity of providing more bank balances for the government in the United States'; to which Cunliffe 'would reply invariably, "Mr Chancellor, this is a matter of exchange, and the responsibility here lies with me."' Indeed, that autumn, the governor secured a significant victory when he successfully insisted that the newly formed London Exchange Committee – a consortium of bankers charged with securing as favourable an exchange as possible and empowered to take under its control all available gold as well as foreign currency – not only have himself as chairman but be run out of the Bank. The governor by this time had a new deputy, Cokayne, unexciting but appreciably more efficient than his port-wine predecessor; while Cokayne in turn employed from January 1916 one of the Bank's directors for day-to-day 'devilling', a director who had just made a clean break from his own firm. 'There goes that queer-looking fish with the ginger beard again,' Cunliffe was soon heard to say, loudly, on passing Montagu Norman in a corridor. 'Do you know who he is? I keep seeing him creeping about this place like a lost soul with nothing better to do.'

It was Norman who, that spring, made a particular friend of Benjamin Strong, governor of the recently established Federal Reserve Bank of New York, visiting London with a view to establishing closer Anglo-American financial relations. Strong's diary of his trip recorded his first meeting with Norman's chief: 'Lord Cunliffe impressed me most favourably, relishes a joke, and likes to make one. He joshed me when I came in and ... wanted to know why I had not let him know in advance of my coming over.' The American then explained his scheme for more intimate co-operation in exchange matters; and he was careful to show – even though the war was seeing New York increasingly supplant London as the world's leading international financial centre – that he was well aware of the appropriate pecking order:

We [at the Fed] realize, however, the extent to which present conditions imposed responsibilities on the Bank of England, and that they were, so to speak, headquarters, and that our plans should naturally be shaped with due regard to the local conditions here, in which the Bank of England control, not only as a matter of comity but in order that our transactions might be more effective in the future through being conducted harmoniously with headquarters.

Cunliffe in response made reasonably positive noises, leaving Strong to reflect that 'on the whole, I am most favourably impressed with his attitude, which was most friendly'. So the governor was also when Strong called again shortly before heading home, with the Englishman himself just back from a trip to Paris. 'He admitted that the Bank of England was a museum, but that after all they could change when necessity required whereas the Banque de France was much more a museum than the Bank of England and apparently did not have the capacity or courage to change.' In practical terms, the eventual upshot was an agreement between the Bank and the Fed that embraced the opening of reciprocal accounts, the reciprocal buying of commercial bills, and the earmarking and shipment of gold – altogether a signal moment, owing much to Strong's personal initiative, in the still barely nascent story of central banking co-operation.[7]

The rest of 1916 saw general relations between Bank and Treasury increasingly tense – 'tho' knowing jeopardy threatens us in N.Y. one might as well talk to an airball as to them,' reflected in June a disenchanted Norman – just as the Cunliffe/McKenna relationship plumbed new depths, with the governor writing to Asquith in August to accuse the chancellor of having attempted to carry out policies which would 'have seriously endangered the credit of the Country'. Cunliffe claimed to have the Committee of Treasury's backing over this charge, but in truth several of his senior colleagues by this time were finding his governorship (so far renewed each year because of the war) increasingly trying. That autumn a coup was talked about, but failed to come off. 'I feel we owe him a debt of gratitude for sticking to the job, and for the ability he has shown, in his arduous duties,' the former governor Middleton Campbell wrote on 20 October to Cokayne, even though 'he is not the man he was', being 'irritable, & does not like any one differing with him'; while 'of course', added Campbell, 'we all regret the departure of the old Custom, of telling every thing to the Treasury Committee, but this has arisen through extra-ordinary Circumstances'. The immediate outcome was related by Norman four days later in a diary entry pregnant with meaning:

Most of Treas Com having agreed to G. [governor Cunliffe] for another year: he sh^d make a point of regular full disclosure of Bk affairs & of his advice qua Gov. This is due to them as Treas Com (by long custom) & essential now to begin preparation of *united* front, as Enquiry after war is certain – & it will be engineered with main object of substituting State Bank. Such a Bank seems to be in minds of C [chancellor McKenna] & whole Treasury as well as grumblers in City & busy bodies in Parl'ment.

Cunliffe for his part continued to insist over the next few weeks that he would continue only on an unconditional basis, and a state of almost open warfare existed between him and his predecessor Cole, but eventually Norman managed to thrash out with the governor some sort of concordat. Reluctantly, Cunliffe agreed that henceforth a female shorthand writer would attend Committee of Treasury meetings and provide a full précis; that those meetings would be more frequent; that all current business would be considered; that there would be a 'gradual bringing in of younger directors' into the Committee; and that in due course there would 'perhaps' be, on the Court as a whole, 'new directors drawn from Bankers &c'. Norman also recorded how the peacemaker's reward came on 22 November: 'T. Com ... Hatchet formally buried by G [Cunliffe] & ACC [Cole]'.

Soon afterwards, as Lloyd George succeeded Asquith at the head of the wartime coalition, the Conservative leader Andrew Bonar Law replaced McKenna at No 11. 'Friction between Bank & Treasury has wonderfully lessened since Bonar Law became C,' noted Norman in January 1917.[8] Yet some six months later there unfolded an extraordinary episode of high-level rancour – unique in Bank/Treasury annals.[9]

Beginning as a fierce campaign by Cunliffe against what he saw as unwarranted interference in questions of exchange, especially by the Treasury's Sir Robert Chalmers and John Maynard Keynes, it took the form by early July – at a critical stage of the war – of a near-mad attempt to block the government's access to the Bank's gold that was being stored for safekeeping in Canada. The governor acted entirely off his own bat; Bonar Law was incandescent, telling Lloyd George that Cunliffe's telegram to the Canadian government had been 'an act of extraordinary disrespect towards the British Government and a direct insult to me'. At which point the governor's erstwhile ally summoned him to No 10, severely reprimanded him and threatened (according to Cunliffe's report next day to the Committee of Treasury) to 'take over the Bank'. The issue then became – in a correspondence-generating impasse that lasted virtually a month – the nature of Cunliffe's written apology to the chancellor, with Cokayne gamely seeking to mediate between two stubborn men. The governor spent most of that time on a fishing holiday in Scotland; but Cokayne frankly warned him that unless he pocketed his pride and offered to resign, then 'the position will become absolutely intolerable and there is bound to be a sort of public scandal'. Yet for the governor such an offer was tantamount to conceding that 'I simply become a Government Official under [the chancellor's] orders'; and in the eventual letter (drafted for him by Cokayne and grudgingly accepted by Bonar Law) that did at last get sent in mid-August, making an 'unreserved apology for anything I have done to offend you', the offer of resignation was conspicuous by its absence. Soon afterwards, he was back in London – 'looking very blooming', according to Gaspard Farrer of Barings, and promising 'to be good'.

Cunliffe's days as governor, however, were numbered. 'No longer sane – if ever he was,' was the blunt verdict in September of one director, Cecil Lubbock, as his behaviour became increasingly erratic and his bullying increasingly rebarbative. Finally, on 8 November, the Court elected Cokayne and Norman as governor and deputy governor respectively from the following spring. It was a decision that Cunliffe found impossible to accept, mounting a vain campaign over the rest of 1917 to persuade bankers, press and senior figures at the Treasury to try to get Bonar Law to apply pressure on the Court to reverse its vote – a campaign that involved systematic vilification of Norman and others at the Bank. Norman himself recorded Cunliffe's graceless endgame during the early months of 1918. In February a 'clear case of megalomania', following a 'violent display' at the Committee of Treasury, 'behaving like a spoilt child'; and next month, at a meeting of the General Court, reading 'a longish speech – of wh D Gov & Directors knew nothing – i. eulogising the Bankers. ii. bum-sucking the Press,' thereby creating a 'very hot' feeling, with 'even' Cokayne 'much disgusted with such an unfriendly finale'. Norman's damning account chimed entirely with the verdict of his fellow-director Teddy Grenfell, who was also at the meeting and confessed to being 'reluctantly compelled to agree that able & strong as Lord C is, yet he is selfish, disloyal to colleagues & the Bank'. Or in short: 'He has a bad yellow streak & is in no sense a white man.'[10]

Naturally, the gorier details of the latter stages of Cunliffe's governorship were kept wholly out of public view. Even so, as Norman's diary entry of October 1916 had already eloquently suggested with its talk of people wanting instead 'a State Bank', a notion almost inconceivable before the war, the Bank by this time was an institution feeling itself somewhat under siege. 'The Bank of England should take stock of its own position,' forcibly argued the *Economist* in September 1917, 'widening as far as it can the sweep of the net with which it gathers new members into its Court, and modifying the system which puts autocratic power into the hands of the Governor for the time being.' The following month an internal committee, under Lord Revelstoke's chairmanship, was set up to consider 'the Direction and general working of the Bank'.

Top of its agenda was the thorny question of whether joint-stock bankers should at last be allowed on the Court, with the submissions that autumn from existing directors showing opinion divided. 'It would create jealousies,' declared Campbell, while deputy governor Cokayne was adamant that 'so long as none of the banks are directly represented on our Court, our advice (e.g. to the Treasury) on matters concerning their interests will carry greater weight'. On the other side of the argument, Frank Tiarks of the merchant bank Schröders, a director only since 1912, claimed not implausibly that 'the Directors of the Bank have great responsibility and yet the majority know little or nothing of many important matters', so that accordingly 'I have no objection to the Directors of other Banks being elected.' The Committee itself was split, with the decisive intervention probably coming from another merchant banker, Sir Robert Kindersley of Lazards – tall and determined-looking with bushy black eyebrows, and eventually recalled in his *Times* obituary as 'a man with whom it would be safe to go tiger shooting'. The joint-stock banks, he insisted, 'had too much power already'; and 'it was his opinion that a man with such responsibility would naturally consider first the needs of his own Bank and that it would be impossible for him to give a fair and unbiassed opinion on the situation as a whole'. Revelstoke's Committee duly decided against recommending a break with the Bank's traditional principle of debarring clearing bankers, let alone recommending industrialists; but it did successfully suggest that the Committee of Treasury become more youthful in composition and be elected annually by free and secret ballot. The problem was that the right candidates were not always elected. 'The inclusion of WMC [Campbell] than whom no one has been less useful, or more prejudiced or is more out of touch, shows how little value can be put on our plan for free ballot,' noted Norman in March 1918, as the Cunliffe era of almost unopposed autocracy seemingly passed into history. And in April: 'Election to T. Com of LHH [Colonel Lionel Henry Hanbury] … is an admission of seniority as agst brains! LHH admits as much & did not desire election. It shows that Democracy, ie a free ballot by Court, is not bold enough to supply best men …' Democracy and the Bank would continue to be a work in progress.

The other significant aspect to the Revelstoke Report was the recommendation of creating a post at the Bank somewhat comparable to that of the general manager at the big joint-stock banks, in effect as the main institutional link between the staff and the governors; and in May 1918, shortly after Cokayne succeeded Cunliffe, this was implemented, as the highly capable Nairne (chief cashier since 1902) took up the new position of comptroller, in order 'to manage the internal affairs of the Bank and to co-ordinate the two sides [Cash and Stock] and generally to assist the Governors'. Cokayne himself had his first major moment as governor that September, as the chancellor tried to persuade him to lower the Bank rate – again, something virtually unimaginable before 1914. Cokayne refused, informing Bonar Law that he felt 'strongly' that 'it will be impossible to preserve our international credit unless we have comparatively dear money after the War and that the more we artificially cheapen it now, the more difficult it will be to revert to normal conditions'.[11]

Also looking ahead was the government-appointed Committee on the Currency and Foreign Exchanges after the War, meeting regularly from February 1918 under the chairmanship of Cunliffe (who as was customary would remain a Bank director after stepping down as governor) and mainly comprising bankers. Although the Federation of British Industries (forerunner of the CBI) argued in its submission that the key post-war priority should be the achievement of a favourable trade balance, its views were ignored. Instead, insisted the Cunliffe Report, appearing just a fortnight or so before the end of the war in November 1918, what was really 'imperative' was that 'after the war the conditions necessary to have maintenance of an effective gold standard should be restored without delay'; for, it went on, 'unless the machinery which long experience has shown to be the only effective remedy for an adverse balance of trade and an undue growth of credit is once more brought into play, there will be grave danger of a progressive credit expansion which will result in a foreign drain of gold menacing the convertibility of our note issue and so jeopardising the international trade position of the country'. The ultimate crux, in other words, was as speedy a return as possible to a fully operational gold standard – a reassuring prospect broadly welcomed by financial opinion at large. 'Back to Sanity' was the *Economist*'s headline, while *The Times* had no doubts that the City would 'firmly approve' the central objective of 'getting back, after the war, to an unimpeachable gold basis for our currency'.[12] Cunliffe himself may have become a semi-pariah at the Bank, but almost certainly no one there would have disputed the thrust of his Committee's conclusions.

Strong was back in London in July 1919, staying at Norman's house on Campden Hill and receiving in Threadneedle Street 'a very warm welcome' from Cokayne and Nairne. 'They have even been good enough to put a telephone at the desk and a card with my name on the door, something which I have no doubt is without precedent in the history of the Bank.' Even so, the American found the directors, whom he joined for lunch, notably lacking in the joys of peace:

> There is undoubtedly a very blue feeling here in regard to the future. It seems based in part upon the huge governmental expenditures, which still continue largely in excess of revenues; the early maturities of short government obligations, which aggregate between nine and ten billion dollars within eighteen months; the existence of the huge foreign debt, principally to the United States, which they would be glad and relieved to see reduced to more definite terms; the government policy of continuing unemployment wages; and,

more particularly and fundamentally than anything else, the general
unrest and dissatisfaction of labor throughout the country ...

'You know,' Cole told him a few days later, 'England may have a revolution on her hands any day.' But for the governor, whose Roehampton
house Strong visited for a night, there was at least a safety valve. 'I
discovered that business and the Bank of England was taboo in the
family. He apparently makes it a practice never to mention the Bank
when he gets home nor his business, and Lady Cokayne, he says, is
densely ignorant on that subject, and it is one thing which gives him
relief from the anxiety of his work.'

Cokayne stepped down the following spring, to be succeeded
by his deputy, Montagu Norman. The new governor continued to
cultivate a close relationship with Strong. 'Whenever you do come
to London,' he assured him later in 1920, 'let me remind you of your
hotel, of which the address is "Thorpe Lodge, Campden Hill, W8."
The Booking Clerk tells me that an hour's notice will be enough to
get your room ready, or, if you are in a hurry, this can be done after
you have arrived.' It is unclear who exactly coined the term 'central
banking', but by early 1922 the two men were consciously formulating its principles. 'If ever you should feel downhearted,' wrote
Norman, 'just you remember that, economically speaking, there is
only hope through a community of interest & cooperation between
all the Central Banks.' At the core of their shared conception was not
just co-operation between central banks, recognising 'the importance
of international as well as national interests in the re-establishment of
the world's economic and trade stability', but the notion that for those
banks 'autonomy and freedom from political control are desirable'.

Norman's ambitions continued to grow. 'I think that Central
Bankers are destined to play their own great part,' he told Strong
in September 1921 after visiting him in America, while five months
later he predicted to his Dutch counterpart that the time was 'not far
distant when Central Bankers presenting an united front will at last
have an opportunity to play a part in the affairs of the world', in other
words after the politicians had done their worst. Soon afterwards, in
March 1922, he wrote to Strong in revealing terms about how 'two
years' had been 'wasted in building castles in the air and pulling them
down again': 'Such is the way of democracies it seems, though a few

"aristocrats" in all countries realised from the start what must be the inevitable result of hastily conceived remedies for such serious ills.' Strong later that year resisted Norman's idea of a grand conference of central bankers, but undeniably the idea of central banking was by the mid-1920s very firmly established. 'Policy must be considered before profit,' Norman explained in January 1925 to the seemingly backsliding president of the National Bank of Austria, 'and the interests of Publics before those of Shareholders.'[13] In a specifically British context, the Bank of England was now unambiguously, and without reservation, a public-oriented rather than a private-oriented institution, with an increasingly broad view of its responsibilities in an almost wholly changed world. Of course, in that challenging public realm, the exact nature of its relationship with the public's elected representatives had yet to be definitively established; though, however that played out, Norman was unlikely to lose his belief in the free-masonry of disinterested central bankers as a necessary counterweight to grubby, vote-catching politicians.

From the very start – and subsequently sometimes overlooked because of the natural emphasis on the Norman/Strong relationship at a time when American financial power was largely displacing British – there was a crucial imperial dimension to the propagation of the gospel of central banking. Here the key figure was Henry Strakosch: Austrian by origin; London-based managing director of the prominent South African mining house Union Corporation; responsible in 1921 for the creation of the South African Reserve Bank; and described by Norman in February that year as 'the best authority' on 'the principles which should govern the policy of central banks in any country'. The same month, a Bank memo declared that 'a chain of central banks in our various dominions and their co-operation with each other and our own Central institution and those of other countries is of the greatest importance to the smooth work of the world's financial machinery'; soon afterwards, Norman put Strong in the picture about the imminent election to the Court of a pragmatic, self-made Canadian, Edward Peacock, who had gained a high reputation in the financial world at large, including the City:

We are taking him with the view of pushing the Central Bank idea for all the Dominions. You will remember that Australia has a State

Bank which in no sense acts as a Central Bank and which is doing more harm than good. You will also remember that a Central Bank is being set up in South Africa to which we have contributed a Governor, and it is of vital importance that its beginnings should be upon sound lines. You'll know better than I do that Canada is without a Central Bank at all.

I am sure you will approve of our desire to see Central Banks in these various places on right lines; and I think you will agree that it is by the fact of our taking in the best Canadian we can get that we are most likely to influence Canadian opinion without offending their susceptibilities.

The establishment of Canada's central bank would have to wait a decade, but the Bank was indeed applying pressure on the Commonwealth Bank of Australia to become a proper central bank, which duly happened in 1924. As for South Africa in 1921, the pioneer governor whom Norman referred to was William Clegg:

He had been Chief Accountant of the Bank of England at the time of his appointment [recalled half a century later a former director of the Reserve Bank] and lived out that association in every way, setting an example in dignity and dress and tolerating no familiarity. His official residence in Brynterion was called Threadneedle House and in initial discussion with local bankers on local banking practices and desirable policies for the new central bank, I was told these always ended with: 'In the Bank of England we do things so and so' and that would be the end of it.

Unsurprisingly, the two central banks kept in the closest possible touch; and when in 1923 they worked together to resolve a liquidity crisis in the South African commercial banking sector, the *Morning Post* obligingly reflected on how the episode had shown 'some idea of the immense reserve power which is imparted to our banking system throughout the Empire by co-operation between Central reserve banking institutions'.[14]

All this was well and good from Norman's point of view, but his higher priority was the financial reconstruction of Europe, a continent left in a wretched state after the war. There were two major related issues – reparations (where Cunliffe in almost the last significant action before his death had managed through his bull-headed presence at the Versailles peace conference to pitch them injuriously high) and war debts (where Norman was closely involved in early 1923 in Washington negotiations that led to an Anglo-American settlement) – but for the governor the crux was reconstruction itself. He did not underestimate the gravity of the task. 'I have never thought', he wrote to Strong in August 1922, 'the immediate future of Central Europe looked blacker than it now appears to look. I cannot conceive how some sort of a break-up of Austria is to be avoided long before the end of the year; nor do I see how a condition very near to civil war can be avoided in Germany.'

Norman's specific – and not unheroic – contribution to mending that dire state of affairs was to do everything he could to facilitate a series of large-scale reconstruction loans, often in the process having to overcome a degree of resistance from the City as a whole. One by this time had already taken place (to Czechoslovakia in April 1922); then came Austria in 1923 (the Bank itself issuing the £14 million loan); and the following year, with Norman having to strong-arm Rothschilds and Schröders into undertaking it, Hungary. Ultimately, as everyone knew, no country mattered more than Germany. 'The black spot of Europe & the world continues to be on the Rhine,' Norman declared to Strong after the Allied occupation of the Ruhr following the German failure to keep up reparations payments. 'There you have *all* the conditions of war except that one side is unarmed. How long can Germany continue thus?' Then, however, came the great breakthrough of 1924. It began with the new president of the Reichsbank, Hjalmar Schacht, visiting London at the start of the year and being privately acclaimed by Norman as, he informed Clegg, 'a Banker pure and simple with no public position, but financially a man of sound and up-to-date views in the sense you would understand them'; in due course there emerged the Dawes Plan for Germany's reparations payments, crucial to which was the huge 'Dawes Loan' in October, of which some £10 million was taken by the London market, as cajoled by Norman. None of this, of course, was pure altruism on his part. After all, it was obvious enough that the Bank being a leading player in Europe's financial reconstruction would in turn help to re-establish the City's and sterling's international position. But to suggest that that was Norman's *main* motive would not only be cynical but also, almost certainly, mistaken.[15]

Closer to home, these were the years when the Bank, above all through the person of Norman himself, began to exercise a far closer – and more continuous – control over the City than it had ever done before. From 1919 the chairmen of the main clearing banks not only met regularly with the governor but now stayed for luncheon, while the governor would also often summon them or their general managers to discuss those banks' latest balance sheets; a close peacetime eye also started to be kept on the merchant banks, with the Bank from 1922 feeling compelled to carry Huths, one of the inner-City houses; even before Norman became governor, and well aware of the key role of the gilt-edged market (that is, in government stocks) following wartime's tenfold increase in the national debt, Cokayne in early 1920 had instructed the firm that acted as government broker, Mullens, to strengthen its partnership and thus capital; soon afterwards, in relation to the money market, one of Norman's first acts as governor was to implement his diary jotting, 'See about weekly meeting with Ch'man of Discount Mkt'; and as for the capital market, at this stage a particularly important dimension in terms of the bigger economic picture, there was for most of the seven years after the war an informal embargo, largely exercised by Norman, on the issuing in London of foreign loans (excluding colonial and reconstruction loans) – an embargo reluctantly necessitated, in the governor's mind, by the overriding need to bolster sterling and thus quicken the return to the gold standard.

Taken altogether, the Norman approach, heavily reliant on his mixture of charm and force of character, essentially amounted to moral suasion. It did not always work. 'I regret more than I can say,' he complained unavailingly in December 1921 to Sir Newton Stabb after learning that a long-term loan to the Siamese government was going ahead, 'that you should find yourself committed to an issue through the Hongkong Bank [the future HSBC] which actually in the spirit, and practically in the letter, is opposed both to the wishes of the Chancellor and to the policy of the Bank of England.' Nor were the chairmen of the clearing banks – hugely powerful figures in their own right – automatically inclined to bow to all the governor's dictates, with Norman enjoying a distinctly mixed relationship with both Frederick Goodenough of Barclays and, perhaps inevitably, Reginald McKenna of Midland. 'I do not like that type of mind, always anxious to make a personal dash,' was the Norman view of Cunliffe's old friend; while McKenna for his part reckoned the governor 'an intellectual without an intellect'.[16] The Bank/City relationship may have been significantly changing in the first half of the 1920s, but the human factor would always be in play.

It did not help on the Norman/McKenna front that the former politician emerged as one of the two most prominent public critics (the other being Keynes) of the Bank's necessarily deflationary monetary policy – necessarily because it fully accepted the Cunliffe Committee's conclusion in 1918 that in effect that was the only way of restoring gold parity between sterling and the dollar and thus enabling Britain to return to the pre-war gold standard.[17] Unsurprisingly, not least in the immediate post-war context of a spectacular boom rapidly requiring dear-money measures (at this stage supported by Keynes), monetary policy now became increasingly politicised. The stakes and competing interests were clear as early as autumn 1919: wanting an increase in Bank rate, Cokayne warned the chancellor, Austen Chamberlain, that 'the Court regard the restoration of the gold standard and the resumption of free gold exports at the earliest possible moment as of vital importance to the Country as a whole and consider that it is well worth a temporary sacrifice to secure that end'; but when, soon afterwards, the rate did rise from 5 to 6 per cent, Norman was still far from sure that 'the certainty of sound money' was 'definitely settled', expressing to Strong his concern about 'the advocates of expansion and the printing press, which to a considerable extent is the view held by many political leaders'. The denouement to this first post-war phase came in 1920. In April, a fortnight after becoming governor, Norman secured an increase from 6 to 7 per cent; but then in July, pushing for 8, he was informed by Chamberlain that another rise was politically impossible. It was a telling moment. Interest rates, observed Norman in September to a colleague of Strong, 'are now a political as well as a financial question'; and later that autumn he reproachfully told Chamberlain that 'when I call to mind your remark to my predecessor (that an independent Rise in the Bank Rate would be an unfriendly act); when I remember our continuing desire for higher rates ever since last July and indeed long before it, and your continuing unwillingness to consent, owing to political reasons ... I wonder what (in the spirit as well as in the letter) is the meaning of "political pressure"'. Yet in the long run, however much Norman may have wished otherwise, there was no escaping this politicisation – with the price of money now increasingly seen as impacting directly on levels of unemployment, on housing policy and on economic policy in general.

In due course, Bank rate did come down – eventually to 3 per cent by July 1922 – but in many external eyes all too slowly and timidly, given the sharp recession that had followed the boom. Yet, for Norman and his most trusted colleagues, there remained no alternative to deflation if a plausible road map to a return to the gold standard was to be charted and followed. One of those colleagues was the highly regarded international banker Sir Charles Addis, a director since 1918. Giving his presidential address to the Institute of Bankers in November 1921, he saw 'no hope of the restoration of the old standard of living and of comfort for the great middle class of this country until prices are further reduced'; called on the country to 'take a long pull, a strong pull, and to pull all together'; repudiated the 'ingenious and insubstantial nostrums of claustral economics'; and, demanding a return to gold as soon as possible, beseeched, 'Let us have done with short cuts and by-pass and, *ohne hast ohne rast*, bend our energies to return to the old standard.' Norman would undoubtedly have agreed with every word, but it was a strategy that by 1923 was under increasing attack from the fluent pen of Keynes. In July he publicly declared that 'so long as unemployment is a matter of general political importance, it is impossible that Bank rate should be regarded, as it used to be, as the secret *peculium* of the Pope and Cardinals of the City'; later that year he published *A Tract on Monetary Reform* (dedicated, perhaps ironically, to the Bank of England), which consigned the gold standard to oblivion as a 'barbarous relic' and instead advocated a system of managed money through which the central bank would be able to control the supply of credit and thus, in the words of one of his biographers, 'even out fluctuations in business activity'. Norman for his part remained adamant that the Bank's was the only true course. 'We can have & perhaps deserve nothing but troubles until we are again anchored to Gold,' he confided in Strong that autumn, though adding almost despairingly, 'How & when can we do it?'[18]

In practice, that happy day came a little sooner than expected. During 1924, Labour's first-ever chancellor, Philip Snowden, proved surprisingly City-friendly, finding in Norman, he would recall, the very reverse of the 'hard-faced, close-fisted, high-nosed' financier of socialist caricature, but instead someone herculean in his efforts, of international cast of mind and with 'one of the kindliest natures and most sympathetic hearts it has been my privilege to know'. That summer, giving evidence to a parliamentary committee, the suitably encouraged governor calmly addressed the possible sacrifice to be made in the short term by 'the trader' (meaning those in the commercial and industrial world at large, as opposed to the financial) through a return to gold 'at the earliest practicable date':

> I should think the thing is, in every country in the world and in every trade in the world unless he can obtain stability he will not prosper and in order to obtain stability through the only means by which I think it can be obtained, that is the gold basis, it is worth while for him to make once this sacrifice for the good of his business and for his future success, and if he does not make it he will be in a state of uncertainty and at the mercy of other countries until he does.

Furthermore, insisted Norman, 'the danger of waiting is much greater than people imagine, much greater, not to currency, but to the trade of this country, to the financial standing of this country'. The winter of 1924–5 saw not only a new, unexpected chancellor in the person of Winston Churchill, after Stanley Baldwin's election victory, but Strong at last swinging fully behind Norman over an early return at the pre-war parity. Churchill himself remained doubtful and reluctant until almost the last moment – 'I would rather see Finance less proud and Industry more content,' he wrote at one agonised point to his main Treasury adviser, Otto Niemeyer – but was ultimately unable to resist the formidable combined weight of Treasury and Bank opinion. By late March the decision was taken, with the announcement to be made in the budget at the end of April. 'Let us be thankful we have escaped the "managed currency" people,' declared Addis to Strong ahead of the public confirmation; 'a signal triumph for those who have controlled and shaped our monetary policy, notably the Governor of the Bank,' proclaimed

The Times the day after Churchill had informed the world about a fateful step that in the end was as much a moral-cum-sentimental judgement as a strictly economic one; but some ten days later, writing to Strong, the governor himself was in thoughtful and far from triumphalist mode:

> Many of the financial community do not realise the importance and even the possible dangers of the step which has been taken. They have lived for ten years in a dream: they have not had to use their wits ... They ignore the fact that London is probably short of dollars; that India, almost irrespective of the Exchange, is a great absorber of gold; that Australasia is over-borrowed in London and may require the position to be put right, and that such a country as Egypt is not only in a position to draw a great deal of gold from London but for national or political reasons might not be averse from doing so ...

Still, as he had scribbled to Churchill in his congratulatory note on the evening of the announcement, 'Pray count on me to try to do my little bit.'[19]

Having become governor in the spring of 1920, Montagu Norman was still governor when Britain returned to the gold standard five years later, thereby equalling Cunliffe's hitherto record length of tenure; he would still be governor at the end of the decade; and indeed would remain in post until almost the end of the Second World War – altogether, a phenomenal twenty-four years. There has been no single more important person in the Bank's entire history. What sort of man was he? And why did no one else displace him during the 1920s?

'A small, carefully-trimmed beard adds length and distinction to his fine-drawn, sensitive face,' noted a profile in an American paper shortly before the return to gold. 'His hair is brushed back from a high forehead, which is notably prominent just above the dark, searching, thoughtful eyes.' The writer then portrayed Norman in his Threadneedle Street fastness:

In his room at the Bank, he receives visitors with his back to the fire, standing. His characteristic attitude is long legs apart and thumbs stuck in the armholes of his easy-fitting waistcoat. He does not like talking whilst sitting at a desk.

Talk to him, and you get his measure. His physique may not be powerful, but his brain is a vibrant dynamo. He speaks in a soft voice and each of his words is significant. 'What d'you want?' he will often ask people who come to see him. He never uses conventional phrases.

As for his life outside the Bank:

He goes for long walks, and he works in the garden. This is his only exercise, for sport has no attraction for him. He neither hunts, golfs, shoots, nor rides.

He reads much. Kipling is his favourite, and he is himself an earnest believer in the Empire idea and the Kipling man. He collects etchings, and is a connoisseur of silver-points.

No governor before, and possibly since, was the subject of more newspaper and magazine profiles than Norman over his long governorship, notwithstanding his own intense secretiveness; and this was one of the better ones.

Contemporaries whom he encountered were almost invariably fascinated. A selection from their descriptions and assessments gives us a three-dimensional (if occasionally contradictory) sense of a remarkable, enigmatic man who combined charm and steel in roughly equal measure:

He appears to have stepped out of a Van Dyck painting; elongated figure, pointed beard, a big hat; he has the bearing of a companion of the Stuarts. It is said that Israelite blood flows in his veins. I know nothing of this, but Mr Norman seemed, perhaps because of it, full of contempt for the Jews about whom he spoke in very bad terms ... He adores the Bank of England. He told me: 'The Bank of England is my only mistress. I think only of her and I have given her my life.' *(The Bank of France's Emile Moreau on meeting Norman in Paris in 1926)*

His beard and hair though greying are still mainly black or give that impression. His flashing eyes are probably brown but leave the impression of being black. His broad brow is of the kind one sees in the Dutch masters but rarely in real life. His movements are graceful and flowing and he has a voice of a singularly compelling and attractive timbre ... I doubt if this man has an equal, never mind a superior, at controlling situations and putting the men who come to meet him where he wants them firmly and kindly but ever so effectively. *(The Manchester Chamber of Commerce's Raymond Streat after seeing Norman at the Bank, 1931)*

He could enlist warm friendships and elicit the most devoted service, yet he could seriously upset the nerves of some of his most faithful collaborators. He disliked politicians as such, but found a congenial soul in Baldwin [a cousin of Kipling]. He was a mystic and read widely, but he had no clear-cut views on some of the most profound issues of thought. Although he disliked explaining himself to more than one person at a time, his written communications were admirably expressed. He could never have been a success on television. He would have despised it ... *(The veteran economist Sir Theodore Gregory, writing in the 1960s)*

He had funny little tricks, he was vain – but it wasn't the sort of vanity that mattered at all. And he was always using strange expressions. I remember he said to me once about someone, 'Your friend's a bit hairy in the heel, eh?' The one thing Monty never wanted to be asked was why he did anything. He didn't really know quite, but he had this extraordinary intuition ... He never made jokes or anything of that kind. He was just amusing. A continual bubble of wit. *(George Booth, a director of the Bank throughout Norman's governorship)*

He was a great banker, banking was his life, he created the 'mystique' of the Central Banker. But he did not look like a banker at all. There was something of the actor in him – but he did not act a part, he was very much his own real self. He had the touch of the artist in dealing with situations and people – he was not an artist. Intuition guided him but he was very rational and reasoned in his conception of problems. He was a traditionalist with an entirely unconventional approach. He exerted power but always through influence. He was, in every respect, immensely interesting. *(J. W. Beyen, a Dutch banker who got to know Norman in the 1930s)*

We see Norman in daily action through his desk diary (now access-ible online) – invariably crisp, sometimes cryptic, in its judgements on his many visitors. The characteristic flavour comes through in a December 1922 entry: 'Rob Martin. Fluff.' Or the following autumn: 'Dufour: a miserable man "with a tale of woe".' Of course, a request to attend the governor was almost a royal command. 'A summons would come to Alfred Wagg,' recalled Lawrence Jones of the merchant bank Helbert Wagg, 'who must put on a top-hat in which to obey it, for the wide-brimmed soft hat that hung outside Mr Governor's room would tolerate no rival.' That hat became part of City lore, with Norman travelling on the Underground each day to the square mile with his ticket stuck in the hatband, before at the exit he bowed his head for the collector to remove it.

Every now and then, amid Norman's voluminous correspondence, there is a moment of apparent revelation, a moment when we seem to draw close. Take a trio of examples from the 1920s. 'Hawtrey is extraor-dinarily clear and clever,' he wrote in 1922 to Benjamin Strong about the senior Treasury figure R. G. Hawtrey, 'but he seems to me to treat his subjects as if they existed in a vacuum; whereas, as we see more and more, Currency and Finance are continually at the mercy of political and psychological and international and incalculable influences.' It was a distinctive and perhaps very English approach, prompting in the 1960s one exasperated economic commentator, Andrew Shonfield, to recall Norman as 'the apotheosis of the English cult of the adminis-trator as artist-leader – a kind of *Künstlerführerprinzip*'. The second example came in January 1928, as the bachelor governor, writing again to his American friend, let himself go about the Bank's recent recruit from the Treasury insisting on taking his wife with him on a working trip to New York: 'Niemeyer pretends to me that he will be as free with a wife as without: that she will sit in the hotel & twiddle her thumbs & ask no questions: I might just as well pretend to be the same with the toothache as without it – he is trying to prove that you can serve God & Mammon – I don't believe it.' Echoes indeed of 'the Bank of England is my only mistress' ... Finally, also to Strong but the previous summer, this from on board the ship as he left New York after a difficult visit: 'What about it? Where does it all lead & what can we do? I always come away with the same thoughts – flies in a web: can lift one (but only one) foot clear: hard work to keep steady:

the personal touch largely usurped by the mechanics of the web: & so on.'[20]

There is little doubt that, despite precedent and despite occasional protestations to the contrary, Norman during the 1920s was determined to stay on as governor for as long as he could – and, broadly speaking, his colleagues fell into line with that in the overriding context of the very changed post-war financial world, though not without some perturbation on the way. 'I earnestly hope you may be persuaded to serve for at least another year,' his deputy, the merchant Henry Trotter, wrote to him during Norman's third year as governor. 'I am convinced it would be in the best interests of the Bank and the Country.' Norman himself conceded soon afterwards to Strong that 'people prefer the Rotation', before adding: 'But how swap horses just now?' Trotter's successor from 1923 was Cecil Lubbock – managing director of the brewers Whitbread and a classical scholar, though not really governor material in the new world – before in 1925 an altogether tougher egg, the ambitious shipper Sir Alan Anderson, became deputy. 'A masterful & strong man,' Norman had already informed Strong, and Anderson by October 1925 was insistent that he would not stay on as deputy governor unless (recorded the director Charles Addis) 'assured of being made Governor in a year'. Norman held firm – 'the trouble is', he informed Strong, 'not that he is not clever & courageous & a good fellow but that his wishes are contrary to our ideas & the whole of our tradition & while we admit they may perhaps be suitable for a shipping business we are sure they are not suitable for a Central Bank' – and the outcome was that Trotter agreed to return as deputy in spring 1926, but only on the basis of a moral undertaking that he would become governor in 1927. Autumn 1926 was decision time, and once again Norman declined to play the rotation game. 'We tried to get him to accept Trotter for a year,' Edward Peacock told Strong, adding that Norman had been adamant that if he stepped down as governor but continued at the Bank under Trotter, 'it would break down within three months'. As the Committee of Treasury's support for him crumbled, Trotter accepted the inevitable outcome graciously enough – assuring Revelstoke that 'we must retain the master hand' and that he was 'without one particle of feeling of having been let down' – but his cousin Robert Boothby would subsequently relate how not becoming governor 'broke' him.[21] As for the deputy governorship, the musical chairs continued with Lubbock succeeding Trotter in spring 1927.

By then, during the winter of 1926–7, a committee under Trotter's chairmanship had been in action, seeking to stand back and look at the whole question of the governorship in a larger perspective. The evidence it took revealed a strong continuing attachment to the principle – if not hitherto in the 1920s the practice – of rotation, with a particularly thoughtful contribution coming from Baron Cullen of Ashbourne, as Cokayne had been since stepping down as governor. Expressing himself 'greatly impressed' by the argument of his fellow-director Sir Robert Kindersley that 'if the Governorship of the Bank became a life, or even a long term, appointment it would be impossible long to resist pressure from the State – from whom the Bank derive their chief powers – to force its own nominee or nominees upon them', he advocated a return to rotation from March 1928, noting pointedly that 'any opposition to that course the present Governor could do much to prevent or allay'; and he went on to describe himself as 'oppressed by the thought that even now we may, by departing for so long from the policy of our predecessors in this fundamental matter, have forfeited the magnificent legacy of independence which their prudence and altruism has secured for the Bank'. Cullen concluded with a not very soft impeachment, declaring of the period since 1920 that 'if our action should lead to some loss of the Bank's independence, posterity will assuredly say that it was forfeited by the laziness of the Court who found a "willing (and most capable) horse" and got him to do all the work rather than take their turn at the wheel'.

The Committee's eventual report – calling for rotation to resume in 1930 – went to the Committee of Treasury in September 1927 but never made it to the Court. Instead, the real battle was fought in autumn 1928, as Norman pushed hard for Sir Ernest Harvey (Nairne's successor as chief cashier, then comptroller) to succeed in 1929 to the deputy governorship on a permanent basis, with – it was tacitly understood, given that he had come up through the ranks – no realistic prospect of succeeding to the governorship. Initially, there seemed to be a critical mass of opposition on the Court, as Cullen put forward a resolution proposing a return to rotation and Anderson was (in Revelstoke's words) 'condemning' of 'M.N. and all his works'. Yet again, however, Norman got his way, making at the following week's Court 'a most conciliatory speech', as Cullen's motion was defeated by a majority of two.[22] Henceforth, the main internal threat to Norman's position would be his own health, psychological as much as physical.

From the point of view of many of the directors, there were arguably three main problems during these years. One of course was the absence of rotation: not only in flat contradiction to over two centuries of Bank custom, but directly detrimental to their own chances of advancing to the top position. They may have accepted the logic – in Addis's words, in a lucid, influential memo in September 1926, 'the old familiar ways of finance are abandoned, and it is mere illusion to suppose that we can ever return to them ... we have reached a critical stage ... there is much to be said for allowing a craftsman to complete his own work' – but only with considerable reluctance. The second problem was Norman's almost congenital disposition to hold all the cards that mattered as close as possible to his chest. 'Of course he will have to reform his ways about keeping things to himself,' Peacock wrote to Strong later in 1926 after the Trotter challenge had been seen off, but there is little evidence that Norman did so. Finally, there was the problem of the rise of the expert. The governor himself had few doubts that this was the way to go. 'We were late in building up a body of professionals drawn from outside,' he conceded privately in 1928, but certainly by the mid-1920s he was vigorous in taking belated action, with senior recruits including Sir Otto Niemeyer and Harry Siepmann (both with a Treasury background) and the American economist Walter Stewart, none of them at this stage on the Court. The director giving Norman the strongest backing in this initiative was Frank Tiarks of Schröders. Half a dozen or so 'experts', he told the Trotter Committee in 1927, 'should meet daily and reports of their Meetings should be available every week for all Members of the Court', in which way 'the interest of all Directors in the affairs of the Bank would be increased and the weekly Meetings of the Court would be become much more interesting'. Addis and Cullen were markedly less enthusiastic. 'The proper place for an expert', the former informed the Court the following year, 'is to assist and advise, but it is for the Merchant Directors to determine the policy of the Bank, and it is the belief that that policy is so determined which has won for the Bank its traditional authority and prestige'; while Norman's predecessor stated frankly at the same time, 'I do not believe that the Trade of the Country will long be content to see the Central Bank controlled by financial experts,' as opposed to the tradition of ultimate internal control resting with 'a Board or Court of Directors consisting not of Bankers nor financiers but of sound and high-class business men'. Given that in English cricket it would still have been unthinkable not to have an amateur as captain of his county, let alone his country, a certain resistance to the professionalisation of the Bank was perhaps hardly a surprise.

The coming of the expert did not mean a significantly new, more open attitude to the outside world. With the odd exception (such as the trusted A. W. Kiddy, City editor of the *Morning Post*), Norman continued to hold the financial press in even more contempt than he did most politicians. 'A second class sheet which prides itself on irritation and sore spots and tail twisting,' was how in 1927 he characterised to Strong the City's actually rather staid and respectable pink bible, the *Financial Times*. In practice, the reality of the underlying culture was a little more complicated, though a degree of disdain was seldom quite absent. From an essentially kindly but nevertheless insightful perspective, Michael Thornton in the 1970s would describe the Bank of the Norman era as

an institution pragmatic, idiosyncratic, inarticulate, rather highly strung; knowing better than many of its critics its own strengths and weaknesses, and therefore often mistaking criticism for ignorance – and anyway deaf to both; never letting go of a sound argument when it had one; prepared to skip the high debate, act on instinct, and not be too troubled by the post-hoc rationalisers; but above all adaptable, because it was largely unhampered by doctrine, principle, or even tradition.[23]

What matters is what works. Yet by the second half of the 1920s, the big problem in Norman's life was the consequences of the return to gold; for *that*, sadly, had been a decision – in its strong emotional desire to return to the pre-1914 world – that transcended empiricism.

The consequences themselves have been keenly debated ever since, but two aspects were immediately and undeniably apparent: that the recent catastrophic slump in foreign demand for coal (still the most important of Britain's industries) was further exacerbated by the 10 per cent increase in cost automatically ensuing upon return to gold at the pre-war parity; and, more generally, that the pound could stay on the gold standard – crucial, in Norman's eyes, to the City's international business, as well as 'knave-proof' against politicians – only if foreign funds were attracted, which in practice meant high (or certainly not low) domestic interest rates, inevitably impacting on industry at large. The flashpoint came as early as December 1925, when Churchill learned that the Bank, faced by large quantities of gold leaving London and rates rising in America, was minded to increase its own rate from 4 to 5 per cent. The chancellor at once telephoned the governor, warning that in that case he would have no alternative but to inform the Commons that he had not been consulted and that it had been against his wishes. Whereupon Norman called his bluff, raising the rate and telling Churchill that if he made such a statement it would be 'unprecedented'. The chancellor duly kept quiet, but for Norman it proved in practice a pyrrhic victory: henceforth, the possibility definitively no longer existed, in the context of unemployment of over a million, of Bank rate policy operating in its traditional pre-1914 ring-fenced political vacuum; while over the next few years (as Bank rate stayed largely unchanged, with Norman unable to bring it down but reluctant to raise it and risk another stand-off), not only did Keynes continue his campaign against the gold standard regime and what he regarded as the Bank's malign influence on monetary policy, but he was increasingly joined by the Midland Bank's McKenna. As for Churchill, all his frustrations were poured out in a memo that he sent to Niemeyer (about to move from the Treasury to the Bank) in May 1927, a year after the General Strike had sundered the country:

> We have assumed since the war, largely under the guidance of the Bank of England, a policy of deflation, debt repayment, high taxation, large sinking funds and Gold Standard. This has raised our credit, restored our exchange and lowered the cost of living. On the other hand it has produced bad trade, hard times, an immense increase in unemployment involving costly and unwise remedial measures, attempts to reduce wages in conformity with the cost of living and so increase

the competitive power, fierce labour disputes arising therefrom, with expense to the State and community measured by hundreds of millions ... We have to look forward, as a definite part of the Bank of England policy, to an indefinite period of high taxation, of immense repayments and of no progress towards liberation either nominal or real, only a continued enhancement of the bondholders' claim. This debt and taxation lie like a vast wet blanket across the whole process of creating new wealth by new enterprise.

Things even started to get personal, as Churchill, according to his private secretary, 'got into the habit of almost spitting out comments on the presumed enormities of "that man Skinner"' – Ernest Skinner being the governor's private secretary in whose name Norman used to reserve his passages across the Atlantic. Nor was Churchill in later years inclined to forgive. 'The biggest blunder in his life', his doctor noted him declaring in 1945, 'had been the return to the gold standard. Montagu Norman had spread his blandishments before him till it was done, and had then left him severely alone.'[24]

A significant side-effect of the politicisation of Bank rate was the need for Norman to continue to keep a tight rein on London as an international capital market. Back in July 1925, during the post-return honeymoon period, the Committee of Treasury 'discussed the embargo on foreign and colonial issues', Anderson reported to the absent governor, 'and everyone agreed that the sooner we could get back to freedom the better', with the result that four months later the formal embargo on foreign loans (in place for the past year) was lifted. Yet from the start London in its attempt to regain lost ground on New York was operating with one hand tied behind its back, as Norman, well aware even before the December clash with Churchill that a high Bank rate was political dynamite, was understandably concerned about the gold-exporting implications of an avalanche of foreign loans – for all his keen desire to help the City reassert itself. The consequence, as caught by his diary, was a prolonged exercise in encouraging a significant degree of self-denial:

2 Rothschilds. ? Loan to Poland for Tobacco Monop & Exch. I say in confidence that they sh[d] avoid all such transactions: not even worth discussion at present. *(2 December 1925)*

London the 21th day of June 1694

63	*[handwritten subscription entry]*	2000
66	*[handwritten subscription entry]*	5000
75	*[handwritten subscription entry, John Smith of Beaufort Buildings]*	10000
76	*[handwritten subscription entry]*	10000
77	*[handwritten subscription entry, John Smith of Beaufort Buildings]*	2000
78	*[handwritten subscription entry, John Smith of Beaufort Buildings]*	4000
79	*[handwritten subscription entry, John Smith of Beaufort Buildings]*	2000
73	*[handwritten subscription entry, Thomas Walkes of London]*	1000
80	*[handwritten subscription entry, Thomas Tipping]*	1000
81	*[handwritten subscription entry, John Knight]*	5000
68	*[handwritten subscription entry]*	2000
82	*[handwritten subscription entry]*	600
83	*[handwritten subscription entry]*	4000
84	*[handwritten subscription entry, Richard Leach]*	500

Extract from the original book of subscriptions, June–July 1694

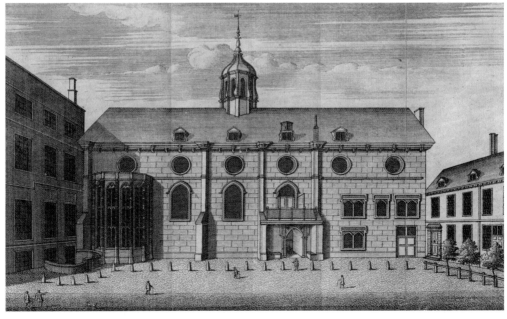

The Bank's second home, December 1694–June 1734: Grocers' Hall, Poultry

Dominant early figures:
Sir John Houblon (*right*),
the first governor;
Gilbert Heathcote (*below*),
the only man to be
governor twice

The original west wing, built 1783–6 by Robert Taylor after the demolition of the church of St Christopher le Stocks

The Pay Hall, 1808: engraving by Auguste Pugin and Thomas Rowlandson

Two men who demanded
high standards:
Samuel Bosanquet (*right*),
portrait by Charles Turner
after George Romney;
Abraham Newland
(*below*), portrait by
Henry Spicer, c. 1800

James Gillray's other 1797 take on the Bank's subjection to William Pitt the Younger

Soane's Bank: Rotunda (*right*); Accountants (later £5 Note) Office (*below*); curtain-walled Threadneedle Street front (*far right*); Bank Stock Office (*far bottom right*)

Over 90 years on the
Court between them:
Samuel Thornton (*right*),
study by Anton Hickel,
c. 1795;
John Horsley Palmer
(*below*), drawing by
James Swinton, 1851

Two upstanding governors:
William Cotton (*left*),
1850s; William Lidderdale
(*below*), c. 1890

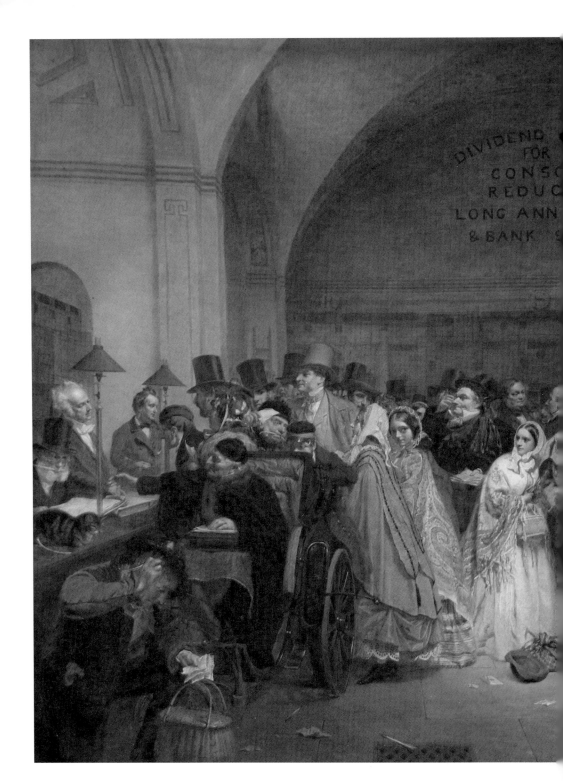

G. E. Hicks, *Dividend Day at the Bank of England*, 1859

Front Courtyard, 1894, with entrances to Pay Hall and Stock Offices

Consols Office, 1894

The Bank *en fête* for Queen Victoria's Diamond Jubilee, 1897; the wording above the Portico reads, 'She Wrought Her People Lasting Good'

A touch of *Mary Poppins*, albeit by the Royal Exchange, not St Paul's: the Threadneedle Street south front, from across the steps of the Royal Exchange, prior to inter-war demolition

Watching the gold: the Court, 1903, with the governor (Samuel Morley) fourth from left

Staff singing the National Anthem, 4 August 1916, the second anniversary of the start of the Great War

Fleischmann [of the merchant bank Seligman Brothers]: considering Loans here for 1. Central American Country & 2. Italian Industrial. I say free market – OK, BUT many more foreign issues – mean gold exports & higher B Rate & an end of such business. *(8 October 1926)*

A de Rothschild ... He protests bitterly agst continued embargo on French Loans ... *(4 October 1928)*

Norman tended to look more liberally at potential foreign issues if they fitted in with his picture of the ongoing European reconstruction jigsaw. These included a series of German loans (arranged by Schröders) in 1925–6, a major loan for Belgium in October 1926, and in late 1927 an Italian stabilisation loan. Norman had initially declined to give the last his blessing, telling an American banker that in Mussolini's Italy 'opposition in any form is gone: freedom of speech, opinion, criticism and press – even private life as we understand it'; but eventually he changed his mind, asserting to Strong that although 'Italy is not a free country in the usual sense of the word', nevertheless 'the fact remains that she has made economic and financial progress and is probably making social progress too'.[25]

So much, in Norman's eyes, still depended on his harmonious relationship with the New York Fed's chief and the other key central bankers. 'The main object' of 'the encouragement of close co-operation among Central Banks' was, he spelled out to Schacht barely a week after the return to gold, 'in order to secure regulation of rates of interest and exchange – and so prices of gold and commodities – and by these means the improvement of international trade'. He certainly put in the time and effort. 'We are staying here rather longer than I had expected or wished but that can't be helped,' he reported to Anderson not long afterwards, in July 1925, from Berlin's Hotel Adlon. 'B.S. likes to go into everything with a gimlet, as well as a good deal of talk, which takes time. He & Schacht are making friends & a good feeling is growing up from which much else may follow, sooner or later.' There followed, in response to a query from his deputy, some dense paragraphs infinitely suggestive of Norman's perplexing preoccupations:

Now as to Gold: see Schacht's telegram of the 11th & mine of 13th. When I came away from London I supposed that Schacht still had to buy Mks 200/250 mil (i.e. the Mks 300[m] mentioned in their telegram

last month less our later purchases) for which he w^d have to pay in
the form of valuta [foreign notes] – or exchange.

In the last 2 or 3 weeks the position regarding their gold needs
has changed for 2 reasons – first: They have bought from Switz^d &
Norway (in connection with Gov^t operations) Mks 50 mil – German
gold coin – & may buy a similar amount more: secondly – they have
had to repay short foreign Loans to German Bankers &c of about
Mks 200 mil, directly or indirectly arising out of the Stinnes affair.
This reduces their stock of valuta & as later they may perhaps have
to find money to repay other short foreign Loans (made by N.Y. or
London) they cannot contract to buy Clegg's Gold during several
months for fear of running short of valuta. (*This* valuta or exchange
belongs of course to the Reichsbank: they hold other exchange as
proceeds of Loan &c, of which they cannot dispose.)

Thus Schacht must go slow & see what happens: he will also have
to restrict Circulation as much or more than of late, because he has
to hold a Gold Reserve of 40% agst all *his* Notes (of wh 10% may
be in Exchange) & now he has not much more than enough Reserve
for present size of circulation.

Generally it looks as if Schacht was going to have a difficult time
with shortage of Note-cover. If necessary Strong or we will have to
lend him some money again.

'I hope this is clear,' he added, 'but I doubt it! Letters don't suit such
a subject.'

Norman's dearest hope, as he explained to Siepmann two months
later, was to see the 'inauguration' of what he called a 'private and
eclectic Central Banks' "club", small at first, large in the future' – a
club with 'subscriptions in the shape of exclusive relations; appropriate balances with other Central Banks; proper ratio of free balances
and earning assets in each market; no undue regard for profit; political
freedom by right or by custom; credits when there is bad weather in
any particular place; and so on'. By summer 1927 it looked as if the
dream of institutional central banking co-operation was on track, as
there assembled the so-called Long Island 'Club', comprising Strong,
Norman, Schacht and the Bank of France's Charles Rist (deputising for Emile Moreau); but that dream soon foundered, in large part
because of Moreau's fear of Schacht and resentment of what in his

wonderfully readable diary he called 'the Bank of England's imperialism'. 'England,' he explained to prime minister Poincaré in February 1928, 'has managed to install itself completely in Austria, Hungary, Belgium, Norway and Italy. It will implant itself next in Greece and Portugal. It is attempting to get a foothold in Yugoslavia and it is fighting us on the sly in Romania. Should it be allowed to go forward?' The answer was obvious, and over the next few months, supported by Strong, the very capable Frenchman, having already stabilised the franc and accumulated for his bank large sterling balances, successfully squeezed out Norman from a major loan to Romania. Strong, hitherto Norman's staunchest ally, justified his change of tack to the American economist Walter Stewart who had recently gone to the Bank: 'For some years past it has been more than current in Europe, both in political and banking circles, that Governor Norman desired to establish some sort of dictatorship over the central banks of Europe and that I was collaborating with him in such a program and supporting him.' Norman was forgiving ('think no more about Romania'), but that was the last letter between them before Strong died in the autumn. He departed at a pregnant moment. The previous year, at a point when the US economy had needed a firm touch on the monetary brake, he had pushed through a cut in New York interest rates in order to help the Bank of England support sterling without having to raise its own rate; but by late 1928 and going into 1929 Wall Street was enjoying an extraordinary credit boom. 'Both financially and politically,' Norman wrote to a correspondent in March, 'the prospect has rarely seemed to me more obscure than it does now'; and he referred darkly to how in New York 'the Stock Market is playing ducks and drakes with their own and other people's money'.[26]

Nor was that all that troubled the governor. 'In a few weeks,' he added in the same letter, 'we are liable to be tossed hither and thither by a General Election'; and, as he perhaps suspected, the outcome was the fall of Baldwin's Conservative ministry and the arrival in June 1929 of a second minority Labour government under Ramsay MacDonald, again with Snowden at No. 11. Neither politician was disposed to nationalise the Bank (notwithstanding a recent Labour policy document advocating it), nor indeed to stray from the path of financial orthodoxy, but Snowden in particular was acutely aware of the political sensitivity of Bank rate decisions. Almost certainly, this sensitivity was becoming greater than ever. Norman in 1927 had told Moreau frankly that he could not raise Bank rate 'without provoking a riot', given that a rise would 'intensify' industry's 'burden'; the following year, Cullen had conceded to the Court that 'we hear not a few whispers of complaint that our monetary policy is determined too much in the interests of finance and not sufficiently in the interests of Commerce'; and earlier in 1929, in February, Norman had managed to push through a small rise (to 5½ per cent) only because he had correctly guessed that Churchill was unlikely so soon before an election to make a public fuss. That summer saw delicate discussions between chancellor and governor (faced by a continuing drain of gold), culminating in early September in a concordat reached at Snowden's country cottage in Surrey:

> The Chancellor was persistent for a long time [recorded Norman] that a higher rate was no remedy; would harm trade; would be bitterly criticised; and would itself lead to still higher rates elsewhere and eventually here ... The Governor said that his was the technical and financial side – the Chancellor's was the political and fiscal side. On this basis the Chancellor must now leave the Bank rate to the Governor, to which the Chancellor agreed, stipulating that the Governor should see him next week; the Governor promising that he would not this autumn put up the Bank Rate for fun but only when it was essential ...

Eventually, with Snowden's reluctant consent, Norman later that month raised the rate to 6½ per cent – and the result was an intensely hostile reaction, not only from the left. 'The Governor may be in touch with the volume of banking advances and trade bills,' declared the *Evening Standard*, 'but he is out of touch with the flesh and bones of industry.'

Firmly on the table by this time was the possibility of a major monetary inquiry, a prospect seriously displeasing to Norman and prompting him to try, shortly after the Bank rate hike, to put the frighteners on Snowden via the Treasury's Sir Richard Hopkins:

> I rather fear that the Congress [that is, the Labour Party conference] which is to be held at Brighton this week may be made the occasion

for a general attack on the Bank Rate; credit policy: the effect of dear money on unemployment and other kindred subjects; and that in such event the attack might be met by some Minister present by a promise that the cabinet would at once set up a Committee to enquire into these subjects. I wish to impress upon you as definitely as possible that the mere promise of any such Committee under present conditions would of itself endanger our financial position, both at home and abroad. Indeed, the maintenance of the gold standard itself might by such action be suddenly and dangerously threatened.

To no avail: Snowden on 3 October announced to the party faithful that he would shortly be appointing a committee to inquire into the relations between finance and industry. His speech was deliberately low key – prompting Norman to congratulate him on how 'it seems that you have got the extremists at both ends on your side' – but at least as much to the point was the question put to the chancellor soon afterwards by his private secretary: 'Is there not some danger of giving the impression that the Governor is being put in the dock?'

That, however, was probably not Norman's greatest anxiety at this particular moment. 1929 was the year that the virtuoso, high-profile financier Clarence Hatry hit the rocks – confirmed by Norman's refusal to help, despite a personal appeal – and then succumbed to the temptation of authorising the forgery of scrip certificates. A very public fall was played out during September ('this Hatry affair has smirched us all,' reflected Norman), for a time plunging the stock market into free fall.[27] Then in late October came one of the seminal events of the twentieth century: the Wall Street Crash. All bets, whether for Norman or anyone else, were off.

Away from market ups and downs, the Bank by the late 1920s was in fact starting to get significantly involved in the problems of British industry.[28] 'In general I believe that the great industries can only be satisfactorily re-established by means of rationalisation, and this is slowly coming to be recognized in textiles, in iron and steel, and to some extent in coal and shipbuilding,' Norman wrote in November

1928 to a Foreign Office mandarin. 'In particular I am interested in the reorganisation of Armstrong, Whitworth & Co and its allied undertakings.' That indeed was true – with Norman, Peacock and a 'company doctor' called Frater Taylor, an unsentimental Aberdonian, having already spent much time on the financial reconstruction of the troubled Tyneside armaments firm, eventually leading to the creation of Vickers-Armstrong, a pooling with the naval-shipbuilding business – but increasingly what concerned the governor by the end of the decade was the wretched state of the Lancashire textile industry. The conventional wisdom of the day was that the route to economic salvation lay in large-scale mergers in order to increase efficiencies and reduce over-capacity; and though both the Midland and Barclays banks declined to back the proposed Lancashire Cotton Corporation, intended instrument of rationalisation, the Bank stood firmly behind the LCC and made a series of temporary advances. Norman undeniably had misgivings, admitting to bankers and others in December 1928 that he 'was not anxious for this business, which was entirely outside the normal sphere of the Bank of England'; but at the same time, he explained, 'the Cotton Industry was not the only one in need of rationalisation, and he looked to any scheme for the rationalisation of the Textile Industry to lead the way and set the type for schemes of rationalisation in other industries'. The details of the LCC were announced soon afterwards, prompting rare public praise from Keynes about how 'this incursion of the Bank of England – somewhat late in the day but wholeheartedly in the end – into the field of Rationalisation is in itself a matter of much interest and, in my opinion, of congratulation'.

What were Norman's broader motives in his industrial initiative more generally? It is hard to imagine that he was unaware of the possibility that it might play well in the wider world, at a time of mounting criticism of the City's neglect of industry and of the Bank's industry-insensitive monetary policy; there is also evidence that through the 1920s he had been under increasing Treasury pressure for the Bank to become more constructively engaged in this whole area; yet equally, rather as with his commitment to international financial reconstruction, he did believe for its own sake in what he was trying to do, in the context of the deep problems faced by British industry, especially in the traditional exporting sector. What he did *not* want was for the Bank either to exercise managerial control or to be permanently involved, candidly telling Peacock in August 1929 that his ultimate goal was to get all the various industrial questions out of his room 'and on a self-supporting and conducting basis'.[29]

The stakes were undeniably high. When in November 1929 the Bank established Securities Management Trust (SMT) – essentially a group of outside experts to advise the governor and see through rationalisation schemes – Norman explained to the Court 'at considerable length the present position in regard to industry generally and his views as to the necessary steps to restore it to a healthy condition by private enterprise and without government intervention'. Two more Norman initiatives followed in quick succession: in January 1930 he sought to strengthen the national credit machinery, and simultaneously to keep government out of the money market, by sanctioning a major injection of capital into the City-based United Dominions Trust (UDT), offering hire-purchase finance along American lines; and three months later he established the Bankers' Industrial Development Company (BIDC) – 'a new private Company to finance rationalised industry' (as he informed the Treasury), mainly comprising merchant bankers but with Norman as chairman, and with its £6 million capital coming partly from the Bank itself (£1½ million) but mainly from the suitably cajoled clearing and merchant banks. As all this unfolded, not every industrialist was convinced that Norman and his colleagues were the solution. 'In their own affairs they have never given more employment than that vouchsafed to gardener, chauffeur, and valet,' reflected after a visit early that year to Threadneedle Street a disgruntled twenty-seventh Earl of Crawford, with his family firm, the Wigan Iron and Coal Co, about to be 'rationalised' and become part of the Lancashire Steel Corporation. 'They are,' he went on, 'too much detached from the realities of production with its tremendous problems; they are usurers and nothing else ... The banks sail serenely above the tempests of industrial trouble.'

The first year or so of the new institutional dispensation tended to confirm the sceptics rather than the believers. As the LCC struggled – gaining for itself the reputation of being (in Norman's regretful words) an 'association of lame ducks' – so the BIDC came under public fire in August 1930 from a local Conservative MP, who accused it of 'a wilful lack of knowledge of the existing situation in Lancashire and of the practical difficulties that have to be overcome'; at the BIDC itself, the

day-to-day leadership of the merchant banker Sir Guy Granet proved
ineffectual, so that it soon became known in the City as the 'Brought
in Dead Company'; and in spring 1931 the LCC's long-awaited
debenture issue, made under the Bank's auspices, flopped. Ultimately
the problem was that the Bank found itself uncomfortably exposed,
in the middle of a vicious circle. 'Very large sums of money must be
forthcoming if we are to make the slightest impression on the re-organisation of our basic industries,' noted SMT's managing director,
the experienced iron and steel manufacturer Charles Bruce Gardner,
on the occasion of BIDC's first anniversary; but, as he added, 'experience has shown that in most cases it will be impossible to help those
industries to formulate schemes that can guarantee to the investor
their interest and sinking funds and the money provided …'[30]

A few weeks before the Wall Street Crash, in September 1929,
Norman had his initial sitting for what would become a controversial
portrait by Augustus John. The painter was struck by the governor's
preoccupied air, 'as though he was troubled by graver problems than
beset other men'; and over the next year and a half there was ever
more to be preoccupied by, as much of the world slipped into what
would become the great depression of the early 1930s. A rare source
of solace for Norman was the establishment in April 1930 of the Bank
for International Settlements (BIS), enabling central bankers to mix
on what he commended to Snowden the previous autumn as 'neutral
soil' (in the event, Basle) and thus provide 'the only way for Europe
out of financial chaos'. It was not an easy birth – tangled up as it was
with the whole reparations question – but Norman was hopeful at
the outset, telling the BIS's first general manager, Pierre Quesnay, that
the new institution should aim 'to direct short-term capital towards
long-term markets by coordinating the policies of central banks, their
discount rates, and by increasing the control each of them has over its
own market': in other words, an essentially supra-political approach.
Elsewhere, difficulties continued to mount, including in Australia,
with its economy in particularly dire straits because of the gathering
world slump. The Bank's answer (on a request from Canberra) was
to despatch Niemeyer, who arrived in July in full deflationary mode,

ready to recommend to the Labor government there the unappetising steps, especially in the form of wage cuts, that it needed to take so that its increasingly onerous financial obligations in London might be met with the Bank's assistance. 'I hope our good Niemeyer will succeed in converting these remote Australians to economic sanity and indeed to reason,' observed Norman some weeks later to a London stockbroker, 'but they have a long way to go'; and indeed the unbending, somewhat high-handed Niemeyer proved an intensely divisive figure down under, so that it was not until several months after the end of his mission that a compromise settlement was reached. As for Norman himself by this time, a certain understandable weariness was perhaps setting in. 'As regards the Serbian negotiations, both the Serbs and the French have been very troublesome,' he grumbled in November 1930 to Peter Bark, the last finance minister in Tsarist Russia and by now, as a Central European expert, one of the handful of people on whom the governor most relied. 'The longer I go on,' he added, 'the harder do I find the path of an internationalist!'[31]

Casting a further shadow for Norman over this year and a half was the Committee on Finance and Industry that Snowden had set up. Its chairman was the Scottish lawyer Lord Macmillan, while members included Keynes, McKenna, the strong-minded trade unionist Ernest Bevin, and Lubbock for the Bank. 'Whatever the outcome of the Committee may be, we at any rate have nothing to fear,' the deputy governor, Sir Ernest Harvey, assured his chief in December 1929 after giving five days of very capable evidence, concentrating mainly on explaining the mechanics of the Bank rather than attempting to elucidate or justify questions of high policy; but for Norman himself, giving evidence one morning in March 1930 after an earlier postponement because of a physical-cum-nervous breakdown followed by a convalescent cruise in the Mediterranean ('I have been away for a month to get my fire-box patched because the fire burnt it through'), the whole thing was a considerable ordeal.

Much of the session turned on the increasingly debated question of whether the Bank's traditional threefold prioritisation – defence of sterling, adherence to the gold standard, maintenance of London's position as an international financial centre – was to the detriment of the domestic economy. 'I think that the disadvantages to the internal position are relatively small compared with the advantages to the

external position,' insisted the governor, before Macmillan courteously pushed a little further:

> What is the benefit to industry of the maintenance of the international
> position? – This is a very technical question which I am ill equipped
> to explain, but the whole international position has preserved for
> us in this country the wonderful position which we have inherited,
> which was for a while thought perhaps to be in jeopardy, which to a
> large extent, though not to the same extent, has been re-established.
> We are still to a large extent international bankers. We have great
> international trade and commerce out of which I believe consider-
> able profit is made; we do maintain huge international markets, a
> free gold market, a free exchange market – perhaps the freest almost
> in the world – and all of those things, and the confidence and credit
> which go with them, are greatly to the interest of industry as well as
> to the interest of finance and commerce in the long run.
>
> One of the criticisms which has been made is that while the policy
> pursued may have been excellent from the point of view of the finan-
> ciers of the City of London, it has not benefited the industries of
> this country, that the considerations which have moved that policy
> have been directed rather to the financial side than to the plain man's
> industry? – Yes. Of course, industry has had ill luck, shall I say, and
> has been in a very unfortunate position and from one reason and
> another has suffered particularly. I agree; I am sure that is true.
>
> There has been no doubt a conspiracy of causes at work? –
> Almost; yes.

At which point, a clearly frustrated Bevin pressed Norman to
concede that the decision to return to gold at the pre-war parity had
played a major part in industry's misfortunes; to which the governor
responded, 'I do not attribute the ills of industry in the main to that
change.' Unconvinced, the trade unionist made a suggestion:

> Having regard to the fact that the workpeople at home have to
> suffer the biggest blow of unemployment and the depression of
> their standard of life, can you see any way to separate the national
> and the international policies, so that the effect of restoring the gold
> position internationally can be in some way modified in its effect

upon British industry? – I believe it is absolutely impossible to have two separate policies …

Supposing, for instance, you have to stop your gold flowing out, and therefore restrict credit, is it not possible to have a conscious direction of credit under those circumstances to the home market? – And to maintain, as it were, two separate supplies of credit at different rates?

Yes? – I do not think so.

Overall, the session left Norman in a depressed state, having held his ground but failed to articulate satisfactorily what in the end was instinctive behaviour and assumptions. At one moment during the session, the Committee's secretary would recall, he had been asked how he knew something – to which he had simply replied by tapping his nose three times.

In any case, that proved to be Norman's main appearance, though in February 1931 he did give two final and less challenging days of evidence, accompanied respectively by Granet and O. M. W. Sprague, his new American economic adviser. The Committee itself, meanwhile, spent part of the interim in private sessions, with Keynes inevitably to the fore and, equally inevitably, expressing the hope that the Bank would at last engage in 'a more open discussion' about matters of policy. 'If at every stage in the last ten years,' he went on, 'the Governor of the Bank of England had stated publicly what his object was and what he thought the things he was doing were likely to result in and how he assessed the advantages and disadvantages of his policy, if he told us what he was aiming at and what his method was and what he thought his method would cost in order to gain the advantages he was seeking, then it would be possible for public opinion of an informed kind to be crystallised on the point whether his policy was wise and successful.' McKenna for his part put it more crisply: the governor was guilty of 'a mute and irresponsible despotism'. A further private session, in December 1930, included this piquant exchange:

Keynes: I should like to see our Report centre round the magnification and evolutionary enlargements of the functions of the Bank of England … so that by the time her new mansion is ready for her [a reference to the physical rebuilding of the Bank], she must be no longer the 'Old Lady of Threadneedle Street' gathering her skirts round her, but some new image must be thought of appropriate to the occupant of the new palace.

Macmillan: A bright young thing?

Keynes: I hardly know what – perhaps Mr Lubbock can suggest something?

Lubbock: Well, I am one of the old timers.[32]

So he was, though that did not stop him, ahead of the report and surrounded by Keynes *et al*, from fighting a quietly effective rear-guard campaign on the Bank's behalf.

All this was against the background of a seriously struggling British economy. Bank rate did steadily come down – from 6½ per cent before the Wall Street Crash to 3 per cent by May 1930, where it stayed for over a year – but in the eyes of many too slowly and not far enough. 'The Bank's policy,' observed a Treasury insider in February 1930, 'seems to me quite inexplicable except by an unreasoning terror of cheap money,' and it was a plausible assessment. Nor, as unemployment climbed rapidly during the rest of the year (by the end of 1930 up to 2.7 million, compared with barely a million in summer 1929), did Norman deviate from his belief that nothing mattered more than Britain's capacity to stay on the gold standard; and at the start of 1931 he warned Snowden that 'if loss of gold, Budget prospects, socialist legislation or any other cause' appeared likely to trigger a flight from sterling, then he would have no alternative but to raise Bank rate in order to bring pressure to bear upon what he termed 'the unsatisfactory position'. In short: the Labour government had to retrench on expenditure or accept the consequences; and a few weeks later, in February, Snowden took the cue and agreed to establish an Economy Committee (to be chaired by Sir George May, a distinguished actuary) that would search for places to make spending cuts – a search under way even as Norman-endorsed foreign loans, symbolically so important to the international-oriented City, enjoyed that spring a last hurrah.[33]

The 1931 financial crisis began for real in mid-May with the failure of Austria's largest commercial bank, Credit Anstalt.[34] 'A monetary breakdown in Austria might quickly produce a similar result in several countries,' the governor was soon warning his opposite number at the Fed, George Harrison; and although the Bank did what it could – including a £4.3 million credit to the Austrian central bank – financial instability spread rapidly to Hungary and Germany. Some of the City's biggest names were heavily exposed in the latter, with Norman, umbilically committed to the international economy, now applying strong pressure on them to keep credits running. 'Germany – sh^d they withdraw Credits &c as others are said to be doing,' he noted in his diary on 10 June after a visit from Eric and Charles Hambro of the family bank. 'I say Germany is a good bet in the long run & needs help & comfort rather than worrying.' Briefly in late June the German situation seemed to have stabilised – helped by the provision to the Reichsbank of a $100 million credit from the Bank and other central banks – but Norman was far from sanguine in his update to Clegg at the start of July: 'You can really have little idea of the times through which we have been going here lately, during which as near as no matter Austria, Hungary and Germany – indeed Eastern Europe – went over the dam; and we are not by any means clear of trouble yet …' Nor were they. That same day, 1 July, a new run of foreign withdrawals began from German banks; and a week later, the news from the Reichsbank was of the German financial system in a state of crisis.

Back home, the name of the game during June was getting the politicians to face the facts – or, more specifically, softening them up ahead of the anticipated findings of May's Economy Committee. An exchange of letters between Norman and MacDonald, with that politician thoroughly apprehensive and not knowing which way to turn, was revealing about who called the shots. The prime minister began by wondering, in the wake of recent gloomy speeches by the Bank's Professor Sprague, whether the central banks could not do more, co-operatively, to stabilise prices and thus prevent the appalling unemployment consequences of severe deflation. 'I hope,' he added, 'you will not resent my intruding in these technical fields. I scarcely dare to contemplate, however, what it will mean for the world, and for this country in particular, if all prices and wages have to be forced down to meet the fall in commodity prices.' Norman in his reply stated flatly that the prospect of central banking co-operation raising commodity prices was a chimera, while as for Sprague, 'if his utterances may seem to some to have been on occasions hard, crude or ruthless, may it not be that having convinced himself that the true facts and difficulties of the position have too long been unperceived or faced in this and other countries, he finds it necessary to paint the colours with a heavy brush if he is to succeed in forcing home on unwilling minds the facts as he sees them?' MacDonald's apologetic response was almost abject: 'I am constantly being bothered about this matter, and it is a subject which I have never really studied and therefore know nothing about.'[35]

Events at large continued to pick up speed from mid-July. On Monday the 13th, the publication of the Macmillan Report (with little critical about the Bank, and mainly remembered for its identification of the 'Macmillan gap', that is, in the financing of small to medium-sized firms) was overshadowed by news that one of Germany's largest banks, the Darmstadter, had suspended payments; next day it emerged that the merchant bank Lazards was in trouble (as a result of fraud), requiring in due course a £3½ million loan from the Bank; and, increasingly, well-founded anxiety about London's German exposure saw gold flowing out from the Bank, some £22 million in the course of a week. Norman himself was under huge pressure, and eventually buckled. '12.30 about – left C. Treas^y and went home about 3 o'clock,' recorded his diary on Wednesday, 29 July. 'Queer.' Thereafter, he was only a bit-player as the rest of the crisis unfolded, with his capable deputy, Harvey, stepping into the breach and at once on the 30th ensuring a rise in Bank rate, from 3½ to 4½ per cent, to try to stem the gold losses.

Next day, Friday the 31st, was pivotal. Not only did Harvey inform MacDonald that the Bank's reserves had fallen by an alarming £55 million since the middle of the month, but the long-awaited May Report was published, claiming that the budget deficit was likely to be £120 million (an alarming figure at the time) and strongly recommending that the government achieve a cut in unemployment benefit of £67 million – a recommendation that over the next few weeks the Bank did not deviate from supporting, insistent that on international confidence in sterling depended the very fate of Britain's indispensable maintenance of the gold standard. Harvey spelled it out to Snowden on 6 August:

> I wish to explain to you that in less than four weeks we have to date lost more than £60 millions in gold and foreign exchange and, apart from the credits, we have virtually no foreign exchange left. If the flood does not abate we cannot maintain ourselves long ...

We are doing all that we can but our power to act is rapidly diminishing. As I tried to explain to you last week, the reports which reach us all show that the sign which foreigners expect from this country is the readjustment of the budgetary position, and this attitude on their part has again been forcibly expressed today in messages from both Paris and New York. I am most anxious not to step beyond my province but I feel I should be failing in my duty if I did not say that with the prospects as they present themselves today the time available for the government to reach decisions on this subject (as a means of safeguarding the value of sterling) may be much shorter than recently seemed likely.

The sense of urgency was palpable. Speaking to the Committee of Treasury on 11 August, Harvey 'feared that neither the Prime Minister nor the Chancellor were yet prepared to face the position and from certain information which he had received he feared that the Chancellor might even be considering the advisability of an abandonment of the Gold Standard'; a day or two later, the absent Norman, about to leave for Canada and convalescence, was asked if the country would 'pull through' and he replied, 'Yes, if we can get them frightened enough,' with little doubt about the identity of 'them'; or as Harvey expressively put it to a former Treasury chief on the 17th: 'We are having a desperate struggle in the hope that the government, on whom we are keeping a strong pressure, will adopt and announce this week a programme of financial reform which will sufficiently restore confidence abroad ... At the present moment it looks like being a neck and neck race ...'[36]

The political denouement would enter the history books. On Tuesday, 18 August, in a further stiffening letter to Snowden, and almost certainly in the knowledge that the Cabinet's own economy committee was in the process of finalising its proposed package of cuts, Harvey warned that 'everybody' in the City was 'anxiously awaiting the announcement of the Government's programmes', adding that 'so long as the present tension lasts there must always be the danger of a sudden break taking place in some quarter and becoming the signal for a general sauve qui peut'; two days later he sanctioned a telegram from Morgan Grenfell in London to Morgans in New York, exploring whether the British government might be able to place there a $250 million loan, but only if it first made a 'satisfactory announcement as regards balancing Budget'; and next day the deputy governor and Peacock candidly informed MacDonald and Snowden not just that the Cabinet's so-far-agreed cuts of £56 million would be insufficient to enable further credits to be secured from abroad, but that such was the current flight from sterling, and accompanying desperation of the Bank's exchange-support operation, that its reserves were likely to be exhausted in only four days.

Decision time arrived on the evening of Sunday, 23 August. Harvey passed on to MacDonald the crucial message from the Morgan partners in New York, namely that a major short-term credit was available to the British government within days provided that 'the programme under consideration will have the sincere approval and support of the Bank of England and the City generally';[37] the prime minister put this to the Cabinet; around half the Labour ministers refused to support the proposed cut in unemployment benefit that would enable such a programme to be implemented; later that evening, intending to resign, MacDonald (accompanied by Harvey) went to the Palace, where King George V was dining with his financial adviser, Peacock; the prime minister was persuaded to defer his decision; and late that night, accompanying him back to Downing Street, Harvey and Peacock sought to convince him that he could still serve the country by taking his place at the head of a National government – a government, of course, fully committed to the enhanced programme of cuts. Next day, that duly happened, as the Labour government fell and the King asked MacDonald to form a National government (inevitably Conservative-dominated) instead.

Had the whole thing been a 'bankers' ramp', as the accusatory phrase now went? In some fundamental sense not: the Bank's unwavering priority had been to save the pound and thus stay on the gold standard, with a sincere belief that the only way to achieve this was through major cuts in government expenditure; whereas it had not been the aim to force the Labour government from office – and indeed the plausible belief was that the necessary cuts would be more generally accepted if they were implemented by Labour. Even so, for anyone reflecting on the balance of power between elected politicians and unelected central bankers, including the ability of the latter to frame the arguments and give the former little room in which to manoeuvre, there was much to ponder.

That was not, in any event, the end of the crisis. International confidence in sterling continued to diminish, even after Snowden (who had stayed on as chancellor) delivered on 10 September an emergency budget more or less following the lines of the cuts package that the Labour government had failed to agree upon; while the Bank's gold reserves ebbed away during the first half of September, before a conjunction of difficult circumstances – reports from Invergordon about a possible mutiny of naval ratings over pay cuts, a poor show by ministers in the Commons of toughing it out, the imminence of a general election, a new and serious Dutch banking crisis – led to a run of sharp losses: £3½ million on the 16th, £10 million on the 17th, and a demoralising £18¾ million on Friday the 18th. Late that evening Harvey and Peacock met MacDonald at No 10, in effect telling him that there was now no alternative but to go off gold; the prime minister 'agreed that if one could not see one's way through it was better to acknowledge it now'. Whereupon discussion turned to practicalities:

> The Deputy Governor stated that it was better to stop on Monday morning as that would give time to warn the press, and the public could be stopped from rushing the banks ... The Prime Minister asked what would the effect be on things in general, particularly on the internal situation, of this upset? Mr Peacock replied that it would be an awful blow to everyone, but that the banks would loyally support one another in trying to keep working, and if the press played up, appearances at home might not be too bad ... Mr Peacock went on to explain the shock to our people all over the world in Ireland, Egypt, India and so on: in every village a bill on London was looked upon as cash – and it would be cash no longer.

As the meeting ended, Peacock observed that 'no one could accuse this country of not having made every effort before letting the pound go'; and 'it was pointed out' – by Harvey? by Peacock? by MacDonald? – 'that by having balanced the Budget, whatever happened, this country had at least demonstrated her will to play the game at all costs'.

A formal announcement to the press was made on the Sunday, shortly after Harvey had sent a deliberately cryptic cable to Norman, returning home from Montreal: 'Sorry we have to go off tomorrow and cannot wait to see you before doing so.' Norman, understandably, was somewhat puzzled. In the event Monday, 21 September, with the Stock Exchange closed, was less troubled in the City than some had feared, no doubt helped by the press that morning resolutely looking on the bright side. 'NO JUSTIFICATION FOR ALARM' declared the *Daily Telegraph* on its front page, adding below, 'A Speedy Return to the Gold Standard Assured'; *The Times* predicted the same, once the new government had done its work of 'retrenchment and reform'; while for the *Daily Mail*, coming from a different angle, suspension of the gold standard was nothing less than 'a blessing to British industry': 'The country was rashly hurried into it in 1925, against this newspaper's protests. It has cost us tens of millions and almost ruined us. Now that it has gone we may breathe more freely.'

Undeniably, whatever the rights and wrongs, it was a major moment. 'You will see by this morning's papers that after all our struggles we are driven off the gold standard,' lamented Teddy Grenfell (still on the Court) to Vice-Admiral Sir Aubrey Smith. 'It has been rather a losing fight for some time – one rung a day – until the Navy business knocked us clean off the ladder. England was represented to the foreigner by the Navy and the Bank of England. It is all very bewildering and distressing.' An ill-judged attempt to return to the prosperous certainties of the pre-1914 world had definitively failed, and a last word goes to Keynes's friend Virginia Woolf. 'We're off,' she scribbled in her diary, 'and I write about Donne. Yes; & what could I do better, if we are ruined, & if everybody had spent their time writing about Donne we should not have gone off the Gold Standard – thats my version of the greatest crisis &c &c &c – gabble gabble go the geese – who cant lay golden eggs.'[38]

Look Busy Anyway

The inter-war Bank was a significantly larger organisation than its pre-war counterpart. It was also much more mixed-sex. In 1914 there had been about 1,000 clerical staff, of whom only about 60 were women; by 1927 there were about 3,400 clerical staff, of whom some 1,270 were women, mainly employed either as shorthand typists or in connection with the progressive mechanisation of office work. Much of the increase in overall numbers was attributable to the tenfold rise in the national debt as a result of the war, a rise that in particular directly led in the immediate years after 1918 to the creation of the so-called 'Hump' – a mass of rather hastily recruited men who had only limited promotion prospects and who over the ensuing decades would block the path of the more able generation coming up behind them. The cause of the Hump's creation might not only have been the suddenly bloated national debt; it was said (though not documented) that there also was informal pressure from government, anxious to keep down unemployment figures at a time when the world was palpably not fit for heroes.

Across the inter-war period as a whole, male recruitment continued for the most part along broadly traditional and non-specialist lines. A would-be recruit (who was seldom a graduate) still needed to secure a nomination from a director, which in practice meant that the overwhelming majority of clerical staff came from a middle-class background, albeit quite often lower middle class. Cricket helped. Leslie O'Brien, leaving grammar school in the mid-1920s, managed to obtain a nomination from Lord Revelstoke on the basis that his father had played with a Baring; some ten years later the Bank's favourite game made all the difference in the life of a public schoolboy, David Harris:

> My father [he recalled] was the 'beak' at Thames Police Magistrate's Court and commuted by steam train from Woking to Waterloo. Among his regular travelling companions was Basil Catterns [a director and until recently chief cashier]. One morning Dad, buried in his *Times*, spotted that I had made 126 not out for Sherborne against Westminster and proudly drew his attention to it.
>
> 'Well done,' said Catterns. 'What is he going to do when he leaves school?'
>
> 'He has not made up his mind yet,' replied my father.
>
> 'Well,' said Catterns, 'the Bank cricket team has not been performing very successfully of late and could do with some fresh young blood. I would be very happy to give him a nomination if he would be interested in a career in the Bank.' He had never met me.

Even so, that was a more direct route to the indispensable nomination than for many. Nigel Spelling's, for instance, was achieved in the summer of 1939 'by an uncle who had a connection with a man who knew ... who knew ... who knew a senior in the Bank who knew a Director – or something like that ...' But after whatever route, there followed a two-day series of exams in Orthography, Arithmetic, English Composition and either General Knowledge or a foreign language; also required was a handwriting certificate from the London Chamber of Commerce, which usually disqualified left-handed writers. The exams themselves were not hugely demanding, and seem to have had high pass rates, but still had their moments of strain. 'The spelling of twelve "hard" words must nearly have been my undoing,' remembered Ted Bellamy about the early 1920s, 'for although I had no trouble with eleven of them, I stupidly misspelt that one word so prominent in the Bank vocabulary, the word "Principal".'[1]

For all the Bank's increased numbers, its organisational structure between the wars remained largely familiar. Two expanding areas by the 1930s were Economics and Statistics (where a newly recruited Cambridge economist, Humphrey Mynors, began to make his mark) and the Foreign Exchange Office (where the emerging force was the incisive, highly energetic George Bolton); while in 1932 the Special

Committee on Organisation, under Peacock's chairmanship, success-fully recommended the creation not only of two new departments – Overseas and Foreign, coming out of the pioneering central banking co-operation of the previous decade, and Establishments, taking over responsibility from the secretary for the Bank's domestic organisation – but also of a cadre of executive directors. All these were signifi-cant developments, yet taken as a whole the Bank was still by the Second World War a markedly federal animal, with individual heads of department tending to rule the roost along unashamedly hierar-chical lines, notwithstanding the efforts of Establishments and/or executive directors to achieve a more centralised approach. The key battleground tended to be promotions policy. Peacock's Committee had hoped that future promotions would be 'submitted to the Staff Committee by the Chief of Establishments in collaboration with the Heads of Departments'; but doubtless following informal pressure from those heads it had soon been settled that submissions for higher appointments, the ones that really mattered, were to be 'by the Heads of Departments in collaboration with the Chief of Establishments'. Promoting their own men, preventing them from going elsewhere, and largely determining the size of their staff, these departmental heads were the local Threadneedle Street equivalent of all those men on the spot who in effect still ruled the British Empire.[2]

One area where the writ of Establishments did not even theoret-ically run was the Printing Works. From 1920 these were no longer a department in the Bank itself, but instead one mile away in Old Street – inside the former St Luke's Hospital for Lunatics, built in 1782 by George Dance junior, to whom Soane had been a pupil. In the context of rapidly rising note circulation from the war years onwards, the principal task at St Luke's Printing Works was the printing of banknotes; and that became even more so from 1928, when following the long-desired amalgamation of the Bank and Treasury note issues, as well as the demise seven years earlier of the last of the country banks to issue its own notes, the Bank finally assumed entire responsibility for the note issue of England and Wales. The immediate consequence was the launch in November 1928 of the Bank's own newly designed £1 and 10 shilling notes: both with the somewhat amply proportioned Britannia as depicted by Daniel Maclise back in the 1850s, but the £1 note printed in green with a tint of blue and the 10 shilling note printed in red with a mauve tint – the Bank's first coloured notes. As would increasingly become the case at such moments, reaction was mixed. 'A strange and somewhat foreign appearance,' complained the *Liverpool Post*, while the *Glasgow Evening Times* reckoned that 'adulation of America may go too far', given they were so 'bilious-looking'; but at the more business end of the new note issue the *Financial Times* sought reassurance by submitting the signature of the chief cashier, C. P. Mahon, to a graphologist, who on the basis of magnifying it twenty times stated his conviction that it 'revealed characteristics of stability, solid reliability, and great experience of routine work'.[3]

Among the branches, those Cinderellas of the Bank, there was little change between the wars. Manchester, Birmingham, Liverpool, Bristol, Leeds, Newcastle and Plymouth were all open throughout, as was the Law Courts branch; the Western branch was sold in 1930 to the Royal Bank of Scotland; the Hull branch closed in 1939; and a new branch began to be built in Southampton (eventually opened in 1940). 'Senex', joining the Plymouth branch in 1920, would recall what was for the most part an undemanding, unambitious jog-trot:

Banking hours were ten till three, except Thursdays (market day) 10–4, and Saturdays 9–1, and the staff were required to sign on fifteen minutes before opening time, when the vault was opened. The staff consisted of the Agent, the Sub-Agent, the Chief Clerk, about six men, four women, and C. E. Phillips the messenger. The Agent, Sub-Agent, and the Messenger all lived on the premises, and the remainder of the staff within walking distance, or at the most fifteen to twenty minutes tram ride away. The Agent's house adjoined the Branch, with direct access to the office through an internal door, whilst the Sub-Agent lived in a flat above the Bank with similar access.

All money, etc, was conveyed into and out of the vault by means of a hand-operated lift. In winter the office was heated by a large fire and there was great competition to get near this in the lunch hour, when the Agents were in their respective homes. Except for certain times of the year (e.g. when dividends, etc, were heavy or when the Dockyard and Customs accounts were drawn on heavily) the hours were good, and at slack times if no one was on Governor's Leave a round of 'offs' was worked, which meant that one could leave at 10 am for the rest of the day provided the Auditors had not decided to visit the Branch.

The high sum Bank Notes were counted and examined by the Cashier, whilst the 10/- and £1 Currency Notes paid in daily by the local banks were dealt with by the women, who were granted an 'off' for every forgery they discovered. All the paid Currency Notes were subsequently cancelled, two corners being cut off by means of a guillotine, manipulated by the junior. Cancelled Notes were made up into parcels of 5,000, and sealed with sealing wax.

From time to time by arrangement with the Branch Banks Office cancelled notes were sent to Head Office and new notes received. We had no Bullion Yard in those days, and the Great Western Railway van would pull up at the front door, usually at about 8.30 or 9.00 am. The packing cases of notes would be brought up, about six at a time, in the lift and taken to Millbay station accompanied by a clerk and a messenger.

These 'Treasure Journeys' were much sought after as it meant a day, or possibly two, away from the Branch, and also a small fee …

Threadneedle Street's detailed inquiries in 1936–7 into the branches found that by this time they fulfilled three main functions: providing clearing facilities for local banks; collecting government revenue; and – by some way the most important – acting as reception and distribution centres for banknotes (Manchester, top of the league, dealing with ninety-three million paid £1 and 10 shilling notes annually). Apart from the Hull and Southampton decisions, the key recommendation coming out of the inquiries was that the Victorian premises of the branches were no longer fit for purpose and that it was now necessary to consider 'a programme of reconstruction'.[4] But for reasons beyond any committee's control, such a programme would in the event take a quarter of a century even to begin to implement.

'After St Paul's, the Tower and the Guildhall it probably stands more for London than any other structure, the exterior is known to everybody and I believe, in some unrealised way, is loved by all!' Such was the tribute paid in June 1921 to the Bank's home by W. R. Lethaby after two recent visits. He was writing to his fellow architect Herbert Baker, who was himself in the process of being appointed to undertake a major rebuild – the first since Sir John Soane had stepped down in the 1830s.⁵ Why the rebuild? And why Baker?

The reason for the rebuild was obvious enough, lying mainly in the hugely increased size of clerical staff following the war and the accompanying desire to have everyone working on the same site; as for the choice of architect, it reflected Baker's own 'imperial' qualifications (including his important work with Sir Edwin Lutyens on the government buildings in New Delhi), as well as a personal connection with Cecil Lubbock, chairman of the Special Committee on Rebuilding the Bank. Lutyens himself was dismayed at not landing the commission, but reputedly had forfeited his chances by jesting to Norman that the Soane halls were just the place for a *thé dansant*. From the start, Lubbock's committee emphasised to Baker the need for the 'reconstruction' to be 'satisfactorily carried out consistently with the general appearance and style of the building being preserved'; in accordance with this sentiment, Baker reassured the Committee that it was 'unnecessary for me to add my advocacy to the widely-acknowledged importance from the points of view of archaeology, architecture and historical association of the retention of as much of the old building as may be possible without too great a sacrifice of the other vital considerations involved'. The architect also (he would relate) asked Lubbock what the Bank of England stood for. 'Not the amassing of money, I was told; but rather that invisible thing, Trust, Confidence, which breeds Credit ...'

Things moved up a gear in 1922 with the publication of Baker's plans. 'An entire reconstruction of the interior will be necessary,' the Bank's recently started house magazine, the *Old Lady*, informed staff that autumn. 'But in order to preserve as far as possible the style and character of the existing building it is proposed to keep the present outside walls with as many of the old rooms behind them as possible; to continue a similar series of top-lighted Offices round the site, and, inside the enceinte thus formed, to raise the building to the height of four or five floors.' The staff's response is unrecorded, but inevitably there was concern from the Soane trustees, not just because it was clear from the start that the Rotunda would have to go. 'It is the intention to keep all of Soane's banking halls which lie comfortably with the exterior wall,' Baker wrote soothingly to Lubbock. 'There are three such halls and the entrance vestibule.' Even so, he was compelled to add that 'the remaining two of Soane's Banking Halls which lie uncomfortably with the outer wall must, unfortunately, if any plan like mine be adopted, be rebuilt'. The other external pressure came from the City Corporation, wanting the western wall withdrawn in order to allow the widening of Princes Street; while parliamentary legislation was required to enable the clearing (human bones and all) of the ancient graveyard of St Christopher-le-Stocks, which had long provided an attractive garden court within the Bank. By April 1925 demolition had begun and rebuilding about to start, and a few weeks later a model of the proposed new Bank was put on public display at the Royal Academy. The *Architects' Journal* offered an early assessment, praising 'the luxuriant combination of wings, domes, and porticoes', but arguing that Baker's final design was 'marred by the superaddition of the standard London County Council two-floor dormer roof, a feature into which no architect alive could breathe a tolerably individual spirit'. Nevertheless, the overall verdict was that 'the building promises to be one of considerable distinction'.[6]

Work was soon fully under way. 'A combined impression of the ruins of Carthage, the fall of Jericho and the after effects of an air raid,' reflected one observer, as each day a small crowd gathered in Bartholomew Lane to watch the demolition of the Stock Offices. Probably few imagined at this point that the entire process of rebuilding the Bank would take seventeen years, including a new wave of air raids over London. For those at the coalface, it could be hard and sometimes furtive going. 'It was the most difficult job I have tackled,' remembered John Chitty in the 1940s about the erection of a glistening dome over the re-creation three storeys down of Taylor's Treasury:

There was so much moulding and panelling. It was done without the use of solder or brazing. Everything had to be panelling ... The old outer walls were left standing when the reconstruction work on which I was engaged took place. The reason was that if the foundations of the outer wall should be broken the City Council would be likely to step in and claim street widening ... The new vaultage of

the Bank was kept a secret, and the men working in it were sworn
to secrecy.

For Baker himself, these were occasionally fraught but mainly satisfy-
ing years. 'I go happily [on his way to India] having seen the portico
finished,' he wrote to George Booth (Lubbock's successor) in January
1931, hours after the formal unveiling of the six buttress figures
sculpted by Charles Wheeler above the architect's new Threadneedle
Street entrance. 'I only hope,' he added, 'the music won't be a terror
to face! ... My wife sends her kind regards; and says she is proud
that Baker now rises above Soane.' The following year, when George
Bolton joined the Bank's Foreign Exchange Office, temporarily
housed 'in two contractors' sheds in the Chief Cashier's Garden
Court', he was disinclined to mourn the passing of the familiar. 'The
old Soane structure,' he unsentimentally recalled several decades later,
'was not only an anachronism in terms of internal services, office
efficiency and flexibility, but was becoming a ruin; the ceilings, for
example, were prevented from falling on staff and customers alike by
festoons of chicken wire draped in cobwebs that had the appearance
of grubby Spanish moss hanging from trees in a deserted Carolina
plantation.'

April 1933 saw the building of the first half of the new Bank
completed – with departments moving in at nights and over week-
ends – and Baker took the opportunity to issue a comprehensive press
statement. The 'several old Soane Banking Halls,' he noted, had been
rebuilt 'not as separate disconnected units as before, but on the same
axis and opening into each other'; moreover, 'owing to improvements
in the design of the lighting it has been possible to remove the ugly
iron and glass skylights which had been built above his circles of
columns and caryatides, and to replace his solid domes thus restoring
to their original design the most beautiful feature of his halls'; and
altogether 'it may be truly said that the Soane Banking Halls can now
be seen to better advantage than ever before'. Baker had plenty of
other progress to report. He referred to 'the great Garden Courtyard,
half of which has now been built'; 'the Court Room is being built
on the first instead of the ground floor as before'; 'the treatment of
the new Parlours' was, it had been decided, to be 'in the same familiar style as the old'; the 'skill and craftsmanship' of the Boris Anrep

mosaics on the ground floor were self-evident; while as for 'the walls, and the domed and vaulted ceilings of both the inner and outer halls', these had been 'built in solid stone from the Hopton Wood quarries in Derbyshire', involving with such hard-as-marble stone a quality of masonry that 'has perhaps never been equalled and reflects the very highest credit on the British masons of today'.

The Times soon afterwards also accentuated the positive: 'Within the enclosing walls the transformation that has taken place is, ignoring style, something like that of the medieval fortress in the Renaissance mansion. A good deal of the reconstruction has taken the form of the simplification and tidying up, with improved lighting, of cellular structure.' In architectural terms, the last significant development was unveiled in October 1936 with the formal opening of the controversially reconstructed Tivoli Corner – a reconstruction necessitating, in response to traffic requirements, a pedestrian passage through new archways, but going beyond necessity in Baker's cavalier decision to remove Soane's crowning attic. 'This tomb-like superstructure,' claimed his retrospective justification, 'the design of which Sir John Soane let his fancy play with, however suitable it might have been as seen against the skyline of a one-storey building, would lose all its character and appropriateness – or meaning if it ever had any – in relation to and as seen against the high building behind it.'[7]

By this time, even before the completion of all the work, Baker's critics were starting to sharpen their pens – none more so than C. H. Reilly, a professor of architecture who wrote regularly in the *Banker*. A building 'which was once majestic' had been transformed, he declared in 1937, into 'the overgrown private residence of some plutocrat of more than Rockefeller proportions'. Especially regretting the Tivoli Corner reconstruction – formerly 'a thing of complete and strange and unexpected beauty to find in the City', now 'a commonplace little cupola above a low dome' – he concluded bitterly enough: 'I see nevertheless after all this, the Bank has erected a statue to Soane. When one has destroyed a man's best work, I suppose it is the gentlemanly thing to do.' Eight years later, shortly after the publication of Baker's self-justifying memoirs, which misleadingly emphasised the retention and incorporation of Soane's best features, the aesthetically discerning diarist James Lees-Milne was shown round:

To my surprise there is absolutely nothing left of Sampson, Taylor or Soane's work inside, and outside only Soane's outer wall. And that has been mutilated by Sir Herbert Baker. I was disgusted by the re-erection of the Taylor court room, which Baker tampered with to suit his own devices. Had he demolished the whole building and built anew from the foundations I should have respected him more, but he has compromised by reproducing Taylor vaulting and Soane motifs in the basement. Yet Baker is a distinctive architect and craftsman. His lapses into Kraal detail are undignified in classical work.

The most influential of the public attacks was made in 1957 by Nikolaus Pevsner in *The Buildings of England*. He asserted that 'Baker's superstructure is not only oppressive but – which is worse – lacks grandeur'; he deeply regretted the destruction of 'Soane's interiors with their infinite variety of domes, every one original and interesting, and several of a very high and exacting beauty'; and over-all, taking the first half of the century as a whole, he reckoned that it was, even allowing for the Second World War, 'the worst individual loss suffered by London architecture'. The centenary of Baker's birth failed to shift what had become a hostile consensus. 'Now that Soane is esteemed as one of Britain's great and original architects, we find it difficult to forgive Baker for his treatment of the Bank of England, Soane's masterpiece,' solemnly stated *The Times* in 1962. 'Baker was more ruthless than he need have been. He gutted the whole interior, sweeping away all Soane's and Sir Robert Taylor's unique, original courts, and he built inside Soane's peripheral wall a multi-storey block that was self-confidently elaborate where an architect with a true artist's humility would have been content to be discreet.'[8]

More recent opinion has been mixed. Simon Bradley, authorita-tively updating and revising Pevsner in 1997, was unwilling to retract the great man's damning verdict ('Pevsner's judgement still stands'). In terms of the exterior, asserted Bradley, 'Baker's vocabulary gener-ally appears not as a considered response to particular circumstances, in the way of Soane's restless endeavours, but as a kit of parts to be deployed complacently and regardless of context,' with 'the recurrent motif everywhere a singling out of odd principal windows by rather weak aedicules, or by a favourite Baker form with segmental head and foot', both of them 'entirely out of sympathy with Soane's style – as is the gruesome hipped pantiled roof'; as for the interior, he regretted the way Baker, though reproducing the Old Dividend Office 'almost exactly', had nevertheless 'sabotaged the proportions by adding at either end a version of the domed centre bay of the Old Colonial Office'. Admittedly, he conceded, 'the new top-lit banking halls of the perimeter are more faithful to Soane's models than is commonly realized', yet overall 'the distinction between his architectural personality and Soane's is a matter not of taste, but of the gulf between talented professionalism and imaginative genius'.

The real reputational recovery came in 2005 with Daniel Abramson's magisterial *Building the Bank of England*, which included a sensitive and archivally based appraisal of the actual – often difficult – circumstances in which Baker did his work. 'Throughout the process of rebuilding,' he notes, the architect was 'faced with striking a balance between tradition and modernisation', with the latter a clear and inescapable competing priority, whatever anyone's understandable attachment to the former:

> Functionally the old Bank of England had become obsolete. The major construction campaigns of the eighteenth and early nineteenth century had culminated more than a century earlier in a more or less public complex housing some thousand staff without electricity, telephones, plumbing and other modern technologies and amenities. The new building, on the other hand, would have to house an organisation that was not only four times larger, but whose work had changed fundamentally, now being much more clerical and less publicly oriented [in the sense of daily customers calling at the Bank], and directed by a professional executive corps.

Abramson further emphasises that during the 1920s and 1930s Baker and the Bank's directors and public opinion generally were all more or less as one, in that they 'accepted the Bank's practical requirement and felt, too, that Baker's design work and re-creations of some interior Soane spaces represented a respectful enough continuation of the classical tradition, of Soane's aesthetic and of the Bank's architectural history'. Moreover, he points out, 'as eventually constructed the rebuilt Bank contained numerous preserved, altered and re-created "gems" set into the fabric of the new building' – gems such as Taylor's sculpted twisting and flowing 1730s figure of Britannia or various of Soane's transfer hall lantern columns or the replication on the third floor of his Doric vestibule, even as elsewhere in the Bank such thoroughly modern and utilitarian developments were being introduced as its own generating station, engine room and 800-foot deep water well, not to mention, behind the Lothbury front, a high-tech, horseshoe-shaped Bullion Yard able to accommodate turning motorised vehicles.

Altogether, while not denying Baker's 'seemingly gratuitous fiddling with his predecessors' work', typified by 'the alterations to his replica of Taylor's Court Room', and rightly critical of his 'claims to be respecting Soane's real intentions', it is a persuasive defence; and Abramson quotes with tacit sympathy Baker's own comparative verdict in relation to the newly built (1921–4) Federal Reserve Bank of New York: 'It was a veritable fortress of wealth. But its interior had none of the welcoming appearance of a house of city merchants, which is the tradition of Threadneedle Street.' Perhaps that was a stretch – Baker's Bank was also a deliberately formidable, unyielding symbol of the financial power at the very heart of what was still the British Empire – yet over the years a certain domesticity, epitomised by the new Garden Court, would even in its twentieth-century garb help to make the Old Lady an institution capable of commanding affection as well as respect.[9]

What was life like in the Bank between the wars? It certainly did not start on a harmonious note. On a Saturday afternoon in February 1919 a crowded meeting of the staff was held in the Court Room and addressed by Wilfred G. Bryant, a 1st-class clerk in the Branch Banks Office. He began by thanking the governors for their 'magnanimity and kindness' in allowing 'the use of this beautiful room'; and he emphasised 'the gratitude we all feel for the very many privileges and blessings we enjoy in the service of the Governor and Company'. But his tone soon darkened: 'It has come to pass that because we are in the service of the Bank, the Bank claims the right to commandeer, if it thinks fit, the whole of our waking life and to recompense us for the sacrifice of all our leisure on its own terms. Is it any wonder that human nature has rebelled against this worse than slavery?' And: 'For years past the whole system of promotions has caused comment and disaffection. Men are passed over without a cause assigned and are barred accordingly from legitimate advances.' And again: 'How many men in this room could give a complete list of our Directors? Or tell aught about their personalities? Not one in ten. Yet they are our masters ...' Strong words, yet Bryant (speaking as a member of the self-styled 'Committee of Delegates') was just as harsh on those gathered around him:

> We have not received from you, although we have been fighting your battles, all the sympathy that we deserved. There is a terrible amount of snobbery in the Bank. There is an extraordinary ability to sit upon fences. There is a remarkable shrinking from compromising your dignity or your fancied position with the authorities. There is the strangest aversion to putting your names to documents. There is an appalling lack of brotherly feeling among you. There exists a most utter callousness to any sort of *esprit-de-corps*.

Suitably stung, the meeting agreed to send a memorandum, 'respectfully addressed to the Governor and Directors of the Bank of England by the staff of the same', demanding the establishment of a standing committee of directors and staff, on the grounds that 'in no other way does it seem possible that difficulties can be brought to light and alleged grievances ventilated'. The deputy governor was unsympathetic – Norman in his diary calling it a 'Grumblers Meeting' – but the Court as a whole responded by appointing a Special Committee on Grievances.

Over the next few months it heard many grumbles. No doubt there was a self-selecting and not necessarily representative element to those who spoke up; but cumulatively the eloquent evidence was of a far from happy workforce:

> I am of opinion that the men who were promoted on the Stock side last October were very largely in one particular clique and that undue influence was exercised. *(William Challis, 1st-class clerk in the Dividend Accounts Office)*

I was eleven years in the 4th-Class, which was most disheartening, and I thought that once I got out of that Class things could not be worse; I have, however, been 13 years in the 2nd Class and I am still there. I am nearly 54 ... I believe my case is the worst in the Bank. *(Henry Onyon, 2nd-class clerk in the Dividend Pay Office)*

I may say that there are many men who would like to come before you but are afraid to do so, partly because they are not sure what their reception will be, and partly because they fear that a black mark would be put against them. *(Frederick Rumsey, supernumerary 2nd-class clerk in the Dividend Pay Office)*

Since I was demobilised on the 12th December last, my average time of leaving on Saturday has been 3 o'clock ... I used to play Rugby football and often I did not arrive on the field until half-time. *(Arthur J. F. Bond, 4th-class clerk in the Private Drawing Office)*

May I say that I am loath to be thought a man with a grievance ... I think the Class system works unfairly in that men have to depend largely on chance for their promotion. If promotion is stagnant at the head of an office it means that through no fault of their own the men in the office are kept back. *(Wilfrid M. Acres, 1st-class clerk in the Branch Banks Office and future historian of the Bank)*

I may say that I came into the Bank in 1882 and since then I have not spoken to a Governor or Director. *(Henry H. Lempriere, 1st-class clerk in the Dividend Pay Office)*

A man never knows his character in the Bank. If a man wants to know his character he has to ask his Principal, who may or may not tell him. Any secret system is liable to abuse, as it places the Principal in an autocratic position ... *(James R. Sugars, 3rd-class clerk in the Accountant's Bank Note Office)*

I have to work late on every possible occasion in order that I may be able to give my family the bare necessities of life ... The Bank have always been particular as to the type of men they elect into the Service; they come from decent homes and have the habits and tastes of gentlemen and I think the Bank should put them in the position to gratify those tastes. *(Cuthbert Pearce, 4th-class clerk in the Dividend Accounts Office, aged twenty-nine and married with small twins, on a basic salary of £290)*

We don't want the Bank run on the lines of a factory and we fully appreciate the benefits we enjoy in the Service. We don't expect anything unreasonable. We don't want to be paid double for half the work or anything of that sort. But if the Staff are treated with sympathy and consideration you need have no doubt whatever that they would respond to that treatment ... If the Authorities will endeavour, when considering problems connected with the Staff, to put themselves in our places and think what they would feel if they were in our position they need have no fear as to the result, nor need the Staff. *(James Harrison, 4th-class clerk in the Private Drawing Office)*

Reassured by what Bryant described as 'the extreme repugnance among our men to have anything to do with Trade Unions', the Court in July set up an Advisory Council of Directors and Staff.[10] The Bank would remain for a long time a decidedly hierarchical organisation; but the old days of seemingly arbitrary autocratic rule had gone for ever.

The end of autocracy did not mean the end of paternalism – far from it. Even before the war, in 1908, the Bank had provided the eighteen-acre ground (off Priory Lane in Roehampton) for a staff sports club; and in July 1919 – only months after the 'Grumblers Committee' and amid rising industrial tension in the country at large – the visiting Ben Strong, following lunch at governor Cokayne's Roehampton home, went on to the 'field day' at the nearby Sports Club:

They have a cricket field, bowling greens, tennis courts, etc, all in beautiful order and in every way a desirable adjunct to the Bank. There were nearly 6,000, each man taking some lady friend and each of the girls in the Bank taking some man. The entertainment consisted of cricket games, tennis, bowling, a band concert and dancing in a big open air tent. I was very greatly impressed with the general appearance of the people, resembling in many respects the type which we employ in New York. A number of the directors of the Bank were there with their families, and, as in America, the dancing proved a great attraction.

'Cokayne told me,' added Strong, 'that steps were being taken by the bank employees in London, including the Bank of England, to get up some sort of a general protective organization, not quite along the lines of the labor union, but, I gathered, with the expectation that ultimately it will amount to the same thing. He viewed the movement with some concern.' In the event the recently formed Bank Officers' Guild failed to secure a meaningful foothold in the Bank, but directors like William Douro Hoare and Cecil Lubbock now started to spend significant amounts of time on matters of staff welfare, with Hoare's cricket match against the Bank 1st XI remaining the centrepiece of the annual summer garden party until his death in 1928, when a governor's team took over, usually fielding a Test star or two. Other indications of the enhanced paternalism between the wars included the start in 1921 of the *Old Lady* (albeit seldom a forum for the venting of grievances), the establishment in 1934 of a Superannuation Fund for pensioners (replacing the old system of pensions being granted 'at the pleasure of Court'), and, especially valued by current staff on a daily basis, the creation in 1927 in Tokenhouse Yard of the Bank of England Club, featuring a bar, a coffee room and a meeting room as well as dining rooms – 'Every stick and stone of which,' reported the *Old Lady*, 'has been ungrudgingly given by the Governor and Company.'[11]

The third floor at Tokenhouse Yard was reserved for women clerks, while at Roehampton the women had from 1921 their own separate Sports Club. What there does not seem to have been – in the early 1920s anyway, and probably throughout the inter-war period – was parity of esteem. 'Experience has shown,' declared a January 1920 memo about the Secretary's Office, 'that although Women Clerks perform straight-forward work very satisfactorily they are unable, with rare exception, to carry out any intricate work without supervision and they suffer from a lack of adaptability ...' Moreover: 'Women Clerks cannot be employed on the work of the Bank Provident Society, or the Income Tax, which involve private affairs of members of the staff, as the staff will not consult them. The work of the counter, involving as it does on many occasions criminal questions, is also unsuitable for women.' A memo later that year from the principals of the Correspondence Department was if anything even less enthusiastic:

> We are of opinion that a given number of men will get through considerably more work than an equal number of women; & that speaking generally the standard of their work will be higher ... The value of the work of Women Clerks is lessened because of their frequent absences, because they are emotional & easily upset & also

we think because there is a tendency amongst the younger ones not
to look upon their work as their career in life.

The key report was that of March 1921, as the House Committee
submitted to the deputy governor its views on 'The Future
Employment in the Bank of England of Women Clerks', in other
words in the larger context of men's post-war return to work. After
noting that 'the disparity, under existing conditions, in the absolute
efficiency of the two sexes is sufficiently obvious in our opinion to
justify the relegation of women in the mass to the work for which
they seem specially adapted', the report went on:

> Without expressing an opinion upon the abstract merits of Equality
> of Service, we do not consider that the service of the Bank admits the
> practical application of a principle of equality because the continu-
> ity of the subordinate and administrative careers implies eligibility
> for either, but the woman's eligibility for the administrative career
> is qualified by uncertain duration of service: a disqualification, in
> fact, that we would make apparent during her subordinate career
> by *restriction* to a particular class of work and render perhaps less
> objectionable by *segregation* from men. Nor although there may be
> women whose capacity equals or exceeds that of the average clerk
> do we think that it would serve any useful purpose under present
> conditions to engage such women exceptionally upon the work
> which we propose to confine to men.

'Shorthand and Typewriting; Currency and Bank Note work;
Machining and sorting dividend warrants and coupon work; General
Card Index work' – such were the functions, concluded the report, to
which women in the future were to be confined, with of course the
rule staying in place that a woman had to leave at once if she married.
Nor was there significantly more freedom sartorially. Hat and gloves
on arrival and departure were compulsory for all female staff; a notice
was issued forbidding make-up, especially lipstick; and when in the
1930s a female clerk in the Dividend Office dared to wear a blouse
with a bow at the neck showing above her stipulated dark-navy overall, a superintendent in the War Stock Office took exception and
formally complained.[12] Women may have comprised over one-third

of the workforce, but in all essentials and outlook the Bank remained
– as Janet Hogarth had realistically anticipated – almost as male-
dominated an institution as it had always been.

First impressions can be the sharpest, and a trio of male reminiscences evoke the flavour of a place that was still, in many other sorts
of ways as well, traditional and unchanging:

The twenty young hopefuls who made up my 'Election' [in 1921]
were paraded in the Court Room and subjected to the usual scrutiny before being walked round the Bank and dropped off in ones
or twos in various offices. My destination was the old Private
Drawing Office, which in those days faced north and overlooked
the old Bank Garden ... The Superintendent of the G-O section, on
which I worked, was Charlie Butterworth. Clad in a frock coat and
wearing elastic-sided Victorian boots he seemed to me to be a very
old gentleman ... The Drawing Office then was a noisy, busy place.
Ledgers, cash books, pass books and waste books were all hand
written and at around 3.00 pm and again after 4.00 pm there were
furious rushes to enter the 'Town Clearing' and then the bundles
of Bank cheques ... The countermen were noisier and used louder
and coarser language than in later years. Especially I remember a
couple named Troughton and Olivier, the latter said to be the son
of a bishop. Olivier had a habit of leaving the counter and passing
through the office, pinching or annoying some woman clerk on his
way, to bait an inoffensive colleague named Grugeon who worked
on the Bankers counter. (C. D. Garton)

My first impression on entering the Bank in 1926 was of a number
of bearded old gentlemen and an equally elderly messenger standing in front of a large coal fire in the Treasury – on the right of the
main entrance. It was all very Dickensian ... On reporting to the
Chief Cashier's representative, I was instructed to walk across to
the Stock Offices in Finsbury Circus. I soon found myself working
in the 5% War Stock Office on the ground floor. The Principal was
named Delamere. His first words, delivered rather pompously, were
'Have you had any indulgences?' I was completely nonplussed. It
turned out that he wanted to know if I had had any leave. This
was the only time he ever took any notice of me, but in those days
Probationers and Third Class Clerks did not expect to be noticed,

much less spoken to, by Principals and Superintendents. They never appeared to do any work, so being too busy was no excuse. Two Superintendents in an office on the first floor woke each other up during the morning by exchanging newspapers; another telephoned his friend in another office every day. 'Bowler or topper?' he asked, nothing more. The conversation was to decide upon the appropriate headgear for their trip to the Wine Lodge. *(F. R. Levander)*

The Bank was then [in 1936] heavily rule- and image-ridden. It was made clear that one wore a bowler hat, a stiff collar and a waist-coat. We were also required to look busy all the time. This was a problem in the War Stock Office: when the market was quiet we had virtually no work. So, to create the impression of industry – until 3.55 when we got on to the starting blocks – we devised a system in which each of us filled in a batch of the Inland Revenue's nasty little buff forms, then passed the bundle of forms and transfers to the next chap. He would tear up the forms and start again! *(Jasper Hollom)*

'But one was working with an agreeable bunch of young people,' added the subsequent deputy governor, 'and with the much narrower range of entertainment in those days, the Sports Club was a great advantage.'[13]

Across the Bank as a whole, most of the dullest and especially repetitive work was on the Stock rather than Cash side. There must have been moments in the Accountant's Department – between the wars mainly situated in Finsbury Circus – when some of those employed lost the will to live. 'Looking back to my early days,' recalled R. B. Charsley in the mid-1970s half a century after joining the Power of Attorney Office, 'I seem to remember masses of sheer pen pushing in the Stock Offices – "entry", abstracts, ledgers, white sheet, circulars, etc, also adding up long columns of figures without the help of a machine, and going down to the vaults to agree signatures on Powers, Deeds, Div. Requests, etc.' But there could be tedium too on the Cash side, with another pensioner of the same vintage, M. H. Browning, looking back on the Dividend Pay and Loans Office:

All Bearer Bonds were recorded by Bond number and denomination in the Bond ledgers with columns indicating the dividends represented by the coupons attached. Coupons when paid, were listed on numbered sheets which were then taken to the ledgers for the sheet number to be inserted against the Bond number and under the appropriate Dividend column. Bonds surrendered for inscription in the Bank's Books were first sorted and checked to see that coupons not yet due were still attached, and then also listed. These lists were taken to the ledgers and red lines drawn opposite the Bond number from the next dividend column onwards to ensure that no more coupons could be cashed. Every posting and red line was counted and your month's total was reported to you together with the number of mistakes you had made, and woe betide you if this figure amounted to more than one per thousand. Ten thousand postings in a month was considered reasonably good and often exceeded in June and December when War Loan paid and we were very busy. At other times already sorted Bonds were taken away, unsorted and given out again to be resorted, and failing all else one was expected to be seen writing something – even with the wrong end of one's pen!

Or take the sometimes vexed matter of flyleaves. The *Old Lady* from 1932 ran a column called 'Flyleaf', and it was an apt enough symbol of the day-to-day clerical routine – involving endless precision and endless chatting – as Frank Dancaster explained many years later:

The 'flyleaves' of the old manuscript ledgers were with pages somewhat smaller than those of the ledgers tucked into stout pockets, pasted inside the front outer covers of the parent volumes, to prevent them from straying. When one of them did stray panic reigned until it was found, for it was an adjunct essential to the system then in use. Stock accounts have, of course, to be altered sometimes – when, for example, an address was changed, a stockholder altered her surname on marriage or a nominee for the receipt of dividends was appointed – every such alteration had to be 'flyleaved' and anyone who 'forgot to flyleaf' was due for a kick in the pants. A flyleaf page was divided into three (or it may have been four – I forget which) main columns, each of which was subdivided into four smaller columns. The first of these was for the folio reference to the altered account, the second for the correspondence 'mark' under which the alteration was made, while the third and fourth much narrower sub-columns were headed 'done by' and 'checked by' (dawn at last begins to break). A few weeks before a dividend was due, an operation – itself known as 'the flyleaf' – was performed by a couple of clerks. One extracted the slips which required alteration from their slip-box, altered them and initialled in the column headed 'done by' against the corresponding folio and reference mark entries; the other checked the alterations and similarly initialled the column headed 'checked by'. The slips were large cards, made of thin, tough cardboard each bearing an exact copy of its corresponding stock account. The accounts in the manuscript ledger were, of necessity, all higgledy-piggledy being raised in the order of their dates of opening. It was therefore impossible to use these immensely heavy and bulky volumes directly for any such purpose as the preparation of a dividend but the slips were, in effect, a duplicate of the ledger in loose-leaf form which could be sorted in dividend-book order. When the 'flyleaf' was completed the bundles of altered slips were sent to the Printers so that the necessary amendments could be made to the dividend-books, the postal warrants and the envelopes containing them. On their return they could be easily sorted back into the main body of 'slips'.

A degree of mechanisation, though, was on its way: Mercedes accounting machines were in widespread use by the mid-1930s, as well as special fanfold typing machines, using continuous stationery, and the Hollerith system of punched cards. 'I and other clerks were trained how to operate the Burroughs Adding Machines,' recalled Naree Craik about their coming in 1934 to the Dividend Preparation Office at the St Luke's Printing Works. 'The large sheets, which already had the names and addresses printed on them, were rolled into the machine. The capital, interest, tax and net amount were copied from stiff slips. Then, the sheets were added up by hand and proved with various tables. Each clerk was expected to do not less than 750 entries a day. Whenever work was slack, we read or knitted, but if anyone was visiting the office, we added trip sheets from old ledgers, proved them, rubbed out the totals and began again.'

The probability is that many found in the Bank a safe and adequately fulfilling berth, at a time of insecurity and high unemployment in the world outside. Certainly the pages of the *Old Lady* in the 1970s and 1980s would be full of essentially cheerful reminiscences. Take Neville Goodman's 'Happy Memories', written in 1982, sixty years after he had 'entered the Service' as a seventeen-year-old probationer:

There were some bizarre characters among us. There was, for instance, the occasion at the Silver Refinery (housed in the printing works in Old Street) when a young clerk turned up in a 'shock-ing-pink' shirt. This so outraged his colleagues that they took him into the 'cloaks', divested him of the offending garment which they tore into shreds and conveniently disposed of, hung an oval wooden seat, which lay handy, round his neck and pushed him, thus adorned, into the Principal's sanctum. Shirts were the subject of another episode which occurred in the Dividend Pay Office: one of our number arrived one morning wearing the usual collar and tie – but no shirt. He explained that he possessed only one and that was at the laundry. Here, again, his fellows took matters into their own hands by painting alternate stripes of red and black ink down his chest, thus making him appear respectable – at a distance.

Still in the D.P.O., we suffered from a superintendent named Gardiner – known as 'Goat's Milk Gardiner' as he was reputed to rely on that product for his sole means of sustenance. Rather austere and feared by some, he nevertheless had his mellow side. On one occasion two of us were on our way out by the side door for an illegal 'cuppa' when we had the misfortune to run full tilt into G., returning, no doubt, from some similar refreshment. Using his most awe-inspiring tone, he addressed us: 'Don't imagine that I am unaware that you indulge in this clandestine habit – but don't let me see you and, for God's sake, WEAR YOUR HATS!' (In those days, we were not allowed outside the Bank bare-headed.) ...

In the Bill Office, we had a superintendent named Williams – a strict disciplinarian. He noticed that one of our number habitually arrived late in the morning and decided to confront him. 'Yer not doing yer duty by yer Masters; yer not doing yer duty by yer colleagues,' said W., to which the offender replied: 'I acknowledge only one Master, and He's above.' 'Is that so?' said Williams. 'Well, I'm quite certain that He is the first to disapprove of yer goings on.' Also in the Bill Office, there was a rather scruffy individual who wished, one day, to make some complaint to the Principal. On his entering the sanctum, the Principal (one Dalrymple-Hay, affectionately known as 'Daddy-Winkle') eyed him up and down, gave him a shilling and told him to go and get a hair-cut and a shave, after which, he would be prepared to see him ...

I cannot vouch for the following story, but it was told as fact at the time. The Rotunda included an upper gallery in which some of the clerks worked, including two chicken-fanciers. One of these two was extolling the merits of a new breed he was trying and he offered to bring a specimen to the Bank to show his friend. The next morning he placed a hamper on his desk and opened the lid for his colleague to examine the contents. At that very moment someone slammed a ledger; the bird took flight and flew over the balcony and down into the Office below, causing a great commotion. The chicken was eventually retrieved and the Principal, on his return from luncheon, was surprised to find an egg lying on his desk ...

I may give the impression that the young Staff in my time were a bit irresponsible, but we did no real harm, respected (most of) our seniors and, in spite of – or perhaps, because of – the fact that we had no Union, there was an atmosphere of mutual trust between the Bank and its Staff. We worked hard and long when required, including Saturdays. If Christmas Day fell on a Sunday, that was our bad luck, as we had only Christmas Day and Boxing Day 'off'.

'The things I have recorded,' reflected Goodman, 'helped one to survive the monotonous tasks we had to perform. I posted ledgers (by hand, of course) for eight solid years and, when I asked my Principal (Whiting) if I could have a change of occupation after so long a time, he chid me for my impatience, saying, by way of comfort, "*I* posted ledgers for *eleven* years – and look at me now!"'[14]

In practice, few did make it to principal; and, more generally, there was a darker side to the inter-war Bank. 'So every pre-war clerk became a person of great authority, wearing a top hat in the office, enthroned in a raised stall; and able to make or break any junior at will,' recalled Leslie Bonnet about the absurdly overmanned Accountant's Department of the 1920s. 'Results were ludicrous. Some of these old men were of feeble intellect. Some were more numerate than literate. Many were just plain stupid. And why not? They hadn't been chosen for initiative, or intelligence. Good handwriting was their best commendation. And so, confronted by this seething cauldron of ambitious, clever, young men, it is little wonder that they feared and hated the newcomers.' It would of course be wrong to suggest that merit and ambition (qualities not as uniformly on display as Bonnet suggested) went entirely unrewarded: Kenneth Peppiatt, who had joined the Bank shortly before the war, enjoyed an almost meteoric rise, becoming chief cashier in 1934 when barely in his forties; while Leslie O'Brien, following his cricket-based recruitment in 1927, became only fifteen years later Norman's last private secretary. These, however, were exceptions. The most revealing – and in its way disturbing – evidence comes from Reay Geddes, who after Rugby and Cambridge joined the Bank in March 1933 and spent almost two years there before deciding, at the age of twenty-two, that it was not the place for him. Son of the businessman-cum-politician Sir Eric Geddes, and not lacking in self-confidence, he took the opportunity to send to the chief of Establishments what he called his 'sincere but untutored observation from the lowest rank'.

Noting at the outset that 'the boys who the Bank enlist have a good general standard of education, no experience other than that of school and holidays, and no definite bent', and that 'the vast majority do not come at their own express request, but on the choice of their Fathers, who are glad to find a gilt-edged investment for the capital represented by a son who is "developing rather late"', he went on to explain how – because of the policy of deliberate overmanning in order to be able to cope with the occasional brief rush – the new recruit found himself not only quickly bored but also corrupted:

> For half the day, men are, to a greater or less extent, idle. Any attempt to interest himself in a book, be it novel or text-book, on the part of a recruit is frowned upon as much as any desire to make suggestions or try to see something of another section's work. The command to 'Look busy anyway' is no uncommon one. Its continuation is 'or they may take men away and we will have to work late' …
>
> It is quite inevitable that the recruit should start work in one of the outer offices. There he meets and works beside 'Disappointed men' who are always willing to tell what dreadful luck they have had at the hands of God, disease, the war and the Bank's complete

disregard for merit. These gentlemen have one curious loyalty: if their superior winks at the custom of coffee or tea being taken during office hours, it is quite understood that each clerk enjoys these pleasures entirely at his own risk, if there are complaints from the 'case'. The recruit then learns that the foremen allow rules to be disregarded, but deny any knowledge of such transgressions. This cannot increase the recruit's respect for his superior. Apart from this loyalty, the disappointed ones have had none. With their mocking of keenness, their obstruction of questions and their eyes on the clock, they are a strong and undesirable influence on boys fresh from school, during the latter's almost inevitable periods of doubt and apprehension.

Inevitably, disillusion sets in – exacerbated, according to Geddes, by older clerks often saying to the recent recruit, 'Does it ever strike you that you will be like me one day?' And as a result, he calculated, some 2,000 men, roughly half the total workforce, were condemned 'to work at which their education only serves to make them uncomfortable – either openly discontented or passively awaiting a pension'. Accordingly, he recommended that it would be altogether more desirable if the work was done by those better suited to it:

The objections to a cheaper grade of labour than the Bank employ at present are behaviour, appearance and intonation. A visit to the Clearing House would show how difficult it is to pick out Bank men [as opposed to those employed by the clearing banks]. This is not to suggest that the Bank's standard is lower than in years gone by, but that mass-produced clothing and general knowledge have spread a certain 'savoir faire' which used only to be obtainable in conjunction with expensive education.

'While the men are here,' concluded Geddes, 'let them work. If they are temporarily surplus, they are better playing golf at home than dominoes in a "Mecca" café.'[15]
Geddes himself had a notable business career ahead; his report was carefully filed away, to gather dust; and it would be a while yet before the Bank became an environment that nurtured rather than stifled what Keynes would call capitalism's necessary 'animal spirits'.

The Dogs Bark

Despite the national humiliation of going off the gold standard in September 1931, only six years after the return to gold, Montagu Norman would remain as governor for the rest of the decade and indeed beyond. Later that autumn he successfully resisted a final threatened coup – 'some of us,' reflected Addis, 'would like to see him retire, but I fancy he will get his own way in the end' – by dint of verbally promising to depart in 1933, a promise carrying so little weight in subsequent practice that as early as July 1932 the Court formally told him that henceforth there would be 'no restriction' on his 'length of service'. It is likely that Norman was being less disingenuous when in July 1936 he informed the Committee of Treasury of his wish to step down by 1938, prompting over the next twelve to fifteen months a serious search for a successor. Four possibilities were considered: one, W. H. Clegg, back at the Bank since 1932 after his stint in South Africa, decided in 1937 on health grounds to leave the Bank altogether; another, the merchant banker Charles Hambro, who had become a director in 1928, regretfully decided that he could not permanently detach himself from the family firm; a third, Sir Otto Niemeyer, was ruled out by Peacock on the basis that 'the name would not be easily swallowed in several quarters'; and the last one, Lord Catto (formerly Thomas Catto), a highly regarded partner at Morgan Grenfell, was for the moment inadmissible because that merchant bank already had a presence on the Court in the person of Lord St Just (the former Teddy Grenfell). Hambro came nearest to replacing the seemingly irreplaceable, with the approach to him representing an attempt (in the words of Norman's first proper biographer, Henry Clay) 'to find

a candidate who satisfied *both* the Governor, who wanted a "professional", and the old gang on the Treasury Committee, who wanted a
traditional-type merchant-banker'. Yet whether Hambro anyway had
the stomach for it, quite apart from his other commitments, is another
matter. 'I am not fit to be Governor,' he frankly admitted to Peacock
even before the approach in September 1937, 'because I loathe a row
and have not the guts to see it through.'¹

Norman himself remained one of public life's most distinctive
figures. Geoffrey Madan – reluctant City man, but celebrated connoisseur of aperçus – described him travelling on the Central Line in
1932. The governor boarded at Bond Street 'in a state of high tension'
and 'lay back looking half strangled, as if fallen from a great height';
during the journey to Bank he 'glared round with the queer look of a
man swelling with laughter and longing to share it with someone else,
or groaned aloud in pain'; and on arrival, after pausing 'for a leisurely
and mournful study of an advertisement on a wall', he 'strode on and
mounted the escalator, alone, like the bridge of a ship, striking a glorious pose – portrait of an admiral in China seas', reminding Madan of
'the Treasury saying, that the Bank of England acts like a commander
in the days before strategy was thought of'. For Norman the man,
the major event of the decade was his marriage in January 1933, at
the age of sixty-one, to the thirty-three-year-old Priscilla Worsthorne.
'He wore a check scarf flung carelessly around his neck,' reported
a London evening paper about the ceremony at Chelsea Registry
Office, 'and the black trilby hat that has become familiar with him.'
It seems to have been a happy marriage, and before long featured a
touching moment engineered by his colleagues:

> On the appointed day [his widow would recall after his death] I was
> driven to the Bank by our chauffeur, Tom, in the white-topped Ford
> Lincoln and ushered into the Governor's room. This had two doors,
> one leading into the passage and the other into the Court Room. I
> was alone for what seemed a long time. Suddenly I panicked and I
> had a feeling that this episode might ruin my marriage. I was making
> for the exit door when the other one opened and Mont came in
> alone. He stopped and said, 'What the devil are you doing here?'
> My heart missed a beat! The Deputy [Sir Ernest Harvey] was close
> behind him and said 'Mr Governor, I am responsible for this. Your

colleagues want to be introduced to Mrs Governor.' He took me kindly by the arm and led me into the room to meet the Directors, who were all standing in a circle. Mont then took me by the hand and introduced me to each one, giving an amusing thumb sketch of each. I remember one rather aged director bursting into tears. Of course this set me off, and Mont too had tears pouring down his cheeks! Looking back, it was an extraordinary emotional scene and one that only Mont's personality could have evoked. Like me, the directors were all a little apprehensive, wondering if they had been wise to take this secret step. However, the ice was broken and I had got into the Old Lady's parlour. I was offered a glass of sherry and then courteously despatched home. I returned to a lonely lunch but felt very happy, although overwhelmed by the ordeal ...

Marriage only partially softened Norman. 'I find it's difficult to take my mind off work,' Harvey in the mid-1930s confessed to a Treasury acquaintance as he recuperated from a nervous breakdown. 'Even in my dreams I can't seem to escape from the Governor's eternal harangues.' And in Norman's desk diary, crisply summarising his interviews with the daily stream of visitors, the tone was still laconic, sometimes sardonic. 'P. A. Carmine: as he asked in Letter of 24^(th),' he jotted down one fairly typical day in May 1934. 'Swiss natural^(d) 1912. Disc^(t) and, post-war Exch Broker. Business gone: misery come: starvation coming.'[2]

Significant institutional change – and load-sharing – was meanwhile happening around Norman. If the mid- to late 1920s had seen the emergence of the specialist adviser, the early to mid-1930s saw the arrival of the full-time executive director. The immediate catalyst was the Peacock Committee of 1931–2, a forum for the old guard on the Court to have their full and uninhibited say for perhaps the last time:

If whole-time Directors were appointed the management of the Bank would largely fall into their hands and the power of the Court and of the Committee of Treasury would to a great extent disappear. (*Arthur Whitworth*)

The Public, or at least the City Public, much prefer to have City Merchants or Business men of experience rather than expert Financiers or Theoretical Economists. They have much more confidence in the former and I have already heard several complaints of appointments lately. *(Colonel Lionel Hanbury)*

The whole question of the Direction [that is, the composition of the Court] of the Bank is, in my view, bound up with the maintenance of its historical link with the City. I think it imperative that this link should be maintained, and that if it is weakened or broken the Bank will lose the confidence of business men, and will more or less rapidly become a Government institution, apt to run in a rut and deprived of the prestige and confidence which it now enjoys. This aspect of the matter appears to me so important that I should be prepared to sacrifice a certain amount of abstract technical efficiency rather than weaken the position referred to. *(The Hon Alexander Shaw)*

It does not follow because an Expert is well versed in the details of finance that he is therefore equipped with the width of outlook and the diversified experience required in determining a sound financial policy. In reality, it is the contrary which is more commonly met with … There is often to be found in business men a native shrewdness of judgment, a natural instinct for affairs, almost a sensory touch of market conditions, qualities in fact which are none the less valuable because they are partly inarticulate and should not, therefore, on that account be outweighed by mere expertise. *(Sir Charles Addis)*

Inevitably Frank Tiarks disagreed – 'the Bank should be re-organised on lines similar to those of many important undertakings at home and abroad with a certain number of ordinary Directors selected as at present and, say, six or seven permanent whole-time working Directors, who would each have his special Department, for which he would be directly responsible to the Governors' – but so too, crucially, did Norman. His oral evidence advocated the introduction of 'executive Directors' who would 'devote their whole time to highly-paid work for the Bank'; they would be 'experts', with 'the majority' having had 'outside experience', including 'at least one to deal with the Industrial questions'; and 'these executive Directors would undertake much of the work now performed by the Governors who would then be free to devote their time to constructive thought'.

Peacock's eventual report came down cautiously on Norman's side, successfully recommending the appointment of initially only two executive directors, on the grounds that 'a considerable number of Executive Directors giving their whole time to the affairs of the Bank would tend to reduce the influence of the other Members of the Court and to diminish living contact with the commerce and trade of the Country'. Even so, with the appointment of Clegg and Hambro as the first two, the key principle was now established, and over the rest of the decade several more executive directors were appointed. The *Evening Standard* in May 1939 profiled three of them:

Sir Otto Niemeyer is 56 years old, with a rugged demeanour, an untidy boyish appearance and a breeziness of manner which conceals an icy clearness of vision and the effortless superiority of a Balliol scholar. Foreign statesmen have been seen to quail beneath the bluffness of his questioning, and it is said that a distinguished Rumanian was once found weeping after an interview with him.

Mr Edward Holland-Martin is 39 years old and is known to his friends as Ruby, a name which he inherited, together with his red hair, from Mr G. E. Martin, whose initials spelled Gem, and who first acquired the nickname. Apart from banking his greatest interest is horses. He is a fearless rider and has several times ridden round the National course at Aintree in the Foxhunters' Steeplechase.

Mr Cameron Cobbold is known as Kim, has a fresh complexion, a boyish demeanour, and a beautiful wife, Lady Hermione Cobbold, who is a daughter of Lord Lytton.

The last, still in his thirties, was very much a Norman protégé and had come up on the international side, particularly in relation to Italy. 'Cobbold was a staunch traditionalist and faced the future as a complete and unrepentant pragmatist, determined to salvage as much of the past as he could.' The retrospective verdict belonged to George Bolton, another rising star and blessed with a particularly powerful mind, but born on the wrong side of the tracks. It was probably not too difficult in the late 1930s to guess which of the two would rise the higher.

In general, looked at from the top, the Bank was becoming in the 1930s a significantly more sophisticated institution – an institution in which the importance of the Court, and probably also the Committee of Treasury, was diminishing, as key decisions and business were undertaken by what has been called 'an entourage or Cabinet' of some fifteen or twenty generally youngish, well-qualified people, operating mainly on the international side and reporting directly to Norman. One should not exaggerate the modernity of it all. Norman's own belief in the primacy of instinct, his dislike of theory and an at times almost mystical belief in the wisdom of the City's markets all remained strong, influencing not only the circle immediately around him but even subsequent generations at the Bank. 'The Economics Section', the executive director Basil Catterns told a former colleague in 1935, 'tell me that they are very happy; much used by Henry Clay and myself, not to mention Siepmann and Skinner; but I am told that the Governor has not yet heard of it!' Or, as Norman himself had, two years earlier, famously informed his eventual biographer: 'Mr Clay, we have appointed you as our economic adviser; let me tell you that you are not here to tell us what to do, but to explain to us why we have done it.'[3]

Going off gold was one of those watershed moments. In Norman's eyes, the City (and perhaps even the Bank) could never be quite the same again, while he also became ever more aware that the moment marked a decisive shift in the already increasingly unfavourable (from the Bank's point of view) Bank/Treasury relationship. Back in 1926 he had told a royal commission that, though he looked upon the Bank as 'having the unique right to offer advice and to press such advice even to the point of "nagging"', that advice was 'always of course subject to the supreme authority of Government'; but in 1937, even as he continued to insist on as high a degree as possible of operational autonomy for the Bank, he would unambiguously state to the governors of the Empire's central banks that 'I am an instrument of the Treasury.' What about post-1931 policy? In November 1931, at a board meeting in Basle of the Bank for International Settlements, the BIS's Per Jacobsson asked him if, two months after going off gold, he had a 'plan' for sterling's rehabilitation:

Norman: No, I have no plan.
Jacobsson: But isn't that terrible, considering that not only Great Britain but the whole world economy is affected by the movements of sterling? And now you tell me you don't know what to do!

Norman: I didn't say that I don't know what to do. In fact, I have
made a list of some twelve points, and there is a great deal that I
want to have done with regard to each of them; I can only hope that
if there is some improvement under each of these heads there will
also be some considerable improvement in the position as a whole.

Yet incrementalism only went so far, and often for Norman at this
difficult time it was a case of looking through a glass darkly. 'The difficulties are so vast, the forces so unlimited, so novel, and precedents
are so lacking, that I approach this whole subject not only in ignorance, but in humility,' he would admit in frankly confessional mode
in October 1932 at the lord mayor's annual Mansion House banquet
for bankers and merchants. And he went on: 'It is too great for me – I
will admit for the moment the way, to me, is not clear.'[4]

In fact, and far from entirely to Norman's liking, there had taken
place by that autumn a major reshaping of British economic and
monetary policy. What one might call the 1932 settlement had four
main pillars. The first was protection, with the new chancellor, Neville
Chamberlain, announcing in February a 10 per cent general tariff, while
six months later the Imperial Conference held at Ottawa saw a system
of imperial preference formally agreed. The City was broadly happy,
but Norman himself remained an unabashed free trader. Pillar two
was the creation in April 1932 of the Exchange Equalisation Account:
essentially, the Treasury's mechanism for the management of sterling
and avoidance of undue fluctuations in the value of the currency – a
mechanism that in effect not only made the Bank the Treasury's agent
in the foreign exchange market (acquiring foreign currency from
British banks in return for Treasury bills), but more or less killed off
Norman's fond hopes of a return to the gold standard. The third pillar
was less clear-cut, being the emergence in the course of the year of a
de facto sterling area – conducting its external transactions in sterling
as well as holding its external reserves in sterling – that comprised
most of the British Empire as well as the Baltic States, Egypt, Iraq
and Argentina. Initially reluctant to accept the concept, presumably
viewing it as a rival to the gold standard, Norman eventually came to
see its potential for helping to restore the City's international position. Finally, there was cheap money, now possible after those years
of adherence to the gold standard necessitating high interest rates.

Bank rate started 1932 at 6 per cent, but by the end of June – with the Treasury driving the policy – was down to 2 per cent. What degree of reluctance Norman felt as he implemented this policy, regarded by the Treasury as vital to the revival of trade, is frustratingly hard to gauge from the sources.[5]

Probably more to his taste, directly involving him from an early stage of the negotiations and enabling one of the great Bank set-pieces, was the massive and challenging exercise that followed in July, by which the bonds of the giant War Loan of 1917 (comprising some 40 per cent of all quoted government securities) were successfully converted from a 5 per cent basis to 3½ per cent, thereby producing lower long-term interest rates to complement the lower Bank rate.[6] Richard Sayers would memorably write of how the episode revealed the Bank's 'determined exercise of all the power derived from its position in financial markets, the extent and the limits of its persuasion in informal contacts in the City, its quick adaptability in the face of unforeseen technical problems and – perhaps for the last time in its history – the fewness of the men who participated in the discussions and took the crucial decisions'. Not everyone, despite the press's loud beating of the patriotic drum, played the game; and although Norman managed to lean on the discount market to convert its share, he was compelled by Reginald McKenna's obstinacy at Midland Bank to buy £25 million out of Midland's £30 million holding of the stock. For the Bank's footsoldiers, these were days, nights and weeks of intense and continuous strain, as they coped with a veritable mountain of clerical tasks. 'L stands for Late-work, horrid and chill' ran part of 'The Conversion Alphabet' published in the next (understandably delayed) issue of the *Old Lady*, and Norman was doubtless pleased to circulate the grateful message he received from Chamberlain: 'Long hours of work and much personal inconvenience also were demanded from the staff in all ranks, and I learn with satisfaction that all concerned bore these discomforts cheerfully and threw themselves heart and soul into their work, in a manner worthy of the highest traditions of the Bank.'[7]

In general, the City's Pope still largely – if for the most part informally – ruled the roost in the square mile.[8] In relation to the Stock Exchange, Norman's central concern was naturally the gilt-edged market, an informal patronage vindicated as well as demonstrated by his adroit handling of the leading gilt jobbers and brokers during the conversion operation. 'Long talk,' he noted in 1932 after he had in effect cross-examined a possible future partner, Ted Cripps, at the government brokers Mullens. 'Satisfactory in all ways, e.g. manner, ideas, Natl Service capacity – but? health.' He also kept a close eye on the institution as a whole, for instance in 1934 giving it a steer to open on Saturdays ('their monopoly sh^d be exercised in interests of the Public – or their historic freedom may come to be lost'), as well as continuing to be particularly watchful about the flotation of foreign loans, largely discouraged by the Treasury. 'As regards your Turkish proposal, I think from your angle it is little less than silly,' he curtly informed none other than Charles Hambro that same year. 'There is nothing to be said in favour of the Turks; they have nothing to do with you; and if they need financing for orders they place here it is up to the Government and not to the City.' There were other areas of the Bank's sway during the 1930s. Norman resisted as far as possible, though not always successfully, the spread of speculative forward dealings in the foreign exchange and gold markets, while Bolton in particular did much to clean up the former market and make it better regulated; on the discount market, the governor still kept the closest possible tabs through his Thursday-afternoon tea-parties for the market's representatives, as well as brokering a trio of gentlemen's agreements between the clearing banks and the discount houses to ensure that the market was running at least a modest profit; the clearing bankers themselves (even McKenna as the decade went on) were now markedly more susceptible to Norman's mix of charm and forcefulness, perhaps reflecting their own sense of having permanently 'arrived' on the London financial scene; and as for the merchant banks, traditionally so resentful of the provincial upstart clearers, they were in no position, as much of the City's foreign business almost dried up, to argue the toss, with Norman insisting – as the quid pro quo for the members of the Accepting Houses Committee (formed in 1914) receiving from the Bank the finest rediscounting terms – on regular sight of their balance sheets. The governor even poked his nose into the commodity markets. The pepper scandal of 1935 was a complicated and colourful story, involving a corner that failed (because the fact that black pepper was capable of being processed into white was carelessly overlooked), an embarrassing exposure for Midland, and the prospect of many of Mincing Lane's brokers and traders being ruined.

At which point Norman stepped in decisively, twisting the bankers' arms to make the necessary advances to key firms and enabling the formation of a pepper pool, which over the next six years disposed of over 20,000 tons of pepper. The main villain of the whole piece was one John Howeson, a middle-aged financier. In 1936, not long after he had been sent to prison for publishing a false prospectus, the question arose of what he should do when he came out. 'Go far East, or far West,' responded Norman. 'Never show his nose in London: he can & sh^d have no moral standing & is not welcome here, ever.'[9]

The Bank's ability to make the weather – or at the least get out the umbrellas – was altogether more limited in its continuing industrial role. 'The more I look at this L.C.C. [Lancashire Cotton Corporation],' observed Norman in 1932, 'the more do I believe in the rightness of its origin and purpose and in the difficulty of its future!' It was a fair call. Even though the Bank that year, in tandem with Barings, success-fully shook up the LCC's management, and in due course its financial performance picked up, the necessary scrapping of some ten million surplus spindles did not get very far, with on the one hand the banks professing to lack the means to drive through amalgamations in the cotton industry's spinning section, on the other Norman baulking at statutory compulsion, in his eyes a wholly unacceptable solution striking at the very roots of private enterprise. The other main indus-try of Bank involvement was steel, where several times in the course of the decade it dipped into its own pockets, including major infusions of capital into new works at Corby, Jarrow, Ebbw Vale and Shotton, but was generally unwilling to assume the responsibility for rigorous, co-ordinated restructuring. There were some other industrial initia-tives during these years – notably the creation in 1936 of the Special Areas Reconstruction Association (SARA) that made some, albeit not huge, progress in granting medium-term credits to industries in the most depressed areas of Britain – but by 1939 there was on the part of the Committee of Treasury an almost valedictory tone in discussions about this distinctive phase of the Bank's history:

Walter Whigham: Position of control which the Bank has had to assume is dangerous: renders them still more vulnerable to attacks from the 'Left'. City would assist sound concerns; if unsound, better that they should crash and reorganise. Each industry should work out its own salvation. Present tendency is to bolster up bad management.

Peacock: Consider B.I.D. [Bankers Industrial Development Company] as carried on for some time useful, but disturbed at its becoming more and more a Nursing Home … Any company in good order able to obtain its finance from City.

Norman: Speaking broadly, the Bank's policy over the past years has proved to be a right one. Companies necessary in the public interest have been saved from extinction and Government intervention has been avoided.[10]

So it had, but it was arguably an achievement of only limited relevance in the larger economic context.

That context was of course mixed. 'We seem to see in this country,' Norman wrote in December 1933 to a correspondent in Siam, 'the beginnings of a recovery which, though it may be precarious, is real.' In truth, the recovery would be profoundly patchy in this decade of the Jarrow March: real enough in some parts of the country, invisible in others, as mass unemployment came down only with painful slowness. Undoubtedly cheap money – with Bank rate held at 2 per cent from June 1932 to August 1939 – made a positive difference, especially in stimulating the housing sector; but this remained very much the Treasury's policy, with Norman periodically warning in vain about the inflationary and speculative consequences of excessively easy money. Either way, however, monetary policy was no longer at the centre of economic debate or policy-making. Instead, the focus, whether hostile or favourable, was now much more on Keynesian doctrines. Addressing in 1933 (three years before his path-breaking *General Theory*) what he termed 'the control of the business cycle', Keynes insisted that 'circumstances can arise, and have recently arisen, when neither control of the short-rate of interest nor control of the long-rate will be effective, with the result that direct stimulation of investment by government is a necessary means'. For its part, the National government, and Chamberlain in particular, continued to follow – cheap money notwithstanding – its essentially orthodox and deflationary approach to macro-economic policy, with balanced budgets at its heart. Norman naturally applauded – and came down hard on deviants within his orbit of influence. 'Our troubles &

embarrass[t] from time to time by his writings & speeches in opposition to Chancellor's policy,' he noted in January 1934 after giving a
dressing-down to Sir Basil Blackett, a Treasury man who had become
a Bank director and was the author of a recent treatise called *Planned
Money*. 'Bk & all members of Court,' added Norman, 'sh[d] support
in public tho' they may urge & nag in private.' The most emblematic issue was public works, which saw the governor non-committal
(at least in public) even as some of his advisers, including Clay, were
supportive; towards the New Deal and its architect, he was distinctly
hostile, observing that Roosevelt reminded him of no one so much
as Lloyd George (not a compliment in Norman's book) – while the
American politician came up with 'Old Pink Whiskers' as his unflattering epithet for the governor.[11]

Against a largely discouraging and increasingly autarchic backdrop,
Norman remained in the 1930s a convinced if pessimistic internationalist. 'No stability', 'no international trade', 'econ. Nationalism': such
were some of his jotted-down headings in 1933; as for the future,
his stark heading was 'Hang together or hang separately'. Almost
certainly his favourite part of the job became the regular gatherings
of central bankers at the Bank for International Settlements in Basle;
but as BIS's historian, Gianni Toniolo, points out, in practice it acted
during these difficult years of fast-diminishing central bank independence and power as a locus less for 'actual co-operation' than for 'the
exchange of information and opinions'. That the world had fundamentally changed for central bankers was graphically demonstrated in
the summer of 1933 by the failure of the World Economic Conference
in London. The assembled bankers may have hoped to reach a temporary agreement to stabilise the main currencies; but those hopes were
brutally nullified when a message arrived from Roosevelt (who a few
months earlier had taken the dollar off the gold standard in an attempt
to end deflation) declaring that 'the old fetishes of so-called international bankers are being replaced by efforts to plan national currencies
with the objective of giving those currencies a continuing purchasing
power'. It would, in effect, be each currency for itself – with conclusively no going back to the pre-1914 international gold standard.
Over the next few years, foreign exchange and gold markets became
increasingly turbulent, until the reaching in September 1936 of the
Tripartite Agreement, a stabilisation accord between London, Paris

and Washington. Bolton would recall it as 'the first sign of monetary sanity', as something that, 'like a candle in a window, threw a flickering light on the gloomy scene of international monetary and political convulsions'; yet not only would those convulsions far from go away, but, specifically from the Bank's perspective and notwithstanding Cobbold's significant contribution to the negotiations, the sobering fact was that the agreement as a whole was largely the work of the treasury representatives of the respective countries.

A major consolation – if occasional headache – was the Commonwealth and, associated with it, the sterling area. Contact was regular and continuous: during 1936 some 2,230 cables of a routine nature passed between the Bank and the five 'Empire central banks'; the following year, coinciding with George VI's Coronation, Norman assembled the leading central bankers of the Dominions at an Imperial Conference. A prime example of the governor spreading the gospel was India: there, the Reserve Bank of India opened in 1935 very much under the Bank's auspices, with relations close thereafter. China, of course, was not in the Commonwealth, but Norman put considerable effort, prior to the Japanese invasion of 1937, into ensuring a series of sterling loans to it, in the belief that this would strengthen China's position within the sterling area and thereby reduce the spread of American financial influence. It was a particular disappointment to the governor in these years that Canada preferred to stay out of the sterling area. 'Are we to have a Norman Conquest of Canada?' asked one prairie politician, and overall Canada remained in the American financial orbit.

More generally, in terms of the world at large, the newly established Overseas and Foreign Department began to put fingers in more pies than the Bank had ever done before. Take the experiences of one of its young men, Gordon Richdale. In 1934 he was sent on a mission to El Salvador to sort out that country's banking problems, a mission that featured a hurricane so devastating that he and his colleague were cut off from the outside world for six weeks; two years later, just prior to the Spanish Civil War, he spent a long time in Madrid helping the Bank of Spain implement a recent trade and payments agreement concerning British exporters; then came Bucharest, negotiating a similar agreement with the Romanian government, followed in 1937 by a mission to Rome seeking to reopen normal trade channels in the wake of the Abyssinian war; and in 1938 he and Humphrey Mynors were in

Salisbury, drafting the constitution of the Rhodesian Currency Board, subsequently converted into the Bank of Rhodesia and Nyasaland. On his return to London, he would recall many years later of the Rome mission, 'I was awarded a special bonus by the Bank in recognition of my services – as far as I know the only time it had ever done such a thing.'[12]

———

One country dominated the international scene: Germany. 'I believe the interests of the B.I.S., the Reichsbank and the Bank of England to be identical,' Norman informed a fellow central banker in September 1933, adding that 'I do not think any of them should act without the others ...' Germany, the country whose fortunes he had done so much to try to rebuild during his early years as governor, remained in his eyes the symbol, and to a significant degree the substance, of economic internationalism, if that creed was to have any meaning. It is undeniable that for much of the decade this blinded Norman to the reality of Nazism. 'A Hitlerite,' he claimed in early 1934, was someone who 'accepts private initiative subject to public advantage'; and later that year, on a visit to New York, he spoke frankly to a Morgans partner, who summarised his thoughts: 'Monty says that Hitler and Schacht are the bulwarks of civilisation in Germany and the only friends we have. They are fighting the war of our system of society against communism. If they fail, communism will follow in Germany, and anything may follow in Europe.' As ever, all hopes were pinned on Schacht, minister of economics from 1934 as well as president of the Reichsbank; and underlying everything was an understandable hope-cum-conviction that the world could not be so foolish – so economically irrational – as to plunge into another catastrophic conflict so soon after the last one. A revealing moment occurred in April 1935, as a BIS meeting in Basle coincided with Anglo-French (and indeed Italian) condemnation of Germany's repudiation of her Treaty of Versailles obligations. 'There was,' Norman confided in Addis on his return, 'only one subject of conversation from Boulogne back to Calais ... which seemed in everyone's thoughts – war, war, when, where, how. And practically today all due to Nerves: at least I believe it to be as remote as the Millennium. And so does Schacht ...'

By 1936, the year of Hitler's occupation of the Rhineland in defiance of Versailles, Norman's pro-German approach was operating under certain external constraints – political opposition preventing him from either pushing hard for Germany to become a member of the sterling bloc or backing credits and advances to German borrowers beyond existing agreements – but the stance itself remained essentially unchanged. In March 1937 the *Old Lady* published without comment a six-page article by Dr Hermann Willke, editor of the *Staatsbank*, the Reichsbank's equivalent house magazine. '*The feature of the leisure of the German official is his work for his people and for his State,*' began his peroration on the final page:

> If he would be worthy to receive his bread from this State he may not merely passively allow things to happen of themselves; he must actively collaborate in building up the nation. Not only employers and employed but also the whole body of German officials accept the view of this necessity, and every section competes with every other in the model fulfilment of its duty. For it is *not compulsion* that determines the conduct of the individual but his *own free will* from which alone the great deeds, which are necessary for the material and spiritual liberation of the German, can be born. So long as we still have to endure bitter anxiety for our daily existence we cannot think of the light-hearted leisure hours spent by the official of the Bank of England. It is our firm conviction that our people, working indefatigably to this end, and with them the officials of the Reichsbank, will also reach the happy position of our professional colleagues on the other side of the Channel. The plans announced by our Leader at the Reich Party meeting for the development of German resources and for the improvement of the living conditions of the German people are colossal tasks, especially for the officials of the German Reichsbank.

'This man has, however, led Germany from hope to faith,' concluded Willke, 'and this faith will also cause foreign countries to recognise that Germany desires nothing more than to do her work in tranquillity as an equal among the nations of Europe and thereby to serve the peace of the world.'

Importantly, there was a limit to Norman's wishful thinking about Anglo-German financial and economic co-operation, mainly through the good offices of Schacht, and an eventual return to something like the pre-1914 world they had grown up in. A significant, very hush-hush development was under way from autumn 1936, with the authoritative inside account coming from Bolton:

The Governor, for reasons never revealed, let it be known to Siepmann, Catterns, Cobbold and Edward (Ruby) Holland-Martin that a war book might be prepared but that he was not to be officially informed or consulted. There was a very precise understanding that this was to be an entirely normal Bank precaution against an emergency never likely to happen: moreover, the circle in the know was to be the smallest possible, no secretaries were to be used and we must make doubly sure that nothing leaked to the Press, to Whitehall and especially not to Ministers. Siepmann and I had a series of discussions on strategy and tactics but conclusions were hampered by his conviction that no one could cater for chaos ...

In consequence, Cyril Hawker and I talked about the possibilities and, despite his personal revulsion against any idea that his hockey-playing friends in Bonn University would support or even welcome a Second World War, we began to hammer out a series of ideas to deal with the problems of financing our imports of basic necessities in time of war ...

After weeks of laboured consideration, Hawker and I decided to recommend a total mobilisation of resources, without any consideration of the rights of the individual, and comprehensive exchange control with the aim of conserving for as long as possible our exiguous foreign exchange purchasing power. The consequential interference with private business and financial life raised problems of great magnitude; although our self-imposed terms of reference appeared superficially to concern, say, the foreign exchange market, overseas finance, commodity markets, gold, portfolio investment etc., the execution of our projected measures would require official interference with practically every aspect of personal and institutional activity. But we plunged ahead undeterred ...

By June 1937 a lengthy memorandum on 'War Measures' had been prepared, followed towards the end of the year by a rough draft of an Exchange Control Act.[13] Norman himself, for all his day-to-day distance from this secretive process, remembered all too well the financial chaos of August 1914, and he was determined to avoid a repeat if the worst happened.

The worst nearly did during the Czech crisis of September 1938. Norman missed it, convalescing after a bad attack of shingles during the summer (a summer that featured the first practice air-raid alarm sirens sounding at the Bank); but shortly before the crisis broke he assured the South African statesman General Jan Smuts of his support for the appeasement policy of Neville Chamberlain, describing the prime minister as 'not being deluded like an ostrich but rather in his wisdom has been facing facts and, in spite of what may be thought of the autarchic rulers, trying bravely to reach a solution with them on all outstanding questions'. For those at the sharp end in the Bank, it was a crisis to remember. 'Mr Bolton called [by phone] at 9.30 [US time] this morning,' noted Bolton's counterpart at the Fed in New York on 24 September, after news that Chamberlain's talks with Hitler at Bad Godesberg had failed. 'It had taken them nearly half an hour to get the market under control and altogether they had had to sell $35,000,000 ... There had been such a tremendous demand for dollars at times that all sorts of rates had been quoted. Selling had been of a panick stricken nature and had originated everywhere but particularly in Switzerland.' Eventually, of course, Munich and peace for our time saved the day; and by early November Norman was informing the British ambassador in Berlin of his intention to go there in a godfather capacity for the christening of Schacht's grandson, arguing that 'the more the intercourse between London and Berlin the better'. At the start of 1939 he duly paid his visit, against the wishes of the Foreign Office and failing, despite catching the Dover train from Cannon Street rather than Victoria, to escape the attentions of the press. On his return, unrepentant, he reported to the Foreign Office. 'He was not optimistic,' recorded the official there, 'about the possibility of finding a solution to the European question; but he does not believe in the likelihood of war this year.' As usual, he emphasised the importance of Schacht as a moderating influence; but later in January Norman's friend received the order of the boot from his Nazi masters. Not long afterwards, the governor penned a private tribute to Schacht – 'a good German but a true internationalist, who wishes to increase world trade, to pay debts, to get rid of exchange restrictions, to be decent to the Jews'. That last point of praise was especially noteworthy, given Norman's undeniable streak of anti-Semitism. And Norman added that he looked upon Schacht as '*the* sane man among a party of dangerous totalitarians'.

Norman himself obdurately continued to hope for the best – 'War not inevitable at all,' he told Joseph Kennedy at the American Embassy in February – but Hitler's annexation the following month of what remained of Czechoslovakia was a bad blow, stiffening even Chamberlain. Norman too, perhaps still more so, now shed his illusions. In early June the passionately pro-Hitler Duke of Buccleuch asked the governor to call on him at Grosvenor Gardens. 'I reserve my opinion, contrary to his, that Hitler and Co are liars,' was Norman's summary of the conversation. And in terms of war preparations, the Bank by this summer was at full stretch, including shipping to Canada a huge amount of both its gold and that belonging to customer central banks. 'We took enormous risks,' remembered Bolton, 'and when the war actually began we had about £500,000,000 of gold afloat in ships of 5,000 tons upwards.' Other aspects of preparation involved, with the Bank working closely with the clearing banks, the detailed establishment of the appropriate machinery for exchange control; ensuring that the clearing system (to be transferred to Trentham Park in Staffordshire) would work smoothly; and a thousand and one other matters.

On 26 August, Norman wrote to the Home Secretary, enclosing a letter from H. Lipschutz and requesting his naturalisation: 'There is no doubt in my mind that Mr Lipschutz is an uncommon good oculist: he was put on to me by another non-Aryan – a Doctor – and probably saved the sight of an eye.' It was too late. On 2 September, the day after Germany's invasion of Poland, Norman had no alternative but to break the news to Lipschutz himself. 'I have to admit,' ended his regretful, dot-filled letter, 'that there is nothing I can now do towards giving effect to your suggestions. And, while I have been searching, the sands of peace have been running out … so that there is no more for me to say … except to wish you well.' Next morning, Britain's ultimatum to Germany expired and Chamberlain gravely spoke on the wireless. 'From now on,' a mordant Norman announced to his secretary during that lovely sunlit Sunday, 'we shall be simply rubber stamps.'[14]

The severe economic depression generally of the early 1930s, and specifically the profound political fall-out from the 1931 financial crisis, had impacted in a major, long-lasting way – transcending matters of war and peace – on external perceptions of the Bank. The tone of the debates in the Commons in February 1933 – in the context of the Austrian Loan Guarantee Bill that in effect involved the British government making it financially possible for Austria to repay to the Bank what it had urgently and unilaterally lent following Credit Anstalt's failure – would have been hardly thinkable a decade earlier. Strong criticism came from MPs sitting on both sides of the House. Rhys Davies condemned 'a sordid international financial transaction'; George Lambert did not see why 'my [Sheffield] constituents, many of them struggling men, should be called upon to pay Income Tax in order to buttress the dividends of the stockholders of the Bank of England'; Sir Stafford Cripps reckoned of the £4½ million now going to Austria that 'the country will never get it back again until they nationalise the Bank of England and get it in that way', adding darkly that 'whether this item will then be traceable in the accounts, it is impossible to say'; Brendan Bracken, friend of Churchill and dominant figure at the *Financial News*, called it 'practically a Bank of England Relief Bill', observing that 'we are always being told by the Government that they cannot afford a penny to get rid of our suppurating slums, or for any sort of social service, but they are quite willing to march forth with £4,500,000 to help the Bank of England'; and Sir William Davison wanted 'a change in some of the governors of the Bank', declaring it 'high time' that the Bank 'stopped putting up its hands to shield itself from the camera of criticism, saying, "We are sacrosanct – you must not ask us any questions"'. Some of the most memorable invective came from the future creator of the National Health Service:

Austria was in danger of defaulting [in the early summer of 1931]. The Bank of England, closely associated with the City of London, closely associated with the people who had lent money to Austria, saw the difficulty, and they did what they always have done – they rushed to their friends in the City and said: 'We cannot allow Austria to default, otherwise all the people who have been lending money to Austria will lose their money.' Therefore, the Bank of England stepped in to support the credit of Austria for the purpose of supporting their friends in London. That is perfectly proper for the government of the Bank of England to do. They have always done it. They have only been international buccaneers.

As for the present proposed arrangement, Aneurin Bevan vainly asked the financial secretary, Leslie Hore-Belisha, 'to take the House into his confidence and to tell us why we are asked to raise this money to reimburse the Bank of England'. 'Is it', wondered the eloquent Welshman, 'as a wedding present to the Governor?'[15]

Such parliamentary criticisms coincided with the publication of J. R. Jarvie's *The Old Lady Unveiled*, a serious if hostile prosopographical examination of the Court. 'The Bank of England is dominated by men whose interests are not primarily British but international,' contended Jarvie. 'Their main occupations are the financing of foreign states and distant enterprises and the earning of profits from monetary transactions which may easily be, and indeed often are, inimical to the economic health of our country.' He also attacked the Bank's lack of accountability:

> The essential facts concerning the Bank are impenetrably veiled. It is preposterous, for example, that the files cannot be inspected as with a public limited liability company ... The directors neglect, even, to let the public hear occasionally an explanation of the more important moves made in the name of British banking and finance. Fugitive antics by Mr Montagu Norman and peep-bo frolics with the Press photographers are apparently thought to be adequate gestures.

Over the next few years, the attacks mounted. From the left, G. D. H. Cole, the Labour Party's prime academic economist, accused the Bank on the wireless in 1934 of paying 'far too much attention to what they regard as sound finance, and far too little to industry and to the need to getting the biggest possible output of goods and doing all that can be done to prevent unemployment'; the following year, Labour's leading figure on financial matters, Hugh Dalton, argued in the *Banker* that 'the only choice' was 'between private politics, played by an irresponsible Governor, and public politics, played by accredited Ministers directing the Governor'; and in 1937, *Labour's Immediate Programme* explicitly committed a future Labour government to turning the Bank into 'a Public Institution', which 'will be administered by practical and experienced men under the general direction of the Government', thereby enabling 'credit' to be 'controlled in the interests of trade and employment'. Another critic, from somewhere in the political centre-ground, was Cunliffe's old mucker. The Bank, Lloyd George told an audience at Nottingham in 1935, had been guilty of 'cumulative blunders' that had 'cost the nation during the past 12 years more than would have sufficed to put through a gigantic scheme of industrial, agricultural and social reconstruction'. Nor was the Bank entirely spared by Conservatives. That same year, Harold Macmillan's *The Middle Way*, a key text published in 1938, wanted the Bank to be made a public institution in order to be able to 'influence the *direction* of investment' in addition to just its volume; and the following year, a treatise called *Managed Money*, by Major J. W. Hills (a well-respected MP and financial expert), not only accused the Bank of being unhealthily obsessed by the exchange rate as opposed to concentrating on being 'the judge of the money which trade, industry, and commerce require', but concluded that there was no chance of the Bank becoming an adequate 'Currency Authority' unless its 'controllers' were 'drawn from a wider area'.[16]

The Bank was broadly unrepentant about its approach to the outside world. Its time-honoured custom, Harvey had explained to Keynes during the Macmillan Committee's inquiry, was 'to leave our actions to explain our policy' – adding that 'it is a dangerous thing to start to give reasons'. Notwithstanding the severe blow to the Bank's prestige caused by going off gold, Norman saw no reason to change. 'I console myself with this thought,' he ended in October 1933 his annual Mansion House speech, 'that the dogs bark but the caravan moves on.' All his listeners understood this application of an old Arab proverb: the dogs were the Bank's critics, the caravan was the Bank, and the governor's words were a polite version of a two-finger sign. Even so, the continuing attacks from all sides – stimulated by that PR disaster – did eventually make a difference, with the executive director Ruby Holland-Martin given the job of speaking to the press. Unfortunately, 'though a most affable character' (recalled the future Labour politician Douglas Jay, then working in the *Daily Herald*'s City office), 'he turned out to know more about horsemanship than public relations'; and accordingly Norman's rising star, Kim Cobbold, was deputed instead 'and made a very much better job of it'.

Norman himself, in the twentieth year of his governorship and seventeen years after the start of the BBC, took to the airwaves, giving in March 1939 a radio talk about the Bank. The first part was historical, the second an uncontroversial survey of its main activities, and the third a look at how it was run, including the assertion that 'you will find now that more than half of the directors come from trade and industry, commerce and shipping, and barely a quarter are merchant bankers'. Then, towards the end, came the big picture:

> In monetary as in other matters the Government of the day must have the final word, and this is fully recognised. The essence of this system of management is that the Bank is able to give independent advice to the Government, with whom the final decision must rest. On the other hand it is not controlled by bankers, nor does it compete any longer with them. This means that we get real co-operation from the banks and bankers in carrying out policy, a co-operation which is also fully shown by the imperial and foreign banks in London. For my part, I would sum up the vital characteristics of the Bank as: experience in affairs; co-operation, on all sides; independence of judgment. But these three things – experience, co-operation, independence – are no good unless people have confidence in you. I like to believe that the Bank with its long history and tradition, stands high in the public esteem; but only by service to the public can that esteem be maintained through times good and bad.

'I should like you,' concluded Norman, 'to believe – and please to remember – that we value and are always trying to justify the confidence and the esteem, perhaps indeed the affection, which surely are summed up in the name "The Old Lady of Threadneedle Street".'[17]

A resonant message, but by this time it did not help the Bank's reputation that Norman in particular was often viewed as excessively pro-German. Two months before his broadcast, the governor's unauthorised visit to Berlin provoked the leading trading unionist Ernest Bevin into publicly warning about the harm being done 'to the cause of Democracy and Freedom', while the *Evening Standard* ran a very hostile cartoon by Low; and then in the early summer of 1939 came the damaging affair of the 'Czech gold'. This was largely down to the brilliant and relentless investigative work of the financial journalist Paul Einzig, who from mid-May exposed how the BIS had successfully instructed the Bank to hand over to the Reichsbank a gold deposit of some £6 million belonging to the Czechoslovak National Bank. A 'breach of trust' to 'the Czech people' was one accusation made in the Commons on 26 May; while specifically in relation to Norman and Niemeyer, the Bank's two directors on the BIS board, Bracken declared that 'they came, they saw and they capitulated', before accusing them of 'a very squalid form of financial appeasement'. The controversy reverberated. By 6 June the *New York Times* was reporting a widespread cross-party feeling in Britain that not only should the BIS be 'liquidated' before it 'furnished any more sinews of war to Germany', but that 'the odd relationship between the British government and the Bank of England should be re-examined without delay'; and that same day, in the Commons, one MP frankly put the question, 'May I ask the Prime Minister why he does not make the great Mr Montagu Norman Chancellor of the Exchequer?' The Bank for its part – despite Norman privately informing the actual chancellor, Sir John Simon, that 'the Bank of England are not aware whether gold held by them at any time in the name of the Bank for International Settlements is the property of the National Bank of Czecho-Slovakia' – declined to engage in a public defence. What that public must instead 'settle', Sir Alan Anderson (still on the Court) observed in early June to Norman, 'is whether they wish – in finance – to maintain the machinery of international discussion instead of force. If they do then the umpire must be left free to decide & sometimes he will decide against us …' Yet the fact was that the rules of the game had changed; and as Einzig would reflect many years later, the Bank would have been far less bruised by the episode if it had brought itself to depart from its adamantine policy of 'never explain, never apologise'.[18]

War in September 1939 meant evacuation: somewhere between a third and a half of the Bank's regular London staff, including almost everyone on the Stock side, decamped to rural Hampshire.[19] 'There are wash-houses some 200 yards away, with limited hot water and *unscreened* baths,' an appalled J. A. Mulvany wrote to his family on the 9th, the day he arrived at Hurstbourne Park near Whitchurch, the estate belonging to Lord Portal. 'The girls,' continued Mulvany, 'are better off, being mostly put up in the mansion, as their billets were found to be lousy! Principals and the like also have rooms in the mansion.' Further missives over the next six months continued to paint a distinctly critical picture:

Work started at 8.15 – the whole Stock-Side, including Chief Accountant's, in a glass-covered sort of factory shed 90 yards square. I was at first drafted to Passing, but Berry soon came and grabbed me in exchange for another, so that I found myself back on my own joint with my machinist, Miss Graham. Spent a long day till 5 getting my account pages in order. We are not straight yet – as a whole – and the arrears of work is colossal. They say it will be weeks or months before we catch up, if we do. *(10 September 1939)*

Holland Martin has been round and it is rumoured that he has insisted on everyone having proper *beds*!... *(14 September 1939)*

I can't get any certain news about the weekend: we can only hope for the best. The Bank Policy seems to be to make things as difficult and unpleasant for the staff as they possibly can. If we were really conscripts we would receive more considerate treatment ... *(20 September 1939)*

The latest totalitarian pinprick is a system of categories by which the staff are *compelled* to feed at certain allotted times whether suitable or not. I needn't add that no one is consulted as to times that might suit ... *(4 October 1939)*

The sensation was a 'riot' and 'strike' at Overton (Div. Prep.) over their Gratuity. Most of them were offered about £3 or less – and refused to accept it! Next day they staged a genuine sit-down strike until Holland Martin arrived post haste, harangued them, and promised that if they'd sign for the paltry bonus their grievance would receive every consideration. *(7 November 1939)*

Late work looks like going on and on and on and on – the girls are getting very fed-up. *(27 February 1940)*

The Governor is here today on an 'informal' visit – he has been strolling round the factory with an entourage of satellites, and 'chatting' with a few carefully selected (beforehand) members of the staff. I only hope he has to eat the same lunch as was the fate of the masses. Not b----- likely! *(19 March 1940)*

Mulvany may have been more disgruntled than most about his enforced exile, but it is possible anyway that the women had a jollier time. Naree Craik, hitherto at St Luke's, was among the several hundred female clerks despatched to Hampshire right at the start of hostilities, in her case soon living in one of the purpose-built chalets (each housing twenty-four women and a senior clerk) overlooking Overton Village, near to Whitchurch. 'As the men were called up for war duties,' she would recall, 'the women took over the working of the machines':

The Addressograph cut the names and addresses of stockholders on small metal plates. Those were fed into another big machine of that make, which printed the information on large sheets. Those were checked, then passed on to the Sensomatic Ledger Posting operators. I learned to operate all three. A Chambon machine printed the basic warrants. Each warrant had to be 'protectographed' through a small machine which wrote the net amount in words. Finally, the finished warrants were checked by other clerks, folded and placed in envelopes. Those were then inspected, counted or proved to be sure the address and totals were correct. We were expected to do 1,600 a day. Warrants going to foreign addresses bore asterisks and had to be removed from the bundle separately; presumably payments were suspended.

When there was a lull at work, any girls who wished were allowed to help the farmers who were short-handed. I learned to bind and stook the corn, to build a haystack, to thin beet, and to pull up charlock. It was hard work but interesting for a town girl like me. I felt I was doing my bit towards the war effort ...

   Films, table tennis and dances were arranged for our entertainment. Airmen and soldiers from local camps came over for dances
(and we went over to the camps by courtesy of the CO's). The girls
would line the walls waiting to be asked to dance. The men stood
in huddles eyeing us and plucking up courage to approach us. For
some reason, many of us thought men wearing brown shoes were a
superior type …

It doubtless also helped female morale that strict sartorial rules were
relaxed – 'Women staff in Hampshire,' noted an order in September
1942, 'may now wear slacks during office hours.' Yet locally these
women may not always have been flavour of the month. 'Hundreds of
girl clerks are being supplied with four meals a day at the canteen – and
also drawing their rations,' reported the *Daily Mail* in August 1942,
by when women formed the majority of the 2,000 Bank employees
based in Hampshire. 'Housewives in neighbouring villages who see
"the young ladies of Threadneedle-Street" queuing up at the weekend for sugar, tea and butter to take home on leave are complaining
bitterly about their privileged position.' And indeed, added the *Mail*'s
man from '"Bank of England Camp," Southern England': 'Sometimes
the girls have had taunts and sarcastic remarks flung at them as they
have waited at the grocers' counters for their rations.'[20]
   Meanwhile, the financial core of the Bank's activities stayed firmly
put; and when during the early months of the war the Stock Exchange
authorities sought to move their trading floor to Buckinghamshire,
the gilt-edged jobbers successfully resisted that plan, such was the gilt
market's umbilical cord to the Bank and its transfer facilities. It was
not, of course, an easy time in Threadneedle Street for anyone, but the
underlying mood was neatly summed up by George Bolton. 'We will
get through,' he assured the Fed's man during a transatlantic phone
conversation in July 1940. Two months later saw the start of the Blitz:

   All clocks & nearly all windows facing on Bank crossing blown
   right out. Threadneedle Street and Cornhill barricaded off – I
   had to show my Bank Pass and put out my cigarette before I was
   allowed through. Then I saw the cause of the damage: a vast crater
   in Threadneedle Street between NW corner of Exchange & the
   Bank walls, extending the full width of the roadway, & perhaps 20′

deep, rimmed with huge blocks of concrete, chips of Bank walls and pillars, & some yards of balustrading blown away. The shops opposite quite wiped out.

Inside the Bank a terrible mess. Every one of the great windows round the central well blown in, curtains in ribbons, massive bronze window frames twisted & bent like so much soft lead. Only one lift working. On every floor the same ruin of windows. Arrived on the 6th I was confronted with the big surprise – a direct hit on the Bank phone exchange. It had penetrated the roof & burst on the 7th floor, blowing out a large hole. I went & stood in the Directors' Kitchen on the 6th floor amid lumps of concrete and pools and leaking water, immediately under the hole in the ceiling above & the roof above that. So one can say that the Bank is bomb-proof from the 6th Floor downwards. The bomb exploded only some 30 yards from my desk on the 6th Floor & glass splinters were lying in my basket. The wooden & glass partitions in our office were blown down; and with all windows out it was necessary to move us all down to the sub-vault Lecture Hall, for the day at any rate. Even down there, 10 floors below, glass & frames were smashed. All clocks in the Bank stopped at 16 mins. to 4 this morning.

Only cold lunch available ... *(9 September 1940)*

The writer was John Mulvany, who to his relief had been transferred back to Head Office in the spring; and over the next year or so, before he was called up, his diary provides a unique contemporary record of life at the Bank during the Blitz:

Detailed to spend night at Bank, took up attaché case and staked claim in sub-vault during day. Signed-on in Establishments at 4. Shopping in Holborn & cinema at Dominion ...

Arrived Bank 8.30. Drew 3 blankets. Groped up to 3rd in inky blackness for towel (none provided – nor sheets – nor pillows). Washed & shaved and in bed by 10.30. Dozed fitfully. Narrow camp bed & noise of 40 other sleepers & of air-conditioning plant made good sleep impossible. *(23 September 1940)*

Endured the tedious ordeal of 3 days and 2 nights at the Bank, 50′ below ground level. Worked 9–9; no Overtime to be paid! ... Carried my bed & blanket down to sub-vault, and slept in the same spot as I worked at by day. Was ages getting to sleep on Wed., thanks to girls in gay gowns tripping past the open door of the vault. My first taste of roof-spotting 4–5: at dusk in a chill N. wind, with only my raincoat & steel helmet as protection and no scope for exercise. I have never passed a longer or more painful hour. Was frozen stiff by 4.30 and lasted-out till 5 only by fierce endurance & power of will. Could barely stagger down from the Crow's nest – only to find it was too late to get tea anywhere, in the Bank or outside! *(27–29 November 1940)*

Dull & cold. Had to make a long detour to approach the Bank. After viewing the scenes of destruction from the Oak Room spent the whole of my Roof Spotting Hour gazing in harrowing fascination into the world's largest artificial crater, some 50 yards across and 15′–20′ deep, created in an instant of time at 8.30 p.m. on Saturday [two days before this Monday diary entry] by 1 of Hitler's Angels of Destruction – a truly appalling sight. The bomb fell plum in the centre of the Bank Crossing, penetrated the roadway & exploded in the Bank Station Booking Hall, blowing out the entire subway Roundabout, shops & all. The effect of the blast in that confined space was terrific, but above ground, apart from damage at exits, man-holes etc., there was no damage to buildings, Statue, or even windows …

Hayes told me how on Sunday, Norman was with him & others on the Balcony of the Oak Room, watching the scene. His comment was: 'There's no telling what That Man won't do!' When presently a body was brought out of the debris – it was enough for Norman – he retired from the balcony. *(13 January 1941)*

Fire-watching … Caught 4.14. Arrived Victoria 5.15 & Bank 5.45. Supper at 7. Practice at 8.15 … Bed 11. At 12.45 roused by sudden 'Stand To!' followed at once by 'Take up positions!' Never dressed so quickly in my life: in 5 minutes from sound sleep all 24 of us, including Deputy Governor Catterns, were at the assembly point, only to be told it was merely a 'test'! The rottenest practical joke I have ever been victim of. It gave me a shock & I was ages getting to sleep again. *(2 June 1941)*

For most of the war, the majority of staff worked below ground during the day; while on any one night up to some 500 slept in the Bank, either in camp beds by their desks or in the now relatively empty vaults or in the nearby vault corridors. Fun or amusement was on the whole in short supply, and some thirty years later an *Old Lady* contributor would recall without any misplaced nostalgia 'those airless vaults it was part of our fate to endure, on one of those nights which were a mixture of extended hours of work, interrupted by meals, with an occasional spice of danger but mostly made up of hours and hours of empty boredom'.[21]

A crucial new reality – and almost from the start a major source of employment – was exchange control. 'Suddenly,' remembered Leslie O'Brien, 'everyone was on our doorstep with questions of bewildering complexity':

> We made up rules as we went along and we made them fast under the pressure of insistent enquiry and the threat of unjustified loss for the enquirer. To those in the Bank who liked the challenge, and that was most of us, the exchange control was highly stimulating. Many of us excelled ourselves, even over-reached ourselves, as never before. Long hours meant nothing in such a vibrant community which for some years worked and slept in Threadneedle Street. As the machine necessarily expanded with new offices being created, promotions and appointments came thick and fast and they caused some uneasiness, if not jealousy.

The contrast was stark – for elsewhere in the Bank, added O'Brien, 'there was little of our excitement to be found', with 'numerous women' having 'taken over jobs formerly the male preserve as men were released for war service'. Inevitably, exchange control in its strict wartime form was incompatible with the continued operation of London's foreign exchange market, and the Bank softened the blow by recruiting some seventy-five foreign exchange brokers to come and help on the exchange control side, as well as selecting four firms to be retained as sub-offices of the Bank in case its telephones were put out of action. The guiding spirit was one of flexibility, epitomised by the fact that the man in day-to-day charge of exchange control, Harry Siepmann, had on his wall what would become a celebrated notice: 'Freedom is in danger, Defend it with all your might.' Even so, building on Bolton's important preparatory work before the war, there was a determination not to allow any loopholes. An impressed outsider was Keynes. In May 1940, having submitted a lengthy memorandum on the whole subject of exchange control, he visited the Bank to meet Clay, Siepmann and Bolton. The ensuing dialogue, he informed Clay next day, 'was one of the most heartening I have enjoyed for a long time', for 'it was extraordinarily agreeable to discover for once people in executive positions who were in a drastic state of mind, seemed completely competent and equal to their job and were *not* enjoying living in a perpetual twilight, dim and incomplete'. A copy of Keynes's letter went to Norman, who scribbled on it some words that for most of the previous twenty years would have been unimaginable: 'He must come again: his support of Exch policy will be most important under new Cabinet [Churchill had just succeeded Chamberlain]. Treas^y have neither time nor knowledge to help – but feel bound to interfere!'[22]

In fact, in the dominant context of war, the two men had already started to become reconciled. Keynes in February 1940 published his pamphlet *How to Pay for the War*, advocating a policy of compulsory savings (in the form of deferred pay) and explicitly seeking 'an advance towards economic equality greater than any which we have made in recent times'. Such an approach was anathema to the City at large, but Norman invited his old antagonist to the Bank in early March. The conversation went well, and soon afterwards Keynes noted with pleasure that their 'long estrangement' was over. The economist (based in the Treasury for the duration of the war) and the central banker were also singing from the same hymn sheet over the related question of war loans. There, for all his qualms about the high-tax implications, Norman accepted that it needed to be a cheap-money war in which, unlike before, there were no politically unpopular high returns for bondholders; and accordingly the principle was established by March 1940 of a '3 per cent war', with the governor doing much to persuade a doubtful City that there was no realistic alternative. All of this made possible the election in autumn 1941 of Keynes to the Court. It was a richly symbolic moment. 'At last,' he remarked, 'orthodoxy has caught up with me.' And: 'I do not know if it is I or the Old Lady who has been made an honest woman of.' Keynes also reflected that although 'the old villain' (that is, Norman) 'loves his *institution* more than any doctrine', nevertheless in terms of the Bank as a whole 'the balance of sympathies and policies is widely reoriented'. Soon he was a regular attender at Court on Thursdays, usually staying on for lunch afterwards. 'I do enjoy these lunches at the Bank,' he declared after one visitation, as he slumped back in the car he was sharing with a fellow-director. 'Montagu Norman, always absolutely charming, always absolutely wrong!'[23]

Norman himself reluctantly but more or less uncomplainingly accepted that the war further tipped the scales of power away from the Bank and towards the Treasury. Nor was it only the Treasury to which Norman found himself having to be subservient. In February 1940, shortly before an issue of War Loan, he saw someone from the dreaded Ministry of Information. 'He is settling details for next week,' noted Norman, '& I promise to obey his orders!' Yet during that same first winter of the war, he seems to have been reinvigorated by the new situation. Sayers portrays the sixty-eight-year-old governor as 'tireless in his calls upon Ministers and the Treasury to get moving with an adequate economic policy':

> He went far beyond any normal bounds for a central bank. Though sometimes he would confine himself to urging adequate Ministerial guidance in the rationing of exchange resources, at others he would launch out into advice on labour supplies, unemployment benefit, control of commodity prices, and a great deal else. In the first months of war, the Governor and Cobbold were wanting a drive for more exports, though there was little satisfaction to be had from the President of the Board of Trade. Norman was impatient, too, at the laggardness of the development of the new Ministry of Supply, and poured into Ministerial ears suggested names for important posts in it. Above all, he chafed at the weakness of the Chancellor ...

In the event, Simon stayed on at No 11 until the change of government in May 1940 – a change in the political landscape that could not but be a serious blow for Norman. 'Now I know that I shall never cross the threshold of No 10 again,' he accurately predicted on hearing the news, well aware that Churchill would never forgive him for his part in the ill-fated return to gold in 1925. That did not, however, dilute one jot his commitment to doing all he could in the wider war effort. 'Ruin?' he expostulated in early 1941 to Wendell Willkie, when that visiting American politician mentioned the economic cost to Britain of resisting Hitler. 'Go to hell,' went on Norman. 'We must win.' And in the Bank itself he remained an alert and vital – if sometimes irascible – presence, often sleeping there two or three times a week and readily distinguished by a dressing-gown emblazoned with a dragon.[24]

Even more than in peacetime, Norman was now acting as 'the bridge' – as he called it himself – between Whitehall and the City. A significant constitutional moment occurred as early as the fourth week of the war, when the chancellor wrote to the governor asking him to ensure that the clearing banks confined their advances to such war-oriented purposes as the needs of armaments and the export trade. Norman in turn passed on Simon's letter to the chairman of the Committee of London Clearing Bankers; and thus was established what would become the firm unwritten rule that all communications between the Treasury and the clearing banks were, in either direction, to be mediated by the Bank. Norman also increased, if anything, his number of fingers in City pies. In March 1940, for instance, he saw the Stock Exchange's deputy chairman and tersely recorded, 'No fortnightly settlements'; some three months later, he insisted to the merchant banker Helmut Schroder that for the rest of the war he be 'neither seen nor heard in any way by anybody anywhere'; and the ailing discount market was the subject of his constant attentions, as was the struggling, often undercapitalised merchant banking sector, where he came tantalisingly close in 1942 to acting as midwife to a grand if improbable union between Rothschilds, Barings and Schroders. Norman that year even tried to stop a Jew becoming lord mayor, with his diary giving his reasons as 'bait for Hitler' and 'black market'; but to no avail. This did not stop him being, at a big Mansion House lunch soon after Sir Samuel Joseph had assumed office, 'somewhat embarrassingly audible, in view of a very Jewish-looking old boy sitting opposite, in voicing his preference for Christian over Jewish Lord Mayors', according to the Tory politician Leo Amery sitting next to him.

Even amid a broadly unifying national struggle for survival, the political climate remained chilly – despite the Bank at last in March 1941 recruiting Bernard Rickatson-Hatt from Reuters to become its first press officer. 'Yes, whether we like it or not, we've got to have Mr Montagu Collet Norman as the man in charge of Britain's money-bags for another eighteen months,' declared the *Sunday Pictorial* in September 1941. 'For he has just calmly announced that he is going to be re-elected governor of the Bank of England next April. Which means that nobody can get rid of him until April 1943.' And the Sunday version of the *Daily Mirror* went on: 'ALTHOUGH HE IS OVER 70 YEARS OLD AND BY THE RULES OF THE BANK OUGHT TO RETIRE AND ALTHOUGH HIS FINANCIAL DICTATORSHIP FOR THE LAST TWENTY-TWO YEARS HAS BROUGHT NOTHING BUT MISERY TO THE PEOPLE'. Siegmund Warburg would not have been so demotic, but that gifted and driven Jewish merchant banker, who before the war had fled from Nazi Germany, was almost equally critical of the Bank. In October 1942 he sent a candid memo to his friend the Labour politician Manny Shinwell:

> The Governor and the directors of the Bank of England ... should be appointed by the Treasury and should not be chosen preferably from representatives of the City. The Board of the Bank of England should of course contain a number of experienced bankers, but the majority should consist of industrialists, trade unionists, accountants and economists. The result would be that the Bank of England would be a centre of British economic life which would stimulate commercial and social progress instead of being a bulwark of reaction as it is today to a considerable extent ... As to the actual policy of the Bank of England, its chief aim should be to prevent inflation in times of prosperity and deflation in times of depression. Unfortunately during the twenty years before the war the Bank of England did usually just the opposite, mainly in times of prosperity they allowed over-investment, and in times of depression they accentuated the crisis by restricting the flow of credit.

Robert Boothby, a Tory radical with a flair for publicity, also weighed in, demanding in the *New Statesman* the following spring that 'the grip of what is usually called finance capital upon the economic system must be broken'; and that accordingly the Bank 'will have to be converted into a public corporation, owned by the State', with 'representatives of industry, of agriculture, of the trade unions and of the consumers' to be appointed to its Court.[25]

Inevitably, indeed, the great looming question for the Bank was nationalisation. 'Like many of the institutions that form the mainstay of this country,' observed a defensive internal memo drawn up not long after Rickatson-Hatt's appointment, 'the Bank has reached its

position by a process of growth and whilst, in theory, it may seem
to be open to criticism on this ground or that, in practice – like the
Common Law of England – it works'; in spring 1942 the election to
the Court of the leftish pottery manufacturer Josiah Wedgwood V,
author of *The Economics of Inheritance*, was a deliberate attempt to
defuse external criticism. What did Norman himself think? About the
same time as Wedgwood's election, he frankly told senior colleagues
not only that 'in his view it had seemed for a long time past increasingly likely that some form of nationalisation would be applied to the
Bank, not long after or even during the war, whatever the political
party in power', but also that 'the interests of the Country and Empire
and the maintenance of the credit structure and of a valuable tradition
would be best served by the conversion of the Bank into a public utility corporation ... perhaps the sooner the better'. Yet a year and a half
later, at the *Economist*'s centenary lunch, he gave a 'very short' speech
that, noted one of those present, 'traced the community of interest
over the 100 years between the *Economist* and the Bank of England –
both privately owned but both, he thought, rather the better able on
that account to serve the public interest'.[26] In short, it was a case of
head versus heart: not unusual for Norman, and perhaps hardly to his
discredit.

   That was in September 1943, with Norman of course still governor,
but now more or less accepting that he really would retire in 1945. Early
in 1944, however, his health decisively gave way, and only penicillin – a
remedy then available to few – kept him alive. 'One thing that would be
intolerable would be to go back to work,' he wrote in March to Peacock
during his protracted convalescence, '& then to crack again.' Soon
afterwards, Peacock and Holland-Martin saw Norman's two doctors,
who informed them that the governor would not be fit to resume his
duties even in three months' time. It was a verdict that he yielded to
with infinite reluctance. 'It's not going back that will kill me,' he told
Peacock, but on 6 April the Bank let it be known that Norman was
finally retiring, with a successor to be in place the following week. 'We
could never build the new Britain with Mr Norman in Threadneedle
Street, so there will be no tears among the people at this parting,'
declared the unforgiving *Sunday Pictorial*; but the *Financial News* was
kinder, reckoning that he was leaving behind 'a tradition of service, efficiency and sincerity which will long be an inspiration to those who

follow'. What no one could deny was his place as the dominant figure in the Bank's history; some time afterwards, Humphrey Mynors whiled away a few idle minutes by computing that the span of the Bank's first quarter of a millennium was virtually covered by only six members of Court: Gilbert Heathcote (1694–1733), William Hunt (1728–63), Richard Neave (1763–1811), John Horsley Palmer (1811–57), James Pattison Currie (1855–1908) and of course Norman (1907–44).

All this was little consolation to either the man himself or his ninety-six-year-old mother. 'They should have let him finish his twenty-five years,' she grumbled; and it was with some lingering bitterness that in February 1945 the ennobled Norman, writing to a former colleague now at the BIS, referred to how he had been 'turned out a year ago'. Ultimately, as he left the stage, he believed himself to have failed – unable to re-create the world economy's (and the City's) golden age, let down by nationalist demagogues, vote-grubbing politicians and ill-tutored democracies. Until his death in 1950, he remained unsparing on himself and indeed his generation of central bankers. 'As I look back, it now seems that, with all the thought and work and good intentions which we provided, we achieved *absolutely nothing*,' he reflected in 1948. 'By and large nothing that I did, and very little that old Ben did, internationally produced any good effect – or indeed any effect at all except that we collected money from a lot of poor devils and gave it over to the four winds …' Yet there is truth also in what his one-time private secretary, Ernest Skinner, wrote twenty years later:

> When the dogs have ceased to bark (!), I think we shall be left with the lasting impression that Montagu Norman –
>
> (1) was conspicuously a great public servant of unquestioned integrity;
> (2) at a critical juncture (with his customary vision) evolved a new structure for the direction and higher management of the Bank;
> (3) by his initiative galvanized central banking throughout the world and gave it the international outlook from which we are now in benefit.

'The records,' added Skinner with a not wholly ill-founded degree of optimism, 'provide the proof.'[27]

Back in 1941, the *Economist* had devoted a lengthy editorial to the question of what sort of person should succeed Norman. It offered three broad criteria: that, with rotation in effect dead, the appointment should be on a more permanent basis; that, in the context of the passing of the gold standard and accompanying need to 'husband the gold reserve', the next governor should be 'an economic statesman', preferably with a 'dominating interest in the finance of British industry', rather than an out-and-out 'financial expert' as such; and thirdly, that he should be 'a young man', not least because of the 'revolution' in the past ten years in monetary 'thought and practice', given that 'for any banker or financier whose mind was set before 1931 it is almost impossible to change such beliefs as, for example, that exchange stability in a free market is the only natural state of the foreign exchanges, or that dear money has a higher ethical justification than cheap money'. With Niemeyer a no-go because of Churchill's undying hostility (1925 again) and Cobbold too young (not yet forty), a serious executive search began in May 1943, as the chancellor, Sir Kingsley Wood, pushed hard (probably influenced by Keynes) for the Bank of Canada's Graham Towers. That autumn saw, however, not only Wood's death but the Committee of Treasury deciding that the Canadian was unsuitable on several grounds: as an outsider, not qualified to be '"Confidant and Confessor" to the City'; the fear that his appointment 'would be regarded either as a political appointment, thus bringing the Bank right into the political arena, or as confession that both the Bank and the City of London were so bare as to provide no adequate candidate'; the accompanying worry that, Towers having presided over the Bank of Canada during its nationalisation, 'his appointment might well be regarded as a pointer towards a similar change here'; and finally the disconcerting fact of his 'essentially "dollar" background', which made him 'publicly committed to post-war plans which many of us feel would prejudice the international position of sterling'. Or as Norman characteristically put it in his diary that day, Towers was altogether 'too much JMK & $'. Instead, the focus switched to Thomas Catto, from 1936 Lord Catto of Cairncatto, who in 1940 had at last succeeded his Morgan Grenfell colleague Lord St Just as a director of the Bank. During the war he was based in the Treasury, where, though forging a close alliance with Keynes ('Catto and Doggo' as they were known), he was trusted

by Norman to protect the Bank's interests. After Norman's illness
hastened events, the only realistic alternative to him was the deputy
governor, Basil Catterns; but when Peacock in March 1944 consulted
the chancellor, Sir John Anderson, the latter's distinct preference was
for Catto, on the basis of his greater 'worldly knowledge as to affairs
in general and especially as to Whitehall'.

So Catto it was: born 1879, seventh child of a shipwright, left school
at fifteen, and eventually a successful merchant (first in the Near and
Middle East, then in India) before being based in London from 1929
– a very different trajectory to almost all his predecessors. 'One of the
smallest men I have met,' recorded a diarist in 1945. 'Dapper, alert,
sharp-eyed, Scots accent.' Undoubtedly some of the Bank's permanent officials would come to feel that Catto was over-respectful of the
Treasury, but almost all valued the depth of his commercial experience,
the soundness of his judgement and the fact – at this delicate moment
in the Bank's history – that he was neither a government stooge nor
an entrenched, hereditary member of the City establishment. 'I shall
love the work,' this self-assured, self-made man promised the *Daily
Express* just before he assumed office. 'I love figures, economics and
finance. I never read books except those which deal with these matters,
even when I read for pleasure and recreation.'[28]

In July 1944 the Bank briefly gazed backwards, as it celebrated in a
low-key way its 250th anniversary, but generally the mood during the
closing stages of the war was one of looking forward. Quite apart from
the issue of the Bank's own status, two policy areas were now of particular importance, as indeed they had been towards the end of Norman's
governorship. The first concerned the provision of capital to medium-
sized firms – the so-called Macmillan gap. Norman, writing to a
sympathetic banker at the start of 1944, was frank about his motives
for seeking to fill that politically high-profile gap: '*My purpose is
to satisfy Whitehall*: to keep them out of the Banking Business and
free of malevolence towards the Bankers – which at this moment are
stakes worth playing for.' The eventual upshot in 1945 would be the
Industrial and Commercial Finance Corporation (ICFC, forerunner
of the latter-day 3i), an outcome made possible only by Catto devoting much of his early time in the governor's chair to persuading the
bankers that the gap existed and that they had politically no alternative but to come together and give their financial backing to the

proposed new organisation. 'There is no suggestion,' he assured them, 'that this should not be run on a strictly commercial basis'; and with some reluctance the deal was done, as the 'Big Five' (Barclays, Lloyds, Midland, National Provincial and Westminster) became ICFC's main shareholders.

The other key policy area, playing its part in the blackballing of Towers, was the reconstruction of the international financial order. There, whatever the improved personal relations, a huge gulf remained between Keynes and the Bank: whereas Keynes, in tandem with the Americans, developed plans for an international monetary fund that would be based in the US and apparently transcend existing structures of central banking co-operation, the Bank still tended to hold to a view of the world in which the importance of the sterling area was paramount. 'The Bank is not facing any of the realities,' Keynes complained in February 1944 to the chancellor, arguing that it was failing to allow either 'for the fact that post-war domestic policies are impossible without American assistance' or 'for the fact that vast debts and exiguous reserves are not, by themselves, the best qualification for renewing old-time international banking'. Soon afterwards, he poured out to Beaverbrook frustrations that went back a long way:

> Twice in my life I have seen the Bank blindly advocating policies which I expected to lead to the greatest misfortunes and a frightful smash. Twice I have predicted it; twice I have been disbelieved; twice it has happened ... My conviction is that here is a third occasion. The Bank is engaged in a desperate gamble in the interests of old arrangements and old-fashioned ideas, which there is no possibility of sustaining. Their plan, or rather their lack of plan, would, in my firm belief, lead us into yet another smash.

Ultimately he need not have worried: not even Bank of England obstruction could stop the International Monetary Fund (designed to stabilise exchange rates – 'with the countries experiencing difficulty,' as the historian Forrest Capie puts it, 'having access to adequate international reserves to smooth out short-term problems') from being created; nor indeed its cousin the Bank for Reconstruction and Development (the future World Bank, designed to provide long-term loans). The pivotal international conference was in July 1944 at Bretton

Woods, with the Bank (represented by Bolton) only a bit-player in the process but managing to secure what became known as 'the Catto clause' – in effect a reluctant acceptance by the US that, even in a world run by the almighty dollar, other nations had the right, as a last resort and in consultation with the IMF, to vary their exchange rates. Catto himself was nothing if not a realist. The following spring, in a note on post-war commercial policy, he reflected that it would be 'sheer madness to think the Empire can create a cave where we take in one another's washing and ignore the rest of the world'.[29] Put another way, there was a fundamental choice to be made, financial as well as commercial. Was the whole world to be Britain's (and especially the City's) oyster, as it had been before 1914 and even up to 1931? Or, with the dollar now conclusively dominant in global terms, was the safer – and sentimentally more appealing – course to rely almost solely on the sterling area? One way or another, it was a question that, despite Catto's clear steer, would take the Bank and other policy-makers at least two decades to resolve.

'One pleasant sign of returning normality was the mounting of the Bank of England Guard on September 6th by the Brigade of Guards for the first time since the outbreak of war,' noted the *Banker* in October 1945. 'In wartime, there has been no "March to the Bank", the Guard having been converted into a day and night guard and the duties taken over first by the Honourable Artillery Company and subsequently by the Military Police. Now, once again the familiar spectacle may be seen towards dusk each evening of 24 Guardsmen with fixed bayonets, led by an Officer, marching towards the Bank of England to protect it during the night.' By this time also, the evacuees were back from Hampshire, while among new members of staff was Pat Jarrett, who had been appointed as a 'Woman Clerk' shortly after V-E Day. 'The lunch club was the thing which came into the lives of all of us,' she would explain in 1949 to colleagues at Seattle First National Bank about a stay in Threadneedle Street that lasted only sixteen months but left vivid impressions:

For 20c a year you were a full member and, naturally, everyone belonged. You were provided with an excellent lunch every day, and 'tea' in the afternoon. If you worked late, after 6.30 p.m., there was also a very good dinner.

The club rooms were built on the flat roof of our office building, and were very pleasant. On leaving the elevator one walked right into the Lounge Bar, where one could pass a few minutes in social chatter and refreshment before proceeding to lunch. After the bar the Great Divide appeared – men to the left and girls to the right.

We had a very pleasant coffee room, too, and a reading and writing room in which to pass the remainder of our lunch hour, and I conclude that the men had the same facilities; however, no feminine foot ever crossed the threshold to find out!

Time-keeping was very strict and to-the-minute. Upon arrival we had to sign in a book on the principal's desk, and at 9 a.m. precisely it was whisked away. Anyone who came in late had to go to a special book held by the head of the office and sign in as 'late', and give her reason. Twice was too much for that sort of thing!

Then in the evening one could not leave until a senior clerk stood up to go (which was always on the exact second), and then there was one mad rush for the elevators.

'No one', she almost needlessly added, 'felt inclined to finish the job in hand or give a few extra minutes to anything, for the attitude was one of "come on the minute – leave on the minute."'[30]

Such concerns were not Catto's during the early months of peace. The Bank's future constitutional status was hardly a headline issue during the 1945 election campaign; but whereas Labour was explicitly committed to the Bank's nationalisation, Churchill in his infamous 'Gestapo' radio broadcast sarcastically warned of the dangers of the Bank falling into the hands of 'trustworthy Socialist politicians'. Labour under Clement Attlee won by a landslide, and within days, at the start of August, the governor was stressing to the new chancellor, Hugh Dalton, his hope that 'the method giving the least possible disturbance to the existing set-up would be chosen'. At this critical juncture, Catto received significant help from the permanent officials at the Treasury, where Sir Wilfrid Eady argued soon afterwards that 'there is everything to be said for viewing the Bank as a public corporation, subject to control on policy but not to interference in the running of the machine', given that 'the more the permitted independence on inessentials the easier will it be for the Bank to maintain its intimate relations with other parts of the financial system and with City interests'. From Catto's perspective, there was certainly no point in trying to resist public ownership as such: not only did the government have an overwhelming mandate, but the new leader of the Opposition now changed his tune, with Churchill telling the Commons in mid-August that 'the national ownership of the Bank of England does not in my opinion raise any matter of principle' – a statement prompting an 'Oh' from some MPs.

Serious negotiations were by this time under way between the booming, seemingly self-confident Dalton and the canny, obstinate Scot whom the politician privately described as 'a splendid little asset'. It was with justified pride that Catto would subsequently boast (to a diarist who met him) of 'how he had succeeded in keeping things surprisingly unchanged in daily practice, how he had held to a refusal to disclose secret reserves to the government, how he had got compensation for stock-holders which left their income unaffected, how the "halo" of mystery and power was an asset which he had preserved'; he might also have added that, on the key question of the issuing of directives to the clearing banks, the Treasury would in effect be permitted to do so only via the Bank and not off its own bat. Why did Catto get the better of Dalton? Partly no doubt because the chancellor was underprepared for the technicalities involved, but at least as important may have been the human element. 'Dalton was frightened of him,' reckoned Kim Cobbold in considering the governor's decisive advantage. 'Dalton had a guilt-conscience about his upbringing as a canon of Windsor's son, Eton etc, whilst Catto started work on an office stall in Scotland. Though he was apt to be offensive and overbearing to people of his own background and to "establishment" officials, Dalton seemed to feel that his attacks on privilege, etc, would not stand up to a public row with Catto.'

The Bill was published on 10 October. Apart from the actual transfer of stock and related mechanics, it had three key clauses. The first dealt with the Treasury's power to direct the Bank: 'The Treasury may from time to time give such directions to the Bank as, after consultation with the Governor of the Bank, they think necessary in the public interest.' The second clause dealt with the Bank's authority to direct bankers: 'The Bank may, if they think it necessary in the public interest, request information from and make recommendations to bankers, and may, if so authorised by the Treasury, issue directions to any banker for the purpose of securing that effect is given to any such request or recommendation.' The third clause stated that 'the affairs of the Bank shall be managed by the Court of Directors' – as opposed, implicitly, to being managed by government or any other external agency.

'It is of course evident that with the change of ownership the Treasury must have power of direction (which as a matter of fact it has had in practice for many years past),' Catto wrote that day to his counterpart at the Fed about the Treasury/Bank relationship. 'I regard the requirement to consult the Governor of the Bank as of prime importance: and although no limit is set to the scope of any directions that may be given to the Bank, it may be accepted as the intention that they will cover only questions of financial policy and not internal organisation and administration.' Moreover, he went on, 'the new authority of the Bank with regard to "bankers" makes statutory a position which has hitherto relied on custom and tradition'. In short, the proposed legislation 'preserves to the fullest possible extent the continued existence of the Bank and its independence in the general conduct of its affairs'.[31]

Press reaction to the Bill was reasonably mild. 'It would take a very nervous heart to register a flutter,' observed the *Economist*. 'Nothing could well be more moderate.' And indeed, the whole thing was on Labour's part little more than 'a symbolic sacrifice on the altar of party doctrine'. The *Financial Times* tended to agree, relieved that 'so far as status – apart from ownership – is concerned, the Bank's unique and responsible position is maintained', and adding that 'the City, which is jealous of the reputation of the Bank the world over, will hail that fact with satisfaction'. Perhaps predictably, a more querulous tone came from the *Daily Telegraph*. In an editorial headed 'A Gilded Pill', the paper argued that 'the Bill owes everything to past Socialist chatter about private dictatorship over finance, and nothing to practical experience'; noted that 'though the Bill may only legalise existing practices, it gives them the sanction of compulsion rather than co-operation'; and concluded that altogether it made the Bank 'the Treasury's agent instead of its ally', given that 'theoretically, the Bank will have no right even to discuss the financial measures decided by the Treasury, and its "recommendations" to the Joint Stock Banks will for all practical purposes be orders'.

Later in October, on the 29th, the Commons gave the Bill its decisive second reading. In the course of a fairly low-key debate, Dalton commended 'a streamlined Socialist Statute' containing 'a minimum of legal rigmarole' and offered the double justification for the Bill that it not only brought 'the antiquated and out-moded constitution of the past into a form which fits the practical realities of the present', but ensured 'a smooth and efficient growth of our financial and banking system, in order to meet the new needs of the future'; the previous chancellor, Sir John Anderson (Conservative), called it a 'wholly unnecessary Bill'; a future chancellor, Hugh Gaitskell (Labour), reminded the chamber of the Czech gold episode before contending that 'the real issue' was 'whether this country is to take control of the head and fount of financial power in this country'; and the most memorable – and possibly most telling – passage came from the rogue Tory Robert Boothby:

Mention has been made of Lord Norman. I think that, in some respects, he is the real architect of this Bill. Nobody denies that he was one of the most selfless public servants who ever worked day and night in the interests of this country – or in what he conceived to be the interests of this country. He had only one fault; he was nearly always wrong. He held the Governorship for so many years that he came to be regarded, not only in the City but far beyond its confines, as the embodiment of power without responsibility. I remember an eminent Governor of the Bank of England telling me many years ago that it was essential, if that institution was to remain outwith the control of the Government, that the Governorship should be constantly changed. Prior to Lord Norman's tenure that did happen. You always had a number of ex-Governors, men with great authority and experience, to keep an eye on the Governor; and that system worked rather well, especially during the last century. I remember this Governor [Cokayne?] telling me that if ever the Governorship came to be held for any great length of time by one man, it would be only a question of time before the Bank was nationalised. He has proved to be right.

Boothby ended by quoting Abraham Lincoln: 'The privilege of creating and issuing money is not only the supreme prerogative of the Government, it is the Government's greatest opportunity. Money will cease to be master and become the servant of humanity. Democracy will rise superior to money power.'[32]

The Bank had another central preoccupation this first autumn of peace: Britain's appallingly weak economic situation – and, specifically, the enormous loan from America that Keynes was negotiating in Washington.[33] As with Bretton Woods, the whole process saw the Bank largely sidelined. It had no one present at the key decision-making meeting in London in late August, prior to the delegation sailing; while when in mid-October the recently elected deputy governor, Cameron ('Kim') Cobbold, pushed hard for Keynes's recall, Catto (historically close to Keynes) failed to support him. 'Clearly he does not want any general settlement on the lines contemplated with the Americans,' one of Keynes's colleagues, James Meade, noted of Cobbold's attitude. 'He would like us to snap our fingers at the Americans ... He is a clever ass.' Keynes himself – under huge pressure – was also unimpressed. 'Some fig leaves which may pass muster with old ladies in London wilt in a harsher climate,' he dismissively cabled the Treasury in early November about Treasury/Bank concerns over the sterling area.

For his part, Cobbold of course viewed it all rather differently. The Bank's position, he recalled, was that 'although we should be prepared to move steadily towards "convertibility" and doing away with restrictive "sterling area" and "payments" agreements, it would be madness to accept any commitment which would limit our transitional freedom under Bretton Woods agreements or to give any specific undertakings about writing down or otherwise dealing with sterling area balances' – the last a reference to the increasingly vexing legacy of the accumulation in London during the war of very substantial overseas sterling balances unmatched by external reserves. Cobbold would also come to reckon that Keynes that fateful autumn 'basically agreed' with the Bank's position, but 'gradually got immersed in the Washington atmosphere'; as for ministers, ultimately responsible, they were 'mainly concerned to get the money without too much row with the Americans'. In any case, the eventual upshot was a $3¾ billion loan in return for multilateral trading arrangements, early convertibility of sterling and an interpretation of the Bretton Woods agreement that gave the whip hand to the Americans – a deal accepted in Britain, shortly before Christmas, with the utmost reluctance, encapsulated by the *Financial Times*'s opinion that 'the consequences of present refusal of American aid would be more grievous than the possibility of subsequent failure to live up to its conditions'. As unreconciled as almost anyone was Norman. 'He is entirely opposed to Bretton Woods and the whole of the Washington Loan ramp,' recorded Leo Amery a few months later after a conversation with him. 'In his curiously ingenuous way he said that he did not understand the economics of the matter but that he had a strong hunch that we were being done down and resented it.'[34]

By then the Bank, in its 252nd year, was under public ownership. The vesting date was 1 March 1946, two days after a 'Last Supper' in Threadneedle Street for past and present directors of the Court: native oysters, clear turtle soup, lamb cutlets and fruit salad with ice cream were washed down by 'Old Trinity House' Madeira, Steinberg 1935 hock and Cognac 1884 brandy. 'I am deeply appreciative,' Catto told those present, 'of the manner in which all members of the Court stood solidly behind me in this crisis in the Bank's history':

> A break in our ranks would have enormously increased the difficulties! The policy we adopted has proved its worth and gradually everyone is coming to realise that although the essential principle of Public ownership had to be conceded, on all other matters, particularly those questions concerning the future of the Bank and its management and the protection of the Staff, we put up a fight behind the scenes and obtained every point we considered essential to the well being of this great and ancient institution.

Catto coupled the toast – 'Long live the Bank of England' – with the name of his predecessor who 'has given all the best years of his life in living up to that toast'. Norman replied, apparently in a 'slightly pessimistic' tone; and when asked a few weeks later whether the Bank was still the same place, he replied mournfully, 'They try to pretend it is the same place.'

Yet in truth they did not have to try so hard. Nationalisation involved no vision of how a central bank should function in the new era of a more planned economy; no convincing model of the ideal triangular relationship between government, central bank and commercial banks; and no insistence that the Bank shed its culture of secrecy and deliberate cultivation of mystique. Arguably, however, it was the Bank as well as the Labour government that missed a historic opportunity. 'During the preceding twenty-five years, including the very difficult period of the late 1920s and early 1930s, the Bank had not attempted, under private ownership as it was, to develop a position of public accountability for discretionary monetary policy,' reflects one of the Bank's historians, John Fforde, in a suggestive passage. 'On the contrary, it had cultivated considerable public reticence while in private zealously building up its position as confidential monetary and financial adviser to the Government, its most important customer. Besides suiting Norman's personality, this part was natural enough for an institution whose experience and expertise in monetary policy, though deep, tended to be narrow and technical.'[35] In short, operational autonomy and the right to continue to offer advice from behind the throne – without ultimately being responsible for the consequences of policy – suited well enough during the 1945 negotiations an institution that psychologically had been badly scarred by all the scapegoating, fair or unfair, it had endured. Accordingly, there was little appetite to stake out in a bold, confident way what precisely the Bank *was* now going to be responsible for. At least two generations of politicians would have to do their best and worst before Norman's and Catto's successors even started down that challenging road.

PART FOUR

1946–1997

13

Not a Study Group

'I never use the word "nationalisation,"' governor Catto informed an American audience in October 1946, seven months after that undeniable fact. '"Public ownership" sounds so much better.' Others were less inclined to accentuate the cosmetic. 'The prestige of the Bank is not what it was,' Arthur Villiers of Barings informed an American correspondent in early 1947; next year the *City Press* poured forth an impassioned lament, describing the Bank as 'the East End branch of the Treasury', asserting that the absence of Norman-style 'completely impartial advice' meant that in the City 'there is no confidence in the Bank', and claiming that 'the old hands' in Threadneedle Street were 'very unhappy'; while in 1949 Dalton's successor at No. 11, Sir Stafford Cripps, even declared that the Bank was his 'creature'.

Of course, it all depended. In a purely City sense, Villiers certainly had a point when he elaborated how the changing composition of the Court (now reduced from twenty-four members to sixteen) had impaired standing: 'Various Directors have been appointed for their political views. Some of the Directors are excellent and others just average. To be a Director of the Bank in former times was a considerable honour; today that is not the case.' Two new directors he undoubtedly had in mind were George Gibson, a prominent northern, plain-speaking trade unionist, and George Wansbrough, a left-wing expert in industrial finance; in the event, both were soon caught up in a black-market scandal and stepped down, with the Bank sending neither flowers nor a letter of condolence on Gibson's death some years later. Significantly, the new directors in 1949 included not only another trade unionist, but the first-ever director to be a clearing banker, in the person of Michael

Babington Smith of Glyn Mills. By contrast, one area that saw little change was that of public information. The Bank was now compelled to publish an annual report, supplementing its weekly statement of account; but so unrevealing was its first effort, all of fifteen pages, that as the *Economist* observed in May 1947, 'the Bank has found tongue, but she has hardly yet spoken'. Ultimately, in terms of the new dispensation and how it played out, what mattered most was the calibre of the man in charge. Here, the key figure was Kim Cobbold. In 1946 he stayed on as deputy governor against Dalton's wishes (the chancellor viewing him as too right-wing) but at Catto's insistence; over the next two years or so, he assumed increasing authority within the Bank; and in October 1948 – after Cripps had briefly flirted with John Hanbury-Williams (chairman of Courtaulds and on the Court since 1936) – it was announced that he would succeed Catto the following March.[1] Realistically, the only other full-time Bank person who might have had a claim was George Bolton, though he was even less in tune with leftish notions of how to run the economy than Cobbold was. The choice of governor (for an initial five-year term) was now wholly that of the government of the day; but in practice it was seldom likely to be that straightforward.

Not unnaturally, the Bank during these early years as a nationalised entity went to extra lengths to demonstrate that it was still a major constructive force in the City – a motive reinforced by the fragile state of the City itself, wholly out of sympathy with socialist ministers and operating in the very straitened circumstances of the international as well as British post-war economy. The Bank was especially active in relation to the reopening of London's commodity markets, including coffee, rubber and progressively the various metals markets; in 1947 it in effect acted as midwife for the formation of the Foreign Banks' Association; during the winter of 1949–50, as the City came under fierce pre-election attacks from Labour politicians, Cobbold calmed down the chairman of the Stock Exchange and successfully insisted to other City grandees that they also stay above the party political fray; and the following winter he was in full mediating mode as he more or less kept the peace between the ICFC's Labour-supporting Lord Piercy (who had joined the Court in 1946 and had confidently expected to become governor) and the clearing banks, his main shareholders.

Traditionally, of course, the Bank's very closest links were with the discount market and the merchant banks (aka accepting houses). For the former, it ensured a major injection of capital, over £10 million by 1947; for the latter, it averted a nasty collision of egos in April that year, in the context of the City's leading houses coming together to make a huge £15 million offer for sale of Steel Company of Wales debenture stock, a move viewed as crucial on behalf of British exports. The problem was that Lazards' seventy-six-year-old Lord Kindersley (thirty-two years on the Court before retiring in 1946) had gone too fast without consulting other members of the consortium. Early one morning, in a classic old-City gubernatorial set-piece, Catto telephoned Barings' seventy-six-year-old Sir Edward Peacock (who had also left the Court in 1946):

I said, all right, let us have a meeting in my room at 11.30 this morning. He said he would attend and bring one of his partners with him. I then telephoned to Lord Bicester but he had not arrived, but Mr R. H. Vivian Smith said he was sure Lord Bicester would be glad to attend the meeting. He suggested that as some of the other Houses that were coming would be bringing a second partner with them, perhaps his father [Bicester] would bring him. I also telephoned to Mr Anthony de Rothschild and asked him if he would attend, and he stated he would be glad to do so. (Barings, Morgan Grenfell & Co and Rothschilds being, in particular, the three houses who felt objection to co-operating in the business in the form put forward by Lord Kindersley.) I then telephoned to Lord Kindersley and told him I was ready for a meeting and that Barings, Morgan Grenfell and Rothschilds were each sending representatives. I told him Sir E. Peacock was bringing a partner with him and so was Lord Bicester. Lord Kindersley asked if I would mind if he brought his partner, Mr Horsfall, and I replied that I would welcome that. Later, I telephoned to Lord Kindersley and suggested that perhaps he might feel it helpful to get a partner or two partners from Helbert Wagg. He thanked me and said that would be most helpful and he would arrange it.

The particular problem, following some conciliatory words from Kindersley, was resolved, though it was telling that three years later

Cobbold felt the need to have 'a word' with Charles Hambro (still on the Court) and Hugh Kindersley (next generation down, on the Court since 1947) about the Bank's relations with the accepting houses. 'I have been feeling for some time,' recorded the governor of this initiative, 'that there was a danger of their slipping a little away, particularly having in mind that fewer Accepting Houses are nowadays represented on the Court and also the possibility that future Governors might not have the same personal contacts as hitherto.' Accordingly, he suggested twice-yearly lunches at the Bank, comparable to the regular lunches for the clearing bank chairmen, to which the heads of the accepting houses agreed, no doubt gladly.[2]

What almost everyone in the square mile would have been unanimous about was that a strong pound meant a strong City. Inevitably – in the context of a parlous balance of payments situation and the continuing overhang of the sterling balances, despite the Bank's best efforts to make bilateral settlements with sterling area countries – the early post-war years offered little cheer, with sterling's first great trauma coming in 1947. 'Convertibility and all that' was the title of a Cobbold memo in late April, some two and a half months before sterling was due to become fully convertible into dollars under the US-imposed terms of the American Loan. 'The more I think about this the less I like it, and I think we are in a jam. The fact that we foresaw this and warned the Treasury during the Washington negotiations is not much consolation … Things have moved against us even quicker than we anticipated and we are being forced into a corner.' Was the answer to seek postponement? Cobbold believed not. 'Having accepted the principle of convertibility,' he insisted in late June, 'we cannot in any circumstance cancel convertibility without destroying sterling as an international currency.'

Come 15 July, the due date, and there set in almost immediately an appalling drain of dollars (by far the world's strongest and hardest-to-obtain currency), with little let-up for several weeks. Eventually on 20 August, with Britain virtually out of dollars, Dalton had no alternative but to announce suspension of convertibility. By then, Cobbold had abruptly broken off his holiday in the south of France, flying from Nice to Croydon and then shortly on to Washington, joining the Treasury's beleaguered Sir Wilfrid Eady. According to *Time*, he arrived there 'unshaven and with his old school tie (Eton's black with narrow light blue stripes) holding up his pants', with the American magazine reflecting on the obvious symbolism: 'Not even the Old Etonian belt could disguise the fact that this flurried arrival departed from the tradition of the British Treasury and the Bank of England. Ties as belts were not normal Threadneedle wear, Britain's financial pants for two and a half centuries had been held up by the stoutest braces.' Cobbold himself would never waver from his belief that the convertibility crisis had followed the Loan Agreement 'as night follows day'; and that is surely correct, though it is also possible that for once in its life the Bank had been guilty of not issuing the government with enough dire warnings in advance. Catto for one, however, was disinclined to share in any blame. 'Convertibility very nearly succeeded,' he told Per Jacobsson soon after suspension. 'Had it not been for the crisis in imports and exports, and the government measures [essentially an austerity package] announced by Attlee, it might have come off. We have, of course, hoped that the convertibility would have made people more inclined to hold sterling, but the lack of confidence which arose caused people to leave sterling.'[3] The pound and 'confidence': it was becoming once again a familiar tune.

Not least just two years later. 'I had the Chancellor [Cripps] to lunch alone,' noted Cobbold on 1 June 1949, three months after succeeding Catto. 'We had a general talk, particularly about the external situation. He is very strong and sound against any move in sterling but is fearful of the effects of a prolonged talking campaign.' Against a background of Britain's already threadbare reserves starting to suffer serious losses, the paramount question that summer was whether it would be possible to sustain the existing exchange rate (agreed at the outbreak of the war) of $4.03 to the pound – whether, in short, devaluation was becoming an inescapable reality. Stiffened by Niemeyer ('Jiggling about with devaluation of Dollar exchange will not help us'), Cobbold over the coming weeks took the predictable line that what really mattered to the holders of sterling were indications that the government was taking a firm grip on public expenditure. 'I reiterated the view,' he recorded after a conversation with Cripps on 5 July (first anniversary of the creation of the National Health Service), 'that the main thing necessary to restore confidence was evidence of action about Government expenditure, and that devaluation was not a positive policy but rather a recognition of disagreeable facts.' Even so, it was on the governor's part a careful balancing act, being well aware of the political ghosts of 1931; and in early August, when stressing to Attlee that 'devaluation by itself cannot be a remedy for the present difficulties', he was careful to add that 'it is no part of our submission that the present rate should be maintained at all costs by what may be termed a classic deflationary policy'. That rider was not enough to banish the ghosts. 'Montagu Norman walks again,' Dalton had already privately reflected; and during the three-month sterling crisis as a whole, ministers made a determined, broadly successful attempt to marginalise the Bank.

The end-result was Cobbold reluctantly concurring in devaluation – to which the Treasury ultimately saw no alternative – while achieving little movement in terms of expenditure cuts. On the evening of Sunday, 18 September, just before Cripps broadcast to the nation that the pound would henceforth be worth only $2.80 (a fall of 30 per cent, substantial enough to make the pound appear a little under-valued and thereby create some subsequent headroom), Cobbold spoke to an informal meeting of the Court: 'The one essential thing – and this I repeat and underline – is that devaluation can be done once but can and must not even be in question a second time unless there have been major events such as a world war in the intervening period.' Solemn enough words, and a moment of national humiliation, but in the immediate future life staggered on. 'We are getting back into our stride and trying to tackle the numerous problems in front of us,' the Bank's Jack Fisher (deputy chief cashier and in charge of exchange control) wrote at the end of the month to an opposite number at the Fed. 'The weather is delightful, the children are back at boarding school and I am hoping for a little golf this weekend for a change.'[4]

Either side of devaluation saw the negotiations that eventually led to the creation in 1950 of the European Payments Union – forerunner of the whole European 'project' over the next half-century and beyond. It was a landmark that owed little to the Bank, whose attitude during the protracted discussions was almost uniformly suspicious and negative. 'It no doubt required a considerable effort of mental adjustment in London, the centre of the sterling world, to accept that the tune should at this time be called by a minor power like Belgium,' reflected John Fforde many years later; an even more damning retrospective judgement comes from Charles Goodhart, looking across the whole admittedly difficult phase from the US Loan to the early 1950s:

> It is arguable that the correct way for the UK to have pursued its quest for greater US support was to have put itself in the vanguard of European multilateral solution(s) to the postwar liquidity/convertibility problems. Instead, the Bank (and Whitehall) exhibited devastating Euro-blindness. They could not see much likelihood of joint European initiatives succeeding; they continually feared that any such initiatives would weaken, or complicate, their closer connections with the sterling area. So, although too close to the Continent, and too important, to exclude themselves, or be excluded, from such European negotiations, they were at best half-hearted, often negative and sometimes downright destructive on European proposals.

Accordingly, the assumption in the Bank – as indeed in the City and in British politics at large – was that questions of Empire and the sterling area had a higher importance and priority than those of Europe, that it was sterling and the sterling area that represented Britain's financial ticket to the world's top table. One of the few questioning that assumption was Siegmund Warburg, who in 1946 started his own merchant bank but was still viewed by the Bank with distinct suspicion. 'After the Second World War,' he recalled some thirty years later, 'I said to everyone – I even put it in writing – that we had become a debtor nation instead of a creditor nation, and a reserve currency status [a currency held by central banks and other key financial institutions] doesn't make sense for a debtor country. It's a very expensive luxury for us to have.' Had the Old Lady, asked his interviewer, appreciated that iconoclastic perspective? 'No, the Governor of the Bank of England at the time didn't like this statement at all, it was against the general view.'[5]

As for domestic monetary policy, that remained largely quiescent during Labour's six years in office, with Bank rate staying unchanged at 2 per cent. Enthusiastically espousing cheap money, Dalton received in October 1946 only lukewarm support from the Bank when he decided to convert 3 per cent Local Loans into a 2½ per cent irredeemable Treasury stock (soon nicknamed 'Daltons'), which by the following spring found themselves at a discount – a fate that only deepened the Bank's already well-entrenched suspicions about an academic-cum-politician like Dalton getting involved in the practical niceties of market matters. By the late 1940s, with Cripps at No. 11 and Douglas Jay as economic secretary, the focus was on reducing the money supply in order to check inflation, and during 1948 there took place a lengthy, ill-tempered struggle, as the Treasury leaned on the Bank to in turn lean on the banks to keep their advances and deposits under control. The Bank resisted, for the most part successfully. 'If it is necessary from the angle of credit policy to try to keep advances down,' Cobbold wrote near the end of the year to the ailing Catto, 'I still believe that the only satisfactory way is the old-fashioned one of making borrowing more expensive' – an approach, of course, fatally tarnished in Labour's eyes by its association with Norman and inter-war monetary policy; while Catto soon afterwards from his sickbed sent Cripps the strongest possible memo that not only expressed his 'utmost alarm' about the impracticality of a proposed ceiling for deposits and advances, but declared that 'it is an entire fallacy to suppose that pressure from the Bank of England on the banks could rectify inflationary pressure which comes from overgearing the country's economy'. Why were he and Cobbold so hostile to the quantitative 'ceiling' strategy? Almost certainly their stated arguments were sincere (and indeed correct), but underlying them was a profound unstated anxiety: the existential threat that that strategy posed to the Bank's steadily accrued powers of moral suasion over the banking system – powers that relied heavily on discretion and judgement rather than directives and figures.

The Bank's most serious attempts to get monetary policy conducted the 'old-fashioned' way came during Labour's final year in office, with the arch-Wykehamist Hugh Gaitskell now chancellor and disinclined to be unduly deferential. 'I must say,' he reflected quite early about Cobbold and his colleagues, 'that I have a very poor opinion not only of him – he is simply not a very intelligent man – but of also most of the people in the Bank'; and he added that 'they are singularly bad at putting their case'. In January 1951, and then in June, he faced considerable pressure from the Bank to strengthen sterling and check inflation (against a backdrop of the Korean War) by sanctioning an increase – albeit modest – in Bank rate. Both times he refused, instead

pushing for the banks to restrict their advances and even in July telling Cobbold that he would like to talk directly for himself to the
clearing bank chairmen. The governor was not unnaturally alarmed,
probably not solely because this request threatened the Bank's own
authority in the City. 'I believe in the voluntary system by which our
banking arrangements are run,' he recorded after reluctantly agreeing to arrange a meeting for late September, 'and I believe that once
we get into direct Government interference in the credit system we
run into very deep waters.' In the event, Gaitskell's rendezvous with
the bankers never happened, because instead that autumn he and his
fellow-ministers were fighting a general election campaign. Cobbold's
public – and carefully bipartisan – contribution was his speech at the
Mansion House dinner some three weeks before polling day. 'We
are all in the same boat, capital, management, office, industrial and
agricultural worker,' he declared. 'If the forces of inflation and depreciation were to be allowed to take real hold of our currency, we should
all lose not only what we hope for, but much of what we have. We
have faced stormy weather before and the City is ready, along with
the rest of the community, to face it and come through it.'

The general expectation – certainly in the City – was that the
Conservatives under Churchill would return to power. That was
probably also the expectation at the Bank, where on 22 October, three
days before decision day, the chief cashier, Kenneth Peppiatt, wrote
to 'Gus' Ellen, formerly of Union Discount, asking him to call on the
24th. 'Perhaps I should add that I do not wish the fact you are coming
to see me to be known to your old friends at the UD!'[6] The subtext was
clear enough: with a change of government likely to lead to a return
to old-style, pre-1932 monetary policy, guidance from an old money
market hand was required in order to oil the very rusty mechanism for
Bank rate changes. It was time, in short, to return to the future.

'After the Second World War,' reflects Forrest Capie in recounting the
muted impact of nationalisation, 'the Bank continued to regard itself
as in many ways independent, and frequent appeals to its independence were made. Throughout the 1950s and 1960s, it was left pretty
much alone to manage the exchange rate, manage the government

debt, administer exchange controls, take the initiative in monetary policy, look after the City, and so on.' All that was undoubtedly the case. And Capie quotes Cobbold himself, publicly observing in 1962 that without a significant measure of independence from government – 'both in operations and in policy' – it would be impossible for central bankers (including of course at the Bank of England) to carry out their responsibilities. What were those responsibilities? Soon afterwards, in a chapter on the Bank in a BIS publication, the Bank's John (Jack) Fisher identified eight key tasks or objectives: overseeing the note issue; acting as registrar for the public debt; defending the value of the pound; standing ready to be lender of last resort; supplying expert advice to government; maintaining 'the credit and reputation of the banking and financial system'; promoting 'orderly financial and exchange markets'; and promoting 'the orderly flow of capital in the capital markets'. Fisher seems to have viewed these as perennial, time-honoured responsibilities, 'implicit' in the very existence of the Bank in the second half of the twentieth century; and certainly this noble eightfold path that he outlined was as applicable to the 1950s as to the 1960s.[7]

The 1950s were Cobbold's decade, being governor throughout. He subsequently recalled his own key priorities:

1　The current weakness of the overseas balance and consequently of sterling, largely due to the legacy of debt left by the War.
2　The need for international monetary stability and the fight against inflation.
3　The movement from the controlled economy of wartime to a freer (and hopefully more prosperous) economy of peace.

These were the objectives of someone who was very much his own man, including being significantly more sceptical than some of his colleagues of Keynesian economics, not least theories about demand management and a managed economy. At a more micro level, the flavour of the man and his style comes through in three early snippets, all from 1949. 'I spent a lot of the day talking to Bolton, Wilson Smith and others about the American efforts about European exchange rates, convertibility etc,' he noted only a few weeks after becoming governor. 'Everybody seems rather over-excited and inclined to rush about in aeroplanes and I encouraged them to go away for Easter.' A little later, he summarised a talk he had had with Midland's chairman about the quarterly meetings with the clearing bankers: 'I have a feeling that they are sometimes a little bare and I had in mind, without trying to launch a Debating Society, to say a word or two occasionally about things of particular interest at the time.' And in early July he recorded how the Treasury's Eady had 'mentioned that somebody in the Board of Trade had written to somebody in the Treasury asking if a junior official in the B.O.T. [Board of Trade] could spend a week or so in the Bank of England to get a closer idea of what we do', and how in turn he had reacted: 'I trod firmly on this suggestion.'

Cobbold was not everyone's favourite. A notably harsh verdict (perhaps owing something to having been overlooked for the top job) comes from George Bolton:

Cobbold was a man of violent contrasts and many puzzling contradictions. He inspired loyalty rather than affection among the
immediate circle of his friends in the City and among his colleagues
in the Bank, but as a public figure he appeared remote and cold.
He could be ruthless, too, and was never quite at ease with financial journalists. He enjoyed the respect of Civil Servants and the
City and, to some extent, industry, but was never able or willing to
develop an atmosphere of personal warmth and therefore failed to
get the best out of his relations with his contemporaries.

More favourable is the judgement of John Fforde, who joined the Bank in 1957 as an economist and would subsequently write a detailed history of the Cobbold era:

He was a careful listener and a thoughtful reader. But he was not a
lengthy debater. His meetings were inclined to be short and to the
point. He was determined to maintain the authority of the Governor
as the Chairman and Chief Executive of the Bank. He was certainly a
commanding personality and was to exercise command in an almost
military fashion for over twelve years. He was, however, sensitive
to any questioning of the decisions that he was not slow to take but
in which he may not always have had complete self-confidence.
Once he had firmly declared a point of view he had as often as not

announced his decision, or at least the general shape of it. Persuading
him to change his mind was not impossible but was not a task to be
taken lightly.

Ultimately, Cobbold was someone who was comfortable in his own
skin and slept soundly at night – invaluable qualities in any central
banker. Class helped. Married to Hermione Bulwer-Lytton (daughter
of the second Earl of Lytton), and living from 1947 at her ancestral seat
of Knebworth House, he was a distinctly Etonian Etonian. 'During
my time in the City, those who hadn't been to Eton were striving for
Eton standards and the Eton ethos dominated from Kim Cobbold
downwards,' recalled one leading merchant banker, Michael Verey of
Schroders. 'Good Etonian standards means a total trust – if you say
you'll do something, you'll do it.'[8] Crisp, authoritative, pragmatic, not
always articulate: Cobbold had the stature and the steel for his office.
    Who were his colleagues? Dallas Bernard (1949–54) and Humphrey
Mynors (1954–64) were his two deputy governors: the former's background was Jardine Matheson and the Far East, but he had become an
executive director in 1939; while the latter was of course the Bank's
pioneer economist – though an economist with a marked horror of
the words 'economics' and 'research', and who in 1948 confessed to
Eady that 'I do not move easily in the post-Keynesian terminology,
although I believe it is largely only restating the old truths.' Deeply
unimpressed that same year was Robert Hall, head of the Treasury's
Economic Section. 'It is hard not to get the impression that the Bank
do not think at all about credit control as economists do,' he noted
after a meeting with Mynors, 'and indeed that they don't quite understand what it is all about.' Fforde put it a little more gently. Mynors
had, he insisted, 'a first-class mind' (as well as 'great personal charm'),
but 'he often gave the impression either of keeping his cards very close
to his chest or else of great reluctance to disturb the conventions and
ambience of Norman's Bank'.[9]
    Among the executive directors, meanwhile, were Harry Siepmann
(1947–54), whose 'interests narrowed' and 'attitudes hardened',
according to Fforde, after the 1947 convertibility trauma; Kenneth
Peppiatt (1949–57), who had had a long run as chief cashier and was
an expert on the gilt-edged and money markets, but (again in Fforde's
words) 'would never have regarded himself as capable of arguing

out a particular monetary policy in analytic terms with the university-educated mandarins in the Treasury'; Cyril Hawker (1954–62), who had made his name during wartime exchange control and was renowned (amid stiff Bank competition) for his love of cricket; and Maurice Parsons (1957–66), who was knowledgeable, a lay preacher ('the parson') and an imposing presence, but who in Fforde's judgement found the post 'probably a strain on his underlying capacity', as confirmed by 'his reluctance to work with more than a very few chosen lieutenants at any one time'. The weightiest – and most controversial – of the executive directors was undoubtedly George Bolton (1948–57, knighted in 1950). 'He stood well over six feet tall, had reddish hair, bright blue eyes, a round and cheerful countenance, a deep seductive voice, and all the agility of an exchange dealer,' notes Fforde. 'It must,' he adds, 'have taken skill, courage, and a stern heart to stand up to him,' especially relevant given that 'Bolton's judgement was at times erratic and over-influenced by his personal opinions.' Norman had come to much the same view – 'not balanced, but often a strange insight' – while Hall at the Treasury reckoned him 'essentially an operator' who 'takes snap decisions by instinct and finds any reasons that come into his head to justify them'. Hall would also note in 1952 that, after devaluation three years earlier, Bolton had 'told several of my friends that the Bank had been in favour of it a long time and had wanted a floating rate', whereas 'both statements are exactly the opposite of the truth'.[10] All in all, it would have been an interesting ride if this undeniable visionary, appreciably more aware than anyone else at the Bank of what was needed in order to restore London's position as an international financial centre, had become governor in 1949.

At least half a dozen others were significant figures. Two were advisers to the governor: Lucius Thompson-McCausland (1949–65), an Anglo-Irish classical scholar who, remarks Fforde with evident scepticism, 'had great confidence in his own intellectual powers, moved easily among senior Whitehall officials and economists, and regarded the exposition and indeed the further creation of monetary economics as within his capabilities'; and Maurice Allen (1954–64), a more trained economist whose 'highly expectational, psychological, and non-quantitative approach to monetary economics', including a conspicuous lack of interest in monetary aggregates, did not, asserts Fforde, 'encourage the enlargement of the Bank's statistical

and economic services'. Two others were, in turn, chief cashier: Percy
Beale (1949–55), of 'outstanding technical ability' according to Fforde,
but arrogant, unpopular and in due course shunted out; and Leslie
O'Brien (1955–62), who since the 1920s had worked his way up in the
Bank but may have thought he had reached his ceiling, being informed
by Cobbold on his appointment that it was the Court's expectation
that 'he should have a long tenure of office, perhaps for the rest of his
Bank career, while others may move elsewhere and possibly higher'.

The last two were Roy Bridge and Hilton Clarke, both in some
sense representing the very soul of the Bank and for much of the
decade in charge of the Dealing and Accounts Office and the Discount
Office respectively. Bridge, who had entered the Bank in 1929, was
the master of the foreign exchange scene, ironically enough a mastery
that coincided with sterling's long, unstoppable decline. An appreciative observer was the Fed's Charles Coombs, writing on Bridge's
retirement in 1969:

> He was a familiar figure at Basle, of course, the suave, imperturbable
> negotiator with the air of an experienced old cat quietly apprais-
> ing an unwary mouse. Yet he rarely had an easy negotiating brief.
> But the style he chose, a devastating candour in analysing market
> developments and the issues at hand, saved precious time and
> avoided dangerous misunderstandings. More generally, his opera-
> tional relationships with foreign central bankers were marked by an
> unswerving sense of integrity and fair play. We trusted him.
>
> To some of his foreign central banking associates, Bridge prob-
> ably appeared at his best on his home ground, when we happened to
> be in his office at moments of crisis in the foreign exchange markets.
> Then, we could watch the true professional, alert to all of the tech-
> nical and psychological forces of the market, as he took decisions
> whether to hold a certain rate level, at possibly heavy cost, or to
> retreat and risk even heavier losses. Those were not easy judge-
> ments, but they were made decisively and courageously as he paced
> the floor between crackling telephone calls and snarling commen-
> taries on whatever had brought things to such a pretty pass.

'He was fluent in several foreign languages,' added Coombs. 'Yet
there was no trace in him of the romantic internationalist. No one ever

mistook Bridge for anything but a hard-shelled patriot, who thought of international co-operation strictly in terms of a visible overlapping of national interests.' As for Hilton Clarke, who had joined the Bank just after his eighteenth birthday in 1927, an eventual obituary captured some of the salient qualities of a Bank man through and through:

As principal [of the Discount Office], Clarke was in effect the eyes and ears of the Governor of the day. In his disciplinary role, which he executed with wisdom and good humour, he was the personification of 'the Governor's eyebrows'. Clarke's breadth of acquaintance and his ability to gather City intelligence were legendary. A master of the calculated indiscretion, he would appear to let slip confidential snippets while extracting information from his unwitting interlocutors.

Tall, dapper and resplendent in his silk hat, Clarke controlled the discount market by the force of his presence. His firmness was never resented. When a young bill broker asked for the customary seven-day loan to cover a cash shortage, Clarke replied that the Bank would make the loan for nine days at a punitive rate. When the supplicant protested, Clarke cut him short: 'And it'll be eleven days in a moment.'

Strong-minded, humorous, decidedly non-cerebral, and based in what was sometimes called 'the window in the windowless wall', Clarke was on just the right wavelength to use the most informal but assiduous of methods to uncover and assess the creditworthiness of the City's most sensitive markets and houses.[11]

Taking Cobbold and his top team as a whole, there persisted through much of the 1950s a disinclination to open up to the outside world, epitomised by the blandly uninformative annual report and the infrequency of governor's speeches. The high-profile economist Lionel Robbins, reviewing on the Third Programme in May 1957 Henry Clay's biography of Norman, made a powerful point. After noting that Norman's 'almost aggressive parade of reticence and disguise' had led to 'ignorant people' suspecting 'all sorts of sinister implications which did not exist at all', he called on the present-day Bank to 'remember that, in a democratic age, the preservation of values and the creation of an informed public opinion demand not only intuition and devotion in action but also systematic reason and the frank explanation of policy as it evolves'. Another aspect of this introverted streak was the tendency to keep the Treasury at arm's length (and indeed beyond) as much as possible. Cobbold paid regular visits to the permanent secretary, but the exasperation on Hall's part was understandable when he declared in 1956 that 'it is really almost unbelievable how little co-operation in economic policy we have had from the Bank of England over recent years'.

As for inside the Bank itself, and its capacity or otherwise to contribute to broader policy-making, it is impossible not to quote John Fforde's overview of the institution he got to know soon afterwards:

Norman, it is reported, once opined that the Bank was a bank and not a study group. This adage was often repeated and much admired by many among the generation of officials at the top of the Bank in the forties and fifties. Correctly interpreted, it meant that the Bank should never let its eyes wander from the market-place, whether that be foreign exchange, money, gilt-edged, or banking practice. Wrongly interpreted, it was taken to mean that systematic thought and exhaustive debate were somehow not required and that a wisdom acquired from market experience was an adequate substitute for rigorous analysis. Put these ingredients into a very hierarchical system of management, into a staff mostly lacking in university training, and into an informality of discussion on matters of policy that was confined to a very few at the top and there had to result a tendency to make things up as one went along; admirable in the management of markets or talking to accepting houses, inadvisable when preparing legislation.

Or in the words of Charles Goodhart (who himself got to know the Bank in the 1960s), on the basis of Fforde's study of the Cobbold era, 'a not entirely flattering picture emerges of a tiny group of intelligent officials without a clear strategic grasp of emerging wider politico-economic world trends, eschewing quantitative professional economic advice, and reacting to overwhelming pressures in an unfavourable context by reliance on technical, market virtuosity'. It was a culture with – for good as well as ill – very deep roots. In October 1948, after a year in Exchange Control, the young Stanley Payton entered the Overseas Office, where the work was a mixture of financial diplomacy and international economic intelligence. Having been assigned to the Commonwealth Group, where his superintendent was W. J. Jackson (immaculate suit, stiff white collar, showing Payton early on how to hold a cigarette in a way that would not be thought 'vulgar'), his first job was to write a memorandum on the world production of rice:

> I spent days of research in the files and the reference library and produced what I thought was a masterpiece. Jackson circulated it to a number of big names in the Bank and I thought my reputation was made. After some days it came back with only one comment: 'Monkeys are a menace,' written on the first page by R. N. Kershaw, the Economic Adviser. In the margin of the second page he had added 'monkeys are a menace in India and Burma where they cause great depredation to crops'.[12]

The coming of Churchill's government in October 1951 opened a new phase in Cobbold's governorship. A quarter of a century on from the ill-fated return to gold, Churchill himself still did not feel any great warmth towards the Bank, but it helped that Cobbold's mother-in-law was, in his words, 'a life-long intimate friend of Sir Winston's' and 'I was, therefore, regarded as a near-family friend.' Indeed, Cobbold came to reckon of the prime minister's Indian Summer that 'without his support we should have got nowhere on the reintroduction of flexible monetary policy'. At the time, at the start of November, the governor spoke 'secretly' to the chairmen of the clearing banks on the understanding that what he said stayed in the room. 'The position of sterling was very difficult,' began his summary of the briefing he gave. 'The whole question of monetary policy was under review with H.M.G. [His Majesty's Government] ...' and 'I was particularly anxious to get away from rigidities. If it proved possible to make any move on these lines it would be experimental and the machinery would be rusty. We should need a lot of help from the Clearing Banks ...' A week later, Bank rate rose from 2 to 2½ per cent – the first change since nationalisation, and with the new chancellor, Rab Butler, happy to accept Cobbold's advice. By February 1952, with the balance of payments as well as the sterling position seemingly deteriorating quite quickly, Cobbold was pushing hard for a more substantial rise, to 4 per cent. Again, on 11 March, Butler obliged. Next day, though, the governor was reporting to him 'a lot of sore heads' in the City, with the sorest belonging to the discount market. There, back in November, the Bank's broker (or special buyer), Lawrence Seccombe, had persuaded it to play its part in the so-called 'forced funding' operation. This had involved the take-up, under considerable moral pressure, of a mass of newly issued serial funding bonds; unfortunately, the sharp rise four months later led directly to substantial capital losses for all hold-ers, including Seccombe's own firm.[13] So long absent from the scene, monetary policy – the Bank's special domain – was poised to become increasingly controversial, outside as well as inside the City, as the decade went on.

On the external side, a significant moment was the reopening of the foreign exchange market in December 1951, symbolising a greater freedom for the City under the new government but prompting a sceptical take by 'Sagittarius' in the *New Statesman*:

> The Old Lady has eased some restrictions
>   And opened the Foreign Exchange
> And brokers base joyful predictions
>   On this timely, if overdue, change.
> Spot cash for the forward transaction
>   The Bank will to bankers advance –
> But the citizen sees no reaction
>   In the region of private finance.
>
> The Old Lady is showing her mettle,
>   Resourceful, adroit and resolved,
> And they say that the Market will settle,
>   Though the process is highly involved.
> Return to our banking tradition
>   Our balance of payments will save –
> But the balance of payments position
>   Remains, for the citizen, grave.

Unbeknown to poets and almost everyone else, a potentially far more dramatic development was brewing that winter on the external side, against a background of what may well have been exaggerated fears about the downwards trend in the sterling reserves. This was 'Operation Robot', taking its name from the three officials most closely associated with its formulation: Sir Leslie **Ro**wan (Treasury), **Bolton** of the Bank, and '**Otto**' Clarke (Treasury). In essence, it involved simultaneously making sterling convertible and floating the pound. Bolton, in his key memo of 16 February, made his pitch in typically bold terms, arguing that a fundamental choice existed 'between allowing sterling to become a domestic currency involving the collapse of the international sterling system and the sterling area, or accepting convertibility of non-resident sterling, thus retaining sterling as an international currency'. Given which, he proposed that 'the present policy of partial convertibility and partial inconvertibility should be replaced forthwith by a policy of comprehensive convertibility of all sterling in international use through the machinery of the exchange markets'. What Bolton did not do, however, was discuss the domestic implications – inevitably deflationary – of such a policy.

Very briefly, Robot appeared to have political legs. 'C of E sold, PM interested and great hopes favourable decision,' Bolton buoyantly noted on 20 February, after hearing Cobbold's report on his dinner the previous evening with Churchill and Butler. Soon afterwards, on the 22nd, Churchill received a Bank deputation, headed by Cobbold, formally advocating the plan. According to Donald MacDougall, economic adviser to Lord Cherwell, the paymaster general, Churchill subsequently 'reported that they were a fine, patriotic body of men, anxious to do what was right for the country'. But Cherwell himself – who was in reality Churchill's personal economic adviser and had a distinctly low regard for the Bank – now took the lead in opposing Robot. 'The view of the Bank,' he wrote disparagingly to Butler on the 25th, 'is that there is now such a drain on the reserves that they cannot be held on present policies, and that measures of the kind now proposed are inevitable. I have seen no evidence for this.' The 28th and 29th saw the crucial Cabinet discussions. Churchill deep down was attracted to liberating the pound, but decisive opposition came from his heir apparent, Sir Anthony Eden. 'The country are not ready,' Eden told a colleague, 'to cast away the whole effort of years and return to "Montagu Normanism" without a struggle.' Despite brief and misleading flickers of life thereafter, Cherwell in mid-March put what was in effect the final nail in Robot's coffin. In a brilliantly crafted memo to Churchill that anticipated appalling consequences – 'an 8 per cent Bank Rate, 2 million unemployed and a 3/- loaf' – if Robot was adopted, he took aim squarely:

> Our fundamental problem is that the Sterling Area is spending more than it is earning. We have to put that right by exporting more and importing less. No monetary tricks can overcome this hard fact …
>
> It is at first sight an attractive idea to go back to the good old days before 1914 when the pound was convertible and strong and we never had dollar crises. No doubt the bankers honestly believe that, if only the pound could be left to market forces, with the Bank of England free to intervene when necessary by varying the Bank Rate at their discretion, all would be well. The country's economy, they think, would be taken out of the hands of politicians and planners and handed over to financiers and bankers who alone understand these things …
>
> Sterling, I repeat, cannot be made strong by financial manipulation. It is the real things that count – more steel mills in Britain, more ship loads of British manufactures crossing the Atlantic, more Australian farmers growing wheat and meat for England, more cotton plantations in the Colonies. That is the way to make sterling strong. It is a hard way and it will take time, but it is the only way.

'I trust,' concluded Cherwell, 'we shall not allow ourselves to be persuaded that there is a painless, magical way – by leaving it all to the Bank of England.'

Far from everyone in the know in Threadneedle Street had been convinced of Robot's merits, including perhaps Cobbold by the end; but the episode still left the Bank, in Fforde's words, 'severely bruised', being perceived as having 'rashly attempted to engineer a change of economic and monetary strategy without proper consideration or consultation in Whitehall'. The debate would continue for many years whether the failure to implement Robot was the great missed opportunity of post-war economic history; but in the here and now of 1952 the focus switched to achieving convertibility more gradually, with a new and coherent Bank/Treasury plan ('Collective Approach to Multilateral Trade and Payments', involving American help and European co-operation) in place by the autumn, followed in March 1954 by the reopening of the London gold market and in February 1955 by the de facto (if not yet de jure) convertibility of sterling for non-residents at practically the official fixed rate. 'A long steeplechase course with fences to be jumped at intervals, some stiffer than others, but with a lot of steady plodding in between,' was how Cobbold in 1954 described that route to convertibility, and there was still the odd obstacle ahead.[14]

By then, the Conservative government had successfully denationalised the steel industry, nationalised by Labour. 'I found myself,' recalled Cobbold, 'in the extraordinary position of having to act as adviser and "pusher" to the sellers (Chancellor and Minister of Supply), the intermediaries and agents (Issuing Houses), and the buyers (mainly Insurance Companies), not to mention negotiation with the banks and the Stock Exchange, as well as many of the individual companies.' Indeed, it was the governor who in April 1953 assembled an issuing consortium, comprising the major merchant banks and to be headed by Morgan Grenfell. 'This whole matter is far too political,' complained one merchant banker, David Colville of Rothschilds, to Cobbold's face at a meeting at the Bank of the issuing houses:

> What the Bank of England is in fact doing is to use its influence in the City, acting as the nationalised agent of a government controlled by a political party, to obtain the support of private enterprise to help implement the election promises of that party. In effect, private enterprise is being suborned by a nationalised institution for political ends and the Bank is, moreover, seeking to throw the whole political onus and possible loss on the City, without taking either risk or responsibility.

Colville received little support for this remarkably frank attack, but it was another reminder of that inherently treacherous terrain that the Bank occupied, somewhere between government on the one hand and the City on the other. Undeterred, Cobbold over the next fourteen months continued to play a key role as the sale to the investing public and institutions was undertaken in turn of six of the biggest steel companies: talking to key figures like Carlyle Gifford of the Scottish

Investment Trust, or agreeing to 'have a word with the Chairman of the Pru'; ensuring that the Bank acted as a long-stop in the under-writing process; persuading Butler that, after a poor response to the Lancashire Steel Corporation's offer, the process 'be left to simmer for a bit' and 'that there was nothing to be gained by rushing any fences'; and generally, through deft deployment of his considerable force of personality, leading from the front.

The first privatisation virtually coincided with that disturbing phenomenon, the contested takeover bid, previously almost unheard of in the corporate world. In March 1953, in the context of the hard-bitten outsider Charles Clore initiating a much publicised stake-out for J. Sears & Co (parent company of Freeman, Hardy & Willis), the Bank drew up an internal 'Memorandum on Real and Fictitious Share Bids', arguing that 'this kind of manoeuvre may mean the break-up of businesses which are making an important contribution to the country's needs'. Even so, notwithstanding the concerns of the City establishment at large, there was a limit to how far the Bank felt it could go in preventing such bids, as the senior figure at Morgan Grenfell discovered on a visit to the governor's room that summer:

> Lord Bicester came in to say that he was very agitated about further manoeuvres by Mr Clore and wondered whether I could not suggest to the Insurance Companies that they should not lend him money. I said that I thought this would be extremely difficult. I started by being reluctant to interfere with other people's business. Although I had no love for Mr Clore's activities I found it very difficult to draw a line between what was moral and what was immoral in this field and I certainly had no evidence of any misbehaviour by Mr Clore. Finally I thought that if I talked to people, the nice people would play and lose the business which would be taken by the nasty people ...

The winter after that tellingly Manichean observation saw the battle for the Savoy group of hotels, including Claridge's and the Berkeley as well as the Savoy itself. The aggressor was the property devel-oper Harold Samuel, acting in informal liaison with Clore; and for a moment the government was minded to step in on the Savoy's behalf, until Cobbold pointed out to the minister concerned,

Reginald Maudling, that 'any remedy would cause more trouble than the disease'. Accordingly, the Savoy was left to save itself, which it managed to do with significant help from Anthony Tuke, chairman of Barclays. 'Mr Tuke told me privately that they had fixed up the Savoy business,' noted Cobbold in early 1954. 'The Savoy people had managed to collect some quite good guarantees but it had still meant Barclays taking the shares at 40/- instead of the 30/- they had originally contemplated.' The governor's note at the foot of his memo was Normanesque: 'I am telling HMT [the Treasury] 1st sentence only.'[15]

The previous autumn had seen Bank rate reduced from 4 to 3½ per cent – the first Bank rate change since the war to be announced in the traditional way, with a notice being posted in the front hall of the Bank at precisely the same time that the government broker (Derrick Mullens) arrived on the floor of the Stock Exchange, climbed on to the customary bench, took off his top hat and bawled out the new rate to the assembled gilt-edged market. The question increasingly, though, was whether monetary policy, having been neglected for so long, could carry the load. 'I stressed the danger of thinking that monetary policy could do more than it can,' noted Cobbold as early as July 1953 after one of his quarterly briefings for the clearing bankers. 'The main problems remain those of Government expenditure, taxation and the tendency for wage increases.' Moreover, he was uncomfortably aware that if the Bank was to continue to retain a significant degree of control over monetary policy – squeezing out the Treasury, certainly below the very top level – then that policy had to be seen to be working, the chances of which hinged on a whole range of factors, mostly beyond the Bank's control. By the start of 1955, he found himself in a particularly unenviable position. A summer election was in the offing, the stock market was booming and it would have been little comfort to read the *Financial Times* on New Year's Day assuring its readers that, 'with the monetary weapon available to check inflation', Butler would be free in his budget in the spring to concentrate on tax cuts.[16]

A fateful year played out with an implacable inevitability. Eden was prime minister from early April, not long after Churchill had paid his one and only visit to the Bank, for a farewell dinner. There was some anxiety beforehand – Churchill wanting champagne, as well as worried that Niemeyer might be present – but, recalled Cobbold, 'in any event he came and we made polite little speeches, there was a lot of champagne and a good time was had by all!' On 19 April, Butler delivered his much awaited budget and duly cut the standard rate of income tax by sixpence, while publicly pinning his faith on 'the resources of a flexible monetary policy' in order to counterbalance this fiscal generosity. Already, behind the scenes, the signs were visible of serious trouble ahead. On the Bank's part, Cobbold the day before the budget was trying to nudge the clearing bankers to apply the brakes, telling them that he had 'heard a good deal of gossip round the place that there was little or no change in the attitude of the banks towards lending' and that he 'thought this ought to be put right'; on the Treasury side, Robert Hall was even more critical of the Bank than usual. 'They have never been too keen on being tough with the Banks,' he observed in his diary on budget day. 'Now the Governor tells the Chancellor that he *is* being tough with them, but Oliver Franks (now Chairman of Lloyds) tells me that this is not so ...' And he added ominously that 'altogether we are working up to some sort of *éclaircissement* with the Governor, but whether the Chancellor will support us I don't know – he has always felt that the Governor is in the saddle and that it is a very serious thing to disagree with him'.

Some five weeks later Eden and Butler won their election, which was followed even more predictably during the rest of the summer by serious inflationary and balance of payments pressures. The first crunch came in July. While Butler on the 26th announced a round of credit-tightening measures, Cobbold and the Treasury engaged both before and after (going into August) in a fierce tussle over the governor's exclusive authority to deal with the clearing banks, with the Bank's man successfully counter-attacking through his usual line that a 'credit squeeze' would work properly only if more was done 'to cut back public spending'. The second crunch came in the autumn as severe pressure on sterling led by late October to an emergency budget and significant cuts in government expenditure – though not significant enough for Cobbold, who told Butler soon afterwards that he 'continued to feel doubts whether it was possible to run a defence programme and a social programme of the present size at the same time, without keeping the economy overloaded'. As for monetary matters, the mood in the Treasury remained deeply resentful of what it saw as a tacit conspiracy between the Bank and the banks not to implement credit policy with sufficient stringency – a charge that Cobbold strongly denied, claiming in November that 'in the last few months' the banks 'had done much more than anybody else to fight inflation'.[17] Increasingly, West End was telling East End how to run its affairs, and vice versa: not a happy situation.

Butler, his reputation badly tarnished, was replaced in January by Harold Macmillan. Believing that the debacle of the previous year had been caused less by his predecessor succumbing to the electoral cycle than by 'ignorance, lack of proper statistical information, bad Treasury advice, a weak Governor of the Bank, & resistance of the Clearing Bankers', the new chancellor was soon enjoying personally cordial but professionally difficult relations with the governor, amid a circle increasingly hard to square: the Bank and the banking system wanting to stick as far as possible to a voluntary system of credit control; such a system appearing at best only semi-effective; and naturally the Bank and the bankers looking to shift the blame elsewhere. February, with sterling once again in trouble, saw a temporary accord – Bank rate raised to 5½ per cent, Macmillan acceding to Cobbold's demand for a package of expenditure and investment cuts – but in late March there was an explicit stand-off:

> I am wondering [Macmillan wrote to Cobbold] whether you could not help me, not merely by what you are doing but by getting the full benefit of everyone knowing what you are doing. For it is not only what we are, but what we seem to be, that matters …
>
> The question of liquidity ratio [the ratio of cash held by banks relative to their deposits] seems to be worth considering again from this point of view. I know at present you rely on the banks carrying out your general wishes. But is there not a lot to be said for this system being more regularised? For instance, could I announce in the Budget that the liquidity ratio was now to be imposed by the Bank of England on the banks?

The governor in his reply gave no ground. After arguing as usual that the banks were already being squeezed as severely as possible, and that it was the expenditure side of things that really needed the chancellor's attention, he upped the stakes:

There has been no major banking failure or moratorium in living memory, no Government has had in this country to rescue the banks from unliquid commitments, the banks have survived two great wars and immense economic changes without loss to anybody and they have provided enormous help to the Government of the day in war and peace.

Our banking system is incomparably better co-ordinated, more responsible and more willing (some critics would say too willing) to listen to official advice and requests than any other banking system in the world ...

Macmillan backed off for the moment, but by early May, after further discussion on the vexed subject of liquidity ratios, was noting that 'the Governor is putting a fast one over me, I fear'. Eventually he did accept that a prescribed liquidity ratio was unrealistic (except in an emergency), but at the same time exacted a price for that acceptance. 'I want to *see & talk* to the Clearing Bankers myself,' he recorded in his diary in early July. 'Mr Governor does not like this, as he regards himself as the right person to deal with the Clearing Banks. We compromised. He will see them, & tell them my wishes this week. I will see them later on in the month ...' That meeting duly took place on the 24th – the day after an entry in the governor's diary that would not have surprised the Trollope-reading chancellor: 'I had a talk with Mr Robarts [chairman of the Committee of London Clearing Bankers] and Sir Oliver Franks about tactics at the Bankers' Meeting with the Chancellor.'[18] At which point, late July 1956, Egypt's President Nasser nationalised the Suez Canal Company, and suddenly all that tactical manoeuvring seemed rather unimportant.

Three months later, at the end of October, military action began. A Fed memo on the 31st recorded the gist of Bolton's telephonic commentary on the Suez crisis as seen from Threadneedle Street:

Just don't know how things are going to turn out. If Suez settles down quickly, maybe alarm in the market may also disappear. We now have an open breach between London and Washington and that may have consequences one can't foresee very accurately ... I was quite convinced that something was going to happen – only thing that surprised me was the speed ... I regard that sort of thing as being quite inevitable. Sorry it happened so quickly and also before the [US presidential] election ...

'The pressure on Sterling was considerable,' Cobbold next day told the discount market, adding that he didn't 'wish it to continue in this way for 365 days in the year'. On 6 November, faced by Britain's reserves draining away and the Americans unwilling to come to the rescue by offering dollar loans, Eden announced a ceasefire. That, though, did not halt the run on sterling (not helped by the recent Russian invasion of Hungary), and on the 15th the Fed's John Exter recorded a far-from-buoyant Bolton:

> Sir George seemed tired and harried. He said there was a real war psychology in Europe and that there was strong pressure away from Continental currencies and toward North American dollars. He said that as far as they were concerned in Britain they were very discouraged about the situation and were at loose ends as to what to do. He emphasized twice in the conversation that the deterioration had gone beyond the point where it could be handled by any available techniques. I inquired about direct controls and he indicated that he did not think tighter controls would do any good.

By the time things stabilised, during the second week of December, Britain had lost $450 million of reserves since 30 October – ultimately, the cost of an episode that had marked, with brutal clarity, the end of Britain as a world power.

That episode also now prompted a Cobbold special:

> Whatever longer-term effects Suez may prove to have on the economy [he wrote to Macmillan five days before Christmas], it has certainly had the immediate effect of laying bare to the public eye, both at home and abroad, some of the weaknesses of which we have long been conscious ...
>
> The fundamental trouble is that the economy and the public purse have been over-extended for many years, partly as a result of the war and partly because of the many commitments, social, military and political, which we have since undertaken (most of them

doubtless justifiable on their own merits but adding up to a total bigger than we could afford).

On top of our domestic commitments, we are overstretched by our banking liabilities to overseas holders of sterling ...

Accordingly, he called for 'dramatic, far-reaching and convincing measures in 1957'; and he ended by asserting that 'we are, I believe, at a cross-road, where the whole future of sterling, and everything which that implies, depends on the decisions of the next few months'. Just over a fortnight later, Macmillan replaced Eden. 'Mr Hallett called to say that they were pleased with the way sterling was behaving and that they had been able to acquire some dollars,' noted the Fed's Thomas Roche next day after a phone conversation with Richard Hallett, deputising for Roy Bridge. 'Hallett said that they, in the Bank of England, were of the opinion that the resignation of Eden had cleared the air and they look forward to more settled conditions for the rest of the year.'[19]

The recent Suez drama did not obliterate memories of the monetary system's embarrassing failure in 1955 to deliver the credit squeeze on which Butler's tax-cutting pre-election budget had been predicated; and in April 1957 the new chancellor, Peter Thorneycroft, announced that the eminent lawyer Lord Radcliffe would be chairing a formal inquiry into the working of that system. In mid-May, after a fairly staid, eminently respectable array of Bank-vetted names had been assembled, Cobbold sent Radcliffe 'Some Thoughts at Random':

I hope that the Committee will not feel it necessary to go deeply into relations between Government and Bank. They have worked out happily, much along the lines which you will remember we were hoping for at the time of the [1946] Bank Act; though there is a mild blow up from time to time, the relationship is pretty smooth and pretty well defined in practice. This does not seem to me a matter of much public controversy, and I hope it may be 'taken as read'.

I think you will also find that working relations between the Bank of England and the Banking System are pretty good. The Banks dislike 'directives' and are getting tired of the credit squeeze – but, even so, relations are close and harmonious. The only place I expect you to hear contrary views is among some banking economists who feel that they are inadequately consulted ...

Many people (and some members of your Committee) will press for more information from the 'Authorities' ... We ought not to go too fast or too far. And Heaven protect us from a monthly 'Federal Reserve Bulletin', a duplication of Government Economic services, and a continuous spate of unreliable statistics and prophecies ...

Notwithstanding the Treasury's intense frustration over the previous couple of years with the Bank's unwillingness to instruct the clearing banks to cut their advances by a specific amount, Cobbold was also in productive, pre-emptive correspondence with its permanent secretary. 'Each of us will keep in touch with the other's thinking while we prepare our positions,' Sir Roger Makins assured the governor, who for his part replied, 'We are, I think, in full agreement and I foresee no difficulty in practice.'

Two early sessions in July saw Cobbold giving evidence. Asked about his institution's openness or lack of it, he insisted that the Bank needed to be able to offer its advice to government 'on terms of strictest banking secrecy', adding that 'there is very much to be said for the policy we generally adopt of hammering out any differences of policy or view and by and large leaving it to the Government to explain the decisions finally taken'; even so, he went on, 'on balance the Bank's policy is in fact to be rather more forthcoming than it was, I would judge, in the old days', and he noted that 'it has been my practice to make speeches from time to time – not a great many, perhaps two a year – saying a good deal about the Bank's view on current policy developments'. In short: 'Our view is that it is very much better that we should be able to choose our own time when it would be useful and helpful to the public to say something rather than be forced by some regular monthly or weekly arrangement to say something, or indeed perhaps to say very little, in frequent, regular statements.' Cobbold gave a controlled, measured performance almost throughout, but did allow himself the occasional show of emotion. Given that the Bank was now nationalised, would he equate his position, Radcliffe boldly asked, with that of 'a leading Civil Servant'? To which the governor indignantly replied: 'Not at all. I am a servant of the Bank Court.'[20]

Within weeks of these appearances, sterling was yet again under intense pressure, with reserves tumbling fast. 'We have a difficult time ahead,' Cobbold warned Thorneycroft on 22 August before going on holiday to Sardinia, adding darkly that 'the Germans are going to behave like Germans'. The focus turned to his deputy, Humphrey Mynors. 'We may be in for a real exchange tussle,' Mynors wrote in early September to an absent director (the Court's by now semi-obligatory trade unionist, Sir Alfred Roberts) in response to August's alarming exchange figures. 'I remain convinced that our prosperity and standard of living will suffer a mortal blow if the pound goes again, even though it is not easy to put this across as it is not apparent in everyday life.' Over the next week or so there developed what was tantamount to a constitutional crisis: the chancellor was adamant about the necessity of a 5 per cent reduction in bank advances; the clearing banks were equally adamant that such a policy was not only 'unwise' but also 'unworkable'; and as usual the Bank was stuck somewhere in the middle, though with Mynors making it very clear to Thorneycroft that a) it was highly undesirable that the voluntary approach to bank credit be jettisoned, and that b) under the terms of the 1946 Act the government would require fresh powers if it sought to limit bank advances without doing so via the Bank. That left the possibility of Thorneycroft issuing a formal directive to the Bank to get the banks to do his bidding – a drastic option that in the end he pulled back from. Instead, the inevitable outcome was a major hike in Bank rate, with Cobbold persuading the reluctant politician that there was no alternative to a stiff 2 per cent rise – from 5 to 7 – if the pound was to be saved. Thorneycroft duly made the announcement on 19 September. 'There has recently been a good deal of speculative pressure against the pound,' a Bank spokesman declared in strikingly robust language. 'People have been selling sterling. This will show them "where they get off".'[21]

The hike did its job – pressure on sterling soon easing – but left a vexed Thorneycroft convinced that proper control over the money supply was imperative if creeping inflation was to be mastered. Cobbold, for every reason, was sceptical. 'I do not accept the view that we have lost control of the money supply,' he wrote to Thorneycroft in early October, warning at the same time about the danger of making 'this country the only leading democracy where the Treasury (as opposed to the Central Bank) has powers to direct the commercial banks'. Or again, later that month in a note on a meeting with Thorneycroft ahead of an economic debate in the Commons: 'I hoped that the Chancellor would not allow himself to get pinned down in the Debate too exclusively to his money supply arguments. I thought it would be unwise to get too far into an academic argument anyway and, as he was aware, I did not feel that the total money supply was by any means the whole question.' Such sentiments were entirely consistent with the governor's general reluctance to pin everything on monetary policy, as he explained to the Radcliffe Committee in early November, reflecting on the six often charged years since the reactivation of monetary policy:

> I think, if I examine my conscience, I should find it difficult to feel that we really hoped in any of these Bank Rate moves really to reverse the situation. We have felt throughout this period that we could not reverse the situation by Bank Rate or monetary measures in the private sector unless they were in line with and only used in support of action on a wider field, more particularly on overall Government expenditure. We have felt that it would be not only useless but a mistake to try to overload or overburden the monetary weapon ...

Even so, Cobbold's political antennae told him that it would be a serious error to have a re-run of the September confrontation – and that it was necessary to make a concession on the monetary front in order to avoid the government assuming powers that *would* enable it to issue diktats to the clearing banks directly, in other words circumventing the Bank. Fortunately from his point of view, there emerged during the winter of 1957–8, as the Radcliffe Committee considered 'Alternative Techniques' of credit control, a Bank/Treasury consensus that resisted any extremes of compulsion, with the Treasury explicitly accepting the Bank's emphasis on 'the risks of rigidity and dislocation of bank practice'. Accordingly, the concession itself was relatively minor, namely the introduction in due course of a system of 'special deposits' – deposits placed by clearing banks, on the Bank's instructions, with the Bank itself in order to limit the amount of credit the banks could create. Macmillan and his ministers might have hoped for something more dramatic, but for them there was always the sobering thought of a future Labour government having direct access to the resources of the banking system.[22]

Labour – and specifically, the shadow chancellor Harold Wilson – was also on the Bank's mind during the winter of 1957–8. 'I'm spending far too much of my time on this damned leak business,' Cobbold expostulated to a colleague shortly after the dramatic Bank rate rise in September, with rumours spreading that powerful figures in the City had had advance warning of that rise and had taken advantage of it to sell heavily in the gilt-edged market.[23] Wilson pressed hard for an inquiry, and eventually Macmillan gave way, with a tribunal being appointed under Lord Justice Parker.[24] Two of the Bank's non-executive (that is, part-time) directors now found themselves under enemy fire – the second Lord Kindersley (of Lazards) and W. J. ('Tony') Keswick (of Mathesons) – as evidence was taken at Church House, Westminster during the weeks before Christmas. The case against Keswick was that, while shooting on the Scottish moors in early September, he had heard from Mynors that 'a swingeing rise in the Bank Rate was in the offing'; that on the 16th, in person at the Bank, he had been told again by the deputy governor that this was a distinct possibility; and that next day, two days before the actual rise, he had cabled Jardine Matheson in Hong Kong, anticipating tighter money and recommending that gilts be sold, which they duly were. As for Kindersley, the uncomfortable fact was that the three major concerns he chaired – Lazards, Royal Exchange Assurance and the British Match Company – had between them sold almost £2½ million of gilts during the day and a half before the Bank rate announcement.

Neither man had a comfortable time (Keswick not helping himself by observing that 'it is difficult for me to remember the exact timing of conversation on a grouse moor') as they were questioned by the attorney general, Sir Reginald Manningham-Buller, while Cobbold was also ill at ease. 'The City is in a rage against Ministers over the Bank Rate Inquiry, because they think the Attorney-General attacked the Governor and the Court and let off the politicians,' noted the Treasury's Hall, and indeed there was no doubting the outrage. 'I thought the Attorney General went out of his way to be offensive about the Governor in his big winding-up speech,' Kindersley wrote to Bolton (no longer at the Bank) just before Christmas. 'If he was the next gun to me tomorrow I would certainly use my cartridges in a different direction to the pheasants!!!' As for the outside world, it watched fascinated, with one observer, Mollie Panter-Downes, evoking for her *New Yorker* readers 'a succession of spruce, pink-jowled City gentlemen easing themselves and their briefcases into the witness chair' and speaking a 'totally different language' about '"comparatively small"' deals of a million or so pounds. 'It has all been a revealing glimpse into a special, jealously guarded world ...' And one Labour politician, Michael Foot, made a prediction: 'My prophecy is that this whole amazing story of how the City works is bound to lead, at the very least, to plans for the reconstruction of the Bank of England.'[25]

While Parker over the holiday season pondered his findings, there began to unfold one of the seminal episodes of British post-war political history. 'I am bound to express the view,' Cobbold wrote gravely to Thorneycroft on 27 December, 'that if HM Government accept estimates of the order which you mentioned to me this morning, it will be seen at home and abroad to be in flat contradiction with your statement of 19th September' – a reference to how that statement had featured not only the Bank rate hike but also a two-year standstill in public sector investment. The governor then went on to warn that despite 'a distinct improvement in atmosphere and small increase in the reserves' since those measures, 'there is no prospect that any weakening of policy ... would escape immediate notice and strong criticism'. How much that further fortified an already determined chancellor is impossible to tell; but over the next ten days a bitter battle within the Cabinet culminated on 6 January with the resignation of Thorneycroft and the other two Treasury ministers (one of them Enoch Powell), unable to accept draft estimates for public expenditure for 1958–9 showing an increase of £50 million, viewed by the trio as incompatible with the principle of restraining government spending. 'I myself think he is right,' Cobbold wrote that day to Macmillan. 'I am very sorry, because I felt with P.T.'s courage and with you behind him at No. 10, we were on an improving wicket from the currency's point of view. And I still feel – perhaps I am prejudiced! – that the success or failure of the next two years depends more on the currency than on anything else.' But for Macmillan, instinctively a Keynesian and with an understandable eye on the need for a significant degree of reflation before the general election due by 1960, the priorities were rather different as he prepared to ride out the storm – or what, in his blithely immortal words, he called a 'little local difficulty'. Did the governor, in his sense of regret, have the City behind him? Only up to a point. 'I would like to see the Government cutting every penny off expenditure,' a leading broker reported to the minister charged with gauging reaction there. 'But if it is a matter of political judgement I would prefer to trust Macmillan rather than Thorneycroft.'[26] Put another way, if the socialists could be kept out, then a certain loss of free-market purity was an acceptable price to pay. It was a trade-off that, for almost another twenty years, would continue to govern City assumptions – and could not help but influence those in the admittedly somewhat less tribal and more objective central bank.

By now Lord Justice Parker was ready to pronounce. 'I have just read the Report,' the Treasury's Makins on 10 January 1958 informed his new chancellor, Derick Heathcoat Amory. 'It could scarcely be more satisfactory from the point of view of the government, the Bank of England and the City. Everybody connected with the Government and Bank of England is completely exonerated.' So it proved when the report was published on the 21st. There was, it declared, 'no justification for allegations that information about the raising of the Bank Rate was improperly disclosed to any person'; as for those in receipt of advance warning of the rise, 'in every case the information disclosed was treated by the recipient as confidential and … no use of such information was made for the purpose of private gain'. That evening, returning to London after a Rolls-Royce meeting in Derby, Kindersley was handed a copy at St Pancras Station. 'I am very pleased,' he told a reporter before leaving in a chauffeur-driven Roller to attend a diplomatic reception. 'It is very pleasant indeed.' And next day, Cobbold sent a message to all the staff, noting the complete exoneration of the Bank and acknowledging that it had been 'a very worrying time for all of us'. Certainly that was how it felt in Threadneedle Street – both then and later. In 1987, paying tribute to Cobbold at his memorial service, his successor but one, Leslie O'Brien, recalled the leak and tribunal as a 'damaging affair, in which good men and true were pilloried to provide a roman holiday for lesser men'. Yet looked at from the outside it is quite possible that Keswick and Kindersley got away with it. Forrest Capie, in his successor volume to Fforde, suggests that the latter anyway may have done so, pointing to how the British

Match Company had for several years faithfully held around £250,000 of gilts – until it abruptly got rid of them the day before the Bank rate hike was announced. 'They sold that stock,' the last government broker, Sir Nigel Althaus, would recall almost half a century after the event, 'and that seemed to me the absolute clincher, and I think Lord Kindersley was very lucky.'[27]

At the time, what was unavoidable for the Bank was an intense fortnight or so in the public spotlight, culminating in a two-day debate in the Commons instigated by Labour. Immediate press reaction to the report had a distinctly critical tinge, identifying a whitewash, while the leftish economic journalist Andrew Shonfield gave a radio talk on 'The Future of the Bank of England', in which he deployed evidence from the tribunal to create a verbal picture of a 'slow-footed' institution with 'too little professionalism' where 'the national cult of the not-so-gifted amateur has got out of hand'. Looking ahead, he did not deny that 'a central bank inevitably has a certain measure of independence in some spheres of policy', but demanded a firmer, more precise definition of 'the respective areas controlled by the Bank and the Treasury'; as for the Bank's relations with the City, he argued that because of its reliance on prestige-cum-persuasion, 'it acts, in fact, like a head prefect, whereas the real task of a central bank today is to behave like a headmaster'. Shonfield ended by calling on the Bank to 'now come down firmly on the side of the masters in Whitehall', rather than be 'unduly influenced by its special role in relation to the business interests of the City'.

Early February saw the Commons debate, in which Wilson gave an aggressive, virtuoso performance: disparaging not only the Court ('we cannot defend a system where merchant bankers are treated as the gentlemen and the clearing bankers as the players using the professionals' gate out of the pavilion') but the Bank more generally – 'supposed to be a nationalised industry', but behaving 'like a sovereign State' and conducting its relations with the Treasury 'with too much out-dated stiffness and protocol'. An even more direct broadside came from Harold Lever, in the process of establishing his reputation as Labour's expert on monetary matters:

The policies of the Bank of England directorate have meant that our dollars have been diddled away into the hands of every second-rate currency dealer on the Continent. Every commodity shunter has outwitted them. Every dealer in American stocks and shares appears to have been able to get hold of our dollars. Yet all the time the charades of the Bank are religiously maintained. Simple, honest, patriotic and highly talented people have, with great social discipline, continued their efforts to put the country on its feet again, and all the time their efforts have been frustrated because, at one stroke, these blind doctrinaires have poured out the wealth which our people have laboured so hard, so patriotically and with such discipline to produce.

'Let them answer that one,' called out Labour's Jennie Lee at this point, but sadly no one did.

Less than a fortnight later, speaking at the Guildhall to the Overseas Bankers' Club, the governor sought to answer the critics. After observing that it had recently become a popular national pastime to suggest how the Bank ought to be run, he made a series of assertions: that of the twelve non-executive directors, only three came from merchant banks, while seven 'have their main experience in industry and commerce'; that 'both in everyday business and in top-level contacts' the Bank's relationship with the clearing banks was 'second only in importance to the Bank's relationship with Government'; that although 'the Bank of England must be a bank and not a study group' (a no doubt conscious nod to Norman), the 'charge that the Bank is bereft of economic thinking does not bear examination' (with Cobbold pointing to 'two former dons from Oxford on our senior permanent staff', supplemented by a deputy governor 'who may still remember something from his ten years at Cambridge'); and finally, that the Bank's policy remained that of moving 'gradually in the direction of saying more about what we are doing'. It was a reasoned defence that did its job well enough – albeit one financial editor commented, 'Two economists for the whole Bank!' Even so, more was clearly needed and in May the governor opened up a whole front by agreeing to allow the TV cameras into his room and film him being grilled by Robin Day for the ITN series *Tell the People*. Concentrating mainly on the Bank's functions and carefully elaborating the nature of its relationship with government – that of a 'very dutiful wife' who offered her advice very freely 'as a good wife should' and had even been known to nag – he made a favourable impression, displaying, noted the *Manchester Guardian*, 'none of the starchiness in his telling which people with low bank accounts might have expected'. In addition, clinching this PR triumph after a somewhat harrowing period, 'the beadle, the messenger, even the gentlemen in top hats, entered thoroughly into the spirit of the occasion'.[28]

Radcliffe and his team continued their inquiry through the whole of 1958. 'I personally should think that the more and closer the contacts we have with the Bank of England the better,' David Robarts of National Provincial Bank asserted early in the year. 'That is very important indeed; and we do have them; I am quite satisfied with that. Having arrived at that position, I do not think we want to go and discuss very much the same problems with the Treasury.' Radcliffe's two main monetary experts were the economist Alec Cairncross and the historian Richard Sayers, and that summer the former privately heard from the latter that the Bank 'not only engaged in forward dealings but that they had been very heavily in the market in September 1957 and didn't want this known', with Cairncross reflecting in his diary that 'they must have cleared a big profit'; about the same time, another economist, Harold Wilson's adviser Thomas Balogh, submitted a memorandum of evidence proposing that the Court's chairman should be a senior Treasury official, with the governor relegated to being a member of Court only.

In December – by when it had been announced that Cobbold would stay on as governor until after Radcliffe had published his report – it was the turn of two former chancellors, with Gaitskell (now the Labour leader) appearing at the inquiry on the morning of the 18th and Butler in the afternoon. The main thrust of Gaitskell's evidence was the urgent need to improve the frequency and depth of contact between Treasury and Bank, as well as wanting the Treasury (including the chancellor himself) to enjoy direct access to the leading clearing bankers. Altogether, commented Cairncross privately, 'he didn't try to screen the Bank and yet did not take a position obviously hostile to it'. Predictably, his successor at No. 11 was more emollient, tactfully delineating what he saw as the essential differences between the two bodies that sought in their distinctive ways to serve government:

I think that there are things the Bank can do that the Treasury cannot, and things the Treasury can do that the Bank cannot. The Bank is more instinctively intuitive, and the Treasury is more instinctively deliberative – at least, so it seems to me – and so the two partners rather supplement each other. The management of the day-to-day market, which is the fundamental job of the Bank, apart from their agency functions in relation to the debt, the note issue and so forth, is a different sphere from the more deliberative long-term policy aspect of the Treasury.

Throughout Butler's feline performance there was no hint that the Bank's failure three years earlier to deliver him the monetary conditions it had apparently promised had gone a long way towards costing him the premiership. Or, as Cairncross acutely put it, 'He took pains to defend the Bank and seemed to want to tell us that everything was all right *now*. No question at all that *he* would tell a different story in private.'[29]

1958 was also the year of financial liberalisation – sometimes though not always in accordance with the Bank's wishes. The Stock Exchange, Cobbold warned its chairman in May in the context of a possible return there of option dealing (banned since 1939), would be 'most unwise to hand this particular weapon to their critics'; but to no avail, and option dealing resumed that autumn. He fared better, as credit controls eased, with the burgeoning, barely regulated hire-purchase sector, successfully encouraging the clearing banks to buy into hire-purchase companies as a way of enabling the Bank indirectly to exercise some control; while, as the banks themselves for the first time in their history made a serious effort to reach out to society at large, a year after Macmillan's famous 'never had it so good' speech, they did so with the Bank's blessing, Cobbold broad-mindedly telling the chancellor that 'the more they can attract the new highly paid classes to open bank accounts the better'. Another aspect of financial liberalisation, scarcely noticed at the time but ultimately of huge significance to London's future as an international financial centre, was the emergence in 1957–8 of what would by the early 1960s be known as the eurodollar market – an innovation, according to Catherine Schenk's subsequent analysis, 'tolerated' by the Bank because 'it was not strictly illegal'. No doubt it helped too that the key visionary behind the market was Bolton, chairman of the Bank of London and South America (BOLSA) after leaving the Bank. The final piece in the 1958 liberalising jigsaw was the full convertibility of sterling (that is, of sterling held by non-residents), attained – simultaneously with the French and West German currencies – on 29 December: an achievement owing much in its final phase to Cobbold's insistence that this was crucial for the City's international prestige and his determination to override Treasury qualms about the consequences of an even speedier-than-usual drain on the reserves if the world once again lost confidence in sterling. The most articulate critic of Cobbold's position, arguing that the priority given to the strength of sterling imposed an unacceptable burden on British industry and economic growth generally, was Andrew Shonfield; and earlier that year, a caustic internal note by the deputy governor, Mynors, referred to that journalist (who during the war had served in the British Army as a gunner and intelligence officer) as 'Andrew Shönfeld'. Still, the press as a whole did its patriotic duty and acclaimed full convertibility. 'Pound Flies High' (*Sunday Express*), 'This Proud, Free £' (*Daily Express*), 'The £ Stands Firm on Freedom Day' (*Evening Standard*): this was sterling's rare moment in the sun.[30]

All the time, Cobbold continued to act as the great arbiter of that intimate, personal place that was the old-style City. Take almost at random a couple of typical moments from July 1958:

> Sir John Benn came in to mention one or two possible names for his Board. At his request, I checked up on Sir Henry Warner with Lord Kindersley and gave him a good report. He asked whether I saw any objection to their putting on a sensible Labour M.P. I said 'on the contrary' ...
>
> Sir George Bolton came in for a gossip. He wants somebody to reinforce them at Director level in New York and Bahamas. After a good deal of discussion with his colleagues, he is thinking of Henry Tiarks. I said that, provided he knows what he is buying and squares Helmut Schroder, I had no comment ...

By this time, though, a legendary City episode was looming – an episode that saw not just Britain's first out-and-out contested takeover ('in the modern sense', to quote Niall Ferguson, 'that a controlled shareholding in a public company was acquired on the open market with the conscious aim of ousting the company's management and board'), but the governor's authority significantly undermined. Managing director of the company under attack, British Aluminium (BA), was Geoffrey Cunliffe, son of the former controversial governor; while the rival bidders were on the one hand Alcoa, favoured by BA, and on the other hand an alliance of another American company, Reynolds Metals, and a British one, Tube Investments, with that combination's principal financial adviser being the merchant banker Siegmund Warburg, still regarded with considerable misgivings by the City establishment. During the closing weeks of the year the Bank maintained a carefully neutral position, but became increasingly concerned about the acrimony within the square mile that the 'Aluminium War' was generating. On New Year's Eve, Cobbold spent much of the day trying and failing to arrange a two-month truce, not least with a view to curbing the activities of Warburgs and what he called their 'monkey business'. The early days of 1959 proved decisive, with Warburgs piling into the market to buy shares, even as other combatants held off for apparent fear of upsetting the Bank. 'A troublesome little trouble' was how Cobbold many years later would refer to the Aluminium War; and in retrospect it is debatable whether even his predecessor but one would have been capable of keeping Warburg in check.[31]

Radcliffe, meanwhile, maintained into 1959 its steady, impervious course, with Cobbold submitting on 15 January a written statement that included a paragraph deliberately raising the stakes:

> In a totalitarian state, with private enterprise and markets more or less eliminated, it would make sense for central bank operations to be handled under direct Treasury control, both as to policy and as to detail. For any country operating to a great extent with private enterprise and markets, and working with other countries similarly placed, I should regard direct Treasury control over central bank operations as a major weakness. For a country as dependent as the U.K. on international trade and confidence, it could be a disaster.

'I base these views,' he added, 'on twenty-five years' experience, under Conservative, Labour and Coalition administrations, of the

Bank of England's working relations with Government; and also on a fairly intimate knowledge, over the same period, of the problems and developments in this field in the United States and the principal countries of the Commonwealth and of Europe.' The governor insisted, moreover, that 'the strength and the independence of thought of the Bank derive largely from a Court constituted on present lines', so that accordingly 'if the nature of the Court were to be altered so that it were not to be composed of active practical men of business, or if directors were to become mere figure-heads divorced from the real affairs of the Bank, the standing of the Bank throughout the world, and its ability to perform its public duties efficiently, would both be gravely prejudiced'. Accompanied by his deputy, Cobbold that day also gave oral evidence:

> The Governor [noted Cairncross] talked far more sensibly than his paper ... George Woodcock [the trade union representative on the Committee] asked one particularly sharp question that implied a resemblance between the Bank of England and the House of Lords pre-1911. The Governor obviously disliked a couple of long questions that I put at the end and fell back on his usual stonewalling tactic – put that to the Treasury. Mynors said nothing but nodded agreement once or twice when appealed to by the Governor.

Throughout the lengthy Radcliffe process, Cobbold was absolutely determined not to forfeit the Bank's operational independence; and the following week, in a bilateral communication to Radcliffe himself, he stressed that 'the Bank, to do its job properly, must be a "market" animal and not an "administrative" animal as a Government Department must be'. Furthermore, he went on, there were two 'even more fundamental reasons for favouring a degree of Central Bank independence': first, the desirability of a 'free and intimate interplay of ideas and criticism between Treasury and Bank'; and second, the Bank's role in helping to prevent the 'democratic government' of the day from being 'pushed in directions which will tend to prejudice confidence in paper money, thereby risking inflation, exchange crises and all the social troubles to which they give rise'. Not long afterwards, Radcliffe and his team discussed the governor's evidence. For his part, Cairncross observed that Cobbold seemed 'still to dream of taking monetary policy out of the political arena' and 'to want to exercise more influence on economic policy than was altogether wise'; but his colleagues were significantly less inclined to be critical. 'Radcliffe,' noted Cairncross, 'thought I was "inhuman" and R.S.S. [Richard Sayers] also disagreed, saying that Cobbold saw how things were going but didn't want to go there fast.'[32] Eventually, at the end of April, the Committee heard its final evidence, and there ensued a summer of waiting for the report, mainly written by Sayers.

The other uncertainty that hot summer was political: would it, as the City strongly hoped, be a hat-trick of Tory election wins? Macmillan, abetted by his chancellor, had already laid the economic groundwork. If only ministers were allowed to pursue a Keynesian stimulus to consumption, he told Midland's chairman (the former politician Lord Monckton) early in the year, then 'the Conservative party will be re-elected, prosperity will be secured, the Bank of England will be preserved, and funding in 1960 will be easier than ever before'. During the weeks leading up to the April budget, Cobbold successfully resisted the chancellor's wish to reduce Bank rate, but effectively at the price of allowing by default a distinctly reflationary package. On 7 April – the day after the governor in a speech at Newcastle had called on 'the normal citizen' to 'accept some disciplines and make some sacrifices' for the cause of 'stable money' – Heathcoat Amory duly cut income tax by ninepence and overall released into the economy some £6 billion in present-day values. Sidelined by a strong-willed prime minister (who for monetary as well as fiscal advice looked neither to the Bank nor to the Treasury but instead to the Keynesian economist Sir Roy Harrod) and by the demands of the electoral imperative, Cobbold could do little more over the next few weeks and months than 'warn' the chancellor that if his party was indeed returned in an autumn election, 'it might be necessary to pull in the reins rather sharply'. All this was no surprise to Cobbold (although arguably he might have done more to resist Macmillan). 'The moment unemployment figures become at all menacing,' he had with timeless gubernatorial sentiments observed to a bank chairman exactly a year before his somewhat academic warning to Heathcoat Amory, 'our political friends will wish to jump in in a great hurry and we shall again be cast for the unpromising role of carrying a larger part of the baby than we can handle.'[33]

The Radcliffe Report was finally published on 19 August 1959.
'I have had a private copy,' the governor almost a fortnight earlier
informed one of his directors. 'In general the background is not too
bad but there are a few very tiresome suggestions … As a whole I do
not find the document very constructive – but it is unanimous, which
is important.'[34] William Allen, in his survey of monetary policy during
the 1950s, has called the report 'notoriously hard to summarise', but
from a Bank perspective it had perhaps five main aspects: first, the
recommendation, following the events of 1957, that the Bank's part-
time directors be excluded from Bank rate discussions; second, the
further recommendation that Bank rate changes be made at the explicit
directive of the chancellor of the day; third, the key assertions that
economic policy needed to be integrated, that monetary policy alone
was not enough and should not be permitted to pursue autonomous
objectives, and that within monetary policy interest rate changes were
a more effective weapon than attempts to control the money supply;
fourth, a call to the Bank to provide more statistics and information
generally; and finally, the recommendation that a standing committee on monetary policy be set up, to include representatives from the
Bank, the Treasury and the Board of Trade.[35] Cobbold's considered
reaction to all this took the form of a letter to Makins at the Treasury,
despatched two days before publication. While willing to go more or
less quietly on the recommendations concerning non-executive directors, statistics and public relations, he expressed himself unequivocally
unhappy 'that the full responsibility for Bank rate decisions should be
transferred to the Chancellor' and that 'a Standing Committee should
be appointed in Whitehall to which all decisions on monetary policy
should be referred by the Chancellor for advice'. Instead, he insisted
that 'Bank Rate is an integral part of the Central Bank's own business';
and, though not disputing the fact of the chancellor's 'over-riding
decision', the governor maintained that 'to place on the Chancellor
direct responsibility for what is essentially a market and operational
decision would blur the real responsibilities'.

Press reaction was almost unanimous that the report represented
a significant rap on the knuckles for the Bank, indeed a potentially
significant shift of power away from it. 'The main impression that
emerges,' noted one City commentator, 'is that the power and authority of the Bank of England should be trimmed and the Old Lady be

made more visibly amenable to Treasury control.' Inevitably, the central question now became whether the Treasury and its masters had the desire and the stomach to act on the aspects of Radcliffe that not unnaturally perturbed the governor. The answer soon emerged. By mid-September it was clear that the Treasury had no appetite for a standing committee on monetary policy that involved the Board of Trade; by late October, after the general election, the re-elected Heathcoat Amory was letting it be known not only that there would be no new standing committee, but also that it would only be in a situation of irreconcilable disagreement that the Treasury would publicly reveal that it, not the Bank, was responsible for a change in Bank rate; and by late November, following a dullish Commons debate on the report which showed how relatively little of it was to be implemented, the *Financial Times* was even claiming that the Bank had achieved 'a complete rout of Radcliffe'. In short, monetary policy was to remain primarily the responsibility of the Bank, which would continue to take the initiative, albeit subject to the ultimate say-so of the Treasury; and more broadly, the Bank would continue to enjoy operational autonomy. The setting up by the Bank of a Central Banking Information Department for the collection and publication of statistics, the start (from 1960) of the *Bank of England Quarterly Bulletin*, the recruitment of more economists, the partial easing out of non-executive directors from the interest rate decision-making process – all this was small beer by comparison.

'We here feel that this is a satisfactory outcome, which makes virtually no change in the reality of existing normal practices,' Cobbold assured central bankers around the world on 27 November, the day after the chancellor's formal statement to the Commons about the government's response to Radcliffe; and a week before Christmas, the Bank gave Makins a well-earned dinner in his honour, with his Treasury colleague Hall among those present:

As the governor made clear in his speech, it was a sort of demonstration of appreciation for all the help Roger gave them in the troubled weeks of the Bank Rate Tribunal and of Radcliffe. Almost the whole Court were there ... We were received by swarms of tall footmen in their plush livery and had sherry in the ante-room and dinner in the Court Room, which was comfortably filled but with plenty of room. One large table with a white cloth and a good deal of silver, nearly all bought by the Bank because it was [hallmarked] around 1694 ... All the servants have learned one's name for the occasion and whisper in a friendly manner when they offer you anything. In fact it was rather like dining in one's own College.

The Governor made a little speech about how much their safe survival owed to Roger, and he replied pleasantly. I sat between the Governor and Cadbury [Laurence Cadbury, a non-executive director since 1936] – the former much more talkative than I had ever known before and making slightly malicious sketches of his colleagues. Afterwards we stayed at table and the hosts moved around ... About 9.45 the Governor began to edge us out and it must have been all over about 10. And it was really extremely well done and most enjoyable ...[36]

Honest Money

Cobbold's final eighteen months, at the start of a legendary decade, were not entirely easy. From spring 1960 the post-election brakes on the economy began all too predictably to be applied, with the Bank reluctantly implementing the special deposits scheme in relation to the clearing banks – a move towards the quantitative controls that Cobbold had always dreaded, seeing them as likely to erode the Bank's authority. Then in June, with the balance of payments position deteriorating, not only was a second tranche of special deposits removed from the clearers but Bank rate went up from 5 to 6 per cent. 'There is no crisis,' noted one of the discount market's representatives after their regular weekly meeting with the governor. 'Asked whether he [Cobbold] had not fired two barrels at once, he said that it was no bad idea to discharge an extra round at the retiring enemy.' The relief lasted only until March 1961, when a surprise revaluation of the deutschmark precipitated a sudden surge of pressure on Britain's gold and foreign exchange reserves, in turn leading to Cobbold and Roy Bridge negotiating at the Bank for International Settlements the so-called 'Basle credits', running through to July and totalling some $910 million. 'Parsons felt that the tide had turned, at least temporarily, against the speculators,' recorded the Fed's Charles Coombs soon afterwards about the Bank's reaction; and in the event 'temporarily' proved correct, as another sterling crisis gathered in June, amid what Cobbold called 'the recurrent market rumour about early sterling devaluation', a rumour that, writing to his counterpart at the Fed, Bill Martin, he wholly repudiated: 'We are determined to hold the present position and are most anxious not to give public opinion the slightest excuse for detecting any weakness in that determination.' Cobbold had become governor in 1949 under the threatening cloud of devaluation; now he was leaving under the same cloud, perhaps slightly less threatening but undeniably present. 'It has all been great fun,' he told a leading City figure, and it was to his credit that at least some of it had been.' Over the twelve years he had grown into his office and, through strength of personality as much as anything else, would come to be seen as perhaps the ultimate 'Mr Governor' of the nationalised Bank.

The selection of the new governor – ultimately the government's decision, but intimately involving Cobbold and other senior figures at the Bank – had been far from uncomplicated. The front-runner at the start of 1960, following the Court's recommendation, was Morgan Grenfell's Lord Harcourt, who in the mid-1950s had spent three years in Washington as the UK's economic minister; but Sir Frank Lee, permanent secretary at the Treasury, was soon persuading Heathcoat Amory that Harcourt was not up to it and that instead they should look to Sir Oliver Franks, a brilliant administrator and former ambassador in Washington who was now chairman of Lloyds Bank. Eventually, in September 1960, the new chancellor, Selwyn Lloyd, formally offered the position to Franks. 'The Governor won't like it and the Deputy perhaps will be a bit prickly,' predicted Hall at the Treasury, 'but in nine months' time everyone will be saying what a good thing it is.' The diarist was mistaken, as there took place during October what was in effect a Cobbold-led rebellion at the Bank, with the governor deploying three senior members of Court to make it clear to both Macmillan and Lloyd that Franks was unacceptable. The reasons they gave are apparently unrecorded, but it is a fair guess that they and Cobbold had at least a triple motivation: Franks was someone whom they regarded as essentially a civil servant, not a City man; who was probably too fastidious for the increasingly important public-relations aspect of the office; and who, with his formidable, ultra-analytical intelligence, was ominously likely to turn the Bank into a study group, not a bank. Nor did it help Franks's cause that, if Labour had won the 1959 election, he would have been the unambiguous choice of the new government. Almost certainly Franks got wind of the Old Lady's hostile sentiments, and on 25 October he informed Lloyd that he no longer wanted the position. 'Kim Cobbold,' noted

Macmillan somewhat bitterly after trying and failing to persuade Franks to change his mind, 'is, of course, triumphant.'[2]

Within days, Macmillan and Lloyd made their final decision: Lord Cromer, intimately connected with Barings and currently the UK's economic minister in Washington. Tellingly, as Hall now noted, Cobbold and the Court had been 'plugging' him 'ever since they knew they could not have Harcourt'. Cromer was forty-two (making him the youngest governor for over 200 years); and the *Financial Times* reckoned that 'with membership of the right clubs (Brooks's and the Beefsteak), descended from a family which has combined business acumen and great wealth with pro-consular tradition, and married into one of the great 20th century newspaper dynasties [the Harmsworths], his qualifications must have appeared irresistible to the Prime Minister'. Or as Macmillan himself reflected after Cromer became governor: 'Lord C. has a nose. He is not a Baring for nothing – a long business and financial tradition.' During his governorship, though, he would provoke mixed emotions in Threadneedle Street. To some he was an accessible figure who brought a welcome, indeed novel, degree of verve and imagination to the job; to others he seemed self-important and, in an unwelcome patrician way, lacking in sympathy for life's toilers in the ranks. 'He was an aristocrat,' recalled one colleague. 'He didn't always bother to defend his arguments, I mean he was rather good at stating things ...' Or according to another: 'For me Cobbold is still the great Governor. Cromer was written up enormously because he was very good with the press. But to those of us in the Bank he was an outsider ...' And, even worse, he was 'much more inclined' than his predecessor 'to like to see his name in the papers'.[3] Transcending those judgements is a larger question. At a time when Britain was poised to undergo a social revolution, was this really the right moment for George Rowland ('Rowley') Stanley Baring, third Earl of Cromer, to become the Bank's new public face? In retrospect it is perhaps surprising that Cobbold, largely responsible for engineering the appointment, failed to see the danger.

In July 1961 the new governor – who right from the start, noted the visiting Per Jacobsson, 'seemed as natural as any man could be' – was confronted by a serious sterling crisis. 'Sterling is under extreme pressure and the threat of imminent devaluation is only being held in abeyance by massive short-term support enlisted from other Central Banks,' he bluntly informed Selwyn Lloyd on the 7th, adding that the underlying circumstances were 'more serious in many ways than the previous all too frequent post-war sterling contretemps'. Demanding a comprehensive statement by the end of the month, Cromer then set out his stall. 'Wage and salary increases unrelated to increased productivity' amounted to 'a fraud on other sections of the people'; organised labour was guilty of 'restrictive practices', management of a 'high degree of complacency'; public expenditure comprised far too much 'non-productive investment'; and it was high time to start fashioning a defence policy that was no longer 'a heritage from the great days of our Imperial past'. Over the next two and a half weeks he continued to keep up the pressure, above all insisting – as for so many years Cobbold had done – on the necessity of strong fiscal measures to accompany monetary ones if there was to be, he reiterated to Lloyd on the 19th, 'a reasonable prospect of achieving the object of defending the existing parity of sterling'.

Eventually, on the 25th, the chancellor announced his package: various personal credit and government expenditure restrictions; Bank rate up from 5 to 7 per cent; and a call for a 'pay pause'. As almost invariably was the case in these situations, the Bank would have preferred a still tougher package, even though the *Financial Times* reckoned the measures 'the toughest economic restraints since the austerity period of Sir Stafford Cripps'; and in early September, by when sterling was no longer under pressure but funds were failing to flow to London despite the Bank rate hike, Cromer explained to Lloyd that there still 'unquestionably' persisted 'lack of confidence in our taking measures to increase our competitiveness'. Significantly, one area where Cromer would come to look for sharper elbows was among the cartelised and mainly sluggish clearing banks, publicly raising the question in 1963 (at a Martins Bank anniversary banquet) 'whether the considerable rigidity in interest rates which has grown up in the banking world in the last twenty years or so is an encouragement to the growth of bank deposits' – subsequently described by one commentator as 'a moment of high drama in an industry not unduly given to histrionics', and a pointer to that industry's more dynamic if less stable future.[4]

1961, with the orderly Bretton Woods world of stable currencies palpably starting to come under attack from speculators and hot money in the foreign exchange markets, signified the start of the modern era of central bank co-operation. This took the form first of the swap arrangements involved in the Basle credits and then the inauguration that autumn of the so-called 'gold pool'. The old-style gold standard might no longer exist, but gold was still (in Forrest Capie's phrase) 'the anchor for the US dollar'. Indeed, 'the Bretton Woods system depended on the United States standing ready to buy and sell gold at $35 an ounce.' Even before the pool was formally established in November, essentially as a US initiative to share the cost of intervening on the London gold market in order to stabilise the dollar's gold value, the Bank was working closely with the Fed. 'With respect to the Bank of England activity in the gold market, he said that he saw no reason for anyone getting hysterical if the price goes above $35.20,' noted the Fed's Thomas Roche in September after a phone conversation with the Bank's foreign exchange virtuoso. 'Bridge said that he expects lots of trouble between now and the end of the year and that the Bank of England would use all the artistry possible. Bridge feels that the Bank of England being on the scene must handle the market as they see fit since, in his opinion, it is difficult for us to be of any substantial help at the fixing time, for example, since it would be 5.30 a.m. in New York and we would not be able to get the feel of the market.' February 1962 saw the gold pool's role expanding, with the key central banks agreeing to form a buying syndicate for the co-ordinated purchase of gold on the London market. External reaction was generally favourable, with one of the Bank's executive directors, John Stevens, observing to the Fed that he had been 'gratified' that the London press 'had not tried to delve deeply into some of the figures, especially the matter of the ¼% buying or selling charge'.

All this was consistent with Cromer's strong, Norman-like internationalism, if not necessarily with his perhaps equally strong belief in free markets. 'He had a particularly strong relationship with the Federal Reserve System, both in Washington and through the Federal Reserve Bank of New York, where he counted respectively Bill Martin and Al Hayes amongst his close friends,' recalled an obituarist. 'He built equally good relationships with the Governors of the Group of Ten countries [G10, established in 1962 to boost the

IMF's lending capacity] whom he met regularly in Basle.' A typical moment occurred in July 1963, just before the governor headed off for a three-week holiday in Majorca. The context was the Fed's recent discount-rate action; and, recorded Hayes after his transatlantic phone call, 'I thanked Governor Cromer for the helpful way in which his bank had cooperated in holding things steady during the last hectic day or two – including the gold market.'⁵

Befitting his merchant banking background, Cromer also had a powerful sense of the need to restore London's position as an international financial centre – and, crucially, he stimulated and encouraged his colleagues to think likewise. Emblematic, as well as hugely important in its own right, was the unfolding Euromarkets story. There, as far as the infant but fast-growing eurodollar market was concerned, the Bank's policy remained broadly one of benign neglect. 'However much we dislike hot money we cannot be international bankers and refuse to accept money,' a report to the Treasury stated in October 1961. 'We cannot have an international currency and deny its use internationally.' Undeniably there were qualms, not least during the winter of 1962–3 after Sir Charles Hambro (still on the Court almost thirty years after stepping down as a pioneer executive director) had told Humphrey Mynors that he was getting 'quite alarmed' at the way the market was expanding, a market in which Hambros had a significant stake, and had asked for guidance. After a two-month internal debate at the Bank, the eventual steer was unequivocal. 'It is par excellence an example of the kind of business which London ought to be able to do both well and profitably,' the deputy governor wrote to Hambro in January 1963. 'That is why we, at the Bank, have never seen any reason to place any obstacles in the way of London taking its full and increasing share. If we were to stop the business here, it would move to other centres with a consequent loss of earnings for London.' Similarly, when during the second half of 1963 bank runs on the Continent prompted widespread anxiety about the stability of eurodollar deposits, the Bank held the line, with Bridge (by now an adviser to the governors) asserting that 'the international framework of monetary co-operation which we now have' was capable of dealing with any 'misplaced lack of confidence'. Or as he candidly explained his thinking the following spring to the chief economist of Bankers Trust in New York:

The so-called Euro-dollar market is nothing other than a natural international money market. My point of analysis is that while domestic money markets are subject to the supervision of the monetary authorities and indeed to the banking laws of the countries concerned, there is not in existence any comparable international monetary authority to supervise and, where necessary, regulate the international money market nor, if there were, is it immediately evident by what means it could or would exercise its control.

The key word was 'natural'; as for the lack of supervision, itself a strong attraction at this stage to many of the market's participants, Bridge was not unduly worried: 'There may indeed be some unsound banking here and there. Too much lending long against short borrowings. But this is where the experience and the judgement of the international banker should come in ...'[6]

By this time, moreover, the eurodollar market – essentially an interbank, wholesale money market – was complemented by the newly created eurobond market, essentially a long-term capital market that was likewise based in London and was predominantly dollar-denominated. Its two main architects were George Bolton and Siegmund Warburg, but it was undoubtedly indispensable to their cause that Cromer happened to be in the governor's chair. 'We are sympathetic to this proposal,' he replied to Bolton in July 1962 after the latter (still on the Court, as a non-executive director) had set out the various initiatives in play that would help to restore London's position as a capital market, 'and will give it what practical support we can.' The following summer saw not only the pioneer eurobond issues, but the US administration's fateful Interest Equalisation Tax, doing major damage to New York as an international financial centre; and within weeks, in August 1963 after Morgan Grenfell's Harcourt had inquired about the Bank's attitude to a possible City of Oslo dollar issue in London, Maurice Parsons was stating explicitly that 'we do not put any obstacle in the way of such issues on the basis that London is thereby conducting a brokerage business, which on the whole we are inclined to favour'. 'Admittedly,' continued that executive director, 'we in the Bank would much prefer to see this kind of business done in sterling but unfortunately that is only possible in the case of a limited number of countries ...'[7]

Taken together, the eurodollar and eurobond markets were central to London's re-emergence from the 1960s as a top international player, starting to recover some of the ground it had lost since 1914. What Cromer was unable to engineer, however, was the abolition of exchange controls. 'The restraint on the foreign exchange earning power of the City by the continuation through all these years of the Exchange control mechanism has been insidious and by no means insignificant and that has played its part in diminishing the contribution which the City makes to the "invisibles" element in the balance of payments,' he declared in July 1961 to Selwyn Lloyd in his lengthy remonstrance shortly after becoming governor; in October 1962, in his Mansion House speech, he called for a revival of London's 'entrepot business in capital'; and the following spring, writing to the permanent secretary at the Treasury, Sir William Armstrong, he was adamant not only that exchange control represented 'an infringement on the rights of the citizen, either individually or collectively, to dispose of his own property as he sees fit', but that its continued existence (almost a quarter of a century after the start of the war) 'proclaims to the world at large a sense of our weakness while providing the British Government of the day with a wholly unjustified feeling that in it they have a defence against the consequences of misfortune or mismanagement'. Fortunately or unfortunately, the governor did not get very far. 'Those who think that we are not expanding as fast as we might,' wrote Armstrong in July 1963 reflecting on why he was unable to recommend abolition or near-abolition, 'would say that if we have sufficient resources to be able to devote them to overseas investment, we ought rather to use them for a further reduction to unemployment at home.'[8] In short, the politics did not yet stack up – and would not for another decade and a half.

Cromer also failed to get his way on the home front, certainly once the growth-minded Reginald Maudling had replaced Lloyd at No. 11 in July 1962, just over two years before the latest date of the next general election. 'He is, of course, obsessed with the idea that the international obligations of sterling act as a direct restraint on economic growth and is therefore somewhat impatient of the argument that external considerations have to be taken into account,' Parsons regretfully warned his chief in September after an early conversation with the new chancellor. 'I have been trying to persuade him, and incidentally some of his officials, that no country can ignore the external implications of domestic policy, but he is not altogether convinced.' That was indeed the case, and over the next seven months or so Maudling made his famous – or infamous – 'dash for growth', mainly on the fiscal side but abetted by a falling Bank rate. Ahead of the budget, the governor in March 1963 sent a missive expressing serious concern about the growth in public spending, but Maudling simply ignored him; and in the following month's boldly tax-cutting budget, the Tory politician breezily announced, 'I absolutely reject the proposition that a vigorous economy and a strong position for sterling are incompatible.'

Why had the Bank been unable to restrain what, with some reason, it viewed as a policy of reckless expansion? The economic commentator Samuel Brittan would many years later blame 'the appallingly bad case put up by the advocates of sound money in the Bank and elsewhere' for having made people like himself temporarily succumb to a belief in 'growthmanship, i.e. using rapid demand expansion to stimulate industry into more vigorous performance'; and it is a plausible claim, certainly if one puts any weight on a suggestive 1962 diary entry by Roger Alford, an economist from the London School of Economics (LSE) on a two-year secondment at the Bank:

Talked to John Fforde about the Governor. Ff said that he felt he was a typical product of his environment – he has their moral outlook and prejudices. His stress on honest money is one of these, and (with plenty of inflationists about) probably a good thing. At Birmingham [where Cromer had recently made a speech] he stressed that those putting money into the Post Office Savings Bank ought to be able to withdraw the same real value later. (What are the others? Supremacy of London as a financial centre? Growing role for merchant banks/accepting houses? Independence of the Bank of England? Certainly restraint of government expenditure.) But Fforde agreed with me that the moral basis of such assertions is unsophisticated and not strong – it can always be discomfited by the reply: would you prefer honest money and 10% unemployed to 1% p.a. dishonest money and 2½% unemployed? A governor of the Bank of England must have at least this degree of sophistication surely? Also Fforde agreed that since it is hard to pinpoint any substantial amount of individual hardship due to inflation, such moral fervour may be ineffective.

Cromer was further handicapped by his poor – even dysfunctional – relationship with Maudling, who according to his biographer had 'little personal regard' for the governor, who in turn had 'feelings bordering on loathing' for the chancellor. 'He was very idle, very opinionated and very conceited' would be Cromer's unflattering retrospective verdict; but according to Maudling's private secretary at the Treasury, Tom Caulcott, the governor's dislike was caused by resentment of the other man's obvious intellectual superiority. Something has also to be allowed for the prevailing Zeitgeist. 'The best thing the Government could do for the country's future as well as for its own would be to go all out for a faster rate of economic growth,' announced the *Financial Times* at the start of 1963; and by that autumn, with only a year at the most to go to polling day, Maudling was still going all out, with Mynors sardonically observing to the discount market that 'the car was now going downhill fairly rapidly' and adding that 'before long the brakes may be rather difficult to apply'.[9]

The question during 1964 was whether that crash would come before or after the election, in the event held in October. The backdrop throughout was Britain's rapidly deteriorating balance of payments position and the accompanying pressure on the sterling reserves. As early as February, the opposition leader, Harold Wilson, was only with difficulty persuaded not to go public with allegations that the Bank was 'cooking the books', in the sense of deliberately obfuscating the country's true external situation; by the summer the Bank was not only intervening on a significant scale to support the pound but systematically adjusting the figures in order not to destroy international confidence; Cromer meanwhile continued unavailingly to warn Maudling about his 'considerable misgivings about the direction in which our financial affairs are going'; in September the Bank substantially extended its swap facilities with other central banks; and at the start of October, a fortnight before polling day on the 15th, Cromer found himself at the centre of a political storm, albeit behind the scenes. In the context of Wilson having declared in a speech on 30 September that the latest gold and currency reserve figures, due to be issued on the afternoon of 2 October, were going to 'dominate this Election', the governor rang the office of the prime minister (Sir Alec Douglas-Home) and let it be known that he was 'worried at the possibility of the adjustment of the September figures to take account of Central Bank support becoming a factor in the political situation', in that (the office further noted) 'the extent to which the September figures had been cooked would be clear in due course from the Bank of England Bulletin and the Federal Reserve Bank Review and he might be accused of conniving at a political manoeuvre'. Cromer accepted that 'it was out of the question to think of publishing the true figure but said that the compromise that he had in mind was disclosing it privately to the Leader of the Opposition'. The matter was left to Maudling, who told Cromer later that day that he must not even think of volunteering 'the true figure' to Wilson, and Cromer reluctantly complied. The next day the published figures showed a politically containable fall of £16 million. Perhaps unsurprisingly, when he came a week later to brief the discount market on the general situation, 'the Governor said he thought the outlook was very difficult to assess and not very convincing'.

Throughout all this, and despite mounting evidence that Britain was faced by a fundamental external disequilibrium, one critical issue only occasionally broke cover: was $2.80 to the pound still a realistically sustainable exchange rate without doing major and long-lasting damage to the productive economy? The Bank's position remained unyielding. 'The devaluation of the currency of a major trading nation may be a necessity,' Parsons asserted bluntly in April 1964 to the governor and others, 'but only as a confession of ineptitude and irresponsibility'; in June, when Alec Cairncross (since 1961 the government's economic adviser) did a hypothetical exercise about the consequences of a 10 per cent devaluation, Leslie O'Brien wrote unsympathetically on his first version, 'Not a very happy effort'; and responding in July to a Treasury paper on 'The Next Five Years', the governor himself insisted that, whichever party won the election, the Bank's fundamental priority would remain unchanged: 'Let us be quite clear that the international standing and use of sterling is an inherent and essential part of our external economic relationships, and not merely some out-dated slogan exclusive to "The City" ...' A new recruit to the Bank in September was the youngish Australian-cum-Oxford economist Christopher ('Kit') McMahon, who a quarter of a century later would recall the prevailing temperature: 'It was rather an emotional place then, and merely to mention devaluation was like saying a four-letter word in church.'[10] If that emotion was understandable, so too was any outsider's impatience with the limits of reason.

After Labour had narrowly won the election – a narrowness prompting the Bank's George Preston to reassure the Fed on the afternoon
of 16 October that 'no sweeping changes might be expected' – the
new government's first and most cardinal decision was not to devalue,
notwithstanding the increasingly serious balance of payments situation and accompanying pressure on sterling. After all, Labour did not
want to be seen, following 1949, as the party of devaluation. It was,
Wilson told President Lyndon Johnson soon afterwards, a decision
made not only for 'now' but 'for all time'. Even so, relations between
the Labour government and the Bank were seldom easy almost from
the start, with Cromer later in October expressing his displeasure to
the new chancellor, James Callaghan, after the foreign secretary had
unilaterally told Washington that there would be no raising of Bank
rate in the near future. The clearest sign of trouble ahead came on
3 November. That day, the government announced its intention to
abolish prescription charges and increase pensions; that evening, at
the annual Mansion House bankers' dinner, Callaghan urged the City
to 'harmonise' its 'interests' with 'the needs of the nation as a whole',
as part of a 'joint effort to create a fairer, a more productive and more
progressive society'; while at the same dinner the governor set out
a rather different stall: 'I am convinced that the future prosperity
of this country at home and its power in the world abroad depends
above all on the strength of the pound, and the strength of the pound
depends today, as it always has, on wise and prudent husbandry of
our resources so that they may grow and fructify.' And accordingly:
'We must reduce expenditure in this country which distracts resources
from contributing to the top priority of closing the payments gap.'[11]

A week later on 11 November, Callaghan's emergency budget –
immediately viewed by international financial opinion as inadequate – led to as dramatic a fortnight in Bank/government relations as
anything since 1931 and arguably even since the days of Cunliffe. On
Friday the 13th, with sterling under severe pressure and the Bank's
reserves losses starting to run at their highest since 1961, Cromer
strongly urged Callaghan to raise Bank rate from 5 to 6 per cent in
order to 'mitigate the danger of a further serious fall in confidence';

on the 16th, Wilson publicly declared his unshakeable determination to keep the pound 'riding high', an apparent signal to the markets that the rate would rise on Thursday the 19th; but that Wednesday evening, after telling Cromer to his face that 'the present difficulties' were due to 'the deflationary prejudices' of central bankers, Wilson overrode Callaghan and refused to sanction the rise (partly because of anxiety about American reaction). '£ under immense pressure,' noted Bolton on Friday the 20th. 'Roly trying to educate Wilson & Co about life.' Indeed the governor was, writing that day to Callaghan in the strongest possible terms:

> The situation of sterling is deteriorating disturbingly quickly ... I must emphasise once again to you, Mr Chancellor, that I do not consider that by borrowing alone can we get through this present phase of strain on sterling no matter how much we borrow ... The facts speak for themselves that the Budget has not created the degree of confidence necessary to sustain sterling ... In my opinion, unilateral devaluation of sterling, even due to force majeure, could easily precipitate a world financial crisis for which this country would be held responsible and which could have far-reaching consequences both political and economic ...

That weekend the government gave way, to the extent of agreeing to raise the rate on Monday not just to 6 but to 7 per cent. It was not enough, however, for the markets; and Tuesday the 24th saw an intense and sustained run on the pound, with sterling's spot rate falling to $2.786 despite huge support from the Bank (the chain-smoking Bridge as ever to the fore), by now starting to be in serious danger of exhausting its cash reserves.

Late that afternoon, Cromer and his deputy (Leslie O'Brien, who had succeeded Mynors earlier in the year) were at the Treasury to see Callaghan, who asked them what needed to be done to re-establish confidence on the part of holders of sterling. The governor did not stint himself:

(a) credit squeeze;
(b) demonstrable action on incomes policy, in particular in relation to restrictive practices on both sides of industry;

(c) the fixing of a date for the beginning of a reduction in the level of the import charges;

(d) the naming of a specific figure in the reduction which the Government would bring about in public expenditure;

(e) the deferment of what foreign opinion would regard as some of the more doctrinal elements in the Government's legislative programme;

(f) the provision of more specific information about the Government's intentions on corporation tax and capital gains tax.

The denouement came that evening, at a 10.30 meeting at No. 10 attended by Wilson, Callaghan, Cromer and O'Brien, with prime minister and governor – two men both in their mid-life prime but from very different backgrounds – the key actors:

> Commenting on the suggestion that there might be difficulty in getting central bank assistance the *Prime Minister* said that if central banks and their governors were going to impose a situation in which a democratically elected government was unable to carry out its election programme then he would have no alternative but to go to the country. He would expect to win overwhelmingly on that xenophobic issue and would then be free to do anything he liked – devaluation included. *Mr Governor* said that the rest of the world did not believe that the policies so far put into effect were sufficient to put the economy straight and this was the real issue.

Later in the meeting, Wilson again raised the possibility of 'seeking a mandate for devaluation', to which Cromer replied that 'to go to the country on that issue would mean putting Party before country'. It was a historic stand-off – a stand-off in which ultimately, and perhaps inescapably, the governor blinked first. To quote from Wilson's own account, Cromer expressed himself 'doubtful' whether he could hope successfully to send round the begging bowl to the world's central bankers 'unless he was able to convey to them news of major changes of policy'; but Wilson was adamant that he would not 'sacrifice the constitutional rights of a newly-elected Government'.

In fact, the governor's bowl had already begun to do the rounds, and at 7 pm on Wednesday, 25 November, after another terrible day for sterling, the Bank was able to announce that it had raised a £3 billion credit from foreign central banks – a huge achievement on Cromer's part, involving many phone calls. Or as Cairncross (still the government's economic adviser) nicely put it in his diary, 'it was the old firm that did its stuff', in that 'the Governor delivered the goods, and but for him the Government would have been in a sad way with devaluation inevitable'. So it would; but, as Cairncross recalled many years later, the Bank received 'small thanks' from ministers, despite having put its 'neck on the block'. Over the next few weeks, rumours of imminent devaluation still swirled about and sterling still had some bad days – with an unrepentant Cromer warning Wilson shortly before Christmas that 'we are close to the brink of the abyss' and vainly demanding that he make an immediate TV broadcast announcing major cuts in public expenditure – but by the start of 1965 the worst of the crisis was over.[12]

Over the next fifteen months, as the economy improved sufficiently for Labour to be re-elected at the end of March 1966 with a much increased majority, there remained little love lost. 'I find his speeches tedious, inappropriate and designed to create the maximum embarrassment for Ministers!' George Brown at the newly created Department of Economic Affairs complained to Callaghan in February 1965 after Cromer had publicly urged the government to follow the fiscally prudent policies of some of the countries from which Britain was now borrowing so heavily, even if those necessarily 'disagreeable' policies involved 'deferment of the level of public services they would like to have'. Cairncross observed the resentment at first hand: in March, at a dinner at the Italian Embassy, he watched as Brown 'ragged Cromer unmercifully at the table and passed messages to Lady C. comparing her with Mata Hari', unsurprisingly making the governor 'very annoyed'; while in relation to the late-evening meetings at No. 10 to enable ministers and officials to enjoy uninhibited discussion, he noted that 'the Bank of England are rigorously excluded so that rude comments about the Governor can be freely made'.

There were even two more direct confrontations between Wilson and Cromer. In August 1965, with sterling yet again under significant pressure and the governor demanding an immediate wages and prices freeze as the unavoidable price of other central banks continuing to support the pound, Wilson warned him that 'if the Government were required to abandon normal methods of consultation and to take arbitrary unilateral action of a kind which no other democratic Government had ever taken, they might be forced to consider that it would be wiser to devalue sterling, to let the rate float and to appeal to the Country'; and then in March 1966, three weeks before polling day, Wilson flatly refused Cromer's request that Bank rate be raised in order to protect sterling. 'Deliberate interference with politics,' declared Wilson during another memorable late-night encounter at No. 10, before going on:

> Since the Government were going to win the election anyhow, they would thereafter have to take steps to ensure that a situation of this kind could never arise again. *Mr Governor* asked how this would help sterling. The *Prime Minister* replied that, just as the Bank had to try to cope with irrational people in the money market, so he had to try to cope with irrational people in politics. The plain fact of the matter was that the Government's will must prevail and that, if the Government clashed with the Court, the latter would have to be overruled. *Mr Governor* observed that in that event this country could never again command any international credit.

After being accused of 'an attack on democracy', Cromer asked if he should resign rather than go against his conscience – to which Wilson adroitly replied that 'if the Governor resigned, the pound would be a casualty'. Shortly before the meeting broke up, with Cromer asserting that the Bank had 'a clear statutory responsibility to act independently as well as to advise', the knowledgeable prime minister riposted that if it tried to do so in the present situation 'the history of the Bank of England which had begun with Governor Houblon would end with Governor Cromer'. Next day, a Thursday, Bank rate remained unchanged; and Cairncross the following week reflected that Cromer had 'overplayed his hand', not least 'by suggesting adverse market reactions where none had shown themselves'.[13]

Cromer was by now approaching the end of his five-year term. Late the previous year, following a conversation at Basle about his intentions, he was recorded as 'waiting to see whether an election will be held this spring and, if so, what the results of the election will be, as this could have quite a bearing on his decision'. By March 1966, with Labour on course for re-election, Cromer had probably made up his mind to go, and in April he informed Callaghan to that effect. Would he have been reappointed anyway? At best it is doubtful, and it is also doubtful whether grief was unconfined among many of his colleagues. 'I think various of us felt he was playing the hand wrong,' recalled one of them, John Fforde. 'He was playing it almost as a Tory politician and not as it should be played, with a Labour Government by the Governor of the Bank of England.' Jasper Hollom, who had joined the Bank thirty years before Cromer's departure and was chief cashier during most of his governorship, agreed, reckoning that he had 'become increasingly incapable of a dialogue with Whitehall' as he 'fired off immense amounts of ammunition at them, often actually without cleaning the barrel before he put another round in'.[14] The truism about someone being his own worst enemy does perhaps apply in this case.

It is possible that at least six people were, at one point or another, in the frame as likely successor. One, H. C. ('Nugget') Coombs, was a Keynesian-minded Australian central banker, well regarded by Wilson and backed by the *Economist*; another, the Court's favoured candidate, was John Stevens, a former executive director now in Washington; a third, backed by George Brown, was the highly regarded Sir Eric Roll, currently at Brown's Department of Economic Affairs; a fourth, at least according to himself, was the press magnate Cecil King, a non-executive director since 1965; a fifth was Cromer's deputy, O'Brien; and finally, as sounded out by Callaghan, there was Reginald Maudling, recently defeated (with some covert assistance from Cromer) for the Tory leadership. In the end it went to O'Brien. He had, in Callaghan's admiring retrospective words, 'entered the Bank of England on the bottom rung without the advantage of family or school' and was 'modest, quiet, considerate of the views of others but firm in his own beliefs', as well as 'technically proficient'; O'Brien himself was surely correct in judging that his meritocratic background appealed to Callaghan and Wilson, as did the fact that he was not part of the City establishment in the same way as Cromer. The appointment was announced later in April. 'Good plain cook: won't argue about the menu' was reputedly the reaction of Lord Harcourt (that possible alternative to Cromer), while the *Economist* offered a cautious welcome: 'He becomes Governor because he has fewer enemies than his rivals. The same negative virtues produced surprising results for the Labour party in 1935 ... If Mr O'Brien can be an Attlee of Threadneedle Street, he could find no better model.' Or more succinctly, as the Fed's William McChesney Martin would call him: 'a tough little scrapper'.[15]

O'Brien took his seat in the governor's room in the parlours at the start of July 1966 – a month of English footballing glory offset by a major sterling crisis. 'Sterling has been under speculative pressure in the exchange market, reflecting such diverse factors as the seamen's strike and its high settlement cost, the heavy loss of exchange reserves reported for June, the rather large trade deficit in June, and a renewed discussion in the press about the possibility of devaluation': the sober report by the Fed on the 14th summed up the situation well enough. The new governor had already sent Callaghan a six-page memo, calling for deflationary measures but adopting a notably less hectoring and censorious tone than his predecessor; and on the evening of Friday the 15th, after a rise in Bank rate from 6 to 7 per cent had failed to stop the attacks on sterling (the Bank active all day in the foreign exchange market and losing $140 million), he put his case in person to Wilson and Callaghan:

> If the British Government were to devalue [recorded the official minute], it would be regarded by overseas countries as a device by the Socialist Government to avoid having to face the real decisions which were essential if our payments were to be brought into balance. This view he restated on three occasions, and he used a graphic phrase, namely that devaluation would be regarded as the Socialist Government's 'recipe' for dealing with a situation which in fact demanded unpleasant internal measures. On the other hand, if a Socialist Government could maintain the parity of the £ in spite of the present pressures by introducing tough measures, it would once and for all demonstrate worldwide its determination to solve the problems without recourse to devaluation. From this he believed the Government would gain enormous benefit.

On Tuesday the 19th, following the prime minister's return from Moscow, the Cabinet voted by seventeen to six against devaluation. Next day, Wilson announced a heavily deflationary package – 'perhaps the biggest deflationary package that any advanced industrial nation has imposed on itself since Keynesian economics began', reckoned the *Economist* – and the pressure on sterling began to ease. Wilson would subsequently pay tribute to how, during the crisis, O'Brien's 'calm and reasoned advice' had 'made a deep impression on my colleagues and myself'; and at this critical moment in Labour's history, three and a half months after it had won a commanding majority for the first time since 1945, the governor's apparently not unsympathetic stance – so different in feel if not necessarily substance from his predecessor – may well have been decisive in stiffening ministerial resolve to place the needs of sterling above those of economic expansion.[16]

Through the winter of 1966–7, although O'Brien intermittently succumbed to bouts of governor's gloom ('he harped on the rising tide of Government expenditure,' noted Cecil King in December in his tell-all diary), the balance of payments improved, interest rates fell, and there was less talk of devaluation. Then in the early summer of 1967, not a summer of love in Threadneedle Street, the mood music changed decisively, against a backdrop of sharply deteriorating trade figures, the justified expectation that Britain's application to join the European Economic Community (EEC) would fail, and the Six-Day War, accompanied by the closure of the Suez Canal. 'The press openly discusses devaluation and some of the papers are strongly pressing for it,' observed Cairncross in May, while not long afterwards in Paris, safely away from the Bank for an OECD meeting, Kit McMahon confided in Jeremy Morse (an executive director), 'You know, I think we ought to be devaluing now.'

More generally at the Bank, as the summer wore on and doubts steadily increased about the government's political determination to defend the pound, there existed perhaps three schools of thought: those (exemplified by Parsons, now deputy governor, and Bridge) who, on moral grounds as much as anything, remained implacably opposed to devaluation; those who thought that the time had come to devalue before being forced to do so; and the middle group, which preferred to hold to the parity as long as possible. The governor himself oscillated between the ditchers and the hedgers. 'O'Brien drew me aside after Court to talk about the political situation,' recorded King on 3 August. 'He is acutely unhappy, living from day to day … He is afraid that the idea of devaluation has gathered so much momentum that it

may prove irresistible.' O'Brien was no less pessimistic, even fatal-
istic, by the end of the month, not least following the government's
decision to relax hire-purchase restrictions. 'I think he has given up
hope of maintaining the exchange value of the pound,' recorded King
after 'a long talk' with him. 'He thinks under pressure ministers are
thinking more of full employment and less of our financial position.'
The autumn brought little relief. Bad trade figures, a dock strike in
London and elsewhere, an EEC report questioning sterling's long-
term future as a reserve currency – it was all too apparent that sterling
was now on an irreversible one-way ride towards devaluation. Even
so, when O'Brien saw Wilson on 1 November, with sterling being
sold heavily, he was still unwilling to recommend that fateful step.[17]
Given his perspective on the politicians and what he saw as their lack
of will-power, he wanted them to make the call.

   Over the next few weeks, events moved swiftly – more swiftly,
and unpredictably, than anticipated by the Bank/Treasury group
(code-name FU, short for 'follow up' but accurately reflecting official feelings) that since spring 1965 had been preparing the detailed
mechanics in the event of devaluation. 'After three years of incessant
borrowing and ever-rising debt Jim Callaghan felt he had come to the
end of the road and I agreed with him,' was how O'Brien would recall
his key meeting with Callaghan on Saturday, 4 November. At Basle
over the following weekend, the governor managed to persuade his
fellow central bankers to accept the principle of a 15 per cent devaluation without any retaliatory devaluation by themselves. On Thursday
the 16th, after the final political decision had been taken to devalue
on Saturday the 18th, and after O'Brien had told the Court that (in
King's words) 'money had been pouring out since May' and 'we had
got to the end of our present resources', a question in the Commons
from a Labour backbencher called Robert Sheldon about a possible
$1 billion loan from abroad made it obvious to the rest of the world,
from Callaghan's evasive reply, that devaluation was about to happen,
giving speculators an easy killing next day. The Fed's memo recorded
graphic telephone conversations with those in the thick of the action
at the Bank:

   6.55 a.m. (New York time). Robson said that they were holding the
   rate at 2.7824 with heavy selling going on all day. He said they had

been supporting the forwards to a small extent but had been backing away as the pressure built up. He said that so far they had lost something close to $300 million.

8.45 a.m. Sangster said the money was still going out with the spot total now $600 million and forwards $100 million.

8.55 a.m. Bridge said that gold was now up another $7 million, bringing a total for the day to $43 million. He said that a great deal of sterling was being sold that he was sure people did not have.

10.25 a.m. Sangster said the total was now $800 million spot and $47 million on gold.

Altogether, according to Forrest Capie's account, the Bank spent some $1,450 million defending the rate, for the last time, on this long bad Friday – a day on which Bridge's market report was just one word: 'Crucifixion'. 'The pound was under siege in the world's foreign exchange markets yesterday,' began *The Times*'s patriotic front-page report next day. 'In London, the Bank of England battled courageously, non-stop, in an attempt to beat off the biggest selling wave ever seen.'

On Saturday evening, the Treasury announced the pound's devaluation to $2.40; on Sunday evening, Wilson made his ill-fated broadcast declaring that devaluation did not mean that 'the pound here in Britain, in your pocket or purse or in the bank, has been devalued'; on Monday afternoon, Callaghan announced the accompanying package of measures, involving expenditure cuts significantly smaller than O'Brien had wanted. It was just over eighteen years since the previous devaluation – and, writing to an American correspondent a week or so later, the deputy governor Maurice Parsons, who had been in a state of virtual denial almost up to the announcement, expressed himself 'acutely embarrassed' and 'deeply regretful'. Could the Bank have played its hand better? Quite apart from the larger question of whether it would have been more sensible to have recommended devaluation in July 1966 or even in October/November 1964, which it probably would, 'the immediate timing', reflects Capie in his authoritative account of the devaluation saga, 'was poor even apart from the mess of the Chancellor's response to the parliamentary question' and 'the end of October would have allowed a more orderly process', whereas 'by mid-November it was increasingly costly and difficult to stick to the planned timetable'. His overall verdict, moreover, is damning:

> One of the principal failings in the operation as far as the Bank was concerned was their obsession with psychological warfare. Their pride in market skills and the lack, for so long, of serious economic input contributed to a concentration on manipulating the market. There was no economic model employed in the discussion of devaluation in the Bank. There was no mention of the monetary approach to the balance of payments. The analysis used was the elasticities and absorption approach that had been used in the analysis for the 1949 devaluation.[18]

Or put another way, if the Bank of 1949 had still been recognisably Norman's Bank, the Bank of 1967 was still recognisably Cobbold's Bank.

There was no shortage of alarums and excursions during the year after devaluation – starting with the tumultuous gold crisis of March 1968, as the gold pool (which the Bank had been operating since 1961 on behalf of most Western governments) came under intolerable strain from speculators convinced that the dollar was no longer strong enough to hold gold's price at $35 an ounce.[19] During the week beginning the 11th, so much gold had to be flown from Fort Knox to London that eventually the floor of the Bank's weighing room collapsed; and that Friday, following a request from the Fed supported by O'Brien (but not by Bridge), the new post-devaluation chancellor, Roy Jenkins, agreed to the temporary closure of the London gold market – eventually reopened at the start of April after a meeting of central bankers in Washington, attended by O'Brien, had agreed to a two-tier system for gold, in effect creating an artificial distinction between official and private transactions.[20]

Then, for light relief, came Cecil King's attempted coup d'état in May. A manifestly political appointee to the Court, resented from the start by Cromer and then O'Brien, that non-executive director had become convinced by the spring that there was a conspiracy afoot to conceal the gravity of the financial situation facing the country, specifically in relation to the state of the Bank's reserves. On 9 May, the day before he tried to overthrow the Wilson government via revelations in the *Daily Mirror* about what he claimed was the true position, he tendered his unmourned resignation as a Bank director. 'His scorn for everyone was lofty and unending,' recalled O'Brien. 'Not by a long chalk one of Winchester's most attractive products.' Even so, and despite the almost capital crime of disclosing what had been reported in confidence to Court, King was correct in his allegation that the reserves figures were fixed, especially by the non-reporting of forward transactions which could be huge. Indeed, it was said during this period that at any one time there were at least five versions in play: the position in the dealing room; the position as reported to the chief cashier; the position as reported to the governor; the position as reported to the chancellor; and the position as published.[21]

O'Brien himself, as the summer unfolded, was increasingly preoccupied by the problem of how to run down in as orderly and honourable a fashion as possible the sterling area, whose belated demise had been made inevitable by devaluation. Australia was identified as the key country; and, fortified by the recent Basle Agreement (in effect involving the world's central banks giving the UK a $2 billion credit to enable her in turn to give exchange rate guarantees to all the official sterling holders), the governor set out in late August for secret negotiations, travelling under a false name and smuggled on board a Qantas flight via the freight-loading room at London Airport. The negotiations did the job, with the Australian authorities agreeing not to dump sterling wholesale, and other countries in the sterling area soon followed their example – in effect pledging to keep an agreed proportion of their reserves in sterling and thus allowing the Basle Agreement to come into operation. As for the British economy, in some sense the cause of all these difficulties, it did during 1968 – under the notably harsher regime of Jenkins, much encouraged and applauded by O'Brien – very gradually start to give the appearance of improving. Eventually, by the autumn of 1969, it was reasonably clear that the balance of payments situation had, in Jenkins's retrospective words, 'fairly firmly turned'. And he also remembered an exchange at around that time with O'Brien: 'I said, "Leslie, I think there might be some balance of payments honours. Would you like to be a peer or a privy councillor?" I always treasured the reply. He said, "I'd rather be a privy councillor, I'll get a peerage anyway when I retire."[22]

Honours aside, O'Brien was not just concerned in these years with the travails of sterling. A growing preoccupation was the increasingly vexed area of contested takeovers, which since 1959 had been conducted, in theory anyway, in accordance with the City Code on Takeovers and Mergers, itself the fruit of a working party set up by Cobbold after the Aluminium War. By 1967 it was looking a distinctly threadbare set of guidelines, prompting Wilson that July publicly to demand that the City promulgate 'formal and clear ground rules' about takeover battles and ensure that those rules were carried out. O'Brien responded by rapidly getting the merchant bankers into line, telling one that 'if the City were not capable of putting their own house in order it would be open to me to advise HMG that there was no alternative but to introduce a securities and exchange commission on the American model'. The outcome was a somewhat tougher City Code and the start in March 1968 of what was generally known as the Takeover Panel, both funded and staffed (as well as Mynors being its first chairman) by the Bank.

'It was the blind leading the blind for a while,' conceded long afterwards its first secretary (the Bank's Peter Cooke), and that summer the panel proved itself largely ineffective during the so-called Gallaher Affair – a fierce takeover battle for the Ulster-based tobacco company that saw Morgan Grenfell and its brokers, Cazenove, successfully riding roughshod over the central tenet of the Code that all shareholders in a company being bid for should receive equal treatment. 'Ultimately,' declared the *Daily Telegraph*'s Kenneth Fleet in assessing where the episode left the Takeover Panel, 'it must be replaced with statutory rules interpreted and administered with statutory authority.' That, however, was something that O'Brien, and indeed the City at large with its deep, almost atavistic attachment to being left alone to run its affairs, refused to accept; and by early 1969 he was ready to put in place a beefed-up panel with rather more powers. Not everyone was happy, including the top man at Schroders who was also since 1967 a non-executive director at the Bank:

Mr Gordon Richardson telephoned the Governor to say that he was alarmed at the rumours which were flying round the City

about sanctions in support of the Panel on Take-overs. He personally viewed these developments with apprehension, and felt that
there would be several people in the City who, while supporting
the operations of the Panel, would object in principle to the quasi-
legal status of the sanctions proposed. The Governor replied that he
understood this feeling, but that the only people he had been able
to find to run the Panel were insistent that the Panel be given teeth.
The alternative was an SEC.

O'Brien carried the day, and by spring 1969 the Takeover Panel Mark
II was under way, including tough-minded, non-Bank people now
running it. Even so, *The Times*'s headline was still apt: 'Teeth at last –
but how will they bite?'[23]

All this coincided with significant takeover or would-be takeover
activity on the part of the clearing banks, half a century after it had
seemingly been settled for all time that there would be a Big Five of
Barclays, Midland, Lloyds, Westminster and National Provincial. In
early 1968, with O'Brien and government both supportive, it was
announced that the similar-sized last two would be coming together
to form National Westminster; soon afterwards, in February, a startled City learned of the intention of Barclays and Lloyds to form a
combine, likely to have control of some 48 per cent of joint-stock
banking. Again the governor was on board, explaining in due course
to the Monopolies Commission (to which reference had been made
by government) the key arguments of economies of scale, greater
potential for modernisation, less over-banking, and an enhanced size
and therefore presence in international banking – at a time, he hardly
needed to add, of American banks flexing their muscles, especially in
the context of the Euromarkets. What O'Brien was unable to deny was
either that the creation of three large banks might well lead in time to a
duopoly (that is, if NatWest took over Midland in order to combat the
Barclays/Lloyds giant) or, still more damagingly, that (in the words of
the eventual report) 'a duopoly situation would make nationalisation
of the banking system easier to achieve and would bring that possibility nearer'. In July, the Commission came out against a merger;
and with Jenkins having been told by the governor that although he
'remained on balance in favour' he 'would not feel it necessary to go
to the stake about it', the government accepted that verdict.

By contrast, where O'Brien did not feel at all relaxed was about major tie-ups between clearing banks and merchant banks, especially after he had been almost entirely by-passed in 1967 when Midland took a 33 per cent stake in Samuel Montagu – to his 'extreme displeasure', as he informed Midland's chiefs. Two years later, in September 1969, he spoke frankly to Hill Samuel's expansion-minded Sir Kenneth Keith about why he 'continued to feel that too close an association between individual merchant banks and particular clearing banks was not in the best interests of the City': partly because such association would make it hard for clearers to access across the merchant banking spectrum 'the lion's share of the banking brain power in the City'; and partly because there would be no gain in 'merchant banking personnel being turned into organisation men of the clearing bank type'.[24] In short, the Bank was determined that the City's barriers – in effect an old-style guild system – would remain intact for the foreseeable future.

During the turbulent late 1960s – the Vietnam War intensifying pressure on the Bretton Woods system as well as provoking huge protest demonstrations, before one of which Tariq Ali told students, 'Don't be surprised if the Bank of England is occupied' – the most discontented citizens of the square mile were, irrespective of mergers or non-mergers, the clearing bankers. Liquidity ratios, special deposit schemes, 'ceilings' for lending: one way and another, they had spent most of the decade with one hand tied behind their backs, seldom free from some sort of quantitative lending restraint, and inevitably they came increasingly to feel that the Bank was not doing enough to protect them against politicians too cowardly to make the cuts in public expenditure that were the real alternative to always turning off the monetary tap. 'The co-operation of the banks on which we have relied so heavily for so long is sorely strained,' O'Brien himself warned the Treasury in November 1968, 'and might break if we try to impose a further restraint on their lending,' but in vain as yet another round of credit tightening went ahead; and soon afterwards, the chief cashier, Jasper Hollom, recorded a meeting with Sir Archibald Forbes at which Midland's chairman had 'made some rather wild remarks, e.g. that we still maintain a pretence in this country of having a private banking system but that it might be all for the best if this façade was torn down without more ado'. Was there a better way of organising things? By the end of the decade, recalls Charles Goodhart (who as a youngish economist had come to the Bank in 1968), 'the desire to get rid of direct quantitative credit ceilings, generally seen as distortionary and partially ineffective, was widely shared, not only by the banks and the Bank, but also in the Treasury and amongst politicians of all the main parties'. The task then for the early 1970s, he also recalls, would be finding a satisfactory 'half-way house' between 'direct credit controls' on the one hand and 'pure reliance on flexible interest rates and open-market mechanisms' on the other.

Moreover, complementing this new emphasis on how to implement monetary policy, and perhaps causally related to it, was a new emphasis on that policy itself. 'Monetary policy suddenly became fashionable last autumn,' noted the *Financial Times*'s Samuel Brittan in February 1969; while that same month John Fforde in an internal memo scornfully referred to monetarism (as it was starting to be called by followers of the Chicago economist Milton Friedman) as 'wishful primitivism, born of exasperation with certain intractable economic problems of modern society'. Still, primitive or not, such views, with their stress on watching monetary aggregates and setting monetary targets, could not be ignored. 'The Governor said that, despite some dissenting views in the Bank, he was minded to publish Goodhart's paper in the June Bulletin, with a personal attribution,' noted Hollom in April 1970 after O'Brien's meeting with Jenkins and the Treasury's permanent secretary, Sir Douglas Allen. 'He thought it a subject on which it would be helpful to put out a study which was of an academic nature rather than a set position taken up by the Bank.' Allen gave the go-ahead, and Goodhart's article, 'The importance of money', duly appeared in the June issue of the Bank's *Quarterly Bulletin*. Forrest Capie has called it 'a watershed in the Bank', marking 'the beginning of some monetary economists' influence in the Bank', and so it was. Yet to read it almost half a century later is to be struck by the circumspect tone. 'Monetary policy is not an easy policy to use,' conceded Goodhart towards the end. 'The possibility of exaggerated reactions and discontinuities in application must condition its use.' His final passage lacked nothing in balance:

Professor Friedman has argued that the rate of change of the money supply would be a better indicator of the thrust of monetary policy than variations in the level of nominal rates. To the extent that price stability ceases to be an accepted norm, and expectations of inflation, or even accelerating inflation, become widespread, this claim that the rate of growth of the money stock may be a better indicator of the direction of policy than the level of interest rates takes on a certain merit. As, however, there will always be multiple objectives – for example the balance of payments, the level of employment, the distribution of expenditure, etc – no single statistic can possibly provide an adequate and comprehensive indicator of policy.

Accordingly, he concluded, 'basing policy, quasi-automatically, upon the variations in one simple indicator would lead to a hardening of the arteries of judgment'.[25]

Large and challenging questions of policy and judgement were sadly outside the remit of the Select Committee on Nationalised Industries at a time when select committees were not yet independent of government. Under the vigorous promptings of the left-wing Labour MP Ian Mikardo, that body had long been itching to scrutinise the Bank, and by 1969 they got their wish from Jenkins – though not without a doughty and successful rearguard action from O'Brien, who, threatening not to co-operate, managed to persuade a reluctant chancellor that it should in essence be a narrowly functional inquiry into how the Bank operated as an institution. Chaired by a Tory MP, Colonel C. G. Lancaster, the Committee began questioning witnesses in April 1969; and between then and March 1970, the governor made nine appearances, stressing throughout the paramount need to retain the Bank's operational independence, especially if it was to be able to continue to give worthwhile advice to the government of the day. The end-result was an eminently sober report, published in late May 1970 and recommending that the Bank should behave more like other nationalised industries, with the publication each year of a full set of accounts. 'The Old Lady of Threadneedle Street has been told to strip her bonnet and shawl and put on a see-through dress,' optimistically declared the *Daily Mirror*, but O'Brien soon afterwards told the Treasury that he was 'not too unhappy' with the report and its reception. Or as he would later recall, his only significant disappointment concerned Mikardo, who had used the report's publication to displace Colonel Lancaster and chair a press conference. 'He proceeded to say some pretty rough things about the Bank, not at all in keeping with his courteous behaviour during our long examination. Once again the vulgar political animal had won the day.'

As it happened, the report coincided with a torrent of vulgar politics: the 1970 general election. The Bank of course stayed studiously above the fray, but it was still a resonant moment when on 1 June, just over a fortnight before polling day, Cromer appeared on *Panorama* in order to dispute Jenkins's claim that Britain now had one of the world's strongest balance of payments positions. 'There's no question,' he insisted, 'that any government that comes into power is going to find a much more difficult financial situation than the new Government found in 1964.' Next day, publicly responding to Cromer's comments, Wilson understandably compared the current surplus with the £800 million deficit he had inherited in October 1964. 'I do not see', he declared, 'how the most committed politician could describe that as a worsening of the situation.'[26] Did the former governor's intervention make a significant difference to the outcome? Probably not; but, all things considered, he was presumably less than dismayed as it became clear on the night of 18 June that his old foe would be packing his bags and leaving Downing Street.

'I have never been to the Bank of England before,' recorded one of Wilson's colleagues in his diary earlier that year, 'and one really did have to go through about five great iron gates as if one were entering a prison.' Tony Benn was there for lunch with O'Brien:

> We then went up to the most beautiful dining room. He is a nice man, very agreeable but totally out of touch because he has worked for the Bank all his life and doesn't understand the attacks on him from outside ... He said the usual stupid things about trade unions and wished the shareholders would play a larger part in companies. He lives in a dream world. It occurred to me with a great sort of flash of lightning that this is what is wrong with the City: the people in it don't make any effort to broaden their interests.

Almost a decade earlier, in the early 1960s, another diarist-outsider, in his case on secondment to the Bank, might have broadly agreed. This was Roger Alford, who was particularly struck by the deputy governor, Humphrey Mynors: 'His interest in genealogy and cosy trivia (the holding of Bank of England stock by the professors of divinity in the University of Utrecht) all point to a very limited outlook; but to great capability within those limits. The limits seem to exclude any willingness to really search for the truth or for sound opinions; if it is familiar and satisfies appearances, this is enough.' There was also the question of imaginative sympathy. In November 1966, the financial journalist William Davis wrote in *Punch* an open letter to O'Brien. Noting that the recently appointed governor had had, unlike his two Etonian predecessors, an unassuming suburban school education, Davis then singled out for criticism a passage in O'Brien's first speech as governor, at the lord mayor's dinner, in which he had declared the necessity of having 'to maintain continuously some margin of spare resources until we find out how to keep the economy on an even keel without it' – Bankspeak, observed Davis, for half a million out of work, at which point 'you didn't sound a bit like a suburban school product who understands what happens to men in their fifties (your age group) during high unemployment'. And more generally, added Davis, although 'the Bank has already become a good deal less stuffy' and 'you are less secretive than in the past', nevertheless 'on several major issues your approach seems to be far from progressive', not least the Bank's deeply 'emotional' attachment 'to the word "sterling", and to its role on the world stage'. Empathy was not the concern of Thomas (now Lord) Balogh, the economist closest to Wilson, when he submitted to the Lancaster/Mikardo inquiry a memorandum entitled 'The Bank of England – Some Defects in Organisation and Functioning'. One passage perhaps gave particular offence in Threadneedle Street:

Until the present incumbent [O'Brien], the decisive (almost dictatorial) Governorship was filled from the outside, without any recognisable training either in what has become a recognised economic administratorship. In the U.S., Germany, France, Italy, Australia, Canada and the Netherlands, to name but a few countries, it would be difficult to imagine a non-expert's appointment to this particular function. The present Governor rose from the ranks of the Bank without any general training so much needed by a Central Banker. While perhaps less obviously politically partisan than some of his predecessors he has strongly biased views on the management of the economy.

In short, Balogh's overall impression, looking at the Bank, was one of 'inadequate intellectual ability and political bias'.[27]

Benn, Alford, Davis, Balogh – how fair or accurate was the largely unflattering picture that they drew? Indeed, how ripe for fundamental change was, by the start of the 1970s, the Bank in its higher echelons, both in themselves and in relation to the outside world?

The classical exposition of the Bank's world-view was set out in 1962 by Mynors and the economic adviser Maurice Allen. In the context of an internal course being devised on central banking, they assembled a list of propositions called, with deliberate modesty, 'Opinions Attributed to Central Bankers', propositions that undoubtedly they endorsed:

A central banker needs a sense of smell. Analysis is only theorising but may be encouraged when it confuses critics.

No civil servant understands markets.

Politicians do not sufficiently explain the facts of life to the electorate.

Central bankers should always do what they say and never say what they do.

Taxes are too high.

Bankers are people who do, in the main, what you wish. The rest are fringe institutions. They do not exist.

Wave the big stick if you like, but never use it; it may break in your hand. Better still, try wagging your finger.

In banking, the essence of solidity is liquidity.

Never spit into the wind.

Always lean against the wind.

As for economic policy specifically, a handful of maxims revealed how little, in a supposedly Keynesian age, the Bank's verities had shifted since Norman's time:

All expenditure is inflationary, but government expenditure most of all.

A foreign exchange rate is sacred, to be touched only when all other corrective measures are seen to have failed.

Stability in the value of money helps economic growth.

Confidence in a currency is the first requisite for its stability; weakened confidence can be restored only by policies of a Gladstonian kind.

Other countries do not owe us a living.

None of this would have surprised Anthony Sampson, who had recently spent some time anatomising the Bank and being struck by the rarity of graduates, the profusion of 'inarticulate but confident' market operators, and the way in which the institution embodied 'the unquestioning regimental spirit of the public school proletariat'. Not long afterwards, in the mid-1960s, when an aspiring financial journalist, Christopher Fildes, wrote a piece about how London would soon have a market in dollar-denominated bills of exchange, the rebuke came on high from Hilton Clarke: 'Young man, I would trouble you to remember that this institution has a branded product of its own.'[28]

Nothing, of course, stood entirely still – and, looking at the top personnel, as the Bank passed from the uncertainties of the 1960s into the turbulence of the 1970s, it is tempting to divide them into old school and rather less old school. Undeniably in the former camp were O'Brien, the authoritative but increasingly afflicted Maurice Parsons (deputy governor, 1966–70), and the extraordinarily industrious Jasper Hollom (executive director, 1966–70, then deputy governor). Among the younger generation they were joined by John Page, who rose to become chief cashier in 1970, which in effect made him the Bank's chief executive, with extensive managerial and operational responsibilities. 'He took a very old-style clearing bank Chief Executive approach, very tough, aggressive, down to earth, no nonsense, bugger it kind of line,' recalled a colleague not altogether fondly. Arguably somewhere between old and new schools was the economist John Fforde, an executive director from 1970 (having been Page's predecessor as chief cashier) and possessed of a formidable intellectual grasp, though also susceptible to strong tugs of emotion. Finally, there were the two youngish manifest high-flyers, Jeremy Morse and Kit McMahon, both in their different ways impatient with the Bank's apparent lack of sophistication. Already celebrated as the first winner of the maximum prize of £1,000 on the TV crossword programme *Take a Letter*, and the quintessential cerebral Wykehamist, Morse had become an executive director in 1965, working mainly on the overseas side and winning his spurs above all through his leading role in settling the post-devaluation claims of fifty-six sterling area countries. McMahon (like Fforde an executive director from 1970) was also cerebral, but with a bit more edge, befitting an Australian who, shortly before coming to the Bank in 1964, had written a challenging book called *Sterling in the Sixties*. 'His approach is critical without getting over-doctrinal,' reckoned the *Economist* on his original appointment as an adviser, and that would be a just assessment of his Bank career as a whole.[29]

As had been the case for many years, the executive directors on the Court continued to be heavily outnumbered by the non-executives, as usual by this time coming from a reasonably broad range of backgrounds – including, in 1970, industry (Pilkingtons, English Electric), food (Cadbury Schweppes), mining (Rio Tinto) and of course trade unionism. Three notable recent appointments were Sir Richard Thornton of Barclays (the first time one of the Big Five was represented on the Court), the economist Sir Eric Roll (two years after he failed to become governor) and one of the big beasts of post-war Britain, the National Coal Board's chairman Lord Robens. The last made his mark more than most non-executives, provoking in December 1968 'a rather lively meeting of the Court' (according to Cecil King's inside source) by 'saying that he didn't see why directors of the Bank should be kept in the dark while all those gathered at Basle were given the true figures of our reserves'. Robens generally pushed hard for more information to be given to the Court, as well as for a streamlining of procedures; and by 1977 he would be able to tell the *Old Lady* that in his view the Court had at last become more akin to the board of an industrial company.[30]

In the bigger day-to-day picture, though, more significant was the vexed issue of the role of the executive directors, of whom under the terms of the 1946 legislation there were only four at any one time. Despite the fact they had been in existence for almost forty years, these executives still remained somewhat to the side and not fully integrated into the Bank's workings, certainly in terms of responsibilities. The direct contrast was with the time-honoured chief cashier, who initialled every memorandum to the governor and from whom permission was required, in theory at least, before a member of staff was permitted to talk to someone outside the Bank. The decisive moment – albeit a turning-point that failed to turn – came in September 1969 when the management consultants McKinsey & Co initially wanted to recommend a much expanded role for the executive directors, before O'Brien persuaded them to tone down that advice. Summarising their meeting, McKinseys' Alcon Copisarow noted that the governor had been worried such a recommendation 'might adversely affect the morale of department heads since it could appear to carry with it a downgrading of their position'. And: 'You felt it might overburden Executive Directors by involving them in detailed departmental activities. We agree that these would be undesirable consequences, and fully recognise the vital contribution that department heads – and the Chief Cashier in particular – make to the policies and operations of the Bank … We have therefore modified our organisational recommendations in this area.' Accordingly, the report formally presented to the Bank that autumn, while indeed recommending that executive directors 'should exercise effective supervision over major policy decisions, departmental budgets, the initiation of new programmes, and selected senior staff appointments', at the same time made it clear that 'we do not suggest that Executive Directors should become involved in the detailed administration of departments'. Nor did the report insist on any great urgency:

> Clarifying the role of Executive Directors should be an important medium-term objective for restructuring the organization of the Bank. We recognise that a change of this kind is difficult to implement immediately. Furthermore, the appropriate degree of authority that Executive Directors need to exercise differs between departments. The aim, therefore, should be to move towards this objective of direct executive responsibilities gradually and flexibly.

O'Brien had been bold to commission McKinseys in the first place, not least because of the tricky politics of their being an American firm, but this reassuring sight of the long grass was what he wanted to see.

Or as on one occasion he observed to Morse, with some force, 'Never forget that the Chief Cashier is the third man in the Bank.'[31]

There was only limited progress too when it came to the quality and depth of the Bank's economic analysis. 'This is the sort of analysis which any uninformed person could make from reading the newspapers,' scornfully commented a Whitehall mandarin in early 1961 on the latest diagnosis that Cobbold had sent to Macmillan and his chancellor about the darkening economic situation. Several factors contributed to this general shortfall: an aversion to modern economic thought on the part of Maurice Allen, economic adviser before becoming an executive director (1964–70); an even deeper aversion to economics generally (in terms of that discipline's place in the Bank) on the part of Mynors, so that it was not until after the end of his deputy governorship that the Bank felt able in 1965 to create a bespoke Economic Intelligence Department (EID); an almost atavistic loyalty to practice over theory, to market touch over everything, with Allen proud to describe monetary policy as 'psychological warfare'; the fact anyway that monetary policy as such was wholly secondary to the paramount, even obsessive priority of defending sterling, so that by 1968 the Bank did not yet publish a single monetary statistic; and a slowness to realise that, with the rise of high-class financial journalism, the Bank could no longer claim sole in-the-know authority and needed to put in some hard mental graft. Of course, the odd individual recruitment of economists did make a significant positive difference, notably those of McMahon in 1964 ('one felt like a fish out of water,' he recalled), Andrew Crockett two years later, Leslie Dicks-Mireaux in 1967 and Goodhart soon afterwards. Even so, as late as 1975 it was clear from the review of the EID conducted by Eddie George (who had joined the Bank in 1962) that a certain shortfall persisted. Putting aside the department's already increasingly specialist Economic Section, he observed that although a growing number of staff 'are recruited with specialist qualifications, notably in economics, they are recruited basically for their all-round acceptability to the Bank as a whole, and they do not typically specialise in any particular area or type of work when they arrive'. Accordingly, he went on, 'some sense that the balance has been too much in favour of generalism is shared by many of those interviewed, both within the Department and outside'. And altogether, he concluded, 'the dominant impression to come out of the Review is of E.I.D. at an uneasy stage in a process of transition from a narrow statistical-informational role to a wider role embracing also financial and economic assessment and policy advice'.[32]

Was there also a transition taking place in the Bank/City relationship? The answer, by 1970 anyway, was yes, but only up to a point. 'If I want to talk to the representatives of the British Banks, or indeed of the whole financial community, we can usually get together in one room in about half-an-hour,' Cobbold had famously told the Radcliffe Committee in 1957; and to a large extent the City still remained a village in which the Bank was the acknowledged head. In 2012 a former acting deputy governor, Brian Quinn, would somewhat wistfully evoke that 'stable, clubby environment':

All recognised banks reported to the Bank and came into the Discount Office once a year for a discussion of their returns. There was no unambiguous legal definition of what constituted a bank. It was what the Bank said it was and any prospective new entrant had to be judged fit, usually after having operated with only its own capital for a period of a year or more.

The Discount Office received and monitored banks' financial accounts and, more importantly, kept its fingers on the pulse of what was going on in the City generally. Informal information – including gossip – played an important part in this process. Talk of any unusual activity or questionable behaviour was passed on to the Bank, which, if the rumours had some foundation, would have a word with the relevant management, usually sufficiently early to anticipate problems. Much depended on confidence and trust, on pursuing real and not imagined problems, on not disclosing sources, and on how the action taken by the Bank, though not publicised, could adversely affect reputation. That mattered a great deal.

It was a world, added Quinn, of a banking oligopoly, of tightly controlled credit, of generally stable interest and exchange rates, of little risk-taking, of limited movement of staff around the City ('switching from Barclays to Lloyds, for example, was unheard of, if not treasonable') and of standards of behaviour being 'monitored and enforced by unwritten consent, with the Bank unquestionably the final arbiter'. 'Of course,' he concedes, 'there were occasional transgressions, and the Bank's views were not always accepted without protest, but challenging its role as headmaster of the City carried its own risks.' In the Discount Office itself, Hilton Clarke's successor was James (Jim) Keogh; and the story is told of his decisive intervention on learning that the discount house Gerrard & National were buying a firm of undertakers (apparently on the grounds of synergy – 'something else we can do with our hats'). 'You are not going to do this,' he curtly informed its buccaneering Kenneth Whitaker, 'you are not going to do anything like it, get rid of it now!'

Nevertheless, the traditionally rather feudal relationship *was* changing. Partly this reflected the fact that the City itself was starting to change, especially with the rapid emergence of the Euromarkets and the accompanying arrival of American banks, mainly unsupervised by the Bank. But the bigger cause was growing scepticism on the City's part as to whether the Bank – as ultimately, especially since 1946, an arm of the Treasury – could effectively represent and further its interests. 'One instance of a conflict between a set of City institutions and the Bank of England recently was the conflict between the clearing banks and the Bank of England specifically in regard to their ability to meet the ceilings set on their lending,' the *Financial Times*'s M. H. ('Fredy') Fisher told the Select Committee in February 1970. 'There everyone knew – the Bank knew, the clearing banks knew – that what they were up against was not the Bank of England but the Chancellor. This was apparent all the way through and became immediately apparent once the thing came out into the open.' Another journalist, Anthony Harris of the *Guardian*, elaborated:

> The present ambiguous situation is obviously unsatisfactory in some ways. The Bank tries to act in both capacities. The most clashing one is not an argument with the Government, but technically over its management of the gilt-edged market, since it became less concerned simply to stabilise the market of any time, and more concerned to maximise the amount of public lending taking place. In such a case the ambiguity comes out very acutely. One is not very clear whether the Bank is acting as the guardian of marketability of gilts or as sales agent of the Government. The two worlds to some

extent clash. I do not see an escape from this, but it is causing a lot of uneasiness at the moment.

Later that month, also giving evidence, O'Brien insisted that his 'prime responsibility' was to act 'as agent of Government, to carry out a variety of functions as efficiently as possible in line with Government policy'; and accordingly, 'I am not the representative of the City but I do represent City interests where I think it is right and proper to do so.' He was, in short, the City's 'discriminating advocate'.[33] Given the Bank's continuing insistence that it mediated the square mile's representations to government, as opposed to allowing it direct access, it was not hard to predict further tensions ahead.

What about the Bank/government (aka Bank/Treasury) relationship? 'It would be very helpful to us,' was the message in June 1969 from O'Brien to Al Hayes at the Fed ahead of the Select Committee's fact-finding visit to New York, 'if you could emphasise the difference between your position and ours. We have none of your independent authority and therefore no independent right of action.' In his own evidence, naturally, O'Brien emphasised the necessity of the governor of the day retaining his 'superiority', in comparison to civil servants, 'in the degree of independence'. So too for the Bank as a whole, which according to him (in effect following the Cobbold line to Radcliffe) required operational autonomy if it was properly to fulfil its 'independent advice function' to government. Certainly there was a degree of self-respect involved. 'Central bankers are persons in their own right,' declared O'Brien when asked about how much he consulted ministers before going to meetings at Basle. 'They have views about the future of the universe, particularly in so far as monetary and economic affairs are concerned, and no central bank governor would be prepared to go to such a meeting in such a forum merely as the puppet of someone else; he goes in his own right. After all, he is a central bank governor.' Certainly also, the Bank did continue to enjoy a quite significant degree of day-to-day independence, an independence founded largely on its necessarily highly technical management of the money market (including through its relations with the discount houses), the gilt-edged market and the foreign exchange market – quite apart of course from its key supervisory-cum-macro-economic role in relation to the banking system. In practice, moreover, it tended to be

– notwithstanding the snub to Cromer during the March 1966 election – the dominant party when it came to interest rate decisions. 'I said that the Chancellor had been near to overruling the Governor on a cut in Bank rate,' recorded Cairncross in April 1968 after a conversation with the Bank's Jeremy Morse. 'J. pointed out that it was the Bank's rate and therefore could not be changed without their agreement. I said that this was going too far. He then said that both sides had a veto on moving and that it was usually the Bank that wanted to move. I had to agree that I couldn't recall a specific case where the Bank had been pushed into cutting the rate against its will (or even into increasing it when it didn't accept the need to do so).'

Yet in a larger sense it is hard to avoid the impression of the Bank as somewhat marginalised during the increasingly Keynesian and corporatist 1960s, as demand management flourished and new centres of policy-making influence came to the fore, including the trade unions, the CBI and the National Economic Development Council ('Neddy'). 'It has reached my ears that you are shortly having a cocktail party for employers and the TUC,' Cromer wrote almost forlornly in 1963 to John Hare, the minister of labour. 'With considerable temerity I am writing to ask you whether it might be possible for me to receive an invitation. The reason for this rather odd request is that, in the normal course of events, I have virtually no opportunity of meeting the TUC members and on this occasion I have a particular reason for wanting to contrive a meeting with one or two individuals ...' It was also arguably a problem that O'Brien had spent his career working his way up at the Bank, which perhaps inevitably meant that he tended to view the permanent secretary at the Treasury as his opposite number whereas say Cobbold and Cromer (but not Catto) had instinctively cultivated a more direct relationship with ministers. In any case, by the turn of the decade the feeling at the Bank seems to have been one of some frustration – a frustration that McMahon eventually gave vent to in July 1971, writing a note for O'Brien that apparently applied to recent years as well as 1971 itself:

A number of us have been concerned for some time about the relationship between fiscal policy and monetary policy. For example, in the run-up to the Budget, the following is hardly a caricature of what happens. The broad magnitude of fiscal action is agreed in

the Budget Committee, while the economic forecasts are still being
made. Reference to the possible role of monetary policy at this stage
can be made by the Bank representative, but only in the most general
terms and in any case they are not taken very seriously. Then, when
the national income and balance of payments forecasts are complete,
detailed work goes on in the Treasury, to which we are not privy,
settling particular tax changes agreed upon. At a late stage, when
the Budget speech is already into its third or fourth draft, the financial forecasts are completed, throwing up certain implications for
money supply, the appropriate net sales or purchases of gilt-edged
to the public for the year ahead, etc. It is then decided at a Treasury/
Bank meeting that since it would be absurd for the authorities to try
to operate a monetary policy which was inconsistent with the aims
the Chancellor was trying to achieve by his fiscal policy, monetary
policy should be broadly accommodating.

In short, 'the present situation, whereby monetary policy is effectively a residual in total policy, is very unsatisfactory'; and near the
end McMahon referred with some bitterness to the way the Treasury
'keep us at arm's length in devising their packages'.[34]

Perhaps the area of greatest concern to the Select Committee was
that of accountability. 'It helps you to do good by stealth, in other
words?' asked Mikardo, after O'Brien had sought to justify the Bank's
non-publication of accounts on the grounds that this at times enabled
it discreetly to ensure the stability of the banking system. 'Yes, indeed,'
replied the governor, but the MP for Poplar persisted:

> But does that not also have the corollary that it helps you to drop
> clangers by stealth, to make mistakes by stealth, or, to put it another
> way, this facility of doing good by stealth creates as a corollary a
> situation in which whatever mistakes and however large they may
> be the Bank makes, there is no way in which they are ever publicly
> revealed? – Yes, that is so, but dropping clangers is not a thing which
> the Bank goes in for.

The Committee's report in 1970 was predictably critical on this aspect.
After noting that 'the Bank could go on operating inefficiently for
years without anyone outside knowing about it', that indeed 'for all

anybody knows with certainty to the contrary, it may have gone on operating inefficiently for years', it went on:

> Your Committee have no reason to think that this has been the case. But the fact is that any institution which is protected by secrecy and shielded from scrutiny is in danger of becoming unselfcritical and complacent. This danger is greatly increased in the case of the Bank by the fact that, in many areas of its work, it has been reluctant to apply to its performance and methods the types of objective criteria which are used by other large businesses, public and private. The Bank seems ready to fall back on the broad view that an institution that is nearly 300 years old does not need to use other people's instruments of measurement and control because its longevity indicates that there cannot be much wrong with it: this is a view which Your Committee finds unacceptable. It must be said that there was almost an assumption of institutional infallibility that flavoured much of the Evidence which Your Committee received and the Governor himself was not immune from it.

Various recommendations followed – including not just that the Bank should publish its accounts, but also that in terms of capital expenditure it should be held to the same criteria as other public corporations – but what mattered more was the broad critique. It was a critique in line with Anthony Sampson's charge eight years earlier in his *Anatomy of Britain*: 'The Bank has never accepted the notion of public accountability, and over the past hundred years its activities have become more, not less, clandestine.' And he quoted an anonymous banker as to why the Bank's *Quarterly Bulletin* was so (in Sampson's phrase) 'ingeniously obscure': 'It isn't so much that they don't *want* to tell you what's going on; it's more that they don't know how to explain it: they're like a Northumbrian farmer.' Perhaps in truth it was a bit of both, but either way this absence of transparency was not a helpful contribution to the quality of debate – whether outside or inside the Bank.

Ultimately, like so much else, it came down to culture, and the traditional rather introverted culture of the Bank was very deeply entrenched. Notably revealing testimony, suggestive of a whole mentality, comes from Pen Kent, who joined the Bank in 1961 as a graduate recruit and later that decade was enduring the 'fairly nerve-wracking exposure', as he recalled over forty years later, of preparing the figures for the daily morning meeting in the governor's room. That meeting, attended by the governor and a handful of senior colleagues including the chief cashier, was called 'Books'; and significantly, the all-important leather-bound book had 'precisely the right number of pages to cover the weekly returns for our financial year':

It was this book which you had to complete in manuscript, in special ink made by the printing works, guaranteed not to fade for 200 years. An expensive recipe. And you were not allowed to show or reveal any errors of any kind. Now it's very difficult to imagine that you can fill this in, (a) that the figures are always right, and (b) that you always transcribe them correctly. So techniques had been developed for scratching this rather high glossy parchment-like paper with a scratcher which was supplied as part of your toolkit, it even had an ivory handle. And then you had to polish the paper because if you tried to write with this kind of ink on paper that's been roughed up ... you can imagine. Now that was a completely artificial constraint on your facility and ability to do this efficiently and quickly. And for a long time it was kept deliberately archaic as I think a sort of testing ground for your nerve and your endurance. And it became a kind of joke. But it also developed this mystique because there was a book kept in which there was a photograph of everyone who had managed the Bank of England's books, single-handed on their own, having qualified. And this book had photographs going back to the 19th Century ...

'All the Bank's greats,' added Kent about this ritual which anyone who aspired to high office had to master, 'it was like the Hall of Fame ...'[35]

Entering from Stage Right

The Bank and the Tory government of the early 1970s did not prove to be a love match. At the heart of Edward Heath's initial economic strategy, after the election of June 1970, was the free-market belief that tax cuts and other stimulants of growth would be enough to discourage organised labour from making inflationary pay claims; but Leslie O'Brien, who had actively supported the prices and incomes policy of the last three years of the Labour government, was unconvinced, flatly declaring at the Mansion House in October that he did not 'see how we can expect to maintain a fully employed, fully informed and increasingly well-off democracy, in which the development of wages and prices is left entirely to the operation of market forces' – given that 'the bodies on both sides of the bargaining tables, the unions and employers in both the public and private sectors, are too big and too powerful for such a process to yield us the result most likely to contribute to our general welfare and prosperity'. Presciently, he added that 'if we try to rely on the marketplace and on the strict operation of fiscal and monetary policies, we shall find, I think, that we can achieve price stability only at the cost of unemployment that might be on a very large scale indeed'.

Discord was deepened that autumn by Heath's outright refusal of the governor's request for Bank rate to rise in order to counter inflation and a rapidly increasing money supply; and over the next few months the general assumption was that the new government would decline to renew O'Brien's governorship (due to expire in June 1971) for a further term. Cecil King faithfully recorded the gossip about a possible successor. Initially, Gordon Richardson (despite being 'vetoed by Cromer for health reasons'), Morgan Grenfell's

John Stevens (back on the Court, as a non-executive, since 1968) and – plausibly or not – Cromer himself as the three being bruited as candidates; then the emergence of Heath's friend Lord Aldington, a politician-turned-banker ('thinks he has the reversion to the job'); a strong late run from Richardson ('actively canvassing for the job and may still get it'); and talk at the last of the youngish, energetic merchant banker David Montagu. In the event, there was no vacancy. O'Brien apparently expressed serious regret that he might not be reappointed, claiming it would be viewed as a public humiliation for the Bank; and in early 1971 a compromise was agreed, by which he would step down after a further two years, at the age of sixty-five.[1]

1971 was also the year that saw the start of what became known as the 'Barber boom' – named after the chancellor Anthony Barber, but in practice probably owing much more to Heath. It was certainly a boom cooked up in Downing Street. 'To his eye,' noted Jasper Hollom as early as January of Sir Douglas Allen's views at the Treasury as imparted to O'Brien, 'everything pointed to a repetition of the 1962/64 situation – in which Treasury and Bank caution would be very uncongenial to Ministers and there would be a strong tendency for them to go for growth.' Or as the governor himself explained soon afterwards to the clearing bankers: 'The pressures towards reflation were increasingly to be seen. He made clear his own belief that such moves would not at present be timely, but recognised the influence which the unemployment figures were having on Ministers' thinking.' Barber's tax-reforming budget in March (including the abolition of short-term capital gains tax) duly set off a bull market (property as well as stock market), even as unemployment stubbornly continued to rise. There followed in July a mini-budget full of explicitly reflationary measures, marking the real green light for the Barber boom. 'He was discreet, of course, as usual,' recorded King later that month after calling on O'Brien. 'Straws in the wind of conversation were: (1) no reference of any kind to Barber; (2) Heath was described as "unapproachable". In general terms it became clear that he thought the latest Budget had no economic justification but was forced on the Government by political necessity. Opinion polls had shown the Government in so unfavourable a light that something had to be done, and this was also necessary to get the Common Market [which Britain was moving towards entering] off to a good start.'[2]

The European question was intimately connected to the perceived stagnation and even decline of British industry – a perception already sharpened by the Rolls-Royce debacle. By September 1970 that hugely symbolic company was in serious financial difficulties, resulting in heated negotiations at the highest level over the next two months. 'The initiative in Rolls-Royce now lay very much with Whitehall because of the unwillingness of the City to put up any money,' O'Brien told Lord Poole of Lazards in late October, and increasingly the governor found himself the nut in the nutcracker: trying to get support from government, trying to get support from banks, getting thanks from no one. King recorded in early November the scathing verdict of George Bolton, no longer on the Court and as forthright as ever: 'He said what remained to O'Brien of his prestige had vanished with his clumsy attempts to raise money for Rolls-Royce. He said there is nobody now at the Bank who is taken seriously in the City ...' Eventually, promises of help were secured – £42 million from government, £8 million from the Bank, £5 million each from Midland and Lloyds, plus a revolving £20 million credit from merchant banks – but they failed to prevent the company's collapse in early February 1971, in turn leading to nationalisation. Almost at once, seeing the bigger picture, Heath started pushing for the Bank to reprise its constructive inter-war role in relation to industry. O'Brien responded in character:

> I said [to the Bank person who had informed him of the prime minister's steer] that this yearning to go back to the 1930s was unrealistic. Nevertheless we were considering what might be done to mobilise City views and investment strength, to secure improvement in industrial management, and possibly facilitate the raising of funds in suitable cases ...
>
> This, however, was very much a matter for the Governor, who would be personally identified with any move which might be made. I was not prepared to be pushed from any quarter into what I thought was an inappropriate initiative. My own feeling was that in the matter of Rolls-Royce I had come very near to impairing my influence in the City.

It all took time, and encountered significant resistance from some of the big insurance companies and pension funds, but by 1972 the

Bank-sponsored Institutional Shareholders' Committee was at last in existence. In practice, it punched well below its weight in terms of intervening collectively to improve the quality of industrial management. 'Largely unsuccessful', reckoned *The Times* the following year, while John Plender, in his 1982 study of the rise of the institutional investor, would frankly call it 'an emasculated organisation'.[3]

Any pretence of business as usual was unavailing when it came to the international monetary order, as the early 1970s saw the collapse of the post-war Bretton Woods system of fixed exchange rates – the system that had tied the whole world to the US dollar. In May 1971 both the deutschmark and the Dutch guilder were floated; in August the US itself suspended the dollar's convertibility into gold; and although shortly before Christmas the world's finance ministers tried to put together a new system of broadly fixed exchange rates (the Smithsonian Agreement), it soon became clear during 1972 that a static approach was no longer appropriate for an increasingly uncertain world, not least with the inflationary consequences of the Vietnam War. Emblematically, the first financial futures market, enabling the hedging of currency fluctuation risks, began in Chicago in May 1972; and just over a month later its founder, Leo Melamed of the Chicago Mercantile Exchange, was in London trying to encourage participation in it. During his visit to the Bank, he suggested (probably to Hollom, in O'Brien's absence on holiday in the south of France) that if the Bank really wanted to help the new market it would kindly float the pound. A strained smile greeted the wisecrack – and the next day, 23 June, the newspaper headlines announced (including to O'Brien) that this was what the British authorities had indeed decided temporarily to do, though for different motives. The trade balance had been deteriorating rapidly, and the probability of an imminent docks strike had led to such pressure on sterling that the government decided that floating was preferable to another ignominious forced devaluation. 'IT IS RIGHT TO FLOAT THE POUND' confidently declared *The Times's* main editorial next day. Some in the Bank saw the move as the soft option, a political evasion of the financial discipline of a fixed exchange rate, but by this time the governor was not among them.[4] In February 1973 the yen was floated, soon afterwards the dollar was further devalued, and on 19 March the major central banks formally abandoned their commitment to maintaining their exchange rates within a predetermined band in relation to the dollar. The era of flexible exchange rates – accompanied by the rise and rise of the almighty financial markets – had conclusively arrived.

Nothing, though, defined O'Brien's last years as governor more than four fateful words: Competition and Credit Control (CCC). This new framework for the banking system had its immediate origins in a self-confessedly 'curious and emotional' note to O'Brien and Hollom sent by the executive director John Fforde on Christmas Eve 1970. 'Our responsibility for ensuring, or failing to ensure, the proper evolution of the banking industry is more direct than that of H.M. Treasury,' he declared. 'It is our job to make the running in this field and actively to seek the required over-riding political decision that will govern the future shape of monetary controls. With six years of ceilings behind us, and a new Government in office, this is a responsibility that we cannot put to one side.' As the Bank firmed up its proposals over the next few months, it took care not only deliberately to involve the Treasury at a relatively late stage, but to seek to avoid frightening the horses. 'It does not look likely that anything like the theoretical possible expansion of credit under the new approach would occur if it were introduced,' reassuringly predicted Kit McMahon in March 1971 as he passed the details on to the Treasury.

Overall, the Bank seems to have had four principal motives in mind: first, producing a healthier set of arrangements ('the quantitative restriction of advances imposed on the banking system proper turned good bankers into non-bankers, forced on grounds of public policy to turn away business they would dearly have liked to do,' recalled O'Brien of 'the bad effects on the banking system of the repeated and prolonged periods of harsh credit restraint which had been necessary ever since 1957'); second, encouraging a more level playing field between the hamstrung Big Four and their more liberated competitors, including the increasingly active and barely supervised 'fringe' or secondary banks – with the Bank quite possibly hoping that that would enable Barclays *et al* to put the pesky secondaries out of business; third, the ambition that a single, indivisible market for credit would encourage those trusted Big Four to get into such critical, almost unregulated areas as the wholesale sterling market; and finally, most important of all, the underlying belief that the interest rate weapon was in every way preferable to ceiling controls as the way of maintaining tight control of the money supply, itself an increasingly high priority. But, observes the financial historian Duncan Needham of this last motive behind the new dispensation, the awkward political fact was that Heath was 'implacably opposed to higher Bank rate'. And therefore, he adds in his persuasive analysis, 'the Bank had to dress its proposal up in the language of competition' – in order to 'lull' the Heath government, strong at this stage on such rhetoric, 'into believing it was all about a more competitive banking sector'.[5]

Competition and Credit Control, a four-page consultative document, was published by the Bank on 15 May 1971. It proposed, as far as the clearing banks were concerned, the end of both quantitative ceilings on lending and the interest rate cartel; while *all* banks would maintain the same minimum liquidity ratio, at 12.5 per cent a ratio less than half of the prudential ratio that had previously been required from the clearers. In essence, the deal for the clearers was that in return for agreeing to the abandonment of their cosy, familiar cartel, they would be free to compete on level terms with the secondary banks and others. The document received a generally warm welcome. 'A Keener Edge to Banking' applauded *The Times*, arguing that 'nothing has done more to stifle enterprise than the present system of controls and agreements'; 'Yes, at last, revolution for the City' was the *Economist*'s jubilant headline; and the *Banker* looked forward to 'the habits of the last decade' being 'well and truly buried'. Over the next three months the clearing bankers signified their willingness to accept the thrust of the proposals, while managing to persuade the Bank that building societies and savings banks should not be protected from competition for deposits. At the end of the summer session, Heath addressed his party's 1922 Committee and explained the new policy. 'I looked around the room and wondered how many of the MPs present fully comprehended what he was talking about,' recalled Edward du Cann, a City man as well as a prominent Tory politician. 'I doubt whether more than half a dozen had the least idea.'[6] On 16 September, only a matter of weeks after Barber had pushed hard on the reflationary button, the new arrangements came into force.

It was, to put it mildly, an unfortunate conjunction: following the introduction of CCC, there took place an explosion of more or less uncontrolled lending. 'The freedom that was imposed in 1971 was a tremendous spur to the inter-bank market,' the deputy chief cashier, George Blunden, would recall:

> Many institutions conceived the idea that you could always get your deposits in large wholesale numbers. It became a case of liability management. And with that great growth in liquidity in the banking system, they turned to property. And property prices always went up – at least they had always, since the war. Ultimately, in the early 1970s, there were these two great myths around: that you could always get wholesale deposits and that you couldn't go wrong with investing in property ...

They were an extraordinary couple of years. 'Almost for the first time in the whole history of banking,' a senior clearing banker remembered, 'you found your lending business and then scurried round for deposits.' Between September 1971 and the end of 1973 total sterling bank advances to UK resident borrowers rose by no less than 148 per cent.[7] Crucially, and feeding the frenzy, most of that lending was directed not to manufacturing but to property and finance; undeniably, the prime driver, even if much abetted by CCC, was the Heath government's reckless – however well-intentioned – pursuit of economic growth at all costs. For the Bank, all this meant a loss of control over the money supply, and much else besides, for which it paid a high reputational price. Could it have done more to alter the course of events?

O'Brien would subsequently be criticised for not having fought the Bank's corner harder, particularly in relation to interest rate policy; but in many ways he was powerless, especially in the context of a weak chancellor and an unusually obstinate, determined prime minister. In the first week of 1972, asking Sir Douglas Allen at the Treasury about the government's 'intentions on further reflation', he was told that the minds of Barber and Heath 'appeared to be running on divergent lines, with the Chancellor at present very much less concerned about unemployment'; later that January, he was informed by Allen that, in relation to Bank rate, 'the idea of a reduction had receded for the present' – an explicit indication of where the whip hand lay; by the spring, the word to King (via John Stevens) was that 'the Governor can get no answers from the Chancellor and finds it hard to meet Ted'. Heath did in June reluctantly agree to a rise in Bank rate (from 5 to 6 per cent) in order, stated the official record, 'to curb the rate of increase in the money supply and so damp down inflationary pressures'; but a few days later, responding to a member of the public complaining about inflation, O'Brien's tone was almost one of helplessness, with the role of monetary policy conspicuous by its absence: 'Inflation is certainly a very serious problem, but it is, unfortunately, a very difficult one to solve. I agree with you that we will need new initiatives and approaches. However, the Government is, as you know, engaged in discussions with the Confederation of British Industry and the Trades Union Congress, and we must hope that these prove fruitful.'

That same day, in the wake of the floating of the pound, O'Brien saw Heath, who raised 'the question of bank credit and the disproportionate share of this which appeared to be going to property concerns':

> I explained to him the logic of an easy credit policy in harmony with H.M.G.'s plans for reflation of the economy. I said that inflation was the nigger in the wood-pile. On the one hand, it was holding back the restoration of confidence amongst industrialists, while on the other it was encouraging all and sundry to rush into property as a hedge against inflation. He clearly yearned for the return to qualitative controls. I said that I had seen indications that the banks were feeling that they had put about as much money into the hands of property concerns as they thought prudent. I would, however, take an opportunity of telling the bank chairmen that it would be helpful if they could damp down their property lending as much as possible.

To no avail, even after a formal, old-style request to the banks in August. 'Money out of control' was the title of the *Banker*'s very critical editorial in September marking the unhappy first anniversary of CCC; and the magazine damningly noted that 'for some time now the City has come to assume that the Bank has meekly implemented the Treasury's growth policy against its better judgement', an assumption that was consistent with O'Brien apparently being relaxed, in his conversation with Heath, about 'an easy credit policy'.[8]

The autumn of 1972 saw Bank rate being replaced, after 270 years, by a rather different mechanism. Linked to the market rate for Treasury bills, minimum lending rate (MLR) was a mechanism adopted, the chief cashier John Page explained not long afterwards, 'basically because it was better than having Bank rate completely frozen by Ministers, not because we thought it was technically a superior arrangement'. Inevitably, against a backdrop of deepening industrial as well as economic troubles, a testiness developed in government/Bank relations, epitomised by an episode in November:

> The Governor mentioned the Prime Minister's irritation over the last Bulletin Commentary ... Allen said that the sensitivity of Ministers, and particularly the Prime Minister, on matters of presentation could hardly be exaggerated. References in the Bulletin which did not wholly accord with the Government's own presentation had a serious cost in making Ministers' minds highly unreceptive to Bank advice on whatever subject ... The Governor made it clear that he was not prepared to publish a Bulletin which was subjected to Treasury or Ministerial approval.

As for CCC itself, a beleaguered O'Brien had no alternative by February 1973, with the money supply still out of control and inflation rampant, but to tell the clearing bank chairmen that 'we must face the fact that it is being widely criticised'.[9] He had not, he must have reflected, had the easiest hand to play.

None of which, moreover, helped his or the Bank's standing in the City, with things probably at their worst during the difficult summer of 1972. 'Bank of England resisting pleas to revise gilts policy though jobbers withdraw' was *The Times*'s headline in late July, recording discontent in the gilt-edged market about the aspect of CCC that involved the government broker (traditionally the senior partner of Mullens & Co) no longer supporting the market. The August issue of the *Banker* then drew attention to how, during the June weeks of flight from sterling and the floating of the pound, in turn creating intense pressure on the money markets, the Bank had 'not handled the matter with particular efficiency', not least being guilty of having 'spoken with more than one voice at a critical moment'; while on 9 August, after O'Brien had asked the banking system to 'make credit less readily available to property companies and for financial transactions not associated with the maintenance and expansion of industry', the *Daily Telegraph*'s City editor (Kenneth Fleet) described the Bank as 'tucking her skirt between her ageing knees and trying a handstand', given the obvious contradiction between that request and the precepts of CCC, thereby putting the latter's 'credibility' under 'severe strain'.

A week later, O'Brien circulated to a handful of senior colleagues one of the most heartfelt governor's memos in the Bank's entire history:

> I have become extremely disturbed by the growing volume of criticism of the Bank in the daily and Sunday newspapers, in other responsible journals, e.g. Richard Fry in the Banker this month, and from what we know of unhappiness in various quarters – the discount market and accepting houses, and the gilt-edged market to look no further.
>
> I would not want anyone here to discount these developments as the inevitable process of the central bank being tarred with the brush of failure of Government policies, particularly in the field of inflation. Certainly the inflationary background is the principal enemy with which we have to contend, but against that background we are failing in various respects, not least as the market see it, to give that firm lead and guidance which they expect from us and, indeed, without which they feel as lost as a child whose parents falter in their authority.
>
> Competition and credit control is partly the cause. It was welcomed by the press and embraced by the banking community who then, in some instances, proceeded to let it go to their heads. The market consequences have not been wholly satisfactory. Added to which the monetary authorities appear to have lost their grip of the situation and to have fostered, by allowing an undue expansion of the money supply, the inflation which frightens us all.

Altogether, he concluded, 'I do not think it too alarmist to say that the Bank's whole authority in the City is in some jeopardy ... We pride ourselves on the lack of banking law and specific regulations, and on the superior merits of the Governor's eyebrows. This is only justified if the latter are used with firmness to give clear and unmistakeable messages which are accepted as just and fair by all concerned.'

Those final three words begged a salient question. The Bank had long enjoyed a significant degree of authority over the clearing banks;

but towards the secondary banks its stance was largely one of remoteness, with instead the main responsibility for their supervision resting with the Department of Trade and Industry, which during the Barber boom continued to hand out certificates to 'fringe' banks like confetti, even as their lending increased by three or four times as much as the clearers. Perhaps the sole exception to this detachment was Slater Walker, whose celebrated financial wizard, Jim Slater, fascinated O'Brien, even to the extent of wanting him (before being dissuaded) to join the Court. The consequences of the prevailing detachment would be played out in due course, but during the final phase of O'Brien's governorship it was the Bank's chequered relationship with the traditional City that preoccupied observers, among them the *Telegraph*'s Fleet in February 1973. After noting that 'dissatisfaction' in the City with CCC was 'marked and probably growing', and citing the discount market as a prime example, he went on:

> The real trouble there is that the Bank, despite its apparent conversion to modern 'scientific' credit management, still loves its traditional ways too. It clings to the ancient rituals of 'nod nod, wink wink' but whereas in the good old days a nod was a nod and a wink a wink, now a nod may turn out to be a wink, a wink a nod, a nod 'good morning', and a wink no more than a 'hello darling'. What is more, you can't learn this sign language: it is liable to change every week.

In sum: 'The dilemma for the Bank is between going completely modern, which it has not yet the will to do, and going back, which it can't do. It should face up to it soon.'[10]

Later that month came the announcement that O'Brien would be stepping down at the end of June. Despite the earlier agreement, he had probably hoped to stay on a little longer, until the work had been completed of the IMF's Committee of Twenty, set up the previous year to recalibrate the international financial framework and chaired by Jeremy Morse, who had left the Bank to take on the job. O'Brien had support from Barber, but the prime minister was adamant that the governor had to go, with King subsequently informed by both John Stevens and George Bolton that he had been 'sacked' by Heath. O'Brien himself favoured Morse as his successor – in effect the Bank's 'inside' candidate, having been an executive director from 1965 to 1972

– but instead it was Gordon Richardson (a non-executive director since 1967) whom Heath chose, apparently consulting O'Brien and the Court only after he had reached his decision. Richardson's broad-based experience (including on Neddy) made him, according to *The Times* following the announcement, 'well attuned to the Government'; but in the *Spectator* 'Skinflint's City Diary' was more sceptical, calling him 'hardly the bright new dawn of an economic Renaissance'. For Richardson himself, who had long wanted the position, it was a case of waiting for a few more months. 'Mr Hugh Seccombe of Seccombe, Marshall and Campion Limited, who are, as you know, the Bank's bill brokers, telephoned me today to enquire whether you would like to have lunch with them before you become Governor' was the message in early April from the governor's office. 'He told me that, after you become Governor, they cannot invite you.'[11]

O'Brien's final day in post included a haircut at Geoffrey's, the barber's at the Royal Exchange; and soon afterwards he was on the front cover of the *Economist*, with the accompanying, somewhat hyperbolic words 'A Great Governor'. The largely laudatory assessment inside included a notable, historically informed passage:

Lord O'Brien [as he had recently become] has brought the Bank into its proper role as alternative brains trust and away from any role as emotional right-wing banshee. The role of banshee is still one after which central banks can hanker. Less than 50 years ago, in the aftermath of the First World War, central banks felt so indignant at the risk of being dominated by the swaying financial policies of their governments that an international conference which discussed the subject actually advocated their private ownership. Today, the ultimate political sovereignty of governments over central banks is not in doubt. Even the German Bundesbank, on paper the most unfettered of central banks, knows that it can go so far and no farther. But the idea of alternative brains trusts for policy is gaining in importance and influence ...

Did the Bank in 1973 quite have the brainpower, allied to independence of mind, to fulfil that demanding role? The *Economist* thought so – 'for the first time the Bank's senior executive staff outdo the Treasury in economic sophistication and liveliness; its executive directors are a remarkable team of original, often slightly unorthodox, happily eclectic, and always stimulating turn of mind' – but arguably such claims were exaggerated. 'I was surprised at the absence of economic expertise which I found in the Bank,' recalled Christopher Dow of his arrival as chief economist shortly before O'Brien's departure; while in his congratulatory letter Bolton offered Richardson a robust analysis that may not have been wholly fair but was in essence probably true:

> You have taken over the responsibilities of the Governor of the Bank at a time when few men would welcome the challenge and your position is all the more exposed because, in recent years, the Bank has lost a great deal of power and influence in the City – the reasons being many and varied. Leslie O'Brien did a most remarkable job in helping to restore some of the lost internal morale [following Cromer's governorship] but he never had the experience or the imagination to build up around him a group of independent-minded men who could make an impact both on Whitehall and the outside world.

'The tendency,' added Bolton with salutary intent, 'has been to promote from within and import the ready-made academic mind.'[12]

'It is thought in the City that Gordon is not a good administrator, and not really a banker, but a very intelligent lawyer and a brilliant draughtsman,' noted King after Richardson's appointment was announced. 'Not really a banker' was at most only half fair. Born in Nottingham in 1915, the son of a well-off local provision merchant, he had read law at Cambridge before becoming a successful London barrister specialising in company law. In 1955 he decided to try his luck in the City, going two years later to Schroders and becoming the top man there in 1962. Over the rest of the decade he proceeded to turn it into (in the words of a client and close observer of City matters, Charles Gordon) 'one of the smoothest, best-operated merchant banks in the City', with the general tenor being 'overall expansion, little publicity, less fanfare, superb results'. Befitting an essentially self-made man, he had little time for the Etonian aspect of the City and enjoyed saying things like 'I look at Morgan Grenfell's clients today and say they will be ours tomorrow.' Striving consciously for excellence (with a particular focus on attracting qualified recruits), and developing a wide range of contacts with leading people in politics and industry, he was increasingly seen as the City's coming man, just the right sort of meritocrat. 'Richardson is a highly professional banker, ruthless but fair, opposed to nepotism, and his directorships range from the Royal Ballet to Lloyds Bank,' noted Anthony Sampson admiringly in 1965. Undeniably he was a class act, helped by a handsome, commanding face and bearing, which made him seem significantly taller than he actually was.

The main downside, all his colleagues agreed, was a lawyer's unwillingness to reach a decision that was not on the basis of full information and equally full deliberation. One colleague at the Bank would even compare him to Thomas Hardy's Bathsheba – 'she had to consult her clergyman on financial affairs, her lawyer on medical matters, her doctor on business, and so on, and Gordon normally consulted a tremendous range of the top of the Bank on any issue'. The ultimate upside, comparable in its way to Norman, was the sheer authority-cum-charm of his presence, suggestively evoked by Christopher Dow, writing privately about halfway through Richardson's governorship:

When one first sees him in the morning, almost without fail, however preoccupied or hurried, he smiles and says, 'Good morning, Christopher'. This may seem a small thing; but most of us nod and go on with our trains of thought; I am sure such consistent courtesy does not come without conscious effort and training. I remember the Governor once saying to me, 'I am constantly finding irritation aroused in me by X and Y, and then interrupting myself and saying, "If I ever allowed myself to feel irritation, this would irritate me profoundly."' When he has an address to make, however small, as after a lunch or dinner where an important visitor is present, his words are always carefully chosen, and caressingly enunciated. In working hours he does not drop his courtly manner. When he introduces a subject for discussion at a meeting, or sums up what he wishes to be the conclusion of a discussion that has just taken place, his words are always balanced and elegant – not inarticulate and halting as with most of us; and this elegance, which carries a sensation of his having command over events, increases his authority, like a man who has a good seat on a horse.

Even so, added Dow, 'just as he is always courteous to us, so he, like the Grand Monarch, likes us to be attentive to him, and does not care for disloyalty'. Indeed, analogous again to Norman, the inner steel was never quite absent. 'You know, the Bank has not always been right,' the chairman of Barclays remarked to him on one occasion (as observed by the Tory politician Jock Bruce-Gardyne). 'Oh, when hasn't it?' he asked, with a flash of his blue eyes. 'Well, when you didn't say that our paper was eligible.' To which Richardson responded unanswerably: 'That remains to be seen.'[13]

What could not be gainsaid was that July 1973 was an intensely difficult point to become governor. Twice in his first three months he offered 'directional guidance' to the clearing banks – pointing out that 'personal lending, if not controlled, could come to be the Achilles heel of Competition and Credit Control' – but the underlying economic policy reality was that Heath, Peter Walker and a few other ministers still hoped against hope that, as Heath's biographer would put it, 'the Government was on the brink of achieving its breakthrough, despite the commodity price explosion, the alarming trade balance and the sinking pound'. From October, however, all bets were off, following first Egypt's invasion of Israel and then an alarming rise in the price of oil. At last, on 15 November, Barber informed Richardson that the time had come to rein back the money supply, though with the crucial rider that the prime minister was insistent that this be done without raising interest rates. Orders were orders, but next day, at a meeting at the Treasury, the governor not only argued that 'monetary policy had pretty much shot its bolt', but complained of 'a serious lack of understanding by Ministers of the problems in this field' and emphasised the difficulty involved in achieving 'any sizeable decrease in the potential liquidity of the system'. Later that month, having been briefed by Walker to stress 'the dangers that a further increase in oil prices would present for the world economy', Richardson paid a visit to Saudi Arabia; but to little avail, with OPEC's announcement just before Christmas that the price of crude oil would rise from $5.10 a barrel to $11.65, four times what it had been at the start of the Arab–Israeli War.

By then, the Bank had reluctantly come up with a solution to meet the politicians' wishes, a solution (largely devised by Charles Goodhart) that Barber announced in his emergency mini-budget on 17 December, itself coming shortly after Heath had announced on television the start of the three-day week in order to conserve electricity supplies. That solution was the so-called 'Corset', as coined by the Bank's Gilbert Wood, recalled Goodhart, 'to indicate an external constraint to disguise and conceal internal flab'; officially known as the supplementary special deposits scheme, and marking an end after barely two years of the full-tilt CCC period, it required banks to make non-interest-bearing deposits with the Bank if their interest-bearing deposits increased at more than a specified rate. 'Too primitive an idea' would be the scornful verdict of Barber's successor, Denis Healey, but Goodhart probably had a case when he contended – likewise many years later – that it was 'the best possible answer to a tricky, and unavoidable, problem'.[14]

During the closing weeks of 1973, the Corset was the central preoccupation of neither Richardson nor his deputy Jasper Hollom. Instead, it was the increasingly fraught state of the secondary banks – a sector flourishing since the late 1960s but now suddenly vulnerable because of imprudent loans and heavy reliance for funds on the fast-growing, wholesale inter-bank market. The canary in the mine was London and County Securities: run by the self-promoting Gerald Caplan, and including the Liberal leader Jeremy Thorpe on its board, it was in such serious trouble by early December that, via the good offices of the Bank, it had to be rescued, mainly by its bankers NatWest but in part by a more reputable secondary bank, First National Finance. Soon afterwards, another secondary bank was also known to be in dire straits: namely Cedar Holdings, which specialised in second mortgages and whose quality of business had sharply declined after going public in 1971. For all secondary banks, moreover, Barber's emergency measures of 17 December had – through their combination of immediate credit controls and a pledge to introduce a development gains tax aimed at curbing property speculators, to whom the secondaries had lent so much – potentially lethal implications that were almost immediately recognised. That week before Christmas saw the secondary banking crisis fully under way, a crisis played out, in time-honoured fashion, largely behind closed doors.[15]

On Wednesday, 19 December the Fringe Banks Standing Committee – set up by the Discount Office's James Keogh on the 14th and comprising representatives of the Bank, the four leading clearing banks and Williams & Glyn's – met for the fourth time, chaired in Keogh's absence by his deputy Rodney Galpin. After a discussion about the plight of various of the secondaries (now including First National as well as Cedar), the key moment came when NatWest's Sidney Wild, almost certainly under instructions from his bold and energetic chief general manager Alex Dibbs, 'suggested that a support fund should be set up as a means of providing the potentially large amounts of assistance which could be needed for joint rescue operations' and 'thought it might be no exaggeration to speak of a total of well over £1,000m'. Such was the genesis of what would become known as the 'Lifeboat', some eighty-three years after a similar vessel had rescued Barings. That afternoon, at a secret meeting with the chairmen of the clearers, Richardson mentioned the possibility of a general support operation. Meanwhile, through that Wednesday and long into a memorable night, a series of meetings at the Bank sought specifically to prevent Cedar's immediate collapse. 'Both acted magnificently,' recalled Hugh Jenkins (investment manager of the National Coal Board pension fund, one of Cedar's four main institutional backers) about Richardson and Hollom. 'They knew the nature of the problem and their sang froid was remarkable. They were cool but very firm.' Hollom in particular successfully warned of the domino effect if Cedar went, with the Bank's overall performance marred only by the tactless serving of ham sandwiches to Cedar's mainly Jewish directors, as they waited downstairs for several hours to be brought into the discussions. The public announcement of a support package for Cedar was made on Thursday morning – but, far from reassuring the City, it had the effect, as it sank in that a substantial concern like Cedar had been brought low, of fuelling the rumour-mill and causing the share price of many secondaries to plummet.

Help, however, was at hand. Following meetings at the Bank on 21 and 27 December at which the governor deployed all his formidable powers of persuasion to achieve from the chairmen of the clearers broad acceptance for the principle of a joint support operation, the Lifeboat was launched, with the Bank agreeing to a 10 per cent participation (having initially suggested 7.5 per cent) and the remainder being shared by the clearers. Chaired by Hollom, the first meeting of the Control Committee (as it soon came to be known) took place on the 28th and considered what was to be done in relation to twenty of the secondaries. The Lifeboat may not have been the Bank's idea – indeed, a Hollom memo dated 20 December on 'Rescue Operation' contemplated alternative approaches – but it had rapidly adopted it and given it its imprimatur. 'We had to support some institutions which did not themselves deserve support on their merits and, indeed, institutions which fell outside the Bank's established range of supervisory responsibilities,' publicly explained Richardson five years later:

> But I felt, as I saw the tide coming in, that it was necessary to take the Bank beyond the banking system proper, for which it was responsible, into those deposit-taking institutions, because collapse there was capable of letting the wave come on to the institutions themselves; and the fact that very rapidly we had to extend our support to a wider circle, which included some reputable banking institutions, showed that our instinct that we were on very treacherous ground was sound ... I have absolutely no hesitation in saying that, faced with the same circumstances again – regrettable though they were – I would take the same strategic position and would act in the same way ...

It was a cogent and in many ways convincing rationale, but inevitably there were dissenters. 'Bolton thought the secondary banks should have been allowed to go to the wall,' recorded King some months after the Lifeboat's launch; in October 1974 the *Banker* noted that 'some bankers believe that the operation was misconceived from the start and that more of the bad apples should have been allowed to fall to the ground'; while a year later, a Labour MP, Frank Hooley, wrote to the governor declaring that the whole support operation appeared 'to indicate to the financial "smart Alecs" in this country that they need not worry too much in future about incompetent or shady deals since, at the end of the day, the Bank of England itself will step in and save any outright scandal'.[16]

By August 1974 the Control Committee, very actively chaired by Hollom, had met over fifty times; by June 1975, a hundred times (occasioning a drink). Predictably enough, the Lifeboat in action was a complicated story, full of resentments and cross-currents as well as nobler motives. After only a few weeks, for instance, Hollom noted Eric Faulkner of Lloyds telling him, in relation to First National, that there existed on the part of Faulkner's colleagues 'a good deal of uncertainty about our own [that is, the Bank's] motives and surprise at our championing of Matthews [Pat Matthews, top man at First National], who was after all an appreciable competitor of theirs and was not everybody's favourite character – nor on his record did he deserve to be'. Indeed, Faulkner even suspected that the Bank was trying with First National 'to build up a sixth London clearing bank'. The deputy governor's response was characteristic: 'I said that, though I was not an unbridled admirer of Matthews, I thought he was not as black as he was sometimes painted. Much more important was the fact that, since we felt we could not let First National go or be strangled by its rescuers, the clearing banks had effectively forced our hands by their reluctance to back a less aggressive rescue operation.' And: 'I emphasised that though we felt bound to head the support operation ourselves and meant to make it go, we would be concerned to withdraw again as soon as our prime objective had been secured.'

Transcending such concerns was the broadly agreed need, strongly pushed by Hollom, to keep the Lifeboat afloat – especially in the context of the deep crisis during 1974 in the property sector. 'What it amounted to was really buying time so that the property market could recover' was how John Quinton of Barclays recalled the situation, and he remembered Hollom saying at one point to the clearing bankers: '"Unless we save this bank, then the ripples will hit some of you people round this table". The temperature dropped about 10 degrees and we all said "Yes".' The grumbling persisted of course, though abating somewhat when Hollom in August agreed to an overall limit of commitment being set at £1,200 million – not so far from Wild's original figure, and a limit that by November the joint support operation was close to reaching. Eventually, the secondary banking crisis receded, with some of the fringe concerns allowed to collapse: the Lifeboat peaked at £1,285 million in March 1975 (the Bank having to meet the excess above the agreed limit), before slowly but surely that figure came down. The financial loss sustained by the Bank is impossible to compute retrospectively but was certainly containable;

and the incoming tide had been stemmed, though at one point (late 1974) it lapped alarmingly close to NatWest.[17]

Picking up the tab for the febrile early 1970s also involved concerns outside the Lifeboat's remit. Two in particular warrant mention, the first being the asset-stripping and share-juggling Zeitgeist-reflector that was Slater Walker – up like a rocket, down like a rocket. 'Slater claimed to be massively liquid,' Keogh informed the governor on 21 December 1973 after a meeting at Slater's request, 'but he was obviously worried and spoke very forthrightly about the need to rescue the "fringe" lest there should be repercussions on his own bank.' Over the next year and more, Slater publicly stressed the virtues of 'retrenchment', but was denied in December 1974 when he requested that Slater Walker be added to the Bank's list of eligible names. 'In our view,' pronounced Hollom, 'eligibility is a recognition which has to be built up over a considerable period of time and which may only be considered when a house's acceptance business is judged to be of sufficiently high quality in the eyes of the discount market.' 1975 proved the decisive year. In March, Slater called on Richardson to tell him that he had had an approach from Tiny Rowland's Lonrho about purchasing Slater Walker ('he assumed that we would not accept this and this was confirmed,' ran the Bank's note of the meeting); two months later he was still sufficiently *persona grata* for the deputy chief cashier, Rodney Galpin, to accept his invitation to Slater Walker's cocktail party at the Dorchester; and in October, having first secured the Bank's say-so, Slater abruptly announced his retirement from the City, with James Goldsmith to take over the running of the company. Propped up by the Bank, Slater Walker then staggered on for two more years, before in 1977 a major reconstruction saw the Bank (at considerable, much criticised expense) taking over the banking arm and proceeding to run it down, while other parts of the business were reconstituted under a different name. It already seemed a long time since 'the Master' (as Slater's small shareholders liked to call him) might have joined the Court.

The second concern, also with its element of controversy, was the Crown Agents: ill managed, ill advised, and by 1974 having staggering amounts lent out to suddenly floundering property companies, above all the Stern Group run by the Hungarian-born Willie Stern. The ensuing collapse – necessitating a government rescue – inevitably triggered the blame game. 'We appreciate that the Bank is independent of government,' noted the 1977 report of a committee of inquiry chaired by Judge Edgar Fay, 'but it is government's major contact with the City, and we think it would not have been unreasonable for the Bank to have played a greater part in this affair than it did.' Hollom, however, was unrepentant. After calling the report 'a horror story of the way the Crown Agents swam out of their depth into every kind of speculative venture', his typewritten memo ended flatly: 'To us, throughout, the Crown Agents were part of the Government machine which it was for the Ministry and the Treasury to manage and monitor.' To which, with feelings clearly running strong, the deputy governor added a handwritten sentence: 'The Bank are not to be regarded (as the Committee at times seems to do) as just another part of the Government machine.'[18]

The events of 1973–4 could not but have significant supervisory implications. In June 1974 the governor explained to the Treasury's permanent secretary, Douglas Wass, that his aim was 'to move quietly and steadily since rush and drama would be bad for confidence'; and the following month, the historic Discount Office was closed down – with Keogh, in many ways unfairly given his poorly supported attempts to monitor the fringe banks, made the scapegoat – and replaced by a new Banking Supervision Division, under the ruggedly pragmatic George Blunden and much more heavily staffed. Within weeks, reflecting ultimately a shift away on the Bank's part from the time-honoured virtues of trust, informality and personal judgement, it was insisting on regular prudential returns from all banks. 'A tremendous relief to them, they were delighted – all except one bank ... The oldest bank, Hoares Bank,' recalled Blunden. 'The chairman of Hoares phoned me up, when he had the letter saying we were going to be supervising them, and said, "This is quite absurd, we don't want to fill in forms, and you don't want to waste time looking at forms, and we don't want to come down to the Bank of England to be interviewed. Why don't you agree to come and have lunch with us once a quarter?"' Under the new dispensation, no dice – and indeed there was by now also a changing international dimension to supervision, following the collapse in June 1974 of a leading German private bank Herstatt, prompting Richardson to seize the initiative and, at the following month's Basle meeting of the BIS, persuade his fellow central bankers to adopt the principle of 'parental responsibility', whereby each central bank assumed responsibility for the supervision of foreign branches established by its domestic banks. The final, Treasury-led piece in the new supervisory jigsaw, though it took a considerable time to complete, was the eventual Banking Act of 1979, formally embodying a two-tier system of regulation under the Bank that in effect distinguished between 'proper banks' and licensed deposit takers. Almost certainly, Richardson's preference would have been for the established banks to be excluded from the legislation; but as the chancellor of the day, Healey, realistically said to him, 'Look, I cannot do it, I would like to but you cannot have it.'[19]

1979 seemed a distant date indeed during 1974, a year of intense crisis management – and accompanying political-cum-economic drama – in Britain plc. Rampant inflation, a savage bear market, Labour winning two general elections were just some of the features of twelve months that culminated in the announcement on New Year's Eve, the day after Aston Martin had gone into liquidation, that Burmah Oil was going to have to be rescued by the Bank on behalf of the government. Motivated in part by considerations of sterling plus the City's standing as an international financial centre, it was an involvement that exposed the Bank to significant if misplaced criticism, on the grounds that its purchase of almost £78 million of BP shares hitherto held by Burmah Oil had been unfair to existing Burmah shareholders, with the shadow energy minister Patrick Jenkin even declaring in the Commons that 'lasting damage' had been done 'to the credibility and independence of the Bank of England as a lender of last resort'. During the mid-1970s, however, most of the political flak concerned Labour, whose hostility to the City was matched only – and perhaps even exceeded – by the City's hostility to it. The Bank sought to calm passions. In July 1974 the Stock Exchange's chairman showed Hollom his proposed riposte to Labour's consultative green paper on the reform of company law: 'It was, of course, for them to decide on the tone of the document but I expressed my feeling that a cooler reply might have been more effective.'

What about the relationship between Richardson and the often combative chancellor, Denis Healey? In June 1974, barely three months after the first election, a moment of frisson occurred when Healey, ahead of a visit to the Bank, 'requested meetings with the

Dealers, the Chief Cashiers who are in direct touch with the gilt and day-to-day markets' and 'the principals of the Discount Office, with respect to both their responsibilities for the discount market and banks in general', as well as wanting to meet 'those in the Bank who have direct links with industry'. Reassured, however, by a Treasury mole that the meetings 'may amount to little more than exhibitions of the Chancellor's bonhomie', the governor made no objection, merely letting it be known internally that he 'would not object if the systems were given an extra polish to dazzle the Chancellor'. In general, moreover, it proved to be an eminently workable relationship: although Healey was unfavourably struck at the outset by the Bank's determination to uphold what he called 'the cabbalistic secrecy' of the Norman era, and although Richardson was disconcerted by Healey's insistence on cultivating his own contacts with key players elsewhere in the City, there developed a strong mutual respect, perhaps helped in the early stages by each recognising that the other was learning on the job. In any case, with so many enemies to his left, not to mention the extraordinarily difficult macro-economic situation facing him, Healey was hardly looking for unnecessary opponents. 'Although he could be pretty brutal and rough, throw his punches around, he was a very cautious man when it came to taking on the Governor on a serious matter,' recalled the Treasury's Douglas Wass. 'Time and again he would prefer the Governor's views on a monetary matter or a capital market matter, a gilt issue, to the Treasury's not because he felt the Governor was endowed with greater wisdom, [but] I think because he thought this wasn't worth a fight.'[20]

The documentation is somewhat patchy, but one's sense is of Richardson becoming an increasingly confident and assertive figure in the course of his second year as governor. The turning-point may well have been in mid-December 1974, when in the immediate context of a beleaguered pound (causing the Bank to spend some £1 billion intervening in the foreign exchange market) he frankly told Healey that the time had come for a new economic strategy – which in practice meant a reduced PSBR (public sector borrowing requirement) and the implementation of a statutory incomes policy. Healey had been getting the same message from his advisers at the Treasury and now largely took it on board (involving on his part a conscious repudiation of his Keynesian assumptions), though it took another six months or so for his colleagues more or less to sign up. 'Everyone now admits that you are the best government that we could hope to have at the moment,' the governor remarked in March 1975 (with inflation still roaring ahead) to the paymaster general, Edmund Dell, who was in effect Healey's deputy. 'Why are you doing so many silly things? The NEB [National Enterprise Board, designed to invest public money in industry] will do no good at all ...' Over the next month or so a series of hugely inflationary pay deals revealed the much vaunted Social Contract (the government's agreement with the trade unions over voluntary pay restraint) to be in tatters; but by early June the EEC referendum was safely won and the prime minister, Harold Wilson, was at last willing to take on his party's left wing.

Conveniently for him, for Healey and indeed possibly for the Bank, a major sterling crisis then blew up over the next few weeks. On the 12th the word to the governor from Bolton was that 'the centre of activity in the latest attack on sterling' was 'the Dresdner Bank in Frankfurt', with a spokesman for that bank having declared its belief that 'Britain was crumbling'; the following week, Richardson told the Treasury that 'what was puzzling to outside observers was why it took the Government so long to act'; soon afterwards, a beer-and-sandwiches session in Downing Street earned the railwaymen a 30 per cent pay settlement; and on the last day of June came the denouement, as sterling nose-dived with at this stage perhaps little impediment from the Bank. 'Richardson in with Wass,' crisply noted Healey. '"Sterling collapsing." Tell him to see PM.' Richardson duly went to No 10 – where, shortly before, Wilson had predicted to an adviser, Bernard Donoughue, that they were reaching the 'point in the play when the Governor of the Bank of England enters from stage right'. Donoughue now recorded the words of the 'haughty and patrician' visitor: 'This Government's whole credibility has gone ... We must end this nonsense of getting the cooperation and consent of others, the trade unions, the Labour Party. We must act now.' No doubt there were shades of Cromer in Wilson's mind; but 1975 was not 1964, and the government did act in accord with Richardson's wishes, producing on 11 July an anti-inflation White Paper that included an incomes policy.

What did the future hold? 'The horrible experiences of the past two or three years ought to have given us a unique opportunity not only to see more clearly the monetary problems lying ahead in the recovery phase, but also to obtain and retain governmental and public support for the monetary and fiscal policies that will have to be pursued if the problems are to be overcome,' reflected Fforde in a note to the governors shortly before the White Paper. 'None the less,' he added, 'although the opportunity may be unique, it may not in practice be at all easy to grasp it and keep hold of it.'[21]

Amid the political and economic turmoil, a running sub-plot through the mid- to late 1970s was the City's troubled relationship with British industry.[22] Richardson, who personally knew a wide range of industrialists and maintained his contacts, responded constructively and, like Norman between the wars, did all he could to keep government out of the picture. That constructive response had three main aspects. The first, involving pressure on the often reluctant and sometimes hard-pressed clearing banks, was seeking to expand the role of Finance for Industry (FFI), itself the creation of a recent merger between the Industrial and Commercial Finance Corporation (ICFC) and the Finance Corporation for Industry (FCI); the second, involving in 1975 the recruitment to the Bank of the near-legendary accountant Sir Henry Benson as industrial adviser, was the creation of an Industrial Finance Unit, essentially in its initial stages seeking to improve corporate governance through the influence of the major institutional investors; and the third, also involving Benson, was the launch in 1976 of Equity Capital for Industry (ECI), a Bank baby that struggled to get even the unenthusiastic support of the City. Taken in the round, the evidence is that these three initiatives did between them achieve some useful things, but fell well short of being game-changing. The Bank's contribution to industrial finance was squarely in the remit of the Wilson Committee, chaired by the former prime minister and eventually reporting in 1980 on the functioning of financial institutions. Reasonably supportive, its main criticism of the Bank was to question whether it was yet 'adequately' equipped with 'staff experience and qualifications to match its increased responsibilities'.[23]

For Bank, City and industry alike the scourge of high inflation – never quite Weimar-like, but unprecedented in British living memory – was pervasive and dominant. By September 1975, with inflation running at an annual rate approaching some 25 per cent, a full-scale debate was under way at the Bank about whether the best way to control and check inflation was through targeting monetary aggregates. 'There is some general feeling that we lack a philosophy about monetary policy,' observed Christopher Dow, adding that 'if we could agree on what we did believe in, we could then start to try to put it over in public'. John Fforde, Kit McMahon and Dow himself now all had their say, none of them starting remotely from the position of being convinced monetarists, unlike their colleague Charles Goodhart.

The major, somewhat anguished contribution came from Fforde. He observed that 'there are undoubtedly people of some distinction in the field of economic policy who would respond to an acceleration of monetary growth in present circumstances by advocating precisely the kind of action which every enlightened demand manager [that is, Keynesian economists] would totally reject'; he noted that the high inflation of recent years had 'enabled the monetarists to seize and occupy different strategic ground to the demand managers and to accuse/attack the latter for failing to recognise and to tackle the true nature of the inflationary problem'; he called the existing debate between Keynesians and monetarists a 'dialogue of the deaf'; he accepted that the ultimate 'economic objective' was that of 'preventing inflation from destroying our entire politico-economic structure'; he accepted too that it was impossible to assess the viability in counter-inflationary terms of continuing 'the prices and incomes/demand-management strategy'; and he acknowledged in conclusion that he was finding himself increasingly 'sympathetic' towards 'the monetarist position', in the sense anyway of it being 'a position which the Bank could at least partly adopt, as a means of trying to get what we (and most other people) would want in the prices and incomes and PSBR areas'. Dow in his response then made a pragmatic, not dissimilar 'non-monetarist case for a monetarist line'; as for McMahon, after noting that 'there will be risks that monetary policy will prove a brittle instrument', he asserted that nevertheless he was 'for taking a deep breath and going for relatively tight control of money supply from now on and for as long as we can maintain it'. That was very far from the end of the internal debate – which continued through the winter of 1975–6 and beyond – but clearly the sands were shifting; and although Richardson declined for the moment to commit himself fully to any set position, it was significant that in March 1976 he specifically requested Healey to include in his forthcoming budget 'a firm statement on monetary policy'.[24]

That request was on the 30th – at the end of an extraordinary month in sterling's chequered history. The backdrop was a running Treasury/Bank dispute going back to at least the previous December: in essence, the former wanted to engineer a significant depreciation of the pound in order to make British exports more competitive, while the latter was instinctively resistant. Dow, writing privately a few months later, recalled the tension:

> After a period when the exchange rate seemed to have got stuck on a plateau, the view strengthened, most vocally in the Treasury, that the exchange rate was too high and could with advantage be lower. We [the Bank] should cream off more dollars from the market when the rate was strong, or support it less zealously when it was weak; or we should be less anxious to preserve a favourable interest rate differential against rates abroad. What the external side of the Bank most hated was the Treasury breathing down their necks with the constant cry: 'Go on, get the rate down'. If we tried to get the rate down we were likely to be seen doing it. For the dealers, to accept a fall brought about by events was one thing, but deliberately to worsen one's own rate went right against the grain. To the Governor and others in the Bank, it also seemed close to a breach of faith …

Matters came to a head in early March. On Tuesday the 2nd, following Healey's lunch at the Bank the day before, Richardson reluctantly consented to the Treasury preparing a depreciation strategy involving a mixture of intervention and interest rate policy to get the exchange rate down; but in the event, before that policy could come into effect, the markets themselves took over, as the pound fell sharply on the afternoon of Thursday the 4th, at one point to a record low of $2.0125, amid what *The Times* reported as 'a sudden wave of selling … thought to have largely emanated from London', with currency dealers describing the sudden movement as 'inexplicable'. The Bank would subsequently be blamed (including by Healey) for having sold sterling in a falling market and thus unnecessarily precipitating a sterling crisis; its own defence, which few listened to, was that it had started selling on the 4th as it became known that large buying orders from commercial banks were pushing the currency up, which it knew would displease the Treasury. Next day the pound finished trading below $2 for the first time ever, while over the following fortnight the slide continued. 'Byatt said the Bank of England had done everything it could to steady, to interrupt and to create a sense of hesitation in the decline of sterling's rate today,' noted the Fed record on the 15th of a phone update from the Bank's foreign exchange adviser, Derrick Byatt (subsequent historian of the Bank's note issue). 'But no matter what the Bank of England did, it was not believed in the market ... Today has been a record in every respect. The drop in the rate is the largest ever, to $1.92 ...' And: 'Generally speaking, the market is extremely disturbed by the lack of indication that the Bank of England intends to take a firm stand.' The Treasury, though, had got what it wanted – a substantial depreciation – and could, in Wass's retrospective words, 'hardly believe its luck'; as for Healey, who had always had his misgivings about a deliberate fall in sterling, he took the broad view, privately admitting to 'mixed feelings, like the chap who saw his mother-in-law go over Beachy Head in his new car'. There were few such mixed feelings at the Bank, which felt that its reputation in the foreign exchange market, and accompanying ability to maintain an orderly market, had been seriously compromised.[25]

From early April the occupant at No. 10 was James Callaghan, who would recall his first meeting with Richardson:

It was uncannily like stepping back 12 years and listening to a record of one of my talks with Lord Cromer when he was Governor. The decline in the sterling rate was a direct response to unparalleled uncertainty and loss of confidence. The US was taking a gloomy view of sterling's future and industrialists were saying that all that appeared to be happening was that a bankrupt nation was selling off its stock. The Government's borrowing requirement was too high and in due course would crowd out investment by the private sector ...

For the moment Callaghan would try to shrug this off as 'Governor's Gloom', but in truth the foreign exchange markets had been thoroughly rattled by sterling's debacle in early March. Over much of the next two months – with not only Bank and Treasury mutually failing to communicate effectively, but there developing within the Bank an atmosphere that Dow described as 'one of collective hysteria' – sterling took a battering, so that by Thursday, 3 June, it was down to a new low of barely $1.70. The immediate upshot, as initiated by the BIS and arranged by telephone over the following weekend (largely by the Bank), was a $5.3 billion stand-by credit to enable the Bank to support the pound, with a handful of central banks chipping in as well as the BIS and the US Treasury. Tellingly, Richardson's preference would have been to go in the first place to the IMF for assistance, as the surest way of imposing greater discipline on government policy. Healey duly announced the package on the afternoon of Monday, 7 June, a day with a piquant aspect: the first visit to the Bank of the newish (from February 1975) leader of the Tory opposition, Margaret Thatcher. She came to lunch and it was, recalled Dow, a 'disastrous' encounter: 'We were of course polite but did not take to her, because she spoke her mind in very broad and sweeping terms and gave little opening for anyone to tell her things which we could have told her and which would in fact have been useful for her to know. She sensed we did not like her: "I saw them smiling," the Governor reported her as saying afterwards ...' Nor did it help her mood when she discovered later in the day that she had not been told by the Bank about the imminent stand-by announcement.

The announcement itself just about did its job in terms of stabilising sterling, which gradually rose during the summer to the higher $1.70s. Intrinsic, however, to the massive loan was the assumption on the part of the lenders – and the international financial community at large – that the government would use the breathing space to reduce substantially its projected PSBR for 1976–7 from the £12 billion figure that Healey had given in his recent budget. Richardson for one now pressed that point implacably, visiting the Treasury at least twice later in June in order to demand that £3 billion of public expenditure cuts be made immediately. It was during such a visit that the Court had one of its relatively rare substantive (albeit inconclusive) discussions about a matter of high policy – appropriately enough, given that Richardson's demand was so dramatically at variance with the whole post-1945 social democratic 'welfare' settlement. Dow, by instinct an unashamed Keynesian, recorded the episode:

The Governor missed that meeting: he was with the Chancellor arguing that spending should be cut. Maurice Laing [an industrialist], as senior Director present, asked that the wishes of the Court for his success in these endeavours should be conveyed to him. Sidney Greene [Lord Greene, a trade unionist] looked unhappy and asked a muddled question. Since some dissent had been voiced, I felt I could not stand aside. Though normally it would not have seemed proper for an executive director to criticise the Governor in open session, I raised my hand and said that, as the Deputy Governor (who was in the chair) knew, I had difficulty in fully associating myself with what Maurice Laing had just proposed. The Deputy then invited me – which I had not expected – to explain my view. Eric Roll then spoke up, starting by saying that he agreed with me, though perhaps ending more equivocally; to be followed by Adrian Cadbury [another industrialist], who seemed to be half agreeing, or was it agreeing with everybody? Jasper Hollom then thanked everyone.

Eventually, after protracted haggling between ministers, Healey on 22 July announced cuts of just under £1 billion: appreciably less than the governor had wanted, but still a historic surrender on Labour's part to the power of the financial markets. The chancellor in his speech also touched on the question of controlling the money supply. 'In our judgement,' a Bank paper sent to him three days earlier had asserted (in another clear defeat for Keynesianism in Threadneedle Street), 'a publicly-announced target would do much to allay the generalised fear of excessive monetary expansion, by giving the public a clearer idea of the commitments of policy and greater confidence that action as necessary be taken to achieve the intentions of policy.' In the event, Healey said that, for the financial year as a whole, 'money supply growth should amount to about 12 per cent'. Was that a target or merely a forecast? Or somewhere in between? Theological debate raged – but, whatever precisely it was, undeniably it was another step in the monetarist direction.[26]

The next few weeks provided some brief relief for the Bank if not for the nation's gardeners or groundsmen. 'Byatt said Britain's lack of water now means that sterling can't float very well in the exchanges,' noted his counterpart at the Fed in late August shortly before the drought broke. But for most of the rest of 1976 there were few jokes to be had.

During early September, sterling held steady at around $1.77 only because of heavy Bank support, in turn leading to an increasingly unsustainable drain on the reserves; and by the 10th, against a backdrop of Labour's proposals to nationalise the banks and news of an impending seamen's strike (shades of 1966) combining to push sterling southwards by some 3 cents, not only did the government instruct the Bank temporarily to stop spending money on propping up the pound (with Callaghan still hoping to repay the stand-by loan), but Healey raised MLR to an unprecedented 13 per cent in order to try to get gilt sales moving again after the so-called 'gilts strike' of the summer. Sterling continued to slide, so that by Friday the 24th it was barely $1.70. 'The market seems to be falling into the trap of reacting with excessive pessimism to developments in Britain,' lamented the Bank's Roger Barnes to the Fed that day about what he saw as the irrationality of foreign exchange dealers. The following week was memorable. On Monday the 27th, as Labour's conference at Blackpool began by passing a resolution against any further public expenditure cuts, sterling fell to $1.68; and then next day came the drama tersely captured in Healey's diary entry: 'Packed in morning. £ still falling heavily. Gordon in just before I left Downing St. £ fell the whole morning. Out to airport. Decided to stay. Back to London. Series of meetings, 3% loss.' Healey and Richardson had both been intending to fly that day from Heathrow, with the IMF meeting in Manila their ultimate destination, in the chancellor's case via the Commonwealth finance ministers' meeting in Hong Kong and in the governor's case via a visit to Tokyo. In the event, neither man left Heathrow, with Richardson persuading Healey at the airport – before they returned together to the Treasury – that it would be too risky for the chancellor to be out of contact with the markets for as long as seventeen hours. The markets themselves saw sterling at a little below $1.64, having fallen 8 cents in four days of trading and apparently heading irresistibly towards £1.50.[27] The following day, the 29th, Healey reluctantly announced a $3.9 billion application to the IMF – at the time, the largest-ever application to that body, and a request bound to involve more explicit and more stringent 'conditionality' than that attached to June's stand-by credit.

October proved a nervous, confusing month, pending the arrival in London of the IMF negotiating team. On the 7th, taking Richardson's advice that it was the only way to (in Healey's retrospective words) 'sell enough gilts to get money under control', the chancellor raised MLR to a politically disastrous 15 per cent. This was the somewhat controversial tactic of the Bank's now coming to be known by sceptical observers as the 'Grand Old Duke of York': or in Forrest Capie's words, seeking 'to boost flagging sales of gilts by increasing MLR and then hoping that the ensuing rise in yields would attract buyers', before 'a falling trend in short-term rates was then engineered by the Bank to maintain the interest of gilt investors'. No observer, however, could have been more sceptical than the Labour backbencher Jeff Rooker, who soon after the MLR rise introduced a Prohibition of Speculation Bill (targeted at both currency and commodity speculation) that accused the Bank of being guilty of 'treasonable mismanagement of the money markets'. By contrast, Labour's chancellor and the Bank's governor gave every appearance of complete harmony at the Mansion House on 21 October, with the former explicitly stating his commitment to a monetary target (for £M3, otherwise known as 'broad money', including not just physical money – notes and coins – but also deposits at banks) and the latter warmly supporting him for doing so. This was a carefully orchestrated display, for the benefit of the markets, of what Samuel Brittan in the *Financial Times* scornfully dismissed as 'unbelieving monetarism', declaring that 'they have belatedly and inefficiently been pursuing a money supply policy at the behest of overseas opinion in which they do not have their hearts and are therefore carrying out badly'. In any case, it was a display soon eclipsed by the so-called 'Sabbath thunderclap': this was a *Sunday Times* story on the 24th claiming that the IMF intended to set sterling at $1.50, resulting next day in sterling falling by no less than 7 cents, to $1.55; and by Thursday the 28th it had hit a new low of $1.53. 'Turmoil is everywhere, discussion is confusion and exchange rates move over wider and wider ranges as if capable of being blown almost in all directions at once,' noted without exaggeration an end-October report by Barings.

On 1 November the IMF mission arrived in London. It was headed by an Englishman, Alan Whittome, who had been at the Bank between 1951 and 1965, rising to become deputy chief cashier before moving to the IMF; and, befitting a Bank man, he would be evoked in his obituary as 'elegant, courteous but firm and blessed with a dry humour'. Over the next six weeks, during the negotiations between his team and government, and then within government, the pound remained fairly stable, mainly between $1.62 and $1.67, nudging upwards as it became clear that a package of cuts was going to be agreed in return for the IMF's massive loan. The Bank seems to have been relatively marginal in the process. 'Officials in general,' recalled Dow of both the Bank and the Treasury, 'cut no ice with ministers at this juncture. There had been so much talk of British officials getting together with those of the IMF and agreeing a package they would jointly sell to ministers – talk, after all, not entirely beside the point – that the PM resolved to keep officials right out of it.' The Bank's major formal input came from McMahon, who for all his Keynesian sympathies was adamant that the government had no alternative but to take the IMF medicine and thereby pacify the markets. 'If the markets do not accept that we have done enough and the rate starts to slide,' he reflected in late November, 'there are no shots left in the locker.' And accordingly, he sent a paper to Healey proposing spending cuts of £2 billion and tax increases of £1 billion.[28] In the event, the package of cuts that Healey announced to the Commons on 15 December amounted to £1 billion for 1977–8 and £1.5 billion for 1978–9. Press comment was generally critical, but the markets responded just about enthusiastically enough, with the pound closing the year worth £1.70. Altogether it was, from the Bank's perspective, a tolerable end to a very long ten months.

The mid-1970s, from the onset of the secondary banking crisis in late 1973 through to the succession of sterling crises in 1976, had been in their way as tumultuous as any short period in the Bank's history – and the upshot, perhaps inevitably, was a reputational hit. 'THE BANK OF ENGLAND'S FALL FROM GRACE' was the title in March 1977 of a lengthy article in the American magazine *Business Week*, with the general unflattering thrust being that the Bank had become increasingly aloof, blundering and irrelevant. Among those quoted were the monetarist economist Brian Griffiths and a key figure in the euro-bond market, Stanislas Yassukovich. 'If you take the record of the

Bank of England over the last five years in terms of technical expertise,' declared the former, 'you have to say that it is incompetent.'
While according to the latter: 'There has been a clear-cut diminution
of the Bank's independence. In the past, the Treasury set policy, and
the Bank set tactics. But now the Treasury even sets the tactics.' And
after noting that 'for the first time in memory, banks are beginning to
ignore the Old Lady and talk directly with government departments
in Whitehall', the article concluded portentously that 'the decline of
the Bank of England as paramount central bank in the West casts a
gloomy cloud over the future of The City'. Three months later, on a
Saturday in Basle, the head of *Business Week*'s European Bureau called
on Richardson to apologise for the piece: 'The Governor accepted the
apology, commenting only that he had found it a stupid and ignorant
article.'

The very next day, however, there appeared in the *Observer* a major
broadside entitled 'THE LAX OLD LADY OF THREADNEEDLE STREET',
with the two writers, Robert Heller and Norris Willatt, seeking to
draw a portrait of an institution that 'never locks any stable doors
until far too many horses have bolted'. The relaxation of controls that
had led to the secondary banking crisis, the inflationary expansion
of the money supply, sterling's unhappy experiences on the foreign
exchange markets – all these were blamed squarely on the Bank,
where because of its lack of accountability 'no important heads have
been seen to fall in public'. Further criticism came in October from
the *Guardian*'s influential political commentator Peter Jenkins, who
reacted to Richardson's monetarist-flavoured Mansion House speech
by arguing not only that it was 'unacceptable in its practical implications and presumptuous in spirit', but that it highlighted the Bank's
'unsatisfactory' constitutional position. 'The idea of autonomous
control of money supply is impractical and in spirit antidemocratic,'
he declared, invoking the deflationary ghost of Norman, and added
that the Bank was 'too much of a lobbyist on behalf of City interests
to perform the more independent role envisaged by the Tories [who
had recently been making vague noises to that effect] or to perform
effectively as the agent of the Government'. Jenkins did not explicitly touch in his piece on the question of the renewal of Richardson's
governorship for a second five-year term; but later that autumn 'for
a week or two', in Dow's words, he 'ran a very virulent and personal

campaign against his reappointment'. It is possible that Healey and Callaghan hesitated, but in early 1978 the governor's reappointment was duly announced.[29]

In fact there is evidence to suggest that the Bank – including Richardson himself – retained during the mid- to late 1970s considerable authority, even if life was made significantly more complicated (and liable to interference-cum-politicisation) by managing a floating rate as opposed to defending a fixed rate. The Orion episode in early 1976 was a good example of the governor's eyebrows at their most classically raised. The context was a large UK Electricity Council issue, which was being lead-managed by the consortium bank Orion, relied heavily on Arab money and sought to exclude Rothschilds and Warburgs from the underwriting group. Those two Jewish houses complained bitterly to Richardson, who summoned Orion's William de Gelsey and told him to halt the issue. The latter protested that it was too late, to which Richardson countered, 'I think that you will find that it is not too late.' Orion had no alternative but to change the arrangements rapidly, with lenders found elsewhere and Rothschilds and Warburgs reinstated. Or take the sale in June 1977 of the BP shares that had come into public hands following the Burmah Oil rescue. The world's largest-ever equity offering at the time (£564 million), it hit a serious last-minute obstacle on the afternoon of Monday the 13th, with an underwriting price of 845p settled upon but still needing final government approval. At which point Richardson was asked to go to No. 10, where he was told that some Cabinet members were objecting to the sale. Confronted by this development, Richardson rang the government broker, Tommy Gore Browne, to ask him what the consequences would be of not going ahead. Gore Browne's uncompromising reply was that even a twenty-four-hour delay might well defer the launch for months. As a thunderstorm over London began to build up that evening, the City's key figures in the BP sale waited for another call from Richardson, who in turn was also waiting for the phone to ring. Finally, as recorded by his private secretary, 'the Chancellor called the Governor at 8.30 pm and reported that, with extreme reluctance, the Prime Minister had given his approval for the sale to go forward, at the suggested price of 845'. Richardson duly rang Gore Browne, telling him to proceed, and next day the issue was successfully underwritten by 782 institutions.[30]

Yet overall, notwithstanding these episodes as well as the Bank's successful resistance to index-linked gilts and tender selling (prompting Donoughue's comment at the No. 10 Policy Unit that 'it was clear that the Bank considered its own mode of working both to be perfect and nobody else's business'), there perhaps was some erosion of authority. Within the City, the so-called 'Sarabex affair' was a significant pointer, arising in autumn 1977 when a London-based foreign exchange and money broker, dealing mainly for Middle Eastern banks, filed a formal complaint to the EEC about the restrictive practices operating in London, above all the impossible-to-fulfil, Bank-imposed, catch-22 condition that one could not become a member of the Foreign Exchange and Currency Deposit Brokers' Association (FECDBA) unless one was *already* providing BBA (British Bankers Association) banks with 'a full service' – rather difficult, given that the Bank insisted that members of the BBA and other authorised banks in London solely used members of the FECDBA to conduct their foreign exchange business. The Bank itself, in a public letter to the EEC in November 1977, strongly defended existing arrangements, mainly on the basis that they were necessary to preserve an effective and orderly market; and it now looked to the clearing banks, the main users of the foreign exchange market, for support in this stance. Here, however, it was disappointed, giving the NatWest's Bill Batt (acting head of the foreign exchange sub-committee of the BBA) a difficult meeting with the Bank's John Page. 'I had hoped the clearing banks would support the Bank of England,' remarked the chief cashier frostily but to no effect, and the following year the Bank retreated from its position, with Sarabex becoming a member.[31]

Restrictive practices also operated on the Stock Exchange; and though the Bank added its lobbying support to the Stock Exchange's efforts to avoid having its rule book referred to the Restrictive Practices Court, it was to no avail, with the Labour minister Roy Hattersley formally making the reference in February 1979 – a crucial step on the eventual road to the Big Bang of 1986. Then of course there was the rumbustious Healey:

I did introduce an innovation when I was Chancellor [he told a Select Committee in the 1990s] because before I became Chancellor the Bank would not allow Chancellors to talk to people in the City because it regarded itself as God's appointed ambassador on earth from the City to the Treasury. It is one of the few things I had an argument with Gordon Richardson about ... I said I wanted to hear not from the chairmen of the banks, who are usually time servers, but from the chief executives who are often very, very able indeed like Alex Dibbs who was at NatWest in my time ... I said I wanted to have them in myself and talk to them about their problems. 'Oh, no; this has never happened before'. In the end they agreed but only on condition that I had a spy from the Bank of England, Charles Goodhart, who I like to hope was perhaps a double agent in the end.

The Bank's influence was possibly even waning when it came to honours. 'I said that we were grateful for the work that Mr Goldsmith was doing with Slater Walker,' noted Richardson in early April 1976 after speaking with Wass about the proposed knighthoods in Harold Wilson's resignation honours list, 'but I was very positive that it would be quite unsuitable, and indeed embarrassing for us, for him to be recognised in this way at this particular time.' Sir James, however, it was.

At a more elevated level, these years also saw an agreement, reached between central banks in Basle in early 1977, to run down the sterling balances – an agreement over which, according to Healey, the prime minister was 'unfairly grudging' in his thanks to Richardson for securing it. In effect this meant the running down of sterling as a reserve currency, only two months after the Bank had issued a notice prohibiting the use of sterling as a finance medium for non-UK-related (that is, third-country) trade.[32] Would the demise of sterling's international role handicap London as an international financial centre? It was a sign of how much had changed in the past two decades that most informed people, including at the Bank, were justifiably confident that it would not.

Monetarism, meanwhile, continued to come into increasingly close focus. 'Reflections on the conduct of monetary policy' was the title of the inaugural Mais lecture, given by Richardson in February 1978; and in it he endorsed the phrase of Paul Volcker (soon to be his American counterpart) about the need for 'practical monetarism' and observed that 'formulating a line of practical policy and trying to stick to it, while yet remaining appropriately flexible amid the uncertainties of day-to-day affairs, feels very different from devising ideal solutions in the seclusion of a study'. So no doubt it did, but by this time Fforde, one of the unbelieving monetarists, had already done much to improve the quality of monetary data and their regular monitoring and assessment. Was there a hidden agenda behind Richardson's monetarism? Certainly he believed that Keynesianism and an acceptable rate of inflation were no longer compatible; but there was also a significant phrase in his lecture, where he described monetary targets as representing 'a self-imposed constraint, or discipline, on the authorities'. Presumably 'the authorities' was code for the politicians, and behind them the inflationary demands of a mass electorate. Even so, after Reginald Maudling had written to him following the lecture to express scepticism about monetarist dogma, he was at pains to call the former chancellor and reassure him:

> The Governor took the opportunity to touch on a couple of points arising from the lecture. He said that the emphasis in discussion of monetary policy was invariably in terms of restraint, but pointed out that in each year there had been a planned expansion in the money supply. The stance of monetary policy was thus not directed solely to deflationary ends. He touched also on the inter-relation of the growth in the monetary stock and inflation: the relationship was not mechanistic, but there was clearly an equivalence in the longer run between high rates of growth in the monetary aggregates and high inflation. He stressed the importance the Bank attached to restraining inflation but indicated that the Bank differed from pure monetarists in believing that all means available should be used in tackling inflation – including incomes policy.

By this time the Labour government, whose fortunes had picked up post-1976 amid economic recovery and generally greater stability, was approaching its endgame. That endgame featured of course the 1978–9 'winter of discontent', with the mood in Threadneedle Street little better than anywhere else. 'I recall the Governor being tired and ratty at the beginning of February,' wrote Dow some months later:

> He had been giving too many speeches, a great drain on his energy the way he does them. There was also considerable disagreeableness

among us about the state of the economy, which we discussed one afternoon in the Governor's room. I, of course, deplored having to depress the economy further when it was already depressed, merely to keep public borrowing to last year's figure. The Governor said aggressively that he did not care about the state of the economy. The Chief Cashier said he didn't either. David Walker [recruited from the Treasury in 1977 and now running the Economic Intelligence Department] was also there. I learned afterwards that this line of stupidity by John Page had roused him to silent fury. John Fforde was tense and apocalyptic on the other side and talked of the Governor wanting a return to the recession of the 1930s, something with which he, John Fforde, would want to have nothing to do. I certainly felt out of favour ...

The election was eventually set for Thursday, 3 May 1979, one of the turning-point dates in modern British history. Two days before polling, Richardson characteristically took the trouble to note down what someone had told him about the previous weekend's 'Sunningdale meeting between the Civil Service and Industry':

Douglas Wass had made a remark which had caught wide attention, to the effect that there had been a great political change over the last years, in which the focus of attention had become inflation while the level of unemployment had diminished in importance, so that its rise from its present level still further was not a central preoccupation. Douglas Wass had then said that some of them in the Treasury were now wondering whether this was the right balance or whether the level of unemployment ought not to swing back into greater prominence.[33]

It is impossible to be certain, but the chances are that the governor – despite his 'ratty' remark a few months earlier – would not have disagreed.

16

Sunny Offs

It begins with the usual touch of drama, a ship unloading, a BR van speeding through London until it is ushered through Grandma's back door by the majestic porter in top hat and long fawn coat who usually deals with Rolls-Royces; then we have little wooden cases slipping down rollers, a hatchet lifted – crack, and in each case there glints a couple of gold ingots. We admire the gold, we admire the basement stacked high with stuff, we even swallow the narrator's saliva; but then the film begins. It shows us the Bank glinting in the sunlight, dedicated crowds pouring over London Bridge, Mr Cobbold smiling at Mr Jacobsson, committees meeting, directors in session, Mr Cobbold communing silently with Mr Mynors, hordes of perky girls managing the national debt, hordes of knobbly boys playing hockey, pink-coated waiters, the nightly guard, and a world thrilling to the news of an unchanged Bank rate. But 35 minutes is much too long.

'Each time one thinks that the film is at last dropping off,' added in July 1960 the *New Statesman*'s weary but observant critic of the new colour film about itself that the Bank had commissioned as part of its deliberate opening up following the Bank Rate Tribunal and all that, 'it jerks up again, remembering the weather-vane, or the bust of Governor Norman, or the George Washington share-certificate which we haven't seen yet, eager to show us one more picture of a Comet or a supermarket and hint once again that all the affluence is Grandma's own work.'

A documentary film-maker had plenty of activities to choose from. On any fairly typical working day during the quarter-century or so after the war, these might have involved (in no particular order): monitoring sterling's performance on the foreign exchange market and dealing as required; examining the macro-economic problems of one of the larger Latin American countries; resolving knotty problems to do with contravention of the exchange control regulations; managing the national debt; 'passing transfers', that is, updating the ledgers kept as registrar of government stocks; calculating dividends for holders of government stocks; storing and moving around the gold held in the vaults on behalf of government and other central banks; examining, destroying and issuing banknotes; 'posting' and 'pricking' (in other words, stamping and checking) the Bank Note Registers; training central bankers from overseas; producing balance of payments estimates; borrowing in the money market to meet the government's need for short-term funds; acting as banker not only to the government, but also to commercial banks, discount houses, accepting houses, other central banks and some private customers; implementing the government's monetary policy through operating in the money and gilt-edged markets; executing customers' orders for the purchase and sale of foreign currency and gold; providing special certification facilities for jobbers in the gilt-edged market; enabling discount houses to discount bills or borrow; operating in gold, foreign exchange and foreign securities on behalf of the Treasury's Exchange Equalisation Account; and, often on a deceptively informal basis, attempting to keep an eye on the rest of the City. Each day – as no film-maker could ignore – ended with the Bank Picquet, mounting guard through the night over the Bank, the officer in charge favoured with a suite of rooms, where he was served dinner with claret and port.

The total size of the concern remained broadly constant over the quarter of a century. In 1949 there were 8,263 staff, of whom just over 7,000 were in the offices and the rest were at the Printing Works; by the end of the 1960s, after a decade or so of significant mechanisation in the offices, the aggregate figure was around 7,400, of whom almost 2,000 were at the Printing Works.[1] They were all part of the living but sometimes slumbering organism that was the Bank – and that was still, in many ways, a world of its own.

During these years the most customer-facing part of the Bank's work was through acting as the government's agent in administering exchange control – or, in Stephen Fay's apt words once exchange control was a memory, 'monitoring the export of money from Britain'. By 1950 as many as 1,600 staff were involved in the work, and two years later one of the Bank's non-executive directors, Hugh Kindersley of Lazards, wrote a lengthy letter to an executive director, Harry Siepmann, expressing concern about the way in which 'City houses and their industrial clients' found themselves 'frustrated by the eternal delays which they meet once they have crossed the threshold of the Bank'. The implications, he believed, were serious:

> The technicalities and difficulties faced by the Bank are not appreciated nor understood so that inevitably faith in the Bank as the leader and parent of the City becomes progressively shaken. In other words I believe the reputation of the Bank is at stake and unless something can be done to improve matters and to put things on to a more businesslike footing, also to guide the City as to what is or is not wanted of it, the great regard in which the Bank has been held will gradually diminish and it will come to be looked on as just another Government Department with wheels that turn just as slowly as any other Department. In other words the result of nationalisation as foretold by many in the early days …

Siepmann countered with a robust set-piece defence. After noting that 80 per cent of all letters were answered within eight days of receipt, and 50 per cent of forms dealt with within twenty-four hours, as well as observing that the Bank was left with 'all the difficult cases' after the routine ones had been delegated to authorised dealers, he went on:

> When one considers how arbitrary and tyrannous, how intrusive and impertinent, the foreign exchange control is bound to seem to those who suffer from it, the surprising thing, to my mind, is that we are not more hated and execrated. Partly this may be due to the fact that in some domains we are financially ineffective, i.e. that personal suffering can often be prevented by evasive action. But I believe it is also due to our having realised at the Bank from the very start, that what you do matters, very often, less than how you do it.

Dilatory we may be, where we have not the authority to be prompt and decisive; but if you were to tell me that we are inconsiderate, tactless, rude, or even pert, and that we take sides with the Sheriff of Nottingham rather than with Robin Hood, I should feel deeply hurt …

Through the rest of the decade the work declined somewhat, and staff numbers with it, so that exchange control even became known as 'the Bank's withered arm'; but the sterling crisis of 1961 then gave renewed importance to exchange control, and by 1969 (when almost 500 staff worked there) governor O'Brien was describing it to the Select Committee on Nationalised Industries (SCNI) as 'a regrettable necessity': 'We have it still because we have to have it. If we were to achieve such a change in our affairs that we achieved the strength which some countries not very far away have achieved since the war, we, like them, no doubt, would no longer have exchange control.'

The work itself could undeniably be difficult, requiring a mixture of experience, knowledge and judgement. Around the time O'Brien gave evidence, the chief of Establishments, Ken Andrews, recorded that in October 1968 the superintendents 'working as signatories in the Exchange Control' had requested extra payment (discontinued in 1964) on the grounds of their 'special position'; and that the governors had consented, on the basis of 'the creation of goodwill towards the Bank in a field which is potentially a source of conflict and dissatisfaction and the small proportion of decisions on Exchange Control questions which, in practice, have to be submitted to administrative staff for decision'. Exchange control itself was abolished in 1979, and many years later an old Bank hand, Eddie George, would recall that it had been administered 'in a flexible, sensible way', with 'on the whole remarkably little challenge as to why we are not being allowed to do this and he's being allowed to do that'. The last man in charge – at which point there were more than 200,000 live case files in London alone, quite apart from those being dealt with by the Bank's agents – was the eminently pragmatic Douglas Dawkins. 'If the control was to be acceptable, those who administered the rules also had themselves to be accessible,' he wrote shortly after abolition. 'Over the years, controllers at all levels gave countless interviews and answered countless telephone enquiries. For a controller, face to face contact with an applicant was a salutary experience. Nothing concentrated the mind on the shortcomings of a rule quite like a well-aimed attack on it from an irate applicant across the table. Nothing, on the other hand, boosted confidence quite like a successful defence of the rule and the collapse of the irate party (not that it always happened that way). Most interviews in fact proceeded in a relaxed and friendly fashion ...'

From across a huge range of possible areas ('foreign trade, greenfield investment, take-overs, investment in securities, oil, insurance, shipping, diamonds, films, bloodstock, commodity trading, merchanting, documentary credits, factoring, Euro-bond issues, roll-over credits, cheque cards, bureaux de change, trust law', as listed by Dawkins), a specific if minor example is illuminating and perhaps representative. At some point after leaving the Bank in 1962 and returning to academia, Roger Alford was approached by a postgraduate student, 'very worried and carrying a letter he had just received from the Bank threatening him with dire penalties for breaking the Exchange Control Regulations':

He was Swiss, and he had noticed that in London large, crown-sized, continental silver coins of the eighteenth and early nineteenth century were not popular with British collectors and were considerably cheaper here than they were on the continent. To help pay for his stay at the LSE he began a small arbitrage business, buying such coins, taking them back with him to Switzerland and selling them at a profit. He then remitted these funds to his account in the UK and I think that it must have been at this point that he broke the Exchange Control Regulations by not declaring his foreign currency earnings. I suggested to him the commonsense solution: that he should write a contrite, even grovelling, letter to the Bank explaining that he was only a Swiss student who knew nothing of these regulations, and was deeply sorry for breaking them inadvertently. He should go on to ask if the Bank would be kind enough to tell him exactly what he should do to rectify his position because he was anxious to be on the right side of the law. I explained that the Exchange Control experts in the Bank would enjoy exercising their deep understanding of their own intricate regulations in telling him what he should do. In due course he received a letter back which in a kindly way told him how to put everything right.

The crux was a necessary degree of flexibility. 'Real life stubbornly refused to limit its variety to that provided for in the body of rules as it existed at any one time,' reflected Dawkins. 'As a result, there was a constant need for review and adjustment which was often a ticklish matter since exchange control in its maturity was represented by an intricate network of rules, each supporting, dependent on or derived by analogy from one or more other rules. The art in devising a new rule, or in introducing a relaxation for that matter, was to ensure that the whole corpus remained more or less in equilibrium and that one did not create intolerable anomalies or internal contradictions.' 'Devotees of the old game of spillikins,' he added, 'will recognise the problem.'[2]

The note issue remained of course the Bank's most visible responsibility. 'This new fiver is not a beautiful thing,' commented *Punch* in March 1957 about the predominantly bluish £5 note that now replaced the old and larger white fiver. 'It is rather like a Victorian sampler as seen in a nightmare by the Council of Industrial Design. Amorphous panels sprawl on both sides, vaguely suggesting lacework, commemorative masonry, wallpaper and the covers of old-fashioned exercise books. There is Britannia (decapitated), St George and the Dragon, a loveable old lion mauling a key on a chain, and the magic signature "L. K. O'Brien."' Not everyone would agree. One historian of banknote design, John Keyworth, has called Stephen Gooden's note 'a powerful, confident design exhibiting extraordinary draughtsmanship'; but such was its curtailed size that, as a letter to the press pointed out in 1959, Lear's owl and pussycat would have found 'difficulty in wrapping honey, money or anything else in it'. Either way, its reception was mild compared to that in March 1960 for the new £1 note – the Bank's first note to bear the likeness of a reigning monarch. Outspoken critics included (in a rare show of unanimity) Harold Wilson and Osbert Lancaster, while according to the *Daily Telegraph*'s art critic, Terence Mullaly, 'severe without being stately' was 'not the Queen we know'. The unfortunate artist-designer was Robert Austin. 'He had no previous experience of bank-note design,' ruefully recorded O'Brien (who as chief cashier was ultimately responsible for the new note), 'and found himself severely constrained by the experts in the Bank of England printing works intent upon incorporating every anti-forgery feature they could think of. The result was a note of far from distinguished appearance which lived to haunt me for many years.'

In 1963, on the new blue £5 note designed by Reynolds Stone, a more acceptable likeness of the monarch appeared; but most attention focused on the surprisingly young and even racy Britannia on the back, prompting the *Bankers' Magazine* to reflect that 'we can get used to anything'. A pause ensued, during which the Bank turned to the fine artist Harry Eccleston as its full-time banknote designer. The upshot was the Series D notes: the Bank's first fully pictorial banknotes, featuring the Queen on one side and notable historical figures on the other – William Shakespeare (£20), the Duke of Wellington (£5), Florence Nightingale (£10), Isaac Newton (£1) and Christopher Wren (£50), issued in that order between 1970 and 1981. Artistically the series was a triumph, but the significantly smaller size of the new £1 note issued in February 1978 prompted the president of the Royal Academy, Sir Hugh Casson, to comment that 'it looks cheap, feels cheap and is cheap'.[3] As for the gender aspect of Series D – four men, one woman – that for the moment was the dog that failed to bark.

From 1956 the banknotes were produced at the new, purpose-built Printing Works at Debden. The old works at St Luke's in Old Street had become increasingly beset by capacity and other problems; while the choice of Debden in Essex – a London County Council out-county estate rapidly filling up with young families of Londoners leaving rundown housing in Bethnal Green and elsewhere in the East End – was influenced partly by its greenfield potential, partly by the fact that many of the printers already lived in the north-east London area. 'Compared to St Luke's, it seemed a paradise, with the outlook on open country,' observed a former non-executive director, Arthur Whitworth, following a visit to Debden shortly after the move had been made in June 1956, though graciously adding that 'the grim and grimy St Luke's served its purpose'. The huge main production hall, designed by the leading architect Sir Howard Robertson, had no central roof support, enabling uninterrupted use to be made of its whole area. 'At first sight,' explained the *Old Lady*, 'the interior appears to the spectator to be enormous, which indeed it is, though he may be a little surprised to learn that the areas provided under this roof are not very much greater than the corresponding ones at St Luke's. The clear space, however, makes it possible to arrange the machines more economically.'

Around the time of the move from St Luke's, the decision was taken also to transfer from the Cashier's Department to Debden the task of inspecting, checking and destroying used notes – deeply repetitive and boring work for which the Bank had found it increasingly difficult to recruit female clerical staff whom it regarded as sufficiently well qualified. The Paid Note Building opened at Debden in 1961, with facilities enabling a reduction in the number of examiners needed. 'You seem to have a splendid body of women there,' declared Colonel Lancaster to the governor in July 1969 after he and the rest of the SCNI had visited the Debden complex. 'A lot of them look to me the epitome of honesty … Your system seems such a perfectly splendid one that it did not look as though there was any chance anyhow of getting away with anything. I tried very hard myself and found I could not.' Security at the Printing Works was undeniably stringent, but of course it was always, as O'Brien said in reply, 'a matter of judgement as to what is enough'. Moreover, he went on: 'The Committee will have noticed from walking round, I expect, that the control corridors which might be manned by hundreds and hundreds of people certainly are not. There is an exercise in psychology there.'[4]

Throughout these years, the most populous part of the Bank, excluding the Printing Works, was the Accountant's Department, home of the Stock side, where the already considerable attritional daily workload expanded greatly as a result of the Labour government's nationalisation programme soon after the war. Between the wars it had largely been based in Finsbury Circus; but even before the nationalisation programme fully unfolded it was clear that extra accommodation was needed, leading to the move in 1948 of some offices to the West End's Regent Arcade House, quickly nicknamed 'Spiv House'. In 1951 the decision was taken to purchase a substantial bomb site just to the east of St Paul's, with a view to housing virtually the whole department there; and in due course this became the Bank's New Change building, as designed by the veteran architect Victor Heal (who had been responsible for the Southampton branch just before the war) and situated just slightly set back from a new road (New Change itself) running from Cheapside down to Queen Victoria Street. In its way the ambitious construction, varying between eight and eleven storeys, represented the arrival of modernity at the Bank:

The offices are lit by fluorescent tubes in specially designed fittings [noted the *Old Lady* in June 1958 three months after the department had taken possession]. There are at present three groups of press-button lifts, to be increased to five groups when Phase 2 is complete; each group is controlled by its own electronic 'brain', which sorts out the demands that are made upon the group as a whole and arranges the journeys of each lift so as to provide the maximum service in the minimum time. At first the Staff had some natural scepticism as to the powers of the 'brain', but they were soon reassured, despite a few electronic tantrums in the early days. Some of the older members have been a little embarrassed on finding themselves, as creatures of habit, murmuring 'Thank you' to a non-existent liftman.

Architecturally speaking, however, modernity was hardly the *mot juste*. 'The designer might have pressed for a skyscraper in which case he would have earned the plaudits of the modernists,' gratefully noted the *Financial Times*. 'But he had a greater regard for the precepts of Wren than for those of Le Corbusier.' Inevitably, others were more critical. Professor Anthony Blunt of the Courtauld Institute led the attack on what he saw as the Bank's unimaginative, backward-looking effort, while according to Dr Nikolaus Pevsner the 'vast pile' was 'shockingly lifeless and reactionary', indeed 'almost beyond comprehension'. Certainly, once the asperities of contemporary debate had died down, no one ever claimed it was a great building. Updating Pevsner some forty years on, even the measured Simon Bradley wrote of a 'general stuffiness', of 'silly little semi-period balconies', of sculpture 'in what might be called the George VI style', and of 'a shapeless public courtyard, disastrously bleak despite the plain fountain and lead cisterns, in C18 style but dated 1960, scattered about'. Perhaps so, but the anonymous 1958 writer in the *Old Lady* was also justified in welcoming the way 'at New Change the light and colourful appearance of the offices is making its own contribution – impossible to measure but nonetheless real – to the well-being of the Staff'.[5]

If Debden was an outpost, and New Change sort of an outpost, so too were the branches. 'They were formed in the 1820s for the distribution of the note circulation,' O'Brien explained in 1969 to Colonel Lancaster and his troops:

We now have eight of those branches [Plymouth having closed in 1949]. Their main function is, indeed, to distribute notes to the local Banks and to recover notes from them, to mill them and send them down to the printing works to be destroyed. They also hold the accounts of the local banks, the local government accounts, customs and excise and so forth, and a certain amount of private business still survives, but not very much. The function which they now perform which they have done only since the last war is to act as centres from which our agents make contact with local industry, get to know local industrialists, visit local factories and help us to have a better view of what is happening in industry.

In answer to another question, O'Brien agreed that for the eight cities themselves the Bank's local presence was a valued 'prestige symbol'. 'Indeed recently,' he related, 'we were very strongly pressed by the Corporation of Cardiff to have a branch down there. We examined it with every sympathy, but came to the conclusion it would not be justified, particularly now the Severn Bridge makes it easier for us to look after Wales from Bristol.' Altogether by this time the eight branches comprised some 334 staff, with the recruitment policy essentially being women locally, men from head office, and no graduates. As for the steady jog-trot of life in the branches, the recollections of B. M. Lahee, who as a young man was seconded from London to Newcastle in 1947, are broadly applicable to the 1950s and even to some degree the 1960s:

> It was a small branch: Agent, Sub-Agent and Secretary, about ten of us in the banking hall – Fairmaner and Folliot usually at the counter, Homfray bustling about behind the scenes, machining piles of cheques ('Burroughsing', in Bank parlance) or reading down to find a difference – Philip Smith and a couple of others in the Foreign Exchange room, and, upstairs, a bevy of young ladies who spent their days counting, banking and cancelling used banknotes under the, no doubt, watchful eye of Miss Dick. This was sometimes quite an unpleasant job if the notes had originated in a branch near the fish market.
>
> No computers, of course, only adding machines. Customers' accounts were kept by one of us juniors in hand-written ledgers

and a young lady would come down from upstairs in the afternoon to type the day's debits and credits on customers' statements. The Branch operated accounts for Government agencies, the other banks and a few private individuals. One of the latter was for a single lady who had given standing orders for a number of charities – one called the Fund for Assisting Missionaries to attend the Keswick Convention, and another, the Japanese Evangelical Band, whatever that may have been.

Included in our duties was a daily 'walk' to the offices of the two Newcastle Collectors of Taxes and the Inland Revenue Stamp Office. Two of us – or one with a messenger – would venture into the Newcastle streets carrying a small Gladstone bag to which was attached a chain which we were supposed to fasten round our waist; more commonly we just wrapped it around a wrist. At our ports of call we would count notes and examine cheques, put them in the bag for paying in and continue on our way.

Every morning representatives of all the banks in central Newcastle would come into the Branch and exchange bundles of cheques in a local Clearing House. One of us would supervise this process and see that the net creditor and debtor positions were equal. We were always glad to be able to announce 'House agrees'. Just about the last job on a Saturday morning was to enter the total of the week's clearings on a postcard and send it off to the Clearing House in London.

As before the war, there was also of course a monthly ritual. 'A small group would go down to the central railway station to meet a "Treasure" – a large consignment of new notes sent up in a special van attached to the London train. Closely guarded by one policeman, they would be transferred to a road van and taken to the branch's secure courtyard and we would all lend a hand at getting them down into the vault via a wheezing hydraulically-operated lift.'

The whole feel of the branches, during these immediate post-war decades, remained largely Victorian. 'The banking hall, sombre-furnished and heavy with time, tolerates its visitors with a built-in dignity,' was how the *Birmingham Post* as late as 1970 evoked its local branch in Temple Row. 'Elaborate cornices and Wedgewood-blue ceiling; an atmosphere which feels cloistral, even though it isn't;

a murmurous air of purpose which could just as aptly have been a pen-scratched silence.' Fundamental physical change, however, was already under way. 'Almost all our branches are about 125 years old, built for a different age than the present one,' the governor told the SCNI in 1969. 'Their vault space in particular, due to the growth of note circulation, is entirely inadequate, and the bullion yard space in which vans have to come in with massive quantities of notes is very exiguous indeed.' To this he might have added that the Great Train Robbery of 1963 (£3.5 million in banknotes on their way from Glasgow to London on behalf of the clearing banks) had made a significant difference. 'Before the Robbery, well over half the notes used by the public were drawn by the clearing banks from the Bank in London,' observed the Bank's George Blunden in the 1970s. 'After the Robbery we had to decentralise the operation further, because the banks wanted to withdraw money from our branches. But decentralisation meant larger security vaults ...'

In Bristol there was already a new building – the controversial, unfortunately proportioned Wine Street building, opened in 1963 and described in the *Architects' Journal* as 'an architectural disaster of the first order'; in Liverpool, Charles Cockerell's greatly admired 1848 building was much modernised inside between 1961 and 1965; while in 1967 designs were displayed in Threadneedle Street's Oak Room for completely new and on the whole uncompromisingly modernist buildings in Leeds, Newcastle, Manchester and Birmingham, all of which were duly erected and opened by the early 1970s. 'There is, no doubt, an enormous change in atmosphere between the two offices,' reflected Newcastle's D. J. Baker somewhat regretfully in 1971 shortly after the closure of the old building in Grey Street and the opening of the new one ('pretty dreary and noisy', thought O'Brien) in Pilgrim Street. 'I think that not many of us realised the extent to which the lofty ceilings, polished floors and mahogany fittings affected all who worked within or visited the Branch,' continued Baker. 'This atmosphere at least ensured that the inconveniences of using, for present-day note handling, a building designed for small issues of gold were passed over with courtesies appropriate to an earlier age. The new arrangements are so secure that there is very little possibility of face-to-face conversation with one's cash-handling customers ...'[6]

Everywhere, an obligatory aspect of the modern was computer-isation. 'I remember exactly when it started,' Peter Edgley told the *Old Lady* half a century later. 'It was in 1955, when Ron Middleton and I were both working in CCO [Chief Cashier's Office]. Ron was summoned to see the Chief Clerk and emerged with a bemused expression on his face. "I'm off to America with the Deputy Chief Accountant next Monday, to learn about computers," he told us. Whereupon his audience – supposedly a cross-section of the Bank's finest – turned to each other and chorused: "What's a computer?"' Middleton would be the go-to computer person through to the mid-1980s, with the Accountant's Department to the fore during the pioneer years. In 1959 there began on the fifth floor at New Change the Powers-Samas experiment – named after the British company that merged that same year with British Tabulators to form ICT, later ICL – and essentially involving each holding of stock being stored on the system's 160-column punched cards; the following July, the first 'live' (as opposed to 'dummy') dividend was paid, on 2 Per Cent Consols; by October 1962 cards had been punched for one million accounts (one-third of the total); and in the course of that decade, following the purchase of two powerful and appropriately huge 1301 computers, the process began of putting the stock registers themselves on to tape. 'Computerisation has been undertaken by the Bank on its own initiative and entirely under its own control,' O'Brien told the SCNI in 1969. 'We can claim, I think, that in this sphere we were in the van.'

What about computerisation for the Bank as a whole? 'The first steps were being taken to computerise staff records and payments, much of the processing of statistics, and even our banking operations,' recalled O'Brien of his time as deputy governor in the mid-1960s. 'It was urged by some that a centralised computer service for all departments was the obvious next step, but the Chief Accountant ['Billy' Bardo] was resistant. He had long had a large and efficient computer operation which was vital to the management of the enormous government debt in gilt-edged stocks. He did not want to lose control of this operation and very likely get caught up in teething troubles of more sophisticated computers which the work of other departments would require. This made sense to me ...' Even so, March 1968 saw the official opening by the Queen Mother of the Head

Office Computer Centre, as she pressed the button of an ICT 1904E computer and thereby produced a print-out of Britannia. Already in general the savings through computerisation were considerable; but, quite apart from the obvious manpower implications, not everyone enthused. 'All was fine until the advent of the computer,' was David Harris's wry memory of being superintendent in the Drawing Office at about this time. 'A selected few were sent on courses but on return considered themselves an elite race apart, unwilling to impart their new-found electronic expertise to the old sweats, who were simply told "you will just have to pick it up as you go along".'[7]

A final functional aspect during these post-war, post-nationalisation years was the opaque matter of the Bank's own finances. Asked in 1950 by the Treasury about the possibility of introducing a procedure to vary the fixed half-yearly payment of £873,180 that the Bank made to the Treasury under the terms of the 1946 Bank Act, Cobbold was adamant that he was 'entirely opposed', insisting that he 'did not see how any such discussions could take place without going into the accounts as a whole'. As for the annual report that the Bank was now compelled to publish, the comforting fact that it need not involve a profit and loss account allowed the chief cashier, Percy Beale, to observe in 1953 that 'the Report is as dull and free from controversy as usual – rightly in my view'. Retrospective examination by Forrest Capie reveals the Bank enjoying what he calls 'a very comfortable level of profits' – mainly derived from interest earned on bankers' balances – with gross annual profits steadily rising from somewhat under £5 million in the early 1950s to around £13–14 million during most of the second half of the 1960s. Fielding a question from the SCNI in 1969, O'Brien explained how things evened out:

The Bank's work as bankers to the Government is much less profitable than its work as bankers to other customers, because of the Government's low balance with the Bank of England, but in fact you do not lose money by being bankers to the Government, I take it? – Yes, we do. In agreement with the Treasury we keep the Exchequer balance at the Bank to the lowest figure compatible with efficient operation of those very large accounts, and certainly that balance does not provide sufficient remuneration to cover the cost of those services to us. The banks' balances, on the other hand, are very substantial, and the services we provide for the banks are very small in relation to those we provide for Government, so it could be said that the cost of the work we do for Government in part comes from the banks' balances.

The following year, in its report, the Select Committee successfully recommended not only that the Bank publish full annual accounts, but that it charge the full cost for services performed for government and pay a variable dividend to the Treasury, with that dividend comprising the entire profit apart from agreed provision for reserves and working capital.[8] Less than thrilled by the dawning age of transparency, the Bank had no alternative but to go quietly.

From 1940 onwards, women outnumbered men in the Bank. 'We must be prepared,' reflected an executive director (Dallas Bernard) towards the end of the war, 'to cater for women who are able to and desire to do more important work than has been allotted to them hitherto. It is a grave reflection on the organisation of the Bank that there is no scope for really intelligent women in any capacity other than administration.' Progress after the war, however, was at best patchy, not least because of the continuing deterrent, in terms of recruiting and retaining those with potential, of female staff often being compelled to spend up to five years in the Issue Office examining and counting used notes – tedious, much disliked work. Tom Courtis, in charge of exchange control at the Bank's Glasgow office, saw the bigger picture when in April 1946 he wrote to the chief of Establishments in London:

By adding up various opinions and conversations heard from time to time I get the impression that many girls regard the Bank merely as an interlude (pleasant or unpleasant according to taste) between school and matrimony and that this state of mind arises because of the relatively few good jobs open to women in the Bank by comparison with the numbers employed.

Do you think perhaps that the application to some extent of the doctrine of equality of opportunity as between men and women might be in the best interests of the Bank?

Specifically, suggested Courtis, 'if more good jobs were available, then a large majority of the women in the Bank would do better work'.

In practice, the most positive step taken in these immediate post-war years – during which the existence of the Hump, by now an almost ludicrously big middle-aged cohort, largely blocked progress for everyone else – was the removal of the marriage bar in 1949, three years after the Civil Service had done so but ahead of most of the clearing banks. The change was broadly welcomed, at least among the women, with some 75–80 per cent of female clerks at the Bank having in a recent internal ballot voted for removal 'because they considered that the individual should have the right to choose whether she should continue to work after marriage'. The main dissenting voice, in public anyway, came from L. J. Filewood, who was secretary of the Midland Bank Staff Association and whose daughter was a probationary clerk at the Bank of England – which, he claimed in a letter to the *Manchester Guardian*, 'has taken a step which benefits the exceptional minority presumably on the grounds of current theories of sex equality', despite such theories being 'psychologically and biologically mischievous'. No doubt he would have taken some comfort from statistics produced in 1952 about the three years at the Bank since the removal of the bar: 723 female staff had married, of whom 252 had left the Bank immediately; while, of the 471 staying on, 279 had done so for less than a year – and all but six for less than three years.[9]

'Men were definitely the favoured species, and women either did filing, typing or counting notes,' recalled Anne Skinner some four decades after joining the Bank in 1955 as a 3rd-class clerk (woman). 'I thought that was quite normal.' That same year, though, saw a significant development, with a Special Committee on Women's Work (chaired by the director in charge of Establishments, the formidable Sir George Abell) concluding that a 'gradual integration of the male and female staff of the Bank is practicable and desirable', thereby ensuring that 'women should have the opportunity to graduate from [women's] work to the work done by men and be promoted in competition with men, after an initial period of five years of their service, until age twenty-one or twenty-two, employed on routine work as at present'. It would, emphasised Abell, be gradualist reform rather than sudden revolution. 'Most of the difficult technical and administrative work would probably always be performed by men,' he told (reassured?) the male-dominated Council of Directors and Staff soon afterwards, 'but women would find their own level and there need be no formal limit to their eligibility for promotion'; indeed, 'until the final run-off of the "hump" the amount of progress which could be made might prove to be disappointing'.

In fact, on paper anyway, progress was quite swift. In 1957 – at which point still only about one-quarter of female staff were married – a detailed assessment produced an illuminating breakdown of the 3,880 jobs done by clerical staff (excluding shorthand typists) below administrative rank: 500 were properly the domain of men; 1,900 were properly the domain of women; and 1,400 could as well be done by men or women. Crucially, of those 1,400 'common jobs', 79 per cent were currently being done by men. The upshot was the 1958 Scheme of Classification, described by Elizabeth Hennessy (in her authoritative domestic history of the Bank between 1930 and 1960) as 'the first step towards complete integration of the sexes', meaning that the highest category – Classed Staff, as opposed to the two other categories, the Staff of Women Clerks and Shorthand Typists – would 'consist of men and women working alongside each other under similar conditions of service'. For some female staff, even so, the scheme involved a painful downgrading; while on the pay front the only commitment was that women were to receive not less than 75 per cent remuneration in comparison to men of the same age and seniority.

The issue of equal pay was never likely to go away, notwithstanding Abell's reported response to the news in 1962 that member-countries of the EEC (which the UK was applying to join) had agreed to implement an equal-pay policy by the end of 1964: 'Let us duck our heads until the storm is passed and then survey the landscape!' Britain of course was temporarily thwarted by General de Gaulle's 'Non', but in 1964 a new Scheme of Classification made the first move towards the introduction of equal pay, which from 1968 was phased in over the next four years. By then, there was an exemplar to all women in the person of Aphra Maunsell: the news in February 1967, thirty-one years after she had arrived at the Bank as an eighteen-year-old Irish girl, of her appointment as deputy chief of Establishments, the highest position yet for any woman, received front-page treatment in *The Times*.[10] Nevertheless, few indeed of the 2,700 or so women on the staff in the late 1960s could realistically have hoped for similar

promotion or anything like it. The Bank remained, like corporate
Britain as a whole, fundamentally a man's world; while the notion of
a female director, let alone a female chief cashier or a female governor,
was still strictly for the birds.

More generally, recruitment was a significant problem through these
post-war years, not helped by high levels of employment in the
outside world and a growing aversion to working on Saturday morn-
ings (when the Bank still had a statutory obligation to be open). Abell,
moreover, pinpointed in the mid-1950s the underlying fact of life at
the Bank that the staff 'in the main is required to do comparatively
uninteresting work with practically no chance for women of achieving
real responsibility and only a somewhat hazardous chance of doing so
for the men'; accordingly, 'men of the type we should like to recruit are
not prepared to run the risk of wasting many years as routine clerks
when there are more certain and immediate opportunities elsewhere
for advancement to interesting and remunerative work'. Handsome
career brochures made some difference, as to a greater degree did
advertising in the press, introduced in 1958 after agonising internal
debate, but at all levels the problem far from disappeared. 'Typewriter
manufacturers have succeeded in giving a modern image to electric
typewriters,' noted a 1969 report recommending a move away from
manual, 'and there are indications that firms are using them as bait
to attract typists in these days of shortage of applicants.' There was
also the diversity – or lack of it – aspect. Of the fifteen boys' schools
visited for recruitment purposes during the year ending August 1963,
all were private (apart from two direct grant), ranging from St Paul's
to Chigwell; and it was as late as June 1966, some eighteen years after
the *Empire Windrush* had started significant non-white immigration
after the war, that a note recorded that 'Miss B. Z. Alladin, the first
coloured entrant, will be starting work in the Dividend Pay and Loans
Office.'[11]

What about graduates? From soon after the war, four decades after
the failed pre-1914 recruitment experiment, a systematic approach was
introduced, so that by the end of the 1950s there were almost a hundred
graduates – predominantly Oxbridge, predominantly generalists, often

Greats men – at the Bank. The training programme they received tended to prove a sad disappointment. 'Most of the graduates thought it was pathetic and inadequate,' recalled Pen Kent (who arrived in 1961):

> It consisted really of doing a relatively fast track of what the Bank's own induction process probably had always been, which was a six months spell doing transfer deeds in registrar's department, then moving on to something called chief cashier's school where you learned to do mechanical cash management in an ordinary banking way. It was only after that, that you got posted to a department where you could, if you like, start to use intellectual skills. And that took a whole year to get to, which against graduate training expectations then, was already pretty disappointing and off-putting. A lot of people I think left in frustration. And the senior management of the Bank was not very sensitive to the demands of the new kind of intake that they were having. I can remember having a discussion with Cromer as it happens, just by happenstance that he and I found ourselves in Basle sitting at a coffee table, and he actually said, to my amazement, 'I spent the first six months of my career counting drawing pins in Barings and it didn't do me any harm.'

Things did start to change, though, in the course of the 1960s, partly as times changed and partly because of the impact as it worked its way through of the Radcliffe Report, with its demand for greater economic sophistication giving birth to what has been described as 'a whole range of new analytic "policy-related" jobs and associated "middle management" opportunities'. In 1966, by when there existed an advanced training scheme, about a quarter of the total intake were graduates; and by the end of the decade the Bank was taking each year some twenty-five to thirty male graduates and some five to ten female graduates – still a telling discrepancy – in addition to fifty to fifty-five boys and twenty to twenty-five girls straight from school with 'A' level qualifications. 'Will a feature of your work in the future be recruiting mature specialists rather than trying to train people internally in the Bank?' the SCNI asked O'Brien in March 1970. 'In some spheres undoubtedly,' he replied. 'Indeed, we have for some years past increasingly recruited mature specialists, particularly in the economics sphere. The number of economists in the Bank now is large and they come at various stages of maturity. We shall have to do the same, I think, in the computer sphere and in financial control …'[12]

For many years, against a background of the Hump and the general policy of overmanning in order to cover against emergencies and seasonal fluctuations, the opportunities for promotion were relatively limited. 'We had the regular pantomime called "Black Thursday" aka "The Feast of the Passover",' remembered J. D. W. Raimbach, mainly in the Accountant's Department from soon after the war. 'The Court of Directors assembled on the first Thursday in the month, when promotions, if any, would be announced. This was a sure trigger for the disenchanted to repair to the bar and drown their sorrows, or go sick, or break down in tears … and that was just the men!' Was the Bank a meritocracy between the 1940s and the 1960s? Leaving the Court aside, as well as gender, Forrest Capie argues that it was, citing the examples of O'Brien and Hollom as evidence that it was 'possible for any male clerk to rise to the top'. Some support comes from the recollections of John Taylor, according to whom most staff were interviewed at least once a year in the Chief of Establishments Office, told about their reports (following consultation with the principals who had signed them) and 'asked from time to time which parts of the Bank appealed to them most' – though naturally 'they were not always sent there'. But according to another witness, Tony Carlisle, the reality was rather different, mainly because of the division of responsibility between Establishments and individual departments. This was fine if they co-operated but pernicious if they did not, in which case, 'by denying movements in or out, a department could frustrate the development of its own staff and at the same time, or on other occasions, staff of other departments'; more broadly, in terms of career development, it was not until the 1970s that (in Carlisle's words) 'people were for the first time told frankly how they were getting on and what the future might hold for them, and were consulted about their careers and not merely told to report to a new office on Monday'. As to how objective assessments were (whether secret or revealed), it is impossible to know. In September 1963 four teenage girls on probation were being considered for the permanent staff. One, 'alert and resourceful', did not 'allow herself to be put off by difficult work' and attended 'meticulously to the mechanics of filing'; a second was 'interested, keen and remarkably sensible in her approach to the more advanced work'; a third had 'a tendency to get flustered when pressed'. The fourth, 'employed on Certificate and Fanfold typing', was on the plus side 'enthusiastic and keen' and 'a very fast worker', but against that with 'accuracy inclined to suffer at times'. Still, as a daughter of Lord Kindersley's chauffeur, perhaps she had the edge.[13]

That same year, as the Beatles became a national phenomenon, a future chief cashier arrived. 'What a strange place, looking back, the Bank of 1963 was,' recalled Graham Kentfield. 'In some ways it was like stepping back into what I imagine the world in general was like pre-war: stiff, hierarchical and of course heavily dependent on clerical labour. But at the same time, it was a very easy life, with offices staffed up for peaks which only rarely occurred.' Relevant here is the American social psychologist Douglas McGregor, who had recently identified two distinct management styles, Theory X and Theory Y: the former was authoritarian and assumed that people, with their inherent dislike of work, require a combination of carrot and stick to do it; the latter, assuming the existence of a psychological need to work, was participatory. No one could doubt which style of management the Bank traditionally practised. 'I am sending this to you,' began Courtis's postscript to his 1946 letter to the chief of Establishments, Eric Dalton, about the limited motivation of his female staff, 'because I conceive that it is a Principal's job not only to work on orders from his Chiefs but also to convey to them his impressions of the trend of thought of his own subordinates.' Dalton's reply was to the point: 'I much appreciate your continued desire to help. I hope you will not weary in well doing but on this occasion you have added nothing to the knowledge of this Department ...'[14]

If one figure exemplified the Bank's continuing adherence (if unconscious) to Theory X, certainly the stick aspect, it was perhaps Percy Beale, chief cashier during the first half of the 1950s. 'A rather unpleasant and authoritarian man who could make or break a man's career in the blinking of an eye,' recalled Guy de Moubray:

This happened whilst I was in his office. Every Friday there was a strange ritual of the Treasury Bill tender. Accepting Houses, or indeed anyone with £5,000 cash in hand, could apply for Treasury bills. If one bid £5,000 for a £5,000 bill one was obviously going to get no interest when the bill was paid off 91 days later. So tenders were invited with the highest bidders receiving their application in full. Tenders had to be received at the Chief Cashier's Office no later than 1 p.m. on a Friday. The Chief Clerk, in his case, would ring the recorded time number on the telephone and when it said, 'At the third pip it will be one o'clock precisely,' he would wave his hand to a clerk standing at the door of his case; this clerk in turn would wave to another clerk standing at the office door who would then with a flourish close the door and lock it. On this occasion, however, a messenger from Hambros Bank had still not reached the door when it was locked. So Hambros were denied any bills in that week's tender. But the Chairman of Hambros, Sir Charles Hambro, was the senior non-executive Director of the Bank of England and immediately rang Percy Beale in a fury. Beale not only caved in and allowed their application to be accepted, but sacked the clerk on the door from his office instanter. The poor man had until then a promising career. Now he was finished.

'"Sir" was the order of the day in speaking to one's line supervisor,' and all the more so to 'anyone more exalted such as a Deputy Chief Cashier', remembered John Hill about joining the Bank in the early 1960s. 'Dress was of paramount importance. To approach one's principal without a jacket would have been unthinkable. Shoes were of a strict standard and hair, both length and style, was controlled – shades of the military …' That military element could even be explicit. 'In my new rank I discovered that I was now an alternate member of the Senior Officials' Mess and was allowed to attend for lunch whenever [Guy] Watson or [Roy] Heasman were lunching out,' recalled de Moubray about becoming in 1960 assistant chief of the newly created Central Banking Information Department:

The first occasion was taken very seriously and one of the senior officials introduced me to the others … The procedure was that one helped oneself to a drink (gin & tonic, Bloody Mary or whatever) and then went to sit at one of the three tables. It was strictly laid down by the President of the Mess, Leslie O'Brien, the Chief Cashier, that people should seat themselves in the order in which they had arrived, no doubt to avoid too much chumminess. I soon discovered that it was wise to go to lunch rather later than had been my habit. When I arrived early, I found myself seated at the top of the far table with Douglas Johns, the agent of the Law Courts' Branch, who had some way to walk to the Bank and always arrived first. He was on the verge of retirement. Very often O'Brien would also be there and a few other elderly gentlemen; their conversation seemed to be entirely devoted to golf and to pensions! There was always wine to drink and cigars with the coffee; in later years I was to help myself to a cigar every day, but in 1960 you could not have a cigar unless the Chief Cashier offered you one.

Of course, as in the world beyond Threadneedle Street, things were slowly changing or about to change. 'Responsibility was already being devolved in 1964,' reckons Carlisle, 'so that it was no longer necessary – as it had been some years before – for every communication from the office – letter, memorandum, even a telephone call – to be closely regulated by the most senior people there.' Even so, not only did clerks during the second half of the 1960s still refer to each other by their initials, but as a vivid reminder of traditional authoritarian, top-down ways, there persisted the ritual of the Governor's Charge, in which probationers were paraded in front of Court to hear the Charge read out. The message itself was by now somewhat toned down from its Victorian stern morality ('you are warned against contracting habits of dissipation', and all that), but the ceremony itself – 'with its marshalling, dress rehearsals, dress inspections and rigid formality', in the words of John Footman – felt increasingly out of place in civilian Britain.[15]

Institutionally speaking, labour relations continued to be conducted after the war through the Council of Directors and Staff (the qualifying word 'Advisory' being dropped in 1950), with both Catto and Cobbold successfully resisting attempts by the Bank Officers' Guild (later the National Union of Bank Employees, NUBE) to secure a foothold. Notwithstanding some notable individuals being involved – including by the 1960s Jack Davies (long immortalised for having as a Cambridge undergraduate bowled Don Bradman for a duck) as staff director, Ken Andrews as chief of Establishments, and the leading trade unionist Lord (Bill) Carron who was a non-executive director on the Court – it was not all sweetness and light. In 1957 the

Council was criticised by staff generally as 'unduly ponderous and secretive' and failing to 'move with the times'; while 1968, that year of the street-fighting man, saw an eloquent memo submitted by the eight elected staff representatives on the Council:

> We are now faced with criticism of the present system from all sections of the Staff and certain constituencies have made it abundantly clear that they would not be prepared to return a candidate to represent them on Council in any future election unless an investigation takes place.
>
> Among other things, it has been said that –
>
> 1 The present system is too ponderous and secretive. There appears to be a lack of true negotiation.
> 2 The present system must be held largely responsible for the loss that has occurred in the Staff's comparative standard of living.
> 3 To undertake representative duties is detrimental to an individual's career.

The third charge was especially serious; but the following spring a detailed report by a Council sub-committee found that, in practice, 'service on the Council is not damaging to a person's career' – and that indeed 'we are convinced that in the long term no one would suffer if he or she decided to stand for the Council'. Where ultimately, however, did the whip hand lie? 'The other day you invited our comments on the special pension offer,' noted an August 1970 memo entitled 'Some Views of the Council Representatives' and sent probably to Davies. 'We left that meeting with the feeling that it had been the first attempt by the Bank at "Management by Consultation"; it appeared to be the first occasion on which our opinions had been deliberately sought before a firm proposal had been put to us.' And after citing two recent significant episodes in which 'we have been faced with a virtual "fait accompli"' and in which 'it was clear that the Bank would not move far from their proposals', the memo expressed the hope that 'this first glimmer of joint consultation heralds the dawn of a new era of Staff relations'.[16]

Of course, the other side of stick (and limited consultation) was paternalistic carrot. Shortly before, one of the SCNI's Labour MPs, Russell Kerr, had quizzed O'Brien:

From your remarks it would appear that, despite lack of assistance from the NUBE, a relatively happy set of industrial relations have existed over the years. To what extent would you think that has been due to what I would guess to be a fairly generous wages and salary policy as a result of the Bank having a lot of money lying around? – I do not accept the last phrase.

In the literal sense, I am sure you do not? – It is true that the Bank pay well ... It has been the basis of which we have maintained the higher standards of efficiency and performance in the Bank than one would be likely to see in most other financial institutions in the City. I say this without any disrespect.

The governor also acknowledged that, in the context of the Labour government's incomes policy, 'the Bank staff at the present time do not feel that that differential is being anything like maintained'; but essentially, in relation to the previous quarter of a century as a whole, he was correct, albeit with a fluctuating differential in comparison to the clearing banks. In addition, pension arrangements were reasonably well safeguarded from the ravages of inflation, especially after the decision in 1966 to compensate for three-quarters, as opposed to the previous two-thirds, of the rise in the cost of living since retirement. But it was in fringe benefits that the Bank really scored. These included the Housing Loans Scheme, introduced in 1945 and limited by 1969 to three increases per person during a Bank career (in order to encourage 'careful thought before purchasing a property'); the Educational Loans Scheme, inaugurated in 1957 and disbursing loans over the next fifteen years of nearly £700,000, enabling some 800 children of Bank employees to be privately educated; the handsomely equipped and maintained Sports Club at Roehampton; and active support for a range of officially encouraged extra-curricular activities.[17]

'Ladies of Threadneedle Street Are Right on Their Toes' reported the *Evening News* in February 1956:

When work is over at the Bank of England on Wednesday evenings a group of 20 young girls meet at the Bank Club in Tokenhouse Yard. They go by lift to the third floor and into an improvised dressing-room to change. When they emerge they have all the radiance of a ballet chorus. This is their dancing night. The Bank provides professional tuition for them.

They appear at Bank concerts and are rehearsing for a revue which is to be presented in April. Senior girl of the troupe is 24-year-old Paddy Salter of Harrow. 'I would have taken up dancing seriously but for the war,' she said. 'I joined the Bank instead and now I derive all the enjoyment from dancing as well as having a good job.'

Just around the corner from Tokenhouse Yard, in King's Arms Yard, there was from 1962 a wholly new, purpose-built staff club, which included the now modernised Tokenhouse Yard premises and on any one day could provide over 2,200 subsidised lunches as well as other facilities. 'Each day,' recalled Willie Osborn in 2000, 'there was a ritual in the Chief Cashier's Office':

I refer to the distribution of Tea Tickets which took place around eleven o'clock. One of the 'girls' from *Counter*, which also served as Staff Post, would come round the office with the largest-size bull-dog clip bursting with blue Tea Tickets. 'How many would you like?' she would ask. The innocent would whimper that one would suffice, but the *cognoscenti* would bid for six or more; and a hand-ful – not necessarily counted out – would be duly handed over.

A Tea Ticket was a sort of luncheon voucher that entitled the bearer to a variety of goodies available during the tea break over in the Bank of England Club. Appropriately the goodies included Jacobs Club biscuits, Penguins, more boring specimens like digestive and rich tea biscuits and – the ultimate gourmet experience – poached egg on toast. The value of a Tea Ticket must have changed over the years but I seem to remember it as about 1s 6d. Up to two Tea Tickets could be exchanged in any one transaction but, as there were three floors serving teas in the Club in those days, the bold would visit all three floors and cash in six a day. Why go to Sainsburys to stock up the biscuit tin when you could do it at the Club?

Paternalism took many forms, including 'Sunny Offs', introduced by O'Brien as governor towards the end of a long, cold summer. 'He decided that provided the sun shone, and only then, staff who could be spared should be given an afternoon off, in turns,' remembered Dorothy Binns. 'This was presumably to build up our strength for the coming winter.' Accordingly, 'around 12 o'clock, the principal would personally decide whether or not the sun was shining, and word would go round as to whether the selected few would get their Offs or not'. And unsurprisingly, 'one had been glancing out of the window occasionally with more than casual interest from 11.30 am onwards'.

Intrinsic to paternalism was the fundamental fact that only a tiny proportion of the staff – say two dozen out of a total banking staff of well over 4,000 – had a major decision-making role to play. This meant that the day-to-day work for the overwhelming majority was essentially routine, largely repetitive and often boring. 'Desperately dull' was how de Moubray in the early 1950s found work in the Drawing Office, with it being no more enthralling ('deadly dull, processing exchange control applications') when he moved on to the Securities Control Office.[18] Yet, if much of the work was tedious, not only did the deliberately powerful element of benevolent if strict paternalism help to ensure a generally strong sense of *esprit de corps*, but there still existed many old-style Bank 'characters' to help enliven the atmosphere – arguably the last generation of such characters, before computers replaced clerical grind and the management consultants and the 'study group' arrived in numbers.

A trio of reminiscences gives us a final glimpse of the pre-1970 Bank, not so unfamiliar to the pen-pushers of a century or even two centuries before. Michael Pickering, joining the Bank in 1947, was settled by the early 1950s in the Consols Office – that part of it called the Balance Section, where the changes in stockholders' details were recorded on 'balance slips':

Winstanley [a principal] subsisted mainly on gin and chocolate buns, both of which he consumed in the office. He had a habit – which caused at least one nervous breakdown on the passing section – of standing over people and snorting as they worked; indeed, it wasn't until I encountered him that I realised that people actually did say 'Pshaw!' Sometimes he would bellow a comment, and shouted 'That witness won't do!' and jabbed an indignant forefinger at the transfer under scrutiny. He was once holding a chocolate bun in his hand and the wretched passer had to spend 35 minutes scraping the transfer clean before it could be returned whence it came for the error to be corrected.

There were two first-class clerks called Doak and Pendleton; both were very tall and thin, both had lugubrious countenances, both were susceptible to draughts, and both hated each other. One afternoon they had a furious row about the positioning of a draught screen and Winstanley looked up from his desk to observe them engaged in a frenzied tug-of-war. He leapt into action. 'All right, Pendleton,' he yelled. 'If you want the draught screen, you have it!' Whereupon he seized the screen, which was of the flexible sort, wrapped it round Pendleton and secured it with tape, thus obliging his subordinate to stand rigidly to attention for the rest of the afternoon like a bemused umbrella stand.

The superintendent of the passing section was Cruickshank. He had white hair and a petulant face and didn't like people. He reserved an especial venom for a perfectly harmless first-class clerk called Budgin and persisted in telling him he smelt; the fact that none of the rest of us noticed anything made no difference to Cruickshank, who, if he was in a more than usually foul mood, would make Budgin sit outside on the window-sill dangling his legs over Finsbury Circus …

Christopher Bell towards the end of the 1950s was likewise on the Balance Section, by now located in New Change. There, he encountered 'many men talented in directions far removed from central banking':

One such, a very dapper old Harrovian, was heavily involved with racing, and I particularly recall a quiet and scholarly man whose daily task was of a mind-numbing routine nature, but who devoted his time – and part of his working day – attempting to prove that Bacon wrote Shakespeare … Some, of course, merely took solace in more down-to-earth pursuits such as worshipping at the shrine of Bacchus. One man on an adjacent Section would arise from his desk at 11.30 every morning and announce, in stentorian tones, 'Off to the Halls of Mirth!' It was some time before I discovered that 'The Halls of Mirth' were synonymous with 'Ye Olde Watney', a famous hostelry just a hundred yards or so from the office door and the venue for his morning 'coffee' break.

Also to be found on the Balance Section at that time was an aged First Class Clerk who was inclined to fall asleep at his desk after lunch. His spectacles would invariably slip from his nose and remain dangling from one ear. A little later, the Superintendent would return from his lunch and be confronted by this sight. The balance slips were stored in metal boxes, each about the length of two shoe boxes, with heavy metal lids. It was the sleeper's misfortune to have his desk situated close to some of those boxes. And so, inevitably, the Superintendent, on his return, would lift the lid of the nearest box and drop it forcefully. The effect on the sleeper was, of course, dramatic, and the same routine was played out regularly. All very entertaining to the young and impressionable onlookers ...

As for Threadneedle Street itself, the recollections come from Paul Tempest, a member by 1962 of the Overseas Department, comprising about a dozen groups of four to eight men (each with an adviser and an assistant) and situated in a 'long, low side-lit room on the Third Floor overlooking Bartholomew Lane':

The office was supervised by an elderly superintendent who sat in a glassed-off 'case', gazing gloomily down the long strip of carpet, looking for any sign of disorder. He was flanked by one or two girls plucked regularly for their promise or aspiration from the filing room upstairs or the typing pool downstairs ... Women were, however, in short enough supply for the call 'Murphy's (or Mitchell's) balance' to be still in widespread use throughout the office. This century-old Bank traditional signal – more subtle than the paper dart – attracting general attention to a likely pair of legs or other part of a passing anatomy without giving offence had its own particular variant in Overseas where Group One would call out 'Zwei millionen', to be agreed less coarsely by a francophone 'Trente-huit, vingt-deux ...', the Kremlin would chirrup 'Niet, niet, niet' to the alert of the Arabs or the Hispanics, as the visitor passed by them down the full length of the carpet ...

Humour in Overseas was, in that large open room, more often than not, pure Theatre. For the captive audience, the action unrolled constantly before them down that long central strip of carpet. Initiation horse-play took several forms. A favourite was, once everyone had been alerted, to ring up the newcomer on his first morning from several desks' distance. The voice was made to sound immensely old, senior and Governor-like. 'Is that you,

Jones? Welcome to Overseas. Would you care to come in, please?'
The speaker's receiver would be put down sharply, with a crisp clip.
At the other end, Jones would generally spring to his feet before
realising that he had not the slightest idea where to go or who had
spoken to him ...[19]

Probably the sternest internal critic in the late 1960s of the Bank's
organisation was James Selwyn, justifiably disappointed in 1965 not to
become head of the newly created Economic Intelligence Department
and by now an adviser to the governors. 'Labour in the Bank' was the
title of his January 1968 memo for O'Brien, arguing that in four main
ways the Bank was 'inefficient' in its use of human resources:

(i)   Small volume of output resulting chiefly from frequent breaks
        (coffee, lunch and tea) and a leisurely attitude when on the job.
(ii)   Work being done by people of higher calibre than necessary.
(iii)   Work which serves little useful purpose; i.e. contributes little
        to the fulfilment of the Bank's operations.
(iv)   Increased work and/or hindrance to the smooth flow of work
        because of unsuitable organisation (e.g. inadequate decentrali-
        sation of authority).

The upshot, influenced partly also by the desire for cover against
potential criticism from the SCNI, was the appointment later in 1968
of the American management consultants McKinsey & Co. The serious investigative work began in February 1969. 'I think it would be
right to offer them some limited lunching facilities on the 4th Floor,'
Fforde informed a colleague earlier that month about the two members
of the six-man team who were partners in the firm. 'I will therefore
tell them we would be pleased to see them at lunch from time to time
and will add, tactfully, that we would not expect them to lunch with
us every day they are working in the Bank.'

In the event, although the key recommendation by McKinsey –
involving much enhanced executive responsibilities for the so-called
executive directors, thereby reducing the power of the chief cashier
and departmental heads – was blocked by O'Brien at an early stage,

some other recommendations fared better. These led early in the new decade to various changes, of which probably the most important were the creation of a Management Services Department charged with providing computer and general managerial services; the appointment of a financial controller to ensure budgetary control; the start of a separate research division, the Economic Section, in the EID; and the initiation of a Management Development Division with a view to enhancing performance appraisal, career planning and management training. In the round, though, it was far from a revolution. 'McKinsey's general conclusion is that the quality of the Bank's work and the calibre of the Staff is high,' reflected the Bank itself in January 1970, while soon afterwards a press comment was that McKinsey's had 'discovered some rusty or obsolescent machinery, but no actual corpses buried in the courtyard'.[20] Even so, management-speak had now arrived at the Bank, and there could be no going back.

Undeniably, the Bank during the 1970s as a whole became a significantly more modern institution. The lengthy postal strike of early 1971 may have temporarily led to stockholders or their agents once again personally collecting the dividend warrants, but the general direction of travel was emphatically towards the future, not the past. That same year saw not only the end of the Governor's Charge but the opening of the handsome Reference Library three floors below ground level, and in 1973 the time-honoured Bank Picquet was finally put at ease. Graduate recruitment doubled between the early and mid-1970s; increasingly, in the not altogether gruntled words of John Hill, the Bank looked 'to recruit staff who had been taught the new maths and/or computer studies', meaning that 'the place would never be the same again'; and across much of the Bank, what were known as Clerical Work Measurement (CWM) systems were installed, with those carrying clipboards and stopwatches nicknamed only quasi-affectionately as 'Gerry and the Pacemakers'. That pace of change, though, can be exaggerated. Management as a whole was still relatively unsophisticated, with Eddie George, in the context of his 1975 review of the EID, referring to 'matrix management' as 'apparently quite common' in the outside world; Anne Skinner, from 1974 a junior manager in the Accountant's Department, would recall resistance among men to working for a woman ('trying to cut you out, not telling you what the job involved'); through the decade, a battle for control of staff continued to be waged between Establishments and the other departments; and in 1977 the recruitment at an unusually senior level of David Walker from the Treasury involved the governor eventually overcoming stiff, outspoken resistance from the chief cashier and some of the chiefs of departments, with John Page insistent to the end that 'the Bank is not that sort of place'.[21]

The Bank's own finances entered a new era in the 1970s. Published annual accounts, the Treasury scrutinising the Bank's efficiency, profits largely going to the Treasury – all these flowed directly from the SCNI's 1970 report, while from McKinsey's came much tighter budgetary control. A by-product of the new arrangements were moments of distinct Bank/Treasury tetchiness, including at one point some seven or eight months when Richardson as governor simply ignored a formal request from Wass at the Treasury to be informed of the exact details and extent of the Bank's operations in relation to the Lifeboat and other support initiatives, prompting Christopher Dow to reflect that 'no doubt the central bank has to be left a large discretion', but 'it would have cost us nothing to have made a show of telling the Treasury the essentials'. A further source of potential tension were those quite frequent phases during which the Bank, being in the public sector, was expected by government to moderate pay settlements, even as the Bank sought to ensure that its pay levels were kept competitive with those of the clearing banks. 'We had always paid, and would continue to pay, full regard to official policy but the fundamental position was that we had authority under the Bank Act to run our own affairs,' recorded the note of O'Brien's 'very plain' speaking to a Treasury mandarin in March 1971. 'It seemed that civil servants concerned with incomes policy felt that they could dictate the entire detail of our negotiations with the staff. The Governor was not prepared to accept this for a moment.'[22]

More generally for the Bank's employees – 7,200 by 1979, of whom 4,600 were banking staff, compared to 7,400, of whom 4,450 were banking staff, in 1970 – it was a decade of some austerity, especially as wage levels gradually slipped below those of the clearers, with Richardson perhaps less inclined than O'Brien had been to insist on operational autonomy in this sphere. Even so, the fringe benefits remained enviable and, prior to a certain tightening in 1978, largely untouched: not only subsidised lunches and the Housing and Educational Loan Schemes, but also interest-free loans to meet commuting expenses and unsecured personal loans for 'approved purposes'. Paternalism, in short, still broadly flourished. 'The Governor is very pleased with Tennant,' was the word one crisis autumn about the governor's chauffeur. 'He has remarked particularly on his patience and fortitude during a period when he has had excessively long hours both of waiting and of driving. The Governor welcomed the idea that Tennant might receive some extra reward for his efforts.'[23]

In the world at large the 1970s were of course the decade of sharply deteriorating labour relations, and the Bank could hardly expect to be immune, not least given those eroding differentials with the clearers. In February 1973, after years of increasing dissatisfaction with the Council of Directors and Staff, the banking staff overwhelmingly voted to have their own internal representative body to negotiate direct with management; and by the end of the year the Bank of England Staff Organisation (BESO) was up and running, with the Court palpably relieved by the staff's decision not to seek representation through a national trade union. BESO's regular newsletters soon, though, had a notably sharp tone. 'Well, so what?' asked its general secretary, John Ward, in April 1974 in the context of the Bank having in 1972 fully implemented equal pay for women but continuing to refuse to make housing loans available to married women – on the grounds (in the Bank's words) partly that 'despite some erosion by current social trends, responsibility for providing the marital home still rests primarily with the husband', and partly that 'if all married women took advantage of the Scheme, the additional capital commitment by 1986 would be some £4.5 million'. Ward himself was adamant: 'The Bank can afford it. There may be some employers in the City who cannot afford principles but the Bank is not one of them.' Two years later, in a symbolic action, BESO moved its offices out of the Bank; while by December 1978, during Britain's winter of discontent and with staff temporarily refusing (following a pay claim rejection) to co-operate on efficiency and productivity schemes, the recently appointed chief of Establishments, Rodney Galpin, was looking quite darkly through the glass. 'The present dispute must be seen as an indication that staff relations are in disrepair,' he observed to George Blunden (now the

executive director in charge of staff matters), although he still believed
that 'there remains amongst the staff a basic loyalty to the Bank'. And
Galpin went on:

> Staff at all levels in the Bank are, I judge, to varying degrees now –
>
> (a) demotivated and disillusioned with their lot while blaming it on
>   the Bank;
> (b) uncertain of the commitment which the Bank feel to their staff;
>   and consequently critical of the Bank's staff policies;
> (c) anxious to be further involved.

More serious action was averted, but by spring 1979 there existed,
according to the veteran staff representative Paul Clayton, 'a small but
powerful and vociferous group' within the staff who wanted BESO
to join forces with the national union, NUBE. 'As much as these
people are sincere in their views they are courting disaster,' warned
Clayton in the *Old Lady*. 'In a large Trade Union our small numbers
would be swallowed up and we would have little influence in our
own future.' Accordingly, he counselled 'extreme caution when dealing with "Trade Unions bearing gifts"'.[24] NUBE was soon renamed
the Banking, Insurance and Finance Union (BIFU), and within a few
years had succeeded in absorbing BESO after all.

The employment situation inevitably varied between departments:
whereas staff working in Exchange Control increased from some 500
at the start of the decade to some 700 by the time Clayton was writing,
those in the Accountant's Department declined from around 1,300 to
barely 1,000 – the latter change almost entirely the result of continuing computerisation. Computers themselves were at the centre of
an invidious decision in 1971, ahead of their much greater use in the
banking offices: in essence, the choice between the politically favoured
ICL (British) or the technologically favoured IBM (American). 'Sir
Eric Roll suggested that the timing of a decision in favour of an
American supplier would come especially ill against the Common
Market background and wondered if we should not delay for two or
three months,' noted Jasper Hollom in July 1971 after a discussion
with that non-executive director. 'When I suggested that only a delay
of two years or more would help ICL to compete more effectively he

was half inclined to jump at such a prospect.' The outcome the following month was a nicely judged compromise. After explaining to ICL's
Sir John Wall that the Bank was 'reluctantly' unable to alter its view
that IBM were 'better equipped to satisfy our computer needs at the
next stage', O'Brien went on:

> However we had also to take account of Government policy in this
> field and of the national interest in developing a U.K., or perhaps
> later European, firm as a real rival to I.B.M. The Governor and
> the Court had given the matter the most careful consideration
> and had finally decided on a two-centre solution, entrusting the
> Accountant's Department to I.C.L. and the remainder of the Bank's
> needs to I.B.M. This roughly 50/50 division would, we hoped, spur
> I.C.L. to make every effort to prove themselves truly competitive
> and no one would be better pleased than the Bank if they succeeded.
> Sir John expressed his gratitude for the line the Bank had taken …

As for IBM's reaction, further noted Hollom after their man had called
on the governor, 'they were grateful to us for deciding to entrust to
them the more complex part of our programme'. More generally,
technology mattered ever more. 'Telephones had been giving trouble
in the dealing area and this created grave problems,' John Fforde was
reported as admitting in February 1974 after visiting the Gold and
Foreign Exchange Office. 'Moreover, there was a considerable delay
before new direct lines could be installed. He [Fforde] had been told
that Post Office engineers had intimated that a £200 bribe could expedite matters.' 'If this were in fact true,' added that most austere and
upright of men, 'it was a serious situation.'[25]

Later in the decade Fforde contributed to the *Old Lady*'s regular
'As I See It' column. 'Is the Bank', he wondered at the end of some
stimulating if tortuous reflections about how society had changed so
much during his lifetime, 'an institution that tolerates dissent, fosters
an experimental freedom tempered by effective self-regulation, and
prefers a persuasive leadership that proceeds by consent?' To which he
answered: 'I think it is.' The previous issue's column, earlier in 1977,
was written by Tony Carlisle. Focusing almost throughout on the
Bank itself, and comparing it with the Bank of the mid-1960s, he was
inclined to accentuate the positive: more delegation (partly reflecting

the growth in the overall volume of work) and more personal involvement; lower barriers between different types of staff ('it would have been rare indeed fifteen years ago for the most senior people to join the most junior in the bar to celebrate a birthday or a wedding or a change of work, but this is now common practice'); and discrimination against women 'now a fading memory'. But although relaxed about changing sartorial standards ('white collars, once *de rigueur*, are now a rarity', likewise 'waistcoats, braces, and shoes with laces') as well as hair styles ('it is pleasant to see full scope given to individual choice'), Carlisle did have three gripes: 'idiosyncrasies of spelling'; 'the practice of knocking on doors, wholly unknown here until a few years ago'; and the tendency of specialist recruits (as opposed to 'aspiring central bankers') to be 'sometimes slow to develop a corporate spirit, hitherto one of the Bank's great strengths'. Those were two contemporary assessments in the *Old Lady*. A third, also in the magazine but not until 1985, was more retrospective:

> I have always had the feeling [wrote the editor, David Pollard, who had been at the Bank since 1965] that the Bank was far too slow, particularly in the late '60s and the '70s, to react to the needs of a workforce which was increasingly volatile, drawn from an ever-widening social spectrum, and threatened by the march of technology. My impression was that, bearing in mind the considerable resources devoted to 'man management', the Bank was surprisingly unprofessional in its approach to that particular task. It often seemed that the Staff Principal, instead of being selected on the basis of a natural talent (which some have, but most don't) for staff work, and specifically trained as a specialist in that field, was either a technician who had to do a 'staff job' before moving on to higher things, or just a 'nice guy' ...[26]

Hidden from the pages of the *Old Lady*, and perhaps consciously or otherwise responding to the wider national mood, an agenda for fundamental institutional change emerged during the second half of the 1970s.

Christopher Dow set the ball rolling in April 1976 with a paper on 'Possible Future Lines of Development for the Bank'. In essence, he wanted the Bank to attain 'a role as an adviser to the Chancellor of the Exchequer separate from and roughly parallel to the Treasury' – in effect, 'a claim to "parity of esteem" with the Treasury'. This would involve not only building up greater economic expertise, but also cultivating a more modern public image. 'Even small questions of appearance matter,' insisted Dow. 'It is worth asking whether the Court Room is a good place for a business meeting to take place; whether indeed the Court should be called the "Court"; whether messengers should wear pink coats. The Bank could benefit from a phase of *aggiornamento*.' Further aspects of helpful change might include 'the Bank "distancing itself" somewhat from the City'; a more balanced Court ('Perhaps a possible formula would be three City and Business; three other "rightish"; three TUC and other "leftish"; and three "independent"'); the Court itself being 'used more explicitly as an Advisory Council'; generally, 'more frequent, more extensive and more formal meetings with industrialists'; and even the establishment of 'a formal Industrial Advisory Committee'. In the fullness of time, it would become clear that Dow's was a vision that, taken as a whole, anticipated much of what lay ahead. But in 1976, although Richardson apparently told Dow that he went 'a long way' with the paper, that was less immediately apparent; and with Dow himself, conscious of the waning influence in the Bank of his Keynesian views, letting it be known that he hoped to go to the Treasury but vexing the governor by failing to tell him to his face, his paper failed to build up the necessary head of steam, even after it turned out that he was in fact staying at the Bank.[27]

The next initiative came from Kit McMahon. 'Externalising the Bank' was the title of his June 1977 paper, written in the context of an ongoing internal debate about how – in the wake of the troubles of 1976 – the institution should improve its hitherto not particularly impressive communication skills. There were, he argued in typically robust fashion, seven main reasons why in recent times the Bank had been 'subject to abuse, misrepresentation, belittlement, etc':

(i)   Misunderstanding about our aims, activities, our intellectual quality, the kind of people we are, etc.

(ii) Actual mistakes, bad decisions, bad handling of situations, etc.

(iii) The implementation of decisions of policies which may be appropriate or indeed very desirable on general grounds but which adversely affect vocal individuals or institutions.

(iv) The rise of an extremely vocal and opinionated strain of extreme monetarist thinking.

(v) The now rather widespread view that any obvious manifestation of the Establishment has an inherent tendency to be ridiculous, stuffy, overbearing, well-off, etc.

(vi) Straightforward hostility from the Left to the Bank based on the feelings mentioned above, together with race memories of Montagu Norman, hostility to the City and indeed almost everything to do with finance other than receiving it.

(vii) The failures, apparent or real, of British economic performance and of the authorities' capacity (in the most general sense) to overcome them.

As to what to do about all this, McMahon had a suggestion:

We tend to play our news management extremely straight. Naturally there are very good arguments for continuing to do so but it is a rough world and a gentleman among a lot of players is apt to appear wet and stuffy. We could simply put up with this stoically and perhaps this is what we should do. If, however, we were prepared to be a little more calculating, a little more 'political' in our off-the-record comments, letting journalists know what we were going for and where we were finding obstruction, I think we might find it possible not only to change our image and get ourselves more space in the press and more respect as a motive power in policy; we might also enhance our ability actually to influence policy.

In short, it might be time to start exercising the dark arts. That was indeed the way the world was going; and in the event, it was not long before the Bank's press office started to become far more professional and systematic in its approach.

The third initiative was, in its internal implications, the most important. It began with a memo on 'Organisation' that George Blunden sent to Richardson in August 1978, almost certainly following conversations between the two men about the desirability of a major restructuring. At the heart of Blunden's analysis was the identification of a series of shortcomings. 'On many matters,' he argued, 'Governors and Executive Directors have to rely on "grape-vine" methods to keep themselves informed'; budgetary control had become 'highly centralised under the Deputy Governor', with heads of departments 'inadequately involved'; the chief cashier's role ranged 'too widely to fit effectively in the Bank of the 1970s', with one man being unrealistically expected to be 'deeply involved' in 'the detailed work of credit and monetary policy and in the conduct of monetary operations' at the same time as being 'chief administrator of the Bank'; whereas, by contrast, at least three of the four executive directors 'do not have clear-cut executive roles' and 'tend to form a separate little pyramid under the Governor parallel to the larger one going down through the Chief Cashier and other Heads of Department'. To remedy the situation, Blunden proposed an essentially twin-track remedy: on the one hand, in a clear echo of McKinsey a decade earlier, giving the executive directors proper and meaningful executive job descriptions; on the other hand, seriously reducing the chief cashier's responsibilities. Given that the chief cashier (then John Page) had been at least the third most important person in the Bank for virtually three centuries, this was – as Blunden well knew – potentially incendiary stuff.

Richardson's next step was to commission a more detailed report on the Bank's organisation from Lord Croham, who as Sir Douglas Allen had been head of the Civil Service and who joined the Bank in 1978 as a special adviser. In early April 1979, he sent his draft report to the governor. Pointing, like McKinsey and Blunden, to the long-run failure to integrate the executive directors into the Bank's management structure ('policy co-ordinators without managerial responsibilities'), Croham asserted that 'there is a general feeling in the Bank that the present management structure is unclear and frequently leads to delays in decision making and a misdirection of the efforts of higher management'; and he called for 'an organisation in which the lines of command ran through Executive Directors to areas for which they were responsible for both policy and general management'. Just over a fortnight later, having discussed possible policy options with the governor, Croham in his amended report came up with a solution remarkably like Blunden's twin track. It was not yet, however, a done deal; and in the meantime, there was the small matter of a political and economic revolution for the Bank to handle.[28]

Serious Misgivings

'Proper control of the money supply is unlikely to become a simple matter,' the Bank at the end of April 1979, shortly before the general election, warned the next chancellor. 'With a combination of correct judgement and good fortune, the authorities are able to steer a course that allows the money supply to grow within its permitted range without this being accompanied by unforeseen, unwelcome, or unacceptable behaviour of either the rate of exchange or the rate of interest.' Unfortunately for harmonious relations, the problem was that the new Tory government under Margaret Thatcher had a zealous and unbending streak of monetarism, quite different from the Bank's far more cautious approach.

On Thatcher's part, this streak involved attaching huge importance not only to the meeting of tight monetary targets (especially £M3 targets) but also to the ultimately will-o'-the-wisp doctrine of monetary base control (MBC) – a doctrine based on the theory that (in the retrospective words of her first chancellor, Sir Geoffrey Howe) 'the Bank of England could control the money supply directly by manipulating and targeting the small deposits held by the clearing banks at the Bank'. The Bank was not keen from the start, with a paper by Charles Goodhart and others in the June issue of the *Quarterly Bulletin* arguing that MBC would 'threaten frequent and potentially massive movements in interest rates, if not complete instability', quite apart from serious 'disturbances and dislocations to well-established arrangements'. Undeterred, Thatcher soon afterwards commissioned a joint Treasury/Bank study of MBC, a study that over the next half-year or so moved at fairly glacial speed. Thatcher herself, understandably perturbed by the sharp hike in MLR (14 to 17 per cent) in November after a rapid rise in the money supply had led to a funding crisis, became increasingly impatient. 'Wass noted that the Prime Minister and the Chancellor were continually pressing for progress and made it clear, in answer to a question, that it was the Bank that was seen to be responsible for the absence of faster progress, this being our particular area of responsibility,' ran the Bank's record of a Richardson visit to the Treasury shortly before Christmas.

A deep, immovable scepticism remained, though, the order of the day in Threadneedle Street. 'Precise quantitative control has been shown to be unworkable,' the governor told Howe and Wass in mid-January 1980, adding that MBC 'would not solve the problem of how you get the price of money to a level which restrains demand'; later that month he observed darkly to the Scottish clearers that 'certain proponents' of MBC had 'put their case in a simplified and therefore superficially attractive way'; the following month, Goodhart frankly reflected in an internal note that, in relation to Treasury ministers, 'we are demolishing their hopes for monetary base control'; and in early March, shortly before publication of the much delayed green paper on MBC, the new deputy governor, Kit McMahon, warned a foreign visitor against expecting it to 'spring any great surprises', given that 'highly automatic systems are always very difficult'. So it proved. 'Distinctly cool about MBC' would be the accurate recollection of the then financial secretary to the Treasury, Nigel Lawson; and although Lawson suspected at the time that the Bank's 'root-and-branch opposition' to MBC was caused at least in part by an atavistic desire to preserve the discount market, he did not deny that 'given the Bank's profound antipathy, it would all too likely have proved the disaster they predicted'.[1]

Lawson's own pet project, vigorously pursued, was the Medium-Term Financial Strategy (MTFS) – in effect, a set of strict monetarist rules, to be monitored but not determined by the Bank. To a remarkable extent, notwithstanding its considerable experience during the 1970s in attempting to control the money supply, the Bank was kept out of the loop during the winter of 1979–80, as Lawson, backed by Howe, prepared the new counter-inflationary strategy. Eventually, on 22 February, Richardson was able to say his piece to Howe. Noting that he was 'anxious to have an opportunity to contribute views and comments', he went on:

> The medium term financial strategy was of vital concern to the Bank, and he was surprised that the Prime Minister should have been shown a draft before the Bank had been fully consulted. For his part he had serious reservations about the credibility of the sort of document produced and about the wisdom of publishing it; he was particularly concerned that the Government should not adopt a posture of complete inflexibility about the monetary targets to be followed in each successive year.

The Bank did now start to get more involved, but Richardson was no happier by 3 March, telling Howe that the plan was 'undesirably dogmatic, mechanical and rigid'; four days later, Thatcher as well as Howe was present to listen to his critique:

> The Governor said that he and his staff had had valuable discussions with the Treasury over the past 10 days, and as a result the draft had been softened and the targets made less rigid. But he still had serious misgivings about the whole exercise ... Monetary policy had to be defensible. It was hard enough to set a monetary target for one year ahead: it was much harder for a four-year period. Even with a target range, there was still in his view too much rigidity in the figures. He was concerned at the prospect that wages might not accommodate to the declining monetary path; and that if they did not, the pressure on interest rates and activity might well be intolerable ... The Government had already made clear its strong commitment to getting the rate of monetary expansion down: to publish medium-term targets would add little to this commitment.

At the end of the meeting, summing up, the prime minister said that she 'understood the Governor's misgivings', but stated that she and Howe were 'convinced that it would be right to publish medium-term targets', while hoping that Richardson 'would be able to live with this'. The final act came on 14 March: Howe reported to Richardson that the MTFS had 'given rise to a very intelligent debate in Cabinet', in which 'all the worries, including those expressed by the Bank, had been aired'; but 'in the end and on balance', said the chancellor, 'it had been agreed to go forward'. Accordingly, later that month, the MTFS was duly announced in Howe's budget.[2]

By this time, he and Thatcher had taken a major decision far more to the Bank's liking. 'There could be no doubt about the Government's commitment to a programme of exchange control relaxations as and when circumstances permitted,' Richardson informed the clearing bank chairmen in June 1979, a fortnight after Howe had announced some minor easing in his first budget. At the same time, 'the Governor emphasised that it was only prudent to proceed to relax exchange control in stages and particularly in relation to liberalisation of those transactions capable of producing large volatile flows across the exchanges'. Further relaxations followed in July, compelling the Bank – aware that existing staff might need to be redeployed – to withdraw some 200 job offers to new recruits. During the rest of the summer, the most compelling voice within the Bank in favour of total abolition of exchange controls came from Douglas Dawkins, whose fiefdom it was and who headed the Bank part of a small Bank/Treasury team that had been set up by the strongly pro-abolition Lawson. 'If our experience of the last forty years has taught us anything, it is that exchange control restrictions do not cure problems,' he reflected in August. 'It has also shown that restrictive systems usually have a bias towards becoming more restrictive.' And he concluded: 'I am therefore much in favour of dispensing with controls and the associated machinery entirely.'

That autumn, rather belatedly, the Bank's economists woke up to the possibility that abolition might impinge on the effectiveness of monetary policy; but McMahon by 12 October was taking the robust line that 'it would be wrong, and indeed self-deceiving, for us to believe that we would be able to rely on exchange controls for any lasting help in managing our monetary policy'. The following week, Richardson was present at the critical meeting with Thatcher and her ministerial colleagues. According to one account by a Bank insider, 'it was left to the Governor to make the broad connected case – that there would never be a time without risk, nor a better time; that even with exchange control we had been greatly exposed; and that not much money went out on partial abolition'; according to another Bank insider, 'at the end of the meeting she [Thatcher] turned to Gordon and said: "Now, you are the man who really matters on this, what do you say, do we get rid of it or not?" and Gordon said, "Yes," and she said "Yes," and five days later it was announced'. The announcement itself, on 23 October, stunned many – and 'all evening', reported the *Guardian*, 'the Bank of England was bombarded with calls from people who simply could not believe what Sir Geoffrey had said'.

At the point of abolition, the Bank employed some 750 staff in exchange control (including 100 in the branches). 'Your poor people,' Thatcher said privately to Richardson at the end of their key meeting, 'two months before Christmas too.' Some consolation perhaps was the pre-Christmas 'Valedictory Party for Exchange Control' for around 170 EC staff. 'A full bar and light cocktail snacks at five cold pieces per head will be provided,' noted the governor's office. 'No doubt Mr Groombridge will take the usual steps to ensure that the Court Room is cleared soon after 7.30 pm.' What mattered rather more, though, was the avoidance of compulsory redundancies, through a carefully planned Voluntary Severance Scheme involving resourceful exploitation of the Bank's close links with other City employers. Moreover, when some years later there occurred the collapse of Norton Warburg, a firm of investment advisers and money managers who had been meant to be looking after the severance pay of some of the exchange controllers, the Bank made good the controllers' losses. A last word on exchange control itself, 1939 to 1979, goes to Dawkins himself. 'Now it has all gone,' he wrote in the *Old Lady* soon after abolition. 'What, I wonder, will a future historian make of "matching benefits" or "115% cover" or "switch and surrender"? Will he understand what it was all about and will he detect in the ashes of defunct controversies the fire, passion even, that once animated them? Probably not.'[3]

Within months of the end of its exchange control function, the Bank underwent an even more consequential domestic development. The intellectual heavy lifting had already been done by George Blunden (especially) and Lord Croham between summer 1978 and spring 1979, before on 16 January 1980 the governor announced, in a message to all Bank staff, that from March the institution was to be organised into three divisions: financial structure and supervision (following the 1979 Banking Act); policy and markets; operations and services. 'The chief cashier,' he went on, 'will in future be responsible only for banking work and will no longer be concerned with monetary policy and its execution, and will cease to exercise administrative responsibilities ranging more widely over the Bank as a whole.' In effect, although unstated in the announcement, this severe downgrading of the chief cashier's reach would enable the four executive directors (including the now former chief cashier, John Page) properly to fulfil executive responsibilities; and they would be aided by the newly created posts of associate director (just one, Anthony Loehnis) and – instead of heads of department – assistant director (six of them). Later that month, two bank chairmen (including Sir Jeremy Morse of Lloyds) called on Richardson in order to ask 'what points of contact' for their chief executives would 'principally replace the Chief Cashier', prompting the explanation that one of the new assistant directors, Eddie George, would become their 'best friend'. Taken as a whole, the 1980 restructuring marked probably the biggest internal shake-up in the Bank's history. 'These changes have, in my view, now made it possible for the Bank to become in due course a modern institution,' reflected Christopher Dow later that year. 'The Bank had been run by a dead hand [that is, the chief cashier] from the past, and was certainly by far the most tenaciously conservative institution I have had anything to do with.' Yet observing how 'the detail of the re-organisation created a field day for economists', and even though he was chief economist himself, Dow did have a concern: 'One could not but feel that there had been over-promotion. At the time there seemed too great an emphasis on intellectual advice, as against intuition, practice and experience, with some danger of dividing the Bank.'[4] Almost a quarter of a century after Cobbold had publicly warned that the Bank was not a study group, this was a significant shifting moment.

Government/Bank relations in the early 1980s were as bad as at any time since the days of Cromer, and this time round Labour was not even in power. Howe subsequently wrote that he had come 'to rely a good deal' on Richardson's 'impressively measured wisdom', but no such encomium would appear in Thatcher's memoirs. Those privileged to watch the two of them in uncomfortable action together – the 'canine' politician, the 'feline' central banker – were struck by the hopelessness of the personal chemistry, at least after the initial, quasi-honeymoon phase. He found her strident, impatient and almost wholly unwilling to accept that practicalities, not ideology, should determine the workings of monetary policy; she found him patronising and vain, as well as frustratingly unwilling to take a strong, readily comprehensible line, quite apart from his being tainted as a survivor of the old corporatist order. 'What do you think of Gordon?' she at one point asked her chief scientist. 'Gordon who?' he asked. 'Oh, you know,' she replied, 'that fool who runs the Bank of England.' Nor did two other things help the larger relationship: that Thatcher tried to prevent the well-qualified McMahon, an unabashed Keynesian, from becoming deputy governor in March 1980; and that Lawson as financial secretary successfully insisted on becoming the ministerial conduit between Bank and Treasury, which (in Lawson's words) 'greatly upset Richardson, who felt that, as Governor, his relations should be exclusively with the Chancellor except when he wished to see the Prime Minister'.

By early 1981, the governor was talking to colleagues about resigning ('Can you give me one good reason why I should stay in the job?'), but decided against ('I stay so as to preserve my institution'); and in fact relationships did stabilise over the next couple of years, with instead perhaps greater tensions between Bank and Treasury than between Bank and ministers – tensions not helped by a continuing degree of personal friction between Richardson and the permanent secretary Sir Douglas Wass, both of them alumni of Nottingham High School. Certainly the Treasury was out for its pound of flesh in these years. 'I have to ask you to make a renewed effort to live within the cash limit [imposed on the Bank's charges to the Treasury for doing its business] the Chief Secretary has approved,' Wass wrote to McMahon in April 1982. 'I find it difficult to believe that this cannot be done.' Such an approach, reflected McMahon, involved 'a quite unacceptable analogy between the Bank and a non-departmental body in receipt of a grant'. Not long afterwards, there occurred a notable stand-off over the question of how much the Treasury should know, whether in advance or at the time, about any support operation that the Bank felt compelled to undertake. 'The Governor was incensed,' noted Dow about Richardson's reaction to Wass's demand for greater knowledge. 'It touched intimately the Bank's right to do what it would with its own, and moreover seemed impracticable, since decisions on such matters could have to be made quickly. For many months he refused to reply to, or even acknowledge, Wass's letter, which made Wass berserk.' Eventually, persuaded by McMahon and Blunden, he did reply – stating that (in Dow's summarising words) 'all our support operations (which in truth had not been large recently) had come out of our reserves, and that our accounts had been audited, and had been presented to Parliament'.[5]

The Bank's most uncomfortable year, by some distance, was 1980. In March, even as the world learned of the government's Medium-Term Financial Strategy, the Bank was starting to think about trying to shift some of the focus away from monetary policy and towards the exchange rate – notwithstanding the warning from Thatcher's favourite economist, the hard-line monetarist Milton Friedman, at a No. 10 seminar the previous month attended by Richardson, that it was incompatible simultaneously to pursue targets for the money supply and the exchange rate. Conveniently for the Bank, in terms of seeking to move the focus, there already existed the European Monetary System (EMS), linking the exchange rates of EEC currencies, that had begun in March 1979 without British participation. Now, a year later, McMahon argued that it had 'proved a flexible mechanism' and was 'likely to go on doing so'. He then spelled out the particular attraction:

I think it is fair to say that many of us fear that in due course the overriding position given by the present Government to £M3 targets as the anti-inflationary engine will be weakened by disappointing economic, social and political developments. If this were to occur there could be a strong case for at least complementary support in bringing down inflation through linking our exchange rate to those of a less inflationary group of countries. Some of us would feel that such a constraint would have at least as much a beneficent effect on wage bargaining as the monetary targets. None of us, it should be emphasised, would in this way be looking for an exchange rate constraint as a 'softer' discipline – rather as a possibly more effective one.

A few days later, Richardson told Howe that 'the Bank had always been more favourably disposed towards EMS than the Treasury', adding that he 'thought it inevitable that, sooner or later, the UK would have to join'; while by May, in the context of what had become a punitively high exchange rate for British industry, as well as broader government policy 'obviously coming under great strain', McMahon was raising the possibility that the Bank should 'abandon our hands-off policy and intervene heavily in an attempt at least to prevent further increases in the rate', not least given that an 'incidental advantage might be that this could be a half-way stage towards entry to EMS which I think may turn out to be a useful option for us in the not-too-distant future'.[6] All this was in practice looking ahead to what would unfold over the next ten years or more. But for the moment it was monetarism or bust at No. 10.

On *that* all-consuming front, the subject at times of intense theological debate, the cardinal fact during the summer of 1980 was that, as an inevitable if delayed consequence of the abolition of exchange controls, the Corset – the Bank's supplementary special deposits scheme that had been reluctantly introduced back in the even darker days of December 1973 as an instrument of monetary control – no longer operated from July, immediately causing a dramatic and unwelcome spike in the money supply, as measured by £M3. 'First guess' figures for July itself were available by the 29th of that month, with Eddie George warning Richardson and McMahon that once they became public they would 'come as a severe shock to the markets, abruptly extinguishing current hopes for a further cut in MLR in the next 2–3 months'. Even so, looking at the larger picture, he argued that it would be 'premature to think in terms of more strategic policy reaction', whether fiscal correction or more direct lending controls. And George concluded: 'I believe, on the present information, we need to sit tight.' Thatcher herself became aware on the 31st that there was a serious problem. 'The removal of the corset,' ran the briefing to her from the Central Statistical Office, 'will raise the growth of M3 for a month or two; its underlying trend may be difficult to estimate.' Next to which she simply wrote '!!!'. And by 5 August, the ominous message coming through, in a direct phone call from her private secretary to Richardson, was that 'the Prime Minister wished to see the Governor more regularly'.

More immediately, on holiday in Switzerland, she happened to meet the monetarist economist Karl Brunner and the Swiss central banker Fritz Leutwiler. To both she unburdened herself; from both came the message that the drastic overshoot must be the result of

Bank of England mismanagement. Early September saw the denouement, with August's fast-growing, seemingly out-of-control figures
due to be announced on the 9th. Wednesday the 3rd was Richardson's
longest day. At a 9.30 meeting at No. 11, accompanied by John
Fforde and Charles Goodhart, he was told by Howe that Thatcher
was 'clearly unhappy that the monetary situation seemed to have
gone wrong, and would be looking for reassurance that the Treasury
and the Bank had a grip on the situation'; to which he responded by
asserting that 'the markets were clearly inhibited by the fact that they
no longer knew where they were on the map' and noting that 'the
monetary statistics were undoubtedly in disarray'; while Goodhart
commented that 'changes in £M3 were not reliably related to movements in the real economy' and that '£M3 in recent years had been
much influenced by structural shifts in the financial sector'. At 6
o'clock the governor was back in Downing Street, this time at No. 10
and on his own. 'Her strategy was right ... it was not being properly
operated ... the Bank of England was functioning as a lender of first
resort, not last resort ... the clearing banks were shovelling money
out ...' Richardson listened to it all and more, before eventually the
meeting was adjourned. Two days later, on Friday, the chancellor's
office rang the governor's office to say that the prime minister wished
to resume 'the other day's meeting' on the 8th at 3 pm, only to be told
that Richardson would be in Basel for a BIS meeting. So in the event
that Monday afternoon, with McMahon also away, it was Fforde and
George who arrived at No. 10 to see Thatcher and Howe. 'Who are
these people?' she reputedly said on coming into the meeting room,
and then gave (according to the record by her office) what Cobbold
would have called both barrels:

> The Prime Minister said that she understood that the underlying
> rate of monetary growth was now reckoned to be 15 per cent or
> higher. This was extremely disturbing – given that the 7–11 per cent
> target was the centre-piece of the Government's economic strategy.
> It seemed to her that the Bank had been pursuing an interest rate
> policy rather than a policy to control the money supply ... As long
> as the clearers could rely on the Bank to relieve any pressure on
> their liquidity, they would surely be all too willing to maintain a
> high level of lending ... On monetary control, she was disappointed

that it had taken so long to reach a conclusion on the proposals to change over to a monetary base system. Finally she wondered whether more could not have been done to put pressure on the clearing bank chairmen to get them to reduce their lending.

Howe characteristically tried to calm things down. 'It was easy to be wise after the event,' he observed. 'Not only the Treasury and the Bank, but also most outside commentators, had under-estimated the underlying rate of monetary growth.' And the two Bank men, with George doing most of the talking, apparently did attempt in trying circumstances to mount a defence, noting that the issue of methods of monetary control was 'extremely complex', which presumably went down well. The meeting ended with Thatcher stating that 'it was crucial to get the money supply back under control'. Clearly it was a memorable encounter, naturally mentioned by Dow: 'I got no coherent account of how it went. There was evidently much ill temper and interruption, before which the chancellor apparently bowed his head; and, in effect, so likewise (if one can imagine his silent fury) must John Fforde have done. Terry Burns [chief economic adviser at the Treasury] said afterwards it was a pity no one spoke up against the tirade since the PM had nothing to do but repeat herself, and was left frustrated.' As for Fforde, added Dow, he was so shaken that apparently he returned to the Bank saying that he refused to meet Thatcher again; and it was not long before the word was out about the prime minister's extremely dim view. 'Now we have Mrs Thatcher button-holing all and sundry to proclaim that "it's all the Bank's fault,"' wrote Ferdinand Mount in the *Evening Standard*. 'Any passing Swiss banker or Cabinet sub-committee is treated to a lecture on the incompetence of the present Governor, Mr Gordon Richardson. He has, she claims, totally messed up the money supply; he never tells her a thing; how can you run a country with a central bank which does not understand the simplest things, and so on, and so on.'[7]

The closing months of 1980, and early months of 1981, were an extremely difficult time for all concerned, as manufacturing output rapidly declined and mass unemployment became a reality – a grim state of affairs owing much to what the financial historian Duncan Needham has called 'a misconceived monetary policy'. Indeed, on the final page of his authoritative survey of British monetary policy between the late 1960s and early 1980s, he has this striking passage about Thatcher herself:

> If, instead of simply berating Bank officials, she had listened to their advice, she might have learned that it is not possible to control the broad money supply in the UK and, even if it were, that there is no robust relationship between £M3 and real economic objectives such as price stability and growth. If she and her Treasury team had listened to the Bank in 1979, the British economy might not have shrunk by nearly 6 per cent.

Given that judgement, blessed of course with the benefit of hindsight, it is particularly instructive to look at the memo that McMahon sent to Richardson on 18 September – ten days after the great blow-up, and immediately following another difficult meeting at No. 10 – on 'The Bank's Position on Monetary Policy'. He began by considering the suggestion from Goodhart and Dow that the Bank 'should make some form of apologia to the Prime Minister on monetary policy':

> There is a case for exculpating ourselves from unfair accusations that have been made. Thus we could refer to our record of scepticism and concern about the effects of the corset; the fact that the rollovers and the so-called 'interest rate policy' were a firm Government decision; the difficulties the banks have in reducing rates quickly; the difference between experience here and in the US, etc. My feeling in the light of this morning's meeting, however, is that it might be better not to spend time defending ourselves. The danger is that, to hostile or sceptical eyes, such arguments will indeed look defensive.

Instead, argued McMahon, it was better for the Bank to look ahead constructively to the future and to try to *help* Thatcher: 'I read her as seeing quite correctly what a real (quite apart from presentational) jam we are all in and very much wanting to be shown a possible way towards the shore.' But how? McMahon noted that, at the meeting, she had said, in response to Richardson's explicit question, 'that she would like to have the exchange rate lower than it is so long as (a) it was consonant with the continuance of the existing monetary policy and (b) it did not involve a plunge'; and, added McMahon (no doubt entirely accurately), 'she did not join Lawson's strong rebuttal of the idea of joining the EMS'. That, however, would not be enough in itself: there was also an urgent need for lower interest rates. And here McMahon contended that the Bank's policy should be one of encouraging a reduction in the PSBR in order to achieve those lower interest rates – in other words, through public expenditure cuts rather than monetary policy. There may or may not have been a causal link, but in effect that was what would happen. During the autumn the MTFS turned in practice increasingly into something more like a fiscal than a financial strategy; monetarist dogma from the West End started to be toned down, as policy became looser; and Howe's famous/infamous March 1981 budget savaged the PSBR. McMahon himself was enough of a Keynesian to be having by that time serious misgivings – 'I believe that history will view fiscal tightening now as very misguided indeed,' he predicted in February – but the essence of the government's approach was very much in line with his solution the previous autumn.[8]

Over the next year and a half, there remained in Threadneedle Street only patchy sympathy with the general thrust of the government's economic approach. In May 1981, at the first meeting of the deliberately policy-oriented Deputy Governor's Committee (DGC), McMahon speculated rather wistfully that 'if there was still no sign of recovery by the autumn, the Government might be more susceptible to suggestions for stimulating action provided they could be presented in a way which did not seem too grossly in conflict with the broad strategy'; later that summer, he and Dow were in favour of pursuing what Dow termed 'An alternative policy', essentially reflation through reducing indirect taxes rather than expanding public investment, though with McMahon going somewhat further in wanting to introduce 'a 12-months freeze' (or what he wryly called 'the final heresy'); and in mid-September, Dow was stating frankly that 'the Government's central economic strategy is in some disarray', adding that 'by mid-October Government policy will probably be seen to be in a critical state'. The chances are that Richardson distanced himself somewhat from these viewpoints, and it is perhaps telling that the chancellor would specifically pay tribute to the governor for his contribution during that autumn's 'heavy weather' as sterling continued to plummet from its dizzying 1979–80 heights. 'Gordon

Richardson's advice was always measured,' recalled Howe, 'tempered by long, front-line experience of the need to act more rather than less decisively, above all sooner rather than later in face of unmistakable signals from the exchange markets.' By the following summer, most dispassionate observers reckoned that the economy was at last starting to recover, but McMahon at a DGC in July 1982 declared that it was 'increasingly clear that the UK was on a bad track', before asking: 'What sort of forecast would we want before we would advocate remedial action?' At which point, neither of the Bank's two rising men were willing to back him. It was, thought Eddie George, 'difficult to say', but he 'certainly did not think that the present forecast was sufficient'; while David Walker 'cautioned the meeting against premature urgings for fiscal reflation'. Nor was there much joy for grumbling industrialists when they came later that month to see Richardson. The CBI's Sir Campbell Fraser and Sir Terence Beckett arrived 'in sombre mood', a mood that must have darkened after they had listed their complaints about what was still historically a high MLR: 'The Governor remarked that industry's focus on interest rates was in reality a reflection of the weakness of profits. The truth of the matter, he said, was that the profitability of industry was lamentable and that improvement must come from within companies. Reductions in interest rates were not the way to sustained gains in profitability.'[9]

Over this same year and a half or so, monetary policy continued to become less rigid. Thatcher's favoured monetary base control was by the start already in effect off the table, though August 1981 saw a change to the Bank's operating techniques in the money market – changes scathingly described by Goodhart retrospectively as 'a kind of consolation prize for MBC monetarists (for not getting MBC)', in which 'the authorities agreed that operations could become somewhat more market-oriented with less reliance on discount-window lending'. Or as he explained further:

> The authorities would still set interest rates (with a view to hitting their monetary target), but would, it was suggested, disguise what their interest-rate objective was (the unpublished band), and pretend that it was all the market's doing. Frankly this was confused and silly. In practice it had little effect, apart from being a pretext for the Bank to introduce some reform and widening of British bill

markets, which it wanted to do anyhow for its own purposes. The unpublished bands, etc., never transpired; the authorities went on announcing administered changes in minimum lending rate, and the monetarist overtones in the supposed 'new methods' rapidly became a dead letter and forgotten.

MLR was soon abandoned and replaced by the Bank of England repurchase rate. As for the MTFS itself, it was by spring 1982 palpably losing coherence, diluted by an array of rival monetary aggregates: narrow (M1), broad (£M3), broader (PSL2). Indeed, even before then, in December 1981, a piquant conversation took place between Richardson and Wass. 'He was good enough to say,' recorded the governor for his deputy's eyes only, 'that it was now clear that the reservations that I had expressed two years ago about the MTFS were being shown to have been right.' And increasingly, by that time, the Bank was pushing hard – and even optimistically – for entry to the EMS. 'I believe the tide is now beginning to run in favour,' observed McMahon as early as August 1981, citing the 'growing disenchantment' on the part of Lawson (by now very pro-EMS) and 'to some extent' Howe with 'the existing framework of monetary targets'. Nor in this case was McMahon an outlier within the Bank. 'An exchange rate standard has once again come to seem attractive as a possible alternative anchor for domestic policy,' noted Dow at about the same time. 'This is felt as strongly and explicitly by those on the monetary side – John Fforde and Charles Goodhart – as by those more detached like myself.' The crunch came in January 1982, amid some sudden nervousness. 'There is still very great resistance to joining EMS, especially from the Prime Minister,' conceded McMahon on the 18th. Moreover, 'we should I think have to agree that the present is not a particularly opportune time to join: at around 4.30 the £/DM rate looks too strong', though he was still hopeful of 'finally (?some time in the spring) taking the plunge'. Four days later, on the 22nd, Thatcher chaired a meeting with ministers. Howe was opposed, not least because of a concern that the whole European idea might be soured in British eyes if the EMS appeared to cause high British interest rates; and Thatcher agreed, though for a very different reason, with her dominant anxiety instead being loss of 'freedom to manoeuvre'. Accordingly, to the disappointment of the Bank (including

Richardson), the non-decision was taken to continue to wait until the time was 'ripe'.[10] Rather like Thatcher's premiership itself, this one would run and run.

The early 1980s were an exceptionally troubled time for British industry, which for the Bank meant not just intense debates about high policy but also a notably active role for its Industrial Finance Division under the restlessly energetic David Walker.[11] 'In the past four years,' he recorded in early 1984, 'the Bank has been concerned with more than 150 mainly listed companies, some 50 very closely, where lending bankers were reluctant to increase facilities and, in some cases, disposed to withdraw those already in place.' A flavour comes through in a catch-up note that McMahon sent to the returning Richardson in November 1981. 'We have leapt from crisis to crisis on this,' he wrote about the drama surrounding Sir Freddie Laker and his airline. 'As I have always half expected, the Prime Minister, after taking a ruthless line in the abstract, did a volte face when it suddenly looked as if he was going to have to go. However heroic work by D.A.W. has probably managed to see him through the immediate crisis without any significant Government contribution. The underlying situation of course remains grave.' So it did, with the company conclusively collapsing in early 1982, and inevitably there were mixed fortunes overall. 'Good progress had been made over the last two months towards establishing satisfactory financing arrangements in three important cases,' Richardson told the clearers that summer, 'although others were in worse shape'; and he added that 'the Bank was now continuously involved in an array of smaller cases, the problems of many of which were likely to persist for a long time'. Successes in these years included Turner & Newall, John Brown and Weir Group, while failures included the textile machinery group Stone-Platt Industries as well as Laker. Throughout, the Bank's principles of action remained largely consistent: banging together the heads of the troubled company's creditor banks and sometimes institutional shareholders; if necessary, bringing in new management to the company; and making it clear there would be no government or Bank bail-out. Looking further ahead, the Bank had become increasingly convinced that industry would be on a much sounder footing if it had an improved corporate governance model, resulting in the launch in early 1982 under Bank auspices of Pro Ned (Promotion of Non-Executive Directors). Its brief was to promote the wider use of non-executive directors, and under the leadership of Jonathan Charkham, a skilled networker recruited from the Civil Service, it made significant progress. 'What matters in business is the strength of direction and management,' Walker crisply informed an audience of West Midlands industrialists two years after Pro Ned began. 'This transcends every other consideration ...' But as he was also at pains to emphasise, the non-executive director was in himself (very occasionally herself) 'neither magician nor panacea'.[12]

One episode in the early 1980s was well out of the normal run of Bank activities. This involved a key role in the US/Iran hostage deal of January 1981, by which the release of fifty-two captured US personnel in Iran was secured against some $8 billion in cash, gold and securities. The Foreign Office naturally welcomed the Bank's participation in helping to execute the complex plan, unlike the financial secretary. 'How much profit,' Lawson aggressively asked McMahon, 'are you going to make on this deal?' Shortly afterwards, McMahon himself, accompanied by the chief cashier David Somerset, flew to Algiers, where the Algerian government was acting as an intermediary between the two countries; and over a very long weekend of difficult negotiations, they waited to release the Americans' money when the moment was judged safe. 'There were in practice,' recalled McMahon, 'many problems to solve':

> The size of the operation was daunting, involving as it did (even if only for a short time) a trebling of our balance sheet. Our main aim was to minimise the various risks to which the Bank would be exposed. One important aim was to see that the period during which the funds were with us was as short as possible. Another was to reduce as far as possible our own discretion. To the extent that any scope existed for us to exercise judgement as to whether or when or how any particular payment was made, we could be vulnerable to criticism or legal action if anything went wrong. In addition, even if we had fully secured ourselves legally there were the commercial risks inevitably involved with such large sums and what one might call the political risks: e.g., if something had

happened to the hostages while in flight at about the time we were making the payment to Iran that we were legally required to do, we could suffer great criticism ...

Back in London, meanwhile, the linchpin figure was Derrick Byatt, chief manager of the Foreign Exchange Division and providing the technical expertise to enable the Bank to be escrow agent for the transaction. 'During the final crucial days of the operation,' his obituary would record, 'he was in the office day and night, sleeping when he could on a camp bed in the conference room adjacent to his office.' Undeniably the whole episode was a feather in the Bank's cap – and perhaps much needed, at a time when it was feeling distinctly unloved.[13]

The real international challenge during Richardson's governorship still awaited. 'Almost certainly the most dangerous financial occasion of the second half of the twentieth century,' would be Charles Goodhart's verdict on the LDC (less developed countries) debt crisis that broke out in the second half of 1982, as first Mexico and then Argentina and Brazil were unable to refinance their borrowing. 'If the loans to these countries had been marked to market, some, perhaps a majority, of the major money-centre international banks in the world, and especially those in New York, would have been (technically) insolvent, and the world's financial system would have faced a major crisis.' Not least because he was able to mediate between two powerful but personally incompatible central bankers – Paul Volcker of the Fed and Karl Otto Pöhl of the Bundesbank – it was a situation that brought out the best from Richardson's formidable armoury.

A handful of gubernatorial moments stand out from an immensely complicated narrative. In early September, at the IMF's annual meeting held that year in Toronto a few days after the leading central banks had arranged through the BIS a $1.85 billion bridging loan for Mexico, Richardson was very much one of the 'Big Four' – along with Volcker, the Swiss National Bank's Leutwiler and the IMF's Jacques de Larosière – in not only keeping Mexico (and thus the New York clearing system) going, but starting to apply moral pressure on the commercial banks to limit repayment demands; a day or two later, back in London, Richardson told Volcker on the phone that he was 'haunted with the fear that nothing would happen unless someone was prepared to take a very positive lead' and that 'the time might come when they would both have to take the initiative with the banks'; later in September, as the Argentine situation rapidly deteriorated but the British government felt it impossible so soon after the Falklands War to adopt a constructive position, it was Richardson who paved the way to the UK and Argentina unfreezing each other's assets, thereby making it possible to start dealing with the Argentine debt problem; by October, a dialogue was in train between the governor and the British clearing banks – some of which (above all Lloyds) were horribly over-extended in Latin America – to discuss their provisioning; late that month, a dinner at Richardson's St Anselm's Place home saw Volcker, Leutwiler and the host working out how to co-ordinate Volcker's debt plan, including the vital question of how to bring onside the commercial banks without the central banks themselves providing long-term (as opposed to bridging) loans to the debtors; and on 22 November, this time in the governor's flat at New Change, Richardson gave another dinner, where he, de Larosière, Leutwiler and the Bank's overseas director, Anthony Loehnis, sat down with six leading commercial bankers from around the world, including Morse of Lloyds, and successfully explained that there was no alternative to a cohesive approach from what was in effect the creditors' cartel. Much else still lay ahead – including the formation of co-ordination groups of the principal lenders and eventually the invention of 'the Matrix', an indispensable device in getting the banks not to pull the plug unnecessarily through believing they were going to be at a competitive disadvantage if they did not – but it was starting to become clear that there would be no total meltdown. 'I would just marvel over Richardson's patience and the deliberate care in getting the Europeans on board,' recalled Volcker a decade later. 'My style is to walk into a room and say, "Here's the problem and here are some solutions," and expect everyone to get on board in two minutes. He understood it took two hours of explanation over dinner to get them on board.'[14]

By this time, towards the end of 1982, the international debt crisis so preoccupied Richardson that, although sixty-seven, he hoped to continue to serve as governor for a year or two beyond the end of his second term in June 1983. Given, however, that the final decision rested with Thatcher, that was never a realistic possibility. Nor was it realistic, in terms of the succession, that his deputy, McMahon, would get the job, with Thatcher telling a confidant (according to her biographer, Charles Moore) that 'he'll never be Governor of the Bank of England while I'm Prime Minister'. Or as Dow put it on behalf of the other end of the mutual dislike, 'Kit was too transparently a good and honest liberal, not disposed to like her, nor her ways.' What, for the second time round, about Morse? Howe pushed hard for his school contemporary, calling him 'my brilliant fellow Wykehamist', but to no avail. 'He is clever, anxious to appear so, and never surely a lady's man,' was how Dow interpreted the prime minister's veto, while for all Morse's intellect and international experience it did not help that he had a temperament seldom hot for certainties. The obvious merchant banker candidate was David Scholey – on the Court, one of the City's stars, and by now running Warburgs; but there seems to have been a feeling in the Treasury that he was perhaps a little young and might instead be just the man after the next governor had served a single term.

Who would that be? The announcement, taking almost everyone by surprise, came two days before Christmas: the NatWest's Robin Leigh-Pemberton. In his mid-fifties, 'he seemed too much a gentleman, too little a professional', as Dow reflected, before going on:

> His record would be unlikely even as a caricature of a well-off, traditional conservative: Eton, then Classics at Trinity College, Oxford, after which the Grenadier Guards and the bar; a gentleman farmer with a couple of thousand acres of family land near Sittingbourne in Kent, member of the County Council in the Conservative interest ('but that was a long time ago'), now Lord Lieutenant of the county; Brooks and the Cavalry Guards Club; chairman of a lawnmower firm called Birmid Qualcast, and on sundry government committees; and successively regional, then national, director; then (since 1977 – also a surprise appointment) chairman of the National Westminster.

External reaction was largely negative. 'A cause for concern,' observed the *Financial Times*, while the *Economist* did not try to deny either that he was 'ill-equipped for the job' or that the appointment was 'provocatively political'. Why had Thatcher chosen him? The obvious explanation was that, after the largely unhappy government/Bank relationship of the previous few years, he was someone whom she felt could be relied upon to do her bidding; Christopher Fildes would later surmise that she wanted someone at the Bank who would 'stand up for the right' even if the next general election 'went wrong'; while Dow nearer to the time offered a double theory:

> In the first place, he got on with her. In her feminine way, this seems a *sine qua non*. The qualities that enabled him to get on with her were that he was a conservative, in an entirely natural, robust, and unenlightened way; that he was masculine; and that he charmed her. In the second place, he came from the world of the ordinary banks. The appointment was unconventional in this: he was the first clearer ever to get the post ... She thinks not in niceties, but of the end result – whether the clearers' base rates go up or down. She hankers after a direct lien on them. Why not have someone from that world, who might have some authority over it – and listen to you?

Whatever her motivation, Leigh-Pemberton hardly helped himself with his early public pronouncements after the news had broken. Inflation was 'vastly more dangerous to democracy than Communism'; in relation to the international debt situation, 'If ever there was a crisis it is now over'; and 'Are they ever necessary, these 2 a.m. crisis meetings?' Unsurprisingly, the mood in the Bank was at best cautious, and within months McMahon had revamped the Deputy Governor's Committee, describing the change as 'an initiative by top management of the Bank to take decisions or make recommendations without involving him [the next governor] in a lot of detailed discussion'.[15]

Yet while Richardson was still governor there remained one important area of unfinished business: the square mile itself, where during the early 1980s, as in the 1970s, the signs were mixed about the reality of the Bank's once taken-for-granted authority. Specifically, there occurred in 1981 two episodes throwing serious doubt on that authority. The first was Richardson's failure, despite his best efforts, to dissuade Howe from including in his March budget a one-off levy on the clearing banks, amounting to some £400 million. The very next day, meeting the clearers, he 'expressed regret that his efforts had not been more successful', at which point Morse 'intervened to say that the Chairmen were indeed conscious of the Governor's efforts in this regard, and were grateful for them' – a gracious exchange, but twelve years later it would be a revealing moment when, at a Bank/Treasury meeting, the latter's Rachel Lomax 'recalled that when the wind-fall profits tax was imposed on the banks, Nigel Lawson had been concerned that it would diminish the effectiveness of the Governor's eyebrows'.

The other 1981 episode also involved the question of suasion. This was the question of the ownership of the Royal Bank of Scotland (RBS), with Richardson happy by the spring to see it being taken over by Standard Chartered but deeply disturbed by the arrival on the scene of an unwelcome counter-bidder, the Hongkong and Shanghai Banking Corporation (HSBC). Crucially, meetings between Richardson and HSBC's Michael Sandberg, at which the governor's eyebrows were raised to their fullest height, only entrenched the counter-bidder's determination. The Bank's negative attitude had a rational basis – including concerns that if HSBC (still based in Hong Kong) took over RBS, then the Bank might find itself in a position of 'responsibility without power' in terms of supervision-cum-lender-of-last-resort – but poor personal chemistry between two strong-minded men accustomed to getting their own way also played a part. In the event, both bids for RBS were referred to the Monopolies and Mergers Commission (MMC); and during the summer, Richardson was disconcerted to discover not only that the British clearers intended to stay neutral in the matter (Morse explaining to him that 'the fundamental reason common to all four banks was that they would have to live with HSBC in the future'), but that neither the Treasury nor the City gave encouragement when he tried to push the idea of legislative powers to strengthen the Bank's control over the ownership of British financial institutions. Towards the end of the year, with the MMC's decision imminent, the Bank was coming under significant press criticism, including what McMahon called 'a lot of obviously deliberately leaked stuff that we were being protectionist and stuffy', as well as the *Sunday Telegraph* 'raising the whole question of a potential resignation issue [for Richardson] and also suggesting that the Prime Minister would not be displeased to see us discomfited'. In the *Spectator*, Fildes saw the stakes as undeniably high: 'If the Bank of England loses this battle, its authority will never be the same again. On that authority, much hangs. It is felt throughout the City of London – in the banks and beyond them. It lies behind the whole of the City's system of self-regulation.' Finally, in January 1982, the MMC pronounced that neither bid should proceed, and the government agreed. RBS lived to fight another day, while for Richardson it was perhaps a score-draw: neither the outcome he had originally wanted nor the one he had argued so strongly against. It remained for Sandberg to pay a final visit before flying back to Hong Kong. 'He straight away declared his purpose to be "to doff his hat",' recorded McMahon; and at the end of a 'relatively easy conversation', during which the visitor explained that his bank still hoped to get into UK deposit banking, 'the Governor said that if at any time he had any proposals or ideas he, the Governor, would be glad to hear them and talk them over ...'[16]

Other aspects of the Bank/City relationship in the early 1980s revealed a stronger Bank, not least when in 1981 it determined that it would no longer be solely the prerogative of members of the Accepting Houses Committee – which is to say the leading merchant banks – to have their bills rediscounted by the Bank at its 'finest rate'. 'Here, as in some other areas,' Richardson explained to the clearers, 'the Bank felt a tension between its desire to support the interests of British banks and the need to maintain London as an attractive international centre.' The complaints were predictable, including from Barings, but apart from high-street deposit banking it was starting to become increasingly clear in which direction that tension would be resolved. The importance of London's standing as an international financial centre also played its part in the Bank's initially cautious but ultimately firm support for the start of a financial futures exchange, with Richardson doing the formal honours when LIFFE (London International Financial Futures And Options Exchange) opened for business in the Royal Exchange (moribund for most of the century) in September 1982. There was also the thorny matter of Lloyd's insurance market – traditionally not an area of Bank surveillance let alone interference, but by this time deeply scandal-ridden. Increasingly the feeling at the Bank was that Lloyd's was badly under-managed, needing more independent input; and shortly before Christmas 1982, Richardson asked an outsider, the management consultant Ian Hay Davison, to go there as its first chief executive, having influenced Lloyd's in offering him the job in the first place. With some reluctance, Davison eventually agreed – 'Above all I admired Gordon Richardson and he asked me: I would not have accepted for anyone else' – and that marked the start of the clean-up of one of the City's defining historic institutions.[17]

By this time, however, the Bank's central City preoccupation was on more familiar terrain: the Stock Exchange. This was a story going back to the late 1970s and the decision by the Labour government to refer the Exchange's rule book to the Restrictive Practices Court. The hope was that the change of government in May 1979 would make a difference; but when Richardson two months later emphasised to Wass 'the disadvantages of the Restrictive Practices Court and in particular the time it would take to reach a conclusion and the high costs involved for the Stock Exchange', the deflating response was that the new trade secretary, John Nott, was being 'very rigid on this'. So it proved, and over the next few years the Stock Exchange found itself almost completely hobbled by having the well-intentioned but inappropriate Office of Fair Trading (OFT) on its back, with the eventual court case not expected to be heard before 1983 at the earliest – and with the Stock Exchange expected to lose. By 1981 the Bank was starting to think hard about that institution's future, with McMahon canvassing internally in May the abolition of not just single capacity (that is, member firms having to be brokers *or* jobbers) but also minimum commission, on the grounds that 'the services provided by the broking community – research, analysis, etc – might be improved by the concentration that would undoubtedly occur'. Then during 1982 it stepped up a gear, particularly under the influence of David Walker, newly made an executive director. That summer he sent a key paper to the Treasury, arguing for abandonment of the reference and an urgent inquiry (independent of the OFT) into the single-capacity question and if possible the fixed-commission structure also:

> World securities trading is changing very fast, with a particularly strong push into new areas by American houses such as Merrill Lynch and Salomon Brothers, and if the London market is to avoid relegation to the second or third division in the world league, with eroded invisibles earnings, the Stock Exchange in London needs to be flexible and responsive to the new challenge. The pace is brisk and time is short: very large change is likely on the world securities scene over the three years now in prospect before the Restrictive Practices Court rules. The risk is that, by then, the Stock Exchange will have lost ground to some extent irretrievably.

Additionally, in the context of the Stock Exchange Council having reluctantly raised to 29.9 per cent the maximum external stake in a member firm, Walker highlighted the weak capitalisation of many of those firms. 'It is unlikely that many outsiders, including potentially merchant banks and life assurance companies as well as other foreign houses,' he wrote, 'are likely to commit sizeable amounts to invest in the securities market while the present planning blight persists.' In short, and crucial to London's future as an international financial centre in the new era of borderless capital flows, the Stock Exchange somehow had to be rescued from its insular, debilitating imbroglio.

No independent, non-OFT inquiry took place, but during the winter of 1982–3 the Bank worked hard on the issue. In particular, a clutch of papers by Andrew Threadgold (of the Economics Division) and John Footman (of the Industrial Finance Division) examined the Exchange in fine-grained detail. Their work culminated in February 1983 in the Bank's green paper on 'The Future of the Stock Exchange', produced under the auspices of Walker and Douglas Dawkins. It contained serious warnings about the possible consequences of 'wholesale deregulation', defined as 'the removal of all of the restrictions governing market entry, minimum commission and single capacity'. Such consequences might include the market becoming 'less liquid and prices more volatile' as the result of a diminished role for market-making; 'less unified trading' following the abolition of single capacity (because going off the market floor meant trading was less centralised); and, if market entry was loosened, 'failures and defaults would be likely to increase'. Even so, the green paper still advocated the desirability of an alternative structure to the status quo, one that involved significant deregulation; and commending the paper to Eddie George (another recently appointed executive director), Walker made optimistic noises: 'Getting the Stock Exchange into what I think the Americans call a more dynamic mode will be of great importance. I am confident that it can be done.' Nevertheless, huge uncertainty still existed, not least in relation to what was generally after the abolition of exchange controls a rapidly changing business environment. 'I am trying to find more published material on what outside firms would like to do given a relaxation of the Stock Exchange rules,' Footman informed Walker later that month. 'So far I have seen none. One way of getting a better feel of this is to talk privately to senior officials in the major merchant banks, and possibly to the major US securities firms in London through whom we have, through Gold and Foreign Exchange, fairly close contact. But even so, we will have to rely an awful lot on guesswork.' Moreover, of course, there was still the whole hanging question of the court case. Helpfully, Richardson himself was by now fully engaged and starting a series of constructive conversations with the trade secretary (Lord Cockfield) and to a lesser extent Howe; so that by the time of the general election on 9 June 1983, he and Walker had (according to Dow) 'just about persuaded' them that 'the case should be withdrawn from the Court in return for an undertaking by the Stock Exchange to reform'.[18]

Exactly three weeks after Thatcher's landslide triumph was Richardson's final day in office. It concluded with a dinner in the Court Room for directors and wives, at the end of which there entered 'beneath an enormous busby a vast piper' who, recorded Dow, 'marched slowly round the table, solemnly piping, and slowly back, and slowly round again, finally saluting before the Governor, whom he dwarfed'. That was a relaxed occasion, unlike some other formal meals during his governorship. In 1981, a week after becoming a Treasury minister, Jock Bruce-Gardyne had been 'bidden to luncheon':

> On arrival I was ushered up to Kit McMahon who, after a brief exchange about the weather, took me on to the Governor's sanctum. Once again, a brief word of welcome, and then in we passed to a substantial dining-room. Gathered there were about 16 assorted Bank top brass awaiting our arrival. In silence. A glass of sherry was proffered, and then the Governor took me round the circle of introductions. No one else spoke. We sat down, myself on the Governor's right hand, Lord Croham on his left, Kit McMahon opposite. Apart from these three, and a rare intervention from the head of the Bank's market operations, Eddie George, no one round the table used his mouth for any other purpose than to swallow food throughout the entire meal. One and all stared, as if mesmerised, at my host. I emerged to my waiting car sweating.

In the tradition of Norman, Cobbold and Cromer, if not perhaps Catto or O'Brien, Richardson was the last of the governors to be

treated – and, in his case, sometimes to demand to be treated – as akin
to an Eastern potentate. But during ten of the most challenging years
in the Bank's history, he had in many ways proved himself as one of
the great governors. Perhaps he was vain, perhaps he was arrogant;
undeniably he could take an eternity deciding what to do, resulting
in what one aide called 'paralysis by analysis'; but he had a fine mind,
a deep devotion to duty and an infinite capacity for taking trouble.
Neither the secondary banking crisis of the mid-1970s nor the international debt crisis of the early 1980s would have been resolved nearly
so successfully without those qualities. A final word – to return to
matters of the table – goes to the member of the governor's office
who wrote in March 1981 to Mr Mounce, BE Services Limited, about
'Menus for Court Room Functions':

1 The Governor does not approve of Smoked Salmon for a large
   number of people because of its terrible price nowadays.
2 He feels strongly that the foods which are actually in season
   at the time should be served – e.g. Pheasant is certainly *not* in
   season at the end of April. You cannot go wrong with Asparagus,
   Strawberries and especially Raspberries when they are in season
   over here – but only then.
3 This applies strongly to New Potatoes – but the Governor insists
   that these should be the very small ones. In fact he likes vege-
   tables to be light and simple. He particularly dislikes Broccoli
   and also Courgettes.[19]

'The present Governor is commendably prompt in the despatch
of business,' McMahon in March 1984 told fellow-members of the
Deputy Governor's Committee. So he was, in marked contrast to his
predecessor, but the statement begged the question of precisely what
business passed across Robin Leigh-Pemberton's desk, especially
given the rationale of the remodelled DGC itself. In this potentially
invidious situation, as he gradually grew into a position that had
come to him so unexpectedly, it helped greatly that the new governor brought to bear some impressive human qualities. 'He was a
man of great charm and decency,' Forrest Capie has written. 'He had

complete integrity and was generally relaxed and at ease in what he did. He proved to be much shrewder than many would have thought on his appointment. He could also be strong when required. He knew his limitations but also would not only listen to advice but happily delegate where needed. He did not try to substitute his judgement for others on technical monetary matters. He inspired people to give of their best ...' A trio of brief snapshots from senior Bank people who worked for him help to flesh out the picture:

A lovely man ... the ultimate non-executive chairman. *(Michael Foot)*

Gave people their head, he trusted them and he backed them, and if they asked him to do something to help achieve a goal he would do it very patiently. *(Pen Kent)*

He always stood with his troops. He never cut himself loose ... *(Roger Barnes)*

'I have enjoyed pretty well everything I've done – life is interesting if you take enough trouble to find out the details, the problems, the purposes of whatever it is you're concerned with, it nearly always emerges as interesting, and therefore invokes an enthusiastic reaction,' Leigh-Pemberton himself had told the *Old Lady* shortly before taking office. 'And I find it easy to get on with people and therefore to respond to them – whatever their role.' He certainly did not come out of central casting as the modern technocratic central banker – and Dow soon after his arrival sighed that 'conversation at lunch is less amusing; the other day the new Governor and Charles Goodhart discussed sheep' – but at the top of any institution there is much to be said for the human touch.[20]

What about relations across town? Leigh-Pemberton was so much a political appointment that in July 1983 Bruce-Gardyne (no longer a minister) confidently predicted the governor having 'less tense' times at No 10, but warned that 'relations with the new Chancellor could prove more demanding'. He knew his man. 'Nigel Lawson is an unusual Chancellor,' he wrote a few years later. 'Ever since his years in Fleet Street – as a "Lex" columnist on the *Financial Times*, and subsequently as City Editor of the *Sunday Telegraph* – his admiration for the City and its ways has stopped well this side of idolatry. A politician of exceptional determination, he would have been a cross for any Governor to bear.' In their important 1998 survey, *The Politics of Central Banks*, Robert Elgie and Helen Thompson put it well:

> Apparently unbruised by the failure of the MTFS, Lawson brought to the job an overriding confidence in his own judgement not only about the big strategic issues but the day-to-day operation of policy. In the ensuing years he never waited for the Bank to take the initiative about monetary policy nor bowed to the Bank's technical advice about the exact timing of interest rate changes and government bond issues. On occasions Lawson would even, against all previous protocol, telephone directly the Bank's foreign exchange market operators to give instructions. In all senses, Lawson believed he could decide for himself. As he told the House of Commons Treasury and Civil Service Select Committee, 'we take the decisions but they do the work'.

Thatcher for her part kept a beady, suspicious eye on the Bank – in May 1984 the governor was rung by Lawson to tell him that she was 'strongly opposed' to the raising of fees for non-executive directors – but it was Great George Street that really made life difficult. 'Of course relationships have always been up and down,' reflected McMahon in December 1985. 'But what worries me about the present situation is the amount of evidence we keep getting from friendly journalists of really savage attacks from Treasury officials ...' Not long afterwards, in May 1986, came a serious blow-up, indicative of a mutual lack of trust, following a newspaper article in the context of a major City row about Lawson's proposed charge on the conversion of ADR (American depository receipt) shares to native stock:

> The Governor made it clear that he could not acquiesce in stories of this kind. It was quite unacceptable for the Bank, or for him personally, to be said to be giving wrong and inaccurate advice to the Treasury when this had not been the case ...
>
> The Chancellor said that, far from advising against the 5% rate, David Walker had said that it would be acceptable to the City. The Governor said that this was simply not so, and that the Bank had never agreed that any rate in excess of 3% could be argued for. The

Chancellor said that he distinctly recalled David Walker's having said this at a meeting at which other officials were present, and the officials' memories tallied with his own. He said that if the Bank had not advised him to impose a 5% rate he would not have done so. The Governor made it clear that all the information in his possession suggested that the Bank had not given any such advice to the Chancellor, and at the very most had been forced by circumstances into acquiescing in a rate of 5%.

Almost certainly the early years were the worst in the Lawson/Leigh-Pemberton relationship, with the latter recalling many years later that the politician had been 'initially fairly domineering and so on, but gradually we became quite close, genuine friends'.[21] Even so, those early years left their mark in Threadneedle Street: to be remembered for long afterwards as a low point in the operational autonomy of the nationalised Bank.

Lawson himself played a significant part in the forging of the July 1983 settlement between the government and Stock Exchange – the former getting the court case dropped, the latter promising to reform – that ultimately led to the City's 'Big Bang' a little over three years later. The Bank, which of course had done much to prepare the way, naturally welcomed the deal; and over those three years it equally naturally continued to mediate between government and the Exchange. Within weeks, in September 1983, the governor was reporting to Cecil Parkinson (the trade secretary who had reached the deal with the Stock Exchange's Sir Nicholas Goodison) 'an atmosphere of growing uncertainty and nervousness' in the market about 'the future structure of the securities industry', accompanied by an increasing desire 'for abolition of all minimum commissions in one full swoop, at a date to be announced well in advance'; while next day, amid a growing sense that it was not only minimum commissions that were a dead duck but also single capacity, John Fforde reflected on the broader approach that the Bank should take to the future of the securities industry. It would be wrong, he argued, to give 'the impression that officialdom has the power to *choose*, and to *decide*, and to *implement*, some particular middle-course outcome to a structural revolution'. Instead: 'It would be better to emphasise that a *revolution* rather than an *evolution* is now in prospect; and that officialdom can best help by responding correctly to what happens and consolidating the regulatory apparatus etc when things look like settling down.' By this time, the term 'Big Bang' (coined in this respect by the Bank's Douglas Dawkins) was poised to enter the City vocabulary; and at a meeting in early October, Lawson and Parkinson agreed with Leigh-Pemberton and Walker that 'the "big bang" might in practice make more sense than a phased programme of abolition'. So it would be, with in due course all roads leading to 27 October 1986. 'He found himself open-mouthed at the pace of change he saw going on in London,' recorded McMahon in December 1984 after a conversation with Volcker; and it was indeed a high-speed City revolution – one that in many ways the Bank had spearheaded.

Arguably its most crucial aspect was ownership, the subject of keen debate in the Bank during the months immediately after the Parkinson/Goodison agreement, given that it was already clear that 100 per cent outside ownership of Stock Exchange firms was almost inevitable. 'It is plainly undesirable that the entry of foreign firms to the London market should swamp the UK securities industry, either by taking it over wholesale or by dictating the terms on which business can be done,' argued John Footman as early as August 1983. 'Yet the UK industry looks on the face of it peculiarly vulnerable to both possibilities ...' That was undeniably true, and in mid-September he set out what he saw as the imminent reality:

> A rather stark choice may have to be made between, on the one hand, seeing the Stock Exchange lose market share and dominance, and on the other seeing large parts of it fall into non-member, probably foreign, hands. The balance of disadvantage will be difficult to assess. The preliminary conclusions of this paper [on 'Ownership of the UK Securities Industry'] are that the consequences of a significant foreign investment in the Stock Exchange are by no means as unacceptable as is commonly supposed ...

A colleague, Leslie Lloyd, disagreed. 'You see no reason to suppose that foreign firms could not be relied on to exercise efficient self-regulation,' he responded to Footman. 'I do not find this convincing.' And he went on, specifically in relation to American firms: 'I do not think we can expect them to adapt either to collective self-regulation or to watching people's eyebrows in the way most UK establishments are used to. The consequence of greater foreign involvement would probably tend to be a shift towards greater statutory regulation.' Lloyd raised other objections, including the possible conflict of interest between the UK government and the Bank on the one hand and the parent bank on the other, before concluding:

> While in present circumstances one may confidently expect foreigners to play the game, we are talking about a blue-print for a long-term scheme ...
>
> While not noticeably xenophobic I tend to see a case for favouring courses of action which, while welcoming foreign participation, preserve indigenous control for an indigenous core of the UK securities industry.

A few days earlier, Walker and Dawkins had received a visit from Christopher Reeves of Morgan Grenfell, with that British merchant bank already in discussions with several Stock Exchange firms and now wanting to discover whether the Bank foresaw any 'impediments'. In reply, Walker pointed to how full external ownership 'would of course open the Exchange to Morgan Stanley as well as Morgan Grenfell, and while instinctively we would prefer to see the UK houses providing the capital for and having ownership of securities trading in this country, the logical case for protection was not wholly compelling, and in practical terms explicit protection was probably not acceptable in any event'. The rest of Walker's message to Reeves struck a delicate balancing act. No, 'possible UK entrants could not expect preferred treatment', given 'the evident need to reverse the decline in UK securities trading capability', which 'in practice meant greater competitiveness'; but yes, in the sense that 'within this general concern we wished to be as helpful as we could to UK firms or groupings'.[22] In the event, over the next couple of years or so as the marriage market for Stock Exchange firms went its merry way, there was no bar to foreign ownership; but in relation to the ownership of British banks, a larger – and longer – debate still awaited.

For Eddie George, the executive director responsible for the Bank's gilt and money market operations, the paramount worry by the autumn of 1983 was that the process of deregulating the Stock Exchange might, in his own graphic words, 'bugger up the gilts market'. Accordingly, he set about designing a comprehensive restructuring of that market in order to make it ready and fit for purpose in the coming post-Big Bang world. A report by the Fed's Peter Sternlight, following a series of conversations in London in October 1984, accurately caught the mood as preparations began to be made. At the Bank, Bill Allen acknowledged that 'they face great uncertainty in seeking to launch a rather fully developed system sometime in 1986 rather than see a system evolve more gradually and modify their approach as that process takes place'; also at the Bank, Peter Cooke expressed 'some concerns about the rapid pace of new developments as he sees banks taking on additional obligations and risks'; while outside the Bank the chairman of Union Discount, Graham Gilchrist, was 'quite concerned about profit prospects as they anticipate that there could be many firms battling for a share in a limited market', but David Jones of Goldman Sachs said 'they take comfort from the Bank of England assurances that there will be a level playing field'.

What about the architect himself? 'Mr George's attitude, like that of many market participants, is a mixture of eager anticipation and apprehension':

The apprehension reflects concerns over market safety and stability, hence the desire not to go too fast and to keep some separating of functions [between broker and jobber, in the event impossible]. At the same time, he feels the changes will be beneficial to the U.K. financial markets in the long run. He is not wedded permanently to tap issuance of Treasury debt [where the Bank retained part of a gilt issue for release as and when market conditions were favourable], although he would want to see the new dealer market get started before he would consider switching to auctions ... He likes the flexibility of the tap system and does not see this as a threat to dealers because the past history of the Bank of England's behavior shows it to be reasonable; it won't clobber the market ...

On another topic – the proposed Stock Exchange tape to record transactions – he was pleased to hear my report that market participants are unanimously against such a record. He said he had been arguing this point for some time with U.K. Treasury representatives who claim that it is hard to make the case that a tape record is desirable in the equity market but not in the gilt edge market. It seems to make gilts 'second class', they say. As Mr George views it, however, 'central liquidity' is very much the essence of the gilt market and revelation of all transactions could inhibit dealers' willingness to take long and short positions.

All this was important, technical stuff, of which George was an acknowledged master; and long afterwards, Allen would recall how at that time 'there weren't all that many people even in the gilt market itself who really understood how all the parts fitted together'.

The process was not without controversy. The following summer, the Bank's Hilary Stonefrost attended as observer an FT Conference on 'The City Revolution' – where 'the atmosphere was by no means relaxed' – and noted two interventions by the uncompromisingly self-assured senior partner of the broking firm Greenwell & Co:

> Mr Eddie George set out arguments for separate capitalisation of the gilt market makers. Mr Gordon T. Pepper expressed the view that dedicating capital in this way runs counter to the macro interest of the financial sector as a whole. In his view, while high liquidity and abundant capital enable a supervisor to sleep soundly, both hinder the efficient allocation of resources in the financial sector …
>
> Mr George's comment that letters of comfort would be requested from major shareholders to their gilt-edged subsidiaries also provoked Mr Pepper. Mr Pepper took the line that if the intention was to prevent contagion of financial difficulties between subsidiaries of the same group, then such letters 'should be banned by the Bank, not requested'.

George also gave a keynote address, looking at Big Bang as a whole, in which he 'commented on the prevailing belief in the benefits of competition to lenders, borrowers and intermediaries, and noted that the burden of proof now rests with those who want to stop the change'. 'No one,' recorded Stonefrost, 'rose to this challenge, but the concerns of the speakers and participants seemed to suggest not so much imminent golden opportunities for the financial sector, but the need to negotiate the change with minimum damage.'[23]

That rather apprehensive sense was felt not only in the City. Two months later – in September 1985, just over a year before Big Bang's due date – Leigh-Pemberton had a revealing conversation with Thatcher, recently back from her summer holiday in Austria with the British honorary consul, a local timber merchant. 'It became clear,' noted the governor, 'that the Prime Minister is much concerned that "the reputation of the City is at a very low ebb. Indeed it was put to me in Austria that the City was my equivalent of the Austrian wine scandal."' Unsurprisingly, some governor's reflection followed the conversation:

> Freedom of competition is very much part of the Government's philosophy. It must therefore be ready to accept big changes in the markets, especially with the arrival of international operators, financial conglomerates, high salaries, poaching of key staff, and the risk of some failures in the new markets, which are all features which I think we need to put into perspective since the PM connects all this with the low level of the City's reputation.

By this time, after significant input from the Bank, a Financial Services Bill was going through Parliament that involved a major shift away from traditional self-regulation, involving as it did the creation of the Securities and Investments Board (SIB) that would closely monitor the City's handful of main self-regulatory organisations. 'I believe that the regulatory changes now in preparation are well suited to our great financial centre at a time of continuing change,' Leigh-Pemberton told the Overseas Bankers' Club in February 1986. 'They will help to foster the conditions in which high standards can thrive; and in which the City of London can continue to flourish.' In retrospect, of course, there are questions to ask. Did that shift away from self-regulation go far enough? Would it have been better to go the whole hog and move towards something like New York's Securities and Exchange Commission (SEC)? Instinctively, that was not the Bank's view in the mid-1980s, and it was certainly neither the government's (notwithstanding Thatcher's anxieties) nor the City's at large. 'There is,' Walker in 1984 informed the permanent secretary at the Department of Trade and Industry (DTI), 'a fairly general view that self-regulation should continue to play a major role in the future regulatory structure overall'; and he added that 'this is, as you know, a view in which the Bank strongly concurs ...'

Importantly, Leigh-Pemberton in his speech to the overseas bankers was not just referring to the Financial Services Bill; he also had in mind, he told his audience, 'the Bill to amend the 1979 Banking Act which the Chancellor intends to introduce in the next parliamentary session'.[24] Three words formed the essential backdrop for that other legislative initiative: Johnson Matthey Bankers (JMB) – the Bank's most difficult single episode of the entire decade.[25]

Since the 1979 Banking Act, there had existed a two-tier system of authorisation: recognised banks and licensed deposit takers, with the former category subject to a less onerous range of statutory requirements. Naturally, the recognised banks were keen that the Bank should not lose sight of their superior status. As early as April 1980, at a meeting between the governor and the chairmen of the clearers, Morse of Lloyds made 'a plea for flexibility in relation to capital adequacy and foreign currency exposure', to which Richardson responded by assuring them that, in its general approach to supervision in the new era of the statutory framework, 'the Bank intended to be flexible'. Among the recognised banks was JMB; and almost certainly it was that status that contributed to the Bank failing to realise earlier than September 1984 that it was in a seriously bad way – poor management, inadequate controls and most immediately two highly questionable loans to Third World borrowers standing at the equivalent of 115 per cent of its capital. Crucially, JMB was one of the five London banks authorised to deal in the London gold market. That fact determined much that ensued.

The archival trail begins on Wednesday, 26 September, when McMahon – with Leigh-Pemberton away at the IMF's annual meeting in Washington – called on the Treasury's permanent secretary Sir Peter Middleton to tell him 'something of the Johnson Matthey developments': specifically, that 'a large part (but not all) of the bank's capital had been lost' and that the Bank was 'exploring ways of putting the situation right before news breaks and a run develops'. The deputy governor's note for record included a revealing rider: 'I thought it appropriate to tell him this much because Johnson Matthey is a recognised bank and because things might develop in such a way as to call for a Bank of England guarantee. Fortunately, however, he did not raise this last question in any guise. Nor did I.' Next day, following a meeting with the senior general managers of the clearers, McMahon was back at the Treasury to see the permanent secretary:

> I told him that while we were still working for a clean solution which would probably involve the purchase of the bank from the Group [the parent group Johnson Matthey] against warranties, we could not be sure that we would have achieved this before the week-end (or of course even later). If the news broke, we needed to be in a position to stop a run on the bank. To this end we were putting together a standby facility with the clearers, backed by some form of indemnity from the Group. The terms of this standby would be those hallowed by the lifeboat [a reference to the secondary banking crisis]: i.e. the clearers would be involved in proportion to their eligible liabilities as to 90% and the Bank of England would be in for 10% of a total of £200 million.

To this, noted McMahon, the response from Middleton was that the Bank was 'doing the right thing'.[26]

Then, over the next few days and with rumours inevitably starting to circulate, the focus was on who might be JMB's new owners, with the main hope being that the Bank of Nova Scotia would put in a bid, against certain indemnities from other banks; on the morning of Saturday, 29 September, representatives of Rothschilds and Kleinworts – two of the other four banks authorised to deal in the London gold market, the latter through Sharps Pixley – made it clear to McMahon that there was a real danger to the London gold market, and possibly even the London inter-bank market, if JMB was allowed to go. Nor was that all: another of the banks dealing in the gold market was Midland (through Samuel Montagu), and McMahon was well aware of its seriously weakened financial state as a result of its ill-advised purchase three years earlier of the American bank Crocker, an awareness that made him fear a possible domino effect if JMB went. In the course of Sunday the 30th, with the Bank by that evening full of representatives from all possible interested parties (including London's clearing banks), it emerged eventually that the Bank of Nova Scotia was not willing to take on JMB, having failed to receive adequate indemnification from other banks against potential

lawsuits; and at some point before midnight, McMahon took the decision that systemic risk was involved and that therefore there was no
alternative to the Bank itself acquiring JMB.

The governor himself was present by midnight, following a weekend in Kent, and 'at about 3.00 am' he rang the chairmen of the clearing
banks 'to ask for their co-operation in agreeing to indemnify the Bank
for part of the JM bank loan book', saying that he was 'looking for a
£70mn contribution'. If he was anticipating a smooth relaunch of that
celebrated Lifeboat, he was in for a shock:

> **Lord Boardman [NatWest].** Very reluctant to participate because
> of difficulty in justifying it to shareholders. But would stand their
> corner if all the other clearers took their share.
> **Sir Donald Barron [Midland].** Knew very little about Johnson
> Matthey. But provided there were no open-ended commitments on
> the gold market, would reluctantly come in – again provided that
> the others did likewise.
> **Sir Jeremy Morse [Lloyds].** More banks should come in – e.g.
> Standard Chartered and the Scottish clearers. Lloyds in a weak
> position, but would come in to a maximum of £5mn on public
> duty grounds *provided* that the list of contributors was widened.
> Meanwhile, the Bank of England should carry the extra load.
> **Sir Timothy Bevan [Barclays].** Initially refused to contribute –
> impossible to justify to shareholders. After much persuasion agreed
> to £5mn.

Soon afterwards, at about 4 am, 'the Governors and those Executive
Directors still in the Bank rang all the other Members of Court that
could be contacted'. They explained the state of play since the Court
meeting the previous evening – no outside buyer of JMB; instead, the
Bank to acquire JMB 'for a nominal sum'; the parent group Johnson
Matthey to 'put £50mn into the bank' – and noted circumspectly that
'indemnities were being sought from the gold market and the clearing banks against a proportion of the remaining loan book'.[27] Why
were those banks proving so recalcitrant? Perhaps because, contrary
to Morse's warm words at the time, they really did feel let down three
years earlier by Richardson's failure to prevent the draconian one-off
levy; but perhaps more because, when it came to it, the Bank could no

longer, for a mixture of personal and institutional reasons in the new City that was so rapidly taking shape, realistically expect to exercise its familiar powers of moral suasion.

Once day had broken, there were three significant moments that Monday morning. The first was Leigh-Pemberton and McMahon going to No. 11 at 7.30 and putting Lawson (who had also been in Washington the previous week) in the JMB picture – very belatedly, as Lawson felt it, though with his retrospective account not discussing whether his permanent secretary should have mentioned something already. The chancellor was also told that an announcement would have to be made by the time the London market opened at 8 o'clock. 'As a result,' recalled Lawson, 'I was being given only a few minutes to decide whether or not to give an open-ended guarantee of taxpayers' money in support of a rescue about whose wisdom – as I made clear to Robin and Kit at the time, and subsequently in a minute to Margaret – I was far from convinced. I had to make up my mind with no time to secure the information on which to base a considered decision. In the circumstances, I had no option but to rely on the Bank's judgement.' The second moment was the announcement itself: a blandly drafted press release, about the Bank 'acquiring' JMB consequent on 'problems' in the latter's commercial lending book, that was received reasonably calmly. And the third was an awkward telephone call from Morse to Leigh-Pemberton:

> He had seen the Press Notice that the Bank had put out and he wondered how much had been arranged in terms of indemnities and standby facilities.
>
> The Governor explained that the clearing banks were committed for indemnities totalling £20mn, with £5mn from both Barclays and Lloyds; the gold market were providing £30mn and Johnson Matthey PLC £50mn ...
>
> Sir Jeremy's response was that he had thought that there would be a wider circle of banks involved in providing indemnities and that, as the picture was not as he expected it to be, he could not yet commit the bank even to £5mn, although he was not actually withdrawing the offer he had made. The Governor made it clear that he regarded Lloyds as fully committed for £5mn, as the other clearers had all agreed to play their part in providing support.

Even so, £20 million from the clearers: that, to put it mildly, was well short of the £70 million that the Bank had hoped for.

'All the various hitches have been overcome,' an exhausted McMahon was relieved to tell the governor and senior colleagues on Tuesday, 2 October, 'and we have now bought the bank (out of IFD's petty cash!).' IFD was the Industrial Finance Division, with its petty cash box being conveniently at hand to be raided by Walker for a pound coin as a somewhat theatrical gesture. Within days, the Bank's Rodney Galpin was ensconced as executive chairman at JMB, where in his obituary's words he 'swiftly sacked the top three executives, recruited their replacements and steadied the ship' – so successfully that the Bank would finally lose only about £30 million as a result of its acquisition. This was little thanks to the clearers, who remained in entrenched, unhelpful mode, not least when the governor and his deputy summoned Bevan and Boardman to the Bank on the 11th. After Leigh-Pemberton had told them that he wanted the clearers to double their proposed contribution of £20 million, McMahon explained that the Bank had received £10 million from the merchant banks and 'probably' £10 million 'from the Scots and Standard Chartered', and then 'went on to spell out for them the consequences of an ultimate very large loss for the Bank of England, viz either or both inability to play a credible role in future banking crises, or calling for a retrospective Treasury bail-out which would put the Treasury in the driving seat of banking rescues forever afterwards'. Unfortunately, reflected McMahon in his note, 'none of this seemed to make much impression'. That meeting was of course below the public radar, but a week later the governor gave an altogether more harmonious impression at the lord mayor's dinner for the City's bankers. It had been, he emphasised, 'a collective operation' in which 'a large number of banks came together and quickly subordinated their direct and immediate interests to those of the wider system' – in short, 'the rescue operation was characteristic of the City of London'.[28]

Very soon afterwards, the political dimension began to come into play. 'Treasury ministers,' reported the *Financial Times* on 22 October, 'have made known their major reservations about the Bank's handling of the events leading up to JMB's collapse and of the rescue itself'; while at a luncheon meeting that day Lawson told Leigh-Pemberton that he was 'concerned' that some of the governor's remarks in his recent speech 'might be interpreted as giving too liberal an approach to Bank rescue policy'. Next day saw an improbable alliance working together. The left-wing Labour MP Dennis Skinner, motivated by what he saw as the hypocrisy of public funds being used for unprofitable banks but not for unprofitable coal mines, asked Lawson in the Commons if public money had been employed in the JMB rescue; and the leader of the Social Democratic Party, David Owen, in a letter to the chancellor, not only pursued that tack, but argued that the danger to the gold market had been seriously overestimated and that the Bank's decision to take over JMB was mistaken, especially as 'such treatment has not been accorded to a number of other and much larger industrial and commercial companies which have also collapsed in recent years'. Lawson, already irked by being left in the dark in late September, dead-batted as best he could, but over the next few weeks Owen continued his campaign, amid gathering talk of an establishment cover-up. By mid-December, moreover, the ominous word from the *Financial Times*'s Peter Riddell to a member of McMahon's office was that ministers felt that the Bank had 'acted too much on its own' and presented them with 'a fait accompli'. Lawson himself tried to take the political heat out of the situation by announcing to the Commons on 17 December that he was setting up a joint Bank/Treasury inquiry into the system of banking supervision. By a cruel stroke for the Bank, he was asked by the Labour backbencher Robert Sheldon (seventeen years after his costly question to Callaghan) what exactly the Bank's liability was. Wrongly believing that the Bank's only significant liability with regard to JMB was its half-share of a £150 million indemnity, and not having been told that on 22 November the Bank had transferred to it £100 million of liquid (sterling) reserves as working capital, Lawson gave a reply that inadvertently misled the House. When that emerged he understandably (if mistakenly) 'felt badly let down, as I made clear when I learned about it'. As every so often at that time of year, festive cheer and goodwill did not abound, as spotted by Christopher Fildes at the Stock Exchange's Christmas lunch: 'The Chancellor showered Sir Nicholas [Goodison] with praise, said not a word about the Bank or the Governor who was sitting by his side, and then left, pleading an engagement at Westminster.'[29]

Six months later, in June 1985, the report of the joint inquiry (chaired by Leigh-Pemberton himself) appeared. Its proposals included ending the 1979 Banking Act's two-tier system; its replacement with a single authorisation to take deposits, thereby giving the Bank broader powers over all banks; regular dialogue between the Bank and the banks' auditors; and the Bank's much criticised supervisory staff (for instance by *Euromoney* in its recent investigative piece, 'How the Bank of England Failed the JMB Test') not only to be increased, but to be given commercial banking experience. Lawson himself, in his accompanying statement to the Commons, did not deny the Bank's culpability: 'On this occasion the Bank did not act as promptly as it should have, and to some extent fell down on the job.' These were carefully measured words, but there was at least one person who wondered whether the Bank should even retain its supervisory role. Leigh-Pemberton the following month recorded a characteristic encounter with Lawson:

> He opened by wishing to speak to me privately and went on to say that he had had a difficult time with the Prime Minister on the question of banking supervision. She was arguing that the function should be taken away from the Bank of England, but he said that he had succeeded in dissuading her from this, largely on the grounds that it would detract from the Bank's standing. I went on to say that it was not likely to make much difference whether the function was in the Bank or not in terms of the people who had to do it, since there was clearly a limited cadre of qualified personnel. He cut me short and said there was no need to argue the merits of the case since he had dissuaded the Prime Minister, but he wished to emphasise to me the need to 'sharpen up' the supervisory function.

Leigh-Pemberton, thinking about it afterwards, was a little sceptical. 'I am inclined to wonder just how deeply the Prime Minister's attack really went,' he reflected. 'Information reaching me from No. 10 suggests that the Bank is still held in reasonable esteem there and I think I have to make up my mind about the extent to which the Chancellor may be both using and exaggerating this threat.' That was probably unfair to Lawson, given that when two months later the governor was given the treatment by the prime minister in her fiery, post-Austria mood, she not only requested 'a paper on banking supervision' but 'seemed to feel that the Bank of England was barely adequately equipped to supervise the City and that we should need "some system of inspection"'.[30] In any case, Lawson's White Paper on Banking Supervision appeared in December 1985, embracing much of the substance of the June report and directly creating the path to the 1987 Banking Act.

Newly in charge of the Banking Supervision Division by this time, having sorted out JMB, was Galpin. 'JMB has left its imprint,' he observed in January 1986 after two months in post, pointing to how 'particularly among the younger members of the Division there is a desire for more bureaucracy and more ratios with a consequent loss of flexibility – and some danger of eroding one of the strengths of the system'. Other causes of concern were that 'the search for consensus leads to policy decisions taking far too long to establish'; that 'there is no clear sense throughout the Division of the direction in which Banking Supervision is moving'; that 'the records of prudential interviews while generally of high quality do not always comment on those issues which should be of primary concern such as liquidity, capital adequacy and the quality of assets etc'; and that 'though welcome, the 25% increase [announced the previous September] in staff resources is not, at working level, regarded as sufficient', with Galpin wanting 160 people, as opposed to the 125 currently budgeted. Just as after the secondary banking crisis, there had, perhaps inevitably, been a post-JMB scapegoat: this time Peter Cooke, moved to concentrate on coordinating international bank supervision, particularly in Basel. Cooke himself, renowned for his objectivity, would in later years recall the difficult hand he had been dealt in the early to mid-1980s. 'One of the big problems was that the resources simply were not available to do the work, which patently we knew needed to be done, in order to block all the holes up ... We were constantly on short rations and constantly really stretched ... I think the juxtaposition of "let's trust management" on the one hand and "let's be professional about this" on the other was being bridged slightly uneasily at times ...' It was indeed an uneasy bridge, and the fact was that until the JMB disaster there was still, again to quote Cooke, 'a fairly strong ethos within the Bank, and within banking supervision, which derived from as it were the environment of the 70s, which said that the essential issue for supervisors was good judgements of management'.[31] Judging management? Or poring over all the figures? For better or worse, it was now going to be a swing to the latter.

In another area altogether, but of equally pressing concern to the
Bank, the mid-1980s confirmed that the question of Britain's membership of the ERM (the Exchange Rate Mechanism, the operating arm
of the European Monetary System) was coming to matter more
than the arcane shibboleths of monetary policy. 'Monetary targets
were adopted in the belief that the relationship between the monetary aggregates and nominal incomes, the velocity of money, would
be reasonably stable and predictable,' recalled Leigh-Pemberton
in an important lecture at the University of Kent in October 1984.
However, he went on, 'the hopes of those who looked for a simple,
close and reliable relationship, that would hold even in the short term,
have not been fulfilled'. What, then, was the alternative 'in place of a
monetary domestic target'? Noting that 'the adoption of an exchange
rate objective, through a pegged relationship with a foreign currency,
or in earlier times with gold', had 'tradition' behind it, the strongly
pro-Europe governor wondered aloud whether 'for the United
Kingdom with its close political and economic ties with our European
neighbours, there could be a number of attractions in taking a full part
in the exchange rate mechanism of the EMS'. Within the Bank, he had
support from McMahon and Loehnis; and from early 1985, if only on
a provisional basis, from the hitherto sceptical George, for whom the
sterling crisis that January – threatening to create the one-dollar pound
and causing a serious hike in interest rates – may perhaps have been a
signal of the desirability of a collective attempt to tame the financial
markets. On 6 February, ahead of a 'seminar' at No. 10 the following
week, McMahon put the case on paper – for internal consumption.
Acknowledging that the question of joining the ERM was 'a complex
one, which has been argued back and forth in the Bank for more than
five years, and on which a very large number of complex considerations
can be adduced on both sides', he nevertheless argued unambiguously
that 'we should join now', noting that 'it is hard to believe that, whatever happens after joining, developments in our exchange rate would
be less welcome than they have been from time to time in the past'.
Among the positives he cited were that 'we would be linking ourselves
with a demonstrably anti-inflationary bloc' and that 'the public at
large understand better the anti-inflationary constraint of holding
the exchange rate than they do one of holding the money target'.
Moreover: 'Floating exchange rates seem to me demonstrably getting

out of control and producing economic disequilibria and policing difficulties for the world's major economies which by now are surpassing those distortions and difficulties provided by the Bretton Woods system in its late and damaging phase.'[32] The understandable desire, in short, was to return to the once familiar certainties of a more orderly framework.

At the 15 February seminar – the first of the three ERM political set-pieces during 1985 – both Lawson and Leigh-Pemberton argued for joining, though not necessarily immediately, while Thatcher for her part (recalled Lawson) 'chose to dwell on the consensus that now was not the right time to join, and ignored the majority feeling that the right time was not far off'. Ironically, in the weeks that followed, Leigh-Pemberton then became anxious – with the ERM question in abeyance – about Lawson ditching prematurely in the MTFS the significance of the broad aggregates as monetary indicators. 'While we wholly understand the present discomfort over broad money,' he wrote to him in March, 'we do not think that broad money can be simply set aside'; and he warned against anything that could be seen as 'a significant weakening in commitment to monetary discipline with potentially substantial adverse market consequences at a time when we need to do all that we can to re-enforce credibility'. Some four months later, in July, McMahon expressed similar anxiety. 'The Chancellor wished to discard £M3 as a target,' he told a briefing meeting at the Bank, and accordingly he was 'concerned that targets for the monetary aggregates would lapse without an alternative discipline being in place, such as joining the ERM'. But lapse they would: in October, in his Mansion House speech, Lawson announced that he was dropping the £M3 target, declared that henceforth 'the inflation rate is judge and jury', and in effect abandoned monetarism. Leigh-Pemberton at the same dinner made tactfully sympathetic noises – 'real life is far too complex for absolute rules' – but no mention of the ERM as a possible alternative anchor.

By this time, in fact, the second ERM summit at No. 10 had already taken place: on 30 September, with the governor accompanied by McMahon, Loehnis and George. After Lawson had made his case for joining, above all in terms of reinforcing the government's anti-inflationary strategy, 'Robin strongly supported me, claiming that the need to make subjective judgements about the interpretation of the monetary indicators, coupled with our resistance to the increasing pressure from the market to disclose an exchange rate "target", were undermining the credibility of policy.' Thatcher, however, remained unconvinced, though agreeing to a further meeting on the subject; following a post-mortem lunch with Lawson, the governor reflected that 'it seems that we [Bank and Treasury] may have overplayed our hand at the last meeting and appeared to be "ganging up" on the PM'. The final summit, involving a broader spread of ministers, was on 13 November, with Leigh-Pemberton again present, this time flanked by George. As usual, Lawson put forward his pro-joining arguments; other ministers now had their say, on the whole in favour of join-ing; and Leigh-Pemberton asserted that (in Lawson's words) 'the difficulties of sterling outside the ERM were greater than they would be inside the ERM'. The crunch came at the end. 'If the Chancellor, the Governor and the Foreign Secretary are all agreed that we should join the EMS then that should be decisive,' declared the deputy prime minister, Lord Whitelaw. 'It has certainly decided me.' To which Thatcher instantly responded: 'On the contrary: I disagree. If you join the EMS, you will have to do so without me.' End of meeting – and, according to Lawson's retrospective account, end of 'an historic opportunity', when 'the time really had been right'.[33]

All this, with the JMB episode starting to recede, probably brought chancellor and governor rather closer together; and during the next sterling crisis, in January 1986, the two men were allies as they tried to persuade Thatcher that there was no alternative to an interest rate rise:

> I told her [recalled Lawson] that the pound was under severe pressure, and I was afraid that if we did not act that day the bottom might fall out of the market. She insisted that it was quite unnecessary, that it would be a positive disaster, and much else in the same vein. Eventually, after a particularly unpleasant harangue, she concluded, 'Go ahead if you insist, but on your own head be it'. After we had left her room, Robin said to me, 'I don't know how you put up with this sort of thing'. I explained that she had a great deal on her mind.

As it happened, it was all for nothing. Leigh-Pemberton returned to the Bank, discovered that pressure on sterling had eased, and rang Lawson to tell him, leaving the chancellor to inform a 'suitably pleased' prime minister that they would not now be going ahead with the interest rate hike.[34]

By this time there was a new deputy governor. In September 1985 it was announced that McMahon would be leaving at the end of the year to go to Midland – in effect, to try to dig it out of its deep hole – and that his successor would be George Blunden, who had retired in 1984 as an executive director but was still on the Court. Why Blunden? There were perhaps three main reasons. Firstly, because of the impossibility of choosing between David Walker and Eddie George – the former the Bank's principal architect of the City revolution and manifestly energetic, capable and ambitious, the latter increasingly respected by the Treasury for his technical expertise and calm judgement, with Lawson by now asking the governor to bring him along to meetings at which interest rates and the money markets were under discussion. Secondly, because one of the more influential non-executive directors, Sir Hector Laing, who was close to Thatcher, pushed hard for the appointment. And thirdly, above all, because Blunden was generally seen as the man, following the JMB trauma, 'to impose discipline and restore morale' (as Stephen Fay put it in his 1987 study of the Bank, *Portrait of an Old Lady*). Certainly Blunden's qualities were considerable: a silver-haired, avuncular look hiding a tough, thick-skinned operator; a dry sense of humour; a ferocious disciplinarian; a good, pragmatic mind; and a Bank man through and through. 'He will bring authority, entangling humour (he is a gladiator who prefers the net and trident), and banking skills and experience which have long earned him a position of respect among bankers, central or commercial,' commented Fildes at the time of his appointment, and all that proved to be the case.[35] His return to Threadneedle Street proved a particular boon for Leigh-Pemberton, who had not warmed to the more overtly intellectual McMahon; and together, during the second half of the decade, they formed an increasingly effective double act, starting the long haul of restoring the Bank's rather battered (fairly or unfairly) standing.

Much of 1986 was dominated by the looming Big Bang. On the gilts side, all proceeded reasonably smoothly: over two dozen market makers, many of them non-British, limbering up for what was anticipated as a highly competitive marketplace, possibly a bloodbath; and in the Bank itself, the successful completion of a state-of-the-art dealing room, where from March the Bank conducted its own gilt-dealing operation and thereby, after 200 years, took over from the government brokers Mullens the conduct of official business. More generally, the process continued of gearing up intellectually for the new world – not least the vital and sensitive question of whether the Bank would be content in that new world to see foreign ownership of British banks. In terms of the clearers, Leigh-Pemberton reminded an internal meeting in January, the Bank was already publicly committed to opposing any foreign takeover, whereas Lawson was seemingly more relaxed. 'The Chancellor's view might not be widely shared by the electorate,' argued Blunden, adding that 'to the "man in the street" the ownership of an industrial conglomerate was usually immaterial, but if the High Street bank came under foreign control, he might feel very differently'. Walker likewise 'disagreed with the Chancellor's argument that a bank should not be treated differently from an industrial company, as the systemic influence of a major bank in the economy was very much greater'; but George 'said that he was not entirely persuaded that there were no circumstances in which foreign ownership could be envisaged'. What about the merchant banks? 'It would be sad if the five largest all became foreign-owned,' remarked Blunden, but again it was George who took the less protectionist stance: 'The larger Accepting Houses were in a quandary. They were neither sufficiently small simply to be specialists in a particular area, nor big enough to compete globally ... It was therefore arguable that their prime need was for more capital ... So a "British-only" policy might not be in the Houses' best interests.'

The whole ownership debate still had a way to run, but more immediate was the necessity of calming the politicians' nerves. Thatcher called for a pre-Big Bang seminar at No. 10 in early June, and the governor a week before asked Lawson what her purpose was:

He said quite simply, 'What is likely to go wrong between Big Bang and the General Election?' I told him that my main anxiety would be operators dropping out of the market as a result of competitive pressure, lack of volume and, I hoped least likely, bad judgement. The Chancellor said that the important thing would be that the losers should not be widows and orphans ... I said that I was also anxious that large operators from overseas might adopt a loss-leading policy which could have serious effects on UK operators, but I had not been able to think of any means whereby this could be checked. Discriminatory restrictions would hardly be consistent with our philosophy and would be extremely difficult to operate.

The seminar itself, attended by Leigh-Pemberton and Walker, was notable for Lawson's frankness. After agreeing with the prime minister 'that the Big Bang posed risks', he went on: 'Some things were bound to go wrong. But the changes were inevitable if the City was to maintain its competitiveness.'[36]

The final stages had their moments. 'The Times had a very silly and totally incorrect article about gilt-edged market unpreparedness for Big Bang,' Blunden updated Leigh-Pemberton in late August. 'We are trying to feed correcting stories to the FT and Telegraph.' A month later saw a devastating fire at the Bank, starting in contractors' huts and gutting much of the east side, including the International Divisions area on the third floor. And on 16 October, the governor in his Mansion House speech solemnly declared that 'it will be vital for all market participants to exercise a degree of restraint'. The following week, his internal message was also heartfelt:

After some three years of intensive efforts on the part of so many different departments and divisions in the Bank and so many individual members of staff, we completed the second dress rehearsal of the new gilt-edged market arrangements very successfully on Saturday. Big Bang is now only a few days away. Whatever now happens I cannot think that there is anything more we could have done to have been better prepared for the change ...

It has been Bank-wide co-operation at its best, and that best has been magnificent. It has brought home once again to everyone concerned the total interdependence of all parts of the Bank, and the dedication at all levels which is such a valuable asset.

Yet of course, quite apart from the institutional changes about to come into effect on 27 October, the new world was already becoming a reality – and, from the perspective of politicians, central bankers and commentators, often a disturbing reality. Back in July, in a note to the governor for his eyes only, Walker related how he had been rung the day before by Fred Vinton of Morgan Guaranty, to inform him that 'a proposition' had been put to two of his bank's 'young capital markets Group traders' that 'they should leave MG and go as a team at a salary for each of £400,000 a year with a minimum two-year contract, with provision for bonus payments on top'. The rest of Walker's note reflected the Bank painfully starting to wrestle with an increasingly mobile, avaricious world where the City was no longer a club and where club rules no longer applied, let alone Cobbold-style Etonian standards:

> Vinton said that he was not asking the Bank to intervene to seek to abort this proposition, but felt that we should be aware ... I thanked Vinton and said that I fully shared his concern that remuneration on this scale marked an extraordinary escalation beyond anything that I had previously encountered.
>
> Vinton told me this afternoon that the house is Kleinworts and that the deal has now been done ...
>
> All this seems to me to represent a very unsatisfactory state of affairs, and I have no hesitation in recommending that you or the Deputy call in Michael Hawkes [of Kleinworts] for a sharp word. We have of course accepted realistically that City remuneration in internationally competitive business has had to go up and you have gone to considerable trouble to explain this to sceptics and to the City's many detractors. But performance-linked remuneration on this scale for two under-30-year-olds takes the inflation into a quite different league from anything seen hitherto. It suggests that Kleinworts are envisaging a pace of activity and turnover that, *prima facie*, might give supervisors cause for concern; it gives a quite unhealthy inducement to the young individuals concerned to think that they can walk on water, a dangerous state for executives in any business; and it is hardly likely to reflect well on Kleinworts' judgement or the reputation in the City when, as seems certain, the terms of this transfer become publicly known.[37]

On 7 November, a fortnight into the Big Bang era, the Bank's Ian Bond briefed Blunden: 'It is already clear that the objectives of the changes have been met: the equity market is more liquid and deals are more keenly priced. The gilts market passed its first test – with the tender offer – very well.' The gilt-edged market was of course the Bank's particular responsibility; and Ian Plenderleith, head of Gilt-Edged Division, would describe the immediate prelude to 27 October and its reassuring reality once that half-dreaded date finally arrived:

> I promised the banks that if ever the world came to an end and something went terribly wrong, we'd have what came to be called an 'Armageddon button', which they could ask us to press, which would bring the whole thing to a grinding halt, which would have been terrible but was some sort of comfort to them. And when Big Bang started the banks very kindly got together and gave me a wooden plaque with a brass door bell on it with a little thing saying 'the Armageddon button', and I used to keep it in my room.

If that was gratifying, so too was election night in June 1987, as Thatcher won her third decisive victory, the market shot up and the Bank's gilt-market dealers spent the night in the dealing room, with the Bank issuing stock at 2 am. 'It sold out straightaway,' recalled Plenderleith, 'and we issued some more at about 7 am and that sold out straight away, and by the time we went off to breakfast we had sold about 5 billion gilts during that night and done about 10 per cent of the year's borrowing requirement, which I regarded as a great coup.' More generally, the Bank felt able by early 1989 to publish a positive report on the first two and a bit years of the gilt-edged market since Big Bang. Liquidity had improved; dealing costs had declined; despite fierce competition, there were still almost two dozen market makers (compared with what was virtually a jobbers' duopoly prior to Big Bang); the Central Gilts Office Service, a joint venture between the Bank and what was now called the International Stock Exchange, provided 'computerised book entry transfer facilities and assured payments arrangements', operating with 'a high degree of reliability'; and in terms of official operations, the market's ultimate rationale, the new structure had 'enabled the authorities to extend the range of their funding techniques, eg through the use of auctions'.[38]

Infinitely less satisfactory in the Bank's eyes during these years was the City's reputation: high in profile but low in esteem. As early as December 1986 the Guinness affair (involving a share-support operation earlier in the year) was making the headlines; and the following month, possibly after a degree of government prompting, Blunden successfully demanded the resignations of two top people at Morgan Grenfell, the merchant bank most heavily implicated. Soon afterwards, in February 1987, Leigh-Pemberton accepted in an interview that standards were coming 'under great strain', and that it was 'inevitable' that 'we are going to have to have more bodies, more rules, and more law'. One of those new bodies was the Board of Banking Supervision: set up by the 1987 Banking Act, and part of the Bank (in the same sense that the present-day Monetary Policy Committee is part of the Bank), its stated purpose was advisory, reviewing decisions rather than making them. In practice, the banks still essentially looked for their supervision to the Bank's more familiar supervisory faces, with Morse that February, in his capacity as chairman of the British Bankers' Association, paying a telling visit to the governor, in which he emphasised that 'the problem of secret and confidential information and the close relationship between supervisor and supervised' meant that 'there was no other alternative'. What about SIB? 'I am increasingly coming to the view that it would be desirable for Kenneth Berrill [its first chairman] to go as soon as we have a successor,' Leigh-Pemberton wrote in September 1987 to Lord Young at the DTI. 'I sense a distinct hardening of opinion in the City on this question, not only among those who have always been sceptical or opposed to the SIB.' The governor was soon taking soundings. 'I am told that what is most important is that the new Chairman should listen to advice from practitioners,' he informed the minister – as opposed, he added, to someone who 'spends his time asking his in-house lawyers for advice'. In the event, the person chosen was one of the Bank's own, David Walker, who became SIB's new chairman in 1988: a victory for the City, undeniably, although Walker was hardly a man for the easy life or soft option. The scandals, meanwhile, continued to come. One was the investment firm Barlow Clowes, which collapsed in May 1988 some eight months after Blunden had issued a written early warning, ignored by the DTI; another, more intimately concerning the Bank, was the Blue Arrow scandal, involving a share-support operation in September 1987 hatched by NatWest's merchant banking arm. The DTI very belatedly launched an investigation in December 1988, and two months later Blunden learned from the Treasury that 'there are those in the DTI who are not adverse to seeing this as an opportunity to put the Bank into as embarrassing a position as they have found themselves over Barlow Clowes'. The report was published on 20 July 1989, and soon afterwards Lawson observed to Leigh-Pemberton that 'it was very important to maintain the prestige of the Bank of England, and of the Governor in particular, and this would be reinforced if it was known that the Bank had acted firmly in this case'. The Bank did act accordingly. NatWest's chairman, Lord Boardman, resigned next day; a week later he was in the governor's office, complaining to Leigh-Pemberton about the Bank's 'press treatment' and declaring that in the whole Blue Arrow affair he had been 'constantly wrong-footed by the Bank in terms of public relations'.[39]

NatWest and the other main clearers were presumably paying attention when the governor in October 1987 spoke in Belfast about the ownership and control of UK banks. 'We are now seeing London emerge,' he told an audience of local businessmen, 'as a focal point of the world's financial markets; and this is due, in no small part, to our willingness to see foreign companies come to the United Kingdom to do banking business and, on occasion, to take control of British institutions. In my view that policy invigorates the London markets and their participants.' He went on, however, to assert his conviction that 'it is of the highest importance that there should be a strong and continuing British presence in the banking system of the United Kingdom', given that 'it runs counter to commonsense to argue that the openness of the London market must be carried to the point where control of the core of our financial system – the payments mechanism, the supply of credit – may pass into the hands of institutions whose business aims and national interest lie elsewhere'.

That would remain the Bank's formal position, but two years later saw further significant internal debate. At a first meeting, it was generally agreed that there existed a UK banking 'core' of the ten or twelve largest banks and building societies, with the merchant banks being outside that core and not necessarily to be given the protection more likely to be accorded to the core institutions. At a follow-up meeting, discussion opened up. Brian Quinn, an economist at the Bank who was now in day-to-day charge of banking supervision, declared that, quite apart from possible 'prudential considerations or economic arguments in the traditional sense', he 'felt that there was something special about the banks at the centre of the credit and payments system'; Leigh-Pemberton said that he 'broadly agreed'; but George countered that he not only 'found it extremely hard to envisage circumstances in which the UK national interest could be damaged by foreign-owned core banks', but 'believed it was important not to damage the interests of shareholders by preventing takeovers by foreign institutions willing to pay the highest price'; and Andrew Crockett (recently returned to the Bank, after some sixteen years at the IMF, to be in charge of the international side) agreed that 'only in very rare circumstances would a foreign takeover of a core UK bank be liable to damage UK interests', noted that he was 'concerned that our policy might be swimming against the tide of history', asserted that 'the trend was towards fewer, larger, multi-national institutions', and concluded that 'competition between cultures could be beneficial to the UK'.[40] All these were revealing observations, on the cusp of the decade of globalisation.

Back in 1987, Leigh-Pemberton's Belfast speech had a particular context. Late that July, the governor received a visit from Midland's Sir Donald Barron, who told him that the bank (once the world's largest) had received an unwelcome takeover approach from the advertising agency Saatchi & Saatchi. Maurice Saatchi, reported Barron, had said that he 'felt capable of handling the management and financial side of Midland Bank, though admitted to some ignorance of the supervisory requirements'. Next day, the governor passed on the news to Lawson, who 'said that on the face of it, it was difficult to take this bid seriously'; a month later, Blunden informed the governor that Rodney Galpin had been asking Saatchi 'a number of searching questions'. Even the venerable Jasper Hollom, seven years after leaving the Bank, was drawn into this episode of pure top-of-the-market froth, with Blunden noting in mid-September that the former deputy governor had called in to see him, apparently 'in his new role as adviser to Maurice Saatchi on his determination to enter the financial sector'; but, added Blunden, it had been made clear to Hollom that 'we would be determined to resist a move such as that threatened against the Midland'. Unsurprisingly, the brothers did not get very far with their audacious initiative, but Leigh-Pemberton still made a point in his Belfast speech not long afterwards of emphasising that he would 'need some persuading before an industrial or commercial company is allowed to take control of a bank'.[41]

That was on Tuesday, 13 October. Later that week, on the Thursday night, the great storm caused scenes of devastation across much of southern England, including the loss of many of the finest trees on the governor's Kent estate. That Friday, with the City barely functional, Blunden was to be seen wandering around asking whether any of the juniors knew how to call a Bank Holiday – no one did. A deceptively calm weekend ensued, before on Monday the 19th and Tuesday the 20th came the greatest crash, across the stock markets of the world, for over half a century, a long overdue correction of overpriced shares exacerbated in New York by waves of automatic selling from computerised program traders. That week, Leigh-Pemberton was mainly in the Balkans, deciding not to cut short his prearranged trip; so that left Blunden in charge, as he and his colleagues worked harmoniously with the Treasury and the deputy governor himself stayed in constant touch with Gerald Corrigan at the New York Fed. Led by the Fed's Alan Greenspan, and generally supported by the politicians, this generation of central bankers consciously sought not to repeat the mistakes following the Wall Street Crash of 1929, but instead relaxed monetary policy and pumped large volumes of liquidity into the system. Panic was thereby averted, but it was still a line in the sand. '1987 was the first time that central banks and governments ran scared because of concern for securities markets,' Robert Pringle (founder-editor of the magazine *Central Banking*) would write five years later. 'Someday they will have to stand and fight ...'[42]

In any case, in October 1987 itself, Bank/Treasury harmony failed to last the month. The cause of a new if temporary bout of friction was the controversial fate, following the market crash, of the government's huge privatisation issue of $7,250 million of BP shares – fully underwritten the week before the crash, despite the obstinate Sir John Nott, now at Lazards, resisting Leigh-Pemberton's personal plea that the issue would not be complete without the participation of that merchant bank. As markets plunged, Lawson came almost immediately under pressure, particularly from the North American underwriters, to pull the issue. At a meeting on the 20th, he was supported by Blunden in his instinctive determination not to, though with the Bank compelled by the terms of the underwriting agreement to be playing the role of neutral umpire between the Treasury and Rothschilds, whose silky-tongued Michael Richardson spoke for the underwriting group. With dealing in the new shares due to begin on the 30th, the pressure on Lawson to save the skin of the underwriters was almost unrelenting. On the 27th a tantalising might-have-been occurred when Blunden took a phone call from Robert Maxwell, offering to put together a consortium of 'five or six people' to cover the issue. 'He said that this group', noted Blunden, 'would be "buyers of last resort" and would be motivated by the dual opportunity of profit and service.' The deputy governor 'thanked Mr Maxwell for keeping us informed, adding that he would not seek to discourage him from this initiative'. The crunch came on Thursday the 29th. Some six hours late – to Lawson's considerable annoyance, given that he was due to inform the Commons that evening how he proposed to resolve this intensely invidious situation – the Bank shortly after 6 pm faxed through its five-page recommendation, mainly written by George. The chancellor's vexation increased when he read it: the Bank's first preference was to pull the issue; its second preference was for Lawson to institute a buy-back (or 'floor') arrangement that would save the underwriters roughly three-quarters of the £1,000 million that they stood to lose. Thoroughly unimpressed, he rejected both solutions and announced a far more robust compromise, by which the issue went ahead but with a much less generous buy-back arrangement. In this he was strongly supported by Thatcher, who was as disappointed as her chancellor was by the Bank – perhaps unduly influenced by Richardson – seemingly giving so little weight to the sanctity of contract and the international reputation of the City. In the event, Lawson's scheme proved a resounding success: so much so, indeed, that in an ill-advised initiative the Bank's press office sought to claim the public kudos for the Bank, something which the chancellor not unnaturally found a bit rich and which prompted him to ring the governor at his Kent home. 'He was genuinely horrified,' recalled Lawson, 'and I am sure was entirely innocent.'[43]

During the dramas that autumn, Leigh-Pemberton perhaps took comfort from the progress being made on a vital – if far less high-profile – international front.[44] Since the mid-1970s the Basel Committee on Banking Supervision, chaired by the mid-1980s by the Bank's Peter Cooke, had been addressing the question of capital

adequacy, with an increasing emphasis on the question of harmoni-
sation of standards in order to ensure a level playing field for global
banks. The critical impetus, though, came in 1986 from a Fed/Bank
bilateral initiative, with a Leigh-Pemberton/Volcker dinner at New
Change early that autumn starting to get things moving. The original
push was from the American, much concerned about global economic
imbalances, but the governor responded positively, not least in the
context of the imminent Big Bang; and quite suddenly, the road
opened to a common regime for bank-capital adequacy that would
spur wider international agreement. 'An audacious political choice
disguised as a technical regulatory matter,' is how Steven Solomon
would describe the logjam-breaking move in his 1995 account. 'It was
tantamount to a ganging up by the two leading international financial centers. The implicit threat was that other nations would either
submit to the US–UK capital definitions and standards or face exclusion of their banks from London and New York. In one bound it
by-passed the multilateral negotiations going on within Peter Cooke's
G10 Basel supervisors committee as well as within the EC [European
Community] ...' Crucially, it worked: in January 1987, the Fed and
the Bank went public with their accord; and a year and a half later, in
June 1988 following much cajoling of the Japanese by the Fed and of
the Europeans by the Bank, the Basel Accord (subsequently known as
Basel I) was formally agreed by the world's leading central banks – in
effect committing internationally active commercial banks to minimum capital worth 8 per cent of risk-weighted assets, with at least half
of that capital to be Tier 1 ('pure') capital. Inevitably, weaknesses in
Basel I would subsequently emerge, such as imprecise risk-weighting
methodology, susceptibility to regulatory capital arbitrage and inadequate focus on market and interest rate risk as opposed to simply
credit risk; but it was still an important, pioneering agreement doing
much to enhance the general authority of central banks, an authority
increasingly under challenge since the 1960s and the slow death of the
Bretton Woods system; while at home the Bank would make the Basel
Accord the cornerstone of its supervisory regime.

Leigh-Pemberton by this time was about to start his second five-year
term. It is possible that back in 1983, at the start of his governorship, he had anticipated just a single term, but that the various slings
and arrows directed at him, especially during the difficult Johnson

Matthey period, made him determined to serve a second. Certainly the question of his reappointment was a live issue, involving considerable press speculation that in turn prompted the Treasury in late July 1987, with almost a year to go of his first term, to issue a press notice in which Lawson expressed his complete confidence in the governor. That very evening, in the anteroom of No. 10 following a drinks reception, an important but very private exchange took place. 'Quite casually,' as Leigh-Pemberton afterwards informed Blunden, the chancellor said to him: 'Anyway, if you want to go on, I am perfectly content for you to do so.' A full six months later, the reappointment was publicly announced, and thereafter the governor was psychologically as well as politically in a stronger place. As it happened, this development roughly coincided with a significant shift in the Bank itself. 'Availability and Deployment of Economists' was the issue of the key meeting in June 1987. 'It is perhaps time for a step change in the Bank's attitude to the recruitment of economists,' asserted Blunden. 'We have clung for too long to an approach to staffing which favours the amateur, generalist recruit as against the specialist. This contrasts sharply with the policy of many other central banks, where an economics background is regarded as virtually essential.'[45] That indeed would be the future direction of travel – and doubly telling, given that Blunden himself would instinctively have sympathised with the Cobbold dictum about the Bank being a bank, not a study group.

This last year or so of Leigh-Pemberton's first term also marked the zenith of Lawson's chancellorship. 'Finally, and by far the most important item,' noted Blunden in a May 1987 update for his chief, 'the Chancellor came in this week with a new bouffant hairstyle with a series of waves rising up from his forehead to give him a sort of halo appearance!' Soon afterwards, his successful stewardship of the economy was the prime reason for Thatcher's third election victory; and by the following spring, at the time of his boldly tax-cutting budget, his reputation stood higher than that of almost any post-war chancellor. Seemingly, unlike his predecessors, he had cracked the problem of simultaneously achieving high growth and low inflation. The reality, though, was an unsustainable boom – a boom that by 1989 was clearly starting to be followed by a hard and very painful landing.

What had gone wrong? Inevitably there would be many retrospective analyses, putting the blame on different factors: whether excessive financial liberalisation, or sterling's exaggerated depreciation during 1986, or the exchange rate policy from early 1987 of shadowing the deutschmark, or an overly loose monetary policy (especially after the October 1987 stock market crash), or even that 1988 budget. Lawson himself, in his remarkably detailed 1992 account of his chancellorship, spread the blame generously, with of course the Bank getting its share. 'The only occasion in all my years as Chancellor when the Bank can be interpreted as having wanted a tighter policy than I was pursuing,' he wrote, was in 'the difficult period' after the stock market crash, when 'Eddie George argued that sterling should be allowed to rise'. Lawson went on:

> Everything else that has emerged from some Bank quarters since my resignation [October 1989] amounts to an attempt to rewrite history with the benefit of hindsight; an understandable activity, but scarcely a commendable one. It is, I suppose, theoretically possible that the Bank from time to time believed that monetary policy should be tighter, but refrained from telling me – even at the markets meetings I regularly held with the Governor and his senior officials. But that would have amounted to a dereliction of duty so grave as to be unthinkable.

That broad thrust may well be accurate, though there is some evidence that in early 1988 the Bank was warning that the expansion of credit, especially after the crash, had become excessive and that there existed a serious danger of overheating. Specifically, the first issue that year of the Bank's *Quarterly Bulletin* noted that the growth of domestic demand immediately before the crash had been 'significantly stronger than many had thought – indeed, unsustainably rapid'; claimed that the effects of the crash had been overstated; and argued for monetary policy to adopt a 'non-accommodating stance'. But in any case Lawson had a further grievance – namely, the Bank's general unwillingness, especially in the summer of 1988, to lean on the clearing banks and try to persuade them to be more circumspect in their mortgage lending. According to Lawson, the Bank gave a threefold justification for its refusal to act on his wishes: that the lending involved no risk to bank depositors; that it likewise involved no systemic threat to the banking system; and that mortgage lending ('bricks and mortar') was intrinsically safe. 'While there was undoubtedly substance in all these arguments,' observed Lawson, 'I believe that at the more fundamental level at which central bank thinking ought to be pitched the Bank was both unimaginative and misguided'; and with some justification he pointed to how 'the credit-based house price bubble of the late 1980s, by creating an exaggerated impression of personal wealth and prosperity, led to a great deal of other borrowing and lending of a less secure nature'. His final point was also perhaps valid. 'The Bank's strongest argument for inaction was probably the one that it left unsaid: that the commercial banks, driven by a desire to maintain and if possible increase their share of the mortgage market, come what may, would have taken no notice of a call for greater prudence and caution from the Governor of the Bank of England.' Yet was that truly the case? Lawson thought not. 'Although it was true that the Bank's authority had diminished over the years, I very much doubt if it had vanished completely. And if the worst came to the worst, it would have been better to have tried and failed than not to have really tried at all.'[46]

The chancellor's controversial policy between spring 1987 and spring 1988 of shadowing the deutschmark was a further source of tension. 'That experience, I have to say, was disastrous,' publicly recalled George in the mid-1990s with perhaps surprising candour. 'We began to shadow the DM after an exaggerated fall in the exchange rate, in 1986, from DM 3.56 to DM 2.82/£. This depreciation generated an inflationary impulse, which we then locked in to the domestic economy by refusing to allow the exchange rate to recover to above DM 3.00, even though this involved an excessive loosening of monetary policy. The result was a violent inflationary boom.' George, with overall responsibility by 1987 for foreign exchange as well as gilts and the money market, was cross at the time on at least three levels. First, because he thought it a bad policy – at odds with market realities and a potential threat to the prioritisation of domestic inflation objectives; second, because of Lawson's lack of consultation with the Bank about the policy as such ('At no point,' he told colleagues, 'did Nigel Lawson tell us there was to be a policy of shadowing the Deutschmark'); and third, because of Lawson's overbearing interference with the policy's execution ('I think that decision can be left to us, Chancellor,' he snapped at one point). Such was the scale and frequency of intervention, irrespective of the policy's wisdom or otherwise, that these were

King George V and Queen Mary leave the Bank after their visit, December 1917; the governor, Lord Cunliffe, holds his top hat

Soane's Bank demolished, 1920s: Bank Stock Office (*above*), many years later recreated in the Museum; Rotunda (*top right*), including its lunettes; caryatids, made in 1795, being taken away (*opposite*) from the Consols Transfer Office, though eventually restored to the Museum

Printing dividend warrants at St Luke's, 1920s

Committee of Treasury, painted by A. K. Lawrence, 1928; the governor, Montagu Norman, third from right

Taking the Paris air, May 1930: Norman in the centre, with the Bank's lawyer, Sir William Leese of Freshfields, on the right

Baker's Bank: Portico
(*right*); Front Hall (*below*);
Court Room (*far top right*);
Garden Court (*far right*)

Bomb damage to Bank station, January 1941

On the seventh floor,
c. 1942: Messengers'
Quarters Kitchen

Waiting for nationalisation:
Lord Catto, 1944

Bank Note Office, 1942: prickers and stampers

Bank Note Office, 1961–2: paid notes for destruction

Bullion Office, 1960s: gold vault

Dividend Preparation Office, New Change, 1962: the Bank's first computer

A future governor, Leslie O'Brien, holding aloft a presentation book of signatures to the retiring governor, Lord ('Kim') Cobbold, June 1961

Lord Cromer, 1961, with Pitt the Younger continuing to keep an eye on the Old Lady

Personification of
the Discount Office:
Hilton Clarke, 1967

Printing works at
Debden, c. 1960

Governors during
turbulent years:
Gordon Richardson
(*right*), July 1973;
Robin Leigh-Pemberton
(*below*), c. 1990

South front, 1990s

The first two post-independence governors: Eddie George (*right*), 1990s; Mervyn King (*below*), April 2013. (The painting above George is Johann Zoffany's portrait of Abraham Vickery.)

demanding months. With dealing in foreign exchange continuous around the clock, Michael Foot – then head of the Foreign Exchange Division – would recall sometimes having to ring up George in the middle of the night, in the context of the money negotiated with the Treasury ('always too small') having run out: 'One of the things he was wonderful about was never complaining; he knew that if you rang him up it was because you had a good reason, it was never a difficulty. And he would then talk to the Treasury if need be ...'

The shadowing policy eventually ended – at the insistence of Thatcher, supported by the Bank – with the uncapping of the pound in March 1988 and the prime minister herself famously telling the Commons that 'there is no way in which you can buck the market'. Was that old warhorse, the ERM, a possible way? Lawson still hoped so, despite Thatcher's 1985 veto on UK participation; but, well aware of the intensifying conflict between No. 10 and No. 11 on the subject, Leigh-Pemberton by May 1989 was instructing Blunden that the Bank's 'clearly defined stance' on the issue needed for the time being to be one of 'neutrality'. Addressing the Institute of Economic Affairs two months later, the governor turned somewhat wearily to the 'particularly vexed, if also well-worn, question of the timing of our entry into the ERM'. Not only could there be 'no assurance that we would enter at an approximately appropriate rate', given that it had 'to be remembered that too low a rate would have damaging implications for inflation, just as too high a rate could have severe effects on activity and investment'; but also it remained the case that 'there is a difference in the cyclical position of the UK economy relative to the major member countries'. Altogether, in short, 'the problem is not easily solved'.[47]

That would also be true of another, less immediate monetary arrangement sometimes conflated in sceptical British eyes with the ERM: namely, European economic and monetary union (EMU). 'The terms of reference of the Delors Committee quite deliberately make no mention of a central bank or a single currency,' Thatcher told Leigh-Pemberton in person in July 1988 after the previous month's Hanover summit had agreed to the establishment of a committee 'for the Study of Economic and Monetary Union' chaired by the European Commission's strongly federalist president, Jacques Delors, and mainly comprising the European Community's twelve central bank governors. 'Consequently,' she went on, 'these are not topics on which the Committee should feel obliged to give a verdict … It is entirely premature to talk about a single currency or a [European] central bank …' More followed:

> The Prime Minister felt that the Governor's general attitude to the Committee's work should be 'if we were actually to have European monetary union then the following conditions would have to be satisfied and the following consequences tolerated …'
>
> She privately warned the Governor to be extremely careful of Delors, whom she described as a 'Jekyll and Hyde' character. He will appear to be very co-operative at the meetings and agree to confine the discussions to pragmatic steps – but will then make public speeches or work in the background to achieve quite a different objective. And 'Don't forget Delors is a socialist'.

Leigh-Pemberton himself would recall his negotiating instructions from Thatcher being boiled down to a simple injunction: 'Well, if we stride along with Karl Otto Pöhl [still head of the Bundesbank], that must be the right thing to do.'

September saw the start of the Committee's deliberations, against from Leigh-Pemberton's perspective an ominous political backcloth as Thatcher in her famous Bruges speech warned against 'a European superstate'. By early November the governor was giving a heads-up to Middleton at the Treasury that 'now that the drafting stage was getting near it was becoming increasingly evident that there might be pressure from the "idealists" in the Committee to suggest a greater degree of early change than might be acceptable to the "pragmatists"'. A month later an early draft of the report was in circulation. 'We should make it clear what *we* were aiming for,' Lawson having read it told Leigh-Pemberton, adding not only that 'the report might seem so extreme as to play into our hands, in that it gave us a better opportunity to work towards a minority report or to express reservations', but also that 'the combination of bad drafting and the influence of Delors might give us an opportunity to dissociate ourselves altogether from the whole exercise'. The governor for the moment kept his counsel, but soon afterwards told Middleton that it would be wrong for ministers to assume the inevitability of a dissenting report from himself. That was ahead of a key meeting on 14 December, where in essence both

Thatcher and Lawson told Leigh-Pemberton to stiffen his sinews, stay close to Pöhl – whom (in the prime minister's subsequent words) 'we considered strongly hostile to any serious loss of monetary autonomy for the Bundesbank' – and ensure that the eventual final report 'would make it clear that EMU was in no way necessary to the completion of the Single Market [due by the end of 1992] and would enlarge upon the full implications of EMU for the transfer of power and authority from national institutions to a central bureaucracy'.

Both central bankers, in her and Lawson's eyes, let them down. Leigh-Pemberton recorded on 16 February a very difficult meeting the day before at No. 10 with Lawson and the new foreign secretary (John Major) as well as Thatcher. She, having read the latest displeasing draft, took the line that she had agreed to the formation of the Delors Committee 'only on the understanding that it would not deal with a European Central Bank or a single currency'. To which the governor ruefully added in his note: 'In some way this has not emerged in the published version and she is now seeking for this omission to be rectified by the Committee – or at least one member of it!' He also noted that in the meeting all three ministers 'believed that the draft was so pitched as to be irredeemable by drafting amendments'. Feeling somewhat put upon, having duly stayed close to Pöhl, the governor now wrote to the prime minister, stating that 'while I shall do my best to comply with the requirements suggested to me and to avoid embarrassment to the UK government, I must be left a proper measure of my personal integrity on a body consisting of my colleagues on which I am acting in my personal capacity'. When in due course, in April 1989, the report was formally unveiled, it not only in Thatcher's words 'confirmed our worst fears', but featured no dissenting report from the governor. Official Bank policy on EMU remained that it was 'a matter for the politicians' – as Leigh-Pemberton next month put it to Blunden – but Thatcher never forgave him, freezing him out during the rest of her premiership.[48] Nor was the governor forgiven by her successor: when Major blocked his chairmanship of the G10 governors, a position that Richardson had enjoyed, that was little short of devastating.

In the bigger picture, though, it was a minor consideration compared to the great prize for the Bank that somewhat unexpectedly began to hover in the mid-distance during Leigh-Pemberton's second term. The prize was independence, albeit from the start there would be debate about what precisely that four-syllable word meant; and unexpectedly because of the generally bruising time that the Bank had had during Thatcher's decade. 'The traditional role of the Bank as a voice to advise and warn government has been reduced,' commented the *Financial Times* in January 1988 on the occasion of Leigh-Pemberton's reappointment, 'and its utterings now come more from the wings than from centre stage. The Bank's function has become limited to the more technical one of administering policy in the markets. Its ability to influence strategy has been further reduced by the personality of the Governor ...' So why independence? A significant early voice was that of the trenchant, sound-money City economist Tim Congdon. 'Britain should follow West Germany's example by giving the Bank of England as much independence from government as is currently enjoyed by the Bundesbank,' he declared in the *Spectator* in June 1987, against a background of what he called Britain's biggest-ever credit boom, with its accompanying threat of serious inflation. It was an argument, Congdon wrote, underpinned by his 'deep scepticism', after the previous forty years, 'about the ability and willingness of British governments to conduct financial policy in a consistent, stable and non-inflationary way'. There followed an attractively rigorous, puritanical vision:

> In a well-ordered country, decisions on monetary policy should not be subject to the vagaries of the electoral cycle and fluctuations in credit growth should not reflect politically motivated calculations about house price increases and the voting propensities of home-owners.
>
> The Bank of England should be privatised, its autonomy from government should be protected by statute, and both the tactics and strategy of monetary policy should be determined by the Governor of the Bank of England in consultation with its Court of Directors. The Chancellor of the Exchequer would be left with the humdrum but necessary task of keeping the Government's finances in good shape.

Congdon concluded with the long view. 'Before 1946 Britain had its own independent central bank,' he reminded readers; and during those fabled times, 'Britain's currency was the hub of a major international trading area' and 'Britain's inflation record had long been better than that of any other European nation.'

The ghost of Montagu Norman perhaps twitched – and would have twitched again if it had been privy to the remarkable memorandum that Lawson in November 1988 sent to Thatcher, proposing 'to give statutory independence to the Bank of England, charging it with the statutory duty to preserve the value of the currency, along the lines already in place and of proven effectiveness for the US Federal Reserve, the National Bank of Switzerland, and the Bundesbank'. He went on:

> Such a move would enhance the market credibility of our anti-inflationary stance, both nationally and internationally. It would make it absolutely clear that the fight against inflation remains our top priority; it would do something to help de-politicise interest rate changes – though that can never be completely achieved; above all there would be the longer-term advantage that we would be seen to be locking a permanent anti-inflationary force into the system, as a counter-weight to the strong inflationary pressures which are always lurking.

It was not, Lawson stressed subsequently, that he had any 'illusion that the Bank of England possesses any superior wisdom'. Instead, the benefit lay in 'the logic of the institutional change itself', through which an independent central bank would necessarily enjoy a far greater degree of market credibility than a government ever could; and 'this extra market credibility is what would make the successful conduct of monetary policy less difficult'. Thatcher was appalled:

> My reaction was dismissive ... I did not believe, as Nigel argued, that it would boost the credibility of the fight against inflation ... In fact, as I minuted, 'It would be seen as an abdication by the Chancellor ...' I added that 'it would be an admission of a failure of resolve on our part'. I also doubted whether we had people of the right calibre to run such an institution.

Faced by Thatcher's insistence that the control of inflation was ultimately a political problem, not amenable to institutional solutions, Lawson was compelled to let his secret proposal rest.

Less than a year later, however, the genie was out of the bottle. The context was Lawson's resignation in October 1989, a resignation that quite apart from the independence issue had two piquant Bank aspects: the day before he went, Thatcher tried in vain to dissuade him by dangling the prospect of becoming in due course the next governor; while when it was clear he was going, but with nowhere to live in London, the present governor generously offered the temporary use of his flat in New Change. On the 31st, five days after resigning, Lawson gave his resignation speech in the Commons, touching briefly on his rejected proposal to the prime minister for an independent Bank as a way in which 'anti-inflationary credibility might be enhanced in the eyes of the market'. Reaction was mixed. 'It is an excellent idea,' pronounced Credit Suisse First Boston's influential economist Giles Keating. 'The only tragedy is that it was not considered a long time ago.' The shadow chancellor, John Smith, took a wholly different view, stating categorically that Labour 'would not be willing to accept any system of central banks which would be independent of political control, just as we strongly oppose an independent status for the Bank of England'. And somewhere in the middle, but leaning to the positive, *The Times* devoted an editorial to 'A Freer Bank?':

> There is no reason to suppose that it would not rise to the challenge. One cannot judge its capacity by the advice it may have given in the different circumstances of its present enabling role. The exact nature of its obligation would be a matter for careful thought but it would almost certainly need to be a general responsibility for the value of the currency rather than responsibility for any more specific intermediate target such as the money supply.
>
> Yet there is a conundrum at the heart of the proposal. Why if monetary policy is so important should it be taken out of the hands of elected representatives? Put another way, if monetary policy is too important for the politicians, why not fiscal policy and many other aspects of economic affairs? ...
>
> The answer may be that monetary policy is the rock upon which all economic transactions in a modern economy are founded. Unsound money will undermine all other aspects of economic policy. Ways of improving on our capacity to achieve it cannot be dismissed without the most careful consideration.[49]

Welcome and Long Overdue

By the early 1990s the cult of the central bank was gathering global momentum. 'By far the most persuasive case for central bank independence was the rise of stateless money and global financial market integration,' Steven Solomon would convincingly argue in retrospect about the growing trend since the 1987 crash. 'Broadly put, in a landscape in which tears anywhere in the interwoven financial fabric or abrupt alteration in the direction or size of international capital flows could disrupt prosperity across borders, it served the enlightened self-interest of citizens and capitalists everywhere to pool their sovereignty through the upgraded independence of all central bankers.' Examples of this new prominence included preparations for an eventual European Central Bank, the creation of authentic central banks in Eastern Europe after the fall of the Berlin Wall, and the well-publicised, fully transparent development in New Zealand, where from 1990 the governor of the central bank was given an inflation target and required to adjust monetary policy to meet it. 'The Triumph of Central Banking?' was the bold if necessarily provisional title in September 1990 of Paul Volcker's Per Jacobsson lecture in Washington. 'I am convinced,' declared this fairly recently retired central banker who had won renown as the great inflation-slayer, 'there is objective reality in my impression that central banks are in exceptionally good repute these days'; and he looked ahead with a reasonable degree of confidence to a time when few would disagree with the proposition that 'an effective central bank must be a strong central bank, with substantial autonomy in its operations and with insulation from partisan and passing political pressures'.

That was not quite how at least two prominent British politicians saw it. Not only did Thatcher in her last year in office not change her mind about independence, typically pushing through in October 1990 an interest rate cut against explicit Bank advice, but she kept as tight a grip as ever on Bank appointments. 'I think that the Chancellor really has battled hard on our behalf to secure an industrialist,' noted Leigh-Pemberton in February 1990 after lunch with Nigel Lawson's successor, John Major. 'The Prime Minister, however, has decided that she would like to have an economist on the Court and Mervyn King is her choice. I said that I was content to accept this ...' Moreover, despite his help on this occasion, Major when it came to the bigger question was on the other side. 'He said that he doubted whether there was much support in the House of Commons for an independent Central Bank,' the governor also recorded after that meeting with the chancellor; while in his autobiography Major would be bluntness itself: 'I considered giving the Bank of England independence over interest rate policy, as Nigel had wished to do ... I dismissed the idea because I believed the person responsible for monetary policy should be answerable for it in the House of Commons.' Nor was there any sign of that adamantine stance altering after he succeeded Thatcher at No. 10 in November 1990, albeit by the second half of 1991 his own successor at No. 11, Norman Lamont, was picking up on the New Zealand model and starting to try to engage him on the independence issue.[1]

At the Bank itself, much discussion naturally ensued after Lawson's resignation speech had revealed his unsuccessful initiative. From the start, there were some vexed, difficult aspects to consider, and not only the obvious ones of remit and accountability. 'Would greater autonomy over monetary policy make it likely/possible that some functions would be taken away from the Bank?' asked the governor's private secretary Paul Tucker on his behalf in February 1990. 'Specifically, would we lose the debt management function and/or the industrial finance or bank supervision functions, or anything else?' And beyond that, really drilling down to fundamentals: 'Do we believe that greater autonomy would be a good thing?' Over the next half-year, at least three intense meetings sought to get to grips with what was at stake.

At the first, an informal Court discussion, the main voice was George Blunden's, essentially a warning one. The Bank, he argued, not only in practice already enjoyed considerable operational autonomy, but 'was almost unique in that its functions were not laid down in statute'. Nor could it be automatically assumed, he went on, that 'placing a central bank under a mandate to pursue price stability would *guarantee* a better inflation performance'; while crucially the British public did not yet share the 'strong aversion to inflation' felt in Germany and Switzerland, 'the two obvious countries where success was combined with considerable independence' – indeed, 'on the contrary, public opinion probably regarded a bit of inflation as no bad thing', given that 'a wage offer of less than five per cent was widely viewed as insulting'. Blunden as it happened was about to step down as deputy governor, and it was the deputy designate, Eddie George, who later at that meeting took a strongly pro-independence line, especially on the grounds of clarity of both objectives and responsibility. 'Who,' he asked, 'was responsible for the policy mistakes of the past few years – Bank or Treasury officials, the Chancellor, the Prime Minister or the Cabinet?' And he declared: 'Placing the central bank under a mandate to pursue price stability would resolve both these difficulties.'

The second meeting, two months later in April 1990, saw a continuation of the Court's informal discussion. Sir David Scholey, by now one of the senior non-executives, was 'inclined to think that it was better for the Bank to settle for something short of independence and statutory accountability for monetary policy, and rather to continue to work behind the scenes'; Leigh-Pemberton, like George, reflected on 'the unsatisfactory position whereby it was unclear who was responsible for determining monetary policy in the UK'; a pair of non-execs, the trade unionist Gavin Laird and the industrialist Brian Corby, tended to agree with Scholey, with the latter warning that 'it would be the worst of all worlds for the Bank if it were given responsibility for bringing down inflation but could not succeed because of public attitudes'; David Walker (no longer an executive director, but still on the Court) deemed it 'important that the Bank should not be constrained from continuing with its present wide range of roles and that, in consequence, careful consideration should be given to any prospective trade-offs before pressing for a change', as well as noting that he 'thought it inconceivable that government (any government) would give up ultimate responsibility for monetary policy'; the new boy, Mervyn King, 'said that there was no doubt at all that a greater

role for the Bank in monetary policy was definitely on the agenda',
pointing out that 'it was quite something when the Economics Editor
of the *Guardian* and the IEA [the free-market Institute of Economic
Affairs] shared an economic policy objective'; and George concurred,
reflecting that he had been 'quite surprised by the extent of support
for the idea of making the Bank statutorily accountable for monetary
policy, both in the City and in Parliament', where a recent survey had
'suggested that seven out of ten Conservative MPs would support a
change'.

Finally, in July, a handful of senior executives assembled. They
began with Leigh-Pemberton and George accepting that no fundamental change was likely in the near future, but with George stating
that he 'nevertheless believed that the Bank could help to improve
the climate as regards the Bank's constitutional position by continuing to press the point that price stability was an absolutely essential
pre-condition of stable long-term growth and the proper functioning
of the economy'. Attention then turned to various possible models
for the Bank/Treasury relationship, as well as the question of whether
enhanced responsibility on the monetary side might lead to the
removal of other Bank functions, including bank supervision. Two of
those present, Andrew Crockett and the economist John Flemming,
agreed that this might well be the case; but George for his part 'did
not believe there was a logical case for removing functions from the
Bank', and Leigh-Pemberton broadly concurred, adding that the
Bank should 'resist' any attempt to remove functions. There was, in
short, all still to play for.

Publicly, of course, the Bank played a pretty straight bat on the
whole issue. 'Talking about an independent central bank may not be
the best way of describing it,' the governor told an interviewer that
summer. Instead:

The question to think about is rather whether the central bank as a
free-standing body should have some sort of statutory accountability for monetary policy. Is there something about the operation of
monetary policy that makes it quite different from other elements
of economic policy or indeed other elements of government policy?
If you believe this is true, it is a highly political question. This is
something politicians will have to make up their minds about.

Indeed, he seems to have gone to some pains at this stage to ensure that the Bank was seen not to be canvassing for independence – whatever that word meant – too blatantly, especially after a steer to that effect in 1991 from the broadly sympathetic Lamont, well aware of sensitivities at No. 10. Even so, for both governor and deputy that was now the goal. 'In some senses,' Leigh-Pemberton revealingly observed to George in March 1992 a fortnight before Major's somewhat unexpected election victory over Labour's Neil Kinnock, 'the most unsatisfactory outcome would be a hung Parliament, but in a narrow sense I think that it could actually create an important situation and even an opportunity for us, as there may be a need in those circumstances for the politicians to announce that the monetary reins had been placed in our hands ...'²

Increasingly the pivotal day-to-day figure at the Bank during these years was Eddie George, deputy governor from March 1990. Reputedly the Treasury was not keen, taking the line that his appointment should not be viewed as automatically presaging his governorship, while Leigh-Pemberton would have preferred Crockett; but the probability is that Thatcher and her economic adviser Sir Alan Walters pushed it through, encouraged by the pro-George lobbying of her confidant at the Bank, the non-executive director Sir Hector Laing; while Blunden had already paved the way for George by ensuring that David Walker was safely parked at the SIB. Undoubtedly the old deputy recognised in the new deputy not only a hugely capable operator but also, like himself, a Bank man to his core; and in his first message to staff, George wrote wholly sincerely of his pride in working for 'an institution with a long tradition of solid values as well as solid achievements'. He went on:

> *Those values must not change.* The trust essential to all our dealings has been built up over years on the basis of integrity and discretion: without that it could be rapidly destroyed. The authority we enjoy, and sometimes need to exercise with firmness, can only be effective if it has at least the tacit support of those it affects: this we will retain only if we are prepared to consult, listen and understand, and to persuade rather than dictate. And it is our style to seek to further the public good by stealth rather than self-promotion.

The new order at the Bank coincided with the protracted and painful recession of the early 1990s, but prompting little support from

George for what he saw as soft, politically motivated options. 'There was no way of curing cost-push inflation other than severe pressure on margins and thus an increase in unemployment,' he told the clearers in September 1990, adding that 'he conceded that this was a hard approach but he thought it had been proved to be the only way'. Similarly, almost two years later, in the context of possible fiscal-stimulus action, he observed to the Treasury's Alan Budd that 'while, to date, most emphasis in the public debate had been on actions specifically targeted at the housing market, he felt that the distress in the housing market was a symptom rather than a cause of the problem and it made no economic sense to focus relief on house owners'. As usual with a government in an economic hole, the prime minister of the day (now Major) sought to blame the banks; and in his memoirs, Lamont recorded No. 10 putting pressure on him in 1991 to put pressure on Leigh-Pemberton to put pressure in turn on the clearers to change their lending practices. 'I have to say the Governor was not very pleased with me, since he felt the banks should not be made scapegoats for the recession. He did not know that I very much sympathised with his view.'[3]

The banks were closely involved, albeit mainly behind the scenes, in what became known during the early 1990s as the 'London Approach' – a significant Bank initiative, largely driven by Pen Kent and inevitably with echoes of the Bank's activities in industrial finance during the mid-1970s and early 1980s. Against a deteriorating economic background (including an increasingly troubled UK corporate sector), and well aware that the Bank no longer necessarily possessed quite the same feudal authority in the City that it had once commanded, Kent in July 1990 argued that the Bank now needed formally to promulgate some rules about collaborative rescue action for struggling companies that were nevertheless essentially sound. 'I have to say I take an extremely cautious view of this,' observed a somewhat sceptical George; but that autumn, in a speech to the annual dinner of the Equipment Leasing Association, Leigh-Pemberton set out the three key principles:

> The first is that, when difficulties arise, a lending standstill should be considered so that a proper analysis can be made of whether continuing support – and particularly additional financing – is justifiable. Secondly, the fullest possible information should be gathered

to support that analysis and the subsequent judgement. And thirdly, there is a very important role for the lead bank. Whatever its size or home base, the lead bank needs to ensure that all interested bank creditors are informed of the company's position at the earliest possible stage, and are *kept* informed. This is of help to all creditors, and particularly the smaller banks. No one should be – or feel – disadvantaged through lack of information.

The governor added that while the Bank was willing in principle to act as 'a neutral chairman', depending on the circumstances, it would not 'seek to protect or favour any particular group of banks or other creditors' nor would it 'dictate that a rescue must be agreed', given that 'it is the creditors' money that is at stake'. Even so, the Bank now found itself actively engaged in a whole range of support-cum-restructuring cases – as many as fifty new ones between January 1991 and March 1992, including such names as Nissan UK, Vestey Group and Maxwell Communications. By November 1992, looking back on almost three years of sustained corporate workouts, Kent felt able to conclude that the London Approach continued to enjoy 'widespread acceptance in the banking community because it is seen to be fair and flexible'; and that 'a large number of companies owe their survival to their banks, and thus, indirectly, to the London Approach'.[4]

Predating that initiative but overlapping with it, probably nothing on the corporate front occupied more of the Bank's time than the Eurotunnel saga. Back in the early days, following the Anglo-French treaty of February 1986 that established the project, it was Walker who made much of the running, not only getting a grip on the equity financing but seeking to strengthen the Eurotunnel board and management; crucially, it was his suggestion to bring in the determined if sometimes abrasive Alastair Morton. Progress, though, was seldom straightforward, not least in the company's relationships with banks and contractors. 'At times our discussion, which lasted an hour, became rather sharp,' noted Leigh-Pemberton in January 1990 after a difficult meeting with Morton, 'and I told him that, while I did not take it upon myself to make judgments in the matter, I thought it would be useful for him to give due consideration to the impressions I had formed as a result of my discussions with the other parties.' The following month saw a heads-being-banged-together summit, chaired by the governor and featuring one moment of lightish relief. 'Sir Robert Scholey [chairman of British Steel and a Eurotunnel director] commented, apropos of nothing in particular, that it was bizarre to be in the Bank of England discussing management structures and organograms. The governor responded that he quite understood the point but sadly it was *not* trivial. A great deal turned on the intentions of the parties and the understandings between them.' Finally, an agreement was signed – 'there is only one copy of this in existence (i.e. no photocopies) and this is held in the GPS safe', noted the governor's private secretary – but soon afterwards Morton was back to playing hardball with the contractors. 'A plague on both their houses – I ought not to allow myself such a sentiment but it is tempting,' Leigh-Pemberton found himself expostulating to Kent. 'I agree with you that this latest issue is not for us: but how can we generate good will or good faith in such people!' Further dramas lay ahead – including later in 1990 a decisive intervention with the Japanese banks, in 1993 some tricky arbitration manoeuvres overseen by Kent, in 1994 a quiet but timely governor's word with Salomon Brothers to ensure completion of underwriting – before eventually the project was brought to full fruition.[5]

A further element during the generally fraught early 1990s was the small-banks crisis. By all accounts it was the opportunity for George to provide a master class in crisis management, resulting in the safe winding up of many of the banks and the merger or acquisition of others. In late 1993 he made public the broad outlines of an episode that had unfolded largely in secret:

> We had during 1990 been conscious of growing pressures on a sizeable group of smaller banks. They had some retail deposits, but were generally heavily dependent on large wholesale placers of funds: building societies, local authorities, big industrial companies, as well as other banks. All of these were under pressure of some kind and withdrew funds from the wholesale markets. Meanwhile, the assets of the smaller UK banks were becoming increasingly vulnerable to the recession, particularly as it affected the property values supporting their loans.
>
> In early 1991, three small banks – Chancery, Eddington and Authority – closed their doors, after significant loan losses that

were followed by a shrinking of their deposits. At that stage, we saw no clear evidence of systemic fragility so we did not intervene.

The wholesale markets continued to tighten. This process accelerated when BCCI [Bank of Credit and Commerce International] was closed later in the year, trapping some large local authority deposits. Meanwhile – and there is always a meanwhile for banking troubles come in a crowd – there was, quite coincidentally, a run on a building society and growing talk of banks in difficulties overseas.

We had been engaged in prophylactic supervision for some time. But as the bigger picture got more threatening, one particular institution [National Mortgage Bank, a subsidiary of National Home Loans] did run into an immediate liquidity crisis: its auditors could not certify that it had enough assurance of liquidity to allow it to continue to trade. It was then that we decided to provide support to that and to a small number of other banks.

It is, of course, impossible to be sure what would have happened if we had not provided support in this, or any other, particular case. It is easy to slip into the position of the man on the train to Brighton who kept snapping his fingers out of the window to keep the elephants away. Since he saw no elephants, his technique was self-evidently effective. But in the early 1990s, we were quite clear that had we failed to intervene, the pressure would have spread and we would then have found it harder to stop. It was the first time since 1973–74 that we had offered such widespread support ...

Overall, reckoned George subsequently about the crisis as a whole, 'we were monitoring 60-odd institutions and I think we lent to about seven or eight'; in the case of National Mortgage Bank, the Bank eventually acquired it for £1, thereby assuming some £100 million of losses on its balance sheet that in due course were worked out.[6] Throughout the ultimate fear was contagion, and among bigger houses giving cause for concern was the merchant bank Kleinwort Benson. But, as so often in these situations, the Treasury was inclined to suspect the Bank of being trigger-happy: it was a thought that lingered in the institutional memory.

One bank above all, though, really worried the Old Lady in the early 1990s. 'It is a bank which is shrinking and will continue to do so,' declared *The Times* in December 1990 after the increasingly enfeebled Midland had suffered the humiliation of its main minority shareholder, HSBC, deciding temporarily to walk away from a long-mooted union. Or as the *Investors Chronicle* put it: 'Midland is now fully exposed for what it is: a troubled, financially weak, second-rank clearer.' The following month, in January 1991, the governor and his senior colleagues met to consider Midland's future – a far from easy meeting that ended with a decision in effect to withdraw support from McMahon, its beleaguered chairman and chief executive. Within weeks the Bank had put in place a duo – Sir Peter Walters from BP and Brian Pearse from Barclays – to replace him. 'Sir Kit indicated that he did not necessarily agree with the need for such radical changes but had seemed to accept the Bank's right to impose them,' recorded the tactful note of the conversation in which the governor indicated to his former deputy that he had run out of road. Market reaction was positive; and indeed, before making his move, Leigh-Pemberton had carefully checked with the senior partners of Cazenove that it would be.

The new team at Midland made a good go of it in impossible circumstances, but by the closing weeks of 1991 it was clear that both HSBC and Lloyds were seriously interested in taking over the ailing, recession-hit bank. In Threadneedle Street, the preference was unambiguous. 'A merger with HSBC would not produce the same economies as would a merger with one of the clearers,' George in late November frankly told Pearse, adding that HSBC 'could not provide the same degree of credit rating enhancement as one of the clearers'. By contrast, he continued, the Bank would be 'fairly supportive' of a bid from Lloyds, not least since an ensuing merger would be 'in the family'. Shortly before Christmas, the two men met again, with George emphasising to Pearse that, as far as HSBC's top man William ('Willie') Purves was concerned, the Bank 'were', noted Pearse, 'determined to see him off' – some ten years after the far-from-forgotten episode of HSBC's blatant defiance of Richardson's wishes in relation to RBS. Everything changed, however, in the early months of 1992. The Bank reluctantly came to accept the near-certainty of a bid by Lloyds being referred by government to the Monopolies and Mergers Commission; Midland itself started to cool towards Lloyds; and on the vexed matter of 'Hong Kong risk', three years after the Tiananmen Square massacre and five years before Hong Kong's handover to China, Quinn by early

March was telling Leigh-Pemberton and George that 'as he and the supervisors studied the Hong Kong situation more carefully, they were becoming slightly less concerned about the problem, especially given the integration of Hong Kong with the South Eastern PRC [People's Republic of China]'. Soon afterwards, Midland's board finally came down on the side of an HSBC bid, leading in turn to a series of increasingly harmonious discussions between the Bank and HSBC. For its part, the Bank laid down certain conditions: all major non-Hong Kong subsidiaries (including Midland) to become subsidiaries of HSBC's UK-based holdings company; the 'mind and management' of HSBC Holdings to be exercised in London, which meant in practice that Purves and his top team would have to leave Hong Kong and become resident in the UK; the Hong Kong businesses to be entirely funded from local sources; and the Bank to be the overall lead regulator for the HSBC Group. HSBC was happy to accede on all these points and on 13 April the Bank gave an informal green light to its bid. That bid duly went ahead; the City's institutional investors had their say; and Lloyds pulled out in early June, with its chairman, Sir Jeremy Morse, adamant that his bank had not been leaned on by the Bank to do so.[7] Undeniably the outcome, whatever the Bank's initial scepticism, strengthened the British banking system – and importantly, left it with four main high-street clearers, not three.

The other big banking story in the early 1990s, but going back a long way, was of course BCCI. Founded in 1972 by a charismatic Pakistani, Agha Hasan Abedi, the Bank of Credit and Commerce International expanded rapidly around the world (mainly servicing Muslim and Third World clients) and, although registered in Luxembourg, had London as its international operating headquarters. The Bank cast a beady eye. 'I gave him a frank account of our reasons for taking a distinctly cautious view of BCCI and for impressing on them the need to pause for consolidation,' noted Jasper Hollom in 1979 after a visit from the Conservative politician Julian Amery, hoping to become a consultant at BCCI. 'I had no doubt that while Abedi would pay some heed to our advice, it would go against the grain with him and we should therefore have to continue to rein him in.' Nor physically was BCCI allowed in the heart of the City: when the following year Royal Insurance was looking to develop an empty site at 1 Cornhill into a prestigious banking hall, and the only serious offer came from BCCI, the decisive word from across the road was that that bank would not be an acceptable tenant. Then during the rest of the 1980s, as BCCI lost huge amounts through ill-judged proprietary trading and looked increasingly to provide money-laundering services to Latin America's drug barons, while at the same time its structure became ever more byzantine, the Bank continued to view its UK activities with considerable mistrust. 'Bank's [that is, Bank of England's] locus technically confined to UK branches of Luxembourg bank, and objective the protection of UK depositors,' recorded a retrospective internal memo in July 1991:

> Bank anxious to avoid being dragged into becoming supervisor for group world-wide, given the complexity and opacity of the group and the false comfort that could have been taken by depositors and the market.
>
> Nevertheless, Bank's supervision consistently more rigorous than for any other branch operation. In the last ten years, six special visits by Bank teams and six reports (by reporting accountants) commissioned under the Banking Act. Nothing material discovered; any remedial action quickly taken. Since October 1988, weekly statistics and monthly meetings with UK management.

That anxiety about taking on global supervisory responsibilities was for a long time very real. 'We have a difficult matter over BCCI where Lord Callaghan [the former Labour prime minister] came in to try and persuade Brian Quinn and myself to allow BCCI to register in London and to come under B of E supervision,' Leigh-Pemberton informed Blunden in May 1989. 'We both feel that we must resist this, but this particular request from this particular source may need careful handling.'[8]

The endgame came fairly swiftly. To quote again the Bank's July 1991 retrospective:

> Firm evidence of dishonesty in the group emerged in 1988/89 through the Tampa drug-money laundering trials and, separately, in 1990 through evidence that BCCI had acquired control of a Washington-based bank by deception. In the first of these cases, there was no demonstrated link with UK management or with senior

group management, but rather the evidence was that the problem was specific to Miami. And in the second case, the American investigations are still under way; no charges have yet been brought. We have been co-operating with the relevant US authorities.

Evidence of financial malpractice and fraud involving the UK operation was first suggested to us at the beginning of this year and this was immediately investigated by Price Waterhouse, with a section 41 report [under the Banking Act] being commissioned by the Bank in March. This was received 10 days ago, on the basis of which co-ordinated action was taken urgently by the main supervisory authorities concerned.

The global closure of BCCI in July 1991 was a huge event – though with only 6,500 of the bank's 150,000 depositors being in the UK, and with no systemic threat to the British banking system, there was no real question of a government or Bank bail-out. 'The Governors felt that this would not be appropriate,' noted Leigh-Pemberton's private secretary of the possibility of offering financial help to British depositors. 'There was nothing obvious to distinguish BCCI from other deposit-taking institutions in this respect, so that offering help would be unjustified on its merits, could set an unfortunate precedent and might even prompt commentators to suggest that the Bank felt a degree of culpability.' But was the Bank culpable? 'Ministers are standing well back,' and 'none has had a word to say for the Bank', observed Christopher Fildes in the *Spectator* later that month, adding that Leigh-Pemberton was looking 'an isolated figure – flying to the Gulf to mollify the sheikh [in the context of BCCI having in 1990 moved its headquarters to Abu Dhabi], hauled to Westminster once a week for a grilling from backbenchers'; while, as Lamont had already told the governor, Major was 'adamant' that there had to be a formal inquiry into the closure of BCCI, with Lord Justice Bingham soon commissioned to produce a report.[9] In the event, there would be no fewer than three reports on BCCI – from the House of Commons Treasury Select Committee and from the US Congress as well as from Bingham – and in all three the Bank featured prominently.

The British parliamentarians were in action, as Fildes intimated, within weeks of the enforced closure. Against a backdrop of mounting press criticism – typified by the *Sunday Times*'s claim that 'even armed with a

file of press cuttings the Bank of England should have done a better job'
– they interviewed the governor, accompanied by George and Quinn,
over a two-hour session. Predictably, some of the most hostile questioning came from two Labour MPs. 'Let me ask you this,' Diane Abbott put
it to the Bank team after summarising some of the information contained
in two audit reports the previous year by Price Waterhouse on BCCI. 'If
10 per cent of your [BCCI's] capital base is shovelled out in unsecured,
undocumented and dodgy loans does that not amount to evidence of
fraud on a scale which justifies revocation [of BCCI's licence]? How
much of your capital base does, in fact, have to be shovelled out in dodgy
loans for the Bank of England to raise an eyebrow?' 'I think the answer
to Ms Abbott,' replied George, 'is it is actually possible with a sophisticated fraud of this kind for that sort of thing to go on undetected for
a considerable period.' The other MP, Brian Sedgemore, made much of
how when several years earlier Leigh-Pemberton had appeared before
the Treasury Committee (on that occasion with Blunden and Rodney
Galpin) he – Sedgemore – had referred to BCCI's West African desk
as 'a financial cesspit'. That comment, responded the governor now,
'would have been noted down', but it was 'not the sort of evidence on
which we can safely embark to revoke the licence of a bank'. Sedgemore,
previously a vocal critic of the Bank in relation to the Johnson Matthey
episode, was predictably unimpressed:

> When somebody in a quasi responsible position, not obviously a
> complete lunatic, has had the benefit of a massive British education,
> when they gave you this warning – I did not think it up off the top
> of my head, I had a source obviously – did anybody around the
> Bank ever think to say, because they did not at this meeting: 'What
> is their evidence'? Nobody wrote to me.

'I am afraid we did not think of saying that,' replied the governor.
'Part of the difficulty of this is that the West African branch of a bank
incorporated in Luxembourg is rather remote from the jurisdiction
of the Bank of England in England.' Further exchanges followed,
ending with Sedgemore accusing the Bank of 'a cover-up'. That was
the Bank's main evidence, but seven months later, in February 1992,
the Bank's two top supervisors, Quinn and Roger Barnes, appeared
before the Committee. 'We had no shortage, if I may use that term, of

allegations and accusations about BCCI,' accepted the former about the period going back to at least the mid-1980s. However, he went on, 'Allegations and accusations are one thing. The provision of evidence on the basis of which we can act is something very different.' And later Quinn elaborated:

> The Section 41 report completely transformed our view of BCCI. What we had seen hitherto had been indications. We had seen suspicions voiced by the auditor. We had seen concerns expressed by the auditor. What we saw in June 1991 was hard evidence for the first time that fraud had been conducted and supporting information to corroborate that: information that could trace the money flows, could show how accounts in one institution were used, indeed established, to keep accounts in other institutions current and alive. It was a complete picture and the picture it painted was of widespread pervasive fraud over a long period of time ...

The Treasury Committee, though, was unconvinced. Its report the following month accused the Bank of having been neither 'adequate' nor 'speedy' in its remedial action prior to July 1991; and in particular, it focused on how the Bank had failed to respond satisfactorily to the Price Waterhouse audit report of April 1990 identifying BCCI transactions, mainly booked offshore, that were either 'false or deceitful'.

The other two reports appeared in October 1992. The Congressional inquiry had some unpalatable words for the Bank: it had 'colluded in the suppression of the true facts concerning BCCI's financial status and its involvement in fraud'; it had been a 'partner not in crime but in a cover-up' by discounting for too long evidence of fraud and not objecting to Abu Dhabi's capital injection into BCCI; it had attempted to throw a 'veil of secrecy' over its actions; and altogether, its regulation of BCCI had been 'wholly inadequate' to protect depositors and creditors. As for the Lord Justice's findings, perhaps the most lucid summary came from Quinn, once he had sight a few weeks ahead of publication:

> The Bingham Report criticises the Bank for lack of alertness in picking up signs of fraud in BCCI; for failing to follow-up warnings given by others; for inadequacies in communicating with other

agencies, here and abroad, which had knowledge of, or interest in, BCCI's activities which were relevant to our or their statutory responsibilities; and for a general lack of suspiciousness in our dealings with BCCI.

On the other hand, he noted gratefully, the report 'acknowledges the exceptionally complex nature of the BCCI affair and sees it as in many respects unique'. During the days immediately before publication, internal discussion turned to the press: the *Telegraph*, it was agreed, 'would need special handling', while 'there was little point in seeking to influence the *Guardian*'. The fourth estate did not disappoint, exemplified by another excoriating piece in the *Sunday Times*, referring scornfully to Leigh-Pemberton's 'patrician amateurism' and claiming that Bingham had compelled the Bank to move in a single week 'from the 1950s into the 1990s, wiped clean of its traditional arrogance'. The shadow chancellor, Gordon Brown, called for the governor to go, but Lamont insisted that he still had 'every confidence' in him, emphasising that the report showed no evidence of duplicity or bad faith on the Bank's part. Even so, it was still a very dark moment.

Perhaps unsurprisingly, all things considered, BCCI as an episode did not go quietly into the good night. In January 2004, over twelve years after the plug had been pulled on the bank, which left undeclared debts of £7 billion and some 80,000 depositors out of pocket, BCCI's liquidators, Deloitte & Touche, brought a case in the High Court endeavouring to prove that the Bank had committed 'misfeasance in public office' in its supervision of BCCI. The Bank fought the charge vigorously; retired officials gave lengthy evidence; and eventually, in November 2005, the liquidators dropped the hugely expensive case and paid the Bank's costs. All that, though, was only a minor footnote, compared to the significant reputational damage suffered by the Bank in 1991–2. In retrospect, amid the overwhelming mass of documentation, arguably one particular exchange stands out. Early in 1987, in a note on BCCI's management, a Bank supervisor reflected that 'the style of supervision customarily applied to British banks, based as it is largely on trust, would be totally inappropriate'; to which Leigh-Pemberton minuted, 'Haven't we got to make up our minds one way or another about this bank?' Four years later, the Bank still had not made up its mind. Of course there were many understandable reasons for continuing indecision, not least towards the end the genuine international supervisory progress being made towards breaking up BCCI into separately capitalised and ring-fenced UK, Hong Kong and Abu Dhabi banks; but that indecision, ultimately the governor's responsibility, was the fatal error.[10] It is tempting to speculate that in an earlier, more Normanesque era, when banking supervision did not involve statute, the governor of the day would simply have followed his nose and sought, once and for all, to expunge the bad smell.

There was one other crucial element in the challenging early 1990s kaleidoscope. 'Thank God – now down to some strong discipline,' applauded the *Sunday Telegraph*, as Britain in October 1990 at last joined the Exchange Rate Mechanism (ERM). The decision was taken by Major as chancellor and reluctantly acquiesced in by Thatcher, with the Bank playing 'very little role', reckoned Charles Goodhart. 'Its views were anyhow mixed. It recognised the risks of a pegged, but adjustable, exchange rate; on the other hand there was a need for a nominal anchor for policy.' Among those instinctively at the more sceptical end of the spectrum was George, though grudgingly coming to accept there was perhaps no alternative; whereas the governor was entirely sincere when in his Mansion House speech, ten days after entry, he declared that membership of a fixed-rate regime was 'necessary to get us back on track – to restore the conditions for sustainable non-inflationary growth' through providing 'a discipline on policy-makers, on lenders and borrowers, and on wage bargainers'.[11]

It did not quite work out. George would look back on the fateful episode in a 1996 lecture:

At the time of our entry into the ERM our policy needs appeared to coincide with those of our partners. The economy was responding to the high though falling level of interest rates and inflation was coming down. In principle, it seemed possible that with the enhanced policy credibility that ERM membership was expected to bring, we could hope to complete the domestic economic stabilisation with lower interest rates than otherwise, and so at less cost in terms of loss of output …

In the event, reunification meant that Germany needed to maintain a tight monetary policy at a time when the domestic situation in a number of other ERM countries, including the United Kingdom, required an easing of monetary policy ...

It can certainly be argued that the problems within the ERM – including our own problem – could have been avoided by timely adjustment of the relevant parities. And so in principle they could. But in practice it is never as easy as that makes it sound. By the time the developing tension became apparent, the Deutsche Mark anchor was already entrenched as the absolutely key element of the monetary policy framework in other member countries – on which their anti-inflationary credibility crucially depended. To give that up, without a real fight, would have imposed real economic costs. These costs might have been less if it had been possible to agree upon a unilateral Deutsche Mark revaluation – making it clear that the root of the problem lay in the exceptional circumstances of German reunification. But that approach could not be agreed.

We were then confronted with a situation in which raising interest rates made no economic sense in terms of our domestic conditions and so we sought to maintain the parity [back in October 1990, an unfortunately high DM2.95 to the pound] through intervention in the hope that the pressures in Germany would ease ...

That was essentially the situation by the late summer of 1992, a situation not helped by the Danish referendum in June rejecting the European Community's Maastricht Treaty and thereby increasing tensions within the ERM. During July and August, sterling was under serious pressure, as concerns grew about the likelihood of a French rejection of Maastricht, with the referendum due to be held on 20 September. The August issue of the Bank's *Quarterly Bulletin* soberly noted the ERM's 'strains', but sought to calm markets by emphasising the importance of the credibility derived from the authorities' macro-economic policies.

The crunch was inexorably coming. In an update for George on 7 August, Leigh-Pemberton noted that the Bank's Anthony Coleby had recently attended a meeting at the Treasury which had 'included a discussion to the effect that the only alternative to the present policy was to leave the ERM, unilateral devaluations and a realignment being out'. A palpably disconcerted governor went on: 'He [Coleby] spoke as though Treasury officials thought it prudent to prepare for such a drastic reversal of policy as a precaution. Presumably they have more experience than we do of Ministerial jitters but I simply cannot believe that such a reversal of policy would be indulged in by the PM.' Just over a fortnight later, on the 24th, three days after the co-ordinated intervention of eighteen central banks proved unable to bolster the US dollar and thereby weaken the deutschmark, George himself was discussing market developments with the Treasury's permanent secretary, Sir Terry Burns. 'The Deputy Governor noted that he was reluctant to initiate overt intervention in support of sterling at this stage. This was partly because pushing sterling through $1.9725 would be equivalent to pushing sterling uphill.' That afternoon, the deputy was on the phone with the chancellor. When Lamont asked George what he proposed to do 'in the event that concerted intervention did not materialise', the reply was that he proposed to continue with 'covert intra marginal intervention to keep in touch with DM2.81, but being ready to go overt should the exchange rate fall close to DM2.805'; and Lamont said he was willing to spend up to $1.5 billion 'in the covert intervention phase'. Three days later, George and Burns were on the phone: they 'discussed the forthcoming reserves figure and agreed to publish a figure of £1280mn'.

The pace of events then quickened during the first half of September. At the start of the month, sterling went to its lowest level against the deutschmark since May 1990; barely a week later, Major publicly insisted that 'the soft option, the devaluer's option, the inflationary option, would be a betrayal of our future' and was therefore 'not the government's policy'; over the weekend of 12–13 September, the Italian government decided to devalue the lira by 7 per cent against all other ERM currencies; and on the afternoon of Tuesday the 15th, in a development that genuinely shocked the British authorities, it emerged that Dr Helmut Schlesinger, president of the Bundesbank, had given an interview to a German newspaper stating that 'the tensions in the ERM are not over' and that 'further devaluations are not excluded'. Major did not exaggerate when he recollected in only semi-tranquillity that 'such views from one of the most influential central bankers in the world sent out only one message to the markets: "Sell sterling"'. That same day, George gave a journalist a defiant update on the previous week or so – 'it's been a bit of a battering but we're still in there with our troops intact!' – but this changed everything.[12]

Next day was of course Black Wednesday, the day that the pound took such a heavy, intensive battering (costing some £3.3 billion) that the UK government had no alternative but to suspend its membership of the ERM. For the Bank, inevitably somewhere near the eye of the storm, it was a day with three main components: the markets; the fellow central banks; and the politicians.

Heavy selling of the pound (both by speculators such as George Soros and by institutions such as banks and pension funds) duly began first thing that Wednesday morning, immediately prompting massively expensive intervention by the Bank, as agreed the previous evening with Lamont in the wake of the Schlesinger bombshell. 'We went into the market very early,' recalled Ian Plenderleith (the associate director responsible for market operations), 'did a substantial amount of buying of sterling, and it was the most extraordinary feeling, I remember describing it to Leigh-Pemberton, that the rate lifted off the bottom for a few seconds and then just slipped down again, and I said it's exactly like driving a car and you suddenly realise that the steering wheel has come away from the column ...' At 11 o'clock there was a belated rise in interest rates, from 10 to 12 per cent. Lamont was watching the Reuters screen at the Treasury as the announcement was made: 'The pound did not move at all. From that moment I knew the game was up ... I felt like a TV surgeon in *Casualty* watching a heart monitor and realising that the patient was dead.' Over the next few hours, pending a conclusive decision from the West End of town, the Bank had no alternative but to continue to spend Britain's currency reserves at an alarming rate, before Major further delayed that decision by going for a final throw of the dice, with a 2.15 pm announcement stating that interest rates would rise next day from 12 to 15 per cent. Again, the move was viewed by the foreign exchange markets as a sign of weakness, not strength (George had been opposed to it for that reason); and after sterling had staged a tiny, flickering rally the Bank was soon buying yet more pounds. 'That afternoon,' Soros recollected, 'it became a veritable avalanche of selling.' 'It was the most bizarre experience,' remembered the Bank's Michael Foot of that afternoon in the dealing room, 'because there was a bank of phones basically with every light blinking, every light of course being a sell order for sterling at the minimum rate, and the dealers had no choice but to accept this, they could be a little bit slow picking up the phone, but that was it, that was all they could do.' Eventually, at 4 o'clock, with the UK's obligations under the ERM at last ended for the day, it was agreed to let sterling go. 'Suddenly the Bank of England wasn't supporting pounds,' recalled Mark Clarke of the Bank of America from a dealer's perspective. 'Instead of a load of noise coming out of the voice boxes and everything, and around the dealing room, everyone sat in stunned silence for almost two seconds or three seconds. All of a sudden it erupted and sterling just free-fell. That sense of awe, that the markets could take on a central bank and actually win. I couldn't believe it ...' Three and a half hours later, Lamont stood outside the Treasury and announced to the television cameras that, following 'an extremely difficult and turbulent day', UK membership had been suspended – a de facto devaluation.[13]

What about the other European central banks as the ERM drama unfolded? In the course of that afternoon, Leigh-Pemberton, George and seven senior colleagues assembled three times for a telephonic 'concertation' with the various top central bankers on the Continent. To judge by the rather muted official record, the Bank's men did not get all that much joy. During the first one, at 2.15, Leigh-Pemberton began by explaining that 'the drain from our reserves was barely sustainable'; and added that if the second interest rate rise failed to stem the outflow, 'we would need to look to the other central banks in the system for help in the form of intervention on their own account in substantial amounts', given that otherwise 'the UK government was going to need to contemplate suspending its ERM obligations, and an announcement to that effect might have to be made during the afternoon'. The overall response was that 'the UK should be contemplating realignment within the ERM rather than a suspension of its obligations outside the rules'. The second concertation followed soon afterwards, at 3.15, during which a range of views was given to Leigh-Pemberton about the possibility of a UK realignment, with the governor observing that 'suspension was very likely to have to be accompanied by realignment if sterling could manage to rejoin after the weekend'. Finally, at 6 o'clock, the governor informed his fellow central bankers that 'the UK government had reached the conclusion that the turbulence in exchanges was such that there should be a general suspension of ERM obligations', but added that 'if that did not prove acceptable, the UK had decided that it must in any case suspend its own ERM obligations for the time being'; to which the Bank of France's Jacques de Larosière responded by stating that 'it would be impossible for the French to accept a general suspension of ERM obligations', which 'would have dramatic and negative consequences for the market and for the general climate in France before their Referendum at the weekend'; thereupon 'Duisenberg [Wim Duisenberg of the Dutch central bank], Tietmeyer [Hans Tietmeyer of the Bundesbank] and Doyle [Maurice Doyle of the Central Bank of Ireland] agreed with Larosière, whereas Ciampi [Carlo Ciampi of the Bank of Italy] and the Portuguese argued for a generalised response to the market turbulence, and impliedly a general suspension.' Overall, the weight of opinion was towards UK suspension alone; and within weeks, Lamont was making a Eurosceptic speech to his party conference, observing sardonically of that Continent's ambition to become a state that 'no one would die for Europe'.

Could the Bundesbank in particular have done more to help? Jim Trott, the Bank's chief dealer, would add an intriguing tailpiece to this central banking aspect of the day. 'The cavalry were the Bundesbank,' he recalled about those hours during which the Bank was furiously buying sterling, but the Bundesbank was notably reluctant to sell deutschmarks. 'We kept on looking over the hill, but there was no dust and there were no hats and no sabres. And then later at the conference call they suddenly didn't speak English, which was extraordinary. So we were kind of stretched on that day.'[14]

Ultimately, it was with the chancellor and his Cabinet colleagues that the buck stopped that very long Wednesday. At an early stage, George was trying to push Lamont towards a 4 per cent rate rise, but Lamont argued that 'the markets would regard 4 as excessive and so would lack credibility', and in the end they settled on 2 per cent, with the announcement then significantly delayed by Lamont having to persuade Major. Further delay in resolving the whole issue of British membership came with a lengthy lunchtime ministerial meeting, attended by Leigh-Pemberton and George. By this stage both the Bank and Lamont wanted immediate withdrawal from the ERM, but to their frustration – certainly to Lamont's, probably to the Bank's also – the broad consensus, supported by Major, was to keep going until at least 4 o'clock, while announcing at 2.15 the second interest rate rise. That frustration would provoke a telling passage in Lamont's memoirs:

Later on Kenneth Clarke [like Michael Heseltine and Douglas Hurd, refusing to accept immediate withdrawal] claimed, 'The whole thing was taken out of the hands of the politicians by the technicians. We were just there to sign on the dotted line.' The opposite was the truth. It was the politicians who had interfered with the technicians and only succeeded in making things even worse with their amateur and bungling intervention. Later on Kenneth Clarke also claimed the meeting had no information from the outside world and that we were cut off from the markets. In fact Eddie George had with him a pocket Reuters monitor that told him the value of sterling every minute. In no way were we cut off from the markets. But you didn't need a TV to know what was happening: the pound, having been in free fall, was now stuck at DM 2.7780, at which we were obliged to pay out to all those speculators who had sold sterling short. We were bleeding to death, and all we were doing was talking. We had clearly lost the battle but the generals refused to recognise it.

George, like Leigh-Pemberton, was back at the Bank at around 2.45 when he had a long telephone conversation with Lamont. George pointed out that the already substantial loss of reserves could become 'much heavier' in the quarter of an hour or so before 4 o'clock; and in answer to a series of specific questions, he reckoned it 'very unlikely' that a realignment could be achieved that evening, reassured Lamont that up to 4 o'clock 'the authorities would be able to raise sufficient liquidity to withstand the outflow, though it would be extremely painful', and promised that he would 'advise the Chancellor if he felt that the UK was being irresponsible in continuing to meet its obligations until the end of the official ERM day'. Finally, at around 3.45, Leigh-Pemberton and George were back in the West End, joining the ministerial meeting at which the decision was conclusively taken to suspend that evening, as well as to announce that the second interest rate increase would be rescinded. At that point at least two ministers, Clarke and Heseltine, wanted the first rise also to be scrapped; but partly under pressure from the Bank, aware of the possibility of sterling once again going into free fall, that decision was apparently parked for the morrow.[15]

That Thursday morning, amid a general sense of national humiliation and government incompetence, saw a vivid coda to Black

Wednesday. As early as 7.50, George was on the telephone to Burns, having learned that Major and Lamont had agreed the previous evening to cut interest rates back to 10 per cent before the Cabinet met at around 9.30. Such a move, he explained, 'would be disastrous, giving an impression to the markets of total confusion among the authorities'; and he added that he was 'not in principle averse to reducing rates to 10%, but it was extremely important that it should be done in an orderly manner'. Half an hour later, Burns phoned back 'to say that the Chancellor was content for the announcement of the interest rate reduction to be delayed until Friday', but that Alex Allan in the prime minister's office 'was much more resistant for presentational reasons'. Straightaway, George was on the phone to Allan, reiterating that reducing interest rates to 10 per cent that morning would, in the view of the governor as well as himself, 'give an impression of panic and gross incompetence on the part of the authorities and could produce a massive over-shoot in the exchange rate'; but Allan, after asking George not to repeat to Lamont what he had to say, told the deputy that 'for political reasons the Prime Minister was adamant that interest rates should be reduced before the Cabinet met that morning', adding: 'If the Chancellor made the interest rate announcement before the Cabinet meeting, he could regain some of the initiative. But if he waited until later it would look as if he had been forced into doing so by the Cabinet.' The conversation ended with George remarking, perhaps rather grumpily, that 'someone, whether the Chancellor or the Prime Minister, needed to give the Bank a direct instruction to make the rate reduction'. The rest of this chamber drama played out in three more phone calls:

> **8.35.** Sir Terry Burns telephoned the Deputy Governor to say that he had just received a message from Number 10 to the effect that, unless there was an announcement before 9.15 am, that there would be a reduction in rates to 10% either that day or on the following day, the Chancellor would not survive the Cabinet meeting. The Deputy Governor asked whether that was an instruction to the Bank to make the change and Sir Terry replied that it was not clear; the Chancellor was not aware of the message and had previously said he would be content for the announcement to be made on the Friday. It was agreed that Sir Terry would consider how best to approach

the Chancellor and in the meantime the Deputy Governor would think about how best to carry out an instruction to reduce rates.

8.45. The Deputy Governor telephoned Sir Terry to say that, after taking advice, he had concluded that if a rate cut was to be announced that day, it would be best to implement it straightaway rather than announce it that day to take effect on the following day; this would have the minimum disruptive effect on the markets.

9.07. Sir Terry telephoned the Deputy Governor to say that the Chancellor had agreed that the cut should be announced that day at 9.30 am, just before the Cabinet meeting began.[16]

Black Wednesday in September, the Bingham Report in October – the autumn of 1992 was hardly a happy moment as the Bank began to think about how to mark its imminent tercentenary. In a highly critical assessment in the *Spectator*, Stephen Fay argued that the ERM debacle owed at least something to the Bank's 'culture of secrecy', a culture resistant to explaining to the outside world either motives or arguments and reasons; as for Bingham, that had revealed the Bank as 'an introverted organisation, unwilling to trust outsiders, especially from abroad, and reluctant to take advice'. A member of the Treasury Select Committee, Giles Radice, was similarly critical. 'We are astonished by the complacent attitude of Eddie George,' he recorded in his diary a few days later, after the deputy governor had given evidence about the Bank's handling of BCCI. 'In the end, after persistent questioning, he admits that mistakes may have been made. He would have done well to say that at the beginning.' Yet, even during that autumn, developments were under way that would transform the very nature of the Bank by early in its fourth century; and within weeks, there were some insiders who were privately referring to the tumultuous events of 16 September not as Black Wednesday but as Grey or even White Wednesday.

The charting of a new course started, albeit somewhat uncertainly, as soon as Thursday the 17th. 'Yesterday was, in an obvious sense, a crushing defeat for policy,' began George's memo to senior colleagues. 'But it also presents us with an opportunity to break free from the intense conflict between domestic and external objectives which ERM membership in the exceptional circumstances of German re-unification has involved us in over much of the past year.' Thus, in the welcome absence of monetary policy having to be 'directed solely towards maintaining the exchange rate', necessitating 'interest rates at levels which were inappropriately high in relation to domestic inflationary pressure and domestic activity' – in turn resulting in fiscal policy being relaxed by government 'to a degree that would otherwise have been clearly inappropriate', indeed even leading to the Bank itself 'untypically' advising the chancellor 'to undertake further fiscal expansion' – George instead looked forward to a post-ERM context in which 'the opportunity now presents itself to revert to a more appropriate policy mix'. Another memo came from Mervyn King, who since the previous year had been chief economist and an executive director. 'If we remain outside the ERM, and there is no independence for the Bank,' he concluded, 'a clear and coherent framework for the formulation of monetary policy will be necessary, in my view, to restore any semblance of credibility to our policy stance. Otherwise, we shall have to hope that we shall be given the opportunity to build up credibility by the pursuit and achievement of price stability.'

That afternoon, the Bank's top men assembled to discuss what, in the vacuum left by the suspension of ERM membership, the framework for UK economic and monetary policy should be. The first speaker was King:

It would not be enough to cast policy in terms which boiled down to an assurance that the authorities would make the right judgements, since ultimately these judgements would fall to politicians and be prey to the political pressures which they inevitably face. Independence would be an ideal outcome but absent that a new framework was needed. In response to the Deputy Governor [George], Mr King offered monetary aggregates as one possible candidate and said that a 'trust us' approach would have zero credibility. If an alternative framework could not be found, the arguments for going back into the ERM were, in his view, strengthened.

Others present expressed their views. Crockett said that he was 'anxious that the Bank should not simply abandon the objective of using the exchange rate as some sort of guide for monetary policy';

Plenderleith observed that if the choice of 'framework' – defined as 'a published definition of policy from which the authorities could not easily depart' – lay between adherence to the ERM or what 'might be no more than a statement of intent to pursue a policy designed to produce stable non-inflationary growth', the reality was that 'either approach needed to enjoy broad-based credibility and legitimacy', adding that 'it was clear that the public had not been persuaded that the ERM was the right way of pursuing growth'; while Leigh-Pemberton, after noting that in the short term 'the inflationary bogey was not that great', accepted that 'we plainly did need to have a framework and it would not be good enough to rely on "seat of the pants" judgements and to encourage the market to "trust us"', but was disinclined to change horses, telling his colleagues that he 'continued to find the exchange rate a potentially attractive criterion, since it was a visible and well-understood indication to the market and the international community of our position and policy'. Accordingly, the meeting ended with the governor expressing his belief that 'the ERM remained a potentially attractive framework once conditions had improved'.

A week was a long time in central banking that autumn; and exactly seven days later, amid the ongoing policy vacuum and an increasing realisation-cum-acceptance in both the Bank and the Treasury that Britain's ERM era was over, King had an important message for the Court:

> Our immediate problem is that we need a nominal anchor. This takes us to the old debate between rules and discretion for the conduct of monetary policy. Until last week we had a rule – our ERM parity. We now have total discretion but precisely for that reason no credibility. The policy of 'trust us we are clever' is associated with Mr Lawson. And look where that got us. But I do not want to pretend that there is any new simple rule – such as a monetary or other aggregate – that would carry conviction. The obvious alternative, and one that has been canvassed by most academic and journalist commentators, is independence of the Bank of England.
>
> In the meantime, it would make sense to focus directly on the objective most relevant to a central bank, namely the rate of inflation. We have a target path for the inflation rate that leads us to price stability. We also have a number of indicators of inflationary trend.

These can be weighted together by the information content in each indicator. And the Economics Division is carrying out the statistical analysis necessary for this. Policy then compares the expected inflation rate with its target path, and monetary policy is tightened if expected inflation exceeds the desired target range. In one sense that is the usual discretionary policy which in practice we followed for some time before entering the ERM. But it has a much more precise focus because it is clearly targeted on inflation. That should be the main responsibility of the central bank. The immediate problem, however, is to find a way of restoring some semblance of credibility to UK economic policy.[17]

Inflation targeting, in short, was moving towards the centre of the picture; but it was not quite there yet.

King himself was emerging as the key Bank figure during this tantalisingly – but also seductively – blank-canvas phase. An academic economist for most of his working life before coming to the Bank full-time in March 1991, initially on a two-year contract, he more than anyone seized the moment, in the process doing much to raise the standing within the Bank of the Economics Division. That was not an uncharged matter. Back in 1983, an earlier chief economist, Christopher Dow, had listened to 'an hour's quiet monologue' from George about how the economists in Threadneedle Street were as a species 'incapable of being useful to him' and how 'he would not trust them with information anyhow'; King himself had already ruffled some feathers by restructuring the division so that, in his subsequent words, 'those dealing with the analysis of financial markets and those dealing with economic analysis worked together', with the aim of ensuring that 'the analysis matches the operations', as distinct from there being 'just a group of economists working on a large econometric model'; while when in June 1992, during the annual review of 'Objectives and Resources', Leigh-Pemberton asserted that 'it was important for the Bank to recruit economists, but the Bank should not restrict itself to economists, because we would then lose some of the most able generalists', and added that he 'wondered whether the policy of concentrating on economists was short-sighted', King countered by saying that he 'thought non-economist graduate recruits should be willing to become economists and that that should be made clear to them before recruitment'.[18] Traditionally, of course, the Bank had always prized the generalists. It was an irony of the situation that King himself, heading the economic specialists, possessed one way and another an appreciably broader hinterland than some of the generalists.

Late September and early October inevitably involved, whether at the Bank or the Treasury, considerable discussion about the future direction of policy. King went to the Treasury and floated to Burns the idea of putting considerable focus on the inflation target; Burns responded quite positively; and in due course, he and the Treasury's chief economic adviser, Alan Budd, sought to persuade their political chief to go down that road. Even so, there were still some distinct qualms at the Bank. On 6 October, two days before Lamont was due to unveil the government's new, post-ERM economic strategy, George rang Burns to say that he and the governor were 'very exercised about the possibility that future monetary policy would become set in stone before the Bank had had a chance to give its input'; and he added that 'the Bank was keen to be able to line up side by side with the Government on any new policy statement, but if this were to involve specific inflation or monetary aggregate targets, the Bank would find it very hard to support'. Understandably, after his various experiences going back to the early 1980s, George had no great fondness for targets – whether of a monetary or an exchange rate nature – and, befitting his own technical virtuosity, instinctively preferred discretion to rules as the basis for policy. Even so, the tide was now irresistibly flowing towards a new orthodoxy: based not on the money supply, not on the strength or otherwise of sterling, but on the requirements of the inflation target. On 8 October, in a speech to the Tory conference at Brighton and in a letter to the chairman of the Treasury Committee, the chancellor set out his stall, at the heart of which was an inflation target in the range of 1–4 per cent, to be reduced by the end of the Parliament (probably 1997) to a range of 1–2.5 per cent. Such an approach, Lamont assured the faithful, would restore the confidence of the markets. And if the government failed to hit its inflation target? 'It will have a duty,' he pledged, 'to explain how this had arisen, how quickly it intended to get back within the range, and the means by which it could achieve this.'

A certain whiff of Mr Solomon Binding was undeniable, to sceptics anyway; but just under a fortnight later, on 19 October, Burns visited Leigh-Pemberton to put forward a proposal, duly summarised by the governor's private secretary:

> Treasury Officials, impliedly although not absolutely clearly with the Chancellor's support, were giving very serious consideration to the 'openness' issue and the general arrangements by which monetary policy decisions were formulated and reached. In particular, Burns envisaged a monthly monetary policy meeting between the Chancellor and the Governor, each supported by Officials, to review the economic and monetary situation on the basis of a [Treasury] paper which would be published …
>
> The objective would be to make it much more difficult for No 10 to intervene in interest rate decisions, and make it similarly difficult for a non-orthodox Chancellor to make interest rate movements which were – or at least whose timing was – motivated by political considerations …

Next day, at an internal meeting, George supported the idea of a monthly chancellor/governor discussion of monetary policy and suggested that the Bank undertake for public consumption a quarterly 'Inflation Report' – a report, insisted King, that would be 'entirely free from Treasury comment'. A week later, on 27 October, two days before the chancellor's Mansion House speech, Lamont, Burns, Leigh-Pemberton and George gathered to discuss its intended proposals 'for greater openness and accountability in the conduct of monetary policy'. After observing that they would be 'very welcome' from the Bank's point of view, the governor additionally proposed as part of the package the Bank's own quarterly inflation report, a suggestion that the chancellor 'welcomed'; and both sides agreed that, in Leigh-Pemberton's reported words, 'the validity of the inflation report would depend in part on acceptance in the markets that, in the end, the inflation report represented the opinions of the Bank and not the Treasury'. On the 29th, Lamont spelled it all out, with one or two extra twirls, to the City's bigwigs: the Bank, as monitor of the government's progress in meeting its inflation target, to publish a quarterly inflation report assessing 'thoroughly and openly' the outlook for inflation; the Treasury to have an early sight of that report, but no powers to change it; monthly meetings between chancellor and governor, with the dates to be revealed in advance; a report of each meeting to be published by the Treasury; and a panel of seven independent economic forecasters to be established which 'would publish regular assessments of economic conditions'.[19] Greater credibility, greater openness – those by now were the government's buzzwords, and the almost inevitable implication was an enhanced role for the Bank.

On 11 November the governor gave the inaugural LSE Bank of England lecture, written for him by King and in effect laying out the underlying long-term economic justification for the new emphasis on price stability:

> In this country, inflation became a serious problem only after the Second World War. Creeping inflation at an average rate of around 3% a year in the 1950s and 1960s caused concern but little revival in official circles of the traditional view that inflation was a monetary phenomenon. In the 1970s inflation rose rapidly and prices more than trebled. Progress was made in the 1980s with the adoption of firm counterinflationary policies. Nevertheless, we should not forget that prices rose by more between 1970 and 1990 than they had done in the previous 200 years. Some of you here tonight are part of a generation – the inflation generation – which grew up believing that rapid rises in prices were an inevitable feature of a growing economy. I want to persuade you that inflation is not a natural condition. Far from it. It is a condition which derives from a combination of outdated economic theory and flawed policy implementation. And now that both theory and practice have been immeasurably improved, it is a phenomenon which should be confined to the history books once more.

Some serious economic history followed – invoking such names as Irving Fisher and Bill Phillips as well as Maynard Keynes – plus a lengthy disquisition on both the explicit and hidden cost of inflation. 'The simple choice,' declared the governor, 'is between a variable and unpredictable inflation rate caused by instability in monetary policy, and a more stable monetary policy framework that delivers price stability.' His preference was of course for the latter, and near the end, in ringing tones, he committed the Bank to an 'unwavering effort' to direct policy towards price stability. Almost a month later, on 10 December at 8.30 am, the first 'Monthly Monetary Meeting' between chancellor and governor took place at the Treasury, with Leigh-Pemberton accompanied by Crockett, Coleby, King and Plenderleith; two months later, in February 1993, the Bank's first publicly available Inflation Report appeared, at this initial stage as part of the regular *Quarterly Bulletin*.[20] It was very much King's baby: he gave a press conference and privately took satisfaction from the fact that the report's abundance of charts and suchlike had largely thwarted any potential editorial interference by the Treasury.

What about independence as such? 'One cheer for the chancellor' was the title of the *Financial Times*'s leader on Lamont's institutional reforms announced in his Mansion House speech. 'What is needed is comprehensive reconsideration of the roles of the Treasury and the Bank of England. Mr Lamont wishes to persuade the world that the citadel on Great George Street still knows best. It does not. As the whole world now knows all too well.' The Bank itself was disinclined to campaign at this point – so soon after BCCI and Black Wednesday – with an internal note shortly before Christmas recording that George had 'come to the view that the only way to make progress is through an evolutionary (i.e. non-statutory) approach'. Instead, the great – if at this stage covert – champion of the independence cause was Lamont, who despite the opposition of his permanent secretary (Burns) submitted two papers, one in November 1992 and the other in January 1993, that followed Lawson's example by calling for statutory independence over monetary policy, predominantly on counter-inflationary grounds. Just as in September 1991, when Lamont had made a similar initiative, Major refused to budge. Not only did the prime minister continue to believe that the person responsible for monetary policy should be directly answerable to the Commons, but he (in his subsequent words) 'also feared that the culture of an independent Bank would ensure that interest rates went up rapidly but fell only slowly'. To which he might have added that he also had no appetite for needlessly vexing his backbench Eurosceptics, inclined to view Bank independence as a sinister step to meeting the Maastricht criteria for monetary union. Moreover, in the here and now of a hostile political climate, Major badly wanted to keep monetary policy in his own hands, not even the chancellor's – and twice, in October 1992 and January 1993, he unilaterally imposed interest rate cuts, the second time despite that cut's clash with the Bank's attempts to hold an important auction of gilt-edged stock. 'For the future he thought that interest rate moves should be related more closely to the economic events that determined them,' recorded in guarded language Leigh-Pemberton's rebuke to Lamont (the innocent party) at their monthly meeting in early February. 'Any gap between the event and the move leads to suspicion in the markets.'[21]

The governor himself was approaching the final months of his second term. Who would succeed him? The fullest account of a tricky, invidious process comes from Lamont's memoirs, revealing that although he and the Court wanted George to step up from deputy, Major 'kept repeating that he wanted "a man of stature"'. One of those possible men, as in 1983, was David Scholey – pushed by the *Sunday Times* as 'the obvious candidate with the standing, weighty personality and skill to restore the Bank's credibility', but in his own mind certain that George was the right man; while Major himself had an inclination for JP Morgan's Sir Dennis Weatherstone, a British meritocrat after his own heart. In the end, Lamont managed to persuade the prime minister that there was no realistic alternative to George; and the announcement, generally welcomed, was made at the end of January. Even so, Major was insistent that George's replacement as deputy governor must be an outsider; and between them, Lamont and Sarah Hogg (running the No. 10 office) settled on Rupert Pennant-Rea, who had worked in the Bank's Economics Division in the 1970s but was now the forty-five-year-old editor of the *Economist*. 'He could be a splendid fellow and a fountain of ideas and a breath of fresh or hot air, but that in itself would no more qualify him to be Deputy Governor than to fly a Boeing 747,' commented a fellow-journalist Christopher Fildes, while *Banking World* noted that 'there are some in the Bank who secretly express doubts'. *Central Banking*'s Robert Pringle was more generous. 'Why not a journalist?' he asked, and penned Pennant-Rea an open letter in which he explained how the new deputy governor could not only help the Bank cope with the increasing publicity attendant on being a central bank in the 1990s, but also 'help them to get onto terms with the baby-boomers who are inheriting the world (the Clintons, Larry Summers, Michael Portillos)', whom he described as 'a different breed – and a very strange species to most central bankers, who come from another generation'. Pennant-Rea himself had been given only four hours to accept the job, but apparently had done so readily.[22]

The independence question continued to preoccupy during the spring and summer of 1993. 'The Governor should not pull his punches in making the case' that 'operational autonomy for the Bank was the best way to achieve price stability', argued King at an internal March meeting about how best to proceed; Leigh-Pemberton for his part 'noted the list of political moves on interest rates – the most recent cut to 6%, cuts made at the time of municipal elections, cuts at the time of the row about coal mines, cuts to coincide with the Conservative Party Conference and with the presentation of the Budget'; while George 'felt it was not necessary to mount a public campaign for independence, but if asked the Bank should continue to explain its view', adding that 'the objective was to persuade the Prime Minister to agree to think about the topic seriously once Maastricht was behind him and before the next election'.

In late May the prime minister and the governor had a face-to-face on the issue. Major asserted that, while he 'recognised the arguments for independence on anti-inflationary grounds', he was 'not at all sure that Parliament would agree to such a change'; observed that 'even if it did, it was bound to insist on much more oversight of the Bank'; noted that 'interest rates were particularly sensitive in the UK because of the link to mortgage rates'; and held out the somewhat distant carrot that 'if low inflation and economic growth were maintained and the Government were in a stronger position politically, it might be possible to contemplate a change'. After Leigh-Pemberton for his part had pointed to 'the prospect of Britain becoming the only major country where the markets perceived a risk of short-term political interference in monetary policy and demanded a risk premium accordingly', the prime minister 'repeated that greater independence could only be contemplated from a position of strength':

The first step was to convince political and market opinion that the Government's economic policies were credible in their own right and that economic recovery was happening because of these policies, not in spite of them. It needed to be clearly established that recovery had begun before Britain left the ERM – and indeed that recession began before we joined it. The more the Governor and Deputy Governor could do to reinforce the message in speeches and in the Bank of England Quarterly Bulletin, the better the prospects would be.

Shortly afterwards, Kenneth Clarke replaced Lamont at No. 11, and on 3 June the governor called on the new chancellor for 'a very relaxed, informal and open discussion'. Specifically on independence, Clarke said that he 'was not himself particularly opposed to the possibility', but 'felt that it was not an issue for him to raise with the Prime Minister in the immediate future'. Six days later, in a notably plain-speaking resignation speech to the Commons, Lamont à la Lawson publicly revealed his unsuccessful attempts to convince the prime minister of the merits of independence – to which Major almost immediately responded in the chamber by highlighting his 'very real concern' about 'the need for accountability to Parliament for decisions on monetary policy matters'. Back behind closed doors, that left Leigh-Pemberton and Clarke to bat around the issue a second time, on 17 June. 'The Chancellor said that he was temperamentally inclined to the position that both Norman Lamont and Nigel Lawson held. He believed, however, that the party was evenly divided and that it would therefore be some considerable time before constitutional change could be achieved.' And the two men agreed that 'the next step in the process' was likely to be the Treasury Select Committee's report on the issue, expected by the end of the year.[23]

Robin Leigh-Pemberton, with a life peerage in the Queen's birthday honours, retired at the end of June. 'It was generally acknowledged,' noted *Central Banking* soon afterwards, 'that he handed over the Bank in good shape to his successor; it now has a mandate to fight inflation and a more open relationship with the Treasury than at any time in its history.' Subsequent views of his governorship were mixed. According to someone who worked for him, his gentlemanly approach and predominantly non-executive role made him analogous to the non-playing captain in the Davis Cup; according to someone else, who worked for him more intimately, his outstanding qualities of 'integrity, dignity, resilience, toughness, decency, good judgement and leadership' all contributed to a central banker who possessed 'a deep commitment to stability' and 'a strategic cast of mind' (the latter attribute often overlooked), as well as being 'an extraordinary team builder' and 'an internationalist'. Somewhere in the middle, the verdict recorded in his 2013 *Times* obituary is perhaps about right, namely that at the end of his ten years 'it was widely agreed not only that he had comfortably exceeded the experts' low expectations of him but also that he had in fact coped gracefully with a series of stern challenges'.[24]

His successor, Eddie George, was of course an altogether more professional operator, now becoming governor almost thirty-one years after joining the Bank; like Leslie O'Brien he was a lifer who had risen to the top, though in George's case, as a Cambridge graduate in economics, he did not start from such a lowly position. Technically expert across the field (whether macro-economics or markets or financial institutions or financial infrastructure), possessing formidable policy intelligence as well as remarkable powers of concentration, a skilled chairman of meetings, principled but with a degree of flexibility if circumstances changed, not afraid of tough judgements of people, often charming outside the Bank if more seldom inside – George was in many ways the central banker's central banker. 'Part of his success was undoubtedly attributable to the good personal relations he established with bankers, central bankers, and civil servants,' Forrest Capie would observe. 'From his time as Assistant Director onwards he would drop in on his counterparts in the Treasury in the evening, drink whiskey, smoke cigarettes and talk about their respective approaches.'[25] Perhaps above all, no one could doubt the depth of his attachment to the institution itself – 'You know,' he once remarked to a journalist when off duty (relatively speaking), 'I really love this place.' At one of the cusp moments in its history, the Bank could hardly have been in more capable hands.

'Would you be in favour of a stronger, more independent role for the Bank of England, together with a specific brief from Parliament to fight inflation?' George was asked in one of his first interviews as governor. 'Yes, I would,' he replied, and the rest of his answer carefully set out what had become the Bank's studiously crafted official position, a position that in essence held through the mid-1990s:

I have said very publicly, very often, that the really important thing is stability. That is the big issue and if the present arrangement can achieve that then I shall be entirely happy with that. The institutional question is subordinate to that, because if you don't have broad public and parliamentary support for the idea of stability and actually having an independent mandate, firstly it is not likely to happen but, secondly, if you were to have it, it could prove to be a poisoned chalice, because the moment you did what was necessary you would run into broadly-based opposition.

The issue is whether having a change in the institutional arrangements would make it more likely that on balance and over time you would be more successful at controlling inflation, and therefore actually have a more successful economy. There is a presumption that if you had a mandate from Parliament to achieve and maintain price stability, properly defined, and that if you were accountable directly or indirectly to Parliament, then the likelihood is that you would be more successful. This is not because we have any particular expertise that is not available elsewhere, but because policy-making is all about balancing risks on either side.

With a clear mandate from Parliament actually to deliver price stability, one would always tend to take the risk a little bit in favour of stability and that would produce a more consistent performance over time. The other thing is that with a clear measurable mandate, and pure accountability, there would be nowhere for us to hide if we got it wrong. That concentrates the mind wonderfully and although it wouldn't be comfortable for the Bank, it would actually be healthy.

'I claim no monopoly of wisdom for central bankers,' George wrote during his first month to one of his predecessors. 'I do believe, however, that on balance and over time the cumulative decisions of an autonomous central bank are more likely to lead to stability than those taken by the government of the day whose decisions would be more likely to lean towards exploiting the short-run trade-off between inflation and growth.' Lord O'Brien, though not disagreeing with the principle, was understandably sceptical. 'My doubt,' he replied, 'is whether, when it comes to the crunch, Ministers will be able to surrender control over this important part of economic policy.' Another sceptic, but for a different reason, was Sir John ('Chips') Keswick, chairman of Hambros and recently appointed to the Court.

'I would like to make a plea with regard to the independence debate which is hard to articulate,' he wrote to the new governor in late July:

> I am concerned that the executive [of the Bank], in a very civilised way, underestimates its cohesive strength and diverse achievements. I believe it would be very foolish to abandon some parts of the Bank, i.e. Supervision, International and Industrial, as part of a package to secure independence. The quality of economic analysis, in my judgement, is only as good as the quality of real activities which it rubs against. Please do not be persuaded that apparent flying buttresses should be dispensed with – you would be less effective in the round without them.

It was a resonant plea. But when, three months later, Pennant-Rea reported to the executive about the state of play in the Court's discussions on the independence issue, he noted 'fairly widespread agreement that a Bank with full responsibility for conducting monetary policy might find some of its current functions a distraction, and might want to give them up to concentrate on the crucial task the Bank had been given'.

During much of 1993 the Treasury Committee, chaired by John Watts, heard evidence on 'The Role of the Bank of England'. 'You do take the point,' one of the MPs, Diane Abbott, put it to George (the day before he became governor), 'that one of the reasons people are slightly wary of the Bank of England, which has no democratic controls at all, is that you do lead relatively cloistered lives, you do earn these huge salaries and do not appear to be quite in touch with the effects of your policies on people who earn slightly less than a quarter of a million a year?' 'I would dispute a great deal of that with the greatest possible respect,' answered George. 'Our contacts with industry and business are very strong at every level, from the Court down through our agencies, to our contacts here in London. We understand just as much as anybody else the impact that it has on people who lose their homes and lose their jobs. As a matter of fact I think many of us are affected in terms of our own families. So I rather resent the suggestion that simply because we work in the Bank we are not sensitive to the impacts of the policies that we pursue.' Later, he emphasised the importance that the Bank attached to the phrase 'statutory accountability' – in order 'to try', as he put it, 'to get rid of this idea that independence, which is the popular name for the debate, is about a lot of appointed bureaucrats exercising arbitrary powers'; and he added that he would have no problem at all with a statutory provision giving the chancellor of the day the ultimate power of over-ride, as long as that provision was 'open and explicit'. O'Brien did not give evidence, but his successor did. 'I am not quite certain from your evidence so far whether or not you are in favour of a more inde-pendent central bank,' a mildly exasperated Giles Radice observed at one point, but in the fullness of time Lord Richardson did explain that he was indeed in favour of greater Bank autonomy in the oper-ation of monetary policy: 'If it could be established, if it could gain a reputation and you really built through time that deeper and more intense consensus about inflation, then I think it would be vital.' By contrast, the definitively retired Sir George Blunden stuck to his by now well-established line that the Bank already enjoyed a consider-able degree of autonomy and that it might lose influence and freedom of action more broadly if it demanded that its role be rigidly defined by statute.

Two former chancellors also gave evidence. 'I think the markets are going to feel that there is something sinister almost about any govern-ment that does not confer independence on its central bank,' declared Lord Lawson, adding that under the present system the Bank had 'much too easy a time', enjoying 'considerable influence' but subject to 'virtually no accountability at all'. 'There really is no point,' he argued moreover, 'in saying we have an inflationary culture so there is nothing we can do. You have to ask what the best institutional arrange-ment is that we can have ... You will not create a Bank of England which has the credibility and public esteem of the Bundesbank over-night but you have to make a start somewhere.' His predecessor but one could hardly have disagreed more strongly. Lord Healey began his typically trenchant evidence by asserting that the fashion for inde-pendent central banks was essentially a gimmick; attacked the Bank's recent record (not only failing to control 'the explosion of irresponsi-ble lending and borrowing' that had led to the Lawson boom and bust, but also the previous September throwing away 'a large part of our reserves in a clearly doomed attempt to save sterling'); and finished with a stirring defence of the need not to be enslaved by the markets, which 'we talk about as though they were God in heaven, but they are numerous men in red braces in dealing rooms who talk Cockney working for a lot of men in grey suits with red bow ties'.

'I am sitting on the fence and I have not reached a hard and fast opinion on what is usually called the independence of the Bank of England,' the current chancellor told the Committee. But in December 1993, five months after Clarke's uncharacteristically hesitant words, Watts and his colleagues came off the fence in their report. They wanted 'the maintenance of price stability' to be 'the primary objective of monetary policy'; pronounced in favour of 'institutional change', involving 'the transfer of authority from the Treasury to the Bank', in turn leading in the latter to 'the creation of a strong and independent Monetary Policy Committee'; and accepted that, subject to parliamentary approval, the government 'should have power to override the Bank's objective of price stability temporarily and in exceptional circumstances'. Critical, insisted the report, was 'the establishment of clear lines of accountability and answerability to Parliament', and it offered two instructive comparisons: 'There is no such provision in the German arrangements and, however acceptable they may be in their own context, we do not believe that they would be acceptable or workable in the United Kingdom. The lack of direct answerability to Parliament, as distinct from the Executive, also seems to us to be a serious drawback in the New Zealand arrangements, which in other respects have clear attractions as a model for the United Kingdom.'[26]

The overall direction of travel was becoming clear enough, not only in Britain. 'The demand for greater independence of the central bank has come to be the most popular answer to the problem of inflation that was once reserved for the ERM,' the Treasury's Burns rather tartly observed in print that year, in the context of Belgium and France liberating their central banks, with Spain and Portugal preparing to follow suit; while in his valedictory *Financial Times* interview, Leigh-Pemberton noted that central bank independence was an idea that was 'gathering momentum all round the world'. There were two other especially telling indicators, the first being the surprising degree of movement on the Labour side. 'It is now time to reform radically the Bank of England and the conduct of monetary policy,' declared the shadow chancellor, Gordon Brown, in the 1993 document *Labour's Economic Approach*. 'The Bank must be made more accountable and its decision-making bodies be made both more open and more representative.' Here the key influence was the young Ed Balls, who the previous year had written a Fabian Society pamphlet, called *Euro-Monetarism*, in which he argued that an independent Bank, properly accountable to Parliament, would give a future Labour government anti-inflationary credibility with the financial markets and thereby provide the opportunity to concentrate on fiscal and supply-side policies. The other indicator was the impressive cast – including Charles Goodhart (no longer at the Bank), Sir Peter Middleton and Sir David Walker – that assembled as an independent panel under the chairmanship of Lord (Eric) Roll, president of Warburgs, to produce a report, *Independent and Accountable: A New Mandate for the Bank of England*, that appeared shortly before the Treasury Committee's findings. 'Eventually,' declared the City's great and good in their concluding passage, 'a monetary framework with a stronger foundation will be required. The best time to put that system in place is now.' But perhaps inevitably, given its importance, the debate was not yet over. 'An issue that won't go away', 'The smell of a red herring', 'Providing a stable framework', 'Time to counter the fashionable folly', 'Government's job is to govern' – such were the titles of some of the articles that appeared in early 1994 in Parliament's own *The House Magazine*, with the respective authors being Lord Kingsdown (the former Leigh-Pemberton), Lord Healey, the MPs Alan Beith and Austin Mitchell, and Labour's chief secretary to the Treasury back in the 1970s. 'Eddie George, the new Governor of the Bank of England, is a very nice man, and more able and experienced than many of his predecessors,' began Lord (Joel) Barnett, 'but should he have control over much of the British economy?' To which he answered at the end: '"Nice" Eddie George must not be given control. That has to be the proper responsibility of government.'[27]

Whatever the swirling debate, the government – and Major in particular – remained immovable. 'He was pretty blunt about how the government would handle the independence question,' Pennant-Rea reported to George in November 1993 after a conversation with Burns. 'No real interest; no plans for much of a response to the TCSC [the Treasury and Civil Service Committee, due to report in December]; Ministers hoped and expected that the issue would go away.' Two months later, when the Treasury Select Committee sponsored a private member's bill to implement its recommendations, the absence of government support meant that it got nowhere, though there was time for Diane Abbott, who had dissented from the report, to make a fierce anti-independence speech. Soon afterwards, in February 1994, Burns was again the messenger, this time on the phone to George:

> Sir Terry said that it was now the perception of Number 10 that the Governor was actively campaigning on independence. The Bankers Club speech and the Walden Interview [on television] seemed to confirm this. The Governor explained that Walden had been fixed up when he first became Governor and that he had tried very hard indeed to emphasise the importance of stability as the essential end result and not independence per se. He said that he was very sensitive to the issue and that the Bank would now go below the surface on it: it was not in the interests of the Bank or the Governor to campaign for independence. Sir Terry added that the Chancellor was more relaxed than Number 10.

So he was, with Clarke happy enough at this stage to play his own game, which – in the specific context of a still uncomfortably high PSBR necessitating enhanced market credibility if interest rates were to be brought down – essentially consisted from autumn 1993 of taking incremental steps to increase the Bank's authority. By the end of the year, not only was the Treasury no longer seeing the Bank's *Inflation Report* ahead of publication, but the Bank had been given control over the precise timing of interest rate changes determined by the chancellor; while in April 1994, following months of negotiations and dummy runs, publication began of the minutes of the monthly Clarke/George meeting.

This was indeed a development with a history. As early as the previous September, the chancellor had told the governor that he was 'inclined to think publishing minutes would help underline the absence of political motives in monetary policy decisions', as well as helping to 'defuse controversy on Bank independence'; the media in early 1994 was full of damaging reports about George being forced to accept an interest rate cut against his better judgement, causing markets to plunge; and in March, a month before implementation,

Clarke explained his reasoning to a no doubt sceptical – but ultimately consenting – prime minister:

> Publication of minutes will undoubtedly on occasion be uncomfortable initially. But over time markets and commentators should be reassured by more openness from us about the reasons for monetary policy decisions. This happened at the February discussions in advance of the last cut in interest rates on 8 February. Rumours of disagreement have been widespread in the press. I believe that publishing these minutes would help rather than hinder market sentiment, by giving a fuller background to the decision, and by airing the economic arguments for and against the cut. I think publication would add to the credibility of our monetary policy.

Accordingly, he proposed a regular process by which 'the minutes of each meeting would be published about 2 weeks after the *subsequent* meeting had taken place'; and he assured Major that he would make it publicly clear that 'this has no implications for the question of Bank independence'. Reaction to the April announcement was broadly positive, while George saw it as a helpful step – in terms of greater transparency and accountability, as well as making the Bank further raise the level of its analytical work – towards independence. Yet whether the change really enhanced the credibility of monetary policy is perhaps a moot point. Right at the outset, one market participant, John Sheppard of Yamaichi International, warned that 'the risk with this whole process is, if we do get to the situation where the Bank is pushing for a rate increase and the Treasury is resisting, sterling is going to be vulnerable because of the market's dislike of political interference'.[28] In the old behind-closed-doors days the central banker had often won the argument; now, with the new transparency but no shift of ultimate power, the finance minister had significant personal capital invested in the outcome. Arguably it was the worst of both worlds.

On 9 June 1994, some seven weeks ahead of the actual tercentenary anniversary, more than 130 governors or former governors from central banks around the world gathered at the Barbican Centre for a symposium, staged by the Bank, on the future of central banking. 'I would not really be surprised if Montagu Norman were to make a guest appearance,' remarked John Major as he opened proceedings.

'It is, I am told, the largest gathering of central bankers ever to meet completely free of the restraining influence of finance ministers.' As for the question on everyone's mind, certainly among the home team, he merely observed that 'the relationship between central bank and government is one in which some tensions are bound to arise, whether or not the Bank has some measure of independence in the discharge of its functions', adding with little fear of contradiction that 'what central bankers are for is to work for stable money – for a sound financial system – in whatever constitutional and political framework they find themselves'. Two papers were given, of which that on 'Modern Central Banking' by Stanley Fischer, an economist who was about to become the IMF deputy managing director, had the greater immediate impact. An intellectually heavyweight piece of work, claiming that 'the evidence leaves little doubt that, on average, economic performance is better in countries with more independent central banks', it concluded with a sentiment that the prime minister was no longer present to hear: 'On her 300th birthday, it is time to allow the Old Lady to take on the responsibilities of independence.' Reporting on the symposium, the deputy governor's old shop remained on the side of the sceptics. 'Banks such as the Fed and the Bundesbank have shown that a consensus can be established (partly by means of political accountability of one sort or another) to allow them the freedom they need – and the economic benefits look attractive,' reflected the *Economist*. 'Before that was accomplished, an independent Bank of England, taking a tough new line on inflation, could have rioters on its doorstep. That would be some birthday present.'

The tercentenary celebrations were naturally extensive. Quite apart from the symposium on central banking, they included a conference on the Bank's own history (a boiling day in the Oak Room), the release of a new £50 note carrying a portrait of Sir John Houblon, and on 27 July itself a service of thanksgiving at St Paul's – where a packed congregation, including the Queen, listened to the governor reading the lesson from Mark chapter 10 ('Go sell all you have and give it to the poor'). The press that day also accorded the Bank the full treatment, inevitably with the main focus on the independence issue. 'The chances must be,' predicted Philip Coggan in the *Financial Times*, 'that it will take another failure of economic policy – for example, a long period in which inflation exceeds the present 1–4 per cent target – before there is a real chance of the Bank getting its wish.' The present author, at the end of a historical piece in the *Daily Telegraph*, offered another prediction: 'Gladstone's ghost stirs uneasily. The conduct of monetary policy cannot but have profound political and social implications. Whatever the inbuilt safeguards for accountability, unelected central bankers will not be immune from coping with those implications.' In short: 'The Bank's fourth century may be its most testing yet.'[29]

The Bank had long been proud of its history, but for many years its Museum, sited in the Rotunda designed between the wars by Herbert Baker, was accessible only by appointment. 'Except for visitors on a guided tour of the Bank,' noted a memo in 1965, 'we have made no provision so far for members of the general public to view the museum; nor do I think it right to allow casual visitors to the Bank to be admitted there.' Even so, the memo suggested that a certain opening up would be in order, provided that all visits were authorised in advance; and a scribble on the memo agreed that this was 'a good idea, as long as the casual rubberneck is kept out of the museum'. Two decades later, the decision was taken to construct a much expanded, up-to-date (interactive video screens *et al*), fully accessible museum – a museum that would retain the Rotunda but in which the outstanding architectural feature would be a meticulous reconstruction of Soane's Stock Office of the 1790s. By early August 1988, just over three months ahead of opening, concerns had moved on from the architectural. 'We are going to have to steer a clever course between making the Museum popular and a success without belittling the dignity of the Bank,' Leigh-Pemberton observed to Blunden, adding that he had been 'rather horrified' by the proposed list of items to be sold in the Museum shop. 'The only thing I have agreed from the shop while you have been away,' the deputy governor reported back later that month, 'is to approve some very nice chocolate bars reproducing a traditional Britannia which Terrys will make for sale in gold paper – not, I think, undignified.' The governor annotated this reply with 'Good!' The Queen undertook the opening ceremony in November, and the following summer a very positive assessment of the work of the curator, John Keyworth, appeared in *Country Life*. 'The Bank's history is presented instructively in a popular style, using both Victorian display techniques (as in the tableau of the Bank ablaze) and advanced technology,' noted Giles Waterfield. 'An ingenious sequence of "period" interiors – looking, it must be said, rather like film sets – compresses considerable information into a restricted area.' His only anxiety, given the Stock Office's marvellous austerity, was that 'the gift shop which has insinuated itself into a corner of the room (presumably as a contribution to the reduction of the national debt) should not be allowed to spread further'.[30]

The Museum's screens mirrored the inexorable rise and rise of information technology across the Bank as a whole during the 1980s and 1990s. Two particular projects, in both cases responding to failure elsewhere in the City, saw the Bank in notable high-tech action. The first, following the demise of LondonClear (administered by a panel of market representatives), was the creation in October 1990 of the Central Moneymarkets Office (CMO) – in essence, a computerised settlement system for sterling treasury bills, certificates of deposit, bank bills and other money market instruments. Earlier that year, a City messenger had been robbed in the street of £292 million of bearer securities, though in fact the decision to develop CMO had already been taken; and during the early 1990s, the daily physical carrying of £30 billion worth of money market instruments around the square mile was gradually phased out. The other project involved the Stock Exchange, which back in 1981 had started work on a computerised share-settlement system called TAURUS – a system that had still not come to fruition by March 1993, when the Exchange at last pulled the plug. That allowed the Bank to step in; and it successfully developed a paperless system, known as CREST, which became operational in August 1996. 'What the Bank brings to the party is benign dictatorship,' aptly commented Gordon Midgley, head of Management Services Division, in 1994. 'Someone has to sit there and say no, without necessarily having strong reasons to do so.' More generally, he also noted how the Bank's IT philosophy had by then radically shifted: away from mainframe economies of scale, and instead towards cost savings through distributed computing. 'Traditionally it was always the information technology department that had to justify how much was being spent,' reflected Midgley. 'Now it is the business managers. The information technology department will pay for the running costs, but that is all.' The mid-1990s also of course saw the arrival of the Internet. 'Now anybody anywhere in the world with a PC connected to a telephone line and the right software program can call us up and learn all about the Bank,' helpfully explained the *Old Lady* in June 1996 in the context of the Bank's first stab at a website. 'But the Internet is not simply an encyclopaedia – it is also a communications channel,' added the magazine. 'You can send messages around the world for the price of a local telephone call using the "net". We had hardly been on the "net" a day before the first e-mail arrived.' Appropriately, it came from California, home of the micro-computer revolution. 'Our enquirer was puzzled by the concept of legal tender. Public Enquiries Group promptly e-mailed back a reply. Those in Public Enquiries Group are now becoming adept at answering all sorts of questions across cyberspace.'[31]

There were changes too during these decades in the nation's money. In November 1984, just over a year and a half after the introduction of the £1 coin, the Printing Works at Debden produced the final £1 note – a moment accompanied by plenty of ceremony (noisy 'banging out'; printers wearing top hats, black ties and armbands; a coffin and wreath on display), but causing some 300 redundancies. Four years later, in the context of new printing technology offering a compelling combination of enhanced security and significant savings, it was announced that the 'D' Series notes would be phased out and replaced by an 'E' Series, sticking to the four existing denominations but in reduced size. The new notes would also feature a fresh portrait of the Queen. 'She had been disappointed, though prepared to live with it as a matter of duty,' had earlier, in late 1987, been the word from the Palace after she had been shown a proof; and in their discussion Leigh-Pemberton and Sir William Heseltine had agreed that 'the photograph itself was not unflattering, but both the likeness and charm had deteriorated with each stage of the process', in other words between the photograph and the engraving. Happily, in the event, veteran engraver Harry Eccleston was brought back from retirement, the plate was re-engraved, and the new portrait gave general satisfaction. The series was steadily rolled out in the new decade: the £5 note (George Stephenson succeeding the Iron Duke) in June 1990; the £20 note (Faraday replacing Shakespeare) in June 1991; the £10 note (Dickens for Nightingale) in April 1993; and a year later, ahead of the July tercentenary, Wren making way on the £50 note for the Bank's first governor. All this was rather happier than the story of the so-called Debden Four – a quartet of employees who, working in the incinerator plant, conspired between 1988 and 1992 to steal more than £600,000 worth of banknotes that were due to be destroyed. After unwisely big-number cash deposits at the Ilford branch of the Reliance Mutual Insurance Society, arrests soon followed; 'Banknotes "stuffed in woman's underwear"' was one of the more graphic headlines coming out of the ensuing judicial process; and the story was the subject of the 2008 feature film *Mad Money*, starring a well-known Essex girl, Diane Keaton.[32]

The tercentenary in 1994 was not the only anniversary that year; it was also 100 years since the recruitment of the first women to the Bank's clerical staff. By this time there were some distinct signs of progress – Merlyn Lowther was made deputy chief cashier in 1991; Frances Heaton, director general of the Panel on Takeovers and Mergers, became in 1993 the first woman to be appointed to the Court; Carol Sergeant later that same year was promoted to the rank of senior official, as deputy head of Banking Supervision – but overall the Bank remained a very male-dominated organisation. 'There is still a glass ceiling,' Anne Skinner told the *Old Lady* in 1992 as she prepared to retire, having risen to become head of the Administration Division and also a senior official. 'Men choose men.' Her interviewer asked why that should be. 'They feel more comfortable,' was her incontrovertible reply.[33]

Irrespective of gender, the big domestic picture in the 1980s and 1990s was of the Bank starting seriously to slim down. During 1979 the average number of staff employed (banking staff plus technical and services staff plus Printing Works staff) was 7,700; during tercentenary year, the equivalent figure was 4,440. Two years later, in May 1996, a lengthy paper on severance by Sue Coffey (an analyst in Personnel) provided helpful context:

As with many organisations operating in dynamic business environments, the Bank has been forced to streamline its practices, upgrade its technology and, consequently, to reduce numbers. Largely, this has been achieved through natural wastage and voluntary severance schemes, although it has been necessary to raise the question of enforced redundancies on a number of occasions – following the relaxation of exchange controls in 1979, closure of note-centres at Newcastle and Glasgow in 1981 and the closure of the Liverpool and Southampton Branches in 1987 and, of course, at present, the rationalisation of the remaining branches.

The branches indeed seemed during these decades under almost permanent review. 'Changes by the clearing banks in the way in which they handled notes, involving in particular the increased deployment of used note sorting machines, were beyond the Bank's control,' Blunden pointed out in 1986 to a union representative, adding that 'it was an unfortunate fact of life that the present areas of growth in the Bank's work were concentrated in the regulatory and supervisory realms and were essentially London-based'; three years later, he observed to senior colleagues that 'our banking work there was declining, partly because an increasing amount of Government work was put out to tender', leading in turn to 'over-staffing'; and in 1996, the year that Newcastle was closed, George explained to the chancellor how the Bank was 'rationalising' the role of its branches: 'They were pulling out of banking business and their role in the note issue would be substantially reduced. However, he wanted to strengthen their role in gathering economic intelligence. The net effect would be to reduce significantly staff and office space in the regions, but the number of agencies might be increased.' In London itself, an emblematic moment was the complete departure by 1992 of the Accountant's Department – following years of falling numbers because of computerisation – to a new home in Gloucester, leaving just the odd Bank outpost at New Change. More generally, what had traditionally been an organisation long in tooth – prizing above all else the wisdom of practical experience and institutional memory – became during this period distinctly less so. 'The Bank has experienced a significant reduction in its older workforce in the last few years,' noted a senior executive in May 1997, offering a twofold explanation. 'Firstly, the Bank needed net reductions in staffing to cope with reduced workload in some areas (notably exchange control and gilt registration). But, secondly, the skill mix required in the Bank was changing quickly. Many of those who had been working here for a large number of years were not equipped with the kinds of analytical skills which are in the greatest demand across the institution at the present time.'[34]

Little of this was brilliant for staff morale. Back in September 1983, shortly after becoming governor, Leigh-Pemberton had a lengthy encounter with Ray Shuttleworth of the Bank of England Staff Organisation. 'Although his manner was entirely affable,' the note for record observed of BESO's man, 'he was unable to avoid a slightly didactic approach, with a good deal of finger-wagging.' As for substance:

> Shuttleworth freely acknowledged the difficult position of the Bank with regard to cash limits [imposed by the Treasury on public bodies since 1980]. Nevertheless, many Bank staff felt that over the last three or four years their pay had fallen noticeably behind that of their traditional analogues. He thought that middle and senior management were particularly affected by this. As a result, considerable resentment was building up. On the other hand, Shuttleworth admitted that the Bank remained an attractive employer in today's circumstances.

Tellingly, he added that he 'regretted the increasing tendency for the Bank to act not as one integrated institution, but as a series of individually-directed components'.

More broadly, with promotions blocked and pay differentials (especially with the Treasury) eroded, just as the City at large was starting to revel ostentatiously in serious money, the Bank in the mid-1980s found itself the subject of some rather fundamental soul-searching. Admirably the *Old Lady* published during these years a trio of notably objective assessments.

'Few of us in the Bank, if we are really honest with ourselves, have much to complain about with regard to the dissatisfiers, such as salary and working conditions,' reflected Mark Stephenson in December 1984. 'The Bank, even in these days of public sector wage restraint, have always been a good employer, endeavouring to pay us fairly for what we do and to take a keen interest in our welfare.' Even so, he accepted that 'the log-jam in promotions' was having detrimental consequences for 'ambitious people' at the Bank: 'They see no prospect for self-realisation because there is little recognition of achievement nor evidence of advancement. This has a counter-productive affect because these people no longer approach their work in a creative manner. They begin to tick over, doing just enough to stay out of trouble but never injecting any new ideas into the job. Confronted with the prospect of waiting many years until the next promotion, there remains little incentive to work harder because, no matter how good your reports, promotion will not come until you reach the median age for someone of your potential.' A year later the magazine's editor, David Pollard, declared that, in comparison with the 1960s, 'there can be little doubt that the bulk of the staff are less satisfied with their lot now than they were then'; and the final paragraph of his editorial had a particular personal resonance:

> Perhaps the greatest change that I think I can see is the loss of the pride, if that is the word, on the part of the staff that my father felt in working for the Bank. His Bank was more than adequately resourced, its image in the outside world was impeccable, its staff were molly-coddled and therefore its greatest ambassador. The leaner, meaner Bank we know today seems somehow to have jettisoned the staff's goodwill and pride in the establishment, the sense of humour of old has been replaced by cynicism. But lean, mean commercial companies, driven by the profit motive, do increasingly imbue their workforce with a corporate loyalty (and not just in Japan); it can be done, it is imbued professionally and presumably it is cost-effective, so when will *we* see it again?

The third of the trio was Michael Pickering, whose letter to the *Old Lady* in March 1986 was sent from the Register Office. Not only did he deny that 'the gravy train' had 'hit the buffers at 50 mph', as opposed to having 'undoubtedly slowed down', but he called on fellow-staff to stand back a little as they contemplated their situation:

> Unlike a large proportion of the working population we don't have to pay the full market rate for our housing loans; unlike teachers we don't have to suffer abuse from a hostile press and an uncomprehending public for demanding a reasonable salary for a thankless task; unlike transport workers and nurses in casualty wards we don't spend much of our working time in fear of being beaten up; unlike miners (and others) we aren't at risk of industrial disease; unlike workers in private enterprise we don't live in fear of being

eased out of our jobs through takeovers or through a simple failure
to deliver a maximum performance at all times.

'Yes – we *sometimes* think about the outside world,' he concluded in
Eliotic mode, 'but not all that often, because "human kind cannot bear
very much reality" and if we thought about it all the time we should
probably cease to function.'[35]

Over the next seven or so years, neither Leigh-Pemberton as
governor nor Blunden and George as successive deputy governors
were inclined to pursue a major internal shake-up. But in 1993, with
the arrival of Pennant-Rea as a deputy governor eager to exercise an
outsider's dispassionate perspective, that changed. In August, barely
a month after starting, he shared his early impressions at an Executive
Committee (EXCO) meeting. He 'wanted to avoid giving the impression to the Bank's staff that the Executive was only interested in
shrinking the Bank'; but, he went on, 'the ratio of support staff to
total staff in the Bank seemed very high', given that he would have
expected a figure like 15 per cent though it was in fact 30 per cent; and
he noted that he 'found the Bank's approach to surplus support staff
hard to understand', in that 'we were honest in identifying staff who
were not needed, but did not then ask them to leave'.

That autumn saw two significant papers, in the context of an 'away
weekend' having been arranged by Pennant-Rea for later in the year
to discuss the Bank's organisation. One, co-written by Pennant-Rea
himself, began with some striking assertions:

The Bank has long seen itself as a centre of excellence, whose
comparative advantage is partly in market expertise but also in
intellect. That requires staff who are bright and versatile. Such
people are in short supply and the subject of fierce competition.
Moreover, in our recruitment of graduates we have narrowed the
field by concentrating mainly on economists rather than on the full
range of university disciplines.

Apart from the narrowing of our catchment area, three things
have changed recently. First, our salaries are increasingly uncompet-
itive, certainly with the best firms in the City. Second, new graduates
have a new attitude: fewer now look for long-term careers. The
increase in job-hopping means that the Bank's offer of job security

is no longer the pull that it used to be. Third, significant over-staffing in the past enabled the Bank to cope with relatively few people of high ability and a large number of moderate performers. Today, the Bank is leaner: the fewer the people, the better they must be.

The paper also offered a cultural analysis. 'Many decisions' were 'routinely taken at a higher level than is actually necessary'; it was 'still far too common' for individuals 'to produce pieces of work without having much idea of the underlying purpose or, indeed, ever getting a clear feel for how that information is used'; and 'the balance between praise and blame is wrong', attributable partly to 'the Bank's traditional concept of excellence, in which mistakes are not easily tolerated and perfection is taken as the common currency'. The other paper was by someone, Pen Kent, who was wholly an insider, albeit a notably cerebral insider:

> The Bank must be as near a perfect example of a classical bureaucracy in the jargon of management theory as it is possible to create. Bureaucracy has become a term of abuse, but it need not be. It embodies values and behaviours which have a reason peculiarly apt for the Bank because of its role. These include a hierarchical structure calculated to produce consistency of product and accountability. It does not do for a public body for example to seem arbitrary in its application of regulation. This concern, taken to an extreme, can lead to upwards delegation so that only the seniors have the power to communicate with the outside world. Do you recall the ban on anyone below the rank of Zone 1 (b) signing a letter leaving the Bank, which only ended within our own career span? Another value is that of perceived equity of treatment for all Staff – to protect individuals from favouritism or victimisation – hence the elaborate rituals of appraisal, now called assessment. This combination of hierarchy and equity makes our staffing arrangements relatively inelastic, as we are now finding out to our cost. It is possible that a culture change could deliver more efficiency gains than any reorganisation.

'However,' concluded Kent, 'our international stature as a central bank far exceeds the UK's global weight. We must be doing something right!'[36]

The brainstorming weekend took place in December at Ashridge Management College in Hertfordshire; over the next few months, three working groups, reporting to Pennant-Rea, thrashed out details; in April came the announcement to staff; and from 4 July 1994 – just over three weeks before the tercentenary – the Bank had a new structure, amounting to the most significant internal shake-up since 1980. In essence, its activities were now divided into two broad wings, supported by a central services area. One wing was concerned with monetary stability; the other wing was concerned with financial stability, including the supervisory aspect; and the casualty was the International Divisions, with some of their members allocated to the two new wings, but also involving a degree of 'letting people go' hitherto not seen at the Bank. Undoubtedly it was Pennant-Rea who particularly pushed through the restructuring, but it is likely that he had the wholehearted support of the governor. 'There has for many years,' George had observed in 1992, 'been something of a struggle to persuade the people in International Divisions of the relevance of much of their work to the work of the rest of the Bank. This is, in my view, partly because historically the work has been to study overseas economies etc almost for their own sake.' Pennant-Rea himself told an interviewer, shortly before the restructuring took effect, that there was a threefold rationale:

> One of the things that struck me when I arrived – and has struck other people as well – is that quite a few people here do not see the connection between what they do and the Bank's ultimate purposes. I think the Bank's employees would like to know where they fit into its ultimate goals. So that's one important focus.
>
> Secondly, we will bring the operational work and the analytical work closer together. Very often you have had people doing things – say in monetary policy or banking supervision – and some distance away you have a bunch of people of shouting 'Watch out for this!', 'Watch out for that!' These are the analysts looking at, say, the economic background; and the distance between them and the operational people means there is a risk that their words get lost in the wind. As far as one can, one needs to get them working close together so that the operational person can turn to the analytic person sitting at the next desk for his views. Those links are there in

the reality of our work and we needed to find ways of making them as close as possible in the structure of the organisation.

Thirdly, we will make sure that we have the staff – numbers and quality – in the right places to match the demands made on them. One of the features of a well-established, multi-winged bureaucracy is that you tend to get an imbalance between resources and needs. This is difficult to change within an existing framework, but once you shift that framework, you have a once-in-a-decade opportunity to get the balance right.

Sadly or otherwise, an in-house foreign office no longer had a place in the trimmer, more focused Bank of its fourth century. 'It will be some time before the effects of the Ashridge restructuring become clear,' noted the *Financial Times*'s Peter Norman on tercentenary day. 'But it would be unwise to assume it marks the end of change at the Bank.'[37]

Would there be parity of esteem between the two wings? Pennant-Rea's interviewer put it to him that 'all the glamour goes to people involved in monetary policy and all the brickbats to people in supervision'; but the deputy governor was adamant that 'the two sides will be seen as of equal importance in terms of numbers, intellectual content and public profile', adding that 'there is no sense in which one is the Cinderella'. Within weeks of the new structure becoming operational, EXCO had a revealing discussion. Expressing concern about the possible creation of 'two banks with little mobility between them', George was worried about a situation in which graduates recruited as economists would tend not to move from monetary analysis to financial stability, while non-economist graduates (by this time usually less than half the annual graduate intake) would likewise tend not to move in the reverse direction. 'Mr Sweeney [Tim Sweeney, management development manager] said this was the reality already. Many economists, especially MSc economists, already wish to work only in areas involving primarily economic analysis.' On which Mervyn King, the executive director in charge of the monetary analysis division of the Monetary Stability Wing, commented: 'The challenge was for the Bank to motivate them [the graduate economists] to be interested in central banking through the work that they were given. At present the prospect of making what was perceived to be a big switch from economics to other work was terrifying for many junior staff.'

For all these understanding words, King himself remained uncompromising about what he wanted in his own patch. 'A priority would be to recruit quality from outside,' he told Pennant-Rea later in 1994, adding that in terms of the initial two-year training period for graduate recruits 'he would also like people to spend more time in his area when they first joined the Bank in order to properly consolidate what they have learned at University', while 'looking ahead to the future, he said that he would like to recruit more PhD students'. Two years later saw another telling moment:

> Mr King noted [at a meeting with the governor and deputy governor] that he was aware that some people in Monetary Analysis were thought to be arrogant and did not communicate adequately with the Bank. Allied to this was a reported feeling in some quarters that Monetary Analysis is a clique. He felt that such arguments were exaggerated …
>
> Mr King said that he was still worried about any plan to bring substantial numbers of non-economists into FSW [Financial Stability Wing] who would have no Bank-wide utility. He firmly believed that economics was the right qualification for people joining both wings of the Bank.

Undeniably the economists were buzzing in the mid-1990s. Among those recruited in 1994 was the former *Guardian* journalist and future government minister Ruth Kelly, who for two years was part of the team compiling the quarterly *Inflation Report*. 'Being offered a job at the Bank was an unprecedented opportunity,' she recalled in 2002. 'I was hugely impressed with the rigour with which Bank staff approached issues – very different from the way journalists approached them.'[38]

Tercentenary celebrations and growing influence notwithstanding, these were not happy times across the Bank as a whole. 'EDP Talks Break Down' was the main front-page story in March 1994 in the first issue of a new staff paper, *The Bank Fortnight*, detailing how BIFU was that week balloting the Electronic Data Processing staff on strike action over the Bank's proposals for a new pay structure. In the context of management having written to each member of EDP staff, 'inviting them individually to indicate whether they were willing to accept the Bank's package and whether they wished this to be reflected in

March salaries', a BIFU press release accused the Bank of 'living in the 17th Century'. A year later the Court formally endorsed an end to the traditional approach to personnel matters. 'The shift from a 1950s paternalism (with its implication that there was automatically a job for life) has left a vacuum, with staff expectations that are inconsistent with 1990s economic realities,' observed Pennant-Rea in the key paper. 'There is thus some distrust of the Bank as an employer.' And: 'Post-Ashridge changes have brought to the surface some sizeable staff mismatches, with more limited senior opportunities; a move away from paternalism; the absence of effective management development programmes; continuing relatively low staff turnover but above-average absence rates caused, in part, through additional stress; and inconsistent messages to staff.' What was now needed, in order 'to attract, retain and motivate quality people' – in a larger context in which 'the majority of staff cannot have, and should not expect to have, continuous advancement over 30–40 years' – was 'a commitment by the Bank instead to help the continuous personal development and re-skilling of staff'.

Soon afterwards, one of the senior banking supervisors, David Swanney, had a heart-to-heart with his chief, Brian Quinn:

He [Swanney] said he thought the concept of the reorganisation of the Bank was good, but had not been well handled, particularly the treatment of people; and he mentioned the treatment of some long-serving staff as having been particularly brutal. He said that in his experience people were complaining but still got on with the work. Nevertheless, we could no longer rely upon their commitment ...

There had been too abrupt a change of culture from the old Bank to the new approach, by which he meant that people had been obliged to accept a very rapid switch in their career expectations and outlook. He thought this might have been introduced more gradually ...

He said he was acutely aware he was not an economist, not because he felt that it exposed any great deficiency in his ability to do his job, but really because he thought it might cause an obstacle to moves in other parts of the Bank in the course of his career. He asked whether there might be any short courses available for people like him so that he might do something to fill in the gap.

At the heart of the new personnel strategy was internal appraisal. 'We managed,' the governor was informed in June 1995 after a negotiated settlement with BIFU, 'to get the union to "accept" that the principle of merit bonuses will be a main element of our remuneration structure from now on'; though the following February the new deputy governor, Howard Davies, was lamenting the lack of frankness in performance appraisals and noting how the recent round of comments on the forms 'suggested that all was for the best in the best of all possible worlds, and that the performance of HoDs [Heads of Division] was almost entirely even across the Bank'.

Another difficult area in this changing environment was the delicate and emotional issue of voluntary severance. 'Many staff (particularly those approaching mid-career) have factored the expected severance windfall into their long-term planning,' observed Sue Coffey in May 1996; she also highlighted 'the reactions of those satisfactory and good performers who have been refused severance', even leading to 'protracted depressive illnesses brought on by the refusal'; and finally, there was what she called the 'morbid fear of redundancy', or in other words 'the cultural difficulties for some staff who, even with the support of the Transition Centre, an exit secondment and the severance package, are unwilling or unable to accept leaving the Bank'. A Darwinian might have argued that the underlying problem for those unfortunates was that they had existed too long in an unnaturally sheltered, monocultural environment. 'What I found disappointing,' recorded Davies later in 1996 after a visit to the soon-to-close Birmingham branch, 'was that most of the staff, even long-service career staff, had done no external training whatsoever' to improve their subsequent job prospects. And he reflected: 'I imagine that this is a side-effect of the "cradle to grave" proposition which the Bank has made to staff in the past.'[39]

It was an indication of how seriously the Bank took all these related matters that in 1995 it commissioned its first comprehensive (though excluding the Printing Works) staff attitude survey. The process, undertaken by International Survey Research Ltd, began in May with fifty-nine diagnostic interviews with a cross-section of staff. Some of the reactions were positive:

The re-structuring has given people a much clearer focus on their own and the Bank's roles.

The Bank has a very collegiate culture. The atmosphere is a supportive, co-operative one, with very little backbiting or politicking.

The Bank is still the most amazingly generous employer, and in that respect I'm very pleased to work here.

Staff are still delivering the goods to a very high standard. If something needs to be done everybody will rally round.

This is an exciting time for the Bank. We have a prominent role in influencing policy, and we seem to be getting it right for a change.

The great majority of quoted reactions, however, were at the more negative end of the spectrum:

The Bank's real structure is a number of fiefdoms. The reorganisation hasn't changed that.

What we do in the Bank is conceptualise, analyse and criticise. What we don't do is do. We're reactive, not proactive. We can't institute change and we can't manage it.

Staff are now very cynical. The traditional Bank culture is being eroded but nothing positive is being put in its place.

The problem isn't the 'reactionary old guard'. Many of them genuinely care about their staff. The problem is the 'uncaring new guard'. Most of them don't give a damn.

The Bank is very hierarchical. People are sometimes inhibited from responding to senior management by a feeling that to do so would be disrespectful.

The smallest possible minutiae are passed right up the line. Responsibility rests entirely at the top.

If you want to retain capable people in a Mateus Rosé structure you have to delegate authority.

Everything the Bank does is geared to the Officials. The Officers are an afterthought. [The officials/officers terminology was a short-lived replacement for the previous distinction between principals and clerks.]

Staff aren't recognised for good work. They're not penalised for bad work either. It doesn't matter what you do really.

The pyramid has narrowed, but we still have too many people in senior positions who are past their sell-by date.

The Bank is seen to have acted in bad faith by abandoning the 40 year career.

We've managed to keep people so far by a mixture of job interest, career mobility and camaraderie. But we're now dealing with Thatcher's children. We must find some more money from somewhere.

We give people generous appraisals, and then fail to meet their expectations due to budgetary constraints. We therefore have a morale problem which is entirely of our own making.

Nobody is ever praised. We never say 'thank you'. It's alien to the ethos of the Bank.

We've had 15 years of death by 1,000 cuts. It's bitten deep into the psyche of the Bank. Morale is shot to pieces.

A final comment was, in its way, perhaps as damning as any: 'I don't boast about working for the Bank as much as I did.'

Then later that summer, between late July and early September, came the full-scale survey, with 3,010 questionnaires sent out and 1,911 returned. What emerged, as summarised in October 1995 by ISR's managing director, Roger Maitland, was a mixed and even contradictory picture. Seven areas coming out broadly on the plus side of the ledger were followed by nine that clearly raised troubling issues:

Employees are proud to be associated with the Bank.

They understand the Core Purposes of the Bank and believe that it is highly regarded by its customers.

Downward communications are rated relatively favourably.

Divisional management are viewed in a relatively positive light.

Employees are involved in their work and their contributions are recognised.

Employees understand how their job performance is assessed and believe that it is assessed fairly.

Pay and benefits are responded to favourably.

The Bank is seen as being poorly managed and as lacking leadership and direction.

Teamwork across the Bank is seen as being poor, and employees are not well informed about the work of other Divisions.

The culture of the Bank is seen as being 'closed' and as resistant to challenge and innovation.

Bureaucracy is felt to be rife and decision-making to be too slow.

There is a lack of delegation and employees feel that they are not respected.

Technical skills are valued at the expense of people management skills.

Performance management is felt to be poor. Neither superior performance nor expertise are adequately recognised.

Opportunities for either personal or career development are seen as being very limited.

Confidence in the future is low, and senior management are felt to be doing a poor job of managing change.

Tellingly, only one in six believed that action would be taken to address the issues raised by the survey; as for those replying in the affirmative to the question of whether they thought that morale could be said to be good across the Bank as a whole, the figure was a devastating 4 per cent.

Later in October, an early high-level reaction to the survey came from King, who had seen a disaggregation of its results:

There are significant differences between Officials and Officers ... What is striking is that in *both* wings [monetary stability and financial stability] those primarily involved in analytical jobs respond much more favourably, especially towards 'change in the Bank'. The least favourable responses come from EDP staff, Property Services staff, and Bank Officers generally. This is not surprising. Since Ashridge we have done nothing on pay and career structure for Officers. And the Bank has been contracting steadily since exchange controls were abolished in 1979. There *are* management problems in the Bank ... But I feel the impression given to Court that the morale position is uniform across the Bank is in fact misleading.

The final sentence of King's memo drew short shrift from Sue Betts, a senior manager in HR. 'This is pure rubbish,' she scribbled on her copy. 'Only 76 people commented favourably on morale – even if all were Officials (the only group M. is interested in) the result would still

be very bad indeed.' Her broad thrust was surely correct: the following month, at a meeting with Davies to discuss the survey, the heads
of division 'described the reactions they are encountering from staff
– fatigue, resistance, distrust etc'. What was to be done? 'There are no
easy, pat answers,' Davies confessed in the *Old Lady* the following
spring. And though he took comfort in the fact that 'we are not alone',
given the 'mounting evidence that employee satisfaction across the
UK has declined markedly in recent years', and also pointed to the
irrefutable truth that 'by most external standards the Bank of England
is still a very stable culture, with a great number of long-serving staff,
and relatively low turnover', he did not seek to deny that 'a dangerous gap has opened up between the managers and the managed in the
Bank, a gap which urgently needs to be closed'.

That would be the challenge ahead – a challenge in an environment
in which, as Davies succinctly put it, 'the number of essentially administrative and executional jobs is on the decline, while the number of
analytical occupations is rising'. Yet, however that challenge played
out, the Bank would still be the Bank. A small but emblematic issue
arose in February 1997: what was the Old Lady's attitude to be towards
Red Nose Day? 'The Governor and Deputy Governor agreed that the
Bank could not be involved in an official capacity.'[40]

Back in the early 1990s, the collapse of BCCI in July 1991, followed
in October 1992 by the Bingham Report, inevitably had regulatory-
cum-supervisory implications. 'Alertness is something which the Bank
has had cause to address,' acknowledged Leigh-Pemberton immediately after Bingham. 'The criticisms of lack of vigour in pursuing signals
of possible fraud have been well publicised,' he went on to note in his
Mansion House speech, 'as I trust has our response involving establishing a Special Investigations Unit and a Legal Unit under seasoned
experts recruited from the professions; strengthening our capacity
for on-site examination; enhancing the training of our supervisors;
increasing the use we make of the Board of Banking Supervision; and
participating in the new machinery which the Chancellor has set up to
co-ordinate responses to fraud amongst supervisors, and other prosecuting authorities.'

Would it be enough? 'Supervision: recognise need for open financial centre with sensible regulation, but does not want crooks or scandal,' was the crisp summary in September 1993 of Kenneth Clarke's views to the governor, while three months later George and Quinn were at the Treasury to discuss a recent study it had undertaken on banking supervision. George moved quickly on to the front foot. He was 'surprised that the Bank was characterised as being entirely reactive'; he observed that the study failed to emphasise 'the dogs that did not bark, such as the LDC debt crisis'; he argued not only that 'not every bank failure should be seen as a scandal', but that 'expectations were too high, the question was how to anchor them'; while as for the Bank's style of supervision he pointed to how, inescapably, 'there was a conflict between the need for confidentiality and the need for accountability'. There ensued some dialogue with the Treasury's Rachel Lomax. She 'said that there remained a perception, stemming from the Bank's history, that the Bank was the head of the City club'; George 'denied that the Bank was protective of banks', adding that 'the Bank's relationship with the commercial banks was quite different from a decade ago'; with which she 'agreed', noting that 'there was now very limited scope for suasion'. Discussion then turned to the balance between the formal and informal approaches to supervision, starting with George:

The Bank favoured the supervisory approach, rather than the regulatory approach, and this had been endorsed by Bingham. What the Bank had learned from the BCCI episode was that the informal system worked well where a basis of trust existed, but that the Bank had to be very sensitive to when that relationship had broken down, and to maintain an ability to change gear. But the trend was towards regulation.

Mr Quinn said that the Bank was now more systematic in distinguishing between whether or not its powers were exercisable and whether they should be exercised. This meant that the Bank thought very carefully about whether it was deliberately pursuing a voluntary remedial path, rather than a path involving using its powers.

Mrs Lomax agreed that she had seen a pronounced change in the Bank's attitude. She thought that there had been a distaste for using powers in the mid-80s.

The meeting ended with the question of the extent of the Bank's responsibilities:

> The Governor expressed his concern about the trend towards more consumer protection legislation. In the banking industry it was leading to the expectation that banks would never fail. Finance was a risk business. The degree of protection given to customers, however, was a political judgement. The Bank's role was to point out that there were two sides to the regulatory ledger. Mrs Lomax agreed. She said regulation was increasingly governing the relationship between a bank and its customer, but the Bank's real interest was in minimising systemic risk. Mrs Lomax asked whether, if the Bank wished to avoid retail regulation, it would wish to supervise only big banks. The Governor said systemic problems could well start in small banks. The issue was the scope of supervision.

All of which was manifestly sensible and proportionate, but of course, out there in the global financial world, the pieces kept moving. 'Good progress is being made in capturing and confining the risks which arise from derivatives operations,' Quinn in July 1994 reassured the Annual Managed Derivatives Industry Conference in New York. 'The supervisors and regulators in the main centres are working hard in specialised groups to find solutions that deliver regulation without strangulation. Perhaps equally important, the market is developing its own form of safeguards by insisting on greater disclosure and transparency, improved accounting rules, collateralisation and margining requirements that protect both them and the ultimate users of the product.' And he concluded that 'the earliest apprehensions about derivatives have been replaced by a methodical analysis of the possible sources of difficulty'.[41]

Yet should the Bank still be undertaking banking supervision? In the twin context of BCCI and the gathering independence debate, that was becoming by 1993 an increasingly asked question. Taking evidence that year, the Treasury Select Committee heard some views arguing in the negative. 'The problem about having supervision,' reflected Sir Peter Middleton (former permanent secretary at the Treasury, now deputy chairman of Barclays), 'is that it detracts from the Bank's credibility as a counter-inflationary body because people will always think it is more interested in maintaining the banking system than it is in pursuing its own counter-inflationary objectives'; according to the former chancellor, Lord Lawson, another financial scandal like BCCI could 'undermine the respect and authority of the Bank of England in the eyes of the financial markets and public opinion in general, and this respect and authority is important to the successful conduct of monetary policy in the real world'; while even Quinn conceded that 'if the central bank as supervisor gets a sustained hammering in the public domain for its activities there, then that cannot help the authority of the institution'. In November, well aware that the Treasury Committee was considering its report, George used the second of the governor's LSE lectures – a year after Leigh-Pemberton's important one on price stability – to press the case that the close, two-way interdependence with monetary stability meant that the preservation of financial stability was inevitably a matter of close concern to a central bank. Moreover, he implicitly argued, no one could do it better:

> The central bank has a vital duty to support the soundness of the financial system. We are clear about our objective: it is not to prevent each and every failure, but to ensure that, when a systemic threat arises, it is dealt with quickly and efficiently. We have the ability to do this because we know a lot about all the institutions and markets through which threats can materialise. We get our information largely from the process of supervision – from being a direct supervisor ourselves, and through our involvement in the markets, and through our contacts with other supervisors at home and overseas. And, in our central banking role we have the resources to do this job – not just money, but also the technical skills to manage out difficult positions, and the reputation for impartiality which enables us to co-ordinate commercial solutions.

The following month, the Treasury Committee more or less agreed that the Bank should not go down a Bundesbank-style road. 'On balance,' stated its report, 'we conclude that there is no overwhelming case for separating out the responsibility for prudential supervision to a separate body'; and the report added that this was likely to remain its view 'even if the Bank gains greater autonomy in monetary policy'. That, however, was far from ending the debate. 'A super supervisor?'

was the *Economist*'s headline in May 1994, noting the publication of a paper from the Centre for the Study of Financial Innovation with a double proposal: the Bank to give up its supervisory role, concentrating instead on monetary policy; and a super-regulator to be created, known as the Financial Services Supervisory Commission. For the Bank's 250 supervisors, overseeing the operations of 488 domestic and foreign-owned banks in the UK, the premium on 'alertness' merely grew by the day.[42]

Such was the state of play at the point of the tercentenary, and in the event the next financial scandal, intimately affecting the Bank, was not long in coming.[43] 'Peter Baring, Andrew Tuckey and Peter Norris met the Deputy Governor, Mr Quinn, Mr Foot and Mr Reid on Friday 24 February at 12.00 pm to make them aware of a major problem in Barings' Far East operation which had emerged over the previous 24 hours,' recorded the deputy governor's office in early 1995. 'Mr Baring said that if the group survived, it would need substantial recapitalisation,' while 'Mr Tuckey noted that the rest of the business was in very good shape.' In essence, the unwelcome news that the men from Barings imparted was twofold: first, that a Barings derivatives trader, operating from the Singapore futures exchange (SIMEX), had run up huge, fraudulent losses, possibly of at least £400 million; second, that Barings itself – after an impeccable, blameless 105 years since the previous Barings crisis (governor Lidderdale and all that) – was in deep trouble. George had just left for a skiing holiday in France, but at once flew back. On Saturday morning, he spoke to Derek Wanless 'to ask if NatWest were interested in buying Barings', but 'Wanless said the answer was no'; he then 'asked if NatWest might be prepared to put up some equity along with others', to which 'Wanless said it would depend on the deal.' George and his colleagues then spent most of the day arranging for a mixture of clearing bankers and merchant bankers to assemble at the Bank on Sunday the 26th to see if any collective rescue could be arranged of the City's oldest merchant bank, if no longer its most important. The deadline set for any rescue was 10 pm that Sunday – before the Japanese market, in which most of Barings' positions were open, began trading again.

An epic day unfolded, mainly in Threadneedle Street but including occasional gubernatorial forays outside. At the first, calling on the chancellor around lunchtime, George took the line that although it would be 'a big shock to the markets' if Barings were not bailed out, never-theless the risk in his judgement was not systemic – to which Clarke agreed. Would Barings be bailed out? As early as mid-morning, David Scholey was observing to the governor, after a lengthy meeting of the proposed consortium of supporting banks, that 'as the positions were so big and as they were open-ended, it would be very difficult to final-ise the deal'. Essentially, that remained the case throughout the day and into the evening. Meanwhile, hope flickered that the Brunei Investment Agency might perhaps be willing to cap Barings' liabilities – before eventually at around 8.30, an hour and a half before the deadline, the news came through that Brunei was unable to help, on the understand-able grounds that the envisaged deal was 'too complicated, involving too much risk and with too little time'. By 9.45 the governor was at No. 11, informing Clarke that it had proved 'too complicated' to try to save Barings in the time available. They agreed that George should appear on the *Today* programme at about 7 the following morning; and the governor said that he would emphasise 'the control failure'.[44]

Next day, George duly gave a round of media interviews insisting that the problem was specific to Barings and that that bank's failure posed no systemic threat to the banking system as a whole. Should the Bank have done more? William Rees-Mogg in *The Times* on Tuesday thundered about its 'grotesque timidity', arguing that it had 'avoided risking at most a few hundred million pounds', whereas 'the credit of London, which has been put in jeopardy, may be an unquantifiable asset, but it must be measured in hundreds of billions of pounds of Britain's future earning power'. He concluded gravely: 'The Bank of England exists to protect British credit. In this instance, it has failed in its prime duty.' The same paper's Graham Searjeant and Anthony Harris took a similar line, as did its leader writer; but John Plender in the *Financial Times* persuasively countered the Bank's critics:

> It is, of course, a case of mistaken identity. A City whose good name has been so dreadfully traduced no longer exists. London's compet-itive advantage in international finance has little, if anything, to do with the older cohorts of the merchant banking fraternity who financed world trade in the 19th century. For the best part of two decades the powerhouse of financial innovation has been located largely in the foreign banking and securities community ...

Moreover, he added, 'in the absence of a club, successful lifeboats are not easily launched'. By the end of the week there was widespread agreement that George had got it right. 'The external impact of the crisis has so far been successfully contained, vindicating the decision not to rescue Barings,' the *Independent* noted on Saturday, while next day the *Sunday Telegraph*'s Bill Jamieson argued that 'if the impression got around that domestic banks could be counted on to be bailed out by their central bank, that would suggest a playing field so tilted as to drive out every non-resident bank'. And, he asked rhetorically, 'where would the City be then?'[45]

By this time, not only had the 'rogue trader', Nick Leeson, been identified and remanded, but a buyer, the Dutch bank ING, had been found for Barings, priced at an attractive £1. In the course of that process, George firmly declined an invitation from ING's advisers, Flemings, either 'to take on the risk of any potential subsequent claims from SIMEX or the Japanese' or 'to pick up (in an indemnity fashion) some form of *capped* liability in relation to possible claims from Tokyo and Singapore in order to give their client comfort'; but quietly and behind the scenes the Bank did take on Barings' swap exposures and some custodial responsibilities, as well as providing liquidity for ING to acquire Barings. A fortnight or so after the main drama was over, George spoke – at length and privately – at the annual dinner of the Cornhill Club, a City-based dining club. 'It has been a torrid time,' he acknowledged. 'Emotions have understandably run high and a good deal of uncertainty has been generated.' Why had the Bank 'been unable to orchestrate a rescue by the rest of the banking community'? The answer, he asserted, was not any waning influence on the part of the Bank, but rather because commercial banks 'do not easily act against their perceived commercial interest just because the Bank of England asks them to'. 'That probably always was true,' he added. 'It certainly is true. And long may it continue.' Why, then, did not the Bank 'ride to the rescue itself', in other words as lender of last resort, or 'persuade the Government to do so'? 'No financial institution has a right to support,' the governor declared. 'It is deliberately intended that there should be constructive ambiguity about whether or not in any particular situation we would be prepared to support any particular institution. If that weren't the case, and any institution felt that it was guaranteed, then that would introduce, of course, a great deal of moral hazard into the monetary system.' Accordingly, given that the specific 'solvency problem' faced by Barings was in the Bank's judgement 'unlikely to have very major systemic risks', he and his colleagues 'could see no basis for suggesting to the Government that they should write the blank cheque that would have been necessary to produce the cap on the liability'. And, he went on, 'whatever you may read in some newspapers, the knock-on effects were in fact both limited and short-lived'. George finished by looking ahead: 'The shock of Barings' failure will take time to pass. But in the end the reputation and the prosperity of London, and of the British banks operating out of London, will depend much more fundamentally on the quality of the services which they provide.'[46]

He was speaking on Thursday, 16 March. Three days later, a Sunday tabloid's lurid, but in the circumstances irresistible, headline – 'The Bonk of England' – was accompanied by the revelation that a journalist, Mary Ellen Synon, had been smuggled into the Bank under an assumed name and that she and the deputy governor had made love on the carpet of the governor's dressing room. Briefly it seemed that Pennant-Rea might survive, as the quality papers temporarily declined to touch the story; but then the *Financial Times* gave it a seven-column splash, and very soon the deputy was penning his resignation letter. 'Montagu Norman,' he reflected, 'once said that "the dogs bark, but the caravan moves on"' – though quite what the great defender of the Bank's honour would have made of it all rather beggared belief. Brian Quinn briefly stepped in as acting deputy governor, until the appointment of Howard Davies, director general of the CBI and already in his mid-forties a man for all seasons, having worked previously in the Foreign Office, the Treasury, McKinsey and the Audit Commission. An almost absurdly classic meritocrat – son of a publican; Manchester Grammar School; Oxford – he had been, he told Ruth Kelly in an interview for the *Old Lady* before he took up his position in September 1995, 'circling round the Bank for the past twenty years'.[47]

The Pennant-Rea episode was particularly ill timed. The Bank's decision not to bail out Barings may have been vindicated, but there remained the troubling, high-profile matter of whether in the first place it had been negligent in its supervisory capacity. In early April, barely a month after the spectacular collapse, George faced aggressive interrogation from the Treasury Committee's Brian Sedgemore about how subsidiaries of Barings had lent £330 million of Barings' own funds to Baring Futures in Singapore:

> Am I not right in thinking that if you transfer the whole of a company's shareholders' capital, the Bank of England has to be notified? — The Bank of England has to be notified as a matter of law if a company wishes to advance more than 25 per cent of its capital to a single counterparty.
>
> My question, Mr George, is this: were you notified? — We did not know as of 27 February that [£330 million] was advanced this way.
>
> So effectively you are saying to the Committee quite honestly that you have a supervisory system which is incapable of informing the Bank of England that a sum in excess of the whole of the shareholders' capital has been transferred out of the country. Is there not something wrong with the supervisory system? — We do not know day by day the details of every exposure taken.
>
> We are talking about rather a lot of money, Mr George, in relation to the size of the bank. — Of course we are, but how can we be certain to know about the large amount of money unless we are monitoring every day the small amounts of money? It is a criminal offence –
>
> Or unless the internal or external auditors tell you. It is a criminal offence …? — It is a criminal offence not to inform us; to advance this money without notifying us.

Three months later, in July 1995, the Board of Banking Supervision – of which the majority of members were independent of the Bank – issued a report acquitting the Bank of culpability over its ignorance of the transfer of substantial funds from London to Singapore in the early weeks of the year and asserting that the Bank had 'reasonably placed reliance on local regulators of the overseas operations', as well as having been 'entitled to place reliance on the explanations given by management as to the profitability of these operations and on the other information provided by Barings'. The Bank, in short, could not have prevented the collapse. The report did offer some constructive criticism – recommending that the Bank should 'go further in its role as consolidated supervisor' and 'should seek to obtain a more comprehensive understanding of the non-banking businesses in a group' – but broadly was viewed as being something of a whitewash; or, as the *Financial Times* put it, of being 'woefully soft' on the Bank.

The day after the report's publication, George and Quinn gave evidence to the Treasury Committee. Chris Thompson, the senior manager in charge of merchant banking supervision, had resigned ahead of the report, but the two men were adamant that the Bank, whether by commission or omission, had done little or nothing seriously wrong, while George did not hesitate to raise the emotional temperature. After conceding that such was 'the intrusive British press' that he now found 'extremely tempting' the proposition that 'if your reputation in the monetary policy area is damaged by every failure in banking supervision, you would be better off without it', he turned to the fundamentals of the supervisory role itself:

George: I am sure I have said to this Committee before that if you wanted us to guarantee no banking failures, frankly I think we could have a shot at that and we could give you a guarantee. It would mean that everybody's deposit had to be matched by a government liability of precisely the same maturity. Of course the bank could not make any money on that basis and of course it would not do the economy much good, but you have to understand and I am very anxious to really persuade you of this point that there is a trade off, there is a balance that has to be struck between the extent of regulation and the cost of regulation in a direct sense but also in terms of the effect it has on the ability of the financial system to support the wider economy. So you cannot say to me, 'You shouldn't care about that at all. All you should care about is stopping banks going bust'. If you meant that, you would not have provided deposit protection in the Banking Act. You clearly recognise that there has to be some kind of balance. We do not have any clear guideline on whether it is acceptable for one bank to go bust every 20 years and whether it is a bank of £5 million or £5 billion. These are judgements which are actually intrinsic. You can say to us that we must do better. You can say to us we must spend more money. You can say to us we must introduce more restrictions. All I say to you is that you look on the other side and say, 'What is going to be the effect?' I am in full flood now so if I may just make one other point because it is absolutely tremendously important to us as well as to you, and that is that actually getting able people to do this job is becoming damn difficult. Mr [Nicholas] Budgen was asking whether or not we should be getting new people into the Bank to do this kind of thing. How on earth do you think we are going to get people in to come and do this kind of lose-lose job when we go through this kind of procedure every time there is a problem? I do not resent it. I understand precisely that this is the way –

Radice: What kind of procedure?

George: Where every time there is a problem, there is a great investigation, you want blood –

Abbott: You are accountable to Parliament.

George: I have just said I do not object to this procedure. All I am trying to say is do understand –

Sedgemore: You said that sarcastically.

George: I did not say that sarcastically. I am not a sarcastic chap.

Sedgemore: You did not mean it.

George: I did mean it. I accept this kind of procedure and I accept that it has to apply a 100 per cent standard, but I tell you this, if you want better regulation you have got to take account of the fact that this kind of witch hunt every time something goes wrong is going to make it very difficult to get people to do it.

The following week, back in the calm of EC2, George observed to Quinn that 'the real substance of the criticism of the Bank related to its understanding of – and supervision of – securities business'; while in early September, meeting with Quinn and Foot, he noted that 'it was clearly important that the Bank should have expertise in new products as, for example, in the traded markets/models area' and said that he was 'very conscious' of 'the criticism that the Bank knew all about banking but not securities markets'. At the same meeting, Foot pointed out that 'typically experts had backgrounds in accountancy, maths or economics' and that 'the difficulty was in recruiting people with direct Treasury or capital markets experience who were generally too expensive'. Undoubtedly, the Bank was under some pressure. 'Trying times on Threadneedle Street' was the title of a major piece in the September issue of *Institutional Investor*, concluding unenthusiastically that, in the absence of a radical redefinition of the Bank's role, 'the Old Lady will likely continue to muddle through in her traditional manner'.[48]

Over the next year and a half, the Bank tried hard to raise its supervisory game and quieten the critics. In July 1996, following input from Arthur Andersen, it announced risk-assessment models that would 'bring the line supervisors into direct contact, on site, with a wider range of management'; that it would 'promulgate a clear summary of standards it expects to apply'; and that from September its Supervision and Surveillance Divisions would be restructured, enabling the Bank to, among other things, 'improve and harmonise the assessment of risks to which banks are subject', 'recruit more specialists and experienced bankers from the market', and 'develop further co-operation with other regulators at home and abroad'. Later that autumn, Davies launched the Bank's own publication, *Financial Stability Review*, seeking to stake the intellectual high ground (not least in an article by Christopher Huhne on rating sovereign risk); in mid-November, the governor again gave evidence to the Treasury Committee, continuing to insist that, though the Bank was steadily improving in its supervisory capacity, expectations of supervision needed to be realistic; early in December, the deputy governor gave a lecture at the Chartered Institute of Management Accountants, setting out in some detail the Bank's approach ('as far as possible, a light touch ... an approach based on the principle that market participants can do what they want unless we say that they can't, rather than that they can only do what we say they can'); and a fortnight before Christmas, the Treasury Committee published its own rather belated report on the Barings disaster and its implications. Criticism of the Bank was plentiful. As 'a cheerleader for the City', it remained exposed to the danger of 'regulatory capture'; it was not yet 'apparent that the banking sector has earned the soft touch provided by the Bank'; and the post-BCCI supervisory culture of relying less on trust 'did not apply in the case of Barings'. 'The Bank needs to demonstrate,' concluded the report, 'that it is able to separate its supervisory activities from its other functions and avoid any possible weakening of its regulatory effectiveness due to its proximity to the day to day banking market. Otherwise it may be that in order to bring about the necessary cultural change banking supervision will have to be taken away from the Bank of England.'[49]

Earlier in 1996, in the last of the LSE lectures, George had spoken about the Bank's 'three core purposes'. The first, obviously, was 'maintaining the integrity and value of the currency', aka monetary stability; the second, indeed, was 'maintaining the stability of the financial system, both domestic and international'; while the third was 'seeking to ensure the effectiveness of the United Kingdom's financial services', which in practice largely meant seeking to protect and enhance the competitiveness of London as an international financial centre. On this last aspect, George's strictly unsentimental approach – almost unreservedly accepting the forces of free-market globalisation – had been exemplified the previous year by the Bank's policy towards the merchant banks, once so umbilically attached to the Bank itself. Not only did he let Barings go, but soon afterwards he did not seek to intervene as Warburgs, Smith New Court and Kleinwort Benson all passed into foreign ownership. The crux was Warburgs, so long the leader – the national champion – in the field. 'The most important factor was that any deal was commercially realistic,' he told Warburgs' David Scholey in April 1995 after Scholey had asked if the Bank had any preference between the two front-runners – NatWest and Swiss Bank Corporation – to take over his beleaguered firm. 'If both parties believed it to be so he could see the argument in favour of establishing two strong British houses, other things being equal. But he would not wish a deal to be undertaken for emotional reasons. Sir David asked whether the Bank's experience of Morgan Grenfell [the merchant bank acquired by Deutsche Bank in 1989] suggested that life was more complicated where there was an overseas parent. The Governor said that this was not his impression ...'

Elsewhere, a similar lack of sentiment informed the Bank's money market reforms, aimed at enabling the Bank to trade debt through a much broader spectrum of institutions, while at the same time enhancing the liquidity and depth of the gilt market. 'The [discount] houses were fairly depressed because our proposals went further than they had expected in cutting off their access to late lending after the transition period, and by the open access rather than club approach to OMO [open-market operations] counterparties,' reported Plenderleith to the governor in December 1996. 'They saw the prospect of diminished privileges as threatening their credit standing ...' George was unmoved, and in March 1997 the Bank duly ended the privileged position of the discount houses by switching its daily open-market operations to a gilt repos system open to all-comers; Union (the former Union Discount) announced that it was winding down its positions prior to putting itself up for sale; and the following year the last discount house returned its licence to the Bank.

What about the impending euro? As early as September 1996, more than two years ahead of the eventual launch, George insisted that whether Britain was in or out of a single currency, the City would thrive. 'The euro is just a bigger Deutschmark,' he declared. 'We have seemed to do perfectly satisfactorily handling the mark, just as we have the dollar and yen. I am sure that the City will cope.' Few observers believed that George himself was an enthusiast for British participation in economic and monetary union – the prospect of the Bank of England becoming a branch office of the European Central Bank was hardly likely to enchant a Threadneedle Street man. But it was becoming clear that the new currency was going to happen, and the Bank devoted considerable time and resources to ensuring that, irrespective of the question of British membership, the City was fully prepared. 'We aim to identify any initiatives where we at the central bank need to take the lead to provide system-wise facilities, and these we have in hand,' Plenderleith in November 1996 assured participants at the City of London Central Banking Conference. 'Interlinking the individual RTGS [real-time gross settlement] payment systems in TARGET [the euro payment system] is one. Discussion with market participants of the appropriate legal framework for the euro, and of bond market trading conventions, are two other areas. This exercise to prepare wholesale market activity for the euro is now proceeding on a broad front in the UK and we are pleased with the concrete progress being made. We will continue to be active as a catalyst ...'[50]

By the mid-1990s it was the Bank's first core purpose that had become most core of all. 'Do inflation targets work?' was the title of King's September 1995 address to the Centre for Economic Policy Research, and his conclusion was that they had led over the past three years to 'a more systematic and focused discussion of the monthly decisions on monetary policy, both inside and outside government'; while in March 1997, profiling King, the economic journalist David Smith declared 'without hesitation' that 'Britain's inflation performance in the 1990s has been better than for 25 years' and argued that inflation targeting had played its part – not only by forming 'the basis for all the monetary policy discussions between Chancellor and Governor', but also by helping to create 'a climate in which low inflation is seen as the norm'. It was not, at the Bank end of the process, necessarily painless. 'You discussed at some length the preparation of the Bank's forecast and the press briefing for the Inflation Report,' began a note to King from the governor's office in November 1994 after his recent meeting with George:

> The Governor said that he had not realised that he and you feel differently about the immediate outlook. He felt that the Inflation Report had been too sanguine. You thought that there were significant and asymmetric risks on the upside but nevertheless that the central forecast was plausible. There was no point doing careful analysis if it was ignored and the published forecast drawn on the basis of a hunch. The Governor said that the forecasters could not expect to dictate the Bank's policy stance but, of course, their analysis was a very important input into the process. It was agreed that the Governor should be involved in the preparation of the forecast at an earlier stage …

King himself had a clear vision of how the formation of monetary advice-cum-policy should operate, and some two years later, in a presentation to senior colleagues, reiterated his 'determination for the Bank to retain the intellectual leadership in the debate on monetary policy'. Turning to ongoing activity, he then gave some specifics. 'Work in the group of small models had largely been completed, and major progress had been made in the work on the accountability and credibility framework of monetary policy'; as for forecasting, he asserted that one of the Bank's 'major achievements' was its 'relative openness in describing the uncertainty and balance of risks surrounding our forecast'.

Soon afterwards, in his November 1996 lecture at Loughborough University, George carefully set out all the various elements involved in the post-ERM monetary policy framework. On the *Inflation Report* side, these included transparency ('the Bank's professional reputation is on the line as never before'), its forecast of inflation two years ahead ('we now illustrate the extent of our uncertainty by displaying the forecast as a probability distribution, a sort of open fan on its side – with the uncertainty typically increasing though not necessarily symmetrically'), and intense discussions ahead of the forecast (including about 'the behavioural assumptions in the light of past relationships and the news in the current data'). On the regular chancellor/governor meetings side, he emphasised that for all their relative brevity, they had been preceded by a sustained, multi-element process – including in the Bank an internal 'Monthly Economic and Financial Report'; followed by a Monetary Review Committee chaired by the deputy governor and attended by some fifty officials; followed by a meeting of the Monetary Policy Committee (MPC, not to be confused with the post-independence MPC), recently established to determine the Bank's line each month, chaired by the governor and attended by about a dozen; followed by the Bank's assessment being sent to Burns at the Treasury; followed by a Bank team of seven or eight led by the deputy governor meeting their Treasury counterparts; followed by preparation of the draft speaking note for the governor; followed by a further meeting of the MPC to agree the text of the speaking note; and then at last the more or less monthly chancellor/governor summit, with the latter accompanied by his deputy and the two directors (King and Plenderleith) of the Monetary Stability Wing. 'This meeting is sometimes represented as a rather casual affair lasting no more than an hour at which we might almost toss a coin,' observed George. 'The reality is not quite like that.'[51]

In truth, the 'Ken and Eddie show' – Clarke's ironic coinage, in reference to their regular press conferences – was a source of some vexation to George, and not only because its very existence confirmed that the Bank had not yet achieved independence. Ostensibly the two men got on well, but ultimately the governor, as a deeply engaged technician, was frustrated by the politician's almost entire lack of comparable depth. 'I don't know why I bother,' he even remarked on one occasion as he was driven back to the Bank. In general the pair were seldom radically opposed in terms of what they wanted – 'Eddie and I never got more than twenty-five basis points [0.25 per cent] apart,' Clarke would recall – but their instincts and approach throughout remained essentially different.

The key episode, graphically revealing how far the Bank was from genuine autonomy, came in May 1995, against the background of

appalling election results (both local and European) for the Major
government. On the late afternoon of Thursday the 4th, polling day
itself and the eve of the monthly meeting, George was on the phone
with the permanent secretary:

Sir Terry told the Governor that the Chancellor, having slept on
it, was inclined not to increase interest rates the following day. He
was aware of the importance of the decision and felt that he could
not win either way, but in his heart of hearts he was not persuaded
of the case for an increase [from 6.75 per cent to 7.25 per cent] now
… This was not the Chancellor's final decision, but it was 'pretty
final' …

The Governor asked whether the Chancellor understood the
full extent of the risk he would be taking. There was a real chance
that even before he appeared at the press conference [to explain the
no-change], the exchange rate would have fallen very sharply. There
was no doubt that an increase in rates had already been factored in
to the current exchange rate. The Governor said of course he could
not know for certain what would happen, but he had a duty to say
that there was a significant possibility (which he put at least at a 1
in 3 chance). The Governor stressed that it was by no means a black
and white decision, but the point was that the Chancellor would be
overriding almost everyone's advice and the risks were asymmetric.
This could be deeply damaging to the policy-making framework.

George added that 'taking such risks with inflation is precisely what
had undermined UK economic policy-making so often in the past';
and he finished by asking Burns to tell Clarke that, in relation specifically to sterling, 'he [George] was extremely nervous about the
position'. Next day, 'Ken and Eddie' duly met – and the chancellor
decisively rejected the case for an interest rate rise, a stance widely
interpreted (especially after the publication of the minutes six weeks
later) as an assertion of his authority over policy. George in public
would utter some emollient words, for instance declaring in a speech
in Manchester that their 'disagreement about the inflationary outlook'
had been 'well within the reasonable range of uncertainty'; but the
reading by Anatole Kaletsky, that he had 'clearly expected Clarke to
blink', and had subsequently been disconcerted by the lack of reaction

from the markets to the chancellor's metaphorical shrug of the shoulders, was probably not far off the mark.

Perhaps inevitably, tensions also featured during the run-up to the May 1997 general election, as at four consecutive monthly monetary meetings Clarke, fortified by sterling's strength, rejected George's advice for a 0.25 per cent rise and bluntly insisted that he saw no sign of inflation. He even, in January 1997, publicly criticised the Bank, telling the *Financial Times* that it 'took too much notice of predictions in the financial futures markets that interest rates would have to rise' and claiming that 'it was usually wrong to assume that the markets had a feel for the real economy which the Treasury lacked'. By its last curtain call, it was a show that probably neither performer was much enjoying.[52]

The Bank's tercentenary virtually coincided with the creation of New Labour. Crucial to that project's architects were a desire for economic credibility; a fear of the destructive power of the markets, as evidenced by Black Wednesday; and a historical awareness (especially on Gordon Brown's part) that previous Labour governments had suffered from their troubled relationships with the City. With no possibility of Major changing his stance towards the Bank's position, and presumably struck by the opposition's handsome lead in the opinion polls, George and his colleagues spotted an opportunity. A starter of cream of chicken and sweetcorn soup, a main course of fillet of sole with scampi and lobster claws in white wine sauce, a dessert of lemon meringue pie – such was the fairly conservative menu, chosen by the governor, for a getting-to-know-you dinner at New Change in February 1995, to be attended by Tony Blair, John Prescott, Robin Cook, Alistair Darling and Andrew Smith as well as the shadow chancellor Brown. 'EG said to TB the City was not worried about a Labour government provided it was TB's government not Old Labour,' noted Alastair Campbell next day on the basis of Blair's account. 'JP then proceeded to play up to his Old Labour label, e.g. when house prices were being discussed, why do you people talk about housing in terms of house prices not homelessness. TB said Robin C was not far behind. He laughed and said "I'm sure I heard Eddie say get me the BA emergency desk as we left."'

Some appearances notwithstanding, things were about to move. 'Ed Balls [Brown's economic adviser] did a good presentation on Bank of England independence,' recorded Campbell the following month, with Balls in essence rehearsing the credibility-enhancing theme of his 1992 pamphlet; and in early May, during the VE Day 50th-anniversary celebrations, George had a quiet word with Blair that led to 'a private meeting' being set up for the 15th between George, Brown and Balls. Blair himself told Campbell on the 12th that he was 'sure', in relation to the Bank, that 'independence was the answer'; but three days later at the Bank, it was a rather cagier affair:

> Brown asked the Governor about his objectives for independence and whether there were any further evolutionary steps that could be taken in that direction. The Governor thought that it was difficult now to take a small step without taking the fundamental step of statutory autonomy. He explained that he did not campaign for independence as such but for stability. He said that monetary policy decisions were seldom clearcut – they involved a balancing of risks, but independence would affect where that balance was struck.

Then, after Brown had asked whether the Bank had 'sufficient sources of advice' and 'whether the Governor's regional advice was adequate':

> Brown said that he wanted to run with the debate about the status of the Bank of England rather than trying to anticipate it. He wanted the Labour Party to accept the changes that had already been made in party policy, and the need for continued change, but he did not want to move faster than he could carry the party. The Bank should look at proposals affecting the Bank of England in the round rather than at specific rhetoric. Some of the proposals might, for example, be couched in terms of 'reforming the Bank of England' but the substance was likely to be broadly acceptable to the Bank.

The timing was significant, because two days later Brown was due to give a big-picture speech, 'Labour's Macroeconomic Framework', to his party's Finance and Industry Group. In it he talked of a 'prudent' fiscal strategy, unveiled 'the golden rule of borrowing' he would be following in government ('over the economic cycle, government will only borrow to finance public investment and not to fund public consumption'), committed himself in monetary policy to inflation targeting and enhanced transparency, and declared that he was intending 'to consider whether the operational role of the Bank of England should be extended beyond its current advisory role'. That tantalising hint came, however, with two riders. First, 'we are not in the business of depoliticising interest rate decision-making only to personalise it in one independent Governor'; and second, 'the Bank must demonstrate a successful track record in its advice'.[53]

Regular contact between the Bank and New Labour continued, and in November 1996, with the election less than half a year away, George gave a positive update to the Governors' Committee (GOVCO, comprising King, Kent, Plenderleith and Foot as well as Davies and himself):

He believed that the Bank was well plugged into the thinking of the Labour Party. On monetary policy, he interpreted Labour as being clearly committed to having an inflation target, and being prepared to move further towards independence. They had floated the idea of a Monetary Policy Council, although as yet their thinking on this was imprecise. He thought that their ideas were running along the lines of some form of delegation to the Bank which would not require legislation, but on the basis that the Bank would create a Monetary Policy Council. He had made it clear to Gordon Brown that it was not acceptable to have such a Council comprise representatives of interest groups who would be imposed on the Bank. We must have professional people on the Council, and this would mean primarily academics, plus some people with a financial and/or industrial background who did not have a conflict of interest. The Governor said that he thought the Labour Party understood this point. There was clearly a long way to go, but the basic proposition being put forward by Labour was not unreasonable, and it could lead to an outcome anywhere in a range from something along the lines of the current arrangements to at the other extreme a statutory change towards independence.

By January the proposed advisory body was being called the Monetary Policy Committee (MPC), and King and his most senior colleagues were discussing possible external members. 'Reputation and the absence of any controversy surrounding the name' were King's criteria, while in response to Davies wanting at least one woman he countered that 'we should not compromise on quality, and we should put forward the best names irrespective of their sex'. For his part, Foot 'wondered whether we could think of any high-quality former politicians, including people who would leave political life at the election', but 'admitted that he could not think of any, and GOVCO agreed with him'.

In early February they returned to the subject of the putative MPC. Their working assumption was that Labour envisaged 'an initial phase of an advisory MPC', prior to 'operational autonomy' for the Bank; but they wanted 'as a minimum' during that transitional advisory phase that 'the Chancellor [that is, post-election Brown] should make a statement clarifying that the advisory phase, including a Monetary Policy Committee, was part of a process intended to lead to operational independence' – and that 'this should convey the message that the process involved altering the balance of power between the Bank and the Chancellor'. GOVCO also had a couple of further MPC wishes: not only 'no voting', on the grounds that 'voting would foster division not cohesion, and the outcome of voting would be more likely to leak', but also that its composition should be four Bank people and three externals. Next day, 6 February, George formally told Brown and Balls that the Bank welcomed the creation of an MPC, to which Brown responded by agreeing that 'the advisory stage should be a stepping stone to operational independence' and that 'it was important to avoid interest group representatives', while at the same time observing that 'both sides should be in agreement on the appropriateness of appointees'. By the end of the month he had publicly committed himself to an advisory MPC, and in early March the governor met with King to fine-tune his thoughts:

The Governor said that he was very excited about the prospects for upgrading the presentation of data at the first round Monetary Policy Committee meeting. In fact, he wanted to think about the idea of creating an MPC room which would be fitted out with the necessary technology.

The Governor added that, as part of the presentation of data and analysis, he wanted to make more of the markets analysis than we do at the moment. He had been very interested by WAA's [Bill Allen's] material on the shape of the yield curve ...[54]

Soon afterwards, the date of the election was set – 1 May – and no one expected other than a change of government.

During all this, the main focus on both sides was on the monetary policy aspect – but what about the supervisory? 'Darling confirmed that Labour was minded in due course to transfer supervision to a separate agency,' reported *Central Banking* after interviewing the party's spokesman on the City in early 1995 (probably before Barings), 'but emphasised that there would be no "wholesale tearing up" of the regulatory system.' Definitely post-Barings, Brown told George in May that year that 'the Labour Party was leaving open for the present the question of the regulatory structure for financial services'; George 'thought this was wise – there were many aspects to this question'; and the governor 'explained the advantages for the central bank of having some involvement in supervision to pursue its financial stability objectives'. That sounded reassuring enough, while a year and a half later George still seemed reasonably sanguine. 'We could see the case for Labour's suggested consolidation of securities regulation,' he observed in November 1996 to GOVCO, 'but he thought that that would be quite enough for them to be going on with. We would resist absorbing banking regulation into securities regulation ...' Three months later, in his February 1997 meeting with Brown, the issue was very much the tailpiece of the dialogue. 'Finally, Brown mentioned financial regulation,' noted the governor's private secretary, Andrew Bailey; and the shadow chancellor 'stressed that Labour did not favour major change'.[55] There, to all intents and purposes, the matter apparently rested until the election.

Later that February, on the 20th, Brown was in New York and met, not for the first time, the by now renowned head of the Fed, Alan Greenspan. Brown was accompanied by Balls and Geoffrey Robinson, and the latter would record how all three of them had been struck by Greenspan's remark that it was 'unfair' to expect politicians – as opposed to central bankers – to take unpopular interest rate decisions. The official policy position, however, did not change. Although Blair in January had remarked to Campbell that 'the way to really fuck the Tories was to announce during the campaign that we would make the Bank of England independent', Labour's election manifesto went no further than affirming a commitment to 'reform the Bank of England to ensure that decision-making on monetary policy is more effective, open, accountable and free from short-term political manipulation'. On 23 April, just over a week before polling day, Davies reported to colleagues what Deryck Maughan of Salomons had just told him: 'He [Maughan] had recently talked to Brown ... He [Maughan] had argued strongly that he [Brown] should move on Bank independence as quickly as possible. Brown said there was a problem with "public opinion".' In fact, perhaps influenced by that conversation, the plates were about to shift. The exact timings are not yet documented, but the probability is that it was on the 28th, the Monday of election week, that Brown in effect said to those around him, 'Let's go for independence'; and over the next couple of days, Balls was mainly responsible for drafting a letter to the governor setting out the new government's plans not only to make the Bank independent, but also to move banking supervision to a new statutory regulator.[56] The Bank, meanwhile, continued to assume that what lay ahead, in the short term anyway, was a purely advisory MPC.

New Labour duly won its May Day landslide, and by the afternoon of Friday the 2nd Brown and his men were occupying the Treasury. The new chancellor's preference was to go for the big-bang approach, announcing simultaneously the following week that the Bank would be gaining independence over monetary policy but losing banking supervision. In many ways regrettably, given what transpired, he was persuaded by his permanent secretary, Burns, to split the draft letter into two, with the supervisory aspect of the announcement to be delayed. Another Treasury official exercising influence over Brown was Gus O'Donnell, who apparently persuaded him to add to the monetary policy part of the original letter the stipulation that debt management would be moved from the Bank to the Treasury – a turf desire deeply entrenched in the latter's institutional wish-list, while also playing to Brown's and Balls's concern that the new Bank did not become an overmighty subject. Meanwhile, the governor was invited to come to the Treasury early on Monday the 5th, a helpfully timed bank holiday; and Brown on the Sunday afternoon checked with the new prime minister that he was content with the proposed arrangements and that there was no need to consult the Cabinet – in both cases, no problem.

On that historic Monday morning, Brown handed over two letters to a much surprised George (expecting to be discussing the composition of the advisory MPC), one that would be for public consumption the following day and the other very much not. The first letter – headed 'The New Monetary Policy Framework' and stating that 'the Government intends to give the Bank of England operational responsibility for setting interest rates', in order 'to achieve an inflation target which the Government will determine' – noted that the governor would be supported by two deputy governors; that 'operational decisions on interest rate policy will be made by a new Monetary Policy Committee' (five internals and four externals), meeting monthly; that the Court would be reformed in order to broaden its representativeness; and that 'the Bank's role as the Government's agent for debt management, the sale of gilts, oversight of the gilts market and cash management will be transferred to the Treasury'. The governor apparently took that last aspect wholly on the chin and was delighted by the larger sudden development: for him, control over monetary policy, as the best means of checking inflation and providing stability, had long been *the* prize.

The second letter – headed 'Banking Supervision', dated 6 May (like the first letter), and signed by Brown in red Biro – took rather a lot for granted:

> As you know, our Business Manifesto commits us to restructuring the regulation of financial services. It is the Government's intention to introduce the necessary legislation at an early date. I stated that it was the Government's intention to consider transferring part of the Bank of England's responsibility for banking supervision to another statutory body.
>
> I am pleased that you agreed that consultation will now start on this basis.

A brief exchange between governor and chancellor about the implications of the second letter then apparently ensued. What we know for certain is that George left the meeting not only jubilant that the supreme prize had been secured, but believing that the Bank would be fully consulted about the issue of its supervisory role – a belief arguably at some variance, surprising in such a realist, with the letter itself, but perhaps at less variance with Brown's oral assurance, unless of course that assurance was actually more ambiguous ('shifty', according to one unsympathetic observer) than George heard it to be. Given his presumably heightened emotional state, that may well have been what happened. In any event, later that day senior colleagues were summoned to the Bank to be told the great but still confidential news, while on the supervisory side George assured them that the Bank would have a proper opportunity to make its case before a final decision was reached.[57]

Remarkably, there were no leaks. 'The effect was electric,' recalled the *Observer*'s William Keegan about the impact of Brown's announcement of Bank independence at the press conference on the Tuesday morning. 'I want British economic success,' declared Brown himself before turning to the specific Bank aspect, 'to be built on the solid rock of prudent and consistent economic management, not the shifting sands of boom and bust'; after spelling out the changes, he characterised them as 'British solutions, designed to meet British domestic needs for long-term stability'. During the questions that followed, he was asked, 'Can we assume that the Bank's supervisory role will now be hived off to a new organisation?' To which Brown replied: 'There will be further discussion, as we said in our manifesto, about regulatory responsibilities generally and the conclusions of these discussions will be reported at the appropriate time.' That exchange received little attention, but the granting of monetary policy independence received a great deal – most of it positive. 'GB,' recorded Campbell next day, 'got a terrific press re Bank of England independence, deservedly, though there was too much "it was Ed Balls' idea" around.' The *Independent* set the tone ('Welcome to the modern world'), while from opposing flanks came obliging noises from the *Daily Telegraph* ('a cautious welcome') and the *Guardian*'s Will Hutton (looking ahead optimistically to 'a Bank of England that is more distant from the "gentlemanly capitalist" culture of the financial system than any we have so far experienced'). Critics included Keegan ('I believe, with only modest reservations, that Labour has taken leave of its senses') and *The Times*'s Anatole Kaletsky (claiming that Brown was 'locking the pound in a golden casket and throwing away the key'). Perhaps the weightiest of the early verdicts was the *Economist*'s. 'The move is welcome and long overdue,' reflected its editorial about what it called 'an astonishingly bold start for the chancellor'. But in practice, it warned, 'the Bank will be engaged in the highly political task of choosing how many jobs to sacrifice in order to hit the inflation target quickly rather than slowly'; and accordingly, 'the true case for independence is not that there is no democratic loss, but that the loss is more than matched by the economic gain'.[58]

In the Bank itself during the week and a half after Brown's bombshell, some very mixed feelings were almost certainly in the air. As early as that Tuesday afternoon, when George chaired a meeting of senior officials to discuss the way forward, one participant was struck by the depressed body language of quite a few of those present, especially among 'the generalists'. Nor is it psychologically impossible that the governor himself, with his beloved Bank on the cusp of fundamental change, was coming down from his high. When he heard the following week that the Monetary Analysis Division 'wished to host an academic conference associated with the work on openness and growth (which was going very well)', and that 'as a part of this they wished to hold a dinner in the Court Room', it was perhaps telling that his reaction was that 'this was inappropriate' and that indeed 'he was not sure that a dinner was necessary at all'. Unsurprisingly, given his own particular background in the Bank, his main focus was on debt management and related activities, where it seems that his initial acceptance of what Brown and the Treasury were proposing soon became quite heavily qualified. At a meeting with Burns on 9 May – which included the nugget that 'Burns had mentioned to the Chancellor the possibility of changing the Bank's name, but the Chancellor's initial response had been that Bank of England was a good brand name' – he observed that he 'could not think of another central bank that did not act as government banker'; while at GOVCO a week later he took a forceful line: 'It was important that we began by considering which functions and activities we thought were the key to preserving the Bank's status as an institution. A key element was a presence in the markets. And there were links between debt management and monetary policy which we should not ignore ...'

That evening, Davies had a 'lengthy discussion' with Burns, resulting in a note 'about debt management, and all that', that was for the governor's eyes only:

The position remains rather unclear and in many ways unsatisfactory, though some of the worst possibilities do not seem to be on the agenda ...

Terry has attempted to engage Gordon Brown in discussion on the details, but so far without success. He [Brown] has continued, however, to repeat his view that he wants strategy, tactics and *operations* to move from the Bank to the Treasury. That is what he said in his letter (as he interprets it) and that is what he thinks is going to happen. Terry has attempted to get him to focus on the implications of this and particularly the possible movement of CGO [Central Gilts Office] and Registrar's which it would imply, but so far without much success.

Burns hoped, went on the deputy, that ministers would agree 'to take out the "thinking" bits of the operation, but leaving at least CGO and Registration with the Bank, and possibly the management of primary auctions (roughly on the French model)'; as for cash management, the latest from Burns was that ministers 'wished to separate the management of government cash from monetary policy operations'; and finally, ministers were showing 'no desire to move the government's account away from the Bank of England'.[59]

What about supervision? 'The fact that the Government is consulting on the future of banking supervision will soon become known,' Davies wrote to George on 6 May, as part of his list of issues to resolve. 'We need to decide how strongly we need to argue for retention of a function in the Bank, whether there are halfway houses which would appeal to us and how far we should properly seek to mobilise opinion elsewhere in support of our cause.' Quite apart from the question of what Brown had or had not said on the 5th, unbeknown to the governor there would soon be a development at the other end of town. The lord chancellor, drawing up the Queen's Speech with its list of bills through to autumn 1999, had left space for only one Bank of England bill; and unless the Treasury moved swiftly – it now realised rather late in the day – it would be in danger of missing the legislative bus for changing the overall regulatory and supervisory structure.

Brown accordingly asked George to come to see him on Monday the 19th, with the latter again expecting to be discussing the MPC's composition. Instead, he learned that the Bank would be losing its role as banking supervisor, which would be given instead to a much expanded version of the Securities and Investments Board (SIB), to be headed – if he agreed – by Howard Davies. The governor said little in response, and was quiet in the car; but back in the Bank his mood was sulphurous, with only the occasional moment of black humour – 'not even Leigh-Pemberton lost this lot,' he said at one point. Several times he threatened to resign there and then, and it took a considerable effort by the Bank's senior non-executive director, David Scholey, to persuade him not to. George's anger was not because of the loss of supervision as such, but because he believed he had been misled by Brown into promising the staff that there would be full consultation ahead of a final decision. As for Davies, he was in Buenos Aires, addressing a banking conference; later that day, he received the offer by phone, responding to an initially mysterious message, 'please call Mr Braun'; and, after protracted discussion with George (the deputy running up a $2,000 phone bill), he accepted it. Next day, Tuesday the 20th, prior to Brown making his Commons statement about the proposed new structure, George wrote to the chancellor about how the Bank would be reacting to it:

> I have discussed this with the members of Court who have asked me to express to you their dismay that the Bank was not consulted on the substance of your decision to remove responsibility for banking supervision from the Bank. Both they, and I, had clearly understood, both from our conversation on 5 May and the terms of your side letter to me on 6 May, that the Bank would be consulted.

But, after referring to 'what will inevitably be seen as a precipitate decision', the governor went on: 'What is important now, however, is that we work together to make a success of the new arrangements.' Brown duly made his statement that afternoon, noting that he intended to involve the Bank fully in drawing up the detailed proposals, as well as generally relying upon the expertise of the Bank's staff. The following day, George's tone to the chancellor was warmer: 'I spoke to all the staff in the supervisory area yesterday [in a hastily convened meeting at the Guildhall soon after Brown's statement], and I am confident that we will all do everything that we can to make the new arrangements work.'[60]

Everyone of course was more or less in the dark as to precisely what those 'new arrangements' would be, not least what part the Bank would play. The central bank still needed, noted the Bank's press notice on the 20th after Brown's statement, to 'be able to monitor, through the new regulatory body, the financial condition of individual institutions, as well as that of the system as a whole'. In the statement itself, Brown asserted that 'the Bank will remain responsible for the overall stability of the financial system as a whole', while at the same time 'the enhanced Securities and Investments Board will be responsible for prudential supervision and, in due course, for conduct of business rules'. Relatively few tears were shed for the loser. 'The Bank of England deserves to be shorn of responsibility for the prudential supervision of banks,' declared the City editor of *The Times*. 'The roll call of UK bank failures, although spectacular, is short. But the public lost faith in the central bank's supervisory skills, because they were clearly the poor relation in the Old Lady's family of priorities.' And he added that 'top Bank people' had 'long gravitated to the more glamorous world of macroeconomic policy and international currency affairs'. Naturally, views differed within the Bank itself. George had reached a point where he was relatively agnostic; King was frankly relieved, having consistently argued that a continuing supervisory role would represent a serious impediment if and when the Bank received statutory responsibility for monetary policy; and among the 425 supervisory staff, the mood was reported by the *Sunday Times* as 'black'. As for the City at large, it was difficult to disagree with the view of an investment banker quoted by the same paper: 'It will certainly diminish the role of the Bank as a spokesman for the whole of the London financial community. Its leadership role will be undermined ...' From the fourth estate, a last word at this stage went to the *Economist*: 'Achieving the right balance of separation and co-operation between the Bank and the SIB will be difficult.'[61]

The next few months were spent establishing the new settlement, not helped by a distinctly mistrustful Bank/Treasury relationship. As early as 27 May, the governor was expressing to Brown his 'concern about the preparation of the Bank of England Bill' and identifying 'radical differences of approach' between Bank and Treasury officials about 'the extent of the Bank's role outside the monetary policy area'.

His letter tried to get the new chancellor to see the big picture from the Bank's perspective:

> In essence the Bank's credibility and authority as a central bank depends upon its ability to act, with a degree of independence – accountable to and through Court – across a range of functions which give it the necessary overall critical mass. It is possible in relation to any individual issue to take a minimalist view, but the cumulative effect of doing so would then be to diminish the standing and reputation of the Bank, in the eyes of our counterpart central banks overseas, of the world's financial markets, and of the British public, to the point where it would find it difficult to carry out its remaining functions effectively. I am sure this is not your intention because it would substantially undermine what is, and has the capacity to continue to be, an important national asset.

In the sphere of debt management and such, the Bank largely lost: soon after George's missive, Brown made it clear that the Treasury was not going to relinquish its desire to have a considerably more hands-on role. Even so, the Bank still managed to keep a reasonable presence in the markets. 'Our money market operations continued as before,' a senior official told Keegan not long after the new settlement was in place, 'and, although we have less of a role in gilts, we have quite a portfolio of gilts for our own customers, and we continue operating (for the Exchange Equalisation Account) in the foreign exchange market.' Over the Bank's day-to-day financial independence from the Treasury a keen, hard-fought tussle took place, eventually won by the Bank, while much time was spent on the issue of lender of last resort and the Bank's general operational freedom as overall guardian of financial stability.

By the end of July – as the parties concerned moved somewhat acrimoniously towards agreeing a Memorandum of Understanding (MoU) that would embody the new supervisory tripartism (Treasury plus SIB, soon to be called the Financial Services Authority, plus Bank) – the governor was taking his case in person to No. 10, having initiated the meeting 'to ensure that the Prime Minister was personally aware of the issues at stake and the seriousness with which he [George] viewed them'. The governor accordingly outlined to Blair how he had 'envisaged a system where the SIB, as supervisor of individual institutions, would probably first pick up signs of a problem that might raise systemic issues, would bring it to the Bank so that the systemic aspects could be discussed, with the Bank having the primary responsibility for deciding how to act and on what terms'; and he added that 'as he understood it the SIB had no problem with the Bank's proposed model'. However, he went on, 'the arrangements proposed by the Treasury ... would split responsibility in an artificial way between the Bank and SIB', so that 'he feared that they would blur accountability dangerously, and by diminishing the Bank's capacity to act as a central bank, could reduce its ability to respond effectively to a crisis'. Moreover, George further complained, the ceiling proposal ('some £70 million') by the Treasury on how much risk the Bank 'could accept' was 'so low as to be almost useless in a crisis', compounded by the fact that 'the mandatory tripartite consultation requirement above this low ceiling could introduce dangerous delay'. In short: 'It seemed perverse to choose now to put new limitations on the Bank's ability to provide rapid and discreet support in future.' Blair's emollient response was to assure the governor that he would 'make sure' that the chancellor 'was aware of the strength of the governor's concerns'; and indeed, when the MoU was eventually published it contained nothing specific about limiting the Bank's freedom of action to mount an operation 'in exceptional circumstances'.[62]

On the ground, meanwhile, the Bank's supervisors either moved to the FSA in Canary Wharf or remained in Threadneedle Street as part of the Financial Stability Wing, with none made redundant. And of course the MPC, ultimately the rationale for all the upheaval, took shape – remarkably quickly – and got down to work. A crucial prior question was the exact definition of the inflation target it would be set. George's concern, he told Brown in late May, was that 'the surrounding language ... accurately reflected the way in which we took account of the balance of risks'; and he noted that 'the previous Chancellor had muddied the waters with his reference to inflation normally being in a zone of 1–4%'. In the event, Brown in his Mansion House speech in June announced that he was setting the Bank an inflation target of 2.5 per cent, with the requirement that the governor write an open letter to the chancellor if inflation strayed by more than 1 per cent either side of that target. As for the MPC's preparations, orchestrated by King, there seems to have been relatively little blood spilled over the Treasury's appointment of externals, but the harder task was getting George to agree to the principle of voting, which he eventually did. His deputy was now leaving the Bank, to head the FSA; and in late July it was announced that the two new deputy governors would in due course be King (heading monetary stability) and David Clementi (heading financial stability), the latter having made his name at Kleinwort Benson masterminding much of the government's privatisation programme, though not personally known to an initially suspicious George.

Tuesday, 28 October saw simultaneously the Bank of England Bill – formally giving operational responsibility for interest rates to the new MPC – having its first reading in the Commons; the MoU being published; and the new super-regulator, the Financial Services Authority, being launched – and indeed christened – by the chancellor. 'These reforms,' declared Brown, 'provide the platform for long-term monetary and financial stability'; while in Threadneedle Street, a couple of miles upstream from Canary Wharf, the 303-year-old Bank stood poised to play its part in this brave new world.[63]

You Just Don't Know When

Taking as a whole the years 1997 to 2013 – the last six years of Eddie George's governorship and all ten years of Mervyn King's – one event dominates that historical landscape: the banking crisis that began in the summer of 2007 and peaked in the autumn of 2008. Its economic consequences were profound. Some six years later, King's successor noted that if that crisis had not happened, UK output by 2014 would probably have been 15 per cent higher than it actually was; or put more intimately, each person would have been on average £3,750 a year richer. This postscript is different in kind to the preceding chapters. They are largely based on the Bank's archives; this is not (with the exception of certain records released online in 2015 covering 2007–9). Instead, it is based on material already in the public domain and some two dozen conversations. 'The important thing,' observed King himself to *The Times* in 2012, 'is that all the papers and documents will be available to the historians in 20 or 30 years' time and they will be the people who will form the judgement. You have to have someone who wasn't involved, who is dispassionate.'[1] The present author trusts he is dispassionate; but, absent the key archives, any judgements can only be strictly provisional. The authoritative account of the Bank during this period remains to be written.

———

From 1997 the public centrepiece of the newly independent Bank was of course the Monetary Policy Committee. Initially, it proved a distinctly uncomfortable ride, especially during 1998 as the inflation-busting

MPC stubbornly kept interest rates high despite the palpable damage being inflicted on some sectors of the British economy by a strong pound. The consequence was the Bank being uncomfortably exposed to forceful, at times even vicious, attacks – from both sides of industry, from columnists and cartoonists, even from trade union demonstrators gathered by the Duke of Wellington's statue outside the Royal Exchange. By the new century, though, the tide had almost wholly turned. Polling by NOP in February 2001 revealed not only that 55 per cent of people were satisfied with the way the Bank was doing its job and just 10 per cent dissatisfied, but that four times as many people would prefer to see interest rates rather than prices go up – from the Bank's perspective, a gratifying indication that inflationary expectations had at last been anchored. Later that year, an MPC member, Sushil Wadhwani, publicly noted that whereas inflation had averaged around 7 per cent during the 1980s, and around 4.25 per cent over the 1990–7 period, the average between May 1997 and March 2001 had been 2.4 per cent; soon afterwards, the shadow chancellor, Michael Howard, announced that the Conservative Party no longer opposed Bank independence; during 2002 the UK, unlike the US and Germany, avoided recession, prompting the chancellor, Gordon Brown, to assure fellow-MPs that 'the Bank of England has the capacity to make the right decisions at the right time for the long-term interests of the British economy'; while in 2003, shortly before stepping down as governor, George reflected on how, since the start of inflation targeting in the wake of 1992's Black Wednesday, 'we've now had over 40 successive quarters of positive growth … you can't ask for anything more really'.[2]

King's first speech as governor was in October that year, at a dinner in Leicester co-hosted by the Bank and the East Midlands Development Agency. Looking back over the ten years since late 1992, following the adoption of an inflation target, he declared that the UK had 'experienced a non-inflationary, consistently expansionary – or "nice" – decade'. And he went on to describe it as 'a decade in which growth was a little above trend, unemployment fell steadily, and, supported by the improved terms of trade, real take-home pay rose without adding to employers' costs, thus allowing consumption to grow at above trend rates without putting upward pressure on inflation'. A benign picture indeed. 'Will the next ten years be as nice?' King then asked, to which he answered, 'That is unlikely,' for reasons that included the probability of less favourable terms of trade and already a reduced margin of spare capacity. Even so, he emphasised that 'the macroeconomic framework of this country is sound and proven'; while what most listeners and commentators took away from the speech was that seductive four-letter acronym.

Inevitably there was a temptation to believe that the magic formula had been found. Although fully conceding that 'we cannot prevent boom and bust in particular sectors', the Bank's Paul Tucker, an MPC member since 2002, told the Treasury Committee in October 2005 that 'we should be able to prevent boom and bust across the economy as a whole in the way that we experienced all too many times in the past'. The MPC's tenth anniversary fell in 2007. In February the deputy governor for monetary policy, Rachel Lomax (who had moved from Whitehall), reflected in a speech at Leicester on how 'the so-called Great Stability of the past decade has bestowed on the MPC the great gift of credibility – a golden halo which eluded monetary policy makers in the United Kingdom for most of the 20th century'; in May the governor, King, gave an address to the Society of Business Economists that similarly pointed to 'our new-found stability' (average growth over the ten years of 2.8 per cent, above the post-war average; 'not a single quarter of negative growth'; average deviation of inflation from target of 'just minus 0.08 percentage points'); and in September, in its formal assessment of the MPC's first ten years, the Treasury Committee pronounced that 'the monetary policy framework of the last decade has been broadly successful' and that 'while it is difficult to quantify the contribution made by the Monetary Policy Committee to maintaining a low inflation rate over the last decade as distinct from the effects of wider changes in the global economy, the Monetary Policy Committee deserves a significant amount of credit for ensuring that inflation over the last decade has been both lower, and less volatile, than in preceding decades'.[3]

That same September 2007 report noted 'the recent rise in asset prices', one of the 'factors' that had been drawn to the MPs' attention 'suggesting the possibility that the economic climate over the next ten years may not be as benign as that seen over the last decade'. And it went on:

One possible response by the Monetary Policy Committee would be to target such rising asset prices by 'leaning against the wind'

– raising interest rates to deflate the bubble in those prices. However, such a move would presuppose the successful identification of such a bubble. On the evidence we have received, this is not possible with certainty. Furthermore, the only instrument available to the MPC is moving the interest rate, and increasing interest rates to counter a rise in certain asset prices could hamper economic growth across the economy, not just in the markets with rising prices. For such a policy to be worthwhile, therefore, the risk to the economy of a rapid fall in asset prices would have to exceed the actual cost of raising interest rates to counter the rising asset prices.

By this time the banking crisis was actually under way, and over the ensuing years the question was naturally raised – inevitably with the wisdom of hindsight – whether indeed the MPC should pre-crisis have curbed credit growth through having higher interest rates. Among those reflecting were Kate Barker (an external member of the MPC from 2001), the Bank's Charles (Charlie) Bean (chief economist from 2000, before becoming deputy governor for monetary policy in 2008), and King himself. In a valedictory speech shortly before stepping down in 2010, Barker remained broadly unrepentant, but did accept that she had 'seriously underestimated the scale of the downside risks from a potential financial crisis'; while soon afterwards she identified 2005 – when house prices kept rising, but there was only a single quarter-point move upwards – as the year when with 'some signalling', in the form of raising interest rates, 'you would have sent out through doing that, that things weren't quite right', which 'might have been helpful'. In that same interview, she also pointed to how the MPC's unrelenting emphasis on medium-term inflation, central to its remit, 'encouraged too much focus on exactly hitting the target at exactly the two-year horizon and I think that distracted us perhaps from wider strategic issues'. Bean, while not saying he would have done anything differently, likewise accepted there was a lesson to be learned from the pre-crisis experience. 'Hitting the inflation target is not enough to guarantee economic stability,' he observed in 2012 on the MPC's fifteenth anniversary. 'Long periods of stability encourage house-holds, companies and investors to extrapolate such conditions into the future, to underprice risks, and to increase leverage, so increasing the vulnerabilities in the system.' As for King, who during the pre-crisis period had more than a dozen times voted in a minority for higher interest rates, he emphasised the inherent difficulty of the policy-making situation. 'We did talk in the Bank of England about whether we should have had much higher interest rates before the crisis,' he told BBC radio listeners some six months after leaving office in 2013. 'If we had done that, we undoubtedly would have had a downturn, probably a recession even, unemployment, and inflation well below the target.' Moreover, he added, 'we as one country could not have stopped the financial crisis occurring, so I think we should have been shooting ourselves in the foot, even if you could argue that if every country had done that it may be we would not have been in such a difficult position'. As he also put it, 'the real problem was a shared intellectual view right across the entire political spectrum, and shared across the financial markets, that things were going pretty well'.

Even so, and as King fully acknowledged in his stimulating, elegantly written 2016 treatise *The End of Alchemy* (not a history of the crisis, but inevitably touching often on it), there had been pre-crisis a significant debate. Arguably the crucial years were the early 2000s, when overly loose monetary policy contributed significantly to the ensuing asset price bubble of the mid-2000s. 'In the view of some members,' recorded the MPC minutes for February 2002, 'rising debt levels risked increasing the volatility of output and so of inflation,' whereas 'other members placed little or no weight on this'. The underlying problem was the two-speed UK economy: high domestic consumer demand, but weak global demand for British exports. 'In effect we have taken the view that unbalanced growth in our present situation is better than no growth,' George candidly stated that same year, while in early 2003, shortly before becoming governor, King looked ahead:

> The challenge is that by building up the imbalances in order to have some average growth rate close to trend and keep inflation close to the target, you know that at some point a correction will come, and when it comes, it could be very sharp. The difficulty for us is that we simply don't know how big that correction will be, when it will come, how sharp it will be and whether, in fact, it would be difficult to offset.

King was speaking to *Institutional Investor*; and he added that using monetary policy to control asset prices was 'never likely to be successful, because you'll never know by how much you need to raise interest rates in order to reduce asset prices'. And: 'What is the theory that tells you how a small movement in interest rates affects irrational behaviour? There isn't one.'[4]

Not everyone agreed. In particular, Andrew Crockett, former Bank man and now general manager of the Bank for International Settlements, warned in February 2003 that if the central bank, exclusively focused on 'inflation control', failed to 'tighten monetary policy sufficiently preemptively to lean against excessive credit expansion and asset price increases', then the overall consequence would be 'insufficient protection against the build-up of financial imbalances that lies at the root of much of the financial instability we observe' – a perspective on monetary policy almost immediately condemned by Bean, in a speech at Basel, as 'the heterodox view'. That same year, an unidentified 'senior and influential director' of the Bank spoke to the journalist Robert Peston, though what he said would not become public until 2012:

> My view on asset prices is pretty clear ... The reason we care about these evolutions is that they have implications for inflation and activity further down the road. If you build up a bubble in asset prices now, when it implodes that is normally associated with a sharp fall-off in activity, financial distress, all that sort of stuff. You can encompass all those sort of things into what I think inflation targeting is all about. Some people have a narrow conception of what inflation targeting is all about, which is focusing on the target two years out. Now that is not something I would sign up to. Typically these sort of concerns about asset price bubbles leading to financial imbalances that create problems further down the road may require you looking beyond the two-year horizon. Often you know these things are going to unwind but you just don't know when ...

Eventually, in November 2003, after two years of rapidly rising house prices fuelled by low interest rates, monetary policy was somewhat tightened – but by then the horse had bolted.[5]

Over the next three and a half years, the issue broke cover every now and then. In March 2004 Sir Andrew Large, David Clementi's successor as deputy governor for financial stability, publicly argued for a longer time-horizon than two years and noted that 'each month when we on the MPC make our policy decision I am conscious of the debt situation', in particular 'the possibility that the potential vulnerabilities stemming from higher debt levels do in fact crystallise at some point and trigger a sharp demand slowdown'; during 2005, it was mainly he and Tucker who voted in vain for higher interest rates, while in August they were joined by Lomax and the governor himself in unsuccessfully voting against a 0.25 per cent reduction; and at the end of that year, Large gave another speech, this time valedictory but again arguing (and again, as far as one can tell, largely ignored in the Bank itself) that 'there are circumstances which can justify monetary policy being tightened in advance of potential shocks, a form of insurance or risk management if you like'. So too in 2006. May's *Inflation Report* noted that 'broad money growth is currently well above its equilibrium rate', but more or less left in the air how much that mattered; in September, nine economists, including Charles Goodhart, Gordon Pepper and Tim Congdon (the initial drafter), wrote a letter to the *Financial Times*, highlighting the dangers of high money growth; around the same time, John Nugée (a former Bank man, but now of State Street Global Advisors) observed in *Central Banking* that central banks stood 'at the pinnacle of their reputation' following a decade or more of low inflation, but drew on history – not least the Wall Street Crash of 1929 – to argue that 'price stability is not sufficient to ensure general financial stability'; and in December, delivering the Roy Bridge Memorial Lecture at the Honourable Artillery Company, Tucker explained the rapid growth in UK broad money (up more than 25 per cent since the beginning of 2005), but did not really push through the implications in policy-making terms.[6]

What about the fateful year, 2007 itself? In January, after a surprise 0.25 per cent rise (to 5.25 per cent), the *Independent*'s Jeremy Warner wondered whether the move 'might signal a generalised "get tough" stance by central bankers keen to stifle excess liquidity and overexuberance', but was doubtful, noting also that 'in real terms, British rates are not particularly high by international standards, even after yesterday's rise'; in early May, in his 'ten years on' lecture about the MPC, King devoted a lengthy passage to 'the practical problem facing all central banks' of 'how to distinguish between shocks to the demand for money and shocks to its supply', but was unable to promise more than that the Bank was 'trying to develop models' to help it make that distinction and that 'we shall be devoting more resources to this task, including our new Credit Conditions Survey'; later that month, when asked at the *Inflation Report* press conference whether central bankers generally were concerned that 'they may have contributed to very frothy asset prices around the world through over-lax monetary policy', the governor did not deny the broad concern, emphasising that 'asset prices in the UK can be heavily influenced by what is happening overseas, independently of UK monetary policy'; in June he failed to persuade the MPC to vote for a 0.25 per cent rise, before soon afterwards making a Mansion House speech that only marginally addressed the monetary policy aspect of credit growth; in early July the MPC did raise interest rates by 0.25 per cent (to 5.75 per cent, at last making them relatively high in international terms); in early August it unanimously voted for no change; and on 8 August the quarterly *Inflation Report* press conference was held. Strikingly, in retrospect, only one journalist, Bloomberg's Jennifer Ryan, focused at all closely on the credit aspect; and in his reply, King insisted that 'monetary policy is set to meet the inflation target', that 'it's based on a macroeconomic judgement of the outlook for inflation', and that accordingly 'developments in credit conditions' would 'matter only in so far as they affect the macroeconomic outlook'. Was that now the case? 'I don't think there's any real evidence here,' he observed after noting continuing signs of bad loans in the US sub-prime mortgage market, 'of a fundamental challenge to the macroeconomic outlook.'[7] The following day, the credit crunch began.

Inevitably, as the crisis played out, attention also turned to the pre-crisis performance of the Bank's other wing, charged as it was with seeking to uphold financial stability, though of course no longer – since the 1997 tripartite settlement – undertaking banking supervision as such. As a largely negative consensus soon emerged and in due course became orthodoxy, the underlying assumption was that the Bank had been guilty of significant sins of omission. 'It is now obvious', declared the economic commentator Will Hutton in 2012 in words that relatively few observers would have disagreed with, 'that the Bank should have pressed for controls on the amount banks themselves were borrowing, on the proportion of loans that could be lent against property collateral (loan-to-value ratios), and even on the crazy system of pay and bonuses that encouraged such wild risk taking.' While that same year, giving his much publicised *Today* lecture (followed next morning by a lengthy interview on the radio programme itself), King for his part made a notable public confession: 'With the benefit of hindsight, we should have shouted from the roof-tops that a system had been built in which banks were too important to fail, that banks had grown too quickly and borrowed too much, and that so-called "light-touch" regulation hadn't prevented any of this.'

The external explanation for the Bank's pre-crisis failings has been predominantly threefold. Firstly, there has been the perception that not only were the 1997 tripartite arrangements intrinsically flawed, being embodied in a Memorandum of Understanding (MoU) that fudged crucial matters of objectives and responsibilities, but also that the Bank failed to communicate as much as it should have with the Financial Services Authority (FSA) – a failure that went to the highest level – and in general was unnecessarily nervous about stepping on the FSA's toes. Adding to the picture of no one ultimately in charge was the 2016 revelation of Ed Balls, with Labour's former City minister recalling the episode of 'a dangerous and fast-changing financial war-game scenario' during the winter of 2006–7, which showed a fundamental divergence of approach between on the one hand himself and the FSA's head, Sir Callum McCarthy, and on the other hand the governor. The minister and McCarthy, according to Balls, wanted to guarantee the deposits and provide emergency resources to the fictional large British clearing bank that had become over-exposed to a near-bankrupt building society and now risked running out of money overnight; whereas King 'was clear that bailing out the clearing bank risked what the economists call "moral hazard"'.[8] It should be noted, though, that not all participants remember that particular episode the same way; while at least one recalls the governor urging the Treasury to start work on a legal resolution regime to deal with a failing bank (as in the US: arrangements for winding up banks without interfering with their ability to carry on day-to-day business) – work which the Treasury had failed to do by August 2007.

As for the second strand of explanation, it was crisply summarised as early as 2008 by the financial journalist Alex Brummer in his reading of why the Bank 'fell short': 'Under Mervyn King the Bank became so wedded to its role of controlling inflation that ensuring financial stability assumed a secondary function, inadequately staffed and without real decision-making powers.' The following year, a review of tripartism by Sir James Sassoon similarly found that during the mid-2000s the Bank 'significantly downsized the resources devoted to monitoring and analysing changes in the structure of the financial system and assessing their implications for its stability, efficiency and effectiveness'; that it 'lost and did not replace critical financial market expertise among its senior executive team'; and that it 'narrowed the focus of its Financial Stability Reviews', which in turn 'meant that the Bank was actually, and mistakenly, lessening its engagement with the markets in the run-up to the financial crisis'. In November 2010, the FSA's Hector Sants stated to the Treasury Committee that 'the level of communication, and the level of interest, from the central bank in financial stability issues was recognised by all to have been very low, to say the least, in the pre-2007 period'; while in 2012 a close examination by the *Daily Telegraph*'s Philip Aldrick of the Bank's annual reports revealed that whereas in 2003–4 the budget for financial stability was £30.6 million, two years later it was £1.5 million smaller (compared to the monetary policy budget's £2.4 million increase) – and that even when in 2006–7 financial stability received a £6 million budget hike, it was only half that for monetary policy.

The final strand of explanation focused even more specifically on King: in essence, that his relations with the City – above all the leading bankers – became remote; and that almost irrespective of what the banks were or were not doing, his attitude towards them was somewhere on a spectrum between detached and unsympathetic. Tellingly, subsequent analysis by Goldman Sachs demonstrated that in the course of thirty-four speeches between 2000 and 2006, whether as deputy governor or governor, King spoke the words 'banks' or 'banking' a mere twenty-four times.[9] Whatever the rights or wrongs of the matter – and King as governor consciously sought to distance the Bank from its traditional role as spokesman-cum-special-pleader for the City – this was an approach that most of his twentieth-century predecessors would have found almost wholly baffling.

King himself led the case for the defence. As early as April 2008, appearing before the Treasury Committee in the context of his re-appointment by the Labour government for a second term, he explained that 'the big concern that I had before the events of last August, which led to the rewriting [in 2006] of the Memorandum of Understanding, was that the Bank was assumed to have responsibilities which it could not deliver because it had no powers or instruments to do so' (with the new MoU saying no more than that the Bank sought to 'contribute' to financial stability); justified the reduction of staff numbers on the financial stability side, from 180 to 120 during his first term, by noting that 'the only powers we had really were to make speeches, write reports and draw attention to the risks, so we re-organised the work in order to focus very much on how we would identify the main risks'; stated that 'what we did in the Bank was in a generalised way to ask questions about what has happened to the banking sector as a whole and what were the characteristics of some of those developments that we thought most risky'; added that 'we did write a number of reports and spelled out in our financial stability reports and our speeches that we did think excessive reliance on wholesale funding, for example, relying very much for funding on selling into markets for instruments that could become illiquid, was a risky strategy, and we made that clear on a number of occasions', but at the same time emphasised that having raised such questions 'it then requires the regulator [the FSA] to go into an institution and obtain much greater detail in order to find out how risky that institution actually is'; and finally, pointed to how 'on day one when I was Governor, I said to Paul Tucker, "I want you to create a new market intelligence function"', and added that Tucker had done this, creating a function that 'is highly respected in the markets and has a lot of information that it makes available and feeds into all our decisions on this'.

The governor would continue to put forward these and similar arguments to the Treasury Committee on future occasions, while to *The Times* in 2012 he wondered aloud whether anyway the Bank pre-crisis would have been able to use interventionist, risk-reducing powers even if it had possessed them: 'My guess is that that would have produced a chorus of complaints from banks, politicians and, dare I say, even the media about trying to restrain the extent to which our most successful industry wanted to expand.' After leaving the Bank, he still reflected on the pre-crisis period. 'Did anyone try to link what was happening in CDO [collateralised debt obligations] land to the macroeconomy? With hindsight, the answer is not enough,' King observed to Gillian Tett for her 2015 book *The Silo Effect*. 'But the question is what follows from that? It was not because people were not studying CDOs ... [But] there were too many people focused on detail and there was so much paper produced that it was impossible to see the woods for the trees.' And he went on: 'Most public sector institutions suffer from the problem of an excess of bright young people and too few experienced people with the ability and perspective to see what detail matters and what does not. Our biggest problem with analysis was the difficulty in persuading young people to see the big picture and their managers to draw out the big picture.'

The other main internal defence-cum-explanation came from a rising younger colleague, Andrew (Andy) Haldane, by 2010 executive director for financial stability. Speaking that year to *Central Banking*'s Robert Pringle, he claimed that the Bank's pre-crisis reports (first in the *Financial Stability Review*, then in the *Financial Stability Report*) 'did a reasonable job of identifying the key financial fault lines', and he continued:

> At the Bank we even tried to quantify the impact of those fault lines using, at the time, a relatively untested approach – aggregate, system-wide stress tests. The estimated losses were large enough to chew up a chunk of the banking system's capital. But, individually, those fault lines did not appear to be life-threatening for the global financial system.
>
> So what went wrong?
>
> Two things. First, the authorities perhaps discounted too easily the possibility of these fault lines being exposed if not simultaneously then at least sequentially. In the financial system, everything and everyone is connected. Those holding subprime securities also had exposures to various financial vehicles: structured investment vehicles, collateralised debt obligations, monolines and various other nasties. This interconnection across assets, institutions and countries is one reason Lehman's failure [in 2008] brought the entire globe down to earth with a bump at precisely the same time.

Given this interconnectivity, the probability of simultaneous financial earthquakes is many times greater than if you simply multiplied their individual probabilities together. Cumulative pre-crisis losses of many of these financial earthquakes would have been life-threatening for the world's banking system. For UK banks at the end of 2006, the Bank's *Financial Stability Report* stress test estimated total losses in the region of £100 billion. We had the analysis, and even the numbers, roughly right. But pre-crisis, they were viewed through too rose-tinted a lens.

Second, even if we had had the right lens, this would probably not have altered the course of the crisis. The Bank, and others, spoke with increasing forcefulness about potential stresses in the system from 2003 onwards. We were dogs barking at the passing traffic. As the cars drove past at increasing speed, these barks grew louder. The drivers of some of the cars took notice, but they did not slow down. Why? Because they knew the dog's bark was worse than its bite.

What was needed in this situation was someone to slow the traffic, all of the traffic, for the game being played was a collective mania. These manias are founded on a desire to keep one step ahead of the opposition. This results in a race to the bottom which, although individually rational, is collectively calamitous.

His insightful analysis might also have mentioned the sheer scale of derivative instruments in the system, seemingly impossible for the authorities to do anything about and making it very difficult to assess a bank's true financial state. In any case, what, he asked rhetorically, was 'the solution'? The answer to Haldane was clear: 'A watchdog with teeth.'[10]

Prior to summer 2007, the Bank's three loudest barking dogs were Andrew Large, his successor Sir John Gieve (coming, like Rachel Lomax before him, from Whitehall) and Paul Tucker. Speaking at the LSE in January 2004, Large warned about the financial system's increasingly dangerous 'opacity' – the consequence 'of the sheer complexity, speed of movement of risks, and in some cases obfuscation through Special Purpose Vehicles, or other off-balance sheet devices'. He went on: 'The existence of new concentrations of risk might not matter if their new holders are fully aware of the risk. But new holders of such risk may not have the same understandings of what the risks consist of, as those who generate them. And accordingly they may behave in unexpected ways when shocks arise.' Similar speeches and warnings followed over the next two years before Large left the Bank early, in January 2006. Shortly before doing so, he not only rang the *Daily Mail*'s Alex Brummer to (in Brummer's words) 'express concern that banks, given the volume of transactions in which they were now involved as well as the complexity of the transactions, did not hold enough liquidity in the event of a swing in mood in the credit markets or an unexpected calamity'; but he also wrote a piece for *Central Banking* about his growing anxiety that, behind the 'benign exterior' of the current 'financial and economic environment', there were 'vulnerabilities mounting' that might 'one day crystallise when a bigger shock arrives that the market simply cannot absorb', not least because of the increasing concentration of banking firms – and therefore risks – in the global financial system. Gieve's main warning came at a July 2006 roundtable at the Centre for the Study of Financial Innovation. Vulnerabilities that he identified, potentially amounting to systemic risk, included new products like structured credit derivatives ('we simply do not have experience of how they behave in the full range of market conditions'), rising competition between financial firms to establish positions in new and fast-growing markets ('the business risk not just of losing profits this year but of being left behind in the longer term by competitors looms large at the moment'), ill-conceived bonus structures ('rewards from generating "excess returns" far outstrip the penalties for poor performance'), and the way in which 'the more aggressively management pursues short-term shareholder value in the form of rates of return on equity, the greater the motivation to build leverage to meet its targets'.

As for Tucker, the part of his December 2006 lecture at the Honourable Artillery Company where he focused on broad money growth included the revelation that almost half that recent growth 'is accounted for by the money holdings of so-called Other Financial Corporations'; while four months later, addressing a Merrill Lynch conference, he sought to unpick what 'Other Financial Corporations' really meant:

The key intermediaries [in finance] are no longer just banks, securities dealers, insurance companies, mutual funds and pension funds.

They include hedge funds of course, but also Collateralised Debt Obligations, specialist Monoline Financial Guarantors, Credit Derivative Product Companies, Structured Investment Vehicles, Commercial Paper conduits, Leverage Buyout Funds – and on and on ... SIVs may hold monoline-wrapped AAA-tranches of CDOs, which may hold tranches of other CDOs ... and hold LBO debt of all types as well as asset-backed securities bundling together house-hold loans ...

All these other-worldly terms and acronyms would soon become all too familiar; but in April 2007 this was pretty much *terra incognita* to the great majority of journalists and economists, not to mention central bankers. And as Tett would reflect in 2015, the reports of Tucker's speech – which also dealt with such relatively straightfor-ward matters as the housing market, inflation trends and interest rates – almost entirely missed that crucial dimension.[11]

What about King himself? The governor's annual set-piece speech had long been at the lord mayor's dinner for the merchants and bank-ers of the City of London, traditionally held in the autumn but from 1993 in June; and at the last one (as it turned out) before the crisis, on 20 June 2007, he gave – unlike in previous Mansion House speeches – full-frontal treatment to the stability or otherwise of the financial system. After he had explained how securitisation had been 'a positive development' because it had 'reduced the market failure associated with traditional banking', in other words 'the mismatch between illi-quid assets and liquid liabilities', his central passage – giving rise at the time to some audible disapproval from parts of the audience – would become over the years much quoted:

But the historical model is only a partial description of banking today. New and ever more complex financial instruments create different risks. Exotic instruments are now issued for which the distribution of returns is considerably more complicated than that on the basic loans underlying them. A standard collater-alised debt obligation divides the risk and return of a portfolio of bonds, or credit default swaps, into tranches. But what is known as a CDO-squared instrument invests in tranches of CDOs. It has a distribution of returns which is highly sensitive to small changes in the correlations of underlying returns which we do not understand with any great precision. The risk of the entire return being wiped out can be much greater than on simpler instruments. Higher returns come at the expense of higher risk.

Whether in banking, reinsurance or portfolio management, risk assessment is a matter of judgement as much as quantitative analysis. Ever more complex instruments are designed almost every day. Some of the important risks that could affect all instruments – from terrorist attacks, invasion of computer systems, or even the consequences of a flu pandemic – are almost impossible to quantify, and past experience offers little guide.

Be cautious about how much you borrow is not a bad maxim for each and every one of us here tonight …

The development of complex financial instruments and the spate of loan arrangements without traditional covenants suggest another maxim: be cautious about how much you lend, especially when you know rather little about the activities of the borrower. It may say champagne – AAA – on the label of an increasing number of structured credit instruments. But by the time investors get to what's left in the bottle, it could taste rather flat. Assessing the effective degree of leverage in an ever-changing financial system is far from straightforward, and the liquidity of the markets in complex instruments, especially in conditions when many players would be trying to reduce the leverage of their portfolios at the same time, is unpredictable.

'Excessive leverage is the common theme of many financial crises of the past,' concluded King. 'Are we really so much cleverer than the financiers of the past?'

Yet, whether from the governor or his colleagues, the barking was sometimes muffled, sometimes absent. Take half a dozen moments from the year or so before the crisis broke. In July 2006 the Bank's *Financial Stability Report* (*FSR*) noted that 'the UK financial system as a whole has been remarkably resilient over recent years'; and it added that 'several structural developments have helped improve that over time, including high profits and capital, continued improvements in risk management and more sophisticated ways of distributing risk'. Two months later, in the course of an interview with the *Banker* in which he mentioned that the gathering of market intelligence absorbed up to a third of his time ('the MPC obviously takes priority over everything else'), Tucker made positive noises about the risk-reducing potential of new products and the arrival of new market participants – 'there is no doubt that hedge funds and leveraged players can offer a positive dynamic' – before emphasising that he was not losing sleep over fears that the credit markets were over-extended: 'Some people say that, at some point, those chickens must come home to roost in the form of defaults. That may well be true but there are now many more distressed funds out there to help absorb the situation ... The truth is, it is impossible to predict. Global capital markets have changed a lot in the past 10 years.' The following spring, the April 2007 *FSR* began with the most reassuring of statements – 'the UK financial system remains highly resilient' – and although it observed that since 2000 the balance sheets of large financial institutions had more than doubled, it failed to go on to urge that banks should significantly reduce those balance sheets and thereby their vulnerability to shocks, not least if the inter-bank market (for wholesale lending and borrowing) suddenly dried up. That same month, Tucker in his speech at the Merrill Lynch conference did indeed try to chart the murky world of what he called 'vehicular finance', in which risk was transferred beyond banks; but he confessed himself 'not so sure' as to whether 'the variety of vehicles and their use of risk transfer instruments' was necessarily 'a *bad thing*', leaving his listeners with the cautious prediction that 'in ten years' time ... we may be better informed on whether the changes in the structure of our financial markets help or hinder the preservation of stability'.

The penultimate moment came on 11 July, when Haldane introduced to the Court's committee of non-executive directors (NedCo) a paper on the Bank's 'restructured approach to its financial stability work' – 'aimed at providing a more analytical and rigorous approach to risk assessment' and involving a set of carefully targeted modelling techniques. 'In relation to the collaborative modelling work with commercial banks,' recorded the minutes, 'it was asked if the approach had revealed different insights about risks in the financial system. In response, it was highlighted that the work was at an early stage and there was considerable diversity in existing practices. It had not identified any looming gaps.' Finally, there was the *Inflation Report* press conference of 8 August. A few minutes after replying to Jennifer Ryan about credit-related concerns, King took a question from the BBC's Stephanie Flanders. 'Is the greater complexity and international nature of financial instruments and the ways that risk is now being passed across the system,' she asked, 'making it harder for you to assess financial conditions here, liquidity conditions and indeed any systemic risk that might arise?' 'Yes and no,' answered the governor:

Yes, because I think as I said in the Mansion House speech, a common theme in many financial crises in the past was excessive leverage. And it's not entirely easy to work out precisely how much leverage there is in the financial system when the instruments have become so complicated. And the fragility of institutions becomes much more difficult to judge.

But I think against that it is very important to set a very, very key point here, which is that our banking system is much more resilient than in the past. Precisely because many of these risks are no longer on their balance sheets but have been sold off to people willing and probably more able to bear it.

Now some have always had a preference for a banking system in which all the risks are concentrated there. But I think then you create extraordinarily risky institutions with highly illiquid assets in the form of loans to households and medium-sized business, matched by highly illiquid liabilities. And that's a very risky system ...

We don't have a system that is as fragile as that now. The growth of securitisation has reduced that fragility significantly. So that's a very big plus to set aside the difficulty that we face in trying to assess the degree of leverage both because of the complexity of instruments and the wider ownership of those instruments, but also because as you say it's become much more international.

And I think it's quite difficult to imagine a major financial crisis now that would be relevant to us in a systemic sense that wouldn't have a major international dimension. And that's why both in international meetings but also in collaboration with our colleagues elsewhere we have tried to work together to think about how such a problem would be managed in exactly the same way that the Tripartite Standing Committee [Treasury, FSA and Bank] here has regularly carried out exercises to make sure that we are well equipped to co-operate and work together to manage any problems that might arise domestically.

These press conferences were not a forum for debate or even follow-up questions, and no one pressed him further.[12]

Irresistibly, one comes back to assumptions and mental parameters. Much would be said and written about the pre-crisis period – not all of it mindful that in history real-life people act and take decisions in real time – but one retrospective assessment had perhaps a particular resonance. It came from John Gieve, speaking four years after he had left the Bank in 2009, following a little over three years in charge of financial stability: 'The big macro variables which we concentrated on, particularly inflation, were not sending signals of danger, and the truth is that we thought we had cracked it.' And he added: 'We were expecting a shower, not a hurricane.' Few if any believed with more certainty that they had cracked it than the Bank's new priesthood: the economists. 'With focus comes clarity,' an MPC external, Adam Posen, told *Central Banking* in the early summer of 2007 for a tenth-anniversary feature on independence. 'Both internally and externally, the concentration of the Bank on its core role has given it greater authority to carry out its monetary policy mandate.' Indeed, he went on to claim, the Bank's 'virtuous self-restraint' in areas outside of monetary policy had 'caused the rest of the government to raise its game'.[13] No one is immune from wishful thinking; but events would soon prove that this was wishful thinking, almost certainly shared by his fellow-economists, on a heroic scale.

———

The credit crunch began on 9 August 2007, as risk-aversion gripped the international money market and fears about counter-party exposure to subprime assets led banks to stop lending to one another.[14] Immediately at the European Central Bank (ECB), and very soon at the Fed, the reaction was to provide emergency liquidity; but the Bank declined to follow suit, refusing either to ease collateral requirements or to waive the traditional penalty rate of 1 percentage point above Bank rate (the term had come back into general use in 2006, very much on King's initiative), but instead relying on its recently introduced system of liquidity facilities, by which commercial banks were able to determine the size of their own reserves with the Bank – in effect, a mechanism by which the Bank could routinely provide more liquidity to the banks as and when they needed it. On 14 August the FSA informed the Treasury and the Bank that it had serious concerns about Northern Rock, the Newcastle-based mortgage lender that had expanded rapidly on the back of heavy borrowing in the now seized-up inter-bank market and was now not only inadequately capitalised, but faced by a fundamentally broken business model. King at the outset informed Northern Rock's chairman that the Bank would be prepared to act as lender of last resort, but emphasised that if Northern Rock was to have a long-term future it would have to find new sources of funding. By early September the possibility had emerged of Lloyds acquiring Northern Rock – though only if it (Lloyds) was guaranteed a hefty stand-by facility, something that neither the new chancellor, Alistair Darling, nor King thought was an acceptable use of public money, given that the motives of Lloyds were essentially commercial and that the offer would not be made available to other banks. On Sunday, 9 September a four-way telephone conversation – Darling and King plus McCarthy and Sants of the FSA – saw the Lloyds initiative removed from the table, while at the same time the governor confirmed that the Bank was prepared, if necessary, to give emergency support to Northern Rock in its capacity as lender of last resort.

Over the next couple of days, as Northern Rock's share price plummeted and funds flowed out, King finalised a lengthy memorandum for the Treasury Committee, ahead of his scheduled appearance on 20 September with other members of the MPC. Entitled 'Turmoil in Financial Markets: What Can Central Banks Do?', it argued that 'the source of the problems lies not in the state of the world economy, but in a mis-pricing of risk in the financial system'; it emphasised the importance of preserving the concept of moral hazard, noting tartly that 'the provision of large liquidity facilities penalises those financial institutions that sat out the dance, encourages herd behaviour and increases the intensity of future crises'; and it concluded that although 'the current turmoil' had 'disturbed the unusual serenity of recent years', nevertheless, 'managed properly, it should not threaten our long-run economic stability'.

First thing on Wednesday, 12 September, shortly before King's public statement was released at 10 am, the Court's NedCo had the opportunity to discuss it with him and his executive colleagues. Although 'several Directors congratulated the Governor for setting out a rigorous intellectual underpinning of his position', the tone of the meeting was not entirely easy. One questioner from the non-execs 'wondered if there was any thought about, or pressure to, accept lower-quality collateral'; another observed that 'when the current market turmoil had subsided it would be important to assess whether the tripartite institutions were sufficiently alert to the development of non-banks through some conduits, SIVs and hedge funds that were not regulated but which were essentially providing banking-type functions'; and a third asked 'if the risks associated with moral hazard vs the potential damage to the financial system were thought to be asymmetrical'. The minutes do not divulge the names of speakers, but the sentiments of the reply to that last question were undoubtedly the governor's: 'The Executive felt that was difficult to judge but suggested that in the careful assessment that needed to be done it was important that someone should ensure that there is a voice for the moral hazard concerns. There needed to be accountability by policy makers for decisions and the outcome not only in relation to the current crisis, but also for the longer-term consequences.'

Yet, for all that, King in his memo did leave the door slightly ajar, noting that central banks, in their traditional lender-of-last-resort role, could lend 'against good collateral at a penalty rate to an individual bank facing temporary liquidity problems, but that is otherwise regarded as solvent'. By Thursday, 13 September, with Northern Rock's situation deteriorating by the hour, a rescue plan was in place, agreed with the Treasury and the FSA, and to be announced before the markets opened on Friday the 14th. That evening, shortly after the BBC's Robert Peston had revealed to the world that Northern Rock had successfully applied to the Bank for emergency aid, the Court met in emergency session formally to authorise the Bank to proceed, on the basis of a penalty rate of 1.5 percentage points over Bank rate as well as collateral 'at an appropriate margin'. Members of the Court were 'told that both the Bank and the FSA were in total agreement that if Northern Rock was allowed to fail it would create serious economic damage'; they were also informed that in the tripartite press statement first thing the following morning, the wording would say, 'In its role as lender of last resort, the Bank of England stands ready to make available facilities in comparable circumstances, where institutions face short-term liquidity difficulties'; as to the 'potential for some commentators to suggest that the Governor was doing a U turn', there was 'a clear distinction to be drawn between the moral hazard of a general bail-out to banks, e.g. by relaxing interest rates to try to influence inter-bank lending rates, and the type of collateralised assistance considered here'. Altogether, this would be, the executive told the Court before the latter gave its go-ahead, 'the most significant lender of last resort facility since the lifeboat episode in the 70s – when times were very different'.

The memorable Friday the 14th saw powerful TV images of the run on the Rock, as alarmed depositors queued to get out their money. A difficult weekend ensued, with King pushing strongly the necessity of government giving a full guarantee to all Northern Rock deposits; and Darling duly announced that in the late afternoon of Monday the 17th, thereby ending the run. Two days later, in what the *Economist* immediately described as 'a breathtaking volte-face', the Bank announced not only that it would through an auction process be injecting £10 billion into the money market, but that it would be doing so 'against a wider range of collateral, including mortgage collateral, than in the Bank's weekly open market operations'.[15] As for Northern Rock, it eventually passed in February 2008 – after several months of major liquidity assistance, with the Bank managing the Liquid Support Facility on the Treasury's behalf – into reluctant public ownership.

In September 2007, the most wounding instant verdict came from the *Economist*. The front cover of its issue dated the 22nd featured a carefully chosen photograph of a rather anxious, slightly puzzled-looking King, alongside the words 'The Bank that failed: How Mervyn King and the government lost their grip'. Inside, the editorial verdict was damning. The paper did not necessarily agree with the governor's critics who claimed that if he had 'acted more promptly to restart seized-up lending markets', then 'Northern Rock might have muddled through', observing that 'no one will ever know whether that is true'; but it did argue that 'the lurches in the central bank's policy leave Mr King looking either as if he made a mistake, or as if he cannot stand up for his views', with 'neither characteristic' being 'much sought after in a central banker'. And it concluded: 'Nobody trusts politicians. Regulators are always disliked. But central bankers are held to a higher standard; which is why Mr King is the past week's main victim. He has lost credibility; and a central banker without credibility is not much use.' Four months later the Treasury Committee's report, 'The run on the Rock', did not go so far as to argue that Northern Rock would not have needed specific emergency support in September if the Bank the previous month had undertaken the kind of open-market liquidity operation being asked for by at least several banks. Nevertheless: 'We are unconvinced that the Bank of England's focus on moral hazard was appropriate for the circumstances in August. In our view, the lack of confidence in the money markets was a practical problem and the Bank of England should have adopted a more proactive response.' Later in 2008, Alex Brummer's account of *The Crunch* did not spare the governor – 'King's early approach was quickly exposed as wrong-headed. It increased jittery nerves rather than calming them ... Ultimately, King's refusal to pump money into the markets after 9 August made a bad situation worse ... Whatever excuses are made for King, the fact is that the hero of the fight against inflation had not proved adept at battling turmoil in the markets and the most dramatic run on a British bank seen in modern times ...' – while towards the end of his governorship, in 2012–13, retrospective verdicts on this episode remained generally critical. 'Sir Mervyn's [he had been knighted in 2011] response to the unfolding run on Northern Rock was tardy and unsure' (*Times*). 'His initial reaction was ill-judged ... Talking about abstract economic concepts in the teeth of the crisis made him look out of touch' (*Economist*). 'The effect was rather like a fireman worrying about the moral implications of dousing an arsonist's blaze: fine, until the entire street is engulfed in flames' (*Guardian*).[16]

Unsurprisingly, that was not King's perspective. On 20 September 2007 – only three days after Darling's guarantee to Northern Rock depositors – he made a robust appearance before the Treasury Committee. In the face of some hostile questioning, he argued that for the Bank to have undertaken in August a large-scale liquidity operation 'would undoubtedly have been a signal that the authorities were deeply concerned about the entire UK banking system' – a signal that would have been 'wholly unfounded', given that 'the UK banking system as a whole is well-capitalised' and 'there is no threat to the stability of the banking system'; in relation to Northern Rock specifically, he pointed out that the European Union's Market Abuse Directive of 2005 meant that 'we were unable to carry out a covert lender of last resort operation in the way that we would have done in the 1990s'; he denied that, during the past week, he had been leaned on by government ('I can assure you that the operation we announced was designed in the Bank'); he also denied that moral hazard was 'just some dry academic concept', insisting that 'it is moral hazard that has actually led us to where we are'; he linked his refusal to 'provide ex post insurance' to the banking system to how 'the whole regime of monetary policy that we have put in place has been to demonstrate that taking the easy option and giving in in the short run without looking to the long-run consequences of those actions is damaging'; and he described the previous day's announcement of a £10 billion liquidity facility as the result of 'a balance of judgement' – on the one hand, 'designed and structured in a way that minimised the moral hazard', on the other hand, providing 'some liquidity to the markets' in the context of 'strains' in those markets seeming 'somewhat greater'.

Over the next year, until the crisis moved decisively to its climax, the governor continued to make his case. 'Nothing would have been easier than for the Bank of England to lend freely without a penalty rate,' he told the Northern Ireland Chamber of Commerce in October 2007. 'Almost every actor in this drama saw advantage in cheap money and plenty of it. The role of the central bank is to ensure that the appropriate incentives are in place to discourage excessive risk-taking and the underpricing of risk, and in so doing to avoid sowing the seeds of an even greater crisis in the future.' As for the analogy that commentators were drawing between the Bank and a fire service, he did not quarrel with fire departments who 'put out fires started by people who smoke in bed'; but at the same time he observed that 'fire services do not offer free insurance for people who smoke in bed or set fire to their own house, thereby encouraging them to take risks that endanger others'. In November, interviewed by Peston for a BBC radio *File on Four* special, the governor reiterated that 'the role of the Bank of England is not to do what banks ask us to do, it's to do what's in the interest of the country as a whole'; appearing again in December before the Treasury Committee, he denied that there was ever a firm Lloyds bid for Northern Rock on the table and described the latter's pre-crisis business model as 'fatally flawed' on the borrowing side, for all its excellence on the lending side; in April 2008 his reappointment session with the Treasury Committee included two explicit admissions – that 'during August when the events in the financial markets started to unfold, I think I made a mistaken judgement that I did not want to add to the cacophony of voices which seemed to me not to be shedding light but raising concern', and that he also regretted 'the failure to press early enough for a guarantee to be announced when the lender of last resort operation for Northern Rock was implemented' – but was otherwise unapologetic, with as usual an emphasis on how the Bank 'had no responsibility for individual institutions'; while that July, appearing once more with feeling before the Treasury Committee, he stressed 'the absence of any Special Resolution Regime', which if it had been in place the previous year would have allowed Northern Rock 'to have been dealt with immediately'. Almost eight years later, in March 2016, King was still fighting his corner. 'A very odd myth persists about the ECB,' he told the *New Statesman*'s Ed Smith. 'They announced that they would lend over €100 billion, and the next day they would lend €95 billion. Everyone thought, "Gosh, they're lending vast amounts." After one month, the amount of lending to the banking sector was precisely zero. They lent a hundred billion for one day, 95 billion for one day. After one month they had extended no net liquidity. The Bank of England had.'[17]

Although much criticised by the press, King also had his defenders in the public prints. 'For the top management of Northern Rock to seek to pin responsibility for the disaster that befell the institution for which they were responsible on others, such as the Bank of England, is an example of financial illiteracy,' declared *Central Banking* at the outset, adding that 'there was no justification for them to expect the Bank either to lower its lending rate or weaken its collateral just to help the stricken lender'; in the same magazine's next issue, Charles Proctor (a partner in Bird & Bird, specialists in financial regulation) broadly backed King's claim that various existing legislative or quasi-legislative aspects – including corporate insolvency laws, deposit-protection provision and the Takeover Code as well as the Market Abuse Directive – had collectively placed significant obstacles in the way of a properly structured solution to Northern Rock. In later years, writing the first drafts of history, the *Telegraph* stable offered the most sympathetic assessments. 'In the end,' asserted Jeremy Warner in 2011, 'the debacle of bailing out Northern Rock had little to do with either a failure in judgement or the tripartite regime of split responsibility between the Bank, FSA and Treasury. Rather it was the absence of an effective resolution regime, compounded by inadequate deposit insurance.' So too Liam Halligan. 'I believe he was correct, when the credit crunch first hit, to make the banks sweat, questioning unconditional root-and-branch bail-outs,' he argued the following year as he appraised King's record. '"Moral hazard" isn't an academic parlour game. It's the reason why the Western banking system collapsed and why, unless drastic reforms happen, it will ultimately collapse again.'

The debate will no doubt continue to run, especially once full Bank records become available in the late 2020s. Yet, as many remarked – both at the time and subsequently, and often not unsympathetically – a sharp, unexpected crisis was probably not the ideal milieu for King. A deeply methodical man, and an intellectual thoroughbred, all his instincts were to think things through carefully and make sure he got them right, as opposed to taking any hasty, impromptu action. Hypothetical thoughts inevitably turned to his predecessor, Eddie George; and over the years it would become the conventional wisdom that if he had still been governor in 2007 he would have ignored tripartite constraints and forcibly banged heads together in order to get the Northern Rock situation sorted out quickly. It is a tempting scenario, but almost certainly exaggerates the freedom of manoeuvre available for finding a buyer for Northern Rock. Perhaps more tenable is the other aspect of the conventional wisdom: namely, that George as governor in 2007 would have had a more acute 'nose' for the banking system's true condition, in comparison to King's assertion that September to the Treasury Committee that it was 'very well capitalised' and 'very strong'.[18] Yet, as ever with counter-factual history, there is simply no way of knowing for certain.

––––––

'Things have improved significantly since August,' King told Peston in early November 2007. 'We're not back to normal in terms of a number of important financial markets, but things are improving. And I think that most people expect that we have several more months to get through before the banks have revealed all the losses that have occurred, have taken measures to finance their obligations that result from that. But we're going in the right direction.' For the bankers themselves, in some but not all cases struggling with lack of liquidity, this was not a mellow autumn, and often they directly blamed King – with one, half jokingly, claiming that it was the governor's revenge for their failure to read his speeches. King himself denied that the Bank was not doing enough, assuring the Treasury Committee a week before Christmas that through its money market operations it was now supplying £6 billion more to the banking system each month than at the start of August, an increase of 37 per cent. Even so, the perception remained that lack of liquidity was a key issue; and indeed, earlier in December, five major central banks, including the Bank, came together in concerted action to try to unblock the world's credit markets through an emergency injection of £50 billion (£10 billion from the Bank). Significantly, concerns by this point were not just about liquidity. 'The action was being taken,' the Bank's executive informed NedCo on the day of the joint announcement, 'to address the credible scenario that saw a serious downturn in the world economy inevitably leading to losses in the banking system. This, coming on top of the losses that may result from the current repricing of complex financial instruments, would pose a challenge to the capital base of the banks.' Preceding weeks had already seen significant bank losses and write-downs (including Citi, Merrill Lynch and UBS), and King in his pre-Christmas evidence to the Treasury Committee twice mentioned the importance of the banks rebuilding their balance sheets; over Christmas, mulling things over, he came increasingly to the conclusion that what the West's banking system faced was not just a liquidity problem, but in essence a solvency problem.

In early 2008 the liquidity aspect, though, did not go away; and eventually on 21 April – just over a month after a deputation of senior bankers had pleaded with King to inject further extra liquidity into the market (with one complaining to the press that the Bank had 'a much tighter definition of the collateral that it will accept' than other central banks), which in turn was just a few days after the collapse of the American investment bank Bear Stearns – the Bank announced its Special Liquidity Scheme (SLS). 'The Bank,' reported the *Financial Times*, 'will offer to acquire asset-backed securities from banks in

exchange for Treasury bills,' with the Bank expecting to swap £50
billion of assets in the first couple of months. 'Bank of England's
Clever Swap Shop' ran the headline to the paper's editorial, which
joined in the generally warm response (albeit some critics wishing
it had come significantly earlier) but reflected that the SLS was not
necessarily *the* answer:

> A moment of truth is arriving in the credit squeeze: a clear empirical
> test of whether it is a problem of bank liquidity or bank solvency
> is about to begin. The Bank of England's new Special Liquidity
> Scheme is a cleverly designed and welcome move to ease liquidity
> troubles. It should lower the three-month interbank lending rate.
> But if the real fear is solvency – that too many bad loans were made
> at too low an interest rate – it will not make mortgages cheaper or
> release wholesale funding for the banks.

Indeed, King himself at the press conference announcing the scheme
made much the same point: its purpose was 'to take the liquidity issue
off the table in a decisive way'; but it was 'not available for failing institutions' and would not, he insisted, address the solvency of banks.[19]
    What would? By mid-March, increasingly frustrated by the G7's
quasi-dysfunctional meetings, King was talking about the US, the UK,
Switzerland and perhaps Japan coming together to attempt a simultaneous recapitalisation of all major banks; while later that spring he sent
a handwritten letter to the prime minister, Gordon Brown, urging
recapitalisation of the British banks. At this point, undoubtedly, the
governor was well ahead of the curve, having arguably been somewhat behind it during the early months of the crisis. Yet of course
in practical political terms it required something truly alarming to
happen – with Bear Stearns being not quite enough – for externally
imposed recapitalisation to be a serious runner. And anyway, perhaps
all would be well without it. 'The most likely outcome,' predicted the
Bank's April 2008 *FSR* (published shortly after the SLS announcement), 'is that market conditions improve in the period ahead,' though
not denying that 'tail risks' to financial stability remained; and some
four years later, looking back in his *Today* lecture, King reflected that
'we tried, but should have tried harder, to persuade everyone of the
need to recapitalise the banks sooner and by more', adding that 'we

should have preached that the lessons of history were being forgotten – because banking crises have happened before'.

Over the summer of 2008, noises off were seldom reassuring. During the preceding month, noted the minutes of NedCo's meeting on 11 June, 'monoline insurers had been downgraded which had implications for some of the largest financial firms; Lehman's had been the subject of rumour and speculation over a few days, which fortunately had been so far contained; and in the UK, Bradford and Bingley served as a reminder that the situation remained fragile'. Altogether: 'Although there was still some sense that the worst had passed, it was liable to remain a bumpy ride and, depending on the scale of the bumps, the destination might be changed.'[20] Further ominous news followed: later in June, 5 per cent of the rights issue made by Royal Bank of Scotland (RBS) being left with the underwriters and Lehman Brothers reporting a serious second-quarter loss; in July, the announcement by the US Treasury of a rescue plan for Fannie Mae and Freddie Mac; and in early September a complete bailout for both those huge mortgage-providing institutions.

Domestically, the principal issue was whether, against gathering economic as well as financial storm clouds, the MPC was unduly prioritising the countering of inflation at the expense of the countering of recession. 'I would gradually expect the events of the last few months to have an impact in reducing the growth rate of consumer spending,' King told the Treasury Committee at the end of April. 'Remember, this is something that I have been expecting, and, indeed, perhaps hoping for, for some time, a rebalancing of the economy, and I think we would expect over the next two years that there would be some rebalancing of the economy. But that would also be accompanied by a slowing of growth, so the economy would grow below its long-run average for a couple of years. But that is not a disaster in itself, we were growing above the long-run average for a number of years before that ...' In mid-June, in his Mansion House speech, the governor specifically addressed those commentators and others wanting monetary policy to be significantly eased:

Target growth not inflation is the cry. I could not disagree more. This is precisely the situation in which the framework of inflation targeting is so necessary. Without it, what should be a short-lived, albeit sharp, rise in inflation, could become sustained. Without a clear guide to the objective of monetary policy, and a credible commitment to meeting it, any rise in inflation might become a self-fulfilling and generalised increase in prices and wages. And surely the lesson of the past 50 years is that, when inflation becomes embedded, the cost of getting it back down again is a prolonged period of sluggish output and high unemployment. Price stability – returning inflation to the target – is a precondition for sustained growth, not an alternative.

Among the external critics was the *Daily Telegraph*'s Damian Reece, who in early July was prompted by grim manufacturing figures to assert that 'it's clear to me we're headed for recession and as soon as that fact dawns on the MPC it should cut rates without delay'. The Bank, however, remained unmoved, with its *Inflation Report* in August not even mentioning the word 'recession' and arguing that although the risks 'from a more pronounced slowdown in demand' had become greater, nevertheless that was a lesser consideration than the 'possible impact of elevated inflation on pay pressures and infla-tion expectations'. The MPC's meeting on 5 September saw rates held at 5 per cent, and soon afterwards King uttered a striking pronounce-ment before the Treasury Committee: 'I do not really know what will happen to unemployment. At least, the Almighty has not vouchsafed to me the path of unemployment data over the next year. He may have done to Danny, but he has not done to me.'

'Danny' (a reference to the legendary Spurs footballer of the 1960s) was David Blanchflower, a UK-born but US-based economist who had become an MPC external in June 2006 and, after a lengthy period of largely voting in vain for rate cuts, had gone public with his prediction that Britain was heading for mass unemployment. In September 2009, four months after leaving the MPC, Blanchflower wrote candidly in the *New Statesman*:

In my view, and as I have consistently argued over the past two years, the economy would have been in much better shape today had the MPC not kept interest rates so high, especially from the beginning of 2008. House prices had peaked by the end of 2007 and business and consumer confidence surveys had collapsed. By the second quarter of 2008, based on both output and employment, the UK economy had moved into recession. But my colleagues on the MPC did not join me in voting for rate cuts until October 2008.

So why did the Committee get it so wrong? From my perspective, it was hobbled by 'group think' – or the 'tyranny of the consensus'. Mervyn King, with his hawkish views on rates, dominated the MPC. Short shrift was given to alternative, dovish views such as mine. I focused on the empirical data suggesting Britain was heading for recession; Mervyn and the rest of the Committee focused on their theoretical models and the (invisible) threat of inflation ...'[21]

To which, the defence would be that the inflationary threat was far from 'invisible' – approaching 5 per cent by the autumn – and that the all-important oil price was rising sharply. It was, as ever, a matter of judgement.

'Presently there was considerable nervousness around Lehman Brothers which would announce results today,' Tucker told NedCo on 10 September 2008. 'Whatever those results, it was thought that markets would remain tense. No matter what actions were taken by the authorities, market participants appeared to think that there was always one more significant institution to worry about.' There was indeed, and the headline events of that unforgettable early autumn amounted to the biggest financial crisis since the 1930s, perhaps even earlier. Five days later, on 15 September, Lehmans filed for bankruptcy and Bank of America rescued Merrill Lynch; next day, the Fed announced a rescue plan for the world's biggest insurer, AIG; on the 18th, it was announced that Lloyds was taking over the struggling Halifax Bank of Scotland (HBOS), while the Bank concluded a reciprocal swap agreement with the Fed, enabling the former to provide US dollar funding to RBS without either central bank taking an exchange rate risk; on the 28th, Fortis was rescued by the Benelux governments; next day, the mortgage lender Bradford and Bingley was nationalised; in early October, a $700 billion rescue bill for the American financial system passed into law; on the 7th, the Icelandic government rescued that country's second-largest bank; next day, the UK government announced its rescue package for the UK banking system – involving an injection of up to £50 billion capital into UK banks, a doubling of the SLS to £200 billion, and a new credit-guarantee scheme of up to

£250 billion – while at the same time the leading central banks undertook co-ordinated rate cuts; and five days later, on the 13th, the UK government's specific capital injections were announced, amounting to a total of £37 billion into the beleaguered RBS as well as Lloyds and HBOS. Two days afterwards, on 15 October, the Bank's executive team told NedCo that 'the corner had been turned in relation to the banking system', but that there now existed 'a significant macroeconomic risk as the major economies entered recession'.[22]

This is not the place for a blow-by-blow account of those charged weeks, but it is clear in retrospect that the Bank made two overwhelmingly important contributions: predictably enough, one relating to capital, the other to liquidity, with both being pushed hard by King towards the end of September. On the liquidity front, mattering hugely in the short term while recapitalising arrangements were negotiated and took effect, the crux was not just the doubling of the SLS (for which the Bank, two days after the Lehmans shock, had extended the drawdown period), but the Bank's wholly covert Emergency Liquidity Assistance (ELA), coming into operation at the start of October. In the event, RBS's use of the facility peaked on 17 October with some £36.6 billion being borrowed, while HBOS's peaked on 13 November with £34.5 billion; and though initially the Bank lent against bank collateral, soon it had no alternative – given the numbers – but to seek a government indemnity. As for capital, it was very much the governor who continued to take the lead, persuading government (Brown perhaps more receptive than Darling) and helping to face down the often unconvinced, resentful commercial bankers, who continued to insist it was essentially a liquidity problem. He spoke quite frankly at the end of September:

> We have been dealing with the gravest financial crisis since 1914. We have been on the precipice. When we started this crisis there was a widespread view that banks were well capitalised. But now we realise that the problem was that assets sitting on their balance sheets which were supposed to be risk-free, carried a lot of risk. Perceptions of the value of those assets and the risks changed radically. What has become clear is that you cannot deal with this problem just by providing more liquidity to the banks. That just addresses the symptoms …

Importantly, during the four days or so of intensive international meetings – national leaders, finance ministers, central bankers *et al* – following the UK's 8 October announcement, it was King's doctrine about the paramount necessity of recapitalising the banking system that was spectacularly taken to heart; and at NedCo's meeting on the 15th, sober satisfaction was expressed that, 'in the wake of the UK plan', there had been at those meetings 'a real sense of urgency'.

Six days later, the governor gave a well-publicised and very characteristic speech in Leeds. He began with some local flavour, recalling how as a boy, half a century earlier, he had been taken by his father to Headingley to see New Zealand bowled out for 67 by the English spinners; he took his listeners through the causes of the crisis; and he explained why the scale of support, from governments and central banks, had been 'unprecedented'. King's crucial passage focused on why 'a major recapitalisation of the banking system was necessary, was the centrepiece of the UK plan (alongside a temporary guarantee of some wholesale funding instruments and provision of central bank liquidity), and was in turn followed by other European countries and the United States':

Securitised mortgages – that is, collections of mortgages bundled together and sold as securities, including the now infamous US sub-prime mortgages – had been marketed during a period of rising house prices and low interest rates which had masked the riskiness of the underlying loans. By securitising mortgages on such a scale, banks transformed the liquidity of their lending book. They also financed it by short-term wholesale borrowing. But in the light of rising defaults and falling house prices – first in the United States and then elsewhere – investors reassessed the risks inherent in these securities. Perceived as riskier, their values fell and demand for securitisations dwindled. For the same reason, the value of banks' mortgage books declined. Banks saw the value of their assets fall while their liabilities remained unchanged. The effect was magnified by the very high levels of borrowing relative to capital (or leverage) with which many banks were operating, and the fact that banks had purchased significant quantities of securitised and more complex financial instruments from each other. Not only were these assets difficult to value, but the distribution of losses across the financial system was uncertain. Banks' share prices fell. Capital was squeezed.

Markets were sending a clear message to banks around the world: they did not have enough capital. At the Annual Meetings of the IMF and World Bank in Washington ten days ago, the message was reinforced by our colleagues from Japan, Sweden and Finland, who, with eloquence and not a little passion, reminded those present of their experience in dealing with a systemic banking failure in the 1990s. Recapitalise and do it now was the lesson. Recapitalisation requires a fiscal response, and that can be done only by governments.

Confidence in the banking system had eroded as the weakness of the capital position became more widely appreciated. But it took a crisis caused by the failure of Lehman Brothers to trigger the co-ordinated government plan to recapitalise the system. It would be a mistake, however, to think that had Lehman Brothers not failed, a crisis would have been averted. The underlying cause of inadequate capital would eventually have provoked a crisis of one kind or another somewhere else.

'With the bank recapitalisation plan in place,' the cricket-loving governor concluded, 'we now face a long, slow haul to restore lending to the real economy, and hence growth of our economy, to more normal conditions. The past few weeks have been somewhat too exciting. The actions that were taken were not designed to save the banks as such, but to protect the rest of the economy from the banks. I hope banks will come to appreciate, just as the New Zealanders at Headingley in 1958, the Yorkshire virtues of patience and sound defence when batting on a sticky wicket.'[23]

The Bank received considerable plaudits for its role in the October measures, with King himself as the semi-acknowledged hero of the recapitalisation moment; but he himself was subsequently to express some regret. Would the UK, he was asked in May 2013 in his final press conference on the economy, be in a better position if that recapitalisation by government had been on a larger scale? 'The answer to that is yes, and we did say so at the time,' he replied. 'Not publicly, but we did make it clear that a more radical recapitalisation was necessary.' If that was a minority argument, given the political difficulties of tapping the taxpayer even more than was done, so too was the persistent criticism mounted by the economist Tim Congdon. 'Is the Government's rescue programme beast or beauty for Britain's banks?' he asked in *The Times* as early as 15 October, two days after the specific capital injections were announced. 'The leap in share prices has been beautiful for short-term investors in the stock market. But a strong case can be made that the Government has been beastly to the banks, with dangerous long-term consequences for our financial sector.' He went on to argue that 'for all their faults Britain's banks are not insolvent or unprofitable'; that the terms of the deal, with the UK banks being able to access capital only 'if they handed over to the Government chunks of their equity', meant that they would now 'compete head-on with banks from other countries, where the governments are being more lenient'; that it 'would have been better if the Bank of England had reacted to the recent troubles in the same way that it did, so brilliantly and effectively, in past crises', which is to say 'the support should have been pre-emptive and low-key, and it should have come as a traditional lender-of-last-resort loan'; and finally, that the consequence of hasty, ill-judged nationalisation was that Britain's leadership in 'international financial services' was 'now in extreme peril'. Congdon continued to beat his particular drum for at least the next seven years, culminating in a 2015 article in *Standpoint* in which he accused the October 2008 recapitalisation of 'far from stimulating extra bank lending to the private sector', but being instead 'a vicious deflationary shock to the British economy, at just the wrong moment in the cycle'.[24]

Another retrospective strand of the autumn 2008 drama concerned LIBOR – the average interest rate calculated through submissions of interest rates by major banks. For quite some time there had been concern about the possibilities of manipulation. 'The LIBOR rates are a bit of a fiction,' the treasurer of a large UK bank told the *Financial Times* in September 2007; the following spring a Treasury Committee question to King referred to 'the criticisms of the accuracy and credibility of LIBOR that have been raised by the Association of British Bankers'; and that May, RBS's chief treasurer emailed Tucker as well as fellow-treasurers to suggest how the process could be reformed in order to prevent traders and managers from inputting artificially low or high figures in order to improve profits or give a misleading impression of their bank's financial strength. Tucker himself, as head of markets, was in almost daily communication with the City's CEOs; and on the announcement in late 2008 that he would be succeeding Gieve as next deputy governor for financial stability, the *Financial Times* noted that 'he has been at the forefront of Bank efforts to ease the strains in the banking system as financial conditions deteriorated this year, repeatedly modifying the Bank's money-market operations'.

He was still deputy governor when in summer 2012 a sudden storm broke above his head, prompted by the disclosure by Barclays – which had just been fined huge amounts for systematic misconduct relating to LIBOR – of an email sent on 29 October 2008 from its chief executive, Bob Diamond, to other senior officials at that bank. It read in part:

> Further to our last call, Mr Tucker reiterated that he had received calls from a number of senior figures within Whitehall to question why Barclays was always toward the top end of the LIBOR pricing. His response 'you have to pay what you have to pay'. I asked if he could relay the reality, that not all banks were providing quotes at the levels that represented real transactions, his response 'oh, that would be worse' ...
>
> Mr Tucker stated the level of calls he has received from Whitehall were 'senior' and that, while he was certain we did not need advice, it did not always need to be the case that we appeared as high as we have recently.

In July 2012, Tucker appeared twice in quick succession before a Treasury Committee investigation into what had become the LIBOR scandal. He stated that the email's final sentence gave 'the wrong impression' ('It should have said something along the lines of, "Are you ensuring that you, the senior management of Barclays, are following the day-to-day operations of your money market desk, your treasury? Are you ensuring that they don't march you over the cliff inadvertently by giving signals that you need to pay up for funds?"'); he acknowledged that he and his colleagues at the Bank were anxious that October about the strength of Barclays, which had controversially refused to take capital support from the government, but he denied categorically that any minister or civil servant had asked him to get Barclays to lower their LIBOR submissions or that he had personally issued any such instruction; and after observing that the key message he wished to convey to Diamond was to make 'sure that the senior management of Barclays was overseeing the day-to-day money-market operations and treasury operations and funding operations of Barclays so that Barclays' money desk did not inadvertently send distress signals', he explained: 'In actual paying up for money in terms of what you borrow, you do not need to be at the top of the market all of the time. It is very important not to come across as desperate.' It did not help Tucker's cause that coinciding with his second tranche of evidence was the revelation of a warm email sent to him by Diamond in December 2008, the day after his appointment to the deputy governorship – a warmth at least partly explained by the fact that Diamond had been one of his two referees for the position.

The Treasury Committee reported in August 2012. 'We will never know the details of the discussion between Mr Tucker and Mr Diamond,' it noted. 'What we do know is that Mr Tucker denied ever having issued an instruction to Barclays whilst Mr Diamond denied having received an instruction from Mr Tucker.' And after regretting that Tucker had 'failed to make a contemporaneous note of the conversation' – an omission 'explicable' given the 'unprecedented pressure on senior Bank of England staff at this time' – the report concluded: 'If Mr Tucker, Mr Diamond and Mr del Missier [Jerry del Missier, then president of Barclays Capital] are to be believed, an extraordinary, but conceivably plausible, series of misunderstandings and miscommunications occurred. The evidence that they separately gave describes a combination of circumstances which would excuse all the participants from the charge of deliberate wrongdoing.'[25]

Back in the autumn of 2008, it became indisputably clear during October that the UK economy was moving into extremely choppy waters. On 6 November the MPC unanimously voted for a 1.5 per cent cut to interest rates – the biggest cut since 1981, and taking them to 3 per cent. 'Some MPC members were somewhat uncomfortable about their earlier judgements,' the new chief economist, Spencer Dale, told NedCo the following week, though adding that 'it was certainly not the case that a small reduction in Bank Rate over the summer would have prevented the financial crisis and its impact on the wider economy'. The new rate of 3 per cent was the lowest since the mid-1950s, but early December saw a further cut to 2 per cent, following a sharp deterioration in the global economy. 'A nasty recession looks increasingly inevitable,' observed *The Times*'s David Wighton. 'Perhaps we will look back at yesterday's cut as the beginning of the end of the downturn. More likely, it is the end of the beginning.' He was correct. Output plunged during the first quarter of 2009, as the UK economy entered a deep recession; and in response, three successive cuts by the MPC took rates by 5 March to a record low of 0.5 per cent, amid general praise for the rapidity and decisiveness of its action. Yet during these unprecedented times – certainly in the working lifetime of anyone at the Bank – the need was palpable for unconventional (or at least apparently unconventional) as well as orthodox instruments of monetary policy.

'Bank could inject cash directly into economy' was the *Daily Telegraph*'s headline in December 2008, reporting that the Bank was considering 'engaging in so-called "quantitative easing"'; and the following month the government paved the way for QE by announcing the Asset Purchase Facility, not only authorising the Bank to buy up to £50 billion of private sector assets in an attempt to unblock the supply of corporate credit, but also giving the MPC the option to extend the scheme at a later date and pay for assets not with Treasury bills but with newly created money. 'In contrast to much of the post-war period when the need had been invariably to reduce the supply of money to bring inflation down,' the governor explained at NedCo's next meeting, 'the problem was now a need to increase the money supply and nominal spending. The APF provided a framework to do that.' That was on 12 February, and a fortnight later he told the Treasury Committee that he had formally asked the chancellor 'for powers to engage in asset purchases in order to increase the amount of money in the economy', while emphasising to the MPs that 'we are not going to allow a great inflationary surge'. Decision day was 5 March 2009, when the MPC unanimously pressed the anti-deflationary QE button as well as making the historic interest rate cut. 'Quantitative easing is new territory,' noted the *Economist* later that week. 'The Bank of England will buy gilt-edged government securities as well as private assets to the tune of £75 billion, and, crucially, will pay for this with its own money. That alarms many people, who fear that the border being crossed may be an inflationary rubicon. For though the Bank of England will pay for the purchases by crediting the accounts of commercial banks, it is creating money just as surely as if it were printing notes.'

'New-fangled' was a favourite term used by commentators to describe QE, but perhaps they exaggerated. 'Open-market operations to exchange money for government securities have long been a traditional tool of central banks,' King would point out in 2016, 'and were used regularly in the UK during the 1980s, when they were given the descriptions "overfunding" and "underfunding". What was new in the crisis was the sheer scale of the bond purchases ...' Would it work? Dale publicly admitted later in March to 'considerable uncertainty over the timing of the impact of the monetary expansion on nominal spending', while Vince Heaney offered in *Financial World* a sceptical analysis of the efficacy of creating new electronic money. The Japanese precedent, he argued, was far from conclusive evidence for this otherwise 'untested policy tool, which some fear at its logical extreme could unleash Zimbabwe-style hyperinflation'; moreover, 'nobody knows how much quantitative easing is required', given that 'increasing money supply in the hope of boosting nominal demand can only succeed if the rate at which money circulates (velocity) does not fall'; there was also the possibility that 'banks looking to shrink their balance sheets might hoard a lot of the new money, rendering much of the potential stimulus ineffective'; 'the impact on long-term borrowing rates is not clear-cut either'; and in short, concluded Heaney, 'QE is no panacea and it will not ensure a return to growth at anything like the pace the Bank is hoping for.' Among the cheerleaders, however, was Congdon, who as a veteran monetarist was pleased to see money back in the centre of the policy picture, albeit concluding that QE should have begun the previous autumn – instead of recapitalisation. 'Although the cash injected into the economy by the Bank of England's quantitative easing may in the first instance be held by pension funds, insurance companies and other financial institutions,' he wrote in optimistic mood two months or so after QE was under way, 'it soon passes to profitable companies with strong balance sheets and then to marginal businesses with weak balance sheets, and so on. The cash strains throughout the economy are eliminated, asset prices recover, and demand, output and employment all revive.'[26]

The financial-cum-banking crisis as such, which had started with the credit crunch and Northern Rock in August–September 2007, ended in spring 2009 when the dangerously exposed Dunfermline Building Society – Scotland's largest – underwent a forced sale of much of its business to Nationwide, with the Bank deploying its recently granted Special Resolution Regime powers. Over the next few years, the question became increasingly insistent – especially from the Treasury Committee's chairman, Andrew Tyrie – of whether the Bank would undertake a full-scale inquiry into how it had performed during the whole crisis, including the lead-up to it, while Tyrie also pressed for the Bank to reveal to him and his fellow-MPs the minutes of the Court between 2007 and 2009. In both cases the Bank declined to play ball, but it did in May 2012 announce that it was commissioning three reviews into specific aspects of the Bank and the crisis: by Ian Plenderleith (who had retired ten years earlier) into the Emergency Liquidity Assistance; by the banker Bill Winters into how the Bank's money market operations had functioned; and by David Stockton, a former chief economist at the Fed, into the Bank's record of forecasting inflation and growth. 'The Court of the Bank of England believes it is important for the Bank,' declared the Court's chairman, Sir David Lees, 'to learn practical lessons from past experience in order to improve the way it operates in the future.' That threefold move failed to mollify Tyrie: 'What is needed is a comprehensive review by the Bank of its performance through the course of the crisis from which we can all draw lessons. That review should have been done much earlier …' Lord Myners, former City minister and once on the Court himself, agreed: 'I would say there is a feeling of teeth being drawn and the governor selecting which teeth he's allowing to be removed.'[27] The trio of reviews duly appeared in October 2012; and for all their competence, they undoubtedly did not add up to a 360-degree conspectus of the Bank during the crisis years. As for Court minutes during that period, the Bank did eventually in January 2015 release them (online, in somewhat redacted form); but inevitably, in the absence of the record of the key meetings held between the key executives, and of day-to-day exchanges of views and information, their contribution is relatively marginal to our understanding of how it all unfolded in Threadneedle Street. For the moment, the rest is silence.

The financial crisis could not but have a raft of consequences, not least in relation to regulation and supervision. In early 2009 the shadow chancellor, George Osborne, commissioned the Sassoon report into the tripartite system that the current prime minister, Gordon Brown, had established in 1997. Sassoon's verdict, delivered in March 2009, was as damning as perhaps Osborne had hoped for: poorly defined powers and responsibilities in terms of taking pre-emptive action; the absence of appropriate instruments to mitigate risks; inadequate enforcement of existing prudential regulation; and a glaring lack of co-ordination. His main proposal was that the Bank should have 'the primary responsibility for evaluating systemic threats to financial stability'. Three months later, the City veteran Sir Martin Jacomb produced for the Centre for Policy Studies a report boldly entitled 'Re-empower the Bank of England' – calling tripartism 'a disaster' and arguing that 'the central flaw in the restructuring was the removal of the Bank of England's role in supervising individual banks' – while in July the Tories published a 'White Paper' that declared the party's intention to abolish the FSA and to give enhanced powers to the Bank, including the establishment there of a Financial Policy Committee (FPC) that would complement the existing MPC. The general election of May 2010 brought the Tories to power as the dominant coalition partner, and the following month the new chancellor used his Mansion House speech to confirm the abolition of the FSA and to explain that prudential regulation would return to the Bank (in the form of a subsidiary organisation), feeding intelligence back to the new FPC, which in turn would be given tools to halt a dangerous build-up of credit or asset bubbles. 'Only independent central banks,' declared Osborne, 'have the broad macro-economic understanding, the authority and the knowledge required to make the kind of macro-prudential judgements that are required now and in the future.'

For all Bank-watchers, it was a dramatic turn of events. 'Does the Bank of England Deserve More Power?' asked Richard Northedge in the *Spectator* as early as June 2009 – a question he answered only marginally in the affirmative, while soon afterwards the *Evening Standard*'s Anthony Hilton responded to the ersatz 'White Paper' by not only itemising the Bank's pre-1997 'disasters' (secondary banking crisis, Johnson Matthey, BCCI, Barings) but also asking the pointed question of his own, 'What Bank will jack up interest rates for the good of the economy if it thinks such an action will bust half the banks it is supposed to be supervising?' The commentariat also offered a degree of scepticism after Osborne's Mansion House speech, typified by Chris Blackhurst in the same paper. The Tory abolition of the FSA was, he surmised, 'politically motivated', with 'Brown's creation always going to be in their sights'; the Bank had done no better than the FSA in anticipating the banking meltdown, with the governor 'appearing just as startled as anyone else by the swiftness of events, both here and in the US'; and altogether, 'the nagging worry about the Osborne model is that it won't change very much'. A month after Osborne's speech, the Treasury produced a consultation paper. 'The Bank will be pretty much in charge of everything,' commented the *Independent*'s Sean O'Grady. 'Indeed, this is much more than a return to the pre-1997 position, when the Bank was solely in charge of banks' supervision. It now has insurance firms, hedge funds and who knows what else under its wing, bodies that were under an alphabet soup of "self-regulation" agencies in the old days.' A last word at this point went to Charles Goodhart, by now a professor at the LSE. 'There is a danger,' he told the press in September 2010, 'when you are putting so much power in one institution.'[28]

What part if any had the Bank played in the death sentence for the FSA and the return of supervision? The simple answer is that we will not know until the full records become available – and that assumptions of turf wars, power grabs and party-political manoeuvring may well be far from the whole truth. Indeed, the run of records we do have, primarily the NedCo minutes during the crisis, suggests a significant division of opinion at the Bank, at least at one stage. Those minutes for April 2008 reveal the non-executive directors 'agreed that there was a powerful case for the Bank to take a greater role in prudential supervision', but that 'that was not supported by the executive management'. The latter, with King almost certainly to the fore, spelled out their case:

The potential reputational damage to monetary policy from a central bank having responsibility for supervising financial institutions was one of the main motivations behind the current UK regime. Although related, there were important differences between monetary and financial stability. In a fundamental sense, it was possible to achieve the former but not the latter. No regulatory regime could ensure that there would not be another financial crisis or bank failure. It was possible to limit the impact and improve regulation, but financial crises were endemic. A second argument was that it would be difficult to identify a set of institutions that the central bank could plausibly regulate on a day by day basis, while maintaining the focus of the senior team on monetary policy. It will always be likely that, in retrospect, the criteria were judged to be wrong ...

Later that month, asked by the Treasury Committee about what he understood to be the government's thinking, the governor answered carefully but firmly: 'I think that there is agreement that, if the Bank is given powers, then it will require the resources and be held accountable for the exercise of those powers. What I think we cannot do is to accept a responsibility for something that we are in no position to deliver ...'

Of course, that year's autumn traumas still lay ahead, and it is possible that by the early months of 2009 there was a greater appetite at the Bank for an enhanced role, especially in the context of that year's Banking Act giving statutory form to its existing financial stability functions. NedCo in February continued to discuss its concern about 'the Bank's ability to meet its responsibilities for financial stability with limited powers and without direct access to information', noting that 'the inability to drill down to the level of an individual institution's accounts and balance sheet in order to build up a picture of the system as a whole remained a large deficiency'; Tucker the following month gave a speech addressing in some detail various key issues in micro-prudential regulation, including the need to have supervisors with the bottle to face down bank management where necessary; and at NedCo in April, 'it was stressed that the Bank was in a hazardous position at present', given that 'it had to progress the debate without putting itself in the position of either being or being perceived to be a shadow supervisor'.

Then in June 2009 came King's controversial Mansion House speech, rightly or wrongly interpreted by the press as a bid for greater supervisory powers. One passage received particular attention:

> To achieve financial stability the powers of the Bank are limited to those of voice and the new resolution powers. The Bank finds itself in a position rather like that of a church whose congregation attends weddings and burials but ignores the sermons in between. Like the church, we cannot promise that bad things won't happen to our flock – the prevention of all financial crises is in neither our nor anyone else's power, as a study of history or human nature would reveal. And experience suggests that attempts to encourage a better life through the power of voice is not enough. Warnings are unlikely to be effective when people are being asked to change behaviour which seems to them highly profitable. So it is not entirely clear how the Bank will be able to discharge its new statutory responsibility if we can do no more than issue sermons or organise burials.

Soon afterwards, the governor emphasised to the Treasury Committee that 'what matters is that powers and responsibilities must be aligned' and that 'I am not forming any judgement about what powers the Bank of England should have at all.' The Tory 'White Paper' démarche followed in July, and finally of course, eleven months later, the new chancellor's Mansion House speech.

King in his response welcomed the announcements; promised that the Bank would 'bring its own central banking culture' to the new dispensation, seeking 'to avoid an overly legalistic culture with its associated compliance-driven style of regulation'; and observed that 'just as the role of a central bank in monetary policy is to take the punch bowl away just as the party gets going, its role in financial stability should be to turn down the music when the dancing gets a little too wild'. Did he have any qualms? Next month, the Treasury Committee's Chuka Umunna asked him 'to set the record straight as to whether you did actually want to take on oversight of financial regulation' – to which the governor replied that 'I changed my mind after the crisis when I saw that, first of all, despite the fact that we have absolutely no responsibility for banking supervision, it seemed to make absolutely no difference to the degree of reputational contamination and that, more importantly, when big banks did get into trouble, as a lender of last resort, the central bank was inextricably drawn into the minutiae of dealing with the regulation of liquidity and capital of those banks'. He responded to another questioner: 'We have quite deliberately not put consumer protection or market conduct in and the responsibilities are limited to prudential because that is what a central bank can do, so I think it is clarity of responsibility ... it is asking the central bank to do what the central bank can do and not go beyond that.'[29]

Although an interim Financial Policy Committee (a mixture, like the MPC, of internal and external members) started to meet in June 2011, it was not until April 2013 that the new set-up came fully into effect, with the Prudential Regulation Authority (headed by Andrew Bailey, private secretary to Eddie George back in those very different May 1997 days) open for business at 20 Moorgate, once belonging to Cazenove. Intimately involved at the Bank was Tucker as deputy governor for financial stability, and towards the end of May 2013 he spoke to the Institute for Government about the new system. The text released by the Bank made use of bullet points, around which he framed his remarks, first about the PRA:

- Bank of England is once again the prudential supervisor of banks. And this time of building societies and insurance companies too.
- Prominence given in public debate to the Bank absolutely not adopting a 'tick box' approach, but instead a 'judgement-based' approach. This has been widely applauded.
- In fact, market practitioners tend to be schizophrenic about it. For a couple of decades at least, they have called for 'certainty' whenever any specific, isolated policy area is being reformed; i.e. clear and complete rules. But taking the resulting monstrous rule books as a whole, senior practitioners rightly condemn the 'tick box' regulation that almost inevitably results.
- And leaders of firms have hardly stopped their staff from making a living finding ways around rules: endemic regulatory arbitrage was at the heart of so-called 'shadow banking' in the run up to the crisis.
- Step back to consider the public policy purpose. Contrast prudential supervision with securities regulation as traditionally

conceived. Latter works on basis of: write rules; check compliance with those rules; punish breaches. If the rules proved to be flawed, they should still be enforced, for credibility's sake; but later changes should be made to the rules.

- Animating spirit of 'prudential supervision' is completely different. Impossible to write down a complete (or even adequate) set of binding rules on the financial health of a bank (or on the substance of the professional competence of bankers). Instead, things like capital ratios or liquidity ratios are really *indicators* of financial health.

- This is reminiscent of an old debate in monetary policy. Thirty-odd years ago, policy was meant more or less mechanically to follow targets for broad or narrow monetary aggregates. It didn't work: the economic world was not sufficiently stable. Since we adopted inflation targeting, central banks have had an eclectic approach to indicators. We are constrained by a clear medium-term objective (2% CPI target), but do *not* use a set of supposedly fool-proof core intermediate indicators.

- No more can we write down hard and fast rules on bank balance sheets.

- Nor, consistent with Parliament's wishes, is the Prudential Regulation Authority seeking to achieve a zero-failure regime. The failure of individual firms has to be an acceptable outcome so long as they can be wound down in an orderly way.

- So the PRA's approach to prudential supervision entails making judgements of the kind:
  – your bank isn't as strong as you think it is
  – cut back on the risk in your book
  – I'm afraid you're not fit to run the bank
  – your business could not be resolved in an orderly way if it fails.

- This shift from rules to judgement changes the relationship between the regulator and business.

- Challenge is how to make a judgement-based approach acceptable when we use it in earnest. Is our society really ready again for judgements from the Old Lady?

Later in his talk, he turned to macro-prudential policy, in the form of the FPC (no longer interim):

- … Can view the role of the FPC as being to ensure that the need for stability in the financial system is not overlooked. Looking ahead, this will mean keeping the regulatory regime up-to-date as the financial system evolves and, when the time comes, 'taking away the punchbowl' before the next party gets as dangerously out of control as the last one did.
- The case for operational independence here is just as strong as for monetary policy. Taking Away The Punchbowl is something that requires a medium-term orientation. Parliament can tie us to the mast and rely on us not to seek to wriggle free.
- But, as with monetary policy, this makes it vital that Parliament frames the objective and that we are sufficiently transparent to enable ex ante public accountability.
- Objective: The legislation governing the FPC is clear that resilience of the system as a whole is the primary goal but that we must not aim for the stability of the graveyard. Resilience is not quantified, however.
- Transparency: While respecting the confidentiality of data on individual firms, FPC is required by Parliament to be as transparent as possible – via the Published Record of our policy meetings and the twice-yearly *Financial Stability Report*.
- This is the background to the FPC calling on the Bank to develop a regime for stress testing to be used for both micro and macro prudential supervision.
- One possibility is for FPC to use stress tests to define the degree of resilience the system needs. Maybe that could become to financial stability what forecasting is to monetary policy. In the USA and elsewhere the results of such stress tests have been published.
- That represents quite a change in regime for regulated firms. But neither the markets nor the public was comfortable with the degree of secrecy on these matters in the past.

It all added up to a major moment. 'Supervision and central banking grew apart in this country and they're now being reconnected,' Tucker told the *Guardian* earlier that spring. 'Given where this country finds itself, that is a very good thing. It was always the historic mission of the Bank of England to look after stability.' And in June, less than a fortnight before the end of King's governorship, the impact was considerable when the PRA published its stress-test findings, revealing that five out of the eight major UK banks and building societies fell short of the PRA's required standard for capital resources.[30]

The first four post-crisis years – summer 2009 to summer 2013 – also saw a sustained focus on the Bank's role in seeking to support and nourish the British economy as it only slowly and patchily recovered. Three areas were arguably key, with each provoking significant external criticism: lending; QE; and monetary policy more generally.

'It is heartbreaking sometimes,' was how King in July 2010 described to the Treasury Committee his experience of hearing from small to medium-sized companies across the country how hard they were finding it to obtain bank loans, even if they had built long-term relationships with those banks. 'It is a lot harder to run a business out there', he added, 'than it is to stay in London and just trade away and make what appears to be millions one day and minus millions the next.' King did not blame the banks alone. By October 2011 he was criticising the Treasury for failing to insist that the big lenders it owned – RBS and Lloyds Banking Group – increased their lending to SMEs (Small and Medium Enterprises); while in March 2013 he reiterated an earlier call (expressed soon after the bank's collapse) that RBS should be broken up, in effect into a 'good' bank doing normal business and a 'bad' bank housing the troublesome loans (inevitably involving for government a big, up-front loss), so that the 'good' bank could become 'a major lender to the UK economy' and rapidly return to private ownership. Largely off its own bat (though in collaboration with the Treasury), the Bank's key initiative came in June 2012 with the announcement of a scheme known as 'funding for lending' that would come into operation in August and in essence provide banks with cheap funding in exchange for a commitment from lenders to provide cheap loans to ordinary businesses and households. 'The question is whether the cost of funding is the binding constraint on lending by banks,' observed the *Financial Times*'s Martin Wolf. 'Far more important, I suspect, are the risk aversion of banks and the state of potential borrowers: those who are credit worthy do not wish to borrow; those who want to borrow are not credit worthy, at least in the current enfeebled state of the economy.' In the event, the majority of the £80 billion scheme went during its first year to homebuyers, not small businesses – which was not quite the original intention. The Bank was also becoming vulnerable to criticism on the score that its insistence (whether through the FPC or the PRA) on banks holding sufficient capital perhaps acted as a significant deterrent to their lending. 'The idea that banks should be forced to raise new capital during a period of recession is an erroneous one,' declared Vince Cable in March 2013; but King was adamant that 'a weak banking system does not expand lending' and that 'the better-capitalised banks are the ones expanding lending'. Some months later the business secretary would be using and endorsing the phrase 'capital Taliban' to describe Bank officials, though by then a new governor was in post.[31]

Elsewhere on the policy front, 'new-fangled' quantitative easing became during these years a semi-fixture. Having started in March 2009 with the Bank committing to the purchase of £75 billion in assets (mainly gilts) through the creation of electronic money, the programme continued later in 2009 with a further £50 billion in May, £50 billion in August and £25 billion in November – taking the QE total to a fairly staggering £200 billion, equivalent to 14 per cent of nominal GDP. Expert opinion was broadly, if far from unanimously, positive about this attempt to achieve higher asset prices, thereby reducing the cost of funding and increasing the wealth of asset holders, in turn boosting spending and increasing nominal demand. A typically measured assessment came in March 2010 from the City economist Roger Bootle, who concluded that the Bank had been right to launch QE ('the only game in town') and that it had helped significantly to strengthen asset prices and to counter the deflationary threat. In due course, the Bank itself offered some hard figures, claiming that its first full round of QE had boosted Britain's GDP by up to 2 percentage points and inflation by up to 1.5 points.

'Open the taps' was the *Economist*'s cry at the start of October 2011, against the background of what it called 'a sickly economy'. Within a week the MPC obliged, starting a new round of QE (soon known as QE2) with £75 billion of asset purchases, followed in February and July 2012 by two further tranches of £50 billion – taking the grand total, since March 2009, to £375 billion. A fresh round sparked fresh appraisals, prompting one economist, Richard Barwell, to devote an article in *The Times* in February 2012 to debunking five 'QE myths': namely, that 'printing money inevitably leads to rampant inflation'; that QE was 'a cunning plan concocted by the Bank and the Treasury to inflate away the Government's debt on the sly'; that QE was 'ineffective because asset purchases have no impact on the real economy'; that QE was 'ineffective because the money that the MPC created is being hoarded in bank vaults'; and finally, that 'asset purchases suffer from diminishing returns – that is, the more the Bank buys, the less impact each billion of purchases has'. Predictably enough, dissenting voices remained. Soon afterwards, Robert Skidelsky and Felix Martin argued that, although it had done good initial work to 'stop the slide into another Great Depression', QE's fatal double flaw 'as a recovery policy' was that 'its effect on aggregate demand is weak and uncertain', with new money failing to be translated into increased spending, and that 'QE does nothing to improve longer-term growth prospects', given that it 'simply freezes the existing [imbalanced] structure of the economy at a higher level of output'; while also that spring one of the most persistent attack dogs on QE, the *Guardian* columnist Simon Jenkins, was unequivocal that the policy had indeed done no more than fill bank vaults – 'it has helped banks back to profitability but there is no sign the policy has had any impact on credit to businesses, let alone on domestic money supply' – and he called it 'the costliest fiasco in regulatory history'.[32]

In any case, there were before long increasing signs of a loss of confidence in QE at the Bank itself. QE had, Tucker publicly admitted in October 2012, 'lost its bite'; and by June 2013 the MPC had voted against more QE for eleven consecutive months. Looking ahead that month to the policy options facing King's successor, the prominent City economist George Magnus bluntly stated that 'QE cannot address the dearth of investment, low productivity, weak trade or the handicapped financial system.' What about King himself? Had QE, he was asked by Martin Wolf in a valedictory interview, worked as he had hoped? 'I've always seen this as a way of increasing the broader money supply,' replied the governor. 'And the thing that's so extraordinary is that, for the past few years, the banking system, which is normally responsible for creating 95 per cent of broad money, has been contracting its part of the money supply. And since we at the Bank only supply about 5 per cent of it, the proportional increase in our bid has to be massive to offset the contraction of the rest.' Wolf then queried whether the Bank should have been more adventurous and purchased riskier assets. 'No, right from the beginning I said that if other assets should be purchased, and I took no view as to whether they should or should not, then the government should decide on which assets are purchased, and we would finance it. I think that's the right division of labour between central bank and the finance ministry.'

There was also the whole matter, when it came to assessing QE, of unintended consequences. 'QE', declared Ros Altmann (pension expert and director general of Saga) in November 2010, 'is the worst thing that could happen to pensions, it is devaluing and destroying pensioners' income'; and the following autumn, Tucker felt compelled to argue not only that pension assets would have been 'potentially worth much less' if the Bank had not acted, but also – in response to complaints from savers generally – that 'to have allowed the economy to lurch down into a spiral or vortex would have been hugely destructive for savers'. Particularly outspoken was Nassim Taleb, author of the bestselling *Black Swan*. 'Quantitative easing is a transfer of wealth from the poor to the rich,' he asserted in February 2012. 'It floods banks with money, which they use to pay themselves bonuses. The banks have money, and assets, so they can borrow easily. The poor guy, who is unemployed and can't borrow, is not going to benefit from it. The state is subsidising the rich. It is the top 1 per cent who benefit from quantitative easing, not the 99 per cent.' Indeed, that same year the Bank itself estimated that 40 per cent of the £600 billion increase in the value of stocks and bonds since 2009 had accrued to the richest 5 per cent of households. Or as Magnus would note, 'QE has been called welfare for the rich.'[33] At the least, that uncomfortable fact made it a policy with an uncertain future.

A further source of uneasiness during these last four years of King's governorship was the Bank's somewhat erratic forecasting record – usually underestimating inflation and overestimating growth. It was, moreover, that short-term relationship between those two concerns, inflation and growth, that provided perhaps the hardest judgement calls for King and his MPC colleagues. The early months of 2011 were especially testing. Commentators on the whole backed their decision to keep interest rates at the record low of 0.5 per cent, even as inflation pushed towards 4 per cent. 'What would be absolutely disastrous,' argued for instance Anthony Hilton, 'would be for King and the other rate-setters to give in to the pressure from many who should know better, including the Prime Minister [David Cameron], and lift interest rates to try to stop the current round of price rises. Such an act would be more likely to stifle the economy.' Even so, as *The Times*'s Sam Fleming pointed out, 'the Bank is still living dangerously':

> For 20 years governments and central banks have been basing anti-inflation policy not on a backward-looking model of the economy that reacts to reported trends, but by looking forward. Shaping public and market inflation expectations so that prices do not spiral out of control has defined their strategy. So the suggestion that the credibility of the Bank of England is under question because of persistent inflation overshoots is not an academic debating point, it is a dagger aimed at the heart of monetary policy. Put simply, the longer that inflation exceeds the Bank's 2 per cent target [reduced in 2003 from the original 2.5 per cent], the harder it becomes for Mervyn King and his committee to argue that that target has relevance. This could 'de-anchor' inflation expectations and undermine monetary stability.

Inside the MPC, the most hawkish noises came from an external member, Andrew Sentance, who from summer 2010 consistently voted for higher rates and in February 2011 publicly argued, with a nod to sterling's declining external value and a 1973 Genesis album, that 'by raising interest rates sooner rather than later to help offset global inflationary pressures, the MPC can help reassure the financial markets and the great British public that we remain true to our inflation target remit and are not intent on "Selling England by the Pound"'. King, equally publicly, disagreed. With his own cultural nod (to the Battle of Britain sketch in *Beyond the Fringe*), he declared that to put up interest rates too soon would be a comparable 'futile gesture'. Or as he explained in June in his annual Mansion Speech: 'We could have raised Bank rate significantly so that inflation today would be closer to the target. But that would not have prevented the squeeze on living standards arising from higher oil and commodity prices and the measures necessary to reduce our twin deficits. And it would have meant a weaker recovery, or even further falls in output, despite our having experienced the worst downturn in output and spending since the Depression.' Two years later, on the eve of the governor's departure, the *Economist* paid a notable tribute:

> He has responded adeptly to a nasty combination of economic weakness and price pressures. Oil and regulated prices (things like VAT and university fees) have pushed inflation as high as 5%. Bringing inflation back to the 2% target by raising interest rates would kill Britain's feeble recovery. Some brands of monetary policy, notably the European Central Bank's, have been too hawkish. Sir Mervyn's is more subtle. He has allowed inflation to remain above target for the past four years while frequently confirming his commitment to that target. Somehow this has worked. The Bank's credibility as an inflation targeter is intact: firms and workers still expect inflation to be close to 2%.

All that said, the paper fully conceded that the next governor would find it 'a difficult line to tread'.[34]

Would it be helpful, some wondered, to change the MPC's remit? David Wighton offered in December 2012 a helpful commentary:

> When the Bank of England got control of monetary policy in 1997, it was given a simple goal. It was to set interest rates to meet a 2 per cent target for inflation [in fact 2.5 per cent in 1997]. The arrangement arguably worked pretty well for the first decade. But now the problems facing the economy are so severe that there are increasing calls to change the goal from a simple focus on the control of inflation to one that includes growth.
>
> While Sir Mervyn is against changing the target, the suspicion is that the Bank has already done so without telling anyone. Over the past three years inflation has been more than 3 per cent for 80 per cent of the time but the Bank has seemed more concerned about growth. At times it has appeared that the Bank's target is not inflation but growth plus inflation, or in the jargon, nominal GDP growth. This is just what some top economists think it should do explicitly.

The governor was indeed opposed, telling a Belfast audience in January 2013 that 'to drop the objective of low inflation would be to forget a lesson from our post-war history', reminding them of how 'the painful experience of the 1970s' revealed the 'illusion' of the policy-makers of the 1960s in 'trying to target an unrealistic growth rate for the economy as a whole, while pretending that its pursuit was consistent with stable inflation'. And he asserted unambiguously: 'Wishful thinking can be indulged if the costs fall on the dreamers; when the costs fall on others, it is unacceptable. So a long-run target of 2% inflation should be an essential part of our macroeconomic framework.' Two months later, shortly before the March budget, King was still making similar noises – 'I'm not sure there is any call for major change in the remit,' he told ITV News, adding that 'most important is the commitment to the [inflation] target of 2%' – but the chancellor (whether or not influenced by the governor in waiting is impossible to know) decided otherwise, at least to a degree. 'As we've seen over the past five years,' observed Osborne in his budget speech, 'low and stable inflation is a necessary but not sufficient condition for prosperity. The new remit explicitly tasks the MPC with setting out clearly the trade-offs it has made in deciding how long it will be before inflation returns to target.' It was undeniably a change – but it was not as dramatic a change as some had expected, keeping as it did the 2 per cent inflation target and refraining from nominal GDP targeting in order to prioritise growth over inflation.[35] In short, the cherished 1990s dispensation was still alive, if not exactly well.

Broadly speaking, the post-1997 Bank became not only a leaner organisation (well under 2,000 staff by 2006), but also a less paternalistic and less balanced organisation. In 1997 itself, that autumn saw the closure of the branches in Manchester, Birmingham, Bristol and Newcastle, with only the Leeds branch – becoming the Bank's North of England cash centre – remaining; while the Bank's dozen agents now concentrated on assessing the economy in their own areas, via a range of some 8,000 business contacts across the UK, and in turn reporting direct to the MPC. Six years later, marking the end in 2003 of George's governorship, Elizabeth Hennessy noted some other domestic developments: the printing of banknotes had recently been contracted out (to De La Rue, leasing the Printing Works at Debden for an initial period of seven years); the registrar's department, having moved to Gloucester, was under threat of closure (which duly happened in 2004, its work being outsourced to a normal registrar's company called Computershare); and there was a significantly different daily environment:

> While many of the outposts of the Bank have been closed or, like the staff dining rooms which used to be housed in a building in nearby King's Arms Yard, brought back into Threadneedle Street, the physical workplace has been much improved for the decreasing numbers of staff. Many of the warrens of small offices housing clerks in strict hierarchies have been thrown open into large, light workspaces – no mean achievement considering the feet-thick walls which have to be demolished or penetrated by cabling.

Paternalism had of course been in decline for quite a time, but it now almost vanished. Indicators included the closure in 1998 of the Staff Library; the end around the turn of the century of such key perks as assistance with mortgages and school fees; and in December 2007 the final issue of the *Old Lady*, still loyally read by pensioners but of relatively little interest to current employees. The imbalance, meanwhile, came partly from the loss of banking supervision and debt management, partly from what felt to some like the almost complete dominance of Monetary Analysis. 'I recognise that there are morale issues in Banking Services,' observed in 2004 the new chief cashier, Andrew Bailey. 'Job insecurity has followed from the perception that Banking Services is a declining, fringe area that has suffered from attritional cutting and cutting.' He also reflected that 'the Bank has not served its non-graduate staff well – we have not invested in them as we should have done'. Two years later, an outside consultant, Valerie Hamilton, recorded a telling episode:

> I had been leading a workshop on change management for a group of workers who were confronted with a significant increase in the use of technology in their jobs and a huge shift in the nature of their relationship with the Economists they supported. They were resisting, angry and hostile. When I eventually managed to engage them, one woman thumped the table and declared in opposition to something I had said regarding the needs of 'the Bank', 'We are the

Bank, not the graduates who come and go, get Bank of England on their c.v. and then disappear. We are the Bank.' She of course had a point.[36]

In fact, on the domestic front, there were some positive signs during King's governorship. The Banking Department started to return more to the centre of the Bank; more systematic attention began to be paid to the careers of non-graduates, including career planning for secretaries and a new induction programme; and there was even an apprenticeship scheme for engineers working in the Bank's power plant. As for the economists, they were not exactly returned to the ranks as a result of the crisis, but it was undoubtedly a salutary experience.

What about the thorny issue of diversity? Merlyn Lowther was appointed in 1998 as the twenty-ninth chief cashier – the first woman to fill that time-honoured if no longer so powerful position; while Rachel Lomax in 2003 became deputy governor, the most senior woman yet in the Bank's history. Across the board, however, there was an undeniably long way still to go. 'There aren't enough women at the top; nor are we well represented among the ethnic minorities,' the HR director, Louise Redmond, told the *Old Lady* in 2006. And she explained how a staff consultation survey had highlighted two problems: 'a long-hours culture' and inadequate 'career opportunities and development for our A-level entrants'. Two years later she presented to NedCo the latest staff survey, which to judge by the discussion had produced mixed results. Not so good in terms of recruitment from ethnic minorities (with possible factors including 'some resistance within the British Asian community about entering the public sector in view of the lower earnings potential' and 'the low proportion of Afro-Caribbean students at UK universities'); but greater optimism 'about progress around gender, where the new flexible working programme was due to be launched'. Change then did seem to speed up. 'I recently met with the 2012 new recruits at the Bank of England, and noticed that almost half the people in the room were women and many were also non-white,' noted Gillian Tett in 2013. 'Strikingly,' she added, 'there was also a large number of people who had not studied economics.' Even so, as of late 2012, the facts were that all nine members of the MPC were men; ditto all eleven members of the FPC; of the Bank's three governors (that is,

King and two deputies) and ten other executive directors, only one was a woman, and predictably she was in charge of HR; while on the twelve-strong Court the sole non-male was Lady Rice. There was also the much publicised matter of the £5 note and who would replace Elizabeth Fry, herself one of only two women on banknotes since historical figures had been introduced over forty years earlier. By the early summer of 2013 a brilliantly effective feminist campaign, led by Caroline Criado-Perez, was under way protesting about the choice of yet another man – admittedly Winston Churchill – as Fry's successor. Ultimately, a compromise was achieved: Churchill stayed, but that July it was announced that Jane Austen would become the new face of the £10 note. 'Without this campaign, without the 35,000 people who signed our Change.org petition,' responded Criado-Perez, 'the Bank of England would have unthinkingly airbrushed women out of history. We warmly welcome this move from the Bank ...'[37]

A direct consequence of independence in 1997 was a sustained attempt to become significantly more outward facing, not least through the MPC's members. 'Slowing down demand by raising interest rates involves costs,' Willem Buiter told the *Old Lady* in 1998. 'People are going to be adversely affected, they're going to have bear the costs – and they have a right to complain. We have to be capable of answering their complaints. You cannot just give a "mind your own business, we're looking after the good of the economy, we feel your pain" kind of answer. You have to take these things very seriously and be ready to stand up and explain and defend yourselves.' Ten years later, the outgoing director in charge of communications, Peter Rodgers, summarised for NedCo the broadly encouraging bigger picture since those early days of independence:

It was notable that understanding about monetary policy had increased significantly amongst market and media commentators. In 1998, the MPC had faced intense criticism about its response to the threat of recession. That contrasted with the present debate which, although often critical, was centred on an understanding about the dilemma facing the MPC. The fact that the MPC had undertaken visits around the UK for over a decade had helped establish that it was setting policy for the country as a whole, and was not an ivory tower or representing the City.

The direction of travel was more or less one way. 'A transformation in the Bank's approach to external communications and transparency,' was how Andy Haldane would put it in a 2012 speech:

> Think back twenty years. Then, there were no quarterly *Inflation Reports*, no six-monthly *Financial Stability Reports* and certainly no press conferences to accompany both. Twenty years ago, there were no minutes of the deliberations of the Bank's policy committees. Back then, press interviews were rare and scripted to within an inch of their life. In the past year, Bank officials gave around 65 speeches and over 200 press interviews. In Montagu Norman's day, the combined total was one ... Earlier this year, the Governor gave the Bank's first live peacetime radio address to the nation for 73 years. The Bank tweets, fortunately with rather less vigour than your average premiership footballer. Soon we will have, for the first time in history, published minutes of the Bank's Court of Directors ... In 2011, a word search of 'Mervyn King' in the press revealed more hits than 'Kylie Minogue' ...[38]

King himself took the third word – England – of the Bank's name very seriously, undertaking more frequent engagements in the provinces (and of course Scotland, Wales and Northern Ireland) than any of his predecessors, not to mention speaking at the TUC and appearing on *Test Match Special*. Almost certainly, and accentuated by the crisis, there had been no previous governor as well known to the public at large, with perhaps Norman and George in their very different ways having run him closest.

Central to the repositioning of the Bank was, as Rodgers mentioned, the new distance from the City – the refusal to continue to be identified as the financial sector's invariably protective, sometimes one-eyed 'mother hen'. The key announcement, although to King's subsequent regret not quite spelling out how the Bank was moving away more generally from its 'third' core purpose (essentially interventionist) as established in the early 1990s, came in June 2004 in his first Mansion House speech. After reflecting on how the loss of banking supervision in 1997 had 'inevitably changed the Bank's relationship with the City and the financial sector more generally', he argued that the opportunity now existed to 'restate' how the Bank saw that relationship:

Since Big Bang in 1986, the City has changed beyond all recognition. The so-called 'Wimbledonisation' of the City – hosting a successful tournament where most of the winners come from overseas – has proceeded apace. Some have blamed the Bank, among others, for failing to engineer the promotion of more British institutions to the top ranks of global financial institutions. But in fact there are now some home players in the top ten in the world. And there is little evidence that it makes sense for the public sector to try to identify national champions, as opposed to creating an environment which encourages innovation and provides first-rate infrastructure.

The Bank is, and always will be, deeply involved in the City and those who work here. We operate in markets daily; we stand at the centre of – indeed underpin – the payments system; we have a close interest in settlement systems. But our involvement is from the perspective of the public interest, not the defence of particular private interests ...

If those remarks suggested a new degree of objectivity in relation to the City, that objectivity was taken to a higher level by the crisis. The crucial pronouncement was in October 2009, when the governor told businessmen in Edinburgh not only that 'never in the field of financial endeavour has so much money been owed by so few to so many' (that is, following the bail-outs), but that if banks were 'too big to fail', then there was no alternative but to split them up – remarks that found greater favour with the Tory opposition than with the Labour government, though without a commitment from the former that the UK would strike a unilateral path for narrow banking. King's greatest unpopularity, persisting for the rest of his governorship, was with the bankers themselves. In October 2010 he declared that 'of all the many ways of organising banking, the worst is the one we have today'; the following spring, in a frank interview with Charles Moore, he accused the banks of in effect continuing to be bonus-driven, behaving in risky ways in the knowledge that the state would bail them out – the ultimate one-way bet; in July 2012, something not wholly unadjacent to a raising of the governor's eyebrows played a role in the dramatic departure of Bob Diamond from Barclays; and in June 2013, only days before stepping down, he had strong words to the Treasury Committee for banks which deployed their formidable lobbying powers to put 'tremendous pressure' on politicians to interfere with decisions made by the Bank's newly empowered supervisors.[39] All this, to reiterate, amounted to almost entirely unusual behaviour on the part of a governor.

The crisis, followed soon afterwards by the prospect of the return of banking supervision arguably making the Bank more powerful than at any time in its history, inevitably raised serious questions of governance and accountability. The main focus was on two key areas: the role of the governor; and the role of the Court.

Both areas naturally formed part of the Treasury Committee's November 2011 report on *Accountability of the Bank of England*. As far as the governorship was concerned, it made a trio of recommendations: that instead of a maximum of two five-year terms, future governors be appointed for a single eight-year term, based on the argument that the existing renewal process was vulnerable to 'at least the perception of political interference in the Bank'; that, 'in order to safeguard his or her independence', the Treasury Committee be given 'a statutory power of veto' over the governor's appointment and dismissal; and that, in a crisis situation, the ultimate statutory responsibility for managing that crisis should rest with the chancellor, 'after the formal notification by the Bank of a material risk to public funds'. In due course, the new Financial Services Act, eventually coming into force in April 2013, did incorporate the first and third of the Treasury Committee's recommendations, but – perhaps unsurprisingly – not the second.

Fundamental questions, however, remained open. 'The danger of the proposed expansion of the governor's responsibilities,' reflected Samuel Brittan in April 2012 as speculation grew about the identity of King's successor, 'is that we will end up with a bureaucratic chairman figure, dependent on advice from below that will reflect the conventional wisdom of the moment. The alternative of a dictatorial figure, who claims to know it all, might be even worse.' Some believed that King himself was such a dictatorial figure; and when the *Financial Times*'s Chris Giles sought in May 2012 to examine that issue, involving interviews with almost two dozen current and former Bank officials, he concluded that while King was certainly not 'a tyrant, shouting and banging his fist', nevertheless the reality was 'a Bank honed to deliver to the governor what he wants', accordingly rather different from 'an open organisation with open discussion'. In any case, what was crystal clear was that under the new dispensation the governor of the day would hold formidable powers – chairing the Monetary Policy Committee, the Financial Policy Committee and the Prudential Regulation Authority board. He would also be the chief executive; though at a time when the size of the Bank's staff had quite suddenly almost doubled (up to some 3,500, compared to just under 2,000 at the start of 2012), few quibbled in June 2013 about the appointment of Charlotte Hogg as the Bank's first chief operating officer, assuming from July day-to-day responsibility for matters like divisional performance and organisational structure, leaving the governor in his chief executive role free to focus on strategy. What about the deputy governors, of whom by spring 2013 there were three? James Barty's searching report the previous year for Policy Exchange had called on the next governor 'to become more of a chairman, overseeing the coordination between monetary policy, financial stability and prudential regulation', while the deputy governors became 'the CEO's of the respective parts of the Bank', running them on a day-to-day basis and 'enabling the Governor to take an overview of everything the Bank does'.[40] Only time would tell if that became the new reality at the top.

As for the role of the Court – responsible for 'the affairs of the Bank', as the 1946 Act nicely put it – it had of course become increasingly marginal during the second half of the previous century. 'We only used to meet for about an hour,' recalled Sir David Lees about his time as a non-executive director during the 1990s. 'There were presentations by the executive and then we, lambs to the slaughter, were offered five or ten minutes to talk about that part of industry we represented. I spoke for the motor industry in those days. How much they listened, I don't know. Lunch was good.' From 1998 the Court's main forum for oversight (including of the MPC) was the newly created NedCo, with its own chairman (appointed by the chancellor) and drawing on increased representation from the regions; in 2009, post-crisis, new legislation – in effect initiated by King – saw a non-executive director (Lees) replacing the governor as chairman of the Court; but the external impression remained that the Court still had some way to go on its journey from a lunch club to a properly functioning, properly scrutinising Plc-style board.

In November 2011 the Treasury Committee's report 'strongly' recommended that the term 'Court' be abolished and suggested that it be renamed the 'Supervisory Board of the Bank of England' – a board that in essence would be leaner, more expert, better staffed and in general fully empowered to hold the Bank's executive to account. King's response in early 2012 was to meet the Treasury Committee halfway: the Court to set up an oversight committee to review the way the executive made its decisions, but not to become a supervisory board as such. 'I don't think it makes any sense to have another group of unelected officials to say "actually, we want to second-guess the decisions taken by the first group,"' he told the Treasury Committee. 'If you really believe they are better, you should put them in the first group to start with.' As the new legislation took shape during 2012, the governor largely got his way. The Court's name was not abolished; it remained a unitary body, in other words a mixture of executives (the governor and deputy governors) and non-executives (the majority, but no more than nine, with one of them still as chair); and NedCo was replaced by the Oversight Committee, to be chaired by the chair of Court and accorded statutory responsibility for keeping under review the performance of the Bank in relation to its objectives and strategy. 'The chairman of the Court is not first fiddle, he's second fiddle,' Lees would observe in 2014 shortly before stepping down from his three-days-a-week position. 'The Governor, because of all the policy issues, is first fiddle. The next chairman of the Court has to accept that. It's lower down the pecking order than you would be used to in the corporate sector.'[41]

In 2011–12 neither King nor the Treasury Committee's chairman, the redoubtable and zealous Andrew Tyrie, underestimated what was at stake. 'The Bank of England will play an even more vital role in preventing future crises, yet aspects of its governance appear antiquated,' Tyrie remarked at the time of his report. 'Scrutiny of the Bank should reflect the needs of 21st-century democracy. That means clear lines of accountability and more information made available to Parliament.' Of course, the Bank had become significantly more accountable to Parliament since independence in 1997, including with the Treasury Committee holding confirmation hearings (though not with the power of veto) for MPC and subsequently FPC appointments; but what Tyrie now wanted – and what King more or less successfully resisted – was in effect, as Alex Brummer noted after the report, to turn the Court from 'an extension of the Bank' into 'a conduit to Parliament', including through undertaking and publishing reviews of policy. Inevitably, quite apart from the imminent prospect of the Bank's significantly enhanced powers, there was also a specific political context: in this case, the familiar issue of what degree of authority the governor enjoyed to venture – or, some would say, trespass – on to fiscal domain.

A controversial year and a half or so began in June 2009 with King's Mansion House speech. Before he came to his ecclesiastical analogy in relation to the Bank's financial-stability powers, he included a passage that also made headlines. 'As we emerge from recession, fiscal policy will have to change,' declared the governor. 'Five years from now national debt, as a proportion of national income, is expected to be more than double its level before the crisis. So it is necessary to produce a clear plan to show how prospective deficits will be reduced during the next Parliament ...' The *Daily Telegraph*'s take was predictable – 'Put your books in order, and soon, King warns Darling' – while the following week King himself, appearing before the Treasury Committee, had more to say: 'We are confronted with a situation where the scale of deficits is truly extraordinary. This reflects the scale of the global downturn, but it also reflects the fact that we came into this crisis with fiscal policy on a path that wasn't sustainable and a correction was needed.' And: 'Although we are finding it easy now to finance those deficits by issuing gilts, there could be problems down the road. We need a credible statement of what will guide the deficit reduction.' Given that the Labour government was planning to fight the following year's election on the terrain of investment in public services versus 'Tory cuts', it was hardly surprising that the shadow chancellor, Osborne, seized on King's words to claim that they had 'demolished for good any claim that this discredited government ever had to a credible plan for the recovery'.[42]

The election itself in May 2010 saw the Tories becoming the largest party but without an overall majority. It would later be claimed that, during the ensuing days of talks and negotiations that eventually led to the coalition with the Liberal Democrats, and as markets faltered in the additional context of the Greek sovereign-debt crisis, the governor had played an active role in encouraging that political outcome; but such claims lack any evidence. What was undoubtedly true, though, was that in the immediate wake of the coalition being formed his was a particularly prominent voice for deficit reduction, aka austerity. King's Mansion House speech on 16 June could hardly have been more explicit:

> Monetary policy must be set in the light of the fiscal tightening over the coming years, the continuing fragility in financial markets and the state of the banking system. I know there are those who worry that too rapid a fiscal consolidation will endanger recovery. But the steady reduction in the very large structural deficit over a period of a Parliament cannot credibly be postponed indefinitely. If prospects for growth were to weaken, the outlook for inflation would probably be lower and monetary policy could then respond. I do, therefore, Chancellor, welcome your commitment to put the UK's public finances on a sound footing. It is important that, in the medium term, national debt as a proportion of GDP returns to a declining path.

The following week, Osborne turned his 'commitment' into action, with a budget – described by the *Financial Times*'s George Parker as 'audacious' – setting out how he intended to fill the hole in Britain's finances in one Parliament; and according to Parker, it was the governor who 'played a decisive role in persuading the chancellor that the Budget's priority had to be the elimination of the $155bn deficit': 'The chancellor's team say Mr Osborne's most agonising Budget decision was over the risks to the economy from cutting too deeply and too soon. Mr King insisted it was vital to take questions of Britain's creditworthiness off the table for good.' Certainly, irrespective of the question of his direct influence, King continued through 2010 to bang the drum hard and insistently. Public borrowing, he told the TUC in September, was 'clearly unsustainable', and any government had to have a 'clear and credible' deficit-reduction plan; and he added that he would be 'shirking' his responsibilities if he did not warn his somewhat sceptical audience of the risks – including 'a damaging rise in long-term interest rates' – of failing to tackle the deficit.

The storm came in November. 'Concern as King blurs line on policy' was the *Financial Times*'s main headline on the 10th, with the paper reporting that 'some senior staff at the Bank of England are uncomfortable with Mervyn King's endorsement of the government's public spending cuts, suggesting he has over-stepped the line separating monetary and fiscal policy'. Six days later, appearing before the House of Lords Select Committee on Economic Affairs, the governor sought to brush aside the story:

> I would be concerned if people felt that I or the Bank was behaving politically. I don't believe we are. We are facing the largest fiscal deficit in our peacetime history. I think the surprising thing would be if the central bank had no view that this was a matter of concern. We do believe it is a matter of concern. Of course, in terms of the Bank, I am sure everyone has their own view about the right path. They do on monetary policy; it would be surprising if they didn't on fiscal policy ... I have never commented on anything beyond the overall level of the deficit. I did not endorse the spending review, I did not comment on the balance between spending and taxes as the best way to deal with a fiscal deficit, let alone comment on the individual measures. I have never commented on any other aspect of fiscal policy, other than the concern about the size of the deficit and the need, for monetary policy purposes, to have in place a truly credible, medium-term path – not inflexible, but credible – for reducing the deficit over a horizon which is credible to markets, that is a horizon over which an elected Government can claim to have sway, namely, the length of the Parliament.

Just over a fortnight later, the MPC's Adam Posen, well known as its leading dove, spoke to the Treasury Committee of how back in May, during the preparation of the *Inflation Report*, a minority on the MPC had felt concern about the paragraph 'talking about the particular speed with which to deal with fiscal policy'. 'We were concerned,' explained Posen, 'that the statement could be seen as excessively political in the context of the election. That language was too political, too much of a statement.' Next day, the *Financial Times* quoted a former MPC member, Sushil Wadhwani. 'I think that, rightly or wrongly, Mervyn has come to be seen as being much closer to the Conservative Party than the Labour Party,' he observed. 'No central bank governor should allow this to occur. In the years ahead, we are likely to need a Bank that is seen to be independent. It is a great pity that the perception of independence has been put at risk.' The criticism continued into 2011. 'The last thing you ever want is for the Bank of England to be drawn into the political arena,' the shadow chancellor, Ed Balls, told the *Financial Times* in February, and soon afterwards the prominent American economist Paul Krugman accused King of acting as a 'cheerleader' for the coalition's policies: 'He's wrong on the economics – front-loaded spending cuts are the wrong policy for a still depressed economy – but that's not the key point; rather, the point is that if you're going to have an independent central bank, the people running that bank have to be careful to stay above the political fray.'

The row died down, but the inherent fundamentals of the situation did not magically disappear. 'When fiscal and monetary policy start to merge into one,' Rod Price observed in a May 2012 letter to the *Financial Times* about central banks generally, 'governors are no longer apolitical.' King himself was intensely aware – perhaps no one more – of the preciousness of the 1997 independence prize and the prime importance of not having it tarnished or threatened. His 2016 book, *The End of Alchemy*, included what was clearly a heartfelt anecdote relating to 2007: 'At 12 noon on Thursday 10 May, Tony Blair announced his resignation as Prime Minister after ten years at Number Ten. At exactly the same moment the Bank of England announced an increase in interest rates of 0.25 percentage points. Nothing could symbolise more vividly the change in the monetary regime in Britain than that conjunction.' For, as he explained with his well-developed sense of history, 'before the Bank of England became independent it would have been inconceivable that interest rates would have risen on a day when there was an important government announcement'.[43]

Who would succeed King? Paddy Power offered in April 2012 some odds: Paul Tucker and the FSA's chairman, Lord (Adair) Turner, as joint 5/2 favourites; Lord (Stephen) Green, former HSBC chairman and now trade minister, closely behind at 11/4; Lord (Gus) O'Donnell, former Cabinet secretary, at 5/1; and Mark Carney, governor of the Bank of Canada, at 10/1; while out-and-out long shots included Gordon Brown (200/1) and Fred Goodwin (300/1). In June the *Evening Standard*'s James Ashton saw it as 'a straight fight' between Turner and Tucker; by July, O'Donnell had shortened to 9/4 and Green lengthened to 6/1; in August the *Spectator* called on Osborne to 'scour the globe'; in September the position was, for the first time ever, formally advertised; by October the Treasury had denied reports that Carney had been sounded out, while O'Donnell had dropped out; in its issue dated 24 November, the *Economist* recommended Tucker, given Carney's apparent unavailability; and on Monday the 26th, Osborne made his announcement.

It was, after all the smoke and mirrors, Carney. 'He is quite simply the best, most experienced and most qualified person in the world to do the job,' explained the chancellor about the Canadian, who had accepted the position for a five-year term only and would be the first foreigner to become governor. Press reaction was almost unanimously positive. 'A resounding statement that Britain is ready to hire the best talent for top posts' (*Financial Times*); 'ticks virtually all the boxes' (*Times*); 'as an outsider with fresh ideas, he will be perfectly placed to spur open debate and new thinking' (*Daily Telegraph*). Some seven months later, 30 June 2013, a Sunday, was King's last day, coinciding with the Bank's annual sports day at Roehampton. Cricket that afternoon featured a recent England captain, Andrew Strauss, and an over or two of the governor's teasing slows. Next morning, coming in by tube from west London, the new man was at Bank Station shortly before seven o'clock. Unlike Montagu Norman, he did not have a hat – let alone in the electronic age a ticket attached to it. An understandable topographical struggle ensued about which exit to take, but soon enough the 119th person to be governor had his feet under the table.[44]

The Bank over the previous 319 years had had its share of criticism, but also its share of praise. The greatest of writers on the Bank usually dished out the former, but occasionally the latter. 'Nothing would persuade the English people,' declared Walter Bagehot in *Lombard Street*, 'to abolish the Bank of England; and if some calamity swept it away, generations must elapse before at all the same trust would be placed in any other equivalent.' While still deputy governor, King quoted those words at the August 1999 gathering of central bankers at Jackson Hole, Wyoming. And he went on with words of his own that any governor in any era might usefully have pondered:

Central banks may be at the peak of their power. There may well be fewer central banks in the future, and their extinction cannot be ruled out. Societies have managed without central banks in the past. They may well do so again in the future. The website of my favourite football team [Aston Villa] has the banner 'heroes and villains'. For some, central bankers are heroes – more powerful and responsible than political leaders – and for others they are villains – too fanatical to be entrusted with the world economy. For all our sakes, it is important that central bankers are seen neither as heroes nor villains. They should be modest technicians, striving to improve the way they use the tools of their trade, and always eager to learn. Openness of mind and fleetness of foot will be the best way to avoid extinction.[45]

Notes

ABBREVIATIONS

Unless otherwise stated, all archival references are to the Bank of England Archive.

Abramson	Daniel M. Abramson, *Building the Bank of England: Money, Architecture, Society, 1694–1942* (New Haven, 2006)
Acres	W. Marston Acres, *The Bank of England from Within* (2 vols, 1931)
BEQB	*Bank of England Quarterly Bulletin*
Boyle	Andrew Boyle, *Montagu Norman* (1967)
Byatt	Derrick Byatt, *Promises to Pay: The First Three Hundred Years of Bank of England Notes* (1994)
Capie	Forrest Capie, *The Bank of England: 1950s to 1979* (New York, 2010)
CB	*Central Banking*
Clapham	Sir John Clapham, *The Bank of England: A History* (2 vols, Cambridge, 1944)
Clay	Sir Henry Clay, *Lord Norman* (1957)
Conaghan	Dan Conaghan, *The Bank: Inside the Bank of England* (2012)
DBB	*Dictionary of Business Biography*
de Fraine	H. G. de Fraine, *Servant of This House: Life in the old Bank of England* (1960)
Dow	Graham Hacche and Christopher Taylor (eds), *Inside the Bank of England: Memoirs of Christopher Dow, Chief Economist, 1973–84* (Basingstoke, 2013)
Fay	Stephen Fay, *Portrait of an Old Lady: Turmoil at the Bank of England* (1987)
Feavearyear	Sir Albert Feavearyear, *The Pound Sterling* (2nd edn, 1963)
Fed	Archives of Federal Reserve Bank of New York
Fforde	John Fforde, *The Bank of England and Public Policy, 1941–1958* (Cambridge, 1992)

FT	*Financial Times*
Giuseppi	John Giuseppi, *The Bank of England: A History from its Foundation in 1694* (1966)
Hennessy	Elizabeth Hennessy, *A Domestic History of the Bank of England, 1930–1960* (Cambridge, 1992)
Hewitt and Keyworth	V. H. Hewitt and J. M. Keyworth, *As Good as Gold: 300 Years of British Bank Note Design* (1987)
King	W. T. C. King, *History of the London Discount Market* (1936)
King (1)	*The Cecil King Diary, 1965–1970* (1972)
King (2)	*The Cecil King Diary, 1970–1974* (1975)
Kynaston	David Kynaston, *The City of London* (4 vols, 1994–2001)
LMA	London Metropolitan Archives
Morgan	E. Victor Morgan, *The Theory and Practice of Central Banking, 1797–1913* (Cambridge, 1943)
NA	National Archives
O'Brien	Leslie O'Brien, *A Life Worth Living* (privately published, 1995)
ODNB	*Oxford Dictionary of National Biography*
OHC	Oral History Collection (at Bank of England Archives)
OL	*Old Lady*
Roberts and Kynaston	Richard Roberts and David Kynaston (eds), *The Bank of England: Money, Power and Influence, 1694–1994* (Oxford, 1995)
Sayers	R. S. Sayers, *The Bank of England, 1891–1944* (2 vols, plus appendixes, Cambridge, 1976)

Unless otherwise stated, all books are published in London.

PROLOGUE IT MUST NOW NECESSARILY BE A BANK

1 T. A. Stephens, *A Contribution to the Bibliography of the Bank of England* (1979), p 86; M1/1; E. S. de Beer (ed), *The Correspondence of John Locke, Volume Five* (Oxford, 1979), p 81; Bruce G. Carruthers, *City of Capital* (Princeton, New Jersey, 1996), p 246; Acres, vol 1, pp 12–13; M1/1.

2 *ODNB*, David Armitage, 'Paterson, William (1658–1719)'; William Paterson, *A Brief Account of the Intended Bank of England* (1694), p 1; *ODNB*, Stuart Handley, 'Montagu, Charles, Earl of Halifax', 'Godfrey, Michael'; James E. Thorold Rogers, *The First Nine Years of the Bank of England* (Oxford, 1887), pp 9–12; P. G. M. Dickson, *The Financial Revolution in England* (Aldershot, 1993 edn), p 54.

3 *London Gazette*, 5 July 1694; Acres, p 14; M1/1; ADM30/15; G4/1, 27 July 1694; Byatt, p 11.

4 Clapham, vol 1, p 1; Dickson, p 47; Felix Martin, *Money* (2013), p 116; Anne L. Murphy, 'Demanding "credible commitment"', *Economic History Review*, Feb 2013, p 178; Larry Neal, 'How it all began',

Financial History Review, Oct 2000, pp 123–4; Steve Pincus, *1688* (New Haven, 2009), pp 277, 484, 368.

5 Anne L. Murphy, *The Origins of Financial Markets* (Cambridge, 2009); Larry Neal and Stephen Quinn, 'Networks of information, markets, and institutions in the rise of London as a financial centre, 1660–1720', *Financial History Review*, April 2001, pp 7–14; J. Lawrence Broz and Richard S. Grossman, 'Paying for privilege', *Explorations in Economic History*, 2004, pp 50, 56–7; Michael Collins and Mae Baker, 'Bank of England Autonomy', in Carl-L. Holtfrerich *et al* (eds), *The Emergence of Modern Central Banking from 1918 to the Present* (Aldershot, 1999), p 23.

6 Martin, p 119. More generally, for a stimulating treatment of the Bank's beginnings and early history, bringing out the high degree of provisionality and improvisation as well as putting the Bank in a larger social and literary context, see: Valerie Hamilton and Martin Parker, *Daniel Defoe and the Bank of England* (Winchester, 2016).

7 J. A. Giuseppi, 'Sephardi Jews and the early years of the Bank of England', in Jewish Historical Society of England, *Transactions: Sessions 1955–59* (1960), pp 56–7; Dickson, pp 254–8; Murphy, *Origins*, pp 148–52.

8 J. Alan Downie, '*Gulliver's Travels*, the Contemporary Debate on the Financial Revolution, and the Bourgeois Public Spheres', in Charles Ivar McGrath and Chris Fauske (eds), *Money, Power and Print* (Cranbury, New Jersey, 2008), p 125; Feavearyear, p 125.

9 W. Marston Acres, 'Directors of the Bank of England', *Notes and Queries*, 20 July 1940; Pedro de Brito, 'The Portugal Merchants as Founders of the Bank of England in 1694', in British Historical Society of Portugal, *Annual Report and Review 2008*, pp 72–4; F. M. Crouzet, 'Walloons, Huguenots and the Bank of England', *Proceedings of the Huguenot Society of Great Britain & Ireland*, Summer 1990, pp 167–9; Murphy, *Origins*, p 81; Gary Stuart de Krey, *A Fractured Society* (Oxford, 1985), pp 109–10, 151, 154.

10 de Krey, p 146; *ODNB*, Gary S. de Krey, 'Abney, Sir Thomas', Jacob M. Price, 'Heathcote Gilbert, first baronet'; de Brito, p 75; *ODNB*, H. G. Roseveare, 'Houblon, Sir John'; Crouzet, p 168; *OL*, March 1935, p 8; Claire Tomalin, *Samuel Pepys* (2002), pp 291–2; *OL*, Dec 1922, pp 292–3; Donald F. Bond (ed.), *The Spectator, Volume 1* (1965), pp 10–11.

CHAPTER I SERVICES TO THE NATION

1 Hewitt and Keyworth, pp 21–2; Giuseppi, p 19; Henry Roseveare, *The Financial Revolution, 1660–1760* (Harlow, 1991), p 37; Clapham, vol 1, p 22; Nicholas Lane, 'The Foundation of the Bank of England', *History*

Today, Oct 1957, p 689; James E. Thorold Rogers, *The First Nine Years of the Bank of England* (Oxford, 1887), pp 25–6; *OL*, Dec 1965, p 203; Abramson, p 9.

2   H. P. R. Hoare, *Hoare's Bank* (1955 edn), opp p 27; Hewitt and Keyworth, p 24; Anne L. Murphy, *The Origins of English Financial Markets* (Cambridge, 2009), p 82; E. S. de Beer (ed), *The Correspondence of John Locke, Volume Five* (Oxford, 1979), pp 271–2; Bruce G. Carruthers, *City of Capital* (Princeton, New Jersey, 1996), p 141; Michael Godfrey, *A Short Account of the Bank of England* (Pulborough, 1999, Dragonwheel edn), pp 10, 15, 19.

3   D. W. Jones, *War and Economy* (Oxford, 1988), p 14; Andrew Forrester, *The Man Who Sold the Future* (New York, 2004), pp 75–7; G7/1, 16 May 1695; ADM30/6, Godfrey Family file; Acres, vol 1, p 54.

4   *OL*, March 2005 (Anne L. Murphy), p 17; Victoria Hutchings, *Messrs Hoare Bankers* (2005), p 28; Acres, vol 1, p 68; G7/1, 13 May 1696.

5   Dennis Rubini, 'Politics and the Battle for the Banks, 1688–1697', *English Historical Review*, Oct 1970, pp 702–3; *Locke*, p 540; Acres, vol 1, p 63; Carruthers, pp 141–2; G7/1, 29 April 1696; John Francis, *History of the Bank of England, its Times and Traditions* (1848), vol 1, p 69.

6   Acres, vol 1, p 71; Jones, p 24; Clapham, vol 1, pp 40–1; Acres, vol 1, pp 61, 73; Elisa Newby, 'Macroeconomic Implications of Gold Reserve Policy of the Bank of England during the Eighteenth Century' (Centre for Dynamic Macroeconomic Analysis, University of St Andrews, 2007), p 12; Acres, vol 1, p 73; Henry Horwitz, *Parliament, Policy and Politics in the Reign of William III* (Manchester, 1977), p 188; *Locke*, p 731; Lady Alice Archer Houblon, *The Houblon Family* (1907), vol 1, pp 281–2; Horwitz, p 188.

7   *OL*, March 2005 (Anne L. Murphy), p 17; Anne L. Murphy, 'Demanding "credible commitment"', *Economic History Review*, Feb 2013, p 193; Acres, vol 1, pp 79–80; Murphy, *Origins*, pp 152–4; Acres, vol 1, p 81; G7/1, 16 July 1697.

8   David Scott, *Leviathan* (2013), p 253; H. V. Bowen, 'The Bank of England during the Long Eighteenth Century, 1694–1820', in Roberts and Kynaston, pp 5, 10; P. G. M. Dickson, *The Financial Revolution in England* (1967), p 373; Andrew S. Skinner (ed), Sir James Stuart, *An Inquiry into the Principles of Political Oeconomy* (Edinburgh, 1966), Volume Two, p 618; Acres, vol 1, pp 98–9; ADM30/15, Houblon Family file; Acres, vol 1, pp 99–102; T. A. Stephens, *A Contribution to the Bibliography of the Bank of England* (1897), p 15; D. W. Jones, 'London merchants and the crisis of the 1690s', in Peter Clark and Paul Slack (eds), *Crisis and Order in English Towns, 1500–1700* (1972), p 340. For

a full treatment of the Bank and Exchequer bills during the War of the Spanish Succession, see: Richard A. Kleer, '"A new Species of Mony"', *Financial History Review*, Aug 2015, pp 179–203.

9 Abramson, p 11; Gary Stuart de Krey, *A Fractured Society* (Oxford, 1985), pp 143, 231; Giuseppi, p 34; Anne L. Murphy, 'Learning the business of banking', *Business History*, Feb 2010, pp 154–6, 168; *OL*, June 1928, pp 272–3; Acres, vol 1, pp 144, 151; Murphy, 'Learning', pp 161–2; *OL*, June 1928, pp 271–2.

10 Abramson, p 6; Clapham, vol 1, pp 151, 292; Bowen, p 15; Larry Neal and Stephen Quinn, 'Networks of information', *Financial History Review*, April 2001, p 25; Douglass C. North and Barry R. Weingast, 'Constitutions and Commitment', *Journal of Economic History*, Dec 1989, p 821; Murphy, 'Demanding', p 183.

11 B. W. Hill, 'The Change of Government and the "Loss of the City", 1710–1711', *Economic History Review*, Aug 1971, pp 398–9; Geoffrey Holmes, 'The Sacheverell Riots', *Past and Present*, Aug 1976, p 66; Hill, pp 400–4.

12 De Krey, pp 223–8; Carruthers, pp 143, 247–8; Hill, pp 407–8; Clapham, vol 1, pp 75–6; James Macdonald, 'The importance of not defaulting', in D'Maris Coffman *et al* (eds), *Questioning Credible Commitment* (Cambridge, 2013), p 130; Hill, pp 408–11.

13 Acres, vol 1, pp 107–10; Dickson, pp 81–2; Clapham, vol 1, pp 81–3.

14 Richard Kleer, '"The folly of particulars"', *Financial History Review*, Aug 2012, pp 175, 183–5; John Carswell, *The South Sea Bubble* (Stroud, 1993 edn), p 76.

15 Richard Dale, *The First Crash* (Princeton, New Jersey, 2004), p 92; Carswell, pp 92–4; Dickson, p 100; Carswell, p 94; Julian Hoppit, *A Land of Liberty?* (Oxford, 2000), p 335; Kleer, pp 186–8; Clapham, vol 1, p 84; Dickson, pp 145, 192–3; Carswell, p 135.

16 Hoppit, p 335; Dickson, p 139; Hoppit, p 335; Jenny Uglow, *Hogarth* (1997), p 89; Dickson, p 139; Carswell, pp 150–1; Kleer, p 185; Dickson, pp 165–6; Carswell, pp 164, 168; 11A/107/1, 12 Oct 1720; Giuseppi, p 48.

17 Carswell, pp 169–70; Dickson, pp 179–80, 380; Larry Neal, 'How it all began', *Financial History Review*, Oct 2000, p 128; 10A/61/6, fo 497; Giuseppi, p 45.

18 Daniel Defoe, *A Tour Thro' the Whole Island of Great Britain* (1927 edn), vol 1, p 342; Dickson, p 378; Clapham, vol 1, p 92; Acres, vol 1, p 162; Julia Rudolph, 'Jurisdictional controversy and the credibility of common law', in Coffman, *Questioning*, p 106; Paul Langford, *A Polite and Commercial People* (Oxford, 1989), p 179; Clapham, vol 1, pp 230–1;

11A/107/2, 19 Aug 1731; Ann M. Carlos and Larry Neal, 'The Micro-Foundations of the Early London Capital Market', *Economic History Review*, Aug 2006, pp 498, 500; Dickson, pp 276, 279–80; Norman Hunt, 'The Russia Company and the Bank of England', *Listener*, 3 Nov 1960; *OL*, June 2006, p 52 (Kenneth J. Cozens).

19 Acres, vol 1, pp 152–3; *OL*, Spring 1991, p 21 (Derrick Byatt), June 1933, pp 95–8 (W. Marston Acres); Acres, vol 1, pp 123–4; Hewitt and Keyworth, p 26; Acres, vol 1, pp 158–9, 153–4; 11A/107/2, 25 Sept 1728; *OL*, Sept 1937, pp 216–18 (Acres).

20 Abramson, pp 29–32, 48–9; Acres, vol 1, p 130.

CHAPTER 2 A GREAT ENGINE OF STATE

1 Clapham, vol 1, p 232; *Cobbett's Parliamentary History of England, Vol X* (1812), col 62; Historical Manuscripts Commission, *Manuscripts of the Earl of Egmont: Diary of the First Earl of Egmont (Viscount Percival)*, Vol II (1923), pp 380–1; Historical Manuscripts Commission, *The Manuscripts of the Earl of Carlisle* (1897), pp 182–3; *Egmont*, p 396.

2 G4/17, 5 March 1742; R. D. Richards, 'The First Fifty Years of the Bank of England', in J. G. van Dillen (ed), *History of the Principal Public Banks* (The Hague, 1934), pp 216–17; P. G. M. Dickson, *The Financial Revolution in England* (1967), p 217.

3 *Gentleman's Magazine*, Sept 1745, p 500; G4/17, 26 Sept 1745; *Gentleman's Magazine*, Sept 1745, pp 499–500; Acres, vol 1, p 181.

4 E. L. Hargreaves, *The National Debt* (1930), pp 52–3; G7/3, 31 Jan 1750; *Old England*, 3 Feb 1750; L. S. Sutherland, 'Samson Gideon and the Reduction on Interest, 1749–50', *Economic History Review*, Feb 1946, p 27; *General Advertiser*, 19 Feb 1750; G7/3, 27 Feb 1750; *General Advertiser*, 28 Feb 1750; Dickson, p 236; Acres, vol 1, p 184; Dickson, pp 322–3. In general, the two key accounts of Pelham's scheme and how it played out are those by Sutherland and Dickson.

5 J. A. S. L. Leighton-Boyce, *Smiths the Bankers, 1658–1958* (1958), p 75; Giuseppi, p 56; Acres, vol 1, p 186; Julian Hoppit, 'Financial Crises in Eighteenth-Century England', *Economic History Review*, Feb 1986, pp 49–50; Michael C. Lovell, 'The Role of the Bank of England as Lender of Last Resort in the Crises of the Eighteenth Century', *Explorations in Entrepreneurial History*, Oct 1957, pp 9–17.

6 Abramson, p 60; Joseph A. Schumpeter, *History of Economic Analysis* (1954), p 696; A. Anderson, *An Historical and Chronological Deduction of the Origin of Commerce* (1764), vol II, p 375.

7 Clapham, vol 1, pp 102–3; J. E. D. Binney, *British Public Finance and Administration, 1774–92* (1958), pp 97–100; Abramson, p 70; Anne L.

Murphy, 'Making the Market: Trading Debt at the Eighteenth-Century Bank of England', *European Association for Banking and Financial History (EABH) Papers*, 2014, pp 16–17, 30.

8 Dickson, pp 382–8; Clapham, vol 1, pp 70–1, 174.

9 Elisa Newby, 'Macroeconomic Implications of Gold Reserve Policy of the Bank of England during the Eighteenth Century', Centre for Dynamic Macroeconomic Analysis working paper, University of St Andrews, Feb 2007.

10 J. K. Horsefield, 'The Bank and Its Treasure', *Economica*, May 1940, pp 162–3; Sheila Lambert (ed), *House of Commons Papers: George III, Vol 105, Third Report from the Committee of Secrecy appointed to examine and state the total amount of outstanding demands on the Bank of England ...*, pp 26–7; Clapham, vol 1, pp 171, 173.

11 J. H. Clapham, 'The Private Business of the Bank of England, 1744–1800', *Economic History Review*, Oct 1941, pp 80–2; Lovell, p 12; Philip Ziegler, *The Sixth Great Power* (1988), p 51; Stanley D. Chapman, *Raphael Bicentenary, 1787–1987* (1987), pp 7–8.

12 Clapham, 'Private Business', pp 83–7; Adam Smith, *An Inquiry into the Nature and Causes of the Wealth of Nations* (1976 OUP edn), pp 318–20.

13 W. Marston Acres, 'Directors of the Bank of England', in *Notes and Queries*, 27 July 1940 to 24 August 1940, plus 3 Feb 1951; ADM30/11; *OL*, Dec 2005, p 144 (Kenneth J. Cozens and Suzanne J. Davis), March 1935, pp 13–14 (Acres); ADM30/12; John Thornton (ed), *The Book of Yearly Recollections of Samuel Thornton, Esq.* (Ewell, 1891), p 9; Abramson, p 95.

14 Abramson, p 95; Acres, 'Directors'.

15 Sir Lewis Namier, *The Structure of Politics at the Accession of George III* (1957 edn), pp 341–2; Sir Lewis Namier and John Brooke, *The House of Commons, 1754–1790* (1964), vol II, pp 408–9.

16 John H. Appleby, 'James Theobald, F.R.S. (1688–1759), Merchant and Natural Historian', *Notes and Records of the Royal Society of London*, July 1996, pp 179–89; *Gentleman's Magazine*, Jan 1787, p 94; *OL*, March [?] 1947, pp 4–9, Dec 1947, pp 234–5 (Reginald Saw); Ruth Guilding, *Owning the Past* (New Haven, 2014), pp 165–6, 335; *OL*, Dec 1935, pp 241–4 (Acres).

17 Clapham, vol 1, pp 100–1; *The Parliamentary History of England, Vol XXII* (1814), Commons debate 13 June 1781, cols 523–4; Acres, vol 1, pp 186–7.

18 *London Chronicle*, 30 June 1772; Acres, vol 1, p 200; Clapham, vol 1, pp 245–6; Roger Fulford, *Glyn's, 1753–1953* (1953), p 27; Clapham, vol 1, p 247; Henry Hamilton, 'The Failure of the Ayr Bank, 1772', *Economic History*

Review, April 1956, pp 412–15. See also: Paul Kosmetatos, 'The winding-up of the Ayr Bank, 1772–1827', *Financial History Review*, Aug 2014.

19 Clapham, vol 1, p 175; Acres, vol 1, pp 204–7; Clapham, vol 1, p 176; *Times Literary Supplement*, 29 May 2015 (T. H. Breen); Acres, vol 1, p 202; Clapham, vol 1, pp 251–2; Acres, vol 1, p 208; Larry Neal, *The Rise of Financial Capitalism* (Cambridge, 1990), p 211.

20 Garland Garvey Smith (ed), *Thomas Holcroft's A Plain and Succinct Narrative of the Gordon Riots, London, 1780* (Atlanta, Georgia, 1944), pp 27–8; Abramson, pp 83–4; Jerry White, *London in the Eighteenth Century* (2012), pp 540–1; G8/1, 20 June 1780; Bank of England (John Keyworth), 'As Safe as the Bank of England' (1993); Acres, vol 1, p 210.

21 Clapham, vol 1, pp 177–8; *Parliamentary History Vol XXII*, cols 517, 519, 522–3, 528–9; Clapham, vol 1, p 182.

22 Feavearyear, p 176; Clapham, vol 1, p 255; J. K. Horsefield, 'The Duties of the Banker', *Economica*, Feb 1941, p 45; Clapham, vol 1, p 256; Feavearyear, pp 176–7.

23 Boyd Hilton, *A Mad, Bad, and Dangerous People?* (Oxford, 2006), p 114; Clapham, vol 1, pp 186–7; Lawrence Taylor and R. G. Thorne, 'Thornton, Samuel', in R. G. Thorne (ed), *The History of Parliament: The House of Commons, 1790–1820* (1986), p 376; Clapham, vol 1, pp 188–91.

24 Hoppit, 'Financial Crises', pp 54–5; Clapham, vol 1, pp 258–9; White, *London*, p 548.

CHAPTER 3 A STEADY AND UNREMITTING ATTENTION

1 ADM30/17.

2 John Francis, *History of the Bank of England* (1848), vol 1, pp 168–9; Acres, vol 1, p 169; John Keyworth, 'William and the Bank of England' (1989, supplement to official programme book marking tercentenary of William and Mary's Coronation); Abramson, pp 50–3.

3 Acres, vol 1, pp 188–9; Abramson, pp 61–79.

4 *OL*, Sept 2004, pp 92–3 (Graham Kentfield), Summer 1982, pp 76–8 (John Deacon); Abramson, pp 88–90, 92; A Gentleman of the Bank, &c., *The Bank of England's Vade Mecum; or Sure Guide* (1782), pp 3, 11, 22–3; Acres, vol 1, pp 216–17.

5 M5/471, 30 Sept 1788; M5/748, 15 Oct 1788; *OL*, March 2004, p 25 (John Keyworth), Spring 1982, p 18 (Kenneth Ireland); Abramson, pp 96–9.

6 Abramson, p 99; M5/748, 11 Dec 1788; Giles Waterfield, 'Soane's Stock Rises Again', *Country Life*, 15 June 1989, p 162; Abramson, pp 102–6.

7 Acres, vol 1, pp 228–32; *OL*, Dec 1935, p 244 (Acres); Acres, vol 1, pp 226, 234–5; *OL*, Dec 1932, pp 232–6 (Acres), Sept 1933, pp 179–81 (Acres).

8   Acres, vol 1, pp 254–7; *ODNB*, Anita McConnell, 'Abraham Newland'.
9   M5/451.
10 Acres, vol 1, p 234.
11 The sources for these pararaphs on the 1783–4 Committee of Inspection are: M5/212–13; M5/471; Acres, vol 1, pp 238–43; Anne Murphy, 'Georgian Banking Blunders', *BBC History Magazine*, Jan 2013, pp 42–3, 'Clock-watching: work and working-time at the late-eighteenth-century Bank of England', *Past and Present*, 2017
12 Acres, vol 1, pp 243–50.
13 Acres, vol 1, pp 251–2; *OL*, June 1958, pp 74–5 (J. A. Giuseppi), June 1996, p 51 (John Keyworth).

CHAPTER 4   AN ELDERLY LADY IN THE CITY

1   A. Allardyce, *An Address to the Proprietors of the Bank of England* (1797), pp 8, 10, 30; John Thornton (ed), *The Book of Yearly Recollections of Samuel Thornton, Esq.* (Ewell, 1891), p 82; Frank Whitson Fetter, *Development of British Monetary Orthodoxy, 1797–1875* (Cambridge, Massachusetts, 1965), pp 13–15; Clapham, vol 1, pp 263–5; Stanley D. Chapman, *Raphael Bicentenary 1787–1987* (1987), p 8; ADM30/6, Daniel Giles file, 4 May 1793; *OL*, March 2003, p 11 (John Keyworth).
2   S. R. Cope, *Walter Boyd* (Gloucester, 1983), p 63; ADM30/6, Giles file, 30 July 1795; John Ehrman, *The Younger Pitt: The Reluctant Transition* (1983), p 525; Clapham, vol 1, pp 195, 267; Feavearyear, pp 179–80; M5/472, 2 Dec 1795, 31 Dec 1795.
3   Clapham, vol 1, pp 265–6, 269–70; Walter Boyd, *A Letter to the Right Honourable William Pitt* (1801), Appendix B; *Reports from the Committees of Secrecy (1797) on the Outstanding Demands of the Bank of England* (1826), p 98; Kenneth Garlick and Angus Macintyre (eds), *The Diary of Joseph Farington, Volume II* (1978), p 629; Jagjit S. Chadha and Elisa Newby, '"Midas, transmuting all, into paper"' (School of Economics, University of Kent, Discussion Paper, Sept 2013), p 5; *Farington, Volume III* (1979), p 668; Acres, vol 1, pp 270–1; Ehrman, p 639.
4   *Yearly Recollections*, pp 93–4; Feavearyear, pp 181–2; Clapham, vol 1, p 266; *Reports from the Committees of Secrecy*, pp 103–4; Hiroki Shin, 'Paper Money, the Nation, and the Suspension of Cash Payments in 1797', *Historical Journal*, June 2015, p 423; Feavearyear, p 182.
5   Feavearyear, p 182; M5/472, 26 Feb 1797; Acres, vol 1, opp p 276; Shin, 'Paper Money', pp 432–4; *Farington, Volume III*, p 798; Feavearyear, pp 184–5; Hiroki Shin, 'The Culture of Paper Money in Britain: The Bank of England Note during the Bank Restriction Period, 1797–1821' (University of Cambridge PhD, 2008), p 71.

6   *Reports from the Committees of Secrecy*, pp 12, 14, 17, 37, 22–3, 33, 48, 73.

7   *The Parliamentary History of England, Vol XXXIII* (1818), cols 351, 358, 372–3, 394.

8   Martin Rowson, 'Poisoned pen', *Guardian*, 21 March 2015; *OL*, June 1989, front cover, summer 1983, p 83 (John Keyworth); Shin, 'Culture', p 178; *OL*, March 1927, pp 5–7 (Acres).

9   M5/472, 22 Dec 1803; *Yearly Recollections*, p 151; Clapham, vol 2, p 44.

10 E. L. Hargreaves, *The National Debt* (1930), p 291; Feavearyear, p 193; Roger Knight, *Britain against Napoleon* (2013), pp 390, 392; Ian P. H. Duffy, 'The Discount Policy of the Bank of England during the Suspension of Cash Payments, 1797–1821', *Economic History Review*, Feb 1982, pp 76–7; Elisa Newby, 'Sustainable Monetary Policy: Lessons and Evidence from the Bank Suspension Period, 1797–1821' (University of St Andrews PhD, 2008), p 5; Kwasi Kwarteng, *War and Gold* (2014), p 50.

11 Randall McGowen, 'The Bank of England and the Policing of Forgery, 1797–1821', *Past and Present*, Feb 2005, pp 87–9; Deirdre Palk, *Gender, Crime and Judicial Discretion, 1780–1830* (Woodbridge, 2006), pp 148–51.

12 Virginia Hewitt, 'Beware of Imitations', *Numismatic Chronicle*, 1998, p 200; *OL*, March 1997, p 6 (John Keyworth); Hewitt and Keyworth, pp 53, 67.

13 Feavearyear, pp 191–2; Boyd, *Letter*, pp 7, 57, 65–6; J. K. Horsefield, 'The Duties of a Banker – II', *Economica*, May 1944, pp 77, 83; *Yearly Recollections*, p 112; Henry Thornton, *An Enquiry into the Nature of Effects of the Paper Credit of Great Britain* (1939 edn), pp 109–10; Horsefield, 'Duties', pp 78–81.

14 Fetter, *Development*, pp 39–40; Piero Sraffa (ed), *The Works and Correspondence of David Ricardo, Volume III* (Cambridge, 1951), pp 131–3; R. S. Sayers, 'Ricardo's Views on Monetary Questions', in T. S. Ashton and R. S. Sayers (eds), *Papers in English Monetary History* (1953), p 82; F. W. Fetter, 'The Bullion Report Re-examined', in Ashton and Sayers, *Papers*, p 67.

15 *Report, together with Minutes of Evidence, and Accounts, from the Select Committee on the High Price of Gold Bullion* (House of Commons, 8 June 1810), pp 79, 89, 128, 89–90, 95–6; *Ricardo*, p 369; *Report*, pp 132–3, 143, 146–7, 20–4; Fetter, *Development*, p 61.

16 *Yearly Recollections*, p 150; T. C. Hansard (ed), *Parliamentary Debates*, vol XIX (1812), cols 1061, 1163, 1161; Fetter, *Development*, pp 53–4; Boyd Hilton, *A Mad, Bad, and Dangerous People?* (Oxford, 2006), p 258; Clapham, vol 2, p 28; Hilton, p 258; *Ricardo*, vol III, p 133.

17 Clapham, vol 2, pp 31, 33; David Kynaston, *The Chancellor of the Exchequer* (Lavenham, 1980), pp 20–1; G6/184, 16 May 1815; Clapham, vol 1, pp 37, 39.

18 Abramson, chaps 4 and 5; Abramson, pp 108–10; *Farington, Volume II*, p 638; Abramson, pp 162, 133, 96; *Leigh's New Picture of London* (1818), p 294.

19 *Farington, Volume IV* (1979), pp 1274, 1277; Acres, vol 1, pp 294–8.

20 ADM30/1730/17; Anne L. Murphy, '"Writes a fair hand and appears to be well qualified": the recruitment of Bank of England clerks, 1800–1815', *Financial History Review*, April 2015, pp 19–44; G6/184, 3 May 1815.

21 Acres, vol 2, pp 364–8; *OL*, June 1924, pp 230–4 (B. T. K. Smith), March 1929, pp 12–17, June 1929, pp 75–81.

CHAPTER 5 ALL THE OBLOQUY

1 Piero Sraffa (ed), *The Works and Correspondence of David Ricardo* (Cambridge, 1952), vol V, pp 463–4, vol VI, pp 338, 268; T. C. Hansard (ed), *Parliamentary Debates*, vol XXXII (1816), 13 Feb 1816, cols 461, 463, 477–8, 502, 504, 506, vol XXXV (1817), 19 Feb 1817, col 449.

2 John Thornton (ed), *The Book of Yearly Recollections of Samuel Thornton, Esq.* (Ewell, 1891), p 167; Hansard, *Parliamentary Debates*, vol XXXIV (1816), 1–3 May 1816, cols 160–3, 251, vol XXXV, 19 Feb 1817, col 464; Feavearyear, p 216; Giuseppi, p 80; Clapham, vol 2, pp 64–5; Acres, vol 1, pp 315–16; Huskisson Papers (British Library), Add Ms, 38,741, fos 251–2.

3 Randall McGowen, 'The Bank of England and the Policing of Forgery, 1797–1821', *Past and Present*, Feb 2005, p 87; *OL*, March 1959, p 44 (C. A. West); Abramson, p 123; Virginia Hewitt, 'Beware of Imitations', *Numismatic Chronicle*, 1998, p 211; Frank Whitson Fetter, *Development of British Monetary Orthodoxy, 1797–1875* (Cambridge, Massachusetts, 1965), p 73; Kathryn Cave (ed), *The Diary of Joseph Farington, Volume XV* (1984), p 5318.

4 Fetter, *Development*, p 85; *Minutes of Evidence taken before the Secret Committee on the Expediency of The Bank resuming Cash Payments* (House of Commons, 6 May 1819), pp 26, 51–2, 79; Boyd Hilton, *Corn, Cash, Commerce* (Oxford, 1977), p 46; Hansard, *Parliamentary Debates*, vol XL (1819), col 604; Boyd Hilton, *A Mad, Bad, and Dangerous People?* (Oxford, 2006), p 325; Hilton, *Corn*, p 46; Hansard, *Parliamentary Debates*, vol XL, cols 683, 689, 741, 744, 746, 800. For a close reading of the attitudes towards bullionism of individual Bank directors, see: J. K. Horsefield, 'The Bankers and the Bullionists in 1819', *Journal of Political Economy*, Oct 1949, pp 442–8.

5 *Minutes of Evidence taken before the Secret Committee*, p 157; Hilton, *Corn*, pp 56–7; Huskisson, fos 251–2; Abramson, p 123; Hilton, *Corn*, pp 87–8; Clapham, vol 2, p 75; Hilton, *Corn*, p 89.

6 D. P. O'Brien and John Creedy, *Darwin's Clever Neighbour* (Cheltenham, 2010), pp 244–6; Stephen Fay, 'Runs in the Bank', *MCC Magazine*, Autumn/Winter 2014, p 22; *Darwin's*, pp 253–4; *OL*, March 1932, pp 14–15 (Acres); *ODNB*, A. C. Howe, 'Palmer, (John) Horsley'; *Darwin's*, p 352; UCL/*Legacies of British Slave-ownership*/database.

7 Acres, vol 2, pp 399–400; Anthony Howe, 'From "Old Corruption" to "New Probity"', *Financial History Review*, April 1994, pp 23–41; Sir John Soane's Museum, S.M. Private Correspondence, II.T.7.1; Abramson, pp 177–88; S.M. Private Correspondence, I.B.2.14; *OL*, March 2004, p 25.

8 *OL*, Sept 1929, p 167; Feavearyear, p 233; Clapham, vol 2, pp 81–9, 76; Acres, vol 2, p 419–20; *OL*, Dec 1934, pp 255–61 (Acres).

9 *Yearly Recollections*, p 196; Hilton, *Corn*, pp 202–15; Feavearyear, p 235; K. F. Dixon, 'The Development of the London Money Market, 1780–1830' (University of London PhD, 1962), pp 178–9.

10 Feavearyear, p 236; E. M. Forster, *Marianne Thornton, 1797–1887* (1956), pp 106–14; Clapham, vol 2, p 99; Walter Bagehot, *Lombard Street* (1873), pp 51–2; John A. James, 'Panics, payments disruptions and the Bank of England before 1826', *Financial History Review*, Dec 2012, pp 301–2; Liverpool Papers (British Library), Add Ms, 38,371, fo 77; Francis Bamford and the Duke of Wellington (eds), *The Journal of Mrs Arbuthnot* (1950), vol 1, pp 426–7; Kynaston, vol 1, p 70; *Arbuthnot*, p 428; Clapham, vol 2, pp 100–2; *OL*, Sept 1929, p 168.

11 Morgan, pp 88–9; *Darwin's*, pp 298–9.

12 Morgan, p 100; Hilton, *Corn*, pp 237–8; J. K. Horsefield, 'The Opinions of Horsley Palmer', *Economica*, May 1949, pp 150–2; Feavearyear, pp 245–50; Hilton, *Corn*, pp 239–41; *Darwin's*, pp 350–1; Brian Jenkins, *Henry Goulburn, 1784–1856* (Liverpool, 1996), pp 207–8; M5/201, 23 April 1830; Jenkins, pp 213–14.

13 Acres, vol 2, p 456; *OL*, March 1984, pp 26–9 (David J. Moss); Michael Brock, *The Great Reform Act* (1973), p 298; *Times*, 15–16 May 1832; G8/25, 16 May 1832; Fetter, *Development*, p 135; Brock, p 306.

14 *Report from the Committee of Secrecy on the Bank of England Charter; with the Minutes of Evidence* (1832), qq 72, 178–82, 2341, 5127, 5130, 3689, 4946, 4773, 3395, 3402, 3415, 2878–9; Clapham, vol 2, p 129; Feavearyear, p 252; *Report from the Committee of Secrecy*, qq 2710–11; Feavearyear, p 251; Fetter, *Development*, pp 156–7.

15 Acres, vol 2, p 429; *OL*, June 1926, pp 258–60 (Acres); Acres, vol 2, pp 434, 428; *OL*, June 1935, pp 109–12 (Acres).

16 Dieter Ziegler, 'Central Banking in the English Provinces in the Second Quarter of the Nineteenth Century', *Business History*, Oct 1989, p 38; David J. Moss, 'Central banking and the provincial system', *Financial History Review*, April 1995, p 7; Dieter Ziegler, *Central Bank, Peripheral Industry* (Leicester, 1990), pp 9–31.

17 Ziegler, *Central Bank*, pp 5–6; *Darwin's*, p 299; Clapham, vol 2, pp 138–9; Moss, 'Central Banking', p 20; Ziegler, *Central Bank*, p 9. In general on the branch banks in this period, see also: David J. Moss, 'The Bank of England and the country banks', *Economic History Review*, Nov 1981, 'The Bank of England and the establishment of a branch system, 1826–1829', *Canadian Journal of History*, 1992; R. O. Roberts, 'Bank of England Branch Discounting, 1826–59', *Economica*, Aug 1958; Roy Clifford, *The Birmingham Branch of the Bank of England, 1826–34* (c 1998); M. Collins, 'The Bank of England at Liverpool, 1827–1844', *Business History*, 1972; Jean Welsh, 'A History of Banking and the Bank of England in Newcastle and the North East of England, 1815–1850' (undated dissertation at Bank of England Information Centre).

18 Edward Nevin and E. W. Davis, *The London Clearing Banks* (1970), p 61; T. E. Gregory, *The Westminster Bank* (1936), vol 1, pp 151, 164; J. K. Horsefield, 'The Bank of England as Mentor', *Economic History Review*, Aug 1949, p 84.

19 ADM30/10, James Pattison file; Jessica M. Lepler, *The Many Panics of 1937* (Cambridge, 2013), p 53; The Baring Archive, DEP 74 vol 3, Diaries of Joshua Bates, 17 September 1836; G8/29, 26 Oct 1836; Lepler, p 60; G6/286, items 52–4, 81; Lepler, chap 4.

20 Barclays Archives, 25/265 (286, 278, 286); G4/59, 21 March 1837; D. P. O'Brien (ed), *The Correspondence of Lord Overstone, Volume 1* (Cambridge, 1971), p 221; Lepler, pp 167–72.

21 Muriel Emmie Hidy, *George Peabody* (New York, 1978), p 84; Morrison Cryder records (LMA), Ms 11,720, folder one, 21 May 1837; Barclays, 25/265 (289, 290); G4/60, 30 May 1937; Caroline Dakers, *A Genius for Money* (2011), p 133; Barclays, 25/265 (293); G4/60, 1 June 1837; Barclays, 25/265 (293); *Times*, 27 June 1837.

22 *OL*, Dec 1923, pp 136–7; Acres, vol 2, pp 481–3; Abramson, p 79; G8/29, 26 Oct 1836; Acres, vol 2, p 479.

23 Clapham, vol 2, p 162; The Baring Archive, DEP 74 vol 3, Diaries of Joshua Bates, 20 July 1839; Clapham, vol 2, pp 168–9; Marc Flandreau, 'Central bank cooperation in historical perspective', *Economic History Review*, Nov 1997, p 742; diary of Charles Churchill senior (LMA), Ms 5,762, vol 17; Niall Ferguson, *The World's Banker* (1998), pp 398–9; Stanley Chapman, *The Rise of Merchant Banking* (1984), p 165; Flandreau, p 743.

24 *Overstone*, vol 1, pp 250–74.

25 J. Horsley Palmer, *The Causes and Consequences of the Pressure upon the Money-Market* (1837), pp 10, 33, 42; Samuel James Loyd, *Reflections suggested by a Perusal of Mr J. Horsley Palmer's Pamphlet* (1837), pp 13, 10, 17; *Overstone*, vol 1, p 93; Daniel Hardcastle, jnr, *Banks and Bankers* (1842), p 164; Michael Collins, 'The Langton Papers', *Economica*, Feb 1972, p 59; P. L. Cottrell, 'The Bank of England in transition, 1836–1860', in Franz Bosbach and Hans Pohl (eds), *Das Kreditwesen in der Neuzeit* (Munich, 1997), p 105; *Hansard's Parliamentary Debates*, vol LXXIV (1844), 6 May 1844, col 750. See also: J. K. Horsefield, 'The Origins of the Bank Charter Act, 1844', in T. S. Ashton and R. S. Sayers (eds), *Papers in English Monetary History* (1953), pp 109–25.

26 Helpful summaries of the Bank Charter Act include: Clapham, vol 2, pp 183–4; Fetter, p 185; Feavearyear, pp 272–4; Morgan, pp 115–16.

27 *Economist*, 11 May 1844; Churchill, vol 22; Lytton Strachey and Roger Fulford (eds), *The Greville Memoirs, 1814–60* (1938), vol V, p 173; *Times*, 8 May 1844, 14 May 1844; *Economist*, 18 May 1844.

28 Charles Stuart Parker (ed), *Sir Robert Peel from his Private Papers* (1899), vol II, p 570; *Circular to Bankers*, 14 June 1844; M5/206 (item 65); *Circular to Bankers*, 14 June 1844; *Hansard's Parliamentary Debates*, vol LXXV (1844), 13 June 1844, cols 804, 809–11, 851, 869; *Overstone*, vol 1, p 359; Jenkins, p 308; Clapham, vol 2, p 270; *Overstone*, vol 1, p 363; *Darwin's*, pp xlvii–xlviii.

CHAPTER 6 THE EFFECTS OF TIGHT LACING

1 M5/206, item 79; Acres, vol 2, p 501; Richard Roberts, 'The Bank of England and the City', in Roberts and Kynaston, pp 156–7; W. M. Scammell, *The London Discount Market* (1968), p 147.

2 *Bankers' Magazine*, April 1845, p 53; King, p 134; H. M. Boot, 'The Commercial Crisis of 1847' (University of Hull PhD, 1979), p 369; Clapham, vol 2, pp 199, 213.

3 Rudiger Dornbusch and Jacob A. Frenkel, 'The Gold Standard and the Bank of England in the Crisis of 1847', in Michael D. Bordo and Anna J. Schwartz (eds), *A Retrospective on the Classical Gold Standard, 1821–1931* (Chicago, 1984), pp 245–6; Gareth Campbell, 'Government Policy during the British Railway Mania and the 1847 Commercial Crisis', in Nicholas Dimsdale and Anthony Hotson (eds), *British Financial Crises since 1825* (Oxford, 2014), p 71; D. P. O'Brien and John Creedy, *Darwin's Clever Neighbour* (Cheltenham, 2010), pp 417–18; Feavearyear, p 282; Kynaston, vol 1, p 154; Dornbusch and Frenkel, pp 249–50; Anthony Howe, *Free Trade and Liberal England, 1846–1946* (Oxford, 1997),

pp 55–6; D. P. O'Brien (ed), *The Correspondence of Lord Overstone* (Cambridge, 1971), vol 1, p 383.

4 Feavearyear, p 283; Royal Bank of Scotland Archives PRE/1/2 Partners' meetings minute book of Prescott, Grote, Ames, Cave & Grote, 19 August 1847; Jardine Matheson & Co records (Cambridge University Library), II.A.1.10, reel 300, no 3, 128; *Overstone*, vol 1, p 391; Anthony Howe, 'From "Old Corruption" to "New Probity"', *Financial History Review*, April 1994, p 32; Clapham, vol 2, pp 198–204; King, p 142; Jardine Matheson, II.O.5, private letters from London, 1812–82, reel 463, no P.115; *OL*, Dec 1929, pp 236–7 (Acres).

5 Jardine Matheson, II.A.1.10, reel 300, no 3, 141; Boot, 'Commercial Crisis', p 262; RBS Archives PRE/1/2 Partners' meetings minute book of Prescott, Grote, Ames, Cave & Grote, 21 October 1847; Feavearyear, p 284; *Economist*, 23 Oct 1847; Clapham, vol 2, pp 207–8; Feavearyear, p 284; King, p 146.

6 M5/208, 23 Oct 1847; Clapham, vol 2, pp 208–9; M5/527; Dornbusch and Frenkel, p 252; Feavearyear, p 285; *Overstone*, vol 1, p 397.

7 Boot, 'Commercial Crisis', p 280; Robert Blake, *Disraeli* (1966), p 263; *Economist*, 30 Oct 1847; Feavearyear, p 286; Catherine Molyneux, 'Reform and Process', in Michael J. Turner (ed), *Reform and Reformers in Nineteenth Century Britain* (Sunderland, 2004), p 73; Frank Whitson Fetter, *Development of British Monetary Orthodoxy, 1797–1875* (Cambridge, Massachusetts, 1965), pp 260–1; Feavearyear, pp 286–7.

8 Howe, *Free Trade*, p 56; *Overstone*, vol 1, p 391; *Times*, 14 Sept 1847, 17 Sept 1847; *Overstone*, vol 1, p 395.

9 G4/70, 20 Jan 1848, 3 Feb 1848, 10 Feb 1848; Howe, 'From "Old Corruption"', pp 23–41; J. C. Levenson *et al* (eds), *The Letters of Henry Adams, Volume 1* (1982), p 465.

10 Giuseppi, p 110; *Morning Chronicle*, 11 April 1848; Records of the London Stock Exchange (Guildhall Library), Ms 14,600, vol 20, 10 April 1848; *Morning Chronicle*, 11–12 April 1848.

11 The Baring Archive, DEP 74 vol 4, Diaries of Joshua Bates, 10 October 1852; Feavearyear, p 288; E. J. Hobsbawm, *Industry and Empire* (1969 Pelican edn), pp 139–40.

12 Acres, vol 2, pp 512–14; Dieter Ziegler, 'Central Banking in the English Provinces in the Second Quarter of the Nineteenth Century', *Business History*, Oct 1989, p 44; Feavearyear, p 287; King, pp 161–9.

13 John Brooke and Mary Sorensen (eds), *The Prime Minister's Papers: W. E. Gladstone, Volume II, Autobiographica* (1971), pp 128–9; Richard Shannon, *Gladstone, Volume 1, 1809–1865* (1982), p 289; John Morley, *The Life of William Ewart Gladstone* (1905 two-vol edn), vol 1, p 518;

Clapham, vol 2, p 253; Marc Flandreau, 'Central bank cooperation', *Economic History Review*, Nov 1997, pp 747–8.

14 M5/209; Feavearyear, p 290; *Report from the Select Committee on the Bank Acts* (July 1857), qq 328–32; Feavearyear, pp 290–1; Norman St John Stevas (ed), *The Collected Works of Walter Bagehot, Volume Nine* (1978), p 360.

15 14A185/8, item 71; Clapham, vol 2, p 227; 14A185/8, item 95; Nicholas Dimsdale and Anthony Hotson, 'Financial Crises and Economic Activity in the UK since 1825', in Dimsdale and Hotson, p 39; M5/454, 29 Oct 1857; *Overstone*, vol 2, pp 758, 764–5; Clapham, vol 2, p 229; M5/454, 7 Nov 1857.

16 King, p 198; M5/454, 9–10 Nov 1857; Feavearyear, pp 293–4; 14A185/9, item 140; *Overstone*, vol 2, p 786; Walter Bagehot, *Lombard Street* (1873), p 179; M6/65.

17 Kathleen Burk, *Morgan Grenfell, 1838–1988* (Oxford, 1989), pp 21–2; Kynaston, vol 1, p 197; 14A185/9, item 144; *Overstone*, vol 2, pp 811, 819, 822–3.

18 M5/455, 1 Jan 1858; George J. Goschen, *The Theory of the Foreign Exchanges* (1879 edn of the third edn), p xii; M5/455, 8 Jan 1858.

19 *Report from the Select Committee on the Bank Acts* (July 1858), qq 86–7, 189–91, 394–5; Elmer Wood, *English Theories of Central Banking Control, 1819–1858* (Cambridge, Massachusetts, 1939), p 171; Acres, vol 2, pp 520–1.

20 M5/455, 11 March 1858; *Times*, 15 March 1858; Clapham, vol 2, p 240; *Report from the Select Committee* (1858), q 399; Wood, p 134; *Bagehot, Volume 9*, p 382.

21 M5/457, 31 Jan 1860, 12 April 1860, 14 April 1860, 16 April 1860; 14A185/37, item 418; M5/457, 17 April 1860; Clapham, vol 2, p 244; M5/457, 19 April 1860; HSBC Group Archives, UK M 0005, General board minute book.

22 Howe, 'From "Old Corruption"', pp 39–40; Clapham, vol 2, pp 255–6; Howe, 'From "Old Corruption"', p 39; M5/202; *Daily News*, 8 Feb 1861; Giuseppi, p 117; Morley, vol 1, p 686; Howe, 'From "Old Corruption"', p 40.

23 Geoffrey Elliott, *The Mystery of Overend and Gurney* (2006); John Stephen Flynn, *Sir Robert N. Fowler* (1893), p 150; Bertram Wodehouse Currie, *Recollections, Letters and Journals* (Roehampton, 1901), vol 1, p 61.

24 See generally: Forrest Capie, 'The emergence of the Bank of England as a mature central bank', in Donald Winch and Patrick K. O'Brien (eds), *The Political Economy of British Historical Experience, 1688–1914* (Oxford, 2002), pp 303–5; Marc Flandreau and Stefano Ugolini, 'The Crisis of 1866', in Dimsdale and Hotson, pp 76–93.

25 Philip Ziegler, *The Sixth Great Power* (1988), p 182; RBS Archives GM/1118, letter from Bertram Wodehouse Currie to his father Raikes Currie, 11 May 1866; *Times*, 11 May 1866; RBS Archives PRE/1/6 Partners' meetings minute book of Prescott, Grote, Cave & Cave, 11 May 1866; *Times*, 12 May 1866; *Bagehot*, vol 13 (1986), p 608; Clapham, vol 2, p 264; H. C. G. Mathew (ed), *The Gladstone Diaries, Volume VI* (Oxford, 1978), p 436; diary of Sir Richard Biddulph Martin (Holland-Martin family archives), 12 May 1866; King, p 242.

CHAPTER 7 MATTERS OF CONDUCT AND BEHAVIOUR

1 *The Education of Henry Adams* (1918 edn), p 73; Abramson, pp 200–1; de Fraine, pp 26–8; M5/592, fo 250; E30/1, fo 29; George Santayana, *The Middle Span* (1947), p 37.

2 Clapham, vol 2, p 247; G4/89, 7 Feb 1867; Clapham, vol 2, pp 282–3; M5/489, Hammond Chubb, 'Report of the Expenses of the Bank from 1853', p 5; Clapham, vol 2, p 301.

3 ADM30/17, larger file, immediately after fo 21; M5/489, Chubb, 'Report', pp 10, 3, 12–13.

4 R. S. Sayers, *Lloyds Bank in the History of English Banking* (1957), p 151; Dieter Ziegler, *Central Bank, Peripheral Industry* (Leicester, 1990), pp 37–8; Hewitt and Keyworth, pp 111–12; *OL*, Dec 1995, pp 142–4 (Diana Moore).

5 This account is based on: Judy Slinn, *A History of Freshfields* (1984), pp 122–3; David C. Hanrahan, *The Great Fraud on the Bank of England* (2014); Nicholas Booth, *The Thieves of Threadneedle Street* (Stroud, 2015).

6 *OL*, Dec 1985, p 181 (Derrick Byatt); Hennessy, pp 47–8; Acres, vol 2, pp 538–40; *OL*, June 1921, pp 55–6 (A. G. Rowlett), Dec 1985, p 181 (Byatt).

7 *OL*, Dec 1927, p 165 (Acres); de Fraine, p 7; Acres, vol 2, p 550; M5/593, fos 6–7; E4/15.

8 Philip Kelley and Ronald Hudson (eds), *The Brownings' Correspondence: Volume 3* (Winfield, Kansas, 1985), pp 307–9; Philip Kelley and Scott Lewis (eds), *The Brownings' Correspondence: Volume 13* (Winfield, Kansas, 1995), p 299; ADM30/20, Browning Family file; *ODNB*, Rita McWilliams Tullbelg, 'Marshall, Alfred'; J. M. Keynes, 'Alfred Marshall, 1842–1924', in A. C. Pigou (ed), *Memorials of Alfred Marshall* (1925), pp 1–2.

9 de Fraine, pp 14–15; Byatt, p 80; *OL*, March 1967, p 5; Byatt, pp 102–3; ADM30/26, Matthew Marshall file; ADM30/30, Smee Family file; Byatt, p 96; Giuseppi, p 105.

10 ADM 30/17–18; Giuseppi, p 101; ADM30/17, fo 17; Acres, vol 2, p 557; E30/1, fo 8; ADM30/17, fo 27.

11 Acres, vol 2, pp 484–6; ADM30/17, fo 58A; Acres, vol 2, p 559; Elizabeth Hennessy, 'The Governors, Directors and Management of the Bank of England', in Roberts and Kynaston, p 202; M5/489, Chubb, 'Report', pp 12, 3; OL, Dec 1921, pp 150–1 (William Shand).

12 G4/89, 7 Feb 1867; E4/15; OL, Sept 1969, p 152, March 1965, p 28 (Wilbur C. Fish); de Fraine, pp 4–5.

13 Acres, vol 2, pp 486–7; OL, Sept 1922, p 255 (W. Courthope Forman), Dec 1935, p 263 (C. H. Goodman), March 1930, pp 9–10 (Allan Fea); Allan Fea, Recollections of Sixty Years (1927), p 149.

14 Acres, vol 2, pp 551–2; M5/654; E30/1, fo 37.

15 M5/235, 15 Feb 1858, 23 May 1859; M5/289, 5 July 1861.

16 OL, Sept 1922, pp 256–7 (W. Courthope Forman); M5/604, fos 107–11.

17 OL, March 1950, opp p 313; Giuseppi, p 104; ADM30/17, fo 31; OL, June 1950, p 407 (Giuseppi).

18 E30/1, fo 16; de Fraine, p 79; C82/6, fo 103.

CHAPTER 8 MONEY WILL NOT MANAGE ITSELF

1 Economist, 22 Sept 1866; Thomson Hankey, The Principles of Banking (1867), pp 25–6; Economist, 8 Dec 1866, 22 Dec 1866.

2 Times, 28 May 1869.

3 Times, 12 Nov 1872; Economist, 16 Nov 1872; Hankey, Principles (1873 edn), pp iii–ix; Walter Bagehot, Lombard Street (9th edn, 1888), pp 322, 326–8, 196–9.

4 R. S. Sayers, Central Banking after Bagehot (1957), p 9; Morgan, p 181; Hugh Rockoff, 'Walter Bagehot and the Theory of Central Banking', in Forrest Capie and Geoffrey E. Wood (eds), Financial Crises and the World Banking System (Basingstoke, 1986), pp 164, 172–3; John D. Turner, Banking in Crisis (Cambridge, 2014), p 143; records of Rathbone Bros & Co (Liverpool University Library), files of general correspond-ence, 1851–73, XXIV.1.24 (51–113), 17 Oct 1873; Bagehot, Lombard Street, pp 19–20. See also: John H. Wood, 'Bagehot's Lender of Last Resort', Independent Review, Winter 2003, pp 343–51; Vincent Bignon et al, 'Bagehot for beginners', Economic History Review, May 2012, pp 580–608.

5 Bagehot, Lombard Street, pp 41–2, 73, 230–40; Rathbone, files, 21 Oct 1873.

6 The Rothschild Archive (London), 000/84, 17 Sept 1869; Augustus Muir, Blyth, Greene, Jourdain & Company Limited, 1810–1960 (1961), pp 20,

24; ADM30/6; *Bankers' Magazine*, Feb 1888, pp 147–50; Boyle, pp 10–18; Anon (Wilfred Maude), *Antony Gibbs and Sons Limited: Merchants and Bankers, 1808–1958* (1958), p 27; Rachel Gibbs, *Pedigree of the Family of Gibbs* (1981 edn), p xix; *DBB*, William M. Mathew, 'Henry Hucks Gibbs, 1st Lord Aldenham'; M6/28, pp 18, 23, 26, 33.

7 D. P. O'Brien (ed), *The Correspondence of Lord Overstone* (Cambridge, 1971), vol 3, p 1315; Clapham, vol 2, p 309; Turner, p 85; L. S. Pressnell, 'Gold Reserves, Banking Reserves, and the Baring Crisis of 1890', in C. R. Whittlesey and J. S. G. Wilson (eds), *Essays in Money and Banking in Honour of R. S. Sayers* (1968), p 189; Michael Collins, 'The Bank of England as lender of last resort, 1857–1878', *Economic History Review*, Feb 1992, p 147; Dieter Ziegler, 'The Banking Crisis of 1878', *Economic History Review*, Feb 1992, p 138.

8 Michael Collins, 'The Banking Crisis of 1878', *Economic History Review*, Nov 1989, p 526; William P. Kennedy, *Industrial Structure, Capital Markets and the Origins of British Economic Decline* (Cambridge, 1987), pp 120–34.

9 *Observer*, 9 Oct 2011; Anthony Howe, 'From "Old Corruption" to "New Probity"', *Financial History Review*, April 1994, p 27.

10 Kynaston, vol 1, pp 259–60; R. C. Michie, *The London and New York Stock Exchanges, 1850–1914* (1987), pp 145–7; T. H. S. Escott, *England* (1879), vol 1, pp 190, 192–4; Jacob Viner, 'Clapham on the Bank of England', *Economica*, May 1945, pp 63–4; *Journal of the Institute of Bankers*, 1887, pp 509–10.

11 G15/145; *Royal Commission appointed to Inquire into the recent Changes in the relative Values of the Precious Metals* (First Report, P.P. 1887, XXII), q 5880; Bimetallic League, *The Proceedings of the Bimetallic Conference held at Manchester, 4th and 5th April, 1888* (Manchester, 1888), p 22.

12 This paragraph is based on two papers by Bernard Attard: 'Marketing colonial debt in London' (unpublished); 'Imperial central banks?', in Olivier Feiertag and Michel Margairaz (eds), *Les banques centrales et l'Etat-nation* (Paris, 2016).

13 R. F. Foster, *Lord Randolph Churchill* (1981), p 194; diaries of Sir Edward Hamilton (British Library), Add Ms, 48,644, 3 Sept 1886; David Kynaston, *The Chancellor of the Exchequer* (Lavenham, 1980), p 124; Hamilton, 3 Sept 1886, 3 Sept 1885, Add Ms, 48,647, 31 Jan 1888.

14 Hamilton, Add Ms, 48,648, 4 March 1888; Clapham, vol 2, p 320; Boyle, p 27; Clapham, vol 2, p 318; *OL*, Dec 1932, p 238 (Allan Fea), June 1921, p 56 (A. G. Rowlett).

15 G. A. Fletcher, *The Discount Houses in London* (1976), p 30; *Economist*, 5 Dec 1874; Pressnell, pp 186–9; M6/28, pp 5, 7–8; Forrest Capie *et al*,

'The development of central banking', in Forrest Capie *et al*, *The Future of Central Banking* (Cambridge, 1994), pp 13, 114–15.

16   Niall Ferguson, *The World's Banker* (1998), p 821; Richard Aldous, *The Lion and the Unicorn* (2006), pp 262–3.

17   Clapham, vol 2, p 316; G23/67, fos 135–6, 141–4; Clapham, vol 2, pp 317–18.

18   *Bullionist*, 1 Feb 1890.

19   *DBB*, Sheila Marriner, 'William Lidderdale'; Sayers, vol 1, pp 50–1; Pressnell, pp 191–2; Hamilton, Add Ms, 48,653, 9 Aug 1890; Pressnell, p 191.

20   Arthur D. Elliot, *The Life of George Joachim Goschen, First Viscount Goschen* (1911), vol II, p 169; The Baring Archive, HC3.52.8, Currie to Revelstoke, 23 Feb 1887.

21   Instructive accounts of the crisis include: Clapham, vol 2, pp 326–39; Pressnell, pp 192–207; Philip Ziegler, *The Sixth Great Power* (1988), pp 235–66; Ferguson, pp 864–9; Turner, pp 154–7; Marcello de Cecco, *Money and Empire* (Oxford, 1974), pp 88–98; P. J. Cain and A. G. Hopkins, *British Imperialism: Innovation and Expansion 1688–1914* (1993), pp 153–8, 293–4.

22   G15/192, fo 176; G15/189, fo 15A; Elliot, pp 170–2.

23   Ziegler, *Sixth*, pp 247–8; G15/192, fo 183.

24   G15/189, fo 3; G15/192, fo 177; Clapham, vol 2, pp 330–1; G15/192, fo 179; G15/189, fo 15A; Bertram Wodehouse Currie, *Recollections, Letters and Journals* (Roehampton, 1901), vol 1, pp 92–3; Hamilton, Add Ms, 48,654, 15 Nov 1890; G15/189, fo 15A.

25   *Times*, 15 Nov 1890; G23/85, fo 157; George Chandler, *Four Centuries of Banking, Volume 1* (1964), pp 333–4; G15/189, fo 29A; Clapham, vol 2, pp 336–7.

CHAPTER 9   WONDERFULLY YOUTHFUL IN SPIRIT – CONSIDERING

1   The best treatment remains L. S. Pressnell, 'Gold Reserves, Banking Reserves, and the Baring Crisis of 1890', in C. R. Whittlesey and J. S. G. Wilson (eds), *Essays in Money and Banking in Honour of R. S. Sayers* (1968).

2   Diaries of Sir Edward Hamilton (British Library), Add Ms, 48,654, 8 Jan 1891; G23/85, 22 Jan 1891; *Times*, 29 Jan 1891; Roger Fulford, *Glyn's, 1753–1953* (1953), pp 216–17; Hamilton, Add Mss, 48,655, 24 May 1891, 48,656, 19 Nov 1891; Welby Collection on Banking and Currency (LSE), vol VII, fos 374–97; Pressnell, p 213; Hamilton, Add Ms, 48, 615A, 21 Dec 1891; *Bankers' Magazine*, March 1892, p 378; RBS Archives GM/7,

private letterbook containing copies of Bertram Wodehouse Currie's out-letters from Glyn, Mills, Currie & Co, January 1893; Marcello de Cecco, *Money and Empire* (Oxford, 1974), p 95.

3   Sayers, vol 1, p 17; Hamilton, Add Mss, 48,661, 11 Aug 1893, 48,615B, 19 Sept 1893, 23 Sept 1893.

4   For a reasonably full account, see *OL*, Summer/Autumn 1994, pp 58–9 (Alison Cook).

5   *Bankers' Magazine*, Dec 1889, pp 1490–1; G4/116; G8/47, 8 Nov 1893; Harcourt Papers (Bodleian), Dep 170, fo 55; *FT*, 10 Nov 1893; Hamilton, Add Ms, 58,661, 12 Nov 1893; Harcourt, Dep 396, fos 76–8.

6   *Investors' Review*, Jan 1894, pp 1–17; *Daily Chronicle*, 3 Jan 1894; *Punch*, 8 Jan 1894; *Times*, 8 Jan 1894; Harcourt, Dep 170, fo 78; Hamilton, Add Ms, 48,662, 25 Jan 1894; G15/139; Bo Bramsen and Kathleen Wain, *The Hambros* (1979), pp 334–5; *OL*, Summer/Autumn 1994, p 59 (Alison Cook); *Times*, 16 March 1894.

7   de Fraine, pp 81–3; Harcourt, Dep 416, fos 85–6.

8   Acres, vol 2, pp 560–1; E30/1, fo 45; *OL*, Dec 1936, pp 306–8 (Mrs W. L. Courtney); de Fraine, pp 121–2. See also: *OL*, March 2007, p 11 (Hayley Whiting).

9   *Oscar Wilde's Plays, Prose Writings, and Poems* (1930 Everyman edn), p 369; Bertram Wodehouse Currie, *Recollections, Letters and Journals* (Roehampton, 1901), pp 104–8; Feavearyear, p 331; C. A. E. Goodhart, *The Business of Banking, 1891–1914* (Aldershot, 1986 edn), p 106; Jehanne Wake, *Kleinwort Benson* (Oxford, 1997), pp 201–2; Hamilton, Add Ms, 48,672, 16 Sept 1897; *FT*, 20 Sept 1897; RBS Archives PAB/1/3, Directors' meetings minute book of Parr's Banking Co & Alliance Bank Ltd, 23 September 1897; RBS Archives GM/180/22 File of correspondence from members of the Committee of the Gold Standard Defence Association, Sept 1897.

10 *OL*, March 1965, p 25 (R. C. Balfour); Esther Madeleine Ogden, 'The Development of the Role of the Bank of England as a Lender of Last Resort, 1870–1914' (University of London PhD, 1988), pp 376, 380–1; G15/39; HSBC Group Archives, UK M 0153-0062, Rowland Hughes' notes on National Provincial Bank: commission; Goodhart, p 102; *Bankers' Magazine*, Aug 1899, pp 148–51.

11 J. A. Hobson, *Imperialism* (1902), p 359; *Times*, 17 Oct 1899; *Bankers' Magazine*, Feb 1900, p 313; *Journal of the Institute of Bankers*, May 1900, pp 258–9.

12 G23/87, fos 326–7; HSBC Group Archives, UK M 0153-0067-0002, Rowland Hughes' notes on discounts with brokers; NA, T168/87; Sayers, vol 1, p 16; NA, T168/87.

13 G23/88, 23 July 1900; Jeremy Wormell, *The Management of the National Debt of the United Kingdom, 1900–1932* (2000), p 36; Hamilton, Add Ms, 2 Aug 1900; Wormell, p 37; Papers of 1st Viscount Milner (Bodleian), Dep 177, fo 156, Wormell, p 31; Sayers, vol 1, p 17.

14 Janet E. Courtney, *Recollected in Tranquillity* (1926), pp 155, 164–5; de Fraine, pp 153–5.

15 *Financial News*, 6 Oct 1893; John Pippenger, 'Bank of England Operations, 1893–1913', in Michael D. Bordo and Anna J. Schwartz (eds), *A Retrospective on the Classical Gold Standard, 1821–1931* (Chicago, 1984), p 217.

16 NA, T176/13; *FT*, 6 March 1907; *Chamber of Commerce Journal*, Oct 1907, supplement, pp 11–13; R. S. Sayers, *Bank of England Operations, 1890–1914* (1936), p 69; Dieter Ziegler, *Central Bank, Peripheral Industry* (Leicester, 1990), pp 88–95.

17 Records of Smith, St Aubyn & Co (LMA), Ms 14,894, vol 10, 27 March 1900.

18 Sayers, vol 1, pp 8–9; G23/70, fos 157–8; Arthur I. Bloomfield, *Monetary Policy under the International Gold Standard: 1880–1914* (New York, 1959), p 57; Marc Flandreau, 'Central bank cooperation in historical perspective', *Economic History Review*, Nov 1997, pp 757–9; Sayers, vol 1, p 9.

19 Jonathan Schneer, *London 1900* (New Haven, 1999), p 71.

20 *Economist*, 3 Oct 2015; Peter Clarke, 'Churchill's Economic Ideas, 1900–1930', in Robert Blake and Wm Roger Louis (eds), *Churchill* (Oxford, 1993), p 87; 13A84/7/19, 18 Nov 1895, 11 Sept 1896; G23/87, fos 167–9, 174–6.

21 Hamilton, Add Ms, 48,654, 8 Jan 1891; Youssef Cassis, *City Bankers, 1890–1914* (Cambridge, 1994), pp 87–9, 101–2, 259, 263–4; ADM30/3; G15/131, fo 56A; Clay, p 272; Records of Antony Gibbs & Sons (LMA), Ms 11,040, vol 4, 23 Oct 1902.

22 *OL*, Sept 1931, pp 198–9 (Acres), March 1945, p 2, June 1969, p 96 (J. A. C. Osborne); Sayers, vol 2, pp 609–10.

23 *FT*, 8 May 1903; *OL*, March 1936, p 28 (L. Goodyear); de Fraine, p 125; *FT*, 25 Nov 1903; *OL*, March 2007, pp 121–13 (Lara Webb); *FT*, 3 March 1990 (John Keyworth).

24 *OL*, March 1984, p 37 (Jeremy Boulton); *Bankers' Magazine*, July 1920, p 43; *Journal of the Institute of Bankers*, March 1904, p 154; Hamilton, Add Ms, 48,614, 25 May 1906; records of National Discount Company (LMA), Ms 18,211; *Financial News*, 12 July 1906; *FT*, 19 Oct 1906; Sayers, vol 1, p 55; *Economist*, 19 Jan 1907; C40/314.

25 Sayers, vol 1, p 59; Niall Ferguson, *The World's Banker* (1998), p 928; *FT*, 8 Nov 1907; Sayers, vol 1, p 59; Collin Brooks, *Something in the City* (1931), p 62.

26 *Bankers' Magazine*, Sept 1911, p 406; G4/134, 7 Sept 1911; Tessa Ogden, 'An analysis of Bank of England discount and advance behaviour, 1870–1914', in James Foreman-Peck (ed), *New Perspectives on the Late Victorian Economy* (Cambridge, 1990), p 341; G4/134, 7 Sept 1911.

27 Records of London Chamber of Commerce (LMA), Ms 16,648, 7 May 1913; *Times*, 24 Jan 1914; LCC, Ms 16,648, 10 Feb 1914, 14 May 1914, 22 July 1914.

28 Clapham, vol 2, pp 397–8; ADM30/17.

29 NA, CAB16/18A.

30 Gibbs, Ms 11,115, vol 2, 27 July 1914; Richard Roberts, *Saving the City* (Oxford, 2013), pp 27, 36.

31 Smith St Aubyn, Ms 14,894, vol 24, 30 July 1914; Roberts, p 48.

32 *War Memoirs of David Lloyd George, Volume 1* (1933), p 101; records of Morgan, Grenfell & Co (LMA), Ms 21,795, vol 14, 10 Nov 1908; G23/89, fo 102; Morgan, Grenfell, Ms 21,799, fo 122. See also: *DBB*, R. P. T. Davenport-Hines, 'Walter Cunliffe, 1st Lord Cunliffe'.

33 Hartley Withers, *War and Lombard Street* (1915), pp 10–11; *Times*, 1 Aug 1914; *FT*, 1 Aug 1914; *OL*, March 1939, p 67 (C. Landon); Roberts, pp 57–8, 95–6.

34 Roberts, pp 58–62; Boyle, p 97; Roberts, pp 61, 51–2, 233.

35 Roberts, pp 111–12; NA, T170-14; Morgan Grenfell, private letter books, no 12, 3 Aug 1914.

36 NA, T170/55; Roberts, pp 123, 126; *Journal of the Institute of Bankers*, Feb 1912, pp 50–83.

CHAPTER 10 THE KIPLING MAN

1 Uncatalogued diary (at Bank of England archive); E30/2, fo 83.

2 Richard Roberts, *Saving the City* (Oxford, 2013), pp 119–33.

3 Clay, p 80; Roberts, p 154; Sayers, vol 1, pp 77–82; Roberts, p 189; Jeremy Wormell, *The Management of the National Debt of the United Kingdom, 1900–1932* (2000), pp 85–7.

4 ADM30/4, Lord Cunliffe file; *War Memoirs of David Lloyd George, Volume 1* (1933), pp 113–14; NA, T170/56, 5 Aug 1914; Michael and Eleanor Brock (eds), H. H. Asquith, *Letters to Venetia Stanley* (Oxford, 1982), p 312.

5 E30/2, fos 86, 95; Sayers, vol 2, pp 611, 616; E30/2, fos 107, 111; Sayers, vol 2, p 612; G15/113, 15 Feb 1919.

6   Ian M. Drummond, *The Gold Standard and the International Monetary System, 1900–1939* (Basingstoke, 1987), p 29; Feavearyear, p 347; NA, T176/13, Part 1, 6 Dec 1925; G. C. Peden, 'Treasury and the City', in Ranald Michie and Philip Williamson (eds), *The British Government and the City of London in the Twentieth Century* (Cambridge, 2004), p 123; E. V. Morgan, *Studies in British Financial Policy, 1914–25* (1952), p 187; Richard Roberts, 'The Bank and the City', in Roberts and Kynaston, p 60; Wormell, chap 3, 6, 11 (re war loans); Sayers, vol 1, pp 84–5; Morgan, *Studies*, pp 344, 356; G15/7, 23 April 1918; de Fraine, pp 173–6.

7   *Lloyd George*, p 114; *Lord Riddell's War Diary, 1914–1918* (1933), p 94; A. J. P. Taylor (ed), *Lloyd George: A Diary by Frances Stevenson* (1971), p 53; Stephen McKenna, *Reginald McKenna, 1863–1943* (1948), p 237; Lord Beaverbrook, *Politicians and the War, 1914–1916, Volume II* (1928), p 153; Sayers, vol 1, pp 89–91; Boyle, pp 103–5; Fed, 1000.2; Kenneth Mouré, 'The Limits to Central Bank Co-operation, 1916–36', *Contemporary European History*, Nov 1992, pp 261–2.

8   ADM34/4, 27 June 1916; G15/7, 10 Aug 1916; ADM30/4, Lord Cunliffe file, 20 Oct 1916; ADM 34/4, 24 Oct 1916, 8 Nov 1916, 17/18 Nov 1916, 22 Nov 1916; ADM34/5, 12 Jan 1917.

9   The version of the episode given here is based on the Bank's records, as well as owing much to Sayers, vol 1, pp 99–109. For an alternative version, claiming that Cunliffe had *already* given a resignation letter to Bonar Law (for the chancellor to use as and when he saw fit) before going fishing in Scotland, see Robert Rhodes James, *Memoirs of a Conservative* (1969), pp 61–2, and R. J. Q. Adams, *Bonar Law* (1999), p 252.

10 G15/31, fos 30/42; Private Letter Books of Gaspard Farrer, 15 August 1917 (The Baring Archive, DEP33.18 folio 28); ADM34/5, 12 Sept 1917; ADM34/6, 27 Feb 1818, 22 March 1818; Morgan, Grenfell records (LMA), Ms 21,799, fos 121, 123.

11 *Economist*, 8 Sept 1917; G15/111-12; ADM34/6, 28 March 1918, 25 April 1918; Sayers, vol 2, pp 597, 628–31, 618–20; Clay, p 113.

12 NA, T185/1; Sayers, Appendixes, Appendix 7; D. E. Moggridge, *British Monetary Policy, 1924–1931* (Cambridge, 1972), pp 17–22; *Economist*, 2 Nov 1918; *Times*, 30 Oct 1918.

13 Fed, 1000.3; G35/1, 3 Dec 1920; G35/2, 5 Jan 1921; Sayers, Appendixes, pp 74–5; G35/2, 15 Sept 1921; G3/178, 7 Feb 1922, 22 March 1922; G3/183, 29 Jan 1925.

14 P. L. Cottrell, 'Norman, Strakosch and the development of central banking', in Philip L. Cottrell (ed), *Rebuilding the Financial System in Central and Eastern Europe, 1918–1994* (Aldershot, 1997), pp 29–30; Eoin Drea, 'The Bank of England, Montagu Norman and the internationalisation of

Ango-Irish monetary relations, 1922–1943', *Financial History Review*, April 2014, p 61; G35/2, 14 March 1921; Sayers, vol 1, pp 205–6; ADM30/4, W. H. Clegg file; Sayers, vol 1, p 209.

15 *Economic Journal*, Dec 1953, p 764; G3/179, 26 Feb 1923; G35/3, 9 Aug 1922; Anne Orde, 'Baring Brothers, the Bank of England, the British Government and the Czechoslovak State Loan of 1922', *English Historical Review*, Jan 1991, pp 27–40; Sayers, vol 1, pp 168–9, 171–3; G35/4, 9 April 1923; G3/180, 10 Jan 1924; Sayers, vol 1, pp 181–2; Cottrell, 'Norman', pp 61–2.

16 Sayers, vol 2, p 554, vol 1, p 269; David Wainwright, *Government Broker* (1990), pp 64–5; ADM34/9, 1 April 1920; John Atkin, 'Official Regulation of British Overseas Investment, 1914–1931', *Economic History Review*, Aug 1970, pp 324–35; G3/177, 28 Dec 1921; G35/4, 3 Dec 1923; J. A. Gere and John Sparrow (eds), *Geoffrey Madan's Notebooks* (Oxford, 1981), p 14.

17 The fullest account probably remains Moggridge, pp 37–97.

18 NA, CAB27/72, 25 Sept 1919; G35/1, 6 Nov 1919; Susan Howson, 'The Origins of Dear Money, 1919–20', *Economic History Review*, Feb 1974, pp 100 ff; G3/176, 6 Sept 1920; Clay, p 292; *Journal of the Institute of Bankers*, Dec 1921, pp 382–3; *National and Athenaeum*, 21 July 1923; Robert Skidelsky, *John Maynard Keynes: Volume Two* (1992), pp 153–64; G35/4, 8 Oct 1923.

19 Philip Snowden, *An Autobiography: Volume 1* (1934), pp 613–15; NA, T160/197/F7528/02/1, 27 June 1924; papers of Sir Charles Addis (SOAS), 14/43, 8 Jan 1925; Martin Gilbert, *Winston S. Churchill, Volume V* (1976), pp 97–8; Fed, 1112.2, 14 April 1925; *Times*, 29 April 1925; G35/5, 8 May 1925; Gilbert, *Churchill, Volume V Companion*, p 472.

20 *Star*, 21 Jan 1925; Emile Moreau, *The Golden Franc* (Boulder, Colorado, 1991), p 51; Marguerite Dupree (ed), *Lancashire and Whitehall* (1987), vol 1, p 34; *Lloyds Bank Review*, April 1968, pp 33–4; Duncan Crow, *A Man of Push and Go* (1965), p 168; G15/241 (Bayen); ADM34/11, 6 Dec 1922; ADM34/12, 9 Nov 1923; L. E. Jones, *Georgian Afternoon* (1958), pp 122–3; Crow, p 168; G35/3, 31 Oct 1922; Andrew Shonfield, 'The Plaintiff Treble', in Arthur Koestler (ed), *Suicide of a Nation?* (1963), p 80; G35/7, 3 Jan 1928, 25 July 1927.

21 G15/24, 10 Aug 1922; G35/3, 31 Oct 1922; Charles Chadwyck-Healey, *Cecil Lubbock* (Royston, 2008); G35/4, 30 Nov 1924; Addis, 14/43, 7 Oct 1925; G35/5, 18 Oct 1925; Addis, 14/44, 8 July 1926; Fed, 1112.2, 8 Oct 1926; G15/24, 8 Oct 1926; ADM33/26 (Trotter).

22 G15/252–3; Clay, p 310; The Baring Archive, 101961, 2nd Lord Revelstoke Private Copy Out Letter Book, 22 October & 25 October 1928; G1/204, 25 July 1931 (Newman memo).

23 Addis, 14/454, 28 Sept 1926; Fed, 1112.2, 25 Oct 1926; Clay, p 311; G15/252, 1 March 1927; Addis, 14/456, 17 May 1928; G15/24, 17 May 1928; G35/7, 13 Sept 1927; *OL*, Winter 1976, p 241 (Michael Thornton).

24 Sidney Pollard, *The Development of the British Economy, 1914–1980* (1983 edn), pp 137–41; NA, T176/13, part 1, 3 Dec 1925; G15/7, 4 Dec 1925; Sayers, vol 1, p 216; Gilbert, *Churchill*, vol V, pp 237–8; P. J. Grigg, *Prejudice and Judgement* (1948), p 193; Lord Moran, *Winston Churchill* (1966), pp 303–4.

25 G1/515, 17 July 1925; ADM34/14, 2 Dec 1925; ADM34/15, 8 Oct 1926; ADM34/17, 4 Oct 1928; G3/182, 19 Nov 1926; G35/7, 26 Oct 1927. See also: Bernard Attard, 'Moral suasion, empire borrowers and the new issue market during the 1920s', in Michie and Williamson, pp 195–214.

26 G3/183, 8 May 1925; G1/515, 15 July 1925; G3/184, 9 Sept 1925; Sayers, vol 1, pp 337–41; Moreau, p 430; Clay, pp 265–6; Liaquat Ahamed, *Lords of Finance* (New York, 2009), pp 298–9; G3/195, 28 March 1929.

27 G3/195, 28 March 1929; Moreau, p 295; G15/24, 17 May 1928; G15/7, 4 Sept 1929; *Evening Standard*, 27 Sept 1929; G15/7, 30 Sept 1929; G3/195, 4 Oct 1929; Peter Clarke, *The Keynesian Revolution in the Making, 1924–1936* (Oxford, 1988), p 104; ADM34/18, 5 June 1929, 11 June 1929; G3/195, 27 Sept 1929.

28 For an account of the whole process, see: W. R. Garside and J. I. Greaves, 'The Bank of England and industrial intervention in interwar Britain', *Financial History Review*, April 1996.

29 G3/192, 1 Nov 1928; SMT2/240, 5 Dec 1928; *Nation and Athenaeum*, 2 Feb 1929; Valerio Cerretano, 'The Treasury, Britain's Postwar Reconstruction, and the Industrial Intervention of the Bank of England, 1921–9', *Economic History Review*, Aug 2009, pp 80–100; G3/195, 14 Aug 1929.

30 Sayers, vol 1, p 326; Sue Bowden and Michael Collins, 'The Bank of England, Industrial Regeneration, and Hire Purchase between the Wars', *Economic History Review*, Feb 1992, p 126; SMT2/53, 22 Feb 1930; John Vincent (ed), *The Crawford Papers* (Manchester, 1984), p 531; SMT9/1, 11 April 1930; J. H. Bamberg, 'The government, the banks, and the Lancashire cotton industry, 1918–39' (University of Cambridge PhD, 1984), pp 195–6, 119; The Baring Archive, 200537, Charles Bruce Gardner to Barings, 17 April 1931.

31 ADM30/16, 24 Jan 1986 (Byatt memo); G15/7, 4 Sept 1929; Gianni Toniolo, *Central Bank Co-operation at the Bank for International Settlements, 1930–1973* (Cambridge, 2005), p 57; G3/197, 11 Sept 1930; G1/10, 22 Nov 1930. In general on the Niemeyer mission, see: Peter Love, 'Niemeyer's Australian Diary and Other English Records of

His Mission', *Historical Studies*, 1982; Bernard Attard, 'The Bank of England and the origins of the Niemeyer mission, 1921–1930', *Australian Economic History Review*, March 1992.

32 G1/426, 19 Dec 1929; G3/196, 7 Jan 1930; G1/425, qq 3332–5, 3344, 3403, 3405–6; Sayers, vol 1, p 369; papers of Lord Brand (Bodleian), file 31, 30/31 Oct 1930, 5 Dec 1930.

33 Roberta Allbert Dayer, *Finance and Empire* (1988), p 211; Philip Williamson, *National Crisis and National Government* (Cambridge, 1992), p 200; Atkin, p 331.

34 The crisis has an extensive literature. Two particularly interesting interpretations are: Philip Williamson, 'A "Bankers Ramp"?', *English Historical Review*, Oct 1984; William H. Janeway, 'The 1931 sterling crisis and the independence of the Bank of England', *Journal of Post Keynesian Economics*, Winter 1995–6.

35 Diane B. Kunz, *The Battle for Britain's Gold Standard in 1931* (Beckenham, 1987), p 48; ADM34/20, 10 June 1931; G3/198, 1 July 1931; G15/7, 18 June 1931, 25 June 1931, 29 June 1931.

36 ADM34/20, 29 July 1931; G3/210, 6 Aug 1931; G8/60, 11 Aug 1931; Thomas Jones, *A Diary with Letters, 1931–1950* (Oxford, 1954), p 11; G3/210, 17 Aug 1931.

37 G3/210, 18 Aug 1931; Kathleen Burk, *Morgan Grenfell, 1838–1988* (Oxford, 1989), pp 150, 153.

38 NA, PREM1/97, 18 Sept 1931, fos 84–9; *Daily Telegraph*, 21 Sept 1931; *Times*, 21 Sept 1931; *Daily Mail*, 21 Sept 1931; Morgan, Grenfell, private letter books, no 44, 21 Sept 1931; Anne Olivier Bell (ed), *The Diary of Virginia Woolf: Volume 4* (1982), p 45.

CHAPTER 11 LOOK BUSY ANYWAY

1 ADM30/17, larger file, after fo 21; Sayers, vol 2, p 617; Hennessy, p 12; *OL*, Autumn 1992, p 130 (Tony Carlisle); Cathy Courtney and Paul Thompson, *City Lives* (1996), pp 35–6; *OL*, June 2003, p 72 (David Harris), March 2007, p 8 (Nigel J. W. Spelling); Hennessy, p 329; *OL*, June 1971, p 81 (Ted Bellamy).

2 *OL*, March 1964, p 6 (J. V. Bailey); C160/179, Sir George Bolton, 'Memoirs'; Hennessy, pp 325–7; *OL*, Summer 1982, p 53 (Anthony Carlisle).

3 Hennessy, pp 127–8, 167–8; Hewitt and Keyworth, pp 120–1; Byatt, pp 126–7.

4 Sayers, Appendixes, p 335; *OL*, Spring 1975, pp 33–4; Hennessy, pp 258–65.

5   E28/143, 23 June 1921. The fullest account of Baker's rebuild is Abramson, chap 7, but see also: Sayers, Appendix 34; Simon Bradley and Nikolaus Pevsner, *The Buildings of England: London 1: The City of London* (1997), pp 274–80; Iain Black, 'Imperial visions', in Felix Driver and David Gilbert (eds), *Imperial Cities* (Manchester, 1999), pp 96–113.

6   Charles Chadwyck-Healey, *Cecil Lubbock* (Royston, 2009), pp 56–7; *Telegraph Magazine*, 2 July 1994 (Christopher Fildes); E28/127, 14 April 1921, 6 October 1921; Herbert Baker, *Architecture and Personalities* (1944), p 124; *OL*, Sept 1922, p 240; E28/143, 29 Dec 1922; Sayers, Appendixes, pp 339–40; *Architects' Journal*, 6 May 1925.

7   *OL*, June 1925, p 50; *Hampshire Herald*, 13 Oct 1944; Black, pp 105–6; C160/179, Bolton, 'Memoirs'; E28/130, 27 April 1933; *OL*, Dec 1936, p 280; Abramson, pp 223–5.

8   *Banker*, Aug 1937, pp 198–202; James Lees-Milne, *Prophesying Peace* (1984 pbk edn), p 185; Nikolaus Pevsner, *The Buildings of England: London 1: The Cities of London and Westminster* (Harmondsworth, 1957), pp 164–5; *Times*, 8 June 1962.

9   Bradley and Pevsner, pp 274–80; Abramson, chap 7.

10 G15/113; Sayers, Appendix 5, pp 51–4; ADM34/8, 15 Feb 1919; G15/113.

11 *OL*, Sept 1958, p 183; Fed, 1000.3, 26 July 1919; Chadwyck-Healey, pp 61–2; *OL*, June 1928, p 302, March 1996, pp 14–17; Hennessy, p 343; *OL*, Dec 1927, pp 191–2.

12 *OL*, Dec 1970, pp 223–7 (Cynthia Payne); E4/3, 30 Jan 1920; AC25/26, 15 Oct 1920; E4/3, March 1921; Hennessy, p 13; *OL*, Autumn 1991, p 125 (Carmen Birbeck), March 1985, p 13 (Helen R. Herington).

13 *OL*, Summer 1975, p 81 (C. D. Garton), Autumn 1975, p 151 (F. R. Levander), June 1980, p 53 (David Nye).

14 *OL*, Summer 1976, p 83 (R. B. Charsley), Spring 1976, p 13 (M. H. Browning), Winter 1978, p 154 (Frank Dancaster); Hennessy, pp 53–4; *Bankers' Magazine*, Dec 1981, p 18 (Naree Craik); *OL*, Christmas 1982, pp 162–3 (Neville Goodman).

15 *OL*, Spring 1981, p 28 (Leslie Bonnet), Christmas 1979, p 345 (Roger Woodley); *City Lives*, pp 51–3; E1/5.

CHAPTER 12 THE DOGS BARK

1   Papers of Sir Charles Addis (SOAS), 14/49, 2 Nov 1931, 14/424, 2 Nov 1931; G15/24, 28 July 1932, 1 July 1936; Sayers, vol 2, pp 652–3; G15/24, 27 Aug 1937; Sayers, vol 2, p 653; G15/24, 5 Feb 1954, 27 Aug 1937.

2   J. A. Gere and John Sparrow (eds), *Geoffrey Madan's Notebooks* (Oxford, 1981), pp 101–2; *Star*, 21 Jan 1933; *OL*, Spring 1983, p 37; Boyle, p 295; ADM34/23, 26 May 1934.

3 G15/204; G15/204–5; *Evening Standard*, 25 May 1939, 27 May 1939, 30 May 1939; C160/179, Sir George Bolton, 'Memoirs'; Fforde, pp 1–2; ADM23/1, 8 Nov 1935; Paul Bareau, 'The Financial Institutions of the City of London', in Institute of Bankers, *The City of London as a Centre of International Trade and Finance* (1961), p 15.

4 Sir Theodore Gregory, 'The "Norman Conquest" Reconsidered', *Lloyds Bank Review*, Oct 1957, p 4; G. C. Peden, *The Treasury and British Public Policy, 1906–1959* (Oxford, 2000), p 253; Erin E. Jacobsson, *A Life for Sound Money* (Oxford, 1979), p 103; *Banker*, Dec 1932, p 161; Liaquat Ahamed, *Lords of Finance* (New York, 2009), p 463.

5 Robert Elgie and Helen Thompson, *The Politics of Central Banks* (1998), p 49; Capie, pp 141–2; Clay, pp 409–12; Susan Howson, *Domestic Monetary Management in Britain, 1919–38* (Cambridge, 1975), pp 86–8.

6 The definitive account is Jeremy Wormell, *The Management of the National Debt of the United Kingdom, 1900–1932* (2000), chap 19.

7 Sayers, vol 2, p 431; ADM34/21, 6/7 July 1932; *OL*, Sept 1932, p 164 (J. H. McNulty), p 160.

8 For a fuller treatment of Norman and the City in the 1930s, see Sayers, vol 2, pp 533–46, 552–60.

9 ADM34/21, 2 Feb 1932; ADM34/23, 21 Sept 1934; G3/201, 8 March 1934; Sayers, vol 2, p 470; Richard Roberts, 'The Bank and the City', in Roberts and Kynaston, p 172; ADM34/25, 1 April 1936.

10 G3/199, 29 June 1932; J. H. Bamberg, 'The Rationalization of the British Cotton Industry in the Interwar Years', *Textile History* (1988), pp 95–6; Clay, pp 345–9; Sayers, vol 2, pp 547–50; Steven Tolliday, *Business, Banking and Politics* (Cambridge, Massachusetts, 1987), pp 269–71; Carol E. Heim, 'Limits to Intervention: The Bank of England and Industrial Diversification in the Depressed Areas', *Economic History Review*, Nov 1984, pp 533–50; G14/62, 1 March 1939.

11 G3/200, 5 Dec 1933; Howson, p 95; Robert Skidelsky, *John Maynard Keynes: Volume Two* (1992), p 501; ADM34/23, 4 Jan 1934; Sayers, vol 2, pp 462–3; Boyle, p 288.

12 G1/515, 27 April 1933; Gianni Toniolo, *Central Bank Cooperation at the Bank for International Settlements, 1930–1973* (Cambridge, 2005), p 167; Patricia Clavin, '"The Fetishes of So-Called International Bankers"', *Contemporary European History*, Nov 1992, p 306; C160/179, Bolton, 'Memoirs'; Kenneth Mouré, 'The Limits to Central Bank Co-operation, 1916–36', *Contemporary European History*, Nov 1992, p 278; Sayers, vol 2, pp 526, 519; P. J. Cain and A. G. Hopkins, *British Imperialism: Crisis and Deconstruction, 1914–1990* (Harlow, 1993), pp 253–4; P. J. Cain, 'Gentlemanly Imperialism at Work: The Bank of England, Canada, and

the Sterling Area, 1932–1936', *Economic History Review*, May 1996, p 353; *OL*, June 2002, pp 84–5.

13 G3/200, 30 Sept 1933; G3/201, 23 Jan 1934; Ron Chernow, *The House of Morgan* (New York, 1990), p 394; Addis, 14/459, 14 April 1935; Kynaston, vol 3, p 437; *OL*, March 1937, p 18; C160/179, Bolton, 'Memoirs'.

14 *OL*, Sept 1938, p 284; G3/205, 31 Aug 1938; Fed, box 616999, 24 Sept 1938; G3/205, 2 Nov 1938; *Financial News*, 4 Jan 1939; NA, fo 371/23000, fos 245–6; G3/206, 22 March 1939; ADM34/28, 28 Feb 1939, 7 June 1939; C160/179, Bolton, 'Memoirs'; Sayers, vol 2, pp 567–71, 575–81; Hennessy, pp 83–9; G3/206, 26 Aug 1939, 2 Sept 1939; Boyle, p 309.

15 *Parliamentary Debates: House of Commons*, Fifth Series, vol 274 (1933), 7 Feb 1933, cols 134, 139, 155, 165, 167, 20 Feb 1933, cols 1503, 1511, 7 Feb 1933, col 142.

16 J. R. Jarvie, *The Old Lady Unveiled* (1933), pp 11, 50–1; *Listener*, 4 April 1934; *Banker*, Feb 1935, p 107; *Labour's Immediate Programme* (March 1937), p 3; T. W. Huskisson, *The Bank of England and the Financial Impasse* (1935), p 3; E. H. H. Green, 'The Conservatives in the City', in Ranald Michie and Philip Williamson, *The British Government and the City of London in the Twentieth Century* (Cambridge, 2004), pp 160–6.

17 Sayers, vol 1, p 379; Ahamed, p 487; Douglas Jay, *Change and Fortune* (1980), p 68; *Listener*, 23 March 1939.

18 *Evening Standard*, 6 Jan 1939; *Parliamentary Debates: House of Commons*, Fifth Series, vol 347 (1939), 26 May 1939, cols 2726, 2732, 2734–5; Adam LeBor, *Tower of Basel* (New York, 2013), p 66; *Parliamentary Debates: House of Commons*, Fifth Series, vol 348 (1939), 6 June 1939, col 205; G3/206, 30 May 1939; G1/506, 3 June 1939; Paul Einzig, *In the Centre of Things* (1960), pp 186–94.

19 For a full account of the domestic aspect of the war, see Hennessy, chap 1.

20 *OL*, Autumn 1978, pp 113–17; *Bankers' Magazine*, Dec 1981, pp 19–20; *OL*, Sept 1988, p 106 (Tony Carlisle); *Daily Mail*, 2 Aug 1942.

21 Records of the London Stock Exchange (Guildhall Library), Mss 14,600, vol 136, 2 Oct 1939 to vol 137, 20 Nov 1939; Fed, box 616999, 16 July 1940; *OL*, Spring 1978, pp 21–4, Dec 2000, p 169; Hennessy, pp 15–16.

22 Hennessy, pp 90, 87; Sayers, vol 2, p 571; G1/15, 9 May 1940.

23 D. E. Moggridge, *Maynard Keynes* (1992), pp 629–34; Peden, pp 316–17; Moggridge, p 664; Bareau, p 16; Sayers, vol 2, p 602.

24 DM20/29, 28 Feb 1940; Sayers, vol 2, pp 591–2; Boyle, p 311; Nigel Nicolson (ed), Harold Nicolson, *Letters and Diaries, 1939–45* (1967), p 142; Hennessy, p 15.

25 Clay, p 469; G1/69, 26 Sept 1939; ADM20/29, 1 March 1940, 31 May 1940; Roberts, pp 165–6; ADM20/31, 8 Sept 1942, 10 Sept 1942, 2 Oct 1942, 22 May 1942; John Barnes and David Nicholson (eds), *The Empire at Bay* (1988), p 842; *OL*, June 1958, p 106; *Sunday Pictorial*, 21 Sept 1941; Niall Ferguson, *High Financier* (2010), pp 99–100; *New Statesman*, 15 May 1943.

26 G15/7, 9 Oct 1941; ADM34/30, 22 Dec 1941; ADM20/31, 15 Jan 1942; G15/7, 18 March 1942; Marguerite Dupree (ed), *Lancashire and Whitehall: The Diary of Sir Raymond Streat, Volume 2* (Manchester, 1987), p 144.

27 Boyle, pp 322–3; G15/24, 13 March 1944, 20 March 1944; Boyle, p 324; *Sunday Pictorial*, 9 April 1944; *Financial News*, 11 April 1944; G15/45, 19 June 1944; G15/241, 30 April 1960 (Kershaw); 13A84/5/11, 3 Feb 1945; Boyle, p 327; *OL*, March 1968, p 44.

28 *Economist*, 29 March 1941; G15/24, 6 May 1943, 21 Oct 1943; ADM34/32, 21 Oct 1943; G15/24, 14 March 1944; *DBB*, R. P. T. Davenport-Hines, 'Thomas Sivewright Catto, 1st Lord Catto of Cairncatto'; *Lancashire and Whitehall*, p 245; O'Brien, p 23; *Daily Express*, 8 April 1944.

29 SMT2/308, 7 Jan 1944; John Kinross and Alan Butt-Philip, *ICFC, 1945–1961* (1985), pp 324–7; Moggridge, p 734; Capie, p 143; G18/3, 20 March 1945. For full accounts of filling the Macmillan gap and the new international financial order, see Fforde, pp 31–73, 704–27.

30 *Banker*, Oct 1945, p 38; *Coast Bank* (San Francisco), Aug 1949.

31 *Times*, 5 June 1945; G15/7, 1 Aug 1945; Fforde, p 6; *Parliamentary Debates (Hansard): House of Commons*, Fifth Series, vol 413 (1945), col 94; Ben Pimlott (ed), *The Political Diary of Hugh Dalton* (1986), p 362; *Lancashire and Whitehall*, p 378; G15/19; *Times*, 11 Oct 1945; Fed, box 617031, C261, 10 Oct 1945.

32 *Economist*, 13 Oct 1945; *FT*, 11 Oct 1945; *Daily Telegraph*, 11 Oct 1945; *Parliamentary Debates (Hansard): House of Commons*, Fifth Series, vol 415, cols 43, 46, 57, 88, 113, 117.

33 For a full account, see Fforde, pp 73–87.

34 Moggridge, p 806; L. S. Pressnell, *External Economic Policy since the War, Volume I* (1986), p 315; G15/19; Fforde, p 37; *FT*, 14 Dec 1945; *Empire at Bay*, pp 1052–3.

35 G18/2, 27 Feb 1946; Fforde, pp 30, 15–16.

CHAPTER 13 NOT A STUDY GROUP

1 *American Banker*, 5 Oct 1946; The Baring Archive, 200884 fo 15, American Papers vol 18, 5 February 1947; *City Press*, 1 Oct 1948; Philip Geddes, *Inside the Bank of England* (1987), p 67; The Baring Archive,

200884 f 15, American Papers vol 18, 5 February 1947; ADM30/6, George Gibson file (note by John Keyworth, 8 Sept 1992); *Banker*, April 1949, p xxi; *Economist*, 3 May 1947; 16A48/1; Fforde, pp 366–7.

2 J. F. A. Pullinger, 'The Bank and the Commodity Markets', in Fforde, pp 788–92; Adrienne Gleeson, *London Enriched* (1997), chap 3; G3/103, 6 Jan 1950, 11 Jan 1950; G3/4, 5 Jan 1951; Richard Roberts, 'The Bank of England and the City', in Roberts and Kynaston, p 166; G3/99, 23 April 1947; G3/2, 18 May 1950.

3 Fforde, p 147; P. L. Cottrell, 'The Bank of England in its International Setting, 1918–1972', in Roberts and Kynaston, p 117; *Time*, 1 Sept 1947; Fforde, p 162; Erin E. Jacobsson, *A Life for Sound Money* (Oxford, 1979), p 196.

4 G3/1, 1 June 1949; G1/70, 21 June 1949, 5 July 1949, 3 Aug 1949; Alec Cairncross, *Years of Recovery* (1985), p 176; Fforde, p 300; Fed, box 617031, 30 Sept 1949.

5 Fforde, p 213; *Economica*, May 1993, p 243; *Institutional Investor*, March 1980, p 210.

6 Ben Pimlott, *Hugh Dalton* (1985), pp 463–4; G3/100, 8 Dec 1948; Fforde, pp 367–8; Philip M. Williams (ed), *The Diary of Hugh Gaitskell, 1945–1956* (1983), p 227; G1/71, 3 July 1951, 5 July 1951; *FT*, 4 Oct 1951; G1/71, 22 Oct 1951. The authoritative account of monetary policy during these years remains Susan Howson, *British Monetary Policy, 1945–51* (Oxford, 1993).

7 Capie, pp 773, 58.

8 16A48/1; G3/1, 13 April 1949, 2 May 1949, 8 July 1949; papers of Sir George Bolton, 10 Sept 1962, draft obituary of Cobbold for *The Times*; Fforde, pp 231–2; Capie, p 44; Cathy Courtney and Paul Thompson, *City Lives* (1996), pp 164–5.

9 Fforde, p 218; Capie, p 45; ADM14/4, 12 Nov 1948; Alec Cairncross (ed), *The Robert Hall Diaries, 1947–53* (1989), p 41; Fforde, p 773.

10 Fforde, pp 164, 317–18; *OL*, Spring 1980, pp 9–11 (Roger Woodley); Fforde, pp 546, 196, 548; *Hall, 1947–53*, pp 76, 231.

11 Fforde, pp 322, 613, 373, 628; Capie, p 52; *OL*, Dec 1969, p 224; 'Hilton Clarke', *Daily Telegraph*, 18 Dec 1995.

12 William A. Allen, *Monetary Policy and Financial Repression in Britain, 1951–59* (Basingstoke, 2014), p 205; *Listener*, 6 June 1957; G. C. Peden, *The Treasury and British Public Policy, 1906–1959* (Oxford, 2000), p 440; Alec Cairncross (ed), *The Robert Hall Diaries, 1954–61* (1991), p 65; Fforde, p 778; *Economica*, May 1993, p 242; *OL*, June 1998, p 77.

13 G15/19; G3/4, 1 Nov 1951; G3/107, 12 March 1952; *DBB*, Gordon A. Fletcher, 'Lawrence Henry Seccombe'.

14 *New Statesman*, 29 Dec 1951; NA, T236/3240, 16 Feb 1952; C160/24, 20 Feb 1952; Donald MacDougall, *Don and Mandarin* (1987), p 88; NA, T236/3240, 25 Feb 1952; Peter Caterall (ed), *The Macmillan Diaries: The Cabinet Years, 1950–1957* (2003), p 149; NA, T236/3242, 18 March 1952; Fforde, p 448; Cottrell, p 126; Peden, *Treasury*, p 464; *Daily Telegraph*, 21 Oct 1954.

15 G15/19; Kathleen Burk, *The First Privatisation* (1988), p 95; G3/111, 13 April 1954; G3/7, 25 Feb 1954; Richard Roberts, 'Regulatory Responses to the Rise of the Market for Corporate Control in Britain in the 1950s', *Business History*, Jan 1992, p 187; G3/6, 23 June 1953; G3/110, 13 Nov 1953; G3/111, 13 Jan 1954.

16 Hennessy, p 233; David Wainwright, *Government Broker* (1990), p 83; G3/6, 30 July 1953; *FT*, 1 Jan 1955.

17 G15/19; *FT*, 20 April 1955; G1/73, 18–19 April 1955; *Hall Diaries, 1954–61*, p 33; G1/73, 3 Aug 1955; G3/8, 10 Nov 1955, 4 Nov 1955.

18 Diaries of Harold Macmillan (Bodleian), dep d.26, 21 July 1956, fo 123; G1/74, 23 March 1956, 26 March 1956; Macmillan, dep d.26, 4 May 1956, fos 24, 94–5; G3/9, 23 July 1965.

19 Fed, box 617015, 2 Nov 1956; LDMA1/10, 2 Nov 1956; Fed, box 617015, 15 Nov 1956; G1/74, 20 Dec 1956; Fed, box 617015, 11 Jan 1957.

20 G3/75, 13 May 1957; Alan Booth, 'New revisionists and the Keynesian era in British economic policy', *Economic History Review*, May 2001, pp 356–7; NA, T233/1407, 17 May 1957; Committee on the Working of the Monetary System, *Minutes of Evidence* (1960), qq 753, 762.

21 G1/75, 22 Aug 1957; G14/152, 3 Sept 1957; G1/75, 9 Sept 1957; Fforde, pp 680–4; Capie, p 93; *Evening Standard*, 19 Sept 1957.

22 Allen, pp 133–4; G3/10, 28 Oct 1957; Monetary System, q 2026; E. H. H. Green, 'The Influence of the City over British Economic Policy, c. 1880–1960', in Youssef Cassis (ed), *Finance and Financiers in European Economic History* (Cambridge, 1992), pp 206–7; NA, T233/1410 (memo by Sir Edmund Compton, Dec 1957); Allen, p 136; E. H. H. Green, 'The Conservatives and the City', in Ranald Michie and Philip Williamson (eds), *The British Government and the City of London in the Twentieth Century* (Cambridge, 2004), p 171.

23 Fforde, p 688.

24 *Proceedings of the Tribunal appointed to Inquire into allegations that information about the raising of Bank Rate was improperly discussed* (1958).

25 John Littlewood, *The Stock Market* (1998), p 98; *Hall Diaries, 1954–61*, p 140; C160/149, 20 Dec 1957; *New Yorker*, 4 Jan 1958; *Daily Herald*, 13 Dec 1957.

26　G1/75, 27 Dec 1957; G3/78, 6 Jan 1958; *FT*, 3 Jan 1989.

27　NA, T233/1202, 10 Jan 1958; *Report of the Tribunal appointed to Inquire into Allegation of Improper Disclosure of Information relating to the Raising of the Bank Rate* (1958), paras 115–16; *Daily Express*, 22 Jan 1958; G3/119, 22 Jan 1958; 16A48/1; Capie, p 99.

28　*Listener*, 30 Jan 1958; *Parliamentary Debates (Hansard): House of Commons*, Fifth Series, vol 581 (1958), 3–4 Feb 1958, cols 859–61, 1087; *Times*, 18 Feb 1958; *Manchester Guardian*, 18 Feb 1958; *OL*, Sept 1958, p 131; *Manchester Guardian*, 19 May 1958.

29　Monetary System, q 3825; Sir Alec Cairncross, *Diaries: The Radcliffe Committee and the Treasury, 1961–64* (1999), p 10; Capie, p 109; *Times*, 7 Nov 1958; Monetary System, qq 123–4; Cairncross, *Diaries*, p 15; Monetary System, q 12381; Cairncross, *Diaries*, p 16.

30　G3/119, 12 May 1958; G3/11, 24 April 1958; G3/120, 24 Oct 1958; Catherine R. Schenk, 'The new City and the state in the 1960s', in Michie and Williamson, pp 330, 335; G3/119, 9 May 1958; *New Statesman*, 3 Jan 1959 (Francis Williams).

31　G3/11, 2 July 1958, 11 July 1958; Niall Ferguson, *High Financier* (2010), p 184; G1/179, 31 De 1958; G15/19. For the fullest account of the Aluminium War, see Ferguson, pp 183–99.

32　Monetary System, q 12813; Cairncross, *Diaries*, p 20; G3/82, 20 Jan 1959; Cairncross, *Diaries*, p 21.

33　Keith Middlemas, *Power, Competition and the State: Volume I* (Basingstoke, 1986), p 384; *Journal* (Newcastle), 7 April 1959; Allen, pp 201–2; G3/12, 29 May 1959; G15/19, 29 May 1958.

34　G3/84, 6 Aug 1959.

35　Allen, p 228. In addition to helpful summaries of the report by Allen, pp 228–30, and Capie, pp 112–16, 134–7, see also: E. Victor Morgan, 'The Radcliffe Report in the Tradition of British Official Monetary Documents', in David R. Croome and Harry G. Johnson, *Money in Britain, 1959–1969* (1970), pp 3–21.

36　G3/84, 17 Aug 1959; *Punch*, 26 Aug 1959; Astrid Ringe and Neil Rollings, 'Domesticating the "Market Animal"? The Treasury and the Bank of England, 1955–60', in R. A. W. Rhodes (ed), *Transforming British Government, Volume I* (Basingstoke, 2000), pp 129–30; Capie, p 127; G3/85, 27 Nov 1959; *Hall Diaries, 1954–61*, pp 223–4.

CHAPTER 14 HONEST MONEY

1　Samuel Brittan, *The Treasury under the Tories* (1964), p 206; LDMA1/12, 23 June 1960; John Singleton, *Central Banking in the Twentieth Century*

(Cambridge, 2011), p 160; Fed, box 617015, 14 March 1961; G1/252, 6 June 1961; G3/91, 7 June 1961, 22 June 1961.

2 Alec Cairncross (ed), *The Robert Hall Diaries, 1954–61* (1991), pp 225–52; diaries of Harold Macmillan (Bodleian), dep d. 40, 31 Oct 1960, fo 86.

3 *Hall*, p 252; *FT*, 11 Nov 1960; Harold Macmillan, *At the End of the Day* (1973), p 381; OHC, Sir Jeremy Morse, 15 Dec 1994; OHC, Sir George Blunden, 11 July 2005.

4 Erin E. Jacobsson, *A Life for Sound Money* (Oxford, 1979), p 369; G1/252, 7 July 1961; Capie, p 176; *FT*, 26 July 1961; G1/252, 6 Sept 1961; Richard Spiegelberg, *The City* (1973), p 117.

5 Capie, p 175; R. A. O. Bridge, contribution to *International Central Banking* (Federal Reserve Bank of Boston, 1965), pp 21–2; Capie, pp 157–8; Fed, box 617015, 18 Sept 1961, 23 March 1962; *OL*, Summer 1991, p 100 (Rodney D. Galpin); Fed, box 617015, C261, 23 July 1963.

6 Catherine R. Schenk, 'The new City and the state in the 1960s', in Ranald Michie and Philip Williamson (eds), *The British Government and the City of London in the Twentieth Century* (Cambridge, 2004), pp 332–3; G3/128, 22 Nov 1962; EID10/22, 29 Jan 1963, 5 Dec 1963; C20/5, 16 March 1964.

7 G3/96, 23 July 1962; ADM13/6, 23 Aug 1963.

8 G1/252, 7 July 1961; *FT*, 4 Oct 1962; NA, T295/10, 30 April 1963, T295/11, 18 July 1963.

9 ADM13/5, 25 Sept 1962; Lewis Baston, *Reggie* (Stroud, 2004), p 184; Milton Gilbert, *Quest for World Monetary Order* (New York, 1980), p 65; *FT*, 5 March 1992; Roger Alford, *Life and LSE* (Brighton, 2009), p 288; Baston, p 185; *FT*, 19 Jan 1963; LDMA1/13, 1 Nov 1963.

10 Sir Alec Cairncross, *Diaries: The Radcliffe Committee and the Treasury, 1961–64* (1999), p 91; Baston, p 230; Kenneth O. Morgan, *Callaghan* (Oxford, 1997), pp 193–4; NA, PREM 11/4777, 1–2 Oct 1964; LDMA1/14, 9 Oct 1964; Capie, pp 196–7; NA, PREM 11/4771, 24 July 1964; Fay, p 100.

11 Fed, box 617015, C261, 16 Oct 1964; Capie, pp 199–200; *Times*, 4 Nov 1964; *FT*, 4 Nov 1964.

12 Michael J. Oliver, 'The two sterling crises of 1964', *Economic History Review*, Feb 2012, p 318; G1/260, 13 Nov 1964; NA, PREM 13/261, 18 Nov 1964; C160/36, 20 Nov 1964; G1/260, 20 Nov 1964; Capie, p 202; Oliver, '1964', p 319; NA, PREM 13/261, 24 Nov 1964; Harold Wilson, *The Labour Government, 1964–1970* (1971), p 36; Capie, p 203; Alec Cairncross, *The Wilson Years* (1997), p 18; OHC, Sir Alec Cairncross, 16 June 1994 [1995?]; Capie, p 205.

13 NA, PREM 13/275, 15–16 Feb 1965; Cairncross, *Wilson Years*, pp 47, 54; OV44/125, 5 Aug 1965; NA, PREM 13/851, 9 March 1966; Cairncross, *Wilson Years*, p 121.

14 Fed, box 615848, 27 Dec 1965; *OL*, June 1966, p 67; OHC, John Fforde, 1995, Sir Jasper Hollom, 11 Jan 1995.

15 *Guardian*, 4 Nov 1997 (Christopher Zinn); O'Brien, p 60; *King* (1), p 56; O'Brien, pp 60, 62; Baston, pp 272, 260; James Callaghan, *Time and Chance* (1987), p 195; information from Christopher Fildes ('good plain cook'); *Economist*, 30 April 1966; *Times*, 18 Oct 1976 (Frank Vogl).

16 Fed, box 617031, C261, 14 July 1966; NA, PREM 13/853, 12 July 1966; Fed, box 617031, C261, 15 July 1966; NA, PREM 13/853, 15 July 1966; Morgan, pp 245–6; Wilson, p 251.

17 *King* (1), p 99; Cairncross, *Wilson Years*, p 213; OHC, Sir Jeremy Morse, 1 June 2005; *King* (1), pp 137, 141–2; *Contemporary Record*, Winter 1988, p 51 (Kathleen Burk).

18 Capie, pp 217–18; O'Brien, p 72; *King* (1), p 156; Morgan, pp 272–3; Fed, box 617031, C261, 21 Nov 1967; Capie, pp 242–3, 248; *Times*, 18 Nov 1967; OHC, Sir Alec Cairncross, 16 June 1994 [1995?]; G3/262, 30 Nov 1967; Capie, p 243.

19 Timothy Green, *The New World of Gold* (1985 edn), p 130. For a full account of the gold crisis, see: Arran Hamilton, 'Beyond the Sterling Devaluation: The Gold Crisis of March 1968', *Contemporary European History*, Feb 2008, pp 73–95.

20 NA, PREM 13/2051, 15 March 1968; Cairncross, *Wilson Years*, p 289.

21 NA, PREM 13/2017, 9 May 1968; O'Brien, pp 58–9; information from John Footman.

22 P. L. Cottrell, 'The Bank of England in its International Setting, 1918–1972', in Roberts and Kynaston, pp 136–7; O'Brien, pp 79–80; OHC, Lord Jenkins of Hillhead, 7 Feb 1995.

23 Capie, p 531; *Times*, 18 July 1967; G3/266, 24 July 1967; Capie, pp 331–2; Dominic Hobson, *The Pride of Lucifer* (1990), pp 114–23; *Daily Telegraph*, 14 Aug 1968; G3/269, 25 Feb 1969; Spiegelberg, p 183.

24 G3/267, 23 Jan 1968, 26 Jan 1968; NA, PREM 13/2248, 5 Feb 1968; William Davis, *Merger Mania* (1970), pp 124–5; *Guardian*, 18 July 1968; G3/268, 10 July 1968; G3/266, 19 Sept 1967; G3/270, 10 Sept 1969.

25 *Daily Mail*, 31 May 1968; Rob Stones, 'Government-finance relations in Britain, 1964–7', *Economy and Society*, Feb 1990, pp 174–6; G3/291, 15 Nov 1968; Duncan Needham, *UK Monetary Policy from Devaluation to Thatcher, 1967–82* (Basingstoke, 2014), p 196; Charles A. E. Goodhart, 'Competition and credit control', *Financial History Review*, Aug 2015, p 240; *FT*, 1 Feb 1969; Needham, p 34; G3/271, 29 April 1970; Capie,

p 452; *BEQB*, June 1970, p 180 (C. A. E. Goodhart, assisted by A. D. Crockett).

26 G3/268, 10 July 1968, 9 Oct 1968; G3/269, 3 Jan 1969; Capie, pp 358–9; G3/271, 4 June 1970; O'Brien, p 97; *Times*, 3–4 June 1970.

27 Tony Benn, *Office without Power* (1988), pp 233–4; Alford, p 277; *Punch*, 30 Nov 1966; Select Committee on Nationalised Industries, *Bank of England: First Report* (1969–70, vi), pp 388–9.

28 ADM 12/9, 8 May 1962; Anthony Sampson, *Anatomy of Britain* (1962), p 366; OHC, Christopher Fildes, 28 Jan 1997.

29 Capie, pp 403–4; OHC, Pen Kent, 12 June 2005; *CB*, 2004/5 (4), p 89 (Elizabeth Hennessy); OHC, Sir Kit McMahon, 8 Oct 1996; Kit McMahon, 'John Fforde', *Independent*, 19 April 2000; *Daily Express*, 14 Dec 1964; 'Sir Jeremy Morse', *Daily Telegraph*, 5 Feb 2016; *OL*, Dec 1985, p 189 (Gordon Richardson).

30 Capie, pp 367–8; *King* (1), p 222; *OL*, Autumn 1977, p 97 (David Nye).

31 Capie, p 823; *CB*, 2004/5 (4), p 90 (Elizabeth Hennessy); G39/4, 31 July 1969; GT39/2, 1 Oct 1969; G39/5, 30 Sept 1969; OHC, Sir Jeremy Morse, 15 Dec 1994.

32 NA, PREM 11/3285, 11 Jan 1961; *OL*, Sept 1988, p 135 (Tony Carlisle); Guy de Moubray, *City of Human Memories* (Weardale, 2005), p 209; Alford, p 285; *OL*, Sept 1985, p 143 (Eddie George); OHC, Sir Kit McMahon, 6 July 2005; Capie, pp 130–1; 6A106/1, 29 Sept 1975.

33 Michael Moran, *The Politics of Banking* (1984), p 15; *Financial World*, Sept 2012, p 14; OHC, Christopher Fildes, 5 Dec 1996; *Nationalised Industries*, qq 1819, 1986, 1989.

34 Fed, box 615845, 5 June 1969; *Nationalised Industries*, q 1037; Moran, p 25; *Nationalised Industries*, q 141; Douglas Wass, *Decline to Fall* (Oxford, 2008), pp 30–1; Cairncross, *Wilson Years*, p 297; G3/135, 15 Jan 1963; OHC, Sir George Blunden, 11 July 2005; 6A50/5, 19 July 1971.

35 *Nationalised Industries*, qq 184–5, pp lxxxi–lxxxii, lxxvii; Sampson, p 356; OHC, Pen Kent, 12 June 2005.

CHAPTER 15 ENTERING FROM STAGE RIGHT

1 O'Brien, p 105; Duncan Needham, *UK Monetary Policy from Devaluation to Thatcher, 1967–82* (Basingstoke, 2014), pp 37–8; *King* (2), pp 51, 54, 68, 81; Fay, p 55; O'Brien, p 101.

2 G3/273, 13 Jan 1971, 4 Feb 1971; *King* (2), pp 126–7.

3 G3/272, 21 Oct 1970; *King* (2), p 54; G3/273, 17 Feb 1971; O'Brien, pp 110–11; *Times*, 9 Feb 1973; John Plender, *That's the Way the Money Goes* (1982), p 65. Fuller accounts of the Rolls-Royce episode are in Capie, pp 785–90 and O'Brien, pp 106–8.

4 Capie, p 422; David Kynaston, *LIFFE* (Cambridge, 1997), p 9; Keith Middlemas, *Power, Competition and the State: Volume 2* (Basingstoke, 1990), p 334; *Times*, 24 June 1972; O'Brien, p 124.

5 Capie, p 486; Charles A. E. Goodhart, 'Competition and credit control', *Financial History Review*, Aug 2015, p 241; Capie, p 490; O'Brien, p 114; Charles Gordon, *The Cedar Story* (1993), p 146; Needham, p 45.

6 *Times*, 17 May 1971; *Economist*, 22 May 1971; *Banker*, June 1971; Edward du Cann, *Two Lives* (Upton-upon-Severn, 1995), p 130.

7 Peter Kirwin (ed), *A Tribute to the Bank of England* (1994), p 90; Margaret Reid, *The Secondary Banking Crisis, 1973–75* (1982), pp 59–60.

8 G3/275, 5 Jan 1972, 26 Jan 1972; *King* (2), p 206; Needham, p 56; G3/312, 26 June 1972; G3/275, 26 June 1972; *Banker*, Sept 1972, pp 1131–3.

9 Capie, pp 509–11; Needham, p 59; G3/276, 22 Nov 1972; HSBC Group Archives, UK 0346, Records of chairman (Forbes, Archibald): departmental files.

10 *Times*, 28 July 1972; *Banker*, Aug 1972, pp 1019–22 (Richard Fry); *Daily Telegraph*, 9 Aug 1972; G3/276, 16 Aug 1972; Reid, pp 48–52; information from John Plender; *Daily Telegraph*, 5 Feb 1973.

11 OHC, John Fforde, 1995; Fay, p 55; *King* (2), pp 271, 279; OHC, Lord Jenkins of Hillhead, 7 Feb 1995; Middlemas, p 379; *Times*, 9 Feb 1973; *Spectator*, 17 Feb 1973; G3/277, 5 April 1973.

12 O'Brien, p 138; *Economist*, 6 July 1973; *Dow*, p 35; C160, 7 March 1973.

13 *King* (2), p 263; Charles Gordon, *The Two Tycoons* (1984), p 143; information from Colin Leach; Anthony Sampson, *Anatomy of Britain Today* (1965), p 443; OHC, Sir George Blunden, 20 March 1997; *Dow*, pp 108–9; OHC, Christopher Fildes, 5 Dec 1996. See also: William Keegan, 'Lord Richardson of Duntisbourne', *Independent*, 9 Feb 2010.

14 Capie, p 519; John Campbell, *Edward Heath* (1993), p 530; Capie, pp 520–1; G3/278, 16 Nov 1973, 21 Nov 1973; Goodhart, 'Competition', p 245; John Grady and Martin Weale, *British Banking, 1960–85* (1986), p 58; OHC, Lord Healey, 11 Nov 1997; Goodhart, 'Competition', p 245.

15 The fullest account of the secondary banking crisis remains Reid, but see also Gordon, *Cedar* and Capie, chap 11.

16 HSBC Group Archives, UK 0141-0019, Records of assistant chief general manager (Graham Stuart): working papers; Reid, pp 12, 10; Capie, pp 538–41; G3/278, 20 Dec 1973; Fay, p 62; *King* (2), p 374; Capie, pp 575, 577.

17 Capie, p 542; G3/279, 5 Feb 1974; *National Life Story Collection* (National Sound Archive, British Library), C409/001, pp 72, 74–5; Reid, p 126; Capie, pp 581–3.

18 6A70/3, 21 Dec 1973, 30 Dec 1974; 6A70/4, 14 March 1975, 16 May 1975; Reid, pp 138–43, 183–9; Capie, pp 553–4, 636; G3/363, 1 Oct 1977.

19 G3/279, 28 June 1974; Capie, pp 578-80; Michael Moran, *The Politics of Banking* (Basingstoke, 1984), pp 114-17; OHC, Sir George Blunden, p 9; Richard Roberts, *Take Your Partners* (Basingstoke, 2001), pp 78-9; Moran, pp 118-30; OHC, John Fforde, 4 Dec 1986.

20 Capie, pp 791-801; G3/280, 8 July 1974; G3/279, 6 June 1974, 10 June 1974; Denis Healey, *The Time of My Life* (1989), pp 374-5; OHC, Sir Douglas Wass, 13 Aug 1996.

21 Needham, p 86; Edmund Dell, *A Hard Pounding* (Oxford, 1991), p 135; G3/281, 12 June 1975, 20 June 1975; Dell, pp 162-3; Edward Pearce, *Denis Healey* (2002), p 435; Bernard Donoughue, *The Heat of the Kitchen* (2004 Politico's edn), pp 187-8; EID4/200, 8 July 1975.

22 For a detailed account from a Bank perspective, see Roger Lomax, 'The Bank of England and UK Business, 1930-2003', chaps 3-6.

23 This paragraph is based on: Capie, pp 802-8; Kynaston, vol 4, pp 508-10, 537-41.

24 EID4/200, 19 Sept 1975, 24-26 Sept 1975; Capie, p 657.

25 Douglas Wass, *Decline to Fall* (Oxford, 2008), pp 150-2; *Dow*, pp 45-6; Wass, p 178; *Times*, 5 March 1976; Healey, p 427; Fed, box 617010, 15 March 1976; Wass, p 179; Pearce, pp 456-7; Capie, p 746.

26 James Callaghan, *Time and Chance* (1987), p 415; Capie, pp 747-8; *Dow*, p 53; Pearce, p 463; *Dow*, pp 110-11; OHC, John Fforde, 22 May 1996; Capie, p 750; Needham, p 97; Pearce, p 465; *Dow*, p 60; G3/284, 19 July 1976; Capie, pp 658-9.

27 Fed, box 617010, 25 Aug 1976; Richard Roberts, *When Britain Went Bust* (2016), p 9; Capie, p 750; Fed, C261 England, 30 Sept 1976; Pearce, p 469; G3/285, 7 Sept 1976; *NLSC*, C409/037, Sir David Walker, pp 93-4; Capie, p 751.

28 *Institutional Investor*, June 1987, p 68; Capie, pp 669-70; *International Insider*, 18 Oct 1976; *Dow*, p 69; Capie, pp 751-2; The Baring Archive, 202445, Foreign Exchange Advisers Papers Volume 3, October 1976; 'Sir Alan Whittome', *Times*, 23 Jan 2001; *Dow*, p 70; Capie, pp 754-5; *Dow*, p 69.

29 *Business Week*, 14 March 1977; G3/361, 13 June 1977; *Observer*, 12 June 1977; *Guardian*, 28 Oct 1977; *Dow*, p 110; *Times*, 27 Jan 1978.

30 Roberts, *Partners*, pp 106-7; *Institutional Investor*, Dec 1977, pp 40-4; David Wainwright, *Government Broker* (1990), pp 102-3; G3/361, 13 June 1977.

31 Bernard Donoughue, *Prime Ministers* (1987), pp 143-4; Adrienne Gleeson, *London Enriched* (1997), p 160; *International Insider*, 5 Sept 1977, 12 Sept 1977, 26 Sept 1977; *FT*, 16 Nov 1977; interview with William Batt, 1999.

32 Records of London Stock Exchange, Liaison Committee, 28 Feb 1979; Treasury and Civil Service Committee, *The Role of the Bank of England: Volume II: Minutes of Evidence and Appendices* (1993), q 275; G3/283, 5 April 1976; Healey, p 449; *Euromoney*, Aug 1977, p 78 (Peter Hambro); Morgan, p 553.

33 *BEQB*, March 1978, p 33; *Times*, 18 April 2000 (obituary of Fforde); Frank Longstreth, 'The City, Industry and the State', in Colin Crouch (ed), *State and Economy in Contemporary Capitalism* (1979), p 189; G3/365, 7 April 1978; *Dow*, pp 120–1; G3/372, 1 May 1979.

CHAPTER 16 SUNNY OFFS

1 *New Statesman*, 30 July 1960 ('Taurus'); Roger Alford, *Life and LSE* (Brighton, 2009), pp 254–5; *BEQB*, Sept 1966, pp 233–45; Hennessy, p 136; Capie, p 38; Guy de Moubray, *City of Human Memories* (Weardale, 2005), p 202; Capie, p 40; information from Michael Anson.

2 Fay, p 105; Hennessy, pp 118–23; Select Committee on Nationalised Industries [SCNI], *Bank of England: First Report* (1969–70, vi), q 948; E4/5, fo 94, Sept 1969; OHC, Lord George, 8 Feb 2006; *OL*, Spring 1980, p 5; Alford, p 264; *OL*, Spring 1980, p 6.

3 *Punch*, 13 March 1957; *OL*, March 2003, p 12 (John Keyworth); Byatt, pp 167, 173–4; O'Brien, p 34; Byatt, pp 178–9; Hannah Hawksworth, 'Harry Ecclestone', *Guardian*, 7 July 2010; Byatt, p 197.

4 *OL*, March 1996, p 22 (Teri Brown); Hennessy, p 187; *OL*, June 1956, p 69 (A. F. J. Davies); Hennessy, pp 189–91; SCNI, q 922.

5 Hennessy, pp 63–5, 70–1; *OL*, June 1958, p 64; *FT*, 3 July 1958; Hennessy, p 73; Nikolaus Pevsner, *The Buildings of England: London 1: The Cities of London and Westminster* (Harmondsworth, 1957), p 199; Simon Bradley and Nikolaus Pevsner, *The Buildings of England: London 1: The City of London* (1997), p 456; *OL*, June 1958, p 67.

6 SCNI, qq 150, 2127, 1183, 1168; Capie, p 41; *OL*, Sept 2001, p 128 (B. M. Lahee); *Birmingham Post*, 21 Sept 1970; SCNI, q 1174; Fay, p 41; Hennessy, pp 284–90; *Architects' Journal*, 21 Sept 1962; Hennessy, pp 279–80; *OL*, Dec 1967, p 207 (Roger Woodley), Sept 1971, p 187 (D. J. Baker); O'Brien, p 55.

7 *OL*, Dec 2004, p 125 (Peter Edgley); *OL*, March 2000, pp 8–12 (Ron Middleton); SCNI, q 799; O'Brien, p 55; *OL*, June 1968, p 67; OHC, Sir George Blunden, 1994; *OL*, June 2003, p 73 (David Harris).

8 Hennessy, pp 218, 214; Capie, pp 67–70, 348–9; SCNI, q 1154; *OL*, March 1996, pp 25–6 (John Rumins).

9 Hennessy, pp 333, 352–3; E31/3, 29 Aug 1946, 12 May 1948, 18 Nov 1948, 29 March 1949; E15/10, fo 19A, 21 July 1949; *Manchester Guardian*, 2 Aug 1949; E31/3, 15 May 1952.

10 *OL*, Spring 1992, p 20; Hennessy, pp 354–5; AC25/26, 1 Dec 1955; E31/3, 26 April 1957; Hennessy, pp 355–6; E31/4, 21 Feb 1962; *OL*, March 1969, pp 12–13 (V. K. Bloomfield), Spring 1992, p 21 (Jane Collier); *OL*, March 1967, p 3; *Times*, 3 Feb 1967.

11 Hennessy, pp 354, 357–8; E4/56, fo 69E, 6 May 1969; G9/48, Nov 1963; E4/56, fo 22, 2 June 1966.

12 Capie, p 53; *OL*, Spring 1993, p 4 (John Hill); OHC, Pen Kent, 12 June 2005; *OL*, Sept 1985, p 99 (Roger Barnes); de Moubray, *City*, p 212; *BEQB*, Sept 1966, p 244; SCNI, qq 2131, 2138.

13 *OL*, Sept 1998, p 120 (J. D. W. Raimbach); Capie, p 52; *OL*, Winter 1977, p 156, Spring 1978, pp 13–14 (J. E. Taylor), Summer 1982, p 53, Autumn 1977, p 95 (Anthony Carlisle); G9/48, 17 Sept 1963.

14 *OL*, Sept 1999, p 100 (Graham Kentfield); Elizabeth Hennessy, 'The Governors, Directors and Management of the Bank of England', in Roberts and Kynaston, p 215; E31/3, 29 Aug 1946, 30 Aug 1946.

15 de Moubray, *City*, p 112; *OL*, Spring 1993, p 5 (John Hill); de Moubray, *City*, pp 182–3; *OL*, Autumn 1977, p 95 (Anthony Carlisle), Sept 2005, p 112 (Tim Kidd), Dec 2003, p 147 (John Footman).

16 Hennessy, pp 340–1; *OL*, Spring 1979, p 195 (Paul Clayton); Hennessy, p 342; E15/7, fo 102, April 1969; E15/22, Aug 1970.

17 SCNI, qq 1972–4; Capie, p 55; E4/56, fo 15, April 1966; O'Brien, p 55; Hennessy, pp 344–5; E30/76, fo 17, 27 Nov 1969; G9/11, 30 June 1972; Hennessy, pp 363–4.

18 *Evening News*, 20 Feb 1956; Hennessy, pp 361–3; *OL*, Sept 2000, p 103 (Willie Osborn), Spring 1993, p 3 (Dorothy Binns); Capie, pp 52–3; de Moubray, *City*, pp 111, 113.

19 *OL*, June 1984, p 60 (Michael Pickering), Dec 2006, p 138 (Christopher Bell), Sept 1987, p 126 (Paul Tempest).

20 de Moubray, *City*, p 209; G39/1, 26 Feb 1968; ADM10/1, 21 Feb 1969; Capie, pp 356–8; ADM10/1, Jan 1970 (file 30 Jan 1970); *Birmingham Post*, 3 Feb 1970.

21 *OL*, June 2005, p 38 (R. C. D. Lowry), Dec 2003, p 147 (John Footman), June 1971, p 75; John Keyworth, 'As Safe as the Bank of England' (1993); Capie, p 363; *OL*, Spring 1993, p 4 (John Hill), June 2003, p 83 (Rick Salmon); 6A106/1, 7 Oct 1975; *OL*, Spring 1992, p 21, Autumn 1992, p 130 (Tony Carlisle); *Dow*, pp 78–9.

22 Hennessy, 'The Governors', p 209; *Dow*, pp 105–6; G3/273, 26 March 1971.

23 Information from Michael Anson; Fay, p 104; *FT*, 26 Jan 1978; Capie, p 365; G3/278, 15 Nov 1973.

24 E15/7, fo 156, March 1973, fo 172, 4 Oct 1973, fo 181, 11 Oct 1973; E30/92, April 1974; Fay, p 104; *Daily Telegraph*, 12 Dec 1978; G1/567, 14 Dec 1978; Fay, p 104; *OL*, Spring 1979, p 195 (Paul Clayton).

25 Information from Michael Anson; G3/274, 9 July 1971, Aug 1971; G9/12, 21 Feb 1974.

26 *OL*, Winter 1977, pp 147–8 (John Fforde), Autumn 1977, pp 95–6 (Tony Carlisle), Dec 1985, p 145 (David Pollard).

27 7A127/1, 6 April 1976; *Dow*, pp 58–9.

28 7A127/1, 24 June 1977; G1/567, 8 Aug 1978; Capie, pp 823–4; 7A127/1, 2 April 1979; Capie, pp 824–5.

CHAPTER 17 SERIOUS MISGIVINGS

1 Duncan Needham, *UK Monetary Policy from Devaluation to Thatcher, 1967–82* (Basingstoke, 2014), p 138; Geoffrey Howe, *Conflict of Loyalty* (1994), p 152; *BEQB*, June 1979, pp 153, 156; Capie, p 699; G3/375, 14 Dec 1979; 7A133/2, 17 Jan 1980; G3/376, 28 Jan 1980; 10A114/1, 27 Feb 1980; G3/377, 5 March 1980; Nigel Lawson, *The View from No. 11* (1992), pp 80–1.

2 Needham, p 167; 7A133/2, 25 Feb 1980; Needham, p 149; 7A133/2, 10 March 1980; G3/377, 14 March 1980.

3 G3/372, 26 June 1979; *OL*, Spring 1980, p 7; Capie, pp 768–9; *Dow*, p 143; Capie, p 769; *Dow*, p 143; OHC, Sir George Blunden, 20 March 1997; *Guardian*, 24 Oct 1979; *OL*, Spring 1980, p 5 (Douglas Dawkins); *Dow*, pp 143–4; G3/375, 3 Dec 1979; *OL*, Spring 1980, pp 7–8; *Spectator*, 2 Feb 1985 (Christopher Fildes); *OL*, Spring 1980, p 6 (Douglas Dawkins).

4 *CB*, 2004/5 (4), p 90 (Elizabeth Hennessy); G3/376, 25 Jan 1980; *Dow*, pp 149, 151.

5 Howe, p 139; Jock Bruce-Gardyne, *Ministers and Mandarins* (1986), p 94; Charles Moore, *Margaret Thatcher, Volume One* (2013), p 462; *Dow*, p 147; Lawson, p 84; *Dow*, pp 165, 184; G3/390, 1 April 1982, 4 May 1982; *Dow*, pp 228–9.

6 Moore (1), p 523; G3/377, 11 March 1980, 14 March 1980; G3/378, 30 May 1980.

7 Lawson, p 82; 7A133/2, 29 July 1980; Moore (1), p 525; 7A133/2, 6 Aug 1980; Moore (1), p 530; 7A133/2, 3 Sept 1980; Needham, p 152; G3/380, 5 Sept 1980; William Keegan, *Mrs Thatcher's Economic Experiment* (1984), p 153; 7A133/2, 8 Sept 1980; *Dow*, p 168.

8 Needham, pp 155, 174; G3/380, 18 Sept 1980; Needham, pp 155–9; G3/382, 10 Feb 1981.

9 G3/384, 27 May 1981; G3/385, 25 Aug 1981; G3/386, 14 Sept 1981; Howe, pp 226–7; G3/391, 14 July 1982, 27 July 1982.

10 C. A. E. Goodhart, 'The Bank of England 1970–2000', in Ranald Michie and Philip Williamson (eds), *The British Government and the City of London in the Twentieth Century* (Cambridge, 2004), pp 364–5; *Dow*, p 192; G3/387, 10 Dec 1981; G3/385, 25 Aug 1981; *Dow*, p 187; G3/388, 18 Jan 1982; Lawson, pp 112–13.

11 See in general: Roger Lomax, 'The Bank of England and UK Business, 1930–2003', chaps 6–8.

12 *BEQB*, March 1984, p 74; G3/387, 30 Nov 1981; G3/390, 16 June 1982; Philip Geddes, *Inside the Bank of England* (1987), p 117; OHC, Sir David Walker, 29 March 2011; *OL*, Sept 2006, p 120; *BEQB*, March 1984, pp 75–6.

13 *OL*, Dec 1986, p 182; 13A231/16, 15 June 1983; *OL*, Spring 1981, pp 5–6, June 2007, p 72 (Terry Smeeton); G3/382, 22 Jan 1981.

14 Goodhart, 'Bank', p 347; Steven Solomon, *The Confidence Game* (New York, 1995), pp 204–5, 207–11; G3/392, 9 Sept 1982; Solomon, p 218; G3/392, 20 Oct 1982; Solomon, pp 225–6, 233–6; OHC, Roger Barnes, 8 Dec 2009; Solomon, p 233.

15 *Dow*, p 223; Moore (1), p 531; *Dow*, pp 223–4; *Times*, 10 Feb 2016 (Lord Lexden); *Dow*, pp 222–3; *FT*, 29 Dec 1982; *Economist*, 8 Jan 1983; *Spectator*, 26 June 1993 (Christopher Fildes); *Dow*, pp 222–3; 13A231/1, 6 May 1983.

16 G3/383, 11 March 1981; 13A231/20, 20 Dec 1993; Richard Roberts and David Kynaston, *The Lion Wakes* (2015), pp 68–73, 78–9; G3/387, 25 Nov 1981; *Spectator*, 28 Nov 1981; G3/388, 19 Jan 1982.

17 G3/383, 11 March 1981; David Kynaston, *LIFFE* (Cambridge, 1997), chaps 1–3; Godfrey Hodgson, *Lloyd's of London* (1986 Penguin edn), p 363; Ian Hay Davison, *Lloyd's* (1987), p 6.

18 G3/373, 25 July 1979; G3/384, 22 May 1981; 15A91/1, 21 June 1982, Feb 1983; Margaret Reid, *All-Change in the City* (1988), pp 46–7; *Dow*, p 227.

19 *Dow*, p 232; Bruce-Gardyne, pp 94–5; Capie, pp 829–30; G3/383, 25 March 1981.

20 13A231/2, 23 March 1984; *ODNB*, Forrest Capie, 'Lord Kingsdown'; OHC, Michael Foot, 10 Jan 2011, Pen Kent, 11 Jan 2011, Roger Barnes, 8 Dec 2009; *OL*, Summer 1983, p 57; *Dow*, p 233.

21 *Spectator*, 2 July 1983; Bruce-Gardyne, pp 111–12; Robert Elgie and Helen Thompson, *The Politics of Central Banks* (1998), p 63; 13A231/2, 30 May 1984; 13A231/3, 16 Dec 1985; 13A231/4, 1 May 1986; OHC, Lord Kingsdown, 29 June 2011.

22   15A91/3, 8–9 Sept 1983; OHC, Sir David Walker, 29 March 2011; 15A91/4, 6 Oct 1983; 13A231/2, 13 Dec 1984; 158A91/3, 17 Aug 1983, 12–13 Sept 1983, 9 Sept 1983.

23   OHC, Sir David Walker, 29 March 2011; Fed, box 615845, 19 Oct 1984; Capie, p 107; OHC, William (Bill) Allen, 16 Dec 2009; 15A91/6, 17 July 1985.

24   Charles Moore, *Margaret Thatcher: Volume Two* (2015), p 429; 13A231/3, 9 Sept 1985; *BEQB*, March 1986, p 50; 13A224/2, 14 Feb 1984; *BEQB*, March 1986, p 48.

25   Helpful accounts of the episode include: Fay, pp 141–72; Reid, *All-Change*, pp 224–33; Will Ollard and Nick Routledge, 'How the Bank of England failed the JMB Test', *Euromoney*, Feb 1985, pp 49–56.

26   G3/377, 9 April 1980; John Plender and Paul Wallace, *The Square Mile* (1985), p 238; 13A231/2, 26–27 Sept 1984.

27   Fay, pp 151–2; Plender and Wallace, p 239; 4A69/5, 2 Oct 1984.

28   Lawson, pp 403–4; Fay, pp 153–4; 4A69/5, 1 Oct 1984; 13A231/2, 2 Oct 1984; email from John Footman, 22 July 2016; 'Rodney Galpin', *Daily Telegraph*, 14 Nov 2011; Fay, p 171; 4A69/5, 11 Oct 1984; *BEQB*, Dec 1984, p 473.

29   Reid, *All-Change*, pp 228–9; 13A231/2, 22 Oct 1984; Fay, pp 158–61; 13A231/2, 17 Dec 1984; Lawson, pp 405–6; *Spectator*, 19 Jan 1985.

30   *FT*, 21 June 1985; 13A231/3, 22 July 1985, 9 Sept 1985.

31   13A231/4, 23 Jan 1986; Fay, p 172; OHC, Peter Cooke, 18 Feb 1997.

32   *BEQB*, Dec 1984, pp 475, 478; Philip Stephens, *Politics and the Pound* (1996), p 32; Lawson, p 486; 13A231/3, 6 Feb 1985.

33   Lawon, pp 488–9; 13A224/3, 12 March 1985; 13A231/3, 19 July 1985; Moore (2), p 418; *BEQB*, Dec 1985, pp 534–6; Lawson, pp 494–7; 13A231/3, 23 Oct 1985; Lawson, pp 497–500.

34   Lawson, pp 649–50.

35   William Keegan, *Mr Lawson's Gamble* (1989), p 155; Fay, pp 184–5; 'Sir George Blunden', *Daily Telegraph*, 28 March 2012; *Spectator*, 28 Sept 1985.

36   Reid, *All-Change*, p 65; *OL*, Dec 1986, pp 144–6 (Ian Plenderleith); David Wainwright, *Government Broker* (East Molesey, 1990), p 114; 13A231/4, 28 Jan 1986, 30 May 1986; 15A91/7, 5 June 1986.

37   13A231/4, 28 Aug 1986; *OL*, Dec 1986, p 148; *BEQB*, Dec 1986, p 509; 15A91/8, *c* 22 Oct 1986; 158A91/7, 1 July 1986.

38   13A231/4, 7 Nov 1986; OHC, Ian Plenderleith, 26 Jan 2011; *BEQB*, Feb 1989, pp 49–57.

39   Roger Cowe, 'Sir George Blunden', *Guardian*, 15 March 2012; *Independent*, 11 Feb 1987; Richard Roberts, *The City* (2004), p 260;

13A231/5, 26 Feb 1987; 13A224/5, 25 Sept 1987, 2 Oct 1987; 'Sir George Blunden', *Daily Telegraph*, 28 March 2012; 13A231/7, 14 Feb 1989; 13A231/8, 24 July 1989, 2 Aug 1989.

40 *BEQB*, Nov 1987, p 526; 13A231/9, 12 Oct 1989, 16 Oct 1989.

41 13A231/5, 29–30 July 1987, 28 Aug 1987, 18 Sept 1987; *BEQB*, Nov 1987, p 526.

42 Lawson, p 746; *Spectator*, 7 Nov 1987; Lawson, p 750; Robert Pringle, 'Central Bank Co-operation since 1970', in Roberts and Kynaston, p 148; *CB*, Winter 1992/3, p 56 (Robert Pringle).

43 John Nott, *Here Today, Gone Tomorrow* (2002), p 336; Lawson, pp 757–68; 13A231/5, 27 Oct 1987; Lawson, pp 769–75.

44 This paragraph is largely derived from: Solomon, pp 413–35; John D. Turner, *Banking in Crisis* (Cambridge, 2014), pp 195–7.

45 13A231/5, 28 July 1987, 18 June 1987.

46 13A231/5, 6 May 1987; Lawson, p 639; *CB*, Winter 1992/3, p 56 (Robert Pringle); David Cobham, 'The Lawson Boom', *Financial History Review*, April 1997, pp 86, 77; Lawson, pp 840–1.

47 *CB*, Spring 1996, p 111; Stephens, pp 77–84; OHC, Michael Foot, 10 Jan 2011; Stephens, pp 91–3; 13A231/7, 26 May 1989; *BEQB*, Aug 1989, pp 373–4.

48 13A231/6, 22 July 1988; OHC, Lord Kingsdown, 29 June 2011; 13A231/6, 2 Nov 1988, 7 Dec 1988, 12 Dec 1988; Margaret Thatcher, *The Downing Street Years* (1993), p 708; 13A231/7, 15 Feb 1989; Thatcher, p 708; 13A231/7, 26 May 1989.

49 *FT*, 29 Jan 1988; *Spectator*, 27 June 1987; Lawson, pp 789–91, 1059–60, 868–9; Thatcher, p 706; Stephens, pp 135–6; Lawson, p 1063; *Euroweek*, 3 Nov 1989; Michael King, 'New Lady of Threadneedle Street', *CB*, 2000/1 (4), p 83; *Times*, 2 Nov 1989.

CHAPTER 18 WELCOME AND LONG OVERDUE

1 Steven Solomon, *The Confidence Game* (New York, 1995), pp 501–2; *Spectator*, 31 Oct 1992 (Stephen Fay); *CB*, Autumn 1990, pp 77, 85; Philip Stephens, *Politics and the Pound* (1996), p 169; 13A231/10, 4 Feb 1990; John Major, *The Autobiography* (1999), p 153; Robert Elgie and Helen Thompson, *The Politics of Central Banks* (1998), p 75.

2 13A231/10, 5 Feb 1990, 22 Feb 1990; 13A231/11, 19 April 1990; 13A231/12, 6 July 1990; *CB*, Summer 1990, p 11; Elgie and Thompson, p 75; 13A231/17, 27 March 1992.

3 *OL*, March 1990, opp p 1; 13A231/13, 6 Sept 1990; 13A231/19, 18 Aug 1992; Norman Lamont, *In Office* (1999), pp 97–8.

4 Roger Lomax, 'The Bank of England and UK Business, 1930–2003', p 97; *BEQB*, Nov 1990, p 512; Lomax, p 100; *BEQB*, Feb 1993, p 114.

5 Lomax, pp 105–16; 1A231/10, 16 Feb 1990.

6 *ODNB*, Forrest Capie, 'Eddie George, Baron George'; *BEQB*, Feb 1994, pp 64–5; John D. Turner, *Banking in Crisis* (Cambridge, 2014), p 165. See also: Ian Hay Davison, 'How to rescue a bank', *Spectator*, 19 April 2008; Kushal Balluck, 'The small bank failures of the early 1990s', *BEQB*, 2016 Q1, pp 41–51.

7 *Times*, 18 Dec 1990; *Investors Chronicle*, 21 Dec 1990; 13A231/14, 10 Jan 1991, 23 Jan 1991, 4 Feb 1991, 8 Feb 1991, 13 Feb 1991; 13A231/16, 27 Nov 1991; Richard Roberts and David Kynaston, *The Lion Wakes* (2015), p 188; 13A231/17, 2 Jan 1992, 5 March 1992; Roberts and Kynaston, *Lion*, pp 190–1, 200.

8 G3/375, 5 Dec 1979; *Daily Telegraph*, 3 March 1993; 13A231/15, 8 July 1991; 13A231/7, 26 May 1989.

9 13A231/15, 8 July 1991, 4 July 1991; *Spectator*, 27 July 1991; 13A231/15, 19 July 1991.

10 *OL*, Autumn 1991, p 106; Treasury and Civil Service Committee, *Banking Supervision and BCCI* (1992), qq 48, 50, 113, 120–1, 125, 253, 292, paras 29, 32; *CB*, Autumn 1992, p 3; 13A231/19, 25 Sept 1992, 14 Oct 1992; *Sunday Times*, 25 Oct 1992; *Times*, 23 Oct 1992; *Daily Telegraph*, 2 Jan 2004; *CB*, 2005/6 (2), p 15; 13A231/19, 19 Oct 1992; 13A231/15, 8 July 1991.

11 Major, p 162; C. A. E. Goodhart, 'The Bank of England 1970–2000', in Ranald Michie and Philip Williamson (eds), *The British Government and the City of London in the Twentieth Century* (Cambridge, 2004), p 355; Stephens, pp 152–3; *BEQB*, Nov 1990, p 486.

12 *BEQB*, Feb 1997, pp 99–100, 2010 Q4, p 260; 13A231/18, 7 Aug 1992, 24 Aug 1992, 27 Aug 1992; Major, pp 326, 329; *Daily Telegraph*, 27 July 1994 (Neil Collins).

13 *CB*, 2004/5 (4), pp 7–8; Lamont, p 244; OHC, Ian Plenderleith, 26 Jan 2011; *Black Wednesday*, BBC 1, 16 Sept 1997; OHC, Michael Foot, 10 Jan 2011; *Black Wednesday*, BBC 1, 16 Sept 1997; Lamont, p 255.

14 13A231/19, 16 Sept 1992; Lamont, p 291; *Guardian*, 14 Sept 2012.

15 Lamont, pp 247–8, 250–2; 13A231/19, 16 Sept 1992 (Butler note of 24 Sept 1992); Stephens, pp 251–2.

16 13A231/19, 17 Sept 1992.

17 *Spectator*, 30 Oct 1992; Giles Radice, *Diaries, 1980–2001* (2004), p 285; 13A231/19, 17 Sept 1992; 16A118/7, 17 Sept 1992; 13A231/19, 17 Sept 1992; 16A118/7, 24 Sept 1992.

18 *Dow*, p 247; *OL*, March 1997, p 27; 13A231/18, 5 June 1992.

19 OHC, Lord (Terry) Burns, 22 Nov 2011; 13A231/19, 6 Oct 1992; Stephens, p 152; Elgie and Thompson, p 77; 13A231/19, 19–20 Oct 1992; 10A143/1, 27 Oct 1992; Elgie and Thompson, p 77; *Times*, 30 Oct 1992.

20 *BEQB*, Nov 1992, pp 441–8; 10A143/1, 10 Dec 1992; *Evening Standard*, 14 Feb 2013 ('City Spy').

21 *FT*, 30 Oct 1992; 13A231/19, 24 Dec 1992; Lamont, pp 322–5; Major, p 675; Michael King, 'New Lady of Threadneedle Street', *CB*, 2000/1 (4), p 85; Elgie and Thompson, pp 79–80; 10A143/2, 3 Feb 1993.

22 Lamont, pp 321–2; *Sunday Times*, 25 Oct 1992; *Spectator*, 30 Jan 1993; *Banking World*, March 1993, p 11; *CB*, Winter 1992/3, pp 7, 68; *OL*, Spring 1993, p 24.

23 13A231/20, 10 March 1993; 13A183/5, 25 May 1993; 13A231/20, 3 June 1993; Elgie and Thompson, p 80; 13A231/20, 17 June 1993.

24 *CB*, Summer 1993, p 6; eulogy (Paul Tucker) at memorial service, 6 Feb 2014; 'Lord Kingsdown', *Times*, 26 Nov 2013.

25 *ODNB*, Capie, 'Eddie George'.

26 *Securities & Investment Review*, Sept 1993, p 14; 13A183/5, 26 July 1993, 1 Aug 1993, 29 July 1993, 25 Oct 1993; Treasury and Civil Service Committee, *The Role of the Bank of England: Volume II: Minutes of Evidence and Appendices* (1993), qq 114, 158, 503, 511, 381, 198, 200, 221, 242–3, 295, *Volume I: Report* (1993), pp vi, xx–xxix.

27 *CB*, Autumn 1993, p 7; Elgie and Thompson, p 81; *CB*, Summer 1993, p 6; King, 'New Lady', pp 86–7; Centre for Economic Policy Research, *Independent and Accountable* (1993), pp 73–4; *House Magazine*, 7 Feb 1994.

28 13A231/20, 9 Nov 1993; *New Financial Review*, April 1995, p 3; 13A231/21, 11 Feb 1994; Elgie and Thompson, pp 84–6; 13A231/20, 8 Sept 1993; 10A143/6, 14 March 1994; *CB*, 2000/1 (3), p 23; *FT*, 14 April 1994.

29 Forrest Capie *et al*, *The Future of Central Banking* (Cambridge, 1994), pp 360–1, 300, 304; *Economist*, 11 June 1994; *OL*, Summer/Autumn 1994, pp 66–7; *FT*, 27 July 1994; *Daily Telegraph*, 27 July 1994.

30 ADM10/1, fo 96, 15 July 1965; *OL*, Dec 1988, pp 174–5, 178–9; 13A231/6, 5 Aug 1988, 25 Aug 1988; *OL*, Dec 1988, pp 176–7; *Country Life*, 15 June 1989.

31 *OL*, Dec 1990, pp 170–1 (Caroline Wright); *FT*, 2 Oct 1990; Peter Kirwin (ed), *A Tribute to the Bank of England* (1994), pp 98–103; *OL*, June 1996, p 47 (Chris Bailey).

32 Byatt, p 203; Fay, p 43; *OL*, Summer 1991, p 58 (Shane Sullivan); 13A231/5, 1 Dec 1987; Byatt, pp 219–28; Wikipedia, 'Loughton incinerator thefts'.

33 *OL*, Spring 1993, p 13, Spring 1992, pp 20–2.

34 *Annual Report 1979*, p 27; *Annual Report 1994*, p 22; 13A231/25, 24 May 1996; 13A231/4, 14 May 1986; 13A231/7, 22 June 1989; 7A148/12, 31 Jan 1996; *OL*, Dec 2004, p 130; 4A18/12, 6 May 1997.

35 13A231/1, 19 Sept 1983; *OL*, Dec 1984, p 192 (Mark Stephenson), Dec 1985, p 145 (David Pollard), March 1986, p 9 (Michael Pickering).

36 13A231/20, 4–5 Aug 1993, 7 Oct 1993, 8 Sept 1993.

37 Elizabeth Hennessy, 'The Governors, Directors and Management of the Bank of England', in Roberts and Kynaston, pp 211–13; Elizabeth Hennessy, 'The Georgian era at the Bank of England', *CB*, 2002/3 (4), pp 38–9; 13A231/18, 21 July 1992; *CB*, Spring 1994, pp 30–1; *FT*, 27 July 1994.

38 *CB*, Spring 1994, p 31; 13A231/21, 29 July 1994, 7 Sept 1994; 13A231/23, 25 June 1996; *OL*, March 2002, p 11 (Ruth Kelly).

39 *Bank Fortnight*, 17 March 1994; 4A69/110, 17 March 1995; 13A231/22, 12 April 1995, 30 June 1995; 13A231/23, 12 Feb 1996; 13A231/25, 24 May 1996; 13A231/24, 18 Sept 1996.

40 ARM344957–8; 13A231/22, 7 Nov 1995; *OL*, March 1996, pp 7–9 (Howard Davies); 13A231/26, 24 Feb 1997.

41 *BEQB*, Nov 1992, p 459; 13A231/20, 8 Sept 1993, 6 Dec 1993; *BEQB*, Aug 1994, p 280.

42 Treasury Committee, *The Role of the Bank of England: Volume I*, pp xxv–xxvi; *BEQB*, Feb 1994, pp 60–6; Treasury Committee, *The Role of the Bank of England: Volume I*, p xxviii; *Economist*, 7 May 1994; *FT*, 27 July 1994 (John Gapper).

43 The two key accounts are: Stephen Fay, *The Collapse of Barings* (1996); John Gapper and Nicholas Denton, *All That Glitters* (1996).

44 4A69/109, 24–25 Feb 1995; 4A69/110, 26 Feb 1995.

45 *Times*, 28 Feb 1995, 1 March 1995; *FT*, 1 March 1995; *Independent*, 4 March 1995; *Sunday Telegraph*, 5 March 1995.

46 13A231/22, 1 March 1995; 4A69/110, 16 March 1995.

47 *Sunday Mirror*, 19 March 1995; *CB*, Spring 1995, p 21; *FT*, 22 March 1995; *OL*, Oct 1995, pp 114–16.

48 Fay, *Collapse*, pp 245–6; *CB*, Summer 1995, pp 16–17; Fay, *Collapse*, p 246; Treasury and Civil Service Committee, *Board of Banking Supervision: The Report on the Collapse of Barings Bank* (1995), qq 96, 121–5; 4A69/114, 25 July 1995; 13A231/22, 8 Sept 1995; Clare Pearson, 'Trying times on Threadneedle Street', *Institutional Investor*, Sept 1995, p 102.

49 Treasury Select Committee, *Barings Banks and International Regulation* (1996), vol I, pp xiii–xv; *BEQB*, Nov 1996, p 462; Treasury Committee,

Barings, vol II, qq 1291–412; *BEQB*, Feb 1997, pp 111–12; Treasury Committee, *Barings*, vol I, pp xxxv–xxxvi.

50 *BEQB*, Feb 1996, p 92; Philip Augar, *The Death of Gentlemanly Capitalism* (2000), pp 312, 321–2, 325; 13A231/22, 13 April 1995; *CB*, Spring 1997, p 15; Ian Plenderleith, 'Developments in the Monetary Field at the Bank of England', in World Gold Council, *Central Banking and the World's Financial System* (1997), p 14; 13A231/25, 16 Dec 1996; *Independent*, 26 Feb 1997; *FT*, 23 Dec 1998; *Times*, 17 Sept 1996; Plenderleith, 'Developments', p 12.

51 *BEQB*, Nov 1995, p 393; *OL*, March 1997, p 26 (David Smith); 13A231/21, 10 Nov 1994; 13A231/25, 31 Oct 1996; *BEQB*, Feb 1997, pp 100–1.

52 Conaghan, p 15; 13A231/22, 4 May 1995; Elgie and Thompson, pp 87–9; *BEQB*, Nov 1995, p 389; *International Economy*, Sept/Oct 1995, p 12 (Anatole Kaletsky); Elgie and Thompson, p 90.

53 4A69/109, 7 Feb 1995; Alastair Campbell and Bill Hagerty (eds), *The Alastair Campbell Diaries, Volume 1* (2010), pp 152, 158; 4A69/112, 11 May 1995; *Campbell* (1), p 200; 4A69/112, 15 May 1995; William Keegan, *The Prudence of Mr Gordon Brown* (Chichester, 2003), pp 145, 161–4.

54 13A231/25, 26 Nov 1996; 8A388/36, 24 Jan 1997; 13A231/26, 5–6 Feb 1997; Elgie and Thompson, p 92; 13A231/26, 7 March 1997.

55 *CB*, Spring 1995, p 43; 4A69/112, 15 May 1995; 13A231/25, 26 Nov 1996; 13A231/26, 6 Feb 1997.

56 Keegan, p 157; *Campbell* (1), p 626; Elgie and Thompson, p 92; 4A18/11, 23 April 1997; Ed Balls, *Speaking Out* (2016), pp 138–9.

57 Keegan, p 182; Andrew Rawnsley, *Servants of the People* (2000), pp 31–3; *BEQB*, Aug 1997, pp 244–5; 16A129/1, 6 May 1997; Hugh Pym and Nick Kochan, *Gordon Brown* (1998), pp 72–3.

58 Keegan, p 153; Wilf Stevenson (ed), Gordon Brown, *Speeches 1997–2006* (2006), pp 9, 12; 16A129/1, 6 May 1997; Alastair Campbell and Bill Hagerty (eds), *The Alastair Campbell Diaries, Volume 2* (2011), p 10; *Independent*, 7 May 1997; *Daily Telegraph*, 7 May 1997; *Guardian*, 7 May 1997; Tom Bower, *Gordon Brown* (2007 edn), pp 208–9; Rawnsley, p 37; *Economist*, 10 May 1997.

59 13A231/27, 12 May 1997, 9 May 1997; 8A388/37, 16 May 1997; 13A231/27, 16 May 1997.

60 16A129/1, 6 May 1997; Pym and Kochan, pp 73–4; 16A129/1, 20–21 May 1997.

61 16A129/1, 20 May 1997; *BEQB*, Aug 1997, p 246; *Times*, 21 May 1997; *Sunday Times*, 25 May 1997; *Economist*, 24 May 1997.

62 16A129/1, 27 May 1997; Keegan, pp 187–8; 7A148/12, 29 July 1997; *BEQB*, May 1998, pp 97–9.

63 *CB*, 2003/4 (1), p 8; 7A148/12, 29 May 1997; *BEQB*, May 1998, p 93; Brown, *Speeches*, p 20.

POSTSCRIPT YOU JUST DON'T KNOW WHEN

(Note: post-1997 articles and speeches by the Bank's senior figures are available on the Bank's website.)

1 *Evening Standard*, 27 Nov 2014 (Anthony Hilton); *Times*, 15 March 2012.

2 Richard Roberts and David Kynaston, *City State* (2001), p 130; *BEQB*, Summer 2001, pp 164–8, Autumn 2001, p 351; *CB*, 2001/2 (4), pp 9–10; *Institutional Investor*, Feb 2003, p 26.

3 *BEQB*, Winter 2003, p 477; House of Commons Treasury Committee, *The Monetary Policy Committee of the Bank of England: Appointment Hearing, Volume II* (2005), q 74; *BEQB*, 2007 (1), p 110 (Lomax), 2007 (2), p 273 (King); House of Commons Treasury Committee, *The Monetary Policy Committee of the Bank of England: ten years on* (Sept 2007), paras 7, 14.

4 Treasury Committee, *Monetary Policy Committee: ten years on*, paras 18, 22; Kate Barker, 'Monetary Policy – From Stability to Financial Crisis and Back?', March 2010 speech, p 4; *Guardian*, 25 May 2010; *FT*, 3 May 2012; *Guardian*, 30 Dec 2014; *ODNB*, Forrest Capie, 'Eddie George, Baron George'; Sir Andrew Large, 'Monetary Policy: Significant Issues of Today', December 2005 speech, p 7; Mervyn King, *The End of Alchemy* (2016), p 330; *Institutional Investor*, Feb 2003, pp 30, 32.

5 Howard Davies and David Green, *Banking on the Future* (Princeton, 2010), p 120; Robert Peston, *How Do We Fix This Mess?* (2012), pp 192–3; *Times*, 23 Oct 2008 (Jamie Stevenson).

6 Sir Andrew Large, 'Puzzles in Today's Economy', March 2004 speech, p 13, 'Monetary Policy', Dec 2005 speech, p 7; *Inflation Report*, May 2006, p 7; James Barty, *Reform of the Bank of England* (Policy Exchange, 2012), p 13; *FT*, 27 Sept 2006; *Standpoint*, June 2012, p 24 (Tim Congdon); *CB*, 2006/7 (1), pp 59, 61 (John Nugée); *BEQB*, 2007 (1), pp 122–30 (Paul Tucker).

7 *Independent*, 12 Jan 2007; *BEQB*, 2007 (2), pp 280–1 (Mervyn King); *Inflation Report Press Conference*, 16 May 2007, pp 9–10, 8 Aug 2007, pp 6–7.

8 *Observer*, 6 May 2012 (Will Hutton); Ian Fraser, *Shredded* (Edinburgh, 2014), p 492; Sir Martin Jacomb, *Re-empower the Bank of England*

(Centre for Policy Studies, June 2009), pp 2–5; Ed Balls, *Speaking Out* (2016), pp 296–7.

9   Alex Brummer, *The Crunch* (2008), p 217; Barty, p 36; House of Commons Treasury Committee, *Financial Regulation* (Feb 2011), q 696; *Daily Telegraph*, 4 May 2012; Ivan Fallon, *Black Horse Ride* (2015), pp 164–5.

10   House of Commons Treasury Committee, *Re-appointment of Mervyn King as Governor of the Bank of England* (June 2008), qq 33–4, 51, 113; *CB*, 2006/7 (1), pp 1–2; *Times*, 15 March 2012; Gillian Tett, *The Silo Effect* (2015), pp 122–3; *CB*, 2010/11 (1), pp 61–2.

11   Matthew Hancock and Nadhim Zahawi, *Masters of Nothing* (2011), pp 18–19; *New Statesman*, 20 July 2009 (Alex Brummer); *CB*, 2005/6 (3), pp 24–5 (Sir Andrew Large); *BEQB*, 2006 (3), pp 339–40 (Sir John Gieve), 2007 (1), p 127 (Paul Tucker); Tett, *Silo*, p 124–5.

12   *BEQB*, 2007 (3), p 426 (Mervyn King); Barty, p 14; *Banker*, Sept 2006, pp 66–7; *Guardian*, 29 June 2013 (Nils Pratley); Gillian Tett, *Fool's Gold* (2009), p 183; *BEQB*, 2007 (2), pp 313–15 (Paul Tucker); Court minutes, 11 July 2007; *Inflation Report Press Conference*, 8 Aug 2007.

13   Fraser, *Shredded*, p 492; *CB*, 2006/7 (4), pp 1–2.

14   Helpful accounts of the 2007–8 crisis include: Brummer, *Crunch* (2009 edn); Tett, *Fool's Gold*; Philip Augar, *Chasing Alpha* (2009); Howard Davies, *The Financial Crisis* (2010); Dan Conaghan, *The Bank* (2012); Hugh Pym, *Inside the Banking Crisis* (2014); Fraser, *Shredded*; Fallon, *Black Horse Ride*.

15   House of Commons Treasury Committee, *The Run on the Rock, Volume II* (Feb 2008), pp 214, 217; Court minutes, 13 Sept 2007; Treasury Committee, *Run*, p 217; Court minutes, 13 Sept 2007; *Economist*, 22 Sept 2007, Conaghan, p 150.

16   *Economist*, 22 Sept 2007; *CB*, 2007/8 (3), pp 12–13; Brummer, *Crunch* (2008), pp 123, 125; *Times*, 12 March 2012; *Economist*, 15 June 2013; *Guardian*, 20 June 2013.

17   Treasury Committee, *Run*, qq 4–5, 18, 51–2, 54, 111; *BEQB*, 2007 (4), p 567 (Mervyn King); BBC Radio 4, *File on Four*, 6 Nov 2007; Treasury Committee, *Run*, qq 1665, 1696, *Re-appointment*, qq 55, 116, 65, *Banking Reform* (Sept 2008), q 169; *New Statesman*, 4 March 2016.

18   *CB*, 2007/8 (2), p 1, 2007/8 (3), pp 44–7; *Sunday Telegraph*, 29 May 2011, 6 May 2012; OHC, Michael Foot, p 31; Treasury Committee, *Run*, q 114.

19   'File'; Treasury Committee, *Run*, q 1608; *Guardian*, 13 Dec 2007; Court minutes, 12 Dec 2007; Treasury Committee, *Run*, qq 1610, 1677; Fraser, *Shredded*, p 329; *FT*, 22 April 2008.

20   Conaghan, pp 163–4; Barty, p 23; *Guardian*, 3 May 2012; Court minutes, 11 June 2008.

21 Treasury Committee, *Re-appointment*, q 75; *BEQB*, 2008 (3), p 314 (Mervyn King); *Daily Telegraph*, 8 July 2008; Barty, p 24; *Evening Standard*, 5 May 2009; *New Statesman*, 14 Sept 2009.

22 Court minutes, 10 Sept 2008; *CB*, 2008/9 (2), pp 18–20; Alistair Darling, *Back from the Brink* (2011), p 165; Court minutes, 15 Oct 2008.

23 Barty, p 26; Tett, *Fool's Gold*, pp 282–3; Court minutes, 15 Oct 2008; Mervyn King, 'Speech', 21 Oct 2008.

24 *Times*, 16 May 2013, 15 Oct 2008; *Standpoint*, June 2009, pp 40–5, Oct 2011, Dec 2015, pp 42–5.

25 House of Commons Treasury Committee, *Fixing LIBOR, Volume I* (Aug 2012), p 25; Treasury Committee, *Re-appointment*, q 80; *Times*, 1 Sept 2015; *FT*, 11 Dec 2008; Treasury Committee, *Fixing*, pp 44–5, 47–50; *Times*, 18 July 2012; Treasury Committee, *Fixing*, pp 56–8.

26 Court minutes, 13 Nov 2008; *Times*, 5 Dec 2008; *Daily Telegraph*, 5 Dec 2008; Court minutes, 12 Feb 2009; *FT*, 27 Feb 2009; *Economist*, 7 March 2009; King, *Alchemy*, pp 182–3; *Financial World*, May 2009, p 10; *Standpoint*, June 2009, pp 44–5 (Tim Congdon).

27 Pym, *Inside*, p 187; Conaghan, pp 288–9; *Guardian*, 22 May 2012; *Times*, 22 May 2012.

28 Barty, pp 36–7; Conaghan, pp 245–7; Jacomb, p 1; *Guardian*, 21 July 2009; *FT*, 17 June 2010; *Times*, 17 June 2010; *Spectator*, 27 June 2009; *Evening Standard*, 21 July 2009, 17 June 2010; *Independent*, 2 Aug 2010; *Guardian*, 15 Sept 2010.

29 Court minutes, 16 April 2008; Treasury Committee, *Re-appointment*, q 44; Court minutes, 12 Feb 1009; *BEQB*, 2009 (2), p 139 (Paul Tucker); Court minutes, 30 April 2009; Mervyn King, 'Speech at the Lord Mayor's Banquet', 17 June 2009, pp 7–8; House of Commons Treasury Committee, *Banking Crisis: Regulation and Supervision* (July 2009), qq 117–18; Mervyn King 'Speech at the Lord Mayor's Banquet', 16 June 2010, pp 5–7; House of Commons Treasury Committee, *Financial Regulations* (Feb 2011), qq 20, 25.

30 Paul Tucker, 'A New Regulatory Relationship', May 2013 speech, pp 3–6; *Guardian*, 30 March 2013; *FT*, 21 June 2013.

31 *Times*, 29 July 2010, 26 Oct 2011; Pym, *Inside*, pp 176–7; *Guardian*, 7 March 2013; *Independent*, 15 June 2012; *FT*, 16 June 2012; *Guardian*, 1 Aug 2013, 28 March 2013, 25 July 2013.

32 Michael Joyce *et al*, 'The financial market impact of quantitative easing', *BEQB*, 2010 (3), p 205; *Daily Telegraph*, 8 March 2010 (Roger Bootle); *Economist*, 11 Feb 2012, 1 Oct 2011; *Times*, 20 Feb 2012; *New Statesman*, 5 March 2012 (Robert Skidelsky and Felix Martin); *Guardian*, 25 May 2012.

33 *Guardian*, 28 Sept 2012; *Prospect*, June 2013, p 44 (George Magnus); *FT*, 15 June 2013; *Prospect*, Nov 2010, p 36; *Times*, 29 Oct 2011; *Spectator*, 11 Feb 2012 (Nassim Taleb); *Prospect*, June 2013, p 44.

34 *Evening Standard*, 18 Jan 2011 (Anthony Hilton); *Times*, 24 Jan 2011; *Guardian*, 18 Feb 2011; *Daily Telegraph*, 5 March 2011; *Guardian*, 16 June 2011; *Economist*, 15 June 2013.

35 *Times*, 12 Dec 2012 (David Wighton); *Guardian*, 23 Jan 2013, 16 March 2013; *FT*, 21 March 2013; *Daily Telegraph*, 21 March 2013 (Philip Aldrick).

36 *Financial World*, July 2007, p 11; *OL*, Dec 1997, p 145; Elizabeth Hennessy, 'The Georgian era at the Bank of England', *CB*, 2002/3 (4), p 41; *OL*, Dec 2006, p 126 (John Footman), March 2004, p 11; Valerie Hamilton, 'Moll Flanders and the Old Lady of Threadneedle Street' (University of Warwick PhD, 2013), p 50.

37 *CB*, Nov 1998, p 8, 2002/3 (4), p 3; *OL*, March 2006, p 16; Court minutes, 16 Jan 2008; *FT*, 10 Aug 2013 (Gillian Tett); *Guardian*, 19 Nov 2012; *Times*, 22 June 2013; *Guardian*, 25 July 2013.

38 *OL*, March 1998, p 12; Court minutes, 2008; Andrew G. Haldane, 'The Bank and the banks', 18 Oct 2012 speech, pp 10–11.

39 *BEQB*, Autumn 2004, p 350 (Mervyn King); *Independent*, 21 Oct 2009; *Economist*, 30 Oct 2010; *Daily Telegraph*, 5 March 2011; Peston, *Fix*, pp 436–7; *Guardian*, 29 June 2013.

40 House of Commons Treasury Committee, *Accountability of the Bank of England* (Nov 2011), Vol I, pp 52–3; *Guardian*, 8 Nov 2011; *FT*, 27 April 2012 (Samuel Brittan), 5 May 2012, 19 June 2013; Barty, p 46.

41 *Evening Standard*, 7 Feb 2014 (James Ashton); Treasury Committee, *Accountability*, pp 58–9; *Times*, 18 Jan 2012; Emma Murphy, 'Changes to the Bank of England', *BEQB*, 2013 (1), p 27; *Evening Standard*, 7 Feb 2014.

42 *Guardian*, 8 Nov 2011; *Financial World*, Dec 2011, p 10 (Alex Brummer); Mervyn King, 'Speech at the Lord Mayor's Banquet', 17 June 2009, p 5; Neil Irwin, *The Alchemists* (2013), pp 275–6; *Guardian*, 25 June 2009.

43 *Times Literary Supplement*, 21 Jan 2011 (Peter Riddell); Mervyn King, 'Speech at the Lord Mayor's Banquet', 16 June 2010, p 4; *FT*, 26 June 2010, 16 Sept 2010, 10 Nov 2010; House of Lords Select Committee on Economic Affairs, *Meeting with the Governor of the Bank of England* (Dec 2010), q 14; *FT*, 26 Nov 2010; *Guardian*, 19 Feb 2011; *FT*, 1 May 2012; King, *Alchemy*, p 186.

44 *Guardian*, 19 April 2012; *Evening Standard*, 14 June 2012, 19 Jul 2012; *Spectator*, 18 Aug 2012; *Economist*, 15 Sept 2012; *Guardian*, 8 Oct 2012; *Economist*, 24 Nov 2012; *FT*, 27 Nov 2012; *Times*, 27 Nov 2012; *Daily Telegraph*, 27 Nov 2012; *Times*, 2 July 2013.

45 *BEQB*, Nov 1999, p 411 (Mervyn King).

Acknowledgements

I am grateful to the following institutions, in addition to the Bank of England itself, for allowing me to use their archives: Barclays Bank; The Baring Archive; The Federal Reserve Bank of New York; HSBC Holdings; The Rothschild Archive; The Royal Bank of Scotland; Sir John Soane's Museum.

A lot of people helped to make this book a reality, and I apologise in advance for any inadvertent omissions.

Outside the Bank, I am grateful to an array of archivists and fellow historians for their help and encouragement: Melanie Aspey; Bernard Attard; Forrest Capie; Sally Cholewa; Chris Collins; Valerie Hamilton; Clara Harrow; Elizabeth Hennessy; Boyd Hilton; Pamela Hunter; Harold James; James Mortlock; Susan Palmer; Julie Sager; Hiroki Shin; Maria Sienkiewicz; Tina Staples; Alison Turton; Sophie Volker. I am especially grateful to Anne Murphy, who knows more than anyone about the eighteenth-century Bank and generously put her expertise at my disposal.

The role of direct personal testimony is inevitably limited in the history of such an old institution, but the following kindly found time to discuss with me the Bank's more recent history: Andrew Bailey; Ed Balls; Sir Charles Bean; Sir David Clementi; Sir Howard Davies; Christopher Fildes; Paul Fisher; John Footman; Andy Haldane; William Keegan; Lord King of Lothbury; Rachel Lomax; Ian Plenderleith; Brian Quinn; Sir David Scholey; Sir Paul Tucker.

More generally, I am indebted to many inside the Bank. It is over a quarter of a century since I began visiting there for research purposes, and from the old days I have fond memories of all the help I received from (among others) Kath Begley, Phil Davies, Henry Gillett, John Keyworth, Sarah Millard and Elizabeth Ogden. For this book, I am grateful to Andrew Butterworth, Frances Cassidy, Shahid Nazir and Fiona Platten at the Information Centre for their assistance, but given the archives-based nature of the project my greatest debt is to the Archive team: Mike Anson; Lorna Williams; Ben White; Margherita Orlando (a special 'thank you' for her resourcefulness in coming up with files I only half-knew about); Rachael Muir; Holly Waughman (who also helped with the pictures, as did the Bank's Chris Peacock, Bryony Leventhall, Jenni Adam and Eleanor Paton); Joe Hewson; Sara Brimble. Huge credit goes to Mike and his colleagues for making the Archive an unfailingly pleasant as well as professional environment in which to research.

Also at the Bank, the task fell to John Footman to oversee the book from contract to publication, and he has done so (assisted by his secretary, Sharon Hughes) with patience and humour in addition to insight and objectivity, for all of which qualities I am grateful indeed.

Further heartfelt thanks go to Amanda Howard (Superscript Editorial Services) for her transcribing of my tapes; to Peter James for his copy-edit; to Catherine Best for her proofreading; to Alan Rutter for his index; to Georgia Garrett and Madeleine Dunnigan at my agents Rogers Coleridge & White (where Deborah Rogers was closely involved with the project until her still much-lamented death in 2014); and at Bloomsbury, where Bill Swainson commissioned the book, to Michael Fishwick (my editor), Marigold Atkey and Sarah Ruddick, who as a trio have made the publishing experience enjoyable as well as efficient.

Finally, the deepest thanks go to my wife Lucy, including for her help with research and checking transcriptions. Her great-great-great-grandfather was John Horsley Palmer, one of the most influential governors of the Bank's first two centuries; her great-great-grandfather was Edward Howley Palmer, described by Clapham as a 'capable' governor; this history could not have been completed without her.

Picture Credits

Extract from the original book of subscriptions, June–July 1694 (*The Bank of England Archive (M1/1)*)

Grocers' Hall, Poultry (*Bank of England Museum (0003).*
© The Governor and Company of the Bank of England)

Sir John Houblon (*Bank of England Museum (0248ii).*
© The Governor and Company of the Bank of England)

Gilbert Heathcote (*Bank of England Museum (0244).*
© The Governor and Company of the Bank of England)

The original west wing (*Bank of England Museum (902).*
© The Governor and Company of the Bank of England)

The Pay Hall, 1808 (*Bank of England Museum (0820).*
© The Governor and Company of the Bank of England)

Samuel Bosanquet (*Bank of England Museum (0236).*
© The Governor and Company of the Bank of England)

Abraham Newland (*Bank of England Museum (0498 (i)).*
© The Governor and Company of the Bank of England)

Midas, transmuting all, into paper, James Gillray, 1797 (*The Bank of England Museum (0276). © The Governor and Company of the Bank of England*)

Soane's Bank: Rotunda (*Bank of England Museum (0172).*
© *The Governor and Company of the Bank of England*)

Soane's Bank: Accountants (later £5 Note) Office (*The Bank of England Museum (1993/234). © The Governor and Company of the Bank of England*)

Soane's Bank: Threadneedle Street front (*The Bank of England Museum (0087). © The Governor and Company of the Bank of England*)

Soane's Bank: Bank Stock Office (*The Bank of England Archive 15A13/1/1/4/4*)

Samuel Thornton (*Bank of England Museum (0843).*
© *The Governor and Company of the Bank of England*)

John Horsley Palmer (*Bank of England Museum (0257).*
© *The Governor and Company of the Bank of England*)

William Cotton (*The Bank of England Archive (15A13/13/2/8)*)

William Lidderdale (*The Bank of England Archive (15A13/13/2/1)*)

G. E. Hicks, *Dividend Day at the Bank of England,* 1859 (*The Bank of England Museum (0187). © The Governor and Company of the Bank of England*)

Front Courtyard, 1894 (*The Bank of England Archive (15A13/1/7)*)

Consols Office, 1894 (*The Bank of England Archive (15A13/1/7)*)

The Bank *en fête* for Queen Victoria's Diamond Jubilee, 1897 (*The Bank of England Archive (NON ST 68)*)

Threadneedle Street south front, from across the steps of the Royal Exchange (*The Bank of England Archive (15A13/1/2/11)*)

The Court of Directors, 1903 (*The Bank of England Archive 15A13/13/3/1)*)

Staff singing the National Anthem, 4 August 1916 (*The Bank of England Archive (HOCO/963)*)

King George V and Queen Mary leave the Bank after their visit, December 1917 (*The Bank of England Archive (NON ST 49)*)

Bank Stock Office, 1920s (*The Bank of England Archive (15A13/1/3/18)*)

Rotunda, 1920s (*The Bank of England Archive (15A13/1/3/43)*)

Caryatids, made in 1795, being taken away from the Consols Transfer Office (*The Bank of England Archive (15A13/1/3/63)*)

Printing dividend warrants at St Luke's, 1920s (*The Bank of England Archive (15A13/6/1/11)*)

Committee of Treasury, painted by A.K. Lawrence, 1928 (*The Bank of England Museum (1090). © The Governor and Company of the Bank of England*)

Taking the Paris air, May 1930 (*The Bank of England Archive (15A13/1/3/18)*)

Baker's Bank: Portico (*The Bank of England Archive (15A13/1/2/6)*)

Baker's Bank: Front Hall (*The Bank of England Archive (15A13/1/1/58/6)*)

Baker's Bank: Court Room (*The Bank of England Archive (STAFF 15A13/1/1/67/48)*)

Baker's Bank: Garden Court (*The Bank of England Archive (15A13_1_1_68_41)*)

Bomb damage to Bank station, January 1941 (*The Bank of England Archive (15A13/1/4/39). © London News Agency (LN14213B)*)

Messengers' Quarters Kitchen, c. 1942 (*The Bank of England Archive (15A13/1/4/44)*)

Lord Catto, 1944 (*The Bank of England Archive (STAFF C3)*)

Bank Note Office, 1942: prickers and stampers (*The Bank of England Archive (15A13/1/1/27/4)*)

Bank Note Office, 1962: paid notes for destruction (*The Bank of England Archive (15A13/1/1/27/4)*)

Bullion Office, 1960s: gold vault (*The Bank of England Archive (15A13/1/1/8/31)*)

Dividend Preparation Office, New Change, 1962: the Bank's first computer (*The Bank of England Archive (NC 8)*)

Leslie O'Brien and Lord ('Kim') Cobbold, June 1961 (*The Bank of England Archive (E8/164)*)

Lord Cromer, 1961 (*The Bank of England Archive (STAFF C30)*)

Hilton Clarke, 1967 (*The Bank of England Archive (STAFF C10)*)

Printing works at Debden, c. 1960 (*The Bank of England Archive (BkC001)*)

Gordon Richardson, July 1973 (*Hulton Archive/Getty Images. © Central Press/Stringer*)

Robin Leigh-Pemberton, c. 1990 (*The Bank of England Archive (STAFF L11)*)

South front, 1990s (*The Bank of England Archive (15A13/1/2/57)*)

Eddie George, 1990s (*Getty Images. © Gemma Levine/Contributor*)

Mervyn King, April 2013 (*Getty Images. © Bloomberg/Contributor*)

Index

A Note on the Author

David Kynaston was born in Aldershot in 1951. He has been a professional historian since 1973 and has written nineteen books, including *The City of London*, a widely acclaimed four-volume history, and *WG's Birthday Party*, an account of the Gentlemen v. Players match at Lord's in July 1898. He is the author of *Austerity Britain, 1945–51*; *Family Britain, 1951–57*; and *Modernity Britain, 1957–62*, the first three volumes in a projected series covering the history of post-war Britain (1945–79) under the collective title 'Tales of a New Jerusalem'. He lives in London.

A Note on the Type

The text of this book is set in Linotype Stempel Garamond, a version of Garamond adapted and first used by the Stempel foundry in 1924. It is one of several versions of Garamond based on the designs of Claude Garamond. It is thought that Garamond based his font on Bembo, cut in 1495 by Francesco Griffo in collaboration with the Italian printer Aldus Manutius. Garamond types were first used in books printed in Paris around 1532. Many of the present-day versions of this type are based on the *Typi Academiae* of Jean Jannon cut in Sedan in 1615.

Claude Garamond was born in Paris in 1480. He learned how to cut type from his father and by the age of fifteen he was able to fashion steel punches the size of a pica with great precision. At the age of sixty he was commissioned by King Francis I to design a Greek alphabet, and for this he was given the honourable title of royal type founder. He died in 1561.